Inside Word for Windows® 95

Bill Camarda

New Riders Publishing, Indianapolis, Indiana

Inside Word for Windows® 95

By Bill Camarda

Published by:
New Riders Publishing
201 West 103rd Street
Indianapolis, IN 46290 USA

Printed in the United States of America 1 2 3 4 5 6 7 8 9 0

Library of Congress Cataloging-in-Publication Data

```
Camarda, Bill, 1956-
    Inside Word for Windows 95 / Bill Camarda.
       p.   cm.
    Includes index.
    ISBN 1-56205-355-8
    1. Microsoft Word for Windows 95.  2. Word
processing.  I. Title.
  Z52.5.M523C324  1995
652.5'536—dc20                                   95-38225
                                                      CIP
```


Warning and Disclaimer

This book is designed to provide information about the Microsoft Word for Windows computer program. Every effort has been made to make this book as complete and as accurate as possible, but no warranty or fitness is implied. No validity of sample documents used to illustrate the concepts discussed in the book is implied.

The information is provided on an "as is" basis. The author and New Riders Publishing shall have neither liability nor responsibility to any person or entity with respect to any loss or damages arising from the information contained in this book or from the use of the disks or programs that may accompany it.

Publisher *Don Fowley*
Marketing Manager *Ray Robinson*
Acquisitions Manager *Jim LeValley*
Managing Editor *Tad Ringo*

Product Development Specialist
Ray Robinson

Acquisitions Editor
Alan Harris

Software Specialist
Steve Weiss

Lead Editor
Lillian Yates

Copy Editors
Nancy Albright, Geneil Breeze, Susan Christopherson, Cliff Shubs, John Sleeva, Angie Trzepacz, Lisa Wilson Phil Worthington

Technical Editor
Rob Tidrow

Associate Marketing Manager
Tamara Apple

Acquisitions Coordinator
Stacey Beheler

Publisher's Assistant
Karen Opal

Cover Designer
Karen Ruggles

Book Designers
Paula Carroll
Kim Scott

Photographer
Larry Ladig

Manufacturing Coordinator
Paul Gilchrist

Production Manager
Kelly Dobbs

Production Team Supervisor
Laurie Casey

Graphics Image Specialists
Jason Hand, Clint, Lahnen, Laura Robbins, Craig Small, Todd Wente

Production Analysts
Angela Bannan
Bobbi Satterfield
Mary Beth Wakefield

Production Team
Kim Cofer, Kevin Foltz
David Garratt, Shawn MacDonald, Gina Rexrode
Erich J. Richter

Indexer
Christopher Cleveland

About the Author

Bill Camarda specializes in writing about computing and telecommunications topics for large corporate clients. He is the author of *OS/2 in the Fast Lane, Inside Word 6 for Windows,* and *Inside 1-2-3 Release 5 for Windows,* and coauthor of *Inside MS-DOS 6.22, Inside OS/2 Warp,* and *Inside OS/2 2.1* all published by New Riders. He also is vice president of Camares Communications in Wyckoff, New Jersey, a firm that specializes in marketing high technology products and services.

Trademark Acknowledgments

Dedication

To my wife, Barbara, and my son, Matthew. You bring me joy beyond words.

Acknowledgments

To all the extraordinary people at New Riders who labored long, hard, and well to bring you this book: Lillian Yates, Rob Tidrow, Alan Harris, Steve Weiss, Ray Robinson, Stacey Beheler, Tim Huddleston, Geneil Breeze, Phil Worthington, Nancy Albright, Angie Trzepacz, Susan Christopherson, Lisa Wilson, John Sleeva, Cliff Shubs, and all the coffee fiends in Production.

Contents at a Glance

Table of Contents

Part III: Professional-Quality Word Processing

Part V: Command Reference

Part VI: Appendixes

Introduction

This book is about getting more done in less time.

Word is a truly remarkable word processor. It can follow you around, if you want, fixing your most common spelling mistakes before you know you made them. It can number lists, manage cross-references, automatically number your headings, format your documents for you—even shrink them, if they're too long.

It can create business forms, manage revisions from multiple reviewers, automate the creation of indexes and tables of contents, and send e-mail. For your more creative side, it can create drawings, graphs, even twist your characters into any shape or form you desire.

But you still have to know how to enable Word to do these things for you, which is what this book is for.

Finding the Best Way to Do the Job

There's a hard way and an easy way to do everything. Take, for example, writing business letters. It's a good bet that 95 percent of business letters written today are written from scratch. But you *could* have Word automatically place your name, address, today's date, writer's and typist's initials, and closing in every letter you write from here on. How long would it take to get Word to do that? About five minutes.

You could start with one of Word's built-in letter templates—and, when the time comes, use corresponding Word templates for memos, reports, and other kinds of documents. Suddenly, you've got a complete, unified set of well-designed corporate documents—without hiring a designer to establish your graphic design standards (and paying thousands of dollars).

And there really are scores of examples like this. Often, you can save literally 90 percent of the time and keystrokes involved in a specific Word task if you know the best way to perform that task.

Which would you rather do? Spend all that time keystroking, formatting, and compiling—or learn how to have Word do it for you? So, *Inside Word for Windows 95* doesn't just tell you how to get things done, but how to get them done most efficiently.

There's a lot to tell. Word 95 might just be the most powerful word processor ever created. We're out to help you grab as much of that power as you possibly can—as painlessly as possible.

Who Should Read This Book

This book assumes you've at least installed Word and created some basic documents with it, and you're now ready to go a lot further. But, among the millions of people who fit that description, there are several types of users for whom this book offers specific assistance.

If you're moderately experienced with Word, skim Part I, "Word for Windows 95 Techniques," for shortcuts and concepts you may have missed. Then dive headfirst into Part II, "Word for Windows 95 Productivity Tools."

If you're very experienced with Word, use this book as a comprehensive reference, offering in-depth discussions of all features, including those you only use occasionally.

If you're upgrading to Word 95 from Word 6, keep an eye out for this symbol, which marks coverage of brand-new Word 95 features:

If you're responsible for managing Word at your office, note the extensive coverage of many features that make Word work especially well in a business environment, such as templates (Chapter 8), forms (Chapter 23), and techniques for personalizing Word (Chapter 24), which can help you create a word processor that meets the precise needs of your organization.

If you're planning to use Word for desktop publishing applications, like publishing a newsletter, pay special attention to Chapters 21, "Desktop Publishing and Drawing," and 22, "Using Word's Graphing Features."

If you're planning heavy-duty office work and correspondence, pay special attention to Chapters 6 through 9 and 18 through 20, especially the Mail Merge coverage in Chapter 19.

If you're planning to write a book, study Chapters 6, 8, 10, and 18, and especially Chapter 20, all of which cover features that are helpful for creating long documents.

How This Book Is Organized

Here's a quick look at how we've structured *Inside Word for Windows 95*:

Part I, "Word for Windows 95 Techniques," takes a close look at the fundamentals of working with Word, including headers and footers, tables, printing, file management, and using Word's four built-in literacy aids—spell check, thesaurus, grammar check, and AutoCorrect.

Part II, "Word for Windows 95 Productivity Tools," focuses on the essential Word tools that can dramatically reduce the amount of time it takes to create, format, and compile a document: styles and AutoFormat, templates and wizards, AutoText, fields, and macros.

Part III, "Professional-Quality Word Processing," focuses on Word's features for creating long documents, managing revisions, and generating mass mailings.

Part IV, "Advanced Features of Word for Windows 95," focuses on Word's capabilities to go way beyond traditional word processing, into desktop publishing, graphing, calculating, and forms production. Part IV covers techniques for making Word cooperate with your other software in a real-world business environment, making Word your control center for all your Windows computing, and customizing Word to your own specific work style.

Part V, "Command Reference," is a WordBasic command reference that provides easy lookup of WordBasic commands and functions.

Part VI, "Appendixes," offers comprehensive reference lists of keyboard and mouse shortcuts, toolbars, and information on installing the accompanying CD-ROM.

No Matter How You Learn, Come On In

From teaching word processing—and writing for a living—I've learned that many different kinds of learners are out there. So there's something here for each of you:

- **The keyboarder.** Maybe you're a professional writer or typist who never needed a mouse. Now you're in Windows, and you're still not convinced. *Surprise:* You'll do just fine here with your fingers. Quick keyboard commands are available for just about everything Word does, and this book tells you about all of them.
- **The mouse user.** *Inside Word for Windows 95* is a mouse-lover's paradise.
- **The learner who wants to go further.** In these 1,100+ pages, you can learn the underlying concepts of using Word—and how to find even more.

About the *Inside Word for Windows 95* CD-ROM

Inside Word for Windows 95 comes with a CD-ROM containing useful files and data. On it, you'll find *The New Riders' Professional Solutions Guides for Word and Excel*, a complete book of solutions to the problems Word users have reported most often, and practice documents that can be used to try out techniques shown in nearly every chapter of the book.

Conventions Used in This Book

Most New Riders Publishing books use similar conventions to help you distinguish between various elements of the software, Windows, and sample data. This means that after you purchase one New Riders Publishing book, you'll find it easier to use all the others.

Before you look ahead, spend a moment examining these conventions:

- Key combinations appear in the following formats:

  Key1+Key2: When you see a plus between key names, you should hold down the first key while pressing the second key. Then release both keys.

  Key1,Key2: When a comma (,) appears between key names, you should press and release the first key, and then press and release the second key.

- Windows underlines one letter in all menus, menu items, and most dialog box options. For example, the File menu is displayed on-screen as File.

  The underlined letter indicates which letter you can type to choose that command or option from the keyboard—in this example, F. In this book, such letters are in boldface and underlined: **F**.

- Text you type is in a special bold **typeface**. This applies to individual letters and numbers, as well as text strings. This convention, however, does not apply to command keys, such as Enter, Esc, or Ctrl.

- New terms appear in *italic.*

- Text that appears on-screen, such as prompts and messages, appears in a special `typeface`.

Special Text Used in This Book

Inside Word for Windows 95 uses many special "sidebars," which are set apart from the normal text by icons.

New Features. This icon marks a new feature introduced with Word 95.

Tip. This icon marks a shortcut or neat idea that'll help you get your work done faster or better.

Note. A note includes extra information you should find useful, but which complements the discussion at hand, instead of being a direct part of it. A note may describe special situations that can arise when you use Word 95 under certain circumstances, and tell you what to do.

Warning. This tells you when a procedure may be dangerous—that is, when you run the risk of losing data, locking your system, or damaging your software. Warnings generally tell you how to avoid such losses, or describe the steps you can take to remedy them.

A Note from the Author

These are asides by the author that talk about his personal experience or offer subjective opinions.

This flags sample documents on the *Inside Word for Windows 95* CD-ROM you can use to test the concepts you're learning, as well as other items on the disk that are relevant and valuable.

New Riders Publishing

The staff of New Riders Publishing is committed to bringing you the very best in computer reference material. Each New Riders book is the result of months of work by authors and staff who research and refine the information contained within its covers.

As part of this commitment to you, the NRP reader, New Riders invites your input. Please let us know if you enjoy this book, if you have trouble with the information and examples presented, or if you have a suggestion for the next edition.

Please note, though: New Riders staff can't serve as a technical resource for Word for Windows or for related questions, including hardware- or software-related problems. Please refer to the documentation that accompanies Word, or call Microsoft at (206) 462-9673.

If you have a question or comment about any New Riders book, there are several ways to contact New Riders Publishing. We will respond to as many readers as we can. Your name, address, or phone number will never become part of a mailing list or be used for any purpose other than to help us continue to bring you the best books possible. You can write us at the following address:

New Riders Publishing
Attn: Associate Publisher
201 W. 103rd Street
Indianapolis, IN 46290

If you prefer, you can fax New Riders Publishing at (317) 581-4670.

You can send electronic mail to New Riders at the following Internet address:

`rrobinson@newriders.mcp.com`

NRP is an imprint of Macmillan Computer Publishing. To obtain a catalog or information, or to purchase any Macmillan Computer Publishing book, call (800) 428-5331.

Thank you for selecting *Inside Word for Windows 95*!

Part I

Word for Windows 95 Techniques

New Riders Publishing
INSIDE
SERIES

What's New in Word for Windows 95

If you've used previous versions of Word for Windows, you'll find that Microsoft Word for Windows 95 version 7.0 offers much that's familiar—but also much that's new. This chapter takes a brief look at Word's new features and points you in the direction of more detailed coverage elsewhere in the book.

In this chapter:

- Windows 95 features in Word 95
- New document automation features
- New templates
- Document highlighting
- Better integration with other Microsoft Office products
- New WordBasic statements
- More effective help

Making the Most of Windows 95's Features

Not surprisingly, Word 95 takes full advantage of the capabilities of Microsoft's new Windows 95. Of course, Word has been rewritten to take advantage of Windows 95's largely 32-bit architecture, as well as other Windows 95 features, such as preemptive multitasking. Time will tell, but this should mean more reliable, smoother performance than Word 6.0 provided in a Windows 3.1 environment.

Word 95 also supports Windows 95's more *document-centric* view of the world, in which the *document* you are working on becomes more important, and the *application* you happen to be using with that document becomes a bit less important.

The Windows 95 taskbar contains a Documents list, for example, that enables you to open a recently used Word (or other) document easily, without opening Word first. And, as discussed in the section "Property Sheets" later in this chapter, each Word document has a property sheet you can use to inspect its features and attributes in detail—regardless of whether you're working in Word at the time.

But Windows 95 also shows its presence in a variety of other features, including the following:

- Windows 95 interface
- Long file names
- New common dialog boxes
- Integration with Microsoft Exchange
- Full-featured faxing capabilities
- A direct connection to The Microsoft Network
- Property sheets

The Windows 95 Interface

In addition to a new, more subtle standard typeface for menus and a revised title bar, the standard Word window adds two new Windows 95 features. First, as with all programs running in Windows 95, the Windows 95 taskbar appears at the bottom of the screen.

Click on the taskbar's Start button to access any other program you've installed, to open a recently used document, or to change Windows 95 settings. Currently running programs appear in boxes from left to right to the right of the Start button; controls for speakers, modems, Microsoft Network connections, printers, and the current time and date appear at the right edge of the taskbar. Figure 1.1 shows the taskbar.

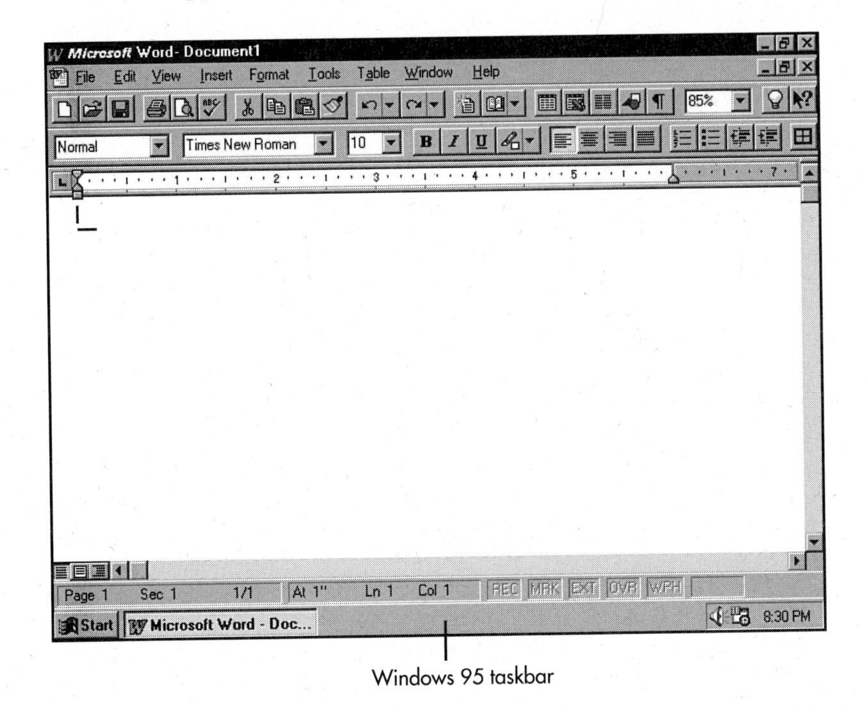

Figure 1.1

The Windows 95 taskbar at the bottom of the Word screen.

Windows 95 also updates the application and document control buttons at the top right of each window, as shown in figure 1.2. Now, there are three buttons:

- **Minimize.** Clicking the Minimize button on the Word title bar reduces the Word screen to a box on the taskbar (while keeping it running in the background). Clicking the Minimize button on a document window minimizes the document to its title bar and displays that title bar just above Word's status bar (unless other documents are open).
- **Restore.** This restores the Word screen or a document window to its previous size.
- **Close.** This button can be used to close Word or a document. If you click the Close button on a document with unsaved changes, Word asks if you want to save the document before closing.

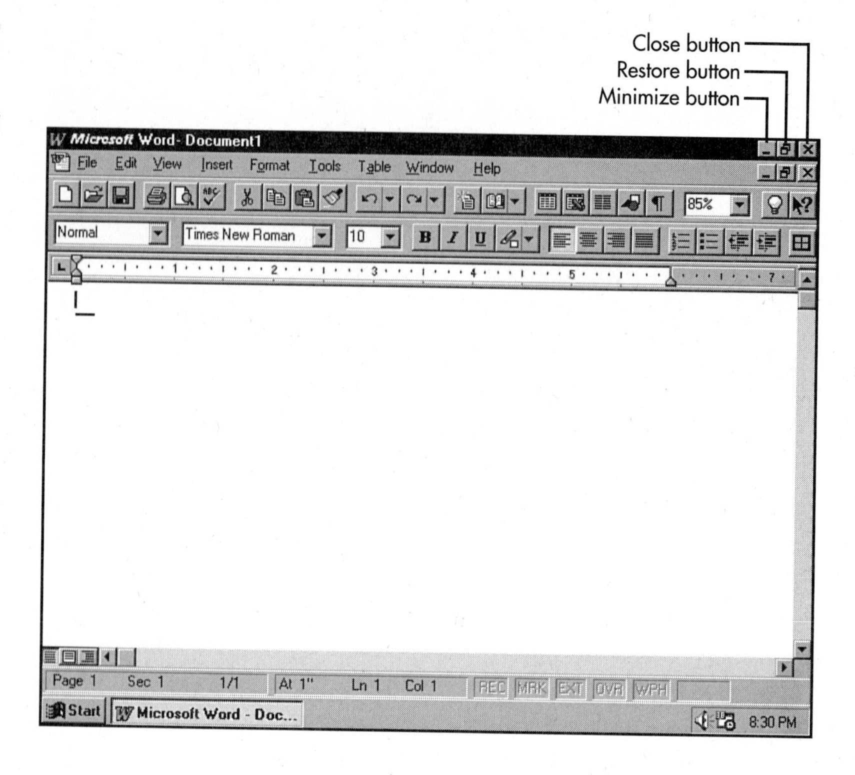

Figure 1.2
New Minimize, Restore, and Close buttons.

Long File Names

Word 95 is the first version of Word to support Windows 95's long file names feature. As with other programs designed for Windows 95, you can use file names as long as 255 characters, excluding only the following characters:

\ ? : * ? " < > |

And, for the first time, spaces are acceptable: you don't have to use underscore characters to simulate them anymore. This means that you can finally use file names others will understand—and you yourself will recognize the names when you come back to these files next year. See Chapter 6, "File Management," for more coverage on long file names.

New Common Dialog Boxes

Word shares new File Open, Save, and Print dialog boxes with other Windows 95 programs. These dialog boxes give you much more flexibility in finding and managing your files. The File Open dialog box, discussed in detail in Chapter 6, appears in figure 1.3.

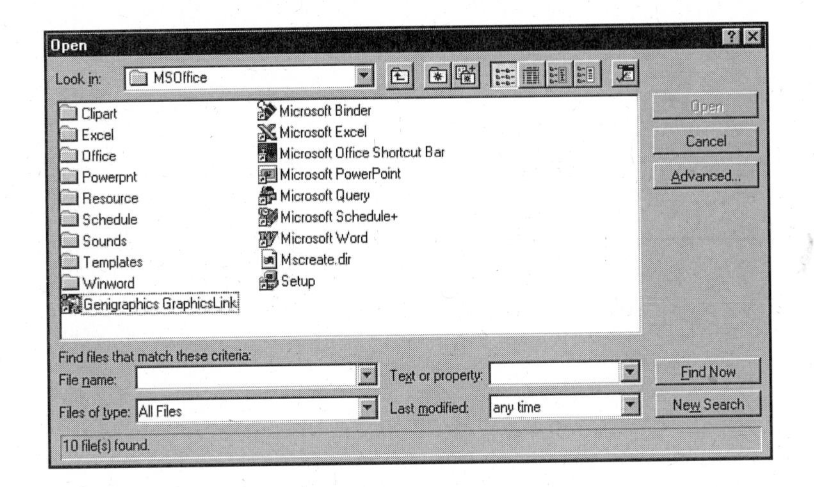

Figure 1.3

The new File Open dialog box.

Integration with Microsoft Exchange

Word 95 integrates with the new Microsoft Exchange e-mail system that comes with Windows 95. If you choose, you can use Word as your e-mail editor. This feature, called *WordMail*, gives you access to Word's powerful formatting and organization features in your e-mail messages. WordMail is shown in figure 1.4 and covered in more detail in Chapter 20, "Word as an Integrating Environment."

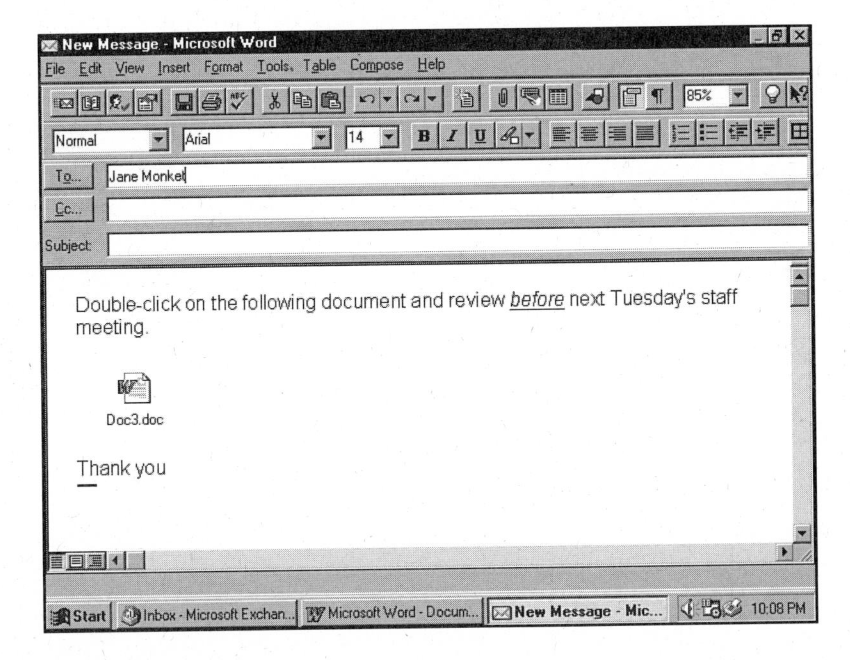

Figure 1.4

Using Word as an e-mail editor (WordMail).

To use WordMail you must have Microsoft Exchange installed on your system. Because using WordMail is essentially the same as opening another version of Word, you'll need at least 12–16 MB of RAM to effectively use WordMail. Otherwise, you can use the simpler but effective built-in editor that comes with Exchange.

Regardless of whether you choose to use the WordMail feature, you can benefit from another new Microsoft Exchange feature: Personal Address Books.

For many PC users, maintaining all address and contact information in one place has been nearly impossible. You can store names in a personal information manager or database program, fax numbers in a fax program, and e-mail addresses in a communications program or front-end programs to information services such as WinCIM for CompuServe.

As time passes, more applications are likely to support the Personal Address Book, as Word 95 does today. Also, Microsoft Exchange is likely to support e-mail connections with more online services. As these two trends proceed, it's possible that you will finally be able to consolidate all your names and contact information in one place accessible to all your applications.

Word can already use Microsoft Exchange Personal Address Books to do the following:

- Address letters (see Chapter 20)
- Act as the data source for mail merges (see Chapter 19, "Automating Mail Merge Tasks")
- Address envelopes (see Chapter 4, "Printing and Faxing")
- Compile labels (see Chapter 4)
- Send faxes (see Chapter 4)
- Insert names, addresses, and other information anywhere in a document (see Chapter 20)

Figure 1.5 shows the Microsoft Exchange window that appears when you ask to use a name from a Personal Address Book.

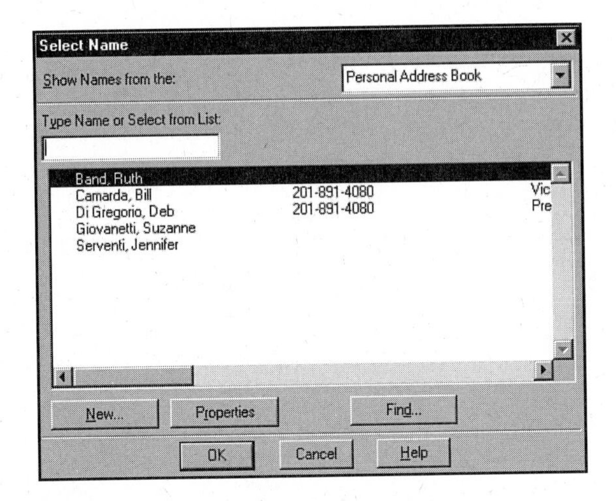

Figure 1.5

The Select Name dialog box from Microsoft Exchange.

Easy Faxing from Within Word

If you have a fax modem and have installed Microsoft Exchange with the Microsoft Fax option, you have easy faxing capabilities from within Word and, as mentioned earlier, you can use your Microsoft Exchange Personal Address Book to store fax numbers.

Faxing from Word is covered in detail in Chapter 4, but briefly, you can send a fax by choosing the Microsoft Fax driver from the list of installed printers in the File, Print dialog box and clicking OK. Word presents the Fax Wizard, which walks you step-by-step through addressing your fax, creating a cover sheet, and sending the fax. The Fax Wizard opening screen appears in figure 1.6.

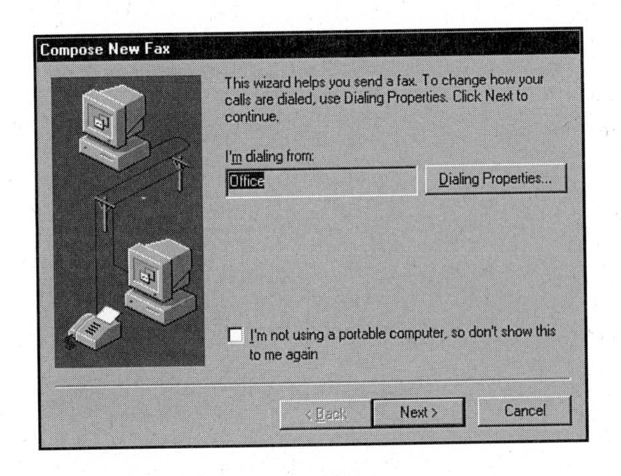

Figure 1.6

The Fax Wizard opening screen.

Direct Connection to The Microsoft Network

You can connect directly from Word to The Microsoft Network's Word Help forum, by choosing The Microsoft Network from the Help menu. Figure 1.7 shows a connection to The Microsoft Network's Help resources for Microsoft products. Of course, you have to be a member of The Microsoft Network. Remember that extensive online help for Word continues to be available on the MSWORD forum on CompuServe.

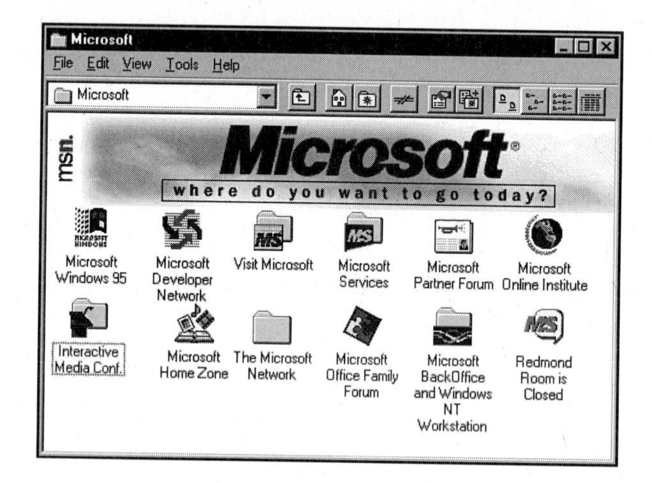

Figure 1.7
The Microsoft Network's Help area for Microsoft products.

Property Sheets

Word documents, like other Windows 95 documents, have property sheets. These *property sheets* are tabbed dialog boxes that enable you to provide and inspect detailed information about a document, regardless of whether you're working in the document, or even working in Word. Property sheets are covered in detail in Chapter 6; Figure 1.8 shows a sample Property tabbed dialog box.

In implementing property sheets, Microsoft has gone beyond the requirements of Windows 95—enabling users to customize any Property categories they need, while automatically tracking detailed document statistics and expanding on the information previously available in Word 6's Summary Info dialog box.

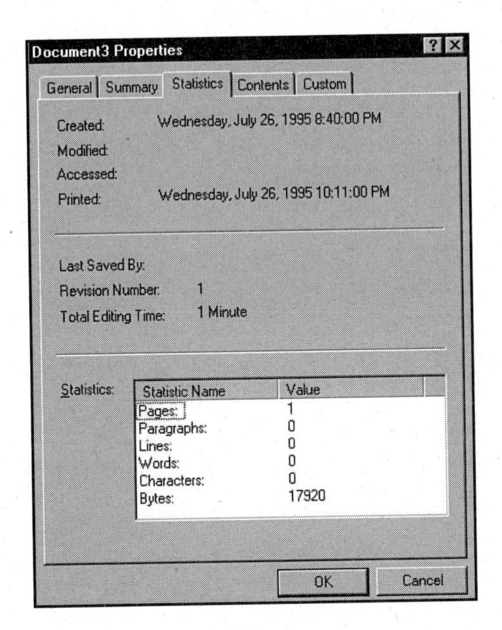

Figure 1.8
A Word document property sheet.

New Document Automation Features

Following in the footsteps of Word 6, Word 95 takes some additional steps toward automating the production of documents. The following are among the new, high-profile features built into Word 95:

- Spell Checking as You Type
- AutoFormat as You Type
- New AutoCorrect options

Spell Checking as You Type

By default, Word 95 tracks spelling errors as you type, marking them with a wavy red underline (see fig. 1.9). You can right-click to select a context menu that enables you to correct the spelling mistake immediately, or add the word to your dictionary so that it isn't flagged again.

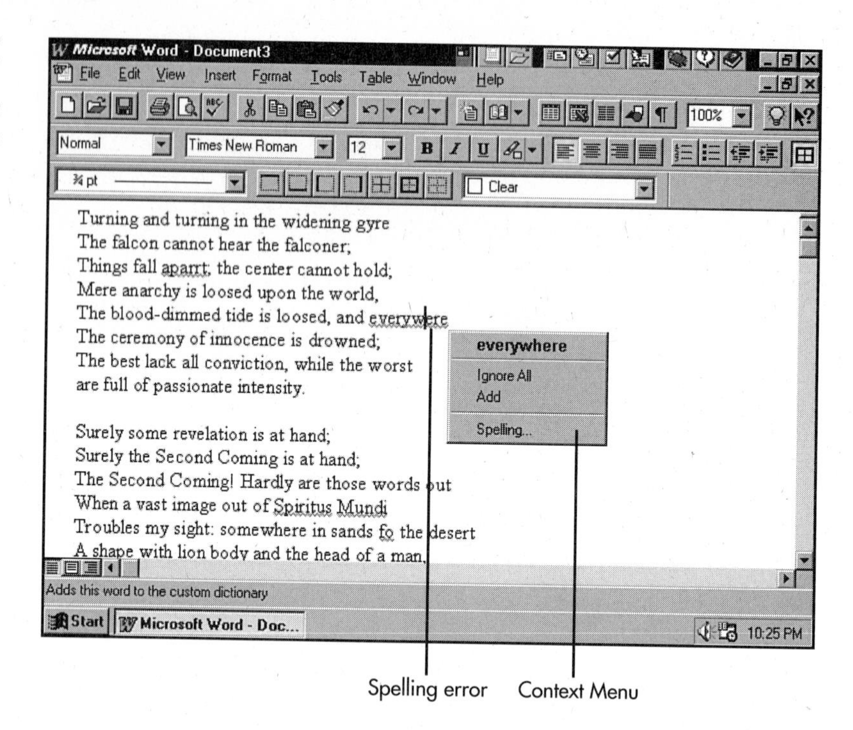

Figure 1.9

Spelling mistakes automatically flagged by Word.

If you find automatic spell checking distracting, you can turn it off and perform spell checking whenever you want, as in Word 6.

AutoFormat as You Type

Word 6 introduced AutoFormatting, a feature that enabled Word to interpret your text entries and apply formatting to them, such as heading styles. Word 95 now applies the same interactivity to AutoFormatting as with spell checking: if you want, Word can now trail behind you, automatically formatting your document as you work. Word also can interpret and autoformat a few more document elements; for example, if you enter a series of dashes, Word can automatically reformat it as a more attractive border.

Figure 1.10 shows Word 95's AutoFormat as You Type feature at work. Notice the *Tip Wizard,* which describes what Word has done and offers you the opportunity to undo it. AutoFormatting is covered in more detail in Chapter 7, "Styles and AutoFormatting."

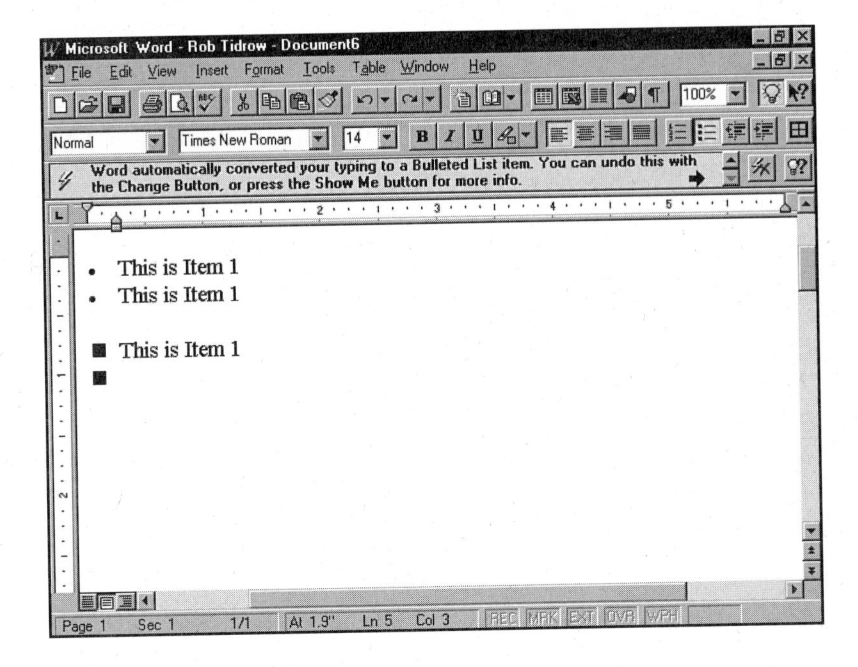

Figure 1.10

AutoFormat as You Type.

New AutoCorrect Options

Word 95 enhances the AutoCorrect feature first introduced with Word 6. First of all, it now comes with a library of 350 commonly misspelled and mistyped words. Second, it converts more combinations of characters like :) and —> to ☺ and →. Finally, AutoCorrect now has the flexibility to enable you to create exceptions for selected words, as shown in figure 1.11.

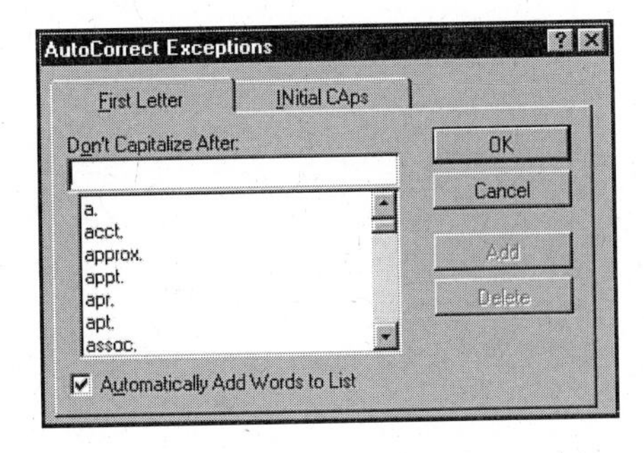

Figure 1.11

The AutoCorrect Exceptions dialog box.

If you use an abbreviation that ends with a period, for example, you can now tell Word not to automatically capitalize the following word as if it were a new sentence. All in all, AutoCorrect should be a much more usable feature in Word 95 than it was in Word 6.

New Templates

Not as well promoted, but perhaps equally important from a business productivity standpoint, the Word 95 template library has been revamped into three coordinated design schemes that are easy to use and will make it appear that your organization has spent thousands of dollars on corporate design standards.

You can choose from among contemporary, elegant, and professional versions of memos, fax cover sheets, reports, press releases, resumes, and other documents. Simply choose the same style for each document, and all your documents will share a consistent look. Figures 1.12 and 1.13 show Word's designs for a professional report and letter, so you can see how they work together. Templates are covered in more detail in Chapter 8, "Templates and Wizards."

Figure 1.12
Professional Report template.

Blue Sky Airlines

Proposal and Marketing Plan

Blue Sky's Best Opportunity
For East Region Expansion

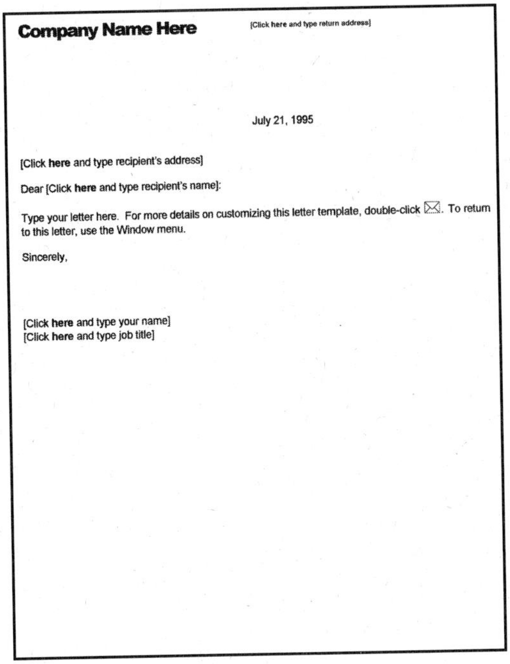

Company Name Here [Click here and type return address]

July 21, 1995

[Click **here** and type recipient's address]

Dear [Click **here** and type recipient's name]:

Type your letter here. For more details on customizing this letter template, double-click ✉. To return to this letter, use the Window menu.

Sincerely,

[Click **here** and type your name]
[Click **here** and type job title]

Figure 1.13
Professional Letter template.

Document Highlighting

Many people learned in school to highlight important parts of a document with a transparent highlighting pen. Now you can do this in Word as well. Select the text you want to highlight, and click the Highlight button on the Formatting toolbar (see fig. 1.14). Word can highlight in 15 colors; choose your color from the list that appears when you click the down-arrow next to the Highlight button. To view more colors, click the down-arrow and then drag the mouse pointer down and to the right.

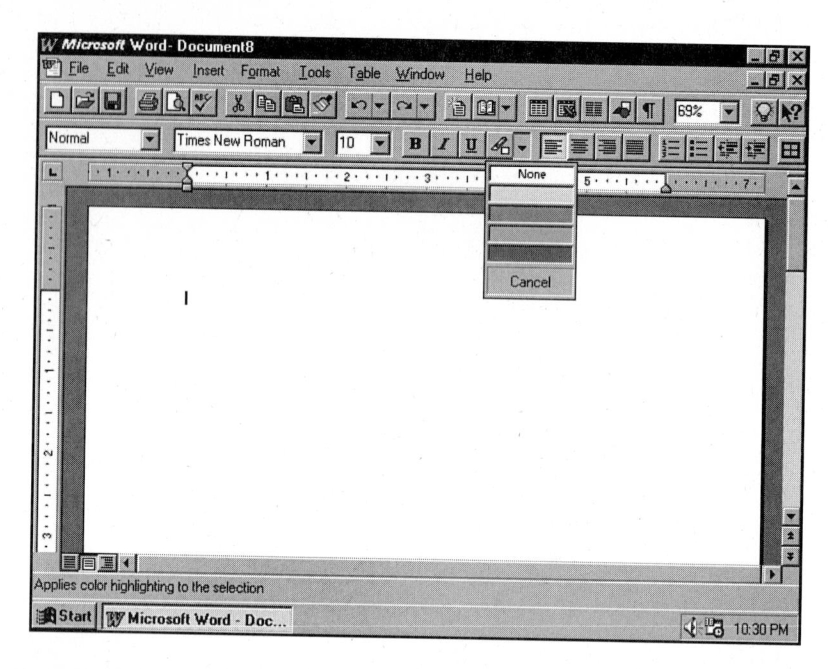

Figure 1.14
Choosing a highlight color.

Better Integration with Other Microsoft Office Products

If you purchased Word as part of Microsoft Office, you can benefit from two new features that help integrate Word with the rest of Office. The Microsoft Office Shortcut Bar, shown in figure 1.15, lets you perform any Office task or open any Office program from icons appearing at the top of your screen (whether you're in Word or another program).

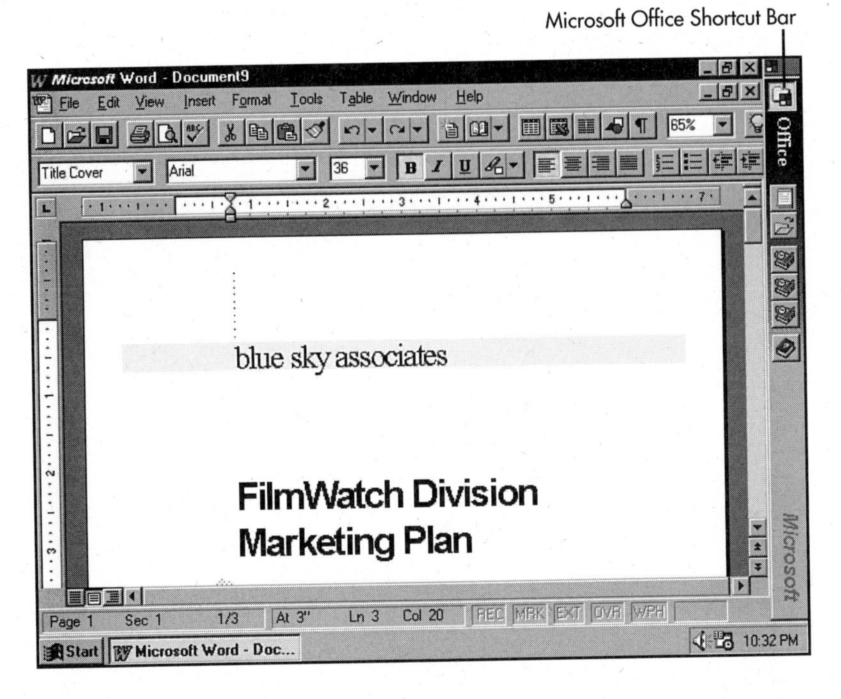

Figure 1.15

The Microsoft Office Shortcut Bar.

The new Binder feature enables you to combine Word documents with each other, or with other Office documents, to create a binder of related documents that can be transported and used together. Office comes with the following built-in binders, as well as a blank binder to which you can add from scratch your own documents and templates:

- Client Billing
- Meeting Organizer
- Proposal and Marketing Plan
- Report

Binders are covered in more detail in Chapter 20. You can choose a binder by clicking on the Start a New Document button in the Microsoft Office Shortcut Bar and choosing the Binders tab. Figure 1.16 shows the binder for developing a proposal and marketing plan.

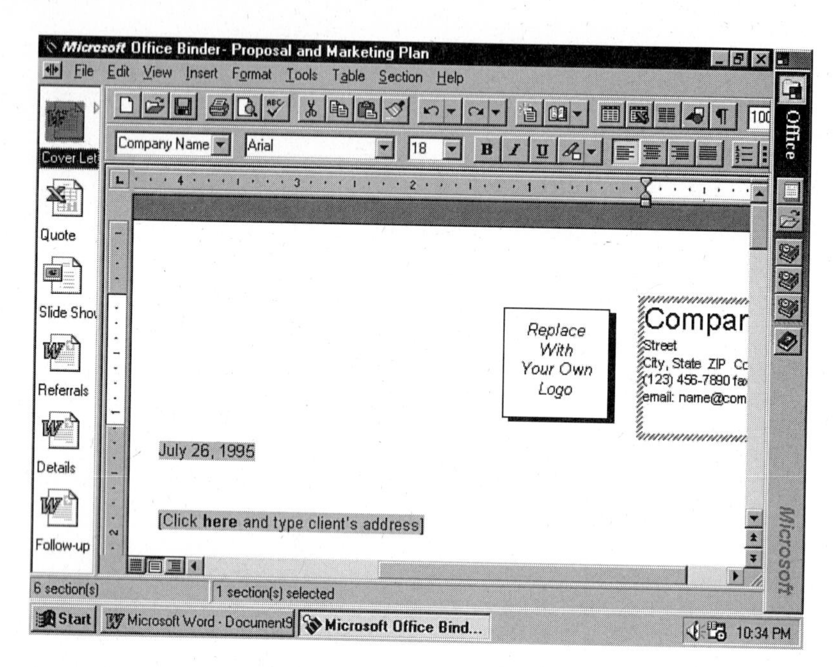

Figure 1.16

The Proposal and Marketing Plan Microsoft Office Binder.

New WordBasic Statements and Functions

If you use WordBasic, you'll be pleased to know that nearly all of Word's new features have corresponding WordBasic statements, so you can automate these features in WordBasic macros. There are nearly 50 new WordBasic statements and functions, and some existing functions take new arguments to handle Word 95 features.

Some advanced users hoped that WordBasic would be replaced in Word 95 by a new version of Visual Basic for Applications (VBA) comparable to (and compatible with) the language used by Microsoft Excel. However, Microsoft decided to hold off on VBA until the next version of Word. According to Microsoft, implementing VBA will require significant alterations to Word that couldn't have been completed in time to meet Word 95's anticipated shipping date. When VBA for Word is implemented, you also can expect Word's file format to change as well.

More Effective Help

Word's Help system has been revamped to comply with Windows 95 guidelines. In general, you'll find more focused help and fewer help screens providing background information. Word's help system includes an Answer Wizard where you can briefly describe what you're looking for and have Word search for the help you need, as shown in figure 1.17:

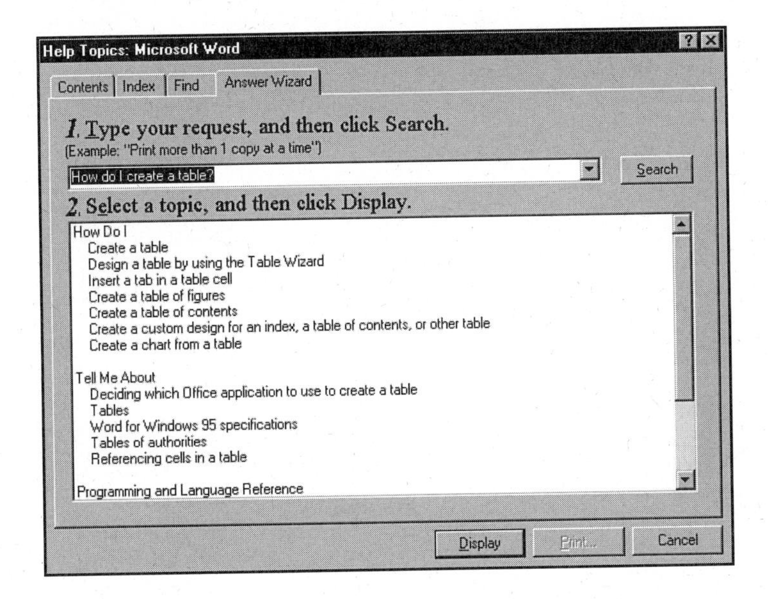

Figure 1.17

The Word Answer Wizard.

In addition, most dialog boxes contain Help (?) buttons. To get help about a specific element of the dialog box, click the Help button and then click the area you want help on.

As mentioned earlier, Word 95 introduces the Tip Wizard, which not only helps you keep track of Word's AutoFormatting, but also watches how you work and presents suggestions on better ways to perform common tasks.

New System Requirements

Unfortunately, as with any software or system upgrade, moving to Word 95 and Windows 95 might mean you will need more hardware than before. A practical bare minimum memory requirement for Word 95 and Windows 95 is 8 MB. In my experience, you get much better performance with 16 MB, especially if you have any intention of running other Windows 95 applications at the same time as Word. Many computers will require hardware upgrades to run the combination of Windows 95 and Word 95.

Things That Haven't Changed

There's also much that hasn't changed since the previous version of Word. The standard Word menus, Standard toolbar, and Formatting toolbar have very few changes. Complex features like mail merge work the same way; Word can still be customized the same way.

Organizations in which some users have Word 95 and others are still using Word 6 for Windows (or for Windows NT or the Macintosh) will be pleased to learn that the Word file format has not changed. Of course, Word 6 running under Windows 3.1 will not support long file names; any long file names you use will be truncated to a short file name equivalent created by Windows 95 for this purpose. There are a few other issues, as well:

- Word 95 stores some document properties that Word 6 cannot store; these are lost if the document is opened in Word 6 and resaved.
- Word 95 provides highlighting; this too disappears if the document is saved in Word 6.
- WordBasic macro commands specific to Word 95 features generally return error messages when run in Word 6.

A Note about Internet Assistant for Word 95

Soon after the release of Word 95, Microsoft was expected to introduce an add-in program, Internet Assistant for Word 95, that would enable Word to act as a basic Internet World Wide Web Browser, and would help you automate the development of Hypertext Markup Language (HTML) documents that can be published on the World Wide Web.

For information on the status of Internet Assistant for Word 95, check Microsoft's Internet ftp server (ftp.microsoft.com); or go MSWORD on CompuServe; or connect to the Microsoft area on The Microsoft Network.

Document Essentials

This chapter brings together several formatting tasks you are likely to encounter on a daily basis: headers and footers, time-stamping documents, adding page numbers, creating bulleted and numbered lists, and using symbols.

As usual, Word not only streamlines these tasks, it also gives you much more control over them than most previous word processors.

In this chapter:

- Using the header and footer window
- Using tabs in headers and footers
- Adding page numbers
- Creating bulleted and numbered lists
- Creating multilevel lists
- Using symbols: the poor man's clip art

Using Headers and Footers

A *header* is text that appears at the top of each page; a *footer* is text that appears at the bottom of each page.

Typically, headers are used to identify chapters, topics, or other information common to part or all of a document. Footers commonly include page numbers. In manuscripts, headers or footers can include the author's name, the date and time, draft numbers, the status of the document, and other information.

These are merely conventions, however—almost anything you can place in a Word document, you can put in a header or footer.

A few things you cannot add to a header or footer are footnotes, bookmarks, annotations, section breaks, multiple columns, and tables of contents.

You might, for example, include your company's logo, as in the sample product sheet shown in figure 2.1.

With information like this already in place, you could start with this document every time you introduced a new product.

Better yet, include additional standard formatting, and turn the document into a template. (See Chapter 9, "AutoText, AutoCorrect, and the Spike.")

On the CD

The accompanying CD-ROM contains a file you can use to practice some of the procedures in this chapter: IWMS2A.DOC.

To insert a header or footer in Normal view, choose **H**eader and Footer from the **V**iew menu. Word switches you into Page Layout View and shows you a screen such as the one in figure 2.2.

As you can see, by default you are placed in the Header area at the top of the current page. For the first time, you can see the context in which your header appears. Your actual document text appears dimmed, in light-gray text, beneath it, as shown in figure 2.3.

We're proud to introduce...

Another safe pesticide from Elkins Environmental

Figure 2.1

Sample product sheet with logo in footer.

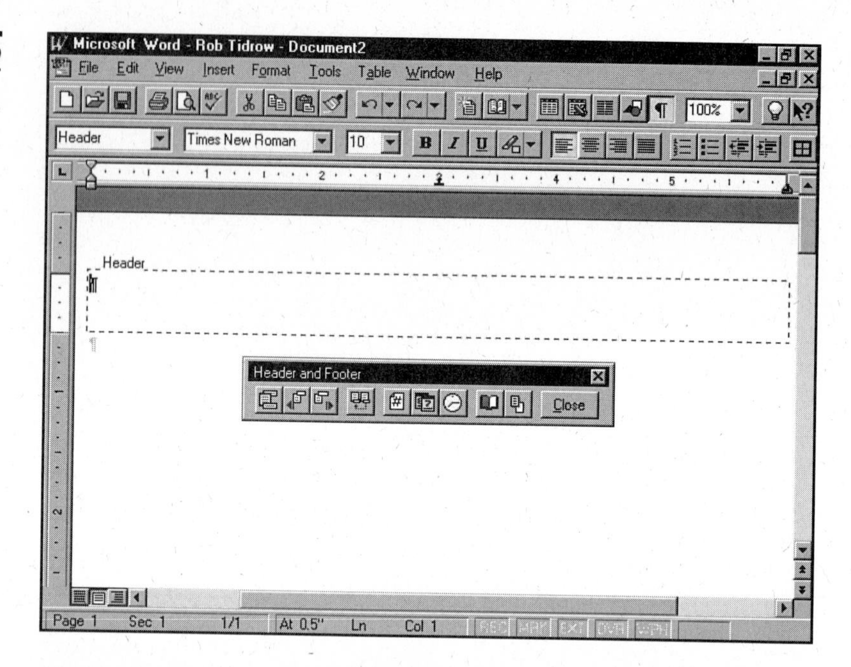

Figure 2.2
The Header area.

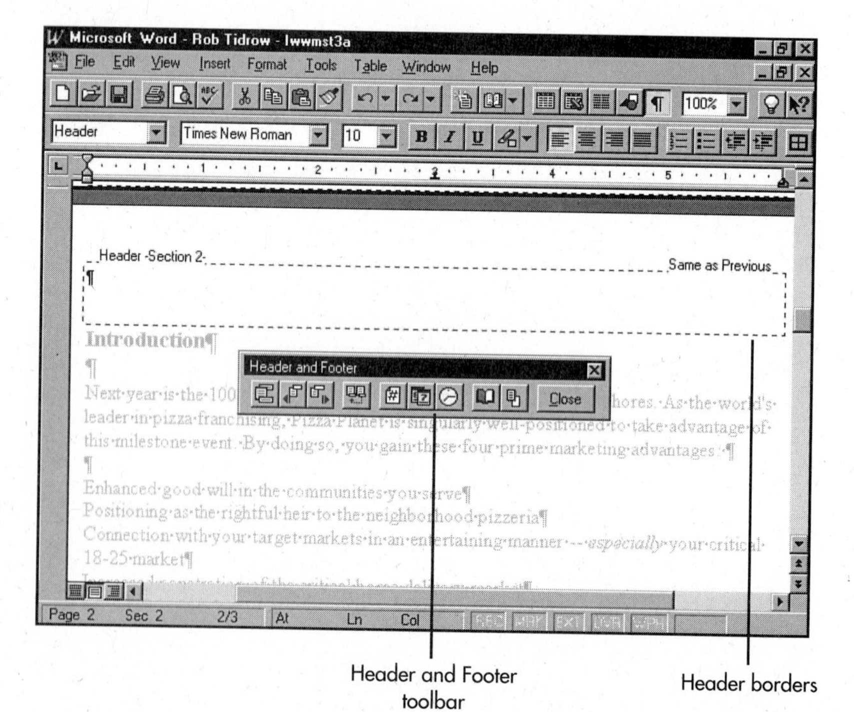

Figure 2.3
Typical Header window.

Word also displays the Header and Footer toolbar. Its buttons are described in table 2.1.

Table 2.1
Header and Footer Toolbar

Button	What It Does
Switch Between Header and Footer	Toggles between displaying header and footer.
Show Previous Header	Shows header associated with preceding section.
Show Next Header	Shows header associated with next section.
Same As Previous Header	Links or unlinks a header from preceding section.
Page Numbers	Inserts a page field.
Date	Inserts a date field. Uses whichever date format you last chose in Insert Date and Time.
Time	Inserts a Time field.
Page Setup	Opens the Page Setup dialog box so you can change margins, paper size, paper source, or document layout.
Show/Hide Document Text	Toggles between displaying light-gray body text in the background and showing no text in the background.
Close	Closes the Header or Footer window.

If you want to work with a footer, click on the Switch Between Header and Footer button.

You can also view and edit your headers and footers by switching to Page Layout View and double-clicking the header or footer you are interested in. The appropriate header or footer area will open.

If you want to work on both the header and the footer in a section, switch to Page Layout View and position your page so that both the bottom of one page and the top of the next are visible. Then double-click either the header or the footer.

continues

If you are in Print Preview, you can edit or move a header or footer by double-clicking on it with the arrow pointer. This opens the header or footer area and displays its toolbar. (If you have a magnifying-glass pointer instead, click on the magnifying glass in the Print Preview toolbar to switch back to the arrow pointer.)

Just about any editing or formatting you can do in a regular Word editing window, you can do in a header or footer area, as well. You have access to all Standard toolbar, Formatting toolbar, and Ruler shortcuts, all basic editing and formatting menu selections, and most keyboard shortcuts.

Word normally styles both headers and footers with left-aligned, Times New Roman, 10-point type. You can change this manually, or by changing the header style, as discussed in Chapter 5, "Spelling and Grammar." You can also use headers or footers to add a graphic that appears on every page. Word calls this a *watermark*.

A Note from the Author

Actually, a true watermark is a translucent image often added to fine paper during manufacture and only visible when you hold the paper up to the light. Nothing Word or your laser printer can do will create that kind of watermark.

More loosely, the term has come to mean any image that appears behind text on every page. Companies often use large copies of their logos this way. Occasionally, a company uses a watermark to make it clear that a document is confidential or only a draft, as in figure 2.4.

Word mentions watermarks in the headers and footers part of its documentation because you can create a watermark only by using a header or footer. Headers and footers are really only the first steps involved in creating a watermark. You need several techniques that are covered in Chapter 21, "Desktop Publishing and Drawing."

After you create the header or footer and move it to where you want the watermark to appear, you can import an image or create a text box by using Word's drawing tools.

Use Word's drawing tools to lighten the image (unless you want it to print black, which would make other text difficult to read). Finally, send the object behind the text layer—another drawing technique that tells Word to print text over it.

President	But you see if I say, "Dean, you leave today," he'd go out and say, "Well, the President's covering up for Ehrlichman and Haldeman" alright. There you are. "Because he knows what I know." That's what he would say. I tried to put -- I mean -- I'm trying to look and see -- John -- what we are really up against. First it was Liddy (unintelligible) scapegoat, now John Dean is.
Haldeman	Well, the answer to that is if he said it publicly, the President is not covering up for anybody, and will not tolerate --
President	The way he's put it to me, Bob, very cute, as I have said, "Son of a gun (unintelligible) in view of what you have told me, if Haldeman and Ehrlichman are willing to resign, and so forth, I too, will resign." In other words, he has basically put the shoe on the othr -- wich of course is what led me to the conclusion that that's exactly what his attorney told him to do. If he can get Haldeman and Ehrlichman, that some way gets him (unintelligible) that's what you have here.
Ehrlichman	Yeah, because then that will be argued back to the U.S. Attorney, "Well you see, the President thought enough of Dean's charges to let these guys go."
President	I was trying to indicate to him that both of you had indicted a willingness to -- in the event -- that you know what I mean.
Ehrlichman	And here's a guy that comes in and in effect, confesses to you the commission of crimes.
President	And charges you.
Ehrlichman	And charges us, that's right.
President	That's right. And I said, "Now wait -- these charges are not --" and you see he also has an alibi in the U.S.Attorney --
Ehrlichman	Small wonders.
President	He's asked (inaudible) Attorney General that the President should act --

TOP SECRET

Figure 2.4
Sample watermarked document.

Opening Headers and Footers from Normal View

Many people who once used Word 2 do not care for the Header and Footer area, in part because it tends to run very slowly. (You have to wait for Word to switch to Page Layout View and then for Word to redraw the entire page each time you move between pages.)

For those who prefer a different way of working with headers and footers, Microsoft has included a macro, NormalViewHeaderFooter, that enables you to edit headers and footers from within Normal View, just as you might have done in Word 2. NormalViewHeaderFooter is located in the MACROS7.DOT file, which is typically installed in the WINWORD\MACROS folder. (If you have installed Office 95, look for the MSOFFICE\WINWORD\MACROS folder.) There are several ways to make NormalViewHeaderFooter available for use; these are described in Chapter 11, "Macros."

These macros are not installed in the default Word installation, but can be included in a custom installation. To install them, run Word's Setup program, choose Custom Installation, and specify that you want to include macros.

The simplest way to make NormalViewHeaderFooter available every time you run Word is to move MACROS7.DOT into the \WINWORD\STARTUP folder. Then every time you run Word, NormalViewHeaderFooter—and all the other macros in MACROS7.DOT—is automatically loaded into memory.

Now that the macro is available, you have to run it. Open the file containing the outline you want to export (you do not need to open the file in Outline view). Choose Macro from the Tools menu. Choose NormalViewHeaderFooter from the Macro Names list, and choose Run.

Word displays a dialog box asking which of your current headers and footers you would like to edit. This dialog box also gives you control over where headers and footers appear on the page and enables you to specify different headers and footers for the first page, or for left- and right-hand pages. Choose your settings and choose OK. A window appears at the bottom of the screen, where you can type your header or footer. When you are finished, choose Close.

Moving a Header or Footer within the Page

By default, Word places its headers and footers outside the top and bottom margins, no closer to the edge of the page than a half inch. Because your default page margins are one inch at the top and bottom, the header and footer areas normally are a half inch deep.

If your header is more than one line, the additional lines move inward on the page, toward your document's text.

If your header or footer extends into the area where document text normally would be printed, Word moves in the document's margins so that the header or footer text does not overlap the document.

The following section tells you how to change nearly everything discussed in this section.

Changing the Distance from the Edge of the Page

To change how close to the edge of the page a header or footer begins, click the Page Setup button in the Header and Footer toolbar. Choose the Margins tabbed dialog box. In the From Edge group (see fig. 2.5), use the spin boxes to set new distances for the Header or Footer.

Note You can use Page Setup Margins to change this setting at any time, not only from within Headers and Footers.

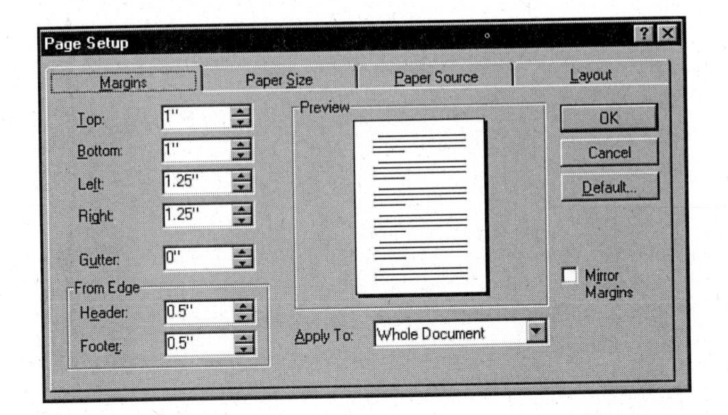

Figure 2.5

From Edge group, Page Setup Margins dialog box.

You also can use Word's vertical ruler to change the location of the header and footer and to change the space made available for it. When you are in a header or footer area, the space set aside for it appears as a white rectangle in the vertical ruler (see fig. 2.6).

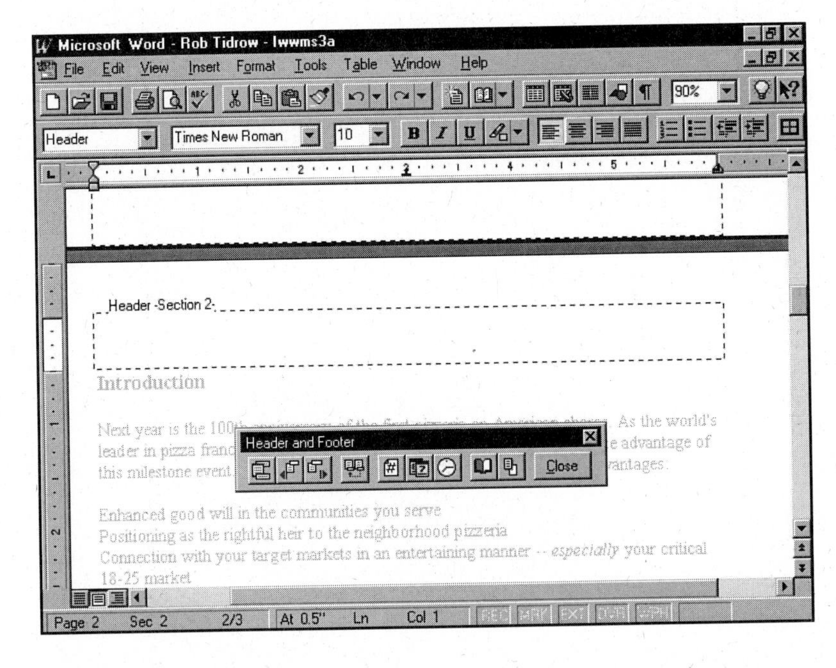

Figure 2.6

Vertical ruler's header area.

To expand or shrink the header or footer area, move the mouse pointer to the top or bottom of this white rectangle, and drag it to the edge. If you expand the header or footer area into an area previously set aside for document text, Word automatically changes your document margins so that the header and document do not overlap.

Using Tabs in a Header or Footer Area

Instead of Word's normal half-inch tabs, Word provides only two preset tabs within its header and footer areas. These tabs provide easy ways to create centered or flush-right headers and footers.

When you press the first tab, your text center-aligns within the area. When you press the second tab, Word aligns the text against the right margin.

As in other parts of your document, you can add custom tabs for the entire header or footer, or only for one paragraph within it.

Creating Additional Headers and Footers

Until now, your document contains only one header and one footer. Many documents require several headers and footers. For example:

- Documents might require headers or footers containing chapter headings or other material that changes throughout the document.
- Books might require different footers on left- and right-hand pages.
- Letters and many other documents use no header or footer on the first page.

Word gives you control over all these aspects of headers and footers.

Using Different Headers and Footers in Each Section

Headers and footers are based on sections. When your document contains only one section, your header or footer appears on every page of the document unless you specify otherwise.

You can split a document into multiple sections by using **I**nsert, **B**reak. Then you can create separate headings for each section, each with its own text, formatting, and location.

Whenever you divide a document or a section into two sections, the second section starts out with the same header or footer as the first.

In early versions of Word, after you split a document into sections, each header or footer had a completely independent existence. That is no longer necessarily true. Because many documents are divided into multiple sections but still carry a single header or footer, Word now assumes that when you make a change in one section's header or footer, you want to make the same change in all your other headers or

footers. In other words, by default, all your headers are connected to each other. Similarly, all your footers are connected to their fellow feet.

You can tell when a header or footer is taking its cues from a previous one, because the words Same as Previous appear at the top right of the header or footer area (see fig. 2.7).

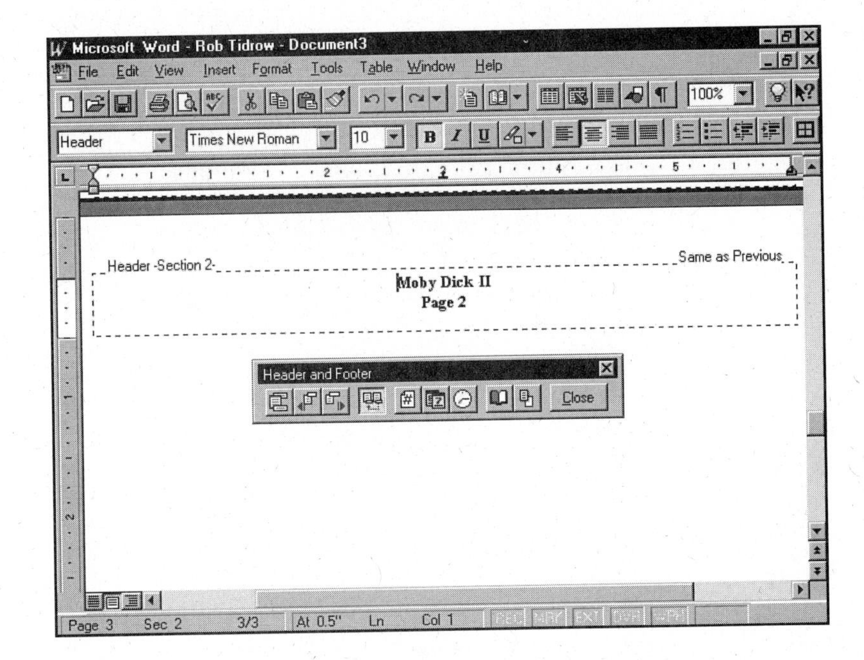

Figure 2.7

Same as Previous header.

In addition, the Same as Previous button is depressed on the Header and Footer toolbar. To change this header or footer without changing others too, click on the button. Now the button is no longer depressed, and your header or footer has been liberated from its shackles.

You can always reconnect a header or footer to the one preceding it in the document. This replaces whatever is in the current header or footer with whatever is in the previous one. Click the Same as Previous button again. You will be asked to confirm the change (see fig. 2.8). Choose Yes.

Word's Header and Footer toolbar makes it easy to move through the document, changing headers and footers. The Show Previous button moves you to the end of the previous section and displays its header or footer. The Show Next button moves you to the beginning of the next section and displays its header or footer.

Because the page's text is visible, it is easier to decide what should appear in the header or footer. You can also use the scroll bars to move through the page, look for a heading, or look for a main point.

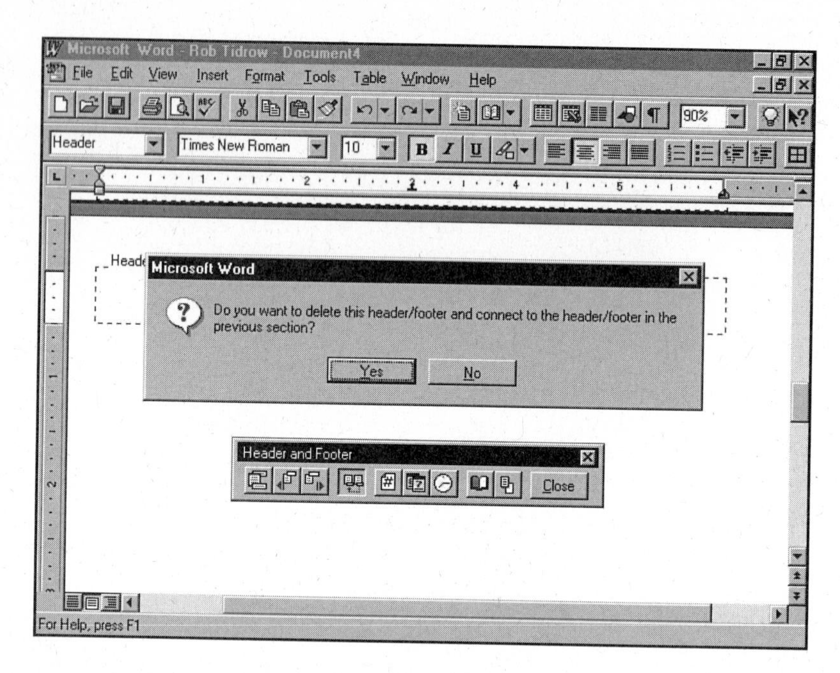

Figure 2.8 *Confirming that you want to reconnect a header.*

If, on the other hand, you simply want to make straightforward edits to existing headers or footers, you might want to speed up Word a bit by pressing the Show/Hide Document Text button. When you do this, Word does not redraw the entire new page before showing your header or footer area.

Changing First Page and Odd/Even Headers and Footers

You can control whether Word allows for different headers and footers on odd and even pages of a section or document, or on the first page. To do so, follow these steps:

1. Open the Page Setup, Layout dialog box.

   (You can do this from within the Header and Footer area by clicking the Page Setup button. From elsewhere, select File, Page Setup, and choose the Layout tab.)

2. In the Headers and Footers group, check Different Odd and Even to set up separate header and footer areas for odd and even pages.

3. In the Headers and Footers group, check Different First Page to set up a separate header or footer for the first page.

4. Click on OK.

When you display one of these header or footer areas, it is identified as in figure 2.9.

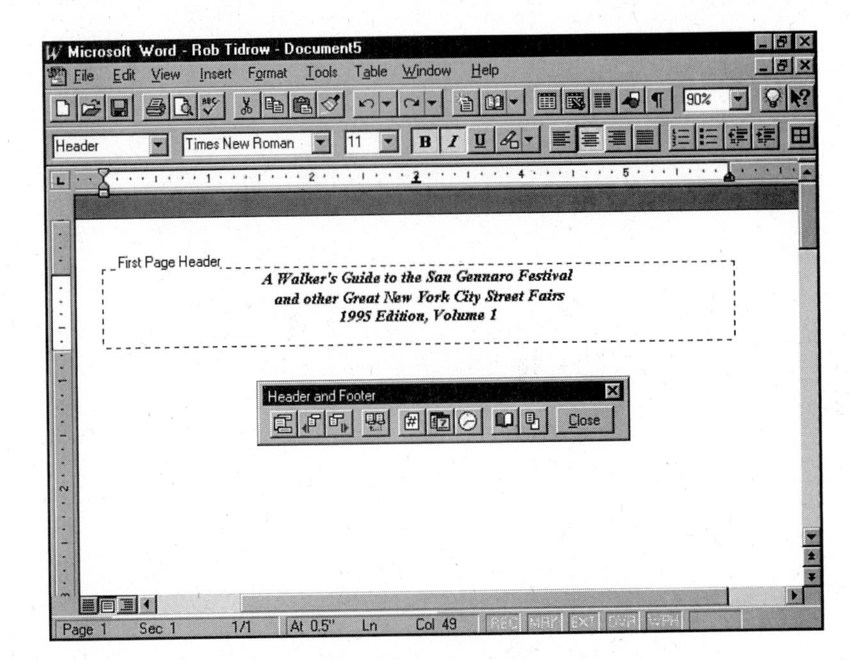

Figure 2.9

First page header.

Time-Stamping a Document

You can add the time or date to a document. In a header or footer, you can use the Time or Date buttons shown in figure 2.10.

The keyboard shortcuts are Alt+Shift+D (date) and Alt+Shift+T (time). As with Alt+Shift+P (page number), these can be used anywhere in a document. You might, for example, use Alt+Shift+D to include a date on a memo or on the cover of a business proposal.

By default, header and footer dates and times appear in the following format:

11/16/93 3:28 PM

You can change this formatting by selecting the entire date or time and choosing Insert, Date and Time. The Date and Time dialog box appears (see fig. 2.11).

Choose a format from the Available Formats list and click on OK. From now on, Word uses this format anywhere you request a date or time, in any document, until you change it again.

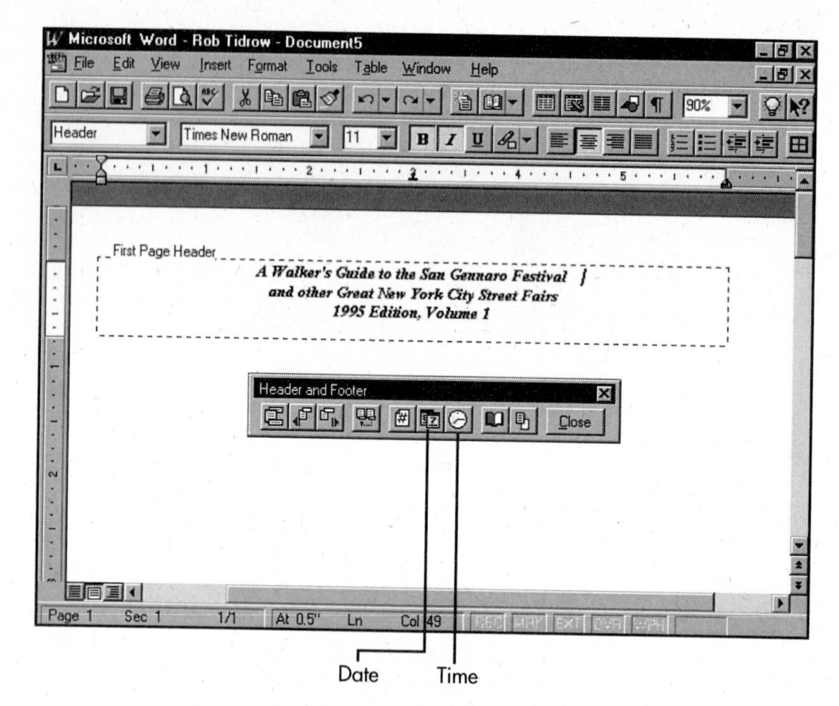

Figure 2.10
Time and Date buttons.

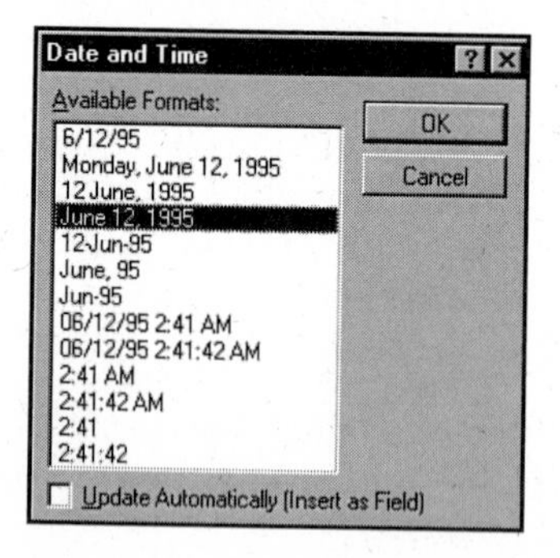

Figure 2.11
Date and Time dialog box.

If you think you might want to update the date and time later, check the Insert as Field box.

What if you always use a different date or time format from the one that Word's Date and Time dialog box presents as the default? By using an obscure macro, RegOptions, which is new to Word 95, you can change the default. RegOptions lets you control a variety of Word settings. Like the macro NormalViewHeaderFooter, presented earlier, RegOptions is stored in the MACROS7.DOT file in the

WINWORD\MACROS folder. Follow the instructions presented there to make it available for use. Then run the macro, choose DateFormat from the Item list box, choose Change, make the change you want in the Value text field, and choose OK.

Updating the Date and Time

Word includes the current time or date as of the moment you insert it. This date or time continues to display in the header or footer area until you update it—assuming you inserted it as a field, as just discussed. (Dates and times inserted with the Header and Footer toolbar buttons are fields.)

To update the date and time, select them and press F9. To update the date and time automatically whenever you print the document, do the following:

1. Choose Tools, Options.
2. Choose the Print tabbed dialog box.
3. Check the Update Fields area.

To prevent the time and date from being automatically updated, do the following:

1. Select the date and time.
2. Press Ctrl+F11 or Ctrl+Alt+F1.

This key combination "locks" the time and date. To "unlock" them, so they can be updated, do the following:

1. Select the date and time.
2. Press Ctrl+Shift+F11 or Ctrl+Shift+Alt+F1.

Time and Date are fields. You can learn more about how to use fields, and how they behave, in Chapter 10, "Field Codes."

One more field, CreateDate, is worth mentioning here. CreateDate enables you to insert the date a document was created—information that Word stores even after the document is revised.

To use CreateDate in a header, footer, or elsewhere, follow these steps:

1. Choose Insert, Field.
2. Choose CreateDate from the Field Names area.

3. If you are satisfied with the default date-time format you have been using, click on OK, and you are finished.
4. To use a different date-time format, choose Options.
5. Choose the date-time format you want from the Date-Time Formats area.
6. Choose Add to Field, and click on OK.
7. Click on OK.

Adding Page Numbers to Your Document

From within the header or footer area, you can add page numbering to your document by clicking on the Page Numbers button in the Header and Footer toolbar.

Tip: You can also add page numbering by using the shortcut Alt+Shift+P. As with the date and time shortcuts, you can use Alt+Shift+P anywhere in a document, not just in header or footer areas.

When you add page numbers by using this method, the number 1 appears at your insertion point in the header or footer area. This indicates the page number format and the starting page number Word will use to number this section. You can, of course, add text to the page number, reformat it, or move it.

Using Insert Page Numbers

By default, Word numbers pages in Arabic (1, 2, 3), beginning with the number 1. If you prefer a different page numbering format—or if you merely want to include bare page numbers, without anything else—there is a better way to do it. Rather than opening a new Header or Footer editing area, choose Insert, Page Numbers. The Page Numbers dialog box appears, as shown in figure 2.12.

First, choose whether you want your page numbers to appear in the Header (Top of Page) or Footer (Bottom of Page). Then, in Alignment, choose where you want your footer to appear: Left, Center, Right, or on Inside or Outside pages. You can control whether a page number appears on the first page by checking or unchecking the Show Number on First Page box.

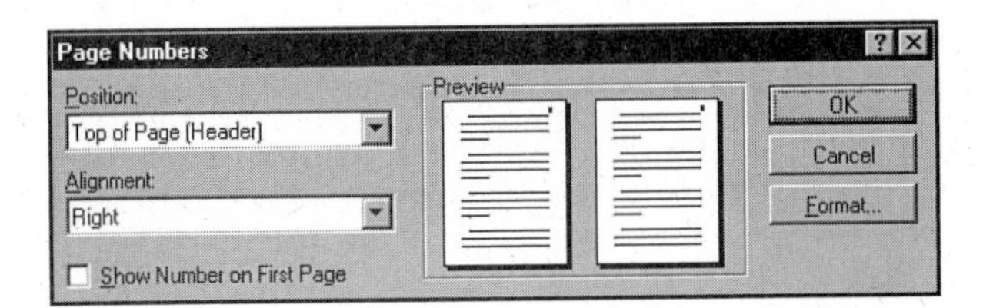

Figure 2.12

Page Numbers dialog box.

If you want to change the format of your page numbers, or your starting number, choose Format. The Page Number Format dialog box appears, as shown in figure 2.13.

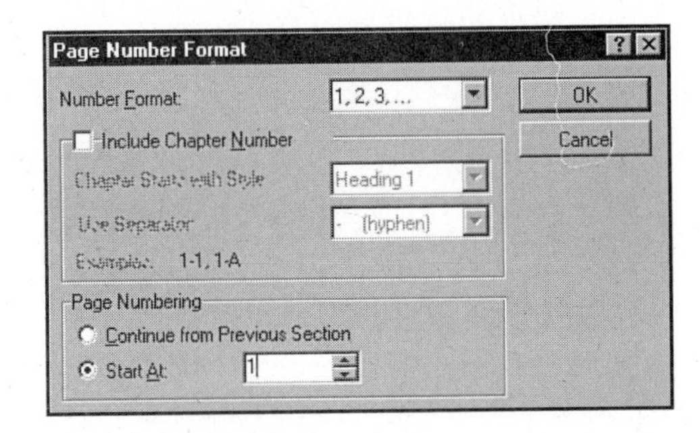

Figure 2.13

Page Number Format dialog box.

The Number Format list area gives you the following five choices:

1,2,3... Arabic numerals

a,b,c... Lowercase alphabet

A,B,C... Uppercase alphabet

i,ii,iii... Lowercase Roman numerals

I,II,III... Uppercase Roman numerals

The most common use for this feature is in a document with a preface or an introduction that uses lowercase Roman numerals.

When you choose another numbering scheme, such as A, B, C, this new numbering scheme appears in the status bar as well (see fig. 2.14).

A Note from the Author

Small but nice improvement. In older Word versions, if you changed the number format of a header or footer area that you had already edited, Word replaced all the additional formatting and text with the new page number. This no longer happens.

continues

continued

Let's say, for example, you insert a Roman numeral page number and format it as 18-point, Arial Bold Underlined. Then you go back into Insert Page Numbers and change it to regular Arabic numbers (1, 2, 3...). The page number remains formatted as 18 point, Arial Bold Underlined—and the other text in the header area is unchanged.

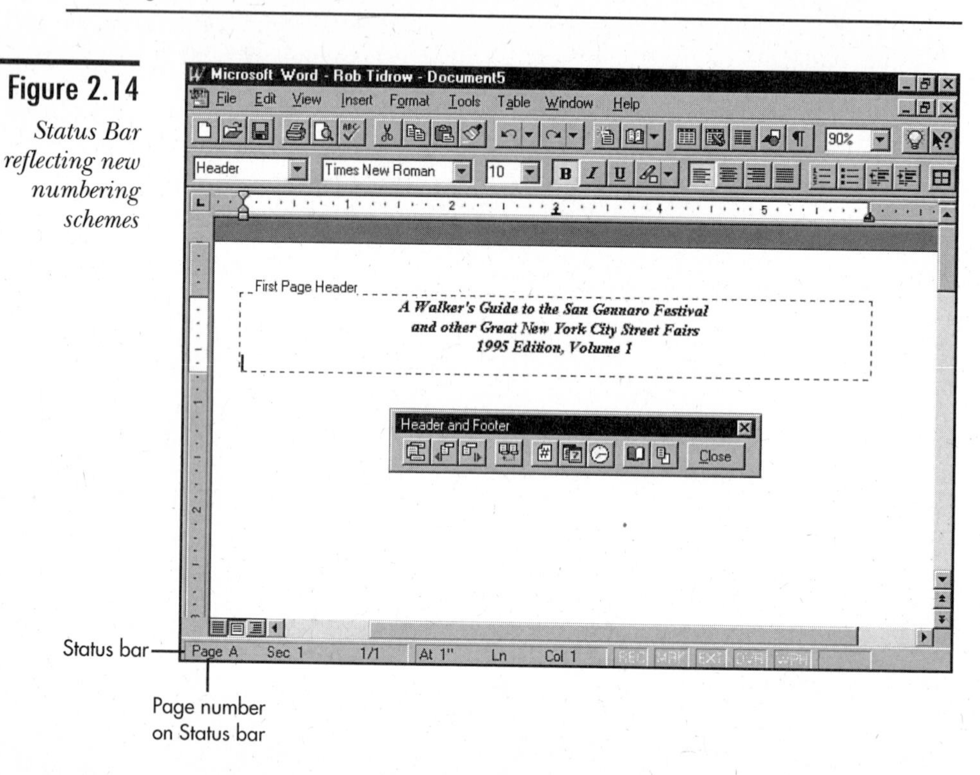

Figure 2.14
Status Bar reflecting new numbering schemes

Adding Chapter Numbers to Headers or Footers

Word makes it easy to add chapter numbers to your page numbering. To do so, you need to include your chapter numbers as text within your document, set apart from other text by a paragraph mark. Then format the text by using one of Word's styles—or one of your own.

Chapter 7, "Styles and AutoFormatting," covers styles in detail. In this example, use Word's existing default style for highest-level headings, which is called Heading 1. (If you don't use Heading 1, you have to use one of the other eight heading styles. You can make them look any way you want, as explained in Chapter 7.)

To specify Heading 1, follow these steps:

1. Select the chapter number in the document.
2. Choose Heading 1 from the Style box on the Formatting toolbar (see fig. 2.15).

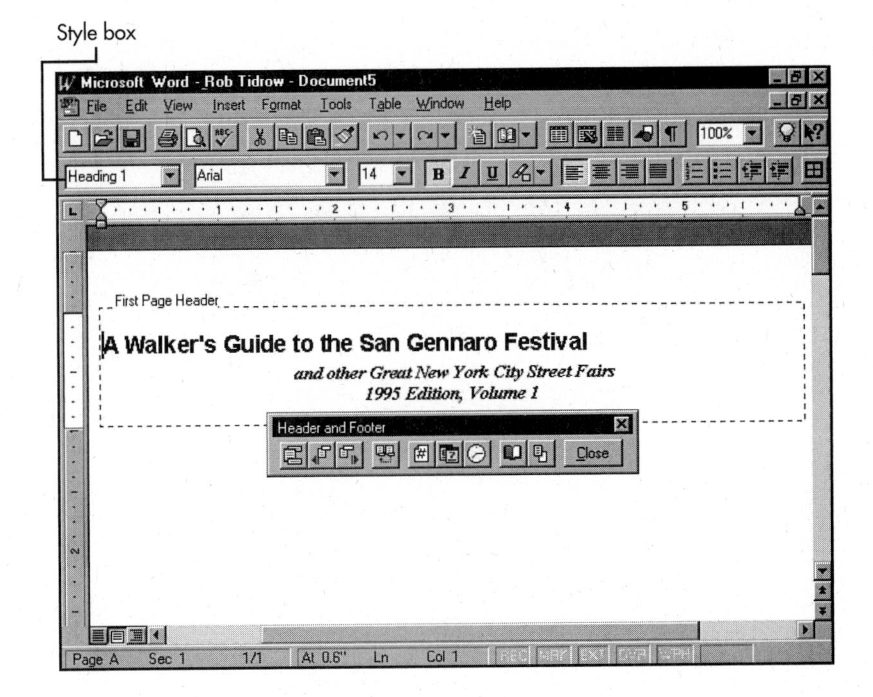

Figure 2.15
Style box.

3. Choose **I**nsert, Page N**u**mbers.
4. Choose F**o**rmat.
5. Check the Include Chapter **N**umber box. The boxes beneath it, Cha**p**ter Starts with Style and Use S**e**parator, become usable.
6. In Cha**p**ter Starts with Style, choose Heading 1 from the list of available heading styles.
7. In Use S**e**parator, pick one of the following characters to separate your heading number from your page number:

   - Hyphen

   . Period

: Colon

— Em dash

– En dash

8. Click on OK.

Having now assigned Heading 1 to chapter numbers, do not use it for anything else, or you will confuse Word unmercifully.

Controlling Starting Page Numbers

You can control the number Word uses as its starting number. By default, Word continues page numbering from section to section. As already mentioned, if you have only one section, Word starts with page 1.

Note: If you have a document with multiple sections, Word will place page numbers only in the sections you select. Unless you tell it otherwise by choosing Start At, Word will take all the document's pages into account when it assigns page numbers.

You can, however, start with any page number. Choose Start At, and type the page number in the list area.

This feature is most commonly used to number a document that is being appended to another document. If you have a 40-page document, for example, you can begin the next document's page numbering with 41.

Note: **The catch.** There is a problem, of course: What if you add a page to the first document? All the documents that follow are numbered inaccurately. There is a solution: Combine several documents into a master document. You learn how to do this in Chapter 18, "Annotations, Revisions, and Master Documents."

If you choose Insert, Page Numbers, you can still open your header or footer editing area later and add text or formatting to the page numbering that Insert, Page Numbers already put there.

Using Bullets and Numbered Lists

Two other very common tasks in creating a document are creating bulleted lists such as the following:

Great Elvis Presley Singles

- ◆ Heartbreak Hotel
- ◆ Don't Be Cruel
- ◆ Hound Dog
- ◆ Jailhouse Rock
- ◆ Suspicious Minds

and numbered lists such as these:

The World's Largest Islands

1. Greenland
2. Guinea
3. Borneo
4. Madagascar
5. Baffin Island

Word streamlines both. This section starts with bulleted lists.

Using Bulleted Lists

As the song says, "everything old is new again." Word for Windows 95 introduces a new feature that takes advantage of the way people created bulleted lists before there were sophisticated word processors.

At the beginning of the first item you want to bullet, type the letter o or an asterisk, as in the following examples:

o This is item 1

or

* This is item 1

Word automatically converts the o or * into a round bullet and continues to add bullets to each following paragraph, formatting each bulleted item with a hanging indent of 0.25" (unless you specify a different hanging indent in Format, Paragraph). To get a square bullet, begin each sentence with a hyphen:

- This is item 1

Samples of Word's automated bullets are shown in figure 2.16.

Figure 2.16 *Samples of Word's automated bullets.*

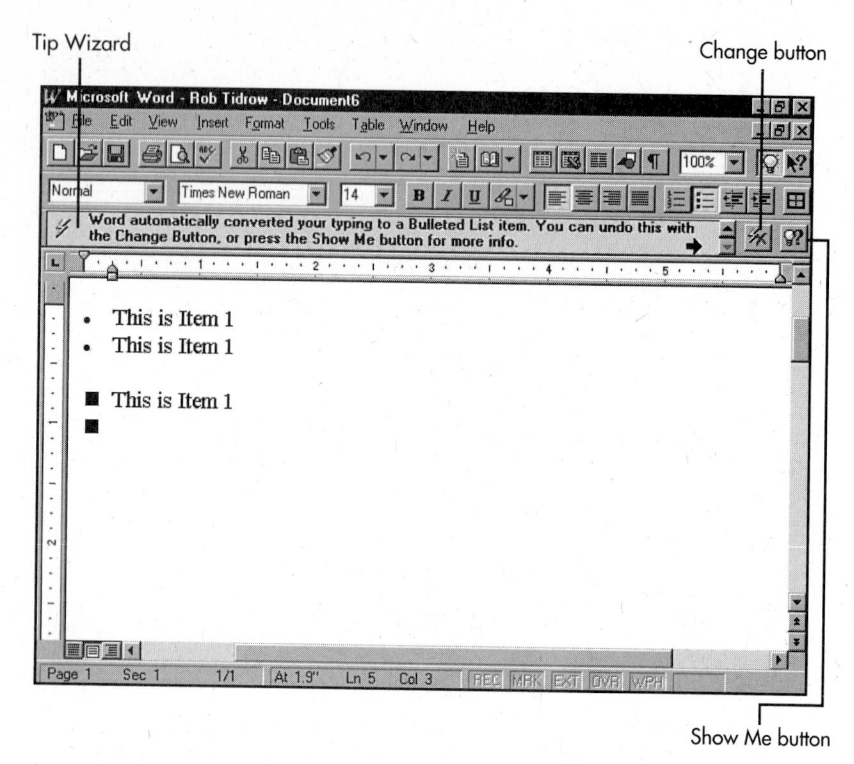

What happens when you do not want Word to automatically start adding bullets to a list? If Francis Scott Key had Word, he would have wanted it to leave his lyric alone:

> O say can you see
>
> by the dawn's early light…

When Word makes its automatic change, the Tip Wizard appears. Normally, the Tip Wizard presents routine tips about using Word more efficiently, but now it shows you the change it has made, and offers you a chance to undo the change. Two buttons appear with the Tip Wizard: the Change button and the Show Me button, as shown in figure 2.16. To tell Word to switch back to your original keystrokes, click on the Change button. If you never want Word to insert bulleted lists automatically, follow these steps:

1. Choose Options from the Tools menu.
2. Click on the AutoFormat tab.

3. Click on the AutoFormat as you Type check box.

4. Clear on the Automatic Bulleted Lists check box.

5. Choose OK.

Word also offers a Toolbar button for bulleted lists. Select the list and click on the button shown in figure 2.17.

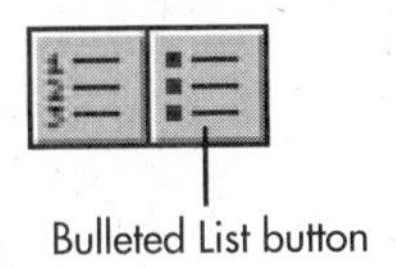

Figure 2.17

The Bulleted List button.

As with Word's automatic bulleted list feature, this button also creates hanging indents. It also uses Word's default bullet (•), which corresponds to character #183 of the Symbol font.

To create a bulleted list with a different hanging indent or bulleted character, first select the text to be bulleted. Then choose Bullets and Numbering from the Format menu. The Bullets and Numbering dialog box appears. Choose the Bulleted tab (see fig. 2.18).

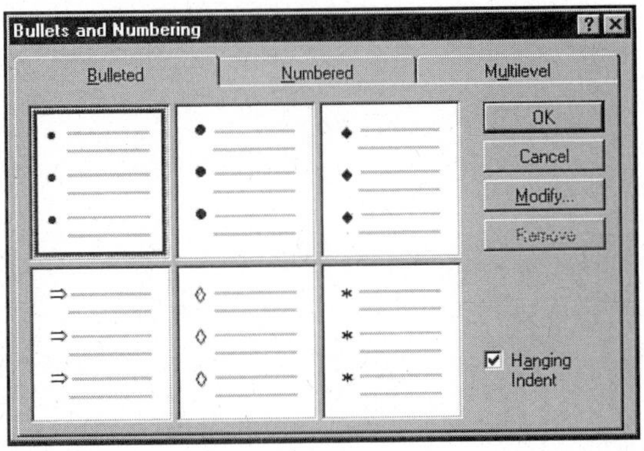

Figure 2.18

Bullets and Numbering dialog box.

To change the bullet character, either choose one of the other five preset bullets, or choose Modify. The Modify Bulleted List dialog box appears, as shown in figure 2.19.

You can specify another common bullet from the Bullet Character group. You can also specify the point size and color of your bullet. (By default, Word makes your bullets the same size and color as the surrounding text; you can change that here as well.)

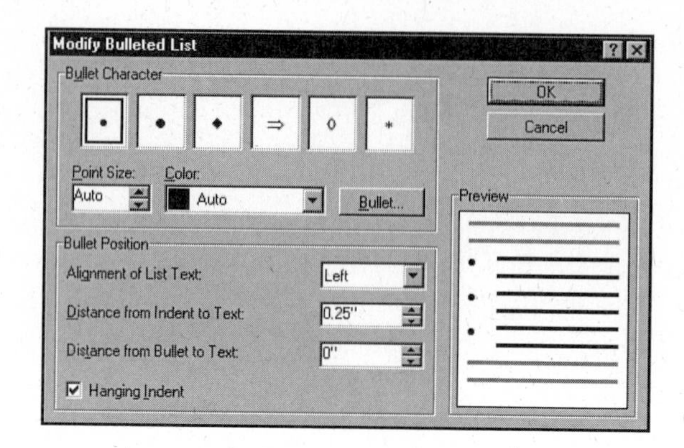

Figure 2.19
Modify Bulleted List dialog box.

In Bullet Position, you can choose from the following aspects of how your bulleted lists appear:

- **Alignment of List Text.** Controls whether the text accompanying your bullets is flush left, centered, or flush right.
- **Distance from Indent to Text.** Sets how much space is placed between the left indent and the first-level paragraphs.
- **Distance from Bullet to Text.** Sets how much space is placed between the bullets and their accompanying text.
- **Hanging Indent.** Specifies whether the bulleted list uses a hanging indent.

Any change you make is immediately reflected in the Preview box.

Changing to Another Bullet Character

Until now, you have focused on Word's six default bullet characters. But you can use any character, in any font, as a bullet. To replace one of Word's six default bullet characters with another bullet, select it in Bullet Character, and choose Bullet.

This displays a complete set of symbols from the Windows Symbol font, as shown in figure 2.20.

If you don't like any of these symbols, click on the Symbols From list for a choice of other fonts that include available symbols. One great source of potential bullets is the Windows TrueType font Wingdings, shown in figure 2.21.

When you click on a symbol, a larger version of it appears. If that is the one you want, let go and click on OK. If not, click on another symbol. To add the bullet, click on OK in the Bullets and Numbering dialog box. (In the section "Using Symbols: The Poor Man's Clip Art," later in this chapter, symbols are discussed in more detail.)

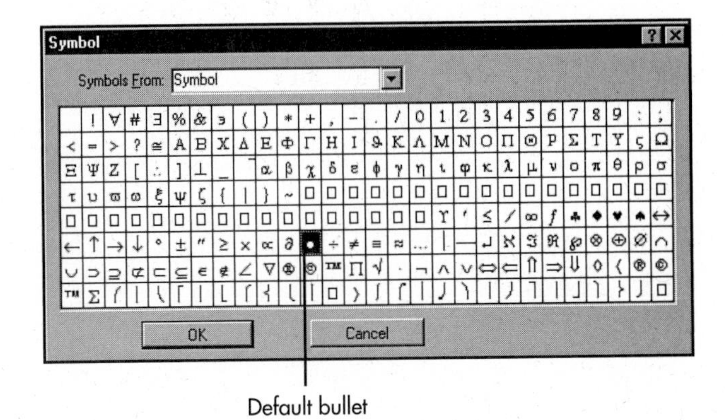

Figure 2.20

The Symbol dialog box.

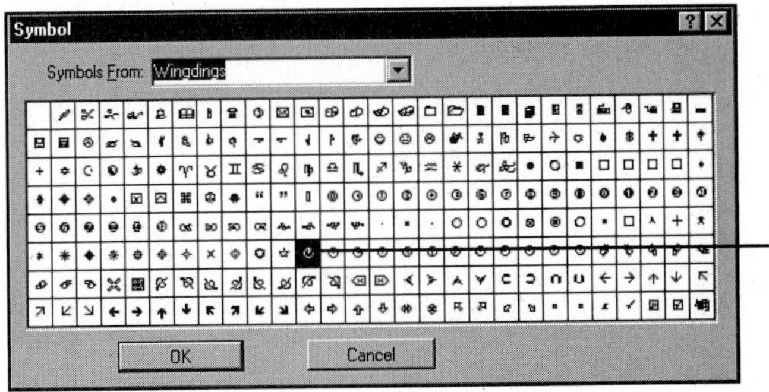

Figure 2.21

The Wingdings font.

Here is a sample of a custom bullet from Wingdings:

Call us!

- Call 1-800-555-1234 for sales
- Call 1-800-555-3577 for technical support
- Call 1-800-555-1969 for service

You can also change a set of bullets that you have already created by selecting them and then following the steps just covered.

How to create a bullet consisting of several text characters is discussed in the next section.

When you create a new bullet, Word uses it as your default bullet until you choose another bullet, either in the Bullets and Numbering dialog box or in the Modify Bulleted List dialog box.

To remove bullets, select the text containing them, choose Format, Bullets and Numbering, then choose the Bulleted tab and choose Remove.

Word 6.0 changed the way bulleted lists behave after you create them. If you go to the end of a bulleted list and press Enter to create a new row, the new row begins with a bullet automatically. Similarly, if you use Enter to create a new row within a bulleted list, it automatically has a bullet.

Using Numbered and Lettered Lists

Numbered lists work much like bulleted lists. First of all, Word for Windows 95 contains a new numbered list shortcut that corresponds to the bulleted list shortcut described earlier. Start a sentence with a number followed by a period, as in the following example:

1. What's the story?

Word automatically starts numbering every sentence that follows, adding a hanging indent. If you choose a number other than 1, Word increments the number by 1 at the beginning of the next sentence. Word also creates consecutively lettered lists as you type, if you start a sentence with A., a., (a), or another letter formatted the same way.

As with bulleted lists, you can countermand Word's action by clicking on the Change button that appears next to the Tip Wizard after Word makes its change. You can also tell Word never to create an automatic numbered or lettered list:

1. Choose Options from the Tools menu.
2. Click on the AutoFormat tab.
3. Click on the AutoFormat as you Type check box.
4. Clear the Automatic Numbered Lists check box.
5. Choose OK.

Word for Windows 95 also offers a Numbered List toolbar shortcut, as shown in figure 2.22. To number a list, first enter the list, then select the text and click on the toolbar button.

If you move paragraphs within a numbered list, Word automatically renumbers them, keeping the numbering consecutive.

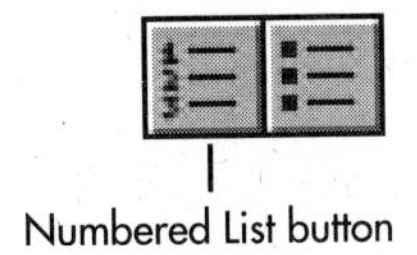

Figure 2.22

Numbered List button.

Numbering numbers. If the first paragraph in your numbered list already starts with a number, Word replaces that number with the first number in its numbered list. This is not always what you want. For example, when you number this list...

Pre-CD record player speeds:

16 rpm

33 rpm

45 rpm

78 rpm

...you get this:

1 rpm

2 rpm

3 rpm

4 rpm

A workaround is to add a nontext character to each line, add the numbered list, and then delete the nontext characters.

For more control over your numbered list, choose Format, Bullets and Numbering, then choose the Numbered tab. The dialog box shown in figure 2.23 appears.

As with bullets, you can choose one of six standard numbering styles. You can also tell Word whether to use Hanging Indents. You can really take control over your numbering options by choosing Modify. The Modify Numbered List dialog box opens (see fig. 2.24).

As usual, Word gives you more formatting control than you might know what to do with. You have several choices for the Number Format:

1, 2, 3

I, II, III

i, ii, iii

A, B, C

a, b, c

1st, 2nd, 3rd

One, Two

First, Second

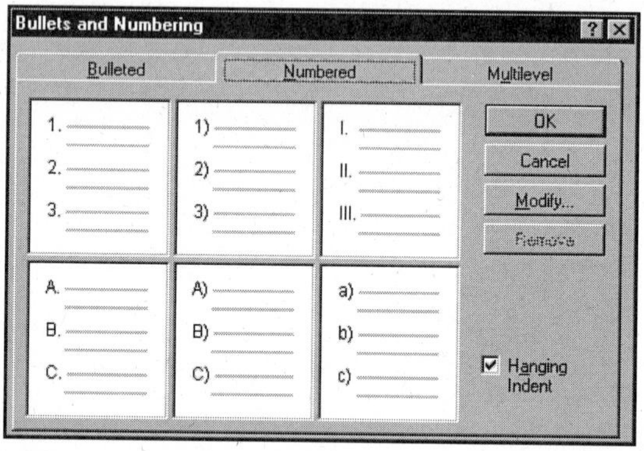

Figure 2.23

Bullets and Numbering Numbered dialog box.

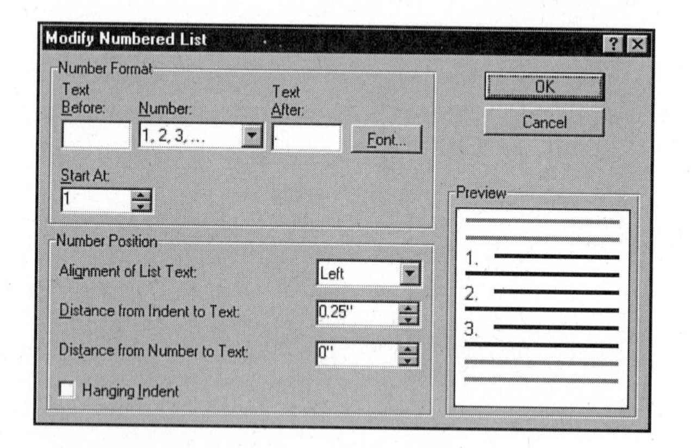

Figure 2.24

Modify Numbered List dialog box.

You can also specify the text before and text after your number so that you can number a list like this:

Chapter 1.

Chapter 2.

Chapter 3.

or like this:

1st Avenue:

2nd Avenue:

3rd Avenue:

If you are creating a new numbered list format, and you want a colon (or other separator) to appear after the number, you have to add it. It does not appear automatically, and this dialog box no longer presents a default separator character.

You can also choose no numbering at all. That is neat; it enables you to type several characters and use them as if they were bullets.

A Note from the Author

Choosing no numbering comes in real handy for me. New Riders Publishing's layout staff recognizes [lb] as the code for a bullet. Finally, I have an easy way to send them bulleted lists like this:

[lb] Microsoft Word

[lb] Microsoft Excel

[lb] Microsoft Access

You can also specify that your numbers appear with different font formatting from the surrounding text. Choose Font, and the Format Font dialog box appears. Here, you can change font, style, size, and effects. Click on OK to return to the Modify Numbered List dialog box.

Assuming that you are using numbers, you can change the list's starting number (Start At). Use this feature when you have already created several numbered lists separated by other text.

As you can see, the Modify Numbered List dialog box also includes the same alignment and distance settings as Word provides for bullets.

Switching between Bullets and Numbered Lists

You can change a numbered list to a bulleted list, and vice versa. To do so, select the list and click on the toolbar button you now want to use—or choose Format, Bullets and Numbering and make your changes there.

Creating Multilevel Lists

Word enables you to create multilevel lists—lists in which each level looks different, or in which subordinate levels include information from higher levels.

To create a multilevel list, first type the list. Use indents to indicate the different levels (no indent indicates a first-level item, one indent is a second-level item, and so on). Choose Bullets and Numbering from the Format menu. Choose the Multilevel tab. As with the Bulleted and Numbered tabs, you are first presented with the six formats you are most likely to use (see fig. 2.25).

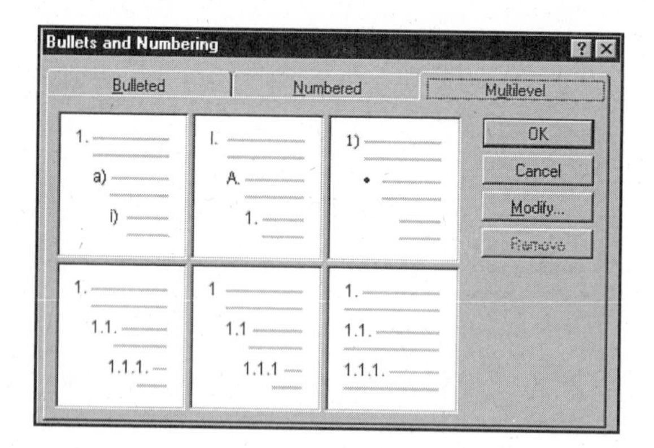

Figure 2.25
The Multilevel tab.

If one of these formats does the job, choose it and click on OK. If not, choose the one that comes closest, and choose Modify. The Modify Multilevel List dialog box appears (see fig. 2.26).

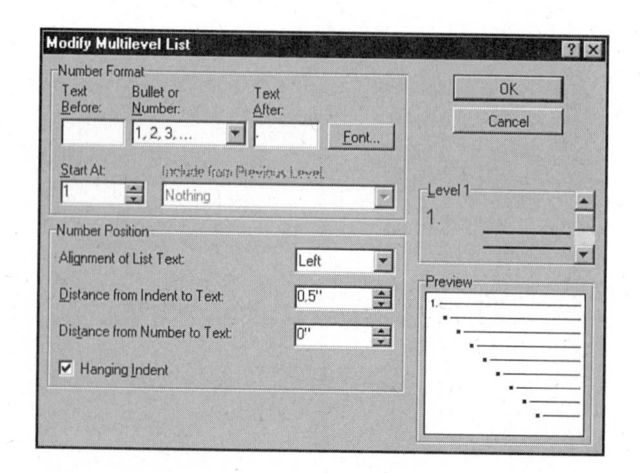

Figure 2.26
The Modify Multilevel List dialog box.

This box is very similar to the Modify Numbered List box. You can place Text Before and Text After your bullet or number. In addition, you can choose a Bullet or Number format. If you use a number, you can specify the first number in your list. You can set alignment, distances, and hanging indents.

There is also one important addition. You can set the format of any of nine levels of your list. Choose the level with the scroll bars in the Level box (see fig. 2.26).

The current appearance of all levels is shown in the Preview box. The text that is added to your current level appears in the Level box.

To work on the second level of the list, scroll to Level 2. Set the appropriate information in the Number Format box. Notice that because you are working on a subordinate level, Word enables you to include aspects of the previous level.

You can include numbers from the higher level so that you wind up with a list such as this:

1. Rocks

    1. a.Igneous

    1. b.Metamorphic

    1. c.Sedimentary

You can include both numbers and position from the higher level, which creates a list such as this:

1. People

1.a. Ingenious

1.b. Metaphysical

1.c. Sedentary

You can also include neither the higher level's position nor its numbers, such as this:

1. Hard Rock Cafés

    a.New York

    b.London

    c.Cancun

When you are finished, click on OK, and Word creates the list.

If you use heading styles, you can have Word create outline numbering for your entire document automatically by using Word's Heading Numbering feature. See Chapter 12, "Outlining," for further details.

Using Symbols: The Poor Man's Clip Art

You can also use the Wingdings and Symbol fonts as a clip art library. To insert a symbol anywhere in your document, choose Insert, Symbol.

The same Symbol dialog box you saw in Bullets and Numbering appears; you can choose a character from any available font, including Wingdings. These characters, like other Word text characters, can be enlarged to 1,638 points—nearly two feet high.

To insert a symbol, click on it. An enlarged version of the symbol appears. Choose Insert.

If you want to insert another symbol without closing the Symbol dialog box, click outside the dialog box and move to where you want the next symbol. Then click on the symbol, and choose Insert again. When you finish adding symbols, choose Close.

Using Special Characters

Word includes many special characters, such as em dashes (—), copyright symbols (©), and ellipses (...). To insert one of these characters from within Symbol, choose Special Characters. The Special Characters tab appears (see fig. 2.27). Word 95 automatically converts some sets of characters to symbols using its AutoCorrect feature, covered in more detail in Chapter 9, "AutoText, AutoCorrect, and the Spike." For example, if you type (c), Word automatically converts this to the copyright symbol "©".

Choose the character you want and choose Insert. Again, if you want, you can switch to the document, move to another location, and add another special character. When you are finished, choose Close.

You will notice that most of these special characters have assigned keyboard shortcuts. (All special character keyboard shortcuts, including foreign-language characters that are not listed in this dialog box, appear in Appendix A, "Keyboard Shortcuts.")

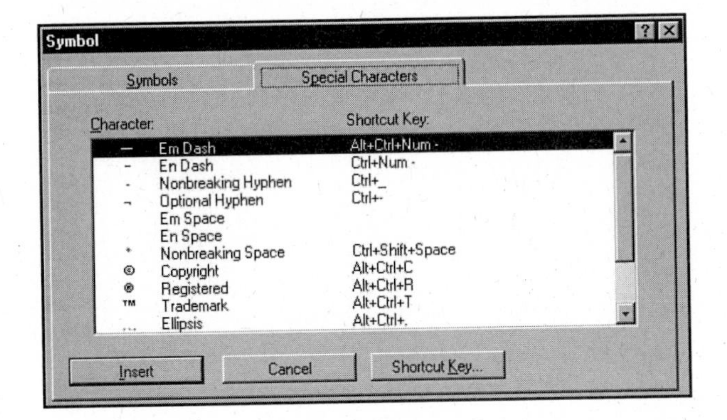

Figure 2.27

The Special Characters tab.

Creating Shortcut Keys for Symbols and Special Characters

If you use a symbol extensively, you can assign it a shortcut key. To assign a shortcut key, follow these steps:

1. Choose **I**nsert, **S**ymbol.
2. From the Symbol dialog box, select the character for which you want to create a shortcut.
3. Choose Shortcut **K**ey.
4. The Customize Keyboard dialog box appears (see fig. 2.28).

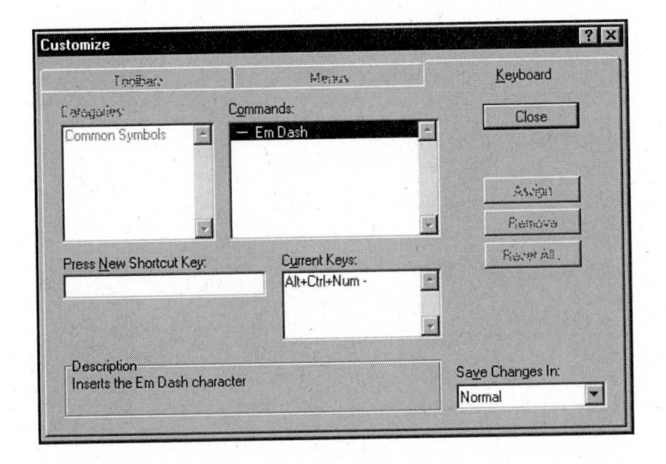

Figure 2.28

The Customize Keyboard dialog box.

5. Enter the shortcut key combination you want to use.

   If you try a shortcut key that is already assigned, Word displays that information in a Currently Assigned To box; you can press Backspace and try another key combination.

6. When you have the key combination you want, choose **A**ssign, and then choose Close.

7. Choose Close again to leave the Symbol dialog box.

You can customize every Word keyboard shortcut, not just those for special characters. To learn how, see Chapter 24, "Personalizing Word."

Tables

Once upon a time, tables were nothing more than rigid rows and columns of information, such as those shown in figure 3.1.

To create a table, chances are you worked with tab settings, and (to put it mildly) there were plenty of opportunities to make mistakes.

Word for Windows 95 has turned the tables, however—turned them into a feature that is so flexible, that you will find yourself using tables for tasks you never even thought were related to tables. Figure 3.2 is an extreme example, but you get the point—these are not your father's tables.

More practically, throughout this book you will learn how Word tables can be used to streamline résumés, forms, scripts, mini-databases, and spreadsheets—and how you can use them to improve your newsletters and other desktop publishing projects. In addition, when all you want is a good old-fashioned table, Word gets the job done lickety-split.

Figure 3.1

Typical traditional table.

Item	Current	Projected
Horseless carriages	25,000	27,000
Telegraph keys	100,00	110,000
Typewriter ribbons	75,000	125,000
Gramophone	30,000	45,000

Figure 3.2

Word can even turn the tables on tables.

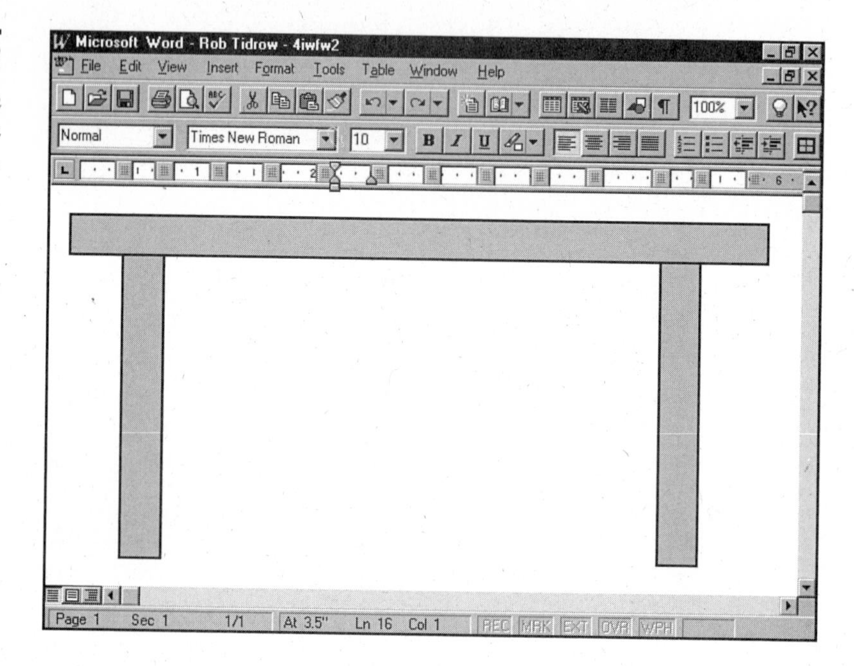

In this chapter:

- Creating a table from the Standard toolbar
- Creating a table with Insert Table
- Editing in a table
- Using the table shortcut menu
- Formatting within a table
- Autoformatting a table
- Inserting and deleting rows and columns
- Changing column width
- Specifying row height

- Adding table borders and shading
- Merging cells
- Converting text to tables and vice versa
- A simple table calculation
- A simple table sort

Creating a Table from the Standard Toolbar

You say for the moment you will be satisfied with a basic quarterly report table?

1. Click on the Insert Table button in the Standard toolbar. A set of rows and columns appears, as shown in figure 3.3.
2. Drag the mouse pointer down as many rows as you need (for this example, drag down four rows). Word automatically adds an additional row as needed. You will see the number of rows highlighted as you go (see fig. 3.4).
3. Still pressing the mouse button, drag the pointer across, covering as many columns as you need. Again, you will see the number of columns highlighted (see fig. 3.5).

Try to have a general idea of how many rows and columns you will ultimately need, but don't worry about it too much. After the table is created, it is easy to add and delete rows and columns.

4. When you are satisfied, let go of the mouse. Word creates a table, as shown in figure 3.6.

Stealth Tables. If by some chance your tables do not appear, make sure a check mark appears next to Gridlines in the Table menu. This places dotted lines around the borders of each cell, as shown earlier. Otherwise the table might be there, but you can't see it.

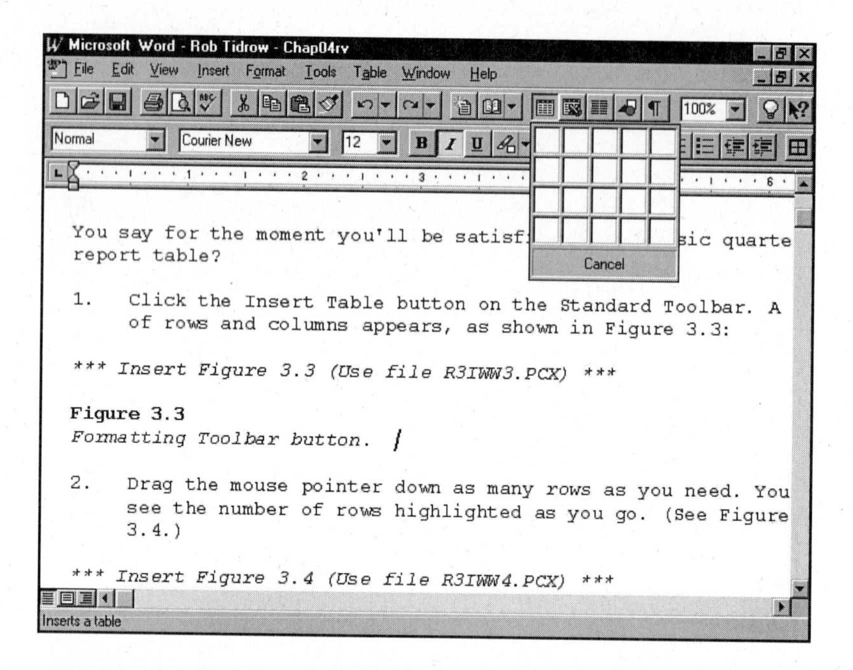

Microsoft Word - Rob Tidrow - Chap04rv
File Edit View Insert Format Tools Table Window Help
100%
Normal
Courier New
12
Cancel
You say for the moment you'll be satisf
sic quarte
report table?
1. Click the Insert Table button on the Standard Toolbar. A
of rows and columns appears, as shown in Figure 3.3:
*** Insert Figure 3.3 (Use file R3IWW3.PCX) ***
Figure 3.3
Formatting Toolbar button.
2. Drag the mouse pointer down as many rows as you need. You
see the number of rows highlighted as you go. (See Figure
3.4.)
*** Insert Figure 3.4 (Use file R3IWW4.PCX) ***
Inserts a table

Figure 3.3

The Insert Table button.

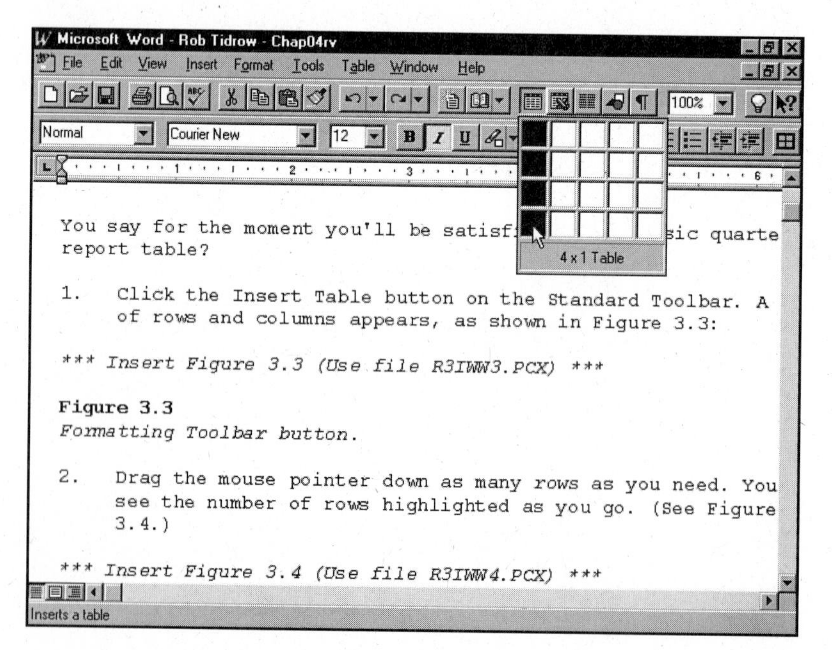

Microsoft Word - Rob Tidrow - Chap04rv
File Edit View Insert Format Tools Table Window Help
100%
Normal
Courier New
12
4 x 1 Table
You say for the moment you'll be satisf
sic quarte
report table?
1. Click the Insert Table button on the Standard Toolbar. A
of rows and columns appears, as shown in Figure 3.3:
*** Insert Figure 3.3 (Use file R3IWW3.PCX) ***
Figure 3.3
Formatting Toolbar button.
2. Drag the mouse pointer down as many rows as you need. You
see the number of rows highlighted as you go. (See Figure
3.4.)
*** Insert Figure 3.4 (Use file R3IWW4.PCX) ***
Inserts a table

Figure 3.4

Dragging rows.

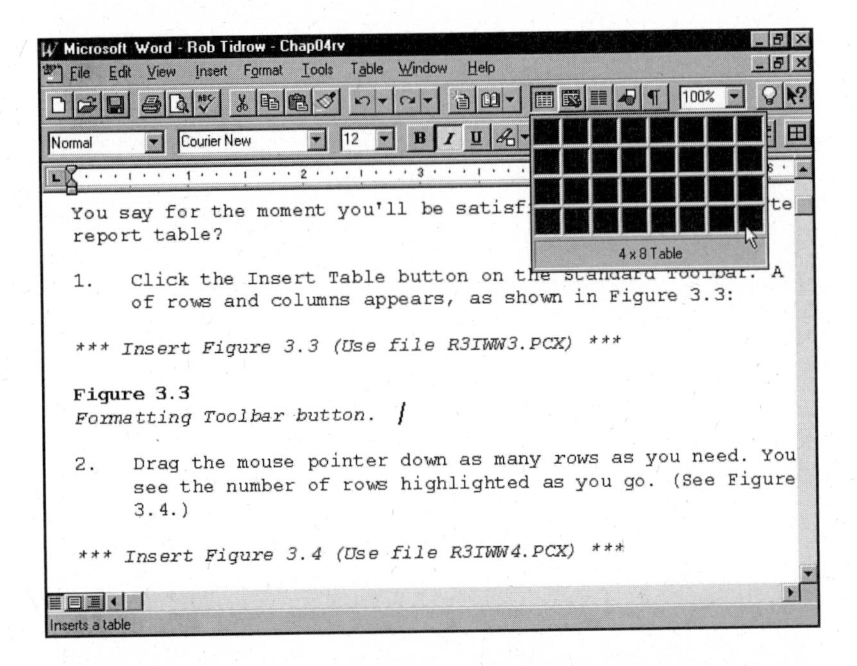

Figure 3.5
Dragging columns.

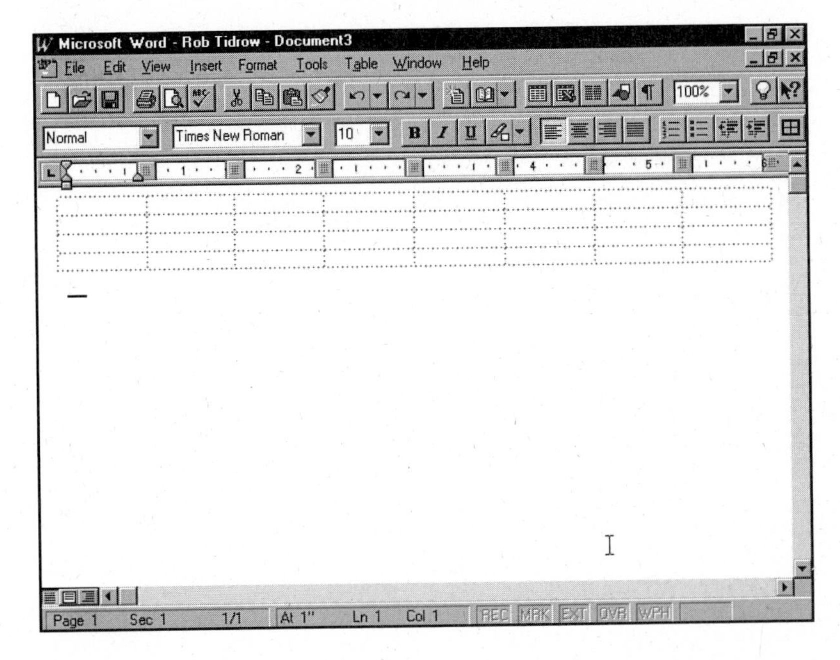

Figure 3.6
Sample 4×8 table.

If you start creating a table by clicking on the Insert Table button and dragging to show rows or columns, you can still change your mind and cancel the table insertion. Move the mouse pointer outside the table matrix (the rows and columns appearing beneath the Insert Table button). When the word "Cancel" appears in the status window, release the mouse button, and the table disappears.

Tip If you need more rows or columns, use Insert Table, which is discussed shortly. If you follow the previous procedure, Word changes the Menu item to Insert Rows.

When you create columns within a row, you are creating cells. A *cell* is the rectangle or box formed by a row and a column (just like a spreadsheet cell). Cells are the basic unit of table formatting. They are similar to paragraphs. Like paragraphs, they have their own markers—*end-of-cell markers*, as shown in figure 3.7.

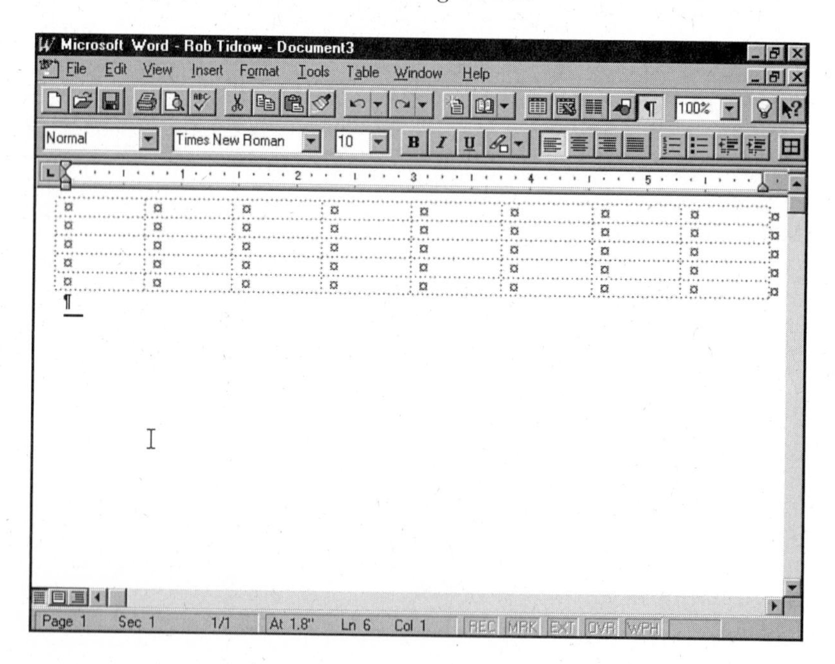

Figure 3.7
End-of-cell markers.

In a blank table, end-of-cell markers appear near the beginning of each cell, to indicate that the cell is empty. Notice that another end-of-cell marker appears after the last cell in a row.

Note If your paragraph marks appear on-screen, end-of-cell markers also appear. If not, you might want to display them, especially while you are reading this chapter and following its exercises.

The quick way to display markers is to click the Paragraph Mark button on the Toolbar, but this also places dots between each word. If you find this annoying, follow these steps:

1. Choose **T**ools, **O**ptions.
2. Choose View to display the View tab of the Options dialog box.
3. Check Paragraph **M**arks in the Nonprinting Characters group.
4. Click on OK.

Word now displays end-of-cell markers, paragraph marks, and line breaks.

In very small type sizes, end-of-cell markers get squished, as shown in figure 3.8.

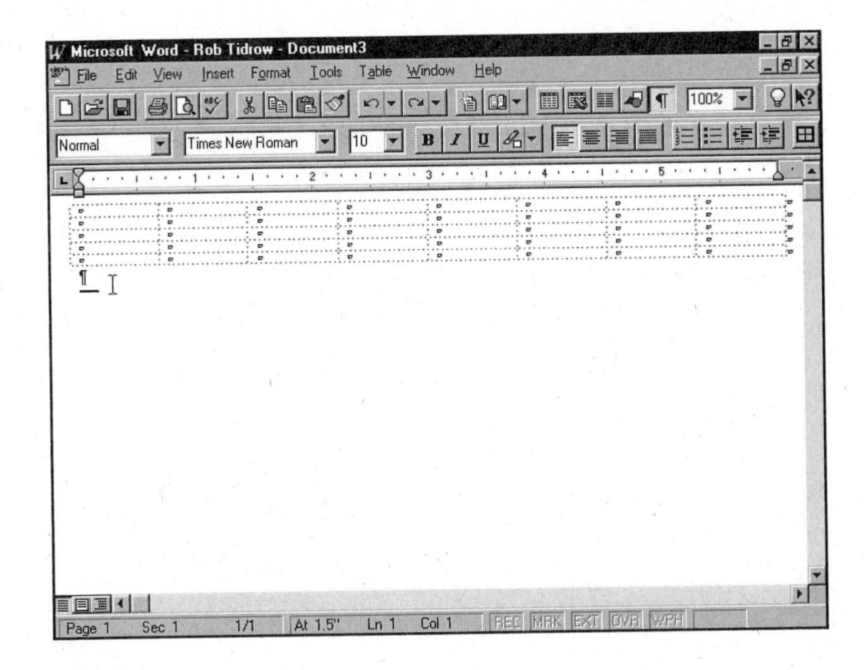

Figure 3.8

Squished end-of-cell markers.

If your table headings are numbered, or contain years, months, quarters, or days, hop over to Chapter 8, "Templates and Wizards," to meet the Table Wizard, who will be happy to type in all that boilerplate for you.

You can get to the Table Wizard from within a document by choosing T**a**ble, **I**nsert Table, Wi**z**ard.

Table Button Default Settings

Like other toolbar buttons, the Insert Table button assumes that you want default settings. When you use it, all cells are created equal. They each have the same width, divided equally from the space between your margins. If, for example, you are using default 1.25-inch left and right margins, that leaves 6 inches of text area. Therefore, if you create a three-column table, Word assigns 2 inches to each column.

Each row also has the same height. Unless you have specified otherwise, row height is one line, based on the line height used in the previous paragraph. Other formatting contained in the previous paragraph carries over, too, including the following:

- Font, size, and character attributes
- Special pagination and line numbering commands
- Tab settings
- Paragraph indents

Stray paragraph indents are some of the most common problems users have with Word tables. A leftover 1.5-inch indent can have the result shown in figure 3.9.

To get rid of the indents, select the entire table, choose F**o**rmat, **P**aragraph, and set From **L**eft, From **R**ight, and any **S**pecial indents to 0".

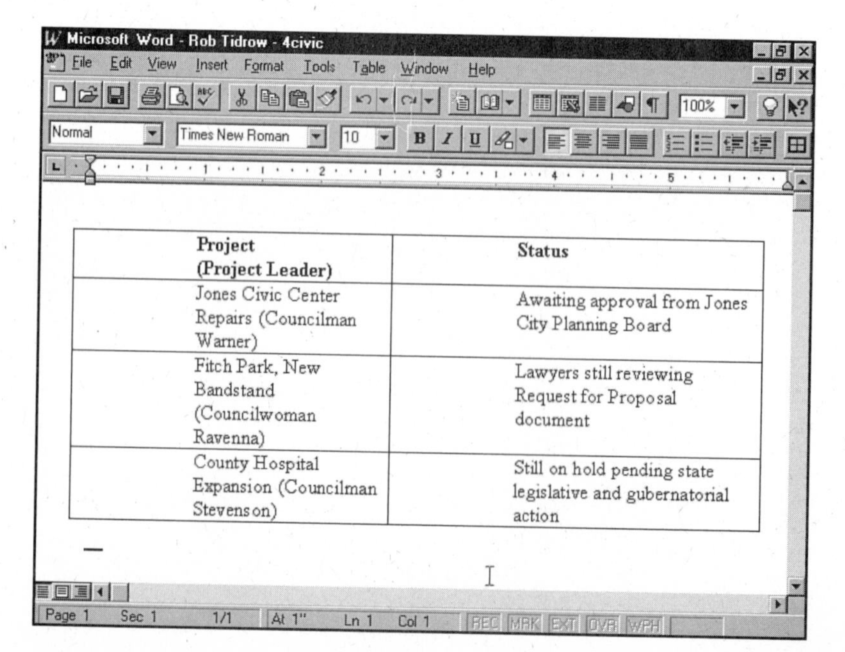

Figure 3.9
Table with unwanted indents.

Creating a Table with Insert Table

If you want more control over your table while you are creating it, or if you need more rows and columns than the toolbar can provide, place the insertion point where you want the table and choose Table, Insert Table. The dialog box shown in figure 3.10 appears.

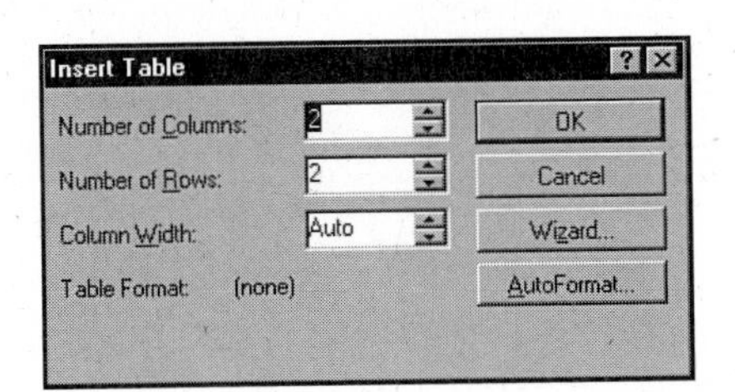

Figure 3.10

The Insert Table dialog box.

The Number of **C**olumns box enables you to create up to 31 columns.

The Number of **R**ows box enables you to create as many rows as you need. (Remember, you can always add rows later.)

The Column **W**idth box enables you to specify the width of all columns. The default setting is Auto, which divides the available space between margins equally among the columns. You can, however, set all columns to a specific width, even if it means they will extend beyond your margins. Columns must be between 0.25" and 10.99" wide.

In the section "Changing Column Width" later in this chapter you will learn how to change the width of a specific column.

The accompanying CD-ROM contains a file you can use to practice some of the procedures in this chapter: IWMS3A.DOC. To see the end-of-cell and end-of-row marks in this file, check Paragraph **M**arks in the View tab of the **O**ptions dialog box, if you have not already.

Editing in a Table

After you create a new empty table, the next step is to put something in it. When Word creates a new table, it positions the insertion point in the table's first cell.

Typing in a table is similar to typing anywhere else in a document, with one major exception: When you reach the right edge of a cell, Word wraps text back to the left edge, as it normally would at the end of a line (see fig. 3.11).

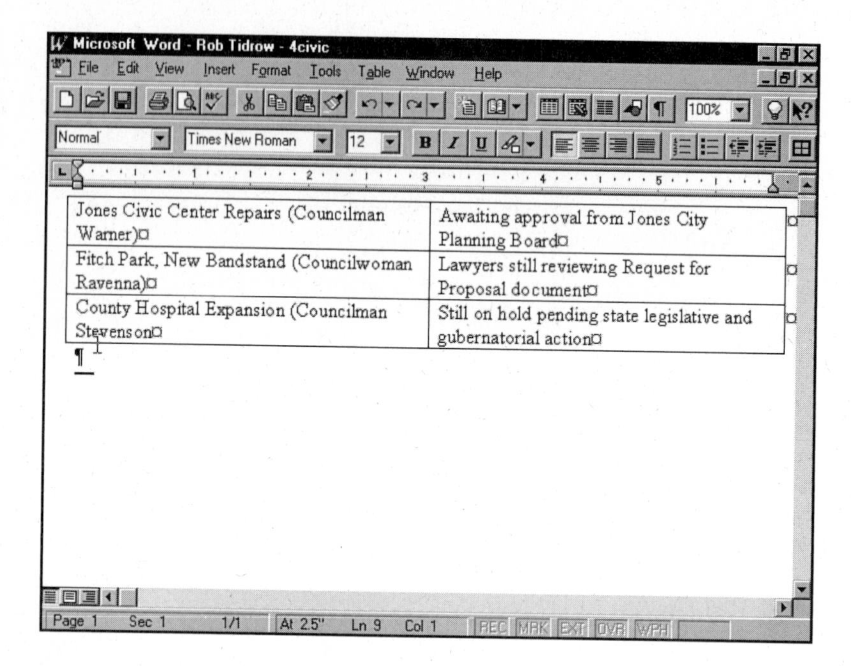

Figure 3.11
Sample table showing wrapped text.

Side-by-side paragraphs. You now can see how tables can be used to present side-by-side paragraphs. These are essential in many kinds of documents. One good example is video script writing, in which video directions often appear on the left, and spoken words appear on the right.

Word also has a very strong multiple-column feature, which is covered in Chapter 21, "Desktop Publishing and Drawing," but that feature snakes text down one column and up to the top of the next. Only tables offer a practical solution for multiple side-by-side paragraphs.

You can enter paragraph marks or line breaks within a cell. These breaks add lines to the row the cell is in, and to all other cells in the same row, as shown in figure 3.12.

Although you cannot have cells in the same row with different heights, you can fake this with borders, as you will see in the section "Using Borders Selectively," later in this chapter.

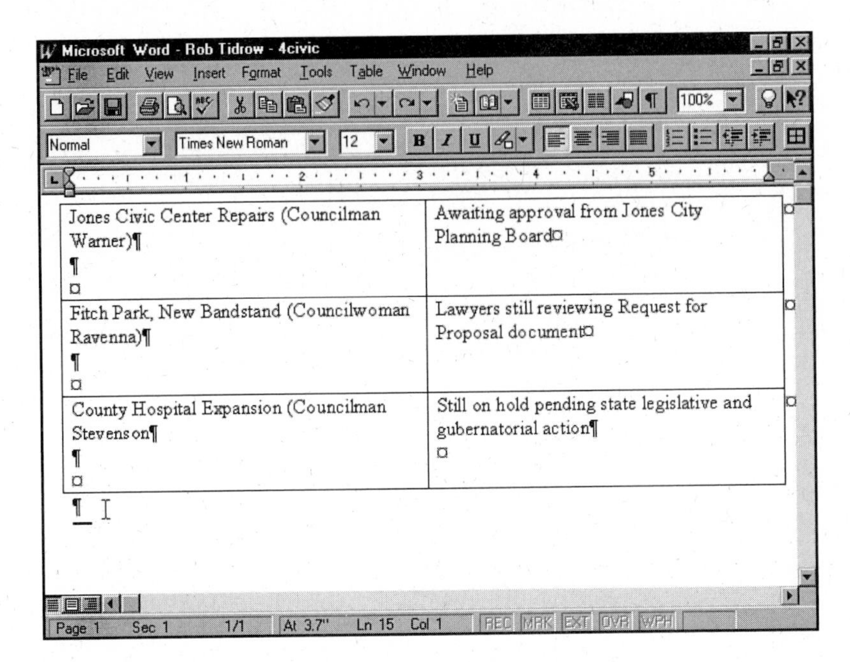

Figure 3.12
Sample table with paragraph marks added.

Moving Around within a Table

To move around a table with the mouse, click the cell you want to go to. Word also offers many keyboard shortcuts. For example, Tab moves you to the next cell; Shift+Tab moves you back. A complete list follows in table 3.1.

TABLE 3.1
Keyboard Shortcuts

This Key	Moves the Insertion Point
Up arrow	Up one line within a cell. If at the top of a cell, up one cell. If already at the top of the table, moves one line above the table.
Tab	To next cell.
Shift+Tab	To previous cell.
Down arrow	Down one line within a cell. If at the bottom of a cell, down one cell. If already at the bottom of the table, moves one line below the table.

continues

Table 3.1, Continued
Keyboard Shortcuts

This Key	Moves the Insertion Point
Left arrow	Left one character within a cell. If at the beginning of a cell, moves to end of previous cell.
Right arrow	Right one character within a cell. If at the end of a cell, moves to start of next cell.
Home	To beginning of current cell.
End	To end of current cell.
Alt+Home	To beginning of first cell in current row.
Alt+End	To end of last cell in current row.
Alt+PageUp	To beginning of first cell in current column.
Alt+PageDn	To beginning of last cell in current column.

Within tables, Word appropriates the Tab key for moving between cells. To actually set a tab within a table, press Ctrl+Tab.

Selecting Text within a Table

Within a cell, Word's normal selection methods apply. With the mouse, you can highlight some or all of the text. With the keyboard, you can press F8 and the arrow keys, or press Shift and the arrow keys.

After you reach the end-of-cell marker, things change. When you select the end-of-cell marker, the entire cell is selected. When you extend your selection beyond the end-of-cell marker, Word selects the entire next cell. When you reach the end of a row, Word selects the end-of-row marker.

When you go even further, either extending the keyboard selection or moving the mouse pointer up or down, Word selects entire additional rows. When you go beyond the edge of the table, Word adds other text to your selection.

For any nontable text you add to your selection, the selection process behaves normally; you can add either individual characters or lines to your selection.

Word offers more shortcuts for selecting text in a table. Alt+5 (on the number pad) selects the entire table. (That is similar to Ctrl+5, which selects the entire document.) In addition, every table cell has its own selection bar. If you move the mouse pointer to the far left of a cell, the pointer changes to a right arrow, as shown in figure 3.13.

Note To use the Alt+5 shortcut, you must have NumLock turned off.

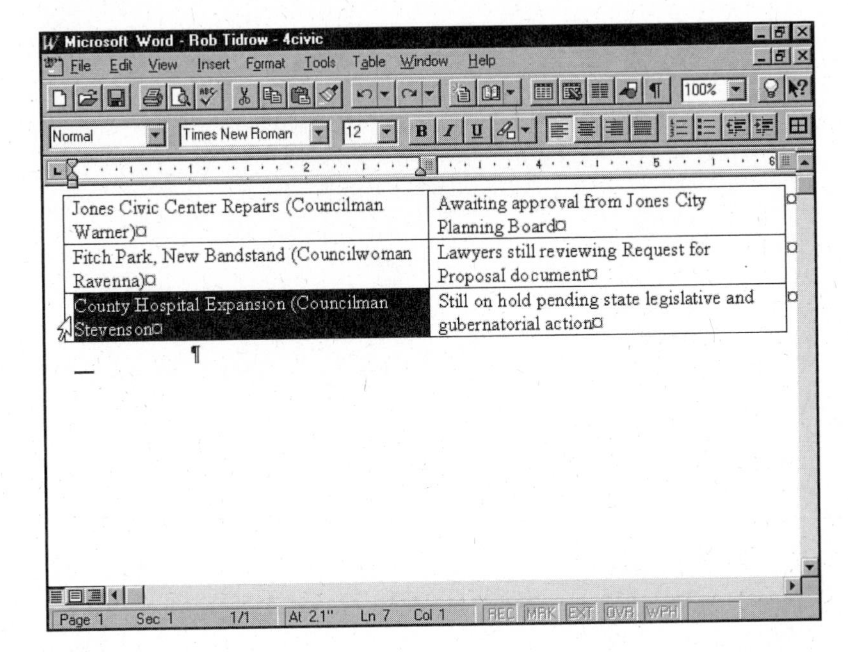

Figure 3.13

Using a cell's selection bar.

Click the mouse, and Word selects the entire cell. Double-click, and Word selects the entire row.

Tip **Try the keyboard.** Because clicking on either the left edge of a cell (its selection bar) or the right edge of a cell (its end-of-cell mark) selects the entire cell, it can be a bit tricky to select the text within a cell without also selecting the cell. You might find it easier to do this with the keyboard, rather than the mouse.

The normal Word selection bar at the far left of the screen also works. Within a table, the selection bar selects rows rather than paragraphs, as in figure 3.14.

You can select specific columns by carefully positioning the mouse pointer at the top edge of the column (see fig. 3.15). When the pointer changes into a down arrow, click the mouse button.

To select more than one column, press the down-arrow mouse pointer as you move left or right to select the other columns.

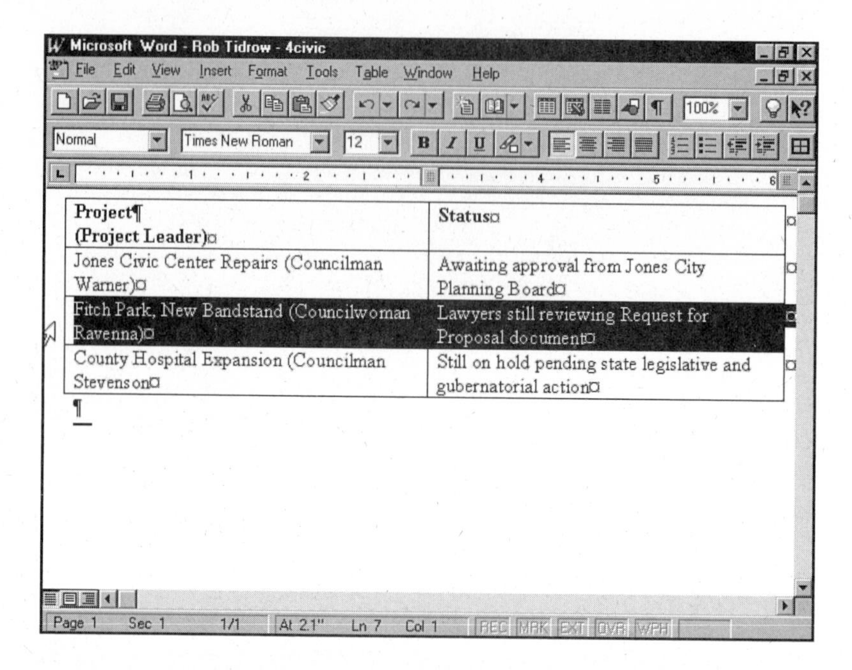

Figure 3.14
Using the Word selection bar to select a row.

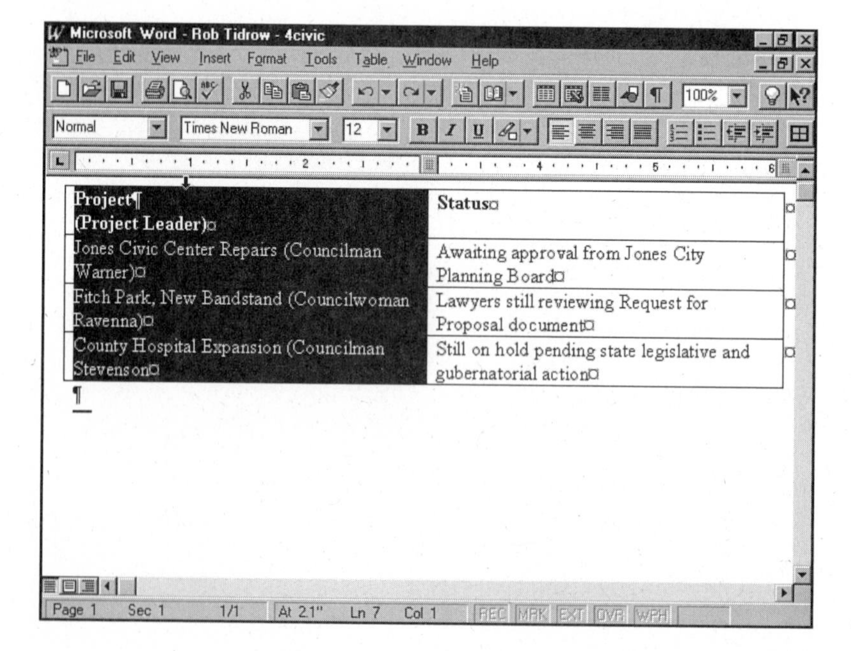

Figure 3.15
Selecting a column with the down-arrow mouse pointer.

Finally, you can select rows or columns from the menu. To select one row or column, position the insertion point anywhere in that row or column, and choose Table, then click on Select Row or Select Column.

To select more than one row, first select individual cells in each row, then choose Select Row. To select more than one column, first select individual cells in each column, then choose Select Column. To select the entire table, choose Select Table.

Using the Table Shortcut Menu

Whenever you are in a table, you can right-click to display a shortcut menu of the commands that Word expects you are most likely to need (see fig. 3.16).

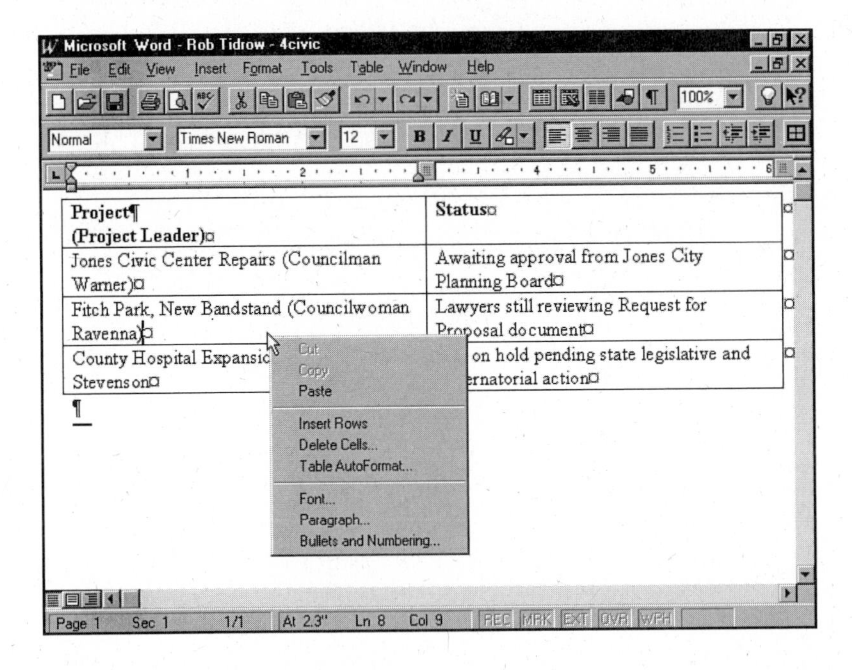

Figure 3.16

The table shortcut menu.

Word does not have a special Table toolbar, but you can build one of your own from the specific table buttons Word provides as part of its customization features. To learn how, see Chapter 24, "Personalizing Word"—or use the NRP Table toolbar created for you on the tutorial disk accompanying that lesson.

Formatting within a Table

As mentioned earlier, when you create a table, it takes on the character and paragraph formatting of the paragraph preceding it. In other words, if the previous paragraph uses Times New Roman 14 point type, double-spaced, so will your table unless you change it. You can change any of this formatting by using the same character and paragraph formatting techniques discussed in previous chapters.

Autoformatting a Table

Word adds a powerful new table feature designed to simplify the creation of good-looking tables. This feature, called *AutoFormat*, enables you to pick whatever elements you want from 37 different formats, as listed in table 3.2.

Table 3.2
AutoFormat Table Formats

Type of Format	Number of Variations
Simple	3
Classic	4
Colorful	3
Columns	5
Grid	8
List	8
3D Effects	3
Contemporary	1
Elegant	1
Professional	1

To autoformat an existing table, place your insertion point anywhere inside the table and choose Table, Table AutoFormat. To autoformat a new table, choose Table, Insert Table, set the number of rows and columns (and optionally the column width), and then choose Table AutoFormat. In either case, the Table AutoFormat dialog box appears, as shown in figure 3.17.

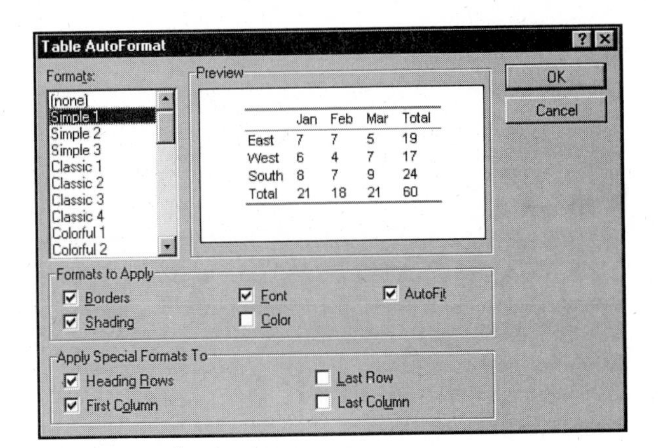

Figure 3.17

The Table AutoFormat dialog box.

You also can run Table AutoFormat by running the Table Wizard (T**a**ble, **I**nsert Table, Wi**z**ard); the AutoFormat options appear after Word creates the table you request.

To choose a format, select it from the Formats list box. By default, AutoFormat expects to apply the **B**orders, **S**hading, and **F**ont elements from the built-in format. (**F**ont does not change your table's text font to Arial, as implied in the Preview, but it does add bold or italic as shown there.)

AutoFormat also expects to use AutoF**i**t, which shrinks or enlarges each column to fit the widest cell contained in that column.

You can turn off each of these features by checking them. You also can add color in those Table AutoFormats that support it, by checking the **C**olor box. Twenty of the formats support color; some of the other formats use more intricate gray or black shading when you choose **C**olor.

Word's Table AutoFormats often include special formatting for Heading **R**ows, and for the First C**o**lumn. These are on by default. Word assumes you are actually putting something special in the top row and first column. If you are not, you can turn them off. You might want that special formatting to appear in the **L**ast Row or Last Col**u**mn—perhaps you are showing a total there. Check the appropriate box to turn these on. Again, the Preview box shows you what to expect. When you have your AutoFormat the way you want it, click on OK.

Inserting and Deleting Rows and Columns

Often, you will have to add a new row or column to your table. In earlier word processors, this was difficult, if you could do it at all. Word makes it much easier.

To add a new row to the bottom of your table, position your insertion point in the last cell and press Tab. A new row appears in the same format as the previous row. To add a new row anywhere else in your table, select the row where you want a new row to be placed and choose T<u>a</u>ble, Insert **<u>R</u>**ow. A new row appears; other rows are pushed down to make room.

To add a new column within your table, select the column where you want the new column to be placed and choose T<u>a</u>ble, Insert <u>C</u>olumn. A new column appears, and other columns are pushed to the right to make room. To add a new column at the right edge of your table, select the end-of-row markers, as shown in figure 3.18, then choose Insert <u>C</u>olumn.

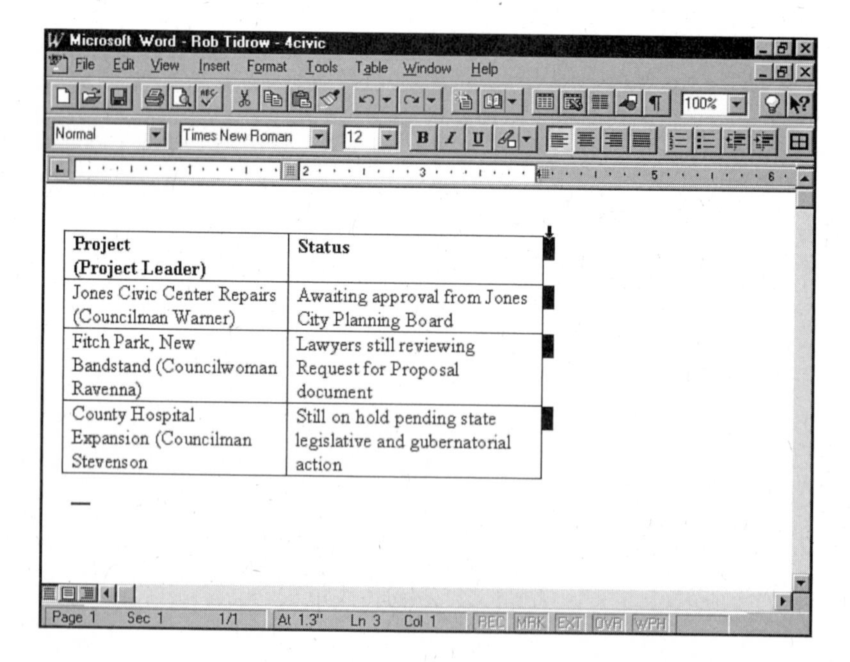

Figure 3.18

Creating a new column at the right edge of a table.

When you insert a row, the new row takes the same height, width, and formatting as the one following it. When you insert a column, it matches the column to its right.

You also can add rows and columns with the Insert Table button. Just position your insertion point and click. Word guesses what you want to do:

- ◆ If you are not in a table, the button assumes that you want to create a table, and it presents you with its row/column matrix.
- ◆ If you select a row, the button assumes that you want to insert a row, and it does so.
- ◆ If you select a column, the button assumes that you want to insert a column, and it does so.
- ◆ If you place your insertion point inside a cell, or select one or more cells, the button assumes that you want to insert cells, and it opens the Insert Cell window, asking you where to move the other cells.

Inserting Cells

You also can insert cells anywhere within a table. Position the insertion point at the point you want to add the cell. Then highlight the cell or cells that are currently in the location where you want to add blank cells, and choose Table, Insert Cells. The dialog box shown in figure 3.19 appears.

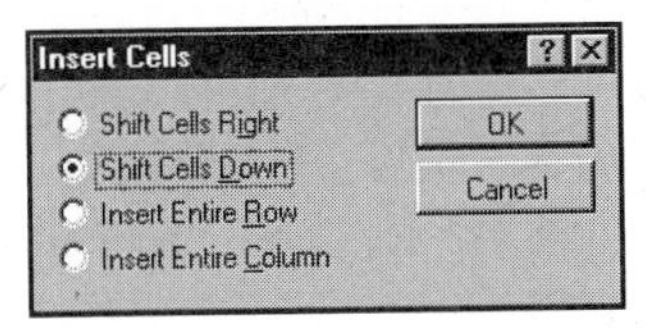

Figure 3.19

The Insert Cells dialog box.

Tell Word where you want to move the cells you are displacing: Shift Cells Right or Shift Cells Down. In either case, Word shifts only these cells—leaving you with a table that has additional cells in some rows or columns, as shown in figure 3.20.

If you are sure that is what you want, click on OK in the dialog box to confirm. Much of the time, you will want to make changes. You might really want to add an entire row or column, so Word also offers these options.

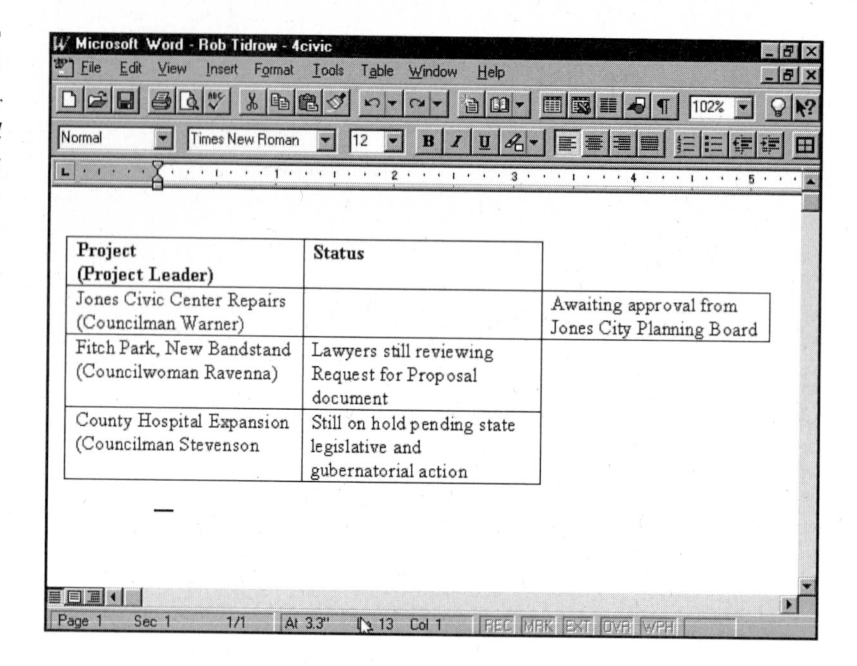

Figure 3.20
Typical table after inserting a cell and shifting cells right.

Cutting and Pasting Cell Contents

As with selecting text, cutting, copying, and pasting within a cell works much the same as it does anywhere else in a Word document. You can use keyboard shortcuts, the toolbar, the menu, or a right-click of the mouse. However, when you select entire cells, rows, or columns, there are a few new behaviors to keep in mind.

Normally, when you cut an entire cell (or multiple cells) into the Clipboard, the empty cell or cells still appear in your table, but the Clipboard also contains cell borders. If you paste the cell or cells outside the Clipboard, they appear as a "baby" table of their own (see figures 3.21 and 3.22).

Tip If you just want to move the text in one cell, you can avoid this situation if you don't cut the end-of-cell marker.

If you paste cells into a table, and the cells require more columns or rows than the table already has, Word adds them. Sometimes this means Word creates new empty cells as well.

You cannot paste both cells and regular (nontable) text into a table at the same time, but you can paste text from outside a table into one cell.

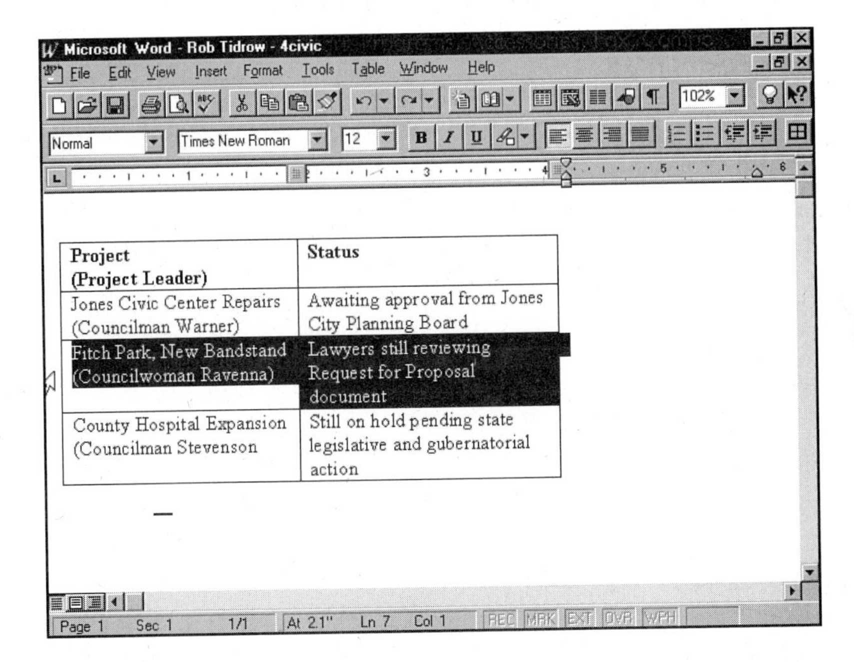

Figure 3.21

Cut...

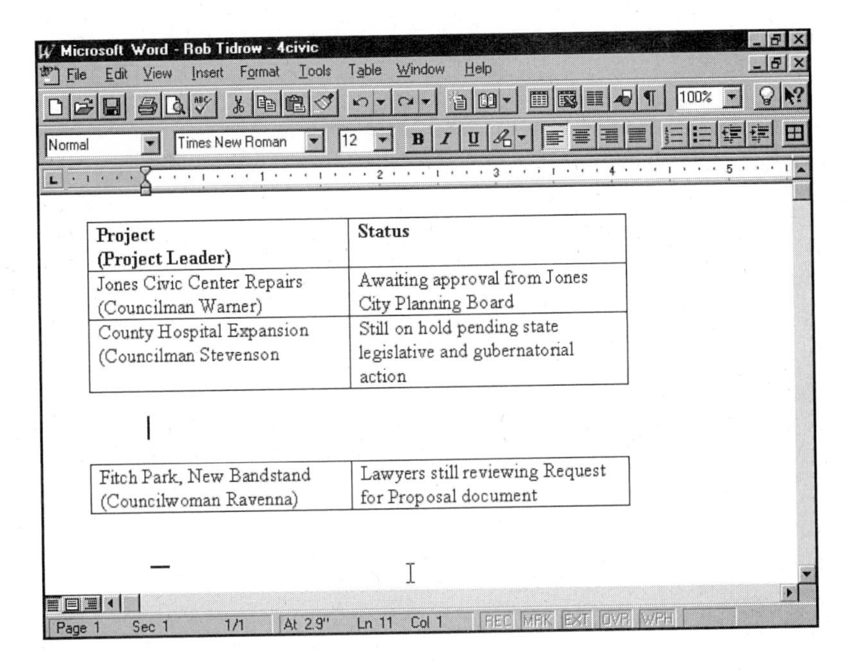

Figure 3.22

...and paste outside the table.

You also can use drag-and-drop to move rows and columns.

Clearing Cell Contents

Sometimes, you might want to eliminate the contents of a cell without storing them in the Clipboard. Select the cell and press Delete, or choose Edit, Clear. You also can use Delete or Clear to wipe out entire rows or columns. As with Cut, the cell borders disappear—and the cells are truly gone.

You can retrieve deleted cells by choosing Edit, Undo Clear, or by choosing Clear from the Undo list box on the Standard toolbar.

Pasting Cells

After you have cut a cell or cells, there are two ways to paste them. You can position your insertion point at the top left of the space where you want to place the cells. Word simply inserts all the cells in your Clipboard—replacing any existing data that might have been in the way. That is the fastest way, but be careful not to destroy any information you needed.

You also can clear a space for the pasted cells. If you cut a 2×5 matrix of cells into the Clipboard, you can select a 2×5 space as their new home. The cut and paste sizes must be identical, or you will see the message shown in figure 3.23.

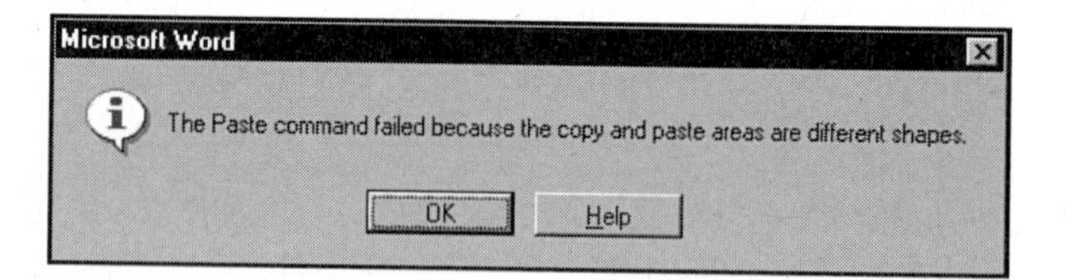

Figure 3.23
Word tells you when the Paste command fails.

The situation is different if you are pasting a complete row. Then, Word automatically makes room. Insert the pointer where you want the new row, and paste. The existing row is moved down to compensate.

Deleting Rows and Columns

When you select and Cut or Delete a complete row or column, Word also removes the row or column borders—eliminating the row or column entirely, and moving the rest of the table to compensate.

You also can use the menu. Select the row(s) or column(s) you want to delete, then choose Table, Delete Row or Delete Column. Similarly, you can delete an entire table by placing the insertion point in the table and choosing Delete Table.

Changing Column Width

Often, making all cells the same width simply does not work. You might have a descriptive first column followed by many shorter columns of numbers, as in the following census statistics:

City	1990	1980	1970	1960
New York, NY	7.32M	7.07M	7.90M	7.78M
Los Angeles, CA	3.49M	2.97M	2.81M	2.48M
Chicago, IL	2.78M	3.01M	3.37M	3.55M
Houston, TX	1.63M	1.59M	1.23M	0.94M
Philadelphia, PA	1.59M	1.69M	1.95M	2.00M

You might also have brief categories followed by lengthier explanations, as shown by this excerpt of a table describing chess moves:

Piece	Moves Allowed
King	One square in any direction
Queen	Any number of open squares in any direction
Rook	Left, right, forward, backward any number of open squares
Bishop	Diagonally
Knight	Any combination of two squares in one direction and one square in a perpendicular direction
Pawn	One square forward, except for its first move, which can optionally be two spaces forward; can capture pieces one diagonal space in front of it

You can, of course, use AutoFit to rearrange this, but you might want to make adjustments. Or, you might not want to take the trouble to clear all the other AutoFormatting elements so that you can use AutoFit.

In either case, as you might be expecting by now, Word offers several ways to change column width without going anywhere near AutoFormat. This section starts with the easiest—the vertical split pointer. To change the width of a column, position the mouse pointer anywhere on the column's right gridline, as shown in figure 3.24.

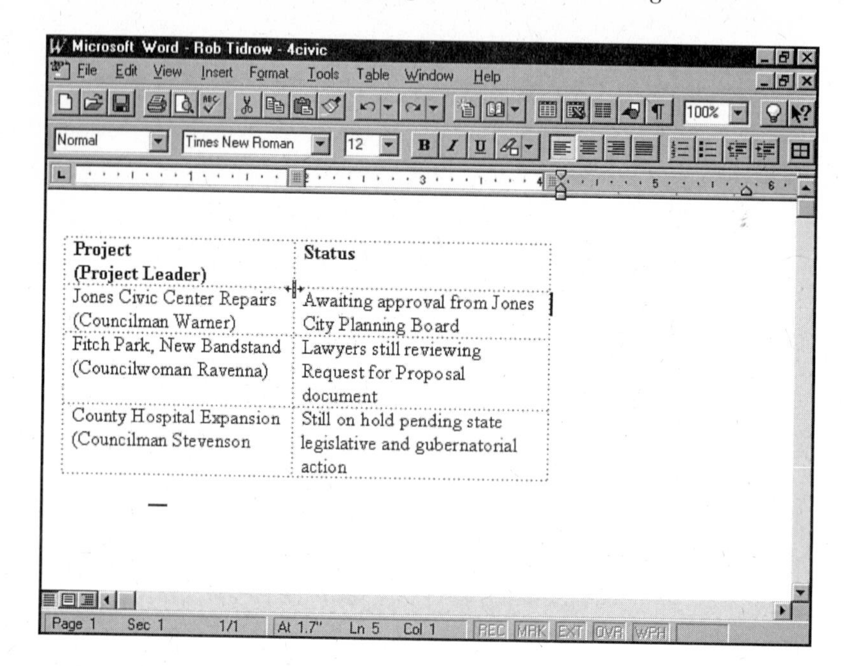

Figure 3.24
Vertical split pointer.

Now drag the gridline left or right to the location you want, and let go. The widths of all the following columns change to compensate, so your overall table has the same width. You can, however, change the last column without affecting the others.

Changing Column Width with the Ruler

You also can change column width with the ruler. As you can see in figure 3.25, when you are within a table, all the table's column borders are shown on the ruler.

You can change these column borders by positioning the mouse pointer on the border shown in the ruler (avoiding the indent markers) and dragging to the new border that you want. As you drag a column border, the new measurements are visible on the ruler. The columns that follow shrink or enlarge to compensate, unless you are changing the last column.

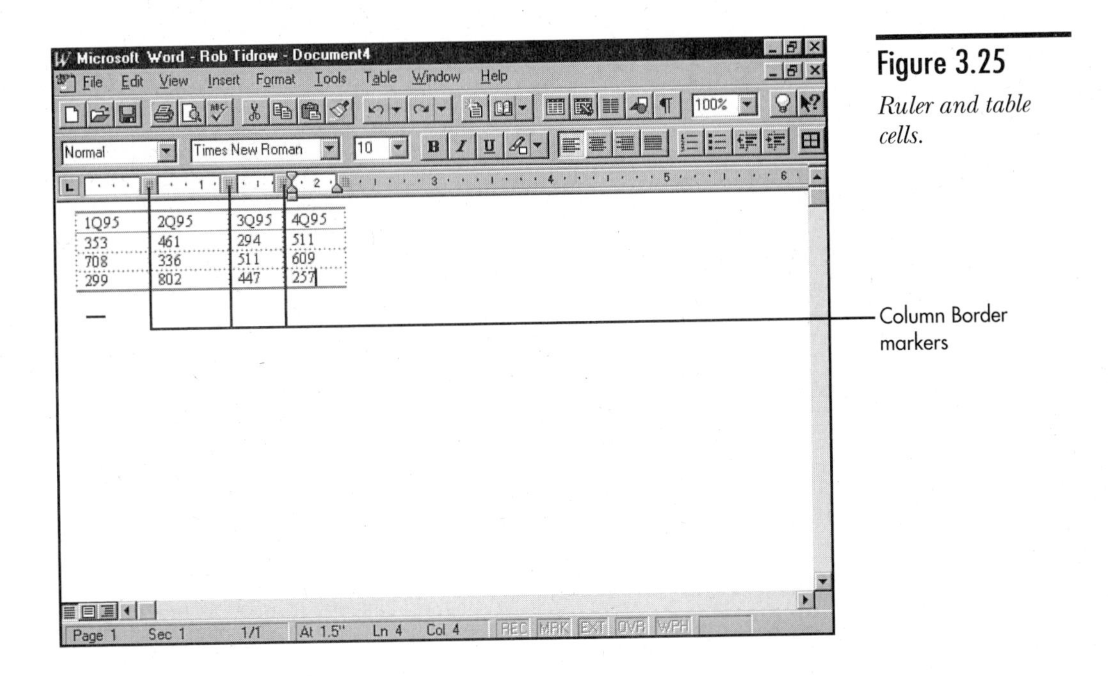

Figure 3.25

Ruler and table cells.

Using Table Cell Height and Width to Change Column Width

If you need more precise control over your column width, if you want to change a column's width without changing the others, or if you want to change the space between columns, work with Cell Height and Width from the Table menu. First, select the column or columns you want to adjust. Then choose Table, Cell Height and Width, and display the Column tab in the Cell Height and Width dialog box, shown in figure 3.26.

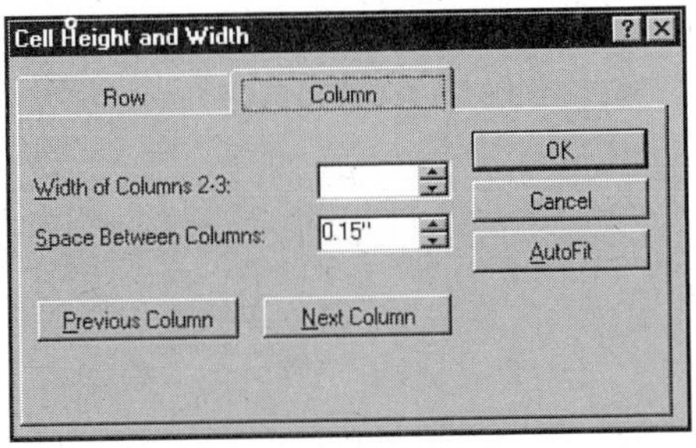

Figure 3.26

The Column tab in the Cell Height and Width dialog box.

As you can see, the box tells you which column or columns you are working with. Type the new width in the **W**idth of Column box, or click on the **A**utoFit button to fit the column around its widest text.

If you want to change the width of another column, you do not need to leave the dialog box. Use **P**revious Column to move to the left, or **N**ext Column to move to the right. When you are satisfied, click on OK.

Changing Space between Columns

By default, Word places 0.15" of space between the end of one column's text area and the beginning of the next column's text area. Notice that the space is not actually between columns—instead, Word moves the cell borders nearer or farther away from the end-of-cell markers. Because you cannot insert text in a cell after the end-of-cell marker, the result is the same.

The difference in approach shows up more clearly when you use borders. You do not see a 0.15" space between columns. Rather, you see 0.075" space between the end of text in a column and the column border. The other 0.075" appears at the beginning of the next column.

In the example shown in figure 3.27, the space between columns has been extended to 0.8", so you can see the 0.4" blank space reserved on each side of the cell's border. (**S**pace Between Columns can now be set to any measurement; in Word 2, you were limited to measurements between 0" and 0.98".)

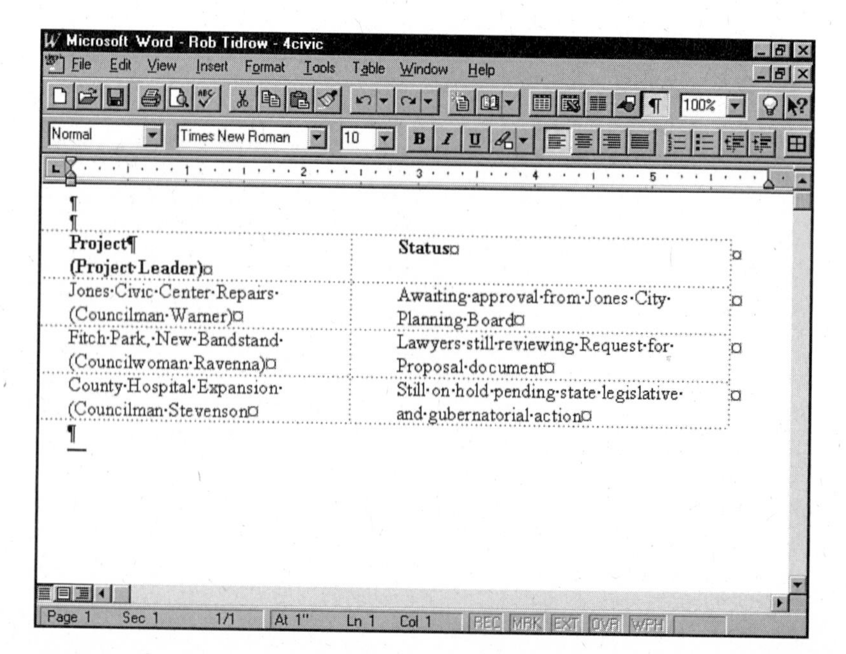

Figure 3.27
0.8" space between columns.

To change the space between all columns, select any column, choose Table, Cell Height and Width, Column, and insert a new value in Space Between Columns. To change the space between all columns in a specific row, place the insertion point in that row, choose Table, Cell Height and Width, Column, and change the value in Space Between Columns.

Specifying Row Height

By default, Word uses a row height of one line. "One line" starts out equal to one line in the previous paragraph. As you work within the table, "one line" can grow or shrink depending on the type size you use on each line. Word always leaves a bit of extra room to accommodate your type. In any case, all cells on the same line always have the same row height.

To control row height, choose Table, Cell Height and Width, and click on **Row** to display the Row tab in the Cell Height and Width dialog box (see fig. 3.28).

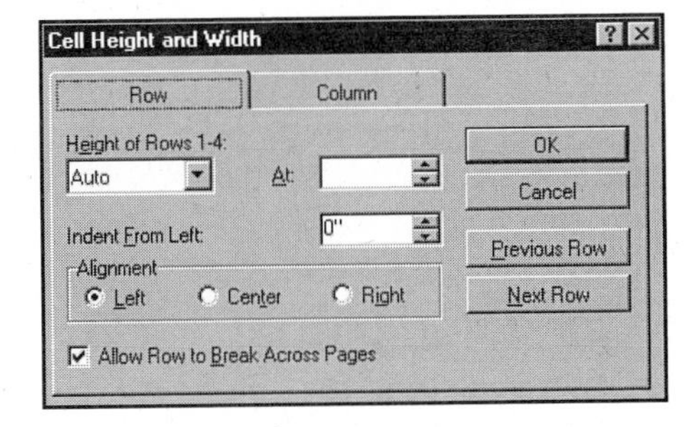

Figure 3.28
The Row tab in the Cell Height and Width dialog box.

Row height is controlled in the Height of Rows box. The list box tells you the row or rows you are controlling. Height of Row gives you similar choices to those in Line Spacing in the Format Paragraph menu:

Auto	Enables Word to control line spacing, setting it at one line.
At Least	Tells Word the minimum row height it should use; however, enables Word to increase Row Height when necessary.
Exactly	Tells Word exactly what Row Height to use, no matter what the type size is.

In the **At** box, you can add measurements in lines (li), centimeters (cm), points (pt), or picas (pi).

If you tell Word to use a row height greater than one line, Word places the extra space after the text. To add space before the text, set **B**efore spacing in the Format Paragraph dialog box.

As with column width, you can use **P**revious Row or **N**ext Row to set the height of adjacent rows without leaving the dialog box to select them. If you use Exactly to set a height shorter than the text in the row, Word cannot display all the text in the row, as shown in figure 3.29. Using At Least avoids this problem and is generally a better choice unless you have specific typographical or design reasons for setting exact measurements.

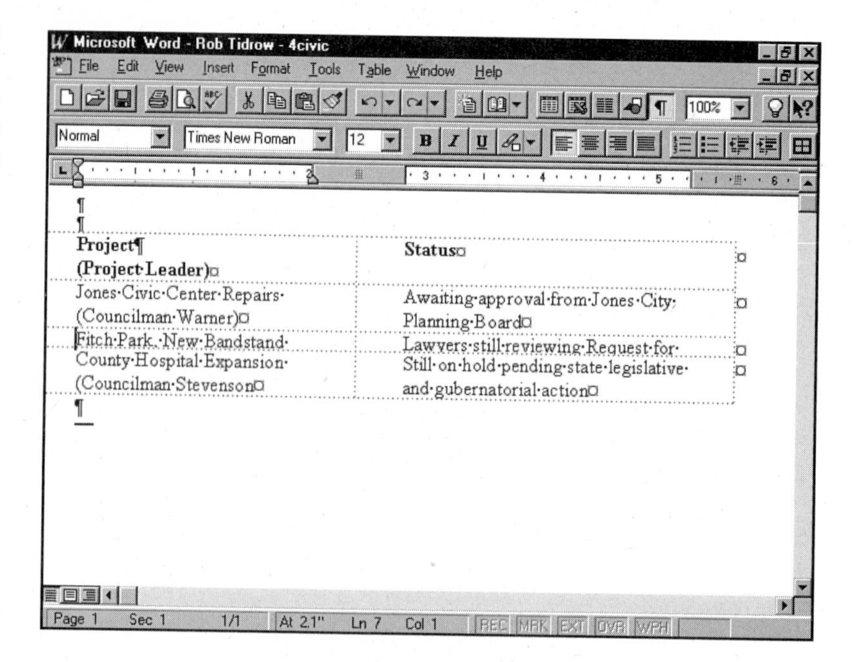

Figure 3.29

Bottom gridline overlaps text that cannot be displayed.

Deciding Whether Rows Can Break across Pages

In Word 2, it was simple: Rows could not break across pages. That simple limitation led to a variety of design restrictions, notably that you often could not use very deep rows.

Now, by default, rows can break across pages. That means you might want to pay attention to the way your page breaks look—widows and orphans in table rows can be even worse than in other parts of your document, especially if you haven't used cell borders to help the reader follow what is going on.

You can select specific cells (or an entire table) and tell Word not to let them break across pages. Choose Table, Cell Height and Width. Choose the Row tab in the Cell Height and Width dialog box, and uncheck the Allow Row to Break Across Pages box.

Indenting and Aligning Tables

You already have seen that existing paragraph indents can affect the location of text within cells. As you will see shortly, you can use the ruler to set indents and tabs within a cell or cells. But what if you want to indent or align the table, or some of its rows?

The Row tab in the Cell Height and Width dialog box contains these goodies, too. First, select the entire table (Alt+NumPad5) or just the rows you want to move. Next, open the Row tab in the Cell Height and Width dialog box. To indent the table, enter a new value in the Indent From Left list box.

To center the rows, click on the Center radio button in the Alignment group. To right-align the rows, click on the Right button. As shown in figure 3.30, these buttons have no effect on the alignment of text within an individual cell; they move the table or selected rows. Alignment matters only if your table is narrower than your margins—otherwise, it has no effect.

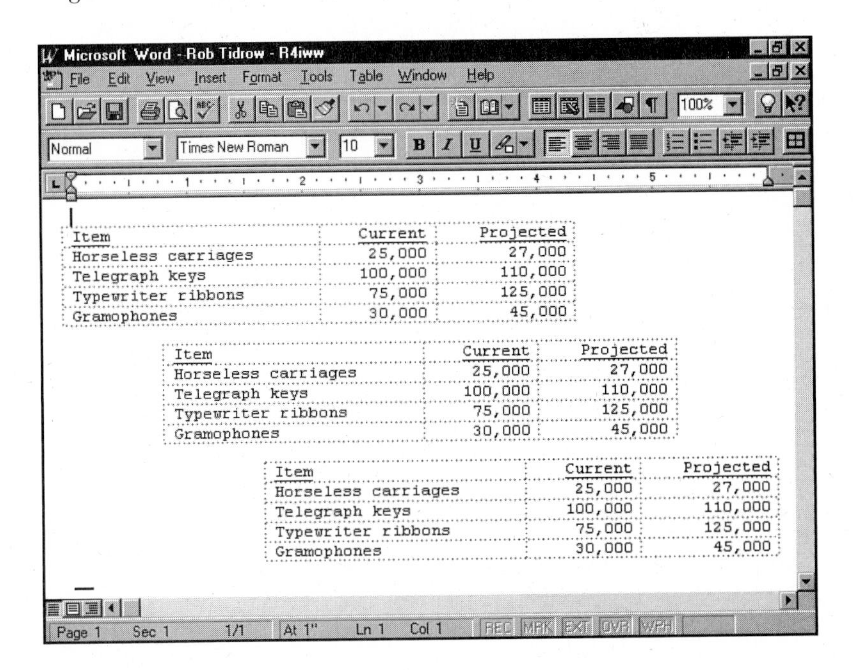

Figure 3.30

Left-, center-, and right-aligned tables.

One common use for center-aligning tables is to create figures. These figures are often preceded by captions, as shown in this book.

To make sure Word always prints the caption on the same page as the table, use the Keep with Next pagination setting in the Format Paragraph dialog box.

Setting Tabs from within a Table

Why bother with setting tabs within a table? After all, the table looks like tabbed text, and you can even use paragraph alignment to create left, center, and right alignments within a cell. It turns out there are several reasons to use tabs within a table, and one of the best is Word's decimal tab feature, which enables you to line up numbers over a decimal point, as shown in figure 3.31.

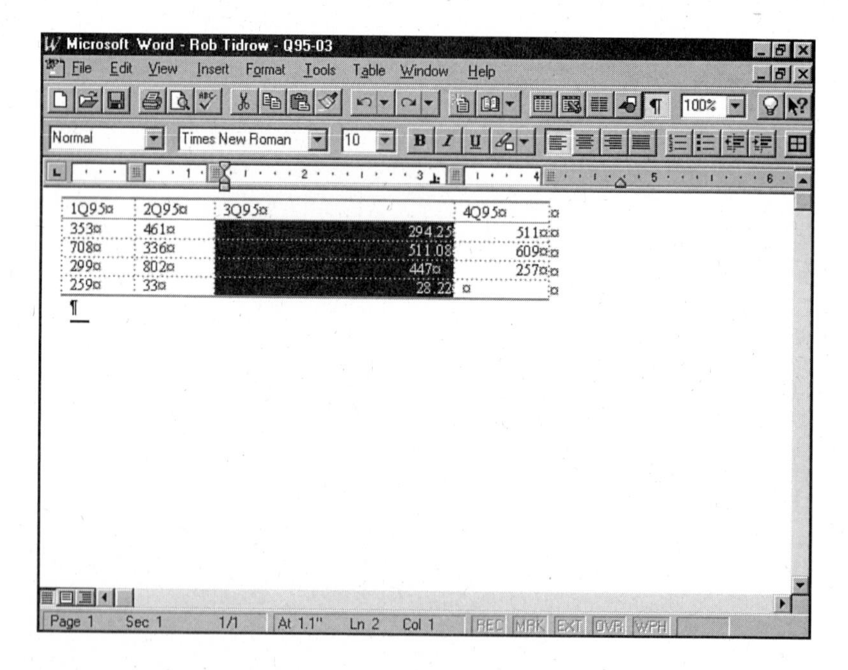

Figure 3.31
Decimal tabs within a table.

Also, you might occasionally have to line up several columns within an individual cell. Often it is easier to use tabs than to add cells and adjust their line widths.

To set tabs in the ruler, select the rows you want to add tab stops for (or press Alt+NumPad5 to select the entire table). Click on the tab box next to the ruler to choose a left, center, right, or decimal tab. Then, as shown in figure 3.32, click in the ruler where you want the tab to appear.

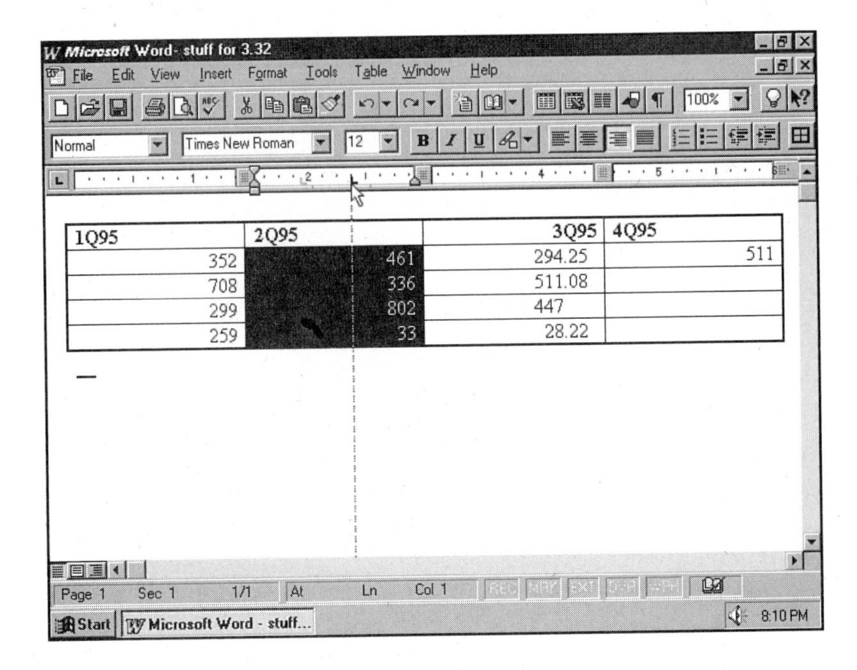

Figure 3.32

Setting a table's tabs using the ruler.

Adding Table Borders and Shading

In the earlier section "Autoformatting a Table," you already saw how Word's Table AutoFormat feature makes use of borders and shading to make tables easier to read and more attractive. You can use borders and shading not only to make your tables easier to read, but also to fool Word into displaying shapes and sizes that cannot easily be created any other way.

To add a border to an entire table, select the table (Alt+NumPad5), choose Format, Borders and Shading, and choose the Borders tab (see fig. 3.33). To add borders to specific cells, select them before choosing Format, Borders and Shading.

At the left, Word presents the three border approaches it expects you to use most often: None, Box, and Grid. None is the default setting. Box places a 3/4-point border around the edge of the table, with no border between cells inside. Grid places a 1 1/2-point border around the edge of the table, and a 3/4-point border around every cell. When you choose any of these three options, a sketch of the results appears in the Border section at the bottom left of the dialog box.

The Grid box appears only if you choose multiple cells within a table and nothing else. If you choose one cell, or if you choose text inside and outside a table, the Shadow box appears instead, as shown in figure 3.34.

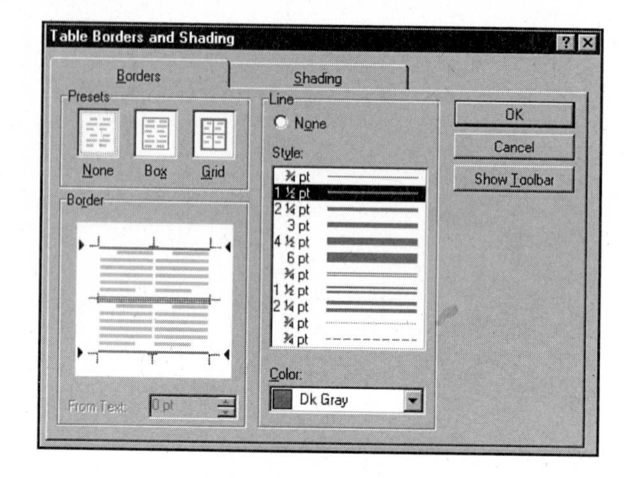

Figure 3.33
The Borders tab in the Table Borders and Shading dialog box.

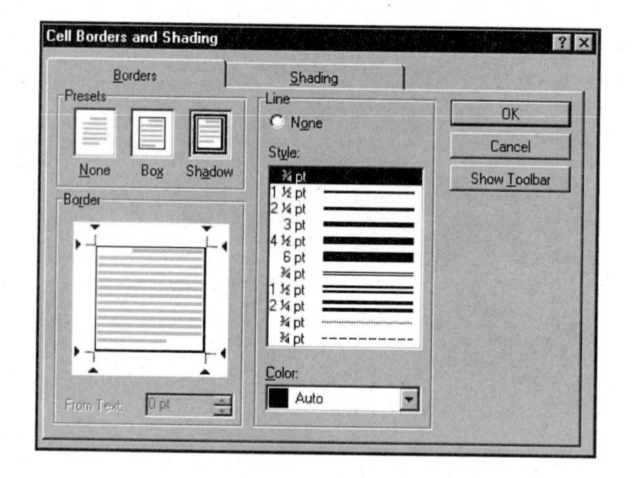

Figure 3.34
The Shadow box.

None, Box, Grid, and Shadow take care of most generic bordering, but you can individually control the left, right, top, and bottom borders of your table—or any cell within it.

To set or change the border of only one side of a table, first click the edge you want to border in the Border box. Then click the border you want. You also can choose a color for your border. Click on the Color list box and select from the options in figure 3.35.

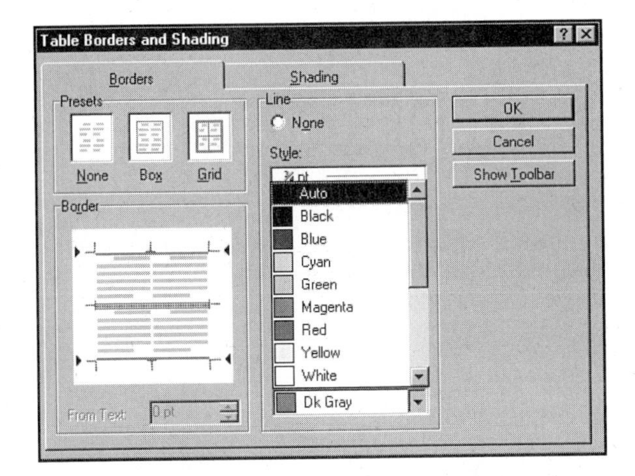

Figure 3.35

Border color choices.

Setting Borders with the Keyboard

With a keyboard, setting borders is clumsier, but still possible. In the dialog box, press R to enter the Border area. A very faint gray dotted line appears near the edge of the area (see fig. 3.36).

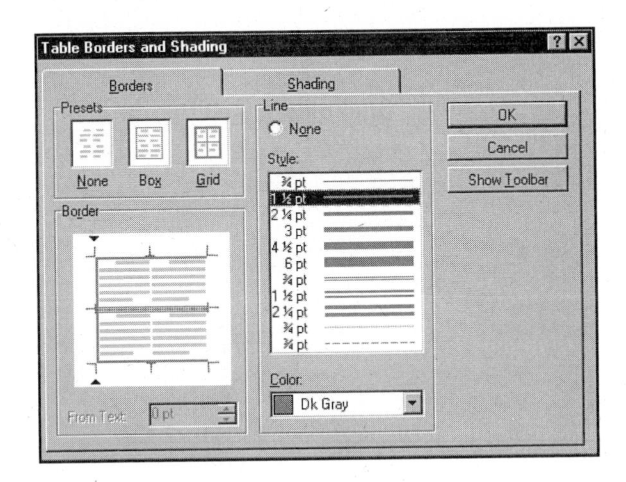

Figure 3.36

Bordering the left edge of a table using the keyboard.

Use the arrow keys to choose the edge or edges you want to border. Then press Y to enter the Style list box, and use the arrow keys to choose a border style.

Changing Preset Boxes and Grids

Although Word has default settings for its boxes and grids, you can change them. To change the Box border, first select it, then choose a different border from the Line area.

To change the Grid area, first select it. To change the outside borders, choose a different border from the Line area. To change the inside borders of each individual cell, click in the middle of the thumbnail sketch, then choose a new border from the Line area.

Using Borders Selectively

Remember, you can create individual borders for every cell. This enables you to perform all sorts of tricks, such as setting up the bowling score form shown in figure 3.37. This table is actually a four-line table, with the first and third lines containing the bowlers' names and pin counts (strikes, spares, and so on). The second and fourth lines contain the running scores.

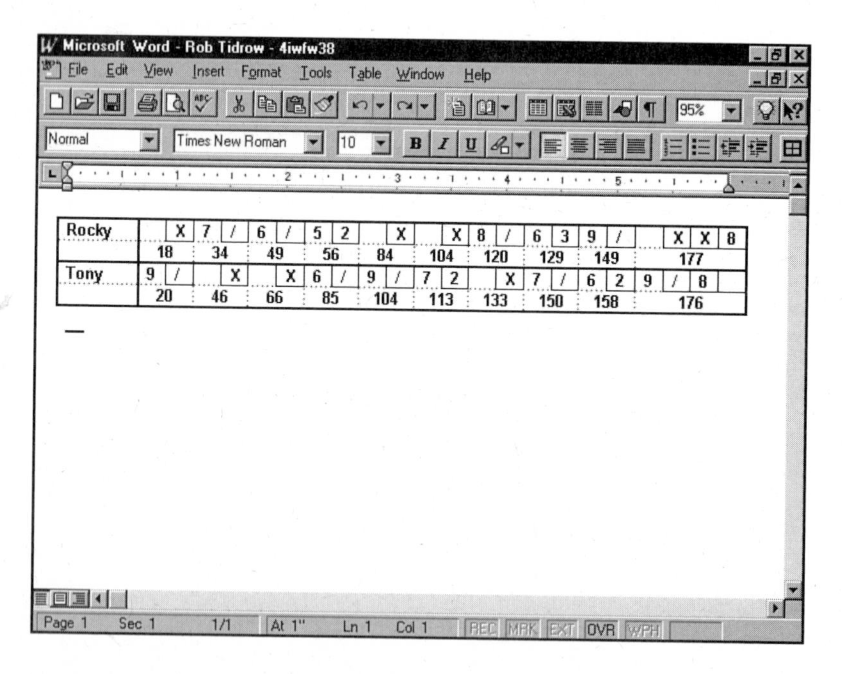

Figure 3.37

Bowling form created with tables.

Except for the column containing the bowlers' names, the first and third rows contain twice as many cells as the second and fourth rows, but each cell is half as wide. That makes it possible to create the small bordered box at the top right in each frame, where strikes and spares are recorded.

This works only because Word handles **S**pace Between Columns the way it does. If it actually placed space between every column, instead of just marking the column edges off-limits for text, the narrower columns would quickly become misaligned.

After the first small box is bordered, all the others are bordered by using the Repeat shortcut command, F4. When complete, the entire table is bordered by using the Bo**x** button.

You also can use selective borders to imitate placing two tables next to each other, something Word does not normally do. Border some cells at left, then border the cells at right, then select cells between them and eliminate their borders (see fig. 3.38).

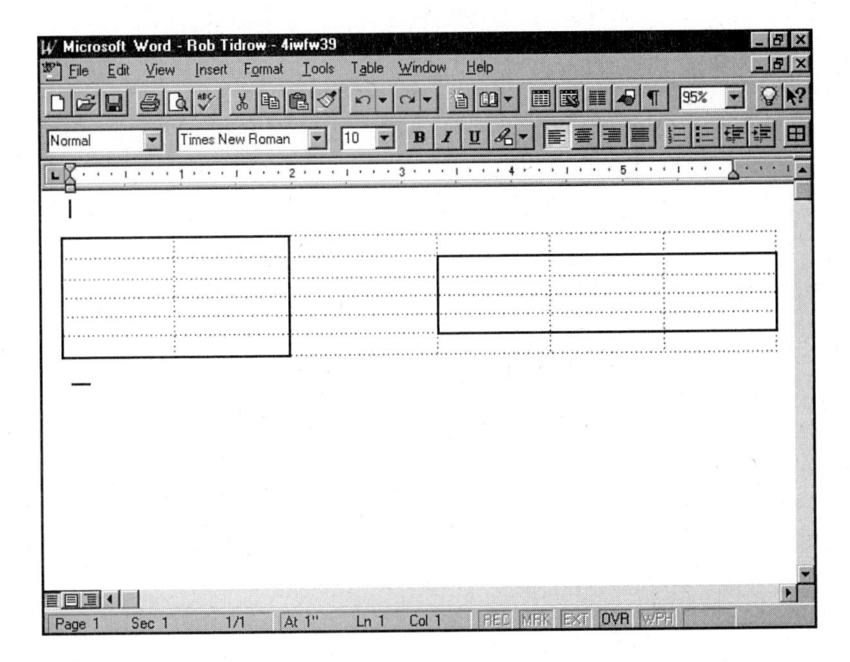

Figure 3.38

Turning one table into two.

Sometimes you might want your tables to stay in a specific location on the page regardless of what other editing takes place on the page. You might want to place a table on the right-hand side, for example, and have your text flow around it. To do that, **F**rame your table (see Chapter 21, "Desktop Publishing and Drawing," for more information).

Shading

As with any other paragraph, you also can create shading in part or all of a table. Select the cell or cells you want; then choose Format, Borders and Shading, and choose the Shading tab, as shown in figure 3.39. Unless you have a color printer, you might not be too concerned about Foreground and Background, which change colors.

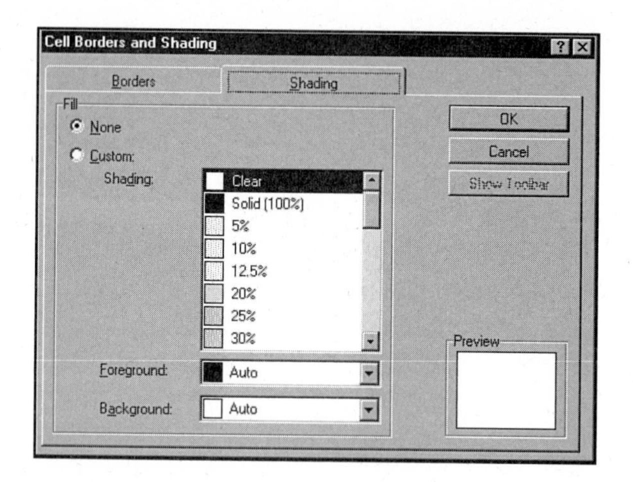

Figure 3.39
Shading tab box.

Even if you don't have a color printer, you might want to experiment; colors might print differently even on a black-and-white printer.

Shading might be more useful than colors on a day-to-day basis. Choosing it enables you to add many different kinds of shading to individual cells. Be careful with shading. Text that is printed over shaded text is much less readable. In general, unless the cell is intentionally left blank (as, for example, some cells on tax forms are), don't use more than 20 percent shading for text to be printed on a laser or inkjet printer.

The readability of shading depends on the quality of your printer. You can get away with darker shading if your text is sent to a Linotronic or other typesetting machine at 1,200 dots per inch. If you are working with a 9-pin dot-matrix printer, you might want to avoid shading altogether, or limit it to 10 percent, or you might want to boldface the text in a shaded area, so it will stand out more.

The Shading list box also provides several custom patterns, as shown in figure 3.40.

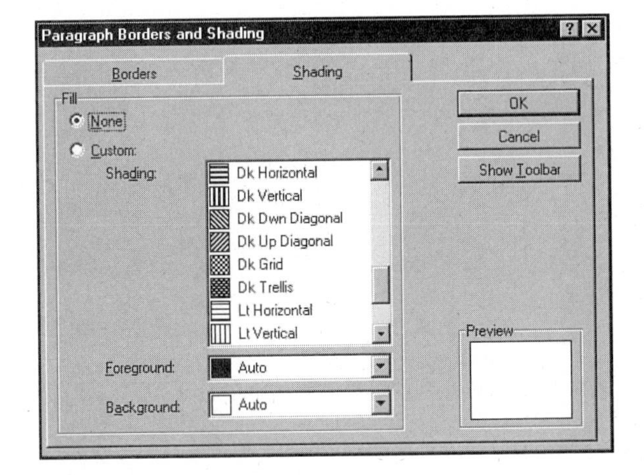

Figure 3.40
Custom shading available.

Merging Cells

Occasionally, you will create a table with information in separate cells and later decide the information should be merged into a single cell. You might, for example, realize you don't have enough room (width) to create all those columns—but you do have room to extend them vertically.

Merging cells solves this problem. Select the cells you want to merge, and choose Table, Merge Cells. Word combines all the selected cells in each row into a single cell. The information that originally was in separate cells is separated with a paragraph marker within each new cell. The new cell is the same width as all the previous cells combined. To narrow it, use the Column Width tools covered earlier. Figures 3.41 and 3.42 show a typical before-and-after example of using Merge Cells.

If you decide to split the cells again, select them and choose Split Cells, which appears instead of Merge Cells in the Table menu. By the way, Word's Split Cells feature can split cells even if they were not previously merged. Select the cell or cells you want to split; choose Split Cells from the Table menu. The Split Cells dialog box opens; specify how many columns you want to split each cell into. After you split a cell that was not previously merged, any text that originally appeared in that cell will appear in the first of the smaller cells you've created.

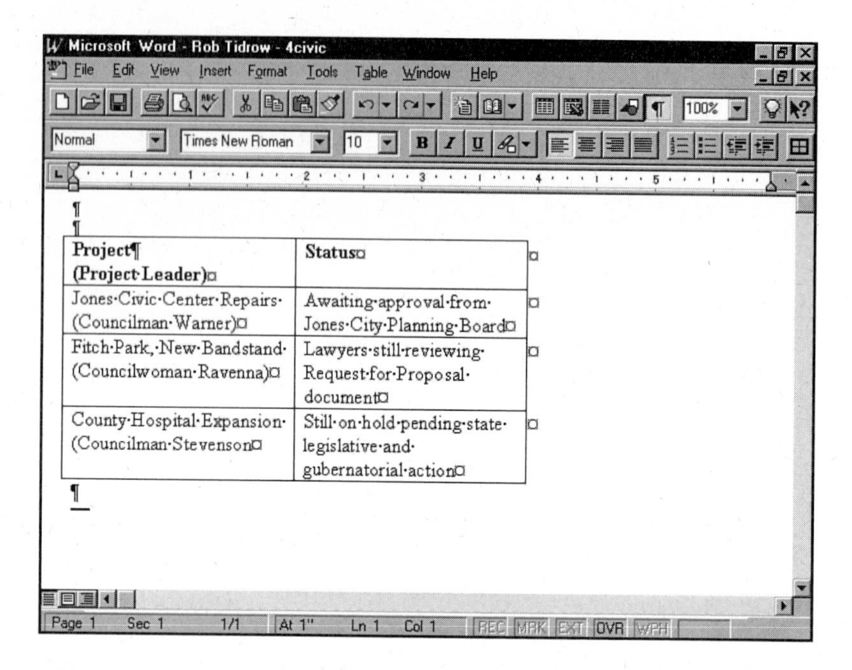

Figure 3.41

Before Merge Cells.

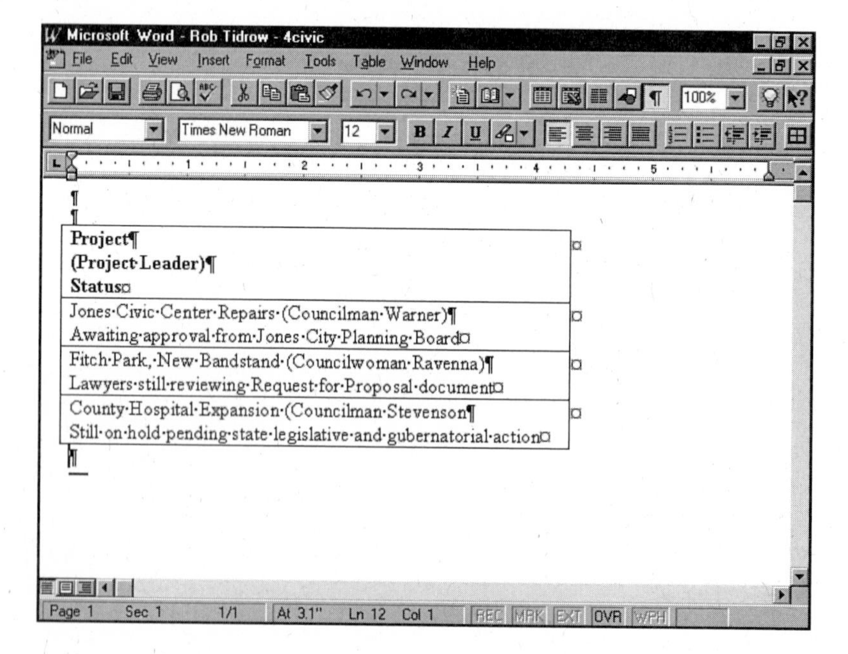

Figure 3.42

After Merge Cells.

Converting Text to Tables and Vice Versa

Sometimes you might want to convert text into a table format, or the other way around. For example:

- You might have an old table created that uses tabs; you now want to revise it, and it is easier to make the revisions by using tables.
- You might have a print merge or database file that was created or exported in tab-delimited or comma-delimited format.
- You might have text that you decide would simply look better in table format.

To create a table by using existing text, select the text, and choose Table, Convert Text to Table. The Convert Text to Table dialog box appears, as shown in figure 3.43.

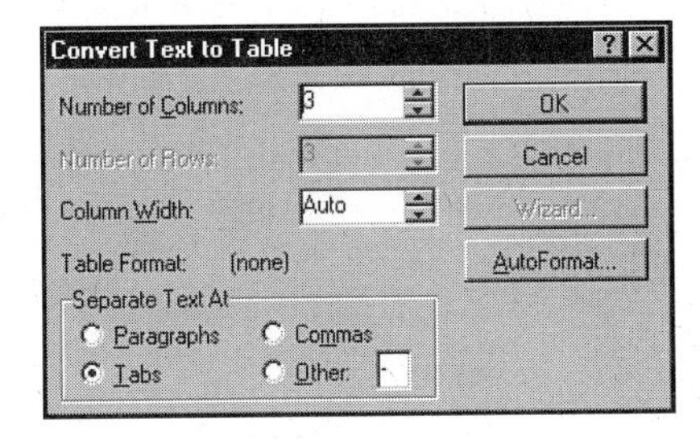

Figure 3.43

The Convert Text to Table dialog box.

When the dialog box opens, Word shows you its best guess as to the number of columns that will be required and how you want the text to be separated. If, for example, you have selected tabbed material, Word will probably think you want to Separate Text At Tabs. If the only breaks Word can find are paragraph marks, Separate Text At Paragraphs is likely to be marked. You can change this and even specify a custom character of your own.

You can either specify the column width yourself or autoformat the table by using Word's borders and shading features and its AutoFit mechanism for specifying column width.

Given a choice, you will generally find it easier to convert text where tabs or commas split cells than where all you have is paragraph marks. First, much of the text you will want to reformat as tables probably was originally created with tabs. (Commas usually are used with exported database files.) A more important reason, however, is the difference in how Word handles the text-to-table conversion.

When you are converting from tabbed or comma-delimited material, Word will recognize a paragraph mark (or line break) as its cue to start a new row. Word also is smart enough to create a table that accommodates the line with the most commas or tabs. All this means you can easily convert long lists of text into tables.

However, if you choose paragraph marks, Word can no longer tell when to end a row. It places each paragraph (or each chunk of text ending with a line break) in its own row. The result is a one-column table.

If you have a table of moderate length, you can use Edit Replace to swap all the paragraph marks (^p) in the selected text for tabs (^t). Then manually restore the paragraph marks where you want each row to end. Finally, use Table, Convert Text to Table.

Text-to-Table Conversions Traps to Avoid

If you are converting from tabbed text, whenever Word sees a tab, it places the text that follows the tab in a new cell to its right. Sometimes people use extra tabs to make sure all the text lines up properly, as in figure 3.44.

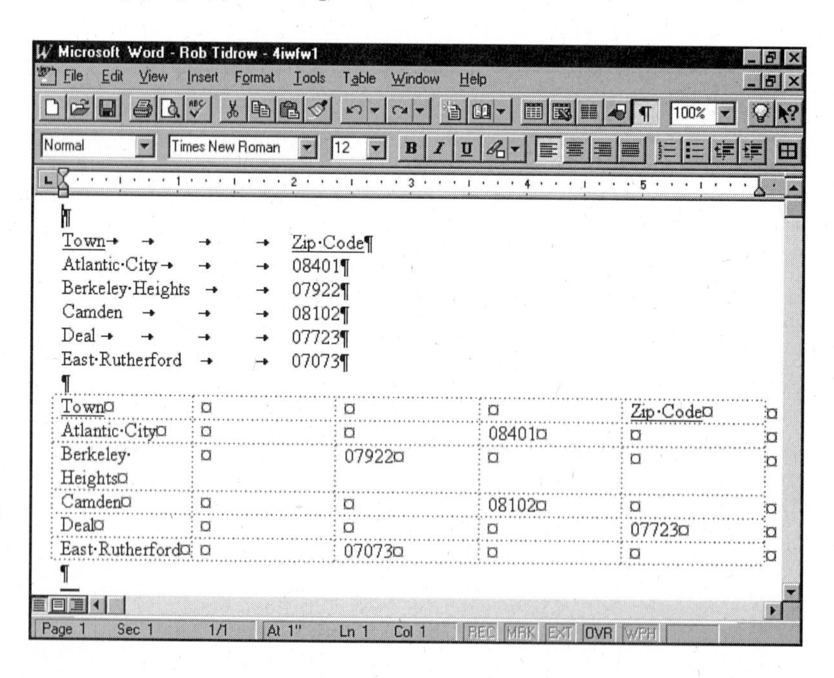

Figure 3.44 *Tabbed copy using uneven tabs, before and after.*

Extra tabs can create havoc when you convert from text to table, because Word will create unwanted empty cells. Of course, this would not have happened if custom tabs were set, rather than using 0.5" default tabs.

If you are converting from comma-delimited text, be careful to make sure that your document contains commas only where you want cell breaks. Sometimes a comma is really just a comma. It is easy to be thrown off by city/state addresses (Fort Myers, FL would be split into two columns) and by numbers (1,000,000 would be split into three columns).

Undoing Text-to-Table. If you don't like the results of your Text-to-Table conversion, use Undo Insert Table immediately. If you change your mind later, you can still revert to text by using Con**v**ert Table to Text, as described next. But you have to accurately specify whether to divide the table by using paragraph marks, tabs, or commas.

If you use tabs, you might also need to adjust the tab settings Word creates, which match the cell borders of the table you just eliminated.

Converting Tables to Text

Word also can convert tables back to text. Select the table (or rows) you want to convert. (Word does not convert only some of the cells in a row.) Choose Con**v**ert Table to Text. The Convert Table to Text dialog box opens, as shown in figure 3.45. You are asked whether to use paragraph marks, tabs, commas, or another character to divide the information in text. Choose an option, and click on OK.

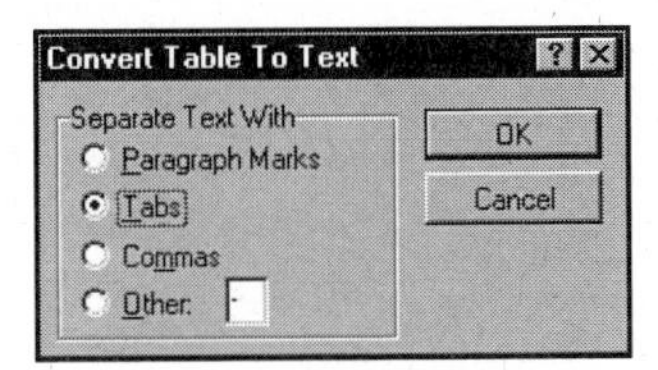

Figure 3.45
The Convert Table To Text dialog box.

Repeating Row Headings on Multiple Pages

What happens when you have several pages of tables, and you would like them all to share the same headings, such as a product list like that shown in figure 3.46? Word has a Headings feature specifically designed to do the job.

To use Headings, first create your table, including the row you want to repeat. Then select the row, and choose T**a**ble, **H**eadings. Now, if the table jumps to a second page, the marked heading repeats at the top of that page.

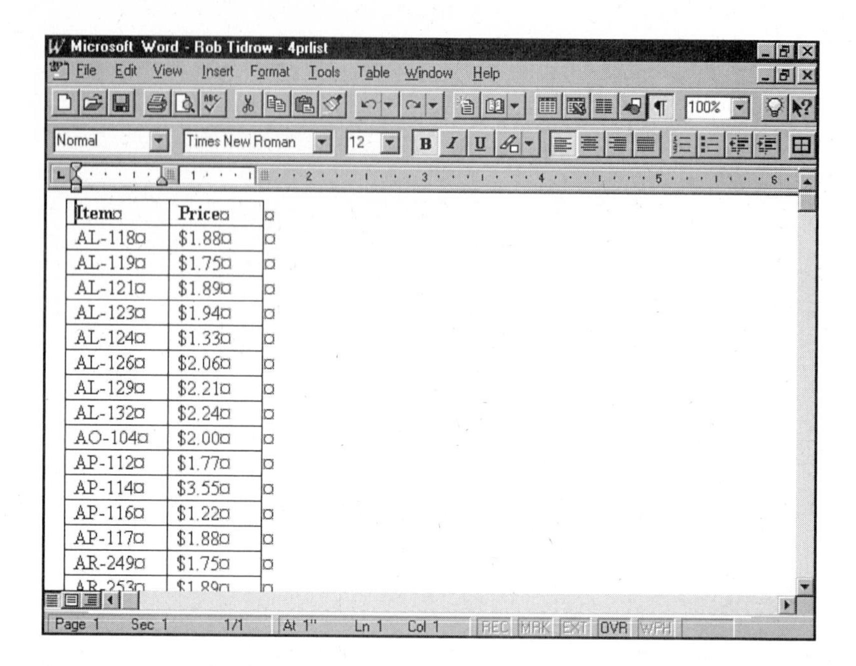

Item	Price
AL-118	$1.88
AL-119	$1.75
AL-121	$1.89
AL-123	$1.94
AL-124	$1.33
AL-126	$2.06
AL-129	$2.21
AL-132	$2.24
AO-104	$2.00
AP-112	$1.77
AP-114	$3.55
AP-116	$1.22
AP-117	$1.88
AR-249	$1.75

Figure 3.46
Excerpt from product list.

To tell whether a heading will repeat on multiple pages, select it and see if Headings has a check mark next to it in the Table menu. To stop a heading from repeating, select it and uncheck Headings in the Table menu.

Splitting Tables to Insert Text

What if you want to include nontable text in the middle of a table? Word provides for that, too. Place your insertion point where you want to add text, and choose Table, Split Table. This splits the table into two parts and places a paragraph mark between them, as shown in figure 3.47.

What happens when you create a table at the beginning of a document, and you then want to write something before it? You can't move your insertion point in front of the table. Even moving to the beginning of the document (Ctrl+Home) won't do it.

The solution? Place your insertion point in the first cell of the table and choose Table, Split Table.

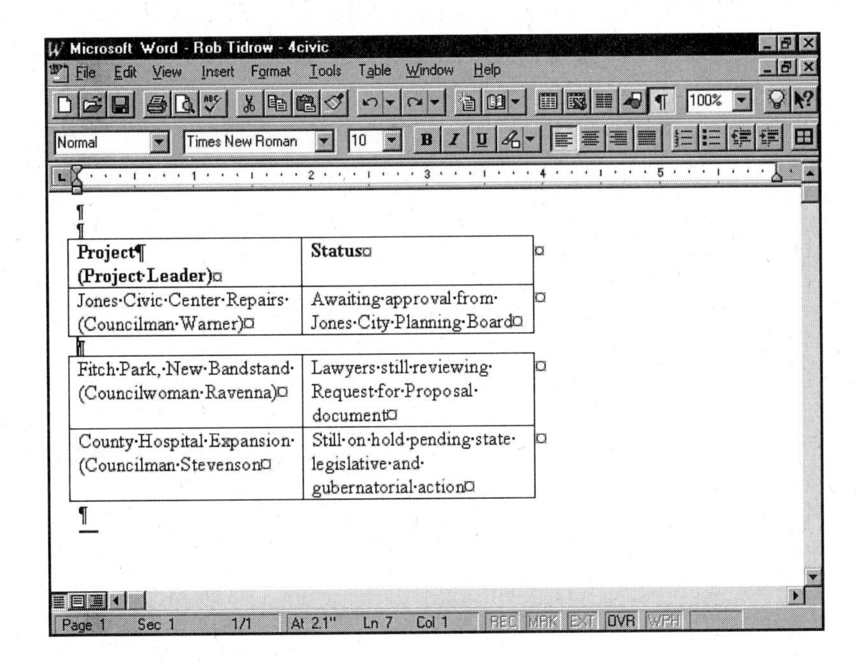

Figure 3.47

Using Split Table.

A Simple Table Calculation

Basic tables look tantalizingly like spreadsheets. In fact, a Word table can actually be made to perform a wide variety of relatively complex calculations. You can open Microsoft Excel, if you have it, directly from within Word and perform every imaginable sort of spreadsheet trickery.

What if you simply want to add up a list of numbers? Imagine you have the table shown in figure 3.48.

To add the numbers, place your insertion point in an empty cell beneath (or to the right of) the list, and choose Tools, Formula. The Formula dialog box appears, already containing a formula such as =SUM(ABOVE) or =SUM(LEFT) (see fig. 3.49).

Click on OK, and Word adds the column or row. You also can choose a Number Format from the list box, which includes dollar and percentage formats.

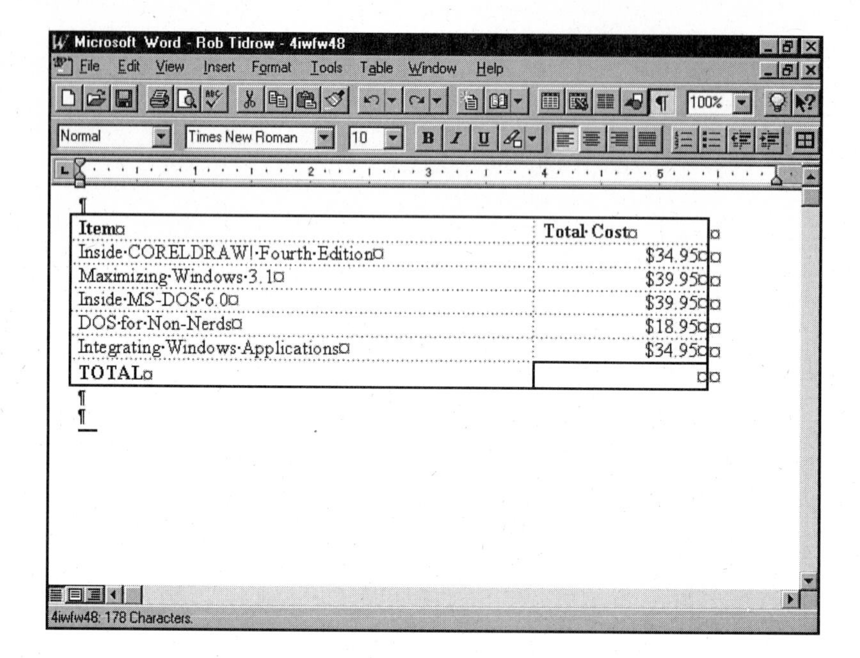

Figure 3.48 *Bill of sale.*

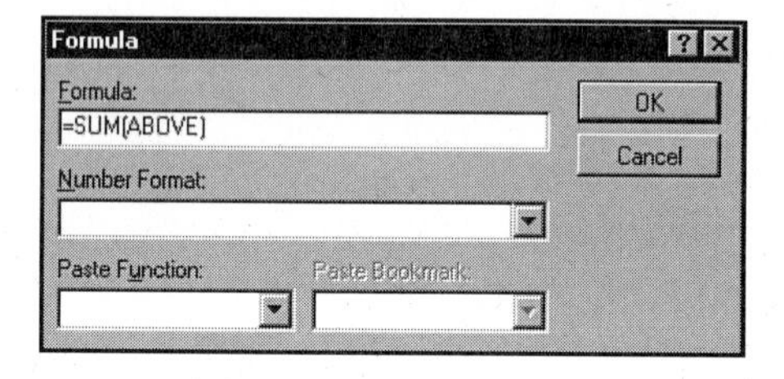

Figure 3.49 *The Formula dialog box.*

From here, you also can write your own formula in any table cell. Word cell references are similar to those in Microsoft Excel; the top left cell in a table is called A1. Rows are numbered, columns are lettered. To subtract cell A1 from cell A2, use the following formula:

=A2-A1

To multiply cell A1 by cell A2, use the following formula:

=A1*A2

To divide cell A1 by cell A2, use the following formula:

=A1/A2

Word offers a variety of functions that also can be used in table formulas. These are available in the Paste Function box.

Finally, your formulas can include numbers from anywhere in your document. Mark the number you want to include as a bookmark. Select it, choose Edit, Bookmark, name the bookmark, and click on OK. Then insert the bookmark in your formula by picking it from the list in Paste Bookmark. (For more on bookmarks, see Chapter 16, "Bookmarks.")

You do not need to be in a table to use the Formula command (although it often simplifies life to work from a table).

Word comes with a built-in macro, TableMath, that can help you with more complex formulas. To install TableMath, follow the instructions in the next section, substituting TableMath for TableNumber.

Automatically Numbering Columns or Rows

This chapter already has mentioned that Word's Table Wizard can automatically insert much of the boilerplate you will want in your tables—inserting, for example, consecutive months of the year. What if you have an existing table and you want to number the rows or columns consecutively? Word comes with a macro, *TableNumber*, that automatically adds numbering to the left, right, top, or bottom of a table.

Before you can use this macro, however, you have to make it available. TableNumber is located in the TABLES7.DOT file, which is typically installed into the WINWORD\MACROS folder. (If you have installed Office 95, look for the OFFICE95\WINWORD\MACROS folder.) There are several ways to make TableNumber available for use; these are described in Chapter 11, "Macros."

The simplest way to make TableNumber available every time you run Word is to move TABLES.DOT into the \WINWORD\STARTUP folder. Every time you run Word, TableNumber—and all the other macros in TABLES.DOT—will be loaded into memory automatically.

Once the macro is available, you still have to run it. Create your table and position the cursor within it. Next, choose Macro from the Tools menu. Choose TableNumber from the Macro Names list, and choose Run. Word displays a dialog box asking where you want the numbering: Number Left, Number Right, Number Top, or Number Bottom. Choose one, and choose OK. Word will add a column or row and insert consecutive numbering in that column or row.

Notice that by default Word numbers the first row of your table; if you are using that row as a header, you might not want it numbered. One workaround to solve this problem is to split the table after the first row; then number the table; then eliminate the space between the first row and following rows so the table once again functions as one table.

A Simple Table Sort

Sorting is another simple trick you can perform anywhere in Word, but you are especially likely to use sorting in tables. Say you wanted to sort alphabetically the list of entertainers in figure 3.50.

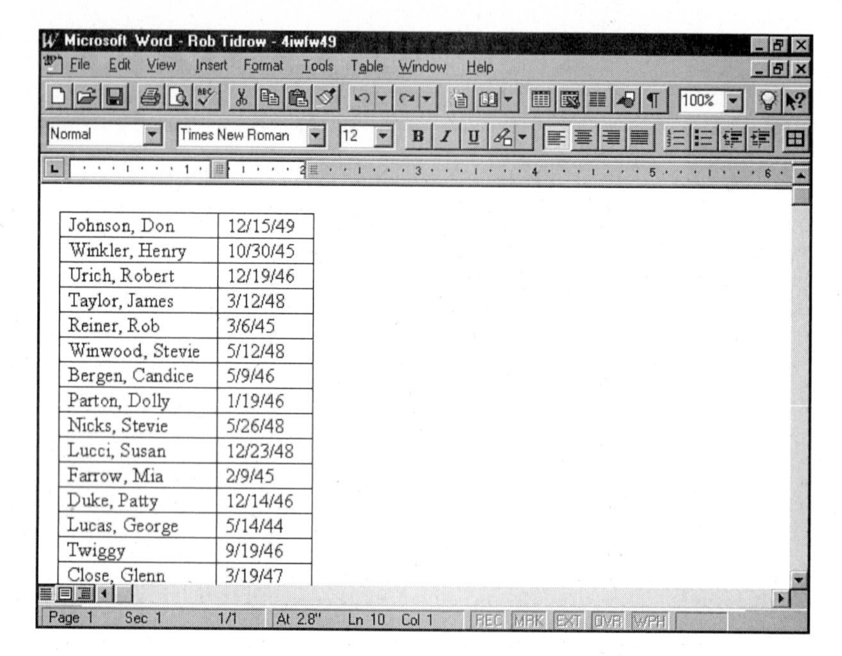

Figure 3.50
List of entertainers.

Select the table and choose T<u>a</u>ble, Sor<u>t</u>. The Sort dialog box appears, as shown in figure 3.51. You can specify up to three levels of sorting. Imagine you have a table in which column 1 includes company names, column 2 includes cities, and column 3 includes names of sales representatives for these companies. You could tell Word to sort first based on company names; after those are in order, to sort based on cities, and finally on the sales representatives' names.

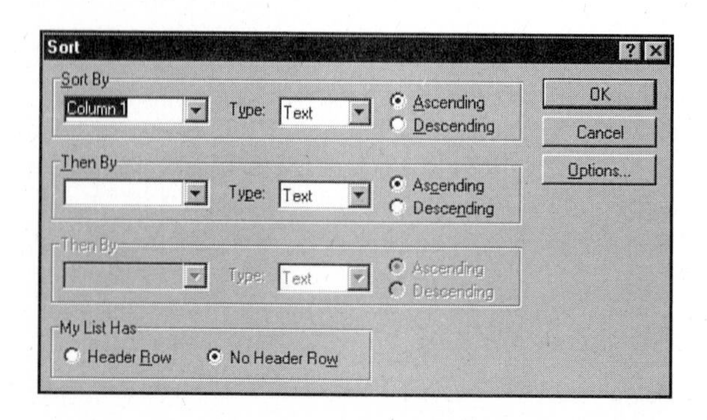

Figure 3.51
The Sort dialog box.

You would get a neatly ordered list of companies, in which each company's listings were sorted by city, and each company's city listings were sorted alphabetically by name.

You also can tell Word to sort a table alphabetically based on text, sort a field based on date order, or sort a field in numeric order. (These sorts can have different results.) You also can specify whether each sort should appear in ascending or descending order.

Word solves an annoying problem: What do you do about the top row? You don't want to sort it, but then you would have to select every line except the top row—a pain in the neck. Now you can tell Word your top row is a Header **R**ow, and Word leaves it alone.

To sort only a single column without moving any text in other columns, select the column, choose T**a**ble, **S**ort, and then choose **O**ptions. The Sort Options dialog box appears (see fig. 3.52). Choose So**r**t Column Only.

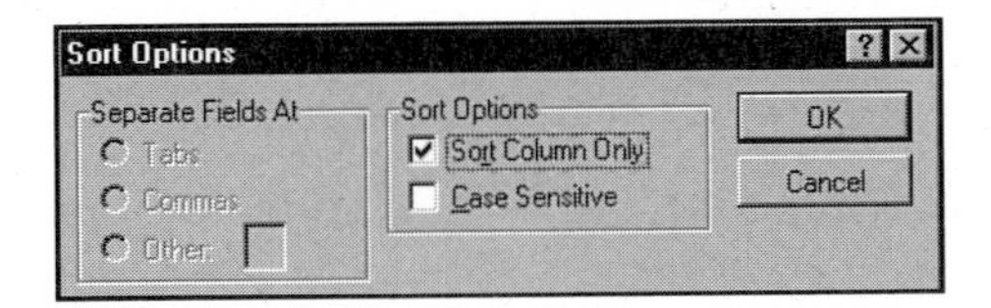

Figure 3.52

The Sort Options dialog box.

Normally, Word sorts are not case-sensitive: march and March are listed next to each other. If you want Word to separate them, listing all capitalized words before lowercase words, choose **C**ase Sensitive in the Sort Options box.

If you are sorting a list that is not in a table, you have to specify a separator in Sort Options: tabs, commas, or another character.

If you want to alphabetize the names in the first column, A to Z, the settings are right. Click on OK. But what if, for instance, you wanted to find the youngest entertainer? For this example, follow these steps:

1. Select the table (Alt+NumPad5).
2. Choose **T**ools, **S**ort.
3. Choose Column 2 from the **S**ort By list box.
4. Choose Date from the Ty**p**e list box.
5. Choose **D**escending.
6. Click on OK.

There you are, youngest to oldest, in figure 3.53.

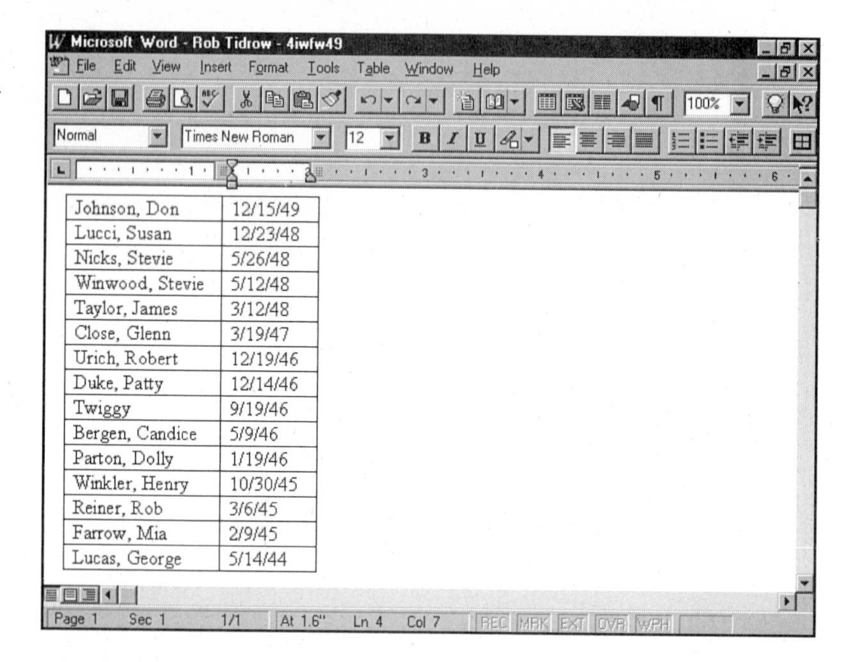

Johnson, Don	12/15/49
Lucci, Susan	12/23/48
Nicks, Stevie	5/26/48
Winwood, Stevie	5/12/48
Taylor, James	3/12/48
Close, Glenn	3/19/47
Urich, Robert	12/19/46
Duke, Patty	12/14/46
Twiggy	9/19/46
Bergen, Candice	5/9/46
Parton, Dolly	1/19/46
Winkler, Henry	10/30/45
Reiner, Rob	3/6/45
Farrow, Mia	2/9/45
Lucas, George	5/14/44

Figure 3.53
List of entertainers, by age.

A Table of Table Uses

The following minitable leads you to chapters that show you how to perform other table tasks:

Task	Chapter
Using tables to build databases for mail merge	19
Using tables with frames in desktop publishing	21
Using tables to build forms	23

Printing and Faxing

Word 95 gives you nearly total control over what you print and where you print it. If all you need to do is print single copies of your current document, one click does the job. But if you want to control highly complex elements of your print job, you can do that, too.

In this chapter:

- Understanding Windows and Word printing
- Printing a whole document
- Printing part of a document
- Printing odd or even pages
- Printing accompanying information
- Setting up a printer
- Printing an envelope

- Printing postal bar codes
- Printing labels
- Printing to a file
- Printing multiple files at once
- Printing in the background
- Troubleshooting printing
- Using Print Preview
- Printing to fax
- Using Fax addresses from your Personal Address Book
- Using Fax security features

Basic Word Printing

Basic Word printing is as simple as it gets. Click the Print button in the Standard toolbar (see fig. 4.1).

Figure 4.1
The Print button.

Doing that prints one copy of your entire document to your current printer (assuming that the printer is turned on and hooked up properly).

Much of the time, maybe *most* of the time, that's all you need to know. Some of the time, printing your document requires more than clicking on the Print button. The rest of this chapter covers those other times.

If you're finding that Word prints too slowly, try disabling background printing (background printing is discussed in detail later in this chapter). In the meantime, follow these steps to disable background printing.

1. Select Options from the Tools menu.
2. Select the Print tab.

3. Uncheck **B**ackground Printing from the Printing Options group.
4. Click on the OK button.

Controlling How and What It Prints

The primary way that Word controls how and what it prints is through the Print dialog box, available by choosing the **P**rint option on the **F**ile menu (see fig. 4.2). Or just press Ctrl+P.

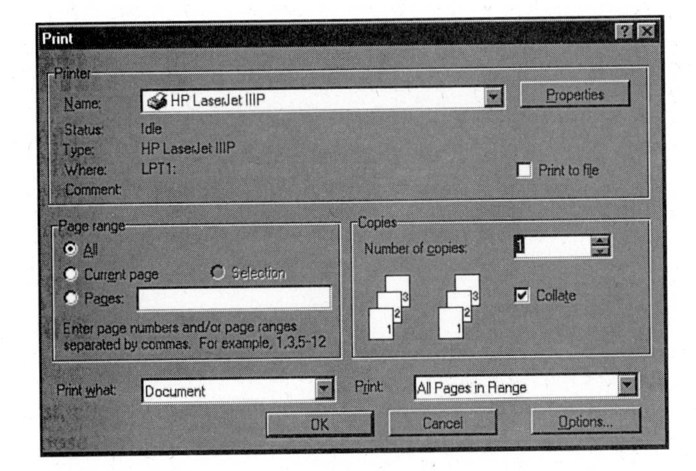

Figure 4.2

The Print dialog box.

If you've used the Word print dialog box before, you can see that it has been revamped in Word 95. Less has changed than meets the eye, however. As before, the simplest thing you can do is print one copy of your document. To do that, just choose the OK button. As you can see, however, you have some other choices.

The choice you might use most often is Number of copies. You can choose to print as many copies as you want. When you print multiple copies, you have another choice to make: Should Word collate the printed copies?

By default, Word automatically collates your documents. As a practical matter, this generally means that Word sends the entire document to the printer, waits a moment, and then sends it again. You get output that's already printed in page order. Because you normally want your document to print in page order, what could be wrong with collated copies?

The only downside of collated copies is speed. Printers process each of the pages in your document separately. When the second copy starts, none of that processing is still there—it has to be done all over again. This can become a significant bottleneck if your documents use extensive graphics or formatting.

Most laser printers can, however, print several *consecutive* copies of the same page without reprocessing them. So if you're willing to manually collate your document, you might get done sooner. To prevent Word from collating your document, uncheck Collate in the bottom right corner of the Print dialog box.

Printing Part of a Document

Rather than printing every page of your document (which is the default), the Print dialog box enables you to control which pages print. You can print just the page the text insertion point is in by choosing Current page from the Page range group, or you can specify a range of pages to print.

The Page range option group at the left-hand side of the Print dialog box enables you to specify the page range you want to print. Specify the pages you want to print in the Pages option box. Word understands hyphens and commas in the Pages option box as in the following examples:

1–3	prints pages 1 through 3
1,2,6	prints pages 1, 2, and 6
1–3,5,8	prints pages 1 through 3 and pages 5 and 8

The accompanying CD-ROM contains a file you can use to practice some of the procedures in this chapter: IWMS4A.DOC.

Printing Odd and Even Pages

If you want to print only odd or even pages, you can make this choice from the Print drop-down box shown in figure 4.3. Choose Odd Pages or Even Pages instead of the default, All Pages in Range.

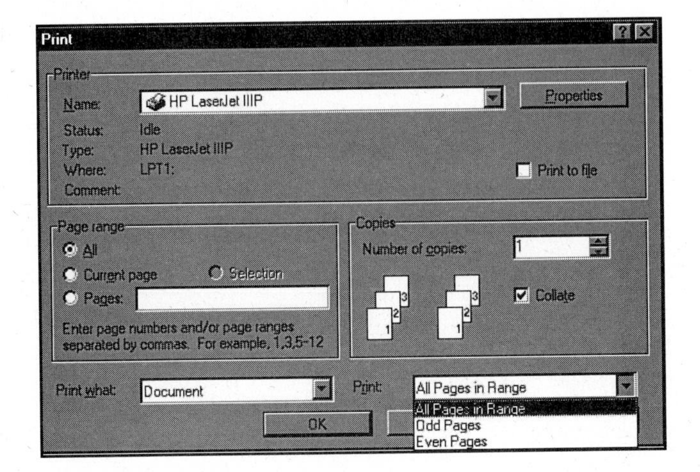

Figure 4.3

The Print drop-down box.

Printing Accompanying Information

Several other elements can be associated with a Word file besides just the document itself. For example, Word stores Summary Info about the document's title, subject, author, and keywords along with considerable space for comments. The Summary Info and other information doesn't print automatically, but you can use a variety of methods to print these elements.

First, you can print the item without printing the entire document. To do this, follow these steps:

1. Select **P**rint from the **F**ile menu.
2. Select the Print **w**hat list box, and choose the element you want to print. As you can see from fig. 4.4, the default element is Document, which signifies the entire document.
3. Click on the OK button.

The second method is to tell Word to print the additional element whenever you print the document. To do this, perform the following steps:

1. Select **O**ptions from the **T**ools menu.
2. Select the Print tab.
3. Check the element in the Include with Document box (see fig. 4.5).

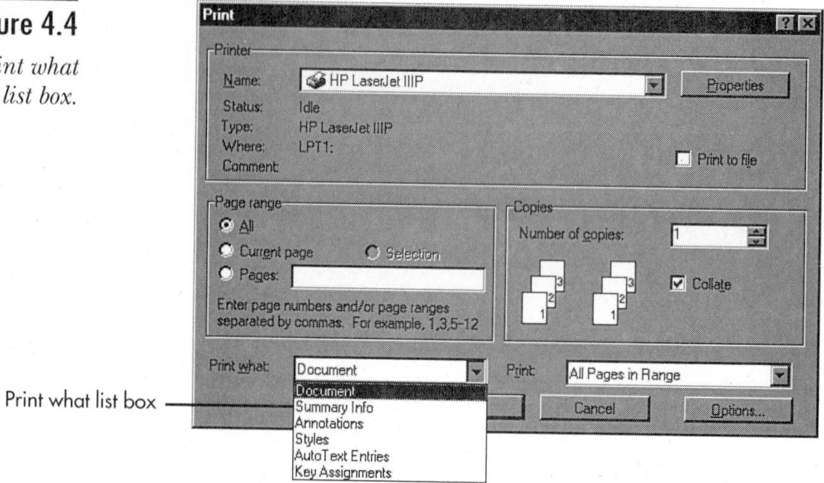

Figure 4.4

The Print what list box.

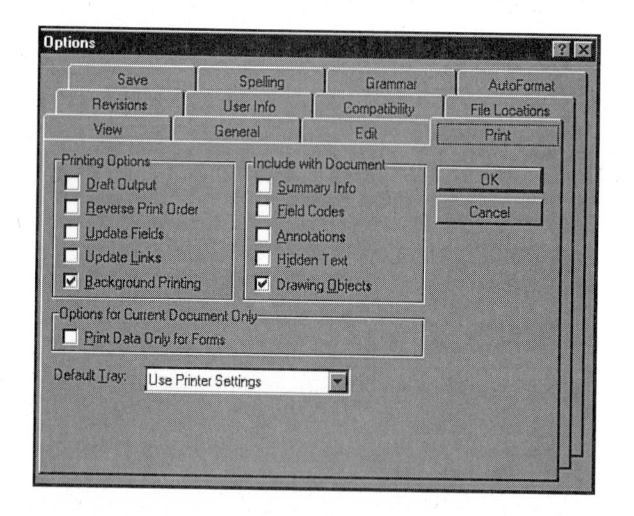

Figure 4.5

The Print tab.

Table 4.1 summarizes how to print each element of a Word file and lists the chapters in which you learn about elements that haven't been introduced yet.

Table 4.1
Printing Elements of Word Files

Element	Include with Document (Tools, Options, Print)	Print Separately (File, Print, Print What)	Display in Document, then Print (Tools, Options, View)	Other
Annotations (Chapter 18)	X	X		
AutoText Entries (Chapter 9)	X			
Envelopes				Covered later in this chapter
Field Codes (Chapter 10)	X		X	
Hidden Text	X		X	
Shortcut "Key Assignments" (Chapters 11, 24)		X		
Revisions (Chapter 18)				Tools Revisions show revisions in printed document
Styles (Chapter 7)	X			
Summary Info (Chapter 6)	X	X		

If you're in the habit of inserting nasty messages to yourself in Hidden Text, double-check Tools, Options, Print to make sure that Hidden Text isn't set to print.

Changing Printer Properties

Like nearly everything else in Windows 95, your printer has Properties. To view or change these properties, choose Properties in the File, Print dialog box. The Properties tabbed dialog box opens (see fig. 4.6).

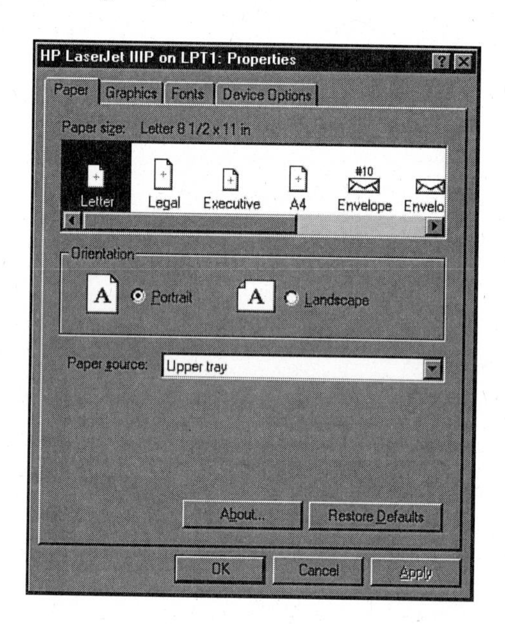

Figure 4.6
A typical Printer Properties tabbed dialog box.

In this typical Properties dialog box are four tabs:

- **Paper**—From where you can specify paper size, paper source, and Portrait or Landscape mode.
- **Graphics**—From where you can specify print resolution, dithering, or intensity. Lower print resolutions can sometimes print more quickly. Dithering blends pure colors into patterns to simulate a wider variety of colors. Choose Line art if your document contains many drawings with high-contrast; choose Error diffusion if it contains many photographs or pictures without sharp, well-defined edges. Choose Coarse if you are printing at 300 dpi or more; choose Fine if you have lowered your print resolution below 200 dpi.

- **Fonts—**From where you can specify whether to download TrueType fonts as bitmap soft fonts (the default), or print them as graphics. Sometimes, choosing to print TrueType fonts as graphics can make your print job faster, especially if your print job has many graphics already. One aspect of Print TrueType as graphics is a drawback or an advantage, depending on your needs. With this feature on, Word "clips" the tops or bottoms of characters if they overlap with other characters, graphics, or table cell boundaries.
- **Device Options—**From where you can specify how conservatively or aggressively Windows 95 should track your printer's memory usage. The more aggressive a setting you choose, the less likely Windows 95 will refuse to attempt a print job due to its complexity—but the job is more likely to fail because your printer runs out of memory.

Setting Up a Printer

Until now, this chapter assumes that you're working with a printer that's properly set up in Windows. But what if you get a new printer? This, too, has been revamped in Windows 95. Microsoft now offers a wizard that walks you through the steps to add a printer.

When you add a printer through Windows 95, it's available for all Windows programs.

First, click the Start button, and choose Settings, Printers. In the Printers dialog box, choose Add Printer. The Add Printer Wizard opens, as shown in figure 4.7.

Click Next. You are now asked whether the printer you want to install is a Local printer (connected directly to your computer) or a Network printer (see fig. 4.8). Assuming that you're connecting to a local printer, choose Local, and click Next.

Windows next displays a list of manufacturers and printers (see fig. 4.9). Choose the Manufacturer that made your printer. Windows displays a list of Printers for which it has printer drivers; choose yours from the list. Click Next.

Next, Windows asks which communications port you want to use; choose from the list of Available ports Windows finds on your system (see fig. 4.10). Then choose Next.

Windows displays the printer's standard name (see fig. 4.11). You can accept it—or change it to a name that may be more familiar to you or your colleagues. In this dialog box, you can also specify whether the new printer will be your default printer, or whether Windows should continue to use the same default printer. Choose Next.

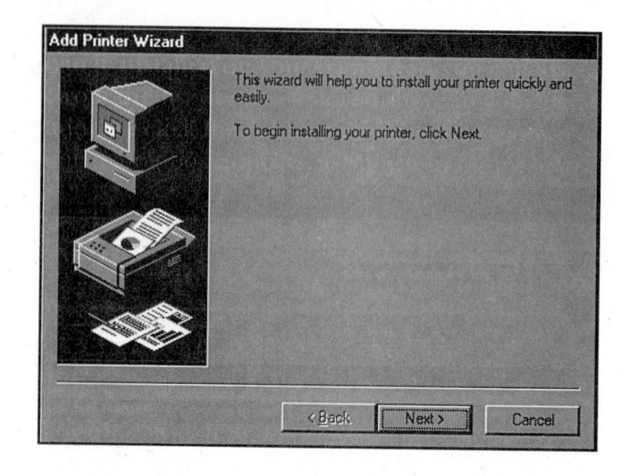

Figure 4.7

The Add Printer Wizard opening dialog box.

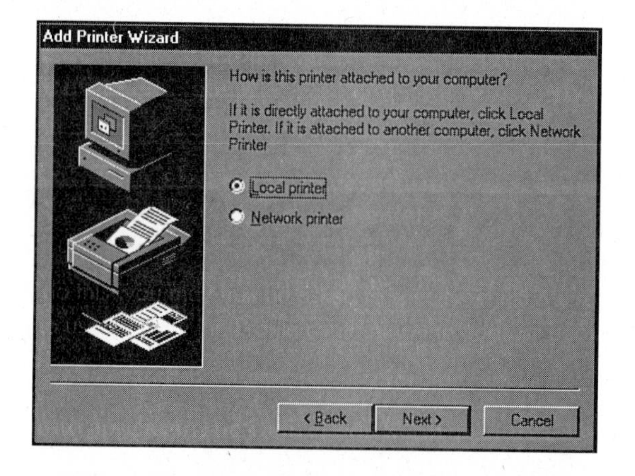

Figure 4.8

Choosing a local or network printer.

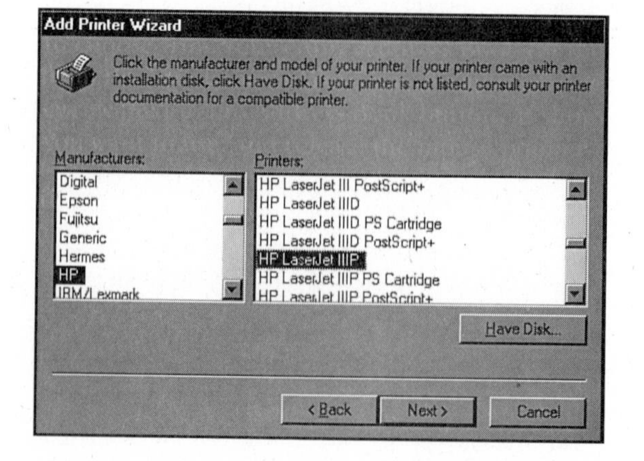

Figure 4.9

Choosing a printer manufacturer and model.

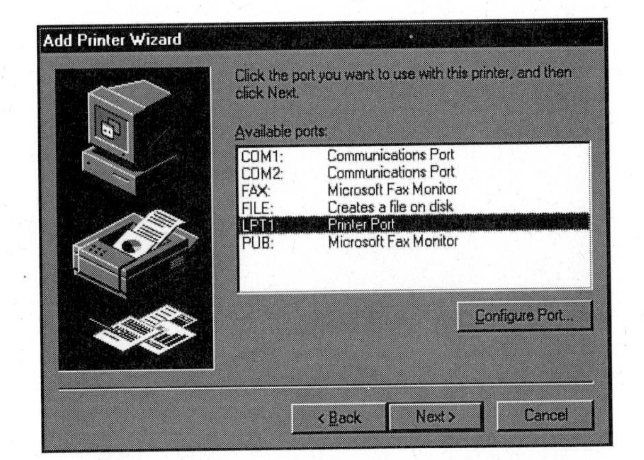

Figure 4.10

Choosing a communications port.

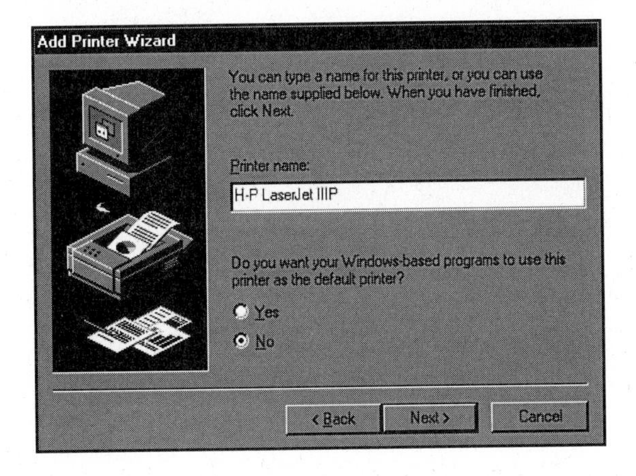

Figure 4.11

Setting a printer name.

Windows offers to print a standard test page. Choose Yes to print the page; choose No if you don't want to. You might choose No if the printer is not actually hooked to your computer. (Perhaps you are installing a driver for your office printer on your home system, so you can make sure that the document prints properly when you bring it to work.) Choose Next. Windows now asks for the disk containing the printer driver (see fig. 4.12). Insert it and click on OK. Windows now installs the new printer driver. After it finishes, the printer driver appears in the list of printers available in Word's print dialog box.

You can install as many printer drivers as you want, regardless of whether you actually have those printers connected to your system.

In fact, there is at least one instance in which you should install printer drivers for printers you don't own. If you ultimately are going to print your document

continues

somewhere else (for instance, you're working on a document at home and you want to print it on the fancy laser printer at work), using that printer's driver while you prepare the document helps you make sure that it prints out as you expect.

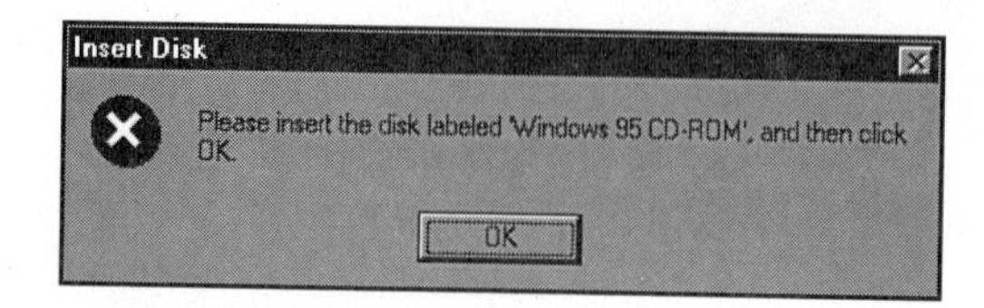

Figure 4.12
Windows requesting the disk or CD-ROM containing your new printer driver.

Switching between Printers

When you have two or more printers installed, you can switch between them from within Word as follows:

1. Select Print from the File menu.

2. Click the down-arrow next to the Name box. A list of currently installed printers appears. Select the printer you want.

Controlling Other Printing Options

You already encountered the Tools, Options, Print tab (refer to fig. 4.5) in the discussion of how to print other elements, such as annotations, along with your document.

You also can control many other aspects of printing by checking or unchecking boxes in this dialog box:

- **Draft Output**—Tells Word to print a document with very little formatting—how little formatting depends on the printer.

- **Reverse Print Order**—Tells Word to print your pages backward.

- **Update Fields**—Tells Word to update all the fields in your document before printing. (See Chapter 10, "Field Codes," for more details on fields. But for now, it is enough to understand that fields include many items you can insert into the text of your document, such as date, time, tables of contents, index entries, and calculations.)

In Word 2, fields were automatically updated by default before printing. Word 95 does not automatically update them unless you check the **U**pdate Fields box.

- **Update Links—**Tells Word to check any DDE or OLE connections you've made with other documents or files. If those connections include text that has changed, Word prints the new text. (See Chapter 20, "Word as an Integrating Environment.")

The last printing option, Background Printing, is discussed a bit later in this chapter.

Changing Paper Sources

Many printers allow more than one paper source. For example, many dot-matrix printers can accept pin-fed paper or manual feed. And many laser printers can have two trays: one for stationery, another for plain paper or envelopes. You can specify a paper source as follows:

1. Choose Page Setup from the File menu.
2. Choose the Paper Source tab (see fig. 4.13).

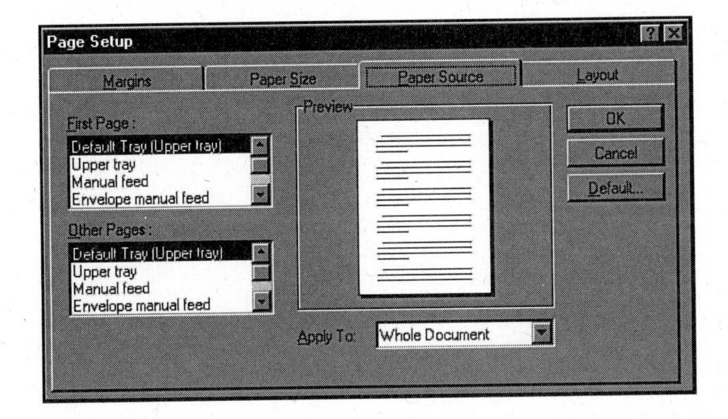

Figure 4.13

The Paper Source tab in File, Page Setup.

Note that you can choose different paper sources for the **F**irst Page and **O**ther Pages. Most business correspondence uses one type of letterhead for the first page, and another (or blank paper) for the following pages. Your choices depend on your printer. If you have a two-tray laser printer, you can instruct Word to load first-page letterhead from one tray, and the remaining sheets from another. Even with a dot-matrix printer, you can often specify manual feed for the first page and automatic tractor feed for the remaining pages. You also may want to use manual feed if you have specified an unusual size of paper that your paper tray cannot handle.

Now that you know how to change the paper source for a specific document or part of a document, here's how to change the default paper source Word uses unless you tell it otherwise:

1. Choose Tools, Options, Print.
2. Select the source you want from the Default Tray list box.

Printing Envelopes and Labels

One of Word's niftiest features is how it automates envelope and label printing. In the simplest example, assume that you've written a letter (see fig. 4.14).

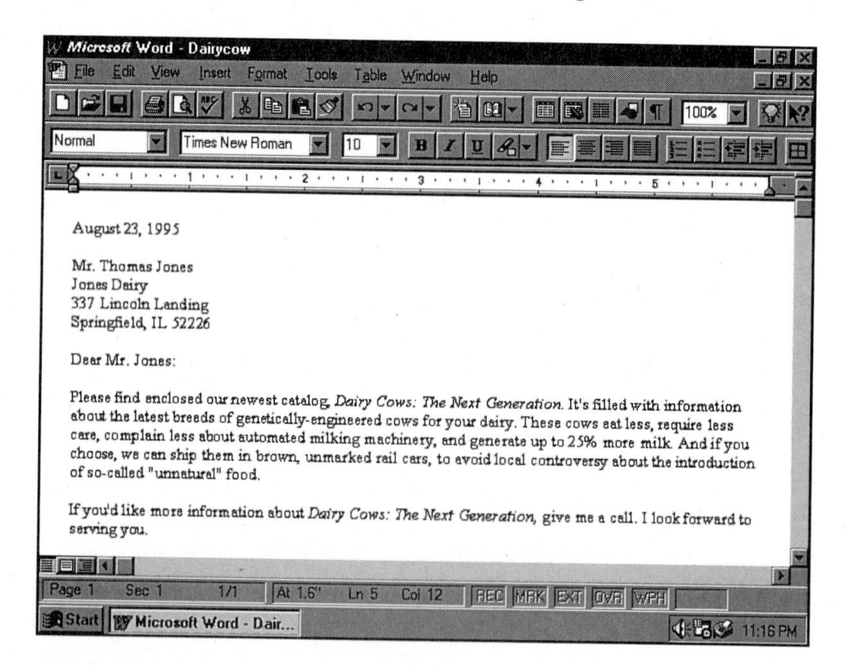
August 23, 1995

Mr. Thomas Jones
Jones Dairy
337 Lincoln Landing
Springfield, IL 52226

Dear Mr. Jones:

Please find enclosed our newest catalog, *Dairy Cows: The Next Generation.* It's filled with information about the latest breeds of genetically-engineered cows for your dairy. These cows eat less, require less care, complain less about automated milking machinery, and generate up to 25% more milk. And if you choose, we can ship them in brown, unmarked rail cars, to avoid local controversy about the introduction of so-called "unnatural" food.

If you'd like more information about *Dairy Cows: The Next Generation,* give me a call. I look forward to serving you.

Figure 4.14
A sample letter.

To print an accompanying envelope, choose Envelopes and Labels from the Tools menu. The dialog box shown in figure 4.15 appears.

Word tries to find the addressee's name and address for you and places this information in the Delivery Address box on the Envelopes tab.

If Word cannot find an address, it leaves the space blank. Occasionally, it may find three *other* lines that seem to fit the general form of an address but that aren't really a name and address. Whether Word's guess is right or wrong, you can edit it in the Delivery Address box.

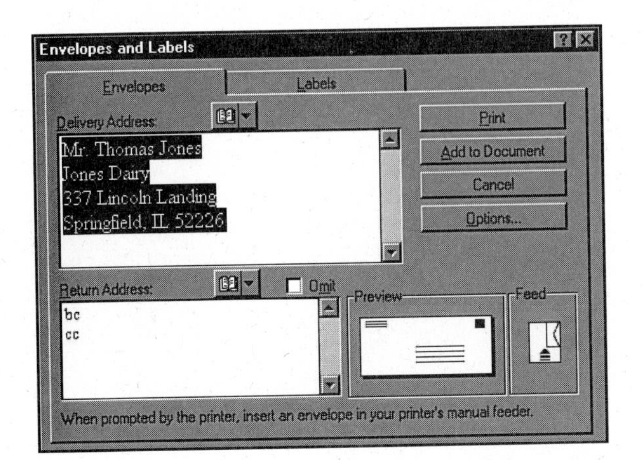

Figure 4.15

The Envelopes and Labels dialog box.

When searching for an address, Word doesn't recognize Shift+Enter carriage returns—only paragraph marks.

Word also pulls your own return name and address from the User Info tab in Tools, Options. You can edit this in the Return Address box, if necessary. If you want no return address, check the Omit box.

You can specify the Delivery and Return Address text if you don't want to let Word find them for you in your document. You can tell Word to flag specific text as the delivery address or return address by using two specific markers (called *bookmarks*) named EnvelopeAddress and EnvelopeReturn. Follow these steps:

1. Select the text you want to use as your outgoing or return address.
2. Choose Bookmark from the Edit menu.
3. In the Bookmark name box, type **EnvelopeAddress** for an outgoing address, or **EnvelopeReturn** for a return address. (Type these as one word, no spaces.)
4. Choose OK.

Bookmarks are covered in more detail in Chapter 16, "Bookmarks."

Word 2's toolbar contained an Envelope button. If you print envelopes often, you either can display that toolbar, or add the Envelope button to another toolbar. (Chapter 24 shows you how.)

Getting a Delivery or Return Address from a Personal Address Book

Windows 95

If you have Microsoft Exchange installed on your computer, you can also get a delivery or return address from the list of names stored there in your Personal Address Book. For either address, click the Address Book icon, as shown earlier in figure 4.15. The Select Name dialog box appears, as shown in figure 4.16.

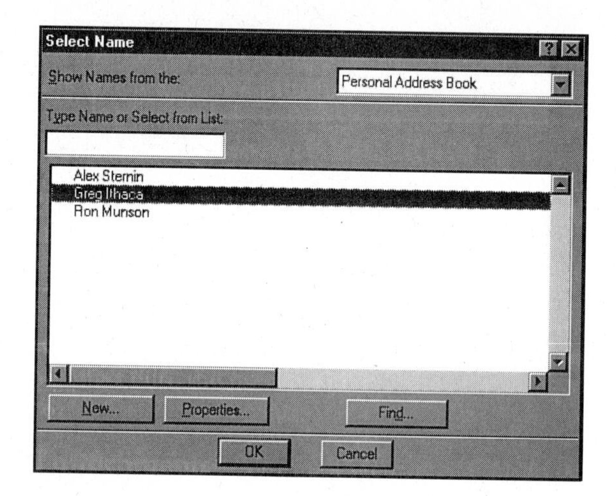

Figure 4.16
The Select Name dialog box.

Note The first time you do this, you may first be asked to specify which Microsoft Exchange Profile to use. Choose the Profile containing the address book with the address you need.

Choose the name you want to appear in the Delivery or Return Address box, and Word inserts it from your Personal Address Book.

As you add names to either the Delivery or Return Address box, Word stores these names, so you don't have to choose from your entire Address Book list the next time you use them. To choose from the list of names Word has already accessed from Exchange, click the down-arrow next to the Address Book button, as shown in figure 4.17. Highlight the name you want to use, and release the mouse pointer.

By the way, Word stores different lists of names for the Delivery and Return Address boxes, so adding a name to one box won't add it to the other.

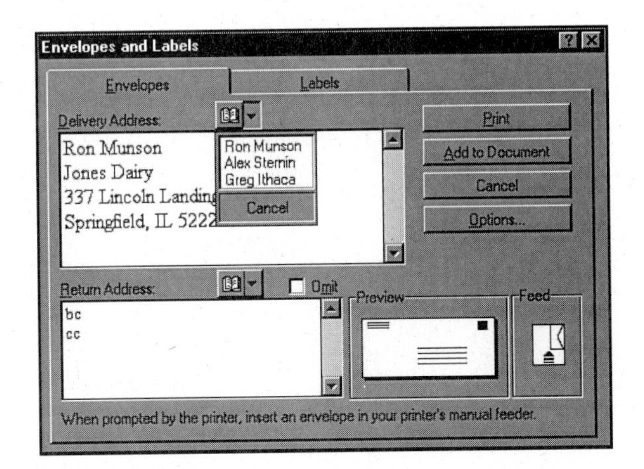

Figure 4.17
Choosing a name by clicking the down-arrow next to the Address Book button.

Printing an Envelope, Now or Later

Assuming that you use a standard (#10) business envelope, and that your addresses are correct, you can simply print the envelope by choosing **Print**. Word prompts you to insert an envelope into your printer's manual feed mechanism.

If you're not ready to print yet, you can tell Word to add the envelope to the beginning of your document as a section. Then, when you print the document, Word prompts you to insert the envelope first. To add an envelope to the beginning of your document, choose Add to Document in the Envelopes and Labels dialog box.

Understanding Envelope Printing Options

You just learned basic envelope printing. But Word provides many options for printing envelopes. You also can control the following elements:

- What kind of envelopes you use
- How the addresses look and where they appear on the envelope
- Whether the envelopes use postal bar codes
- How the envelopes feed into your printer

Changing Envelope Formatting

To change your envelope's formatting, choose the Options button in the Envelopes and Labels dialog box. The Envelope Options dialog box, shown in figure 4.18, opens. It provides near-total control over how your delivery and return addresses look and where they print on the envelope.

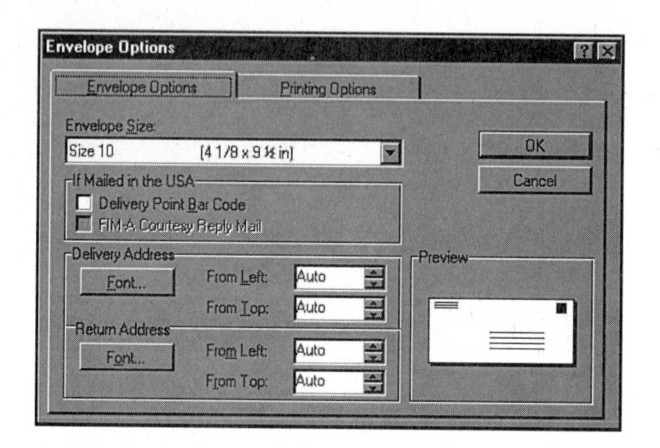

Figure 4.18
The Envelope Options dialog box.

To change the appearance of the typeface used in either the delivery address or return address, choose Font in the appropriate box in the Envelope Options dialog box. The Envelope Address dialog box opens, as shown in figure 4.19. It's much like the Font dialog box you've already seen. You can choose a font, font style, size, and font effects. You also can choose the Character Spacing tab to control letter spacing, height, and kerning.

When you have the envelope address formatting the way you want it, choose OK.

If you want all the envelopes you print with the current template to look like the custom envelope design you've just established, first choose Default. Then choose Yes to confirm the change (see fig. 4.20).

You also can control where the addresses appear by changing the From Left and From Top settings in both the Delivery Address and Return Address boxes.

Notice that the default positions for the delivery and return addresses prevent you from selecting settings that are unacceptable. For instance, you can't set the delivery address to be less than 1 from the left edge or less than 1.5 from the top edge of the envelope. You can, however, override these settings by manually entering positions in the From Left and From Top boxes in the Envelope Options dialog box.

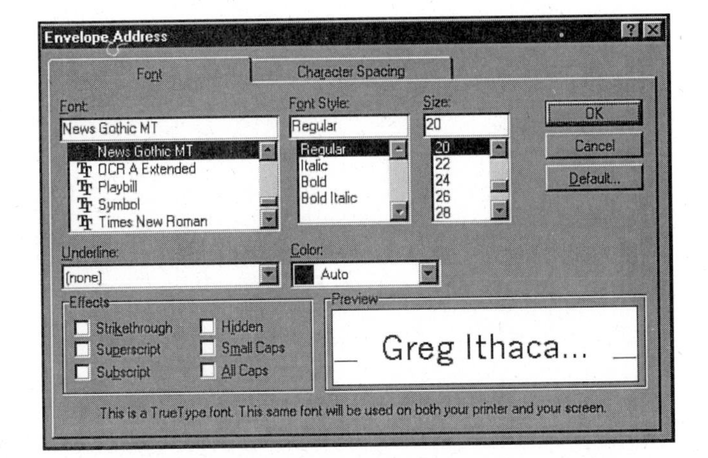

Figure 4.19

The Envelope Address dialog box.

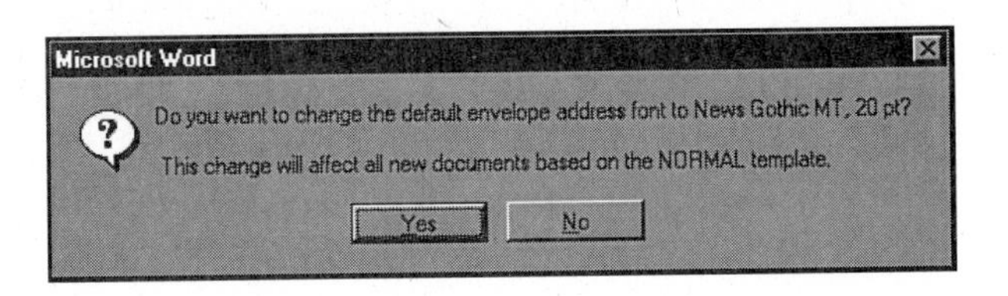

Figure 4.20

Changing the default envelope address font.

In the Feed Method box, you can click on the orientation you want. Word also enables you to insert your envelopes Face Down, or in the opposite direction (Clockwise Rotation).

If, for some reason, you force an envelope orientation that Word doesn't agree with, you'll get a warning message and an opportunity to Reset the orientation to Word's default for your printer. You can ignore this message, if necessary.

Stop You especially want to avoid feeding standard envelopes horizontally into laser printers—they invariably get stuck.

Here's the biggest exception: If your printer has a special envelope tray, you can feed from that tray, instead of using Manual Feed.

Finally, as mentioned, you can feed your envelopes automatically from a tray by selecting another option in the Feed From list box. After you finish, choose OK.

Changing Envelope Sizes

By default, Word expects you to use a standard business envelope—normally referred to as a #10 envelope. Word previews how your printed envelope should look in the

Preview box. If you are using a different kind of envelope, click on the Envelope Preview to get to the Envelope Options dialog box. From the Envelope Size list box, you can choose any of the built-in envelope sizes shown in table 4.2.

TABLE 4.2
Default Envelope Sizes Available in Word

Envelope Name	Size
#10 (Standard)	4 1/8" x 9 1/2"
#6 3/4	3 5/8" x 6 1/2"
Monarch	3 7/8" x 7 1/2"
#9	3 7/8" x 8 7/8"
#11	4 1/2" x 10 3/8"
#12	4 3/4" x 11"
DL	110mm x 220mm
C4	29mm x 324mm
C5	162mm x 229mm
C6	114mm x 162mm
C65	114mm x 229mm

You also can create a custom-size envelope, which you might need if you're designing a special mailing piece.

If you're looking for a way to spend a great deal of money in a hurry, printing nonstandard custom envelopes will do quite nicely.

Choose Custom Size, and the Envelope Size dialog box opens, as shown in figure 4.21. Choose Width and Height measurements and choose OK.

Adding Graphics to an Envelope

Most business envelope stationery includes some form of logo or graphic accompanying the return address. With Word, you can include a graphic next to the return address, without paying for printed stationery. Perform the following steps:

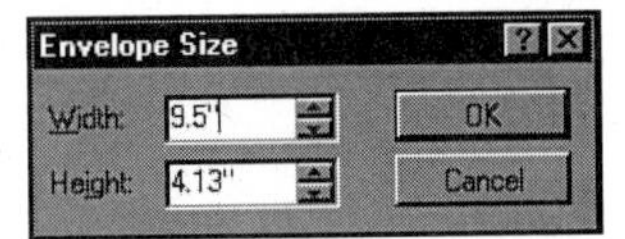

Figure 4.21

The Envelope Size dialog box.

1. Select Envelopes and Labels from the Tools menu.
2. In the Envelopes tab, choose Add to Document. This inserts a new section at the front of your document, containing the envelope copy. (The envelope becomes Page 0, so it doesn't affect the page numbering.)
3. Design and position the graph that you want to appear in your return address.

This could mean importing a graphic from Word's (or another program's) clip-art library—or a scanned logo. Or it might mean using Microsoft WordArt to design special type effects, as in figure 4.22. (WordArt and other Word graphics tools are covered in Chapters 21, "Desktop Publishing and Drawing," and 22, "Using Word's Graphing Features.")

Figure 4.22

Using WordArt to create a custom envelope.

4. Choose Envelopes and Labels from the Tools menu again.
5. Choose Print.

After you create a design for your return address, you may want to include it on all your envelopes from now on. To do this, perform the following steps:

1. Select all the text and graphics you've designed.
2. Choose AutoText from the Edit menu.
3. In the Name box, type **EnvelopeExtra1** or type **EnvelopeExtra2.**
4. Choose OK.

Adding Bar Codes to Your Envelopes

You may have noticed that much of the mail you receive contains special postal bar codes. Two different kinds of these postal bar codes exist, as follows:

- **POSTNET.** These codes are simply ZIP codes translated into bar code language that the U.S. Postal Service's computers can read.
- **Facing Identification Marks (FIMs).** These codes flag different kinds of Courtesy Reply Mail. (Most of us know this as Business Reply Mail, which uses the FIM-A mark.)

You can see the difference between these two types of bar codes in figure 4.23.

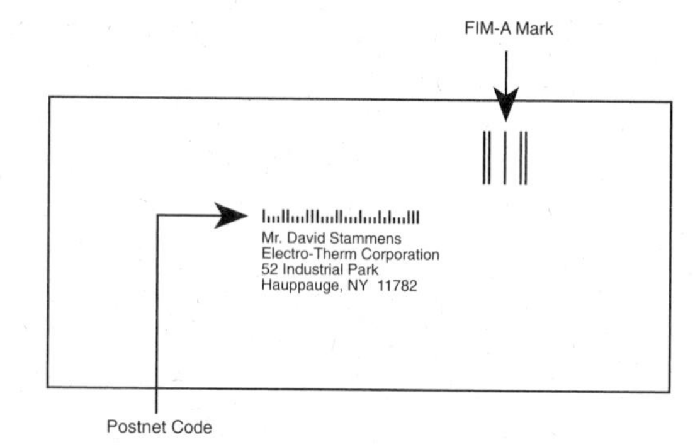

Figure 4.23
Postal bar codes.

Adding bar codes to your mail has two benefits. First, if you're doing mass mailings that qualify, you can get a lower postal rate. Second, bar-coded mail is sometimes delivered more quickly. (That's the theory, anyway.)

Which leads to the obvious conclusion: Word can handle this bar coding for you. To add a POSTNET bar code, do the following:

1. Choose Envelopes and Labels from the Tools menu.
2. Choose Options.
3. In the If Mailed in the USA group, check Delivery Point Bar Code.

   Notice that the FIM-A box now becomes available. That's because you can't have a FIM-A bar without a POSTNET code. (You can, however, use POSTNET codes on standard mail that doesn't need a FIM-A mark.)
4. If you're creating Business Reply Mail, check the FIM-A Courtesy Reply Mail box.
5. Choose OK.

You can't print a FIM or POSTNET bar code with a daisy-wheel printer.

Printing Labels

You also can print a label—or a sheet of labels—using either your outgoing or return address. To do so, choose Envelopes and Labels from the Tools menu; then choose the Labels tab, shown in figure 4.24.

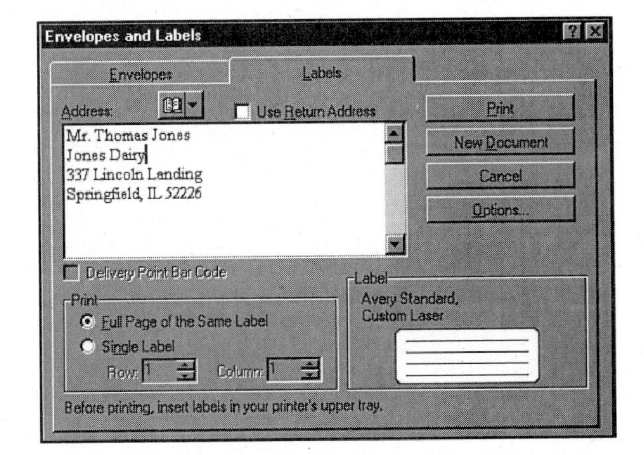

Figure 4.24

The Labels tab.

Word follows the same rules to find an address to include on your labels as it did finding the address for envelopes. If you've already entered a specific name and address in the Envelopes tab, it is here. You can edit it if you want. And as with envelopes, you can click the Address Book button to insert names from your Microsoft Exchange Personal Address Book.

By default, Word assumes that you want the delivery address in the Envelopes, Delivery Address box. If you want Word to import your return address, check the Use Return Address box.

Also by default, Word expects to print a full page of identical copies of the text in the label. Therefore, the Full Page of the Same Label option is automatically selected.

You can, however, print only a Single Label. If so, Word wants to know which of the labels on your sheet it should print. For example, the Avery Standard Custom Laser label sheet has three columns and ten rows of labels (see fig. 4.25).

To print a label in the second row, fourth column, check Single Label. The Row and Column settings become active; enter **2** and **4**, respectively.

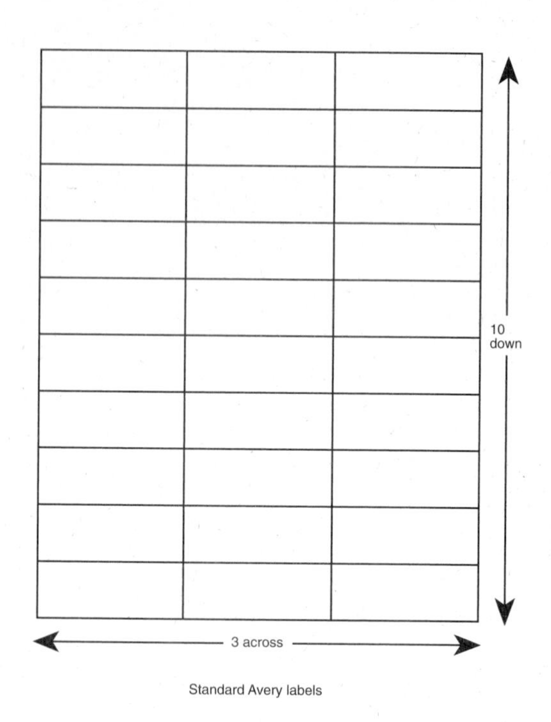

Figure 4.25
Avery Standard Custom Laser labels.

Note Using Word's standard Custom Laser layout (3 across, 10 down), print a sheet containing a single label in the middle of the bottom row. (Use regular paper—you do not need to waste expensive label paper.)

Unlike envelopes, Word assumes that you print your labels from your printer's default paper source—a paper tray or a dot-matrix tractor feed. To tell it otherwise, choose Options. The Label Options dialog box opens, as shown in figure 4.26.

Choose another paper source from the Tray combo box in the Printer Information group.

Choosing the Right Label

Unless you're in the label business, you won't believe how many varieties of labels are available. Word supports most popular sizes of labels, especially the Avery brand of computer labels.

Word's Label Products box contains three groups of laser labels as follows:

- Avery Standard (U.S.)

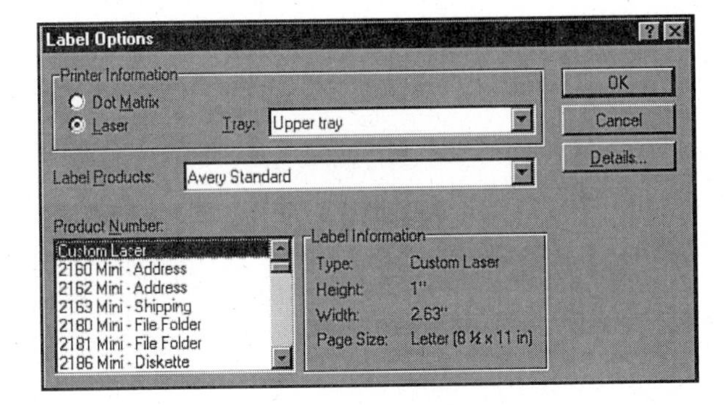

Figure 4.26

The Label Options dialog box.

- Avery Pan European
- Other (includes Inmac and RAJA labels)

And the following three groups of dot-matrix labels are also listed:

- Avery Standard
- Avery Intl (UK)
- Avery Intl (France)
- CoStar LabelWriter

The laser label choices are displayed by default, even if you have a dot-matrix printer installed as the default printer. To select from the dot-matrix label options, you must choose Dot **M**atrix in the Printer Information group.

If none of these labels match yours—hard as it is to imagine—build your own label. Choose **D**etails, and the Custom Laser Information dialog box opens, as shown in figure 4.27 (if you have specified Dot **M**atrix as the printer type, this dialog box is titled Custom Dot Matrix Information, and the picture of the label is somewhat different).

You can set Label H**e**ight and Label **W**idth. You also can set H**o**rizontal Pitch and **V**ertical Pitch, Word's terms for the space between the beginning of one label and the beginning of the next. Labels often have a space between one label and the next or between adjacent labels in the same row.

You also can set **T**op Margin and **S**ide Margin, which tell Word how close the first label should be to the edge of the page. Finally, you can set Number **A**cross and Number **D**own, which tell Word how many labels to place on each row, and how many rows are in a column.

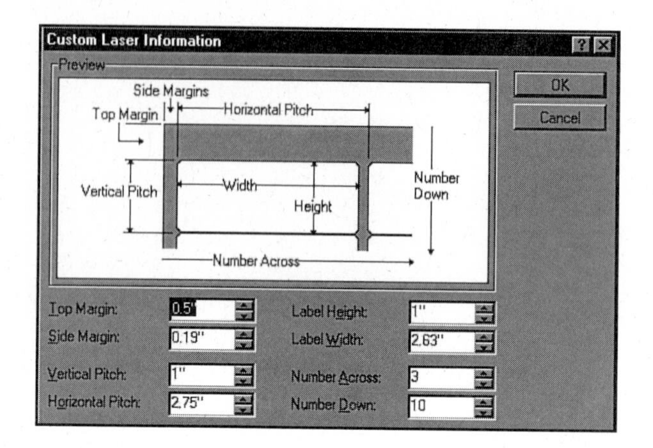

Figure 4.27

The Custom Laser Information dialog box.

As you make changes, the Preview box in figure 4.27 adjusts the picture of the label, showing you the current size and location of your label.

Instead of printing your labels, you can create a New **D**ocument that contains the labels as they would have printed. This enables you to preview the labels, making sure that they print properly. You also can save the new document for printing later.

Printing Several Files at Once

You can print only one file at a time from the Print dialog box, but Word's File Open dialog box, covered in more detail in Chapter 6, "File Management," lets you print many files at once. Assume that you want to print more than one of the Word documents in the same directory. A quick way to do it from the Windows 95 desktop is to drag and drop several files from Windows Explorer (the Windows 95 version of File Manager) to your printer icon (contained in the Printers dialog box that is reachable by clicking Start, Settings, Printers). Here's a way to print multiple files *from within Word:*

1. Select **O**pen from the **F**ile menu to open the Search dialog box.
2. Using the techniques you've already learned, locate and select the first file you want to print.
3. Press Ctrl and select additional files you want to print. All the files will be highlighted.
4. Click the Commands and Settings button or right-click on the selected files, and choose **P**rint from the menu that appears (see fig. 4.28).

5. Click OK. Word displays the Print dialog box, where you can set options that will affect all the documents you're about to print.

6. Click Print.

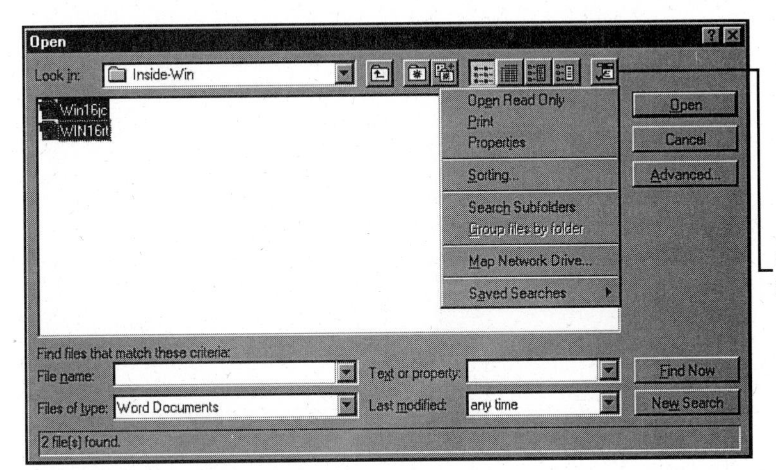

Figure 4.28

The File, Open Commands and Settings button.

Printing to File

Sometimes you may want to prepare a file to print, but not actually print it. (Perhaps you want to take it to the fancy laser printer at the office or to the Linotronic typesetting machine at the service bureau. Or maybe you're just out of paper.)

Word enables you to *print to file*—that is, print the document onto a disk that has all the commands a printer needs to print it. To print a document to file, perform the following steps:

1. Select Print from the File menu.

2. Check the Print to File box.

3. Choose OK. Word displays the Print to File dialog box, shown in figure 4.29.

4. By default, Word places a PRN extension after the file name. Add your file name to it, and choose OK.

You now have a file that can be printed. But how? You can't open it in Word and print it—all you get is text interspersed with printer commands. You can't even drag the file to a printer icon because Windows wants to know what program it should open to interpret the data. If you suggest a program, you're back where you started—text interspersed with printer commands. The solution is a throwback to the oldest days of DOS: copy the file to your printer port, from an MS-DOS command session. Here's how:

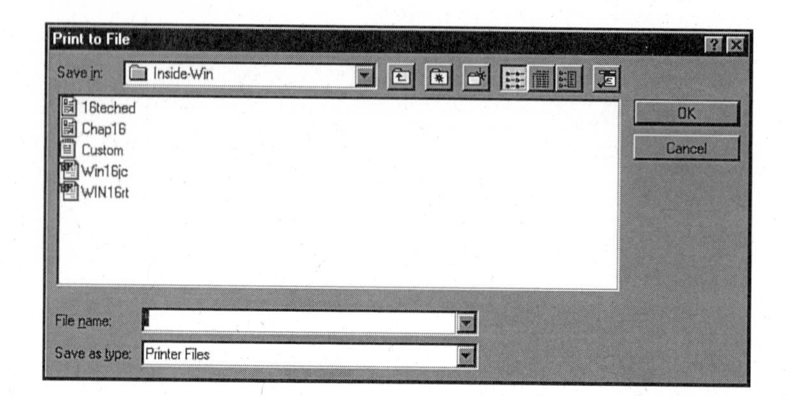

Figure 4.29
The Print to File dialog box.

1. Click Start, choose Programs, and click on MS-DOS Prompt. An MS-DOS window opens, as shown in figure 4.30.

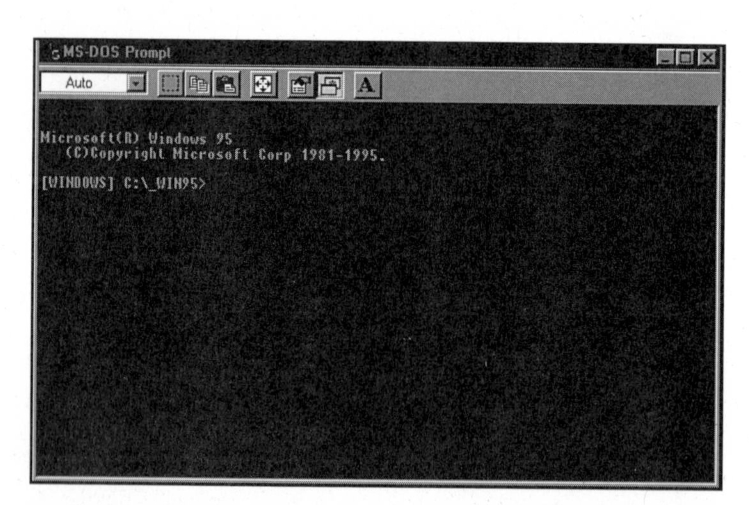

Figure 4.30
Copying a file to a parallel port from an MS-DOS command prompt.

2. At the command prompt, type the following command (where your file name replaces *FILENAME*):

   COPY *FILENAME*.PRN LPT1

Make sure to include the .PRN extension. If you've used a long file name, use the short file name equivalent, for example, SHOPPI~1.PRN for Shopping List.Prn. You can find the short file name by viewing the file's properties.

To see the extensions of your entire directory at once, run a DOS session (choose Start, MS-DOS Prompt), enter the DIR (directory) command, press Enter, and look at the far right of the directory listing that appears—it shows the DOS short file names.

Understanding Windows 95 Printing and Word Background Printing

Traditionally, like most Windows applications, Word depends on Windows 95 to supervise printing. In Windows 3.1, when you sent a document to the printer, the Windows Print Manager program would open. It would start a *queue* of documents, feeding them to your printer one at a time in an orderly fashion. While they're waiting, the documents would be stored on disk, in a process called *spooling*.

There has always been plenty to like about spooling documents. First, if you have the disk storage space, you can send up to 100 documents to print, and stop worrying about them. Second, if you do send a large group of documents to print, you can monitor their status.

Windows 95 retains spooling, but replaces the Print Manager with a series of 32-bit virtual device drivers (VxDs) and dynamic link libraries (DLLs) that are intended to provide better performance and smoother background printing. Now, when you send a document to a printer, a printer icon appears at the right-hand corner of your Windows 95 taskbar (see fig. 4.31).

To see the status of your current print job and others sent to the same printer, double-click on the printer icon. The printer's window opens, as shown in figure 4.32.

In this screen, you can control the print jobs you've sent in the following ways:

- Rearrange them
- Delete them
- Pause them

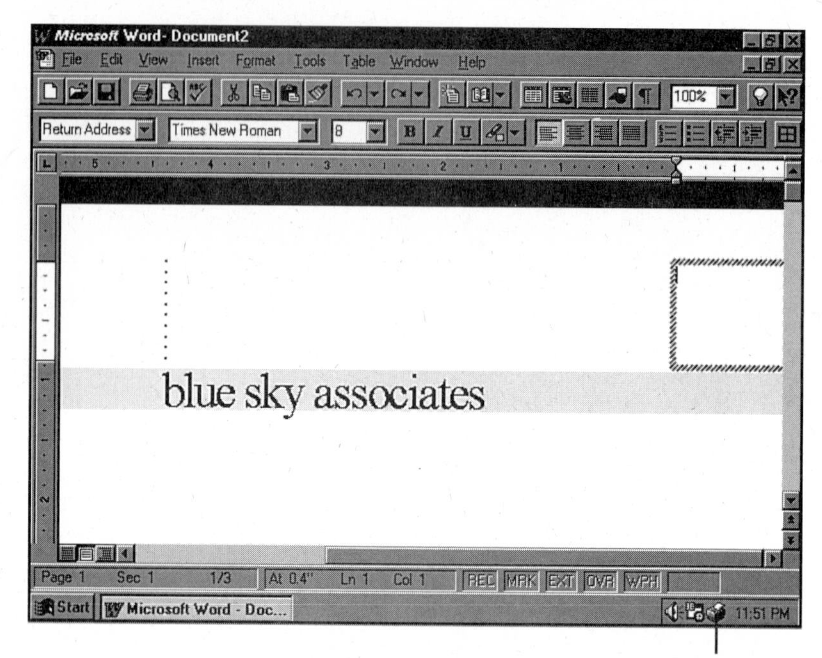

Figure 4.31

Active printer shown in Windows 95 taskbar.

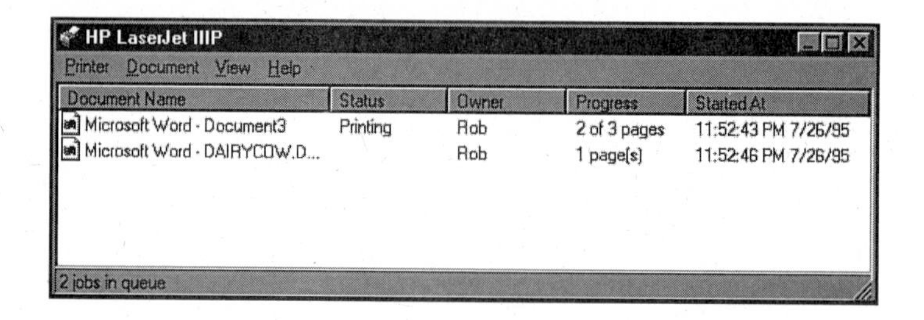

Document Name	Status	Owner	Progress	Started At
Microsoft Word - Document3	Printing	Rob	2 of 3 pages	11:52:43 PM 7/26/95
Microsoft Word - DAIRYCOW.D...		Rob	1 page(s)	11:52:46 PM 7/26/95

Figure 4.32

Viewing status of a printer's current print jobs.

Rearranging Print Jobs

For example, one of the documents you send to your printer is very large. You send a shorter job that you need to have right away. Normally, you have to wait for the large document to finish printing before the short document starts.

Instead, open the printer window. Select the file you want to print first. (Each file is called a *print job.*) When you select a print job, its line is highlighted. Now drag this line to the top of the list. As long as the large job hasn't begun to print, you can drag the small job ahead of it in the queue.

Canceling a Print Job

Sometimes you can send a file to the printer and then change your mind about printing it. (Maybe you think of a few more revisions to make, or decide it isn't such a good idea to send that letter after all.) You can delete a print job by selecting it (be sure you select the print job, not the printer!) and choosing Cancel Printing from the Document menu.

Note: If the job has already started to print, your printer still prints any pages that have already been sent to it.

Pausing Print Jobs

You might want to pause printing temporarily. (Maybe you notice that your ribbon or toner cartridge is getting light and you want to install a new one.) You can pause printing by choosing Pause Printing from the Document menu. A check mark appears next to the Pause Printing menu item; select it again when you want printing to begin again.

Understanding Background Printing

Without background printing, it usually takes a little while for Word to prepare a document to print. If you're accustomed to Word 2 (which didn't have background printing), you're used to that. Word formats one page at a time for the printer, and sends the pages to the print queue; meanwhile, you see a dialog box like the one shown in figure 4.33.

In a long document, this can take a while. Word provides background printing as a solution. With background printing, you can keep working while this document-preparation process happens. The following message appears in the status bar at the bottom of the screen:

```
Word is preparing to background print FILENAME.DOC
```

Then you can start working again.

Unfortunately, background printing has a downside. Background printing requires a substantial amount of memory and processing time. You might find that it slows down your computer unacceptably. If so, follow the instructions at the beginning of the chapter for disabling Background, Printing in the Tools, Options, Print dialog box.

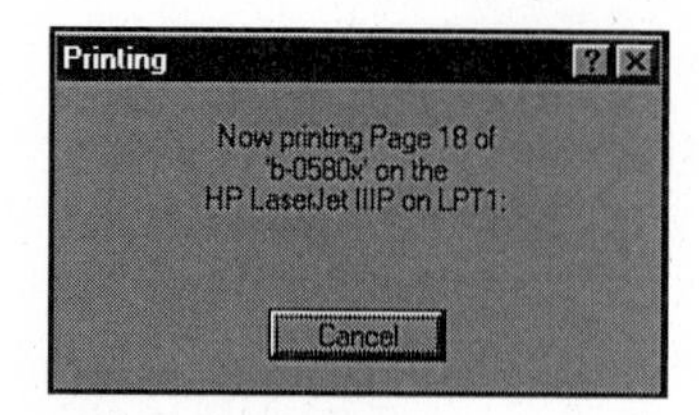

Figure 4.33
Word's Printing dialog box.

Troubleshooting Printing

Here are some things to check if you're not getting the print output you want. Some are obvious—so obvious that you might forget to check them.

If nothing prints, answer the following questions:

1. Is the printer turned on?
2. Is the printer cable connected to the computer firmly, and the cable firmly connected to the printer?
3. Does the name of the printer appear after Printer in the File, Print dialog box? (If not, you might be using the wrong Windows printer driver.)
4. Are you using the same printer port that you told Windows you were using? For example, is the printer connected to LPT2, when Windows thinks it's connected to LPT1?
5. Has your printing been Paused in your Printer's window?
6. If on a network, are you logged on to the LAN? Is the network printer on? Are you currently authorized to share it? (You might have to visit your network system administrator to find out.)
7. Is the paper source correct? Word might be waiting for you to manually feed paper. Check File, Page Setup's Paper Source dialog box, and Tools, Options, Print's Default Tray.

Using Print Preview

When you want to preview a document, you can take advantage of Word's highly flexible Print Preview feature. One quick way to get to it is to click the Print Preview button on the Standard toolbar (see fig. 4.34).

Figure 4.34

The Print Preview toolbar button.

Unfortunately, after you've clicked the button, Print Preview might load fairly slowly. One suggestion: If you need to preview the later pages in a long document, place your insertion point at the beginning of the document, so that Word doesn't have to repaginate the whole document before it displays in the Print Preview screen.

You can perform a wide variety of tasks in Print Preview, including editing. But first, the basics. Figure 4.35 shows the Print Preview screen.

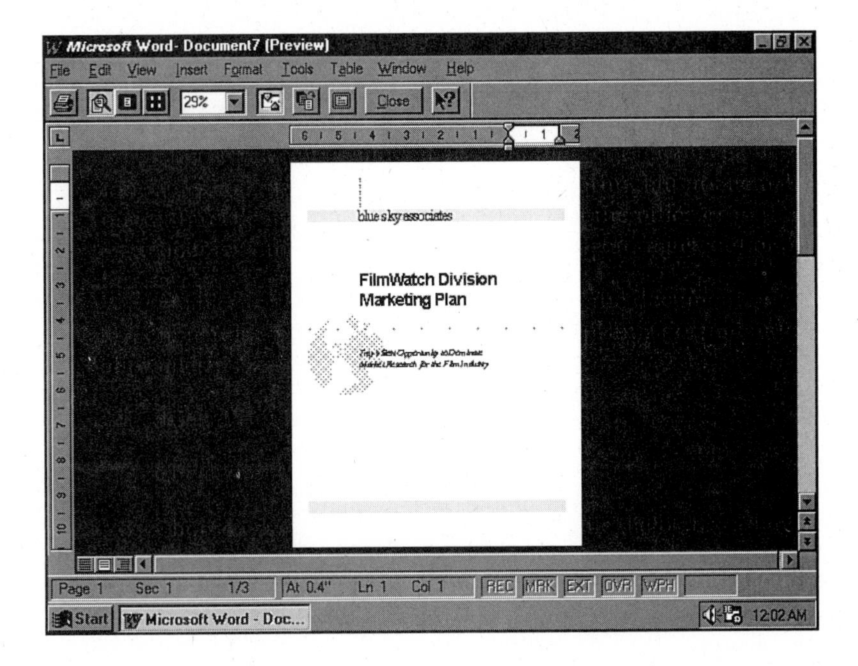

Figure 4.35

The Print Preview screen.

Print Preview contains vertical and horizontal rulers. Your active text margins are in white; nonprinting areas are in gray. Print Preview also has its own toolbar. For example, to print one copy of a document from within Print Preview, click on the Print button. To leave Print Preview without printing, click on Close.

To select options before printing, select **P**rint from the **F**ile menu.

Zooming In and Moving Around

To zoom the document to full size, click on the Zoom button. The mouse pointer becomes a magnifying glass with a plus symbol, as shown in figure 4.36.

Figure 4.36

Magnifying glass mouse pointer.

Move the pointer to the region of the page you want to look at more closely, and left-click. The text enlarges, as shown in figure 4.37.

Figure 4.37

Enlarging text in Print Preview.

If you want to view enlarged text elsewhere on the page, you can get there by using the vertical or horizontal scroll bars. Keep in mind that the scroll bars take you through the entire document, not just to the top and bottom of the visible page.

Note To move forward a page, click on the double down arrow at the bottom of the vertical scroll bar. To move back a page, click on the double up arrow at the bottom of the vertical scroll bar.

When text is magnified, the magnifying glass contains a minus sign. To zoom back out, click anywhere in the page. You can adjust the exact proportion of the text by entering a new percentage in the Zoom box.

You can also make your text appear a little bigger, even in downsized form, by hiding other screen elements that you might not need. To hide the ruler, click on the Ruler button. To hide everything except the Print Preview toolbar, click on the Full Screen button.

Word now enables you to view up to 18 thumbnail pages at once. Click on the Multiple Pages button, and a box opens, as shown in figure 4.38. (Realistically, you don't see much if you display 18 pages, especially if they're text pages.) Select the number of pages you want to appear by dragging the mouse across the selection box. You can display up to three rows of pages in as many as six columns.

Figure 4.38

Using the Multiple Pages button to display six pages at once.

Figure 4.39 shows six pages displayed at once.

To switch back to a single-page Print Preview, click on the One Page button.

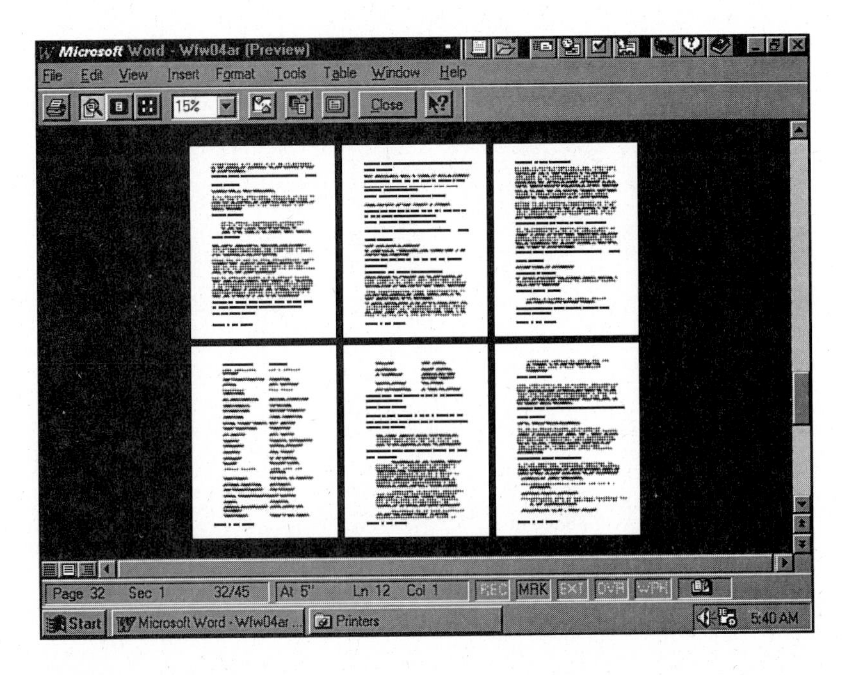

Figure 4.39

Six pages viewed at once.

Shrinking Your Document Automatically

You've probably had a document that was just slightly too long. You thought it was three pages, perhaps, but a few lines jumped onto the fourth page. Often the solution is to slightly shrink the type size and space between lines.

Rather than shrinking your document by trial and error, you can have Word calculate the changes needed. Click on the print preview Shrink to Fit button.

Be warned, though, Shrink to Fit can be a little like a too-hot washing machine. It can shrink text to 4-point without batting an eyelash. Use it just to save a few lines, or it can shrink things way too much. (On occasion, Shrink to Fit gives up and tells you it can't remove a page. But that's rare. It's pretty zealous about trying.)

Editing in Print Preview

Finally, you can edit your document in Print Preview. Choose the magnifier, and place the magnifying glass on the part of the page you want to edit. Then click on the Magnifying Glass button in the toolbar again. This turns the magnifier off, leaving the 100 percent zoom in place. Now you can select text, edit it, move it around, and reformat it as if you had selected Normal or Page Layout in the View menu.

Most of the usual Word menu items are available while you're editing in the Print Preview screen, including Find and Replace, and nearly everything on the Format menu.

You also can edit reduced-size text, if you can see it. One solution for editing in the Print Preview screen is to use the Zoom Control to set the view at 75 percent, so that you can see the entire page left-to-right. Then press the Full Screen button, so that you can see more than half of your page top-to-bottom.

Changing Margins and Indents in Print Preview

You can use Word's rulers to change margins and indents in Print Preview, just as you can in the normal document window. To change any of the page's margins, drag the margin boundary with the mouse. Dragging works for both horizontal and vertical margins, but on the horizontal margins it's easy to accidentally move an indent instead. It helps to see this, so refer to figure 4.40.

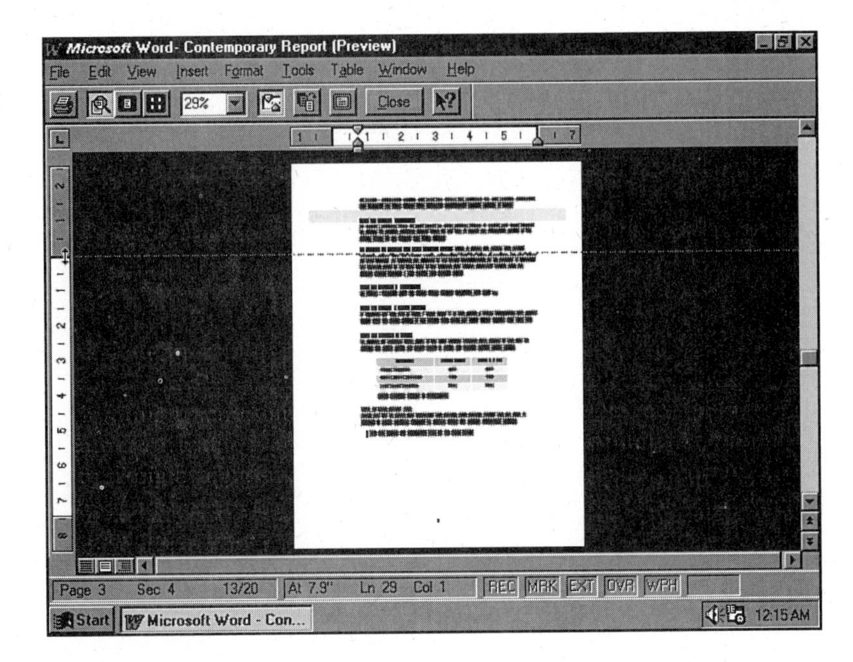

Figure 4.40

Changing margins and indents.

Printing to Fax

If you have a fax/modem, have Microsoft Exchange installed on your computer, and have installed the fax option, Word can fax as well as print.

According to Microsoft, the following fax/modems are incompatible with Microsoft Fax:

Manufacturer	Model
AT&T® Paradyne	Keep in Touch Card 3761
Best Communications	14496EC
BIT	MX-6, XM124S
Cardinal	14400 V.32bis, MB2296SR
CPV Datensysteme	F-1114HV, StarLine
CTK-Systeme	CTK V.32
Datatronics	Discovery 2496CX
DIGICOM	SNM28, SNM41PC

continues

Manufacturer	Model
Digicom Systems, Inc.	Scout Plus
E-Tech Research	E1414MX
EEH GmbH	Elink 301
ELSA	MicroLink, MicroLine
Gateway	Telepath PM144
Hidem	14400 Fax
Kortex	KX PRO 2400
LCE	MiniModem 23
Macronix, Inc.	Maxfax 9624s, VOMAX 2000
Megahertz	P22 Pocket Fax Modem
MultiTech Systems	MT932ba
Nat. Semiconductor	TyIN 2000
Neuhaus Mikroelektronik	Fury 2400
PNB	TT9624
Practical Peripherals	PM2400 FX96SA, V.32 Pocket
QuickComm	Sprint II V.32 Fax
Sysnet	SMF44 Fax
TeleJet	TeleJet 14400
US Robotics	Sportster 28.8 V.FC, Sportster 9600
Woerlein GmbH	M288 Fax
Zoom Telephonics	FC 96/24, VFX 28.8

This section discusses sending faxes through the Word **F**ile, **P**rint dialog box, but if you have Microsoft Exchange, there are other ways to send faxes of Word documents as well. For example:

- You can open Microsoft Exchange and attach a Word document to an e-mail message addressed to a fax number. The Word document is reformatted using Microsoft's Binary File Transfer (BFT) format. If the fax is received by a computer running Microsoft Fax, it can be opened in Microsoft Word by double-clicking on the file attachment. If it is received by a fax machine, it prints just like a typical fax.

- You can choose **S**end from the **F**ile menu, which inserts your current document as an attachment in a Microsoft Exchange message. In that editing window, you can choose a recipient, edit an accompanying message, and send the document via fax through your e-mail system.
- You can send a Word document as a fax from your Windows desktop, by clicking Start, Programs, Accessories, Fax, Compose New Fax, and then running the Fax Wizard, which runs as described in the next few pages and also gives you a chance to attach a document for faxing.

After you choose **P**rint from the **F**ile menu, choose Microsoft Fax from the list of printers in the **N**ame box. Specify any other printing options you choose; then choose OK. The Fax Wizard walks you through the steps required to send a fax; along the way, you'll have the opportunity to set the options you need to fax successfully. Figure 4.41 shows the Fax Wizard's opening screen.

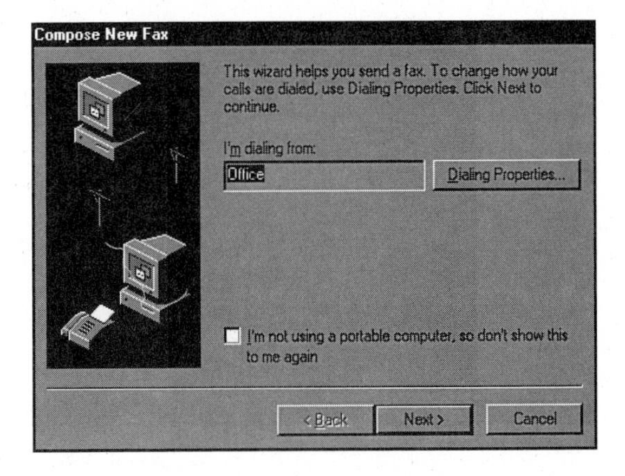

Figure 4.41
The Fax Wizard's opening screen.

You may have already specified your basic dialing information in Microsoft Exchange. If so, you can skip this screen. In fact, if you are working from a desktop PC where the dialing information rarely, if ever, changes, you can tell Word never to show you this screen again, by clicking the **I**'m not using a portable computer, so don't show this to me again check box. If you check this box, you can still adjust your dialing information later in the Fax Wizard if this ever becomes necessary.

Specifying Dialing Properties

If you are establishing your dialing information for the first time, or if you are changing your dialing information, choose **D**ialing Properties. The Dialing Properties dialog box opens, as shown in figure 4.42. Here, you can specify:

- A New dialing location
- A different default Area code where your PC is located
- A different country
- A dialing prefix for local and/or long-distance calls (such as "9" to dial off-premises, or "1" to dial long-distance).
- Whether you use a calling card
- Whether you use call waiting, and if so, which code to use to disable it while you're faxing
- Whether you are using a Tone or Pulse dial phone

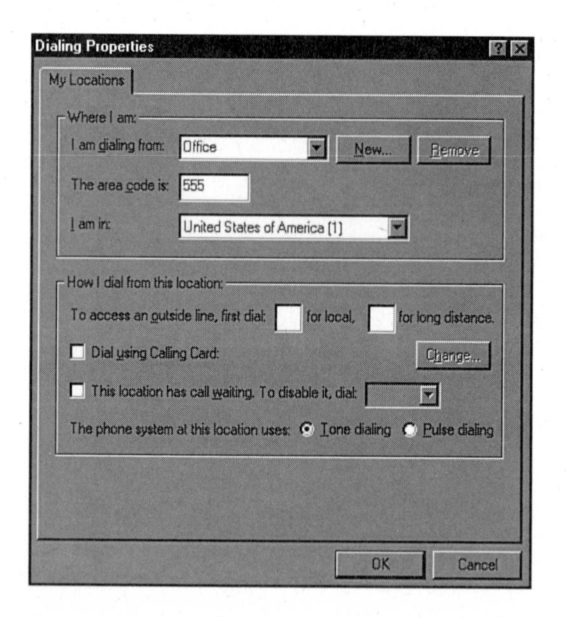

Figure 4.42
The Dialing Properties dialog box.

Addressing a Fax

When you have finished specifying Dialing Properties, choose OK to return to the Compose New Fax dialog box, and choose Next. In the next dialog box (see fig. 4.43), you can specify who will receive your fax.

If you only plan to send a fax to this recipient once, the simplest way is to enter the name and phone number of your recipient in this screen, and click Next. However, if the name of your recipient is in your Microsoft Exchange Personal Address Book—or should be—choose Address Book. The Address Book dialog box opens (see fig. 4.44).

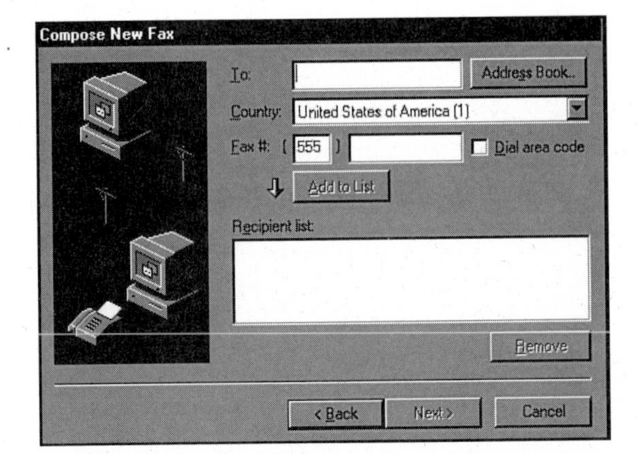

Figure 4.43

Specifying a fax recipient.

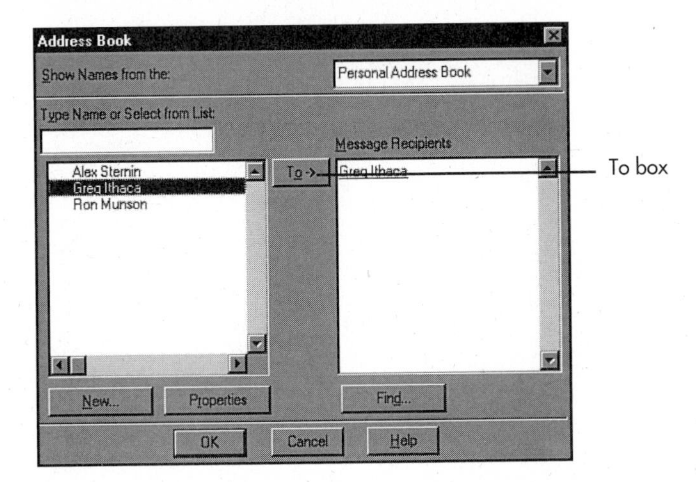

Figure 4.44

The Address Book dialog box.

If the recipient you want appears in the list, highlight the name, and click To. If you want to send the fax to more than one recipient, choose another name and click To again. If you want to send to a new recipient, click New. The New Entry dialog box opens (see fig. 4.45). Choose Fax; then click OK. The New Fax Properties dialog box appears (see fig. 4.46).

Enter the name of the recipient as you want it to appear on the fax; enter the phone number. To add this recipient to the list of people who will receive the current fax, click To. After you've made your selections in the New Entry dialog box, choose OK, then Next.

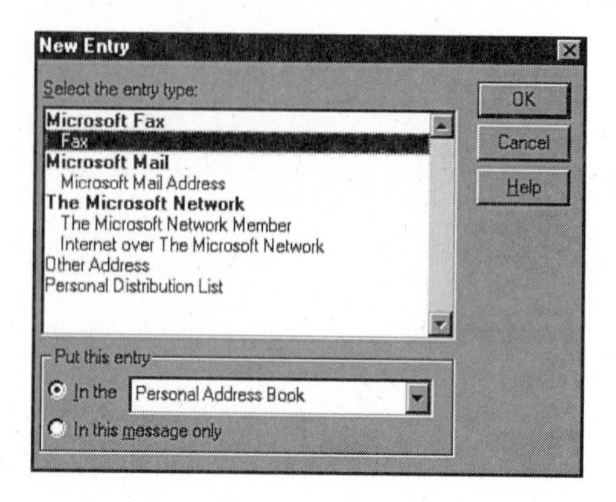

Figure 4.45

Adding a new name to the Address Book in the New Entry dialog box.

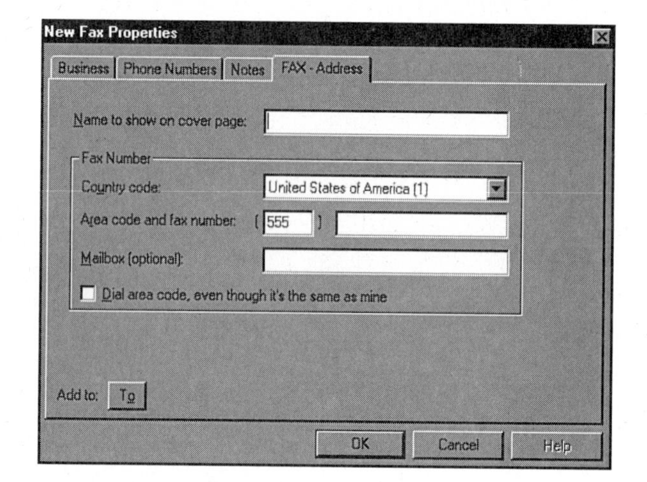

Figure 4.46

Entering information in the New Fax Properties dialog box.

Adding a Cover Page

The Fax Wizard now asks whether you would like to include a cover page. If so, click the Yes radio button, and choose from the five fax cover sheets provided by Microsoft Exchange. (Note that these are not the same fax cover sheets included in Word's library of templates.)

Setting Other Fax Options

If you're sure that you don't want to change any other options, click Next. The Fax Wizard moves to the next step—adding a subject and note to your cover page, if you've chosen to include one.

However, before you skip ahead, take note that you can control many elements of your fax from this part of the Fax Wizard. To review your options, choose Options.

The Send Options for this Message dialog box appears (see fig. 4.47). From here, you can define the following:

- When to send your fax
- What form your fax should take (Message Format)
- Additional dialing options such as call retries
- Security options, if any

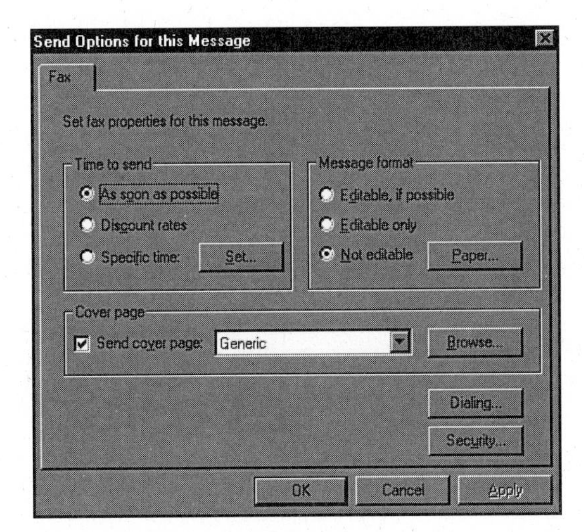

Figure 4.47

The Send Options for this Message dialog box.

Specifying a Time to Send Your Fax

The Fax Wizard allows you to specify when you want to send your fax: as soon as possible, as soon as the telephone rates go down, or at a specific time. To set a specific time, click Set and enter the time in the Set Time dialog box (see fig. 4.48).

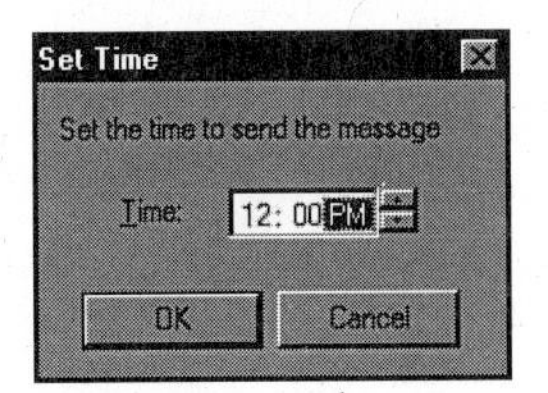

Figure 4.48

The Set Time dialog box.

Specifying a Message Format

If you are faxing to a fax system that supports it, the Fax Wizard allows you to specify a message format that can be edited upon receipt. Choose Editable, if possible, or

Editable only. As mentioned earlier, Windows 95 can send faxes in Binary File Transfer (BFT) format that can be edited if received by another system that understands BFT, such as another Windows 95 computer. Microsoft Fax contains a preprocessor that considers the message format you specify—along with who you're faxing to—in determining which data to send:

- If you choose Not Editable, Microsoft Fax translates the document into a format understandable by standard Group 3 fax machines, unless Microsoft Fax recognizes the recipient as having access to a Microsoft At Work-compatible device—in which case, it uses the Microsoft Fax-rendered format, which is more compact and can be sent more quickly.
- If the recipient has Microsoft Fax, and you select Editable Only form, Windows 95 sends a BFT file only—recognizing that the recipient won't need a standard Group 3 fax transmission.
- If you are sending to several recipients of different kinds, and you check Best Available in the Image Quality box (discussed next), Windows 95 creates both Group 3 and editable versions, choosing the best one to send to each recipient.
- If Windows 95 doesn't know what kind of a fax device the recipient has, it creates multiple formats, making sure that at least one can be used when it establishes a connection.

If you are sending to a fax machine that outputs paper, you can control page size, fax resolution, and whether the pages print in Portrait or Landscape mode. To check or change these settings, click Paper to view the Message Format dialog box (see fig. 4.49).

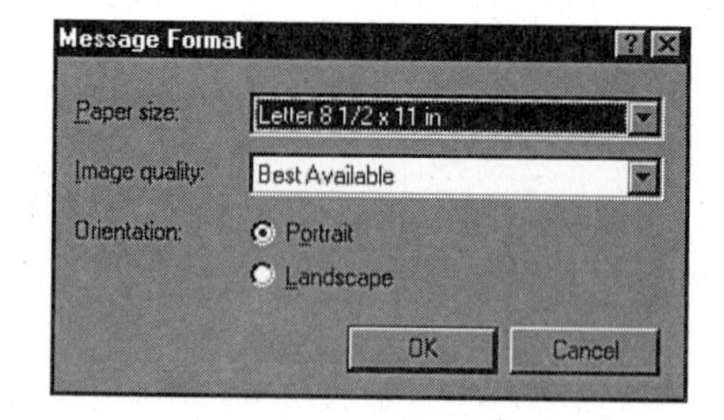

Figure 4.49
The Message Format dialog box.

Setting Additional Dialing Properties

In addition to the dialing properties discussed earlier, the Fax Wizard allows you to set the number of retries after a failed connection, and how long to wait after each retry. To adjust these settings, click Dialing. The Dialing dialog box opens (see fig. 4.50).

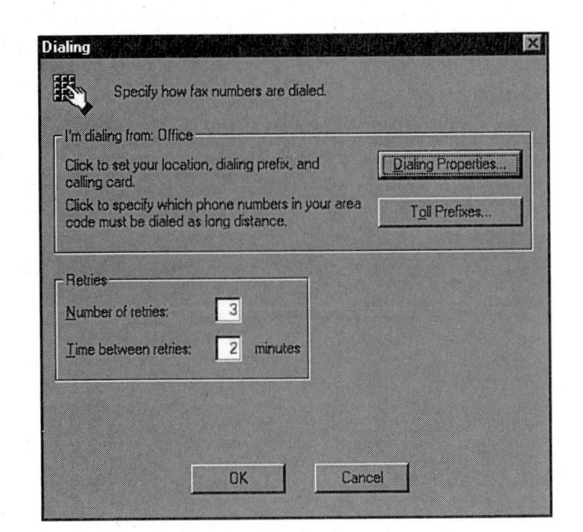

Figure 4.50

The Dialing dialog box.

Notice that you can return from here to the Dialing Properties dialog box discussed earlier. This ensures that the Dialing Properties dialog box is available even if you instructed the Fax Wizard to skip the opening screen, as discussed earlier.

If you live in an area where some of your calls require a long-distance dialing prefix even though they are in the same area code as you, click the Toll Prefixes button in the Dialing dialog box. The Toll Prefixes dialog box opens (see fig. 4.51). From here, you can specify any telephone company exchanges in your area code that require a prefix.

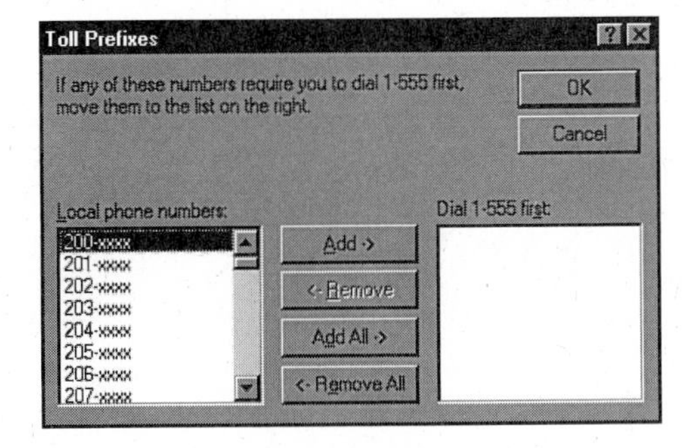

Figure 4.51

The Toll Prefixes dialog box.

Setting Security for Your Fax

The Fax Wizard lets you take advantage of the security options built into Microsoft Exchange's fax feature, if you are sending faxes to systems that support it. You can only secure faxes sent in editable format, not those output on a standard fax machine.

From the Send Options for this Message dialog box, choose Sec<u>u</u>rity. The Security dialog box opens (see fig. 4.52).

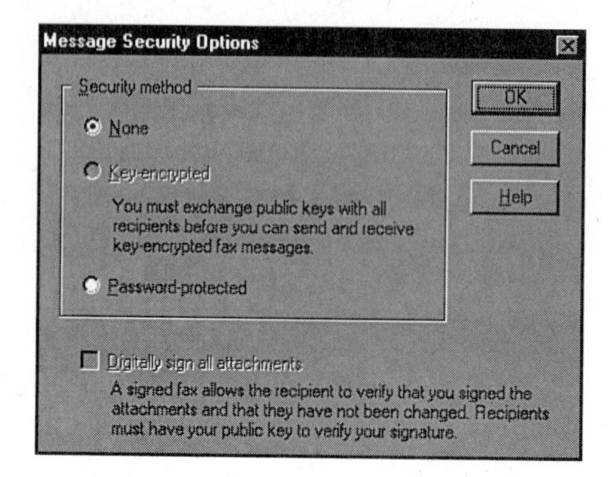

Figure 4.52
The Message Security Options dialog box.

Here, you have four options:

- **None—**The default setting, which provides no security at all
- **Key encrypted—**Allows you to use a public key security system
- **Password-protected—**Allows you to specify a password that travels with your encrypted fax; at the other end, the user must enter the password, or the fax cannot be decrypted
- **Digitally sign all attachments—**A form of security that helps ensure that you, not someone else, sent the fax and its attachments

Next to no security at all, password-protected systems are the easiest to manage. You can simply share your password with the document's recipient, without acquiring or managing a set of public keys. However, they share the drawback of all password systems—passwords have a way of getting misplaced, stolen, or cracked.

Briefly, public key systems work as follows:

1. Two related keys are established: a private key used only by its owner, and a public key available to anyone.
2. To send a message that only a particular person can decipher, you encrypt it using their public key.
3. When the person receives the message, she can decipher it using her private key, but nobody else's private key will do the job.

In the United States, Windows 95's public-key encryption system uses the popular RSA (Rivest-Shamir-Adleman) algorithm—the same algorithm used by the extremely popular Pretty Good Privacy (PGP) freeware package. The encryption generated by PGP is so strong that the United States government prohibits its export.

You can find good discussions of PGP and public-key encryption in the following books: *Actually Useful Internet Security Techniques* (New Riders) and *Protect Your Privacy*, by William Stallings (Prentice Hall PTR).

While reading the following explanation of digital signatures, keep in mind that when you send a secured fax, Windows 95 handles all these details.

Briefly, digital signatures work as follows. You run a *hash program* that translates your document mathematically into a unique *digital fingerprint*—a short pattern of data that can only represent a document containing the precise information contained in the original document. Next, you encrypt this digital fingerprint with your private key. The resulting code is your digital signature. Windows 95 sends it with your document.

When the document arrives, your recipient uses your public key to decrypt the accompanying digital signature. She then runs the same hash program on your document, using your public key—expecting to generate the identical digital signature. If the signatures are identical, you sent the document—no other key could have created the same digital signature. If the signatures are different, either someone else sent the document, or it was altered en route.

To use key encryption or digital signatures, you must first establish security in Microsoft Exchange. To do so, open Microsoft Exchange (double-click on Inbox on the Windows Desktop); choose Tools for Microsoft Fax from the Tools menu; and choose Advanced Security. The Advanced Fax Security dialog box opens; from there, you can create, exchange, and manage public keys.

Adding a Subject Line and Notes

When you finish setting the dialing, security, and cover page options described earlier, click Next. If you have specified a cover page, the Fax Wizard displays a screen where you can enter a Subject line and a Note explaining the fax in more detail (see fig. 4.53). When you finish the note, click Next.

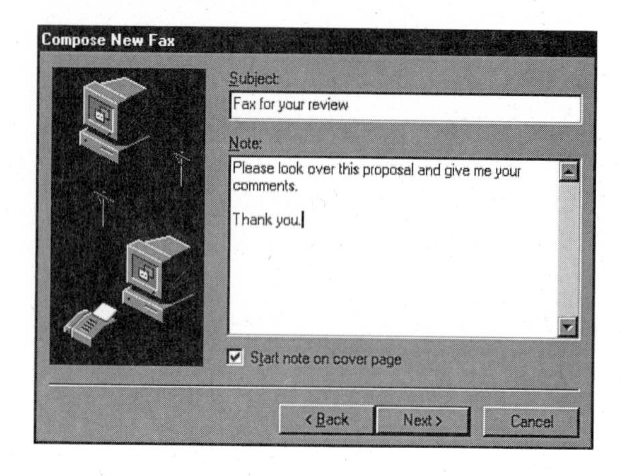

Figure 4.53
Adding a Subject and Note to your fax cover sheet.

Sending the Fax

When you have finished setting options, click OK. At long last, you have made it through the Wizard. (Normally, it's much faster than this, but we stopped at nearly every possible distraction along the way.) Click Finish, and Windows 95 sends the fax (or processes it for sending later, if you made that choice). When the fax is sent, the Microsoft Fax Status dialog box appears (see fig. 4.54) showing the progress of the fax.

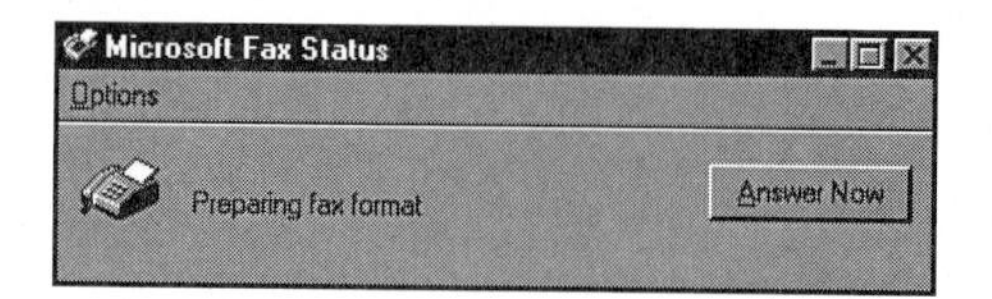

Figure 4.54
The Microsoft Fax Status dialog box.

Tip

People have been known to use printing to fax as an emergency workaround for getting hard copy when no printer is available. If your printing needs on the road are really light, and you are somewhere with a fax machine and two phone lines, you might get away with carrying a modem instead of a printer.

Troubleshooting Faxing

If your fax doesn't fax, start with these troubleshooting ideas:

- Is your fax/modem connected? Check the connections at both ends—modem and phone line.

- Are you sure the wires are OK? Try establishing a modem connection with HyperTerminal or The Microsoft Network or another online service to make sure that Windows 95 is recognizing your fax/modem properly.
- Are you using the correct modem drivers, and are they using the proper serial (COM) ports? You can check this in the Modems dialog box of the Windows 95 Control Panel.
- Is your fax/modem dialing the number but not connecting properly? Check that you are dialing the right number with the right prefixes. (If the name and number come from Microsoft Exchange, check in your Personal Address Book.) Or, if you are using a calling card, is the calling card accepted by your phone company?

Spelling and Grammar

Word offers a complete set of tools to help you improve your writing. Word's *spell checker* contains 104,000 words and can easily be adapted to add or delete words you use in your writing. Word's *thesaurus* contains 200,000 synonyms for 24,000 key words. Word's *grammar checker* tracks more than 40 rules of grammar and style, making recommendations about usage wherever it finds an error.

Together, these tools can serve as your personal system for sharpening your writing—especially as you personalize Word's spelling and grammar checkers to meet your specific needs.

In this chapter:

- Using Word's Automatic Spell Checking feature
- Using Word's spell checker
- Refining a spell check
- Creating and using custom dictionaries
- Creating "exclude" dictionaries
- Troubleshooting the spell checker

- Using Word's thesaurus
- Searching for antonyms
- Using Word's grammar checker
- Understanding Word's grammar and style settings
- Customizing grammar settings
- Understanding Word's readability statistics

Automatic Spell Check

Windows 95

By default, when you open a file in Word for Windows 95, Word runs a spell check and flags all possible errors with a wavy underline mark, as shown in figure 5.1.

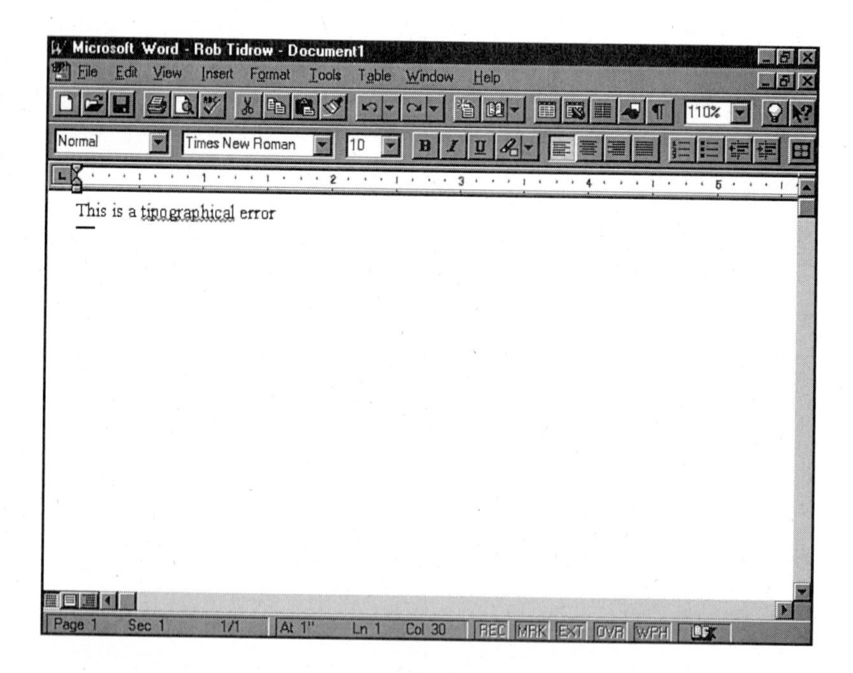

Figure 5.1
Errors underlined by Word's Automatic Spell Check feature.

Word finds any word not in its dictionary—as well as consecutive words, apparent errors in capitalization, and combinations of words with the spaces missing. Of course, sometimes Word flags names or other words that are perfectly fine.

To resolve an error Word finds, right-click on the flagged word. A pop-up menu appears (see fig. 5.2) listing any suggestions Word may have about the correct spelling, as well as the following choices:

- **Ignore All.** Tells Word to disregard all occurrences of the spelling within the current document.
- **Add.** Tells Word to add the spelling to your custom dictionary; once you add it, Word won't flag the spelling as an error anymore.
- **Spelling.** Opens Word's spell checker.

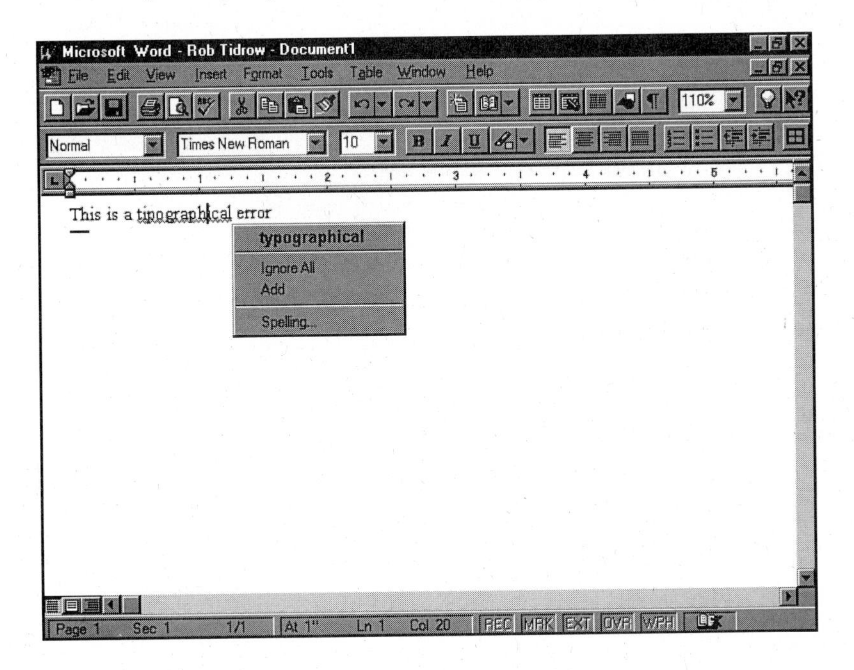

Figure 5.2

The spelling pop-up menu that appears when you press Alt+7.

You also can resolve errors without using the pop-up menu by simply editing the text. Word checks the spelling of the word again as soon as you move your cursor away from it, and if the word is now spelled correctly, the red mark disappears.

Automatic Spell Checking isn't everyone's cup of tea. Many people will appreciate the way it catches typos and other inadvertent errors as you make them—without going through the trouble of a formal spell check. Others will find this feature distracting and will want to turn it off immediately. The feature also slows down Word slightly. If you'd prefer not to use Automatic Spell Checking, here's how to turn it off:

1. Choose Options from the Tools menu.
2. Choose Spelling.

3. Clear the Automatic Spell Checking check box.
4. Choose OK.

You also can allow Word to find all your possible errors but not display the errors until you're ready:

1. Choose Options from the Tools menu.
2. Choose Spelling.
3. Check the Hide Spelling Errors in Current Document check box.
4. Choose OK.

Word offers a new keyboard shortcut for moving through a document from one spelling mistake to the next. When you press Alt+F7, Word moves to the next misspelling and displays the pop-up menu of options there.

Running a Spell Check

If you prefer to spell check your documents conventionally, Word's built-in spelling checker is as close as a pushbutton on the Word toolbar, as shown in figure 5.3.

When you click on this button—or when you choose Spelling from the Tools menu—Word begins the spelling check, starting at your insertion point. You also can press the F7 key to begin a spelling check.

The accompanying CD-ROM contains a file you can use to practice some of the procedures in this chapter: IWMS5A.DOC.

When Word finds a spelling error, the Spelling dialog box opens, as in figure 5.4. Notice that the Spelling dialog box appears toward the bottom of the screen, and the flagged word is highlighted in text, toward the top of the screen. This way, you can usually see the context in which a questionable word appears. If you need to, you can always drag the Spelling dialog box out of the way using its title bar.

Word not only flags misspellings, but also repeated words and capitalization that appear to be incorrect.

Within the Spelling dialog box, the questionable word also appears in the Not in Dictionary box. This means exactly what it says: Word hasn't found the word in its dictionary.

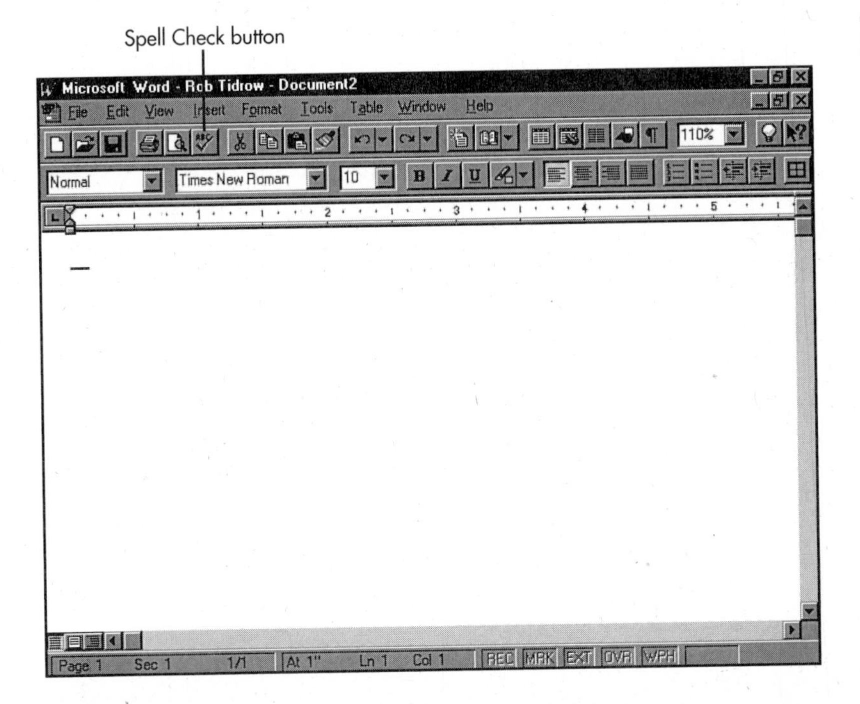

Figure 5.3

The Spell Check toolbar button.

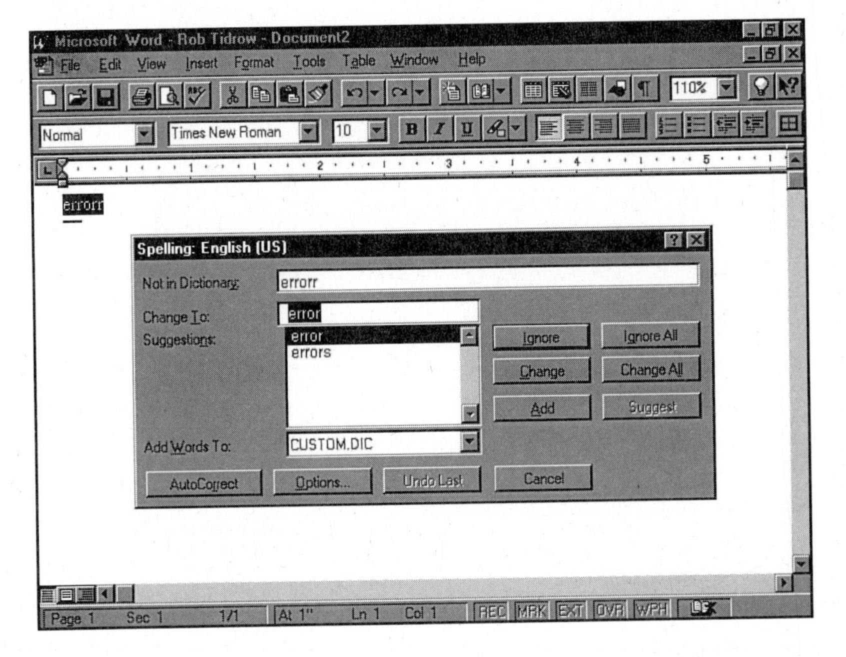

Figure 5.4

The Spelling dialog box.

Word shortage. You'd think with 104,000 listings, Word's dictionary would have all the words you need. But plenty of words you use every day aren't in Word's 104,000-word dictionary. For example:

- Individual, product, and company names (though "Microsoft" has now made it into the dictionary, it wasn't there in some earlier versions of Word!).
- Specialized terms and jargon. For instance, the words "AUTOEXEC" and "386SX" do not appear in the Word spelling dictionary.
- Foreign phrases like "Ichi bieru" are not in the dictionary.

Also, the dictionary can occasionally be capricious. For example, among first names you'll find Susan but not Suzanne, Danny but not Marty.

As we're almost ready to show you, you can add any word you like. But you might also be interested in The Comprehensive Spelling Dictionary, from Alki Software (1-800-NOW-WORD). It adds 74,100 medical, legal, business, financial, and insurance terms to Word's standard spelling dictionary.

Another thing no spelling checker will find is inaccurate homonyms: Did you use "to" when you should have used "two" or "too"?

The Word grammar checker will find many of these errors. If it flags many errors like this, you might set it up specifically to look for them. You learn how later in this chapter.

If the suspected word is correct (for instance, the spell checker stopped on a proper noun), you have three choices:

- Ignore tells Word to skip only *this* reference to a word. You might use it with a name that is spelled correctly in this instance, but might resemble another name with a slightly different spelling.
- Ignore All tells Word to assume that any reference to the word *in this document* is correct.
- Add enters the word in a custom dictionary that Word will also refer to from now on, unless you tell it otherwise.

When you install Word, the custom folder is created for you. If, for some reason, the custom dictionary is moved from its customary location, Word offers to create a new custom dictionary file, called CUSTOM.DIC, for you. Click on the Yes button, and Word proceeds with the spelling check.

Within Word's spelling checker, you can always undo your most recent action—except for adding a word to a custom dictionary—by choosing Undo Last.

You also can undo your entire spelling check—except for any words that you may have added to a custom dictionary—by choosing Undo Spelling from the Edit menu immediately after you finish the spell check. Each time you select Undo Spelling in the Edit menu, one word is returned to its previous spelling. You can't "unspell" the entire document at the same time (though you can close the document without saving any of your changes, including the spelling changes).

Go easy with the trigger finger on the Add button: when you're in a rush, it's all-too-easy to add words to the custom dictionary that shouldn't be there—even typos that may have looked right at first glance. And, as you may have guessed, it's easier to get a word into your custom dictionary than to get it out.

When you Add a word, it goes into CUSTOM.DIC, which may appear either in your WINWORD folder or in the folder C:\WINDOWS\MSAPPS\PROOF.

Making Changes Directly to CUSTOM.DIC

The CUSTOM.DIC file is an ASCII (text only) list of the words you've added. You can edit and resave this document in Word or a plain ASCII text editor like Windows Notepad, adding or deleting words from the dictionary at will. Note that Word stores words in CUSTOM.DIC in alphabetical order, except that all capitalized words appear before all lowercased words.

If you use Word to edit CUSTOM.DIC, be careful not to save it as a Word document. CUSTOM.DIC must be a plain ASCII file in order for Word to use it. As you edit CUSTOM.DIC, place only one word on each line. Don't add any formatting, and don't inadvertently move the file into a working folder.

When you're opening the file, remember that Word normally displays only DOC files. To view a dictionary file in File, Open, first change Files of type to read All Files. The file you want appears with the name Custom, not Custom.dic, because Windows 95 doesn't normally display file extensions.

If you don't want to open CUSTOM.DIC but simply want to know what's in it, you can use File Open's preview feature to do so.

If you are running Word across a network, the network administrator may have set CUSTOM.DIC or its folder as Read Only. If so, you cannot add words to the CUSTOM.DIC dictionary; the Add button is grayed out to tell you this.

Making Spelling Changes

If you spelled the word wrong, again you have some choices. Word does its best to guess what word you're really after. If it "thinks" it has a clue, it places its best guess in the Change To: box. Other options appear below in the Suggestions box.

In my experience, Word guesses right roughly one-third of the time. It generally does best with long words that are misspelled slightly, such as *interchangable* or *tremendus*. Occasionally, a word is so unusual or so badly misspelled that Word just throws up its hands and makes no suggestions.

If Word's best guess is right, click on the Change or Change All button. (Change revises only the current reference; Change All revises all references in the current document.)

If you agree with one of Word's alternative suggestions, select it from the Suggestions box and then click on the Change or Change All button.

Note Word's spelling suggestions are often incorrect in highly technical documents or documents that contain a lot of arcane jargon. It can take Word quite a while to find a suitable suggestion for misspelled words. In the interest of time, you might want to disable Word's suggested spellings to make the spell check run faster.

Choose **Options** from the **Tools** menu. Then choose the Spelling tab in the Options dialog box. Deselect Always Suggest (see fig. 5.5), and click on the OK button. You also can reach this dialog box by choosing **Options** from within the Spelling dialog box.

With Always Suggest unchecked, Word doesn't automatically offer suggested spellings. You can always request suggestions for a single word by choosing Suggest from within the Spelling dialog box.

If the correct spelling doesn't appear in Change To or Suggestions, type it yourself in the Change To box. Then select Change or Change All.

If you've started a spelling check midway through the document, when you reach the end of the document Word automatically wraps to the top of the document and asks if you want to continue the spelling check there. If so, click on the Yes button; if you want to end the spelling check now, click on the No button instead.

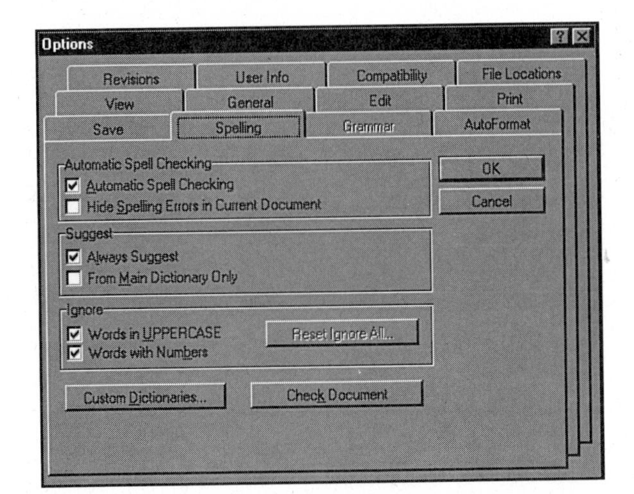

Figure 5.5
The Spelling tab in the Options dialog box.

Spell Checking a Single Word

You've already seen that you can right-click on a word that has been flagged as misspelled to see Word's suggested alternatives. But even if you've turned automatic spell checking off, it's easy to spell check a single word.

Highlight the word by double-clicking on it with the mouse, and press F7. If you spelled the word wrong, Word attempts to provide a list of alternatives. If the word is correct, Word moves to next spelling error it finds and displays the spell check dialog box with a list of alternatives. If you choose, you can instruct the spelling utility to continue spell checking the document, or you can stop spell checking and return to editing the document.

Spell Checking a Text Selection

To spell check part of a document, select the text and click on the Spell Check button on the toolbar. When Word finishes spelling the selected text, it offers to check the rest of the document; to end the spelling check, click on the **No** button.

Spelling Interactively

Often, when you make a spelling change, you'll notice something else in your document that needs changing at the same time. You don't have to close the spell checker to do it.

Click once in the document (or press Alt+F6 or Ctrl+Tab to make the editing window active). Word highlights the flagged word. You can format, delete, or replace it using standard Word commands. The Spelling dialog box becomes grayed out, as shown in figure 5.6, showing that it's temporarily unavailable.

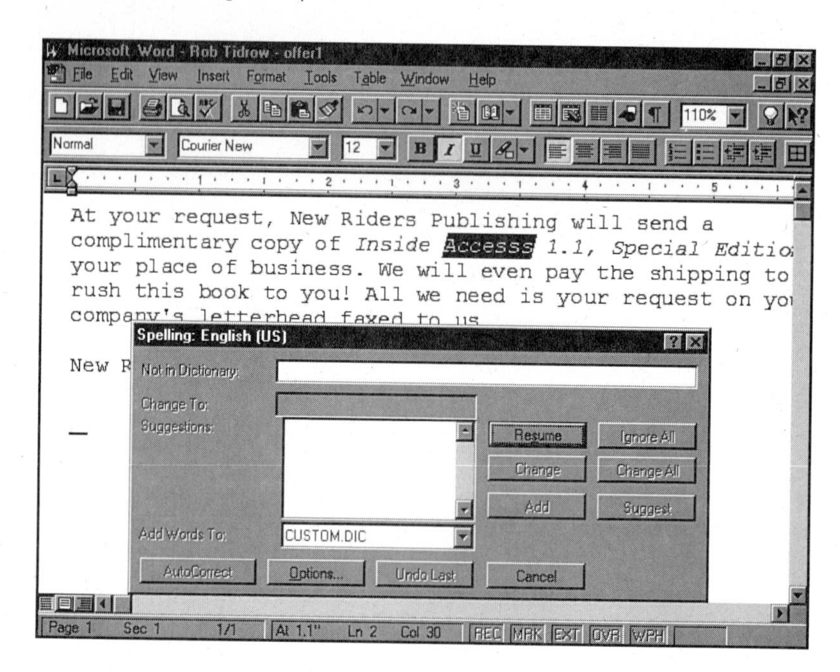

Figure 5.6
Editing from within a spelling check.

Click again anywhere in the document, and the insertion point moves there. You can edit the document normally. When you're finished editing, click on the Resume button in the Spelling dialog box, and the spelling check begins again.

Refining Word's Spelling

Some categories of words cause problems for spelling utilities. For instance, no spell checker understands all acronyms. Because most acronyms are all caps, you can tell Word not to flag words that are all caps. Choose **Options** from the **Tools** menu, and choose the Spelling tab in the Options dialog box. Then check Words in **UPPER**CASE in the Ignore group.

Similarly, many product names combine words and numbers. Suppose that you own a 486SX computer, a DX-677 CD player, and a KFE100 fire extinguisher. Word normally flags these—driving you stark raving mad if you're proofing a price list. You can tell Word to ignore this by checking Words with Numbers in the Spelling options box.

Sometimes, you'll have a block of text that you know is accurate—but you also know that Word will flag plenty of words in it. A list of proper names is a good example. Here's how to tell Word to ignore a specific block of text:

1. Select the text.
2. Choose Language from the Tools menu. The Language dialog box appears, as shown in figure 5.7.

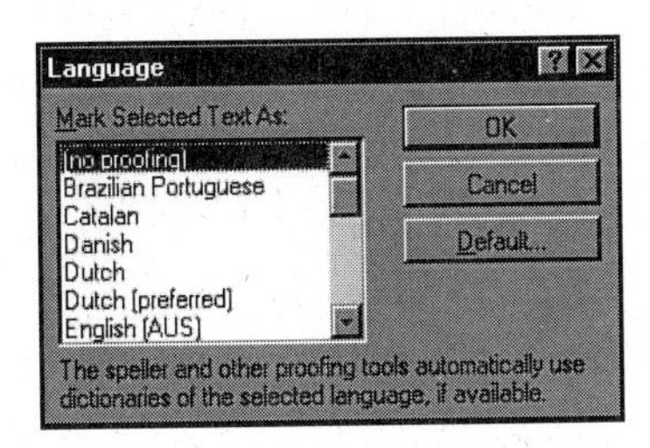

Figure 5.7

The Language dialog box.

3. Choose the (no proofing) item from the Mark Selected Text As list in the Language dialog box (it's at the very top of the Mark Selected Text As list box).
4. Click on the OK button.

From now on, Word skips the highlighted text whenever you check the spelling of the document.

Note Word also skips the highlighted text when you run the grammar check or hyphenation utility.

Using Foreign Language Dictionaries

As you've just noticed, choosing Tools, Language also offers a wide variety of languages besides its (no proofing) option. These work the same way: you select the text you want to proof in a foreign language, and then select the foreign language in the Language dialog box.

There's only one catch: you have to install the correct dictionary. In the United States, you use the English (U.S.) dictionary, named MSSP2 EN.LEX. If you bought your software in another country, that country's proofing tools were most likely included with Word.

Many other languages are available, however, through Aliki Software—the same Microsoft subcontractor that sells *The Comprehensive Spelling Dictionary* already mentioned. The current list appears in table 5.1. At press time, a complete set of proofing tools for any language was $89.95. Except as shown in the following table, these include spell checker, thesaurus, and hyphenation file.

TABLE 5.1
Foreign Language Proofing Tools Available for Word

Language	Spelling	Hyphenation	Thesaurus	Grammar
Danish	Yes	Yes	Yes	No
Dutch	Yes	Yes	Yes	No
English (British)	Yes	Yes	Yes	Yes
English (American)	Yes	Yes	Yes	Yes
Finnish	Yes	Yes	No	No
French (Canadian)	Yes	Yes	Yes	Yes
French (European)	Yes	Yes	Yes	Yes
German	Yes	Yes	Yes	No
Italian	Yes	Yes	Yes	No
Norwegian	Yes	Yes	Yes	No
Portuguese (European)	Yes	Yes	No	No
Portuguese (Brazilian)	Yes	Yes	No	No
Spanish	Yes	Yes	Yes	No
Swedish	Yes	Yes	Yes	No

When Word is checking text in another language, that language appears in the Spelling title bar.

Excluding Words from the Dictionary

Occasionally, you might want to have the spell checker flag a word as a possible misspelling even though the word is in its dictionary. Let's say that you've noticed you often mistype *liar* as *lira*, both of which are spelled correctly. Because you write crime novels, not reports on European currency exchange, wouldn't it be nifty if the spelling utility would always question lira as a misspelling, instead of assuming that you know what you're doing?

You can't remove a word from Word's basic dictionary. You can, however, create a supplemental file, called an *exclude dictionary*, which includes words you want to flag as misspellings even if they're spelled right.

Like custom dictionaries, exclude dictionaries are ASCII files with one word on each line. Exclude dictionaries use the same file name as the main dictionaries with which they are connected, except they have an EXC extension. They are stored in the same folder as the main dictionary.

If you're using the default dictionary for American English, your exclude dictionary will be MSSP2 EN.EXC. Chances are you'll place it in either your WINWORD or C:\Windows\Msapps\Proof or C:\Program Files\Common Files\Proof folder. To create an exclude dictionary, follow these steps:

1. Find your main dictionary. (It'll probably be in the C:\Windows\Msapps\Proof folder.)
2. Create a new ASCII file with the same name as your dictionary and the EXC extension. Use Windows Notepad, Word, or another editor capable of producing a plain ASCII file.
3. Type each word you want to flag, one per line.
4. Save the file into the same folder as the main dictionary. If you are using Word to produce this file, choose Save As from the File menu, and select the Text Only option from the Save as type list box (see fig. 5.8).

If, during a spelling check, you tell Word to **A**dd an excluded Word into its main dictionary, this will have no effect: the word will remain in the exclude dictionary unless you remove it manually.

Save the file as MSSP2 EN.EXC, and place it in the same folder with MSSP2 EN.LEX. Reopen the sample document and run spell check. Notice that "paginate" is now flagged as a possible error.

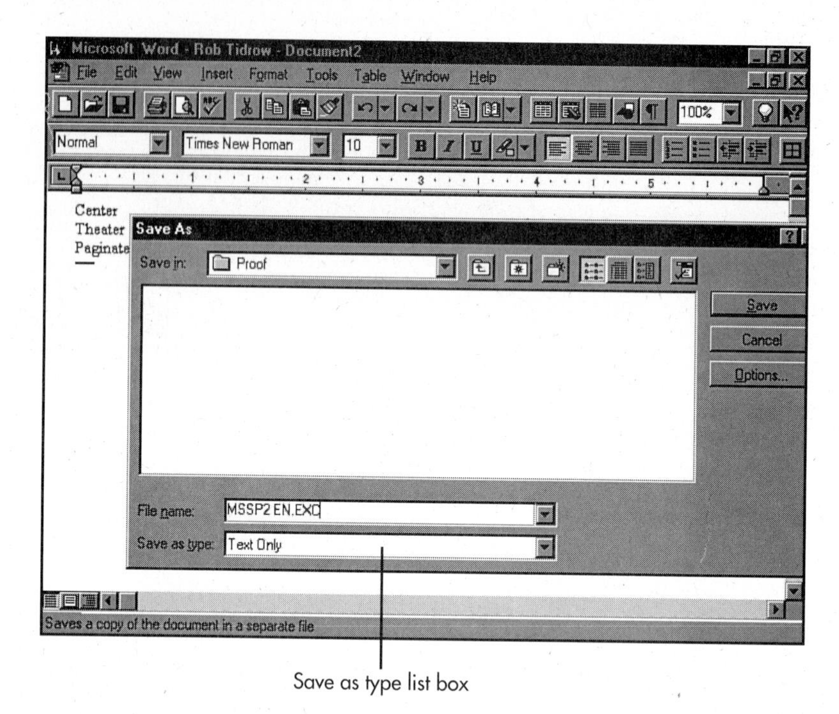

Figure 5.8
Saving the exclude dictionary as plain text.

Adding and Using a New Custom Dictionary

You've already learned that Word creates a custom dictionary, CUSTOM.DIC, to store additional words you want Word to recognize. You also can create specialized custom dictionaries to meet the needs of different kinds of documents.

For example, if some of your documents specifically concern computers, you may want to allow some acronyms in these documents and still flag them as misspellings in other types of documents.

You can do this in two ways. The first is to create the custom dictionary manually, and then copy it into the same folder as CUSTOM.DIC. This makes sense if you already have a pretty good idea of many of the words you want to add. Follow these steps:

1. Open a new file. Use a text editor capable of producing plain ASCII text, like Notepad or Word.

2. Add the new spelling words to this file, one per line.

3. Save the file with a DIC extension, placing it in the same folder as CUSTOM.DIC. If you are using Word, be sure to use Text Only as the format.

A second approach is to instruct Word to create the new folder for you. (Note that this process has changed somewhat in Word 95.)

1. Choose Options from the Tools menu and select the Spelling tab (see fig. 5.9).

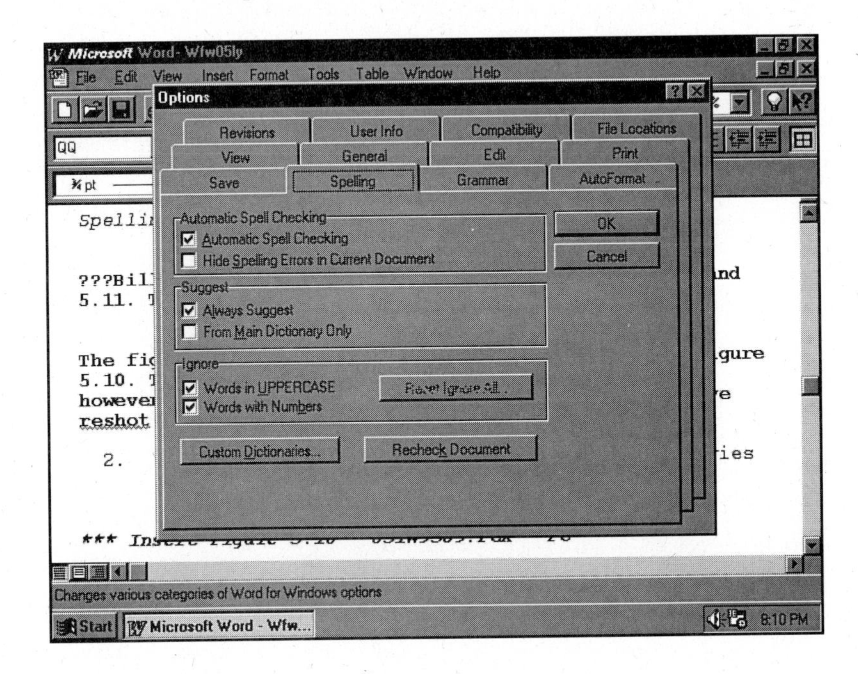

Figure 5.9

Spelling tab in the Options dialog box.

2. Choose Custom Dictionaries. The Custom Dictionaries dialog box opens (see fig. 5.10).

3. Click New. The Create Custom Dictionary dialog box opens (see fig. 5.11).

4. Enter the name of your new custom dictionary in the File name box. This name can be anything you choose, as long as you save it as a Dictionary file.

5. Click on the Save button, and you are returned to the Custom Dictionaries dialog box (see fig. 5.12). Check the box next to your custom dictionary to make sure that Word uses it when you spell check your documents.

6. To add words to this dictionary, click Edit. Word displays the empty dictionary file in a document window. Now you can add words—making sure to place a carriage return after each word. When you're finished, save the file, making sure to save it as an unformatted text file.

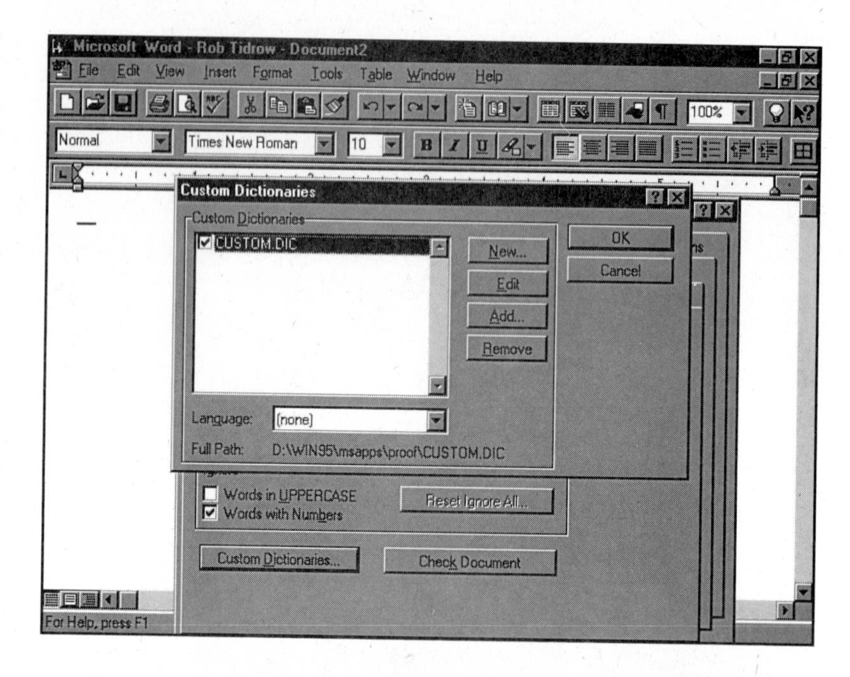

Figure 5.10
The Custom Dictionaries dialog box.

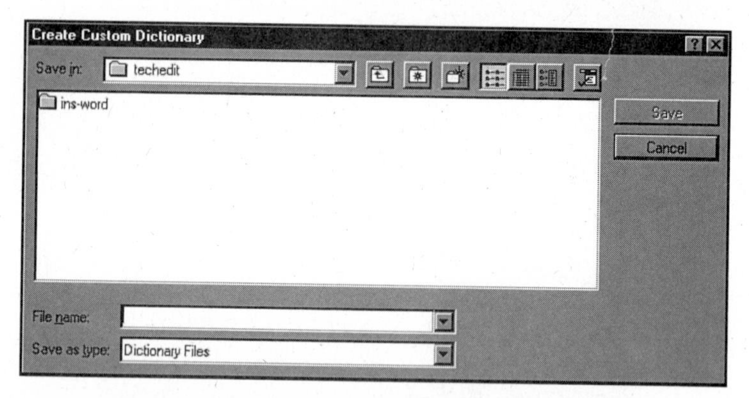

Figure 5.11
The Create Custom Dictionary dialog box.

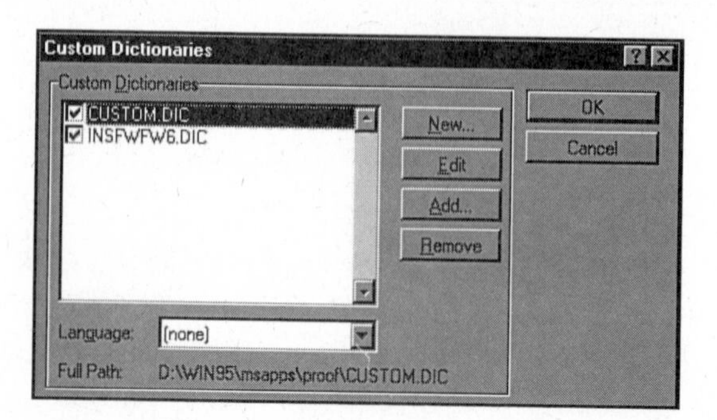

Figure 5.12
The Custom Dictionaries dialog box.

Word uses any custom dictionaries with check marks next to them in the Spelling tab in the Options dialog box. All active custom dictionaries are checked before Word flags a word as misspelled, and you can choose which dictionary to place new words in.

If you deselect a dictionary in the Spelling tab in the Options dialog box, that dictionary will not be available during the spelling check session until you select it again.

Adding New Words to Your Custom Dictionary

To place a new word in your new custom dictionary without manually editing the dictionary file:

1. Run the spell check.
2. When Word flags a word as an error that you know is spelled correctly, choose the new custom dictionary from the Add Words To list box in the Spelling dialog box.
3. Select Add.

Try this: Copy the custom dictionary WORDDICT.DIC into the same folder as your current spelling dictionary (most likely the Word spelling dictionary MSSP2 EN.DIC is in C:\WINDOWS\MSAPPS\PROOF). Choose the Spelling tab in the Options dialog box (under the Tools menu) and see that it appears beneath CUSTOM.DIC as an available dictionary. Highlight it, choose the OK button, and run a spelling check on the sample document. Notice that the Word spelling utility no longer flags "repagination," "386SX," "Wingdings," "WordArt," ".EXC," "WINWORD," or "AUTOEXEC." (These words are included in the custom dictionary WORDDICT.DIC.)

Using the Thesaurus

As you write, you may sometimes find yourself getting into a rut—using the same word or phrase repeatedly, when another word might make your point more clearly. That's what a thesaurus is for, and Word comes with a very good one.

To use the thesaurus, position the text insertion point in (or immediately after) the word for which you want *synonyms* (similar-meaning words). Or, select the entire word by double-clicking on it. Then choose Thesaurus from the Tools menu.

The keyboard shortcut for starting the thesaurus is Shift+F7.

In some cases, Word also recognizes a phrase and provides synonyms for it. For example, if you highlight "speed up," Word recognizes it and presents "accelerate" and other synonyms.

Word highlights the entire word or phrase and opens the Thesaurus dialog box, as shown in figure 5.13.

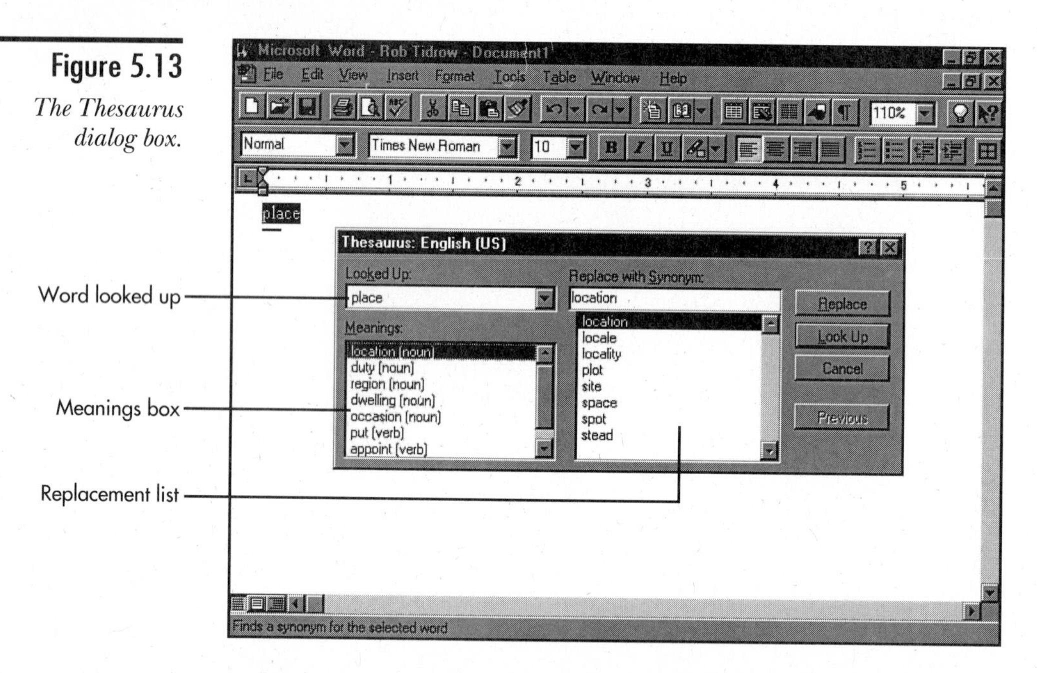

Figure 5.13
The Thesaurus dialog box.

The word you've chosen appears in the Looked Up box. To the right, Word proposes the most likely equivalent term. The example in figure 5.13 asks for synonyms for the word "place," and Word provides "location" as the most likely synonym. It also provides several alternatives in the Replace with **S**ynonym list box.

But "place" is used in several senses, each of which has its own synonyms. These alternatives appear in the **M**eanings box.

For example, if you're using place as a verb ("He was told to place the book on the table"), select the most similar meaning from the **M**eanings box. In this case, you would select put (verb). When you do, new synonyms for "put" will appear (place, deposit, settle, and so on).

When Word presents a list of synonyms, you may decide you would like to review the meanings and synonyms of one of those words. To do so, press the Look Up button. As you can see, sometimes you might follow a trail of several suggested replacements before arriving at the word you want. If you'd like to return to a previous request, you can. Click on the downward-pointing arrow on the Looked Up list box to reveal a list of all the requests you've made since opening the Thesaurus dialog box. Click on the request you want, and those synonyms reappear.

When you do find the synonym you're looking for, select it, and click on the **R**eplace button. Word substitutes the synonym for the original word in your document.

Sometimes Word can't find a synonym. In these cases, Word presents you with an alphabetical list of words with similar spellings, as shown in figure 5.14.

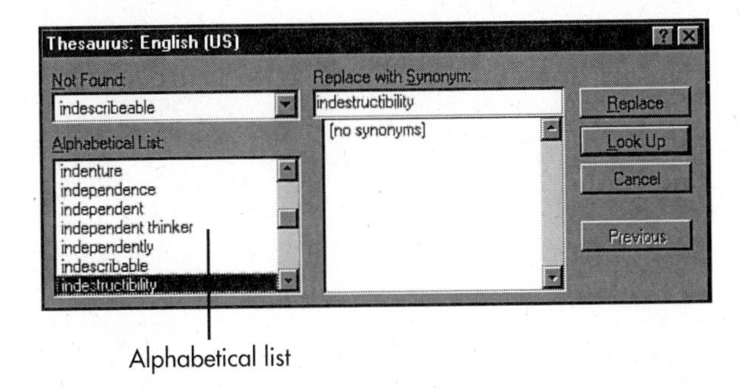

Figure 5.14

An alphabetical list provided by the thesaurus.

If you spelled the word wrong (as in figure 5.14), you may be able to pick the correct word from this list and search Word's thesaurus for it. In figure 5.14, you can see that the proper spelling of "indescribable" appears near the bottom of the alphabetical list.

Multiple Meanings, Antonyms, and Related Words

Many words have multiple meanings, depending on how they are used. In an earlier example, you saw how the word "place" can be used as a noun (where a thing is) or as a verb (to put something somewhere). The Word thesaurus retrieves as many alternate meanings for words you look up as possible. In figure 5.15, the word looked up is "last." The synonyms for last as an adjective are words such as "final," "concluding," and "closing."

Figure 5.16 shows the Thesaurus dialog box with suggestions for last as a verb (as in "Wow! These Swiss army boots sure last a long time").

The Word thesaurus can show you antonyms (opposite meanings) of many words. If a list of antonyms is available, the word Antonyms appears in the **M**eanings list box, as shown in figure 5.17. Select Antonyms to see them.

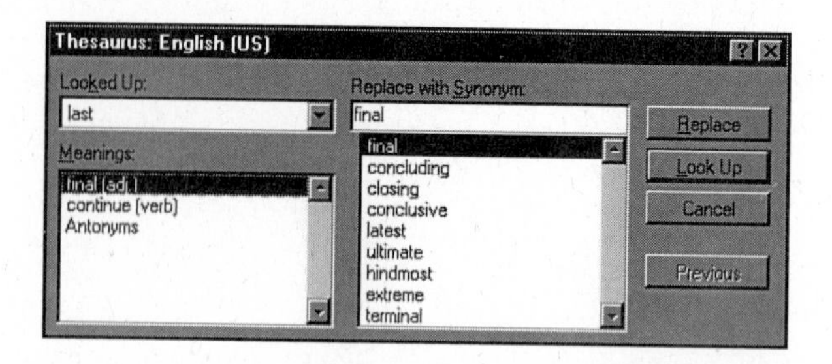

Figure 5.15

Synonyms for "last" when used as an adjective.

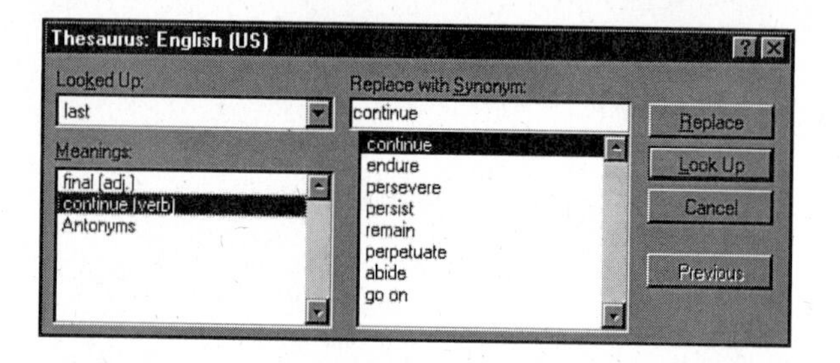

Figure 5.16

Synonyms for "last" when used as a verb.

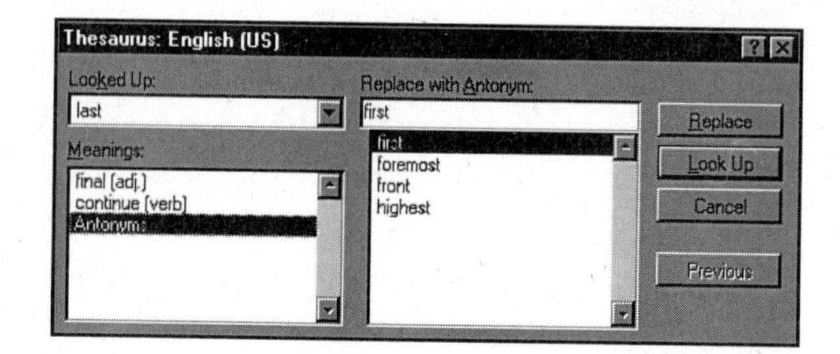

Figure 5.17

Antonyms for the word "last."

Finally, some words in the Word thesaurus have a number of "related words" that you can review. Figure 5.18 shows the list of related words for "transformation." You may find the related words useful if you're trying to think of an alternative to a word you'd rather not use. Generally speaking, using a variety of descriptive words is preferable to using the same words over and over again.

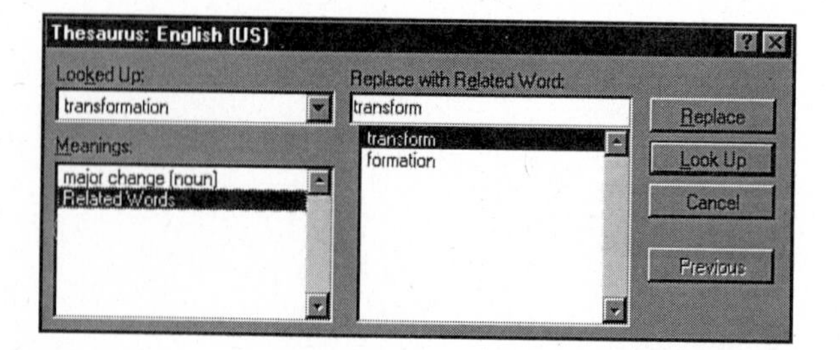

Figure 5.18

Related words for "transformation."

Using Look Up Independently

If you place the insertion point in an area of the screen with no text, Word assumes that you want to look up a word that is not in the document. The Thesaurus dialog box opens with nothing filled into the Looked Up box. Enter the word you want to look up in the thesaurus in the Insert box (see fig. 5.19), and click on the Look Up button.

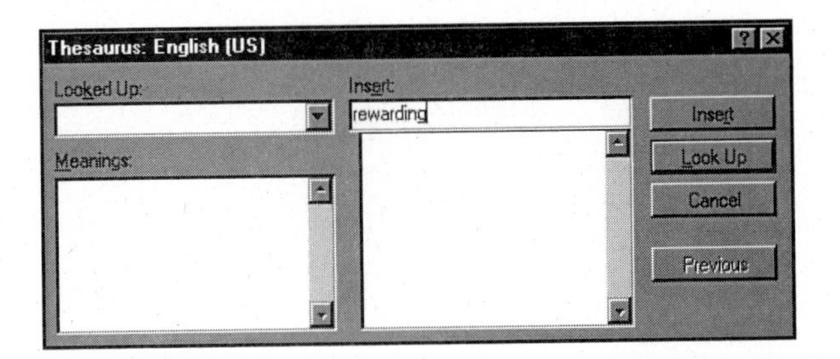

Figure 5.19

Using the thesaurus to look up a word not in the document.

When Word has finished looking up the word (in this case, "rewarding"), the Thesaurus dialog box changes as shown in figure 5.20. The Thesaurus dialog box in figure 5.20 looks as it does when you've looked up some word in your document. You can, if you want, use the Insert button to put the word in the Replace with Synonym box into your text at the insert cursor's location.

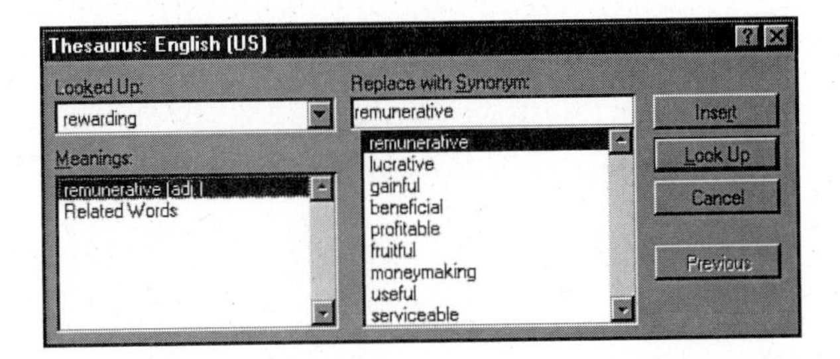

Figure 5.20

The Thesaurus dialog box when look up is completed.

In other circumstances, the Insert box is named Replace With, but you can use it the same way. Type the word you want to search in the Replace With box; then choose Look Up, and Word presents the synonyms it finds.

Grammar Check

Word's grammar checker carefully reviews 42 important rules of grammar and style, making suggestions whenever it believes it has found an error. If you want an explanation of the rule Word thinks you've broken, Word gladly provides one. It's one of the best grammar checkers available. But it isn't perfect—not by a long shot.

Word's grammar checker, like all contemporary grammar checkers, simply follows preprogrammed rules. Of course, the grammar checker doesn't understand a word of what it's reading. Because the grammar checker cannot *really* discriminate between good and bad grammar, many "errors" are flagged that are perfectly OK.

On a bad day, Word's grammar checker creates a lot of extra work for you. Every "error" may turn out to be nothing more than a misunderstanding of your text. But on a good day, the grammar checker will pleasantly surprise you—catching things you would never have remembered on your own. Even better, you can personalize the grammar checker so that it only catches the errors you actually make.

I ran the grammar checker on an early draft of this chapter, and the results were quite instructive. (To me, anyway.)

It found several sentences in the passive voice. I thought I had eliminated the passive voice from my writing. Now I know better, and I know I need to try using a more active voice whenever possible.

The grammar checker fixed incorrect punctuation here and there.

It caught several instances of the overused modifier "actually." I agreed and eliminated most of them.

It caught some cliché phrases, like "in fact," and wordy phrases "once again" and "in addition to."

It also helped out with the difference between "which" and "that"—something I've never learned on my own.

On the other hand, it flagged several instances of an opening parenthesis not followed by a closing parenthesis—unaware that the whole sentence was parenthesized.

Running a Grammar Check

You can run a grammar check on your entire document or any text you select. Word's grammar checker checks only complete sentences—ignoring any text without a period at the end.

This usually makes sense: for example, the grammar checker won't flag items in a bulleted list. On the other hand, whenever it sees a period, Word's grammar checker assumes that the sentence has ended—causing problems with initials, figure numbers, and other items.

The grammar checker starts at the insertion point and continues checking to the end of the document. It then continues at the beginning of the document. When it finds a sentence with a possible error, it highlights the sentence and opens the Grammar dialog box, shown in figure 5.21.

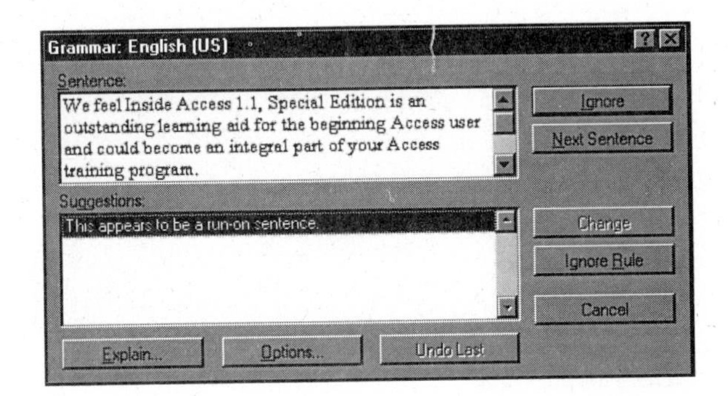

Figure 5.21

The Grammar dialog box.

In the Sentence box, you can see the sentence Word is questioning. If Word questions a specific word or clause, that word or clause would be boldfaced.

In the Suggestions box, you can see the grammar test that the sentence failed. In many cases, Word also provides a specific recommendation.

At this point, you have several choices:

- The Ignore button tells Word to skip this problem and continue with the grammar check. If you choose Ignore, Word might find another problem in the same sentence, or else move on to the rest of the document.
- Next Sentence tells Word to skip to the next sentence, regardless of any more problems that may exist in the current sentence.
- The Ignore Rule button tells Word to skip this error and any other errors resembling it. For example, if Word flags a run-on sentence, Ignore Rule tells Word not to flag any more run-on sentences.
- Explain tells Word's grammar checker to provide a more detailed explanation of the rule it is invoking. A sample explanation appears in figure 5.22. If Word's proposed change is simple enough that it can be made automatically, the Change button will also be available.

For example, if Word recommends a change in usage (as in fig. 5.23), it offers to automatically fix the error. Choose Change; Word revises the document and continues the grammar check.

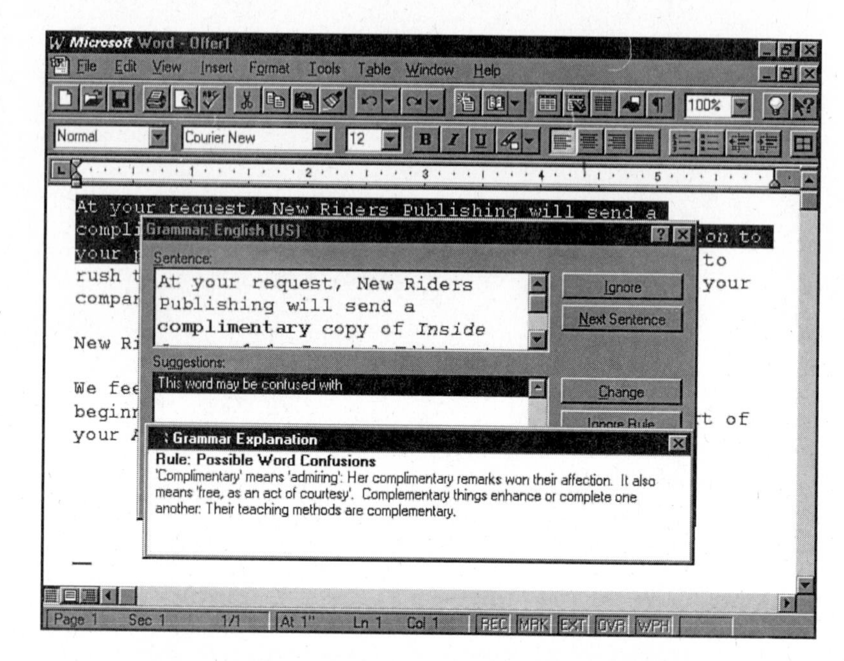

Figure 5.22

The Grammar Explanation dialog box.

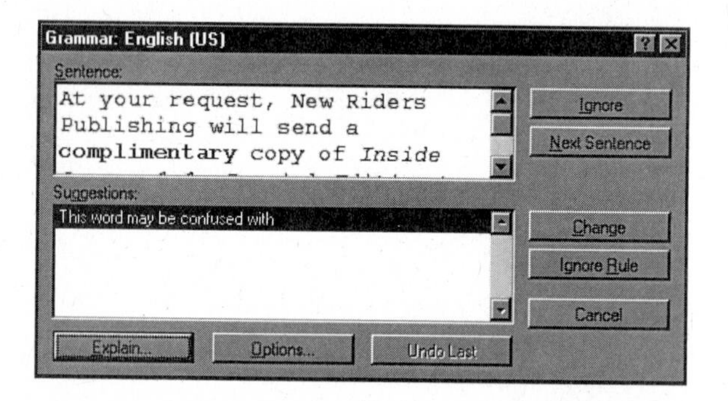

Figure 5.23

Word's grammar checker will suggest simple changes.

As with Word's spelling utility, you can edit the document from within the grammar checker, by clicking in the editing window, or switching to it with Alt+F6 or Ctrl+Tab. The grammar checker will be grayed out, except for a button marked Start. Choose Start to begin checking grammar again.

Choosing Which Rules of Grammar to Apply to Your Work

Word's grammar checker tests your document using any of the following three built-in sets of grammar rules. In addition to these three "standard" sets of grammar rules,

Word provides you with three different "custom" grammar rule sets you can modify to suit your own style:

Strictly	Checks 34 rules of grammar and style
For **B**usiness Writing	Checks *all* grammar rules and *most* of the 25 style rules
For **C**asual Writing	Checks *most* grammar rules and *some* style rules

You can decide how tough you want Word to be on your document. Choose **O**ptions from the **T**ools menu. Then choose the Grammar tab in the Options dialog box (see fig. 5.24). Tables 5.2, 5.3, and 5.4 show a representative set of the rules that Word's grammar checker is capable of reviewing.

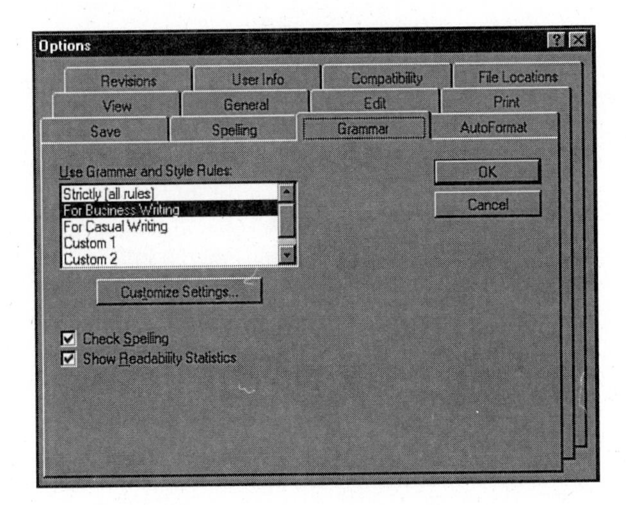

Figure 5.24

The Grammar tab in the Options dialog box.

Table 5.2
Some of Word's Grammar Checker Rules

Rule	Explanation
Noun phrase consistency	Disagreement of numbers within noun phrases; for example, a singular article used with a plural noun
Passive verb usage	Passive voice ("It is to be hoped...")
Subject-verb agreement	Disagreement between verbs and their subjects
Pronoun errors	Errors in case or ordering of pronouns
Commonly confused words	Commonly confused words that are different parts of speech

continues

Table 5.2, Continued
Some of Word's Grammar Checker Rules

Rule	Explanation
Word usage	Confusion between similar words; for example, homonyms such as *too, two,* and *to*
Jargon words	Jargon expressions; that is, *rightsize, activate*
Punctuation errors	Incorrect punctuation, such as wrong placement of commas in specific expressions, or wrong punctuation of parenthetical or quoted material

Table 5.3
Some of Word's Grammar Checker Style Rules

Rule	Explanation
Wordy expressions	Expressions that can be replaced by simpler words or expressions, or eliminated altogether (example: replace "in addition to" with "besides")
Redundant expressions	Needlessly repetitive expressions that often can be revised by cutting part of the expression
Informal expressions	Expressions more appropriate in speech than in writing
Clichés	Overused expressions that can weaken the impact of a sentence
Weak modifiers	Weak or unnecessary adjective or adverb modifiers/ qualifiers, such as "nice" or "pretty"
Misused words	Words often used incorrectly because they are confused with similar words or phrases
Pretentious words	Unnecessarily complex words that can be replaced by simple, straightforward alternatives
Overused phrases	Overused adjective/noun or adverb/adjective phrases
Stock phrases	Overused phrases that can be deleted without changing the meaning or emphasis of a sentence (example: "in fact")

Table 5.4
Other Rules Checked by Word's Grammar Checker

Rule	Business	Casual
Split infinitives	By more than one word	By more than two words
Consecutive nouns	More than three in a row	More than four in a row
Prepositional phrases	More than three in a row	More than four in a row

Where grammar rules come from. If you want more background on Word's grammar rules, you may want to consider the following books that are source material for Word's grammar checker:

Written Word 3, Houghton-Mifflin

The Riverside Handbook, Houghton-Mifflin

The Chicago Manual of Style, University of Chicago Press

The Associated Press Style Book and Libel Manual

The Elements of Style, Strunk and White's small classic

Getting the Most from Word's Grammar Checker

You will probably benefit most from Word's grammar checker utility if you customize its behavior. It is a relatively simple task to modify the grammar checker to trap only those errors that you make most often or are the most common errors made by most people.

Following are some examples of common mistakes that Word's grammar checker seems reasonably reliable at tracking. You might start with these rules, or better yet, run a complete grammar check a few times, and keep track of the recurring problems Word notices in *your* writing.

- Wordy expressions
- Passive voice
- Weak modifiers
- Vague quantifiers

- Jargon words and jargon expressions
- Punctuation errors
- Redundant expressions
- Double negatives

Adapting Grammar Check to Your Personal Preferences

To change any of Word's grammar settings, choose the Grammar tab (see fig. 5.24) in the Options dialog box (accessed by choosing Options from the Tools menu).

Choose Customize Settings. The Customize Grammar Settings dialog box opens, as shown in figure 5.25.

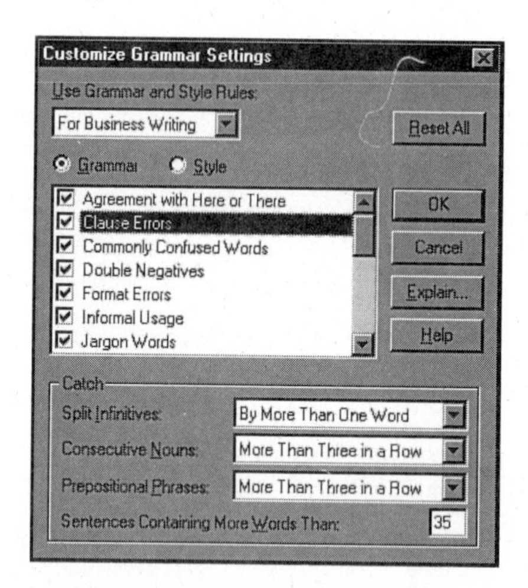

Figure 5.25
The Customize Grammar Settings dialog box.

Using the Use Grammar and Style Rules list box, you can change the way Word interprets Strict, Business, or Casual. Each check box toggles on or off.

Notice also the list boxes in the Catch group, which allow you to control which Split Infinitives, Consecutive Nouns, and Prepositional Phrases will be flagged. You can request an explanation of any rule by clicking on the Explain button. When you've set the grammar checker to catch only the errors you want, click on OK.

Normally, you can reset all grammar checking settings to their "factory settings" by clicking on the **R**eset All button.

Using Word's Readability Statistics

When Word completes a grammar check, it provides several estimates of your text's readability, as shown in figure 5.26. These statistics are based on an estimate of the number of words in an average sentence, and the average number of syllables in each word. The Flesch-Kincaid, Coleman-Liau, and Bormuth grade level indices are an attempt to estimate the school grade level required to understand your text.

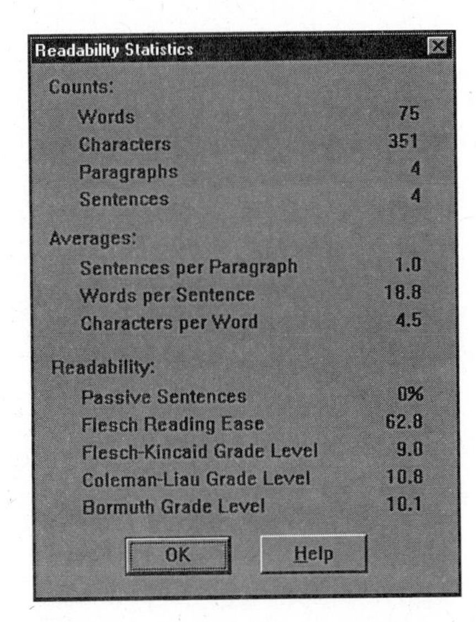

Figure 5.26

The Readability Statistics dialog box.

Of course, like the grammar checker itself, these indices don't take into account the substance of your words. Familiar long words often lead to an estimate of greater difficulty than obscure short words.

File Management

You might already be using Word for Windows regularly, without recognizing its extensive built-in capabilities for working with and managing files. If you learn these capabilities now, you can be more efficient right away, but it really pays off later, when you have hundreds (or even thousands) of documents and need to find a specific piece of information. This chapter covers Word 95's extensive options for opening, saving, locating, and securing files.

In this chapter:

- Opening and working with multiple files
- Saving files in different formats
- Using the Open dialog box to search for files
- Sorting file lists
- Using Properties
- Retrieving recently used files
- Using Word's file security features
- Using Word's file association features

Advanced Techniques for Viewing Files

It's easy to assume that each document always gets one and only one window, but in Word, that's not necessarily true. Using the New Window feature, you can open additional windows on the same document if this makes it easier to move throughout a large document and stay in control of its contents. Using the split box, you also can split a document into two parts and keep both on-screen at the same time.

Using New Window

To open more than one window containing the same file, select New Window from the Window menu, and a second window that contains your current document opens (see fig. 6.1).

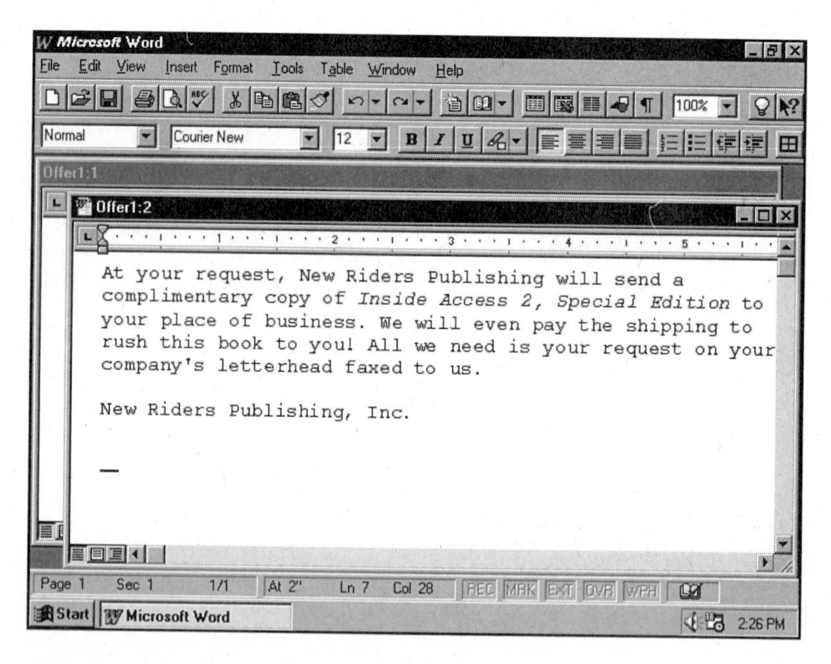

Figure 6.1
Two windows of the same document.

Both windows contain the same contents, and if you change one, the other changes as well. When you Close the file, both windows close. Notice that the title bars of these document windows indicate which copy of the document you're working on. In figure 6.1, the "top" copy is Offer1:2, whereas the one "behind" is Offer1:1.

Note The effect is the same if you open the same document twice with the **O**pen option in the **F**ile menu.

Use New Window primarily when you want to split a document from left to right—for example, to view multiple columns, as shown in figure 6.2. You have to manually arrange the windows

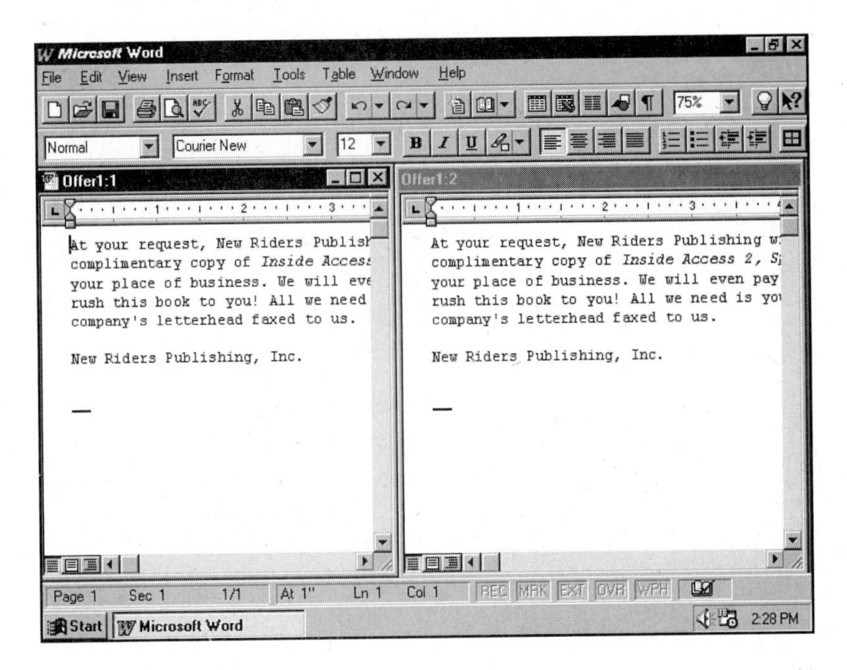

Figure 6.2
Using New Window to view left and right edges of a document.

If you want to split the document horizontally, the split box works better than New Window.

Using the Split Box

The split box is a tiny, nearly invisible 3-D gray rectangle directly above the vertical scroll bar. Figure 6.3 shows the split box. You can use the split box to split your document horizontally in two so that you can view both parts of the document at once.

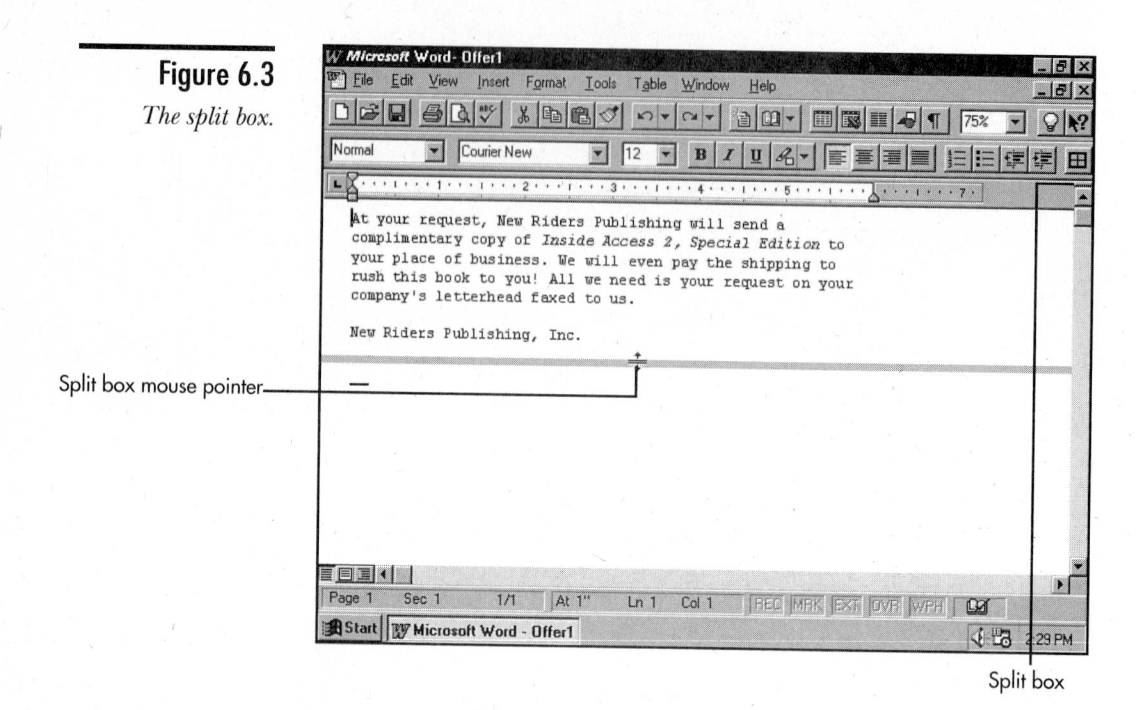

Figure 6.3
The split box.

To use the split box, move the mouse pointer to the split box; the pointer changes shape. Click and drag the pointer to the middle of your screen, to the location where you want the screen to split. Figure 6.3 shows how the screen looks while you are pressing the mouse button and moving the mouse pointer to the location you want. Release the mouse button, and the screen splits into two independent panes, as shown in figure 6.4.

You'll have plenty of opportunities to use the split bar. For instance, you may want to copy text from the beginning of a long document to another location near the end of the document, and still view both parts of the document to make sure that the text fits appropriately—in both places.

If you prefer, you also can split your screen using the keyboard, as follows:

1. Press Alt+W to activate the Window menu.
2. Select Split.
3. Use the up- or down-arrow keys to determine where you want the split to appear.
4. Press Enter.

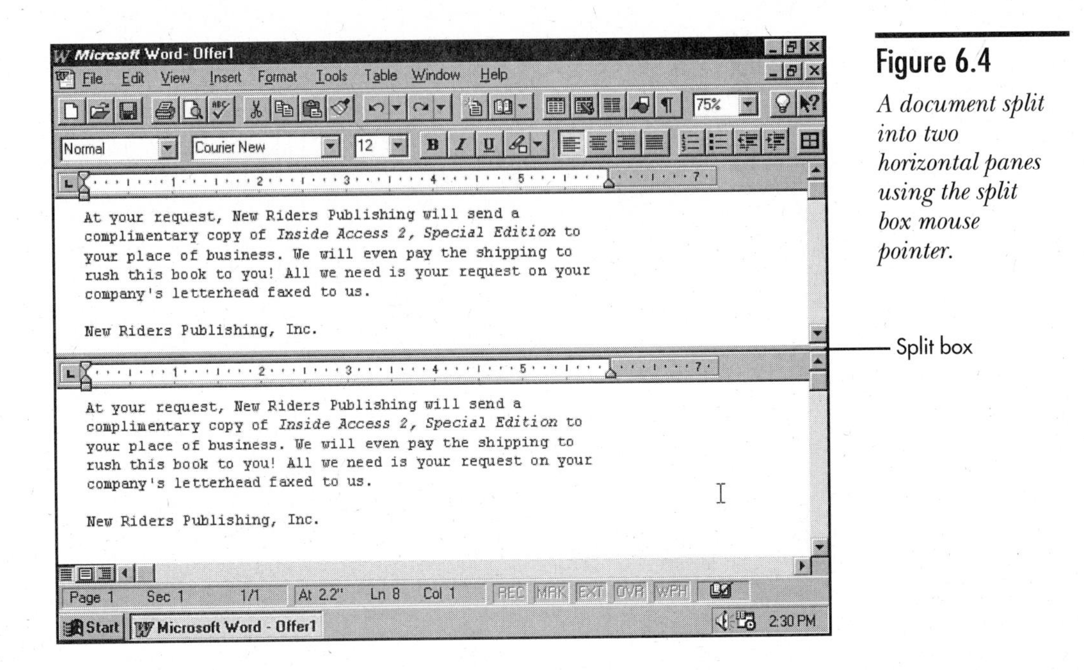

Figure 6.4

A document split into two horizontal panes using the split box mouse pointer.

To “un-split” your screen using the mouse, click on the new split box that appears to the right of wherever you split the window. Then, drag that split box to the top of the screen, above the document window. Using the keyboard, choose Split again and use the arrow keys to move the split bar above the top of the document window.

Opening Several Documents at Once

Most likely, you already know that you can keep several files open at once, and switch among them by choosing the file that you want to view from the Window menu. (Incidentally, you also can move among windows by pressing Ctrl+F6.)

But you may not realize that you can actually open several files in the same folder at once, with one command:

1. Select Open from the File menu.

2. The Open dialog box lists all Word (DOC) files in your current folder (unless you set it to search for something else). I’ll assume for the moment that this folder contains the files you want. Select the first file by clicking on it or using the up- and down-arrow keys to highlight it. Press Shift+F8 to select the file.

3. To choose additional files, press Ctrl while clicking on each additional file. Or, from the keyboard, press Shift+F8, use the up- and down-arrow keys to highlight the next file that you want, and press Shift+F8 again to select it.

4. To open all the files, select **O**pen.

If you inadvertently select the wrong file, you can easily deselect it. If you use the mouse, highlight the file name, press Ctrl, and click. If you use the keyboard, highlight the file name and press the spacebar.

On the CD

The accompanying CD-ROM contains two files you can use to practice some of these procedures in this chapter: IWMS8A.DOC and IWMS8B.DOC.

Arranging Multiple Open Documents

What if you want to view more than one document simultaneously, as you might if you want to check a reference in one document while you work on another? The quickest way to do it is to divide the available screen equally between all active documents by selecting **A**rrange All from the **W**indow menu. Figure 6.5 shows how **A**rrange All looks when three documents are open.

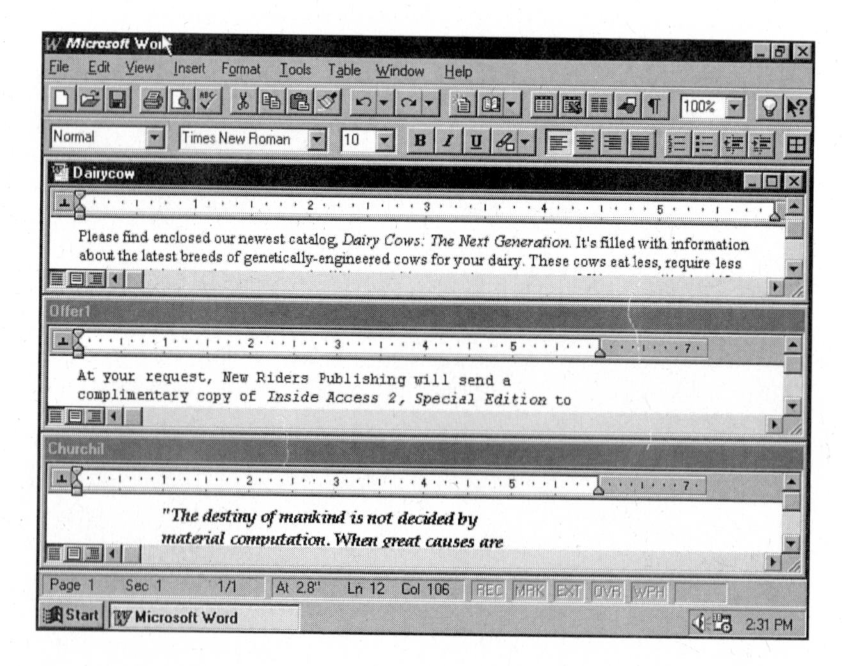

Figure 6.5

Arrange All with three documents displayed.

Cut and paste. You can cut and paste text between documents just as you can within a document. You also can drag and drop from one window to another. See Chapter 10, "Field Codes," to learn how to make one document change automatically because of a change in another.

Saving Different File Types

Having worked with a file, you may want to make it available to a user who works with a different type of word processor, or send it across the Internet in text-only format. Word permits you to save files in a wide variety of word processing formats, through the File, Save As dialog box.

When you save a file in a different format, the original Word file document still exists in memory and remains open after you create the new version. When you attempt to close the file, Word asks whether you want to save changes, even if you just saved the file. This is because the file contains formatting that can't be saved in the format you used: if you do close the file, that formatting will be lost. If you want to preserve the formatting, first save the file as a Word file and then save a separate copy in the format to which you're exporting.

Word can save files in the following formats:

- Word document (DOC). Default format for Word 95, Word 6 for Windows, Word 6 for Windows NT, and Word 6 for the Macintosh.
- Document Template (DOT). See Chapter 8, "Templates and Wizards," for more information on templates.
- Text Only (TXT). This eliminates all formatting, converts section breaks, newline characters, and page breaks to paragraph marks, and uses the ANSI character set. Use this format if you're not sure what computer your file will be used on.
- Text Only with Line Breaks (TXT). Good if you plan to upload the file on an e-mail system, such as MCI Mail, that requires regular line breaks.
- MS-DOS text (TX8, ASC). This format uses the extended ASCII character set used by DOS; it's useful for converting files that will be used by non-Windows applications.
- MS-DOS Text with Line Breaks (TX8).

- Rich Text Format (RTF). A Microsoft standard for exchanging word processing data that preserves most document formatting.
- MS-DOS text with layout. Works like MS-DOS text, except that spaces are inserted to simulate Word's indents, tables, line spacing, paragraph spacing, and tab stops.
- Text with layout.
- Word 2.*x* for Windows.
- Word 4.0 for Macintosh. This export format often is used for sending files to Macintosh QuarkXpress desktop publishing systems because, until very recently, Quark has not had a more current Word document import filter.
- Word 5.0 for Macintosh.
- Word 5.1 for Macintosh.
- Word 6.0 for MS-DOS.
- RFT-DCA (RFT).
- WordPerfect 5.0 for DOS.
- WordPerfect 5.1 for DOS.
- WordPerfect 5.*x* for Windows.
- WordPerfect 5.1 or 5.2 Secondary File.
- WordPerfect 5.0 Secondary File.
- Microsoft Works 3.0 for Windows.
- Microsoft Works 4.0 for Windows.
- Windows Write (WRI).
- Microsoft Works 3.0 for MS-DOS.
- WordStar 7.0.
- WordStar 4.0.
- Normal text.

More conversions. Call Microsoft Customer Service at 800-426-9400 for information about supplementary conversion filters that are free upon request. Information about additional converters also can be found in the Microsoft Word for Windows Supplemental Offers coupon in your Word package.

In some cases, the program that you export to expects a specific extension. In other cases, as with WordPerfect or Microsoft Word for the Macintosh, the program doesn't require a specific extension, but Word assigns one anyway. Because Word displays only Word documents in the Open dialog box by default, files that you save in other file formats may not appear unless you choose All Files in the Files of Type box.

Save Options

In addition to using File, Save As to save a file in a different format (or with a different name or location), Word gives you several options for saving files. You can access these by selecting Options from the Save As dialog box, or by selecting Options from the Tools menu, and then selecting the Save tab (see fig. 6.6).

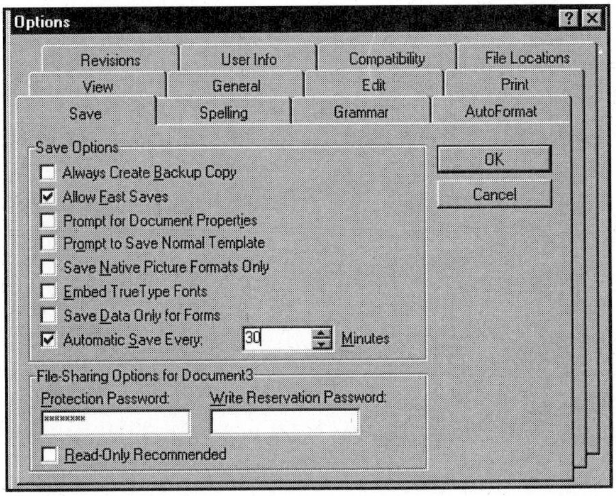

Figure 6.6

Save Options displayed in Tools, Options, Save.

Always Create Backup Copy tells Word to create a duplicate file with a BAK extension every time it saves a file.

Allow Fast Saves permits Word to save only the changes in a document, rather than the entire document. You can choose one or the other, but not both.

Why are Fast Saves so fast? For the same reason that it's faster to throw your clothes on the chair than it is to hang them in the closet. With Fast Saves, Word doesn't actually place the changes in the correct locations within the document. Rather, Word creates a list of changes that aren't integrated until the next time you save normally.

Even if you're using Fast Saves, Word occasionally performs a normal save to take care of all the housekeeping that accumulates.

By default, Word allows Fast Saves. And they really are quick. If you want to use a Word file in another program, however, that program won't know how to clean up the housekeeping that Word didn't do.

So, I prefer not to use Fast Saves unless I run Word on a particularly slow computer, or happen to be saving all my files on a floppy drive.

Two other valuable options are Prompt for Document Properties (discussed in the section "Using Word 95 Property Sheets," later in this chapter) and Automatic Save. No program should be without a feature like Automatic Save. It lets you tell Word to save a file at specified intervals from one minute to two hours. The shorter the interval, the less work you lose if your computer crashes or loses power. The only disadvantage: you can be forced to stop working for a few moments while the computer saves the file.

Retrieving a File That You Recently Worked On

Word, like most Windows applications, keeps track of the last four files that you worked on. These appear at the bottom of the File menu. To reopen one of these files, select it from the File menu. If you use the keyboard, simply open the File menu by pressing Alt+F and using the file's number: 1, 2, 3, or 4.

You might want Word to keep track of more (or fewer) files. For example, you might routinely keep more than four files open and want to be able to reopen any of them directly from the File menu. Or, you might have added commands to the File menu and not even have room for four files without making the menu too long to work with easily. You can change the number of files that Word tracks by choosing Options from the Tools menu and choosing the General tab. Reset the Recently Used File List box to any number from 0 to 9 files.

Remember that in Windows 95, recently used files also are displayed from the Start button, under Documents. If Word already is open, when you open a file from the Start button, it opens into the same copy of Word that you're already running, instead of opening a new copy of Word. This is a sensible change in behavior from Windows 3.1—and a rare acknowledgment that computer users don't have infinite memory resources.

Using Word 95 Property Sheets

As you work, Word compiles comprehensive information about your document and stores it in a *property sheet.* All Windows 95 files and programs have property sheets; even devices such as printers do. Property sheets for Word documents, however, offer more information than most, and Word 95 gives you unprecedented flexibility in organizing and maintaining that information.

Property sheets include all the information formerly collected in the Summary Info dialog box, and then some. This information is organized in five categories:

- General
- Summary
- Statistics
- Contents
- Custom

Note that Word no longer prompts you for detailed information about a file the first time you save it. You might want to change that, however—especially if you are managing document production by a group of people. You can choose to specify exactly what information must accompany each document, and require document creators to provide that information the first time they save.

You might get religion about using Properties even if you never have to share a document—especially when you consider that Word lets you locate documents by searching for any property that you choose. To specify that Word prompts for Document Properties the first time that you save a file, follow these steps:

1. Choose **O**ptions from the **T**ools menu.
2. Click on the **S**ave tab.

3. Check the Prompt for Document Properties check box.

4. Choose OK.

General Information

In the General tab, shown in figure 6.7, Word stores the following general information about every document:

- **Type.** Typically, *Microsoft Word Document.* Word gets this information from the document's file extension. Remember, even though file extensions aren't listed in Word 95 or Windows 95 directories by default, they're still there, stored in the "8.3" short file names that Windows creates so that the files can be accessed by earlier versions of DOS and Windows. You can, of course, open several other types of files and view general information about their properties. For example, if you save a file as a Text Only file in Word, it will be saved with a TXT extension, and that extension will of course be displayed if you view its properties.
- **Location.** Word displays the folder where the file is stored. Note: Word doesn't show the entire path unless the file is stored in the root directory of a drive.
- **Size.** Word provides file size information both in kilobytes (true kilobytes that are 1,024 bytes apiece, not the 1,000-byte kilobytes often used by hard-drive manufacturers) and in bytes.
- **MS-DOS Name.** Word provides the file's equivalent short file name—a maximum of eight characters plus a three-character extension.
- **Created.** Word shows the date, time, and second when the file was created.
- **Modified.** Word shows the date, time, and second when the file was last saved. That's useful information, for example, if you have a system crash and need to know whether recent edits were saved.
- **Accessed.** Word shows the date that the file was last accessed.

No information is stored in the General tab until the first time you save a file. Also, note that you can't edit any of the information stored in the General tab; Word and Windows track this data for you.

Summary Information

In the Summary tab, shown in figure 6.8, Word stores the following Summary information about every document: Title, Subject, Author, Manager, Company, Category,

Keywords, and Comments. Each can be as long as 255 characters. Note that Manager, Company, and Category are all new to Word 95.

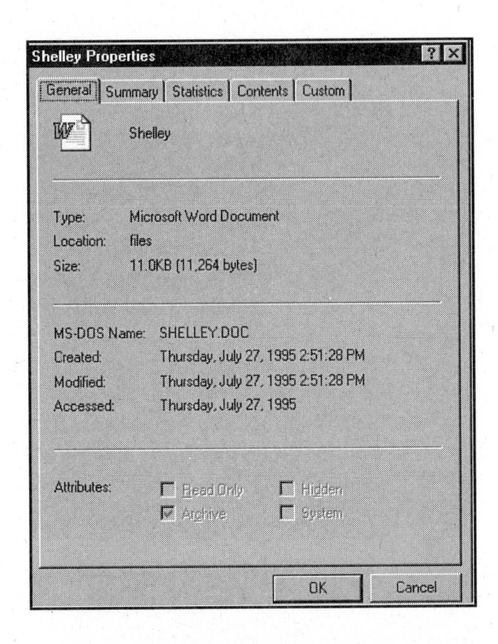

Figure 6.7

The General Properties tab.

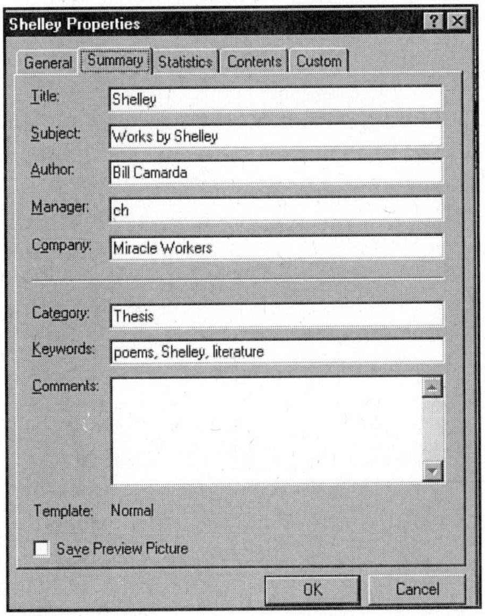

Figure 6.8

The Summary Properties tab.

Using the Title Entry

By default, the first time that you save a document, Word uses the first line of text as the Title of the document. If you later change the first line of text in the document, however, the Title box does not automatically change. Of course, you can edit the document title by placing your insertion point in the Title box and entering new text.

Using the Author Entry

When you open the Properties tabbed dialog box, an author's name will probably already be there. When you installed Word, you may have included your name in the registration information requested by Word. If so, that name was entered into Word's permanent record of User Info. All documents created on this computer carry the same author's name. You can change the author's name for a specific document by changing it in this dialog box.

If you want to change the default author's name, select Options from the Tools menu. Then, choose the User Info tab in the Options dialog box (see fig. 6.9). Type the correct name in the Name box.

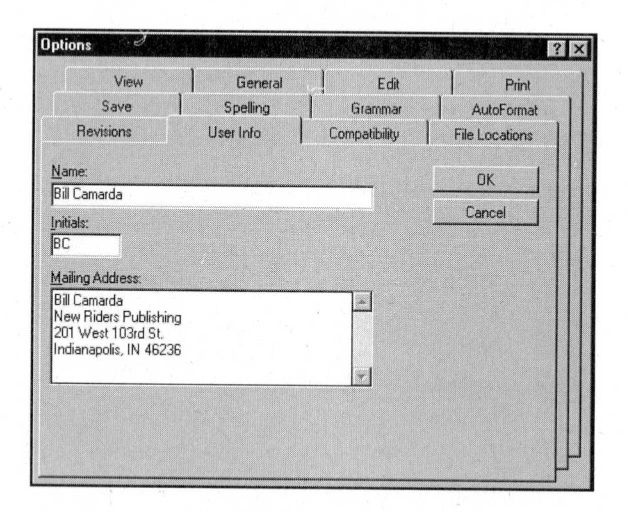

Figure 6.9
The Tools, Options, User Info tab.

If you create a file on one computer, but save it on another, the Author field will not automatically change. But Word does store a different name in the Last Saved By field, which appears in the Statistics box discussed shortly. This will be the name contained in User Info on the computer where the file has most recently been saved.

Using Keywords

You can include keywords to help you search later for documents containing the same important elements. For example, you might use Keywords to name all the

products included in the document, so you can search for all customer-service letters related to a specific project, possibly discovering patterns. Or, you might use them to search for names of people referred to in each document.

Use as many keywords as you want, up to 255 characters. Even if you specify multiple keywords in a single document, you can still search for an individual keyword later, if you separate the words with a space and don't use punctuation.

Document Statistics

The Property Sheet also provides detailed statistics about your current document. Choose the Statistics tab, and the dialog box shown in figure 6.10 appears.

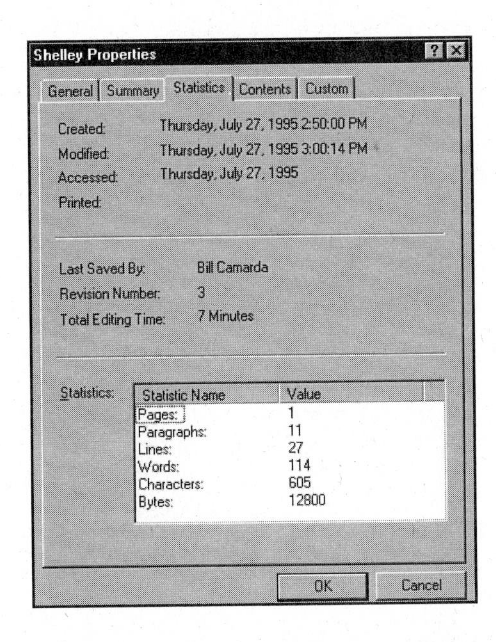

Figure 6.10

The Statistics Properties tab.

In addition to the same Created, Modified, and Accessed information that you've already seen in the General tab, the Document Statistics tab tells you when the document was last printed. It also tells you the following:

- **Last Saved By.** Usually the same as Author in Summary Info, but can be different if the file was created on another computer or loaded across a network.

- **Revision Number.** Tracks the number of times that you saved the file, excluding any Word automatic saves. When you save a file for the first time, your current revision number becomes two. Note, though, that Word counts a revision even if you save a document that hasn't been changed. And if you use Save As to place the file in a new folder, the revision number returns to two.

- **Total Editing Time.** Reflects the amount of time that the document has been open. You can use this feature to track work billed by the hour. Remember that you can always print a Summary Info sheet with your document by checking the Summary Info box in the Print tab in the Options dialog box (found under the Tools menu). By the way, if you are working on Document A, and Document B is still open, Word records that you are editing both documents.

- **Statistics.** Tracks the document's page, paragraph, line, word, character, and byte count, as of the last time you saved the document.

The Summary tabbed dialog box also now enables you to save a thumbnail picture of the first page of your document for previewing in the Open dialog box. You might want to check the Save Preview Picture box if the first page of your document is graphics intensive or uses large headlines that will be recognizable in small print. The preview picture that Word stores is too small to recognize regular-sized text, so you might be better off with Word's standard preview option, which shows the first few paragraphs of text in the document. It can be handy, however, if you use templates or graphics in your documents that are easily recognizable. (The preview capabilities built into the Open dialog box are discussed in the section "Choosing How to View Files," later in this chapter.)

Contents Information

The Contents tab (see fig. 6.11) shows components of a document. In general, there is only one component—the document itself, represented by its title.

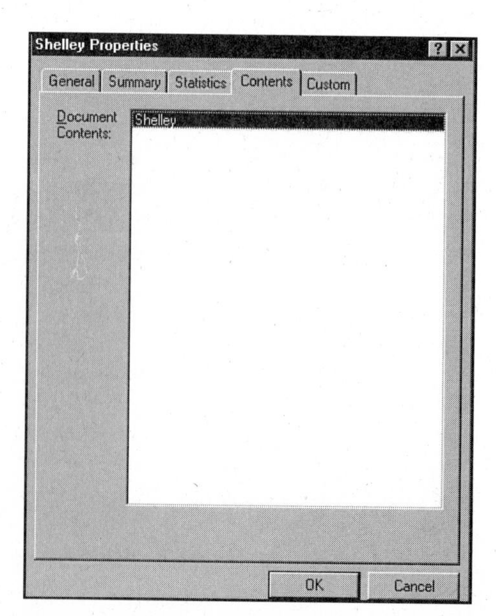

Figure 6.11

The Contents Properties tab.

Creating Custom Properties

In previous versions of Word, the Summary Info feature was helpful in assisting organizations and individual users to keep track of their documents, but users often had to work with categories that weren't quite appropriate for the document tracking that they wanted to do. For example, there was a Subject category, but no category for Client, a category used almost universally by freelance writers and for service businesses.

Word 95 enables you to choose from 27 additional categories, or add categories of your own if Word's don't suffice. To add a category, first choose Properties from the File menu, and choose the Custom tab, as shown in figure 6.12. Choose a category from the drop-down list box next to Name, or place the insertion point in the box and enter a new category name.

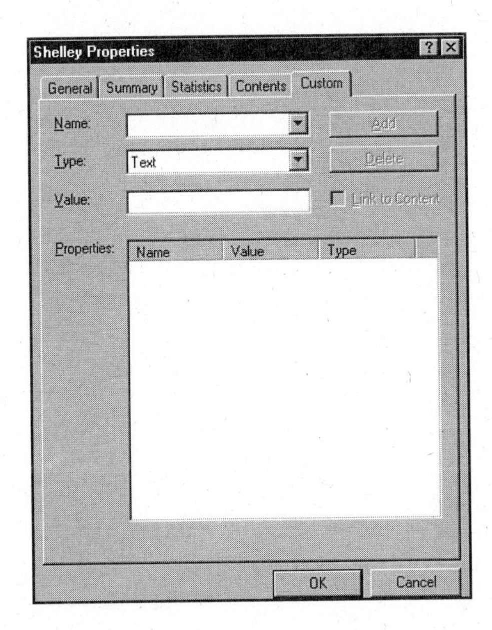

Figure 6.12

The Custom Properties Tab.

Next, choose the type of data that must be entered in this box. For example, you can make sure that where you want to record a date, nobody can enter anything *but* a date. Finally, in the Value box, enter the information that you want associated with this new category. Make sure that the data you enter matches the type you specified. Click on Add and then on OK, and Word adds the new entry. Later, if you want to edit the Value associated with this category, click on the category name in the Properties box, enter the new text, click on Modify, and then click on OK.

To make the most of Custom Properties, you might want to make sure they appear in all your documents. To do so, add the Custom Property to the Normal template stored in Office95\Templates (or whatever default template you use), and then save the edited template. You have to enter a dummy value that users of individual documents will replace. For example, if you add a custom property named Client, you can enter the text Client Name as your value; then when you use this custom property later, you can replace this text with the name of your client.

For more information about editing templates, see Chapter 8.

Linking a Custom Property to Content in a File

You can create a custom property that updates itself when circumstances change. For example, say that your document includes a table consisting of values that are updated regularly. One cell of the table—such as Profits—is recalculated using a Word formula field. (See Chapter 3, "Tables," for coverage of table calculations, and Chapter 10 for more information on using Word fields). Later, in this chapter's "Choosing a Property" section, you learn how to search for documents containing a custom property.

To create a custom property that can update itself as circumstances change, enter the information you want to update into the document itself. Then select that information (which can include text or fields). Next, mark this text with a bookmark. Bookmarks are covered in detail in Chapter 16, but briefly, to create a bookmark, follow these steps:

1. Select the text you want to bookmark.

2. Choose **B**ookmark from the **E**dit menu.

3. Type a name for the bookmark in the **B**ookmark Name box.

4. Choose OK.

Now choose **P**roperties from the **F**ile menu and select the Custom tab if it is not already selected. Check the **L**ink to Content box. In the **N**ame box, enter a name for the Custom Property you want to create. Next, click the down-arrow next to the **S**ource box, and choose the bookmark you've created from the list that appears. Click **A**dd. The new custom property appears with a link icon next to it, as shown in figure 6.13.

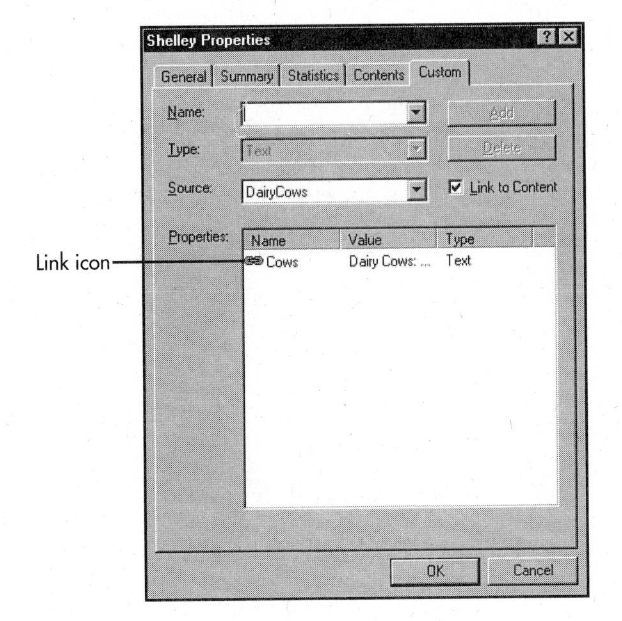

Figure 6.13

Custom property linked to text.

Inspecting a Property Sheet

You already know that you can review the contents of a Word document's property sheet when that document is open, by choosing Properties from the File menu. But you also can review the document's properties from the Open dialog box while you decide whether to open the file. Choose Open from the File menu, and right-click on the document. The pop-up menu appears; choose Properties. The Properties tabbed dialog box appears.

You don't have to be working in Word to inspect most of the contents of a Word property sheet. You might, for example, be organizing your files using the Windows Explorer, Windows 95's replacement for File Manager. Or, you might be looking inside a folder window containing a series of documents. Or, you might have a Word file represented as an icon on your Windows 95 desktop.

In any of these cases, you can right-click on the document icon and choose Properties from the pop-up menu that appears. Windows 95 displays the General, Summary, and Statistics tabbed dialog boxes from Properties. You cannot edit this information outside of Word, however. Note that if the file is a text file that you imported into Word, Summary and Statistics information may not be available because it has not yet been compiled. After you open and resave the file, Summary and Statistics information will be available.

Using the Open Dialog Box to Manage and Locate Files

In Word 95, the Open dialog box has been completely revamped to include all the capabilities that formerly appeared in the Find File dialog box, and then some. Windows 95 offers program developers a new standard Open dialog box. Microsoft Word and the other Microsoft Office programs expand on this new standard to provide extra searching, previewing, and other capabilities. The Open dialog box is discussed here at length, but the Save As dialog box is similar, excluding search features.

You'll be using this new dialog box a lot, so choose Open from the File menu and take a quick look around (see fig. 6.14). At the top left, you'll see the Look in box, which shows you which drive or folder you're looking at—and allows you to specify a new one. To the right of the Look in box, you'll see a set of buttons that you can use to organize how and where your files are displayed. As you'll see later, the last button on the right, Commands and Settings, allows you to perform a wide variety of tasks on your files, including printing and sorting them.

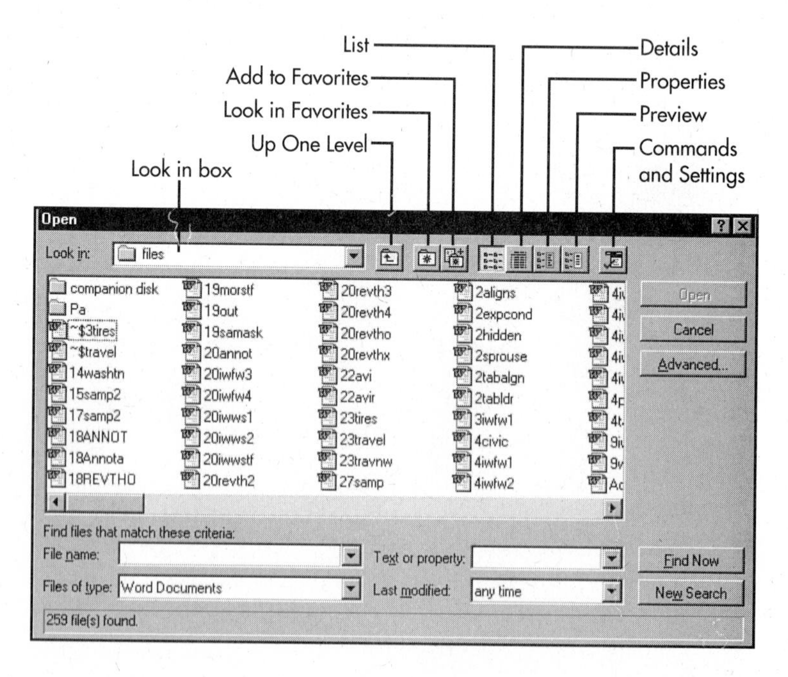

Figure 6.14

Word's new Open dialog box, shown in default List view.

Beneath this row of boxes and buttons are the file and folder listings themselves. Right-click on a file or folder and you'll see that Word provides a comprehensive list of options—from cutting, copying, and pasting files, to quickly viewing the file's contents in draft font, to e-mailing or faxing it to a colleague via Microsoft Exchange (see fig. 6.15).

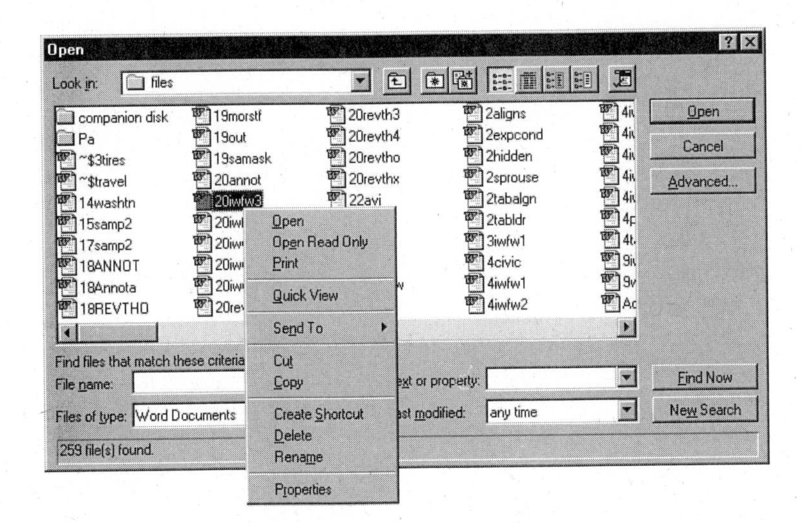

Figure 6.15

Pop-up menu for a file displayed in the Open dialog box.

At the bottom of the window in the Open dialog box are basic search criteria that you can use to winnow out files you're not interested in seeing now—or to find a specific file that you do want to see. If these search criteria aren't enough, Word offers highly sophisticated search capabilities that you can reach by clicking on Advanced. Word's Advanced Find search features are covered later in this chapter.

Be judicious when selecting drives to search. If your network server has a large hard disk, the search can require a long time to perform. Whenever possible, refine the search by selecting specific subdirectories on large drives.

Choosing a Drive or Folder

To choose a file or folder, click on the Look in drop-down box at the top left of the Open dialog box (see fig. 6.16) for a bird's-eye view of your computer: the Windows 95 Desktop, each floppy and hard drive, and any available network resources.

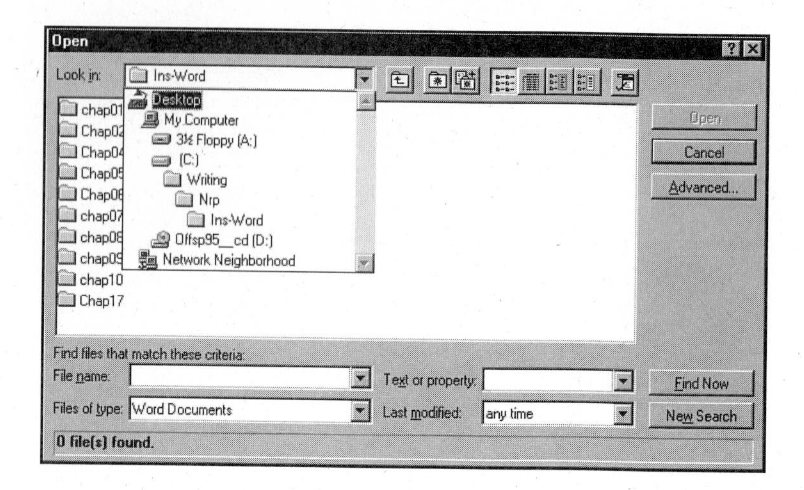

Figure 6.16
The Look in drop-down box.

When you first open it, the Open dialog box displays a list of the Word documents in your default Document folder. This folder is typically C:\Windows\My Documents, unless you change that default setting through the Tools, Options, File Locations tabbed dialog box.

To look in a different drive now, without changing the permanent defaults, choose the new drive from the Look in drop-down list. To view the contents of a different folder, double-click on that folder icon. To return to the folder one level above, click the Up One Level button to the right of the Look in box.

Choosing How to View Files

Once you display the contents of the folder you want to see, Word enables you to view this information in the following ways, each controlled from a button in the row of buttons to the right of the Look in box.

- Click on the List button to view a list of file names and icons, displayed in several columns as shown in the previous figure. This view shows the most file names. It's especially useful when you have a folder containing many files.
- Click on the Details button to view listings of file names, file size, type, and when files were last modified. This can help you track different versions of a file, especially in combination with Sorting features (discussed later). Figure 6.17 shows the Open dialog box displaying Details.
- Click on the Properties button to view a summary of the information contained in the currently selected file's Property Sheet. Figure 6.18 shows the Open dialog box displaying Properties of a selected file.

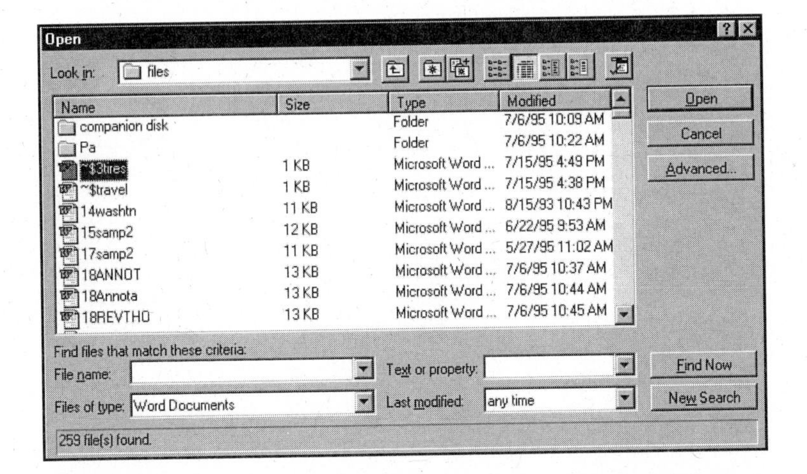

Figure 6.17

Details View, showing names, sizes, types, and when files were last modified.

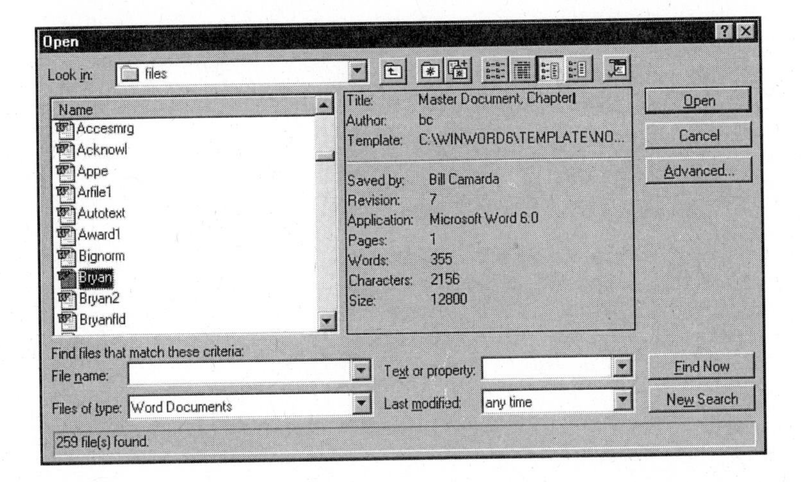

Figure 6.18

Properties View, showing information from the Properties dialog box.

If you want to see all the properties associated with a file, right-click on the file and choose Properties from the pop-up menu that appears.

- Click on the Preview button to view the first few paragraphs of the document, as shown in figure 6.19. Notice that a vertical scroll bar appears to the right of the image; you can scroll through the entire document. Word wraps the document to the width of this window, so there's no need for a horizontal scroll bar.

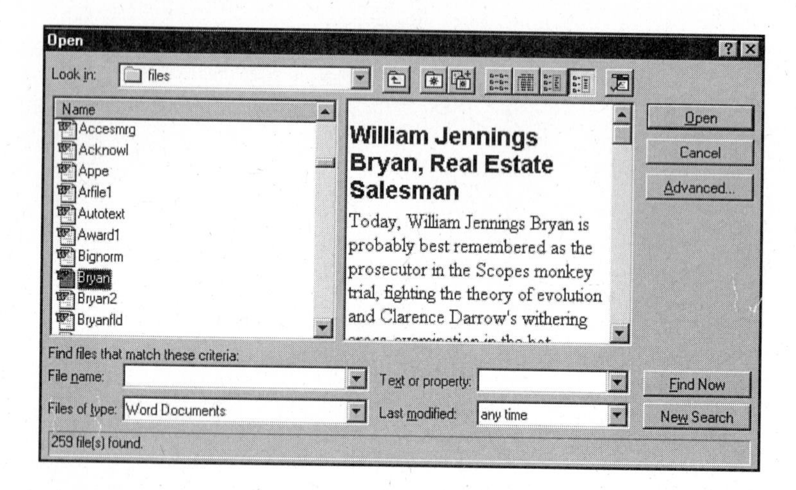

Figure 6.19

Preview view, showing the beginning of a document.

The Preview window displays much formatting information (though not quite all; for example, extra carriage returns are not shown). If all you want to see is text, and you'd like larger type than appears in the Preview window, right-click on the document and choose **Q**uick View from the pop-up menu. The Quick View window appears, as shown in figure 6.20. (Quick View only works if you installed it as part of your Windows 95 installation.)

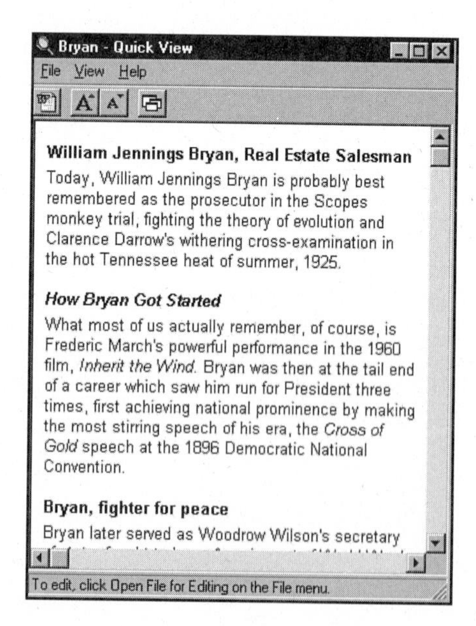

Figure 6.20

The Quick View window.

If you previously saved a thumbnail sketch of the document by checking Save Preview Picture in the Summary tab of File, Properties, this thumbnail sketch will appear instead, as shown in figure 6.21. You can't scroll to any additional pages.

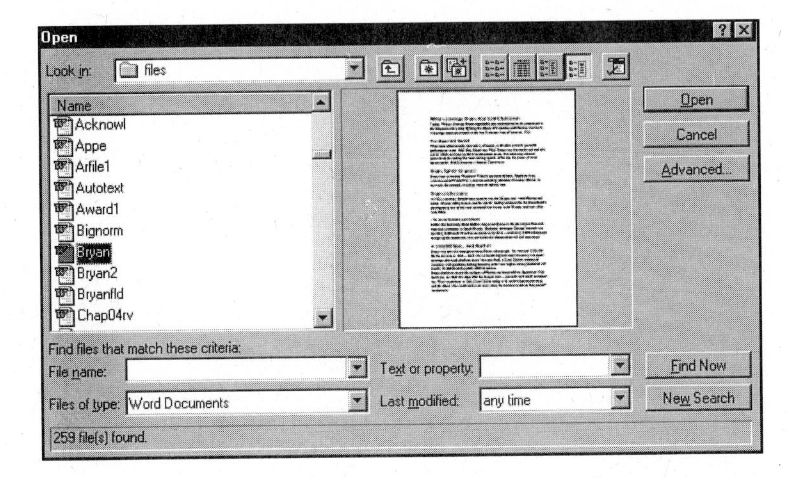

Figure 6.21
Thumbnail preview sketch saved with Properties, Summary.

Choosing Which Files to View

As mentioned earlier, Word defaults to viewing only Word documents—documents that include a DOC extension. You can, however, tell Word to view any category of files in the current folder that you want. Word's Open dialog box provides powerful winnowing capabilities.

To choose a different category of document, such as text files, click the down arrow next to Files of type, and choose from the drop-down list that appears.

You can also choose All Files if you want to view every file in the folder, or if you want to narrow the files down a different way. For example, say that you want to find a PowerPoint file. There's no PowerPoint category in Files of type, but you can select All Files and then use the File name box to specify PPT files. (It's not necessary to enter the "*" wild card.)

Note that Word can use the extensions to search for files, even though it generally does not display them.

You can select three types of file name searches from the File name box drop-down box:

- *.tmp searches for all temporary files, such as the files that Word creates as it works, and leaves on disk after a system crash.

- doc*.* searches for all files saved with Word's default file names, such as Document1, Document2, and so on.
- *.asd searches for all files recovered by Word after a power failure, system crash, or improper shutdown of Word and Windows.

As you perform wild-card searches, your searches are stored in the File name drop-down box, so you can select them again later without re-entering all the information. Note that Word can use not only the "*" wild card, but also the "?" wild card, which represents one specific character in a file name. For instance, a search for CHAP??MG.DOC finds CHAP02MG.DOC and CHAP12MG.DOC, whereas a search for CHAP0?MG.DOC finds only CHAP02MG.DOC.

The File name box has a couple of other tricks up its sleeve. For example, you can type a partial file name and Word will return all names that include the characters you enter. You also can specify more than one search path by spelling out the path names and separating them with a semicolon, as in the following:

```
d:\clients\jones; d:\invoices\1995
```

Viewing Files by Text or Property

You can ask Word to display only files that contain specific text. Enter the text in the Text or property box. Word searches both the document and the Properties you've stored. This is convenient, for example, if you entered keywords that might not appear in the document but would be relevant in helping you find it. For example, a report on the ancient Incas might not include the word *Mesoamerica*, but if you included *Mesoamerica* as a keyword in Document Properties, it would show up here—along with documents on the Maya, Aztecs, and others stored with the same keyword.

After you specify text to be included as criteria, Word stores that text in case you want to use it again. Click on the drop-down box next to Text or property to choose this text.

Viewing Files by Last Modification Date

You also can choose a time criteria to help you narrow down files according to when you created them. The default is "any time," but you also can pick one of these options from the Last modified drop-down list box:

- yesterday
- today

- last week
- this week
- last month
- this month

Note that you can specify more detailed date and time information by using the advanced searches covered in the section "Performing Advanced Searches," which follows.

Performing a New Search

After you perform a search that displays only a portion of the files in your current folder, you can restore the entire list of files—either for another search, or simply to prevent you from "misplacing" files that are in a directory but don't appear in the file list. Click on New Search, and Word resets the search criteria to Word Documents last modified any time—the broadest possible search criteria within the current folder.

Performing Advanced Searches

If you haven't been able to find the file you're looking for using the basic search capabilities built into the Open dialog box, use the more extensive search features available in the Advanced Find dialog box (see fig. 6.22).

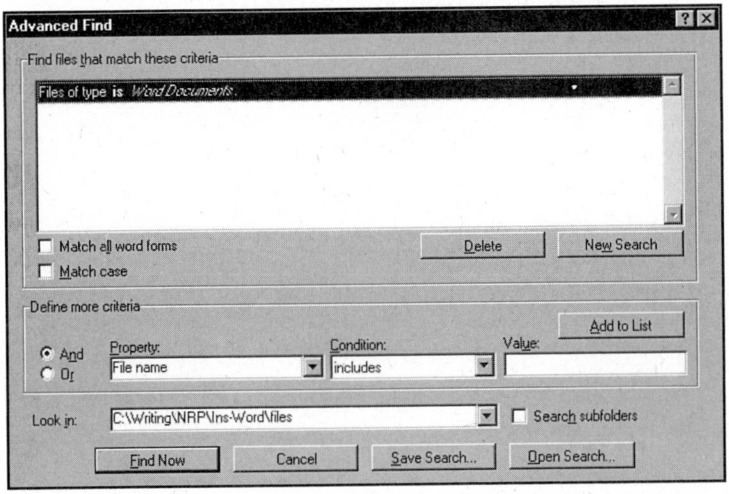

Figure 6.22

The Advanced Find dialog box.

To use Advanced Find, follow these steps:

1. Specify a search criteria in the Open dialog box.

   You might specify only Word documents created during the previous month, for example.

2. Click on Advanced.

   The Advanced Find dialog box opens, displaying the criteria you already set.

3. Build a search by specifying additional criteria:

   a. Choose from the built-in Word properties in the Property drop-down list box.

   b. Specify a condition from the Condition drop-down list box.

      As you'll see, the conditions available to each property vary, depending on the nature of the property.

   c. If necessary, specify a value for Word to search for.

4. Choose Add to List to include this new criteria in your search.

   A line of text describing your search criteria (in English!) appears in the Advanced Find window.

   You can add as many separate search criteria as you want.

5. After you enter all the necessary search criteria, choose Find Now to perform the search.

   Word displays the files it finds in the Name box within the Open dialog box.

The following sections take a closer look at building a search.

Choosing a Property

The Property drop-down list contains all the properties available in Word's Property sheets, plus a few that aren't, such as Slides, which you might use if searching for a PowerPoint presentation file, and Multimedia Clips. (Yes, Word's Advanced Find feature can even search for all documents that contain a specific number of multimedia clips.)

Note that Advanced Find does not limit you to working with Properties stored in the document's property sheet. One of the options available from the Property box is Text or property, which searches the contents of documents as well as their property sheets.

If you want to search for a custom property, type the property in the Property box. Of course, Word can find a custom property only in those documents in which you have assigned the custom property.

Specifying a Condition

After entering a property, enter a condition in the Condition box. The conditions available to you vary widely depending on the property you specify. If you're searching based on file name, for example, you have three options:

- **includes.** The property must include specific text or a specific numeric value. This is the most flexible criterion, because it enables Word to flag documents regardless of where in the file name the characters are.
- **begins with.** The property must begin with specific text or a specific numeric value. This might be useful if you want to search for documents with their file names in series, such as MEMO1, MEMO2, and MEMO3.
- **ends with.** The file name must end with the characters you specify. This is increasingly useful in an age of long file names, when you might be in the habit of naming files like Jones Report, Stewart Report, and so on.

On the other hand, if the property you're searching for contains a numeric value such as total editing time, you'll have the following choices:

- equals
- does not equal
- any number between
- at most
- at least
- more than
- less than

Or, if you've specified a property that consists of a date, such as Last modified, you'll have yet another set of choices:

- yesterday
- today
- last week
- this week

- last month
- this month
- any time
- any time between
- on
- on or after
- on or before
- in the last

Specifying a Value

Most of the time, you also have to specify a value. You don't need a value when you've already given Word enough information. For example, if you've asked Word to search for files created yesterday, Word doesn't need to know what day yesterday was; it can figure that out for itself.

Word is fairly flexible about how it recognizes values. For example, if you ask to search for all files modified between two dates, you can specify the dates in any of the following formats:

May 8 and June 9

5/8 and 6/9

5/8/95 and 6/9/95

Notice, however, that you always have to use the word *and* to separate the two values: "&" or a hyphen won't work.

After you enter a property, condition, and value, if necessary, choose Add to List and Word will include the new criteria in the list to be searched.

Using "Or" Criteria

Typically, when you use more than one criterion in an advanced search, the additional search criteria are intended to narrow the search. If you ask to find files that were created after June 5, 1995 *and* contain the text "Machiavelli," chances are you'll find fewer files than if you used only one criteria or the other. (You certainly won't find *more* files.) By default, Word expects you to build searches this way, which is why the And radio button in the Define more criteria box is checked.

Sometimes, however, you'll want to build a list of several kinds of files. You might, for example, want to see both customer service letters and thank-you letters. Or, you might want to see all the presentation files on your disk, regardless of the software used to create them. You can build a search that captures several different kinds of documents by clicking the Or radio button each time you establish additional search criteria. When you add the new search criteria, the word Or appears at the beginning of the line, as in the following:

```
Application name includes PowerPoint
Or: Application name includes Freelance
Or: Application name includes Harvard Graphics
```

Matching Word Forms and Case

By default, Word searches are case insensitive: if you search for documents containing the name Stone, you might inadvertently also retrieve documents about rocks and gravel. You can choose to make your searches case sensitive by checking the **Match** case check box in the Advanced Find dialog box.

Word 95 also includes a feature that enables you to liberalize searches so that Word finds the word you're looking for whether it's expressed in past, present, or future tense. If you're searching for documents containing the word *write,* you could miss documents that include the word *written.* Check the Match all word forms check box and Word will catch both.

Note that neither of these features works in a search of file names.

Saving and Reusing Searches

Searches can get quite complicated, and recreating them from scratch is a hassle. Fortunately, Word enables you to save searches and then reuse them.

To save a search, create it in either the Open dialog box or the Advanced Find dialog box, and then choose **Save** Search in the Advanced Find dialog box. The Save Search dialog box opens, as shown in figure 6.23; enter a name for this search and choose OK.

You can retrieve a saved search in two ways. In the Open dialog box, click on the Commands and Settings button, and choose Saved Searches from the pop-up menu that appears. A cascaded menu appears, listing all saved searches; click on the one you want. Or, from the Advanced Find dialog box, choose **Open**. The Open Search dialog box appears (see fig. 6.24), also listing all saved searches. Choose the search you want, and choose **Open**.

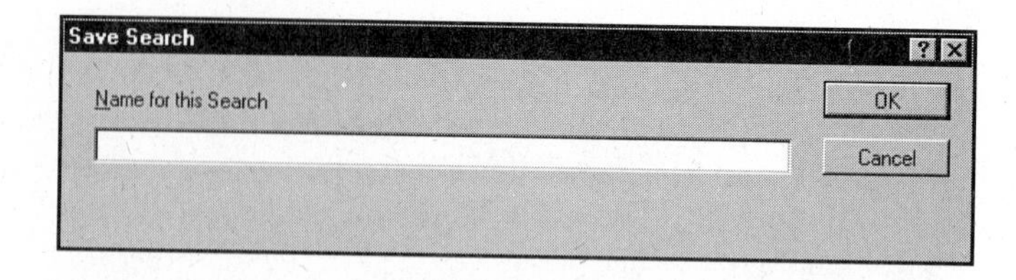

Figure 6.23
The Save Search dialog box.

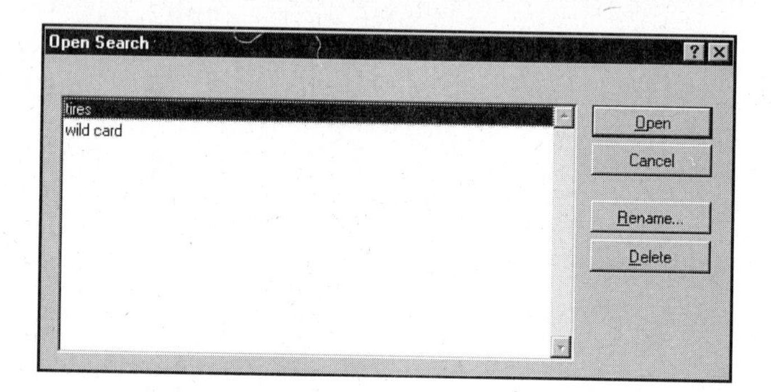

Figure 6.24
The Open Search dialog box.

Using the Favorites Folder

What happens when you regularly need to access the same files, but you store them in different folders? For example, say that you need to access monthly reports for all your clients at once—but you store each clients' files in separate folders. Prior to Word 95, you would have had to open each folder before accessing the files you wanted—or create a complex search for them.

Word 95's Open dialog box solves this problem by taking advantage of a new Windows 95 feature—shortcuts. *Shortcuts* are small files that act as pointers to other files (or programs). When you select the shortcut, the file (or program) opens. You might have already created some shortcuts on your Windows 95 desktop. Word 95 can create shortcuts for you, and store them in a Favorites folder, which it stores within the Windows 95 folder.

Then you can simply open the Favorites folder to access all your most-used documents. Double-click on a document name, and the document will open—even though the actual document still is stored in the same place it was originally, and only the pointer appears in the Favorites folder. You have the best of both worlds—you can keep your actual files in the folders that make the most sense, but get easy access from a central location to the files you use most.

Note The one minor disadvantage to Favorites is that it's buried inside the Windows 95 folder; to return to another folder can require several mouse clicks, especially if the folder is on a different drive.

To create a shortcut and place it in the Favorites folder, click on the Add to Favorites button on the row of buttons to the right of the Look in box. Word displays a pop-up menu with two choices: Add 'Current' Folder to Favorites adds a shortcut to your entire current folder. (The actual name of your current folder appears in the pop-up menu.) Add Selected Item to Favorites adds only the file you select.

Creating Other Shortcuts Within the Open Dialog Box

You can create other shortcuts besides those stored in the Favorites folder. Consider the example used earlier. Imagine that all of a client's information is stored in a folder with her company's name. Now you want to invoice the client. Should you access the invoices in an invoice folder, or in the client folder? Now, with shortcuts, the file can appear in both places. To create a shortcut follow these steps:

1. Select the file you want to create a shortcut for.
2. Right-click on the file, and select Create **Shortcut** from the pop-up menu. Word creates a shortcut in the same folder, adding the words *Shortcut to* to the file name.

That's all well and good, but a shortcut in the same location as the original file doesn't do much for you. In Word 95, however, you can cut, copy, and paste shortcuts and files in the Open dialog box, just as you would text in a document:

1. Select the shortcut (or file) you want to move.
2. Right-click to view the pop-up menu, and choose **Cut**.
3. Use the Look in box to move to the drive and folder in which you want to place the shortcut.
4. Right-click in an empty portion of the destination folder, and choose **Paste** from the pop-up menu. Word pastes the shortcut (or file) in the new location.

Using Commands and Settings

The Commands and Settings button gives you even more control over individual files, and over the way information is displayed in the Name window within the Open dialog box. When you click on it, the Commands and Settings pop-up menu appears. It's something of a catch-all for commands that don't fit elsewhere (though some of these commands are duplicated on the pop-up menu that appears when you right-click on a file or folder). Click on Commands and Settings to see the options shown in figure 6.25.

Figure 6.25
Commands and Settings menu.

Some of these options are relatively straightforward. Print opens the Print dialog box so you can print the file or files you selected. Properties displays the Properties dialog box discussed at length in the section "Using Word 95 Property Sheets," earlier in this chapter. The other Commands and Settings options are discussed in the following sections.

Opening a File as Read-Only

Open Read Only opens a file but does not allow changes to the file. This is relatively weak security, because a user can save the file under another name, make changes there, and then copy the duplicate file over the first one. (You may be able to use the Properties dialog box to sleuth unauthorized changes like this.) Open Read Only *can* help you or a colleague avoid inadvertently overwriting a file you intended to preserve.

Sorting Files

Click on Sorting to display the Sort By dialog box (see fig. 6.26), which enables you to sort the files displayed on-screen in any of the following sort orders:

- **By files of type—**In order of file type, sorted by extension name. This is the default setting, though you might not notice it because Word's default setting shows only Word documents and no other types of files.
- **By file name—**Sorts files by long file name, disregarding extensions.
- **By size—**Sorts files in order of size.
- **By last modification—**Sorts files in the order of the Last Modified date stored in the Properties dialog box.

A radio button controls whether the files are listed in ascending or descending order.

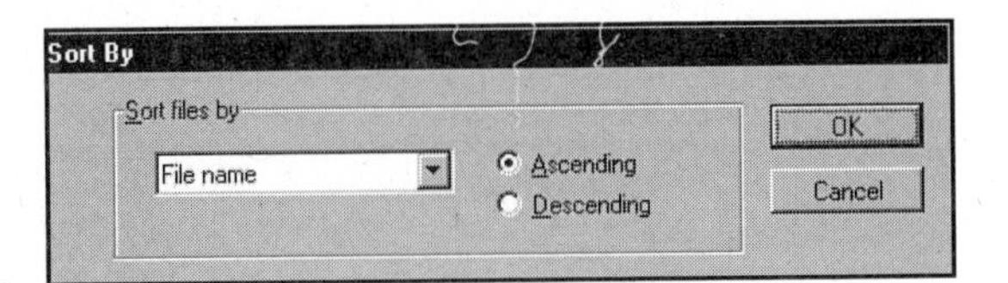

Figure 6.26

The Sort By dialog box.

Searching Subfolders

By default, when Word displays the contents of a folder, it shows subfolders first and then individual files. Sometimes, however, you might want to view the files contained in the subfolders at the same time you see the files contained in the folder itself. Word enables you to do so. Click on the Commands and Settings button, and choose Searc**h** Subfolders from the pop-up menu. Word displays all the files as if they were stored in the same folder. If you would like to see the files organized by subfolder, choose **G**roup files by folder. This option is available only if Searc**h** Subfolders is selected.

Mapping Network Drives

You can review files on a network drive that does not currently appear in the Open dialog box. To do so, map the network drive to a drive letter on your computer. Click on the Commands and Settings button, and then choose **M**ap Network Drive from the pop-up menu to open the Map Network Drive dialog box (see fig. 6.27). Specify the drive name in the **D**rive box.

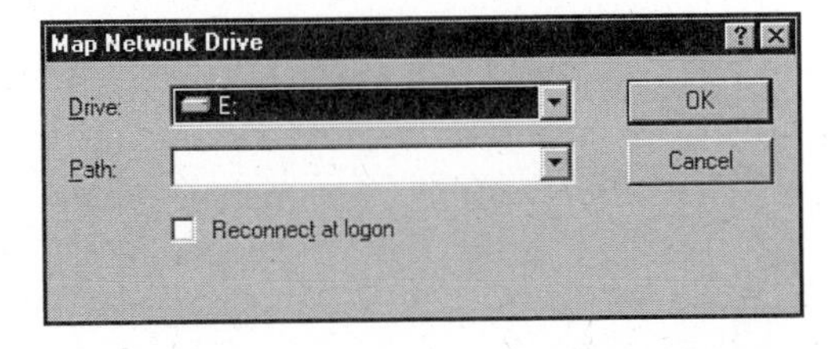

Figure 6.27

The Map Network Drive dialog box.

Sending Files to Disk, E-mail, Fax, or Briefcase

The pop-up menus that appear in Word 95's Open dialog box also can be used to share data with colleagues, either via e-mail and fax or by copying files to disk. Select a file (or files), and then right-click and choose Se**n**d To. A cascaded menu appears with the following choices:

- 3 1/2" Floppy
- 5 1/4" Floppy

- Fax Recipient
- Mail Recipient
- My Briefcase

If you choose 3 1/2" Floppy or 5 1/4" Floppy, Word copies the files to disk. If you choose Fax Recipient, Word opens the Microsoft Fax Wizard and walks you through the steps required to send a fax. If you choose My Briefcase, Word copies the file to the Windows 95 Briefcase, which is used to synchronize files used on both desktop and portable computers.

Sharing a Folder Across a Network

If you have installed Windows 95's networking capabilities, you can share folders with users on computers connected to yours. To share a folder from within the Open dialog box, click on the folder, and then right-click on S**h**aring. The folder's Properties tabbed dialog box opens, displaying the Sharing tab as shown in figure 6.28.

Figure 6.28
Sharing tab of a folder's Properties dialog box.

By default, folders are not shared. To change this, click on **S**hared As. Word suggests a share name, the name by which colleagues will recognize this folder. By default, this name is the same as the current folder name, but you can change this. You also can add a comment about the folder's contents that will be available to other users.

Finally, you can provide three types of access: **R**ead-Only, which enables colleagues to read but not edit your files; **F**ull access, which provides the same access that you have

to the folder's files; or Depends on Password, which enables you to provide full access only to those with the correct password.

If you specify Depends on Password, enter a password in the Read-Only Password box. The password can be up to 15 characters. The Password Confirmation dialog box appears, as shown in figure 6.29. Type the password again for it to take effect. As you type, Word displays asterisks (*) in place of the password characters, so no one can "shoulder-surf" your password by reading the screen while you type.

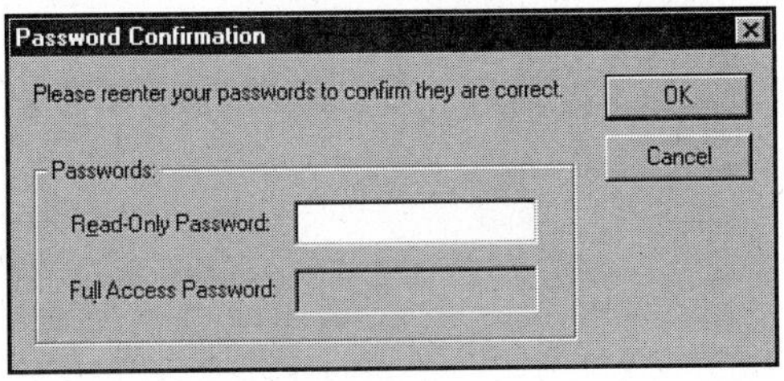

Figure 6.29
Password Confirmation dialog box.

Note that the passwords described here apply only to the folder as a whole. Whether or not you protect a folder, you also can apply passwords to individual files, as discussed next.

Using Passwords

Have a file that you don't want anyone to see? Protect it with a password. When you're ready to save a file, perform these steps:

1. Choose Save As from the File menu.
2. Choose Options.
3. Choose the Save tab.
4. Type the password in the Protection Password box, as shown in figure 6.30. As you type, Word displays asterisks (*).
5. Press Enter.

   Word then asks you to confirm the password by typing it again. If you type it exactly the same way and press Enter, Word accepts the password. If you type it differently, Word asks you to try again.

6. After Word accepts your password, choose OK in the Save As dialog box, and the file is saved with the password.

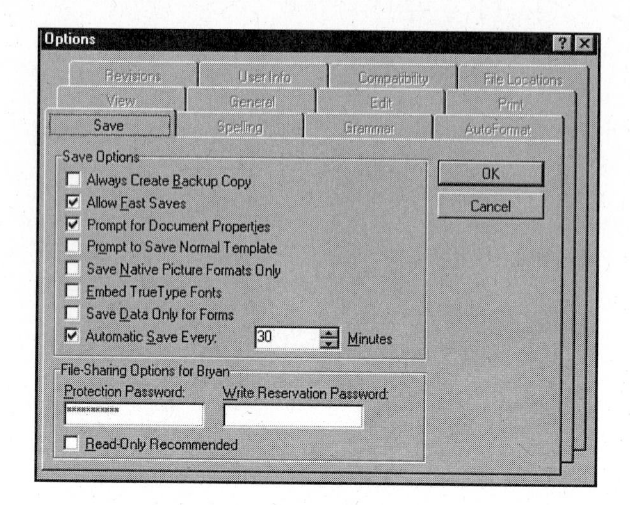

Figure 6.30
Protection Password box in the Save tab.

This is serious password protection. Word actually encrypts the file, so if you open it with another program that doesn't recognize Word's passwords, all you get is gibberish. WordPad can't even open a Word password-protected file, neither can the Notepad text editor that came with Windows 3.1.

Make sure you remember your password—without leaving it in plain sight where someone else can find it. And don't use obvious passwords, like your child's name. Only if you trust yourself not to leave your password where it can be found, you might use a password that serves a different purpose, such as your CompuServe, MCI Mail, or cash machine password.

After you password-protect a file, you can change or delete it only from within the file. Follow these steps:

1. Select Save **As** from the **File** menu.
2. Choose **Options**. The Options dialog box opens with the Save tab displayed.
3. Delete the password.
4. Choose OK.
5. In the Save As dialog box, choose **Save**.

Creating File Types to Be Recognized by Word

Windows 3.1 contains a feature called *file association*, which enables you to associate specific file extensions with specific programs. Windows 3.1 automatically recognizes DOC files as Word documents, for example, so when you double-click on a DOC file, Word opens. That's still the case in Windows 95; however, Windows 95 calls this feature *File Types*.

Say you regularly create reports and want them all to have the extension RPT. You want to place some of these reports on the Windows 95 desktop, and when you double-click on one of these files, you want the file to open in Word. Here's how to associate the RPT file type with Word in Windows 95:

1. Minimize Word and double-click on the My Computer icon at the top-left corner of the Windows 95 desktop.

2. Choose **O**ptions from the **V**iew menu, and choose the File Types tab, as shown in figure 6.31.

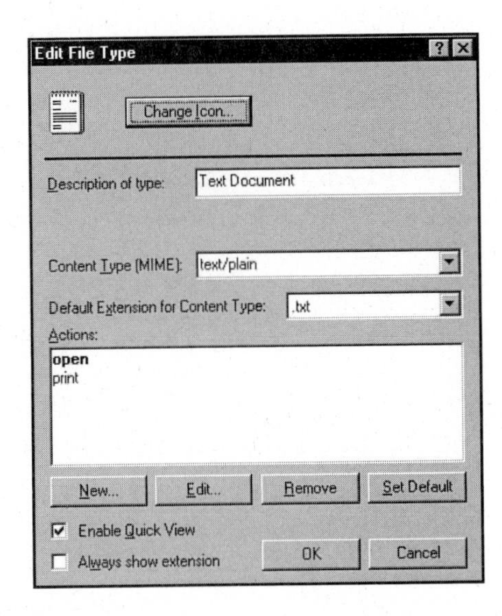

Figure 6.31

File Types tab of the Options dialog box.

3. Choose **N**ew Type.

4. The Add New File Type dialog box opens (see fig. 6.32). In the **D**escription of type box, enter the name of the file type you want to create; in this example, you might use Report.

Figure 6.32

Add New File Type dialog box.

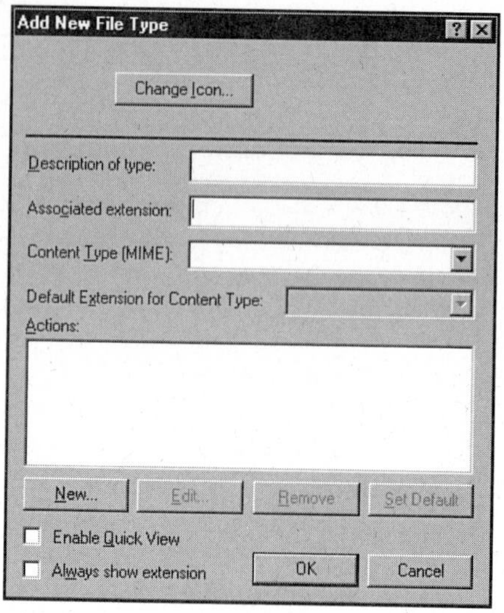

5. In the Asso<u>c</u>iated extension box, type the file extension you want to use; in this example, RPT.

6. Choose <u>N</u>ew to specify the action you want to associate with this file. The New Action dialog box opens (see fig. 6.33).

Figure 6.33

The New Action dialog box.

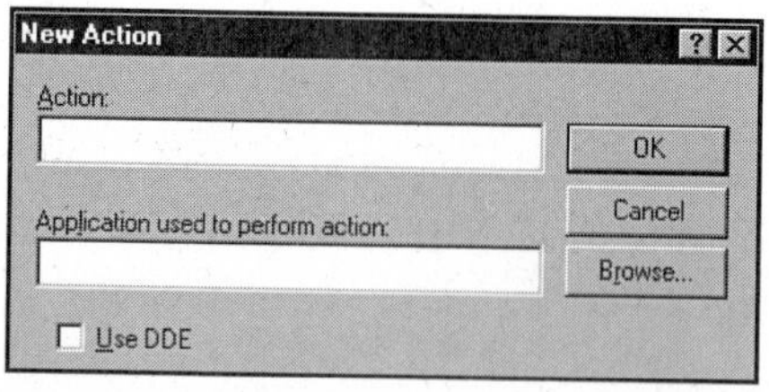

7. In the <u>A</u>ction box, type **Open**. (By doing this, you tell Windows that you want to specify what program to open. If you entered Print, you would be specifying which program should print this file when you drag the file to a printer icon.)

8. In the App<u>l</u>ication used to perform action box, enter the entire path to the Microsoft Word application (or click B<u>r</u>owse and find the Microsoft Word application file in the Browse dialog box).

9. The Add New File Type dialog box reappears with the word Open appearing in the <u>A</u>ctions box, and the Word icon appearing to the left of the Change Icon button. Click Close twice.

Part II

Word for Windows 95 Productivity Tools

New Riders Publishing
INSIDE
SERIES

Styles and AutoFormatting

Until now, you've been working *retail*; that is, you've made only one edit or one formatting change at a time.

The Formatting toolbar and the keyboard shortcuts can make formatting so delightfully easy that many Word users never go any further. But if you always stop at the Formatting toolbar, you're missing out on Word's most impressive productivity tools.

It's time to start working *wholesale*; by using styles, AutoFormatting, templates, AutoText, and fields, you can magnify the results of your efforts dramatically.

Instead of reformatting a document one paragraph at a time, you can reformat tall documents (in a single bound!) by using styles, AutoFormatting, and templates. Instead of rekeying the same text over and over again, you can insert it automatically (faster than a speeding bullet!) by using AutoText.

Best of all, you can use Word as an intelligent assistant that handles the details of keeping your document organized and up-to-date (more powerful than a locomotive!) by using fields.

In this chapter, you start by learning how to use styles and AutoFormatting—Word's features for wholesale text formatting.

Styles are doubly important in Word 95 because so many other features depend on them. For example, Word can add heading numbers to every section in your document, but only if you've added styles to identify your headings. Word can add chapter numbers to all your document's page numbers, but only if you format your chapter heading with a unique style.

Before Word 6, styles were considered an extraordinary time-saver. Now they're the price of admission to many of Word's most exciting new features.

In this chapter:

- Understanding styles
- Using Normal style
- Applying a style
- Creating keyboard shortcuts
- Creating a new style
- Copying a style between documents
- Basing a style on another style
- Automatically following one style with another
- Moving styles among documents
- Renaming or deleting styles
- Clearing manual formatting
- Finding and replacing styles
- Keeping track of styles with the Style Gallery and the Organizer
- Using AutoFormatting
- Working with the Style Gallery

Understanding Styles

A *style* is simply a group of formatting instructions that you can name and assign to as much text as you want. Styles offer you three major advantages:

- Instead of individually formatting every attribute of every paragraph or chunk of text, you can do a great deal of formatting with a single command.
- Your document's formatting can remain consistent because you're using a limited number of styles.
- When you need to change a document's formatting, you only have to change a few styles—not every single paragraph.

The more complex or changeable your document, the more you need styles. Granted, Word isn't quite a desktop-publishing program, but for many complex documents, Word's styles make it *better* than a desktop-publishing program.

Styles are closely related to templates. Templates are covered in detail in the next chapter; for now, think of a template as the overall starting point for a document, including a default style sheet, macro commands, keyboard shortcuts, and other customization, possibly including toolbar and menu changes.

In this chapter, assume that all the style techniques are being used within a single template.

Saving Time with Styles: An Example

Until they see it for themselves, many people don't believe how much time styles can save them. Here is an example:

The *pullquote* paragraph shown in figure 7.1 is designed to call attention to a quotation and add graphic interest to a page.

"I can't live either with you or without you."

Ovid (43 B.C. - A.D. c. 18)

Figure 7.1

A sample pullquote.

Suppose that you want to make this piece of text appear this way, but that you formatted the whole thing manually. You would have to use 18-point type for the quotation itself and 14-point type for the quotation's attribution. A double line at the top and bottom adds a border, and three points of space between these borders and the text makes it easier to read. Finally, you'd have to add one-half a line of blank space between the quotation and the attribution.

This formatting requires 36 mouse clicks and keystrokes. Those 36 clicks and keystrokes would be required every time you created another pullquote.

10 pullquotes×36 mouseclicks = 360 actions

That is, unless you use styles.

With styles, all you have to do is select the quotation, including the top border, and type **Quote** in the Style box on the Formatting toolbar. Then select the quotation's attribution, including the bottom border, and type **QRef** in the Style box.

This nifty shortcut is called *defining styles by example*, and it enables you to create and name both of these styles with only 15 clicks and keystrokes. If you want to use both styles, you need to invest only six more clicks. Because this is a total of only 21 keystrokes, you so far can save 42 percent of your effort the first time you use these styles, and then save 83 percent every time afterward.

10 pullquotes = 75 actions

You can save even more time with styles by telling Word to use QRef automatically as the next style whenever it sees the Quote style. In this real-world example, styles save more than three-quarters of your time and effort.

Using Word's Default Styles

Even if you are not using styles, Word is. When you open a document using the default Normal template, Word opens an accompanying *style sheet*—a set of styles. The default style is *Normal*, which formats your text as follows:

Element	Type of Formatting
Font	Times New Roman, 10-point
Language	English (U.S.)
Alignment	Flush Left

Line Spacing	Single
Pagination	Widow/Orphan Control

This is the format of your text when you first open Word. Three other styles are immediately available: *Heading 1, Heading 2,* and *Heading 3.* Word uses these styles to create three types of headings.

Each heading is based on the Normal style; it uses all the Normal style's attributes except when you specify a different attribute. In essence, any changes you make to Word's default styles are *superimposed* on the Normal style.

Some 70 additional styles are available in the Normal template, even though they aren't immediately shown on the screen.

These styles are divided into *paragraph styles* and *character styles.* In Word for Windows version 2, every style is a paragraph style; that is, it affects the formatting of the entire paragraph to which you apply it. Word 6 and Word 95, however, are more precise. You can create and use character styles that apply only to selected text within a paragraph. Tables 7.1 and 7.2 list all the Word styles built into the Normal template.

TABLE 7.1
Character Styles in the Normal Template

Style Name	Formats This	As "Default Paragraph Font Plus" This Formatting
Annotation Reference	Initials of person making annotation	8 pt
Endnote Reference	Endnote number or custom mark	Superscript
Footnote Reference	Footnote number or custom mark	Superscript
Line Number	Line numbers	No additional formatting
Page Number	Page numbers	No additional formatting

Table 7.2
Paragraph Styles in the Normal Template

Style Name	Formats This	As "Normal Plus" This Formatting
Annotation Text	Text in an annotation pane	No additional formatting
Body Text	Regular body text	Space after 6 pt
Body Text Indent	Indented body text	Indent left 0.25", Space after 6 pt
Caption	Captions created by Word's Insert Caption feature	Bold, Space before 6 pt, Space after 6 pt
Closing	Yours truly, or a similar phrase in the closing of a letter	Indent left 3"
Endnote Text	Text appearing in endnote pane	No additional formatting
Envelope Address	Addressee's address placed on envelope by Word's Envelopes and Labels feature	Font 12 pt, Indent left 2", Position center, Horizontal relative to Page, 0.50" from text, Button vertical relative to margin, Width 5.5", Height: exactly
Envelope Return	Return address placed on envelope by Word's Envelopes and Labels feature	No additional formatting
Footer	Text placed in footer area	Tab stops: 3" centered, 6" right flush
Footnote Reference	Footnote number or character	Font: 8 pt Superscript: 3 pt
Footnote Text	Text placed in footnote pane	No additional formatting
Header	Text placed in header area	Tab stops: 3" centered, 6" right flush
Heading 1	1st-level heading	Font: Arial 14 pt Bold, Kern at 14 pt, Space before 12 pt after 3 pt, Keep with next

Style Name	Formats This	As "Normal Plus" This Formatting
Heading 2	2nd-level heading	Font: Arial 12 pt Bold Italic, Space before: 12 pt, after 3 pt, Keep with next
Heading 3	3rd-level heading	12 pt Bold, Space before 12 pt, after 3 pt, Keep with next
Heading 4	4th-level heading	12 pt Bold, Italic, Space before 12 pt, after 3 pt, Keep with next
Heading 5	5th-level heading	Arial 11 pt, Space before 12 pt, after 3 pt
Heading 6	6th-level heading	Arial 11 pt Italic, Space before 12 pt, after 3 pt
Heading 7	7th-level heading	Arial 10 pt, Space before 12 pt, after 3 pt
Heading 8	8th-level heading	Arial 10 pt Italic, Space before 12 pt, after 3 pt
Heading 9	9th-level heading	Arial 9 pt Italic, Space before 12 pt, after 3 pt
Index 1	1st-level index entry	Indent: Hanging 0.14", Tab stops: 6" right flush
Index 2	2nd-level index entry	Indent: Left 0.14", Hanging 0.14", Tab stops: 6" right flush
Index 3	3rd-level index entry	Indent: Left 0.28", Hanging 0.14", Tab stops: 6" right flush
Index 4	4th-level index entry	Indent: Left 0.42", Hanging 0.14", Tab stops: 6" right flush
Index 5	5th-level index entry	Indent: Left 0.56", Hanging 0.14", Tab stops: 6" right flush
Index 6	6th-level index entry	Indent: Left 0.69", Hanging 0.14", Tab stops: 6" right flush

continues

Table 7.2, Continued
Paragraph Styles in the Normal Template

Style Name	Formats This	As "Normal Plus" This Formatting
Index 7	7th-level index entry	Indent: Left 0.83", Hanging 0.14", Tab stops: 6" right flush
Index 8	8th-level index entry	Indent: Left 0.97", Hanging 0.14", Tab stops: 6" right flush
Index 9	9th-level index entry	Indent: Left 1.11", Hanging 0.14", Tab stops: 6" right flush
Index Heading	Heading separators (these appear after you compile the index)	No additional formatting
List	1st-level item in Word list	Indent: Hanging 0.25"
List 2	2nd-level item in Word list	Indent: Left 0.25" Hanging 0.25"
List 3	3rd-level item in Word list	Indent: Left 0.50" Hanging 0.25"
List 4	4th-level item in Word list	Indent: Left 0.75" Hanging 0.25"
List 5	5th-level item in Word list	Indent: Left 1.00" Hanging 0.25"
List Bullet	1st-level item in Word bulleted list	Indent: Hanging 0.25", Bullet
List Bullet 2	2nd-level item in Word bulleted list	Indent: Left 0.25", Hanging 0.25", Bullet
List Bullet 3	3rd-level item in Word bulleted list	Indent: Left 0.50", Hanging 0.25", Bullet
List Bullet 4	4th-level item in Word bulleted list	Indent: Left 0.75", Hanging 0.25", Bullet
List Bullet 5	5th-level item in Word bulleted list	Indent: Left 1.00", Hanging 0.25", Bullet
List Continue	1st-level item in list continuation	Indent: Left 0.25", Space after 6 pt

Style Name	Formats This	As "Normal Plus" This Formatting
List Continue 2	2nd-level item in list continuation	Indent: Left 0.50", Space after 6 pt
List Continue 3	3rd-level item in list continuation	Indent: Left 0.75", Space after 6 pt
List Continue 4	4th-level item in list continuation	Indent: Left 1.00", Space after 6 pt
List Continue 5	5th-level item in list continuation	Indent: Left 1.25", Space after 6 pt
List Number	1st-level item in numbered list	Indent: Hanging 0.25", Auto numbering
List Number 2	2nd-level item in numbered list	Indent: Left 0.25", Hanging 0.25", Auto numbering
List Number 3	3rd-level item in numbered list	Indent: Left 0.50", Hanging 0.25", Auto numbering
List Number 4	4th-level item in numbered list	Indent: Left 0.75", Hanging 0.25", Auto numbering
List Number 5	5th-level item in numbered list	Indent: Left 1.00", Hanging 0.25", Auto numbering
Macro Text	Text used in macro-editing window	Courier New 10 pt, English (U.S.), Flush left, Line spacing single, Widow/Orphan control, Tab stops: 0.33", 0.67", 1", 1.33", 1.67", 2", 2.33", 2.67", 3"
Message Header	Text in Word message header	Arial 12 pt, Indent: Hanging 0.75"
Normal	All text not assigned to another style	Font: Times New Roman 10 pt, Language: English (U.S.), Flush (Normal style) left, Line spacing single, Widow/Orphan control

continues

Table 7.2, Continued
Paragraph Styles in the Normal Template

Style Name	Formats This	As "Normal Plus" This Formatting
Normal Indent	Indented text	Indent: Left 0.5"
Signature	Letter-writer's name, appearing in closing of letter	Indent: Left 3"
Subtitle	Document subtitle	Arial 12 pt Italic, Centered, Space after 3 pt
Table of Authorities	Entry text in a table of authorities	Indent: Hanging 0.14", Tab stops: 6" right flush
Table of Figures	Entry text in a table of figures	Indent: Hanging 0.28", Tab stops: 6" right flush
Title	Document title	Arial 16 pt Bold, Kern at 14 pt, Centered, Space before 12 pt, after 3 pt
TOA Heading	Heading at the top of a table of authorities	Arial 12 pt Bold, Space before 6 pt
TOC 1	1st-level table of contents entry	Tab stops: 6" right flush
TOC 2	2nd-level table of contents entry	Indent: Left 0.14", Tab stops: 6" right flush
TOC 3	3rd-level table of contents entry	Indent: Left 0.28", Tab stops: 6" right flush
TOC 4	4th-level table of contents entry	Indent: Left 0.42", Tab stops: 6" right flush
TOC 5	5th-level table of contents entry	Indent: Left 0.56", Tab stops: 6" right flush
TOC 6	6th-level table of contents entry	Indent: Left 0.69", Tab stops: 6" right flush
TOC 7	7th-level table of contents entry	Indent: Left 0.83", Tab stops: 6" right flush
TOC 8	8th-level table of contents entry	Indent: Left 0.97", Tab stops: 6" right flush
TOC 9	9th-level table of contents entry	Indent: Left 1.11", Tab stops: 6" right flush

Your current style appears in the Style box (on the Formatting toolbar) unless you've selected paragraphs that have been formatted with different styles. Paragraph styles appear in bold; character styles appear in nonbold type.

Applying a Style

You can see all the styles currently in use, including the three heading styles Word includes by default, by clicking on the down arrow next to the Formatting toolbar's style drop-down list, as shown in figure 7.2. (The keyboard shortcut for access to the style box is Ctrl+Shift+S.)

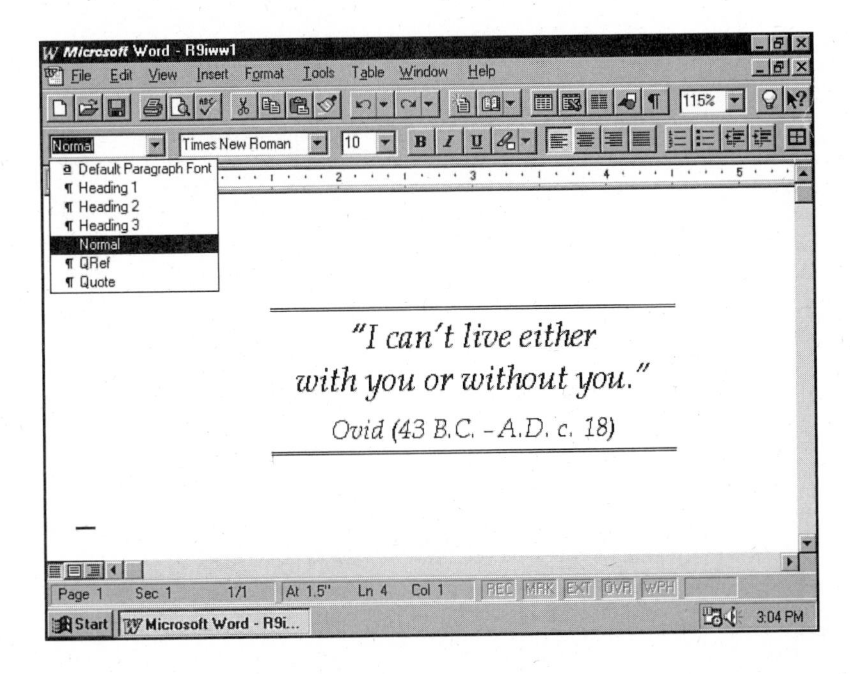

Figure 7.2

The style drop-down list.

To use a *paragraph style* to change the style of your current paragraph, place the insertion point in the paragraph or select the entire paragraph. Then choose the new style from this drop-down list.

You can also type the style name by positioning your insertion point in the style box and keying the new name. (The keyboard shortcut to open the style box is Ctrl+Shift+S.)

continues

Be careful to type the name properly; if you misspell it while text is selected, Word creates a new style based on the current appearance of the selected text.

Typos (mistakes in spelling) are common. For this reason, Word includes a feature, called *aliases*, which enables you to type a brief name that has the same effect as a long style name. Aliases are covered later in this chapter.

No Formatting toolbar, no sweat. If your Formatting toolbar isn't displayed, you can still choose a style name. Select the paragraph(s), press Ctrl+Shift+S, and choose the style name you want from the Style box in the Format Style dialog box. Then press Enter.

You can change several paragraphs at once by selecting them before applying a different paragraph style. If you want to use a *character style*, select the text within or across paragraph boundaries, and choose the replacement style from the style box. In either case, the new style appears in the list box, and the text changes.

Each paragraph can have only one paragraph style. Even if you select only part of a paragraph, when you change its style, the entire paragraph's style changes.

The exceptions in Word 2—footnote, endnote, and annotation reference marks—are now character styles.

The accompanying CD-ROM contains a file you can use to practice some of the procedures in this chapter: IWMS7A.DOC.

Using a Built-In Style That Doesn't Appear in the Style Box

Only the Normal style and three Heading styles appear in the document, but you can use any of Word's 75 built-in styles. Many of those appear automatically when you perform the appropriate task. For example, when you add a table of contents, Word hauls out whatever TOC styles it needs. You can manually access one of these styles in one of two ways:

- Type it in the style box.
- Choose it from the Format Style dialog box.

The Style dialog box is discussed later, but here is a preview. To open it, choose Style from the Format menu, or press Ctrl+Shift+S twice. The dialog box appears, as in figure 7.3.

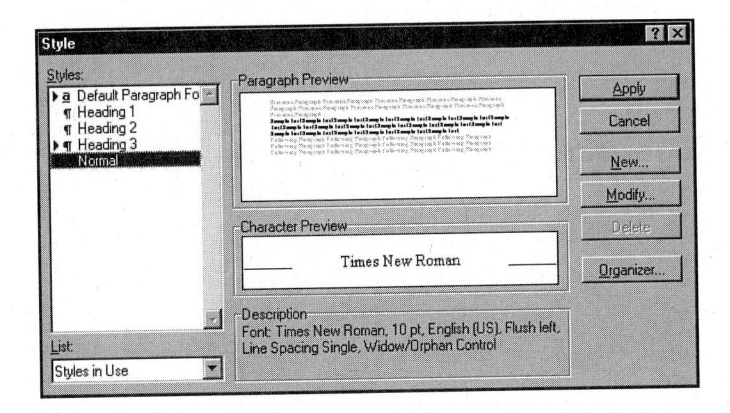

Figure 7.3

The Style dialog box.

If the Format Style dialog box still only includes Normal and the three Headings (a good name for a New Wave doo-wop group), you can choose All Styles from the List box to see all available styles, including the 70+ that Word automatically makes available. Choose a style; then choose Apply. This formats the selected text or paragraph with the style you've chosen.

Using Format, Style is slower than simply picking a style from the toolbar, but it compensates by showing you a painfully detailed written description of your style, plus thumbnail sketches of how it might look on your characters and your paragraphs.

When you choose Apply, the style you've just used (but not the entire list) becomes available through the Style box.

Note If you've created styles of your own, you can tell Word to display only those by choosing User-Defined Styles from the List box in the Style dialog box.

What Can Go into a Style

Most of Word's default styles are relatively simple. Any formatting you can create manually can be included in a style. This includes anything you'll find in any of the Format menu's dialog boxes shown in table 7.3.

Table 7.3
Formats That Can Be Controlled Using Styles

Dialog Box	Contains These Formats
Format, Font	Font Type size Type style Underlining Color Highlighting Super/subscript Type effects Letterspacing Type position Kerning
Format, Paragraph	Indentation Line spacing Paragraph spacing Alignment Pagination Line numbering
Format, Tabs	Tab stop position Default tab stops Tab alignment Tab leaders
Format, Borders and Shading	Edges bordered Bordering line Border distance from text Border color Foreground shading Background shading
Format, Bullets and Numbering	Type of bullet used Type of numbering scheme used Text included with bullet or number Multilevel numbering Bullet/number alignment and indentation
Format, Frame	Text wrapping Size of frame Horizontal and vertical position Distance from text
Tools, Language	Dictionary to be used No proofing option

Word even allows you to include formatting for a bulleted or numbered list in your style.

Normally, you decide what a specific element of a document should look like, and then you create a style with the name of that document element. All the document elements shown in the following list are prime candidates for custom styles, as well as for Word's built-in styles:

Address	Headings
Attachments	Headline
AutoText Entry	Title
Blurb	Index
Body Text	Initial Cap
Byline	List
Captions	Pullquote
City	Quotation
Comments	Salutation
Date	Sidebar
Definition	Sidehead
Enclosure	State
Figure	Subhead
Footer	Table of Contents
Header	ZIP

Word lets you create 4,093 styles for a single document, although you rarely use more than a few dozen. (If your document really needs 4,093 styles, how in the world could you manage *without* using styles?)

Built-In and New Keyboard Shortcuts

Word now comes with several built-in keyboard shortcuts. You've already seen Ctrl+Shift+S, which opens the Style box. Table 7.4 lists the new shortcuts.

Table 7.4
Keyboard Shortcuts for Using Styles

Style	Shortcut
Normal style	Ctrl+Shift+N
Heading 1 style	Alt+Ctrl+1
Heading 2 style	Alt+Ctrl+2
Heading 3 style	Alt+Ctrl+3
List bullet style	Ctrl+Shift+L
List all styles	Shift+Style box down arrow

If you find yourself using a style frequently, you might want to create a keyboard shortcut for it. Here are the steps:

1. Choose **S**tyle from the F**o**rmat menu.
2. In the **S**tyles list, choose the style to which you want to assign a keyboard shortcut.
3. Choose **M**odify.
4. Choose Shortcut **K**ey. The Customize dialog box appears (as shown in fig. 7.4), with the **K**eyboard tab displayed.

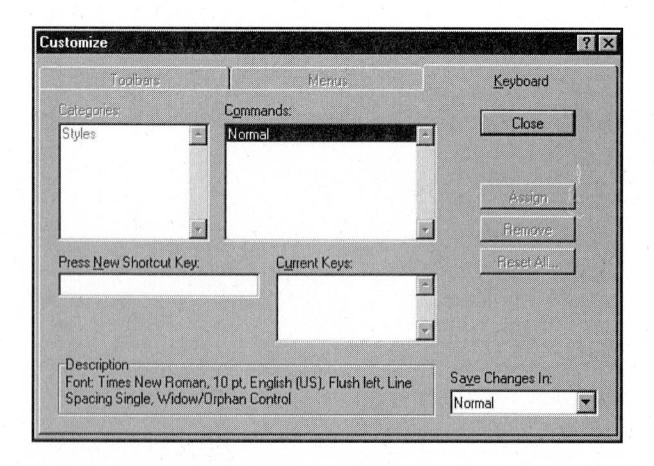

Figure 7.4
The Keyboard tab in the Customize dialog box.

5. Select the Press **N**ew Shortcut Key box, and enter the key combination you want to use. If that combination is already in use, a "Currently Assigned To" message appears. Delete the shortcut combination and try again.

6. Choose Assign.

7. Choose Close.

Try to keep track of how many shortcut keys you use. You might want to save some for later, when you learn macros. (You can learn more about customizing keyboard shortcuts in Chapter 24, "Personalizing Word.")

Creating a New Style by Example

You can create a style in one of two ways:

- ◆ Create the style by example.
- ◆ Use the Style dialog box.

Creating a style by example is the easier of the two methods, because it lets you see exactly what you're doing while you're doing it. To create a new style by example, take the following steps:

1. Format a paragraph or block of characters the way you want your style to appear, and select the paragraph or block (see fig. 7.5).

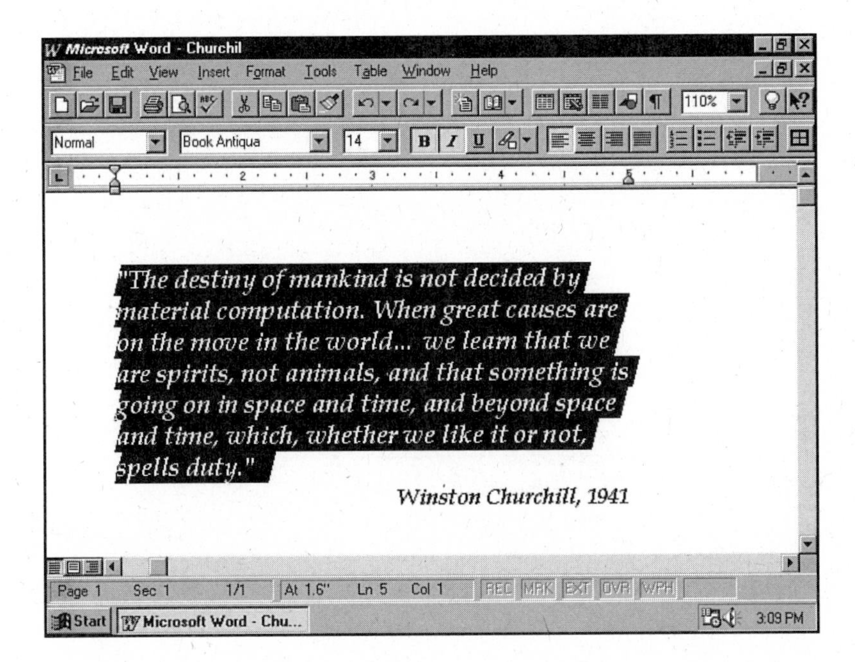

Figure 7.5

Step 1: Format a paragraph the way you want and select it.

2. Select the Style box from the Formatting toolbar, and type the new style name (see fig. 7.6).
3. Press Enter.

Voilà! You now have a new style.

Figure 7.6
Step 2: The new style name appears in the Style box.

Style name

When you create a new style using style by example, Word bases it on the paragraph's previous style.

If you plan to change the style drastically, and you already have a style that's closer to the one you're creating, assign that style to the paragraph first. Then, when you make your style changes, you won't have to make nearly as many.

Creating a New Style with Format Style

Using the Format, Style command is a little more complicated than creating a style by example, but gives you direct hands-on control over every part of your style. Start by

choosing Style from the Format menu. Next, choose New. The New Style dialog box opens, as shown in figure 7.7.

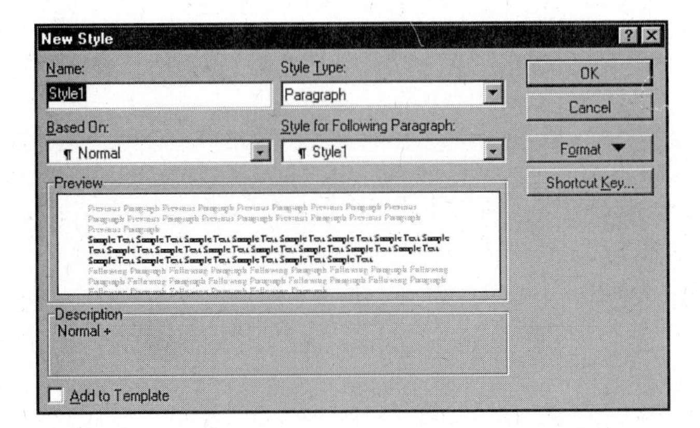

Figure 7.7

The New Style dialog box.

Before you format the new style, however, you have some important choices to make, as described in the following sections.

Choosing a Style Name

Type a new style name in the Name box. Style names can be up to 253 characters long. They can be split into several words, but keep away from these four characters:

\{};

Stay away from commas, too; Word uses them for *aliases*, which you read about in a moment.

All this means that you can now create long, highly descriptive style names. Remember, though, that only about 14 characters fit in the style box. So make sure that you can understand your style name from those first 14 characters.

Name your styles based on the function they serve—not the formatting they contain. Use "Headline" rather than "48 point Machine Bold." You may want to change the formatting of a style later.

Using Aliases

If you like to type your style names, yet you favor long style names that clearly explain the purpose of each style, you may want to use aliases.

An *alias* is an abbreviated style name that Word can recognize in place of the long name. To create an alias, type the style's full name in the Name box of the New Style or Modify Style dialog box, add a comma, and then type your alias. Here is an example:

```
List Bullet,lb
```

Both the full name and the alias appear in the style box when you use the style later, but you only have to type the alias to invoke the style. (By using Modify Style, you can add aliases to styles you already have. You learn about modifying styles later.)

Choosing between Paragraph and Character Styles

In the Style box, specify whether you're creating a paragraph or character style.

Choosing Based on Style

In the Based On box, specify which style you want to base your new style on. (You can also base your new style on no style at all.)

Unless you tell it otherwise, Word bases a new style on the Normal Style—10-point Times New Roman, flush left, English (U.S.). Often, that makes sense. It helps you build a consistent style because the only elements that vary from the rest of your document are those that you consciously choose to vary. You can, however, base your style on *any* style in your current document.

But what if your document won't resemble that in the least? Suppose that you're in the business of creating wedding invitations. In the following example, most of the text is centered and 20 point.

If you use the Normal style as the basis for the styles in this document, you must include all those specifications in every new style you create. Instead, create one new style called Normal Wedding. Then build the other styles on it, as shown in figure 7.8.

In figure 7.8, the Normal Wedding style is the primary style, and the other style—the Bride and Groom style—is based on it. The Normal Wedding style centers the text and sets the amount of space between the lines. The Bride and Groom style does the same, but increases the type size to 28 points.

If you're getting ready to create several entirely new styles, each with similar formatting, you'll find it easier to create one new "base" style first, and use Based On to build the other styles.

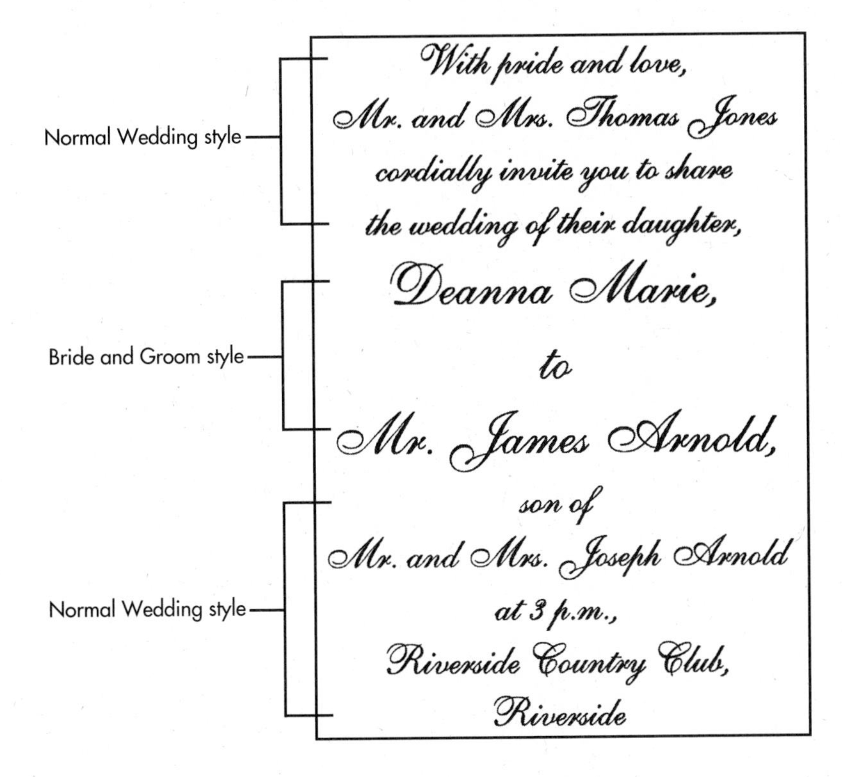

Figure 7.8
Wedding invitation styles.

Note If you know in advance which style you want to base your new style on, choose it in the Style dialog box. It then appears in the Based On box when you open the New Style dialog box.

A Word about Global Style Changes

You've already seen how you can assign a Based On style to any style. In the Normal template, all paragraph styles are based on the Normal style, as you saw earlier. What does this mean? You should be very cautious about making global style changes using the Normal style because the changes ripple through any document you create whenever you use this altered global template. This often creates changes you did not intend.

Suppose that all the type in your document is in Times New Roman. Most styles are based on a Normal style that uses Times New Roman. (This is the case in the Normal template.) If you change the Normal style to, say, Bookman, almost every element of the document changes.

Some headings remain in Arial because they have been specifically redesigned that way. This, too, can cause a problem, because Arial and Bookman don't work together graphically as well as Times New Roman and Arial do.

A more subtle problem is also possible. Different fonts have different widths. Bookman, for example, sets at least 15 percent wider than Times New Roman. If you change a long document this way, you may find that you've lengthened or shortened it by several pages.

The Based On feature is powerful. Don't hesitate to use it on custom templates to make quick and dramatic changes to the formatting of a specific type of document. One way to do this is to base one style on another style that is based on yet another style, creating a hierarchy of styles that changes when the style at the bottom changes.

You're limited to nine levels of Based On styles. For more levels than that, try Nintendo.

Just be aware of the power of Word's Based On feature, and leave the Normal style alone if you can. (You learn more about templates in Chapter 8, "Templates.")

Choosing a Following Paragraph Style

Normally, if you keep typing in a document, Word maintains your current style, applying it to a new paragraph whenever you start one. But what if you want the style to change when you start a new paragraph, and you always want it to change the same way?

This is more common than you might think. For example, most of the time headings are followed by body text; figure numbers are followed by captions. In the example of the wedding invitation described earlier, paragraphs with the Bride and Groom style are always followed by paragraphs with the Normal Wedding style.

Realizing this, Word's designers created a shortcut you can use to assign a style automatically to a paragraph whenever it follows another style. In the New Style dialog box, this feature is called Style for Following Paragraph.

In this box, you can choose the style that Word automatically uses for the next paragraph whenever you use the style you're defining. Remember, you can only use Based On or Style for Following Paragraph if the style you intend to choose already exists.

Style for Following Paragraph is an example of a style attribute that you can't set when you create styles by example. If you have several styles by example, you might think about editing them by using the Format and Style commands so that you can add a Style for Following Paragraph.

Note that Word's new AutoFormat as You Type feature, described later in this chapter, can also handle some style assignments for you automatically.

Choosing Whether to Include the Style in a Template

By default, when you create a new style, it becomes part of your document, but not part of the template your document uses. This gives you more flexibility, but it can get confusing, too. For example, it means different documents using the same template can have varying styles with the same name.

If you believe you will use the new style in other documents that share the same template, check Add to Template. From now on, the revised style appears in all documents you create using the current template. If you only use the Normal template, of course, all your new documents will have access to the revised style. (However, the revisions won't automatically appear in documents already created with this template.)

Save! Each Word document file includes the style sheet for its document. Style-sheet edits are just like text edits: they're not permanent until you save the file.

Formatting the New Style

Now you're ready to create the actual formatting that will become part of the style. Choose Format, and a drop-down menu appears, as shown in figure 7.9.

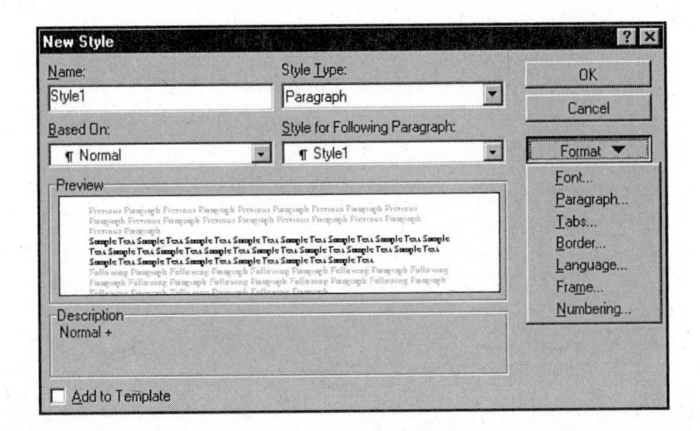

Figure 7.9

The Format button's drop-down menu.

Choosing any of these menu items opens a dialog box that looks identical to the one in the Format menu, but in this case, when you change a format setting, you won't just change the selected text; you may be changing all the text in the document that uses that same style.

If you need to change several parts of a style, make all the changes in one element, such as by choosing Font. Then choose OK. This returns you to the Style dialog box. Select another item from the Format menu, make the changes there, and choose OK.

Each time you return to the New Style dialog box, you can see your revisions reflected in the style description. When you have the style the way you want it, choose OK.

Changing an Existing Style by Using Style by Example

The techniques for changing styles are similar to those for creating new ones. To change a style by example:

1. Format a paragraph or selected text the way you want it.

2. Open the Style box and press Enter. Word displays the Reapply Style dialog box, as shown in figure 7.10.

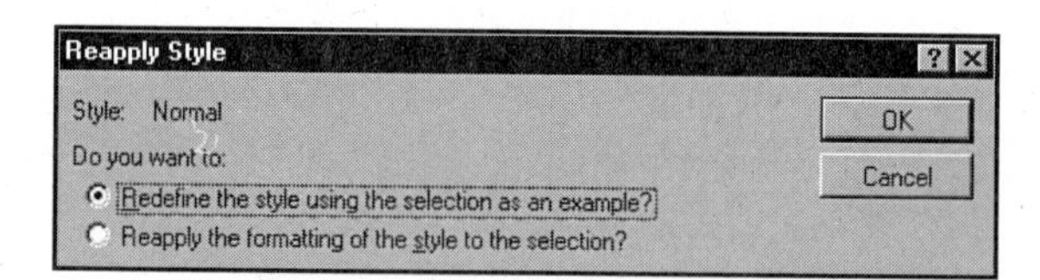

Figure 7.10
The Reapply Style dialog box.

If you want to change the style, be sure to select the button marked **R**edefine the style using the selection as an example?, and press Enter.

If you don't want to change the style, you can return the selected text to its current style, eliminating the changes you were toying with. Choose the button marked Reapply the formatting of the style to the selection?.

If you don't want to do anything, click on Cancel.

A Word about How Word Interprets Formatting in a Redefined Style

Remember that most Word styles are based on paragraphs. What if your paragraph has some stray character formatting that you don't want to include in your redefined style, such as a sentence or two that just happens to be italicized?

Just make sure that the first character is formatted the way you want it. If you choose several paragraphs with different paragraph formatting, Word assumes that you want the formatting from the *first* paragraph.

Changing an Existing Style Using Format Style

Once again, the techniques for changing a style with the Format, Style commands are very similar to the techniques for creating one. To change an existing style:

1. Choose Style from the Format menu.
2. Choose the style from the Styles list. (If you've selected text in the style, it will already be selected.)
3. Choose Modify. The Modify Style dialog box opens (see fig. 7.11). It's a dead ringer for the New Style dialog box you've already seen. It contains options for the following:
   - Setting the style's formatting (through the Format button)
   - Naming the style (or adding an alias to the current name)
   - Choosing between Paragraph or Character style (an option that's not always available)
   - Specifying the style on which it will be based
   - Specifying which style will follow it in the next paragraph
   - Specifying whether the style will be added to the template
   - Setting a new shortcut key
4. When you're finished making changes, choose Apply to apply the style to the current text selection, or Cancel to change the style without applying it to anything.

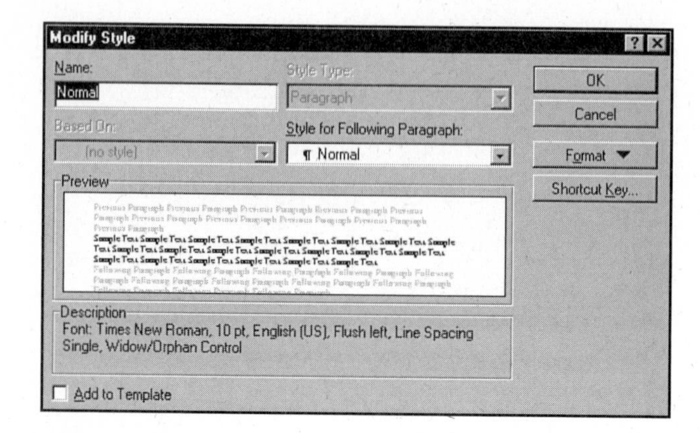

Figure 7.11
The Modify Style dialog box.

Copying Styles between Documents

The easiest way to copy a style between documents is to copy some text with the style into the document where you want the style to appear.

If you chose to practice using the CD-ROM file IWMS7A.DOC, you can copy the text of the file IWMS7B.DOC into IWMS7A.DOC to see how styles import.

Copying text with a particular style has a few drawbacks, however. First, you may not want the text in your document. Second, if you copy text from one document into another document that already has a style with the same name, the text you copy takes on the new style—not always what you had in mind.

Word provides a new tool, called the *Organizer,* which lets you move styles among documents. When you learn how to use the Organizer to manage styles, you'll also know how to manage AutoText entries, toolbars, and macros.

To use the Organizer, choose **S**tyles from the F**o**rmat menu, then choose **O**rganizer. The Organizer dialog box opens, as shown in figure 7.12.

To learn how to use the Organizer in more detail, turn to Chapter 8, "Templates and Wizards."

By default, the Organizer suspects that you may want to move a style you're using in your current document into the NORMAL.DOT template. On this screen, you can copy any style in either direction.

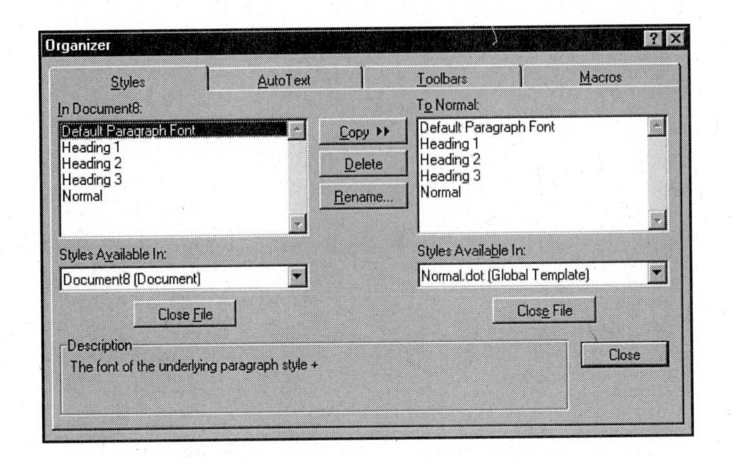

Figure 7.12

The Organizer dialog box.

To copy a style, choose the style you want to copy. A description of the style appears in the Description box. If you want to copy a style that's in the current document, choose it from the **I**n Document *number* list box. If you want to copy a style from NORMAL.DOT, choose a style in the T**o** Normal box. If you want to copy a style from another document or template, follow these steps:

1. Choose either Close File button. The list of available styles disappears, and an Open **F**ile button appears.

2. Choose Open **F**ile. The Open dialog box appears (see fig. 7.13).

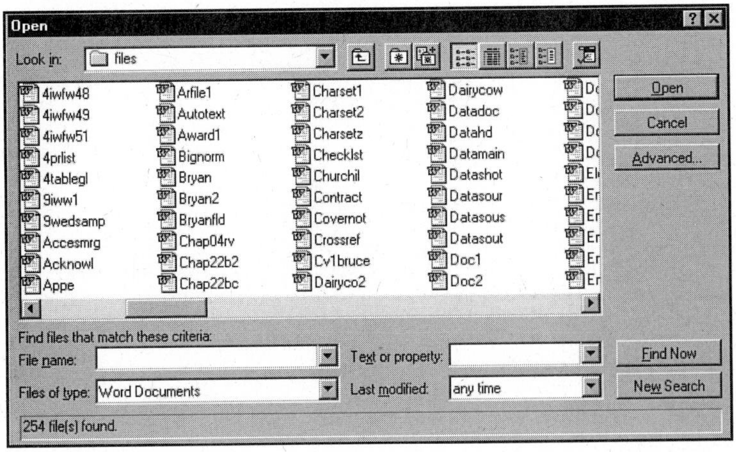

Figure 7.13

The Open dialog box.

3. Choose a document or template the way you normally would. (If you want to move styles from a template rather than a document, choose Document Template from the Files of type box.) Choose OK.

4. Choose the style you want to copy.

5. Choose the destination document or template where you want to copy it. (This might also mean closing the current document or template and choosing a new one.)

6. When you're finished copying styles, choose Close to leave the Organizer.

Changing Styles Globally with the Style Gallery

Ever wonder how a document would look if it were formatted with the styles from a different template? One of the quickest ways to dramatically change the look of an entire document is to change its template.

Style Gallery lets you manage this feat in an easy, risk-free manner. To use Style Gallery, choose Style Gallery from the Format menu. The Style Gallery dialog box opens, as shown in figure 7.14.

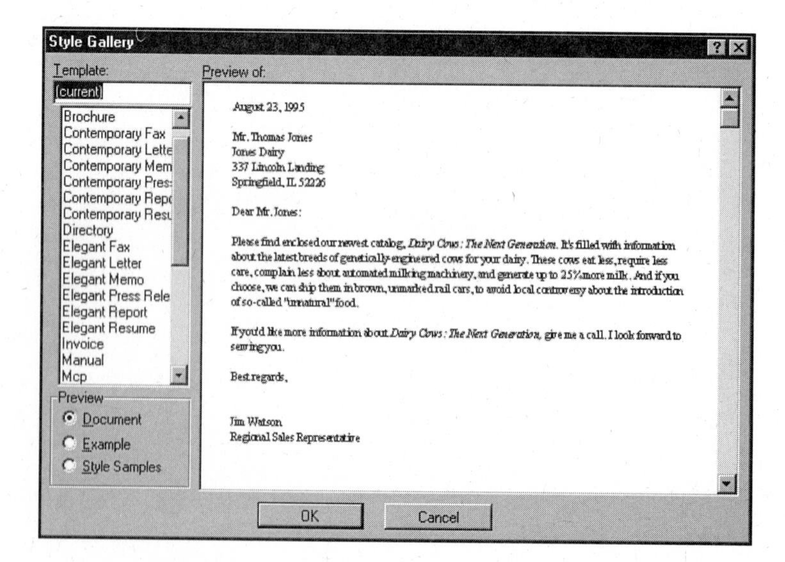

Figure 7.14

The Style Gallery dialog box.

You can see your current document in miniature in the Preview of box. Choose a Template from the list of those currently available, and Word shows you how your document would look if you imported those styles into your document. You can use the scroll bars on the Preview box to scroll through your document to see how the new styles look.

You can see how the styles look in a Word sample document by choosing Example from the Preview box at the bottom left. You can also see samples of each style, along with the names of every style, by choosing Style Samples. If you decide you want to use the styles from another template, choose OK and Word imports them into your current document.

The Style Gallery doesn't actually change the template attached to your document. Rather, it imports all the styles from the template you choose into the currently open document.

Word replaces any existing styles that have the same name as the new styles you import. If you want to keep both styles, rename one before you enter Style Gallery. See the following section for details.

Renaming a Style

You might want to change a style's name to make sure that it is not deleted when you merge styles from another document.

You can't rename or delete any of the 75 styles that are built into Word.

Take the following steps to rename an existing style:

1. Choose Format, Style.
2. Choose Modify.
3. In the Name box, type the new name.
4. Click on OK twice.

Deleting a Style

If you find that you no longer need a style, you can simply delete it. If any existing text already is formatted with the deleted style, Word automatically reformats that text with the Normal style.

Note You can't delete a built-in Word style.

Take the following steps to delete an existing style:

1. Select Format, Style.
2. From the Styles box, choose the style you want to delete.
3. Choose Delete. A confirmation dialog box appears.
4. Choose Yes to confirm the deletion.

If you want to delete many styles at once, use the Organizer as follows:

1. Open the Organizer.
2. Choose the Style tab.
3. Select the first style you want to delete.
4. Press Ctrl and select the next style you want to delete. (If you want to delete several consecutive styles, hold down Shift and select the last style of the group you want to delete. Word highlights all the styles between the first one and the last one you select.)
5. Choose Delete.
6. A confirmation box appears. You can confirm the deletions individually or all at once.
7. Choose Yes or Yes To All. Word deletes the styles.

How Manual Formatting and Styles Interact

You can always add manual formatting to any styled text. The manual formatting is superimposed on the style. If your style calls for 10-point Times New Roman italic, and you boldface it, your type becomes 10-point Times New Roman bold italic. This simple change works the same way for paragraphs, tabs, borders, shading, frames, bullets, numbering, and language.

Manual formatting gets trickier when you start changing your styles. Suppose that you change a style from 10-point Times New Roman italic to 10-point Times New Roman bold italic. What happens to the manual boldface formatting you've already added?

- Should Word keep it bold because that's what you explicitly asked for?
- Should Word change your bold to nonbold to maintain the contrast for which you were probably aiming?

Paradoxes like these caused the mental breakdown of the HAL computer in *2001*. You won't have those problems, however, because formatting problems aren't quite as tough, and your PC probably isn't quite as introspective as HAL. When it comes to bold, italic, and underline, Word maintains the contrast—switching your manual formatting when it needs to.

Things change if you actually *reapply* the style—say, by choosing it again in the Formatting toolbar. Then, the style *overrides*, eliminating any character formatting that conflicts with it.

Clearing Manual Formatting

Occasionally, you lose track of the manual formatting you've added to an underlying style. Word offers two machete-style shortcuts that let you hack through the underbrush and return to your style:

- Ctrl+Spacebar eliminates manual character formatting on selected text. This includes bold, italic, underline, sub/superscript, letterspacing, and everything else in the Format Font tab—plus your Language setting.
- Ctrl+Q eliminates manual paragraph formatting on selected text. These style commands survive: Font, Based On, and Next Style. If the paragraphs you want to clean up have *different* styles, use Ctrl+Q one paragraph at a time. It has the unexpected habit of resetting all your paragraphs to the style in the first paragraph.

Using Ctrl+NumPad5, Ctrl+Q, and then Ctrl+Spacebar unformats your entire document, leaving only the bare styles.

Finding Styles Automatically

Now that you know about styles, you can take advantage of **E**dit, **F**ind's nifty capability of searching for styles and replacing them.

Suppose that you want to search for all major section headings in a document. If they all start with the same letter, no problem. But what if they're numbered? The solution is to format these headings with styles, such as the ones Word includes (Heading 1, Heading 2, Heading 3, and so on). Then you can search for the styles themselves.

1. Select **E**dit, **F**ind. The Find dialog box appears, as shown in figure 7.15.

Figure 7.15

The Find dialog box.

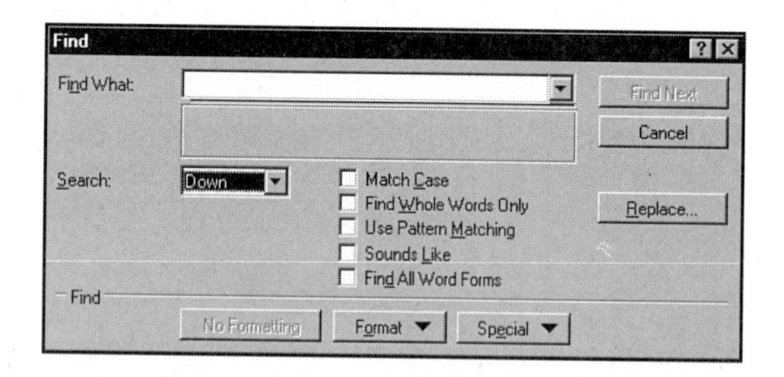

2. Choose F**o**rmat. A menu appears, offering several options.

3. Choose the **S**tyle option from the menu. The Find Style dialog box appears, as shown in figure 7.16.

Figure 7.16

The Find Style dialog box.

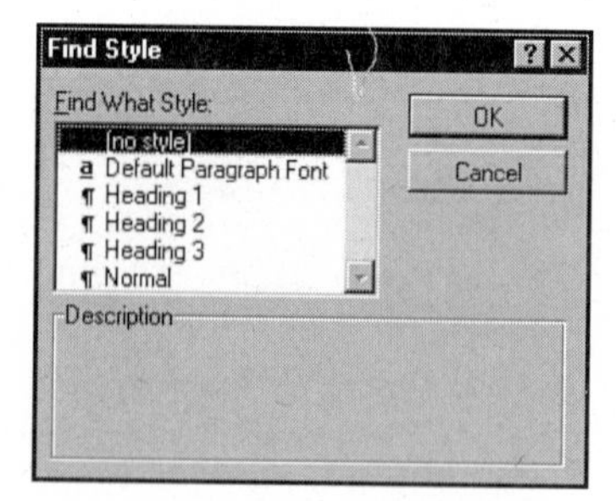

4. In the **F**ind What Style box, choose a style and click on OK.

5. Back in the Find dialog box, make sure that the Fi**n**d What box is empty (unless you are looking for specific text formatted with a specific style).

6. Click on **F**ind Next.

Replacing Styles Automatically

Similarly, you can use Edit, Replace to replace a style. Use this when you want to change the formatting of text from one style to another, while preserving the contents of both styles for future use. Take the following steps to replace a style:

1. Choose Edit, Replace.
2. Make sure that the Find What box is empty; then click on Format.
3. Choose Style. The Find Style dialog box opens.
4. Choose a style to find and click on OK.
5. Now choose the Replace With box.
6. Choose Format again, and choose Styles again. The Replace Style dialog box appears, as shown in figure 7.17.

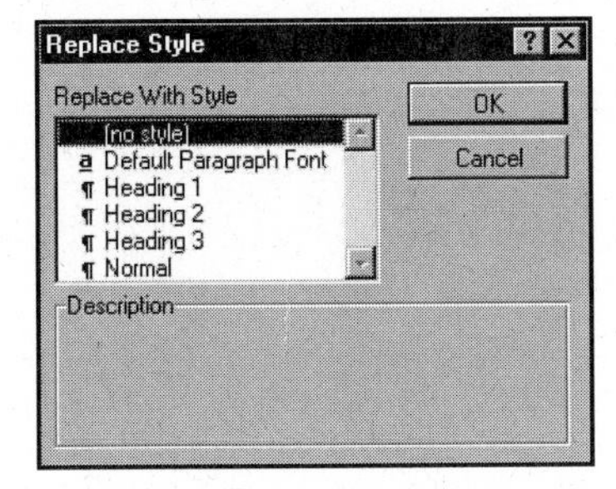

Figure 7.17
The Replace Style dialog box.

7. Choose a replacement style, and choose OK.
8. To replace all examples of the style, choose Replace All. To replace them selectively, choose Find Next, and then Replace only the ones you want to replace.

Keeping Track of Styles

You can always print a style sheet for your document that lists all the styles currently in use. To print a style sheet, take these steps:

1. Choose File, Print.
2. Choose Styles from the Print box.
3. Click on OK.

If you've been busy redefining keyboard shortcuts, you ought to print those out, too. In Step 2, choose Key Assignments rather than Styles.

Another way to keep track of styles is to keep them visible on-screen, next to the paragraphs where they're used. Word provides the Style Area for this purpose. If you want to activate the Style Area on your screen, take these steps:

1. Choose **T**ools, **O**ptions.

2. Select the View tab in the Options dialog box, as shown in figure 7.18.

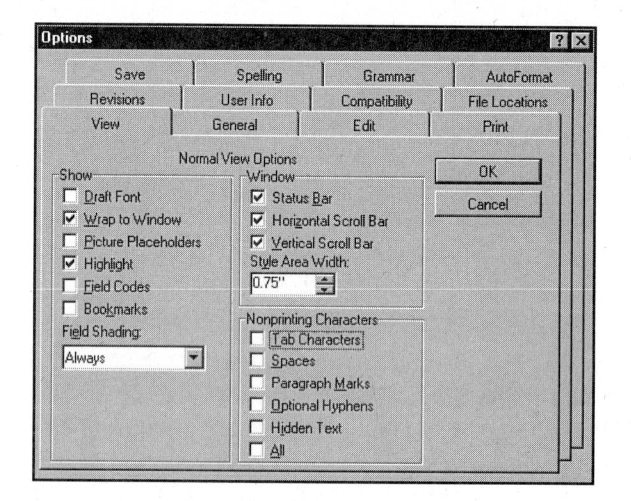

Figure 7.18
The View tab in the Options dialog box.

3. In the Style Area Width box, choose a new width. (The default, zero, means no Style Area. That's why you've probably never seen one.)

4. Choose OK.

Figure 7.19 shows a 0.75" Style Area. 0.75" is a good size because it's wide enough to display most style names without reducing the editing space too much. Any time you want to change the width of the Style Area, you can go back to the View tab and reset the Style Area's width.

The fastest way to change the Style Area's width is to place the mouse pointer on the Style Area's border. When the pointer changes to the vertical split pointer, drag the border to the left or right and let go.

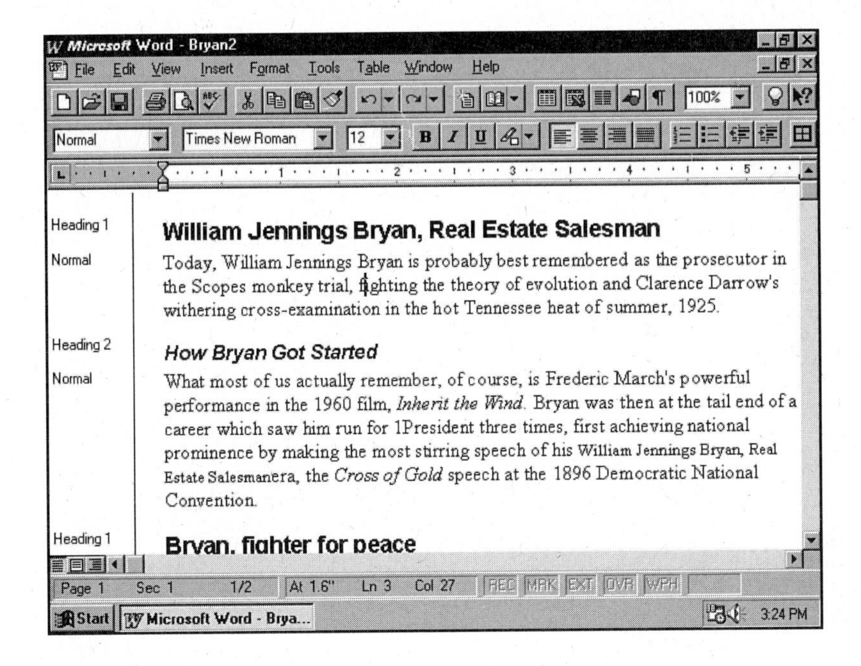

Figure 7.19

A document window with the Style Area set to 0.75".

When the Style Area is open, you can select an entire paragraph by clicking on its style name.

If you have several documents open, setting the Style Area only affects the one you're working in and any additional documents you open during the session.

Checking Styles with the Help Button

Word's new Help button gives you a nifty shortcut for getting detailed information on the styles that apply to specific text. Click on the Help button in the Standard toolbar. Then click on the desired text. Detailed Paragraph Style and Character Style information appears on-screen, as shown in figure 7.20.

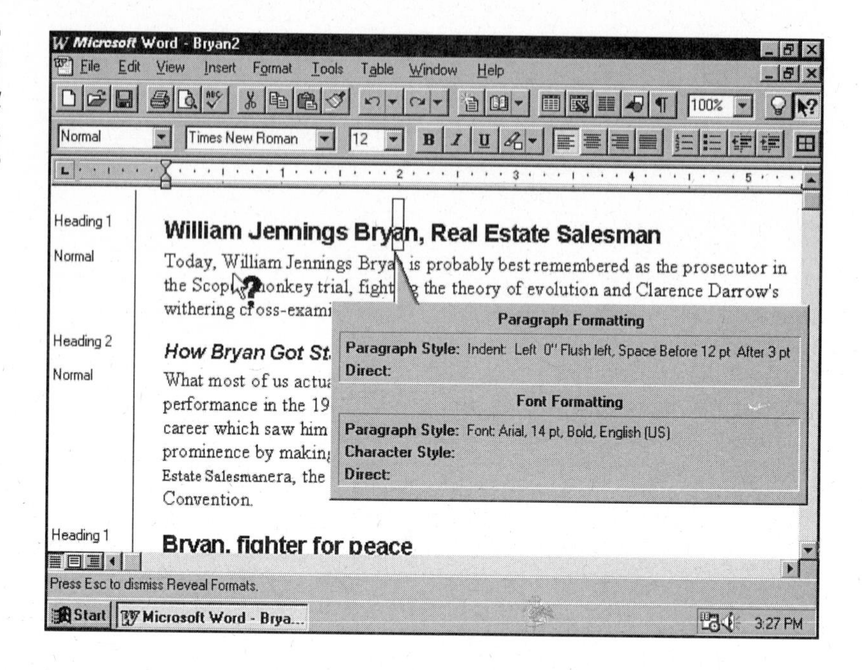

Figure 7.20

Getting detailed style information via the Help button.

Preparing Style Sheets for Export

If you're creating a document that will ultimately be exported to a desktop-publishing program, you may want to prepare a style sheet that can be exported with it.

As of this writing, neither QuarkXPress 3.1 nor PageMaker 5.0 directly converts Word 95 style sheets, but both can convert Word for Windows 2 style sheets. You may have to save your file as a Word for Windows 2 document before converting it, possibly losing some attributes or formatting information in the process.

Tip A preliminary version of a Word 6/Word 95 import filter for QuarkXPress may be found on CompuServe: GO QUARK.

Both QuarkXPress and PageMaker use filters to make their style-sheet conversions. These are similar to the import/export filters Word itself uses to bring data in from other word processors, databases, and spreadsheets. The filter in PageMaker 5.0 actually gives you the option of importing Word's tables, tables of contents, index entries, and page breaks.

QuarkXPress imports only the styles that are actually used in a Word document, ignoring other styles you may have defined but not used. If this is a problem, try saving the Word document as an RTF file; QuarkXPress imports all the styles associated with these files.

If the style sheet does not import properly into your desktop-publishing program, first make sure that the filters are installed correctly and are located where the program can find them.

Using Word's AutoFormatting Feature

If you simply can't be bothered with styles, Word's AutoFormatting feature will be glad to insert them for you. AutoFormat enables you to take a plain document and have Word format it for you by automatically adding styles. AutoFormat can be a big time-saver for you.

To AutoFormat your document, choose AutoFormat from the Format menu. The dialog box appears, as shown in figure 7.21. To begin automatic formatting, click on OK.

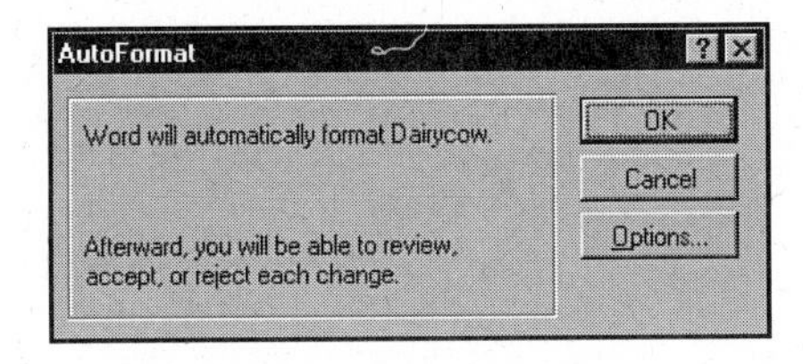

Figure 7.21

The AutoFormat dialog box.

You can also press Ctrl+K to start AutoFormatting with no introductory screen.

Setting AutoFormat Options

You may want to control AutoFormat's options before you turn it loose. Choose Options, and the Options dialog box appears, as shown in figure 7.22. You can turn on or off every part of AutoFormat. If you click on the AutoFormat button, Word displays the changes it can make when you run AutoFormat after creating a document. If you click on the AutoFormat As You Type button, Word displays the changes it can make while you work.

Figure 7.22

Controlling AutoFormat options through the Options dialog box.

The categories are very similar, but not identical. For example, the AutoFormat As You Type feature can turn a row of hyphens into a border, but the regular AutoFormat feature cannot.

By default, if AutoFormat comes across a style you've added to your document, it leaves that style alone. Word figures you know what you're doing. However, Word's AutoFormat may make substantial changes to your document's styles. In some cases, you may prefer to let Word try to make the entire document consistent, by replacing your styles as well. To do this, clear the Preserve Styles check box in Tools, Options, AutoFormat.

Also by default, AutoFormat applies styles to headings, lists, and other paragraphs. You can tell Word to ignore any of these by clearing the appropriate check box. The following provides more information about the changes Word can make when you run AutoFormat after creating a document:

- **Headings.** With AutoFormat headings turned on, Word automatically applies a heading style to any text that starts with a capital letter, does not end with punctuation, is at least 20 percent shorter than the maximum line length, and is set off from other copy with more than one line of space.

- **Lists.** With AutoFormat Lists turned on, Word automatically starts applying Word's built-in list formats (List, List 2, List 3, and so on) to any list of consecutive lines separated by paragraph marks.

- **Automatic Bulleted Lists.** With Automatic Bulleted Lists turned on, Word automatically inserts bullets in place of characters that are often used to substitute for bullets, such as dashes and asterisks.

- **Other Paragraphs.** With Other Paragraphs turned on, Word formats most other paragraphs as body text, while trying to recognize specialized paragraph formats such as letter salutations and apply proper formatting to them as well.

AutoFormat can also change specific characters and symbols, if you specify them by choosing Tools, Options, AutoFormat. These changes lead to a more attractive document, but if you plan to send your document to another computer, such as a Macintosh, you may want to turn these features off—the symbols may not translate properly, leading to errors in your document.

- **Straight Quotes with "Smart Quotes".** Word replaces the default apostrophe (') and inch-mark (") quotation marks with the more attractive (‘’) and (“”) angled quotation marks. This results in a more appealing document.
- **Ordinals (1st) with Superscript.** When Word recognizes that you have typed the word 1st, 2nd, 3rd, and so on, it can automatically replace them with the more attractive 1st, 2nd, 3rd, and so on. This works with any number, but does not work with spelled-out numbers like "twenty-eighth."
- **Fractions (1/2) with fraction character (½).** When Word recognizes that you have typed the fraction 1/4, 1/2, or 3/4, it converts the fraction to the special character ¼, ½, or ¾. Note that these are the only fractions Word can AutoFormat, because these are the only fractions contained in the standard Windows character set. If your document also uses fractions like 5/16, you may want to turn this feature off to maintain consistency.
- **Symbol Characters with Symbols.** When Word recognizes that you type characters that typically are used in place of symbols, such as two consecutive hyphens in place of an em dash (—), it can substitute the proper character automatically.

Note that by default Word changes many other symbols, such as copyright and registered trademark symbols. However, these are controlled through the AutoCorrect feature, which is covered in the next chapter.

By default, Word's AutoFormat feature also eliminates extra unnecessary paragraph marks, such as empty paragraph marks inserted between text paragraphs. Word also replaces extra spaces with tabs, and removes tabs and spaces it doesn't think you need.

When you're done changing AutoFormat options, click on OK. To AutoFormat, choose OK again to close the second dialog box. When Word finishes AutoFormatting, the dialog box in figure 7.23 appears. You can either accept or reject all the changes Word made. More likely, you may want to choose Review Changes. Word then displays the changes that have been made, one by one.

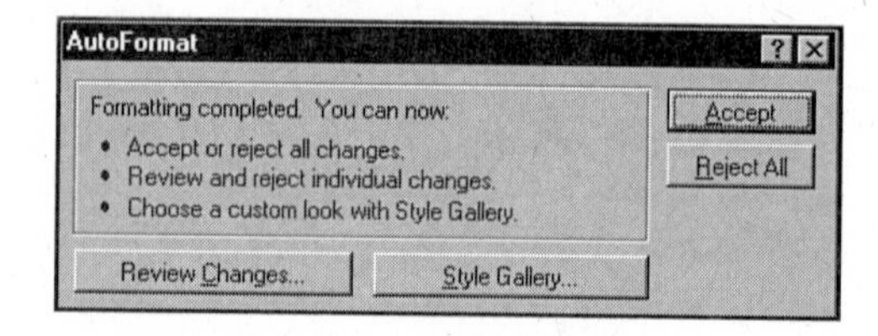

Figure 7.23
The AutoFormat dialog box after AutoFormatting is complete.

Additions are marked in blue and with an underline. Blue paragraph marks indicate paragraphs where Word has applied a new style. Deletions are marked in red and strikethrough. Every line containing a change also has a black bar to its left.

You can manage the review process from the Review AutoFormat Changes dialog box, which opens when you ask to Review Changes (see fig. 7.24). To find the first change, click on the Find button that shows a right arrow. Word highlights the first change and explains the change in the Description box.

Figure 7.24
The Review AutoFormat Changes dialog box.

To reject the change, choose Reject. (You don't actually accept any changes until you're finished with your review.) If you change your mind after rejecting a Word change, choose Undo Last.

To continue to the next change, choose Find again. To return to the previous change, choose the Find button that shows a left arrow. To automatically jump to the next revision after you reject a change, check the Find Next after Reject box. To see how the document would look if you accepted all the changes, choose Hide Marks.

When you're finished reviewing the changes, choose Close or Cancel to return to the AutoFormat dialog box. (Close appears as an option if you have rejected at least one change; Cancel appears otherwise.) At this point, you can accept all the changes you haven't rejected during your review, or choose Reject All to go back to square one.

You also can choose Style Gallery to open the Style Gallery and see if, somewhere else on your computer, there are some styles you might like better than the ones Word has used.

Word's style assignments stay in place, but Style Gallery can assign new formatting to the styles that have already been assigned. In other words, if AutoFormat specifies Body Text for a paragraph, you can change the look of that body text by importing a Body Text style with different specifications from another template. But Style Gallery won't go back and change the style name AutoFormat has already applied.

AutoFormat As You Type

As if AutoFormatting weren't enough, Word 95 goes even further. AutoFormatting As You Type does just that: it makes its changes while you're working, so you don't have to run AutoFormatting separately, and you can decide immediately whether you like the changes Word is making. To specify which types of AutoFormatting you want Word to make while you work:

1. Choose **O**ptions from the **T**ools menu.
2. Display the AutoFormat dialog box.
3. Choose AutoFormat As You Type to display the options for immediate AutoFormatting (see fig. 7.25).

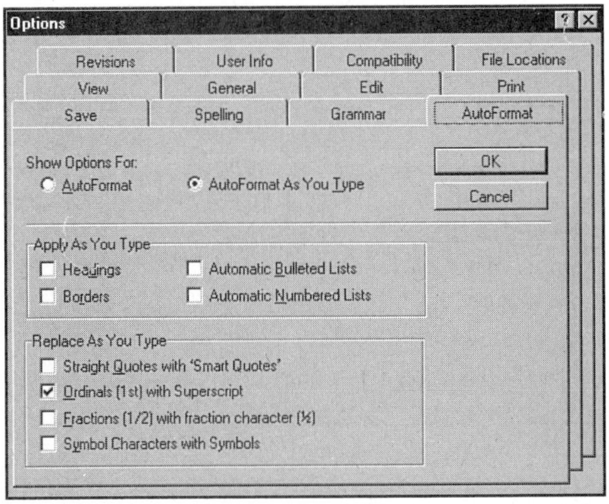

Figure 7.25

Controlling AutoFormat As You Type options from the Options dialog box.

Most of these options are the same as those already discussed in the preceding AutoFormatting section. There are two changes, however. Word doesn't interactively AutoFormat lists or other paragraphs such as salutations. It does, however, automatically add borders in place of rows of hyphens or underlines, and it also creates numbered lists automatically.

Even where the options are identical, you can establish different options for "conventional" AutoFormatting versus interactive AutoFormatting As You Type.

4. Make the changes you want, and choose OK. From now on, Word keeps track of what you're doing and automatically makes the formatting changes you request.

Tracking Interactive AutoFormatting Changes with the Tip Wizard

When Word does make an AutoFormatting change as you type, the Word Tip Wizard displays a note explaining the change it has made and offering to let you undo the change. To undo the change, click on the Change button at the right (see fig. 7.26).

Figure 7.26

Tip Wizard describing a change it has made.

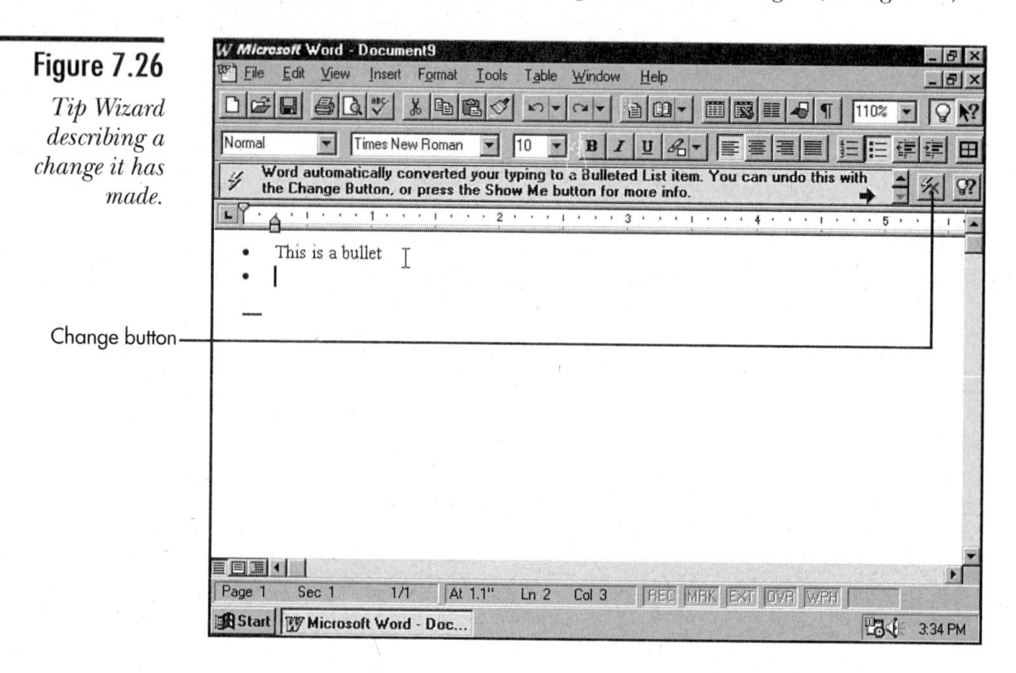

This notification only appears if you are displaying the Tip Wizard. If the Tip Wizard does not appear, click on the Tip Wizard (light bulb) icon on the Formatting toolbar, and the note appears.

If you set AutoFormat *not* to make these changes automatically as you type, the Tip Wizard offers to make the change for you, as shown in figure 7.27. As mentioned earlier, you are only notified if the Tip Wizard is already being displayed.

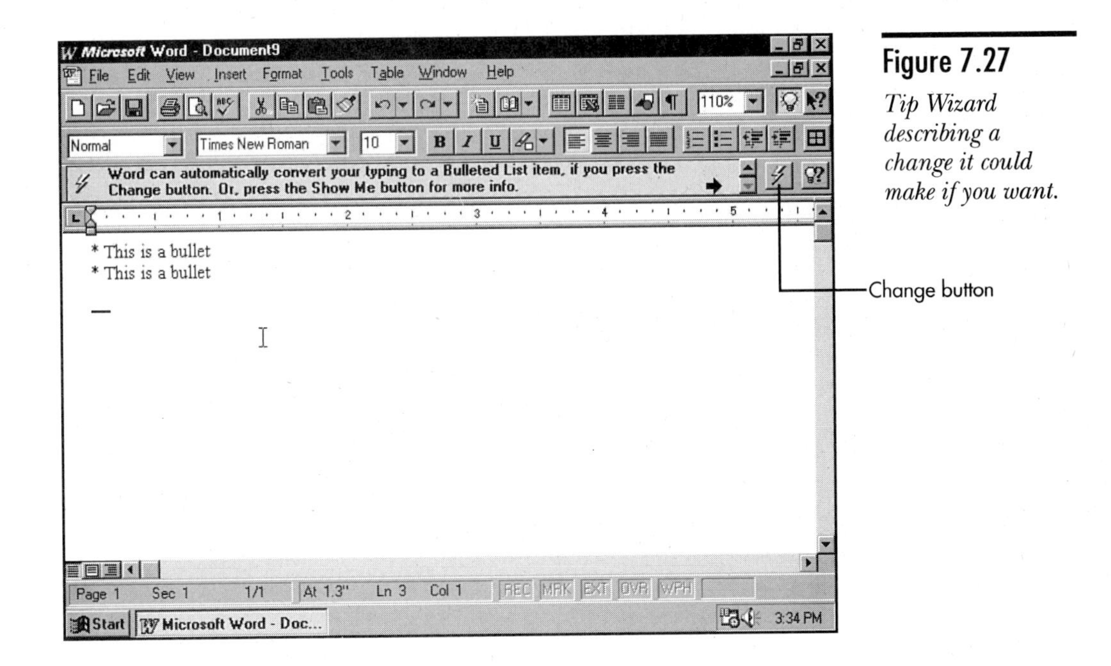

Figure 7.27

Tip Wizard describing a change it could make if you want.

Templates and Wizards

If you've used Word for Windows at all, you've come across the term *template.*

When you create a new Word document, you're asked on which template you want to base your document. At that point, many Word users are relieved to see that Normal is already offered up as the default choice. They press Enter and hurry along to the real work.

By doing so, they miss one of Word's most powerful features—and one that can save them an enormous amount of time.

A *template* is a pattern that tells Word what information should already be in a new document when you open it. (Obviously, any information that Word places in your documents automatically is information you don't have to put there manually!)

Anything you can put in a Word document, you also can store in a Word template, including the following:

- Text
- Graphics
- Automated procedures (macros)
- AutoText (blocks of text that can be called up with a few keystrokes)
- Fields (such as instructions to insert the current date and time)
- Font and paragraph formatting
- Styles
- Customized toolbars, menus, and keyboard commands

If you use templates, you can open your documents with all the boilerplate text and formatting work already done. With templates available, you no longer have an excuse for doing repetitive work to set up a document.

You also can build thoroughly customized work environments into your templates. You can create a template with the built-in text and database connections you need for managing correspondence, for example. Another template might contain the AutoText entries you need to quickly build a new proposal document.

As you see in Chapter 24, "Personalizing Word," each template can even include its own toolbar buttons and menu items.

Templates also are an ideal way of making sure that everyone in your organization prepares consistent documents, and that each Word for Windows user has access to the same shortcuts and macros that you develop over time.

As you build a library of templates, you subtly shape Word to your own work style. At the risk of sounding "cyberpunkish," it becomes an extension of your personality.

But that's all a bit abstract. Word has another feature, *wizards*, which are anything but subtle.

Word wizards are automated procedures that ask you a series of questions, and then build a document based on your responses. You just stand back and watch. Wizards are available for many of the most common kinds of documents. Word's Letter Wizard even comes with 14 prewritten business letters (and one to Mom).

By using the capabilities of Word templates and wizards (after you read this chapter), you should have to create *very few* documents entirely from scratch.

In this chapter:

- Creating templates
- Changing an existing template
- Attaching a new template to a document
- Adding another global template
- Adding a global template permanently
- Using the Organizer to work with templates
- Copying styles among documents and templates
- Copying other elements among templates
- Renaming or deleting in templates
- Using Word's alternate templates
- Using wizards
- Using these individual wizards: Agenda, Calendar, Fax, Memo, Resume, Table, and more

Understanding Templates

As mentioned earlier, a template is a collection of information that Word uses to create a specific kind of document. When you create a new document based on that template, Word places any text you include in your template into the new document.

Word also makes the other information available to your document whenever you need it. A good example of the information available to a template is styles.

All the default Word styles discussed in Chapter 7, "Styles and AutoFormatting," are collected in one template, called the Normal template. (This is the template you use by default when you press the Enter key in the New dialog box without paying attention.)

When you load Word for the very first time, these styles are built right into the program. The first time you make a change to any aspect of Word that is covered by templates, Word saves a template document called NORMAL.DOT. After that, Word looks to NORMAL.DOT for these styles and other default information. If you display a list of Document Templates in the OFFICE95\TEMPLATES or WINWORD\TEMPLATES folder, this template appears as Normal, because Windows 95 does not display extensions by default.

If you delete or rename NORMAL.DOT, intentionally or inadvertently, Word reverts to the built-in settings it had when you first installed the program. This means that deleting or renaming NORMAL.DOT is a last resort for salvaging a hopelessly muddled Normal template.

(As you see later, you can use the Organizer to move any useful AutoText entries, styles, toolbars, and macros to safe harbor before you dynamite NORMAL.DOT.)

NORMAL.DOT is a *global template*, which means it's available to all Word documents, regardless of whether you choose it. Any change you make to NORMAL.DOT affects new documents you create with it later.

What if you open an existing document based on a template you've just changed?

If you create new styles, AutoText entries, or macros, or if you customize Word's toolbars and menu assignments, these new options are available to the old document.

But the old document does not suddenly include changes in formatting or text that you've made to the template.

When you open a document based on *another* template, its customizations also become available. These customizations take precedence when they conflict with NORMAL.DOT. The rest of the time, both templates live together peacefully in memory.

Creating a New Template from Scratch

You can create a new template in two ways. First, you can create it *as a template*. To do this, select New from the File menu. Choose an existing template on which you want to base your new template. (Don't use a wizard.) Then check Template in the New box, and click on OK.

You now have a new template with all the attributes of the existing template. Word identifies it as Template1 until you save it.

If you create a new template based on NORMAL.DOT, it does not include any customized macros or toolbars you've added in NORMAL.DOT.

Typically, you won't notice. Because NORMAL.DOT is still open, they are available to you. However, if you want to share your template with someone else, you have to copy your macros and toolbars into it. To do this, you can use the Organizer, discussed later in this chapter.

Now you can adapt this template any way you like, adding or deleting boilerplate text and other customizations.

When you're finished, choose Save from the File menu. Choose a file name ending with .DOT. (Although you can name a template anything you want, Word displays it in a list of templates only if you choose the .DOT extension.)

Before Word 6, you could save your templates anywhere. Many well-organized users set up a specific template directory and changed their WIN.INI files to tell Word to look in a specific place (path) for these .DOT files.

Now, Word does this for you automatically, placing your templates in the folder WINWORD\TEMPLATE, and graying out any other choices.

Creating a Template Based on an Existing Document

You also can open any existing document and resave it as a template. This is the strategy to follow if you have a document that already contains much of the text and formatting you want to duplicate in other documents.

1. Open the document.
2. Delete anything that's not boilerplate. Adjust any formatting or other document attributes.
3. Save the document using Save As.
4. Choose Document Template in the Save File as Type box. Word automatically switches to the \WINWORD\TEMPLATE directory and assigns a .DOT extension to your current file name. (You may still have to clear your current directory from within the File Name box.)
5. After you have the right file name, click on the OK button.

The accompanying CD-ROM contains a file you can use to practice some of the procedures in this chapter: IWMS8A.DOC.

Changing an Existing Template

As with creating a template, you also can change a template by opening it directly, or by opening a document based on it. If you want to add text to the template, or change its direct formatting, you must open it directly.

To do so, choose Open from the File menu. Specify Document Templates in List Files of Type, so that Word displays DOT files. Click on OK.

Then make your editing and formatting changes. Change the document's other attributes—styles, AutoText entries, macros, toolbars, menu items, and keyboard shortcuts. (These features are covered elsewhere in the book.) Then save the template.

Chances are, you'll often want to change your templates through documents, because that's where you notice that you want to make a change.

Here, things get a bit stickier. Some changes you make in a document are really intended *just* for that document. Text changes are the most obvious example. Other types of information *are* stored in your template—either the global template NORMAL.DOT, or another template.

Table 8.1 shows which document elements are stored in templates and which elements are stored in the document.

Table 8.1
Document Elements Stored in Templates or Documents

Element	Where Stored
Text	Document only
All manual formatting	Document only
Styles	Document only; can be copied into a template using Organizer
AutoText	Template; decide which template (NORMAL.DOT or another open template) when you create the entry; can be copied between templates using Organizer

Element	Where Stored
Macros	Template; decide which template (NORMAL.DOT or another open template) when you record or write the macro; can be copied between templates using Organizer
Toolbars	Template; decide which template (NORMAL.DOT or another open template) when you customize the toolbar; can be copied between templates using Organizer
Menu item changes	Template; decide which template keyboard shortcuts (NORMAL.DOT or another open template) when you customize the toolbar; *cannot* use Organizer to move these among templates

Attaching a New Template to a Document

All documents are attached to the NORMAL.DOT template. If you open a document using another template, your document is attached to that template too.

One way to change a document's formatting quickly and dramatically is to change the custom template to which it's attached. (Remember, this also changes the macros, AutoText entries, and many other items available to your document.)

Before you do so, preview how the document will look when it's reformatted. Select Style Gallery from the Format menu. In the Style Gallery dialog box, click once on the template you want to preview.

If you click twice on a template name in the Style Gallery dialog box, Word copies all the styles from that template into your current template.

This is good to know if you just want to change your styles, and you want to keep the other elements (AutoText entries, toolbars, macros, and so on) of your current template.

To change the template itself, follow these steps:

1. Select Templates from the File menu. The Templates and Add-ins dialog box opens (see fig. 8.1).

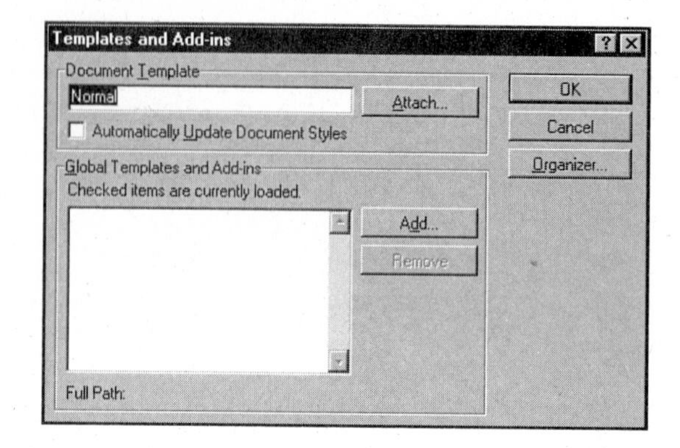

Figure 8.1

The Templates and Add-ins dialog box.

2. Select **A**ttach. The Attach Template dialog box opens (see fig. 8.2).

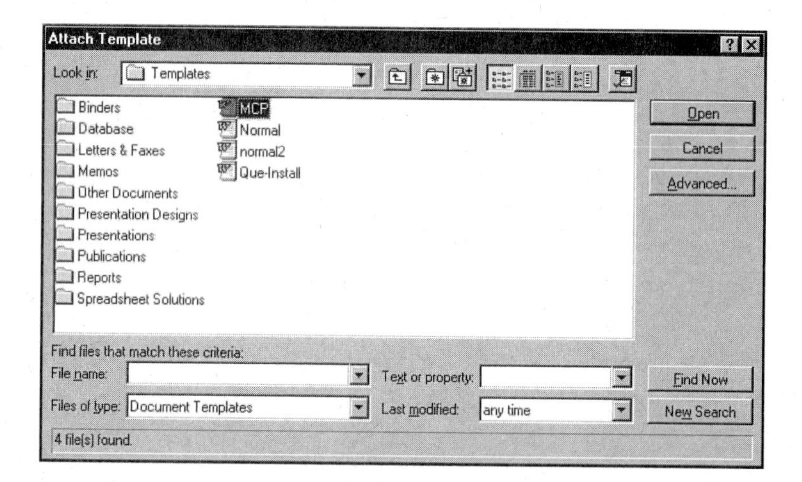

Figure 8.2

The Attach Template dialog box.

3. Select another template from the File **n**ame list, and click on OK.

4. If you want the styles automatically updated, check Automatically **U**pdate Document Styles.

5. Click on OK.

Note You can attach another template to gain access to its AutoText entries, toolbars, and macros. In that case, don't check Automatically **U**pdate Document Styles.

Adding Another Global Template

In versions of Word before Release 6, you could have only one global template: Normal. Now you can have more than one. Each global template's macros, AutoText entries, and command settings are available to all documents you open during your session.

To add another global template, perform these steps:

1. Choose Templates from the File menu.

2. If more than one global template is available, check the one(s) you want in the Global Templates and Add-ins list box.

3. If you want to add a global template that isn't displayed in the Global Templates and Add-ins list box, choose Add. The Add Template dialog box opens (see fig. 8.3).

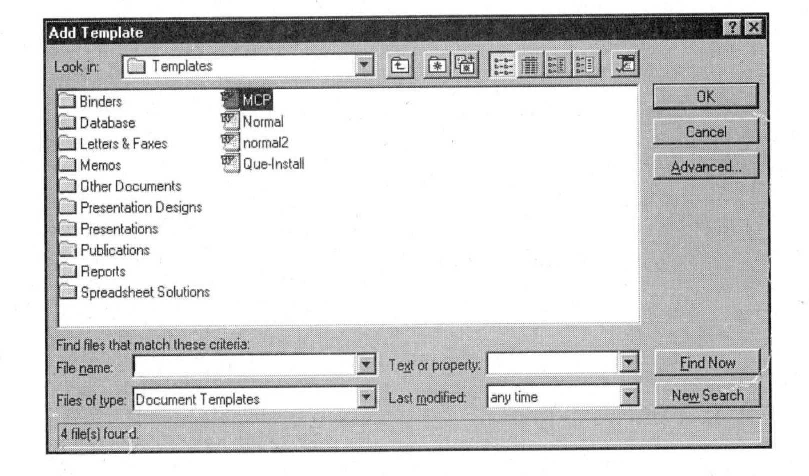

Figure 8.3

The Add Template dialog box.

4. Select the template you want to become a global template, and click on OK.

5. Click on OK again.

Adding a Global Template Permanently

Adding a template permanently keeps it global for your entire session. To make a template global permanently, copy it into your WINWORD\STARTUP directory. Whenever you open Word, it is loaded as a global template.

If you want to make the template unavailable to a specific document, uncheck its box in Global Templates and Add-ins. If you no longer want it to appear as a global template, delete it from the STARTUP directory.

Using the Organizer to Work with Templates

The Organizer has been mentioned several times in this chapter. The Organizer brings styles, AutoText, macros, and toolbars together in one place, where they can be copied between templates. (Styles also can be copied from documents to templates.)

In other words, the Organizer makes it practical to add specific elements of one template to another. If, for example, you have several large blocks of text recorded as AutoText entries in your Letters template, and you'd also like them to be available in your Proposals template, the Organizer makes that possible.

To enter the Organizer, do the following:

1. Select **T**emplates from the **F**ile menu.
2. Choose **O**rganizer. The Organizer dialog box appears (see fig. 8.4).

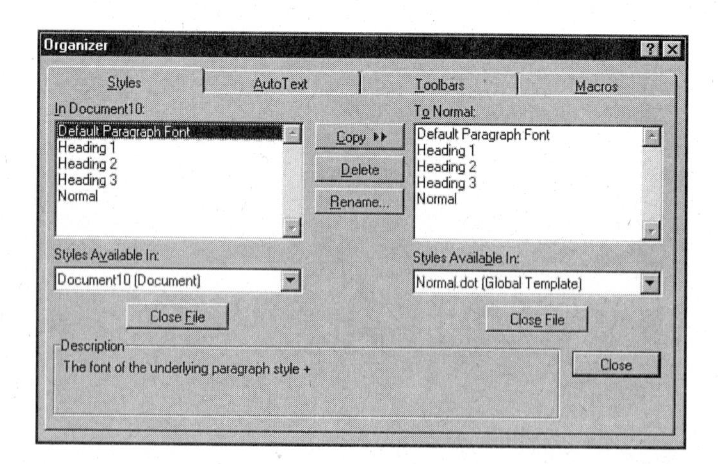

Figure 8.4
The Organizer dialog box.

Copying Styles among Documents and Templates

By default, Organizer suspects that you may want to move a style you're using in your current document into the NORMAL.DOT template. However, in the Organizer dialog box, you can copy any style in either direction.

To copy a style, choose the style you want to copy. A description of the style appears in the Description box. If you want to copy a style in the current document, choose it from the In Document list box. If you want to copy a style from NORMAL.DOT, choose a style in the To Normal box.

If you want to copy a style from another document or template, follow these steps:

1. Click on either Close File button. The list of available styles disappears, and an Open File button appears.
2. Choose Open File. The Open dialog box appears (see fig. 8.5).

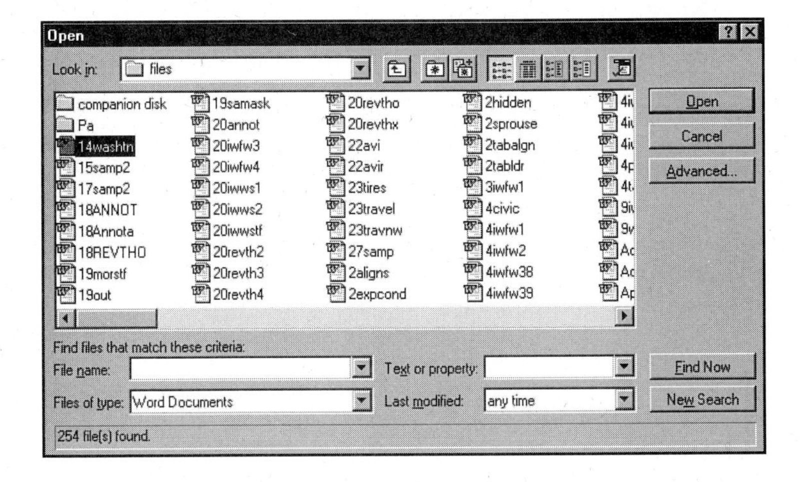

Figure 8.5

The Open dialog box.

3. Select a document or template as you normally do and click on OK.
4. Select the style you want to copy.
5. Select the destination document or template. (This might also mean closing the current document or template and choosing a new one.)
6. When you're finished copying styles, click on the Close button to leave the Organizer.

Copying Other Elements among Templates

Copying AutoText entries, toolbars, and macros is similar. Follow these steps:

1. Open the appropriate Organizer tab (AutoText, Toolbars, or Macros).
2. Select the entry you want to copy. (This might mean closing the existing template and opening a new one.)
3. Select the destination for the object (AutoText, toolbars, or macro).
4. Close the Organizer dialog box or switch to another tab when you're done.

Because AutoText entries, toolbars, and macros all are stored in templates, you can't move them to or from a document. If you choose a document, Word displays the list of available entries in the template to which it's attached.

Renaming or Deleting Elements in a Template

You also can use Organizer to clean up styles, AutoText entries, toolbars, or macros you no longer use. To delete an item, find and select it, and choose Delete. To Rename an item, find and select it, and choose Rename.

Browsing Word's Alternate Templates

Word comes with more than 20 templates that offer internally consistent styles for most kinds of documents. In Word 95, these are organized into categories, and Word takes advantage of long file names to provide a better description of each template. Better yet, you can preview the templates in Word's File, New dialog box.

Table 8.2 lists Word 95's templates.

TABLE 8.2
Word's Built-In Document Templates

Template Category	Template Name
Publications	Brochure Contemporary Press Release Directory

Template Category	Template Name
	Elegant Press Release Manual Newsletter Thesis
Other Documents	Contemporary Resume Elegant Resume Invoice Professional Resume Purchase Order Weekly Time Sheet
Letters & Faxes	Contemporary Fax Contemporary Letter Elegant Fax Elegant Letter Professional Fax Professional Letter
Memos	Contemporary Memo Elegant Memo Professional Memo
Reports	Contemporary Report Elegant Report Professional Report

Notice that the templates are also organized into three graphical approaches: contemporary, elegant, and professional. If you choose one of these styles and use it consistently for all your documents, you'll have created a consistent set of corporate graphic standards with little or no work.

Many of these templates, such as the Fax cover sheets and letter templates, already include text—just substitute your appropriate information. The boilerplate text Microsoft provides even gives you guidance on using the template—in some cases, several pages worth. For example, the Press Release template contains detailed information on how to organize a press release, and the Brochure template explains in detail how to substitute your own copy and make use of the Word features built into the template. Some representative templates are shown on the following pages (see figs. 8.6 through 8.19).

Figure 8.6

Brochure.

To print (and preserve) these brochure instructions, choose Print from the File menu. Press Enter to print the brochure.

HOW TO CREATE A BROCHURE

Using this template, you can create a professional brochure. Here's how:

1. **Insert your words** in place of these words, using and/or re-arranging the preset paragraph Styles.

2. **Print** pages 1 and 2 back-to-back onto sturdy, lettersize paper.

3. **Fold the paper** like a letter to create a three-fold brochure (positioning the panel with the large picture on the front).

WHAT ELSE SHOULD I KNOW?

To change the Style of any paragraph, select the text by positioning your cursor anywhere in the paragraph. With your cursor blinking in the paragraph, select a Style from the drop-down Style list at the top-left of your screen. Press Enter to accept your choice.

To change the picture, click on the picture and choose Picture from the Insert menu. Choose a new picture, and click Open.

&

Bits, Bytes & Chips
123 Main Street, Suite 100
Any City, State 12345-6789
Phone (123) 456-7890
Fax (123) 456-7890

BITS, BYTES & CHIPS
CUSTOMIZED TURNKEY
TRAINING COURSEWARE

Future Solutions Now

Figure 8.7

Directory.

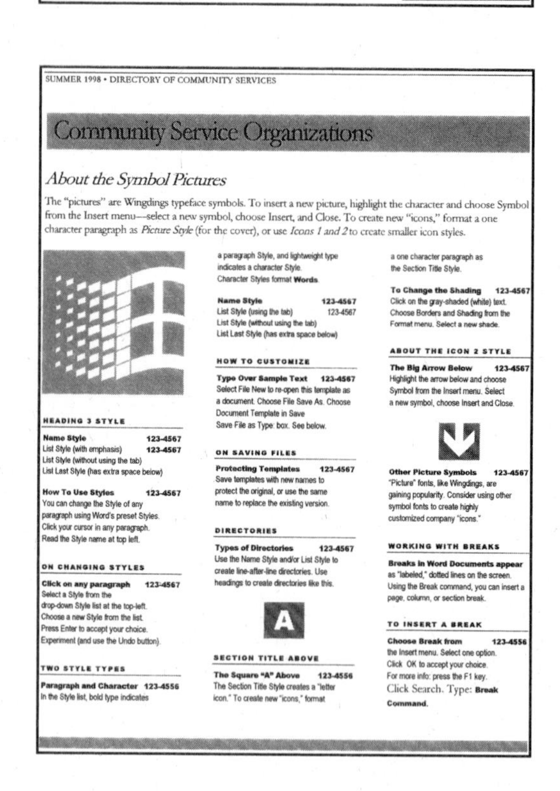

SUMMER 1998 • DIRECTORY OF COMMUNITY SERVICES

Community Service Organizations

About the Symbol Pictures

The "pictures" are Wingdings typeface symbols. To insert a new picture, highlight the character and choose Symbol from the Insert menu—select a new symbol, choose Insert, and Close. To create new "icons," format a one character paragraph as *Picture Style* (for the cover), or use *Icons 1 and 2* to create smaller icon styles.

HEADING 3 STYLE

Name Style **123-4567**
List Style (with emphasis) **123-4567**
List Style (without using the tab)
List Last Style (has extra space below)

How To Use Styles **123-4567**
You can change the Style of any paragraph using Word's preset Styles. Click your cursor in any paragraph. Read the Style name at top left.

ON CHANGING STYLES

Click on any paragraph **123-4567**
Select a Style from the drop-down Style list at the top-left. Choose a new Style from the list. Press Enter to accept your choice. Experiment (and use the Undo button).

TWO STYLE TYPES

Paragraph and Character **123-4556**
In the Style list, bold type indicates a paragraph Style, and lightweight type indicates a character Style. Character Styles format **Words**.

Name Style **123-4567**
List Style (using the tab) 123-4567
List Style (without using the tab)
List Last Style (has extra space below)

HOW TO CUSTOMIZE

Type Over Sample Text **123-4567**
Select File New to re-open this template as a document. Choose File Save As. Choose Document Template in Save Save File as Type: box. See below.

ON SAVING FILES

Protecting Templates **123-4567**
Save templates with new names to protect the original, or use the same name to replace the existing version.

DIRECTORIES

Types of Directories **123-4567**
Use the Name Style and/or List Style to create line-after-line directories. Use headings to create directories like this.

A

SECTION TITLE ABOVE

The Square "A" Above **123-4556**
The Section Title Style creates a "letter icon." To create new "icons," format a one character paragraph as the Section Title Style.

To Change the Shading **123-4567**
Click on the gray-shaded (white) text. Choose Borders and Shading from the Format menu. Select a new shade.

ABOUT THE ICON 2 STYLE

The Big Arrow Below **123-4567**
Highlight the arrow below and choose Symbol from the Insert menu. Select a new symbol, choose Insert and Close.

Other Picture Symbols **123-4567**
"Picture" fonts, like Wingdings, are gaining popularity. Consider using other symbol fonts to create highly customized company "icons."

WORKING WITH BREAKS

Breaks in Word Documents appear as "labeled," dotted lines on the screen. Using the Break command, you can insert a page, column, or section break.

TO INSERT A BREAK

Choose Break from **123-4556**
the Insert menu. Select one option. Click OK to accept your choice. For more info: press the F1 key. Click Search. Type: **Break Command.**

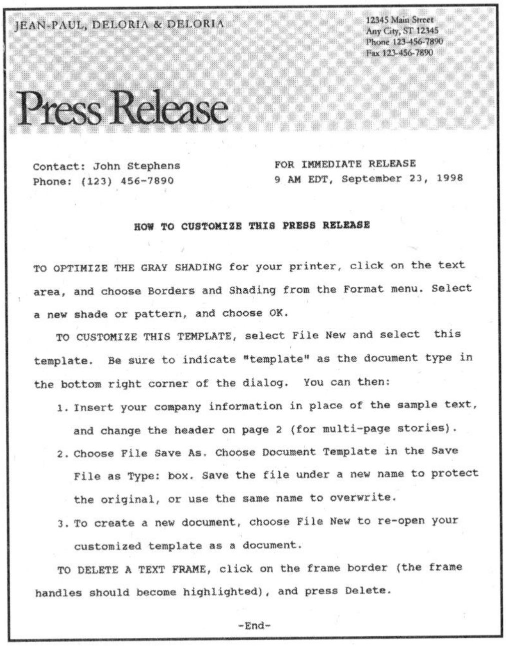

JEAN-PAUL, DELORIA & DELORIA

12345 Main Street
Any City, ST 12345
Phone 123-456-7890
Fax 123-456-7890

Press Release

Contact: John Stephens
Phone: (123) 456-7890

FOR IMMEDIATE RELEASE
9 AM EDT, September 23, 1998

HOW TO CUSTOMIZE THIS PRESS RELEASE

TO OPTIMIZE THE GRAY SHADING for your printer, click on the text area, and choose Borders and Shading from the Format menu. Select a new shade or pattern, and choose OK.

TO CUSTOMIZE THIS TEMPLATE, select File New and select this template. Be sure to indicate "template" as the document type in the bottom right corner of the dialog. You can then:

1. Insert your company information in place of the sample text, and change the header on page 2 (for multi-page stories).
2. Choose File Save As. Choose Document Template in the Save File as Type: box. Save the file under a new name to protect the original, or use the same name to overwrite.
3. To create a new document, choose File New to re-open your customized template as a document.

TO DELETE A TEXT FRAME, click on the frame border (the frame handles should become highlighted), and press Delete.

-End-

Figure 8.8
Elegant Press Release.

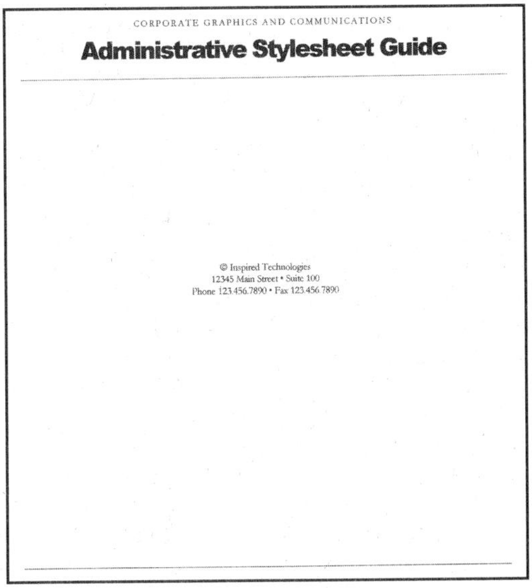

CORPORATE GRAPHICS AND COMMUNICATIONS

Administrative Stylesheet Guide

© Inspired Technologies
12345 Main Street • Suite 100
Phone 123.456.7890 • Fax 123.456.7890

Figure 8.9
Manual.

Figure 8.10

Newsletter.

Highlights

- Secrets To Creating a Professional Newsletter
- Newsletter Tips, Tricks, and Good Advice
- Complete Step-by-step Newsletter Instructions

Inside

1 How To Customize This Newsletter Template
2 How To Save Time in the Future
3 How To Improve Your Newsletter Print Quality

The **Gazette**

The Newsletter of Inspired Technologies
Volume 1 • Issue 7
September 1998

Home delivery service unites with retailers

Offers added value and convenience without increasing cost of goods; sales explode

To re-size a picture, click on it and drag a corner handle. To "re-shape" a picture, drag one of the middle handles. To crop a picture, hold the Shift key down and drag any handle.

How do we customize this design for our own use? I have a color printer and would like to print in color.

To change the shading of text borders, or to remove a ruling line, click your cursor on the paragraph, and, from the Format menu, choose Borders and Shading. Select a new option.

To change the color of text, select the paragraph, and choose Font from the Format menu. Choose a different color from the drop-down color list. Choose OK or Cancel to exit the dialog box.

Section breaks make it possible for various sections to have more than one column. To change the number of columns in any section, click your cursor in the section to be changed, and choose Format Column. Type a new number.

With the Break command, you can insert a page break, column, or section break. Assuming your nonprinting characters are turned on (in Tools-Options-View dialog box), you can identify breaks by the double, dotted lines. To insert a break, choose Break from the Insert menu. Select an option, and click OK to exit the dialog box.

To change/insert a picture, click on the picture, and choose Picture from the Insert menu. Choose a new picture, and click the Link to File box if you would like to save the art with the newsletter.

To change a picture color, double-click on the graphic to activate the drawing layer—where you can group or ungroup picture objects, and re-color or delete objects. Click on an object, and choose Drawing Object from the Format menu. Choose a new shade, and choose Close. To delete an object, press Delete.

Creating Newsletters

When you re-save the template with your changes, future document creation becomes easier. Select File New to re-open your template as a document.

1 With the template open, type your company text over the sample text.

2 Choose File Save As. In the menu, choose Document Template in the Save File as Type: box. (The extension should change from .doc to .dot.) Save the file under a new name to protect the original, or use the same name to replace the existing version.

To create a newsletter from your newly saved template, select File New to re-open your template as a document.

Your company information should now appear in place.

Style Names

There are three ways to view the preset Style names for this newsletter.

- In Normal view, choose Options from the Format menu. Click the View tab. In the Style Area Width box, type a number such as "6" (picas); or
- In Page Layout view, click on any paragraph and view the style name on the Formatting toolbar; or
- From the Format menu, choose Style Gallery. In the preview section, click on Example or Style Samples.

To change the picture background, double-click on the picture to activate the drawing. You'll see a blinking cursor and a paragraph mark. Experiment with that paragraph —alter Format Borders and Shading, and alter the spacing in Format Paragraph.

Figure 8.11

Thesis.

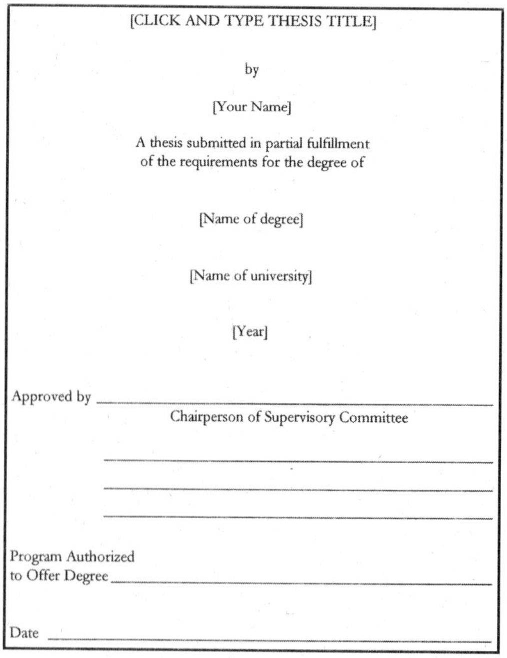

[CLICK AND TYPE THESIS TITLE]

by

[Your Name]

A thesis submitted in partial fulfillment
of the requirements for the degree of

[Name of degree]

[Name of university]

[Year]

Approved by ______________________________
Chairperson of Supervisory Committee

____
____
____

Program Authorized
to Offer Degree ______________________________

Date ______________________________

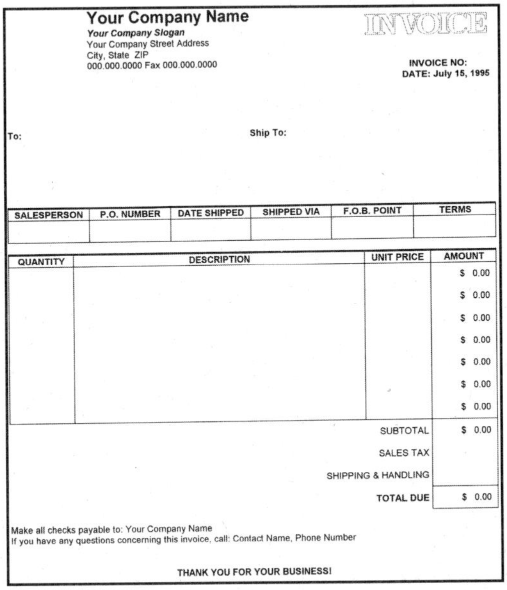

Your Company Name
Your Company Slogan
Your Company Street Address
City, State ZIP
000.000.0000 Fax 000.000.0000

INVOICE

INVOICE NO:
DATE: July 15, 1995

To: Ship To:

SALESPERSON	P.O. NUMBER	DATE SHIPPED	SHIPPED VIA	F.O.B. POINT	TERMS

QUANTITY	DESCRIPTION	UNIT PRICE	AMOUNT
			$ 0.00
			$ 0.00
			$ 0.00
			$ 0.00
			$ 0.00
			$ 0.00
			$ 0.00
		SUBTOTAL	$ 0.00
		SALES TAX	
		SHIPPING & HANDLING	
		TOTAL DUE	$ 0.00

Make all checks payable to: Your Company Name
If you have any questions concerning this invoice, call: Contact Name, Phone Number

THANK YOU FOR YOUR BUSINESS!

Figure 8.12

Invoice.

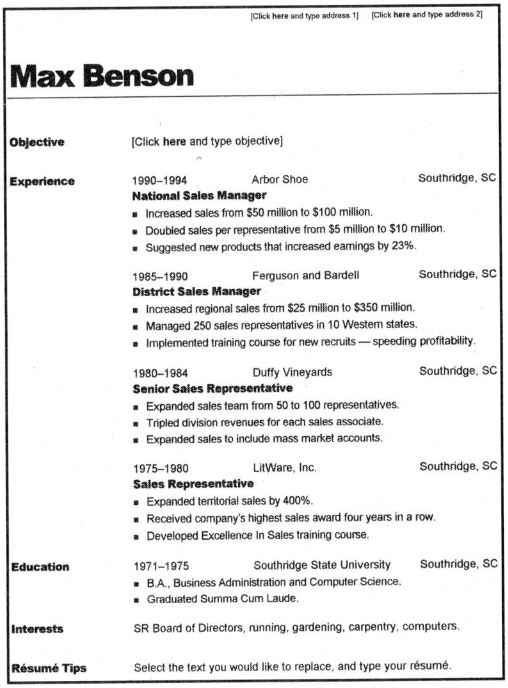

[Click here and type address 1] [Click here and type address 2]

Max Benson

Objective [Click here and type objective]

Experience

1990–1994 Arbor Shoe Southridge, SC
National Sales Manager
- Increased sales from $50 million to $100 million.
- Doubled sales per representative from $5 million to $10 million.
- Suggested new products that increased earnings by 23%.

1985–1990 Ferguson and Bardell Southridge, SC
District Sales Manager
- Increased regional sales from $25 million to $350 million.
- Managed 250 sales representatives in 10 Western states.
- Implemented training course for new recruits — speeding profitability.

1980–1984 Duffy Vineyards Southridge, SC
Senior Sales Representative
- Expanded sales team from 50 to 100 representatives.
- Tripled division revenues for each sales associate.
- Expanded sales to include mass market accounts.

1975–1980 LitWare, Inc. Southridge, SC
Sales Representative
- Expanded territorial sales by 400%.
- Received company's highest sales award four years in a row.
- Developed Excellence In Sales training course.

Education

1971–1975 Southridge State University Southridge, SC
- B.A., Business Administration and Computer Science.
- Graduated Summa Cum Laude.

Interests SR Board of Directors, running, gardening, carpentry, computers.

Résumé Tips Select the text you would like to replace, and type your résumé.

Figure 8.13

Professional Resume.

Figure 8.14

Purchase Order.

Your Company Name
Your Company Slogan
Your Company Street Address
City, State ZIP
000.000.0000 Fax 000.000.0000

PURCHASE ORDER

The following number must appear on all related correspondence, shipping papers, and invoices:
P.O. NUMBER:

To: **Ship To:**

P.O. DATE	REQUISITIONER	SHIP VIA	F.O.B. POINT	TERMS

QTY	UNIT	DESCRIPTION	UNIT PRICE	TOTAL
				$ 0.00
				$ 0.00
				$ 0.00
				$ 0.00
				$ 0.00
				$ 0.00
				$ 0.00
			SUBTOTAL	$ 0.00
			SALES TAX	
			SHIPPING & HANDLING	
			OTHER	
			TOTAL	$ 0.00

1. Please send two copies of your invoice.
2. Enter this order in accordance with the prices, terms, delivery method, and specifications listed above.
3. Please notify us immediately if you are unable to ship as specified.
4. Send all correspondence to:
   Name
   Company Name
   Address
   000.000.0000, ext. ; Fax 000.000.0000

Authorized by Date

Figure 8.15

Weekly Timesheet.

Your Company Name
Your Company Slogan
Your Company Street Address
City, State ZIP
000.000.0000 Fax 000.000.0000

WEEKLY TIME SHEET

Employee Name: Title:
Employee Number: Status: Full-time
Department: Supervisor:

Date	Start Time	End Time	Regular Hrs.	Overtime Hrs.	Total Hrs.
					0
					0
					0
					0
					0
					0
					0
		WEEKLY TOTALS	0	0	0

Employee Signature: Date:
Supervisor Signature: Date:

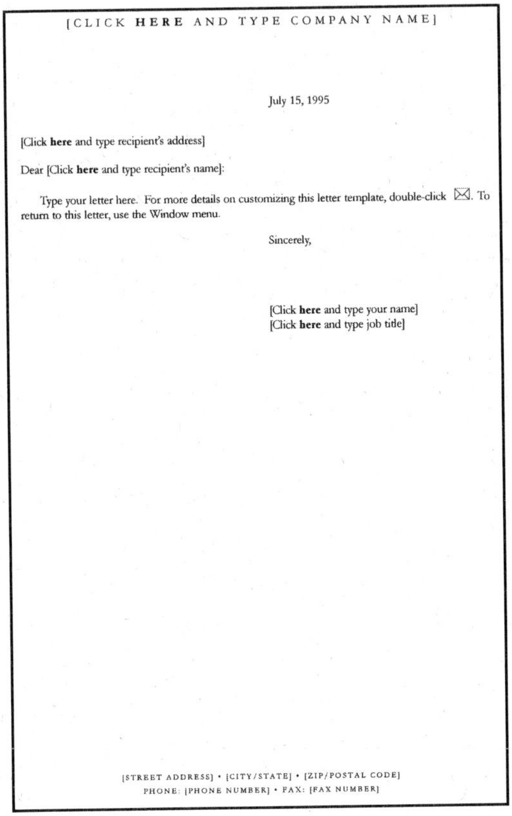

[CLICK **HERE** AND TYPE COMPANY NAME]

July 15, 1995

[Click **here** and type recipient's address]

Dear [Click **here** and type recipient's name]:

Type your letter here. For more details on customizing this letter template, double-click ✉. To return to this letter, use the Window menu.

Sincerely,

[Click **here** and type your name]
[Click **here** and type job title]

[STREET ADDRESS] • [CITY/STATE] • [ZIP/POSTAL CODE]
PHONE: [PHONE NUMBER] • FAX: [FAX NUMBER]

Figure 8.16

Elegant Letter.

Figure 8.17
Professional Fax.

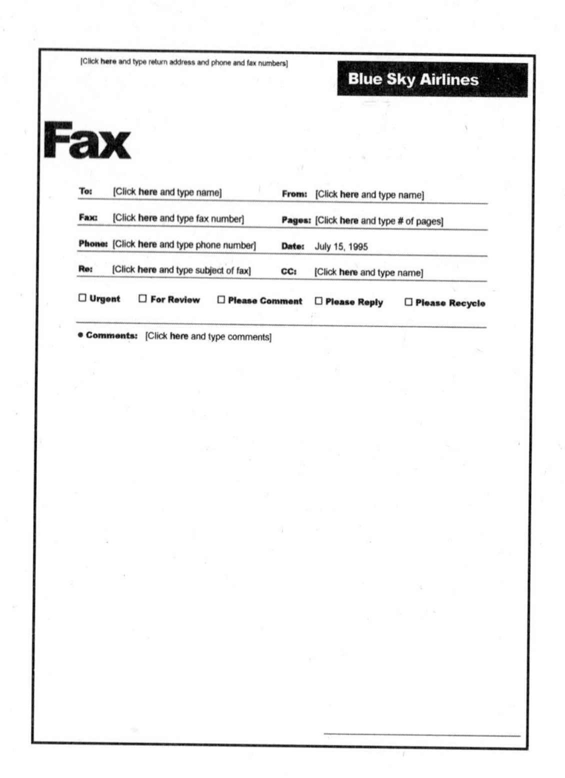

[Click here and type return address and phone and fax numbers]

Blue Sky Airlines

Fax

To:	[Click here and type name]	**From:**	[Click here and type name]
Fax:	[Click here and type fax number]	**Pages:**	[Click here and type # of pages]
Phone:	[Click here and type phone number]	**Date:**	July 15, 1995
Re:	[Click here and type subject of fax]	**CC:**	[Click here and type name]

☐ **Urgent** ☐ **For Review** ☐ **Please Comment** ☐ **Please Reply** ☐ **Please Recycle**

• **Comments:** [Click here and type comments]

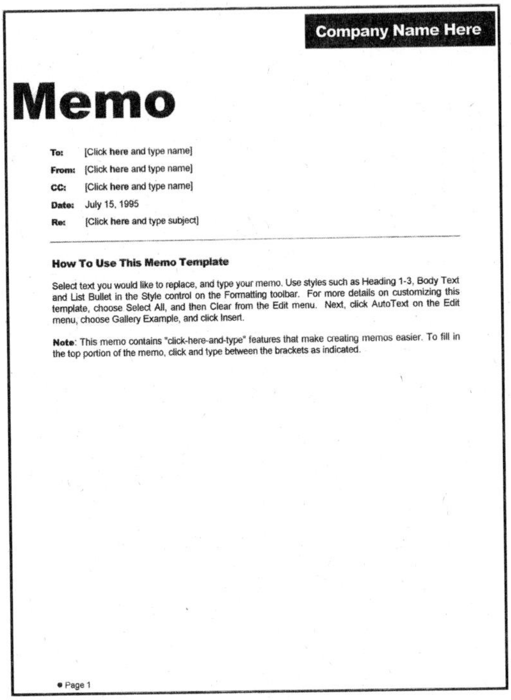

Company Name Here

Memo

To: [Click here and type name]

From: [Click here and type name]

CC: [Click here and type name]

Date: July 15, 1995

Re: [Click here and type subject]

How To Use This Memo Template

Select text you would like to replace, and type your memo. Use styles such as Heading 1-3, Body Text and List Bullet in the Style control on the Formatting toolbar. For more details on customizing this template, choose Select All, and then Clear from the Edit menu. Next, click AutoText on the Edit menu, choose Gallery Example, and click Insert.

Note: This memo contains "click-here-and-type" features that make creating memos easier. To fill in the top portion of the memo, click and type between the brackets as indicated.

• Page 1

Figure 8.18

Professional Memo.

Blue Sky Airlines

Proposal and Marketing Plan

Blue Sky's Best Opportunity
For East Region Expansion

Figure 8.19

Professional Report.

Using Wizards, Word's New Shortcut

Word's *wizards* are built-in programs that ask you questions about how you'd like your document constructed, and then build a document based on your answers.

Depending on the wizard, when you're done you may have a finished document, or just a well-designed framework into which you can add your specific text.

In choosing the ten Word wizards (see table 8.3), Microsoft has focused on the more complex documents you're likely to encounter rather than the more common ones, which are well covered with templates.

Table 8.3
Word's Built-In Wizards

Wizard	Function
Agenda Wizard	Creates a meeting agenda
Award Wizard	Creates customized awards
Calendar Wizard	Creates weekly, monthly, and yearly calendars
Fax Wizard	Creates a fax cover sheet
Letter Wizard	Designs a letter, or enables you to choose from a library of 15 prewritten letters
Memo Wizard	Designs a customized memo
Pleading Wizard	Creates legal pleading papers
Newsletter Wizard	Designs a customized newsletter
Resume Wizard	Creates four kinds of resumes: entry-level, chronological, functional, and professional
Table Wizard	Creates various kinds of tables

Browsing Word's Wizards Library

To open a wizard, choose New from the File menu, choose the category of document you want by clicking on its tab, and select the wizard icon from the box displaying all templates and wizards in that category. Then wait a few moments as Word prepares the wizard for use. (Unfortunately, wizards are among Word's slower features, especially if you have limited memory installed in your computer. You may find Word doing extensive disk swapping to load the wizard into memory and prepare it for use.)

If you need to create a new kind of document once, and you can adapt it on your own later, run the appropriate wizard. Add only the information that appears in all your documents.

When Word displays the document, make any text or formatting changes you need. Then save the document as a template so that you can load it without running the wizard again.

You might even want to go one step farther, and turn the document into a form that can be edited only in the spaces you mark. You learn how to do this in Chapter 23, "Word as a Forms Program."

(In a few cases, such as the Award Wizard, Word wizards place your text within frames. You can't insert a form field in a frame. To view and edit this text, either in the finished document or in a template you create from it, you need to work in Page Layout view or Print Preview.)

To show you how wizards work, the next section walks you through the Agenda Wizard in detail, displaying each screen and pointing out elements common to all wizards.

Agenda Wizard

Agenda is a particularly useful wizard because it requests answers to the questions you really should ask before you call a meeting. *What is to be covered? Who's responsible? Who should be there? How long should each item take to cover?*

In other words, the Agenda Wizard may have the surprising side-effect of making your meetings, not just your word processing, more productive.

To create a document with the Agenda Wizard, follow these steps:

1. Choose New from the File menu. The New dialog box opens.
2. Click the Other Documents tab.
3. Choose Agenda Wizard from the list that appears. Double-click or click on OK to start the Wizard.
4. The first Agenda Wizard screen opens, as shown in figure 8.20. Choose a style for your agenda: Boxes, Modern, or Standard.

   To move forward at any point in a wizard, click on Next. To move back, click on Back. To generate a document without answering any more questions, click on Finish. (If you don't pass through all the wizard's screens, the document may be incomplete.)

   To leave the wizard without creating a document, click on Cancel.

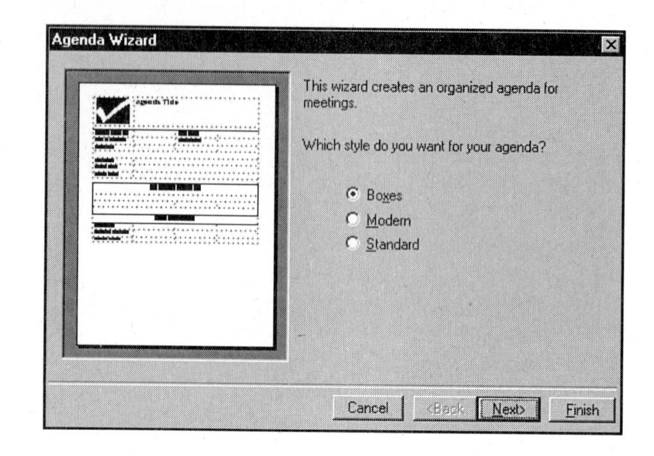

Figure 8.20
The opening Agenda Wizard screen—choose a style.

5. When you click on **N**ext, the date and starting time window opens (see fig. 8.21). Enter the **D**ate and **S**tarting time of your meeting. Click on **N**ext.

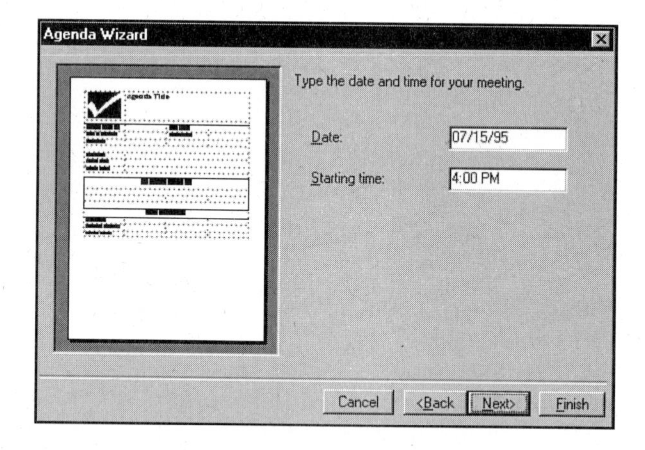

Figure 8.21
The Date and Time window.

6. Next, the meeting title and location window opens (see fig. 8.22). Type the title or main topic of your meeting, and the location of the meeting. Then click on **N**ext.

7. In the next window (see fig. 8.23), tell Word which headings you want on your agenda: **T**ype of meeting, Please **r**ead, **P**lease bring, and/or **S**pecial notes. Then click on **N**ext.

8. In the next window (see fig. 8.24), tell Word which categories of participants should be included on the agenda: **M**eeting called by, Fa**c**ilitator, Note **t**aker, Time**k**eeper, **A**ttendees, **O**bservers, **R**esource persons. You'll add the actual names later, after Word finishes building the document. Now click on **N**ext.

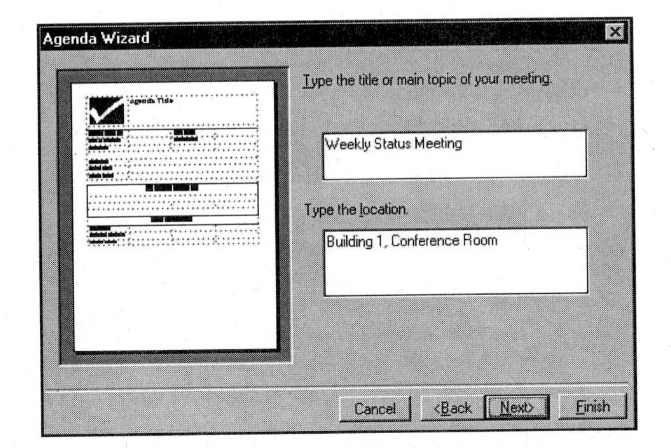

Figure 8.22

The meeting title and location window.

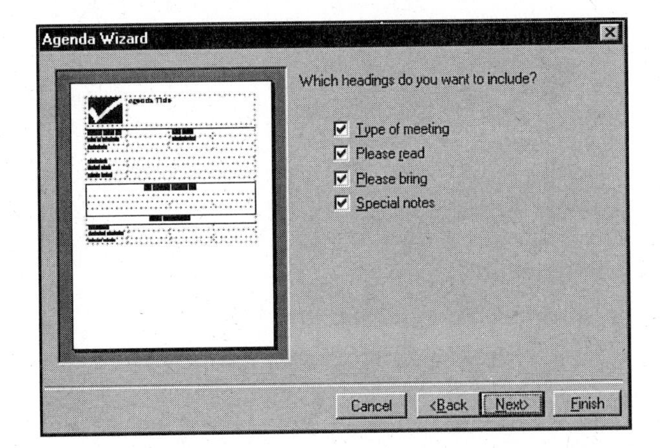

Figure 8.23

Choosing meeting headings.

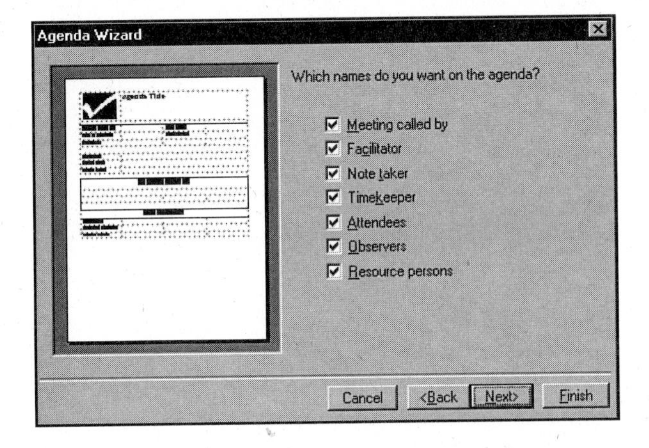

Figure 8.24

Choosing meeting participants.

9. In the next window (see fig. 8.25), list the **A**genda topics, **P**erson responsible, and **M**inutes allocated. If you have even more topics, click on M**o**re Agenda Topics, and another, similar window opens. When you finish building the list, click on **N**ext.

Figure 8.25

Setting agenda topics, times, and responsibilities.

Agenda Wizard

Agenda topic: Person responsible: Minutes allocated:

1 Meeting Overview 10
2
3
4
5

TIP Press the TAB key to move from one box to the next.
Or, click in the box you want. You can rearrange the topics in a moment.

More Agenda Topics
Previous Agenda Topics

Cancel <Back Next> Finish

10. In the next window (see fig. 8.26), rearrange the order of the agenda, if necessary. With an agenda topic highlighted, the Move **U**p and Move **D**own buttons move the topic higher and lower, respectively, in the topic order. When the agenda topics are positioned properly, click on **N**ext.

Figure 8.26

Rearranging the agenda's order.

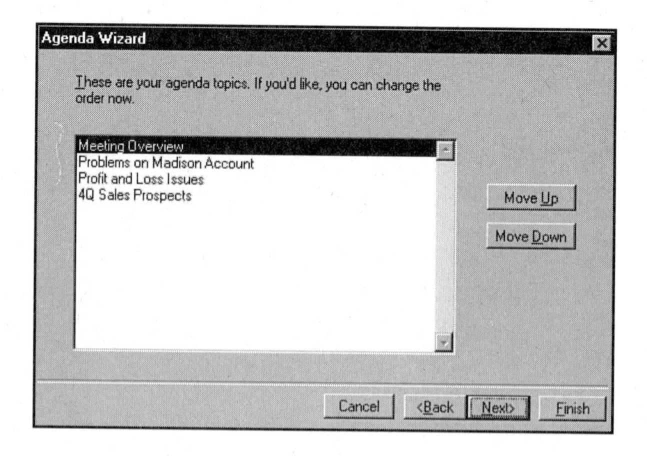

11. In the next window (see fig. 8.27), tell Word whether you want a separate agenda sheet designed for taking minutes at the meeting. If you choose Yes, the Agenda Wizard leaves space below each topic for taking notes during the meeting. Then click on Next.

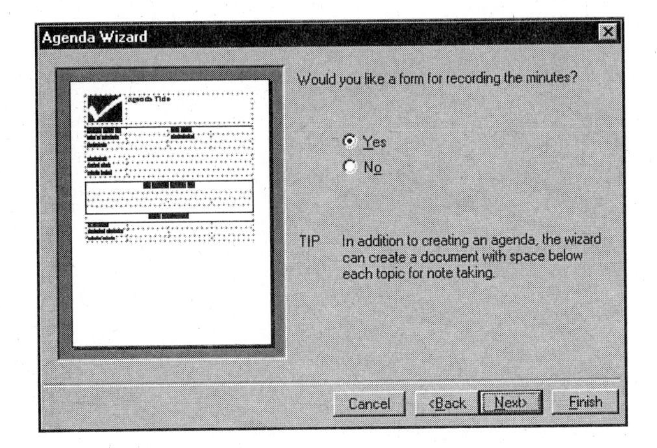

Figure 8.27

Choosing an optional form for taking minutes.

12. You're at the last screen (see fig. 8.28). Think through the answers to your questions; if you need to go back and change anything, now is the time. Then tell Word to Finish preparing your agenda.

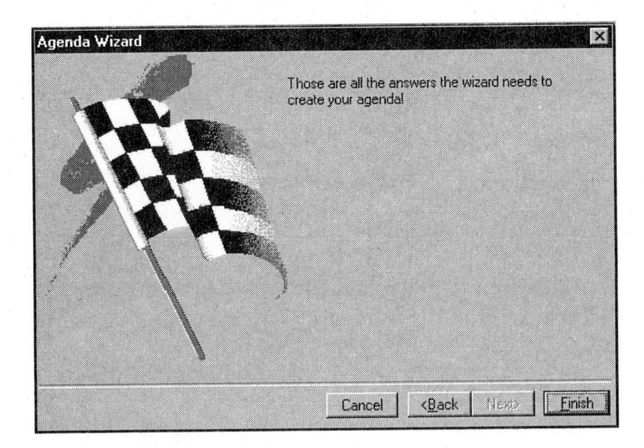

Figure 8.28

The last screen of the Agenda Wizard.

Figure 8.29 shows a sample agenda created in Boxes style.

Figure 8.29

Sample box-style agenda.

Weekly Status Meeting

07/15/95
4:00 PM to 4:40 PM
Building 1, Conference Room

Meeting called by: Note taker:
Type of meeting: Timekeeper:
Facilitator:

Attendees:
Please read:
Please bring:

----- Agenda Topics -----

1. Meeting Overview	4:00-4:10 PM
2. Problems on Madison Account	4:10-4:20 PM
3. Profit and Loss Issues	4:20-4:30 PM
4. 4Q Sales Prospects	4:30-4:40 PM

Other information

Observers:
Resource persons:
Special notes:

Award Wizard

Now that you have seen one wizard in detail, this section quickly steps you through several of the other Word wizards, displaying an example of how each might look when finished.

After you choose the Award Wizard, follow these steps:

1. Tell Word which style of award you want: Formal, Modern, Decorative, or Jazzy.
2. Tell Word whether to print the award vertically (Portrait) or horizontally (Landscape), and whether your paper has a preprinted border.
3. Type the recipient's name and the award's title.
4. Enter the name of the person or persons who will sign the award. (Word uses the name stored in the Tools, Options, User Info tab unless you tell it otherwise.)
5. Tell Word whether to include the name of a sponsoring organization.
6. Type the date of the award and any special text about why it's being given.
7. Tell Word to finish preparing the award.

The results appear similar to those shown in figure 8.30.

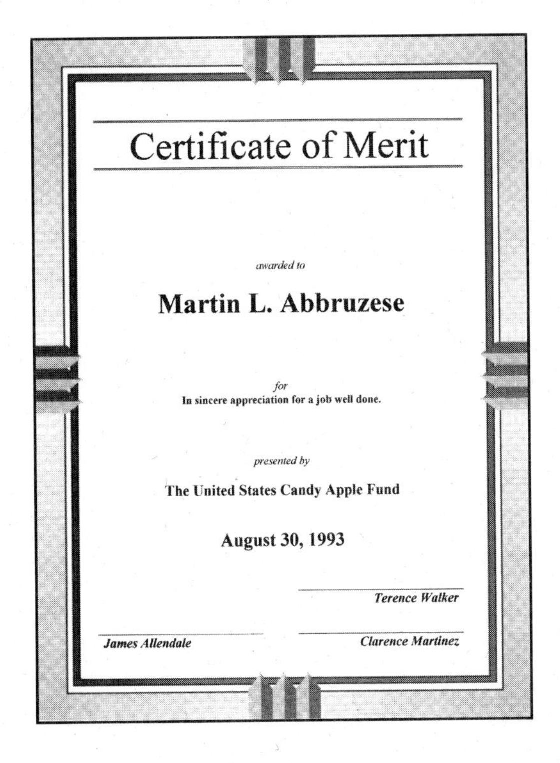

Figure 8.30

The Award Wizard: Typical finished product, portrait orientation, formal style.

Fax Wizard

After you choose the Fax Wizard, follow these steps:

1. Tell Word whether to prepare a vertical or horizontal cover sheet.
2. Tell Word whether you prefer a Contemporary, Modern, or Jazzy design. (Apparently, there's no such thing as a "Classic" Fax cover sheet.)
3. Type your name, your company's name, and address. (Word defaults to the information found in Tools, Options, User Info.)
4. Type your Phone and Fax numbers.
5. Tell Word to finish preparing the Fax cover sheet.

Letter Wizard

After you choose the Letter Wizard, follow these steps:

1. Choose whether to create a letter from scratch or use one of Word's prewritten letters.

2. If you ask for a prewritten letter, choose from the following list of letters, and then go to step 4:

    - Press release: new product
    - Collection letter: 30 days past due
    - Returned check: polite request for payment
    - Credit report: request
    - Complaint under investigation
    - Apology: delayed delivery
    - Announcement: price increase
    - Thank you: for suggestion
    - Resume cover letter
    - Thank you: for applying
    - Thank you: for inquiry (information enclosed)
    - Direct mail offer: product upgrade
    - Letter to Mom
    - Landlord: lease expiring; rent increase
    - Return for credit

3. Choose which elements of a letter to include. For a personal letter, your choices are **P**age numbers and **D**ate; for a business letter, you also can choose Account or document **I**D, **W**riter's initials, **T**ypist's initials, **C**C, **E**nclosures, and **A**ttachments.
4. Choose whether to print the letter on **L**etterhead stationery or **P**lain paper.
5. If you use letterhead, tell Word where the letterhead design appears, and how large it is.
6. Type the recipient's name and address, and edit your return address.
7. Choose a style: **C**lassic, C**o**ntemporary, or **T**ypewriter.
8. Tell Word if you also want an envelope or mailing label. (If so, the appropriate dialog box opens; click on **A**dd to Document to include the envelope or label.)

9. Tell Word to display the letter.

The results appear similar to those shown in figure 8.31.

July 15, 1995

Danny Jones
Unit 42
Stone Landing Condominiums
Arlington, VA 25566

Dear Mom,

How are you doing? Everything is fine with me!

I'm sorry that I haven't written for a while, but I've been really busy! As you know, I really like computers, and I'm spending long hours in front of a screen both at work and at home.

In fact, I just bought a great program. It's really neat — a collection of business letters that I can customize any way I want. For example, there's a letter to people who are late paying their bills and another one that complains about a defective product.

I'm sure it'll save me a lot of time and energy you know how hard it is for me to write letters! Now I'll be able to think about business instead of worrying about what to say in letters.

Too bad they don't have one for writing to you! Ha ha ha. They should also have one for thanking Aunt Patty for the cookies! Nah — form letters could never replace the personal touch!

Gotta run now, Mom! All my love!

Figure 8.31

The Letter Wizard: prewritten letter.

More about Word's Prewritten Letters

As you may expect, Word's prewritten letters themselves are fairly brief and general. You need to replace some words and phrases to make the letter appropriate for your situation. These words and phrases are underlined. You also need to replace the addressee and signature information.

Word's prewritten letters are ideal for the strategy outlined in the preceding tip. Run the wizard once. Edit and format the resulting letter the way you want it, and save it as a new template. You get the advantages of Microsoft's "professionally written" prose, plus your own customization.

Memo Wizard

After you choose the Memo Wizard, follow these steps:

1. Choose whether to use your own preformatted memo forms or enable Word to generate headings of its own.
2. If you're printing the memo onto your own form, tell Word where your preprinted information is located, so that it can move your memo text out of the way.
3. If you use Word's heading formatting instead, type your memo's heading underneath the Yes, using this text box.
4. Tell Word if you want a separate page for your distribution list.

5. Tell Word which items to include in the memo: a Date, To, CC, From, Subject, Priority, and/or A Separator Line. Word assumes today's date; you can change that. Word assumes the memo is from the person listed in Tools, Options, User Info; you can change that, too.

6. Tell Word what information to include at the bottom of the memo: Writer's initials, Typist's initials, Enclosures, and Attachments. (You also can specify the initials to be used or the number of enclosures.)

7. Tell Word which items to place in headers on pages after Page 1: the Topic, Date, or Page Number.

8. Tell Word what to put in the footer on all pages: Confidential, Date, and/or Page Number.

9. Choose a style: Classic, Contemporary, or Typewriter.

10. Tell Word to finish preparing your memo.

The results are similar to those shown in figure 8.32.

Figure 8.32
The Memo Wizard: Contemporary style.

Memorandum

To: [Click here and type name]
CC: [Click here and type name]
From: [Click here and type name]
Date: July 21, 1995
Re: [Click here and type subject]

How To Use This Memo Template
Select text you would like to replace, and type your memo. Use styles such as Heading 1-3, Body Text and List Bullet in the Style control on the Formatting toolbar.

To delete the background elements—such as the circle, rectangles, or return address frames, click on the frame boundary border to highlight the frame "handles," and press Delete. For more details on customizing this template, choose Select All, and then Clear from the Edit menu. Next, click AutoText on the Edit menu, choose Gallery Example, and click Insert.

CONFIDENTIAL 1

Newsletter Wizard

Building a multiple column newsletter with spaces for headlines, tables of contents, and images is one of the more complex tasks you're likely to ask Word to perform. Word 95 contains a Newsletter Wizard that helps you manage the process. After you run the wizard, your format will be essentially in place; you will, however, have to insert your own copy and images, and most likely make some adjustments in layout as well. Notice that the boilerplate copy the Newsletter Wizard includes in your document contains tips and recommendations about how to use the newsletter document itself.

1. Choose between a classic or modern newsletter style (see fig. 8.33).

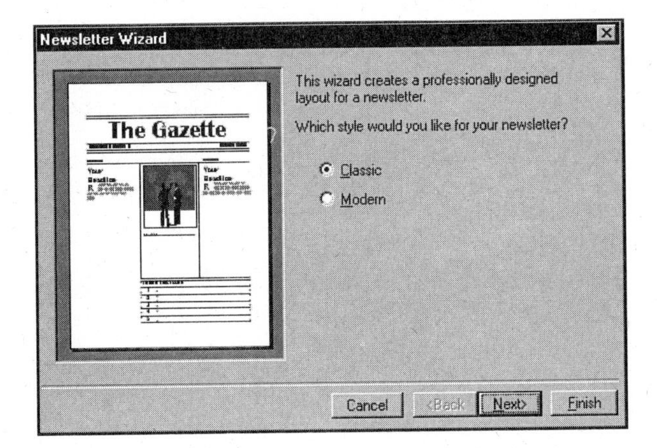

Figure 8.33

The Newsletter Wizard opening screen.

2. Specify the number of columns for your newsletter.
3. Type the newsletter's name.
4. Tell Word whether you want to print or copy the newsletter on both sides of the page.
5. Tell Word how many pages your newsletter will be.
6. Tell Word whether to include Table of Contents, Fancy First Letters, Date, and/or Volume and Issue Numbers.
7. Tell Word to finish preparing your newsletter.

Pleading Wizard

Legal pleadings used by lawyers require special formats that are not common elsewhere, and can vary among jurisdictions. Word's Pleading Wizard helps legal offices build legal pleadings easily by answering a few simple questions.

1. Set font, line spacing, and margins based on your court's guidelines (see fig. 8.34). Then click on Next.

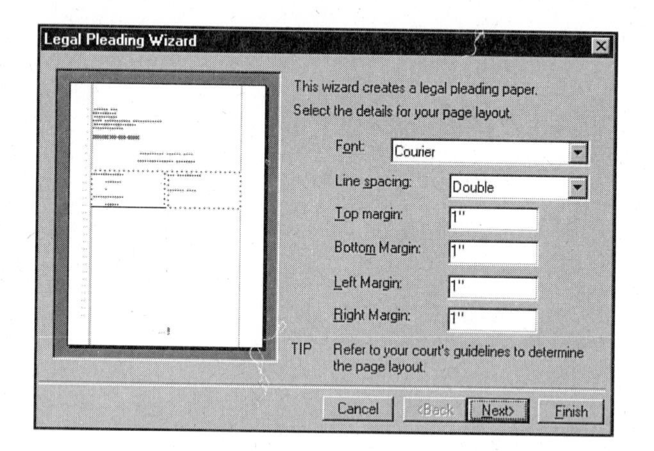

Figure 8.34

The Legal Pleading Wizard opening screen.

2. Specify whether you want a line on the left side of your page and whether you want line numbers.
3. Specify whether you want a line on the right side of the page.
4. Specify whether you want page numbers, and if so, how they should look and where they will appear.
5. Type the attorney's name, address, and phone numbers; type the client's name.
6. Specify where the attorney's address will appear.
7. Type the name of the court and specify where it will appear.
8. Tell Word to finish preparing your legal pleading paper.

Microsoft offers a special Legal Resources Kit with additional information and support for legal offices that use Word.

Resume Wizard

After you choose the Resume Wizard, follow these steps:

1. Choose a style of resume: Entry-level, Chronological, Functional, or Professional.
2. Type your name and mailing address. (Word defaults to the name and address included in Tools, Options, User Info.)
3. Clear any headings that you don't want to appear in your resume.
4. Include any optional headings you may want to include—either those Word offers, or new ones you invent.
5. Rearrange your list of headings, if necessary.
6. Choose a design style: Classic, Contemporary, or Elegant.
7. Tell Word if you also want to write a cover letter.
8. Tell Word to finish preparing your resume.

The results are similar to those shown in figure 8.35.

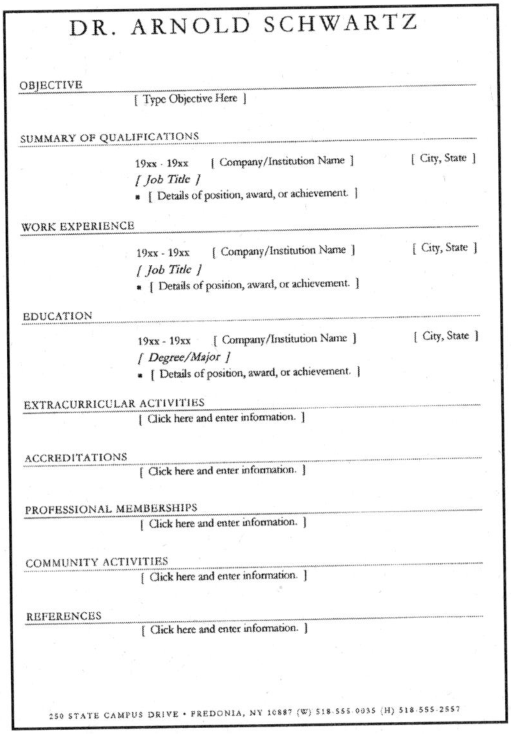

DR. ARNOLD SCHWARTZ

OBJECTIVE
[Type Objective Here]

SUMMARY OF QUALIFICATIONS
19xx - 19xx [Company/Institution Name] [City, State]
[Job Title]
▪ [Details of position, award, or achievement.]

WORK EXPERIENCE
19xx - 19xx [Company/Institution Name] [City, State]
[Job Title]
▪ [Details of position, award, or achievement.]

EDUCATION
19xx - 19xx [Company/Institution Name] [City, State]
[Degree/Major]
▪ [Details of position, award, or achievement.]

EXTRACURRICULAR ACTIVITIES
[Click here and enter information.]

ACCREDITATIONS
[Click here and enter information.]

PROFESSIONAL MEMBERSHIPS
[Click here and enter information.]

COMMUNITY ACTIVITIES
[Click here and enter information.]

REFERENCES
[Click here and enter information.]

250 STATE CAMPUS DRIVE • FREDONIA, NY 10887 (W) 518-555-0035 (H) 518-555-2557

Figure 8.35

The Resume Wizard: Elegant style.

Table Wizard

Unlike the wizards already described, you can use the Table Wizard from within an existing document, as well as to create a new document.

After you choose the Table Wizard, you can choose from six preformatted table styles, as shown in figure 8.36. With Style 1, you can automatically include a consecutive series of column headers, such as numbers or dates.

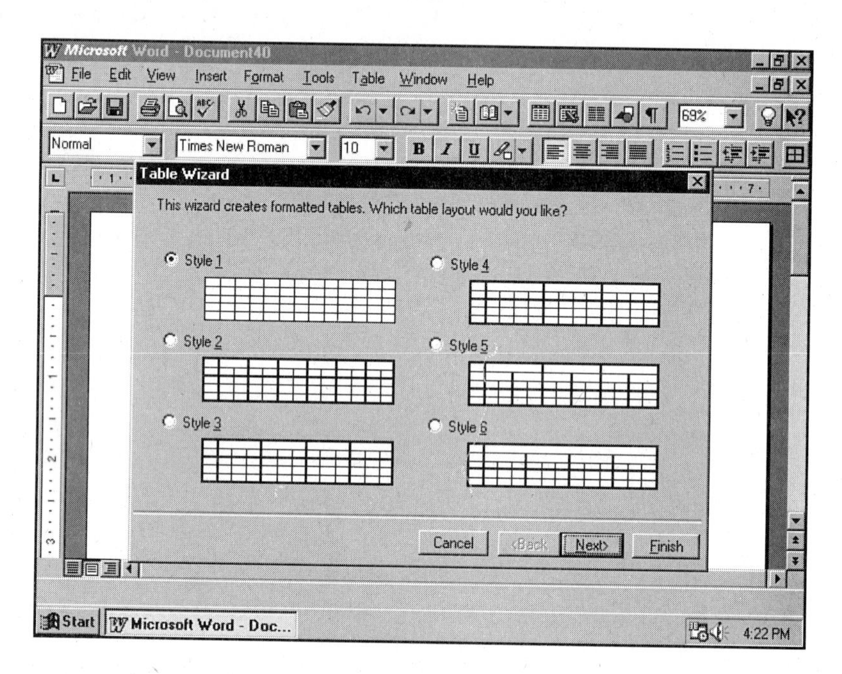

Figure 8.36 *The Table Wizard layouts.*

If you choose Style 1, follow the Style 1 procedure. If you choose another style, follow the Style 2 through 6 procedure.

Table Wizard Style 1 Procedure

To create a table using Style 1, follow this procedure:

1. If you choose Style 1, tell Word whether you want column headings, and how many columns. If you want column headings, choose a type of heading: **M**onths, **Q**uarters, **D**ays, **N**umbers you specify, or **Y**ears you specify.

2. Tell Word whether to repeat that heading on every page, and how the headings should be aligned.

3. Tell Word whether you want row headings, what kind, and how they should be aligned.

4. Tell Word what kind of text you expect to place in most of your columns: **R**ight-aligned numbers, **D**ecimal-aligned numbers, **L**eft-aligned text, or **C**entered text.

Use decimal-aligned numbers for dollars-and-cents information.

5. Tell Word whether the table is to be vertical (**P**ortrait) or horizontal (**L**andscape). If you use an orientation different from the rest of your document, the table starts on its own page.

6. Tell Word whether you want Help displayed as you work.

7. Tell Word to prepare your table.

8. Choose an AutoFormat table design from the Table Autoformat dialog box, and click on OK.

Table Wizard Style 2 through 6 Procedure

To create a table using any of Styles 2 through 6, follow this procedure:

1. Tell Word how many columns you need.

2. Tell Word whether you want to repeat headings on each page, and how your headings should be aligned: **L**eft, **C**enter, or **R**ight.

3. Choose a row heading and alignment.

4. Tell Word what kind of text you expect to place in most of your columns: **R**ight-aligned numbers, **D**ecimal-aligned numbers, **L**eft-aligned text, or **C**entered text.

5. Tell Word whether the table is to be vertical (**P**ortrait) or horizontal (**L**andscape).

6. Tell Word to prepare your table.

7. Choose an AutoFormat table design from the Table Autoformat dialog box, and click on OK.

AutoText, AutoCorrect, and the Spike

Nothing is more mind-numbing and error-prone than typing the same boilerplate text over and over. With Word for Windows 95's tools for reusing text and graphics, you never have to do this again. With just a few keystrokes, you can insert anything you want—text, graphics, field codes, macros—into a document. The insertions can be of any length, provided that you have the disk space and memory.

Best of all, these Word 95 features are exceptionally easy to use. None of the complexities that occasionally creep into document templates or wizards are present. You mark the text or graphic, define it, and use it; that's almost all there is to it. The challenge is to use the new tools to their maximum advantage—determining when it makes sense to use them, and how.

In this chapter:

- Understanding AutoText and AutoCorrect
- Creating AutoText entries

- Using previously defined AutoText entries
- Renaming an AutoText entry
- Deleting an AutoText entry
- Understanding the Spike
- Using AutoText entries with templates
- Creating AutoCorrect entries

Understanding AutoText, AutoCorrect, and the Spike

The new AutoText feature provides a quick and easy way to store text or graphics and, later, paste them into documents as needed.

AutoCorrect, on the other hand, watches as you type text into your document. When you misspell a word that AutoCorrect recognizes, Word automatically corrects the spelling. AutoCorrect enables you to build a library of frequently misspelled words, which reduces the amount of time you spend spell checking your documents.

The Spike complements Word's text storage and retrieval features. Acting much like a multilayered Windows Clipboard, the Spike enables you to set aside any number of different text items and paste them into your document with a single keystroke. You can empty the Spike as you paste the items into your document or preserve them to use again later.

The first and most frequently used of these features is AutoText. AutoText maintains a database of frequently used text or graphic objects that you can quickly and easily drop into your documents.

You can use AutoText to insert long company names, complex scientific terms, or graphics into your documents. For instance, using AutoText, you can replace "nrp" automatically with "New Riders Publishing."

Most people make the same typing errors over and over. For instance, I frequently type "wiht" when I mean "with." The new AutoCorrect feature can automatically correct common spelling errors for you—as you enter text into your document. AutoCorrect can also watch for common capitalization errors. For instance, you can

direct AutoCorrect to always capitalize the first letter of sentences or the names of days of the week.

Like AutoText, AutoCorrect is easy to use. You can add words to the AutoCorrect replacement list with or without formatting. AutoCorrect can handle as many spelling corrections as AutoText.

AutoText and AutoCorrect are stored in an open document template (usually NORMAL.DOT). The items you add to AutoText and AutoCorrect are permanently saved (unless you remove them) and are available whenever you use Word.

Creating AutoText Entries

To create an AutoText entry, prepare the material in your document. Key it in, add any special formatting, and insert any graphics or other special elements. If you add a phrase or a sentence, be sure to add a space after it—that way, you don't have to do it every time you use the AutoText entry.

Then follow these steps:

1. Select the material you want to save as an AutoText entry.
2. Click on the AutoText button on the toolbar or select AutoTe**x**t from the **E**dit menu. The AutoText dialog box opens, as shown in figure 9.1.
3. The bottom part of the AutoText dialog box contains the text you selected for the AutoText entry, whereas the **N**ame field at the top contains the name Word proposes for the entry. In figure 9.1, Word's suggestion is "New Riders," which is a bit long. Enter your own name for the AutoText entry (for instance, "nrp") or accept Word's suggestion.
4. The **M**ake AutoText Entry Available To box permits you to specify in which document template to store the AutoText entry. Choose the Normal template if you want the AutoText entry to be available to all documents, or a Custom template if you want the text available only to documents you create with a Custom template.
5. Click on the **A**dd button.

If you're storing new AutoText entries in the NORMAL.DOT template—or if you're working in the Normal template and haven't defined a document template—Word automatically places new AutoText entries there.

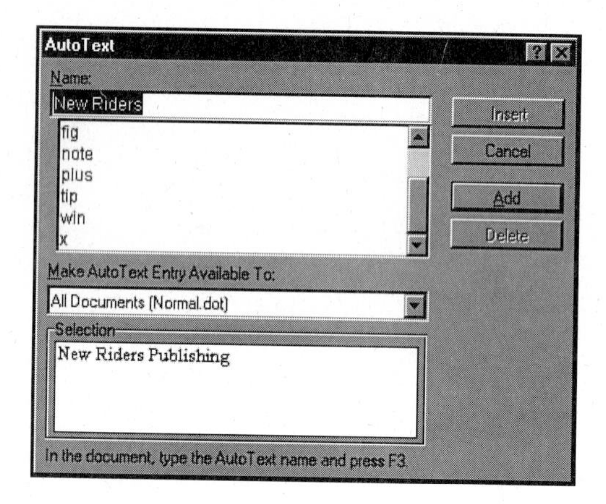

Figure 9.1
The AutoText dialog box.

Naming AutoText entries. In general, use names that are short enough to save you time, but not so short and generic that you can't remember them. (Well, maybe you can get away with a few really short ones, like the stock ticker symbol T, which every widow and orphan knows stands for American Telephone & Telegraph Corporation.)

The longer or more complex the text contained in the AutoText entry, the less you mind a few extra characters in its name.

One other tip: If you have several related AutoText entries, give them similar names.

Using Previously Defined AutoText Entries

The easiest way to use text or graphics saved as an AutoText entry is to type the name of the AutoText entry into the document (for instance, **nrp**) and then press F3. (AutoText isn't case-sensitive—that is, Word ignores distinctions between upper- and lowercase letters.)

Figures 9.2 and 9.3 illustrate using an AutoText entry named "nrp" that contains the text "New Riders Publishing." Word finds the AutoText entry name ("nrp") and automatically inserts the corresponding AutoText entry ("New Riders Publishing") in its place.

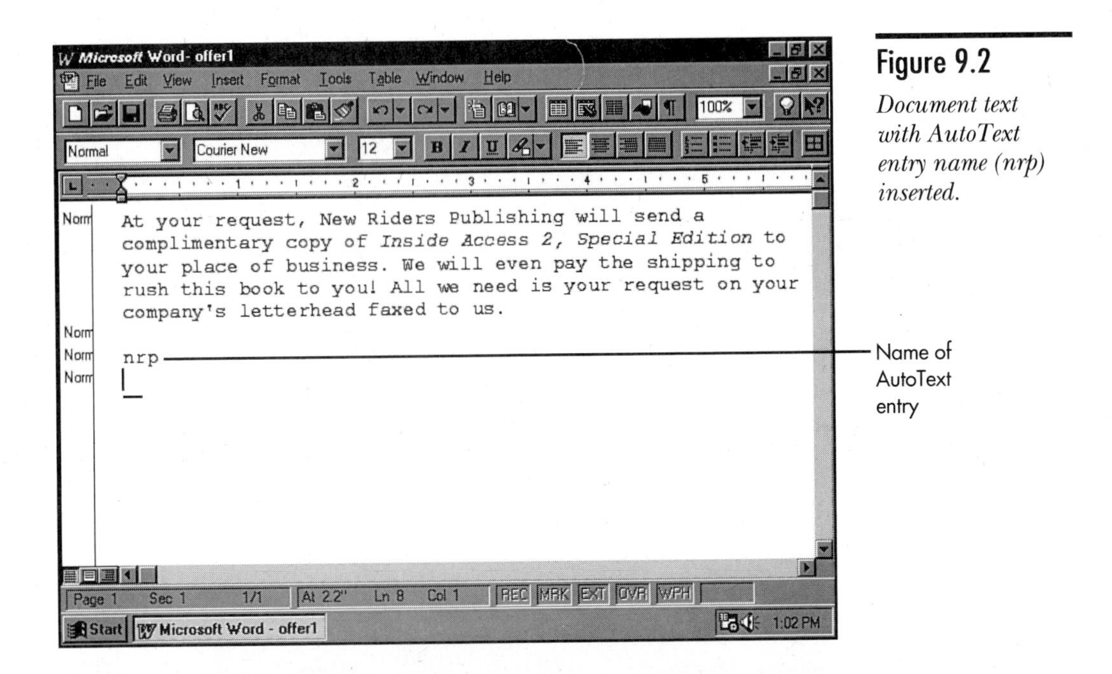

Figure 9.2

Document text with AutoText entry name (nrp) inserted.

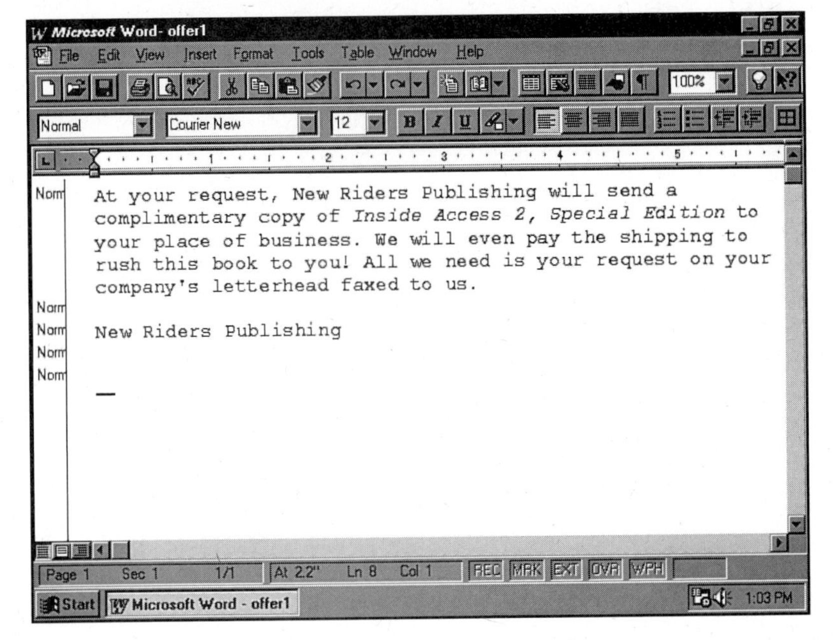

Figure 9.3

The document text after pressing the F3 key.

If you don't remember the name of the AutoText entry, you can refer to the alphabetical list in the AutoText dialog box. Follow these steps:

1. Select AutoText from the Edit menu. The AutoText dialog box appears (see fig. 9.4).

   Notice that several lines of the AutoText entry's contents appear in the Preview box at the bottom of the AutoText dialog box. This is usually enough to refresh your memory about the contents of an entry. (Remember that AutoText entries can be very long; the example here is quite short.)

2. Choose an entry from the AutoText Name list.

3. Choose Insert or press Enter.

After you insert an AutoText entry, you can edit it the same way you edit anything else placed in a document.

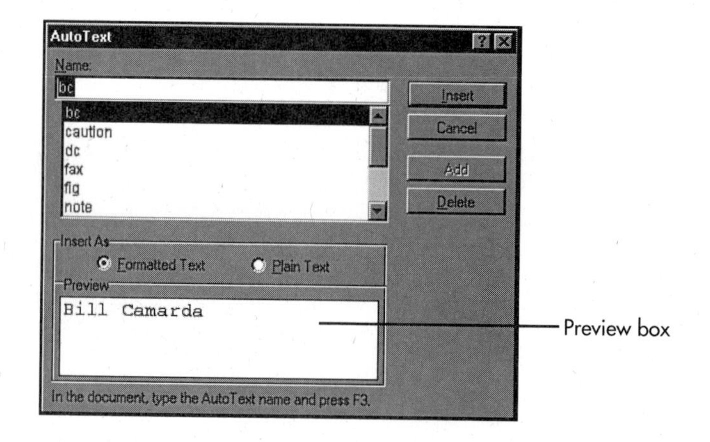

Figure 9.4
The AutoText dialog box showing several AutoText entries.

Formatted AutoText Entries

By default, Word preserves the formatting you give an AutoText entry. When you insert the AutoText into another document, the formatting given to the AutoText in its original document is preserved, no matter how the document into which you insert the AutoText entry is formatted.

In fact, this is a major advantage of Word's AutoText. AutoText relieves you of having to reformat heavily formatted text that might not be appropriate for styles—such as text with many different character attributes in the same paragraph.

But sometimes you want to insert only the content of an AutoText entry, and have that text take on the appearance of the text surrounding it. You can do this by

choosing the Plain Text button in the AutoText dialog box. The Plain Text button can be seen in figure 9.4. By default, the Formatted Text button is selected.

You occasionally might want to change an AutoText entry. For example, a phone number, or company name or address can change. In the following example, you decide to change the AutoText entry containing the words "New Riders Publishing" to "New Riders Publishing, Inc." This AutoText entry is named "nrp."

1. Insert the AutoText entry into your document as you want it to appear in the future. You may want to first insert the *old* AutoText entry, and then modify it in step 2.
2. Revise the entry's contents as you want. In this case, we change "New Riders Publishing" to "New Riders Publishing, Inc."
3. Select the revised entry by dragging the mouse over it.
4. Select AutoText from the Edit menu or click the AutoText button on the toolbar.
5. Select the entry name ("nrp") from the list in the AutoText Name box.
6. Select the Add button or press Enter. The dialog box shown in figure 9.5 opens.
7. Choose Yes.

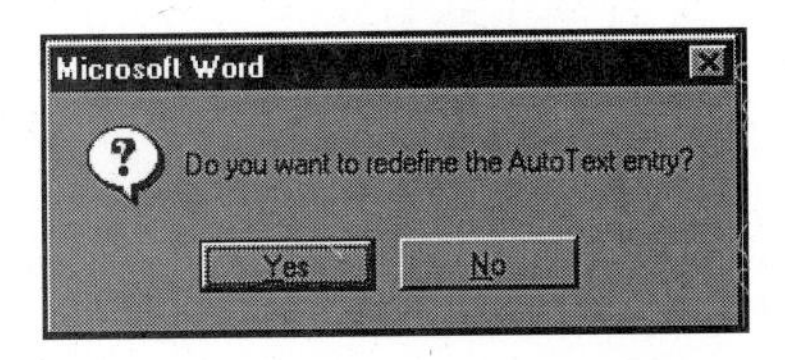

Figure 9.5
Redefining an AutoText entry.

If you change the contents of an entry extensively, you don't have to bother placing it in your document first. Just create the new contents of the entry, go into the AutoText dialog box, choose the same entry name, and confirm the change.

You might notice an oddity about AutoText. If you simply key in the name of the AutoText entry you want to redefine, AutoText creates a second entry that has the same name. If two or more AutoText entries have the same name, only the topmost (that is, the newest) entry in the AutoText Name list is automatically inserted when you press the F3 key.

If you want to use an "older" one, you have to manually insert it with the following procedure:

1. Open the AutoText dialog box by selecting AutoTe**x**t in the **E**dit menu.
2. Select the AutoText entry you want to use by clicking on it in the **N**ame list. Verify that you've selected the correct AutoText entry by checking its contents in the Preview box in the AutoText dialog box.
3. Click on the **I**nsert button.

Notice that you don't have to enter the AutoText entry name (like "nrp") in your document before you manually insert an AutoText entry into your document.

Renaming an AutoText Entry

You also can rename an AutoText entry, although the procedure is a bit complicated.

1. Open the Word Organizer by first opening the Style dialog box (select **S**tyle in the F**o**rmat menu) and pressing the **O**rganizer button.
2. The Organizer dialog box opens with the **S**tyles tab selected. Choose the **A**utoText tab to reveal the AutoText options (see fig. 9.6).
3. Highlight the AutoText name you want to rename and choose the **R**ename button (shown in fig. 9.6).
4. The Rename dialog box (see fig. 9.7) pops up over the Organizer AutoText tab.
5. Enter the new name for the AutoText entry in the New **N**ame text box and choose OK or press Enter.

The newly named AutoText entry appears in the list of AutoText entries at the right side of the AutoText tab (see fig. 9.8).

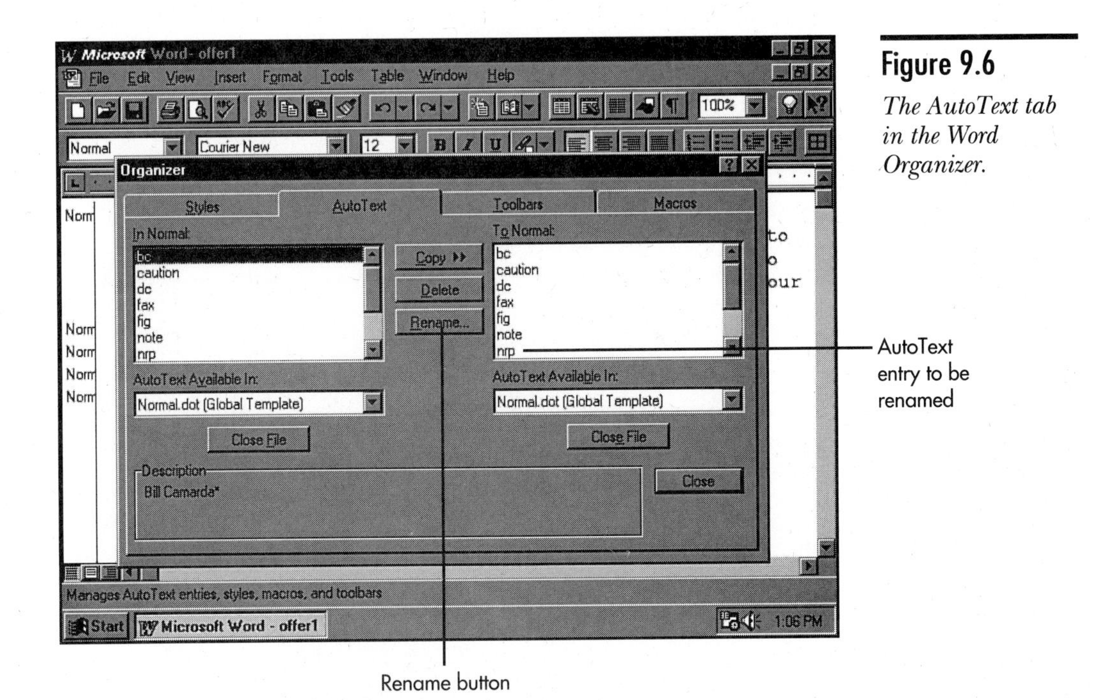

Figure 9.6

The AutoText tab in the Word Organizer.

Figure 9.7

The AutoText Rename dialog box.

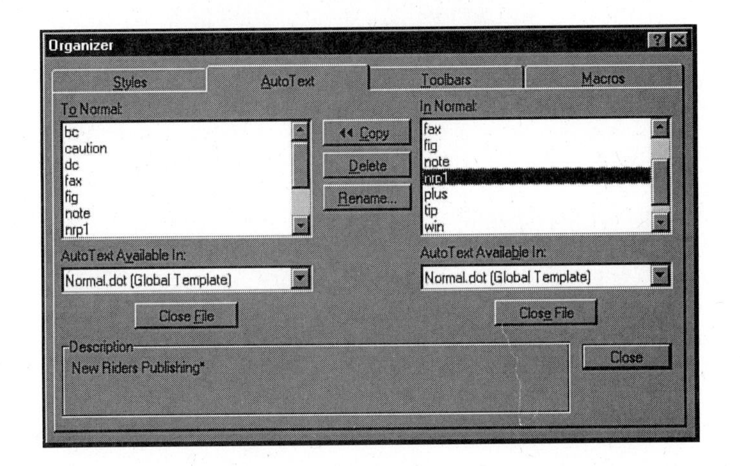

Figure 9.8

The AutoText tab showing the renamed AutoText entry.

Deleting an AutoText Entry

If you no longer need an AutoText entry, you can easily delete it. Perform the following steps:

1. Select AutoTe**x**t from the **E**dit menu.
2. From the **N**ame list, select the AutoText entry to be deleted.
3. Click on the **D**elete button.

Word does not ask you to confirm the AutoText deletion. After you choose **D**elete, the entry instantly disappears from your list and you cannot get it back. If you want to be able to recover accidentally deleted AutoText entries, be sure to read the next section of this chapter.

Recovering Deleted AutoText Entries

AutoText entries are stored as part of NORMAL.DOT, the global document template (or in the template used to create your document). When you delete AutoText entries, you make changes to NORMAL.DOT. By default, when you exit Word, NORMAL.DOT is automatically saved, and you lose forever the AutoText entries you delete during your Word session. Previous editions of Word always asked if you wanted to save NORMAL.DOT, which gave you a chance to prevent Word from saving the changes in NORMAL.DOT, and to recover the entries.

You must explicitly tell Word that you want to be prompted before Word saves changes to NORMAL.DOT. Turning off the NORMAL.DOT "autosave" feature can save you a great deal of trouble if you accidentally delete valuable AutoText entries.

To turn off the NORMAL.DOT autosave (the default setting for Word 95), select **O**ptions in the **T**ools menu; then click on the Save tab. This tab, shown in figure 9.9, contains all the various save options for Word, including the way you want Word to handle changes to NORMAL.DOT.

With the Pr**o**mpt to Save Normal Template box checked, any time you make a change to the document template (including changes to styles, macros, or AutoText), Word asks if you want to save NORMAL.DOT when you exit Word (see fig. 9.10). This option gives you a chance to recover AutoText entries you delete by accident.

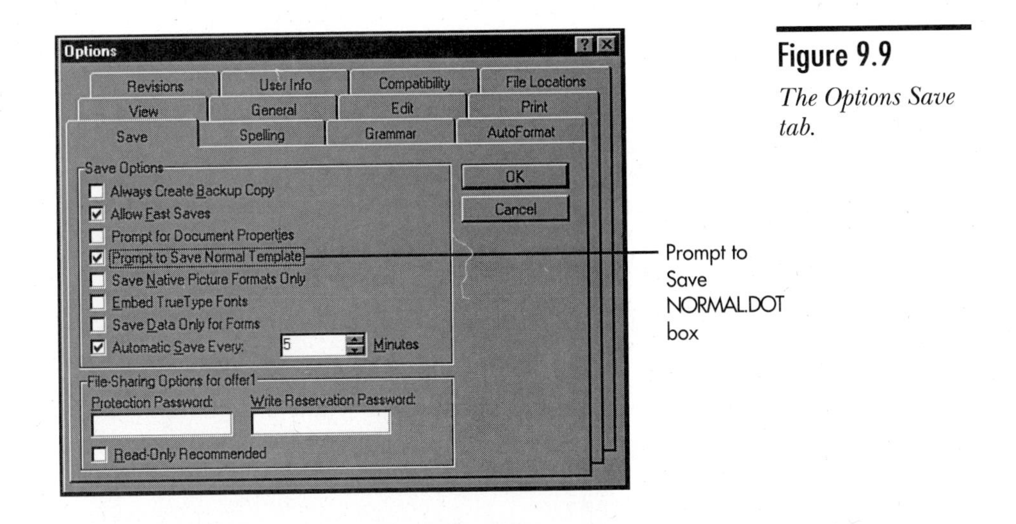

Figure 9.9

The Options Save tab.

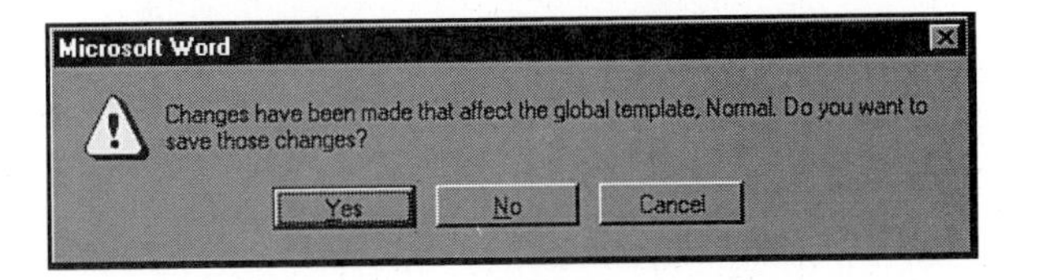

Figure 9.10

Confirmation before Word saves changes to NORMAL.DOT.

Understanding the Spike

Have you ever wanted to "pick up" bunches of text from different parts of a document and plunk them all down in a single location? You can't do it with the Clipboard, which can only handle one chunk at a time. Nor can you do it with a normal AutoText entry. But you *can* do it with the Spike. Think of it as a sticky Clipboard—it holds onto everything you throw at it.

Select the first block of material you want to move, and press Ctrl+F3. That cuts the text into the Spike. Then select another block, and press Ctrl+F3 again.

You can't copy material into the Spike; you can only insert cut material into the Spike.

To get the material out of the Spike, position your insertion point where you want the material to be inserted, and press Ctrl+Shift+F3.

Although you can't copy anything into the Spike, you can copy the contents of the Spike to another location without emptying the Spike.

To do this, type **spike** in your document and press F3. In this case, you are treating the Spike like a special kind of AutoText entry.

The Spike works between documents. For example, you can pick up a clause from one contract, open another and grab one from there, and place them both into a third document.

Just remember these text blocks are being cut from their original documents. If you don't want to lose the text blocks, close those documents without saving your changes.

The accompanying CD-ROM contains several files you can use to practice this procedure if you want. Open IWMS11B.DOC and IWMS11C.DOC, copy both their contents into the Spike, and then paste them into the tutorial document IWMS11A.DOC.

Saving AutoText Entries

Normally, new AutoText entries are saved automatically in the open document template. The default document template is NORMAL.DOT. If you haven't checked the Prompt to Save Normal Template box in the Save tab in the Tools, Options dialog box, NORMAL.DOT is automatically saved when you exit Word.

When you exit Word, you're asked whether you want to save AutoText entries you added during the session only if you have checked the Prompt to Save Normal Template box in the Save tab in the Tools, Options dialog box. If you are prompted to save NORMAL.DOT and choose No, the entries disappear forever. If you choose Yes, your AutoText entries are saved in a template that's accessible to your current document—NORMAL.DOT, or the document template you've chosen.

Printing AutoText Entries

Nobody's memory is good enough to remember every AutoText's name and contents. You might want to occasionally print out your AutoText entries and share them with anyone else who uses them.

1. Select Print from the File menu.
2. In the Print what list box, choose AutoText Entries (see fig. 9.11, which shows the Print What list box in its open position).
3. Choose OK or press the Enter key.

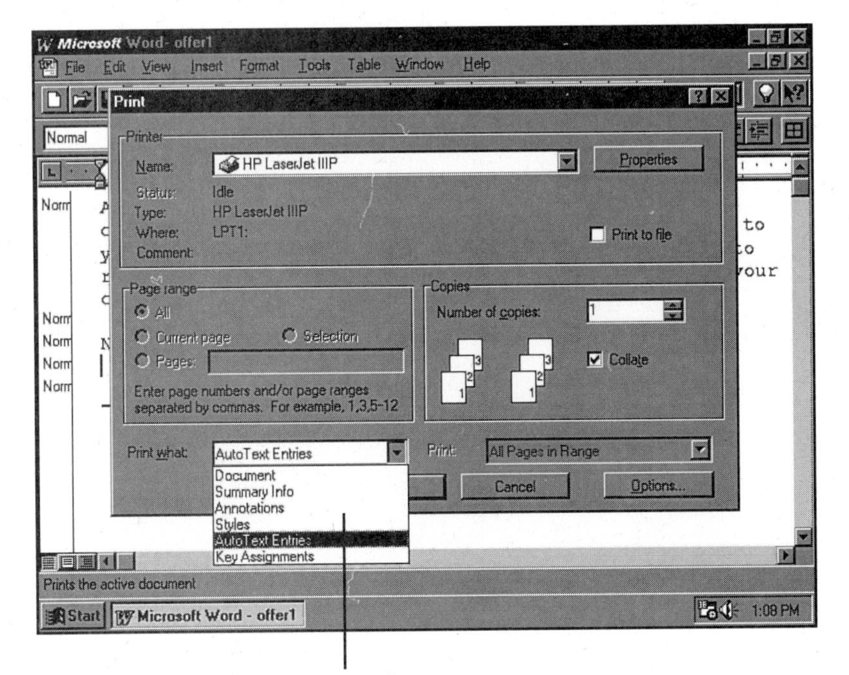

Figure 9.11

The Print dialog box, showing the Print what list box open.

If your document uses a custom template, Word prints out the contents of both the document template and NORMAL.DOT—in other words, all AutoText entries available to the document. If your Spike currently has contents, these are included in the printout, too.

Using AutoText Entries with Templates

You can take advantage of the fact that AutoText entries are stored in templates by including a series of custom AutoText entries with each of your major templates. For example, you might create a template called QUERIES, and include AutoText entries that consist of boilerplate letter copy that responds to the ten most common questions your company is asked.

Consider adapting an existing Word letter template, so that you can take advantage of Word's other automation features, such as dating your letters and storing new names and addresses in your AutoText. See Chapter 8, "Templates and Wizards," for more information about these features.

Or you might want to create a template called Proposals, perhaps based on Word's built-in template. You could build in AutoText entries for:

- Your company's experience in each of your major markets
- Relevant references
- Brief résumés of the people who serve the client
- Illustrations and information about each of your major products

Or you might want to create a template called CONTRACT that always includes your terms and conditions, basic contract language, and a signature page, but also includes AutoText entries with specific boilerplate language related to each service you offer.

If you are creating a new template that contains AutoText entries, follow these general instructions:

1. Create the template.
2. Add any text, graphics, or formatting that you want to always appear in the template.
3. Create the AutoText entries. You might want to import text from other documents using the Spike, as discussed earlier. When asked, assign the AutoText entry to this template only. (If you haven't named the template yet, it's called Template1.)

Remember that the Spike action (Ctrl+F3) deletes text from the document as the text is moved to the Spike. Be careful not to permanently remove important text from your templates or documents.

4. Delete the AutoText text from the document, so it doesn't automatically appear on-screen when you open the template. (Don't delete the entries themselves.)
5. Save the template as a template (using a .DOT extension in the WINWORD/TEMPLATE directory). (In the examples described earlier, the template names would be QUERIES.DOT and CONTRACT.DOT.)
6. When you want to create a new document using this template, select **N**ew from the **F**ile menu, and choose the new template name from the **T**emplate box.

AutoText entries, field codes, and macros. As covered in the next two chapters, AutoText entries are also ideal partners for field codes and macros. You can use an AutoText entry to insert text that includes field codes—such as figure reference numbers that can update themselves automatically.

In Chapter 10, "Field Codes," you learn about the AUTOTEXT field code, which changes a block of text repeatedly throughout a document whenever you change it once.

You also can run macros that insert AutoText entries as they carry out their tasks. (For example, a macro can insert text in a document and then position your insertion point at a specific location within that text.)

Creating AutoCorrect Entries

The Word AutoCorrect feature maintains a short list of frequently misspelled words and automatically replaces these errors with correct spellings as you enter text. The list, which has been expanded in Word 95, appears in table 9.1:

Table 9.1
Words AutoCorrect Fixes by Default

Error	Correct Spelling
adn	and
alot	a lot
don;t	don't
i	I
incl	include
lb	LB
occurence	occurrence
recieve	receive
seperate	separate
teh	the

Using AutoCorrect is quite easy. To add words to the AutoCorrect list:

1. Select **A**utoCorrect in the **T**ools menu to open the AutoCorrect dialog box.
2. Enter the commonly misspelled word in the R**e**place box and its correct spelling in the **W**ith box as shown in figure 9.12.
3. Click on the OK button or press Enter.

Note The Replace **T**ext as You Type box must be checked for AutoCorrect to work.

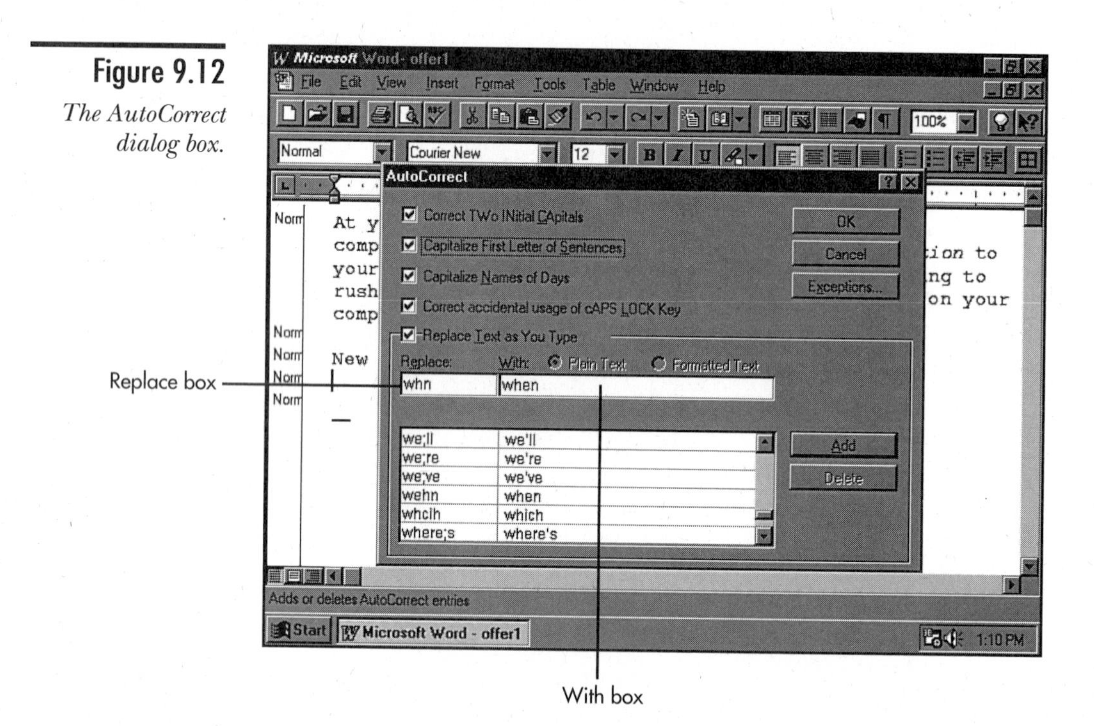

Figure 9.12
The AutoCorrect dialog box.

The next time you misspell the word (in the example illustrated in figure 9.12, the word is "when" misspelled as "wehn"), Word automatically corrects the spelling with the text you entered in the AutoCorrect dialog box.

Note Obviously, you have to be careful not to enter a correctly spelled word in the R**e**place box. For instance, you don't want to enter "tim" in the R**e**place box and "time" in the **W**ith box. Any time you tried to enter "Tim" as a person's name, Word would think it is a misspelling and change it to "Time." Another aspect of AutoCorrect is that it is case-sensitive. If you enter **tim** and **time**, Word won't necessarily change Tim to Time.

Deleting an AutoCorrect Entry

It is easy to delete an AutoCorrect entry:

1. Open the AutoCorrect dialog box by choosing AutoCorrect in the Tools menu.
2. Highlight the AutoCorrect entry you want to delete (see fig. 9.13).
3. Choose the Delete key (or press Alt+D).

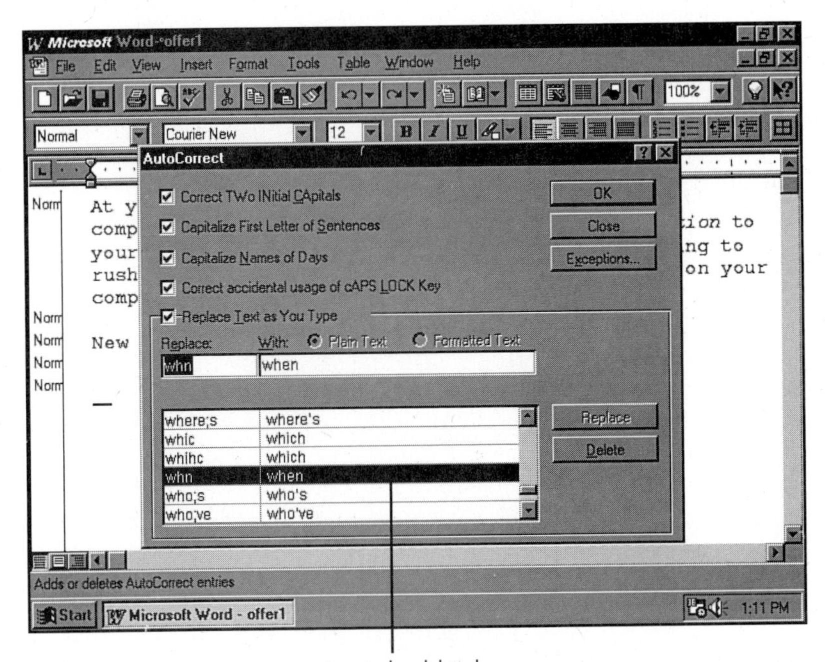

Figure 9.13

Deleting an AutoCorrect item.

The entry is instantly deleted. As with AutoText entries, when you exit Word, NORMAL.DOT or your open document template is updated, and the deletion becomes permanent, unless you've checked the Prompt to Save Normal Template box in the Tools, Option Save tab.

Understanding the Other AutoCorrect Options

You might notice several other AutoCorrect options in figure 9.13. These options specify certain AutoCorrect behavior much like the misspelling replacement described earlier.

- A common error is to capitalize the first two characters of a word that normally has only the first letter capitalized. The Correct TWo INitial CApitals option checks for this situation and corrects it for you.

- Another very common error is to forget to capitalize the first letter of every sentence in a document. The Capitalize First Letter of Sentences option corrects this problem.

- The names of days (Monday, Tuesday, and so on) are proper nouns and should be capitalized in most instances. The Capitalize Names of Days option ensures that the days of the week are capitalized properly. Abbreviations of days of the week (Tue., Wed., and so on) are not checked by this option.

By default, Word 95 corrects one additional common error: inadvertently leaving the Caps Lock key depressed. The telltale symptom is a word that starts with a lowercase letter and then becomes all caps. Unless you clear Correct Accidental Usage of cAPS LOCK key, Word automatically changes:

iNCREDIBLE EDIBLES

to

Incredible edibles

Once Word makes this change, it turns off the CAPS LOCK key.

These AutoCorrect options only affect new text you enter into your document. Existing text is not affected by these options.

Creating AutoCorrect Exceptions

One complaint with Word 6's implementation of AutoCorrect was that it didn't allow the flexibility to create exceptions. In Word 95, however, you *can* exclude specific abbreviations or capitalized terms from automatic correction.

To exclude an abbreviation:

1. Choose AutoCorrect from the Tools menu.

2. Click Exceptions.

3. To exclude an abbreviation from automatic correction, choose **F**irst Letter (see fig. 9.14).
4. In the D**o**n't Capitalize After box, type the abbreviation you want to exclude.
5. Click on Add.
6. Click OK twice.

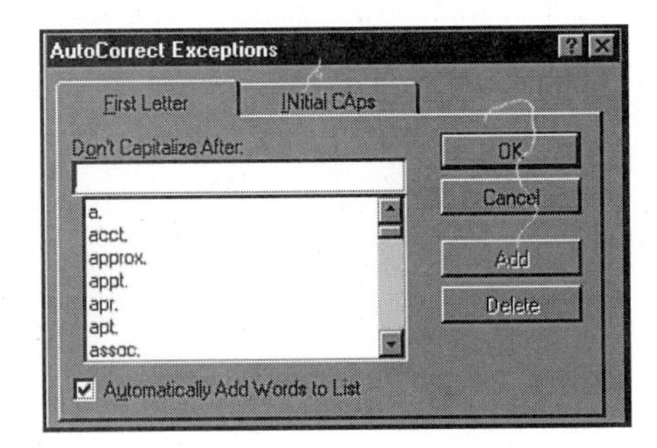

Figure 9.14

Using the AutoCorrect Exceptions dialog box to exclude an abbreviation.

To exclude a capitalized term:

1. Choose **A**utoCorrect from the **T**ools menu.
2. Click E**x**ceptions.
3. To exclude an abbreviation from automatic correction, choose **I**Nitial CAps (see fig. 9.15).
4. In the D**o**n't Correct box, type the abbreviation you want to exclude.
5. Click on Add.
6. Click OK twice.

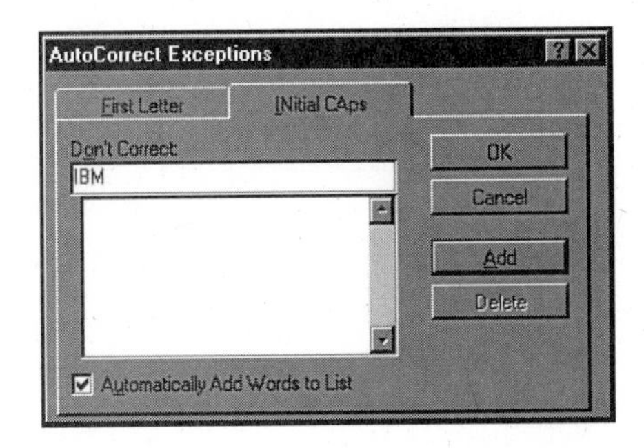

Figure 9.15

Using the AutoCorrect Exceptions dialog box to exclude a capitalized term.

Automatically Creating Exceptions

Windows 95

You can instruct Word to create exceptions automatically as you work. Choose AutoCorrect from the Tools menu; click Exceptions. Check the Automatically Add Words to List box. From now on, whenever Word changes an abbreviation or capitalization you want left alone, press Backspace, and edit the word back the way you want it. Word won't dare to change it again.

Correcting Symbols with AutoCorrect

In addition to correcting more words, Word 95 also increases the number of symbols it will change without being asked. In particular, Word has added a bunch of *emoticons*—those keyboard combinations like :) that have evolved to express emotion over e-mail systems. Those automatic corrections may be a mixed blessing, because the symbols Word inserts can't usually be transmitted by e-mail systems! In any case, Table 9.2 lists the symbols Word changes by default.

Table 9.2
Symbols AutoCorrect Fixes by Default

Original	Correction
(c)	©
(r)	®
(tm)	™
...	…
—>	→
<—	←
==>	➔
<==	🡐
<=>	⇔
:(	J
:)	B
:|	F

Field Codes

Fields are your executive assistant. You can delegate many of the most annoying details of assembling a document to your computer. (Hey, it's a *computer*—it thrives on that stuff.) Meanwhile, you can do the thinking.

Say that you have a document that has figures and tables that need to be numbered consecutively. You can do it manually—and redo the numbering every time you insert or delete a figure or table. Or you can use a field code, and let Word track it all for you.

Word disguises many of its field codes as friendly dialog boxes. When you insert a cross-reference, numbered caption, table of contents, or the current date and time, you're inserting a field code. But you still need to become acquainted with the underlying field codes. You can do many things with field codes that haven't yet been built into neat and clean menu items, buttons, and check boxes.

Suppose that part of your document refers to another part of the document. You can insert a field (called Gotobutton) that readers can click on and go straight to the text you want them to see.)

Even some Word features that have been slicked up with dialog boxes can perform extra tricks if you know how to use field codes. If those tricks happen to be tasks you really need, you'll be glad to know about them.

As with styles, templates, and AutoText entries, fields require a little more forethought—but they pay off handsomely in time savings. And you certainly don't have to understand all of Word's varieties of fields to make good use of them. A dozen fields might be all you ever need.

This chapter covers how to use fields and tries to direct you to the ones you will most likely need. At the end of the chapter, you can find a detailed field reference that has examples of how to use each field.

In this chapter:

- Understanding and viewing fields
- Inserting a field using Insert, Field
- What goes into a field
- Updating fields
- Finding and replacing field contents
- Which fields you need
- Field reference

Understanding Fields

A *field* is a set of instructions that you place in a document. Most often, these instructions tell Word to find or produce some specific text and stick that text where you have inserted the field.

Result Fields

Fields that do just this are called *result fields*, and the information they generate is called *field results*. These "result field field results" can come from many sources, including the following:

- Information stored in the document's Properties or Statistics dialog boxes (such as the author's name)
- Information Word calculates from sources you specify, such as adding a column of numbers
- Information Word requests later
- Information Word produces based on what it finds in your document (such as page counts)
- Information found in other files
- Information found elsewhere in your document

Because your document includes the field instructions, not the actual information, Word can find and insert new information whenever a change occurs. That's the magic of field codes—they handle the details you can easily forget.

Marker Fields

Some fields simply mark text, so that you (or another field) can find it later. For example, the TC field marks entries that later can be compiled into tables of contents.

Action Fields

Finally, some action fields tell Word to perform a specific action that doesn't place new visible text in your document. For example, the Gotobutton field places a button in the text. When you press it, Word goes to the text you specified.

Fields That Might Already Be in Your Document

You've come across several field codes already, although you may not have realized it. When you place the date, time, or page number in a header or footer, Word places a field code in the document. The Date field code checks your computer's built-in clock and inserts the date and time that it contains. You can insert many fields quite easily if you use the specific Word menu commands or toolbar buttons instead of field codes (see table 10.1 for a list).

Even if you enter a field code using a menu command, you might still want to edit it later for precise formatting. But that's still easier than creating it from scratch.

Table 10.1
Menu Command Shortcuts for Some Fields

This Field Command	Corresponds to This Menu
={ Formula }	Table, Formula
{ BarCode }	Tools, Envelopes and Labels
{ Bookmark }	Edit, Bookmark
{ Database }	Insert, Database
{ Date } { Time }	Insert, Date and Time
{ DDE } { DDEauto } { Link }	Edit, Paste Special (Paste Link)
{ Embed }	Insert, Object
{ FormCheckBox }	Insert, Form Field
{ FormDropDown }	Insert, Form Field
{ FormText }	Insert, Form Field
{ IncludePicture }	Insert, Picture
{ IncludeText }	Insert, File
{ Index }	Insert, Index and Tables
{ NoteRef }	Insert, Footnote
{ Page }	Insert, Page Numbers
{ Ref }	Insert, Cross-Reference
{ Seq }	Insert, Caption
{ Symbol }	Insert, Symbol
{ TOA }	Insert, Index and Tables
{ TOC }	Insert, Index and Tables
{ XE }	Mark Index Entry (Alt+Shift+X)

The accompanying CD-ROM contains a file you can use to practice some of the procedures in this chapter: IWMS10A.DOC.

Viewing Fields

Rarely do you see the fields in your document—what you see is the information the fields find or create. Sometimes, however, you want to see your fields. For example, you might want to edit a field so that it presents different information, or presents it in a different format. Or maybe a field isn't behaving the way you expect.

To view all field codes, press Alt+F9, or do the following:

1. Select Options from the Tools menu.
2. Select the View tab dialog box.
3. Check the Field Codes box in the Show area.

Field Code Shading

In early versions of Word, it often was difficult to tell whether text was a field code or just plain old text (until you tried to backspace into it, and your computer beeped, that is).

Word now gives you some help. By default, field codes are shaded in gray when you select them. In the Field Shading list box, you can choose Never (the way it used to be) or Always (field codes always shaded, even when not selected). It's a matter of taste, and now you have a choice.

The shading doesn't appear in Print Preview, and it doesn't print.

If you see field codes rather than field results, press Alt+F9 to toggle them off, or clear the Field Codes box from Tools, Options, View.

You might occasionally want to view the field codes and the field results at the same time. (You might, for example, want to check whether you've formatted a field the way you want.) Open a second window on the same document, as follows:

1. Select New Window from the Window menu.
2. Select Arrange All from the Window menu. Both windows are displayed horizontally.
3. In one window, press Alt+F9.

Your screen displays field codes in one window and field results in the other, as shown in figure 10.1.

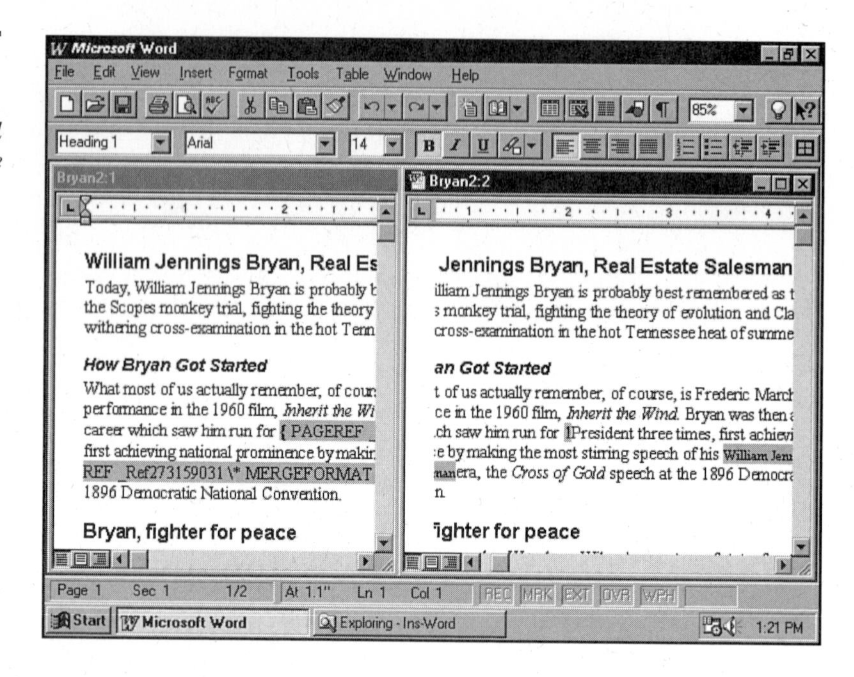

Figure 10.1

Two windows, one with field codes and one with field results.

Inserting a Field Using Insert Field

Although you can enter a field directly, you use the Field dialog box more often. Select Fi<u>e</u>ld from the <u>I</u>nsert menu (see fig. 10.2).

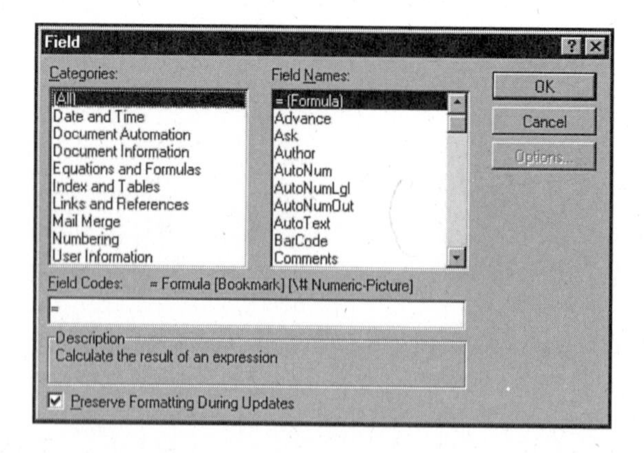

Figure 10.2

The Field dialog box.

The Field dialog box helps you build the field syntax that Word understands and acts upon. Step one is to select a field code. You can select a field code in one of the following ways:

- Select the field code from a list of available fields in the Field Names box.
- If you're not sure of the name of the field code, select a category of fields from the Categories list, and Word lists your choices for you.
- If you know exactly what you want, type it in the Field Codes box. (Unless you're creating a formula, delete the equals sign first.)

Word organizes its field codes into nine categories, described respectively in the following minitable:

Field Category	What It Covers
Date and Time	Fields that include the current date or time, or the date or time that an event relevant to your document took place (for example, the last time you saved or printed)
Document Automation	Compares values and takes an action: runs macros, jumps to new locations, sends printer codes
Document Information	Inserts or stores information about your document
Equations and Formulas	Creates and calculates the results of formulas; inserts symbols
Index and Tables	Creates entries in, or builds, indexes and tables of contents, figures, and authorities (which list by category all citations made in a document)
Links and References	Inserts information from elsewhere in your document, from AutoText entries, or from other documents and files
Mail Merge	Imports information from a data source for a Word mail merge
Numbering	Numbers your document's pages or sections, inserts information about your document's page numbers or sections, or inserts a bar code
User Information	Stores your name, address or initials, or inserts them in a document or envelope

This simple act of organization by Microsoft brings great relief to anyone trying to work with fields for the first time.

Notice the check box in the lower left hand corner of the box. If marked, Word doesn't eliminate any manual formatting you've added when it updates your field.

Look behind the curtain, and you'll see that this switch adds the * mergeformat switch to your field code, another way to say the same thing.

Sometimes, when you choose a field, you're finished. You can choose OK and be done with it. For example, if you want Word to find the user's name stored in the User Info tab of the Options dialog box (accessible by choosing **T**ools, **O**ptions), simply insert the following field:

```
USERNAME
```

Then choose OK.

More often, however, you must tell Word more. You can tell whether you need to tell Word more by looking at the syntax information in light type next to the **F**ield Codes box, as in figure 10.3.

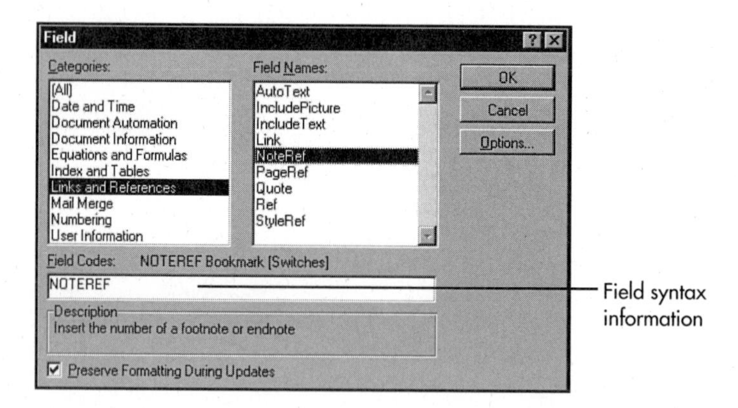

Figure 10.3

Field code syntax information.

Help. To get online help about a specific field, select it in the Field dialog box, and press F1 or click the "?" help icon.

You can also get Field help from elsewhere in Word. Follow these steps:

1. Select **M**icrosoft Word Help Topics from the **H**elp menu.
2. Select Reference Information from the Contents dialog box.

3. Select Field Types and Switches from the Reference Information dialog box.
4. Select Field Types.
5. Select the field you want help with.

What Goes into a Field

This section briefly covers what can go into a field. A more detailed discussion appears later in the chapter.

In the Username field, *USERNAME* is obviously the name of the field—or, as Word puts it, the field type. In this example, Username searches for the name recorded in the User Info tab of the Options dialog box (accessible from Tools, Options), and then inserts it into the document.

But you can also use Username to place a new name in the document and store the same name in the User Info dialog box, as follows:

```
{ USERNAME Robert Smith }
```

The text after USERNAME is a simple example of *field instructions.* Often Word helps you create these field instructions—through a specific menu item, or through the Insert, Field menu item.

In field codes in which you ask Word to refer to text elsewhere in your document, you might have to add a *bookmark*—the name you assign that text.

Bookmarks are covered in Chapter 16, but if you need to create a bookmark so you can add it to a field code, follow these instructions:

1. Select the text you want to mark with a bookmark.
2. Select Bookmark from the Edit menu.
3. Enter a bookmark name in the Bookmark Name box.
4. Choose OK.

If you have to specify text that you want Word to add to the document, this text should appear in quotation marks.

Most of the time you have to specify a *switch*—a command that starts with a backslash, and tells Word to modify the behavior of the field.

Specifying Field Options

If you need to add a switch, or another option, to your field, select **O**ptions. The Field Options dialog box appears (see fig. 10.4).

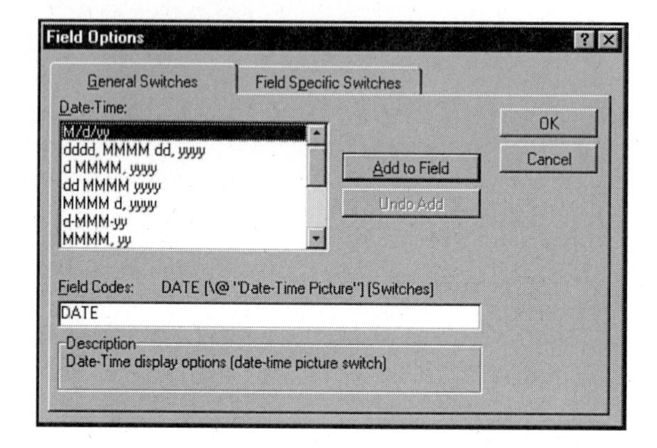

Figure 10.4
The Field Options dialog box.

You can specify either *general switches* (which determine how your field will be formatted), or *field-specific* switches, which change field behaviors that might be unique to the field you're working on. There are four kinds of general switches:

Switch	Name	Does
*	Formatting	Lets you decide how to format inserted text
\#	Numeric picture	Lets you decide how to format inserted numbers
\@	Date-time picture	Lets you decide how to format a date
\!	Lock result	Lets you decide *not* to update some fields even as others are updated

Except for the \! switch, these fields (and all their variations) are available through the Field Options dialog box. You have to add the \! switch yourself.

Not surprisingly, not every field offers all four of the general switches. You can't create a date-time picture for a paragraph of text, for example. For some fields, Word offers these four general formatting switches only. When you select options, a formatting dialog box such as the one shown in figure 10.5 appears.

What's really nice about these formatting dialog boxes is that they display your options in English, and when you select an option, Word's appropriate Field-ese is inserted. You say: format this in uppercase. Word enters: * Upper.

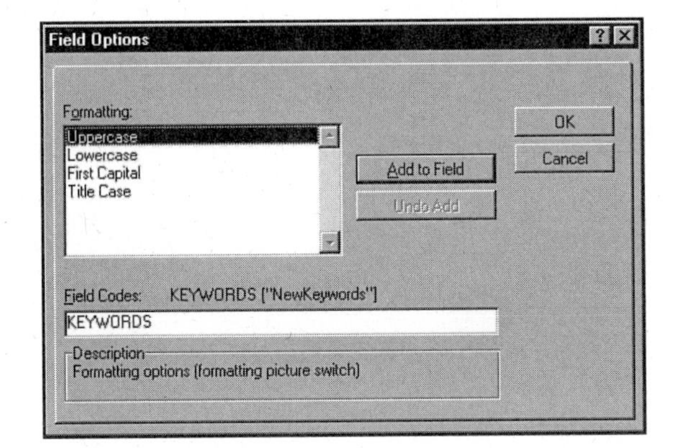

Figure 10.5

Formatting a field using a field formatting dialog box.

In other cases, Word offers field-specific switches that tell a switch to behave in unique ways not relevant to other switches. For example, if you use \t in an XE index entry field, Word knows not to include the page number with the index entry, but to include text instead, which is meaningless in most other fields. Then, when you select Options from the Field dialog box, you can choose from the available switches, as shown in figure 10.6.

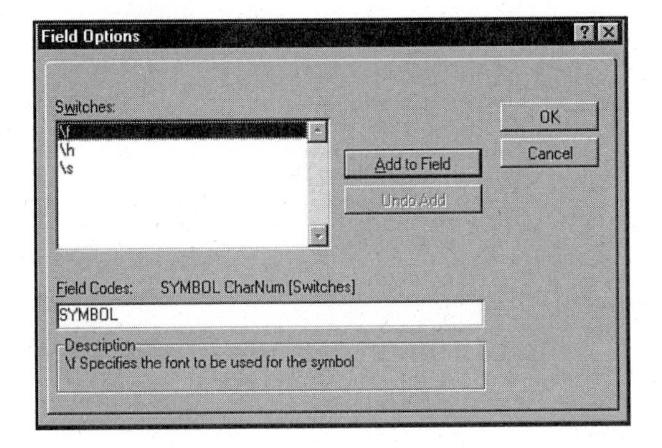

Figure 10.6

The Field Options dialog box, showing available switches.

Both general and field-specific switches are frequently available. In these cases, you see a tab, where one tab says General Switches, and the other tab usually says Field Specific Switches. Select the tab with which you want to work.

Say hosannas for these Field Options dialog boxes, because this is where Word saves you the trouble of memorizing hundreds of switch names.

To add a switch to your field, select it from a box. After you select the field, a description of it appears in the description box. If you like what you see, choose Add to Field.

Some switches require you to add more information. For example, if you're using the Seq field to create a sequence of numbers, you can use the \r switch to tell Word to return to a specific number. You can use \r, and Word inserts it into your field code. But you have to tell Word the number you want to use yourself, by keying it in the Field Codes box after \r.

After you finish, choose OK to return to the Field dialog box, and choose OK again to insert the field into your document.

Inserting a Field Using Field Characters

You can also insert a field directly into your document without using Insert, Field. Press Ctrl+F9 to tell Word you want to edit a field. Word places two curly brackets around your insertion point and colors them gray to indicate that you're in a field (see fig. 10.7).

Figure 10.7

Starting to edit a field within your document.

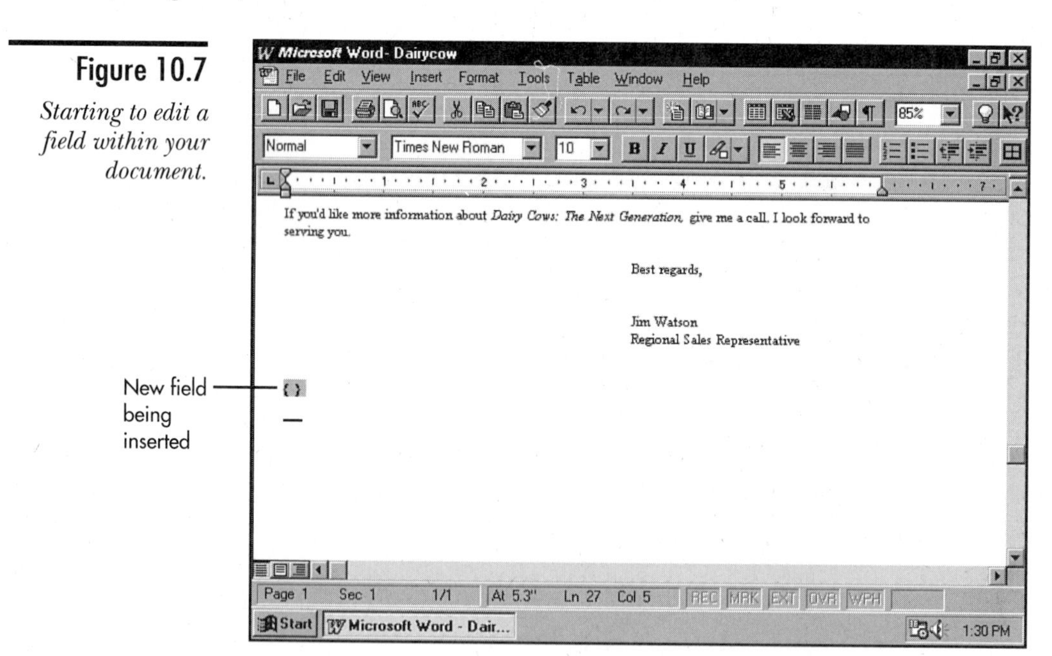

These curly brackets are called *field characters.* The curly brackets on your keyboard don't do the job, however. (If they did, how would Word know when all you wanted was curly brackets? To paraphrase Freud, sometimes curly brackets are just curly brackets.)

Word also adds an extra space after the opening bracket and before the closing bracket. That's why field codes inserted by Word look like this:

```
{ FILENAME }
```

The fields work fine without those extra spaces, and the fields don't have to be all uppercase.

You can then type your field names, bookmarks, quoted material, switches, or whatever, inside the brackets. (You can also cut and paste text into or from the brackets— as long as they're displayed.) Use Insert mode, not Overtype mode. If `OVR` appears in the status bar on the bottom of the screen, press Insert to switch.

Pressing Ctrl+F9 usually makes the most sense when you know exactly what you're going to do—especially if the field is so simple that all you need to enter is its name. For example, the following is all you need to insert a page count within your document text:

```
{ NUMPAGES }
```

Whenever you create a complex field instruction you think you might reuse, make it an AutoText entry. Then you only have to enter it correctly the first time.

When you use Insert, Field to place a field in the document, Word calculates the field at the same time.

Updating Fields

One of the best things about fields is that you can update them without manually changing the text they represent. It's easy, but for most fields, not quite automatic. F9 is the magic key:

- To update a single field, place your insertion point within it, and press F9.
- To update more than one field, select them and press F9.
- To update all the fields in a document, press Ctrl+NumPad5 and press F9. In a long document, this can take a little while. (You can always stop an update by pressing Esc.)

When you insert a field using Ctrl+F9, Word doesn't update the field until you press F9.

Note Updating with F9 doesn't affect the following fields:

Autonum
Autonumgl
Autonumout
EQ
Gotobutton
Macrobutton
Print

Word 2 automatically updated all your fields whenever you printed your document, but no longer. If you want to update fields whenever you print, do the following:

1. Select **O**ptions from the **T**ools menu.
2. Select the **P**rint tab.
3. Check **U**pdate Fields in the Printing Options area.

Locking, Unlocking, and Unlinking Fields

Suppose you want to temporarily prevent a field from being updated, even as you update fields surrounding it. Say you use an Includetext field to display the first quarter results from a table in another document. You might want to update that table at some point, but the first quarter results that appear in your current document aren't likely to change. So you lock the field, which prevents updating.

You might recall that the \! switch enables you to lock a field. But it is easier to lock a field in the following manner:

1. Place your insertion point in the field (or select text that includes several fields).
2. Press Ctrl+F11 or Alt+Ctrl+F1.

When you try to update this field, a message appears in the status bar that it cannot update locked fields. (By the way, the \! switch does not appear in a field you lock like this.)

To unlock a field so that it can again be updated, place your insertion point in the field and press Ctrl+Shift+F11 or Alt+Ctrl+Shift+F1.

You might decide you never want to update a field. For example, you've absolutely finished your document, and you're exporting it to a desktop publishing program that doesn't recognize Word field codes. Word lets you permanently replace the field codes with the most recently updated field results; this is called *unlinking*:

1. Place the insertion point in the field, or select text, including the field(s) to be unlinked.

2. Press Ctrl+Shift+F9.

You can never be sure that the field result is absolutely current unless you press F9 to update the field before you unlink it.

After you unlink a field, the field is gone forever (unless you Select **U**ndo from the **E**dit menu immediately, or close the document without saving any of your changes). If you have any doubts, save a duplicate copy of the file with its fields still in place.

Word's Field Shortcut Menu

When you right-click on a field, the Field shortcut menu appears (see fig. 10.8). This includes two of the most common tasks you might need: Update Field and Toggle Field Codes. (Toggle Field switches between field codes and field results.)

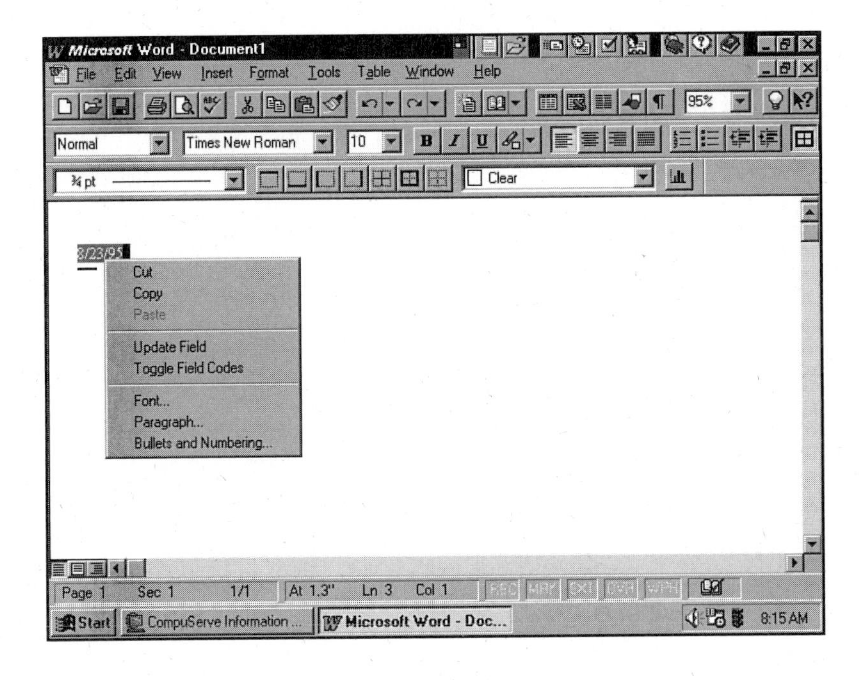

Figure 10.8

Field shortcut menu.

Word Keyboard Field Shortcuts

You've already learned some of Word's keyboard shortcuts for using fields. They're collected in table 10.2.

TABLE 10.2
Field Key Combinations

Task	Key Combination	What It Does
Insert Field	Ctrl+F9	Inserts field characters { } and awaits your field instructions
Update Field	F9	Produces a new field result
Go to Next Visible Field	F11 (or Alt+F1)	Moves to next visible field
Go to Previous Field	Shift+F11 (or Alt+Shift+F1)	Moves to the previous visible field
View/Hide all Field Codes	Shift+F9	Toggles between displaying field codes and their results
Lock Field	Ctrl+F11	Prevents a field from being updated until you unlock it
Unlock Field	Ctrl+Shift+F11	Allows a locked field to be updated again
Unlink Field	Ctrl+Shift+F9	Replaces a field with its most recently updated results, eliminating the field code
Update Source (works with Includetext field only)	Ctrl+Shift+F7	Updates selected text in another document that is connected to the current document by an Include text field
Perform Field Click (works with Macrobutton or Gotobutton fields only)	Alt+Shift+F9	Performs whatever actions you've programmed into a Macrobutton or Gotobutton field
Insert Date Field	Alt+Shift+D	Inserts Date field with default format (06/02/94)

Task	Key Combination	What It Does
Insert Page Field	Alt+Shift+P	Inserts Page field with default format (1, 2, 3...)
Insert Time Field	Alt+Shift+T	Inserts Time field with default format (04:29 PM)

Finding and Replacing Field Contents

Word offers shortcuts for moving among fields. F11 (or Alt+F1) moves to the next field and selects it. Shift+F11 (or Alt+Shift+F1) selects the previous field.

You can also view field codes and then select Find or Replace from the Edit menu to locate or change the contents of field codes. (Find and Replace don't recognize field brackets, only the contents of fields.)

Replace is ideal if you want to change the formatting of a specific kind of field that recurs throughout your document. For example, you could replace all references to { =profit * cardtext } with { =profit * dollartext}.

Display your field codes before you use Find or Replace.

Some fields, such as index entries, are automatically formatted as hidden text. Word's next-field and previous-field keyboard shortcuts normally skip these fields. (Using Find and Replace from the Edit menu skips them, too.) You can show hidden text as follows:

1. Select Options from the Tools menu.
2. Select the View tab.
3. Check Hidden Text in the Nonprinting Characters group.

Understanding More about Field Instructions

You have just completed a brief overview of the elements of a field code. What follows is a somewhat more detailed discussion. Read on if you expect to use field codes heavily, and especially if you prefer to insert them directly into a document.

Field instructions—when necessary at all—can include any of the following elements:

- Arguments
- Bookmarks
- Expressions
- Identifiers
- Text
- Switches

Arguments

Arguments are text, numbers, or graphics that help a field decide how to act, or what information to insert. For example, the following line tells Word to insert "How to Succeed in Advertising" where you place the field, and also in the Summary Info box:

```
{ TITLE "How to Succeed in Advertising" }
```

Note that the field instruction is surrounded by quotation marks. Technically, that's only necessary if the instruction is longer than one word, but it's a good habit to develop.

Once in awhile, you might need to tell Word that you actually want real quotation marks to appear in the document. To indicate this, use backslashes, as in the following example:

```
{ TITLE "Start \"Loafing"\ Around" }
```

You might wonder: What if I need to include a document path, which already uses backslashes? The answer: Use two backslashes wherever you would have used one:

```
{ INCLUDETEXT c:\\reports\\income.doc }
```

Bookmarks

Bookmarks are markers you place anywhere in a document. They identify a location or selected text. You can add a bookmark to some fields, which tells Word to go to that location, or to insert that text. The bookmark name can be only one word, so you never have to worry about quotation marks when you insert a bookmark name in a field. For example:

```
{ REF jones }
```

This tells Word to insert text about Jones that you've flagged elsewhere in the document.

Formulas

You can include a formula as a field code; Word does the math and displays the results. Word formulas start with the = symbol. For example, { =24-8 } displays 16.

But that's an awfully convoluted way of doing math in Word. The real benefit of expressions is that you can base them on other information in your document—and when that information changes, the expression updates itself in your document. The example

```
{ =joesales - bobsales }
```

tells Word to look for a bookmark named *bobsales,* and subtract it from a bookmark named *joesales.*

When all you want to do is calculate a result, your field should start with the = sign. Word can perform a prodigious variety of calculations, covered later in this chapter and in Chapter 3, "Tables."

You can use the If field to tell Word to display one kind of information if it finds one mathematical result, and different information otherwise. Using the joesales/bobsales example, bookmark the expression field. Call it *joevbob.*

This field pats Joe on the back if he outsells Bob. If not, it quietly lets the occasion pass.

```
{ IF joevbob > 0, "Congratulations, Joe_you've made it. Top salesperson of the
month!" }
```

Notice that the expression is now embedded in the field instructions, after If. (The If field is covered in greater detail later.) You can also use cell names (A1, A2, and so on) in place of bookmarks, so that a table can perform many of the tasks of a spreadsheet.

Identifiers

Identifiers tell Word's action fields to recognize specific text to be acted upon. The best example of how identifiers work is the Seq field, which creates and updates sequences of figures, tables, and other elements of your document.

Word's Insert Caption feature has automated figure lists, but suppose that you want to number some other kind of item scattered throughout your document. You can insert a Seq field everywhere you want a consecutive number to appear.

Text

In the context of this discussion, *text* is simply words (or images) that you want to appear in the document or on the screen. As with arguments, text should appear between quotation marks if it's more than one word.

The Fillin field offers a good example of using text. It enables you to display a dialog box that prompts the user to type something:

```
{ FILLIN "What's your sign?" }
```

Fillin has great potential for developing forms.

A Note from the Author

Advanced topic. You can make things even easier for your users—and harder for you—by writing a macro that displays a list box that contains every astrological sign. See Chapter 11, "Macros."

Switches

You might want to change the way a field acts, or the way a field result looks. That's what *switches* do.

If you've ever used a DOS command, like dir /w, you can easily understand the general idea of how switches work. Adding the /w made your directory listing display wide across the screen.

All Word field code switches start with a backslash and appear after your other instructions. For example, \! ensures that a field doesn't change its contents even when all the others are updated, as in the following example:

```
{ INCLUDETEXT january.doc \! }
```

This is called *locking* a field. An easier way is described earlier in this chapter, in the section "Locking, Unlocking, and Unlinking Fields."

Some switches only work with one type of field, but general switches work with nearly all fields. General switches were mentioned earlier in table 10.1. Now, it is time to return to them in a little more detail. There are three categories of general switches:

- Character formatting (*)
- Date-time formatting (\@)
- Number formatting (\#)

Note General switches do not work with these fields:

Autonum
Autonumlgl
Autonumout
Eq
Gotobutton
Includepicture
Macrobutton
RD
TC
XE

Formatting Field Results

Except for \!, each of the general switches has options—for your convenience. Suppose that you make an important point somewhere in your document. You have formatted it in boldface for emphasis. Now you want to bring that phrase into your executive summary, but you don't want it to be boldfaced.

You can reformat or edit any field result manually—but then it reverts to the bold formatting anytime you update your fields. You can lock that field—but if you ever want to update the *substance* of the field, then what? The best solution is to use one of Word's many field formatting options.

Formatting Field Text

If you use a field that consists only of the field name, such as NumChars, it's easy. Format the first character of the field name to look like you want your text. If you want bold italic underlined text, your field should look like this:

```
{ NUMCHARS }
```

If the field also contains instructions, it gets a little more complicated. Again, format the first character of the field name the way you want it. But you have to add the following switch to the end of your field code:

```
\* charformat
```

For instance:

```
{ INCLUDETEXT report.doc \* charformat }
```

Using * mergeformat

You do have an alternative. You can manually format your text, and tell Word not to change the formatting no matter what. You do that with the * mergeformat switch.

The catch is, when you use * mergeformat, Word counts words and takes their formatting literally. If your fourth word is italic, then your fourth word is always italic—even if it's a different word. Let's say the field you insert consists of the following:

> From Paul Dickson's collection, *Words*, comes the word **culacino**, Italian for the mark left on a tablecloth by a wet glass.

Let's say that you changed it a bit. You could wind up with:

> Paul Dickson's collection, Words, *includes* the word culacino, **which** is Italian for the mark left on a tablecloth by a wet glass.

This literalism limits * mergeformat to times when you know your field won't change.

Setting the Case of Field Results

Word also enables you to choose the case of your field results by using the options shown in table 10.3:

Table 10.3
Setting the Case of Field Results with the * Switch

This Switch	Does This	Looks Like This
* caps	Capitalizes each word	Sample Text
* firstcap	Capitalizes first word	Sample text
* lower	Makes all text lowercase	sample text
* upper	Capitalizes all text	SAMPLE TEXT

Formatting Field Numbers

You can use * charformat and * mergeformat to format numbers as well. But numbers present some unique issues. What if a number should appear one way in one place, and another way where a field places it?

The predefined numeric formats in Word's Field Options dialog boxes can handle most of your needs. Think of this as background you can use to adjust those settings when you need to.

For instance, let's say that your source is a numbered list:

Sherby's Laws of Consulting
(source: Gerald M. Weinberg)

1. In spite of what your client may tell you, there's always a problem.
2. No matter how it looks at first, it's always a people problem.
3. Never forget they're paying you by the hour, not by the solution.

Now let's say that you want to use a field to refer to this rule elsewhere in the document, in another context:

> Remember Sherby's third rule of consulting: Never forget they're paying you by the hour, not by the solution.

How can you transpose "3" into "third"? Or, let's say you've got a dollar amount, $32.50, that needs to be placed elsewhere in check format:

> Thirty-two and 50/100

Word offers several field formatting options that can change a number from the way it appears in its source location, or establish altogether new formatting for a number created by a Word field.

Many of these numerical options use the * switch, as shown in table 10.4.

Table 10.4
Numeric Formats Controlled by the * Switch

This Switch	Creates This	Looks Like This	You Might Use It For
* alphabetic	alphabetic (changes number into corresponding lowercase letters)	aa	Catalogs
* Alphabetic	Alphabetic (changes number into corresponding uppercase letters)	AA	Catalogs
* Arabic	Arabic	27	Most applications
* cardtext	Cardinal text	Twenty-seven	Insertion into text, especially numbers below 20)
* dollartext	Cardinal text with fraction	Twenty-seven and 00/100	Checking/ purchase orders
* hex	Hexadecimal	1B	Computing applications
* ordinal	Ordinal	27th	Dates
* Roman	Roman numbers	XXVII	Publication

As usual, the switch is placed after other field instructions:

```
{ =joesales * .05 \* dollartext }
```

Painting a Numeric Picture

You use the * switches to control the kind of text into which your numbers are transformed. What if you're perfectly happy with plain old Arabic numbers (1, 2, 3...), but you want to control how they appear?

For this, Word offers a different switch: \#. You use this switch to paint a numeric picture of how you want your numbers to appear. A *numeric picture* is simply a generic model of how you want to format your numbers. For example, you're using fields to set up a list of numbers. If you use Word's default format, they'll look like this:

327.8

15.96

29

18.223

Sloppy. You want them to look like this:

327.800

15.960

29.000

18.223

You can combine the \# switch with two kinds of placeholders, # and 0, to create a numeric picture of how your numbers should appear. To get the cleaned-up list, use the following switch with each field:

```
\# ###.000
```

Quotation marks are optional unless you're combining the number with text. The # symbol tells Word: If there's no number in that location, insert a blank space. The 0 symbol tells Word: If there's no number in this location, insert a 0.

A numeric picture using # or 0 placeholders rounds off a fractional number that requires more digits than you allowed. For example, the field code { =1/4 } by default displays the result 0.25.

Note Word's default is to round off to hundredths.

But if you add a switch like this:

```
{ =1/4 \# #.# }
```

Word rounds off the last digit, like the following:

0.3

The # placeholders to the right of the decimal point also tell Word to round off any additional digits without a corresponding # symbol. # and 0 are probably the elements used most often. Not surprisingly, Word provides several others as well, all listed in table 10.5.

Several prefabricated # and 0 variants are available through the =expression Field Type box in the Insert Field dialog box.

Table 10.5
Characters You Can Use in Numeric Pictures

This Character	Does This	Sample Usage Field Result	Sample
#	Substitutes a blank space where no number is present. Rounds off extra fractional digits.	{ =1/4 \# #.# }	0.3
0	Substitutes a zero where no number is present.	{ =1/4 \# 00.000 }	00.250
$	Places a dollar sign in your field result.	{ =5/2 \# $#.00 }	$2.50
+	Places a + or – sign in front of any field result not equal to zero.	{ =1/4 \# +#.## }	+.25
-	Places a – sign in front of negative numbers.	{ =1/4 \# -#.## }	–.25
.	Places a decimal point.	{ =1/4 \# #.# }	0.3
,	Places a comma separator.	{ =8500/2 \# #,0 } (note: also use at least one 0 or #)	4,250

This Character	Does This	Sample Usage Field Result	Sample
;	Enables you to specify more than one option for displaying numbers, depending on whether the numbers are positive, negative, or zero.	{ =revenue-expenses \# $###.00; ($###.00); 0 }	$250.00 ($250.00) or 0
x	If placed on the left, truncates digits to its left. If placed on the right, truncates digits to its right.	{ =4875 \# #x## }	75
"text"	Includes text in a picture. Place the entire picture in double quotation marks, and the text in single quotation marks.	{ = "####'lira'" }	3472 lira

Date and Time Formatting

Like numbers, you can format dates and times in many different ways. Usually, the quickest way to format date and time is to create your field with Insert, Field; the Field Options dialog boxes have most of the formats you need. However, it doesn't hurt to know what's going on if you need a specialty format.

The date-time switch is \@. Similar to what you've already seen with numbers, \@ creates a date-time picture—a model of how your dates and times should look. This date-time picture is usable with the following fields:

Date

Time

Created

Printdate

Savedeate

You can use characters in table 10.6 and table 10.7 in date-time pictures. Note that in contrast to numeric formatting, the number of times a character is repeated can change its meaning substantially—as can its case.

Table 10.6
Characters You Can Use in Date Formatting

This Character	Presents This	Sample Usage Field Result	Sample
M	Month in numeric format, 1-12 (M must be capitalized)	{ DATE \@ "M" }	7
MM	Month in numeric format, adding a zero to months that have only one digit	{ DATE \@ "MM" }	07
MMM	Month as 3-letter abbreviation	{ DATE \@ "MMM" }	Jul
MMMM	Month, spelled out	{ DATE \@ "MMMM" }	July
d (upper or lowercase}	Day of month in numeric format, 1-31	{ DATE \@ "d" }	6
dd	Day of month in numeric format, 0-31	{ DATE \@ "dd" }	06
ddd	Day of week as 3-letter abbreviation	{ DATE \@ "ddd" }	Thu
dddd	Day of week, spelled out	{ DATE \@ "dddd" }	Thursday
y	Year (last two digits)	{ DATE \@ "y" }	95
yy	Year (all four digits)	{ DATE \@ "yy" }	1995

Table 10.7
Characters You Can Use in Time Formatting

This Character	Presents This	Sample Usage Field Result	Sample
h	Hour, based on a 12-hour clock running from 1-12	{ TIME \@ "h" }	8
hh	Hour, based on a 12-hour clock running from 01-12	{ TIME \@ "hh" }	08
H	Hour, based on a 24-hour clock running from 0-23	{ TIME \@ "H" }	17
HH	Hour, based on a 24-hour clock running from 00-23	{ TIME \@ "H" }	06
m	Minute, running from 0-59 (lowercase)	{ TIME \@ "m" }	3
mm	Minute, running from 00-59	{ TIME \@ "mm" }	03
AM/PM	Morning/ afternoon data in the format AM and PM	{ TIME \@ "h:mm AM/PM" }	9:30AM
am/pm	Morning/ afternoon data in the format am and pm	{ TIME \@ "h:mm am/pm" }	9:30am
A/P	Morning/ afternoon data in the format A and P	{ TIME \@ "h:mm A/P" }	9:30A
a/p	Morning/ afternoon in the format a and p	{ TIME \@ "h:mm data a/p" }	9:30a

You can add separators, such as the following:

```
:-/
```

wherever you want. For example:

h:mm 9:30

M-d-yy 3-8-56

MM/dd/yyyy 03/08/1956

Notice, that to avoid a conflict, M is always capitalized for Month; m is always lowercase for minute.

You can also add text to a date-time picture by enclosing the text in apostrophes within the field instruction:

```
{ TIME \@ "'This had better be done by' MMMM-d H:mm" }
```

Finally, you can add character formatting to the time or date by adding it to the field characters that represent it. For example, to underline just the month:

```
{ TIME \@ "'This had better be done by' MMMM-d H:mm" }
```

Nesting Fields

If you want the result of one field to affect what another field does, nest one field inside another. This might sound abstract, but it is immensely useful. The logistics are the easy part.

1. Create a field; press Ctrl+F9.
2. Edit the field as much as possible. Then place the insertion point where you want the nested field to appear.
3. Press Ctrl+F9 to insert a new field within your existing field. A sample (and simple) nested field appears below:

```
{IF {DATE \@ "d-MMM"}="25-Dec" "Merry Christmas" "Ho, ho, ho... Not today!"}
```

In this example, the If field checks the date returned by the Date field. If the date and format match 25-Dec, Word reports: `Merry Christmas`. If not, it reports: `Ho, ho, ho... Not today!`

Here's an example of how you can use nested fields to ask a user for an article name and then place that article name in Summary Info and anywhere else in the

document. Start by inserting a Set field, which sets a bookmark on the text that follows it. Call the bookmark Articlename:

```
{ SET ARTICLENAME }
```

Normally, the bookmark is followed by text. However, in this case, you need a Fillin field that asks the user to key in text:

```
{ SET ARTICLENAME { FILLIN "What is the article title?" } }
```

Next, create another nested field that uses Articlename as the document title, and also puts it in Summary Info. If you want the title to appear in your document footer, place this field there:

```
{ TITLE { REF articlename } }
```

With this nested-field technique, you can ask a user for any information and automatically place that information anywhere in the document.

Which Fields Do You Need?

You'll almost certainly never use all 60+ Word fields. The trick is to recognize which fields might help the most with the documents you create. Table 10.8 offers a starter list.

Table 10.8
Which Fields Should You Learn First?

If You Create...	These Fields Might Help You...
Articles	Author Date Edittime Noteref Numwords Ref Revnum Seq Subject Time Title

continues

Table 10.8, Continued
Which Fields Should You Learn First?

If You Create...	These Fields Might Help You...
Books/ Documentation	Noteref Index Pageref RD Ref Seq Styleref TC Title Toc XE
Brochures/ Newsletters	Includepicture Includetext Link Quote Revnum Symbol
Contracts	Autonumlgl Createdate Date Include Link Pageref Printdate Revnum Seq TA TOA
Financial Reports	DDE DDEauto Embed =Expression
Forms	Ask Date Fillin Gotobutton Time Formtext Formcheckbox Formdropdown

If You Create...	These Fields Might Help You...
Letters	Autotext Createdate Lastsavedby Username Userinitials
Print-merged form letters	Ask Data Database Fillin If Mergefield Mergerec Mergeseq Next Nextif Skipif

Field Reference

The remainder of this chapter is devoted to describing each of Word's 60+ fields, explaining usage, and showing examples. Whenever a field is discussed in more detail elsewhere in the book, there is a reference to let you know. Whenever a field can be more easily inserted via a specialized menu choice, you are shown how or told where to look.

Word for Windows 95 includes only one new field: Docproperty, which works with the new File, Properties dialog box.

Date and Time Fields

What they do: The Date and Time fields insert the date and time into the document. The date and time shown are accurate as of when they were inserted or updated.

Syntax:

To view the date or time in default format:

```
{ FIELDNAME }
```

To view the date or time in custom format:

```
{ FIELDNAME \@ customformat }
```

You can use the same custom formats in the date field or the time field. So, while their defaults are different, you can use both of them to return the same information.

Switches: \@ and \!

The Date field offers one additional switch: \l, which tells Word to use whatever date-time format you chose the last time you were in the Insert Date and Time dialog box.

How these fields work (Example):

To insert date and time in the following format:

01/24/94 11:23 AM

Use the following syntax:

```
{ TIME \@ "MM/dd/yy hh:mm AM/PM" }
```

Shortcuts: To display date or time in default format from within the header or footer: click the date or time buttons. To display date or time in any of nine standard formats, select Date and Time from the Insert menu, and choose the Date or Time format you prefer.

More information: Chapter 2.

Other Date-Related Fields

In addition to the Date field, these fields add date or time information to the document, and can use the same formatting options, except for \l. These documents all use information stored in the Properties, Statistics dialog box, accessible from the File menu.

Field syntax:	Corresponds to:
{ CreateDate }	The date and time the document was first created
{ EditTime }	The amount of time the document has been open since it was created
{ PrintDate }	The last time the document was printed
{ SaveDate }	The last time the document was saved

More information: Chapter 6.

Document Automation Fields

Compare

What it does: Compares two values. Returns 1 if the comparison is true, 0 if it is false.

Syntax:

```
{ COMPARE FirstExpression Operator Second Expression }
```

Either expression can be a number, a bookmark, a string, a nested field, or a value. You can also use the ? and * wild cards.

These operators work:

=	Equals
>	Greater than
<	Less than
>=	Greater than or equal to
<=	Less than or equal to
<>	Not equal to

How field works (Example):

To test whether the bookmark revenue exceeds the bookmark costs, and to return 1 if it does:

```
{ COMPARE revenue > costs }
```

Switches: None.

You can also use Compare together with an If field to include certain information if Compare returns 1 and other information if it returns 0:

```
{ IF {COMPARE revenue > costs} = 1 "You're profitable" "You're not profitable" }
```

Gotobutton

What it does: The Gotobutton field inserts a button in text. When you double-click the button, you move to another predefined location in the document.

Syntax:

```
{ GOTOBUTTON destination displaytext }
```

Note that none of these elements appear within quotation marks.

Switches: None.

How field works (Example):

The destination of a Gotobutton can be anything that would work in the **E**dit, **G**o To dialog box, including bookmarks, page numbers, line numbers, sections, footnotes, or annotations.

The display text is the words that appear in the button.

To create a display button that says `Press Me`, and when pressed goes to the bookmark Zap:

```
{ GOTOBUTTON Zap Press Me }
```

To create a display button that says `Go to Page 8` and when pressed goes to page 8:

```
{ GOTOBUTTON p8 Go to Page 8 }
```

Because Gotobutton and Macrobutton don't automatically update, you might want to format them so that they attract attention to themselves—or even embed a WordArt or Microsoft Draw drawing in them.

More information: Chapter 23.

If

What it does: The If field can take one action if a mathematical or logical statement is true, and another if it is false.

Syntax:

```
{ IF test iftruetext iffalsetext }
```

Switches: None.

How field works (Example):

Think of all the times you want a letter to say one thing if one set of circumstances applies, and another if it doesn't:

- Customers who've paid their bills versus those who haven't
- Major customers versus small customers
- Directions to your downtown store or your suburban store
- Information about your premium product line or your discount products

The If field allows you to automate this. If is most often used to test a mathematical statement. For example:

```
{ IF unitsales > 100,000 "Congratulations to
everyone in the department." "We haven't made
our numbers. Come to the next staff meeting
with solutions."
```

In this example, `unitsales > 100,000` is the test. The first statement in quotation marks is the *iftruetext*—what's displayed if unitsales does exceed 100,000. The second statement is the *iffalsetext*—what's displayed if the test fails.

The iftruetext and iffalsetext statements don't have to be quotes. You can use a nested field to bring in information from elsewhere.

Pretend that you own a major league baseball team. Many of your players have incentive clauses that pay extra if they meet certain statistics. If a player bats .300 or better, you want to congratulate him on reaching his incentive. But if not, you want to remind him of the contract language he signed:

```
{ IF batavg >= .300 "Congratulations! The check's in the mail. "Sorry, no
incentive this year. Remember, your contract says: { include contract.doc
incentclause } }
```

More information: In this chapter, related fields include Nextif and Skipif.

Macro

What it does: Runs a macro or Word command when updated.

Syntax:

```
{ MACRO macroname }
```

Switch:

The \s switch, followed by another macro name, runs a second macro whenever any part of the field result is selected.

How field works (Example):

To run the Word command AutoFormat (WordBasic name FormatAutoFormat) whenever you update your fields:

```
{ MACRO FormatAutoFormat }
```

Make sure that the macro is available when it's invoked. Either use a built-in global macro, or make sure that the macro is part of a template always available to you or any of your colleagues who may use this document.

Macrobutton

What it does: The Macrobutton field inserts a button in your text that, when double-clicked, runs a specified macro and inserts the results in the document.

Syntax:

```
{ MACROBUTTON macroname displaytext }
```

Switches: None. (Insert, Field Options box displays your available macro names.)

How field works (Example):

You can use Macrobutton to insert a button that runs any macro you create, or those that come with Word.

To run the macro FilePrintDefault, which displays a message that it can print one copy, and does so when clicked:

```
{ FilePrintDefault Doubleclick to print one copy now }
```

More information: Chapter 11 and Chapter 23.

Print

What it does: The Print field bypasses Windows to send coded instructions directly to your printer. This can be useful to achieve some sophisticated effects on a PostScript laser printer.

Syntax:

```
{ PRINT instructions }
```

The Print field does not update when you press F9.

Switches:

\p	PostScript instructions
\p cell	Prints current table cell
\p page	Prints current page
\p para	Prints current paragraph
\p pic	Prints next picture in current paragraph
\p row	Prints current table row

More information: Chapter 4.

Document Information Fields

What they do: These fields retrieve information about the document, and place it in the document. In some cases, you also can use them to store information you specify in the field, such as the author's name.

Document Information fields are listed in table 10.9.

Table 10.9
Other Fields That Insert Document Information

Field Syntax	Corresponds to	Otherwise Stored in	Switches Available
{ AUTHOR }	The document's author, included in Summary	File, Properties Summary	Character formatting (*) only
{ COMMENTS }	Comments included in Summary	File, Properties Summary	Character formatting (*) only
{ DOCPROPERTY}	*Any* property contained in the Properties dialog box	File, Properties	Character formatting (*) only

continues

Table 10.9, Continued
Other Fields That Insert Document Information

Field Syntax	Corresponds to	Otherwise Stored in	Switches Available
{ FILENAME }	The name of the file, as seen by DOS and in the title bar of the Word screen	Title bar, Properties, Statistics	Character formatting (*) \p \p includes path name
{ FILESIZE }	The size of the file, in bytes	File, Properties, Statistics	Character formatting (*) Numeric formatting (\#), \k displays file size in kilobytes, \m displays file size in megabytes
{ INFO }	Your choice of the other document information fields	N/A	Character formatting (*) list of Info Types including every field in this list, plus: { CREATEDATE }, { EDITTIME }, { PRINTDATE }, { REVNUM }, and { SAVEDATE }
{ KEYWORDS }	Keywords included in Summary	File, Properties Summary	Character formatting (*) only
{ LASTSAVEDBY}	The name of the person who saved the file last (Information originally set in Tools, Options User Info)	File, Properties, Statistics	Character formatting (*)

Field Syntax	Corresponds to	Otherwise Stored in	Switches Available
{ NUMCHARS }	Number of characters in the document	File, Properties, Statistics	Character formatting (*) Numeric formatting (\#)
{ NUMPAGES }	The number of pages in the document Statistics	File, Properties, Statistics	Character formatting (*) Numeric formatting (\#)
{ NUMWORDS }	The number of words in the document Statistics	File, Properties, Statistics	Character formatting (*) Numeric formatting (\#)
{ SUBJECT }	Document Subject included in Summary	File, Properties Summary	Character formatting (*)
{ TEMPLATE }	The template currently attached to the document	File, Properties Summary	Character formatting (*) \p includes pathname
{ TITLE}	Title included in Summary Info	File, Properties Summary	Character formatting (*)

Syntax for fields in this category:

```
{ FIELDNAME \switches }
```

For the following five fields, you can send information back to Summary Info by including it in quotation marks as a field instruction: Author, Comments, Keywords, Subject, and Title.

For the Info field, you must specify which piece of information you want to retrieve. (Your choices are listed in the table 10.9.) You can also use Info to send Author, Comments, Keywords, Subject, or Title information back to Summary Info.

How these fields work (Examples):

To retrieve your document's title from Summary Info and place it in your document:

```
{ TITLE }
```

To use Info to send a document's subject back to Summary Info:

```
{ INFO SUBJECT "Godzilla vs. Frankenstein" }
```

The following also works:

```
{ SUBJECT "Godzilla vs. Frankenstein" }
```

To include information about a document's file size, in kilobytes:

```
{ FILESIZE \k }
```

Shortcuts: If you want to print all Summary Info with your document, you can avoid dealing with fields:

1. Select **Options** from the **Tools** menu.
2. Select the **Print** tab.
3. Check **Summary** Info in the Include with Document group.
4. Choose OK.

More information: Chapter 6.

Creating Formulas with the {=} Field

What it does: Word enables you to perform a wide range of calculations in fields. You can perform these calculations directly on numbers that appear in the field or you can perform them on bookmarks that refer to numbers elsewhere in the document. You can even use cell references (A1) in fields, making Word tables behave much like spreadsheets.

Every field calculation starts with the equals (=) symbol. Fields that start with = are often called =expression fields. After that, you can use the symbols shown in table 10.10.

TABLE 10.10
Mathematical Symbols

Symbol	What It Does/Means
+	Add
-	Subtract
*	Multiply
/	Divide
%	Percentage (multiplies number by 100 and displays result with % sign)
^	Powers (if >1) roots (if <1)
=	Equals
<	Less than
<=	Less than or equal to
>	More than
>=	More than or equal to
<>	Not equal to

A list of mathematical functions are available, too. The best way to understand these is to see examples of how they're used. Word's functions are listed in table 10.11.

TABLE 10.11
Word Functions You Can Use in Fields

Function Name	What It Does	Example of How You Use It	Example of What Returns	Where You Can Use This
abs()	Inserts the absolute (positive) value of a number.	{ =abs(-36) }	346	With bookmarks

continues

Table 10.11, Continued
Word Functions You Can Use in Fields

Function Name	What It Does	Example of How You Use It	Example of What Returns	Where You Can Use This
and(x,y)	Combines two logical expressions. Both must be true for the proposition to be true.	{ =and(sales>costs,profit93>profit92) } (In this example, the statement is true if sales exceed costs *and* profits increased from year to year)	1 if true 0 if false	With bookmarks
average()	Averages as many values as you want.	{ =average (38,52,19,26) }	33.75	With bookmarks and table cells
count()	Counts the items in a list.	{ =count(baseball, football,hockey, golf,basketball) }	5	With bookmarks and table cells.
defined(x)	Checks an expression for potential errors.	{ =defined (revenue - costs) }	1 if the expression could be calculated. (The syntax is OK and the bookmarks exist.) 0 if an error would prevent calculation	With bookmarks
if(x,y,z)	Checks whether an expression is true. If it is, returns one piece of information.	{ =if(revenue>costs,profit, loss) }	1 if true 0 if false	With bookmarks

Function Name	What It Does	Example of How You Use It	Example of What Returns	Where You Can Use This
	If it isn't true, returns another (or none).			
int(x)	Deletes a fraction, rounding down to the next smaller whole number.	{ =int(308.887) }	308	With bookmarks
max()	Inserts the highest value in a list.	{ =max(185,511, 233,300) }	511 (number of highest-selling item)	With bookmarks and table cells
min()	Inserts the smallest value in a list.	{ =min(297,-8, 302,146) }	8 (number of lowest-selling item)	With bookmarks and table cells
mod(x,y)	Divides two numbers and inserts only the remainder (a whole number).	{ =mod(26,3) }	2	With bookmarks
not(x)	If statement is false, returns true. If statement is true, returns false.	{ =not(tapes< CDs) }	1 if false 0 if true	With bookmarks
or(x,y)	Combines two logical expessions. If either is true, the proposition is true.	{ =or(books> records,CDs> tapes) }	1 if either is true; 0 if both are false	With bookmarks

continues

Table 10.11, Continued
Word Functions You Can Use in Fields

Function Name	What It Does	Example of How You Use It	Example of What Returns	Where You Can Use This
product()	Multiplies all numbers in list.	{ =product (2,3,4,5) }	120	With bookmarks and table cells
round(x,y)	Rounds off to the number of places you specify.	{ =round (37.15552,2) } (Second number is the number of decimal digits that will appear.)	37.15	With bookmarks
sign(x)	Displays 1 if the value is positive, -1 if the value is negative.	{ =sign(-2857.2) }	-1	With bookmarks
sum()	Adds a list of numbers.	{ =sum(1,2,3,4, 5,6,7) }	28	With bookmarks and table cells.

Functions followed by an empty parenthesis can use any number of values. Functions followed by (x,y) require two values. The If function, followed by (x,y,z), can take three values.

Word also enables you to compare strings with logical operators. Another change is that Word now uses Excel's A1, B2 formatting for table cell names, instead of the more cumbersome R1C1, R2C2 terminology of olden days.

Syntax/How field works (Example):

A basic =expression field might simply add two numbers:

```
{ =20+40 }
```

This field, of course, displays the number 60 in your document. You're more likely, however, to perform a calculation on a number that appears elsewhere in your document. (That way, you're getting the benefit of fields—when that number changes, your calculation changes as well.)

To do this, mark the number with a bookmark and include the bookmark in your calculation. In the next example, you've bookmarked a number as sales, and you multiply it by five percent to figure someone's commission:

```
{ =sales * .05)
```

To borrow from Einstein's $E=MC^2$, if one quantity is bookmarked mass, and another quantity is bookmarked speed-of-light, you can solve for Energy as follows:

```
{ =(mass * speed_of_light)^2 }
```

Shortcuts: If you insert your =Formula field, using **Insert**, **Field**, you're presented several prefabricated options for customizing the way your field result appears.

If you own Microsoft Excel and you're already comfortable with it, you might not want to bother learning another approach for performing spreadsheet calculations. Instead, embed a spreadsheet in your Word document. With the new OLE 2.0 feature in Word and Excel, double-clicking on the spreadsheet transforms your screen into an Excel display.

In tables, you can use Table, Formula. If you only want to add the cells, select them first, and then choose Table, Formula; the formula will already be in place. Just choose OK.

EQ

What it does: Inserts a formatted mathematical equation in your document.

Syntax:

```
{ EQ switches }
```

Switches:

\a()	Array
\b()	Bracket
\d()	Displace
\f(,)	Fraction
\i(,,)	Integral
\l()	List
\o()	Overstrike
\r(,)	Radical

\s()	Superscript
\x()	Box

Within the parentheses, specify the text you want to include. In some cases, you must specify more than one element. Each switch has its own set of formatting options, which you can see by choosing the EQ field in Word's Search for Help On feature.

Shortcuts: Equations created with this field are compatible with those created in Word's Equation Editor, which is much easier to use.

Symbol

What it does: The Symbol field inserts any symbol you specify.

Syntax:

```
{ SYMBOL charnumber switches }
```

Switches:

\f	Use a specific font
\s	Use a specific size
\h	Overrides Word's Auto paragraph line spacing, so the symbol doesn't affect your line spacing

How field works (Example):

To insert a specific character, use Symbol with the character's number in the ANSI character set:

```
{ SYMBOL 209 }
```

To specify character 209 in the ZapfDingbats font:

```
{ SYMBOL 209 \f "ZapfDingbats" }
```

To specify the same character and font, in 24-point type:

```
{ SYMBOL 209 \f "ZapfDingbats" \s 24 }
```

Shortcut:

You almost always use Insert, Symbol to place a symbol in your document.

More information: Chapter 2.

Index and Tables

XE

What it does: Inserts a hidden index entry that Word finds when you compile an index.

Syntax:

```
{ XE "name of entry" switches }
```

Switches:

\r	Specifies text to be indexed. (\r should be followed by a bookmark identifying that text.)
\t	Specifies text to be printed instead of a page number. (\t should be followed by this text.)
\b	Turns boldface on or off in the entry's page number.
\i	Turns italics on or off in the entry's page number.

General switches don't work with the XE field.

How field works (Example):

First, position the insertion point at the text to be indexed, or select the text. To create an index entry named *Fortress America,* create the following field:

```
{ XE "Fortress America" }
```

To specify an entry that will be subordinate to another entry, use a colon:

```
{ XE "Isolationists: Fortress America" }
```

To specify that the words "See Lindbergh, Charles" appear instead of a page number:

```
{ XE "Isolationists" \t "See Lindbergh, Charles" }
```

Index entries are limited to 64 characters.

Shortcut: Press Alt+Shift+X and mark your index entry in the dialog box that appears.

More information: Chapter 14.

Index

What it does: The Index field compiles an index based on the index entries you mark.

Syntax:

```
{ INDEX switches }
```

Switches:

\b	Indexes only marked text. (Include bookmark name.)
\e	Inserts separator character. (Specify separator character between quotation marks.)
\g	Changes page separator character that normally appears between page numbers. (The default is a hyphen, as in the example 37-38).
\h	Adds characters that display as headings before each new index letter. (Specify characters or empty space between quotation marks.)
\l	Changes character or space to be used between page numbers.
\p	Tells Word to index only part of the document, based on the letters you specify.
\r	Runs sublevel index entries together with main index entries.
\s	Helps insert sequences. (See Chapter 14.)
\d	Changes characters that separate sequence number from page number. (See Chapter 14.)

How field works (Example):

To create a standard index of the entire document:

```
{ INDEX }
```

To index only text marked with the bookmark Columbia:

```
{ INDEX \b Columbia }
```

To index only entries between A and M:

```
{ INDEX \p a-m }
```

To place an empty line between each letter of the index:

```
{ INDEX \h " " }
```

Shortcut: Choose Inde**x** and Tables from the **I**nsert menu and create your index from the Inde**x** tabbed dialog box.

More information: Chapter 14.

TA

What it does: Inserts a table of authorities entry in your document.

Syntax:

```
{ TA switches }
```

Switches:

\b	Boldfaces the page number.
\c	Sets a category for when you compile the table of authorities. (Use the same character for all items in the same category.)
\i	Italicizes the page number.
\l	Defines the text of the long (full) citation.
\r	Includes a page range for the cited text, if you also specify a bookmark.
\s	Defines the text of the short citation.

How field works (Examples):

To boldface the table of authorities page number reference to Smith v. Jones:

```
{ TA \s "Smith v. Jones" \b }
```

In the preceding example, \s "Smith v. Jones" specifies that this is the short version of this reference.

To have your reference include a page range covering bookmarked text you've already marked:

```
{ TA \s "Smith v. Jones" \r smithcase }
```

Shortcuts: Press Alt+Shift+I to open a dialog box that marks your citation.

General switches don't work with the TA field.

More information: Chapter 13.

TOA

What it does: Compiles a table of authorities from marked citations.

Syntax:

```
{ TOA \c switches }
```

How field works (Example):

Switches:

Switch	Description
\c	(Required) Specifies which categories of citations to compile. Use numbers corresponding to the following categories:

Number	Category
1	Cases
2	Statutes
3	Other Authorities
4	Rules
5	Treatises
6	Regulations
7	Constitutional Provisions
8-16	Custom Categories

Switch	Description
\b	Compiles a table of authorities for the part of a document marked by a bookmark
\d	Used with \s, sets separator characters used between sequence numbers and page numbers
\e	Sets separator characters between a table of authorities entry and page number
\f	Clears character formatting from entry, so plain text appears in table of authorities
\g	Sets separator characters for a page range
\h	Adds category headings before each category of citations
\l	Sets separator characters used between page numbers where an entry is referred to on multiple pages

\p	Where an authority has at least five page references, replaces these references with the word *passim*
\s	Followed by a sequence name, includes a sequence number with the page number

How field works (Examples):

To compile a table of authorities consisting of all statutes cited in the document, and to include the word *STATUTES* at the top:

```
{ TOA \h \c 2 }
```

Shortcuts: Choose Inde**x** and Tables from the **I**nsert menu, and choose the Table of **A**uthorities tab. Compile the table from there.

General switches don't work with the TOA field.

More information: Chapter 13.

TC

What it does: The TC field creates a hidden-text entry that can be compiled later in a table of contents.

Syntax:

```
{ TC "Text of entry" switch tableidentifier }
```

How field works (Example):

To create a table of contents entry named *Overview,* insert the following field:

```
{ TC "Overview" }
```

The table identifier \f, followed by a single letter, lets you create multiple tables of contents in a single document. For example, you can add separate lists of figures, illustrations, and tables.

To create a table of contents entry named *Fragonard, Bathers, The Louvre, Paris,* and place it in a separate table of contents for colorplates:

```
{ TC "Fragonard, Bathers, The Louvre, Paris" \f c }
```

In this example, *c* is the one-letter identifier we chose for colorplates.

Shortcut:

Instead of using fields to create a single table of contents, you can use Word's built-in heading levels (styles Heading 1 through Heading 9) as you create the document, and then tell Word to compile them, using the Table of Contents tab in the **I**nsert, Inde**x** and Tables dialog box.

Switches:

\f	Table identifier specifies table of contents this entry should be included in
\l	Heading level
\h	Suppresses page number

General switches don't work with the TC field.

More information: Chapter 13.

TOC

What it does: The TOC field compiles a table of contents from the entries you've specified, or from text in your document already formatted as Heading 1 through Heading 9.

Syntax:

```
{ TOC switches bookmarkname tableidentifier }
```

Switches:

\b	Creates a table of contents based on specific bookmarked text.
\f	Creates a table of contents based on TC fields.
\o	Creates a table of contents based on only certain heading or TC levels.
\s	One step in creating a table of contents with chapter-page numbers, such as 14-2. (See Chapter 13.)
\d	Sets the page number separator. (See Chapter 13.)

How field works (Examples):

To build a table of contents from styled heading levels throughout the document:

```
{ TOC }
```

To build a table of contents from TC fields:

```
{ TOC \f }
```

To build a table of contents from text with the bookmark name partial:

```
{ TOC \b partial }
```

To build a table of contents that only includes first, second, and third level headings or TC entries:

```
{ TOC \o "1-3" }
```

To build a table of contents containing illustrations that have been marked to appear in a separate list, i:

```
{ TOC \f i }
```

Shortcut: Select Inde**x** and Tables from the **I**nsert menu. Select the Table of Contents tab. Choose settings there to compile your table of contents or figures.

More information: Chapter 13.

RD

What it does: The RD field enables you to develop an index or table of contents that includes entries in other documents. Using RD requires substantially less memory than Includetext, because RD inserts only the index or table of contents, not the entire document.

Syntax:

```
{ RD filename }
```

Switches: None.

How field works (Example):

To insert a table of contents or index from the document C:\WINWORD\REPORT.DOC:

```
{ RD c:\\winword\\report.doc }
```

If you want to set starting numbers or sequence values, you have to do that with TC or XE fields and switches in the source document.

RD is formatted as hidden text.

More information: Chapter 20.

Links and References

Autotext

What it does: The Autotext field inserts the contents of an AutoText entry. If the AutoText entry is changed, the field results change when they're updated.

Syntax:

```
{ AUTOTEXT entryname }
```

Switches: General switches only.

How field works (Example):

To insert the text associated with the AutoText entry experience:

```
{ AUTOTEXT experience }
```

More information: Chapter 9.

Includepicture and Includetext

Word provides two basic methods for using fields to display data from other documents.

The first method is to use Includetext to include text from another file, or Includepicture to include a picture from another file. The second, more sophisticated method is to use Object Linking and Embedding to establish ongoing connections between both documents. This method uses the Link and Embed fields.

Linking and embedding is covered in detail in Chapter 20, "Word as an Integrating Environment." Here, the fields each method depends upon are covered.

IncludeText

What it does: The IncludeText field inserts another document, or part of another document marked with a bookmark. IncludeText is often used to create a brief master document that controls the printing of multiple large documents.

Syntax:

To include all the contents of another file, specify the file name. If the file is located in another directory, include the complete path. Remember to use double backslashes (\\):

```
{ INCLUDETEXT c:\\directory\\filename.ext }
```

To include some of the contents of another file, first mark the material you want, and then add the bookmark's name to your field code:

```
{ INCLUDE c:\\directory\\filename.ext bookmarkname }
```

Switch:

\c	Tells Word to run an appropriate conversion filter on the file you're inserting. To insert the file as plain text, use the switch \c text.

How field works (Examples):

To insert selected text, assume that you have a table in another document named C:\REPORTS\SUMMARY.DOC.

You want to include the totals in your current document. Mark them as a bookmark and name it totals. Now return to your current document and insert the following Include field at the location where you want the totals to appear:

```
{ INCLUDETEXT c:\\reports\\summary.doc totals }
```

Shortcut: To insert an entire file, choose **F**ile from the **I**nsert menu. Select a file. (If necessary, change directories or display All Files in the List Files of **T**ype box, to see files without a DOC extension.)

If you want to specify bookmarked text, enter the bookmark in the **R**ange box. Choose OK. If the file is not a Word file, Word asks you to choose a conversion filter.

More information: Chapter 20.

If you insert text from Document A into Document B and then change that text in Document B, the text normally reverts to its Document A form when you update the field. To prevent this, you can lock the field in Document B. Or you can send the changes back to Document A, by pressing Ctrl+Shift+F7.

IncludePicture

What it does: The IncludePicture field enables you to convert graphics files and insert them in your current document.

Syntax:

```
{ INCLUDEPICTURE filename }
```

How field works (Example):

To import the clip art file BINDER.WMF, use the following field code:

```
{ INCLUDEPICTURE c:\\winword\\binder.wmf }
```

To edit a picture imported into Word this way, double-click on it, and Microsoft Draw opens.

Switch:

\d	Prevents Word from storing graphic data in a document, to reduce file size

Shortcut: To insert a picture, select **P**icture from the **I**nsert menu. Select a file. (If necessary, change directories or display the All Files in the List Files of **T**ype box to see files that don't have a DOC extension.) Choose OK.

More information: Chapter 20.

Embed

What it does: The Embed field places an object—such as text, graphics, spreadsheets, video, or sound—into your document.

Syntax:

```
{ EMBED classname switches }
```

Switches:

\s	Lets you scale the embedded object to any size you want
* mergeformat	Applies scaling and cropping of previous result to new result

How field works (Example):

You can't create an Embed field with Ctrl+F9 or Insert, Field (though you can display and edit an Embed field after you created it.

1. Create the object in an application that supports Object Linking and Embedding.
2. Copy the object into the Clipboard.
3. Select Paste **Special** from the **Edit** menu.

Or

1. Select **Object** from the **Insert** menu.
2. Choose the type of object you want to insert. Word opens the application that creates the selected type of object.
3. Prepare the object.
4. Exit the application and return to your Word file.

Here is a sample Embed field:

```
{ EMBED ExcelWorkSheet \s \* mergeformat }
```

More information: Chapter 20.

Link

What it does: Creates a link with text or other material in another file.

Syntax:

```
{ LINK classname filename bookmarkname \format }
```

Switches:

\a	Updates link automatically
\t	Inserts linked object as text
\r	Inserts linked object as RTF-formatted text
\p	Inserts linked object as picture
\b	Inserts linked object as bitmap

How field works (Example):

The Link field contains the type of object (class name), and the file name (including path). If you are only including part of a Word file, specify its bookmark name. Finally, you can specify one of the optional formatting switches given later.

If you use a path name, don't forget the double-backslashes (\\).

Shortcuts:

1. Create the object in Word or another OLE application.
2. Copy it to the Clipboard.
3. Select Paste **S**pecial from the **E**dit menu.
4. Select Paste Link.

More information: Chapter 20.

Ref, Pageref, and Noteref

What they do: The Ref field places the text associated with a bookmark in your document. With Ref, you can copy any text that recurs throughout the document, and when the original changes, all references change, too.

The Pageref field inserts the page number where that bookmark appears in your document. This means you can refer to the location of a document, and the reference remains accurate regardless of any changes you make in the document.

The Noteref field inserts a bookmarked footnote or endnote reference. With it, you can refer to a footnote elsewhere in the document, and the reference remains accurate even if other footnotes are added or removed.

Syntax:

```
{ FIELDNAME bookmarkname }
```

Switches: General formatting switches.

In Ref and Styleref:

\n	Inserts number of paragraph instead of bookmarked text

In Ref:

\f	Includes and increments footnote, endnote, and annotation numbers

How fields work (Example):

To insert a chapter number repeatedly throughout a document, select it and insert a bookmark named *chapnum.* Then, wherever you need the chapter number to appear, insert the field:

```
{ REF chapnum \* charformat }
```

To insert a page number corresponding to the location of the bookmark jonesquote:

```
{ PAGEREF jonesquote }
```

To create a footnote reference, select the footnote reference mark in the document (not the footnote pane). Create a bookmark (westnote), then insert the field:

```
{ NOTEREF westnote }
```

By default, the Noteref reference is formatted as a footnote or endnote reference mark.

More information: Chapter 15 and Chapter 17.

Styleref

What it does: The Styleref field is designed specifically to create the dictionary-style headers that appear on the top of pages in many reference books, for example:

incandescence-incisive

This is a bear of a task in most word processors, because any edit can change the words that appear at the top and bottom of practically every page. The Styleref field doesn't quite make this child's play—but if this is something you need to do, it's enormous progress.

Syntax:

```
{ STYLEREF "stylename" switch }
```

Switch:

\l	Find the last paragraph on a page which uses a specific style. Then display the contents of that paragraph, up to 255 characters, as the field result.

How field works (Example):

The big idea behind Styleref is that the main headings of each item in your text must use a different style from the other text elements. If they do, the next step is to tell Styleref which style name you're using for main headings. Styleref can search for character styles as well as paragraph styles. You have to be using Word styles for this to work—manual formatting won't do the job.

The style name appears in quotes:

```
{ STYLEREF "header" }
```

Left alone, this only picks the first style reference on the page. You probably also want the last. Add the \l switch:

```
{ STYLEREF "header" \l }
```

Styleref is almost always placed in headers and footers, though it can be used elsewhere.

More information: Chapter 2.

Quote

What it does: The Quote field inserts text you specify in the field itself.

Syntax:

```
{ QUOTE "text" }
```

Switches: General switches only.

How field works (Example):

To insert the phrase "When it rains, it pours" into your document:

```
{ QUOTE "When it rains, it pours" }
```

Mail Merge

Mail merge is Word's procedure for printing multiple documents that are individually personalized. Word has refined mail merges to the point where it is now possible to perform very sophisticated merges without directly using fields.

Word's mail merge features are covered in detail in Chapter 19, "Automating Mail Merge Tasks." However, although mail merge has a new, more sophisticated interface, fields are still doing the work behind the scenes. This section covers the fields used in mail merge.

Ask

What it does: The Ask field opens a dialog box that allows a user to type information, which becomes a bookmark that is then placed anywhere in the document you want.

The Ask field is most often used as part of a mail merge, to allow the customization of a letter with information that isn't in a predefined data file. You can't place an Ask field in footnotes, headers, footers, annotations, or macros.

Syntax:

```
{ ASK nameofbookmark "Text you want in the dialog box." }
```

How field works (Example):

Let's say you want to add a personal P.S. to each of your regular sales letters:

1. Insert the Ask field after P.S., using syntax like this:

   ```
   { ASK bookmark "Text" }
   ```

2. Run your mail merge. Before each document prints, an Ask dialog box appears.

Switches:

\d	Assigns default text to print if you don't add custom text when the dialog box appears
\o	Prompts for text only before printing the first document, not before every document

More information: Chapter 19.

Data

What it does: This is an old field that Word 95 does not use. However, if you have it in a Word 2 mail merge document, it still works under Word 95.

In Word 2, Word places the Data field at the beginning of your form letter; it identifies the file that contains the data to be merged. After you attach the data file, the data field is removed.

Syntax:

```
{ DATA datafile headerfile }
```

Switches: None.

Shortcut: Use Word's mail merge feature, described in Chapter 19.

How field works (Example):

If you specify C:\REPORTS\DATA.DOC as your data file, Word inserts this field:

```
{ DATA c:\\reports\\data.doc }
```

If a separate file contains header information, this information appears afterwards:

```
{ DATA c:\\reports\\data.doc c:\\reports\\header.doc }
```

More information: Chapter 19.

Database

What it does: Imports data from a database program.

Syntax:

```
{ DATABASE switches }
```

Switches:

\b Used with the \l switch, tells Word which elements of table formatting to apply. You add up all the formatting elements you want from the following list, and Word deconstructs that number into the formatting elements it will use. (No two formatting combinations add up to the same number.)

0	No formatting
1	Borders
2	Shading
4	Font
8	Color
16	Use Best Fit
32	Heading Rows

	64	Special Format Last Row
	128	Special Format First Column
	256	Special Format Last Column

\c	Prefaces an ODBC query to an external database.
\d	Prefaces the database's path and file name.
\f	Sets a data record from which Word starts inserting data.
\l	Formats the incoming Word data table with a Table AutoFormat format. (Use with \b switch if you only want to apply certain formatting elements.)

Shortcuts: Import database information by using **Insert**, **Database**.

More information: Chapter 19, Chapter 20, and Chapter 23.

Fillin

What it does: The Fillin field prompts the user to insert text in a dialog box, and then inserts that text in the document. It's often used to personalize letters during mail merge, and to make it easier to fill in forms.

Syntax:

```
{ FILLIN "prompt" }
```

Switch:

\d	Gives Word alternative text to insert if the user doesn't enter any text in the dialog box

How field works (Examples):

To present the user with the request "What would you like for breakfast?" enter this field:

```
{ FILLIN "What would you like for breakfast?" }
```

To present the user with the same request, and fill in Oatmeal if nothing is entered:

```
{ FILLIN "What would you like for breakfast? \d "Oatmeal" }
```

More information: Chapter 19 and Chapter 23.

Mergefield

What it does: The Mergefield field places a data file field into a mail merge document.

Syntax:

```
{ MERGEFIELD fieldname }
```

Switches: None.

Shortcut: Use Word's mail merge feature.

How field works (Example):

To specify that the address field should be included in the merged document:

```
{ MERGEFIELD address }
```

More information: Chapter 19.

Mergerec

What it does: The Mergerec field adds the record number to the document.

Syntax:

```
{ MERGEREC }
```

Switches: None.

Shortcut: Use Word's mail merge feature.

How field works (Example): To include consecutive record numbers in your merged letters, insert this field:

```
{ MERGEREC }
```

More information: Chapter 19.

Mergeseq

What it does: The Mergeseq field adds an incremental record number to the document, based on the results of the current mail merge. Whereas Mergerec numbers your merged documents based on the overall number of records in your data source, Mergeseq numbers them based on the number pulled for this mail merge.

Syntax:

```
{ MERGESEQ }
```

Switches: None.

How field works (Example):

You might want a mail merged form to include a document number:

Purchase Order 384

To insert the Purchase order number in boldface, insert

```
{ MERGESEQ }
```

Next

What it does: The Next field tells Word to move to the data file's next record, without automatically starting a new page. You can use it to print lists or address labels.

Syntax:

```
{ NEXT }
```

Switches: None.

How field works (Example):

To start a new address label, place a Next field before the label fields:

```
{ NEXT }
{ SALUTATION } { FIRSTNAME } { LASTNAME }
{ COMPANY }
{ ADDRESS }
{ CITY }, { STATE } { ZIP }
```

You can't use Next in footnotes, annotations, headers, footers, Data files, or in nested fields.

More information: Chapter 19.

Nextif

What it does: The Nextif field tells Word to move to the data file's next record, but only if the conditions you specify are met.

Syntax:

```
{ NEXTIF expression operator expression }
```

Switches: None.

How field works (Example):

To include the next record in a mail merge only if it's been more than 90 days since a payment was received from that customer, add a bookmark, *paydate*, to the field that includes account aging information. Then use the following field:

```
{ NEXTIF paydate > 90 }
```

Nextif and Skipif use the same conditional tests as the If field: = > < >= <= <>

Shortcut: Use Word's mail merge feature.

More information: Chapter 19.

Set

What it does: The Set field places text in a bookmark. After the text is in a bookmark, it appears anywhere a field refers to that bookmark.

Syntax:

```
{ SET bookmarkname "text" }
```

Switches: General switches only.

How field works (Example):

To tell Word to create a bookmark named *lincoln* and insert the text "All men are created equal":

```
{ SET lincoln "All men are created equal" }
```

To tell Word to create a bookmark named *brightideas* and to insert in it whatever text you add to a dialog box:

```
{ SET brightideas { FILLIN "Got any bright ideas?" } }
```

More information: Chapter 16.

Skipif

What it does: The Skipif field skips a record during mail merge, if the record meets a specified condition.

Syntax:

```
{ SKIPIF expression operator expression }
```

Switches: None.

How field works (Example):

During mail merge, to skip records of customers who have paid their invoices in less than 30 days, add a bookmark, paydate, to the field that includes account aging information. Then use the following field:

```
{ SKIPIF paydate < 31 }
```

Shortcut: Use Word's mail merge feature.

More information: Chapter 19.

Numbering Fields

Autonum, Autonumout, and Autonumlgl

What they do: Word provides three fields for numbering text—and renumbering them automatically when you add, change, or delete items. Numbers are placed at the beginning of each paragraph (after paragraph marks).

Autonum provides standard numbering, Autonumout provides standard outline numbering, and Autonumlgl provides legal outline numbering.

Syntax:

```
{ FIELDNAME }
```

Switches: None—not even numeric formatting switches.

How fields work (Example):

Place one of these fields at the beginning of each paragraph or item you want to number. Then, if you change the order of the paragraphs, the fields renumber immediately (even without pressing F9).

Shortcuts: You can perform many of these tasks with the Formatting toolbar's Numbering button, with Format, Bullets and Numbering, and with Format, Heading Numbering.

More information: Chapter 2 and Chapter 12.

Barcode

What it does: Inserts a postal bar code equivalent to a ZIP Code you specify.

Syntax:

```
{ BARCODE "ZipCode" \u }
```

or

```
{ BARCODE AddressBookmark \b \u}
```

Switches:

\b	Tells Word to look for the named bookmark, and use it as the ZIP Code it needs.
\f	Adds a facing identification mark to your envelope. (Used for business reply mail. Specify \f "A" or \f "C" for the FIM-A or FIM-C mark.)
\u	Tells Word that the preceding text is a U.S. ZIP Code.

How field works (Example):

To use the bookmark *addresseezip* as the ZIP Code from which Word creates a postal bar code:

```
{ BARCODE addresseezip \b \u }
```

To include the ZIP Code in the field itself:

```
{ BARCODE "11001" \u }
```

To use a bookmark and also add a FIM-A mark:

```
{ BARCODE addressezip \b \u \f "A" }
```

Shortcuts: For goodness sake, use Tools, Envelopes and Labels. Word finds your ZIP Code in your addressee's address, bookmarks it for you, and inserts the proper {BARCODE} field code.

Page

What it does: The Page field inserts the current page number.

Syntax:

```
{ PAGE numberformat }
```

Switches: General switches only.

How field works (Example):

To insert the current page number:

```
{ PAGE }
```

To insert the current page number in roman numerals:

```
{ PAGE \* roman }
```

Shortcut: To insert a page number in a header or footer, open the header or footer pane, and click the page number button.

To insert a page number anywhere, and to control page number formatting, choose Page Numbers from the Insert menu.

More information: Chapter 2.

Revnum

What it does: Inserts the number of times the document has been revised, as recorded in File, Summary Info, Statistics.

Syntax:

```
{ REVNUM }
```

Switches: * character formatting and \# numeric formatting switches only.

How field works (Example):

To insert the number of times you've revised the file, in Roman numerals:

```
{ REVNUM \* ROMAN }
```

Remember, each time you save the file, Word chalks up another revision number. So this may not capture a true draft number, if that's what you're looking for.

More information: Chapter 6.

Section

What it does: Inserts the current section number.

Syntax:

```
{ SECTION }
```

Switches: * character formatting and \# numeric formatting switches only.

How field works (Example):

To insert the current section number, using a capital letter:

```
{ SECTION \* ALPHABETIC }
```

Sectionpages

What it does: Inserts the total number of pages in the current section.

Syntax:

```
{ SECTIONPAGES }
```

Switches: * character formatting and \# numeric formatting switches only.

How field works (Example):

To insert the number of pages in the current section:

```
{ SECTIONPAGES }
```

Seq

What it does: The Seq field enables you to create sequences of figures, tables, or anything else. These sequences remain in accurate numerical order throughout the document, regardless of editing changes you make in the document.

Syntax:

```
{ SEQ identifier bookmarkname }
```

Switches:

\c	Inserts nearest preceding sequence number (instead of adding "1"). You can use this to make sure that a figure number and its preceding text reference stay in sync.

\n	Insert next sequence number (default setting).
\r	Reset the sequence numbering to a specific number.
\h	Don't show field result. (Ideal when you want a cross-reference, but you don't want a cross-reference number appearing in the document.)

How field works (Example):

To insert a sequence of figure numbers, place the following field next to each figure reference:

```
{ SEQ figure }
```

You can name the sequence anything you like, as long as you use the same name for all items in the sequence. You can create multiple sequences in the same document by using different sequence names.

To create a cross-reference, select a Seq} field and bookmark it. Then place another Seq field where you want the cross-reference to appear, and include the bookmark name in it:

```
{ SEQ figure jones }
```

More information: Chapter 17.

User Information Fields

What it does: Word contains three User Information fields, Useraddress, Userinitials, and Username. These fields retrieve user information stored in the Tools Options User Info dialog box. They can also place information in that box.

Syntax:

```
{ FIELDNAME }
```

or, to place new information in Tools Options User Info:

```
{ FIELDNAME "new information" }
```

How field works (Example):

To insert your initials in the document (as you might at the bottom of a letter):

```
{ USERINITIALS }
```

To change the user's name to Robert Martinez in Tools, Options, User Info:

```
{ USERNAME "Robert Martinez" }
```

Switches: General switches only.

More information: Chapter 6.

Other Fields

Word 95 contains a few other fields not covered here. The Advance field moves text to the left or right, up or down, or to a specific place on the page. In general, you use Word's formatting commands and frames to perform these tasks.

Three Form Fields, FormText, FormCheckBox, and FormDropDown, enable you to block out text areas, buttons, and list boxes that can be used in filling out forms. These fields must be inserted by selecting Form Field from the Insert menu.

Finally, the Private field stores formatting data left over after documents are converted to Word from other file formats. Word inserts this data itself if you request it.

Macros

In this chapter, you first see how far you can get with macros without doing any WordBasic programming. Then, you take a glimpse at how much further you can get with WordBasic programming.

With a macro, you can assemble a set of procedures and run it automatically with a single command. You might have special character formats or paragraph formats, for example, that you would like to set with a keystroke rather than from a dialog box. With macros, you can assemble the procedures that enable you to switch to hanging indentations and then back to normal paragraph style, or from normal text to red, bold, small caps and back. You can assign these procedures to keystrokes so that you can make such changes more quickly than you can using dialog boxes.

The set of procedures can contain several steps and accomplish a great deal of work. You can, for example, create macros that check for matches in paired punctuation marks such as parentheses. To simplify such tasks, Word for Windows 95 contains its own programming language, WordBasic, through which you can develop macros that display dialog boxes, present choices, and execute tasks based on any of the features built into Word. Nearly every Word command has a corresponding WordBasic command that can be written into macros.

You meet WordBasic programming at the end of this chapter. But first, learn all the ways macros can save you time *even if you never write a single line of code.*

Microsoft has announced that it will eventually move from the WordBasic language to a new language, Visual Basic for Applications, which will be common to all Microsoft Office applications. Visual Basic for Applications is already used by Microsoft Excel. Microsoft's current plans are to include Visual Basic for Applications support in the next major revision of Word. Currently, Excel supports both VBA and its previous macro language, so it is reasonable to assume that Word will continue to run macros you write or record in WordBasic for some time.

You can create a macro by *recording* it. The recording process is similar to using a tape deck to record music or a VCR to record a television program. You turn on a device within Word that monitors all your keystrokes and mouse actions. This recording device, the *macro recorder*, translates your keystrokes and mouse actions into WordBasic macro commands. You merely type and click as you ordinarily would to accomplish the task. The macro recorder does the rest, and you have usable macros immediately, all without learning the macro language or how to program.

Making use of Word's macro recorder enables the most complicated actions from the keyboard, menus, or toolbars to be automated into a macro that runs at a single keyboard command.

Think about that the next time you follow the five steps required to transpose two mistyped letters, or insert a page that has to be two columns, or display Print Preview in full-screen mode so that you can see more of your document, or add a footer that contains a title already in your document. Anything you do often is worth recording and automating. This chapter tells you how.

This chapter also shows you more than 25 macros that come with Word. Microsoft's documentation barely mentions them. They aren't installed automatically, but they're easy to use if you know how—and they can make life much more convenient.

In this chapter:

- Understanding macros
- Recording a macro
- Using the macro toolbar
- Deciding what to record

- Assigning keyboard shortcuts
- Running macros
- Creating macros that run automatically
- Using macros that come with Word

Recording a Macro

Before recording a macro, make sure that your document is in the same shape it will be when you *use* the macro. For example, if you are recording a macro that transposes letters, make sure that your insertion point is already just before or after those letters.

In the next example, you record a macro that helps you proofread your documents. Although grammar checkers are good and getting better all the time, they may not find every incomplete sentence in a document. Most grammar checkers miss incomplete sentences that are caused when long introductory phrases have been split off as sentences by accident, as in the following:

- Although grammar checkers are good and getting better all the time. They have difficulty finding every sentence fragment in a document.
- Sitting in the park on a sunny Saturday afternoon and feeding the pigeons popcorn. I felt my mind wandering back to the question of how really to finish the quarterly report.

This sample macro moves you from period to period through the document. It helps you find incomplete sentences by focusing on the punctuation mark that creates them. Reading to the left and right of each period to make sure that a full sentence lies on either side enables you to trap them every time.

To record the macro, follow these steps:

1. Choose **M**acro from the **T**ools menu. The Macro dialog box opens (see fig. 11.1).

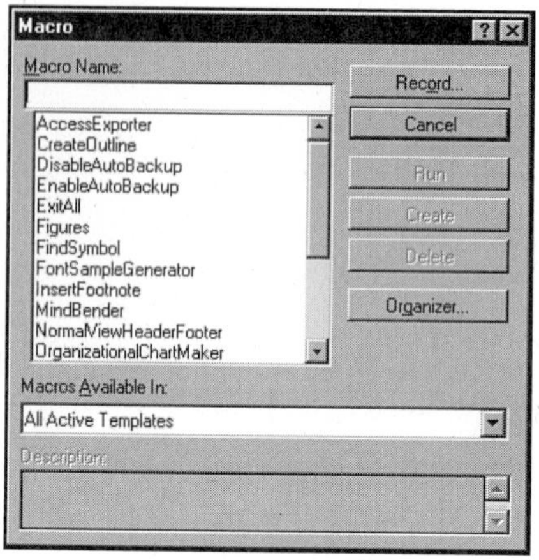

Figure 11.1

Macro dialog box.

2. Click on Rec**o**rd. The Record Macro dialog box opens (see fig. 11.2).

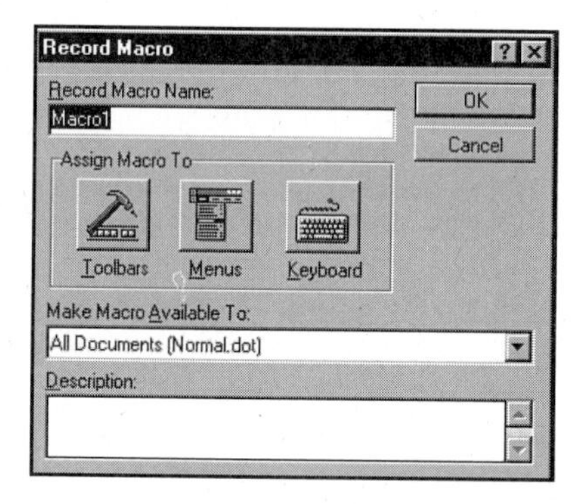

Figure 11.2

Record Macro dialog box.

3. Type a name in the **R**ecord Macro Name dialog box. (PeriodCheck is a good name for this macro.)

   Macro names cannot include spaces. Names must begin with letters of the alphabet, although numbers can be included afterward.

   Mixed caps and lowercase are not only okay, they're required to make your macro names comprehensible, as in this built-in Word command macro:

   DrawBringInFrontOfText

4. In the Make Macro **A**vailable To box, choose where you want to store this macro.

   You can place it in the NORMAL.DOT template, where it is available to all documents, but you run the risk of cluttering up NORMAL.DOT with macros

you use only in rare situations. (If you have lots of little-used macros in NORMAL.DOT, you might lose track of them. It is better to create document templates specific to these rarer tasks and use them to organize your macros. In addition, the more macros you have in a document template, the slower Word might run.) You also can place them in any open document or global template.

Note Fortunately, Word's Organizer makes it easy to move macros among templates, so this decision isn't irrevocable.

5. Type a description of the macro in the Description box. Be specific. Don't skip this step. You'll find it indispensable later when you try to remember what the macro does. (For this example, type **Searches for each period to aid revision**.)

6. Decide from where you want to run this macro. If you do nothing, the macro appears in the Macro dialog box you saw in figure 11.1, and it can be run from there. However, in the Assign Macro To group, you also can place your macro in a toolbar or menu, or give it a keyboard shortcut.

   When you choose one of these options, the appropriate Customize dialog box opens (see fig. 11.3).

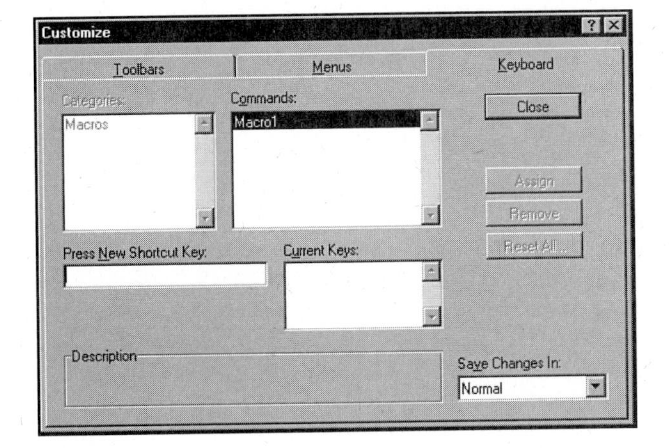

Figure 11.3
Customize dialog box.

Customization is covered in detail in Chapter 24, "Personalizing Word," but before you use it, think of a strategy for where you place your macros.

If you use a macro all the time, you may want to place it in your toolbar or give it a keyboard shortcut. Be careful not to overwrite a built-in Word keyboard shortcut accidentally. (Word shows you which keys are currently assigned to macros under Press New Shortcut Key after the phrase Currently Assigned To.)

If you want other people to use the macro, you can add it to a menu. If you rarely use it, don't clutter your interface. Just go to **T**ools, **M**acro when you want to run it.

7. From Record, click on OK, or from Customize, click on Close. The Macro Record toolbar appears, and your mouse pointer now has an audiocassette tape icon attached to it (see fig. 11.4).

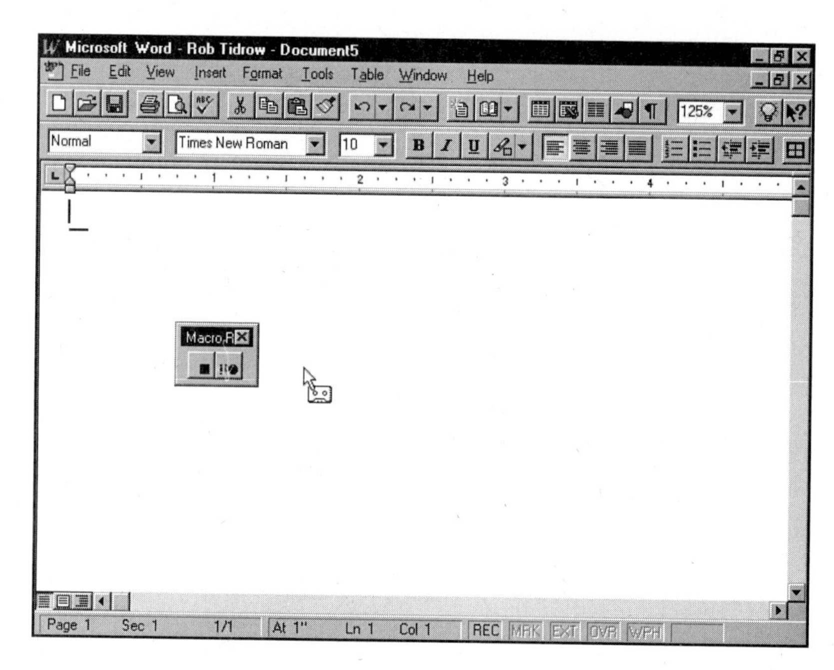

Figure 11.4
Macro Record toolbar and mouse pointer.

8. Now, perform whatever action you want to record. In this case, choose the **F**ind option on the **E**dit menu, press the period key, and click on the **F**ind Next button. If you want to pause recording (while you do something else, perhaps), click on Pause—the right button on the Macro Record toolbar. To stop recording, click on the Stop button—the square button on the left.

   When you choose Stop, the audiocassette icon disappears and your macro appears in the Macro Name list and anywhere else you put it. You can use it immediately.

Note A more detailed macro toolbar opens when you write a WordBasic macro.

The accompanying CD-ROM contains a file, IWMS11.DOT, with 15 prerecorded macros, each with assigned keyboard shortcuts. You can use these macros by loading the IWMS11.DOT template or copying the macros into NORMAL.DOT using the Organizer. These macros are listed in table 11.1.

TABLE 11.1
Macros Included on Disk with IWMS11A.DOT

Keyboard Shortcut	Macro	Function
Alt+A	AlphabetizeSelection	Alphabetizes selected text separated by paragraph marks.
Alt+B	BoldItalicize	Applies bold and italic style to selected text.
Alt+C	ColumnsTwo	Formats selected text in two columns (in its own section).
Alt+F	FootnoteInsert	Inserts a footnote.
Alt+G	IgnoreWhileSpellchecking	Tells Word to ignore selected text while proofing.
Alt+H	OpenHeader	Opens the Header/Footer pane with Header showing.
Alt+L	ColumnsThree	Formats selected text in three columns (in its own section).
Alt+N	NumberListWithLetters	Creates a numbered list that uses the A., B., C. format.
Alt+O	OpenFooter	Opens the Header/Footer pane and switches to Footer.
Alt+P	PreviewFullScreen	Switches to Print Preview and displays in Full Screen mode.
Alt+T	TrademarkSymbol	Inserts trademark symbol.
Alt+U	UnderlineBold	Formats selected text in bold and underline.
Alt+X	BoxBorderText	Borders selected text with a _ point box.
Alt+Y	CopyrightSymbol	Inserts copyright symbol.
Alt+Z	Zoom200Percent	Zooms display to 200 percent.

You might want to combine these prerecorded macros with the custom toolbars and menus in the NRP.DOT template also included on the disk and discussed in Chapter 24.

Running Macros

To run a macro that you haven't assigned to a toolbar, menu, or keyboard shortcut, follow these steps:

1. Select **T**ools, **M**acro.
2. Select the Macro from the **M**acro Name list.

   By default, **M**acro Name lists all macros built into every open template (All Active Templates). If that list is unmanageable, you may want to view the macros in a specific template.

3. Choose **R**un.

One large group of macros is not displayed in the All Active Templates list—the over 500 macros that correspond to Word's built-in commands, many of which aren't on toolbars or menus.

Many of the names of these commands are organized by Word menu category. For example, FileCloseAll is a File-related command that doesn't appear on the **F**ile menu.

To run these Word commands, choose Word Commands from the Macros **A**vailable In box. Then select the macro and run it.

Copy the template IWMS11A.DOT into your WINWORD\TEMPLATES subdirectory. Open a new document based on this template and run the macro.

Creating Macros That Run Automatically

What if you want to run a macro automatically every time you load Word? For example, you can record a macro that opens the document numbered 1 on your file list—the last document on which you worked.

Suppose you want to run a macro every time you create a new document? For example, you can record a macro that displays fill-in fields. The user types the requested information, and that information automatically becomes part of the document.

What if you want to make sure that your Word settings revert to the way they are when you first start Word, eliminating any special settings you temporarily added during a session?

You can make a macro do any of these things if you name it with one of the five special names Word recognizes (see table 11.2).

TABLE 11.2
Macros That Run Automatically

Macro	When It Runs
AutoExec	When you start Word
AutoNew	When you create a new file
AutoOpen	When you open a file
AutoClose	When you close a file
AutoExit	When you exit Word

AutoExec and AutoExit reside in NORMAL.DOT. You can place the others either in NORMAL.DOT or another document template. The advantage of using a document template is that you can choose to have your AutoNew, AutoOpen, or AutoClose macros run only on a specific kind of document.

Finding Good Tasks to Record

As you work, keep an eye out for tasks you perform repeatedly. The tasks are different for everyone, but the following list provides some ideas:

- Formatting, such as Small Caps, and combinations, such as Bold Underline, that don't have toolbar shortcuts
- Closing all open files (create a macro that chooses the FileCloseAll command from the Tools, Macro, Word Commands list)
- Saving a file to a floppy disk

- Changing between two connected printers
- Inserting AutoText entries with a single keyboard combination (create a macro that types the AutoText name and presses F3)
- Displaying the Drawing toolbar and opening the dialog box to choose a picture
- Applying a specific Table AutoFormat
- Compiling an index or table of contents with custom attributes
- Inserting a specific header or footer, perhaps containing bookmark fields that add information from elsewhere in the document
- Showing all field codes
- Displaying hidden text

Moving Macros among Templates

As mentioned earlier, macros live in templates. If you want a macro to be available to a class of documents that doesn't use a specific document template, copy the macro. You use the Organizer to copy macros, much as you did with templates in Chapter 8, "Templates and Wizards." Follow these steps:

1. Choose **T**ools, **M**acros.
2. Choose Or**g**anizer. The Organizer dialog box appears (see fig. 11.5).

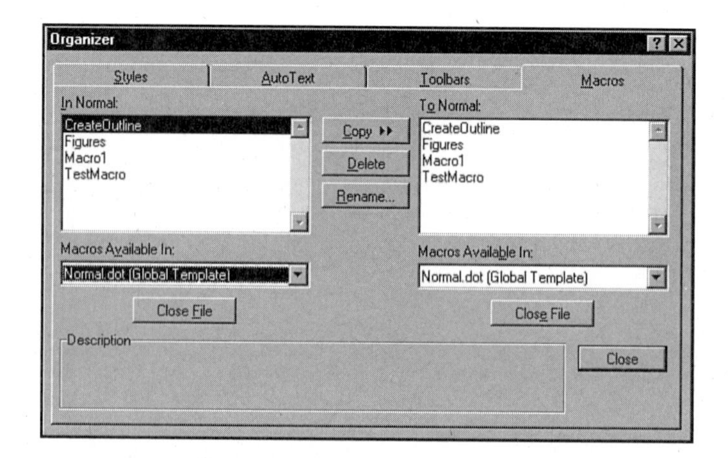

Figure 11.5
Organizer dialog box.

3. Choose the macro you want to copy. (You might have to close the existing template and open another template containing your macro.)

4. Choose where you want to copy the macro.

5. Close Organizer when you finish.

From the template IWMS11A.DOT, copy the PreviewFullScreen macro into NORMAL.DOT.

Using Macros That Come with Word

Word comes with five files of macros. When you install the macro files, they're contained in the WINWORD\MACROS directory. The macro files are not available until you make them available, and you can do this in a couple of ways.

Using the Organizer, you can move some or all of the macro files to NORMAL.DOT, making them available to all documents or to a specific document template. You also can copy one or more of these macro files to the WINWORD\STARTUP directory, where they load as global templates along with NORMAL.DOT whenever you run Word.

When you load a template this way, *all* its macros are available to *all* your documents. More macro code has to sit in memory, however. This is a bit like making Word carry extra suitcases around—it can slow things down.

This book notes the presence of relevant macros throughout, but tables 11.3, 11.4, 11.5, 11.6, and 11.7 provide comprehensive lists, along with occasional pictures of macros that appear especially interesting. Note that, as is the Windows 95 convention, templates in the MACRO folder all appear without the .DOT extension when you access them from the Organizer.

Table 11.3
Macros in MACRO7.DOT

Macro	Function
AutoNew	Displays the Word 7.0 Macros toolbar, with a button that displays a dialog box allowing you to easily choose a MACRO7.DOT macro.

continues

Table 11.3, Continued
Macros in MACRO7.DOT

Macro	Function
DisableAutoBackup	Turns off EnableAutoBackup.
EnableAutoBackup	Starts backing up files automatically to the directory you specify.
ExitAll	Exits Word, first displaying a list of open documents for you to save or discard.
FindSymbol	Finds Symbol characters.
FontSampleGenerator	Prints a matrix containing all of a font's characters.
InsertFootnote	Inserts a footnote.
MindBender	Runs a simple computer game (see fig. 11.6).
NormalViewHeaderFooter	Enables you to edit headers and footers the way Word 2 did it—without having to go into Header/Footer view.
OrganizationalChartMaker	Converts an outline containing information about each individual in your organization into an organizational chart. Each level of employee must be represented by a different heading style for this macro to work.
RegOptions	Views and changes Word options in the registration database.
RunSampleMacros	Displays a dialog box allowing you to easily choose a MACRO7.DOT macro.
SaveSelectiontoTextFile	Saves selected text into a new file attached to a template you choose.
SetPrintFlags	Enables you to change advanced print settings (generally only for technical support).
SuperDocStatistics	Displays a dialog box from which you can display all document statistics, all bookmarks, all fields, all fonts, all grammar rules, graphics, links, objects, sections, and tables contained in your current document; prints a report of these items if you want.
WordPuzzler	Runs a simple word game.

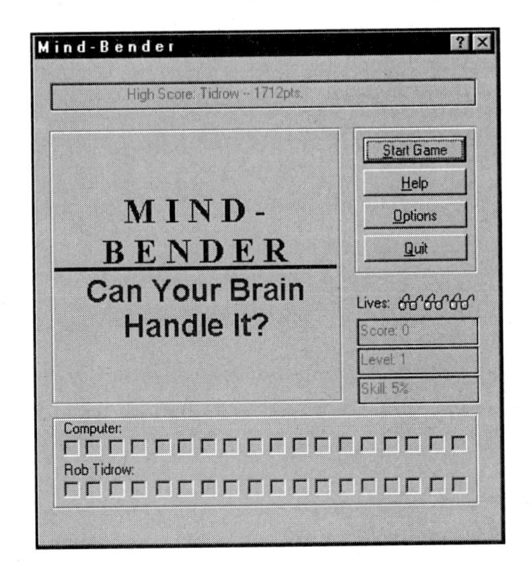

Figure 11.6
Mind-Bender game macro.

Table 11.4
Macros in LAYOUT7.DOT

Macro	Function
ArrangeWindows	Arranges open windows in a tiled, horizontal, vertical, or cascade format.
Cascade	Cascades open windows.
DecreaseLeftAndRightIndent	Unindents selected text 0.5" on left and right margins.
IncreaseLeftAndRightIndent	Indents selected text 0.5" on left and right margins.
OverScore	Adds lines above text you specify.
PrintableCharacters	Creates a table of all printable characters in a font.
SectionManager	Tells you everything you'd ever want to know about the formatting of any section in your document (see fig. 11.7).
TileHorizontally	Splits your screen horizontally between open documents.
TileVertically	Splits your screen vertically between open documents.

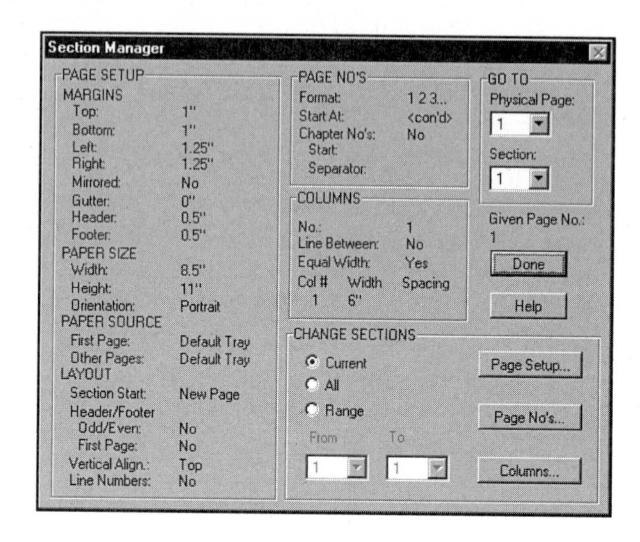

Figure 11.7
SectionManager macro.

Table 11.5
Macros in TABLES7.DOT

Macro	Function
AccessExporter	Exports a table from Word to a Microsoft Access database.
TableMath	Simplifies calculation in tables by providing an easier-to-use dialog box that enables you to identify specific cells and the kind of calculation you want to perform on them.
TableNumber	Inserts a column or row at the left, right, top, or bottom of a table and numbers the cells in that column or row, starting with one.

Table 11.6
Macros in CONVERT7.DOT

Macro	Function
BatchConverter	Runs a wizard that converts multiple text files into or out of Word for Windows format, using Word's conversion filters.
EditConversionOptions	Changes options associated with Word file converters.

TABLE 11.7
Macro in PRESENT7.DOT

Macro	Function
PresentIt	Exports Word outline to Microsoft PowerPoint.

WordBasic: A Brief Introduction

Imagine being able to talk to Word. Instead of selecting menu items with the mouse and typing text with the keyboard, you can control Word's actions. You might say

"Open File MEMO.DOC"

"Type 'Hello there!'"

"Select the text"

"Make it bold"

"Close and save the file"

If you can imagine doing that, you are on your way to using WordBasic, because WordBasic is simply a language with which you talk to Word.

WordBasic is usually referred to as a macro language, but calling it that is like calling Word an electric typewriter. WordBasic might perform a similar function as a macro language, but it can do much more.

The term *macro* originally meant a series of keystrokes that were stored and replayed by early DOS programs to automate repetitive tasks. As software programs became more powerful and more complex, the macro capability within them also developed. WordBasic is an excellent example of a program's macro capability outgrowing the original term macro.

WordBasic is actually a programming language, but don't let that scare you. It is a straightforward language that in some ways simulates the English language. It combines simple BASIC (an established programming language) commands with unique Word commands, enabling you to control Word's actions. You can automate simple tasks or, if you feel adventurous, create complex macros that can communicate with other Windows programs.

WordBasic is made up of three elements:

- Statements
- Functions
- BASIC programming commands and structures

Macros you create can use any or all of the preceding elements.

Statements

Statements are commands that tell Word to do something. `FileOpen`, `InsertFootnote`, and `SelectCurWord` are statements.

Functions

Functions return information or manipulate data. Some functions perform an action and then return the result of that action. `Today()`, `GetDirectory()`, and `InputBox$()` are functions.

Programming Commands and Structures

Programming commands and *structures* enable you to control the execution of statements and functions. With them, you can repeat a statement, add the results of two functions, or stop a macro if an error occurs. `GoTo`, `For...Next`, and `If...EndIf` are examples of programming commands and structures.

FontExample: Recording and Modifying a Simple Macro

To begin, you write a simple macro that creates a document containing examples of all the fonts available on your system.

In this example, you record a macro, as you have already done, and then modify it. Often, it saves time to create a macro in this way, because it lets Word do most of the work. You record the commands necessary to create a new file, insert an example of a font, and save the file. Then you modify the macro to insert examples of all fonts.

All the macros discussed in the following pages appear on disk in the file IWWMS11A.DOT (see table 11.8).

TABLE 11.8
Macros Included on Disk in IWMS11A.DOT

Macro	Function
FontExample	Creates a document that contains examples of all fonts available on your system.
PastDate	Asks you to enter a number and tells you what the date was that many days ago.
SelectAFruit	Displays a simple custom dialog box.

Before you record your macro, make sure the Formatting toolbar is visible. Then follow these steps:

1. Select Macro from the Tools menu. The Macro dialog box appears.
2. Select Record. The Record Macro dialog box appears.
3. Type **FontExample** in the Record Macro Name field. Choose OK.

   Remember, Word is now recording your every move, so be careful. (However, you can start over if you make a mistake.)
4. Select New from the File menu.
5. Choose OK to create a new file based on the Blank Document template.
6. Using the Font drop-down list on the Formatting toolbar, select a font. It doesn't matter which one you choose as long as it is different from the current selection.
7. Type **This is** and the name of the font you have selected. Then press Enter.
8. Type the alphabet, a through z, in lowercase and press Enter.
9. Type the alphabet in uppercase and press Enter.
10. Type the numbers 0 through 9 and press Enter twice.

    Your screen should look something like figure 11.8 (although you may have selected a different font).

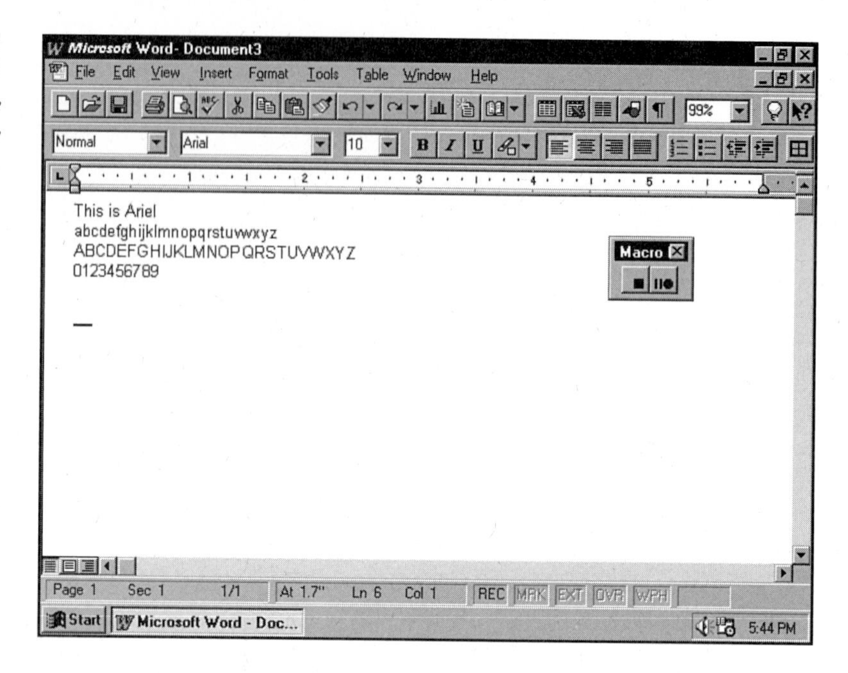

Figure 11.8

Recording the FontExample macro.

11. Select **S**ave from the **F**ile menu. The Save As dialog box appears.

12. Type **FONTS.DOC** in the File **N**ame field and choose OK.

13. Stop recording your macro by clicking on the Stop button on the Macro Record toolbar. It is the square button on the left.

14. Now close FONTS.DOC and use the Delete feature in the **F**ile, **O**pen dialog box (or use Windows Explorer) to delete the file. (For more information on deleting files from inside Word, see Chapter 6, "File Management.")

Now you have the basis for the FontExample macro. Check what you recorded by opening the macro itself:

1. Select **M**acro from the **T**ools menu. The Macro dialog box appears and the FontExample macro is visible in the **M**acro Name list box (see fig. 11.9).

2. Select the FontExample macro. As you do so, notice how the Cr**e**ate button that was deactivated turns into an active **E**dit button.

3. Select the **E**dit button. The FontExample macro appears in a macro-editing window, looking like figure 11.10.

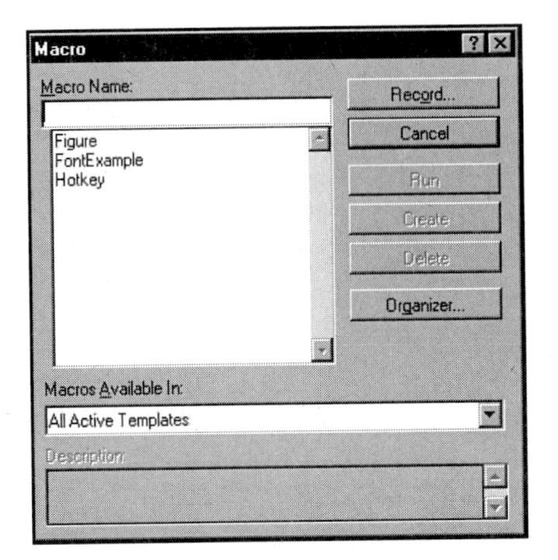

Figure 11.9

Macro dialog box.

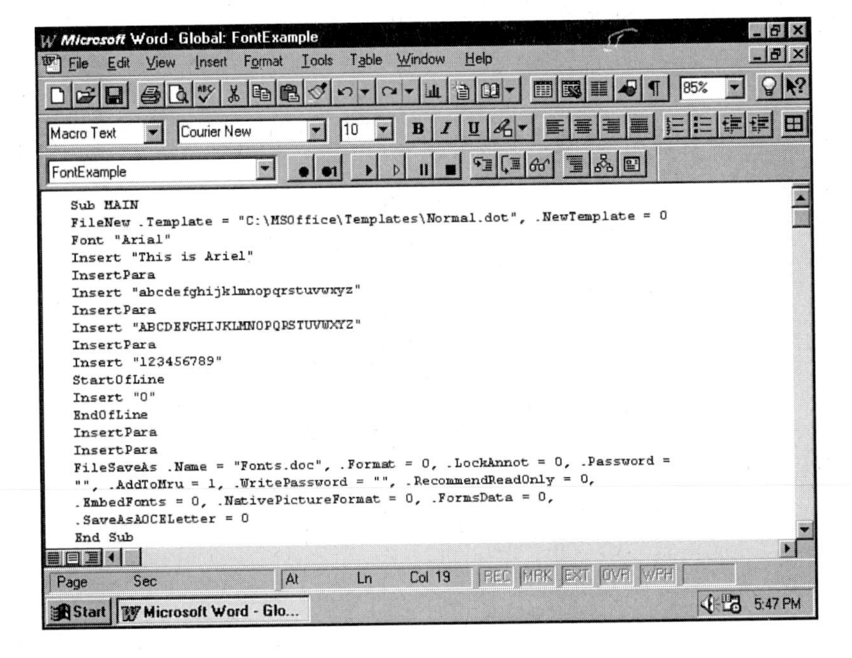

Figure 11.10

Recorded FontExample macro code.

A macro-editing window is like a document window. It can be resized and moved in the same way. You enter macro commands into the macro-editing window by typing them, just as you type text into a document window.

If you take a few moments to examine the macro code, you can see how easy it is to read. Each line matches an action you took. For example, FileNew refers to choosing New from the File menu. InsertPara is WordBasic for Insert Paragraph Marker, which is what you do each time you press Enter.

Now you need to modify this macro by creating a For/Next loop. A *For/Next loop* repeats a set of commands a specified number of times. Follow these steps:

If you begin all your variable names with a lowercase v, it is easier to read your code because you know immediately whether a word is supposed to be a variable or a command.

1. Insert a blank line after the `FileNew` command.

2. Type the following macro code after the `FileNew` command and before the Font command:

```
vNumFonts = CountFonts()
For vNumLoops = 1 To vNumFonts
vFontName$ = Font$(vNumLoops)
```

You don't have to worry about upper- and lowercase when typing WordBasic commands and functions. Word automatically corrects the case of each letter each time you run the macro. In fact, typing all your WordBasic commands in lowercase provides an easy way to spot errors, because Word doesn't fix the case on commands and functions that you mistype.

The first line uses the `CountFonts()` function to store the number of fonts available to Word in a variable called `vNumFonts`. Variables store values for use later in the macro.

Variables can store text or numbers. Variables that store text (for example, `Hello` or `101st Squadron`) are called string variables and must have a dollar sign (`$`) as their last character. Variables that store numbers (for example, `123` or `-15`) are called numeric variables and cannot have a dollar sign as their last character.

The second line is the beginning of the For/Next loop. It uses a variable called `vNumLoops`. This command says, "Repeat the code between this line and the line that contains `Next` as many times as `vNumFonts`."

The third line stores the name of a font in a variable called `vFontName$` using the `Font$()` function. This function returns the name of the font based on its position in the font list. If the first font in the font list is ARIAL, its position is 1. `Font$(1)` is the same as saying ARIAL.

Each time Word executes the commands in the For/Next loop, it increments the `vNumLoops` variable by one. The first time through, `vNumLoops` is set to 1, the next time 2, and so forth, until `vNumLoops` is equal to `vNumFonts`. Thus `Font$(vNumLoops)` eventually returns all the font names in the font list.

3. Now change the line with the `Font` command to read

```
Font vFontName$
```

The `Font` command changes the active font to the font whose name follows. But instead of supplying an exact name (as Word did when it recorded the macro), you are using the `vFontName$` variable.

4. Change the next line, which reads

```
Insert "This is Arial"
```

to read

```
Insert "This is " + vFontName$
```

Just as you used the `vFontName$` variable with the `Font` command, use it here to change the text that Word inserts into the document each time it loops. You are using *string concatenation* to combine the text between the quotation marks with the text stored in the `vFontName$` variable.

You can use string concatenation to combine text strings with other text strings, text strings with string variables, or two or more string variables with each other. You cannot concatenate numeric variables.

When you concatenate strings, don't forget to add spaces before and after variables if you need them. Word does not put spaces in automatically.

5. After the last `InsertPara` command, add a line and type **Next**.

6. Before you run the macro, you need to make it a little easier to read. Add a tab at the beginning of each line between the `For` statement and the `Next` statement. This enables you to see exactly which statements will be run when Word loops through the For/Next loop.

7. On the first line of the macro, above Sub MAIN, add a line and enter the following three lines:

```
REM    Font Example Macro
REM    Written by   <your name>
REM    Version 1.0  <todays date mm/dd/yy>
```

This is the macro title and version information. Starting a line with **REM** tells Word that the following text is a REMARK and should be ignored when Word runs the macro.

Word's new Add/Remove Remark tool on the Macro toolbar simplifies adding and removing remarks from macro code. Highlight the line or lines you want to remark and click on the Add/Remove Remark button. It is the third button from the left. A REM command and a tab are added at the beginning of all lines selected. If a line or lines already have a REM, it is removed.

Your macro should now look exactly like figure 11.11 (except your name and today's date are in the remark!).

Figure 11.11

Completed FontExample macro.

```
Microsoft Word- Global: FontExample
File Edit View Insert Format Tools Table Window Help
FontExample

REM Font Example Macro
REM Written by Bill Camarda
REM Version 1.0 August 15, 1995

Sub MAIN
FileNew .Template = "C:\MSOffice\Templates\Normal.dot", .NewTemplate = 0
vNumFonts = CountFonts()
For vNumLoops = 1 to vNumFonts
    vFontNames$ = Font$(vNumLoops)
    Font vFontName$
    Insert "This is " + vFontName$
    InsertPara
    Insert "abcdefghijklmnopqrstuvwxyz"
    InsertPara
    Insert "ABCDEFGHIJKLMNOPQRSTUVWXYZ"
    InsertPara
    Insert "123456789"
    StartOfLine
    Insert "0"
    EndOfLine
    InsertPara
    InsertPara
Next
FileSaveAs .Name = "Fonts.doc", .Format = 0, .LockAnnot = 0, .Password =
"", .AddToMru = 1, .WritePassword = "", .RecommendReadOnly = 0,
.EmbedFonts = 0, .NativePictureFormat = 0, .FormsData = 0,
.SaveAsAOCELetter = 0
End Sub

Page Sec At Ln Col 1 REC MRK EXT OVR WPH
Start Microsoft Word - Glo... 5:53 PM
```

8. The last step before you run any macro is to save it. Never forget to save. Select Save All from the File menu and choose OK when Word asks whether you want to keep the changes to the FontExample macro.

Because you don't know that your macro will run correctly the first time, always save your work before you try to run your macro. If your computer locks up or you write a never-ending loop into your macro, you run the risk of losing your work.

9. Now run your macro. Click on the Start button on the Macro toolbar—the third button with the small blue arrow.

   Your macro creates a document that has examples of all the fonts on your system.

If an error message appears, don't panic. You probably mistyped a macro command. Word highlights the line that it doesn't understand. Check it carefully for typographic errors. After you correct any errors, click on the Start button again.

After the macro finishes, print the FONT.DOC and keep it nearby. It will save you much time the next time you try to decide which font to use.

The Macro Editing Environment

Before you create more complex macros, it is a good idea to become familiar with Word's macro-editing environment. Word offers a number of powerful features that make it easy to write, run, and debug macros.

The Macro Toolbar

Word's Macro toolbar provides you with various ways to start, stop, and edit your macros. Take a look at each element on the toolbar (see fig. 11.12):

- **Active Macro List.** This drop-down list box displays the active macro. The active macro is the macro that runs if you click on the Start button. You can select any macro that is currently open in a macro-editing window.

- **Record.** This button turns macro recording on and off. Clicking on the Record button on the toolbar is identical to selecting Macro from the Tools menu and choosing Record.

- **Record Next Command.** This is a very useful tool. If you click on this button, Word records the next action you perform and inserts the proper macro command at the cursor location in the macro that appears in the Active Macro list. You can save a great deal of time using this tool because you don't have to look up the syntax for a command with which you are unfamiliar; you can let Word do the work for you.

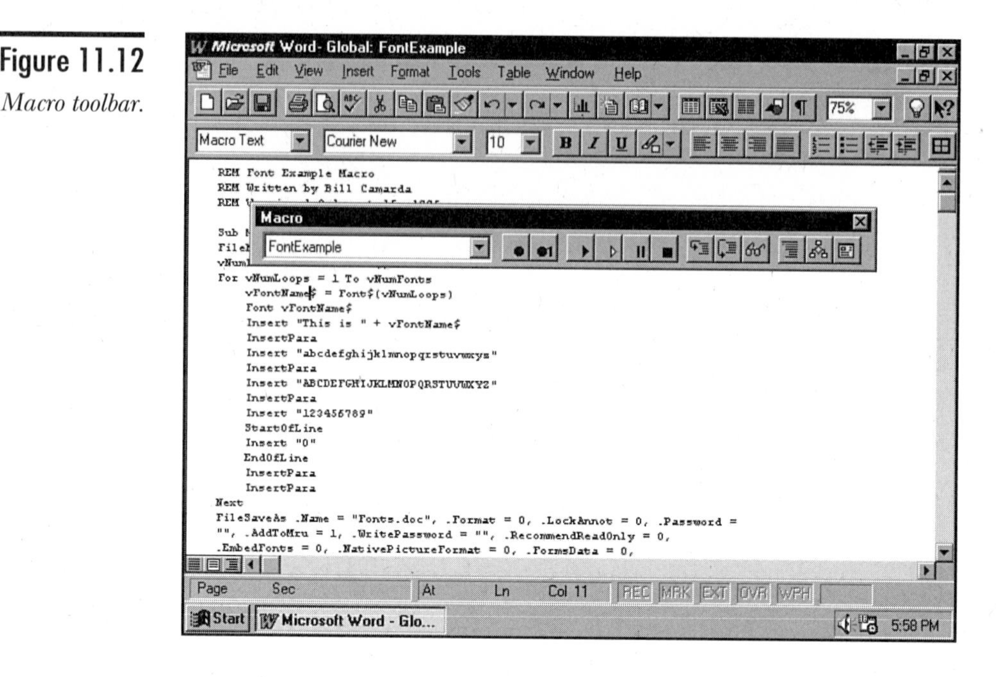

Figure 11.12

Macro toolbar.

If you have to look up a macro command or function, the quickest way is to use Word's online WordBasic help. Type the command or function in a macro window. Make sure the cursor is located somewhere in the text you typed, then press F1. Word opens the help file and jumps to the topic for the selected command.

- **Start Macro.** This button starts the macro that appears in the Active Macro list.

- **Trace.** Selecting Trace causes Word to highlight each line of a macro as it executes that line. Try it out by following these steps:

  1. Open the FontExample macro that you just created.

  2. Type **REM** and press the Tab key at the beginning of the line that contains the `FileNew` command. It should look like this:

     ```
     REM FileNew .Template = "Normal", .NewTemplate = 0
     ```

     You used `REM` on this line because you don't want the macro to open a new document window when you run it this time.

3. Now create a new document by selecting New from the File menu.

4. Arrange the FontExample macro window and the new document window vertically so that they look like figure 11.13.

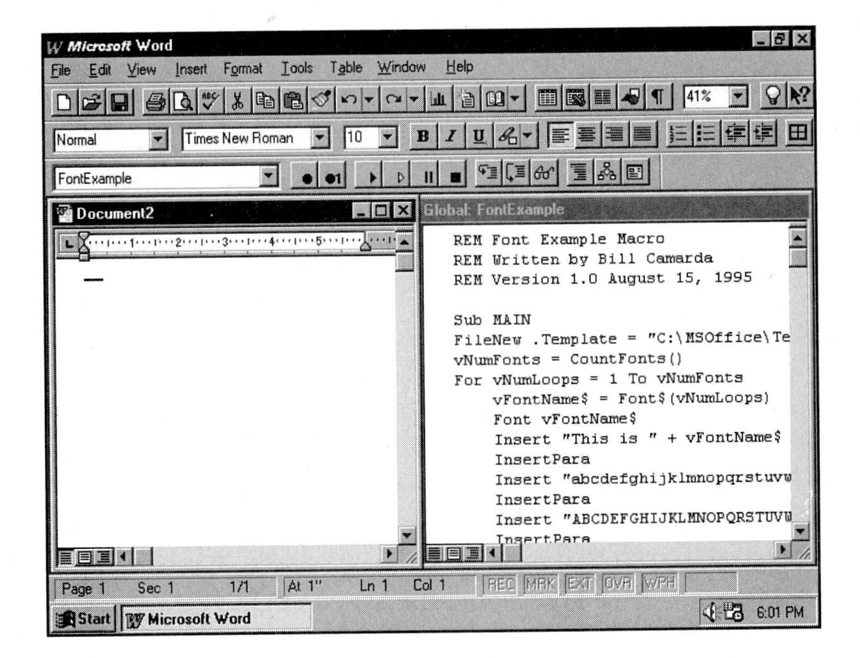

Figure 11.13

Macro and Document windows arranged vertically.

5. Make the new document the active window by clicking anywhere within its borders.

6. Click on the Trace button.

You can watch Word execute each statement and see the effect in the document window. This is an excellent technique to use when debugging macros.

- **Continue.** This button causes a macro to continue running after it has been interrupted. When a macro is running, you can press Esc to stop it. Word halts macro execution at the current macro statement. Selecting this button causes Word to resume macro execution from that point.

When you pause a macro by pressing Esc, you can change the active window, type text into a document window, and scroll or resize document and macro windows. However, if you edit the active macro, macro execution is terminated and you cannot resume the macro. You have to start the macro again.

- **Stop.** This is the same button that appears on the Macro Record toolbar. It stops macro recording.
- **Step.** Stepping through a macro is the most useful way to debug your code. The Step button executes one line of macro code each time you click on it. Try the Step button with the FontExample macro and a new document, (the same way you did with the Trace button).
- **Step Subs.** This button works the same as the Step button, but does not step through subroutines. If your macro does not contain any subroutines or user-defined functions, this button works exactly like the Step button.

Subroutines are separate modules of macro code that you can write to make your macros easier to read and modify. They can make your macros run faster. Subroutines can be called repeatedly from other routines in your macro, so they enable you to write more efficiently by not duplicating macro code. To learn more about subroutines, see "Learning More about WordBasic" later in this chapter.

- **Show Variables.** This is another great tool for debugging your macros. While a macro is paused (because you are stepping through it or because you pressed Esc while it was running), you can click on the Show Variables button to see a list of the variables you have defined and their current values. You can also change the value of a variable and then continue running the macro. Set up the FontExample macro and a new document as you did earlier and try out the Show Variables button:

  1. Step through the FontExample macro by clicking on the Step button. Keep stepping until the macro has looped through the For/Next loop at least once. Stop when one of the `InsertPara` commands is highlighted.
  2. Click on the Show Variable button. The Macro Variables dialog box appears (see fig. 11.14).

     Notice that there are three variables defined. `vNumFonts` is equal to the total number of fonts on your system. Remember this number because you will use it in a moment. `vNumLoops` is equal to the number of times Word executes the For/Next loop. This depends on how many times you press the Step button. `vFontName$` is set to the name of the font currently in use.
  3. Select the `vNumLoops` variable in the Variables list.
  4. Select the Set button. The Set Variable dialog box appears (see fig. 11.15).
  5. Change the number in the Set Variable text box to a value that is 2 or 3 less than the value of `vNumFonts`.

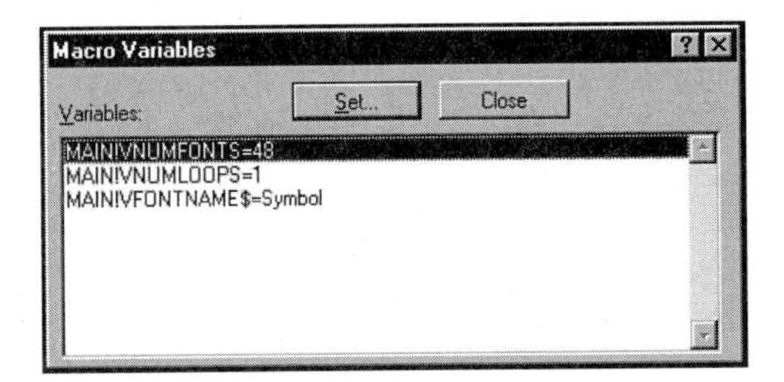

Figure 11.14

Macro Variables dialog box.

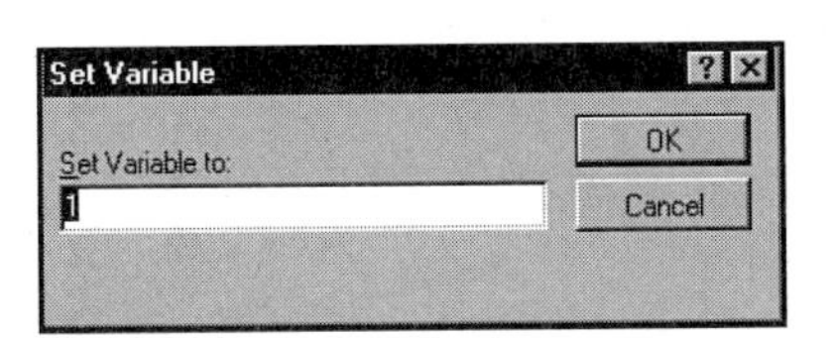

Figure 11.15

Set Variable dialog box.

6. Choose OK and then Close.

7. Now click on the Continue button on the Macro toolbar.

   The macro inserts a few more fonts and then stops running, because you fooled Word by changing the value of `vNumLoops`. Remember that Word loops through the For/Next until `vNumLoops` equals `vNumFonts`. By making the value of `vNumLoops` so much greater, you skipped many of the loops that Word normally would have performed.

- **Add/Remove REM.** This button automatically adds and removes REM commands. When you debug a macro, it is often useful to use `REM` on a section of code that you don't want to run at that moment (the way you did with the `FileNew` command earlier). You can temporarily REM out an entire section of code by selecting the lines and clicking on the Add/Remove REM button. Later, you can remove the REMs by selecting the same lines and choosing the button again.
- **Macro.** This button displays the Macro dialog box.
- **Dialog Editor.** This button launches the Word Dialog Editor. The Dialog Editor is a separate program used to design WordBasic dialogs.

Familiarity with the tools on the Macro toolbar makes writing, modifying, and debugging your macros much easier. You might want to assign shortcut keys to the tools you use the most, or you might want to add a few commands to the toolbar. In order to protect your work, you should use FileSaveAll frequently.

PastDate—Communicating with the User

One of the most powerful features of WordBasic enables you to create macros that interact with the user. You might want to ask the user a question, for example, or display information.

The PastDate macro does both. It asks the user to enter a number, calculates the date that number of days ago, and displays the answer.

Because this macro does not use commands that you can record, you need to start from scratch with a blank macro. To begin, open a macro window:

1. Select Macro from the Tools menu. The Macro dialog box appears.
2. Type **PastDate** in the Macro Name field.

   Notice that the grayed Create button is activated as soon as you begin to type in the Macro Name field.
3. Select Create. A new macro-editing window opens and the Macro toolbar is displayed (see fig. 11.16).

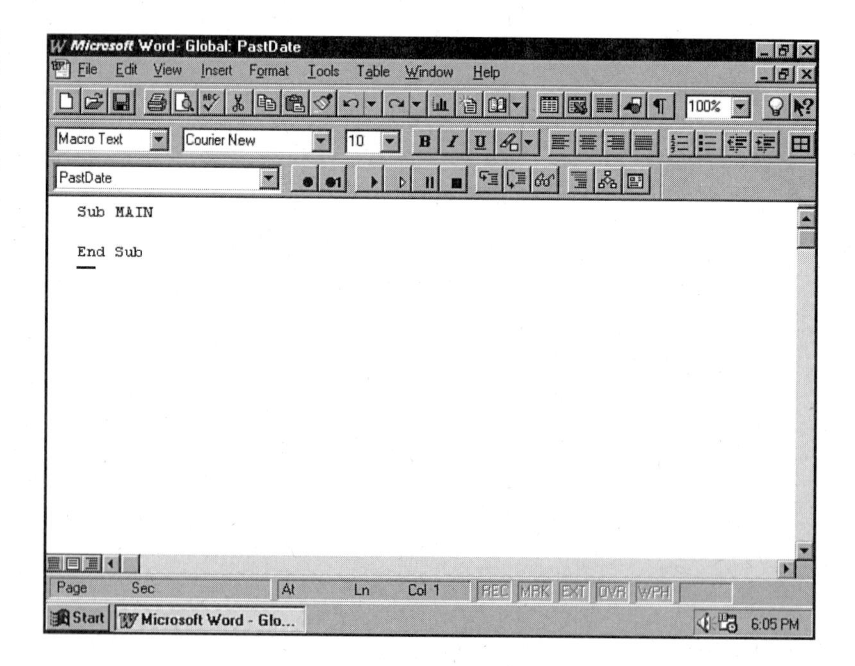

Figure 11.16

New macro-editing window with the Macro toolbar.

A new macro-editing window already contains the following text:

```
Sub MAIN
End Sub
```

`MAIN` marks the beginning of the macro and `End Sub` marks the end. All the macro commands you type are between these two lines (except for remarks).

4. Enter the following text between `Sub MAIN` and `End Sub`:

```
vDays$ = InputBox$("Please enter the number of days before today:")
vNumDays = Val(vDays$)
vSerialEndDate = Today() - vNumDays
vEndDate$ = Date$(vSerialEndDate)
MsgBox "The date " + vDays$ + " days ago was " + vEndDate$ + "."
```

5. Save your macro by selecting Save All from the File menu.

6. Click on the Start button on the Macro toolbar. Your macro runs and an Input dialog box appears (see fig. 11.17).

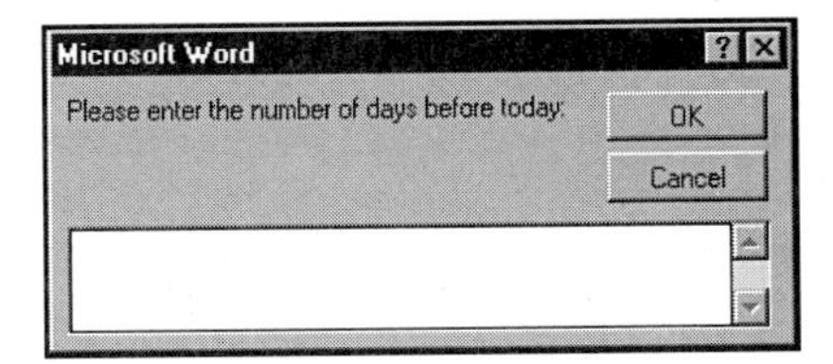

Figure 11.17
PastDate Macro Input dialog box.

If an error message appears, don't panic. You probably mistyped a macro command. Word highlights the line that it doesn't understand. Check it carefully for typographic errors. After you correct any errors, click on the Start button again.

7. Type in a number and select OK. The result appears on-screen as in figure 11.18.

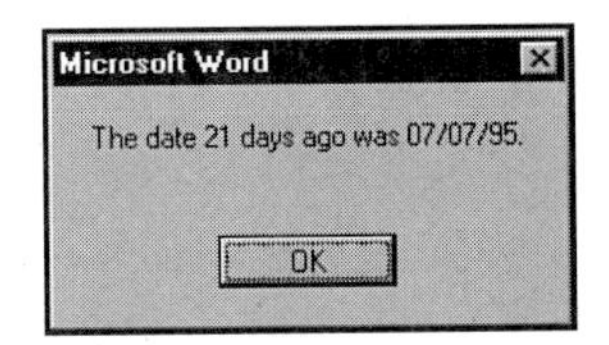

Figure 11.18
PastDate Macro Result dialog box.

8. Select OK and the Result Message box closes.

Take a look at each of the statements in the macro to see exactly what is happening:

```
vDays$ = InputBox$("Please enter the number of days before today:")
```

This statement displays the input box, which asks for the number of days. `vDays$` is a variable.

The `InputBox$` function displays an input box and stores whatever is entered in the variable `vDays$`. You can call the variable `vNumberofDays$` or even `Fred$`. It doesn't matter what you call it as long as you refer to it the same way every time. Because the `InputBox$` function returns a string (even if you enter a number into the input box), the `vDays$` variable has a dollar sign as its last character.

Surrounded by the parentheses after the `InputBox$` function is the string `"Please enter the number of days before today:"`. This is a parameter. Parameters are values that you give to a macro function or command.

Some functions and commands accept parameters. Some parameters are required and others are optional. The documentation for the function tells you which parameters are required and whether the parameters should be text or numbers. Text parameters are always surrounded by quotation marks.

The `InputBox$` function requires a text parameter. This text is the message that appears in the input box when it appears:

```
vNumDays = Val(vDays$)
```

The preceding line uses the `Val()` function to convert the text that was entered into the input box (stored in the `vDays$` variable) into a number. `Val` stands for value. The number it creates is stored in a variable called `vNumDays`. If you want to perform arithmetic on values in your macros, the values have to be numbers, not text strings:

```
vSerialEndDate = Today() - vNumDays
```

Next, the number of days is subtracted from the current day and the result is stored in a number variable called `vSerialEndDate`. The `Today()` function returns the serial date of today's date.

WordBasic can represent the date with a serial number. This is the number of days since December 30, 1899. Thus, December 31, 1899 has a serial date of 1. January 31, 1900 has a serial date of 32 (1 plus the 31 days in January). Serial dates make it easy to add and subtract days without having to remember how many days are in each month or which years are leap years.

The variable `vSerialEndDate` is so named to help you remember that it is storing a date in serial format, not in normal date format:

```
vEndDate$ = Date$(vSerialEndDate)
```

This line takes the serial date stored as a number in the `vSerialEndDate` variable and converts it to text in normal date format using the `Date$()` function. The `Date$()` function accepts a number that represents a serial date and returns text. That's why the `vEndDate$` variable has a dollar sign as its last character:

```
MsgBox "The date " + vDays$ + " days ago was " + vEndDate$ + "."
```

`MsgBox` is a very useful command. It displays a Windows message box filled with text that you specify. You use string concatenation to build the message you want to display.

Besides being able to control what text appears in a message box, you can choose the type of icon in the box, the title of the box, and the amount and configuration of the pushbuttons. Review the `MsgBox` documentation in Word's online WordBasic Help.

You can assign this macro to a toolbar, a menu, or a shortcut key. Select Customize from the Tools menu to display the Customize dialog box.

Dialog Boxes

WordBasic's dialog commands enable you to display dialog boxes that you design. These dialog boxes can be fairly simple, such as the dialog box you create in the SelectAFruit macro, or very complex, as in the Mind-Bender game that you can find in the MACRO7.DOT template (see fig. 11.19).

Dialog Editor

The Dialog Editor enables you to create your own dialog boxes by actually moving and resizing selected dialog box controls on-screen. The Editor then creates the macro commands required to display the dialog.

Dialog box design is one of the most important—and most overlooked—programming skills. Don't forget that your dialog boxes are the primary means of communication between your program and the user. Think about what data and options you want to present. Spend plenty of time experimenting with different designs in the Dialog Editor, and avoid UI (user interface) overload—adding so many controls to the dialog that the user stares blankly at the screen trying to figure out what to do.

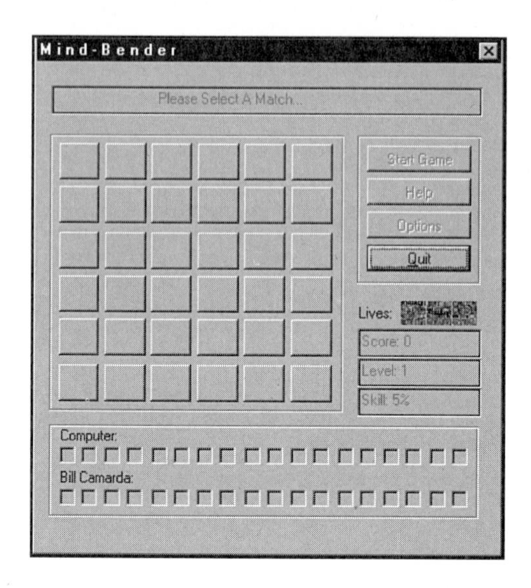

Figure 11.19
Mind-Bender dialog box.

Open the Dialog Editor and examine some of the available controls:

1. If the Macro toolbar is visible, choose the Dialog Editor button. It is the right button on the toolbar. If the Macro toolbar is not visible, you can launch the Dialog Editor by double-clicking on the MACRODE.EXE icon in your WINWORD folder (see fig. 11.20).

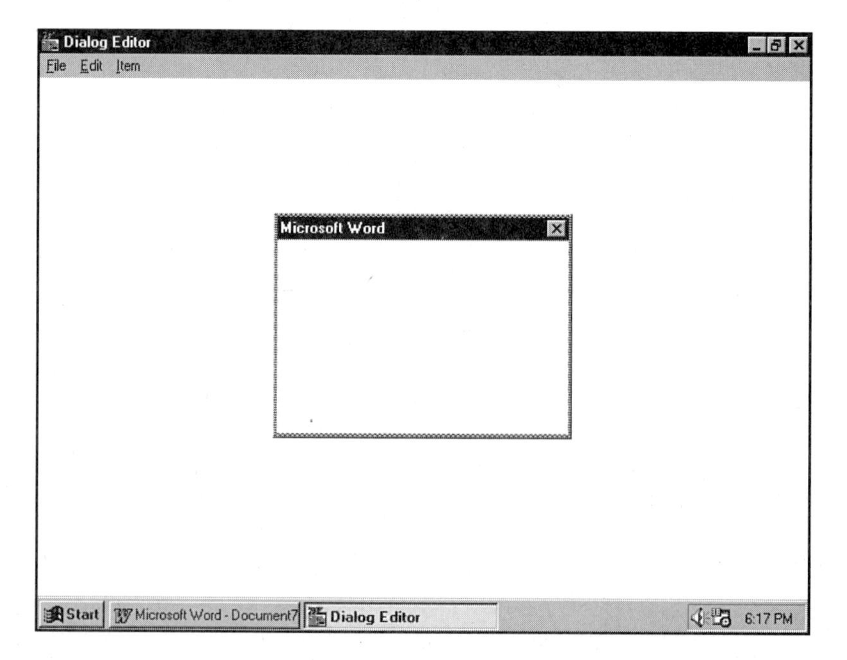

Figure 11.20
Dialog Editor.

2. After you launch the Dialog Editor, a blank dialog box appears. You can resize this dialog box, but you cannot move it. Resize it now by moving the mouse pointer over a corner until it changes into a double-arrow. Hold down the left mouse button while you move the dialog box border.

3. Select Button from the Item menu. A list of dialog box button controls appears (see fig. 11.21).

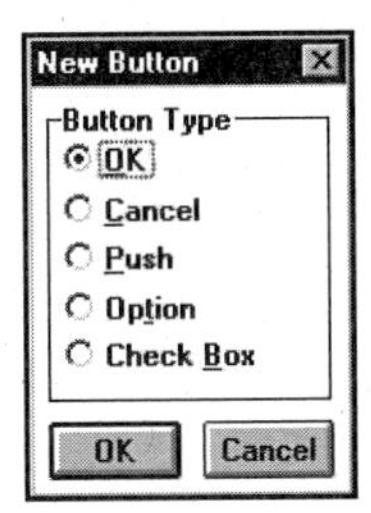

Figure 11.21

Dialog Editor button controls.

4. Choose OK. A new OK button is added to the empty dialog box.

To add a number of buttons to a dialog in the Dialog Editor quickly, add an OK button by selecting the OK Button Type from the New Button dialog box. After positioning the button in your dialog, press Enter. A Cancel button is added just beneath the OK button. Press Enter again to add a third pushbutton. Press Enter after adding other controls in the dialog to find other quick-add shortcuts.

Now take some time and insert different dialog controls. All the controls are available if you select Item from the menu bar. After you place a control on the dialog box, you can double-click on it to display its dialog box. This dialog box presents different options unique to the control you chose. For example, you can set the text of a text control.

The controls available in WordBasic dialog boxes are described in the following list:

◆ **Push Button.** Can be one of three types of buttons: OK, Cancel, or text. You must always have at least one type of button in your custom dialog boxes.

◆ **Option Button.** Use option buttons to enable users to choose one option from several.

◆ **Check Box.** Use a check box to make "yes or no" or "on or off" selections. You'll see check boxes many times when you are setting up environment settings for Word.

- **Text.** Use a text control when you want to display text that the user cannot change, such as a label for a text box.
- **Text Box.** Use a text box when you want the user to input text into a displayed dialog box. You can make the text box hold a single line or multiple lines of input.
- **Group Box.** Usually used with option buttons, group boxes contain a group of option buttons set off for users to select. You also can group check boxes in a group box.
- **Standard List Box.** Use a list box to show a list of selections for the user.
- **Combo List Box.** Use a combo list box when you want to give users a choice to either pick an item from a list or type in a selection.
- **Drop-Down List Box.** Use a drop-down list box when you want a list from which users can choose and you want to conserve space in your dialog box. A drop-down list box can drop down and cover other parts of a dialog box while the user makes a selection.
- **Picture.** Use a picture control when you want to display a picture in the dialog box.
- **File Preview Box.** Use a file preview box (you can have only one in a dialog box) to provide a thumbnail view of any Word document.

You cannot use the Dialog Editor to add File Preview boxes. This control must be entered in the dialog box definition in the macro code. For more information, see the WordBasic online Help for FilePreview and DlgFilePreview.

When you design dialog boxes, review the dialog boxes of programs you enjoy using. Seeing the way other programs solve interface problems can help you design effective dialogs.

Dialog Functions

Dialog functions are powerful functions that you write to control the behavior of a dialog box while it is displayed. For example, you can enable or disable a pushbutton as the user enters or deletes text from a text box. As a another example, the items in a list box can change dynamically as the user selects different option buttons. You even can change the shape and size of a dialog box while it is displayed.

Dialog functions are fairly complex, so you don't work with them in this chapter. (For more information, see "Learning More about WordBasic" at the end of this chapter.)

Creating and Displaying a Dialog Box

The next step is to create and display a simple dialog box to demonstrate how to transfer your work from the Dialog Editor to a Word macro:

1. Open the Dialog Editor. If it is already open, select New from the File menu to create an empty dialog box.

   Now you need to add some controls to the dialog. As you add the controls, you can arrange them so that they look like figure 11.22.

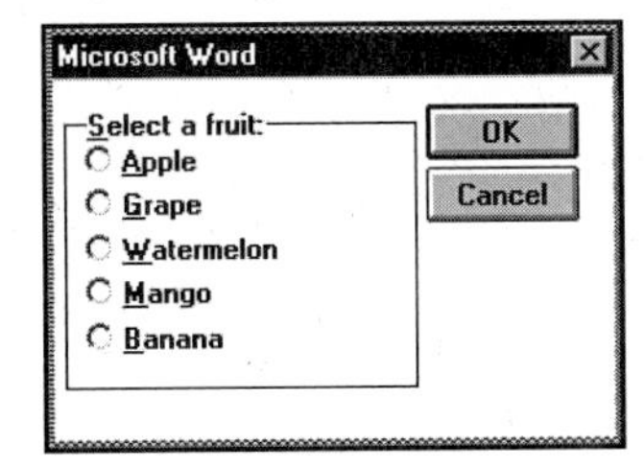

Figure 11.22

Select a fruit dialog box as it appears in Dialog Editor.

2. Add a Group Box by choosing Group Box from the Item menu.
3. Type **&Select a fruit:**. Don't press Enter after you type the text. The Dialog Editor replaces the `Group Box` text at the top of the group box with the text you type. The ampersand before the `S` means that the `S` will be underlined and become the shortcut key for this control.

Tip: If you want to add a real ampersand (&) in a dialog box (for example, Select this & that:), type two ampersands in a row.

4. Select Button from the Item menu. Then select Option. The Dialog Editor puts an Option button in the group box.
5. Type **&Apple**. The Dialog Editor replaces the `Option Button` text with the text you type.
6. Press Enter. The Dialog Editor inserts another Option button. This is one of the quick-add features of the Dialog Editor.
7. Type **&Grape** and press Enter again.

8. Repeat the process for **&Watermelon**, **&Mango**, and **&Banana**.
9. Select Button from the Item menu. Then select OK. The Dialog Editor adds an OK button.
10. Drag the OK button to the upper right corner of the dialog box.
11. Press Enter. The Dialog Editor adds a Cancel button directly beneath the OK button. This is another quick-add feature of the Dialog Editor.
12. Grab the bottom border of the dialog box and move it up just a little to get rid of the extra white space below the bottom of the group box. Move the border up half as far as you think it should go, because the Dialog Editor moves the top border down an equal amount.

Now, to move the dialog box definition into a macro, follow the next set of steps:

1. Select Select Dialog from the Edit menu. This selects the entire dialog box. You might notice that the focus moves to the dialog's borders.
2. Select Copy from the Edit menu, which copies the dialog definition to the Clipboard.
3. Now use Alt+Tab to activate Word.
4. Create a new macro called SelectAFruit. (Display the Macro dialog box, type **SelectAFruit** in the Macro Name field and select Create).
5. When the new macro window appears, select Paste from the Edit menu. The dialog definition is copied into the new macro window (see fig. 11.23).

   Take a few moments to examine the macro code. All the dialog controls you added in the Dialog Editor are present. It was much easier to create this code with the editor than typing all of it in, wasn't it?

To display the dialog box, you need to add two lines of macro code. Type the following code on two separate lines after the `End Dialog` statement:

```
Dim FruitDlg As UserDialog
vDlgResult = Dialog(FruitDlg)
```

The following line creates a dialog record called `FruitDlg`, which holds the definition of the dialog box:

```
Dim FruitDlg As UserDialog
```

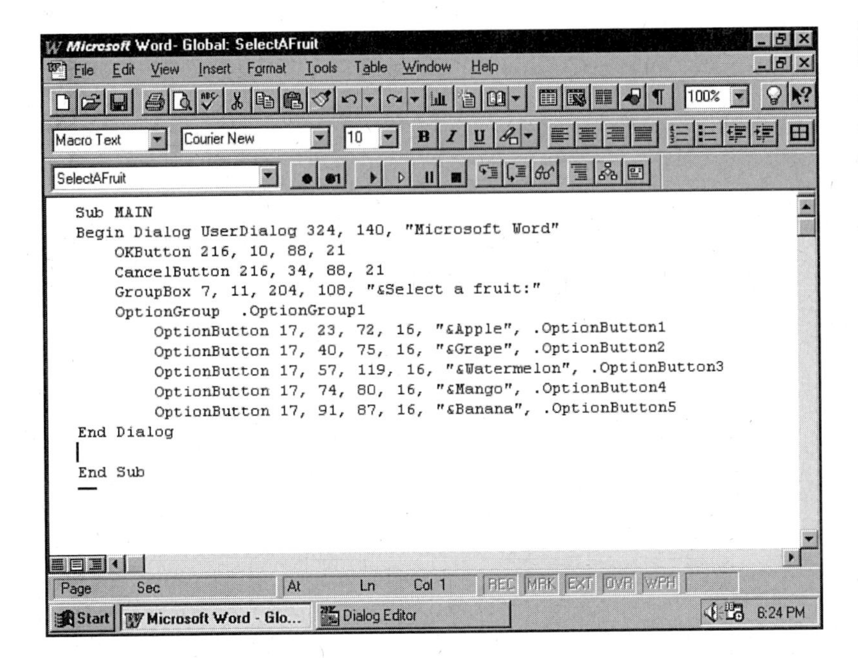

Figure 11.23

SelectAFruit dialog definition statements.

`UserDialog` is the name WordBasic uses to identify a custom dialog box. Notice the reference to `UserDialog` in the `Begin Dialog` statement. You can replace the name of the custom dialog (`FruitDlg`) with anything you want, but you must always use `UserDialog` as it appears here.

The following line uses the `Dialog` function to display the dialog box defined by the `FruitDlg` dialog record and stores the result in a variable called `vDlgResult`

```
vDlgResult = Dialog(FruitDlg)
```

Now try to run your macro. Click on the Start button from the Macro toolbar. The dialog box you create appears, as in figure 11.24. If 3D Dialog and Display Effects is turned on in General Options, the dialog appears with 3D controls that look much nicer than the 2D controls in the Dialog Editor.

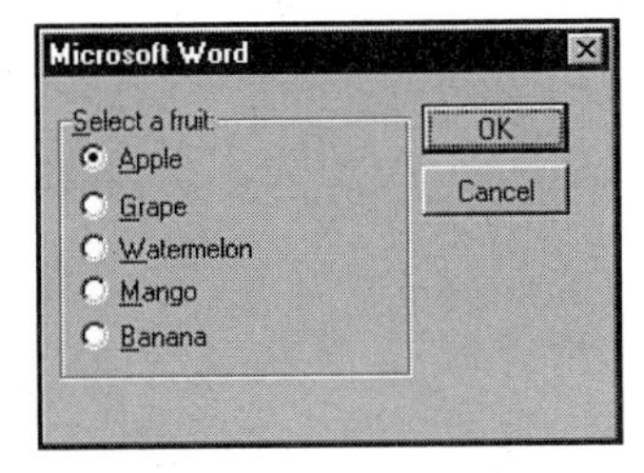

Figure 11.24

Select a fruit dialog box, with apple selected.

Learning More about WordBasic

In this chapter, you just scratched the surface of programming in WordBasic. It can be extremely rewarding. You can automate many of the repetitive tasks you do, create time-saving macros, and add a new dimension to your interaction with Word. With WordBasic, you can see the result of your work almost immediately. You can impress your friends and coworkers, and have fun at the same time.

To learn more about WordBasic, refer to the following source material:

- Part V of *Inside Word for Windows 95*. It features a complete WordBasic command reference.
- Word's online Help. Press F1, choose the Command tab, and select WordBasic Command Reference.
- *The Microsoft Word Developer's Kit* (Microsoft Press), 1995, a complete guide and reference to WordBasic, including disks. To order, call 1-800-MS-PRESS or 615-793-5090.

Part III

Professional-Quality Word Processing

New Riders Publishing
INSIDE
SERIES

Outlining

Even if you don't like to write from an outline, you will find Word's outlines helpful. They make it easy to take a bird's-eye view of your document. Outlines also make it easy to move large chunks of text, quickly restructuring even a very long document. They offer a convenient way to create the styles that can help you build tables of contents. You can even convert Word outlines into PowerPoint presentations.

If you do like to write from an outline, welcome to hog heaven. With Word for Windows 95, you can easily create an outline and then build your document around it, effortlessly modifying your outline whenever you want. You get all the structure you could possibly want.

In this chapter:

- Understanding Word outlining
- Creating an outline
- Editing an outline
- Promoting and demoting outline components
- Switching between Outline and Normal View

- Controlling the way you view your outline
- Adding numbering to an outline
- Customizing your heading numbering
- Printing an outline
- Exporting an outline to Microsoft PowerPoint

Word's Outlining Tools

In Word, your outline is actually a part of your document. To work with it, you just change the way you look at your document. The view you use is called Outline View. To work in Outline View, choose **O**utline from the **V**iew menu, or click on Word's Outline View button on the horizontal scroll bar (see fig. 12.1). A new outlining toolbar appears, as shown in figure 12.2.

Figure 12.1
Outline View button.

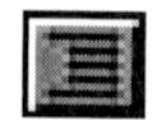

Figure 12.2
Outline View toolbar.

This toolbar contains your tools for working in Outline View. If you are not an experienced outliner, some of these tools might not be self-evident, so a list and explanation of their functions appear first. Later in the chapter we walk you through them.

Tools for Changing Heading Levels

The first three tools at the left of the toolbar enable you to change heading levels, thereby changing the relative importance you give to each element of your outline.

Button	Keyboard Equivalent	Name	What It Does
Left arrow	Alt+Shift+ Left Arrow	Promote	Raises a heading one level (making it more important)
Right arrow	Alt+Shift+ Right Arrow	Demote	Lowers a heading one level (making it less important)
Double right arrow	Alt+Shift+5 on the numeric keypad with NumLock off	Demote to body text	Changes the contents of a heading to body text

Tools for Moving Elements of an Outline

The next two arrows enable you to move outline elements, thereby rearranging your document.

Button	Keyboard Equivalent	Name	What It Does
Up arrow	Alt+Shift+ Up Arrow	Move Paragraph Up	Moves the current outline element (heading or body text) ahead of the previous one
Down arrow	Alt+Shift+ Down Arrow	Move Paragraph Down	Moves the current outline element after the next one

Tools for Expanding and Collapsing Outlines

Expanding an outline means viewing all of its subordinate headings and body text. *Collapsing* an outline means hiding all of its subordinate headings and body text. With the following pair of tools, you can expand or collapse your outline, or any part of it you select. To use the buttons on the numeric keypad, first turn NumLock off.

Button	Keyboard Equivalent	Name	What It Does
+	Alt+Shift+ Plus	Show Subtext	Completely expands any outline element you select
-	Alt+Shift+ Minus	Hide Subtext	Completely collapses any outline element you select

Tools for Displaying Specific Outline Levels

Next, the Show buttons enable you to control just how much of an outline appears. Pressing the button marked 1 tells Word to display only first-level heads; pressing the button marked 2, first- and second-level heads; and so on. Pressing the All button expands the entire document, showing all headings and body text. On the keyboard, Alt+Shift+A toggles between showing all body text and none of it; you can also press * on the numeric keypad.

Sometimes you may want a little more information about what is in a chapter than you can find in the chapter heading. The solution is to display the first line of each paragraph of body text.

You can switch between displaying all text and just the first line of each paragraph by choosing Word's new Show First Line Only button (see fig. 12.3). Alt+Shift+L does the same thing. One last button, shown in figure 12.4, shows or hides character formatting.

Figure 12.3

The Show First Line Only button.

Figure 12.4

The Show/Hide character formatting button.

Note There is one other button, the Master Document View button. Master documents use outlining as a way to streamline the assembly of multiple documents. This topic is covered in Chapter 18, "Annotations, Revisions, and Master Documents."

Looking at a Document in Outline View

Now that you know the outlining tools available to you, look at a typical document in Outline View as shown in figure 12.5. You can see Outline View's differences right away. You are presented with a somewhat stylized version of a typical outline. When subheadings are displayed, they appear indented underneath their major headings. Body text also appears indented under its subheading.

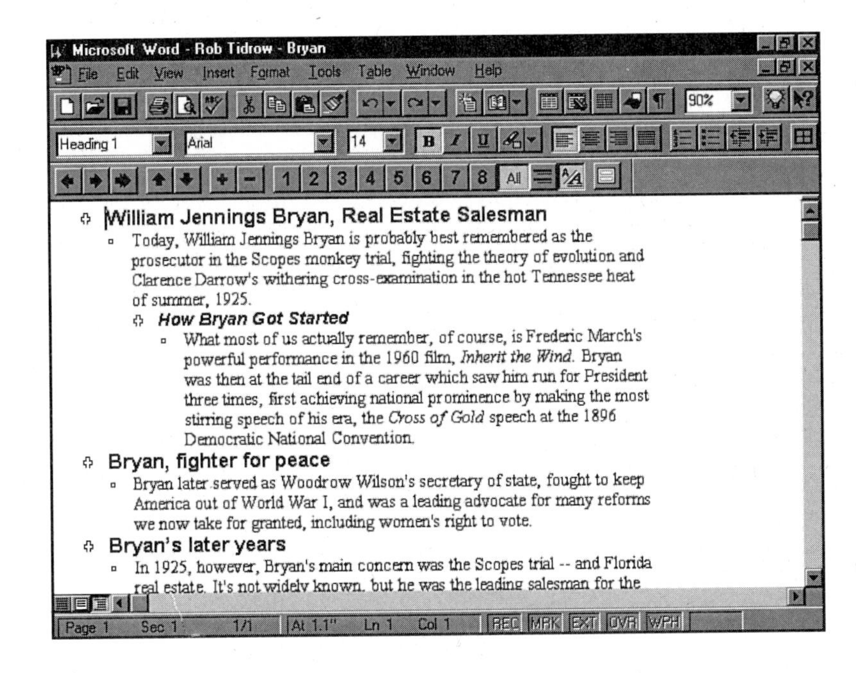

Figure 12.5

A document in Outline View.

In place of outline numbers, however, each paragraph has a plus sign, minus sign, or small square next to it. A plus sign tells you there are subheadings and body text beneath this line or paragraph. A minus sign tells you there are no subheadings or body text beneath this heading. A small square tells you the paragraph is body text. Notice that the plus and minus signs do not tell you which level of heading you are in, but you can always find out by looking at the style box.

As mentioned later in the "Hiding All Character Formatting" section of this chapter, you can also view this information in the Style Area on the left side of the screen. To do so, choose **T**ools, **O**ptions, **V**iew, and specify a style area of approximately .5".

Creating an Outline from Scratch

In this section, you create an outline from scratch. Start by opening a new document and, as mentioned previously, choose View, Outline, or click on the Outline View button.

The accompanying CD-ROM contains a file you can use to practice some of the procedures in this chapter: IWMS12A.DOC.

You are presented with an insertion point that follows a minus sign, as in figure 12.6. The minus sign tells you that no copy appears under this heading. Word assumes that you want to type a first-level heading.

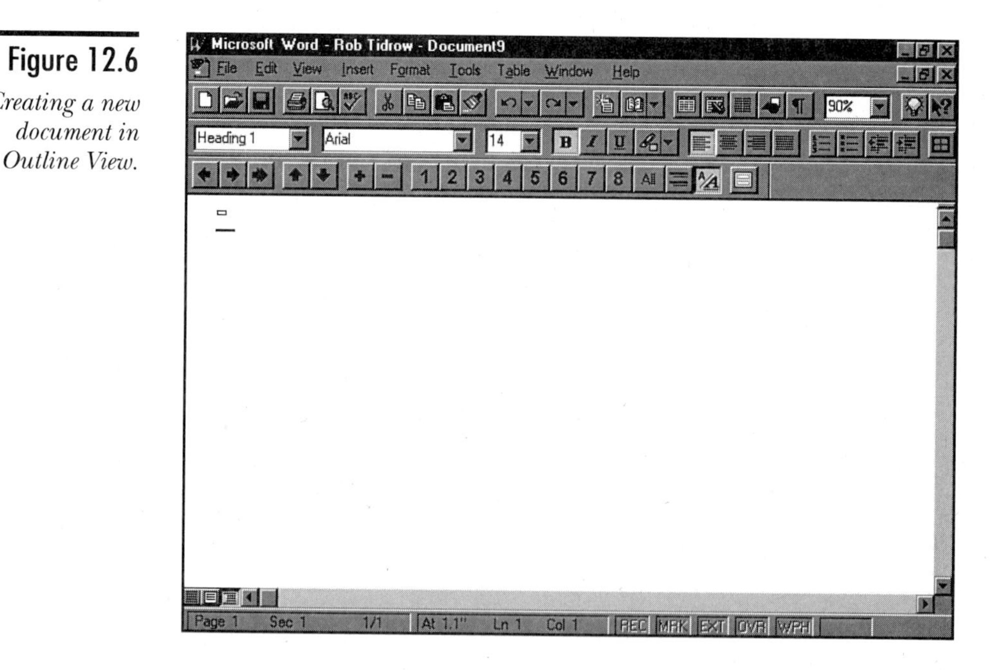

Figure 12.6
Creating a new document in Outline View.

This is a reasonable assumption in Outline View, and it is one way that Outline View differs from Normal View. In Normal View, Word anticipates Normal (body) text unless you tell it otherwise. Now, you can type as you would in Normal View. When you are finished, press Enter. Word starts a new paragraph—also expecting the new line to be a first-level heading.

Entering Subheadings in a New Outline

Now you want to create some subheadings under the main heading you already have. With your insertion point positioned in the line underneath the main heading, choose the right-arrow button, use the keyboard shortcut Alt+Shift+Right Arrow, or press Tab. (Do not use the double-right-arrow button.) As you can see in figure 12.7, two things happen immediately:

- ◆ The preceding heading now displays a plus sign (+), meaning it now contains text.
- ◆ The second-level head is indented.

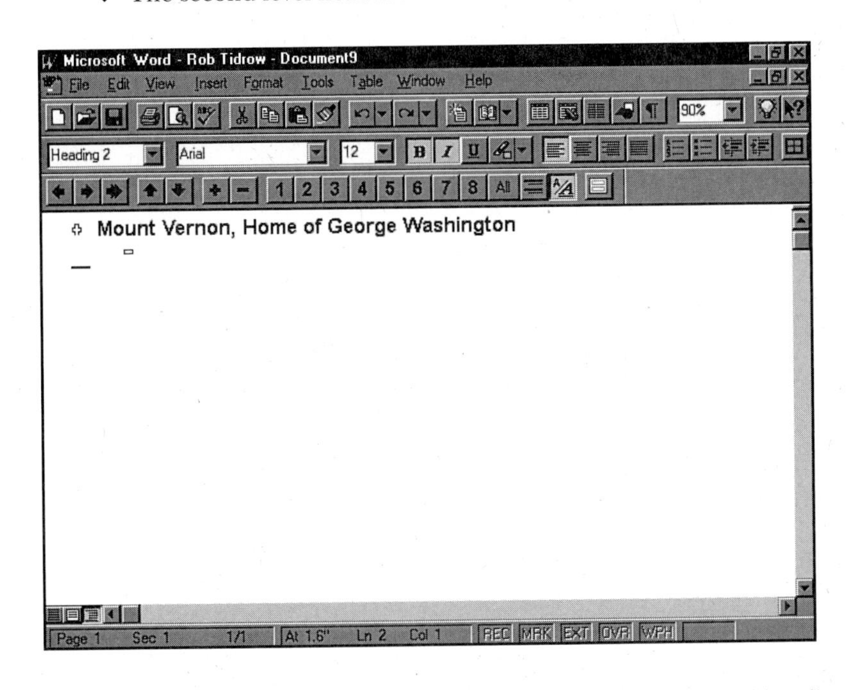

Figure 12.7

Adding a second-level heading in Outline View.

If you press Enter again, Word anticipates another second-level heading. Word always expects the next heading to be identical to the last, although of course you can always change it. This means you can always add another heading or body text paragraph in Outline View by placing the insertion point at the end of the previous one and pressing Enter.

Entering Body Text in a New Outline

You might want to add some body text at this point. Press the double-right-arrow button, or press Alt+Shift+5, using the "5" key on the numeric keypad. (Remember that NumLock must be off.) A square box appears next to your insertion point, and a plus sign appears in the previous subheading, indicating that it now has contents. You can see this in figure 12.8.

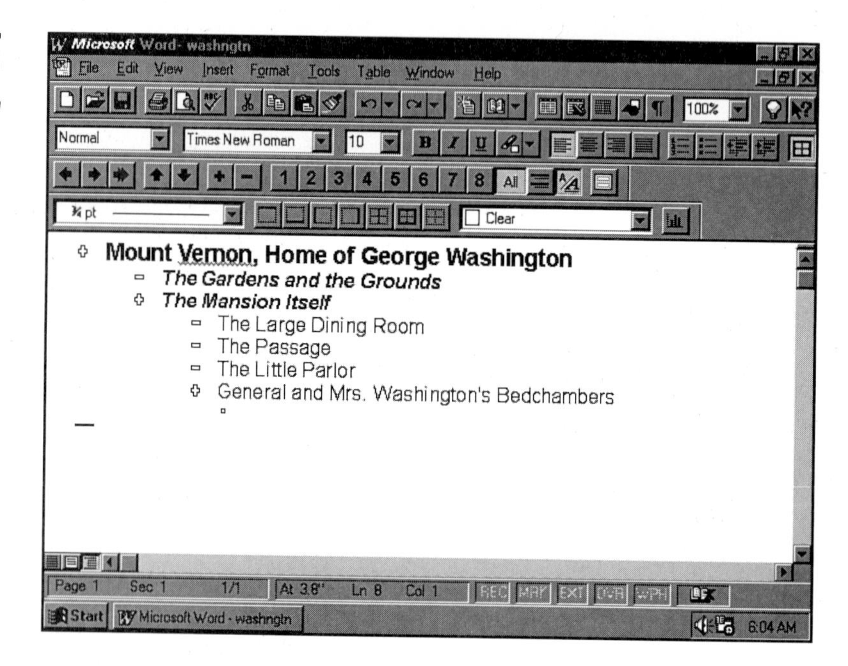

Figure 12.8

Inserting body text.

You can type text here, paste text from another document, import a graphic, use a field code to generate a result, or use character formatting.

The most common editing tasks also are available through the Outlining Shortcut menu, which appears when you right-click in an outline (see fig. 12.9).

Some menu options are not available in Outline View. These include Format Paragraph, Format Tabs, Format Drop Cap, Format Drawing Object, View Ruler, Insert Page Numbers, Insert Form Field, Insert Frame, and Tools Hyphenation.

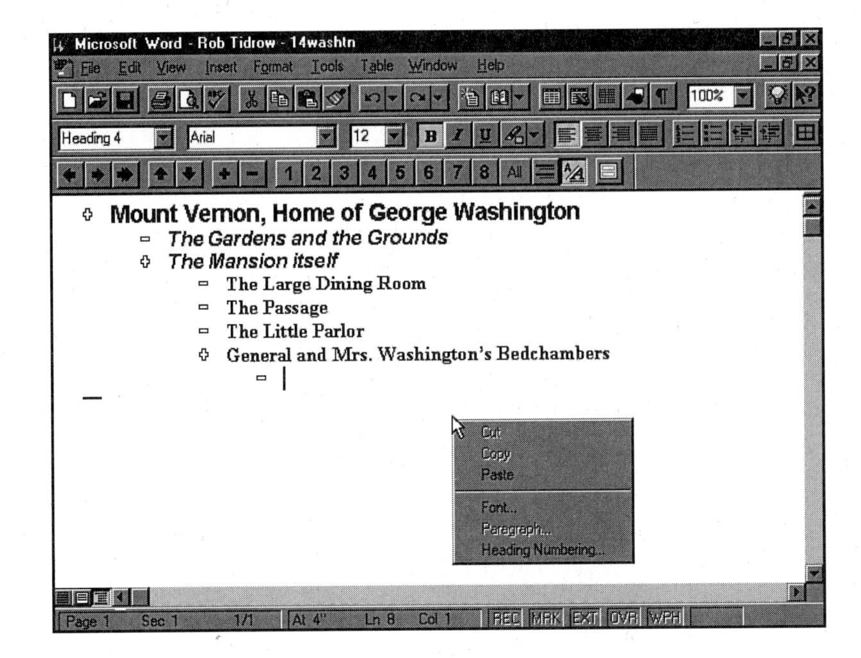

Figure 12.9

The Shortcut menu in Outline View.

Creating and Editing Headings

Now assume you are ready to insert another first-level head. Press Enter to start a new line. Then press the left-arrow key twice. Each time you press it, you are promoting the text by one level: first, from body text to a second-level heading; then, from a second-level heading to a first-level. Your screen should now look like the example in figure 12.10.

To jump straight to a first-level heading, choose Heading 1 in the style box.

You can always choose a heading level through the style box.

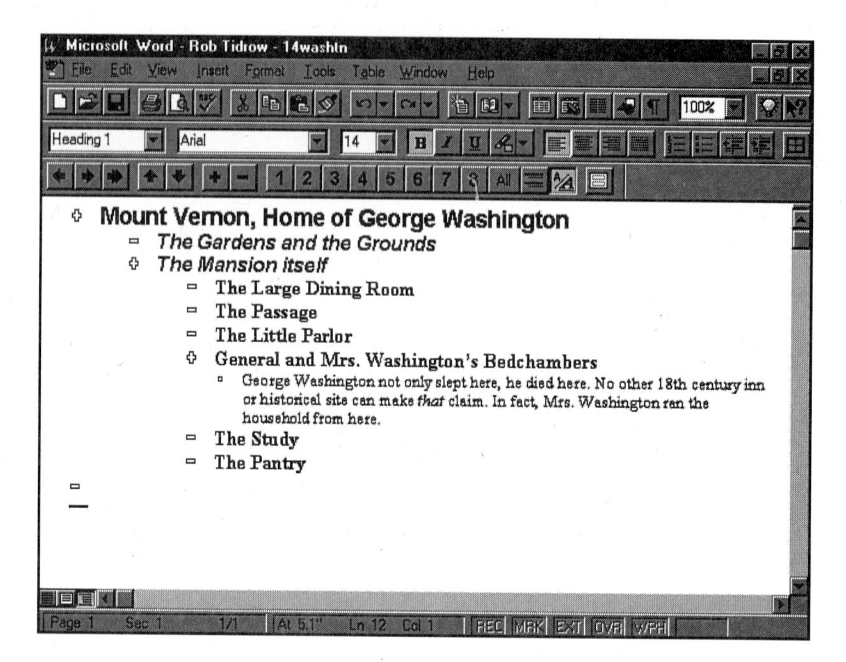

Figure 12.10
Inserting another first-level heading.

Changing Heading Levels

You can promote or demote any heading level by using the left-arrow or right-arrow buttons (or their Alt+Shift+Arrow keyboard equivalents).

If the heading you are changing contains subheads of its own, those subheads do not necessarily change with it. If you promote a second-level head to first-level, all of its third-level heads normally stay put. If you want to move those headings as well, you need to select them all. There is a shortcut, which leads directly to the issue of how you select headings in Outline View.

Selecting Text in an Outline

You can select a heading or body text paragraph by either placing your insertion point in it or clicking on the selection bar (the black left edge of your screen). You can select several headings and act on all of them at once.

You also can select a heading and all its subheadings and body text by clicking on its plus sign. (Your mouse pointer changes to a four-headed outline pointer when you are in the right place.)

Here is the shortcut alluded to earlier. If you select a heading by clicking on its plus sign, you also have selected all its subheadings. If you then promote or demote the

heading, all the others are promoted or demoted, too. Body text does not change, however, unless you specifically select it and change it.

Displaying All or Part of an Outline

Until now, you have been adding new headings and body text to an outline with the whole outline displayed. But one of the advantages of outline view is that you can view your document at any level.

Think of Word's outline display option as a microscope. You can use it to view only the most important topics in your document (first-level headings), or you can zoom in on the entire document, also looking at second, third, or additional headings. You also can zoom in on a specific part of a document, displaying it fully (including body text), while showing only top-level headings in the rest of the document.

To show only the first-level headings, press the 1 button or press Alt+Shift+1 (see fig. 12.11).

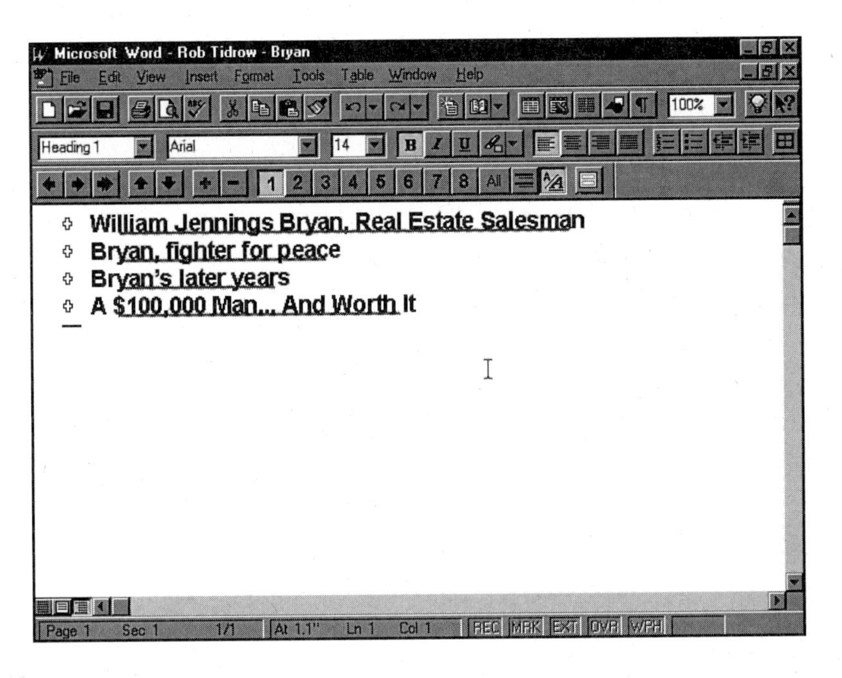

Figure 12.11

A sample document with only first-level headings displayed.

Notice the thick, gray underline beneath most lines. That tells you the heading contains more body text or subheads that are not displayed. You are looking at the top-level view of this document. Even though the document could be dozens or hundreds of pages long, you can see the most important topics at a glance.

You can always switch back to displaying everything by pressing the All button or pressing * on the numeric keypad.

If you are working on a long document in Normal View, you might occasionally switch to Outline View and display only high-level headings just to step back and place yourself in context. It is a way of remembering the forest when you are surrounded by trees and underbrush.

Expanding a Heading to Display All Its Contents

To see all the subheads and text underneath one main heading, select that heading and press the + button (or Alt+Shift+Plus). Your document should look something like figure 12.12.

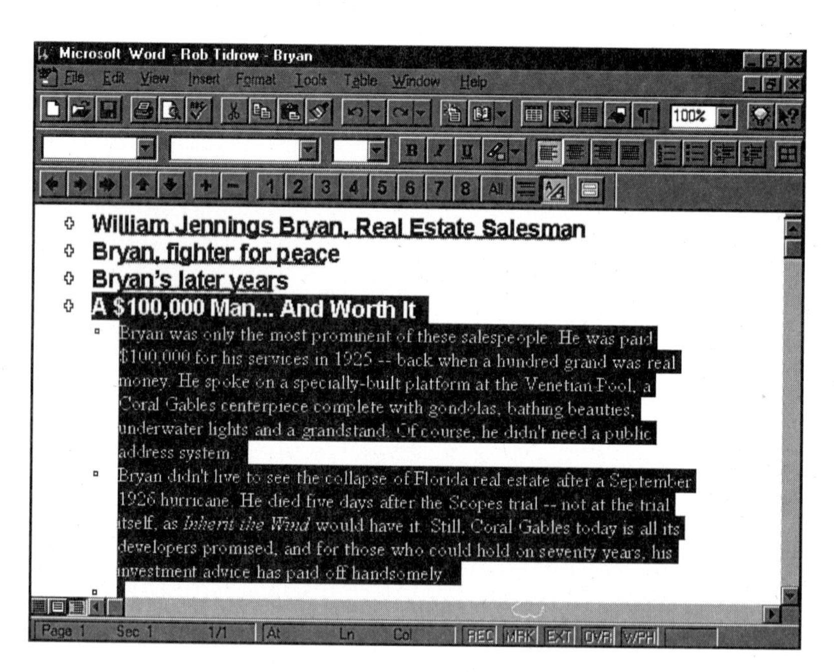

Figure 12.12

Zooming in on the contents of one main heading.

If you have a great deal of body text in these sections, you might want to see only the first line of each body text paragraph. With all body text displayed, press Alt+Shift+L, or click on the Show First Line Only toolbar button. Word abbreviates each paragraph, as in figure 12.13.

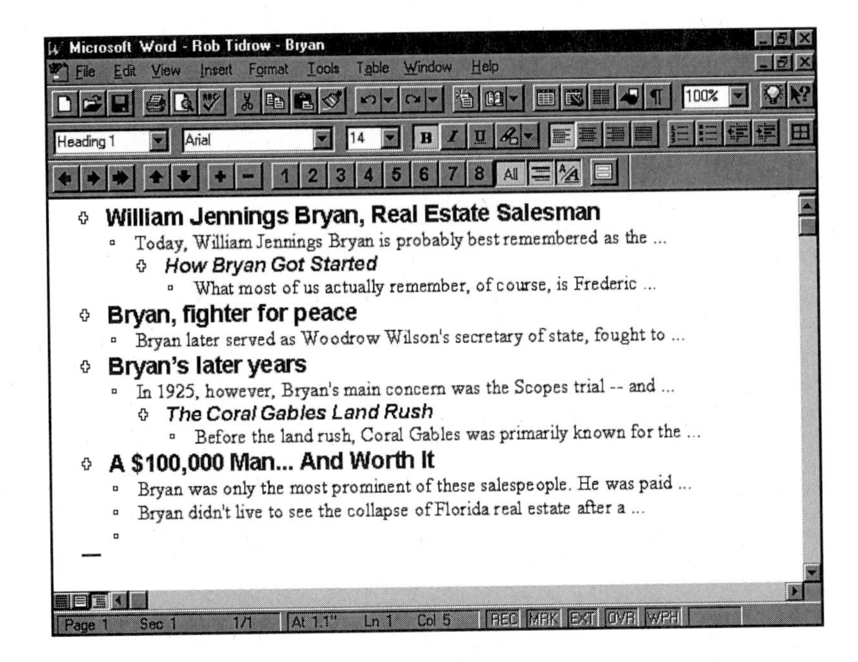

Figure 12.13

Displaying the first line of each paragraph.

Hiding All Character Formatting

Finally, you might be using the outline's styles primarily as a method of preparing table of contents entries or master documents. If so, you might find Word's default heading styles—such as 14-point Arial Bold Underline—distracting. You can turn them off with the Show/Hide Character Formatting button (see fig. 12.14).

Of course, Word's default styles might look just as unhelpful in the final printed document. Many publishers, for example, want to see all their text submitted in Courier—typewriter type, in other words.

You might create a style in which all the headings are simply boldface or underlined Courier. Then, when you demote or promote the headings, they will look the way they are supposed to look. You still benefit from the outlining, table of contents, and heading numbering features, which depend on heading styles.

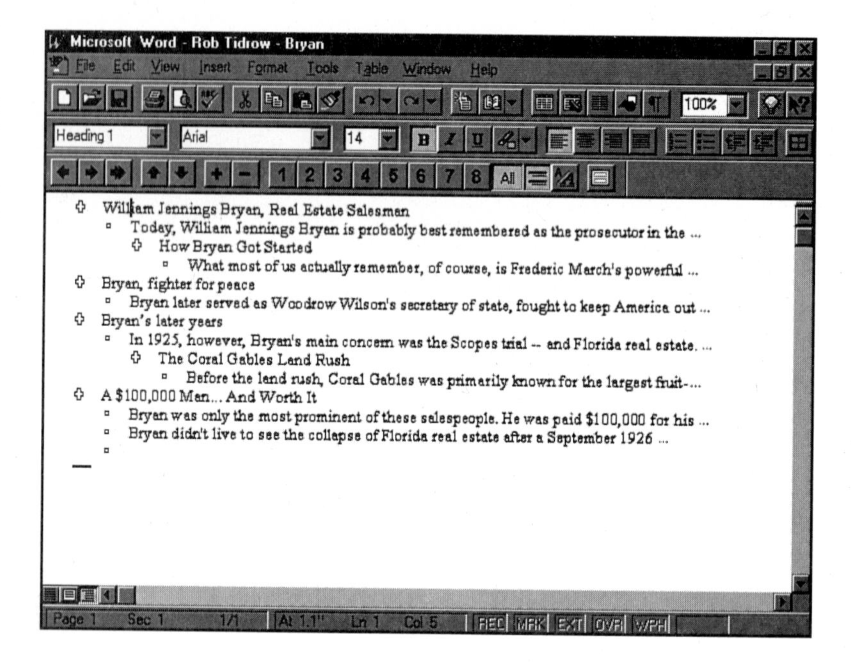

Figure 12.14

Turning character formatting off. Word displays the outline in its "draft" font.

Outline View and Word Styles

Outline View is yet another good reason to use styles. If you use Word's heading styles (heading 1 through heading 9), Word recognizes them when you switch to Outline View.

In other words, if you have used styles, you get all the easy document navigation and restructuring that Outline View provides, without having to consciously create an outline.

Of course, you can do it either way—the result is the same. If you create the document in Outline View, the correct styles are built into the document when you promote and demote headings. If you do it in Normal View, you choose the heading, and Word displays the correct heading levels when you go into Outline View.

Word's increasingly sophisticated AutoFormat feature gives you yet another reason to use Word styles. You can format your document as you normally do, placing your headings on a separate line before your body text. (It doesn't matter if you add lines between headings and body text.)

See Chapter 7, "Styles and AutoFormatting," for more information about AutoFormat.

Viewing the Style Area in Outline View

If you are working in a document with multiple levels, you might want to display the style area to show each heading level, as in figure 12.15. Choose Options from the Tools menu, select the View tab, and set the style area to 0.6".

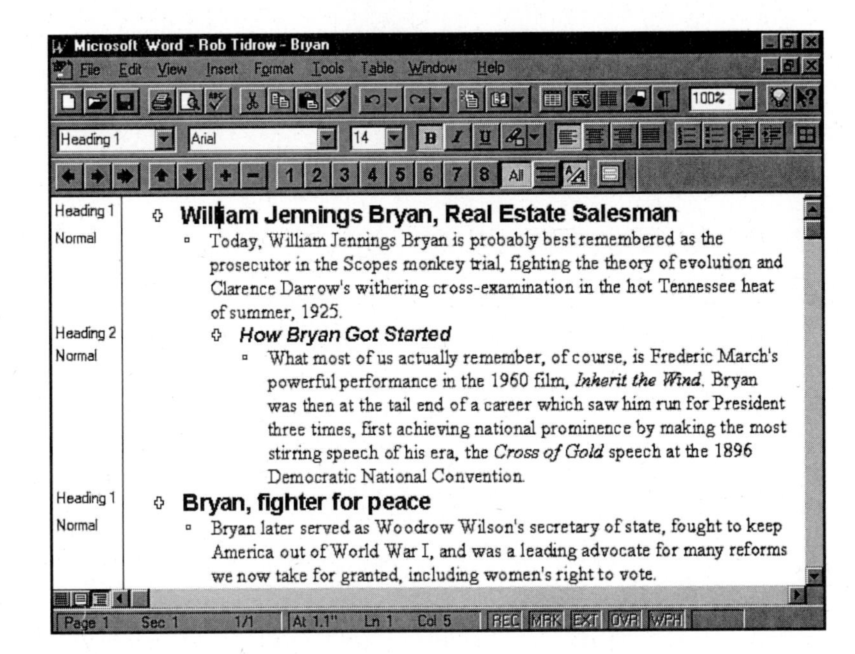

Figure 12.15

Style area displayed in Outline View.

Adding Outline Numbering

If you have spent too many hours trying to insert the proper heading levels in each of your outline headings, you will appreciate this option. After you have promoted and demoted all the headings you want, and the document is organized the way you want, you can delegate the actual numbering to Word.

Choose Format, Heading Numbering. The dialog box shown in figure 12.16 appears.

This works in Normal View, too. You don't have to be in Outline View to use Heading Numbering, as long as you have created your headings with Word's heading styles—or hired AutoFormat to do it for you.

It usually makes sense to work in Outline View, however, because you will be able to see a broad cross-section of your headings. This means you can quickly see if the heading numbers that Word inserts are the ones you want.

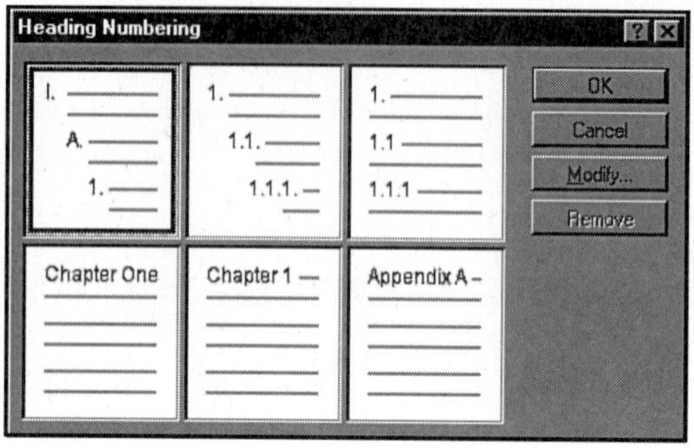

Figure 12.16

The Heading Numbering dialog box.

Creating Custom Heading Numbering

You can choose one of six preset heading formats, or you can create one of your own by choosing Modify. The Modify Heading Numbering dialog box appears, as shown in figure 12.17. In the bottom right corner, Word previews any changes you propose.

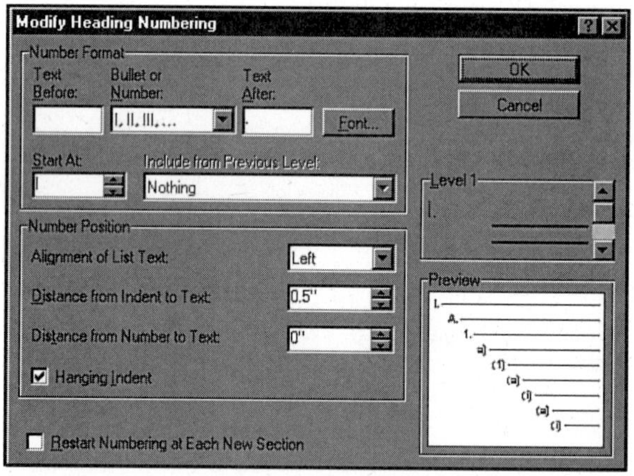

Figure 12.17

The Modify Heading Numbering dialog box.

In Text Before and Text After, you can set additional text that will appear in your outline numbering. For example, say you want your first-level headings to read Main Idea #1, Main Idea #2, and so on. Type **Main Idea#** in the Text Before box.

Notice that a period already appears in the Text After box. This is Word's default setting. You can delete it or add another character. If, for example, you want your numbers to appear in parentheses, you could type (in the Text Before box and) in the Text After box.

You also can set a font for your heading numbers by pressing **F**ont. The Font tabbed dialog box opens, as shown in figure 12.18. It resembles the **F**ont box you use to apply basic formatting, but you cannot choose Superscript, Subscript, Small Caps, or All Caps, and you cannot select a Character Spacing option.

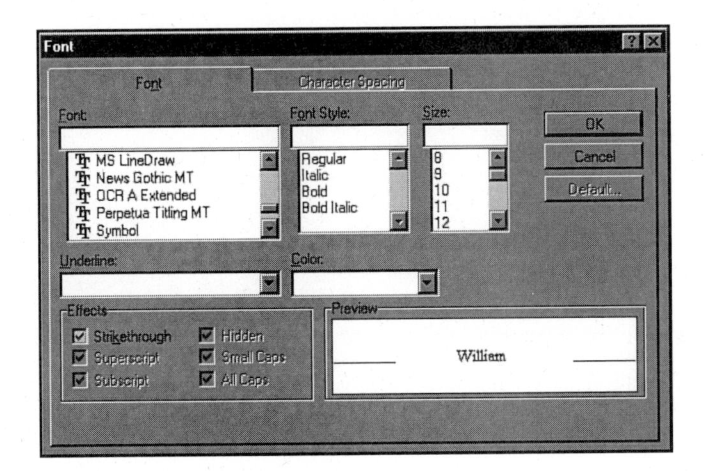

Figure 12.18

The Font dialog box in Heading Numbering.

You also can set a numbering or bullet format, in the Bullet or **N**umber box of the Modify Heading Numbering dialog box. Word's choices include the following:

(none)

1, 2, 3, ...

I, II, III, ...

i, ii, iii, ...

A, B, C, ...

a, b, c, ...

1st, 2nd, ...

One, Two, ...

First, Second...

Several standard bullets also are available. If you want a new bullet, choose **B**ullet, and the Symbol dialog box appears. You can pick any character there.

These numbering schemes accommodate all kinds of uses. A playwright could use First, Second numbering, for example, to accommodate acts and scenes.

If you simply want the same text to recur at every heading, choose (none) in the Bullet or Number list box.

By default, Word starts its heading numbers with 1, but you can change that by entering another number in the Start At box.

Formatting Other Heading Levels

Also by default, Word assumes you want to reformat a first-level heading. You can, however, format any of the nine heading levels available. You can choose another heading level by either using the scroll bar in the Level box or clicking on the heading level in Preview.

When you choose a heading level other than 1, a new option becomes available: Include from Previous Level. If you want previous heading letters or numbers to be part of your subhead numbering, choose Numbers. Here are some examples of headings with Numbers (or letters) included from previous levels:

I.A.1.

4.c.iii.

First Act, Second Scene

Custom-Positioning Your Heading Numbers

Word's default heading numbering also includes settings for the following:

- Alignment of List Text
- Distance from Indent to Text
- Distance from Number to Text

These settings affect all your headings, at every level. You can change any of them. You will almost always want to keep the alignment left-aligned, however.

Also notice that the distance from the number or letter to the text cannot be more than the distance from the indent to the text. If you try to raise it, the indent setting will increase as well. You also can turn Hanging Indent on or off. Finally, you can tell Word to Restart Numbering at Each New Section, by checking the box at the bottom left.

Changing or Deleting Heading Numbering

You can always change or eliminate heading numbering by choosing Heading Numbering from the Format menu again. If you have chosen a standard scheme, it will appear highlighted in the dialog box. If you have customized your heading numbers, none of the six standard options will be highlighted.

To remove heading numbering, choose Remove. To change to a standard numbering scheme, choose the one you want and click on OK. To change the customized scheme you created earlier, choose Modify. Your current settings will appear in the Modify Heading Numbering box, where you can change them.

Printing an Outline

When you print from Outline View, Word prints the outline as it appears on-screen, not the entire document. You can select exactly what part of the outline you want to print, then choose File, Print, and click on OK.

Exporting an Outline to Microsoft PowerPoint

If you use Microsoft PowerPoint for Windows 95 to make presentations, you might want to create the text for your presentation in Word—where you have access to Word's extensive editing capabilities—and then move it into PowerPoint to format it as a presentation. Fortunately, PowerPoint and Word are designed to work together.

Word comes with a macro, PresentIt, which exports a Word outline and then opens PowerPoint and displays your outlined text in a black-and-white overhead format. You can then modify the text and format as you like. To run this macro, however, you have to first make sure it is available.

PresentIt is located in the PRESENT7.DOT file, which is typically installed into the WINWORD\MACROS folder. (If you have installed Office 95, look for the OFFICE95\WINWORD\MACROS folder.) In order for PresentIt to work properly, PowerPoint for Windows 95 must be installed on your system.

There are several ways to make PresentIt available for use; these are described in Chapter 11, "Macros." The method used here makes it available only for the current session, which makes sense if you create presentations only occasionally and do not always want to store this macro in memory.

1. Choose Templates from the File menu.
2. Click on Add. The Add Templates window opens.
3. Click on the Up One Level button.
4. Double-click on the Winword folder.
5. Double-click on the Macros folder.
6. Double-click on the Present icon. The window closes and PRESENT.DOT now appears with a check mark in the Templates and Add-ins Window.
7. Choose OK.

Now that the macro is available, you still have to run it. Open the file containing the outline you want to export (you don't need to open the file in Outline view). Choose Macro from the Tools menu. Choose PresentIt from the Macro Names list, and choose Run.

The PresentIt macro does the following:

1. Saves the outline information in your Word file into a new file named ~PRESENT.RTF.
2. Opens Microsoft PowerPoint.
3. Opens ~PRESENT.RTF into a new black-and-white PowerPoint presentation sized for on-screen display, as shown in figure 12.19.

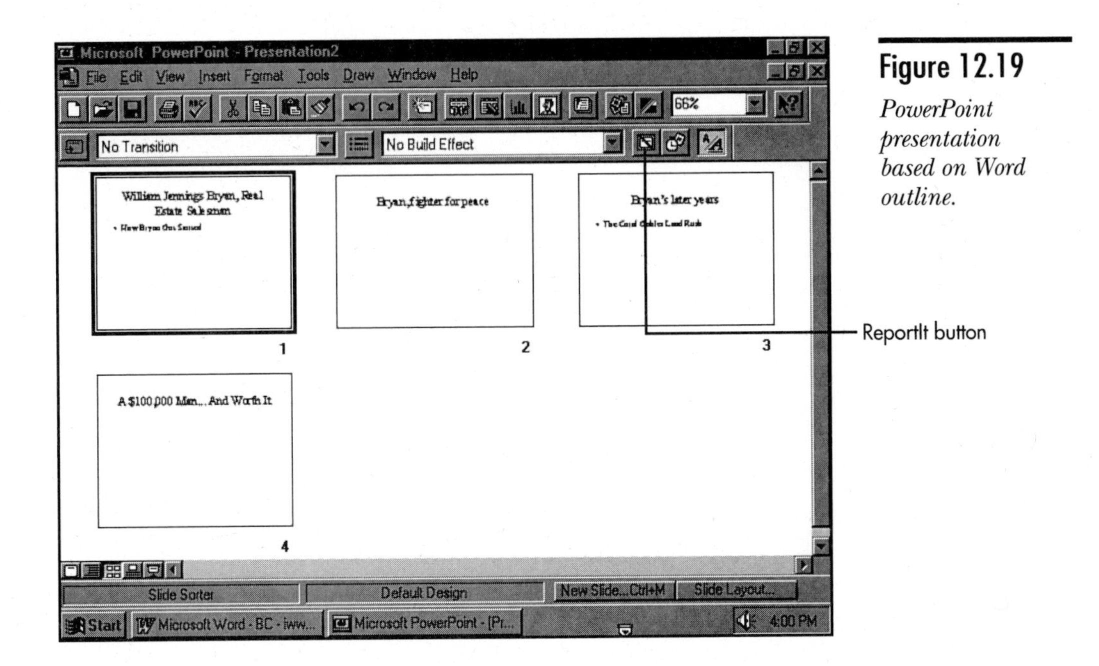

Figure 12.19
PowerPoint presentation based on Word outline.

The Word/PowerPoint relationship is a two-way street: you can click on the ReportIt button on PowerPoint's Standard Toolbar to export slides as an RTF file containing heading styles and display the file in Word for editing.

PowerPoint imports only paragraphs formatted with a heading style such as Heading 1, Heading 2, or Heading 3. Other text in your Word document is ignored.

If you plan to use PresentIt often, you may want to use Word's customization features to add it to one of your toolbars, such as the Standard or Formatting toolbar.

Tables of Contents

The creation of tables of contents used to strike fear into the hearts of document preparers. Today, the process is completely automated with Word. You can do the entire job without ever touching a field code, though they still work if you like them or are already using them. (This chapter describes a few places in which field codes are still indispensable.)

Word for Windows 95 also includes several preformatted Table of Contents styles and dialog boxes that give you much more flexibility in how you compile your table of contents.

Word's separate Table of Figures and Table of Authorities features work much like Table of Contents, but are customized to meet the needs of figure lists and authorities references. You even can use Word's Caption feature to create captions that Word places automatically in its Table of Figures.

In this chapter:

- Building a table of contents from styles
- Formatting a basic table of contents
- Including chapter numbers in a table of contents
- Updating a table of contents

- Using table of contents entry fields
- Compiling a table of contents using the TOC field
- Creating tables of figures and captions
- Using citations and tables of authorities

Building a Table of Contents from Styles

Before you compile a table of contents, you have to create table of contents entries. This can be done in two ways:

- With styles
- With fields

Styles are much easier to use, and fortunately handle most of your needs.

Keep table of contents fields in your arsenal if you need to create table lists different from tables of contents, figures, and authorities, or if you occasionally want to list table of contents entries without their page numbers. You can even build a table of contents that includes both styles and fields.

The accompanying CD-ROM contains a file you can use to practice some of these procedures in this chapter: IWMS13A.DOC.

By default, Word recognizes its first three built-in heading styles, Heading 1 through Heading 3, as likely table of contents entries. The style Heading 1 corresponds to a first-level head, Heading 2 a second-level head, and so on.

You also can add other styles to your table of contents. Often, these will be additional heading styles, such as Heading 4 through Heading 9, but you can include any style.

If you use the Normal template, only Headings 1 through 3 appear in your Style box, but all nine are available.

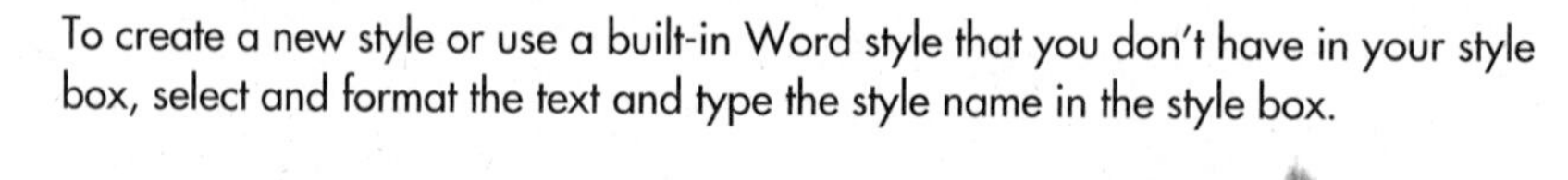
To create a new style or use a built-in Word style that you don't have in your style box, select and format the text and type the style name in the style box.

A Note from the Author

If you want to use styles to compile your table of contents, but you don't like the default formatting Word provides with its styles, you can change the style's formatting.

For example, when I deliver these manuscripts, everything's in 12-point Courier, and all my headings are in boldface. I created a new template where my usual style is Courier 12 point, and all nine heading styles add boldface.

With styles this simple, I'm using the style feature primarily to keep track of headings for when I create tables of contents later.

The simplest way to create a table of contents is to assign a style to any text you expect to include in a table of contents. To assign a style, select the text (you must select at least one complete line) and choose a style from the style box in the Formatting toolbar.

After you assign a style name to every heading you want to include in your table of contents, place your insertion point where you want the table of contents to appear. Then, select Inde**x** and Tables from the **I**nsert menu, and choose the Table of **C**ontents tab from the Index and Tables dialog box (see fig. 13.1).

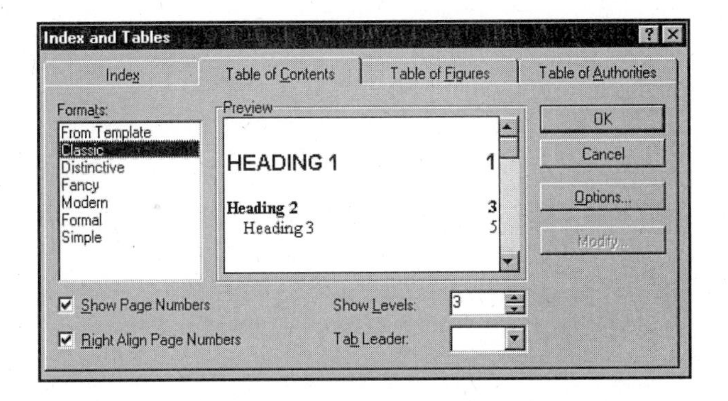

Figure 13.1
The Table of Contents tab.

Basic Table of Contents Formatting

You now have some choices. First of all, you can choose from among six built-in table of contents Forma**t**s: Classic, Distinctive, Fancy, Modern, Formal, and Simple. These are shown in the table of contents gallery in figures 13.2a through 13.2f. Generic versions of these tables of contents appear in the Preview box when you select them. (By the way, *Distinctive* was called *Elegant* in Word 6, but it's the same style.)

New in Word 95, a seventh option, From Template, allows you to build your own table of contents format from a Word template.

Figure 13.2a

Tables of contents based on Word's built-in formats—Classic format.

1. THE COUNTRY, END TO END	1
1.1. Steinbeck's Travels with Charley	**1**
1.1.1. 40 states by truck, in 1960	1
1.2. Gunther's Inside U.S.A.	**2**
1.2.1. All 48 states, as they were in 1947	2
1.3. William Least Heat Moon's Blue Highways	**3**
1.3.1. Finding wonders on small roads, in small towns, circa 1982	3
1.4. William Zinsser's American Places	**4**
1.4.1. Quick takes on the famous places we never really see	4

Figure 13.2b

Distinctive format table of contents.

1. The Country, End to End	*1*
1.1. Steinbeck's Travels with Charley	**1**
1.1.1. 40 states by truck, in 1960	1
1.2. Gunther's Inside U.S.A.	**2**
1.2.1. All 48 states, as they were in 1947	2
1.3. William Least Heat Moon's Blue Highways	**3**
1.3.1. Finding wonders on small roads, in small towns, circa 1982	3
1.4. William Zinsser's American Places	**4**
1.4.1. Quick takes on the famous places we never really see	4

Figure 13.2c

Fancy format table of contents.

1. THE COUNTRY, END TO END	1
1.1. STEINBECK'S TRAVELS WITH CHARLEY	**1**
1.1.1. 40 STATES BY TRUCK, IN 1960	1
1.2. GUNTHER'S INSIDE U.S.A.	**2**
1.2.1. ALL 48 STATES, AS THEY WERE IN 1947	2
1.3. WILLIAM LEAST HEAT MOON'S BLUE HIGHWAYS	**3**
1.3.1. FINDING WONDERS ON SMALL ROADS, IN SMALL TOWNS, CIRCA 1982	3
1.4. WILLIAM ZINSSER'S AMERICAN PLACES	**4**
1.4.1. QUICK TAKES ON THE FAMOUS PLACES WE NEVER REALLY SEE	4

1. The Country, End to End

1.1. Steinbeck's Travels with Charley

1.1.1. 40 states by truck, in 1960

1.2. Gunther's Inside U.S.A

1.2.1. All 48 states, as they were in 1947

1.3. William Least Heat Moon's Blue Highways

1.3.1. Finding wonders on small roads, in small towns, circa 1982

1.4. William Zinsser's American Places

1.4.1. Quick takes on the famous places we never really see

Figure 13.2d

Modern format table of contents.

1. THE COUNTRY, END TO END 1

1.1. STEINBECK'S TRAVELS WITH CHARLEY 1
1.1.1. 40 states by truck, in 1960 1
1.2. GUNTHER'S INSIDE U.S.A. 2
1.2.1. All 48 states, as they were in 1947 2
1.3. WILLIAM LEAST HEAT MOON'S BLUE HIGHWAYS 3
1.3.1. Finding wonders on small roads, in small towns, circa 1982 3
1.4. WILLIAM ZINSSER'S AMERICAN PLACES 4
1.4.1. Quick takes on the famous places we never really see 4

Figure 13.2e

Formal format table of contents.

1. The Country, End to End 1

1.1. Steinbeck's Travels with Charley 1
1.1.1. 40 states by truck, in 1960 1

1.2. Gunther's Inside U.S.A 2
1.2.1. All 48 states, as they were in 1947 2

1.3. William Least Heat Moon's Blue Highways 3
1.3.1. Finding wonders on small roads, in small towns, circa 1982 3

1.4. William Zinsser's American Places 4
1.4.1. Quick takes on the famous places we never really see 4

Figure 13.2f

Simple format table of contents.

By default, Word includes page numbers in its tables of contents. You can omit them by clearing the Show Page Numbers box. In each preformatted style (except Modern and Simple), page numbers are displayed flush-right. You can override the default by checking or clearing the Right Align Page Numbers box.

Also by default, Word shows three levels of headings. You can change this by selecting or typing a new number in the Show Levels box.

Note If you add more levels, Word assumes that you want to use additional heading styles, such as Heading 4 and Heading 5, as the source of these levels. If not, you'll need to tell Word where else to look, as described shortly.

Except for Distinctive and Formal, Word does not automatically include a tab leader in its table of contents formats. You also can control this by choosing a leader from the Tab Leader box.

Customizing a Table's Style

Word provides a common procedure for customizing the appearance of tables of contents, figures, and authorities. Select the From Template option from the Formats box, and then choose Modify. (From Template was called Custom Style in Word 6, but it's the same feature.)

A Style dialog box opens (see fig. 13.3). You're presented with the built-in base styles Word provides for whichever kind of table you modify. These styles are basic. Each style is previewed in Paragraph Preview and Character Preview and described in exhaustive detail in the Description box. To change a style, select it from the Styles box, and choose Modify. The Modify Style dialog box opens (see fig. 13.4).

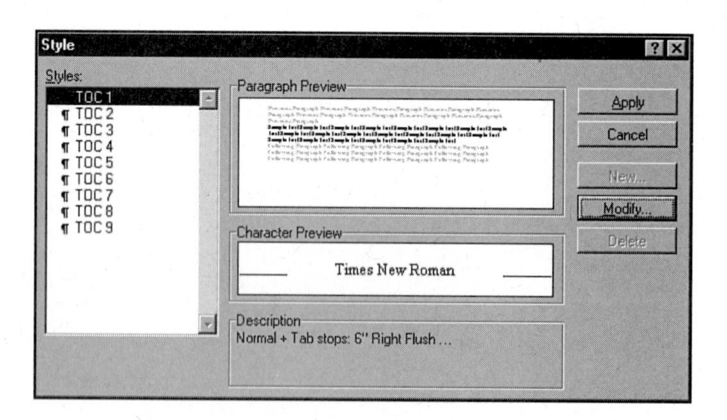

Figure 13.3
The Style dialog box for specifying table of contents formats.

The Modify Style dialog box enables you to specify the style you want the new style to be Based On (right now, the styles are based on the Normal style). Choose Format, and you're presented with a list of all the editable elements of a Word style: Font, Paragraph, Tabs, Border, Language, Frame, and Numbering. In short, you can edit a style here much the same way you'd normally edit a style elsewhere in Word (as described in Chapter 7, "Styles and AutoFormatting").

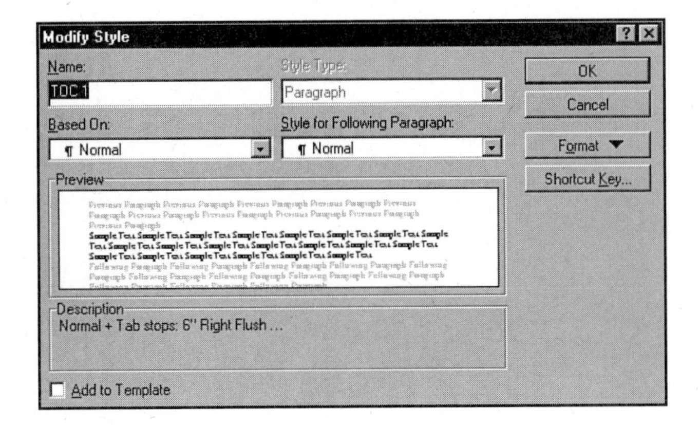

Figure 13.4

The Modify Style dialog box.

After you finish, you can decide whether to add this style permanently to your template. If so, check **A**dd to Template.

Table of Contents Options

Now that your table of contents looks the way you want, you can decide where its entries will come from. Choose **O**ptions from the Table of **C**ontents tab from the Index and Tables dialog box. The Table of Contents Options dialog box appears (see fig. 13.5).

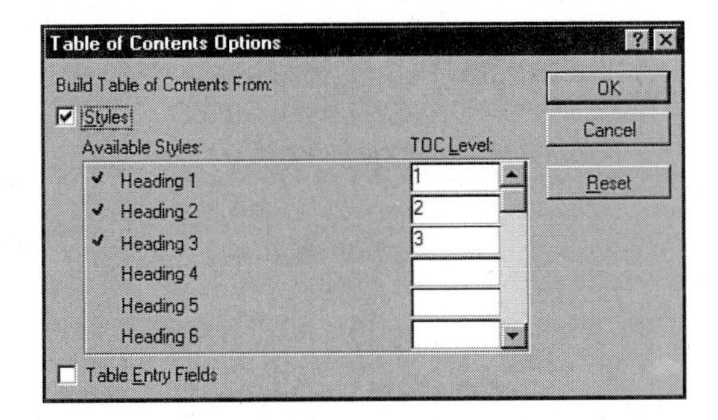

Figure 13.5

The Table of Contents Options dialog box.

Here, you choose the styles that Word looks for when it generates entries for your table of contents. You can choose any style in your document as a table of contents item. You also can rearrange your table of contents entries by typing new order numbers in the TOC **L**evel box for specific styles.

Most likely, you'll specify heading levels starting with 1, but you don't have to. If all your second-level heads were product names, for example, you could compile a list of the products covered in a document by choosing only heading level 2 and clearing the rest. If you also want to add fields to your table of contents, check the Table **E**ntry Fields box.

If you want to keep a custom list of headings permanently, select it and press Ctrl+Shift+F9 to unlink the field. This turns the list into ordinary text. When you next compile a table of contents, this list of headings won't be replaced.

To reset the Build Table of Contents From list to Word's default settings (Headings 1 through 3 only), select **R**eset.

When a table of contents is added, so are the base table of contents styles, TOC 1 through TOC 8. Each style corresponds to as many levels of heading styles as are in your document (up to eight).

After you have a table of contents in your document, you can get to any chapter or heading listed in the document by double-clicking on its page number in the table of contents.

Including Chapter Numbers in a Table of Contents

To include chapter numbers in a table of contents, include them in your document's regular page numbering:

1. Format your chapter number with a style you don't use anywhere else—perhaps an obscure heading style like Heading 9.
2. Choose Page N**u**mbers from the **I**nsert menu.
3. Choose **F**ormat.
4. Check the Include Chapter **N**umber box.
5. Select the style that you've used for your chapter number.
6. Select a separator character; a hyphen is the default character.
7. Choose OK.

Updating a Table of Contents

Tables of contents are fields. You can update one the way you update any field: select it and press F9.

You can have only one table of contents in a document. If you use Insert, Index and Tables to add a table of contents when you already have one, Word replaces the existing one. You can add other kinds of tables, however, such as tables of figures (this is covered later).

Using Table of Contents Entry Fields

You can add field entries to your document that eventually are compiled into your table of contents. This is a time-consuming process that generally is a drag, so why use field entries?

- When you want to include a table of contents entry that doesn't correspond to specific text in the document, such as a paraphrase
- When you want to include a table of contents entry without assigning it a style that Word will flag everywhere it appears
- When you want to suppress the page numbering for a specific table of contents entry

The table of contents entry field is named *TC*. Do not confuse this field with *TOC*, which compiles the table of contents. (TOC is discussed later.)

To insert a TC field:

1. Select Field from the Insert menu.
2. Select TC from the Field Names box.
3. In the Field Codes box, type the text you want to appear in the table of contents entry. Place the text between quotation marks, as in this example:

   ```
   TC "Why Projects Fail"
   ```

4. Specify the level of the entry. Choose Options, select **\l** from the Switches box, and choose Add to Field. Then add a number from 1 to 9 corresponding to the table of contents level you want Word to use when it compiles the table. For example:

   ```
   TC "Why Projects Fail" \l 3
   ```

5. Choose OK to insert the entry, unless you need to add an option:

   Option 1. If you don't want a page number to print with the entry, add the switch **\n**.

Option 2. If you want the entry to appear in another list, not the table of contents, choose Options and add the switch **\f**, along with a letter that corresponds to that list. Here is an example:

```
TC "Why Projects Fail" \f i
```

This example can be used to identify a table list for compilation in a table of illustrations.

You also can enter the field by pressing Ctrl+F9 and keying the field text between the **{ }** brackets that appear.

Also, TC fields are hidden text, which means you normally can't see them even if you're displaying field codes. This can be really bizarre: if you insert a field code using Ctrl+F9 and you type **TC**, as soon as you type the letter C, the field disappears!

To solve this problem, display your hidden text by selecting **Options** from the **Tools** menu and checking the Hidden Text box from the View tab of the Options dialog box, or key the rest of your field text before you insert the letters TC.

If you see the field, but do not see the text that should appear in its proper place, choose **Options** from the **Tools** menu and uncheck the **Field Codes** box on the View tab of the Options dialog box.

The Field Reference in Chapter 10, "Field Codes," also includes more information about the TC and TOC fields, and about using fields in general.

Compiling a Table of Contents Using the TOC Field

The Table of Contents tab in the Index and Tables dialog box contains most of the gizmos you need for compiling a table of contents. When would you ever want to use a TOC field?

- When you want to compile a table of contents from only part of a document
- When you want to create another table list, such as a table of illustrations, that isn't covered by Word's Table of Figures and Table of Authorities features

Compiling Only Part of a Document

Occasionally, you may want to compile a table of contents for only part of a document. Suppose, for example, that you're working on a document, and someone asks you which points you plan to cover on a specific topic. To create a *partial* table of contents, follow these steps:

1. Select the text you want to cover.
2. Select Bookmark from the Edit menu, and type a one-word bookmark name. Click on OK.
3. Position the cursor where you want the table of contents to appear, and then create a TOC field with the \b switch and the bookmark name. The following is an example:

   ```
   {TOC \b vietnam}
   ```

4. Update the field by pressing F9 to see the new table of contents.

You can add other switches to the TOC field, as described in Chapter 10. In the preceding example, you can use the \o switch if you want to print a table of contents for the Vietnam section, but only include heading levels 1 and 2:

```
{TOC \b vietnam \o 1--2}
```

Notice the double hyphens used to indicate a range of heading levels.

Several additional switches are available. In general, you don't need them—you can handle most of these tasks from the Index and Tables dialog box. When you do need them, refer to the Field Reference in Chapter 10.

What if each chapter has its own file? Build a *master document* that creates a table of contents based on all the separate files. Chapter 18, "Annotations, Revisions, and Master Documents," discusses master documents in detail.

Tables of Figures and Captions

As with tables of contents, Word's Table of Figures feature also builds lists based on a style you assign to all your figures. You can decide in advance that all your figures will use a style called Figure. You then format the style and compile it much as you would a table of contents.

There is a pleasing alternative: Word can automatically create your figures and figure numbering for you, using its Caption feature.

Using Word's Caption Feature

To insert a caption anywhere in a document, select Capt**i**on from the **I**nsert menu. The Caption dialog box opens, as shown in figure 13.6.

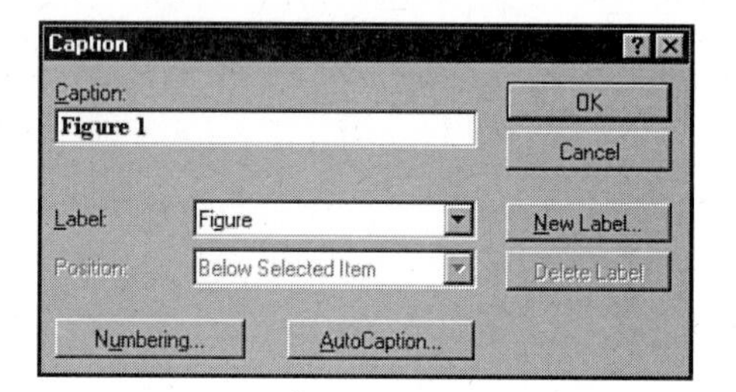

Figure 13.6
The Caption dialog box.

By default, Word numbers figures. The word `Figure 1` appears in the Caption box. You can add any text you like, but you can't edit the text Word has already displayed—you have to change that elsewhere.

If you want a numbered equation or a table, choose these alternatives from the **L**abel list box. If you want to use another label, create it by pressing the **N**ew Label button. The New Label dialog box appears (see fig. 13.7). Key the label in the **L**abel box; then click on OK.

Figure 13.7
The New Label dialog box.

By default, Word uses the numbering scheme 1, 2, 3, and so on. You can choose another numbering scheme by choosing N**u**mbering. The Caption Numbering dialog box opens (see fig. 13.8). This closely resembles the Page Number Format dialog box you've seen in Chapter 2, "Document Essentials," and elsewhere.

Figure 13.8
The Caption Numbering dialog box.

Choose a numbering scheme from the Format list box. If you want to include a chapter number, first place the chapter number in your document and assign it a unique style that doesn't appear elsewhere in the document.

Then return to the Caption Numbering dialog box, and check Include Chapter Number. In Chapter Starts with Style, choose the style name. In Use Separator, choose the character you want to appear between the chapter number and the figure number. Finally, click on OK.

Telling Word to Caption Automatically

If you regularly caption imported objects such as Excel graphs, CorelDRAW! illustrations, or Equation Editor equations, Word can insert your captions for you whenever you add the object to your document. Set up AutoCaptioning when you create a new document. Word can't go back and AutoCaption objects you've already imported.

To set up AutoCaptioning, follow these steps:

1. Select Caption from the Insert menu.
2. Choose AutoCaption. The AutoCaption dialog box appears (see fig. 13.9).

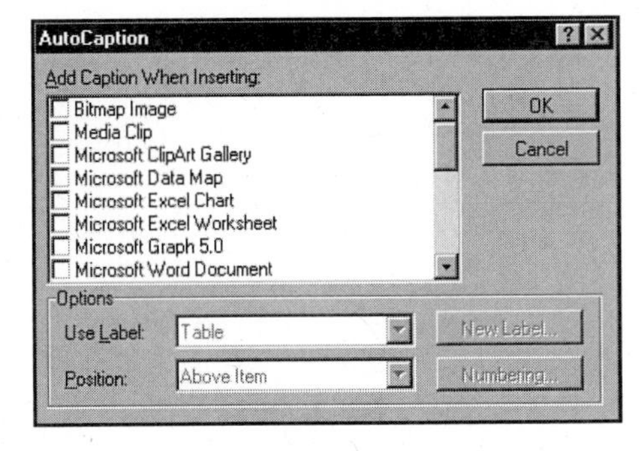

Figure 13.9

The AutoCaption dialog box.

3. In the Add Caption When Inserting box, choose an object type from the list of objects available on your computer.

This list includes object types that appear in your OLE registration database; in other words, programs that registered their OLE support with Windows when you installed them, or had their OLE information migrated to Windows 95 when you installed Windows 95 over an older Windows 3.1 installation.

4. In the Position box, specify whether you want the caption to appear above or below the object you will be inserting.

5. In the Use Label box, specify the label you want to appear when you insert one of these objects. Choose New Label if you need to create another label.

6. Click on the Numbering button to set a numbering scheme, unless you're happy with 1, 2, 3....

7. After you've finished with any New Label-making or Numbering changes, click on OK to activate AutoCaptioning.

Creating a Table of Figures

You can create as many tables of figures as you want in the same document. You can have one table for figures, another for illustrations, and another for tables—you name it!

To create a table of figures, choose Index and Tables from the Insert menu, and select the Table of Figures tab from the Index and Tables dialog box (see fig. 13.10). Much of this will look similar to tables of contents. You can choose to show page numbers, right align page numbers, and include a tab leader.

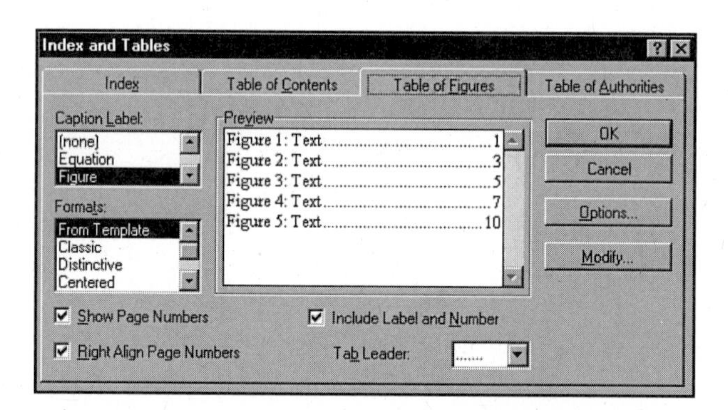

Figure 13.10
The Table of Figures tab.

As with tables of contents, Word provides several standard table of figures formats: Classic, Distinctive, Centered, Formal, and Simple. Each style and any change you make to the style is previewed in the Preview box.

One important addition to the Table of Figures dialog box is Caption Label. In this box, you choose whether to use a caption you've created using Word's Caption feature.

If the captions in your document were created using Word's caption feature, each figure will include a label and number. You can omit these from your figure list by clearing the Include Label and Number box.

If your captions weren't created using Word's caption feature, select (none) from the Caption Label box, and then choose Options. The Table of Figures Options dialog box appears (see fig. 13.11).

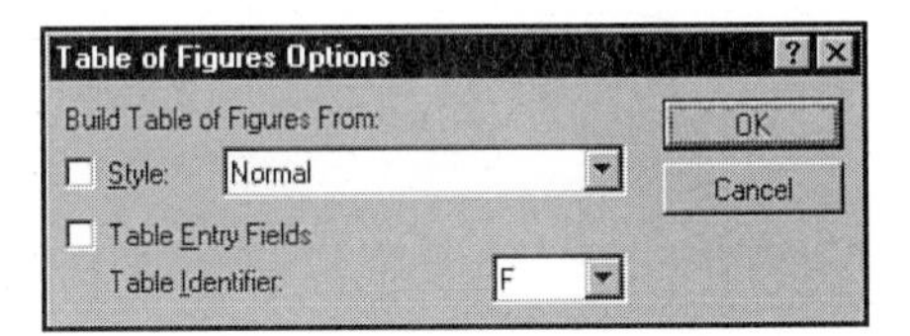

Figure 13.11
The Table of Figures Options dialog box.

If all your figures have been assigned a specific style, check Style and choose the style from the accompanying list box. If you include the list figures you created as TC entry fields, check Table Entry Fields. In Table Identifier, specify the initial you've used for compiling this list. Click on OK to return to the Table of Figures dialog box. Click on OK again to compile your list.

Adding a TC Entry Field to Your Table of Figures

You rarely need to enter field codes directly to create table of figures entries, or to compile a table of figures.

Occasionally, you might want to include a table entry field in your table of contents. For example, if you want only one item to appear in the table of figures without a page number, you'll need to use a field.

In those cases, how do you make sure that the TC entry field appears in the correct table of figures? Add the \f switch. Before you add the switch, the basic TC entry field looks like this:

```
{TC "Text you want to appear in your table"}
```

To this, add the \f switch, followed by an initial representing the table in which you want the text to be included. Word's default is F, for figure. In that case, your table entry field might read:

```
{TC "Text you want to appear in your table" \f f}
```

If you don't include an **\f** switch, the TC entry field appears in your table of contents, not in a table of figures.

Citations and Tables of Authorities

Word also provides a Table of Authorities feature specifically designed to streamline the preparation of legal briefs and other documents that must refer to statutes, rules, and judicial decisions.

Tables of authorities are designed to list all citations made in a document, in alphabetical order within category. Before you can compile your citations, however, you have to mark them.

Marking Citations

To build a table of authorities, first edit your document as you normally would, including citations wherever appropriate. Then scroll through the document, looking for citations.

If all your citations follow a specific format, such as Jones v. Smith, you can search for v. to find the citations.

Whenever you find a citation, select it and press Alt+Shift+I. This opens the Mark Citation dialog box (see fig. 13.12) with the citation already appearing in it.

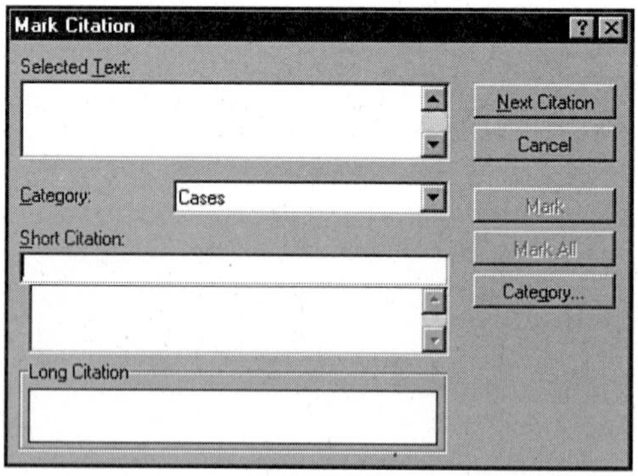

Figure 13.12
The Mark Citation dialog box.

Edit the Selected Text box so that it includes all the detailed information that should appear in a first reference. Your edits don't appear in the document itself, but do appear in the table of authorities.

In the Short Citation box, edit that text, which becomes follow-up references in your table of authorities. Also assign the reference to a Category. Word provides the following seven built-in categories:

- Cases
- Statutes
- Other Authorities
- Rules
- Treatises
- Regulations
- Constitutional Provisions

Adding a new category. Word also provides nine other categories, numbered 8 through 16, which you can replace with real category names. To create a new category name, choose **Category**. The Edit Category dialog box opens (see fig. 13.13).

Choose a category to replace, and type a new name in the Replace **With** box. Choose **Replace**, and click on OK.

Figure 13.13

The Edit Category dialog box.

Now you have a choice. You can mark this citation by choosing Mark, or you can mark all identical citations throughout the document by choosing Mark All. Mark All marks the first reference with the full citation you created in Selected Text; following references to the same case use the Short Citation.

If you'll pardon the pun, legal citations are case-sensitive. The capitalization and text have to be identical for the Mark All option to flag it.

Citations are to fields marked as hidden text. When you mark a citation, Word displays all citations in the document (along with paragraph marks, dots between letters, and some other nonprinting text). To hide the citations, click on the Show/Hide Paragraph Mark button on the Standard toolbar.

After you have created your citations, you can move from one to the next by opening Mark Citation and choosing Next Citation.

Compiling a Table of Authorities

After you finish creating your citations, you can compile them into a table of authorities:

1. Place your insertion point where you want the table to go.
2. Select Index and Tables from the Insert menu.
3. Choose the Table of Authorities tab from the Index and Tables dialog box (see fig. 13.14).

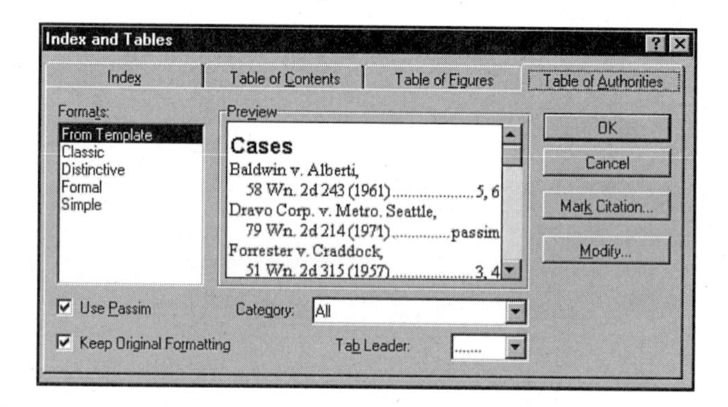

Figure 13.14
The Table of Authorities tab.

As with tables of contents and figures, Word provides several Formats to choose from. There's also a custom style you can adapt by selecting this option and then choosing Modify.

In Category, you can choose the types of citations you want to compile; the default is All. In Tab Leader, you can specify whether you want a tab-leader. Different Formats have different default tab-leader settings.

You have two other choices when compiling your table of authorities:

- **Use Passim.** If Word finds references to the same authority on five or more pages, it can substitute the word *passim,* rather than list the pages. This option is on by default.
- **Keep Original Formatting.** Word retains any formatting applied to the citation in the document itself. This option is also on by default.

4. After you set the table of authorities the way you want, click on OK to compile it.

Indexes

The best indexes are works of art that have been created by people with a wonderful sensitivity to nuance and a finely honed judgment about what's important.

Word for Windows 95 doesn't change that. How good an index will be is still up to the indexer. (This chapter shows you a few clues.) For many documents, a down-and-dirty index is all that's needed. Either way, Word does a masterful job of taking care of the basics: the actual compilation of an index.

As with tables of contents, the idea is simple: you mark index entries, and when the document is finished, you tell Word how you want the index to look. Then you compile the index.

In this chapter:

- Creating index entries
- Marking all references to a text item at once
- Compiling an index
- Creating multilevel indexes
- Using page ranges in indexes

- Using Word's predefined index formats
- Customizing index styles
- Indexing parts of a document
- Including chapter numbers in an index
- Updating an index
- Creating a concordance index

Creating Index Entries

To mark an index entry:

1. Position your insertion point where you want the index entry. If you want to copy words from the document into the index entry, select the text.
2. Press Alt+Shift+X. The Mark Index Entry dialog box opens, as shown in figure 14.1.

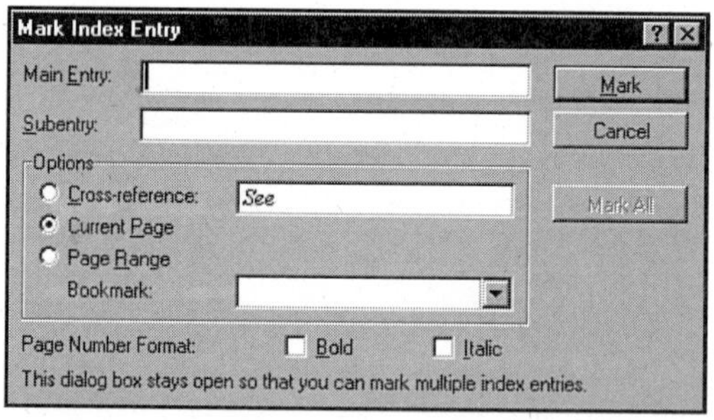

Figure 14.1

The Mark Index Entry dialog box.

3. If you've chosen text, that text appears in the Main Entry box. If not, type in your index entry, or revise what's already there.
4. If the text that you selected contains a colon, Word adds a backslash in the index entry. That's because, as you'll see, Word reserves colons as its way of flagging subentries. (If you *want* a subentry there, delete the backslash, and Word treats the words that follow the colon as a subentry to the words that precede it.)
5. Choose Mark.

Word places a hidden {xe} field in your document, with the index entry text in quotes:

```
{xe "Complementarity"}
```

That's as basic as it gets. You'll wind up with an index such as the following:

Classical physics, 36
Complementarity, 253
Confucius, 117
Consciousness, 406, 432, 477
Copenhagen Interpretation, 43, 45, 51
Copernicus, 227
Decay, 46
Doppler effect, 352

As you can see in the preceding example, all index entries carry equal weight. No subentries are included; no page numbers are boldfaced or italicized; and all references are to single pages.

The Mark Index Entry dialog box lets you change these elements. When you specify an entry, Word inserts a hidden {xe} field in your document. Later, you learn how to control other elements of your index entries by directly editing these {xe} fields, and the {index} fields Word uses to compile its indexes.

Note: You also can get to the Mark Index Entry dialog box by selecting Inde**x** and Tables from the **I**nsert menu, selecting the **I**ndex tab, and choosing **M**ark. Do you see why the keyboard shortcut is recommended?

The accompanying CD-ROM contains a file you can use to practice some of the procedures in this chapter: IWMS14A.DOC.

Boldfacing or Italicizing Page Numbers

Later, when you compile the index, you might want to call attention to a specific entry's page number by using italics or boldface. Open the Mark Index Entry dialog box, and click on **B**old or **I**talic in Page Number Format. Note that clicking on **B**old or **I**talic doesn't boldface or italicize the text itself—only the page number.

Inserting Page Ranges in Index Entries

Often, you may want to create a page range for an index entry, as in the following example:

```
Double-slit experiment, 52-55
```

Before creating the field entry, select all the text you want to include in the entry and create a bookmark. Then open the Mark Index Entry dialog box. Check the Page Range button and choose your bookmark name from the list box beneath Page **R**ange, as shown in figure 14.2. You also can type the bookmark name there yourself, as long as you also click on the Page **R**ange button.

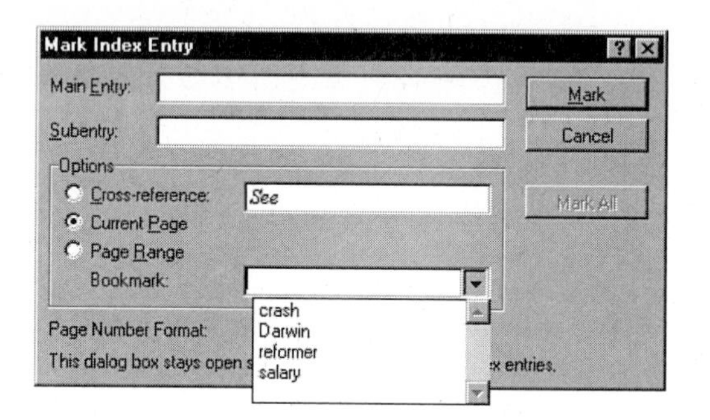

Figure 14.2

A list of bookmarks in Page Range.

Creating Multilevel Indexes

After you catch on to indexing, you'll see that some topics fit naturally as subentries beneath other topics. The process of building an index is similar to building an outline: not everything is a main topic.

Take, for example, the following multilevel index. In that example, "Detergents" is a second-level subentry, and "Dishwashing detergent" is a third-level subentry:

Amway Corporation
    Detergents, 52–54
        Dishwashing detergent, 52
        Laundry detergent, 53
    Soap, 57
Shaklee Corporation
    Cereal, 112
    Vitamins, 39

To create a subentry, first type the main entry that you want the subentry to appear beneath. Then type the subentry itself. If you would like multiple levels of subentry, place them all in the **S**ubentry box, separated by colons:

```
Detergents:Dishwashing detergent
```

Because the Mark Index Entry dialog box stays open as you move around the document, you can move to the document, select text that you want to be included in an index entry, and copy that text into the **S**ubentry box.

You can specify up to seven levels of index entry this way. (That's an awfully cumbersome index, however. You should rarely have to use even four levels.)

If you don't create any entries specifically for the main index entry, the main index entry appears in your index without a page number, as in the example index shown earlier.

Using Text instead of a Page Number

Until now, all the index entries have referred the reader to a page number or a range of pages. But sometimes you come across an index entry such as the following:

```
Alice, see Looking Glass
```

Word refers to this as a *cross-reference.* You can add a cross-reference by opening the Mark Index Entry dialog box, and then clicking on the **C**ross-reference button. The word "See" is already there; type the entry you want to cross-reference. (If you want to use a different word, delete "See" and type the word that you prefer.)

Marking All References to Specific Text

Word's Mark Index Entry dialog box contains a shortcut for marking all references to specific text:

1. Select the text that you want to index.
2. Press Alt+Ctrl+X to open the Mark Index Entry dialog box.
3. If necessary, edit the Index Main Entry and Subentry to read the way you want them to appear in the finished index.
4. If necessary, select a **C**ross-reference or a Page **R**ange bookmark.
5. Choose Mark **A**ll.

Word searches the document—looking for references to the precise text you've marked—and then flags each of the references with an index entry.

If you want to mark all references to several text items at once, use Word's concordance indexing feature, described later in this chapter.

When Mark **A**ll begins running, it immediately displays all nonprinting and hidden characters. If you want to hide them again, you'll have to do that manually after you finish using it.

Creating Helpful Index Entries

In many cases, your index items might be identical to the text you've selected. But you might want to make your index more interpretive. Think about your reader. How would he or she search for information? Consider the ways a reader might think about the following paragraph:

> Miserable in a loveless marriage, Marie Antoinette threw herself into a life of pleasure and careless extravagance. The old story—that upon hearing about peasants without bread, she said, "Let them eat cake"—is most likely false. But scandals such as the Affair of the Diamond Necklace were all too real.

Of course, the preceding paragraph should be indexed under *Marie Antoinette.* But you also might want to flag the quote *Let them eat cake,* perhaps as a subentry under Marie Antoinette. You also can mark the paragraph as an entry in *French Revolution, causes,* or under *ancient regime.* Those three subjects might not explicitly appear in the text, but they might be what your reader is looking for. Similarly, think of synonyms for the index entries you're presenting. (Word enables you to create as many index entries for a passage of text as you like, of course.)

Be sensitive to the relative importance of entries, and use Word's subentry feature wherever appropriate. Even if you create many specific entries, you will help the reader if you also add a broad, conceptual entry that includes them as subentries.

In indexing names, remember that last names should appear first. Word does not invert them automatically. (*Marie Antoinette* is an exception.) Think about phrases that should also appear in inverted form, including the following:

> burial masks
> masks, burial

Finally, when you create index entries that refer to items that can be abbreviated, spell out the entire name. Then include a separate entry, using the acronym or abbreviation, pointing to the main entry:

Confederate States of America, 37, 52, 69, 84
CSA, see Confederate States of America

Compiling an Index

Remember, your index will be created using Word's current pagination. Before you compile your index, make sure that you do the following:

- Complete every aspect of your document, if possible. That includes last-minute items such as the table of contents and figure lists.
- Hide all hidden text. (Select Tools, Options, View; clear the Hidden Text box in Nonprinting Characters.)
- Hide all field codes. (Make sure that there's no check mark next to Field Codes in Tools, Options, View.)

When you're ready, place your insertion point where you want the index. Most likely, that's the end of the document. Then select Index and Tables from the Insert menu, and choose the Index tab (see fig. 14.3).

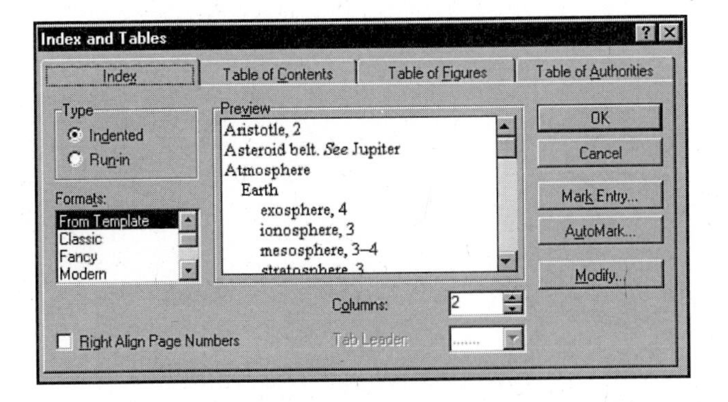

Figure 14.3

The Index and Tables dialog box.

To create a standard index now, click on OK.

From this dialog box, Word offers almost total control over the formatting of your index. Word offers two main Types of indexes. By default, Word creates what it calls an Indented Index: each new entry appears on its own line. You can, however, choose a Run-In Index to save space. The following is an example of what that will look like:

> Amway Corporation: Detergents, 52–54; Dishwashing detergent, 52; Laundry detergent, 53; Soap, 57
> Shaklee Corporation: Cereal, 112; Vitamins, 39

Notice that main entries are separated from subentries with a colon; subentries are separated from each other with a semicolon; the next main entry still appears on a line of its own. In addition, whenever you create an index, Word inserts an index field in your document; if you create a run-in index, Word adds the \r switch. You also can tell Word to place all page numbers flush right by clicking on **Right** Align Page Numbers.

You can divide your index page into multiple columns by selecting a number from 1 to 4 in the Columns box; the default is two columns.

Now that you've made a few basic formatting decisions, Word enables you to choose from six basic index styles: Classic, Fancy, Modern, Bulleted, Formal, and Simple. (These are consistent with the table of contents formats you saw in Chapter 13, "Tables of Contents," except that Bulleted replaces Distinctive.)

As with the table of contents, you can create your own style by selecting Custom Style from the Formats box in the Index and Tables dialog box. Then choose **Modify**. The Style dialog box opens (see fig. 14.4). Select an index style that you want to modify, and choose **Modify** again. The Modify Style dialog box opens (see fig. 14.5).

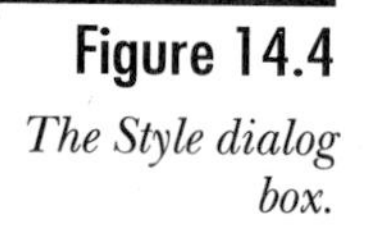

Figure 14.4

The Style dialog box.

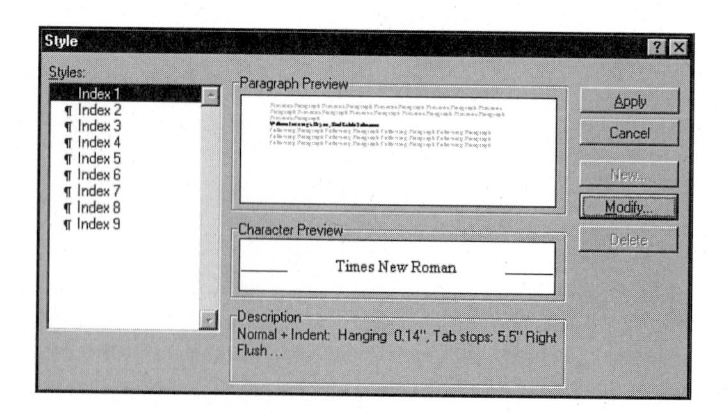

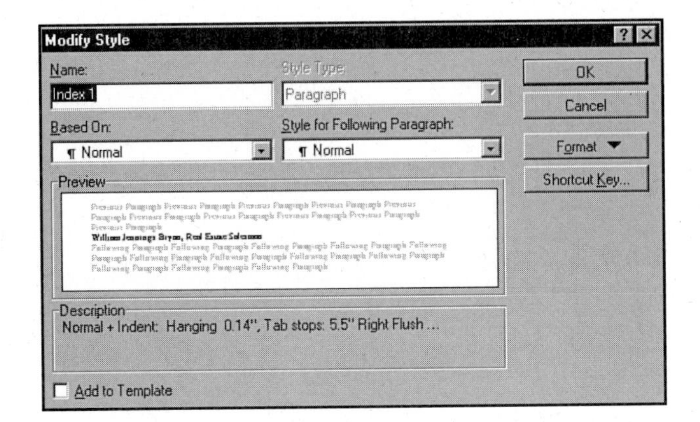

Figure 14.5
The Modify Style dialog box.

The Modify Style dialog box is the same dialog box discussed in Chapter 13; you can use it to modify any aspect of the style you've chosen, and to preview the changes before they take effect. Click on OK when you're finished.

Including Chapter Numbering in an Index

Suppose that you have a document containing multiple chapters, and you want to include the chapter numbers in your index entries, as in the following example:

Elks, 2-9
Kiwanis Club, 4-8
Lions Club, 3-12
Rotary Club, Chapter 6-3; 6-8

Word automatically includes those page numbers in your index, if you use Insert, Page Numbers to add them to your document's numbering.

Indexing Part of a Document

Word's Index and Tables dialog box still doesn't provide a way to index only part of a document. But fields provide three ways to do it. Whenever you insert an index into a document, Word inserts an {index} field. You can modify one that Word inserts, or insert one of your own.

To index only part of a document, do the following:

1. Select that portion of the document.

2. Create a bookmark for that text:

   a. Choose Book**m**ark from the **E**dit menu.

   b. Type a one-word bookmark name.

   c. Click on OK.

3. Next, after deselecting text, insert the **{index}** field:

   a. Choose Fiel**d** from the **I**nsert menu.

   b. Choose Index from Field **N**ames.

   c. In the Field Codes box, after INDEX, type **\b** followed by the name of the bookmark.

   d. Click on OK.

4. Press F9 to update the field.

You can do the same thing directly, by pressing Ctrl+F9 to open a field for editing, and typing **index** followed by the \b switch and the bookmark name, as in this example:

```
{index \b jones}
```

Creating Indexes that Contain Specific Entries

By default, Word indexes contain all the items in the pages being indexed. You can, however, create an index that only contains items that you specify.

After you insert the index entry {xe} fields, display them and add the \f switch to them, followed by an initial. Your field could look like the following:

```
{XE "Bryan, William Jennings" \f x}
```

Add the same switch and initial to every {xe} field that you want to compile. Then, when you want to compile these special index entries into an index, insert an INDEX field with the same \f x switch:

```
{INDEX \f x}
```

Keep in mind a few important points about working with these special index entries:

- Don't use the initial *I*. That's Word's default setting; it'll simply include all the index entries in your index.
- Index entries using \f identifiers other than *I* won't appear in your overall index—only in an index created with {index \f}.

Compiling Only Some Letters of an Index

You can use the \p (partial) switch to tell Word to compile only certain letters, as in the following example:

```
{index \p n--z}
```

Separate the letters with a hyphen. You don't need to place the letters in quotation marks, but do take note of the double hyphen.

Taking Even More Control of Your Index

If you're willing to edit the {index} field that Word enters when you use the Index and Tables dialog box, you also can control the following conditions:

- How (and whether) all the index entries under one letter of the alphabet are separated from the entries for the next letter.
- Which character is used in page ranges (normally, it's a hyphen, as in: 36-42).
- How an index item is separated from its page number.
- Whether sequential references such as figure or table numbers are included in the document.

Customizing the Way Word Separates Each Letter's Entries

You've already seen that the Index and Tables dialog box enables you to choose a blank line or a letter to separate your A entries from your B entries (and C, D, and so on). You can specify more detailed formatting by using the \h switch.

Place what you want to include between quotation marks. For example, if you want to place dots between each letter, type the following:

```
{index \h "........"}
```

To place a letter at the beginning of those dots, type:

```
{index \h "A........"}
```

When you type **{index \h "A........"}**, the resulting index displays separators such as the following:

A.........
Alphabet, 28
Animals, 36
B.........
Barracuda, 52
Bell, 46
C.........
Chimpanzee, 73

Note: Any A-to-Z letter you use after an \h switch is interpreted as an instruction to insert alphabetical letters at every separation. So if you specified something such as the following:

```
{index \h "A entries"}
```

you'd be rudely surprised by:

A AAAAAAA
Alphabet, 28
Animals, 36
B BBBBBBB
Barracuda, 52
Bell, 46
C CCCCCCC
Chimpanzee, 73

All alphabetical characters are capitalized by default. However, you can use the switch * lower to specify lowercase:

```
{index \h "AAA" \*lower}
```

You can tell Word to insert one blank line between letters with the following field:

```
{index \h " "}
```

Changing Page Range Separators

Page ranges usually appear in indexes, as shown in the following example:

Home on the Range, 37–39

On occasion, you might want to change the separator, which is controlled by the \g switch. To display a colon instead of a hyphen, type the following:

```
{index \g :}
```

Changing Page Number Separators

Normally, a list of page numbers is separated by a comma:

Elective surgery, 346, 362, 377, 403

You can change this separator with the \l switch. To specify a semicolon, type the following:

```
{index \l ";"}
```

To add a space after the semicolon, type the following:

```
{index \l "; "}
```

Notice: this one *does* require quotation marks.

Changing the Way Index Entries Are Separated from Page Numbers

Normally, an index entry is separated from its page number by a comma:

British Telecom, 36

You can change this, using the \e switch, and up to three characters of your choice, including tabs. Type the following to add three dots:

```
{index \e "..."}
```

You end up with the following:

British Telecom... 36

Updating Indexes

Even though Word automates the compilation of an index, that doesn't mean that the index it creates will be perfect. You might find when you read your index that certain entries aren't quite right.

Perhaps you indexed MacArthur in one place and McArthur in another. You now realize they should all be MacArthur. Or, more likely, you created a main index entry that, upon reflection, really should be a subentry in another index listing.

In any case, you'll most likely want to proceed systematically through your index, to clean up errors like these. You can do this by setting up two windows: one for the index and one for the document (see fig. 14.6).

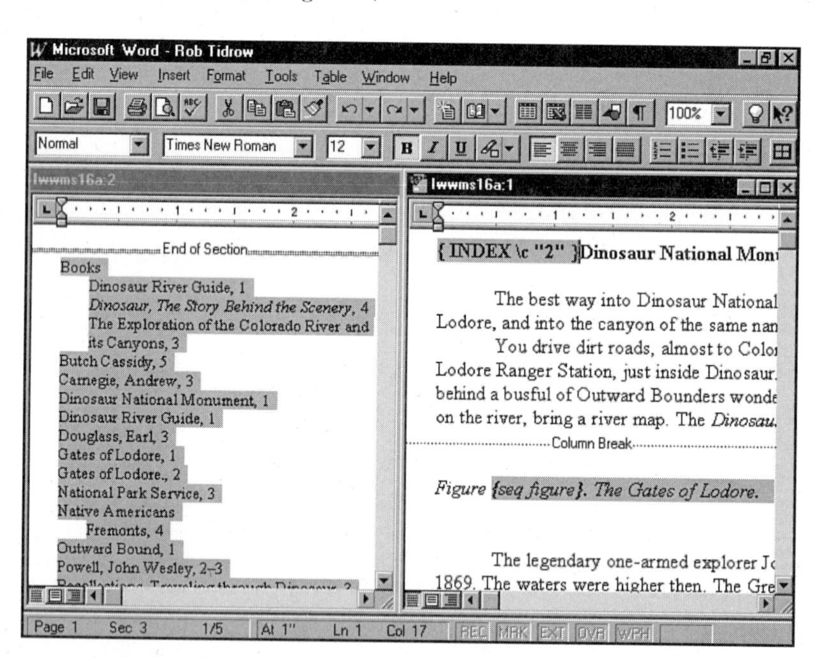

Figure 14.6
Revising an index.

Tip Word's new Wrap to Window feature is invaluable for this kind of work. Select it by choosing Tools, Options, View.

First, display hidden text, so that your index entries will be visible. Then, begin moving through the index. Whenever you see an entry that needs editing, switch windows. In the document window, search for the text of the index entry (or Go To the entry's page). Edit the {xe} field. Switch windows and continue to move through the index.

When you've made all the changes you want, select Inde**x** and Tables from the **I**nsert menu. Select the Inde**x** tab. Click on OK. You'll be asked if you want to replace the current index (see fig. 14.7). Choose OK.

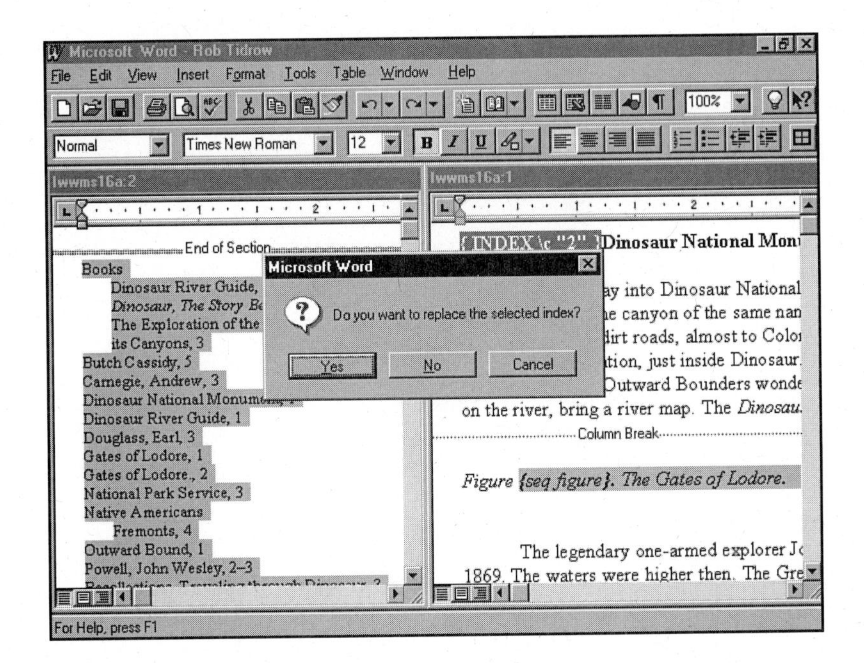

Figure 14.7

Confirming an index update.

Creating a Concordance Index

A *concordance index* (sometimes simply called a concordance) is an alphabetical index of all the words in a text, and it shows every occurrence of each word.

Concordance indexes are most well-known in Bible studies, where—for example—if you're feeling especially put upon, such an index could point you to every reference to Job. Concordance indexes also often are used by academic specialists to study literature, ancient and otherwise.

Word for Windows contains a feature that's capable of doing something very much like the concordance index: AutoMark. To use AutoMark, you open a new file (which Word calls your AutoMark file). Create a two-column table in that file. In the first vertical column, list all the words that you want to index all references to. (Note that unlike a true concordance, this list probably won't contain every single word in your document.)

If you did want to create a concordance index of every word in your document, Word has the tools you need to do it, though it would be a bit cumbersome. You could first use search and replace to change every space to a paragraph mark (^p); then use Word's Table, Sort Text feature to alphabetize all the words; then replace the paragraph marks with spaces again; then write a macro that found and eliminated duplicate words.

In the second column, key the index entry the way that you want it to appear. If you want it to appear as a subentry, key the entire entry—including the main entry—separating each part with a colon. Here's an excerpt from a concordance of Bruce Springsteen lyrics:

Entry	Subentry
Cadillac	Car:Cadillac
fever	Fever
highway	Street:Highway
night	Night
river	River
road	Street:Road
street	Street

Save and close the file. Then, in the file that you want to index, select Inde**x** and Tables from the **I**nsert menu. Select the Inde**x** tab and choose A**u**toMark. The Open Index AutoMark File dialog box opens (see fig. 14.8).

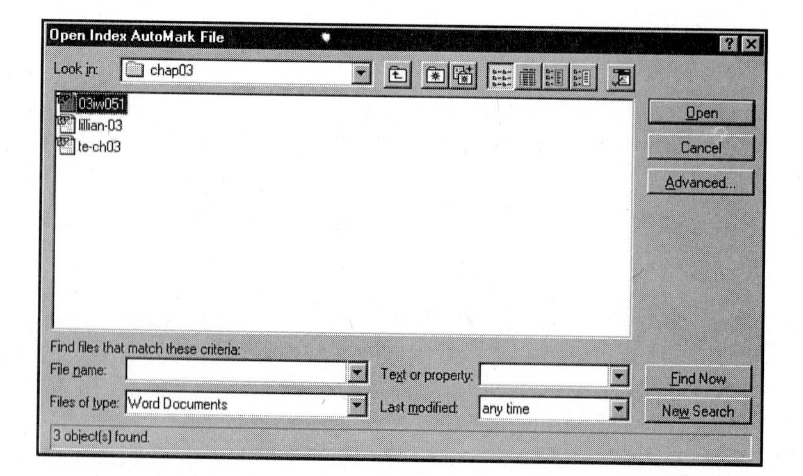

Figure 14.8
The Open Index AutoMark File dialog box.

In File name, find the AutoMark file that you just created. (Change directories or drives if necessary.) Then click on OK. Word generates an index of all references to each word in your AutoMark file.

If Word finds more than one reference to your specified text in a paragraph, it will only create an index entry for the first reference.

AutoMarking is case-sensitive; both lowercase and uppercase must match to be indexed. If you want to AutoMark river and River, include them both in your AutoMark file.

Footnotes

If you've ever tried to leave the correct number of lines at the bottom of a typewritten page for footnotes, you probably know how difficult this can be. Fortunately, you now can delegate that task to Word. Word also gladly keeps your footnotes in order—no matter how many editing changes you make. Just tell Word how you want them numbered, and where you want them to go, and then you can pretty much forget about the process.

If you're willing to do a little footwork, you can even refer to a footnote in text, and have Word update your reference for you if the footnote's number changes. And Word lets you insert both footnotes and endnotes.

In this chapter:

- Using footnotes
- Inserting footnotes or endnotes
- Viewing footnotes or endnotes
- Editing footnotes or endnotes
- Using Go To to find notes
- Moving, copying, and deleting notes

- Formatting notes
- Inserting symbols in footnotes and endnotes
- Positioning notes on page
- Using keyboard shortcuts
- Using separators and notices
- Referencing notes in text

Inserting Footnotes and Endnotes

If all you want is a straightforward numbered footnote or endnote, place your insertion point where you want it, and press Alt+Ctrl+F for a footnote or Alt+Ctrl+E for an endnote.

On the CD

The accompanying CD-ROM contains a file (IWMS15A.DOC) you can use to practice some of the procedures in this chapter.

Word inserts a numbered footnote reference mark in your text and opens a footnote or endnote pane, as shown in figure 15.1.

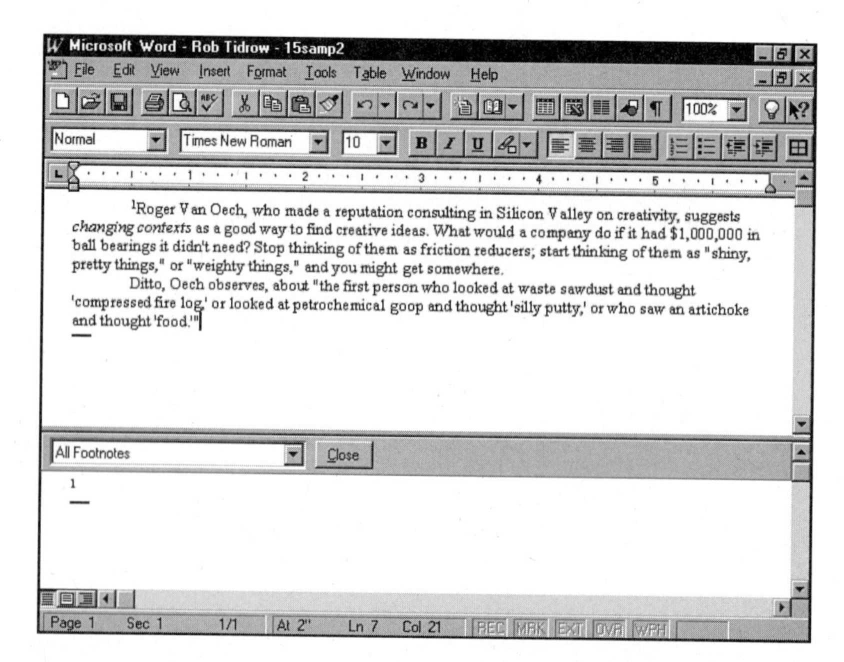

Figure 15.1 *The Footnote pane.*

If you've chosen a footnote, your footnotes will be numbered 1, 2, 3, and so on. If you've chosen an endnote, the note will be numbered i, ii, iii, and so on.

If you're in Page Layout view, the pane doesn't appear; rather, a footnote editing area appears on the bottom of the page (unless you've already moved your footnotes elsewhere). Depending on your position on the page, you might need to scroll down the document to see this area. You can see this in figure 15.2.

From here on, though, assume that you're in Normal view.

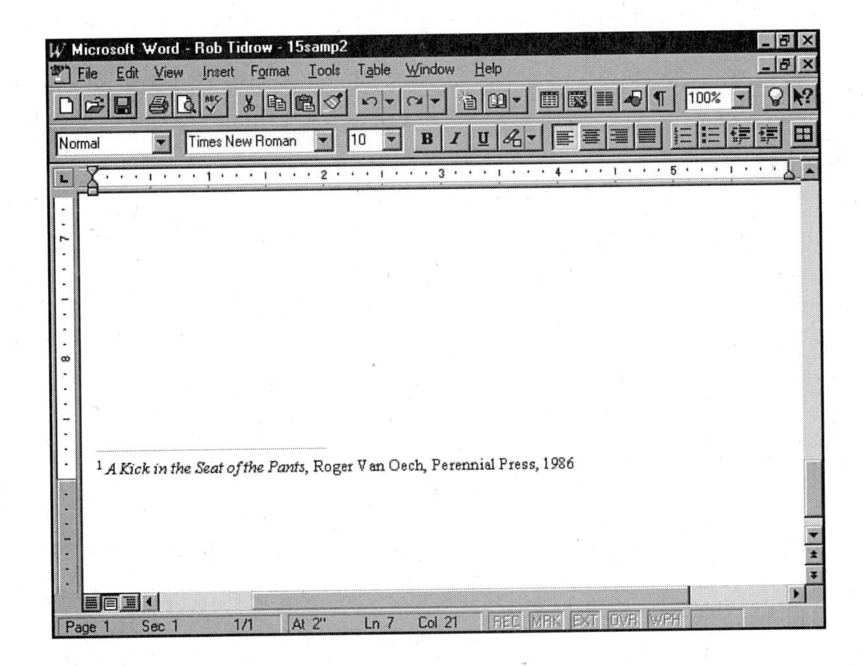

Figure 15.2

Default footnote editing area in Page Layout view.

Editing Footnotes

You can type your footnote text into the footnote pane, or copy it from another document. You can also use REF fields to bring in footnote information from elsewhere in the document, or use the field names INCLUDE, LINK, and EMBED to bring information in from other documents—even across a network. (See Chapter 20, "Word as an Integrating Environment.")

A footnote can include almost anything your document can, including images, sound, and video.

A few fields can't be placed in a footnote pane. These include the following:

- Table of contents entries (TC)
- Index entries (XE)
- Some mail merge fields (such as NEXT and NEXTIF)

When you're done with the footnote text, you can close the footnote pane by choosing Close or pressing Alt+Shift+C.

Getting More Control over Your Footnotes

If you want something other than a simple numbered footnote or endnote—say that you want a custom mark, such as §—choose Footnote from the Insert menu. The dialog box shown in figure 15.3 opens. In the Insert box, choose either a Footnote or an Endnote. Then, in numbering, choose either:

- **AutoNumber.** This inserts a numbered footnote that Word keeps track of as you edit the document.
- **Custom Mark.** Word inserts any symbol you want.

If you select a custom mark, choose Symbol, and Word displays the Symbol dialog box (see fig. 15.4).

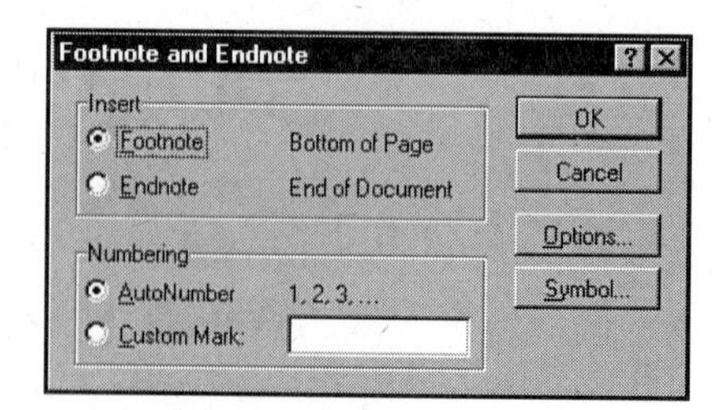

Figure 15.3

The Footnote and Endnote dialog box.

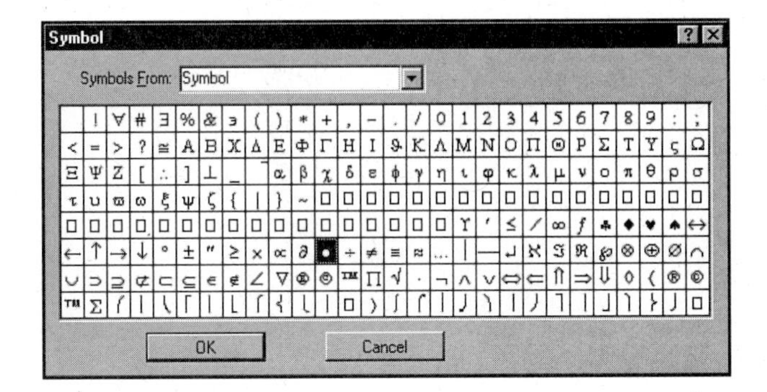

Figure 15.4

The Symbol dialog box.

From here, you can pick any symbol. Word places this symbol in the Custom Mark box. If you use numbered footnotes and custom reference marks in the same document, the numbered footnotes number consecutively, ignoring the presence of any custom marks.

You can also change an existing footnote to use a custom reference mark instead of numbering, or vice versa. Select the footnote, choose Footnote from the Insert menu, and specify the mark you want. Word renumbers all your footnotes to reflect that you've added (or removed) a numbered footnote.

Controlling How and Where Footnotes Appear

By default, Word footnotes appear on the bottom of the page, and Word endnotes appear at the end of the document. You can change this. Choose Insert, Footnote and then select Options. The Note Options dialog box opens (see fig. 15.5).

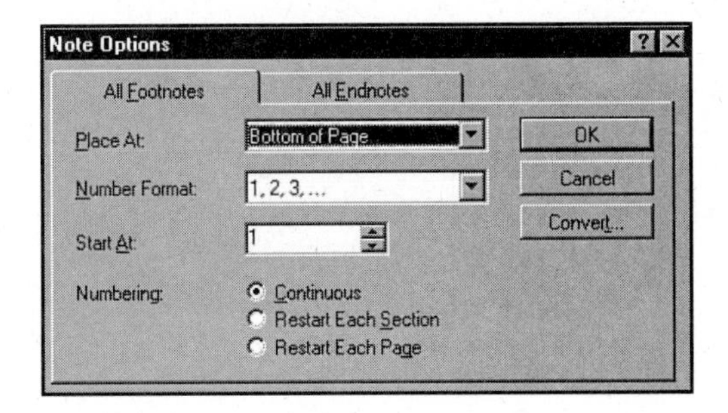

Figure 15.5

The All Footnotes tab in the Note Options dialog box.

Footnote Options

To set options for footnotes, choose the All Footnotes tab. You can do the following:

- Set the location of your footnotes in the Place At box: consistently at the bottom of every page, or directly underneath the last of your text.
- Set a Number Format from among these choices:

    1, 2, 3...

    a, b, c...

    A, B, C...

    i, ii, iii...

    I, II, III...

    *, _, _, §...

If you use custom reference marks, the last choice—numbering with symbols—may be ideal for you. It allows Word to maintain its footnotes in order and saves you the trouble of specifying a symbol each time you add a new footnote.

If you later change your mind and decide to use numbers, Word can display them in order—you don't have to replace each individual custom reference mark.

By the way, after Word inserts these four symbols (*, _, _, §), it doubles them, so your fifth footnote is **, your sixth is __, and so on.

- Set a starting footnote number in the Start At box.
- Set a Numbering approach: either continuous numbers through the entire document, returning to the Start At number for each new section, or returning to the Start At number on each new page.

Endnote Options

To set options for endnotes, choose the All Endnotes tab, as shown in figure 15.6. In the Note Options dialog box are several choices:

- Set the location of your footnotes in the Place At box: at the end of your document, or at the end of each section.
- Set a Number Format. These choices are the same as for footnotes.

- Set a starting footnote number. This option is in the Start **A**t box.
- Set a Numbering approach: either continuous numbers through the entire document, or returning to the Start **A**t number for each new section.

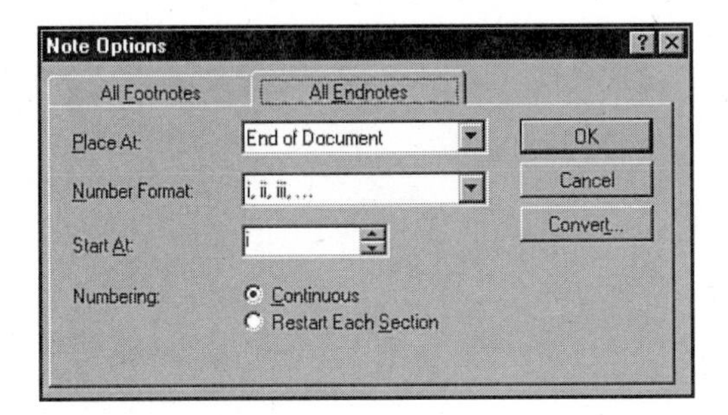

Figure 15.6

The All Endnotes tab in the Note Options dialog box.

Converting from Footnotes to Endnotes and Vice Versa

You can convert your document's footnotes to endnotes, or the other way around. Choose the All **F**ootnotes or All **E**ndnotes tab, depending on the notes you want to convert. Then choose Conver**t**. The Convert Notes dialog box opens (see fig. 15.7). Choose the option you want. (If you only have footnotes or endnotes, but not both, only one option is available.) Choose OK.

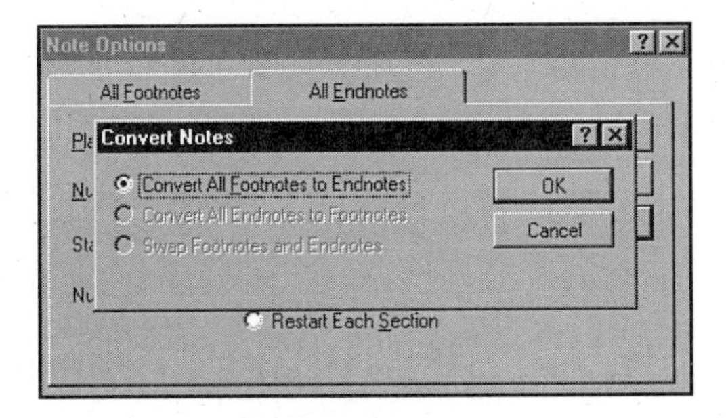

Figure 15.7

The Convert Notes dialog box.

Viewing Footnotes

As you add footnotes and endnotes, they're accumulated in the footnote and endnote editing panes. To open a footnote or endnote pane and view or edit its contents, double-click on any footnote reference mark in the document.

You can also choose **F**ootnotes from the **V**iew menu, assuming that you already have footnotes to view. With the pane open, you can scroll through your footnotes or endnotes, editing them as you want. As you move throughout your footnotes or endnotes, your document scrolls to the locations where the footnotes appear in text. You can switch between viewing endnotes and footnotes by choosing the one you want from the Notes box.

To move between footnote pane and body text, you can click on the pane you want, or press F6. You can copy text between panes using any of Word's cut, copy, and paste techniques.

Now that your footnote pane is open, drag the split bar up (or down) to make it bigger or smaller.

(You can also open the footnote pane by pressing Shift and dragging the split bar down.) If you have no footnotes, Word displays the message box shown in figure 15.8.

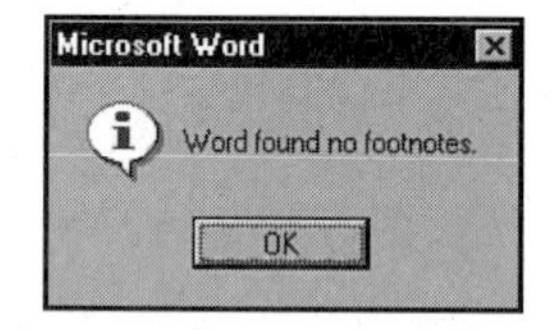

Figure 15.8
Word found no footnotes.

Finding Footnotes

You can always find a specific footnote or endnote by pressing F5, which opens the Go To dialog box (see fig. 15.9).

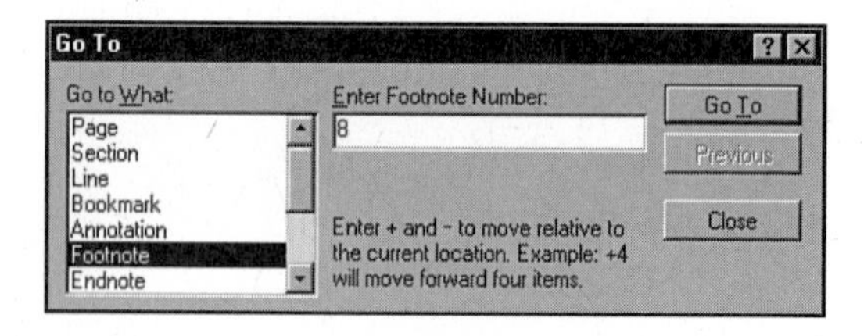

Figure 15.9
Go To a specific footnote.

When it opens, choose Footnote or Endnote in the Go to What box, then do one of the following:

- Go to the next immediate note by choosing the Next button, or the previous note by choosing the Previous button.

- Key in the number of the note you want to see in the Enter Footnote or Enter Endnote box.
- Go forward a specific number of notes (enter + and the number).
- Go back a specific number of notes (enter - and the number).

Moving, Copying, and Deleting Footnotes

Mary had a footnote mark,
Its text was long and low,
And anywhere that marker went,
That text was sure to go.

Indeed. The footnote reference marks that appear in your body text are permanently attached to their corresponding footnote text in the footnote pane.

- **Move.** You can move a footnote reference mark, and the footnote text moves as well, automatically renumbering if necessary.
- **Copy.** You can copy a footnote reference mark, and a duplicate footnote (including footnote text) appears wherever you paste the mark. If the marks are numbered, the new entry receives a new number. If you copy a custom reference mark, the same character appears in both places.
- **Delete.** You can delete a footnote reference mark in body text, and its corresponding footnote text disappears from the footnote pane. (You can't delete a footnote mark from the footnote pane, but you can delete all its text. The footnote mark remains until you delete it from the body text.)

When you copy, move, or delete blocks of text that contain footnotes, the footnotes are also copied, moved, or deleted. Keep an eye out when deleting large blocks of text that might have footnotes.

Changing Footnote Formatting

The normal style for footnote reference marks is 10-point Times Roman superscript; footnote text is 10-point Times Roman. If you use styles to change the Normal font, both footnote styles follow.

However, if you change your body text font without using styles, you'll probably want to reformat your footnote pane as well. You can apply any direct (nonstyle) formatting to the footnote text.

Positioning Footnotes on a Page

Word keeps track of the length of your footnotes. By default, it attempts to leave space for them at the bottom of the same page where they appear in text. If this means jumping body text to the next page, Word does that—following any special Format, Paragraph Pagination commands you may have given elsewhere.

By default, Word normally separates your footnotes from text with a line that stretches two inches from your left margin. For footnotes, this is called the *footnote separator*; for endnotes, quite reasonably, it's called the *endnote separator*.

Occasionally, a footnote is so long that it must be continued on the following page despite Word's best efforts. In these cases, Word normally separates text from footnotes with a line that stretches from the left to the right margin. This is called the *continuation separator*—there's one for footnotes and another for endnotes.

Finally, Word lets you add a *continuation notice*—text that informs the reader that footnotes or endnotes will continue on a following page.

You can change or eliminate any of these six separators and notices. To change any or all of them, open the footnote or endnote editing pane. (The quickest way is often to double-click on a footnote or endnote reference mark; you can also choose Footnotes from the View menu.)

Then, in the Notes box, choose the item you want to change (see fig. 15.10). If you want to change a footnote separator or notice, but you find yourself in an endnote pane, choose All Footnotes first. Then, choose the footnote item you want.

You can edit footnote separators or notices any way you want. You might even want to replace a separator line with text, as in figure 15.11.

When you've finished editing the separator or separators, close the pane. The changes take effect immediately.

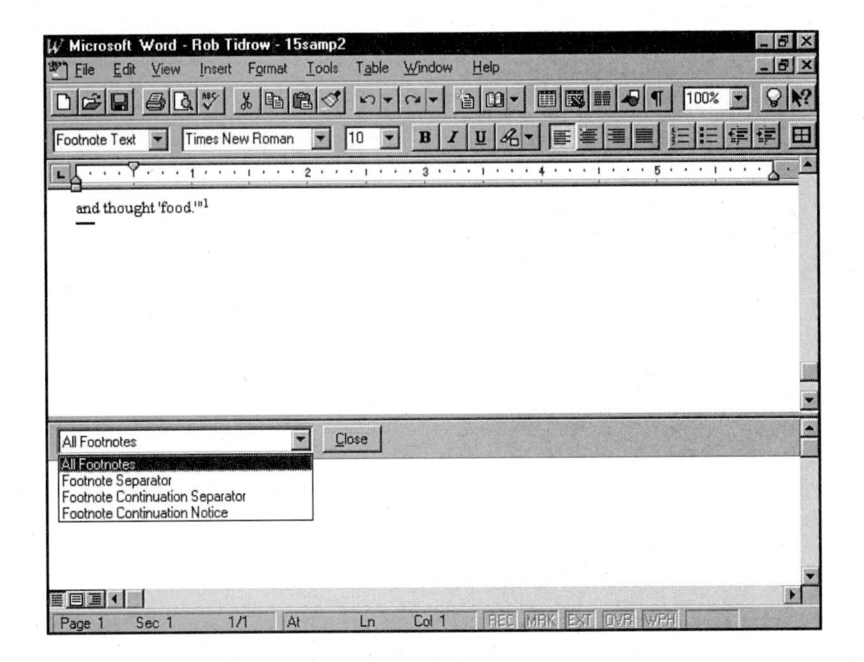

Figure 15.10

Choosing a separator to change.

Roger Van Oech, who made a reputation consulting in Silicon Valley on creativity, suggests *changing contexts* as a good way to find creative ideas. What would a company do if it had $1,000,000 in ball bearings it didn't need? Stop thinking of them as friction reducers; start thinking of them as "shiny, pretty things," or "weighty things," and you might get somewhere.

Ditto, Oech observes, about "the first person who looked at waste sawdust and thought 'compressed fire log,' or looked at petrochemical goop and thought 'silly putty,' or who saw an artichoke and thought 'food.'"[1]

Footnotes...

[1] *A Kick in the Seat of the Pants*, Roger Van Oech, Perennial Press, 1986.

Figure 15.11

A separator line replaced by text.

Referencing Footnotes in Text

You may occasionally want to refer to a footnote in text, as in the following example:

```
For Eisenhower's reaction to MacArthur's
observations, see footnote 12.
```

Word's NOTEREF field (formerly called FTNREF) lets you do this. To use it, follow these steps:

1. Place the footnote in the document.
2. Select the footnote reference mark in the document.
3. Choose **B**ookmark from the **E**dit menu, and name the bookmark.
4. Place the following field where you want the reference to appear:

   {NOTEREF *bookmarkname*}

   Of course, substitute the bookmark name you've chosen.

Another nice thing about NOTEREF is that it lets you reference the same footnote or endnote in as many places as you want, using the same footnote or endnote number or symbol. Basically, the idea behind creating a common footnote or endnote is to:

- Create a footnote or endnote as you normally would.
- Bookmark its reference mark.
- Place the field {NOTEREF *bookmarkname*} wherever you want to reference the same footnote.
- Format the field result in footnote reference style, so that it looks like other footnotes.

Remember, though, if you delete the footnote you've bookmarked, none of the cross-references will work.

If you use NOTEREF to reference a custom reference mark, NOTEREF gives it the next number in sequence. References to numbered footnotes that follow are accurate, however.

If your document contains footnotes 1, §, and 2, NOTEREF returns references: 1, 2, and 2.

Bookmarks

Sometimes, Word's edit and replace function just isn't enough to find what you're looking for—especially in a long document. That's where bookmarks come into play.

With a bookmark, you can name a specific location in a document or a selected portion of a document. When you want to find that location or selected material, you just go to the bookmark.

Use bookmarks to flag any document element you might otherwise have trouble finding easily—for example, an unattributed quote. Use bookmarks to help guide another reader through a document, or perhaps, to flag parts of a document that need more formatting attention.

These are some ways bookmarks can help you directly, but bookmarks also can help you indirectly. They mark text, so that fields can act upon it, and they can simplify many aspects of document preparation, including the following:

- Making internal references and cross-references (see Chapter 17, "References and Cross-References")
- Inserting material from other documents, especially when using DDE to do so (see Chapter 20, "Word as an Integrating Environment")

- Making it easier for a user to add text to an existing structure, such as a form (see Chapter 23, "Word as a Forms Program")
- Placing "buttons" in text that create "hypertext" jumps within your document (this chapter)

This chapter looks closely at the bookmarks themselves.

In this chapter:

- Using bookmarks
- Inserting and naming a bookmark
- Finding a bookmark
- Deleting and changing bookmarks
- Using bookmarks to create hypertext jumps
- Using bookmarks with other fields

Using Bookmarks

If you'd like to follow along with many of these procedures with a disk-based tutorial, open the document IWMS16A.DOC.

To place a bookmark at a location (or on selected text) in a document, follow these steps:

1. Position the insertion point at the location you want to mark (or select the text).
2. Choose **B**ookmark from the **E**dit menu. The Bookmark dialog box appears, as shown in figure 16.1.

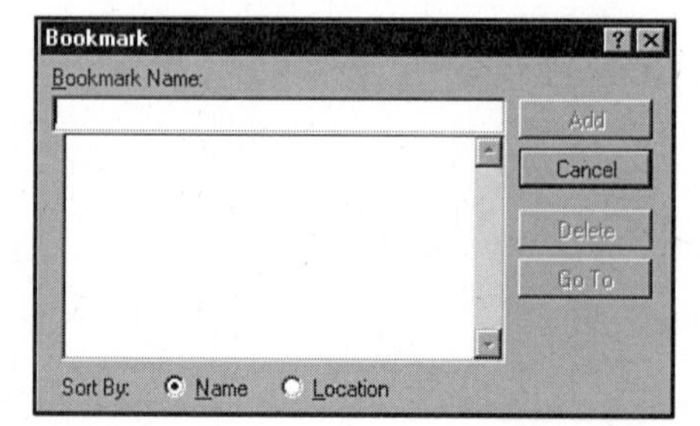

Figure 16.1
The Bookmark dialog box.

3. Type a name in the Bookmark dialog box.

Bookmark names can't exceed 20 characters: letters, numbers, or underscores (_). They must start with a letter, and can't include spaces or punctuation. Also, don't use a name that's already the name of a field that returns document information, such as comments or title.

4. Choose Add.

Insert a bookmark from the status bar by pressing Ctrl+Shift+5 and typing the bookmark name.

You can place up to 32,000 bookmarks in each document.

The accompanying CD-ROM contains a file you can use to practice some of the procedures in this chapter: IWMS16A.DOC.

Finding a Bookmark

Now that the bookmark has been created, you can find it by using Word's Go To feature. If you know the name of the bookmark, press F5; type the bookmark's name; and press Enter. If you don't know the name of the bookmark, choose the Go To option on the Edit menu (or press F5), and then choose a bookmark from the list.

For the first time, Word for Windows 95 enables you to view all your bookmarks at once. Choose Options from the Tools menu, then click the View tab and check Bookmarks in the Show box. All bookmarks now appear in your document surrounded by gray brackets, as shown in figure 16.2.

If you need to list your bookmarks, install and run the SuperDoc Statistics macro in \WINWORD\MACROS\MACRO60.DOT.

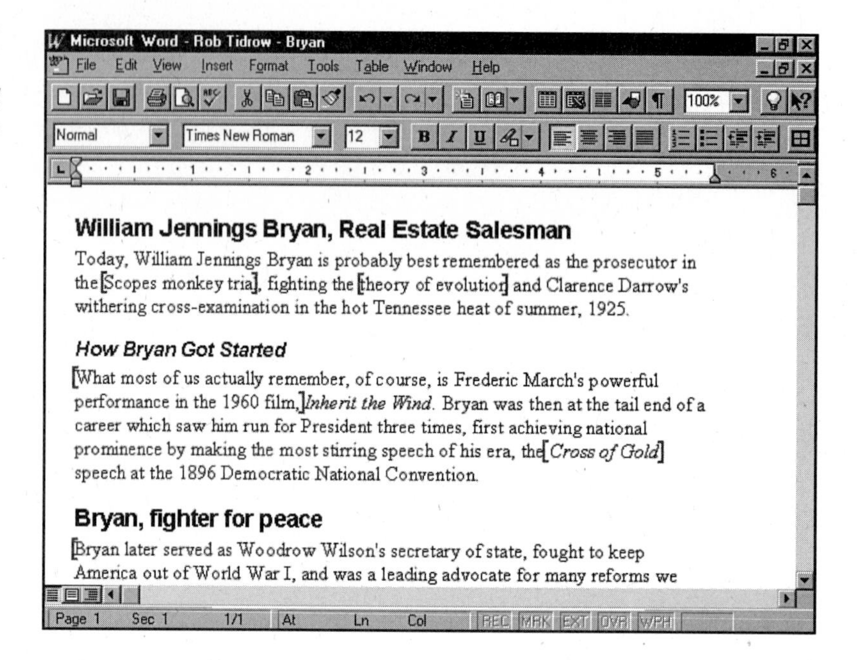

Figure 16.2

Displaying all bookmarks in a document.

Deleting a Bookmark

If you use a bookmark for temporary purposes, such as helping to find a part of a document that needs more work, you must delete the bookmark at some point. Perform the following steps to delete a bookmark:

1. Choose **B**ookmark from the **E**dit menu.
2. Select a bookmark from the list, or type its name.
3. Choose **D**elete.
4. Choose Close to return to your document.

You also can redefine a bookmark by creating a bookmark with the same name as one that already exists. Word does not prompt you that you're about to overwrite an existing bookmark, though, so be careful.

Tip

If you delete text that includes an entire bookmark reference, the bookmark disappears. So, if you're using bookmarks to flag text for editing, select all the text for the bookmark reference, not just a location that might inadvertently be deleted.

Building Hypertext into Your Document

If you're sharing your document with others, you may want to call their attention to certain parts of it. Word provides an easy way to do this: the gotobutton field.

If you've used Word's Help feature, you've seen something a bit like gotobutton—green lines of text that take you to specific help screens if you click on them. That's called *hypertext.*

To create a gotobutton, perform these steps:

1. Place your insertion point at the destination you want to set (or select text there).
2. Create a bookmark.
3. Place your insertion point where you want the gotobutton to appear.
4. Select Fiel<u>d</u> from the <u>I</u>nsert menu.
5. From the Fields dialog box, choose GoToButton in the Fields <u>N</u>ames list box, or type **gotobutton** in the <u>F</u>ield Codes box.
6. If you selected gotobutton in the Fields <u>N</u>ames list box, move the I-beam within the <u>F</u>ield Codes box immediately to the right of gotobutton, and type the name of your bookmark followed by the text that should appear as the button. If you typed **gotobutton**, complete the code by typing the name of your bookmark followed by the text to appear as the button. The following example shows how the field should look for a bookmark named Jones that is the destination for the button. Double-click here for Jones' comments.

```
{gotobutton jones Double-click here for Jones' comments}
```

Notice that, unlike most fields, your text should not appear in quotation marks.

Then, when a reader double-clicks on the button, Word jumps to the text you've specified. (The keyboard equivalent is to place the insertion point within the gotobutton text and press Alt+Shift+F9.)

Of course, the reader does need to know that she's supposed to double-click.

You can tell the reader up front, for example, that every bold underlined item is a hypertext link. Another approach is to create a structure such as the following, in which each gotobutton takes the reader to a different destination:

> Double-click on the college
> you'd like to learn more about:
>
> University of California, Berkeley
>
> Cornell University
>
> University of Chicago
>
> Stanford University

Or, in a corporation that is standardized on Word for Windows:

> Double-click on the benefits package
> in which you're interested:
>
> 401K retirement plan
>
> Medical benefits
>
> Dental benefits
>
> Education benefits
>
> Child care benefits

You also might create an online glossary, in which clicking on an entry in text takes you to a glossary entry defining it, and clicking on the glossary entry takes you back to where you came from.

If you go through all the trouble to create a hypertext document such as this, you probably don't want your readers to edit it and inadvertently mess up your hard work. Choose **L**ock File for Annotations when you save the file (use Save **A**s). The file still can be annotated, but it can't be edited.

References and Cross-References

When you quote text that appears elsewhere in your document, you're *referencing* it. But that's only the most basic example of a reference. You might also reference the page number where the text appears. That way, if the page number where your reference appears changes, Word can automatically change the page number to the new number.

Word helps you automate the process of creating and tracking cross-references, and also provides field codes that allow you to customize your cross-references in just about any way you choose.

In this chapter:

- Creating references
- Creating page references
- Creating page references that change depending on the circumstances
- Establishing a sequence
- Inserting page references

Creating a Reference

A single dialog box manages your cross-references to headings, bookmarks, footnotes, endnotes, equations, figures, and tables. You'll probably most often reference the following:

- **Headings.** Identify sections of your document.
- **Bookmarks.** Identify any specific text you want.
- **Figures.** It's very common to include text references to figures.

Note: Word's features work together very closely—maybe more closely than you expect. For example, Word's Cross-Referencing feature recognizes headings only if you've identified them with one of the built-in heading styles, Heading 1 through Heading 9. It recognizes heading numbers only if you've used Word's Heading-Numbering feature; it recognizes figures only if you've created them with Word's Caption feature.

To create a *cross-reference* (to insert text or other information related to something else in your document), place your insertion point where you want the cross-reference. Type any introductory text you might want, such as **For background, see...** or **This is covered in more detail in...**.

Then choose Cross-reference from the Insert menu. The Cross-reference dialog box opens, as shown in figure 17.1.

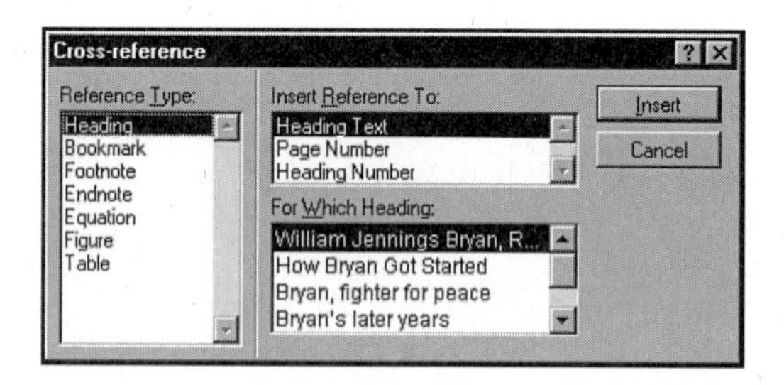

Figure 17.1
The Cross-reference dialog box.

To create a reference to a heading, choose Heading from the Reference Type box. In the For Which Heading box, choose a heading from the list Word displays. This list includes the beginning text of any paragraph styled as a Word heading—other text won't be marked. You may know it's a heading, but Word doesn't—unless you say so.

Finally, in Insert Reference To, Word invites you to choose which aspect of the heading you want to reference. For headings, you have three choices:

- You can insert the heading text itself. In the following reference, what Word has inserted is underlined; Word itself uses the base style of the surrounding text:

  `For more information, see Bryan's later years.`

If you insert a heading into body text formatted with Word's Normal style (10-point Times New Roman), the heading takes on the Normal style.

If you reformat the surrounding text manually without changing the style, however, Word's inserted cross-reference doesn't reflect your manual changes—just the Normal style that's still underneath them.

- You can insert the page number where the heading may be found. For example:

  `This is covered in more detail on page 26.`

  You have to add the word page—Word doesn't do it for you. (You are forgiven for expecting otherwise.)

  If you move the text you're referencing to another page, your cross-reference changes to the following:

  `This is covered in more detail on page 31.`

- You can select the heading number, but only if you've used Word's Format, Heading Numbering feature to set it. For example:

  `See I.A.2 for more about this.`

Heading Numbering is covered in Chapter 12, "Outlining."

By the way, because you can add text to your automatic heading numbering, you can have Word automatically insert words. For example:

`See Chapter I.A.2 for more about this.`

If you choose another Reference Type, such as a Footnote, your choices will be different. Table 17.1 lists what kind of reference Insert Cross-reference can create for each Reference Type.

Table 17.1
Reference Types and Choices

Reference Type	Reference	Or	Or	Or
Heading	Heading Text	Page Number	Heading Number	
Bookmark	Bookmark Text	Page Number	Paragraph Number	
Footnote	Footnote Number	Page Number		
Endnote	Endnote Number	Page Number		
Equation	Entire Caption	Page Number	Only Label and Number	Only Caption Text
Figure	Entire Caption	Page Number	Only Label and Number	Only Caption Text
Table	Entire Caption	Page Number	Only Label and Number	Only Caption Text

Bookmarks are used in this chapter. Refer to Chapter 16, "Bookmarks," for more information about them.

To mark text with a bookmark, follow these steps:

1. Select the text you want to mark.
2. Choose **B**ookmark from the **E**dit menu.
3. Name the bookmark in the **B**ookmark Name box.
4. Choose **A**dd.

The accompanying CD-ROM contains a file you can use to practice some of the procedures in this chapter: IWMS17A.DOC.

Inserting Chapter Numbers and Titles in Headers or Footers

Word's Cross-Reference feature offers an easy solution to the problem of inserting your chapter name and number in a header or footer. Follow these steps:

1. Format the line containing your chapter name and number in one of Word's heading styles.
2. Open your header or footer area.
3. Place your insertion point where you want the chapter name and number to appear in the header or footer.
4. Choose Cross-reference from the Insert menu.
5. Choose Heading as your Reference Type.
6. Choose Heading Text from the Insert Reference To box.
7. Choose the chapter name and number from the For Which Heading list box.
8. Click on the Insert button.

Looking under the Hood

Because cross-references are fields, you can update them the same way you update any other field: by selecting them and pressing F9.

Cross-references are usually {REF} fields. They are {PAGEREF} fields when you ask for a page number; they are {NOTEREF} fields when you reference a footnote or endnote. When you ask to insert a header's text, Word inserts a field that looks like this:

```
{ REF _Ref273159031 \* MERGEFORMAT }
```

The number is purely random, but the * MERGEFORMAT command is Word's way of telling itself that the reference should use the same style as the text surrounding it.

You can display your reference field codes and edit them in any way you want. For example, you can use the Word field-formatting command `\* upper` to specify that a code will insert its text reference in ALL CAPS. (These field-formatting commands are covered in Chapter 10, "Field Codes.")

Using the {ASK} Field to Create References

You've already seen how you can create a reference to specific text by marking the text as a bookmark. But you don't need a preexisting bookmark to create a reference to specific text. You can set up your document so that it actually requests information from the user, assigns that information a bookmark, and inserts that information throughout your document. To do this, use the {ASK} field.

1. Insert an {ASK} field that includes a bookmark name and the question that the field should ask a user. The question should appear in quotation marks.

   In the following example, the user is asked for a client's name, and the client's name is assigned the bookmark *clientname.*

   ```
   {ASK clientname "Who is your customer?"}
   ```

You can instruct Word to insert default text into the document if the user doesn't type any. Use the \d switch, and place the default text in quotation marks:

```
{ASK clientname "Who is your customer?" \d "Client"}
```

2. Now use Word's Cross-Reference feature to insert {REF} fields wherever the client's name should be added to the document.

3. Press F9 to update your fields.

4. Enter text in the {ASK} field, as shown in figure 17.2.

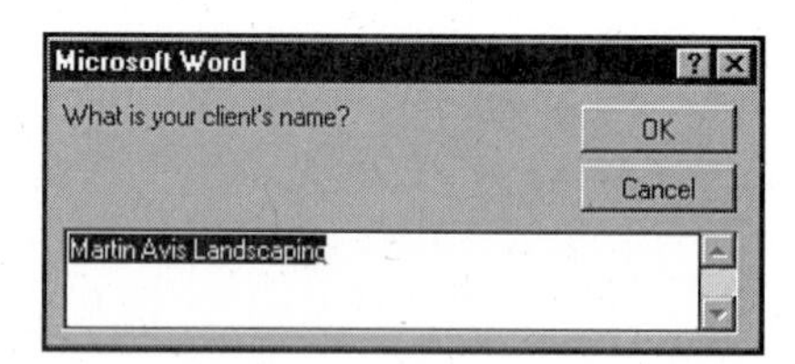

Figure 17.2
A typical ASK dialog box.

In figure 17.3, notice how the {ASK} text has been added throughout the document.

Each time you update your fields, the ASK dialog box reappears, containing the current text. If you want to keep the text you've already added, press Enter.

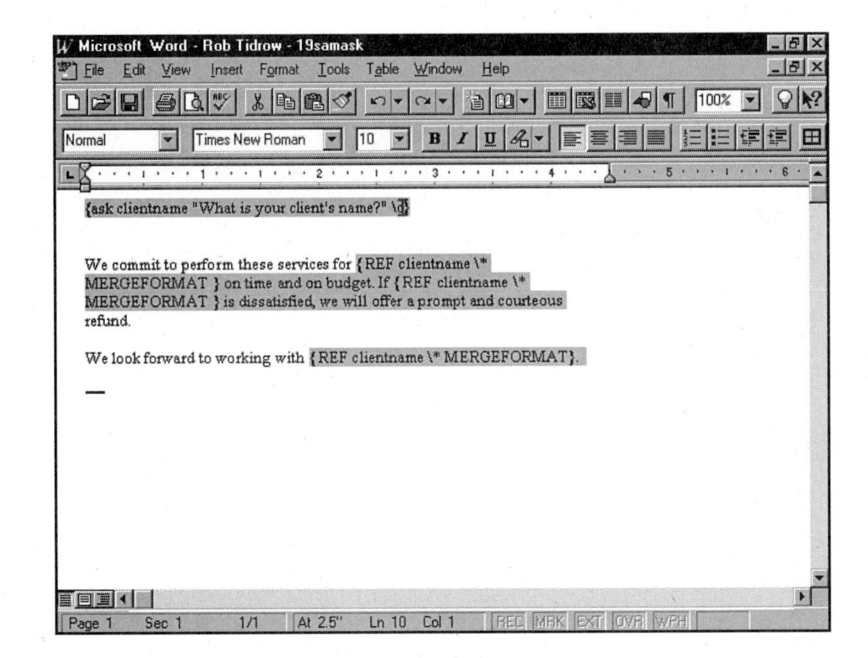

Figure 17.3

A sample document with field codes and ASK references.

A Variation: The {SET} Field

If you don't want the user to be prompted for text, you can use the {SET} field instead. Here, you place both the text you want and the corresponding bookmark into the field code. In the following example, the bookmark name is *state*, and the text you want to include is *New Jersey:*

```
{SET state "New Jersey"}
```

As with the {ASK} field described earlier, the words *New Jersey* will be placed in the document wherever you insert the field {REF state}—either directly or through the Insert Cross-reference dialog box.

Notice that the {SET} field enables you to create a bookmark without including the corresponding text in your document until you're ready. Because you're setting the reference, you don't need to provide an alternate in the event no input is provided.

Choosing Your Reference Based on Events Elsewhere

What if you want one reference to appear in your document if certain conditions are met and another reference if different conditions are met? You can do this by using both the {SET} and {ASK} fields, combined with the {IF} field, which enables Word to make a decision based on what it finds.

Let's use this scenario. You're writing order confirmations. Customers ordering more than 5,000 units automatically qualify for your Frequent Buyer Club, in which they earn credits toward major gifts. Customers ordering fewer than 5,000 units don't qualify, but you'd like them to know about the Club. Maybe they'll place larger orders later.

Start by creating an {ASK} field to input the size of the current order, as in the following example:

```
{ask ordersize "How many units in this order?"}
```

Remember, when the user inputs this information, it's also stored in a bookmark. Here, the bookmark is named *ordersize.*

Now that you have a bookmark that always contains current information about the size of an order, you can build a field that acts on this information. Use an {IF} field, which contains the following:

- The test you want to perform
- The result if the conditions are met
- The result if the conditions are not met

In the example, the test is: *are there at least 5,000 orders?* You know how many orders there are —that number is stored in the bookmark `ordersize`. Therefore, you can write the test as follows:

```
if ordersize >= 5000
```

Now you have to specify what happens if the order is at least 5,000. In this example, these big orders should trigger the appearance of the following text:

```
Congratulations! You've earned points in our
Frequent Buyer Club. Call 1-800-555-5555.
```

If the order is less than 5,000, you want the following text to appear:

```
Have you heard about our Frequent Buyer Club? Call 1-800-555-5555.
```

So the field looks like this:

```
{if ordersize >= 5000 "Congratulations! You've earned points in our Frequent
Buyer Club. Call 1-800-555-5555." "Have you heard about our Frequent Buyer
Club? Call 1-800-555-5555."}
```

The size of each order determines what's displayed in this field.

Now for the final touch. Suppose that you want this information to appear repeatedly throughout the document. (Maybe you want it on the cover, in each footer, and at the end of the document.)

Select the field discussed, and mark it as a bookmark. Call this bookmark *buyerclub.* Now, wherever else you want this text to appear, use this field:

```
{ref buyerclub}
```

That's it. It took a little doing, but you've taken the first step toward building customized documents that present a message tailored precisely for each of your customers.

Annotations, Revisions, and Master Documents

The writer still works alone, but these days, many documents are collaborations. Three Word features are specifically designed to help you work with colleagues: annotations, revision marks, and master documents.

The Annotations feature enables you to mark a document with comments that don't appear in text. You can easily find and read annotations, which streamlines the editing process.

The Revision Marks feature enables you to propose specific changes in a document's text, which can then be accepted or rejected. (You can also use a related feature, Compare Versions, to check changes made between two versions of a document. This can help you determine where a problem arose, or whether a change was missed.)

Finally, Word offers a comprehensive solution for managing large documents: the Master Document.

With Master Document, you can build a document that integrates many other text documents—for example, the chapters of a book, or pieces of a report cowritten by several individuals. Master Document also makes it easy to work naturally in a group, because the feature enables you to split a document into parts that can be worked on individually by various people and then pull the pieces back together when they are finished.

At one time, master documents were only for the very technical or the very brave. Now they have been revamped, and are covered in detail at the end of this chapter.

In this chapter:

- Creating annotations
- Creating voice annotations
- Editing annotations
- Viewing annotations
- Locking documents for annotation
- Printing annotations
- Creating revision marks
- Editing revision marks
- Viewing revision marks
- Merging multiple reviewers' comments
- Comparing documents
- Using Word's Master Document feature

Creating Annotations

Annotations resemble footnotes in many respects. Inserting an annotation places a mark in the document and opens a separate *annotation pane* where you can type comments. To create an annotation use the following steps:

1. Place the insertion point where you want the annotation.
2. Select Annotation from the Insert menu, or press Alt+Ctrl+A.
3. Your initials and the annotation number appear in the document as hidden text. Meanwhile, the annotation pane opens, as shown in figure 18.1.

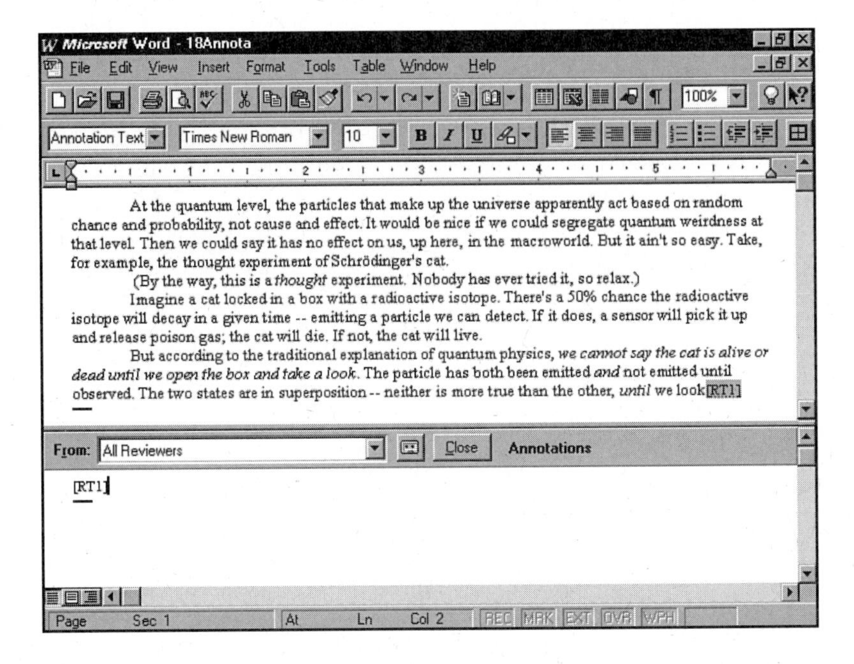

Figure 18.1 *Results of choosing Annotation.*

4. Type and format your comments in the annotation pane.

   As with footnotes, you can do just about anything in this pane—insert graphics, frames, borders. Seven fields, however, cannot appear in an annotation pane: TC, XE, Data, Next, Nextif, Ask, and Set. See Chapter 8, "Templates and Wizards," for details about these fields.

5. If you want to close the annotation pane, click on Close or press Alt+Shift+C. If you want to create another annotation, press F6 to switch panes (or click in the editing pane). Place your insertion point where you want the next annotation, and repeat these steps.

The accompanying CD-ROM contains three files you can use to practice some of the procedures in this chapter: IWMS18A.DOC, IWMS18B.DOC, and IWMS18C.DOC.

Word uses the initials you place in the Tools, Options, User Info tab. If you change them there, all future annotations use the new initials, but annotations already in the document don't change.

The number that appears in the document reflects the sequence in which annotations appear in the document. Word does not number each individual's annotations separately. When you insert a new annotation, any annotations you've created that appear later in the document are renumbered.

Here's one way annotations are different from footnotes: annotations do not appear on the same page in Page Layout view. You get the annotation pane there, too. But only if you ask for it.

Selecting Text for Annotation

In versions of Word through Release 2, you were limited to placing annotations at specific locations in the document. You can now mark the text you want to annotate, so that when a reviewer selects your annotation, he or she can see exactly the text you were commenting on.

To mark text for annotation, highlight the text before you select Annotation from the Insert menu.

Viewing and Editing Annotations

You have to see your annotation marks to know they're there. Annotation marks are hidden text, but Word displays them along with paragraph marks when you click on the Show/Hide Paragraph Marks button on the Standard toolbar.

You can reopen the annotation pane at any time by double-clicking on an annotation in the document. The annotation pane shows all the annotations in a document. You can scroll through them. A nice touch is that when you position your insertion point in an annotation, Word scrolls the document to the matching position.

You can shrink or enlarge an open annotation pane, as follows:

1. Press and hold down Ctrl.

2. Position the mouse pointer on the split bar, and drag it down to wherever you want the border between the annotation pane and the editing window (see fig. 18.2).

The easiest way to find an annotation is to press F5, which opens the Go To dialog box. Then select Annotation. (Your annotations don't have to be visible at the time.)

When you select Annotation, the Reviewers list box appears in the Go To dialog box. You can work with the comments of All Reviewers or only a specific reviewer. To go to a specific annotation by a specific reviewer, select his or her initials and add the annotation number.

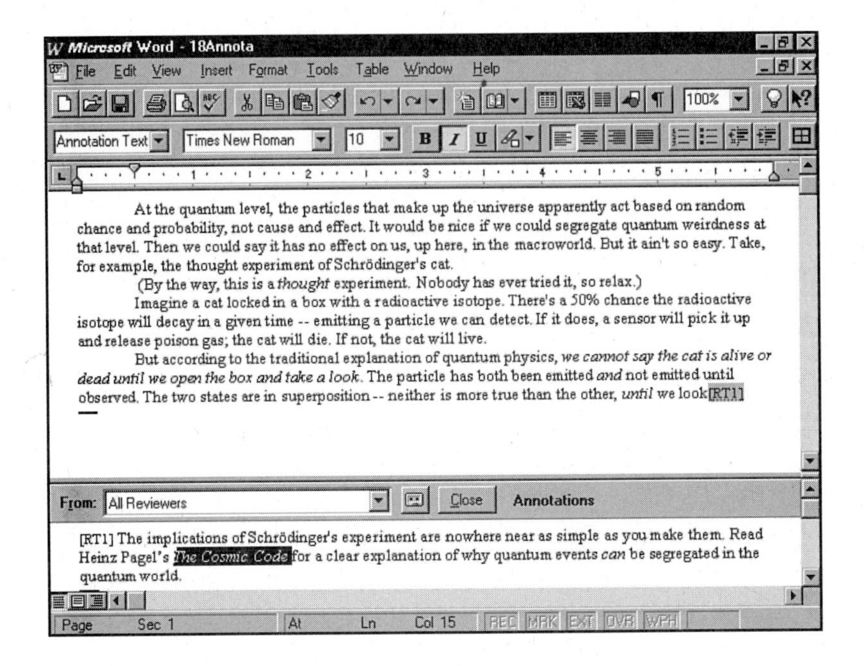

Figure 18.2

Opening the annotation pane with the split bar.

You also can move forward and back a specific number of annotations by typing the reviewer's initials followed by + or - and the number of annotations you want to move forward or backward.

To move to the next annotation in the document, or to the next annotation by a specific reviewer, select the reviewer or All Reviewers, and press Enter. To move to the previous annotation in the document or by a specific reviewer, select the reviewer or All Reviewers, add a minus sign, and press Enter.

If you move to an annotation in the document and double-click on it to open the annotation pane, the pane opens with the following annotation at the top. The annotation must be visible to be able to double-click on it. Just clicking on the area of the annotation won't work.

Reviewing Selected Annotations

Word displays all the annotations in a document by default. But you can tell Word to display only the annotations made by one reviewer. Open the annotation pane. Click on the From drop-down list box, and select the initials of the reviewer whose comments you want to see.

Moving, Copying, and Deleting Annotation Marks

Another way annotation marks resemble footnotes is that you copy, move, or delete them by working with them in the document. Word renumbers annotation marks and reorders them in the annotation pane automatically.

To *copy* an annotation, copy the annotation mark in the document and paste it to its new location. If you prefer, you can also use drag-and-drop.

To *move* an annotation, cut the annotation from the document and paste it to its new location. To *delete* an annotation, delete it in the document. (You can't delete it in the editing pane, although you can delete all the comments associated with it.)

Note To incorporate an annotation into your document, cut the annotation text from the annotation pane, paste it into your document, and then delete the annotation mark.

Locking Documents for Annotation

One of the nicest things about annotations is that they give reviewers a way to comment about your document without actually changing the text. That way, you have complete control of what actually makes it into the document. You can go one step further and prevent reviewers from making any changes to your document *except* for annotations:

1. Select **P**rotect Document from the **T**ools menu. The Protect Document dialog box opens (see fig. 18.3).

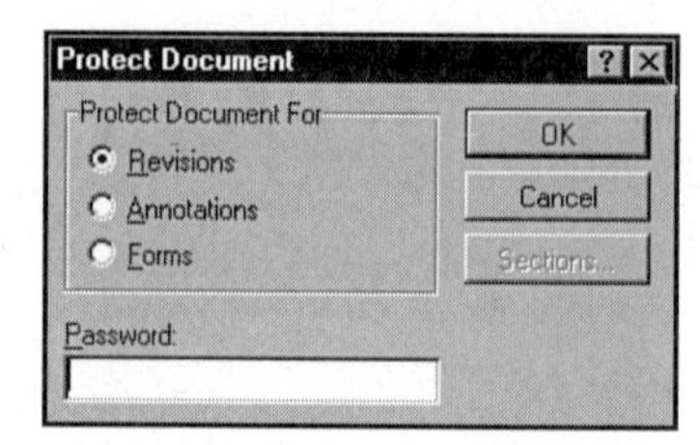

Figure 18.3
The Protect Document dialog box.

2. Choose **A**nnotations.

3. Type a password.

4. Retype the password to confirm it, as requested by Word (see fig. 18.4).

Figure 18.4
Confirming the password.

5. Click on OK.

Inserting a Voice Annotation

If you have a sound board and a microphone, you can insert voice annotations in your document.

1. Place your insertion point where you want to make the annotation.
2. Select Annotation from the Insert menu.
3. After the annotation pane opens, click on the Insert Sound Object (cassette tape) icon.

   A cassette tape icon appears next to the annotation mark in your annotation pane.
4. The Windows 95 Sound Recorder opens. Click the Record button (the red button at the right), and record the annotation.
5. If you're asked to update the object, do so.
6. Close the annotation pane.

Because you're using the standard Windows 95 Sound Recorder, you have access to its features. For example, you can choose Insert File from the Sound Recorder's Edit menu and include a sound file you've already recorded or stored elsewhere.

Listening to a Voice Annotation

If you have a sound board, you can listen to any recorded voice annotation:

1. Select Annotations from the View menu.
2. Double-click on the microphone icon that appears next to the annotation you want to hear.
3. Close the annotation pane after you finish.

Printing Annotations

You can print annotations in two different ways:

- Print the document and its annotations. This method prints hidden text, so you can see the locations that correspond to each annotation. (That means other hidden text appears as well.) The annotations appear on a separate page.

This printout is generated from the annotation pane, which contains hidden field codes that format the page numbers. This means you can reformat the page numbering or add additional text that precedes each page listing.

To print the document and annotations:

1. Select **Print** from the **File** menu.
2. Select **Options**.
3. Check **Annotations**. **Hidden** Text is automatically checked as well.
4. Click on OK.
5. Select **Print**.

- Print only the annotations:

1. Select **Print** from the **File** menu.
2. Select **Annotations** from the Print list box.
3. Choose **Print**.

Understanding Revision Marks

Annotation text isn't included in the main document text. It's well-suited for observations about a document, but less well-suited for specific corrections. For this, Word offers another feature: revision marks.

Marking Revisions

With revision marks, you can specify a correction. Your correction appears in underlined text, in color. Text you delete doesn't disappear, but instead remains in the document, with strikethrough formatting added. Later, the original author can decide whether to accept or reject your corrections—all at once or one at a time.

To begin marking revisions, select Revisions from the Tools menu. The dialog box shown in figure 18.5 appears. Check Mark Revisions While Editing and click on OK. Word begins marking revisions until you tell it to stop. When you add copy, it appears on-screen in color; when you delete copy, instead of the copy disappearing, it appears in color with strikethrough formatting applied.

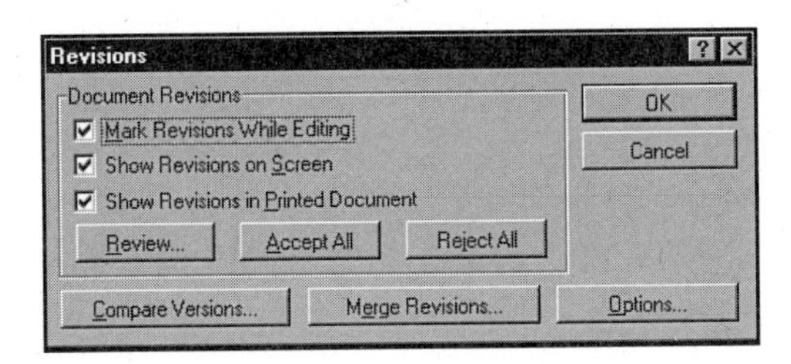

Figure 18.5

The Revisions dialog box.

Meanwhile, as you make revisions, the letters MRK appear in the status bar. Figure 18.6 shows a sample page with revisions marked.

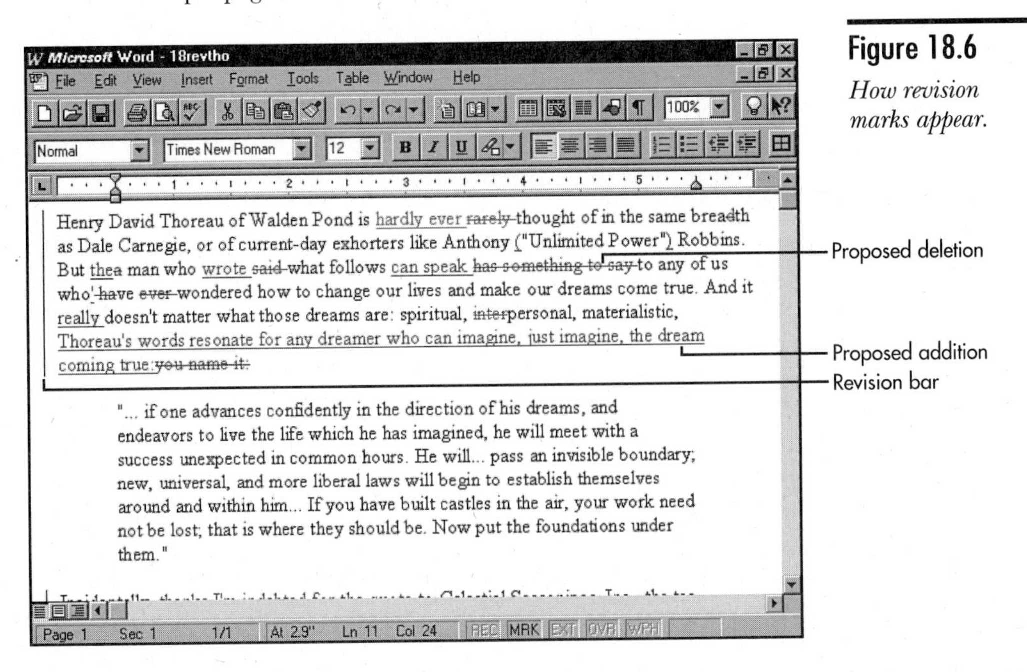

Figure 18.6

How revision marks appear.

To the far left, a vertical *revision bar* appears, extending top-to-bottom next to each line that has revisions. This helps the eye catch revisions that have been made.

If you don't want to bother with individual revision marks, make changes to your heart's content, save the file with a different name, and use the Compare Versions feature, which is covered later.

Tracking Revisions in the Background

If you expect to make substantial changes in a document, it might be annoying to watch all the colored text and strikethrough pile up in your document. To have Word track revisions without showing them on-screen, execute the following steps:

1. Select Revisions from the Tools menu.
2. Select Mark Revisions While Editing.
3. Uncheck Show Revisions on Screen.
4. Click on OK.

Choosing Whether to Print Revisions

By default, your revisions are included in any printouts you make, which you might not want. (For example, maybe you're proposing revisions, but it hasn't been decided whether to accept them.) If you want Word to print the original unrevised copy, uncheck Show Revisions in Printed Document in the Revisions dialog box.

Revision Marking Options

By default, revision bars print on the outside of the page, which means on the left edge of even-numbered pages, and on the right edge of odd-numbered pages. You can specify that they always print on the left, on the right, or not at all.

To make a change, select Revisions from the Tools menu, and then select Options. The Revisions tab of the Options dialog box appears (see fig. 18.7).

In Revised Lines, choose a setting from the Mark list box. You also can change the Color of the revision lines in Revised Lines.

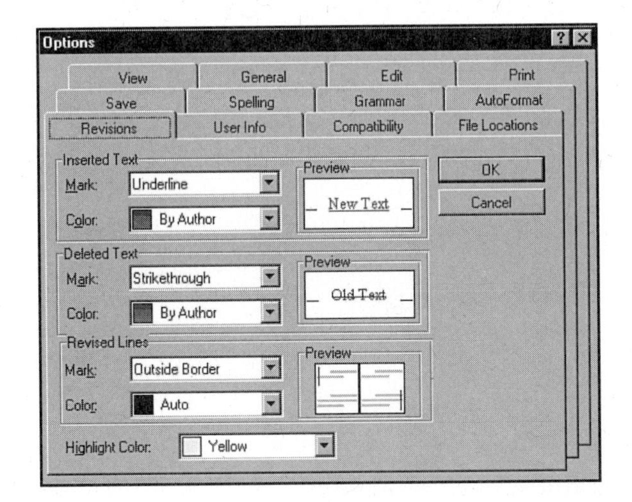

Figure 18.7
The Options dialog box.

Working with Multiple Reviewers

One reviewer per document might be ideal, but in the real world, it's not unusual for several people to review one document. Whenever a reviewer turns on Revisions, Word checks the reviewer's name. If the reviewer hasn't worked on the document before, his or her revisions appear in a different color. Word has eight colors to assign. If a document has more than eight reviewers, the revisions can still be tracked separately, but some will have to share a color.

You can, however, choose a color to use. To choose a color for revisions, select Revisions from the Tools menu; select Options, and then select a Color in both the Inserted Text box and the Deleted Text box.

You can also change the way new and deleted text is marked. By default, new text appears as underline. But if you plan to use underline for other purposes, you can use bold, italic, or double underline. By default, deleted text appears with strikethrough lines. But you can tell Word to make deleted material hidden text. After you make these changes, click on OK twice, and Word will change how it displays revisions.

To stop marking revisions, select Revisions from the Tools menu, clear the Mark Revisions While Editing check box, and click on OK.

Merging Revisions

If you've been handed revisions from several reviewers, you can merge them into a single document where you can decide how to resolve all their concerns. Follow these steps:

1. Open the file that contains your colleague's revisions.
2. Select Revisions from the **T**ools menu.
3. Select **M**erge Revisions. The Merge Revisions dialog box appears (see fig. 18.8).
4. Select the file where you're collecting the revisions.
5. Click on OK.

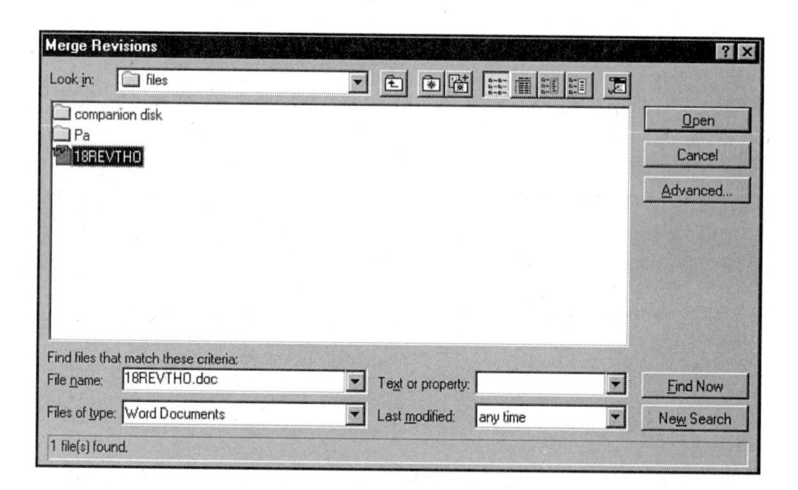

Figure 18.8
The Merge Revisions dialog box.

One by one, you can merge everyone's revisions into a single file, where you can make decisions about which revisions to keep and which to disregard.

Resolving Proposed Revisions

Now that you (and your colleagues) have marked up a document, you need to decide whether to accept or reject the proposed revisions. To make your decisions, open the file that contains all the revisions, and return again to the **T**ools, **R**evisions dialog box.

If you simply want to accept all revisions, which isn't likely to happen often, select **A**ccept All. A confirming dialog box appears (see fig. 18.9). If you click on OK, all

proposed additions and deletions are incorporated into the document. The previous text no longer exists, unless you've kept another copy of the file.

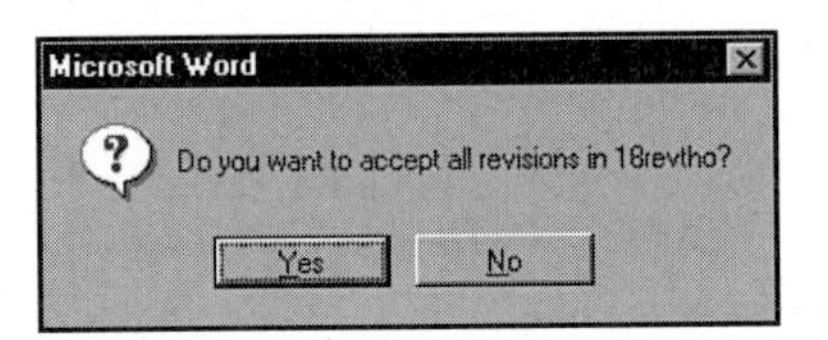

Figure 18.9 *Confirming that you want to accept all revisions.*

Rejecting all proposed revisions is equally straightforward (and equally rare). Select Reject All. After you confirm that you mean it, Word eliminates the revisions.

After you resolve your revisions and leave the Revisions dialog box, Undo cannot bring them back.

Reviewing Revisions Individually

Most often, you want to decide about revisions one at a time. To do so, open the Revisions dialog box, and select Review. The Review Revisions dialog box appears (see fig. 18.10).

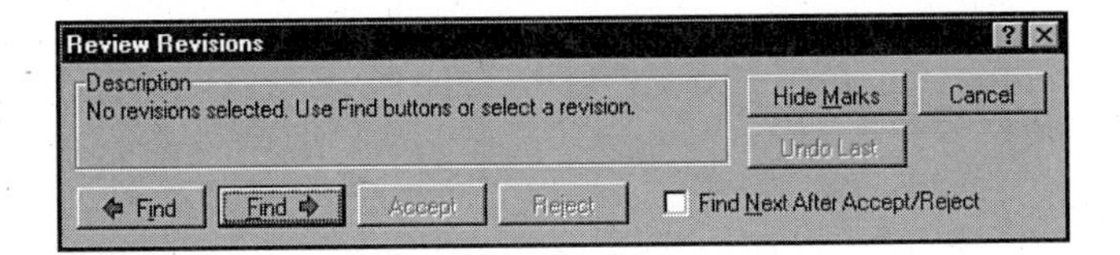

Figure 18.10 *The Review Revisions dialog box.*

If you want to review the document systematically, check the Find Next After Accept/Reject box. Then click on one of the Find arrow keys, depending on whether you want to move forward or backward through the document.

When Word finds a marked revision, the name of the reviewer and the date when the revision was made appears. Select Accept or Reject to accept or reject it, respectively. If you're not sure what to do yet, select Find again to skip to the next revision; you can always come back to this one later.

If you'd prefer to move back and forth throughout the document, don't mark Find Next After Accept/Reject. You can keep the Review Revisions dialog box open while you move around and edit the document. Whenever you highlight a marked revision, you have the choice to accept or reject it. You also can use the Find keys to move from one revision to the next.

If you want a clear view of how the document would look if a revision were accepted, select Hide **M**arks. To return to accepting and rejecting revisions, select Show **M**arks. After you finish, click on Cancel.

Comparing Two Versions of a Document

Suppose that you have two versions of a document and revision marks are not used, but you want to know exactly what changes were made. Word's Compare Versions feature can compare two documents, marking changes much as revision marks does when you edit.

To use Compare Versions:

1. Open the document where you expect to find changes—the most recent version.

You can use the Details button in the new File Open dialog box to see which file has been revised most recently. After you find the file you're looking for, double-click on it to open it.

2. Select **R**evisions from the **T**ools menu.

3. Select **C**ompare Versions. The dialog box shown in figure 18.11 appears.

4. Choose the file that you want to compare to the already open file. (As you can see, this dialog box looks and behaves much like the **F**ile, **O**pen dialog box.)

5. Click on OK.

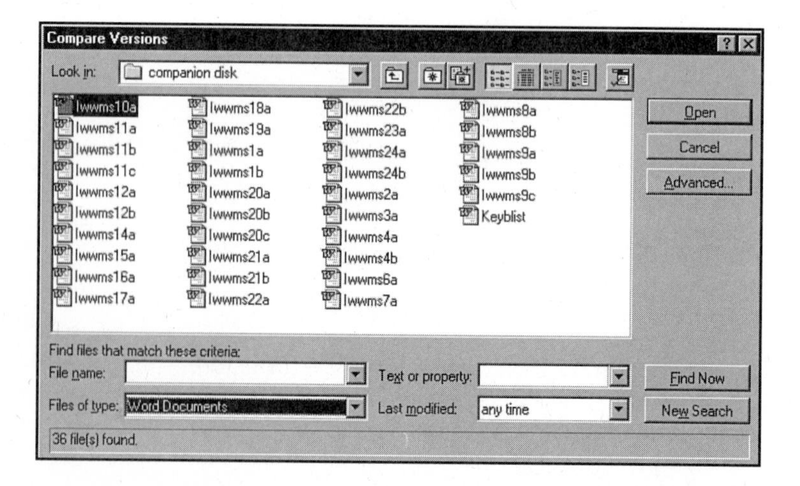

Figure 18.11

The Compare Versions dialog box.

Word moves through the document, adding a revision bar to each line that has changes. This can take awhile in a long document. In the status bar, Word tells you what percentage of the document has been compared.

Word also underlines the changes, as if you had marked them as revisions to be added. You work with these revisions the same way you do when you create them with revision marks. In other words, you can add or remove them to the document one at a time or all at once.

Using Compare Versions rather than Revision Marks

You can use Compare Versions to create revision marks all at once, rather than one at a time. Use the following steps:

1. Create and save your document.
2. Create and save a new copy of your document, with a different name. (Use File, Save As.)
3. Edit your document as you normally do and save it when you're done.
4. Select Revisions from the Tools menu.
5. Select Compare Versions.
6. Select the original file name.
7. Click on OK.

After Word finishes comparing the documents, you have a new document in which all the changes are marked. You can then use Review Revisions to decide which changes to keep and which to reject.

Using Word's Master Document Feature

A *master document* gives you a bird's-eye view of the contents of many small documents that together form a book or other large document. A master document closely resembles an outline, except that the material being outlined can come from many different subdocuments.

You can use master documents to do the following:

- Quickly see where elements appear in a large document
- Move elements around in your large document, even though they're in different files

- Make sure that all parts of your document are formatted consistently, even if they're in different files
- Create cross-references, tables of contents, and other tables that encompass multiple documents
- Send one command that prints the entire document, even though it's split into several files

Master documents also can speed up Word, because extremely large individual documents tend to be cumbersome to work with.

To create a master document, you can build it from the ground up or merge existing documents into a master document, which turns them into *subdocuments.* These subdocuments behave much like Word document sections. They can have their own headers, footers, margins, page size, page orientation, and page numbers. But you can also override differences in sectional formatting by editing and printing from the master document, where the formatting follows a single consistent template.

Creating New Master Documents

To create a new master document, select Master Document from the View menu. The Master Document toolbar appears (see fig. 18.12).

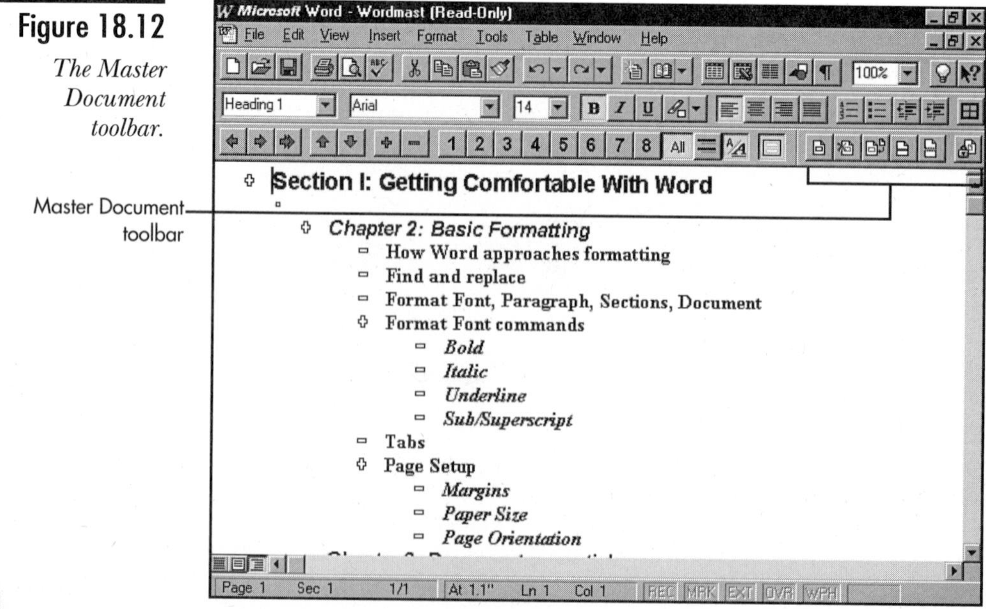

Figure 18.12
The Master Document toolbar.

As you can see, this looks much like Outline view, with the addition of several buttons—the Master Document toolbar (see table 18.1).

TABLE 18.1
Master Document Toolbar

Button	What It Does
Create subdocument	Turns selected outline items into individual subdocuments
Remove subdocument	Removes a subdocument from a master document
Insert subdocument	Opens a subdocument and inserts it in the current master document
Merge subdocument	Combines two or more subdocuments into one subdocument
Split subdocument	Splits one subdocument into two
Lock document	Locks master document or subdocument so that it cannot be edited

Now, begin to outline your document. Use Word's outlining tools and heading styles. Figure 18.13 shows the beginnings of a book outline.

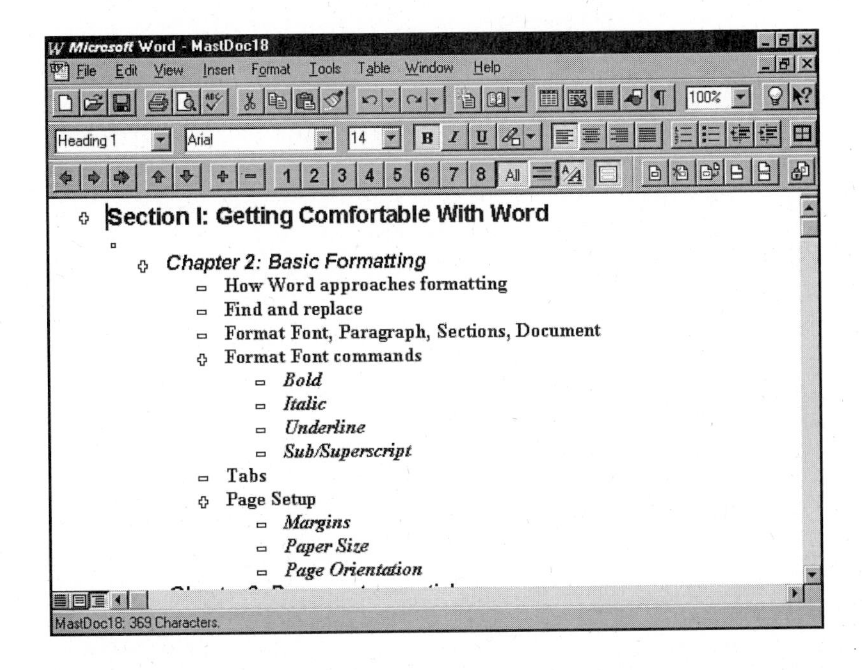

Figure 18.13

Preliminary outlining—no subdocuments yet.

Keep at it until you're ready to split apart the document. For example, if you're writing a book, you might want to finish the entire book outline, get it approved if necessary, and then break apart the outline into subdocuments for each chapter.

Creating a Subdocument

To create a subdocument, select the headings or text you want to incorporate into the subdocument, and click on the Create Subdocument button. A small document icon appears at the top left of the area you select, and a faint box appears around the text (see fig. 18.14).

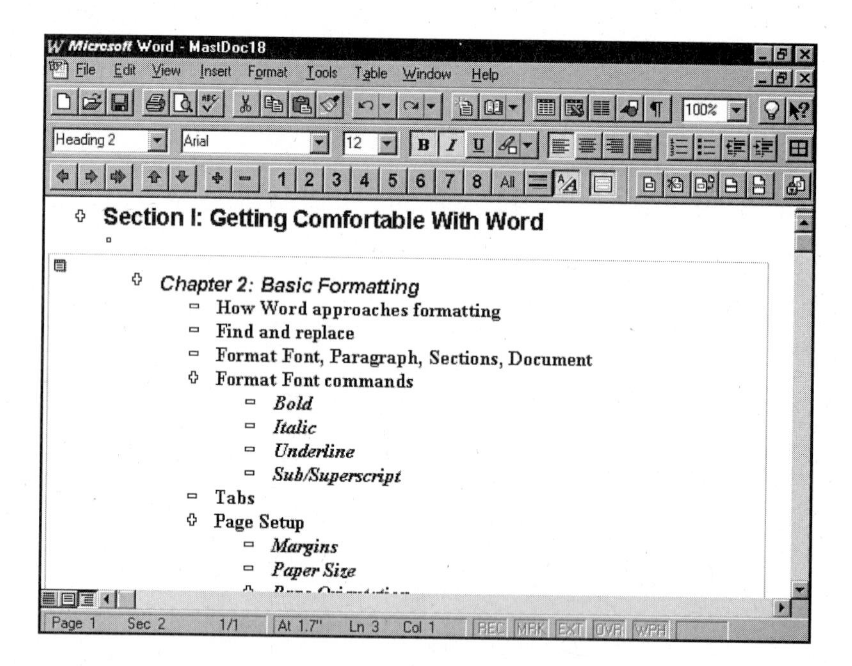

Figure 18.14

A subdocument, viewed in the master document.

You can create more than one subdocument at a time by displaying the outline level where you want the headings to break. In this outline example, second-level headings represent chapter headings. To break the document into chapter-level subdocuments, use the following steps:

1. Click on button 2 to display only first- and second-level headings.
2. Select the entire document. (Ctrl+Numpad 5.)
3. Click on the Create Subdocument button.

Word's official limit is 80 subdocuments and 32 MB per master document. But that assumes that you have plenty of disk space and memory. Your practical limits might be much lower.

Saving a Master Document

When you save a master document, Word also saves any individual subdocuments you create. Word assigns names to these documents based on the first letters of each subdocument's top heading, followed by consecutive numbers.

In the previous example, the first several chapters are numbered CHAPTER1.DOC, CHAPTER2.DOC, up through CHAPTE11.DOC, CHAPTE12.DOC, and so on. However, Word can assign other numbers or text to avoid conflicts with existing files.

After you save it, the text of the subdocument is contained in that subdocument, not in the master document. This has two important implications:

- You can edit subdocuments individually, as if they were regular documents.
- If you delete a subdocument or move it, its text disappears from the main document.

You can rename or move a subdocument as long as you open it from within the master document by double-clicking on its subdocument icon, as long as the master document is still open when you save the subdocument.

If you follow these steps, you can save a subdocument to another workstation on your network, where someone else can work on it, and it still shows up as part of your master document. You might have to log onto a remote drive to find it, however. (See the discussion a bit later about read-write privileges.)

Incidentally, one neat thing is that you can often open a subdocument without knowing where it is.

If you want to edit a subdocument in a way that affects the master document, try to open the subdocument from within the master document, especially if you want to create references that rely on other subdocuments. Unless the master document is open, you get error messages.

Opening a Subdocument

If you've just created a new subdocument, you can edit it in a number of ways. First, you can edit it in the master document. You are not restricted to Outline view; you can switch to Normal view if you prefer. Second, you can double-click on its document icon. That opens a new file that contains only the subdocument.

After you save, you also can close the master document and open the subdocument individually by using the new file name.

Printing Master Documents and Subdocuments

To print all the contents of a master document, switch to Normal view, and print from there. To print only selected contents, or an outline at only specified levels, use Word's Outline view tools. You also can print individual subdocuments by double-clicking on them.

If you print from Normal view, Word places a section break between subdocuments. By default, this section break is also a page break.

If you want the next subdocument to start printing on the same page as the previous one, change your section formatting in the Insert, Break dialog box.

Transforming an Existing Document into a Master Document

You might have already started the Great American Novel without waiting for the new version of Word to arrive. You now have a large document you want to transform into a master document. Easy, as long as you used heading styles.

If you haven't used heading styles, but your document contains text that looks like headings—separate lines of text above paragraphs, for example—you can try AutoFormat. Usually, it turns the correct text into headings, though you have to keep an eye on it.

Another quick way to change manually formatted headings into styles is to use Edit, Replace to find all text with your manual formatting, and replace it with the same text using the style you want.

Open the existing document, and choose Master Document from the View menu. Now select the text or headings you want to make into a subdocument, using the same outlining tools discussed earlier.

After you make the changes you want, select Save As from the Edit menu to save the file under a new name. As with new master documents, Word creates individual files for your subdocuments, and assigns its own names to them.

Adding an Existing Document to a Master Document

You might want to add an existing subdocument to a master document you're constructing. Follow these steps:

1. Open the master document. The Outlining and Master Document toolbars appear.
2. Place the insertion point where you want to insert the new document.
3. Click on the Insert Subdocument button. The Insert Subdocument dialog box appears (see fig. 18.15).
4. Find and select the document you want to insert. Click on OK. The document appears in a box in your master document. To open it, double-click on its subdocument icon.

When Word saves a file that has been turned into a subdocument, the file keeps its original name. If you import a subdocument that uses a different template from the master document, the master document's template applies if you open or print the subdocument from within the master document. If you open your document without using the master document, the individual file's template takes effect.

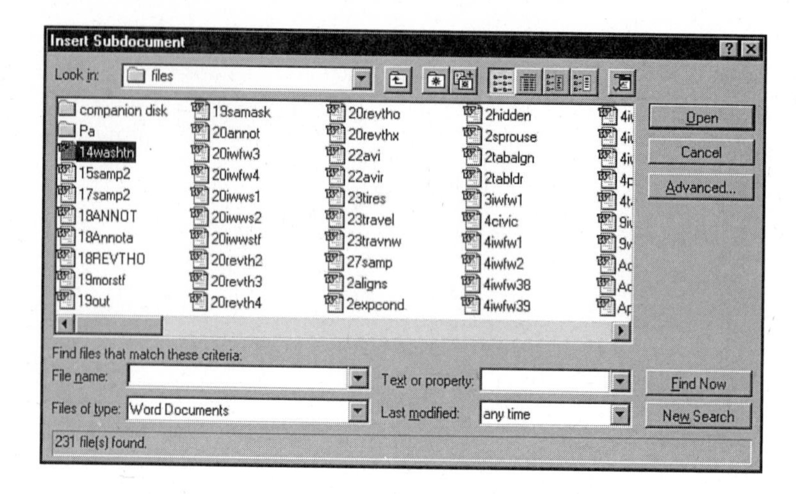

Figure 18.15

The Insert Subdocument dialog box.

Adding an Index, Table of Contents, or Other Table

Master documents make it possible, even easy, to add an index, table of contents, table of figures, or table of authorities that encompass multiple documents. Use the following steps:

1. Open the master document. (Make sure that all subdocuments are present and accounted for.)

2. Switch to Normal view.

3. Place the insertion point where you want the index or table.

4. Choose Inde<u>x</u> and Tables from the <u>I</u>nsert menu, and follow the conventional procedure.

Working with Others on the Same Master Document

Because Word master documents are likely to be used by many people, each responsible for a component, Word makes special provisions for sharing master documents.

When you open a master document, you can edit any subdocument that you created in the first place. You can read the ones someone else created, but you can't edit them without unlocking them first.

To *unlock* a subdocument, place the insertion point inside it and click on the Unlock Document button. No matter what, you can't download and edit a file someone else is currently editing.

To figure out who created a file, Word checks the Author information in the Summary page of the file's Properties. If you change that information, you can change the subdocument's read-write behavior.

Managing Read-Write Privileges

Normally, you can't write to a document if someone else is using it—even if they're viewing it as read-only. If it's critical that you be able to edit a file, you can reserve read-write privileges by setting a password.

1. Open the master document or subdocument and save it by selecting Save **A**s from the **E**dit menu.
2. Select **O**ptions. The Save tab of the Options dialog box opens (see fig. 18.16).
3. If you want to prevent others from writing changes to the file, type a password in the **W**rite Reservation Password text box. Type the password again to confirm it.
4. If you want to discourage but not prevent changes by others, you can check **R**ead-Only Recommended. When the file is opened, the message in figure 18.17 appears.

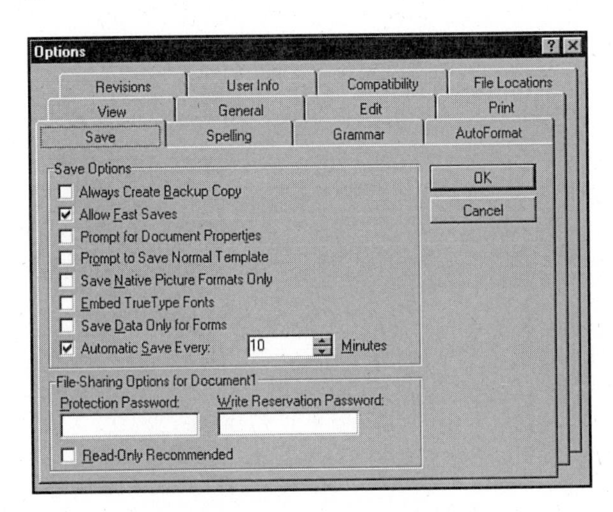

Figure 18.16

The Save tab of the Options dialog box.

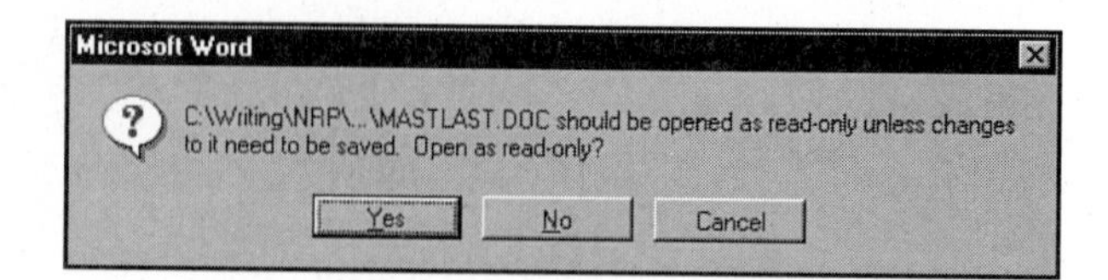

Figure 18.17
The Read-Only Recommended message.

Choosing Yes opens the file as read-only. Choosing No still opens it, but in "locked" condition. Anyone can unlock the file by selecting the entire document (Alt+A) and clicking on the Unlock Document button.

Reorganizing Your Master Document

All the outlining tools covered in Chapter 12 work in master documents. You can move body text and/or headings within a subdocument or between subdocuments. You can promote or demote headings. You can select and move large blocks of copy by displaying only high-level headings and cutting and pasting those.

To select all the contents of a subdocument to be moved or reformatted, click its subdocument icon.

Merging and Splitting Subdocuments

You can combine two subdocuments into one. Or, perhaps you would rather split one subdocument into two when it gets too big or when you want to delegate parts of it to another author. To combine two subdocuments, do the next set of steps:

1. Move both subdocuments next to each other in the master document.
2. Select both subdocuments.

Tip You can select multiple subdocuments by clicking on the first subdocument icon, holding down the Shift key, and clicking the icons of any additional subdocuments (shift-clicking).

3. Click on Merge Subdocument.
4. Save the master document. When Word saves the merged subdocument, it uses the name of the first subdocument contained in it.

To split one subdocument into two, follow these steps:

1. Place the insertion point where you want the subdocument to split.
2. Click on Split Subdocument.

Removing a Subdocument

To remove the subdocument, but keep its text in the master document, click on the subdocument icon, and click on the Remove Subdocument button.

To remove the subdocument and also remove its text, click on the subdocument icon and press Delete. The document file remains on the disk, but no longer is attached in any way to the master document.

Insert File: Another Way to Combine Word Files

If you want to combine several Word files, but you don't need or want them to have an independent existence afterwards, use the Insert, File command as follows:

1. Place your insertion point where you want the file to appear.
2. Select File from the Insert menu. The File menu opens.
3. Select the file you want to open. If it's a Word 6 or Word for Windows 95 file, the file is inserted. If it's not a Word file, Word attempts to convert and insert it, assuming the proper conversion filter is installed.

Unlike in Word 2, you are asked to confirm the conversion only if the Confirm Conversion box is checked.

Automating Mail Merge Tasks

Whether you create direct mail by the hundreds or thousands or just want to mass mail a family Christmas letter, Word 95's mail merge is for you.

Mail merge traditionally has been one of the most complex, error-prone facets of word processing—and the most frustrating, especially after you discover you've printed that whole stack of letters incorrectly. Each version of Word for Windows, however, has made mail merge a little bit easier.

Using the feature still isn't exactly easy, but now if you pay reasonable attention and understand the overarching concepts, you've got a pretty good chance of succeeding the first time. That's the goal of this chapter: for your very first mail merge to be successful.

And after you manage a simple mail merge, plenty more power awaits tapping under the hood. You can, for example, tell Word to make choices about which records to merge or which text to include in a mail merge. And you can create mail merge envelopes and labels, or a catalog in which one merged record follows another on the same page.

In this chapter:

- Using Word's Mail Merge Helper
- Creating a main document and data source
- Inserting merge fields
- Creating a separate header source
- Using an existing Word data source
- Editing a data source
- Using Word fields
- Previewing the Mail Merge
- Merging the main document with the data source
- Printing the output
- Outputting to disk
- Merging to E-mail or fax
- Printing accompanying envelopes and labels
- Importing existing data
- Integrating a Microsoft Access data source

Understanding Word's Mail Merge

Here's the one fundamental concept you need to understand to create a mail merge: You need a main document and a data source.

The *main document* contains the text that you want to remain constant. The main document also contains instructions about *which* changeable text Word for Windows 95 should import and *where* it should import it.

You then need a *data source* that contains the changeable text. That data source normally is just a Word table, although it can be a database file or a Microsoft Exchange Personal Address Book. Each column in the table has a header—a top row—

that tells the main document what kind of data the column contains so that the main document can decide whether to merge that information, and if so, where to merge it.

While you work in mail merge, Word puts a friendly "front end" on your data source table, with dialog boxes that make using it easier. But underneath it all, it's still a table.

This discussion assumes that you are using data created in Word. You also can import data relatively easily from other programs, notably databases. For more information, see this chapter's section, "Importing Data from Another Data Source."

Accessing Word's Mail Merge Helper

To help clarify the mail merge process, Word provides the Mail Merge Helper, which guides you step-by-step through a mail merge, structuring the process for you. To open the Mail Merge Helper, choose Mail Merge from the Tools menu, which brings up the Mail Merge Helper dialog box, shown in figure 19.1.

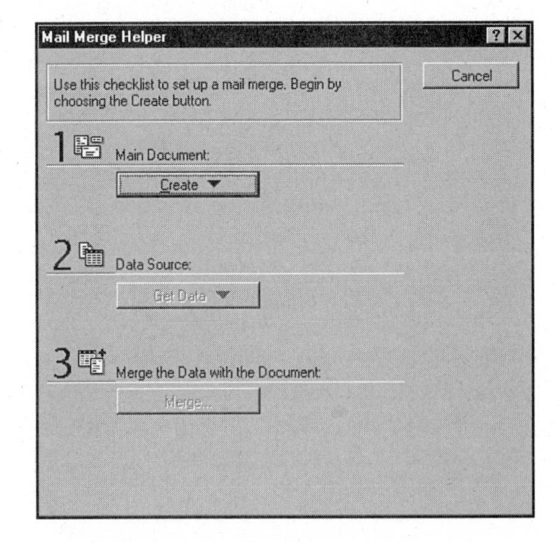

Figure 19.1
The Mail Merge Helper dialog box.

Take a quick look around. The Mail Merge Helper shows the three main tasks you need to perform: creating a main document, creating or getting a data source, and merging the two. Only the tasks you're ready to perform are available. If you haven't prepared a main document and a data source, for example, Word doesn't allow you to use the Merge button.

Creating a Main Document

The first step when you perform a mail merge is creating a main document. (If you want to use an existing document as a mail merge main document, open it before you choose Mail Merge.) To create a main document for a mail merge, follow these steps:

1. Choose Mail Merge from the Tools menu.
2. In the Main Document section of the Mail Merge Helper dialog box, choose Create. A list of options opens, as shown in figure 19.2.

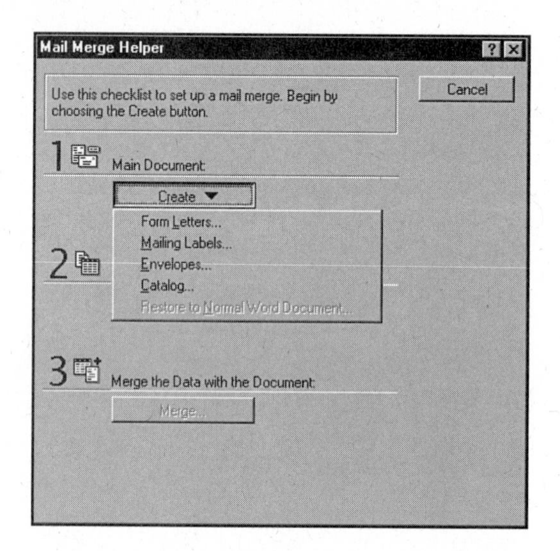

Figure 19.2
Options for your main document.

3. Choose the type of main document you want to create. If you want to print letters, for example, choose Form Letters.
4. From the next dialog box that appears (see fig. 19.3), choose Active Window to use the existing open document, or choose New Main Document to use a new document.

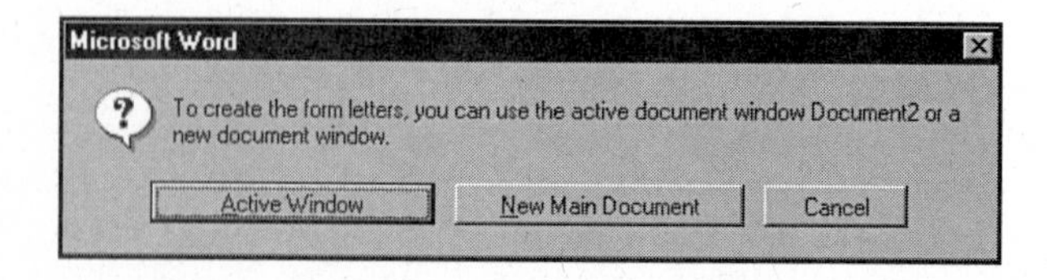

Figure 19.3
Choose to create your mail merge document using the active window or a new document.

5. Whether you choose Active Window or New Window, a new button appears in the Main Document portion of the mail merge window: Edit. When you choose Edit, a list of open main documents appears. (If you've just started creating a New Window, only that New Window document is available. If you're starting the mail merge process for the first time in your current session, you probably have only one choice.)

6. Choose a document from this list to return to that document. You then can edit the new or existing document to include the boilerplate text you want to appear in all copies of the letter.

Before you can tell Word where to place the information to "merge in," you need a *data source.*

The accompanying CD-ROM contains a file you can use to practice some of these procedures in this chapter: IWMS19A.DOC. Open it; then open the Mail Merge Helper and choose this file as your main document.

Choosing a Data Source

The easiest way to create a data source is to go back into Mail Merge Helper *from* your main document. This time, choose Get Data from the Data Source box. The menu in figure 19.4 appears.

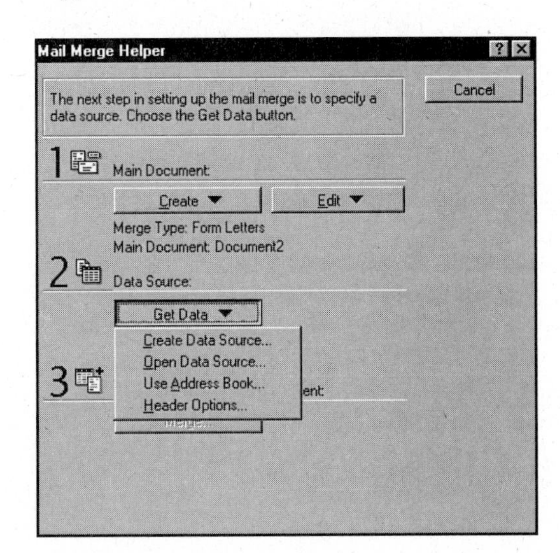

Figure 19.4

Creating a data source.

You have several choices about where to create your data source. If you already have a data source, choose Open Data Source. The Open Data Source dialog box appears (see fig. 19.5). Locate your data source, select it, and choose OK.

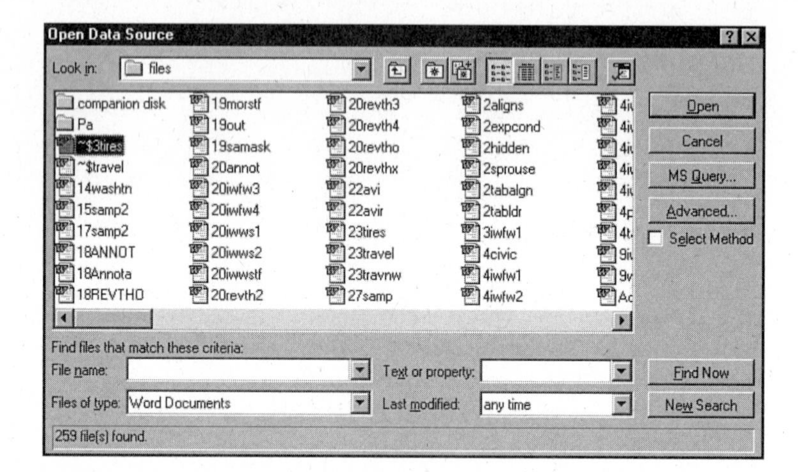

Figure 19.5

The Open Data Source dialog box.

Using a Microsoft Exchange Address Book

In Windows 95, Microsoft introduces Microsoft Exchange to replace the Microsoft Mail program that accompanied Windows for Workgroups 3.1. Among Microsoft Exchange's more interesting features is a centralized Personal Address Book that other programs can use, including Microsoft Word. If you have Microsoft Exchange installed on your computer, you can merge postal, e-mail, and fax addresses from your Personal Address Book into your mail merge documents.

You also can use a contact list from Microsoft Schedule+ as a data source.

To specify that your data source is a Microsoft Exchange Address book, follow these steps:

1. Choose Mail Merge from the Tools menu to open the Mail Merge Helper.

2. Choose Get Data, and select Use Address Book from the list.

3. Choose Personal Address Book from the Use Address Book dialog box (see fig. 19.6).

4. The Choose Profile dialog box appears; choose MS Exchange Settings or a custom profile you might already have created. Choose OK (see fig. 19.7).

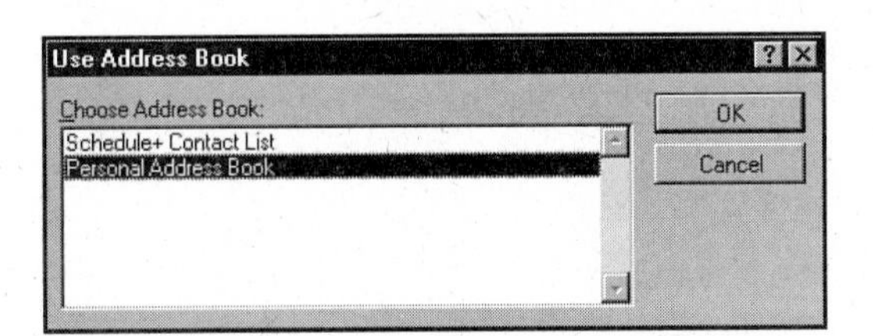

Figure 19.6
The Use Address Book dialog box.

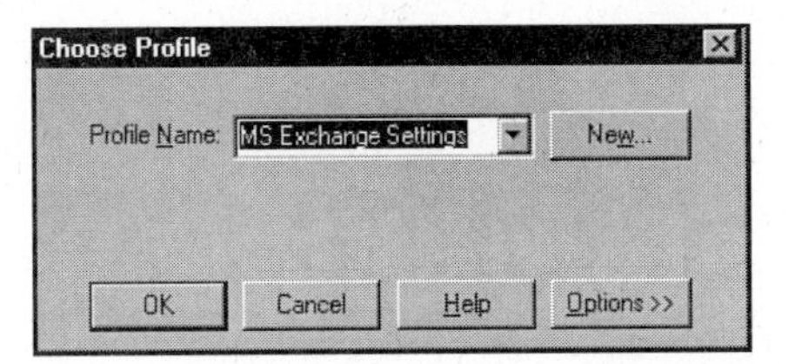

Figure 19.7
The Choose Profile dialog box.

A Microsoft Exchange profile is a set of configuration options that includes data on the information services you use; the location of your inbox, outbox, and address lists; and personal folder files you use to store and retrieve messages and files.

If you want to create a new Microsoft Exchange profile at this stage, click on New to run the Microsoft Exchange Profile wizard, which walks you through the process. If you want to set a default profile so Word doesn't ask you for a profile again, just click on **O**ptions and enable the Set as **d**efault profile check box.

If you plan to merge e-mail to an information service such as The Microsoft Network, you might want to view information about the connections available in your current profile. To do so, after you click on **O**ptions, enable the Show **l**ogon screen for all information services check box.

If you specify the Personal Address Book as your data source before you actually enter any data fields in your merge document, Word opens the dialog box shown in figure 19.8. To begin entering data fields in the main document, choose Edit **M**ain Document.

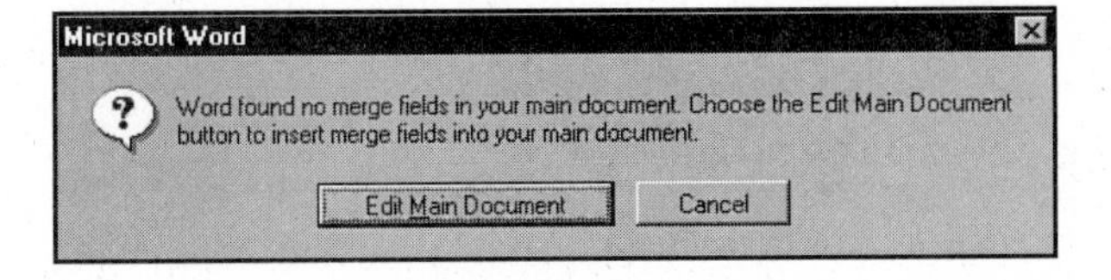

Figure 19.8
Word has found no merge fields.

When you open a Microsoft Exchange Personal Address Book as the data source for a merge document, Word actually creates a "virtual file," which contains a table with the information in the original Personal Address Book.

Creating a New Data Source

Sometimes you need to create new data sources. To do so, choose Create Data Source to open the Create Data Source dialog box (see fig. 19.9).

Figure 19.9

The Create Data Source dialog box.

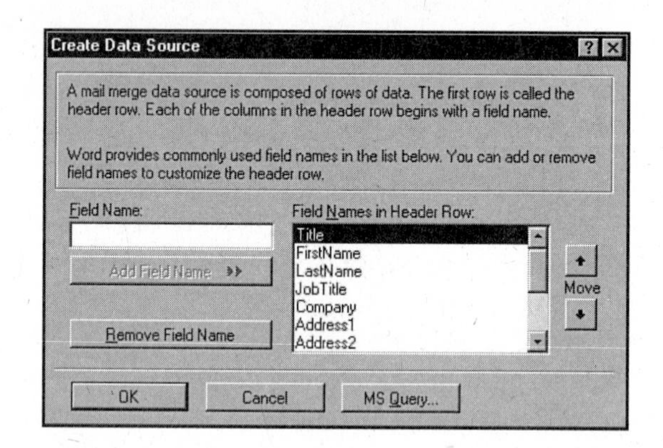

Choosing Categories for the Data Source

You now can choose which categories of data to include in your data source, or as you see later, create your own new categories. As with most databases, Word calls these categories *fields*.

> **A Note from the Author**
>
> These fields are not the same as the fields you learn about in Chapter 10, "Field Codes." (Instead, they're comparable to the fields in a database program.) But, as with other Word fields, they do offer a way for Word to include varying input in a document, depending on other factors—in this case, the differing information contained in different records.

When you create a new data source, Word automatically includes the categories of information you're most likely to use when you merge letters, labels, and envelopes.(As you can see, Word's default data form is set up to track people—after all, that's who generally gets mass mailings. But you could equally well use the form to

track products in a catalog, by creating new categories of data.) These categories are as follows.

Title (for Mr., Ms., Dr., and so on)
FirstName
LastName
JobTitle
Company
Address1
Address2
City
State
PostalCode
Country
HomePhone
WorkPhone

Your job now is to winnow out the categories you don't need, add new categories, and move the categories to match the order in which you want them.

To *remove* a category, select it in the Field Names in Header Row box. Then choose Remove Field Name.

To *add* a category, type a new category name in the Field Name text box, and then choose Add Field Name. Each of these category names must be one word of no more than 40 characters with *no* spaces. The word must *start* with a letter, although you can include numbers afterward. You can use underscore characters to connect words, as in the following example:

```
Last_Called_When?
```

To *move* a category, select it in the Field Names in Header Row box, and then use the up or down arrows to the right of the Field Names in Header Row box to place it elsewhere in the list.

These categories are slightly different from those the Microsoft Exchange Personal Address Book uses.

Specifying Records for the Data Source

After you finish using the Create Data Source dialog box, choose OK. Word prompts you for a file name in the Save Data Source dialog box (see fig. 19.10).Type a file name in the File name box, and choose OK. Word saves the data source file and displays still another dialog box—the one shown in figure 19.11.

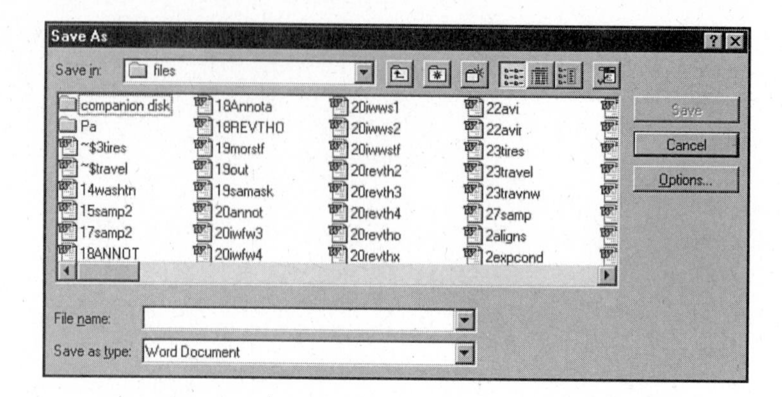

Figure 19.10

The Save Data Source dialog box.

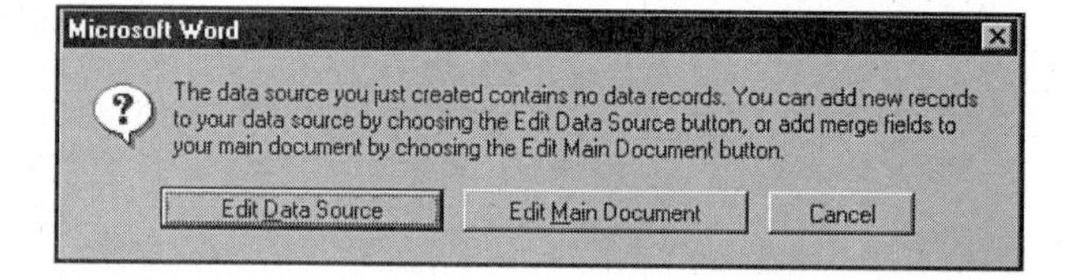

Figure 19.11

Word asks if you want to add records.

Because you now have a data source to accompany the main document you've already created, you could at this point go back to the main document and tell it which data to pull when you run the print merge. This step is called *inserting merge fields.* To insert merge fields, you choose Edit **M**ain Document. For more information on this process, see this chapter's section "Inserting Merge Fields."

Or you could stay in your data source, adding new records to it. To add new records to your data source, choose Edit **D**ata Source. A blank *data form* appears, including the fields you specified a little while ago (see fig. 19.12). Unless you delete several of the default fields, you have to scroll to see them all.

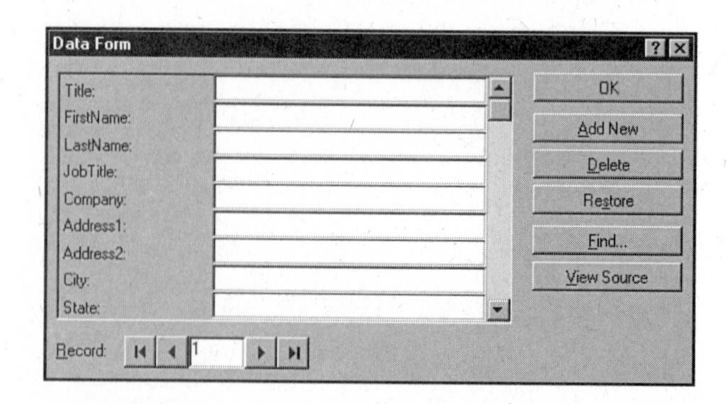

Figure 19.12

The Data Form dialog box.

You are presented here with the first record. A *record* is a collection of information about a specific person or thing.

To fill in the record, click on the field you want to enter (or press Tab to move to it). Then start typing. To move from one field to the next, press Enter or Tab.

After you finish, if you want to create another record, choose **A**dd New and a new blank record appears. If you don't like the edits you've made to the current record, choose Re**s**tore to revert *this* record to its contents before you edited it (in this case, a blank record). If at some point you no longer need a record, choose **D**elete. The record is gone with no further ado.

Re**s**tore doesn't bring back a deleted record, and Word's Undo feature isn't accessible from a data form. Therefore, the only way to bring back a record you just deleted is to close your file without resaving the changes you just made—in which case, you also lose any other changes you made since the last time you saved. The more often you save, of course, the less information you lose. On the other hand, if you set Automatic Save to save very frequently, it might save your changes before you have a chance to close the file—in which case your deleted record will be gone for good!

Finding Information in Records

You can use the **R**ecord box, which always displays your current record, to move quickly among records (see fig. 19.13). You also can search for specific information within the data form. To do so, choose **F**ind. The Find in Field dialog box opens, as shown in figure 19.14.

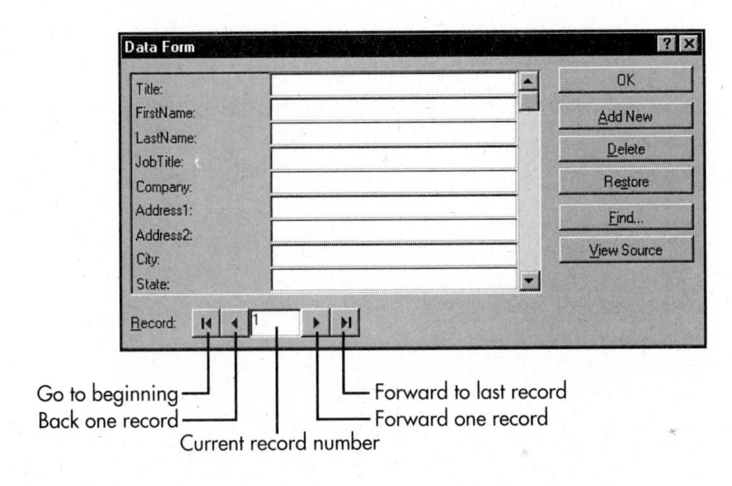

Figure 19.13

The Record box in the Data Form dialog box.

Figure 19.14
The Find in Field dialog box.

Type the information you want to find in the Find What box. Specify the field you want Word to search in the In Field list box. Then choose Find First. Word finds the first reference and displays the Find Next button. To find another reference to the same text, choose Find Next.

Working with the Underlying Data Table and the Database Toolbar

The data form is only a friendly front end patched onto a standard Word table. Not surprisingly, you can do some things from the table that you can't do from the form. Viewing the table also is the only way you can see your data in tabular format, with many records showing at once.

A Note from the Author

A good example: you can search from within the form, but you can replace only from within the table.

Suppose that an area code has changed, and you need to walk through the database, finding references to (212) and deciding whether they should change to (718). That task would be clumsy within the data form. You'd have to find a reference, choose Find and make your edit, choose Find again to locate the next reference, and so on.

In the Word table, however, you can just use Shift+F4 to select the next reference, and overtype the new area code whenever you need to.

To work in the underlying data table, choose View Source from the Data Form dialog box. The table appears and the Database toolbar appears (see fig. 19.15). As you can see, the table might be too wide for your screen, and even so, many words wrap inauspiciously. The aesthetics leave something to be desired, but all your information's there.

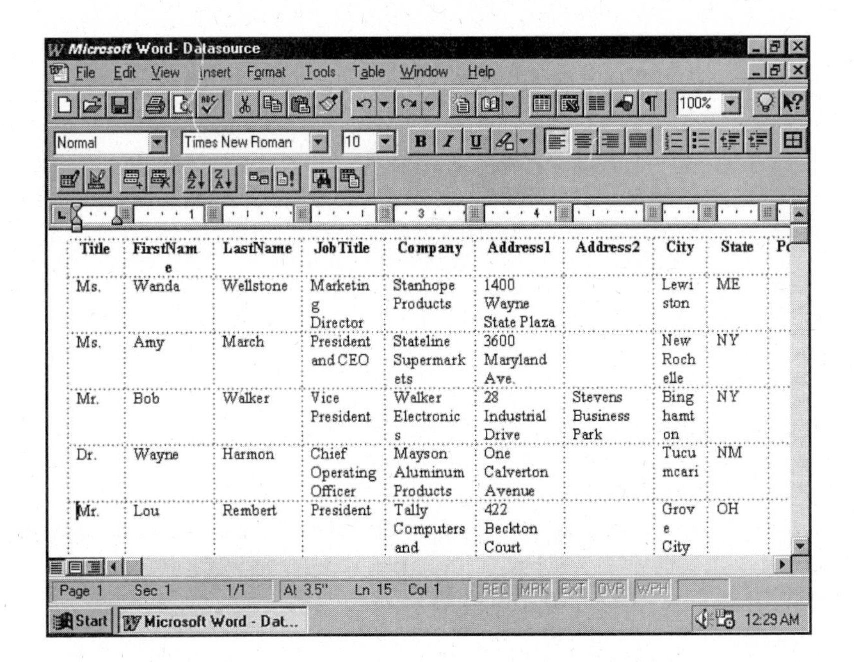

Figure 19.15
Viewing the source table and Database toolbar.

The Database toolbar, meanwhile, contains the shortcut buttons you're likely to need while you work on the data source table. These shortcut buttons are listed in table 19.1.

If you plan to work at length in the source table, you might consider turning off Automatic Spell Checking. It probably will display many names, street addresses, cities, and other data as if they were spelled wrong, because these are not included in Word's dictionary. Automatic Spell Checking can be turned off by choosing **O**ptions from the **T**ools menu; then selecting the Spelling tab; then clearing the **A**utomatic Spell Checking check box.

Table 19.1
Database Toolbar Buttons

Button	Function
Data Form	Returns you to the data form, where you can edit a record
Manage Fields	Adds/deletes a database field
Add New Record	Adds a new record to a database at the insertion point

continues

Table 19.1, Continued
Database Toolbar Buttons

Button	Function
Delete Record	Deletes a selected record from a database
Sort Ascending	Sorts records in A to Z and/or 0 to 9 ("ascending") order
Sort Descending	Sorts selected records in Z to A and/or 9 to 0 ("descending") order
Insert Database	Gets information from elsewhere and places it in the current document
Update Fields	Updates the results of fields you select
Find Record	Locates a specific record in a mail merge data source (opens the Find in Field dialog box)
Mail Merge Main Document	Switches to the main document

The following paragraphs briefly discuss some of these buttons.

Manage Fields enables you to insert, delete, or rename fields. It opens the dialog box shown in figure 19.16, which works like the Create Data Source dialog box, except that you also can choose an existing field and rename it. *New Record* and *Delete Record* do the same thing as inserting a table row or selecting a row and deleting it.

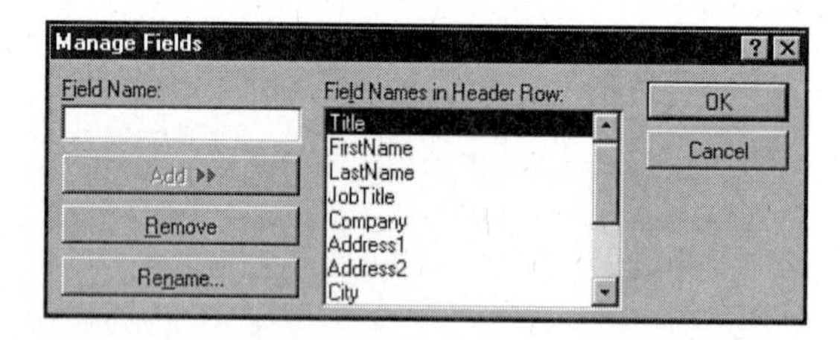

Figure 19.16
The Manage Fields dialog box.

Sort Ascending and *Sort Descending* sort *rows*, based on the contents of the *first* column. (In other words, you can't select a column and ask Word to sort all the rows by the contents of that column.) These buttons ignore the first line, which contains Word's field headings.

Insert Database imports information from other Word documents or database programs; this topic is covered in Chapter 20, "Word as an Integrating Environment." *Update Fields* does just that—updates fields. You learn where you might use fields in merge letters later, in the section "Using Word Fields," but here's an example: you can include a field to add up numbers placed elsewhere in your database.

You can format and print the data source table the same way you would any other table. It still functions as a data source.

You also can use Word's table features (such as the Table shortcut menu) to edit the table. You could, for example, use Delete Column to get rid of a field you no longer need.

Inserting Merge Fields

After you have your data source under control, it's time to return to the main document and insert *merge fields*—the instructions that tell Word what to pluck from the data source and where to put it.

In the Database toolbar, click on the Mail Merge Main Document button, and Word switches to the main document attached to the data source. This document has its own Mail Merge toolbar, shown in figure 19.17. For more information about this toolbar, see the next section, "Using the Mail Merge Toolbar."

Figure 19.17

The Mail Merge toolbar.

To insert your first merge field, place your insertion point in the document at the spot where you want the field. Then click on the Insert Merge Field button. A list of the category fields available in the data source document you've told Word to use appear (see fig. 19.18).

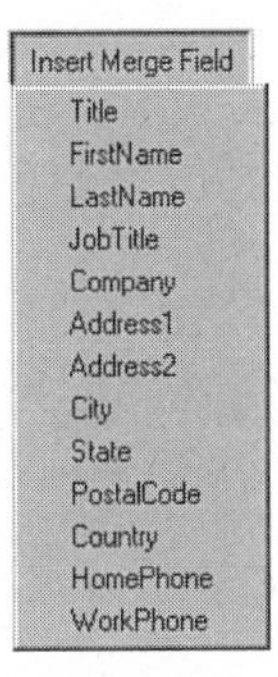

Figure 19.18

The Insert Merge Field list.

You then choose a merge field from the list, and it appears in your main document, as shown in figure 19.19. If you see a field code such as {MERGEFIELD LastName} instead, select it and press Alt+F9 to display the field result.

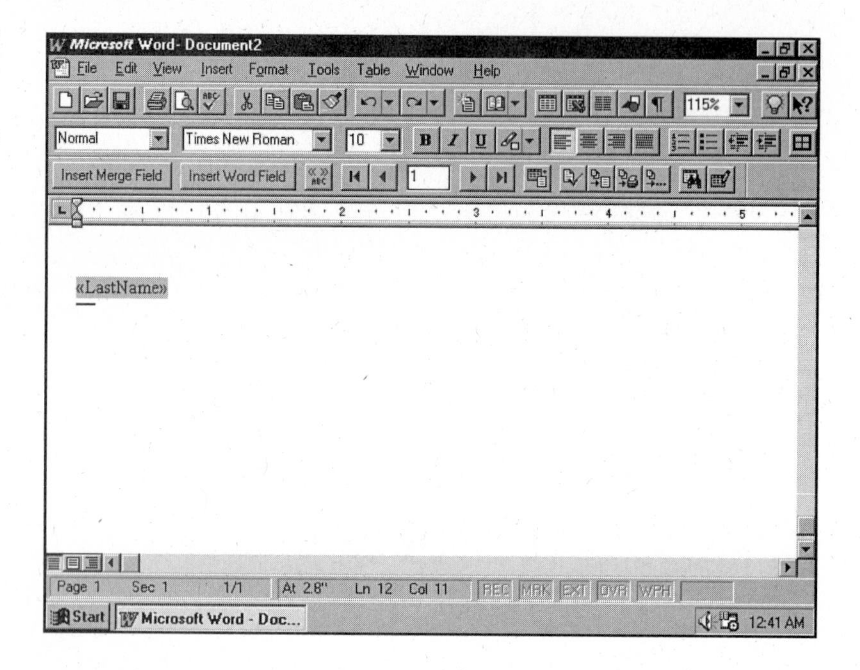

Figure 19.19
A merge field, inserted into a main document.

Each merge field starts and ends with these special "chevron" symbols: << >>. You can't insert a merge field from the keyboard; you have to use Insert Merge Field.

Place each of your merge fields in the correct location. Don't forget to include spaces between merge fields if they are separate words. And remember the punctuation that needs to appear in the finished document.

Look, for example, at this standard letter introduction:

> Mr. Thomas Walker
> Vice President
> Walker Corporation
> Suite 408
> 32 Industrial Drive
> Mission Hills, ND 45881
>
> Dear Mr. Walker:

To get this type of introduction in your merge letter, you need the merge fields and punctuation shown in figure 19.20.

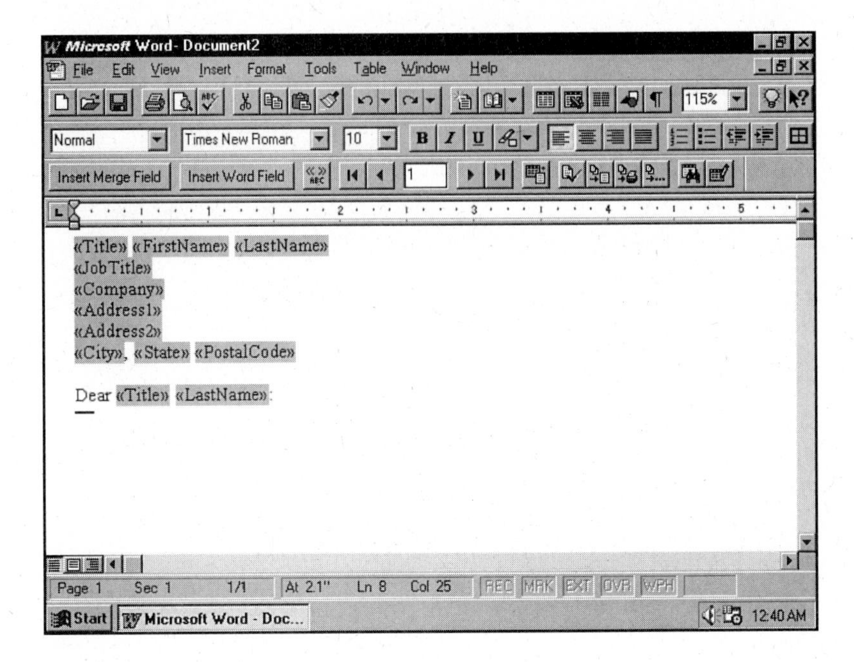

Figure 19.20

Typical merge field introduction.

Tip If you create many letter headings that contain the same merge fields, you might save them as an AutoText entry.

Using the Mail Merge Toolbar

The Mail Merge toolbar contains several tools to help you manage the merge. Table 19.2 summarizes what's in the Mail Merge toolbar.

TABLE 19.2
Mail Merge Toolbar Buttons

Button	Function
Insert Merge Field	Inserts your choice of existing merge fields from the document with which you intend to merge
Insert Word Field	Inserts your choice of these Word fields: Ask, Fill-in, If...Then...Else, Merge Record #, Merge Sequence #, Next Record, Next Record If, Set Bookmark, and Skip Record If

continues

Table 19.2, Continued
Mail Merge Toolbar Buttons

Button	Function
View Merged Data	Displays the merge document as it will appear after you merge it, with the contents of a specific record rather than merge fields
First Record	Shows the first record in the data source
Previous Record	Shows the preceding record in the data source
Go to Record	Shows the current record in the data source; type a new number to go to another record
Next Record	Shows the next record in the data source
Last Record	Shows the final record in the data source
Mail Merge Helper	Opens the Mail Merge Helper dialog box
Check for Errors	Previews the results of your mail merge before you run it so you can identify errors
Merge to New Document	Merges data source and main document to a new file, which appears on-screen
Merge to Printer	Merges data source and main document and prints the results
Mail Merge	Opens the Merge dialog box, in which you can specify where to merge the document (including e-mail) and select from many other options
Find Record	Finds records that contain specific information you choose, in any field you choose (opens the Find in Field dialog box)
Edit Data Source	Switches to data form so you can edit records

Keep in mind that the Merge to New Document and Merge to Printer buttons perform default mail merges, to a document or to your printer, based on your current mail merge settings. Chances are, you'll use these buttons only after you're confident that your mail merge will work the way you want.

The first time around, you need to use the Mail Merge button, which leads you to the climax of this whole enterprise: merging your data source with your main document.

Merging the Data Source with the Main Document

Now that you have your data source and main document in shape, you're just about ready to merge. If you're in the main document, click on the Mail Merge button or choose Merge from the Mail Merge Helper to open the Merge dialog box (see fig. 19.21).

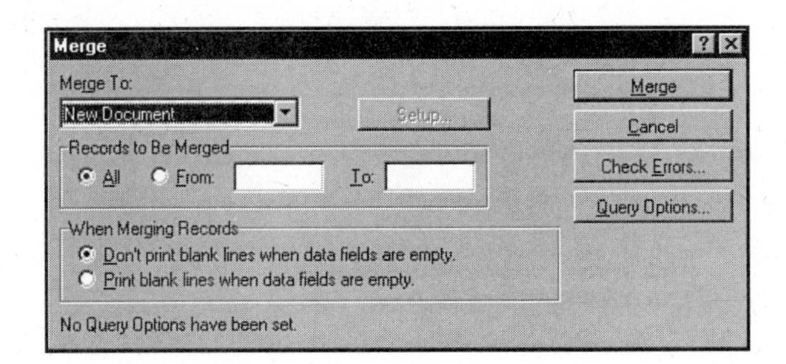

Figure 19.21

The Merge dialog box.

Merging to a Document or Your Printer

Your first option is where you want to merge *to*. You can see Word's default setting, New Document, in the Merge To box. New Document places all the merged documents in a single new document, *Form Letters1*. A section break that starts the next page separates each individual merged letter from the others. After you merge the new document, you can easily print your letters from it.

You also can browse the Form Letters1 document to see whether you want to add any other personal comments to any of the letters. Form Letters1 behaves just like any other Word document.

Obviously, you also can merge directly to the printer. If you prefer to do so, choose Printer in the Merge To box.

Merging to Electronic Mail or Fax

Word also offers one more option in the Merge To box: Electronic Mail. If you have the appropriate network connections or fax/modem, you can use this option to *broadcast* documents to others on your e-mail network or fax machines anywhere in the world.

Electronic Mail is designed for internal electronic mail and fax systems based on either the Messaging Application Programming Interface (MAPI) or the Vendor Independent Messaging (VIM) standard. MAPI and VPI are competing standards; electronic mail systems compliant with the same standard can exchange messages with each other.

Microsoft Exchange is a MAPI product; Lotus cc:Mail and many other e-mail products support VIM. Microsoft Exchange has a fax feature designed to work with Word 95.

If you choose the Electronic Mail option, you need to make sure that your data source has a field that contains the electronic mail or fax addresses you plan to use. You can use an external data source that already contains these addresses, such as a Microsoft Exchange Personal Address Book. Another option is to add an E-Mail Address field to a new data source; when you're ready to merge, tell Word to use that field as its source of e-mail addresses.

To merge to e-mail or fax, follow these steps:

1. Choose **M**ail Merge from the **T**ools menu.
2. Click the Merge button.
3. Choose Electronic Mail in the Merge To box.
4. Click on the **S**etup button that becomes available to open the Merge To Setup dialog box (see fig. 19.22).

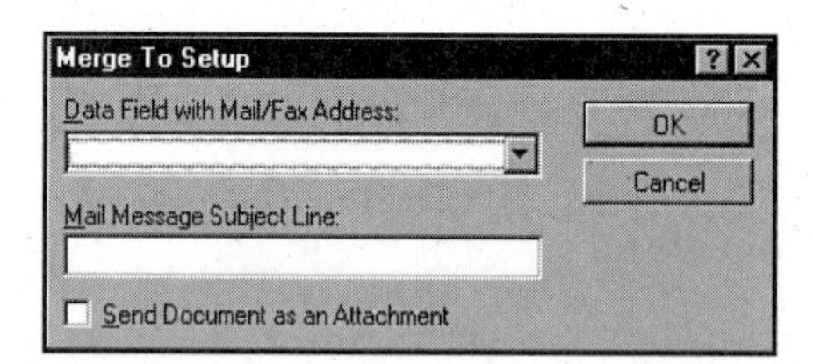

Figure 19.22

The Merge To Setup dialog box.

5. Choose **D**ata Field with Mail/Fax Address, and choose the appropriate data field from the list box.
6. If you send electronic mail, type in the **M**ail Message Subject Line text box a summary of the contents of the message.
7. Most electronic mail systems let you choose between sending the *text* of your file and sending the *document* itself as an attachment that the recipient can store and edit. If you want to send a document as an attachment, enable the **S**end Document as an Attachment check box.
8. Choose OK.

Using Word with Microsoft Exchange for Broadcast Fax

Broadcast fax means sending the same (or similar) faxes to multiple recipients at once. Word and Microsoft Exchange can work together to do just that; you can even use Word's Mail Merge features to personalize the faxes each recipient gets. Because both Word and Exchange support Windows 95's improved multitasking, you can send faxes in the background while you work on other projects.

To use Microsoft Exchange with Word for Broadcast fax, first create your mail merge main document and establish your Microsoft Exchange Personal Address Book as the data source, as discussed earlier in this chapter, in the section, "Using a Microsoft Exchange Address Book." When you're ready to send the fax, follow these steps:

1. Choose Mail Merge from the Tools menu.
2. Click the Merge button.
3. Choose Electronic Mail in the Merge To box.
4. Click on the Setup button that becomes available to open the Merge To Setup dialog box.
5. Choose Data Field with Mail/Fax Address, and choose the Personal Address Book data field that contains your fax numbers—probably Primary Fax Number.
6. Choose OK.

Specifying Records to Merge and Blank Lines to Print

In the Merge dialog box, you also can specify which records you want to merge. Word numbers by rows. The first row beneath a field heading is record #1. The default setting is All; if you want to specify records, choose From, and specify records in a range From a certain record To a certain record.

By default, Word doesn't print blank lines in empty data fields. Why? Some letters have two-line addresses; others have only one. Some recipients might have titles; others might not. Leaving a blank line in an address or other field is a dead giveaway of a computer-generated letter.

On the other hand, you might want the blank line to appear. Perhaps you're printing a form, and you *want* the reader to know that the information is incomplete. (Maybe you want *them* to complete it.) In such a situation, you want to choose the other When Merging Records option in the bottom of the Merge dialog box (Print blank lines when data fields are empty).

Using Query Options to Refine Your Selection

The Query Options button in the Merge dialog box gives you more sophisticated control over which data you output. Choosing Query Options opens the Filter Records tab shown in figure 19.23.

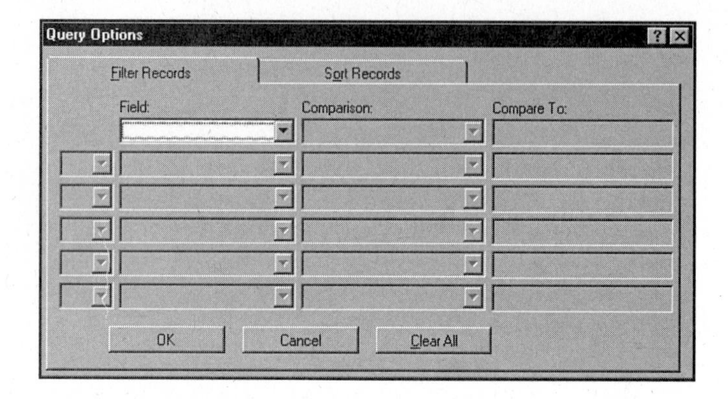

Figure 19.23
The Filter Records tab.

The first tab, Filter Records, enables you to keep some records from printing based on criteria you specify. First, you tell Word the field on which you want to base your selection. Then you tell Word which comparison to make to decide whether to include a record. You can make several kinds of comparisons. Choose one of the following from the Comparison list box:

Equal to
Not equal to
Less than
Greater than
Less than or equal
Greater than or equal
Is blank
Is not blank

In most cases, you not only need to provide a comparison, but you also must tell Word to what it needs to compare the text or number. ("Equal to *what?*")

Note This Query Options feature is similar to the Insert, Database feature discussed in Chapter 20.

Here are a few examples of how filtering records works, first in English, and then in *Word*-lish:

"Print letters for all records where the company name is AT&T."

Field:	Comparison:	Compare To:
Company	Equal to	AT&T

"Print letters for all records where the order size is less than $1,000."

Field:	Comparison:	Compare To:
Order Size	Less than	$1,000

"Print a letter for every record *except* those that don't have a name."

Field:	Comparison:
Name	Is not blank

Using the list box at the left, which specifies And by default (but also can specify Or), you can make up to six comparisons at the same time in the same query. Here's an example using the And operator:

"Print a letter for all records where Postal Code is greater than 11700 but less than 11999." (This query would print only letters addressed to Long Island, New York.)

	Field:	Comparison:
	Postal Code	Greater than or Equal 11700
And		
	Postal Code	Less than or Equal 11999

Here's another example, this time using the Or operator:

"Print a letter for all records where the addressee's company is AT&T, IBM, or General Electric."

	Field:	Comparison:	Compare To:
	Company	Equal to	AT&T
Or			
	Company	Equal to	IBM
Or			
	Company	Equal to	General Electric

If you tell Word to print only records that meet one condition *and* another condition, you almost always get fewer records than if you select records that meet one condition *or* the other.

A bit more subtle tip: the *order* in which you use the Ands and Ors does make a difference. When Word sees an And, the program performs that selection immediately, before doing anything else. Only after the results of *that* selection are firmly in place does Word then proceed to handle any additional Ands or Ors.

An example might help. Suppose Word sees this query:

	Field:	Comparison:	Compare To:
	Job Title	Equal to	Vice President
Or			
	City	Equal to	Cincinnati
And			
	Title	Equal to	Mr.

Word finds all the vice presidents in your database, adds to it everyone from Cincinnati, and then subtracts all the women.

Swap things around a bit, and it's a different story:

	Field:	Comparison:	Compare To:
	Job Title	Equal to	Vice President
And			
	Title	Equal to	Mr.
Or			
	City	Equal to	Cincinnati

Word first finds all the vice presidents in the list, next excludes the women vice presidents, and then adds *anyone* from Cincinnati, without regard to gender.

If you create a set of filtering rules that doesn't work, you can start over again by choosing Clear All.

Deciding the Printing Order for Your Letters

A point or two about sorting are, um, in order. The second tabbed dialog box you can access from the Query Options dialog box is Sort Records (see fig. 19.24), in which you specify the order in which the records should print.

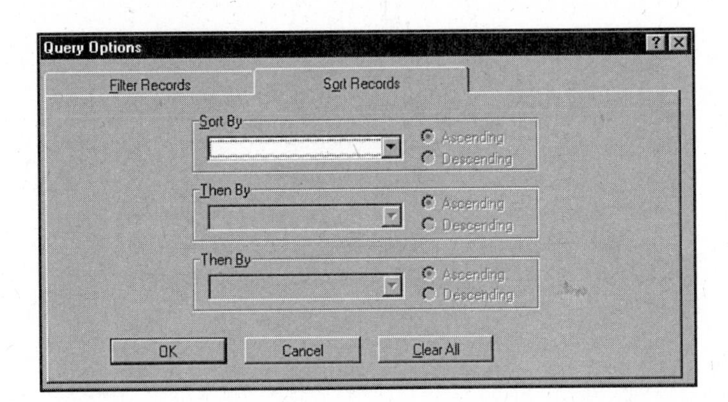

Figure 19.24
The Sort Records tab.

In the basic sort, you choose the field on which you want to sort from the Sort By list box. You also can choose whether to sort in ascending or descending order. Both are relatively simple if your list contains just text or just numbers. *Ascending* sorts from 0 to 9 and then from A to Z (in other words, any entries starting with a number appear before entries starting with a letter). *Descending* sorts from Z to A and then from 9 to 0; in other words, letters appear before numbers.

Word sorts nonalphanumeric characters by their position in the ANSI character set. In that character set, numbers appear before letters. However, as you can see by choosing Insert, Symbol, and viewing the character set, some symbols appear even before numbers: symbols like !, @, and #, which appear at the top of your keyboard. And many other symbols, such as copyright and registered trademark symbols, appear after the letters in the ANSI character set.

You can sort up to three levels, using the Sort By box and the Then By and Then By boxes. Word first sorts by the field in your Sort By box. When that sort is complete, Word sorts by the field in your first Then By box and then by the next Then By box.

Previewing the Mail Merge to Check for Errors

The last step before you merge your document is to check for errors. Errors in field names, such as spaces between words, can prevent a successful merge. Error checking also flags discrepancies between merge fields in the main document and field names in the data source.

To run error checking, choose Check Errors from the Merge dialog box, or click on the Mail Merge Check button in the Mail Merge toolbar, to open the Checking and Reporting Errors dialog box (see fig. 19.25).

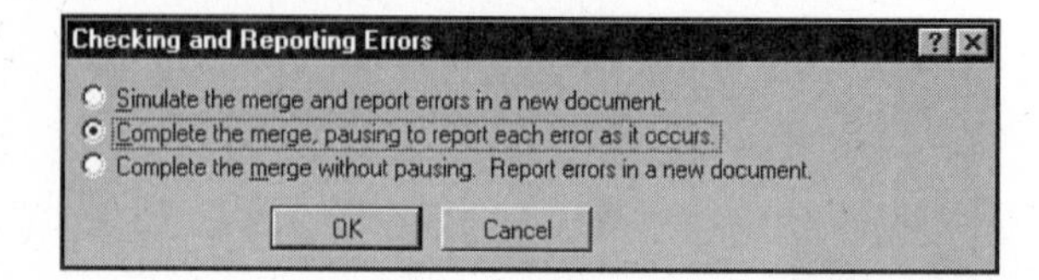

Figure 19.25
The Checking and Reporting Errors dialog box.

You have three choices. The first and third choices list your errors in a new document, named Mail Merge Errors1. The middle choice runs the merge, displaying a message on-screen each time an error takes place. After you complete error checking, choose Merge to run the merge.

Printing Accompanying Envelopes and Labels

If you have a data source, Word enables you to print envelopes or labels along with your letters. You can print matching envelopes or labels for your merged letters by using the same data source with the same selection and sorting options.

Printing Merged Envelopes

To print envelopes, follow these steps:

1. Choose Mail Merge from the Tools menu.
2. In the Main Document box, choose Create; then choose Envelopes.
3. Choose New Main Document.
4. Choose Get Data. Select or create a data source.
5. Set up your main document for envelopes by choosing Setup Main Document from the Mail Merge Helper dialog box. The Envelope Options dialog box appears (see fig. 19.26).

   You can set envelope size, envelope bar codes, fonts, and where the addresses print. In the Printing Options tabbed dialog box, which you access by choosing Printing Options, you can control the way your envelopes feed into your printer.

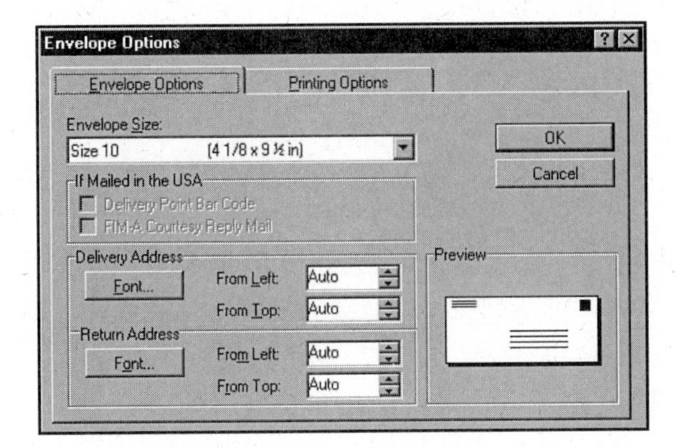

Figure 19.26

The Envelope Options dialog box.

(These Envelope Options dialog boxes are covered in detail in Chapter 4, "Printing and Faxing.")

6. Choose OK. The Envelope Address dialog box opens (see fig. 19.27).

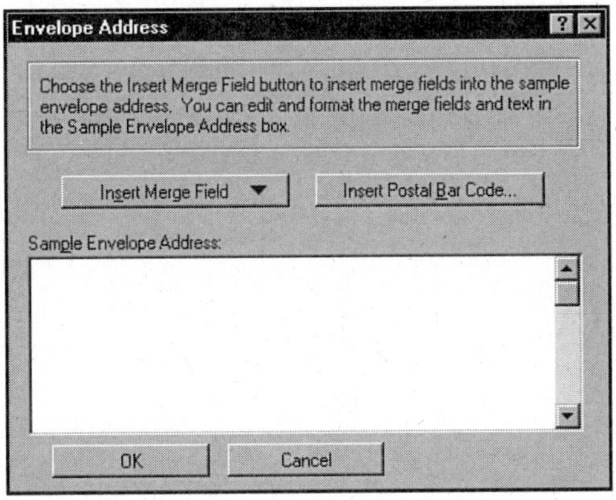

Envelope Address

Choose the Insert Merge Field button to insert merge fields into the sample envelope address. You can edit and format the merge fields and text in the Sample Envelope Address box.

Insert Merge Field | Insert Postal Bar Code...

Sample Envelope Address:

OK | Cancel

Figure 19.27

The Envelope Address dialog box.

7. Create your envelope address by choosing merge fields from the Insert Merge Field box, as if you were working directly in a main document.

8. If you also want to add a POSTNET bar code to streamline mail handling, choose Insert Postal Bar Code. The dialog box shown in figure 19.28 appears.

9. To add the postal code, specify which of your merge fields contain the ZIP code and the street address. Choose OK.

10. Choose Mail Merge from the Tools menu. Then, in the Mail Merge Helper screen, choose to Edit your main document. Your envelope appears in Page Layout view (see fig. 19.29).

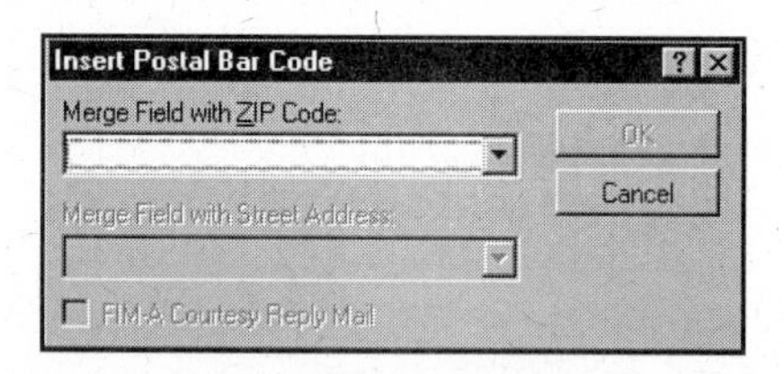

Figure 19.28

The Insert Postal Bar Code dialog box.

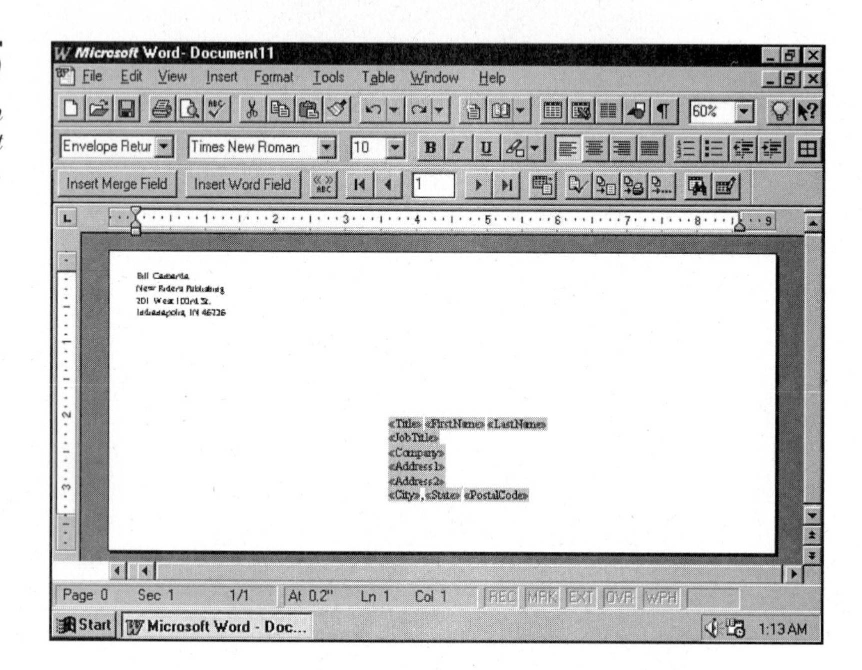

Figure 19.29

An envelope in Page Layout view.

11. If necessary, move the frame that contains your delivery address merge fields.

    Notice that the return address is that shown in Tools, Options, User Info. If you don't need a return address, select and delete it. If the name and address are wrong, you can edit them.

12. To print, click on the Merge to Printer button on the Mail Merge toolbar.

Printing Merged Labels

To print labels, follow these steps:

1. Choose Mail Merge from the Tools menu.
2. In the Main Document box, choose Create, then choose Mailing Labels.

3. Choose **N**ew Main Document.

4. Choose **G**et Data. Select or create a data source.

5. Set up your main document for labels by choosing **S**et Up Main Document from the Mail Merge Helper dialog box. The Label Options dialog box then appears (see fig. 19.30).

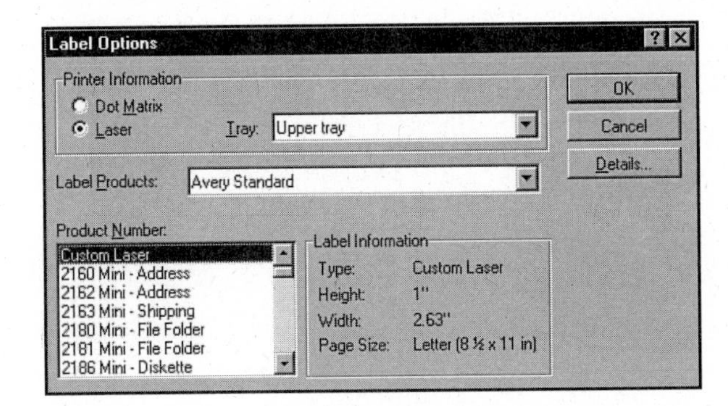

Figure 19.30

The Label Options dialog box.

You can choose a standard label or define a custom label here, and also specify how you want your label to print. (Chapter 4 covers the Label Options dialog box in depth.)

6. Choose OK. The Create Labels dialog box opens (see fig. 19.31).

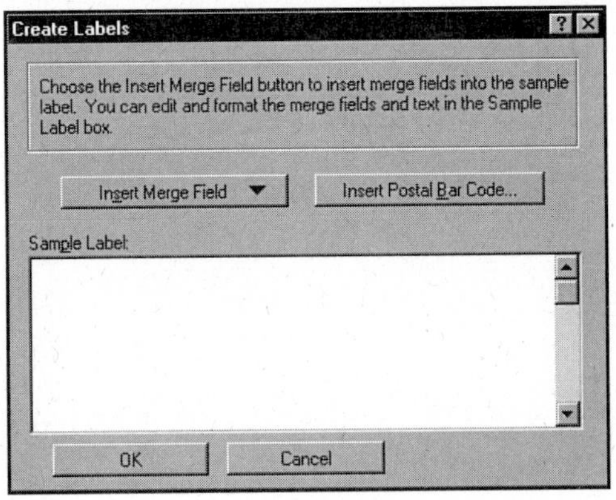

Create Labels

Choose the Insert Merge Field button to insert merge fields into the sample label. You can edit and format the merge fields and text in the Sample Label box.

Insert Merge Field | Insert Postal Bar Code...

Sample Label:

OK | Cancel

Figure 19.31

The Create Labels dialog box.

7. Create your label address by choosing merge fields from the In**s**ert Merge Field box as if you were working directly in a main document.

8. If you also want to add a POSTNET bar code to streamline mail handling, choose Insert Postal **B**ar Code.

9. To add the bar code, specify which of your merge fields contain the ZIP code and the street address. Choose OK.

10. If you want to check the formatting of your labels, choose to **E**dit your main document. Your label fields appear in Normal view (see fig. 19.32). Note that you see the fields, not the finished mail merge.

Note To see the labels as they actually will appear—with data—choose Merge to New Document, complete the mail merge, and view the new document Word creates.

11. To print the labels, click on the Mail Merge button, set your options (including Me**r**ge To Printer), and choose **M**erge.

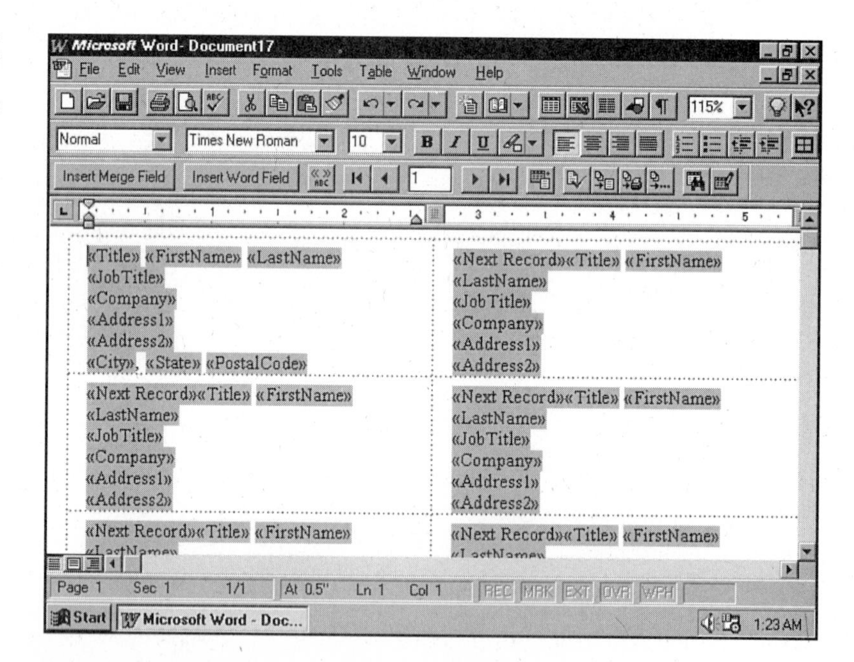

Figure 19.32

A page of labels in Normal view.

Creating a Separate Header Source

Normally, Word takes its merge field names from the top row of your data table or from the field names in the database to which you connect. Occasionally, however, using these merge field names might be inconvenient. You might, for example, want to merge several different data sources that have different field names into a single main document. Or you might use a read-only data source.

For such times, Word enables you to use a separate header source. To do so, follow these steps:

1. Choose **M**ail Merge from the **T**ools menu.

2. Choose **G**et Data.

3. Choose **H**eader Options. The Header Options dialog box opens, as shown in figure 19.33.

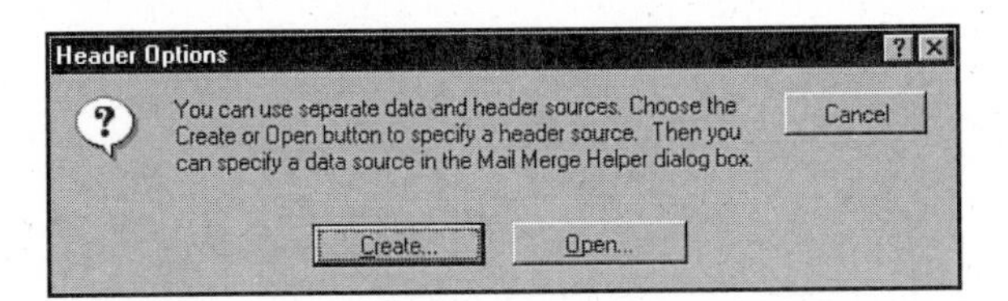

Figure 19.33

The Header Options dialog box.

4. Choose **C**reate from the Header Options dialog box. The Create Header Source dialog box opens (see fig. 19.34).

Create Header Source
A mail merge data source is composed of rows of data. The first row is called the header row. Each of the columns in the header row begins with a field name.
Word provides commonly used field names in the list below. You can add or remove field names to customize the header row.
Field Name:
Field Names in Header Row:
Title
FirstName
LastName
JobTitle
Company
Address1
Address2
Add Field Name
Remove Field Name
Move
OK
Cancel
MS Query...

Figure 19.34

The Create Header Source dialog box.

5. Edit Word's proposed field names by adding new ones in the **F**ield Name box and removing any unnecessary ones from the Field **N**ames in Header Row box. Use the Move keys to rearrange them in the order you want.

6. Choose OK. The Save Data Source dialog box opens.

7. Save the data source with its own file name.

After you establish the header source, you can then create or get your data source and proceed with the rest of your mail merge. Later, you can open and use this header source whenever you need it, which helps you retain the same main documents without having to worry about changing the merge fields.

Using Word Fields

Until now, this chapter has discussed using *merge fields* in a Word mail merge main document. But you also can use the other fields available to Word documents. You can add the current date, for example, by using {date}.

You also can perform a calculation. In the simplest case, suppose that your merge field categories contain dollar amounts. Perhaps you're sending a letter confirming a customer order. You can place these dollar amount fields in a table and use Word's AutoSum field to tally them in each letter.

Finally, several Word fields are designed especially for mail merge. These are listed in table 19.3.

Table 19.3
Word Fields Specially Designed for Mail Merge

Field	Function
Ask	Asks the user for input and assigns that input to a bookmark. With the Set field, you can use that bookmark throughout your document
Fill-in	Asks the user for input at each new mail merge document and places that input in the document
If...Then...Else...	Specifies text to print if a certain condition is met, and different text otherwise
Merge Record #	Inserts the number of your data record in your main document.
Next Record	Tells Word to print the next record without starting a new page. Often used with labels
Next Record If...	Starts the next record on the same page only if certain conditions are met
Set Bookmark...	Marks text as a bookmark that you can insert repeatedly throughout a document
Skip Record If...	Skips printing the current record if a specified condition is met

These fields were all available as far back as Word 2, but Word 6 and now Word 95 make them easier to use by providing the Insert Word Field button in the Mail Merge toolbar and by adding a custom-tailored dialog box as necessary. These Word fields appear in the document enclosed in chevrons, like merge fields, as in

```
<<Merge Record #>>
```

If you choose to view field codes, however, you still see the raw code, as in

```
{MERGEREC}
```

You place a Word field in a main document by clicking on the Insert Word Field button on the Mail Merge toolbar. The list of available fields appears (see fig. 19.35).

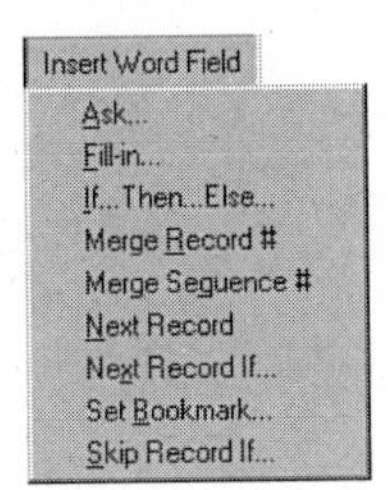

Figure 19.35

Choosing a Word field from the available list.

Using the Fill-in Field

Perhaps the most straightforward Word field is Fill-in. When you insert a Fill-in field, Word stops before printing each document and asks the user for input to place in the location specified by the Fill-in field.

To insert a Fill-in field, click on Insert Word Field and choose Fill-in. The Fill-in dialog box opens (see fig. 19.36).

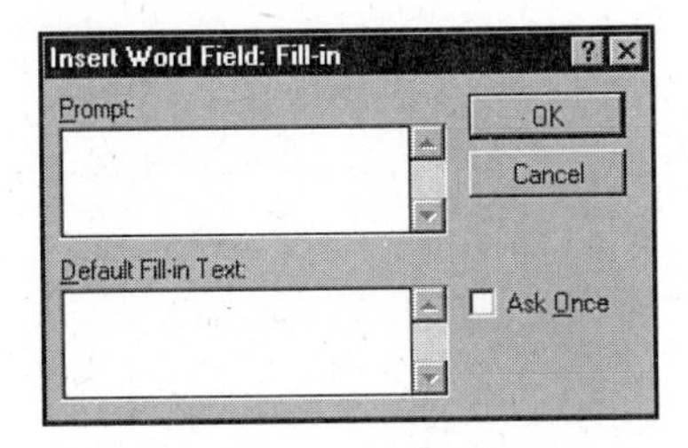

Figure 19.36

The Fill-in dialog box.

In the Prompt box, insert the question you want to ask whomever is running the mail merge—for example, "Would you like to include a special offer in this letter?"

If you want the same text in *every* letter, check the Ask Once box. Then, after the user inserts the information once, Word repeats that information in all letters that the mail merge generates.

To specify default text that prints unless you choose different text for a specific letter, type the default text in the Default Fill-in Text box.

When Fill-in runs, a dialog box like the one shown in figure 19.37 prompts the user to type information in the box beneath the text you've added.

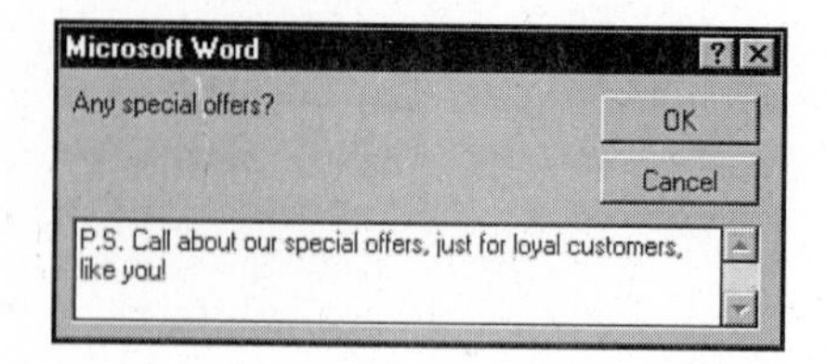

Figure 19.37
The Fill-in prompt dialog box.

Using the Ask Field

The Ask field takes this concept one step further. Instead of placing your response directly in text, the Ask field transforms your response into the contents of a *bookmark*. Wherever you place that bookmark in your text, these contents appear. Therefore, Ask is ideal for inserting the same text repeatedly throughout a letter.

When you choose to insert an Ask field, you also must choose or name the bookmark (see fig. 19.38).

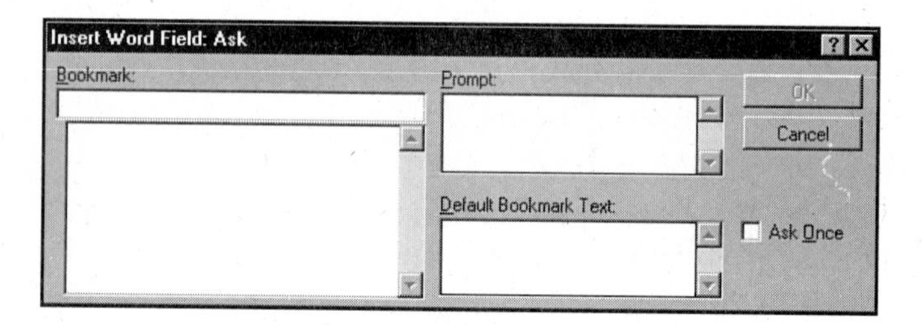

Figure 19.38
Inserting an Ask field.

Because all Ask does is create a bookmark, it doesn't place anything in your letter by itself. You have to place a bookmark field wherever you want the text. In this rare moment, you actually have to press Ctrl+F9 to insert the field manually. The field brackets appear; then you type the bookmark name between them, as in {offer}.

Using the Set Bookmark Field

The Set Bookmark field (known to field code aficionados as *Set*) also sets the contents of bookmarks. But the user isn't prompted for the contents of these bookmarks during the mail merge; *you* set them ahead of time.

Other fields often use bookmarks you create using Set, especially the If...Then...Else field, to decide whether to perform certain actions. In the following example, the Set field creates a bookmark called **threshold** and places the number $50,000 in it.

```
{set threshold "$50,000"}
```

Now you can compare individual records with that number and specify different text for those over and under the number. The following example uses a nested field that also includes If...Then...Else to tell Word to change its response depending on the current contents of the threshold bookmark. Here, if the contents of the yearsales field for this record are less than $50,000, the advice "We have some ideas that could help you increase your sales" is given. If they've sold more than that, they don't *need* any advice, so they don't get any.

```
{if {mergefield yearsales} < {threshold} "We have
some ideas that could help you increase your
sales" ""}
```

Here's how to create a nested field. First display the field rather than the field result. Select the field and press Alt+F9, then place the insertion point where you want the nested field to appear and choose the field you want to nest from the Insert Word Field list.

Chapter 10 covers nested fields in more detail.

Using the If...Then...Else Field

The preceding section alluded to If...Then...Else; in this section, you learn a bit more about it. This field uses the following syntax: *If* such-and-such happens, *Then* do this. *Else* do something different.

This syntax becomes visible when you choose the field from the Insert Word Field list and then see the IF dialog box shown in figure 19.39.

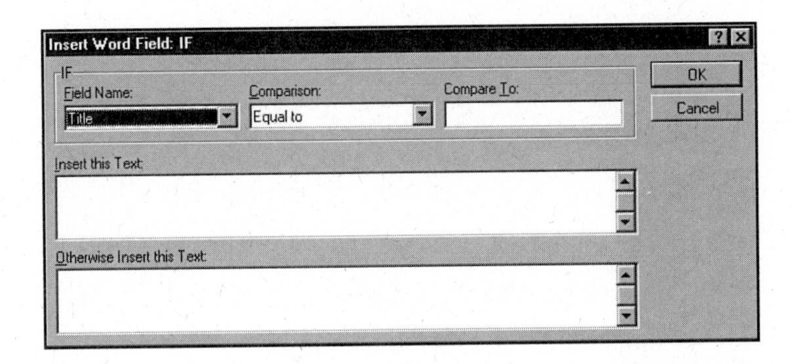

Figure 19.39

The IF dialog box.

In the area at the top, you create the If part of the comparison. First, choose a Field Name from the list box. This field is the category of information you want to compare in each record. Then choose the kind of comparison you want to make.

The comparisons are the same ones available in Query options: Equal to, Not equal to, Less than, Greater than, Less than or equal, Greater than or equal, Is blank, or Is not blank. Finally, unless you've chosen Is blank, or Is not blank, you also need to add in the Compare To box the number or text with which you're comparing the field.

Now for the Then part. In the Insert this Text box, type the text you want to appear if the condition is met. The Else part is the bottom box. In the Otherwise Insert this Text box, type the text you want to appear if the condition is *not* met.

Using the Merge Record # and Merge Sequence # Fields

Inserting a Merge Record # field tells Word to insert a consecutive number in each merged document, starting with 1. The fourteenth document to print would include the number 14.

Inserting a Merge Sequence # field tells Word to include the total number of records merged into the current printout or file.

You could use these fields together to get something like this:

Item 34 of 56

The underlying Word fields are

Item <<Merge Record #>> of <<Merge Sequence #>>

Using the Nextif and Skipif Fields

These two commands are leftovers from Word 2. They determine whether Word should include a given record in the merge. In general, you should use Query Options instead.

Using the Next Field

You can use the Next field to tell Word to print the next record on the same page. But in Word, the Next field has generally been supplanted.

One of the most common applications for this field is catalogs. Accordingly, Word provides a fourth choice, Catalog, for new main documents. When you choose Catalog, Word doesn't jump to the next page when it moves to the next merge record.

Importing Data from Another Data Source

You've already learned how to open an existing data source you might have created earlier using Word's mail merge and database features. But the world is full of database files and relatively few of them started life in Word, much less Word 95.

Fortunately, as you learn in Chapter 20, you can generally import data from other database programs. A Word mail merge can actually *go out and get* data from Access, Microsoft's relational database program, or Excel, Microsoft's spreadsheet program. In these cases, Word initiates a Dynamic Data Exchange (DDE) dialogue with its companion program. In this section, you learn about one example of running mail merge with an external data source, using Microsoft Access (For more information about using DDE, see Chapter 20.)

To import data from Access, follow these steps:

1. Create a main document file the way you normally would: Choose **M**ail Merge from the **T**ools menu, and choose Form **L**etters in the Main Document box.
2. Choose **G**et Data, and choose **O**pen Data Source.
3. Choose Files of **T**ype, and select MS Access Databases from the list. Word then displays a list of all .MDB files available to you.
4. Chances are that not many are in your default Word document directory, so change to the Access subdirectory (see fig. 19.40).

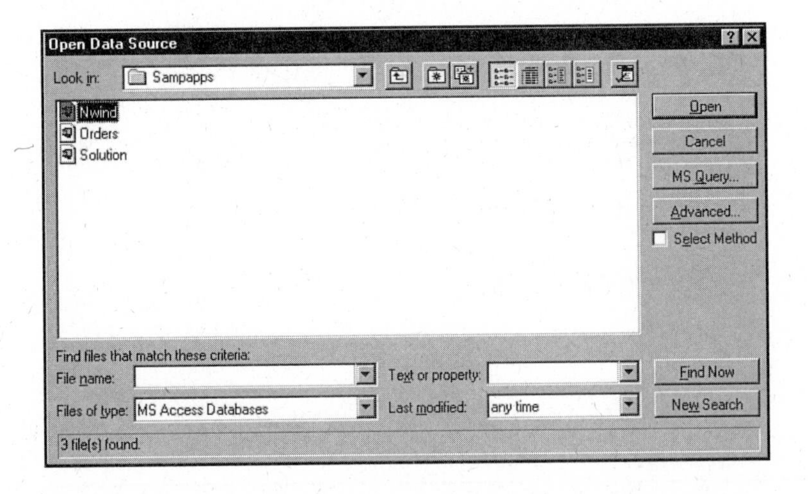

Figure 19.40

Opening the Access database from within Word.

5. Choose the database in which you're interested. This example uses one of the sample databases that comes with Access 2.0: NWIND.MDB, which appears in the SAMPAPPS folder.

   Choosing NWIND.MDB starts the portion of Microsoft Access required for Word to access this database; you might have to wait a little while. Then Word displays a series of tables, as shown in figure 19.41.

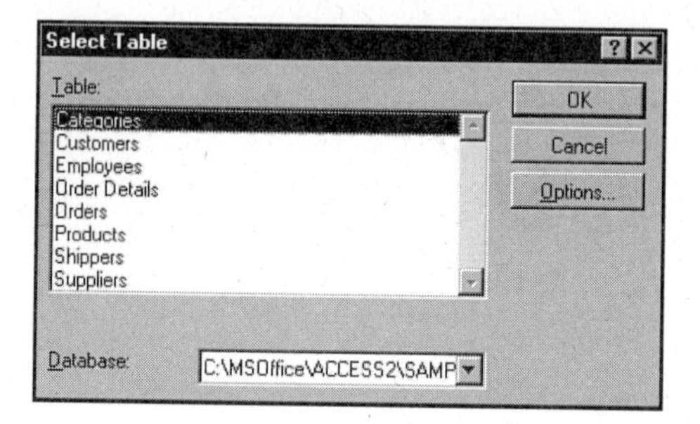

Figure 19.41
The Select Table dialog box.

Access is a relational database; you can access the information in any number of views. The tables listed are the current Access tables that provide views onto the database; you can certainly create others within Access.

If you were using a database of your own, you could define your own table or query within Access, to help make sure that the data that reaches Word is exactly the data you want to merge.

6. When you choose a table (Customers, in this example), Word initiates a Dynamic Data Exchange link with Access. Word then realizes that you're working with a new main document that doesn't have any merge fields in it, so it presents the dialog box shown in figure 19.42.

Figure 19.42
Word asks if you want to edit the main document.

7. Choose Edit **M**ain Document and start adding merge fields. Notice that your field choices are the merge fields from the Access table (Customers in this example). Figure 19.43 shows a dummy document that uses all the Customers fields available.

   Next, you return to the Mail Merge Helper. Because you now have both the main document and data source in place, you're ready to merge.

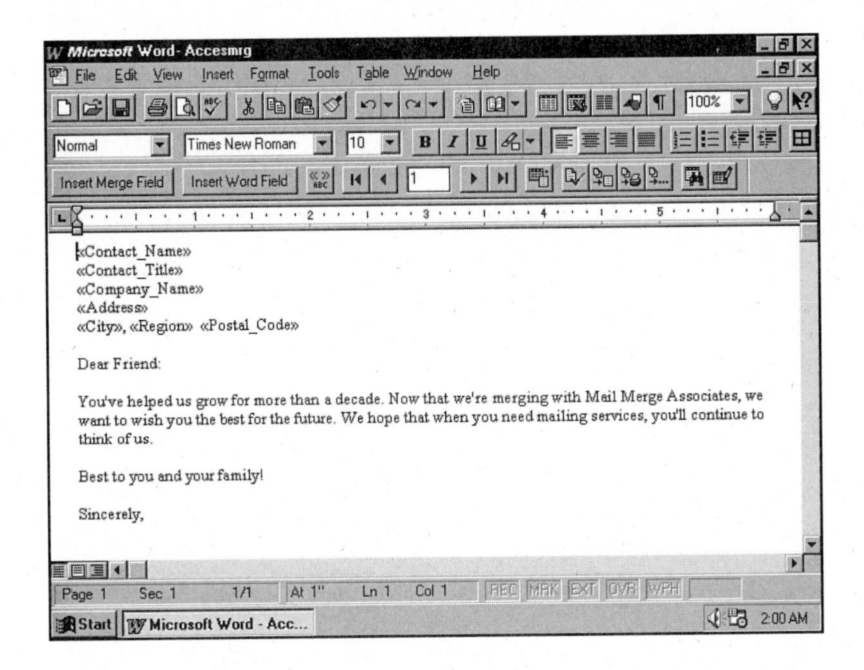

Figure 19.43

A sample document using Access merge fields.

8. Choose **Merge**. Figure 19.44 shows a finished merge as it appears on-screen (merged to a document) in the file Form Letters1.

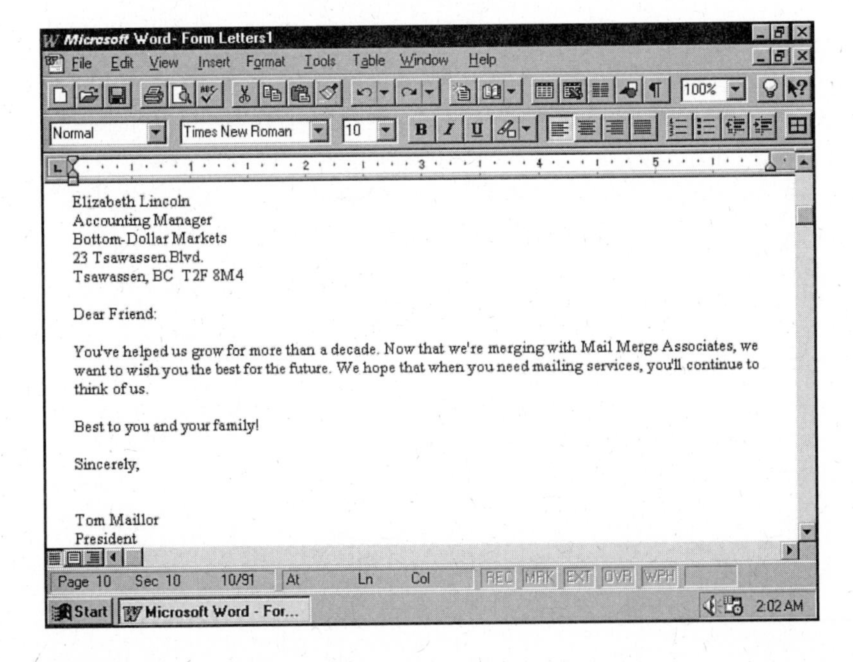

Figure 19.44

Sample merged letters as they appear on-screen.

Part IV

Advanced Features of Word for Windows 95

New Riders Publishing
INSIDE
SERIES

Word as an Integrating Environment

Word 95 is the best available application to act as "Desktop Central" within the Windows 95 environment. Word features not only powerful word-processing capabilities, but also Object Linking and Embedding (OLE), as well as the capability to import database information into your documents.

This chapter covers these features—along with two new Microsoft Office features, *Binders* and the *Office Shortcut Bar,* which simplify the creation of documents you need, leveraging the assistance of other Office applications whenever they're more appropriate.

In this chapter:

- Using Object Linking and Embedding (OLE)
- Creating an object package
- In-place editing via OLE 2.0
- Inserting objects
- Importing databases

- Working with Microsoft Office Binders
- Using the Microsoft Office Shortcut Bar

Exploring Object Linking and Embedding

Object Linking and Embedding (OLE, pronounced "olay") is a Windows communications protocol that enables one application to use the services of other applications. OLE accomplishes this feat by placing information from the source application into the receiving application's document. The application that receives the data is called the *client* and the data source is known as the *server.*

OLE is much more powerful than the Clipboard method of data exchange, because when you change information in the source (server) document, OLE automatically updates the receiving (client) document. In other words, in contrast to traditional cut (or copy) and paste, OLE maintains an ongoing connection between both documents.

Here are some of OLE's advantages:

- **OLE is task-oriented.** OLE enables you to focus on the task rather than the application you need to use to perform the task.
- **OLE is document-centered.** OLE is designed to change the traditional application-centered view of computing that most people have today. After you create a compound document, you can integrate data from a variety of applications. The focus, however, remains on the document—not the source application.
- **OLE is a dynamic form of data exchange.** A linked OLE object can be updated dynamically.
- **OLE is flexible.** An OLE client is an equal-opportunity encapsulater, meaning it doesn't care what objects you embed or link in a document. Nor is it concerned about an object's native format. A compound document, therefore, is assured of compatibility with a future version of a server application.
- **OLE decentralizes your desktop.** OLE enables applications to specialize on a specific task and do it well. An application doesn't have to be a "mega-app" (a word processor, spreadsheet, drawing program, and presentation package all rolled into one). Rather, OLE allows a drawing tool to concentrate on what it does best: drawing. OLE also allows a spreadsheet to concentrate on what it does best: crunching numbers.

Of course, OLE's alleged capability to make modular miniapplications remains more theory than reality. Aside from small programs like Visio Express, which installs into Word and adds business diagramming capabilities, most applications keep getting bigger and more full-featured. Case in point: Word itself.

A World of Objects

As you work with OLE, you first need to get used to the term object, the focus of attention when you talk about OLE. An *OLE object* is a data element that you can display or manipulate. An object can range from a spreadsheet file, a word processing document, an audio or video clip, to a bitmapped image. Figure 20.1 shows a Word document with a number of OLE objects.

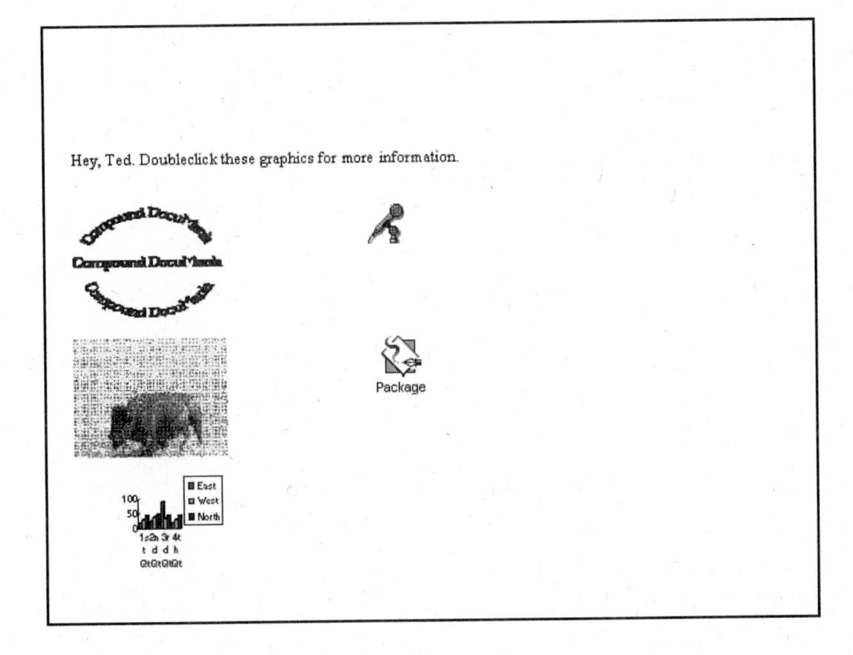

Figure 20.1
Word document that contains multiple OLE objects.

You place OLE objects in a document known as a compound document (or container document). The client application maintains the *compound document,* which can receive objects from one or more server applications. The server provides data in the form of an object to the client and when called upon, allows users to play or edit these objects. You must install a server application on a user's system, although you can place a server document on a LAN.

Note When you use OLE in a networked environment, you need to have a server application on your local drive. You can have a server application on a networked drive, however.

All objects are not the same. Different objects perform different functions, and you work with them differently. Although you play or edit a video clip, you just edit an embedded spreadsheet. The actions an object performs are called *verbs.* In the video clip example, double-clicking on the object causes it to play, so play is the primary verb.

Linking and Embedding Objects

When you place an OLE object in a compound document, you can either *embed* or *link* it:

- **Embedded object.** When you embed an object into an application document, you physically store that data into the receiving application so that it becomes a part of the document. The data contained in the object includes:

    1. Data in a form the client can understand to display the object.
    2. Data to associate the object with the application that created it.
    3. Native data passed to the server application to edit the object. You can place an embedded object by copying and pasting to and from the Clipboard or by using the Insert Object command from the client application's menu.

- **Linked object.** When you link an object, the actual data remains separate from the client document. Instead, a pointer to that data is stored in the compound document and a representation of that object appears. The actual object data remains in its original location.

    A linked object enables you to continue to work with it within the server application apart from the client application. A linked object remains independent of the compound document, whereas an embedded object exists only within the confines of the compound document. You must copy and paste a linked object using the Clipboard—just the way you create a DDE link. If the client application supports OLE, it treats the data as an OLE object.

Note The key difference between embedded and linked objects lies in the storage method for each. An embedded object doesn't exist outside of a compound document, whereas a linked object does. As a result, a linked object requires much less storage space. The difference between a linked and embedded object should be seamless for the user, however, because double-clicking on a linked or embedded object invokes the source application to play or edit the object.

Object linking is advantageous in a networked environment because you can maintain a single source document and have it represented in many compound documents throughout the network. An embedded alternative could be a nightmare. Suppose, for example, that you embedded a video clip in an electronic mail message to 10 people in your workgroup. The video clip is rather lengthy and takes up 5 MB of space. Because the object is embedded (that is, the video clip is stored within the mail message), the mail message becomes 5 MB.

Thus, as you send that message to ten people, the network has 50 MB of space devoted to that single 5 MB message. If you store the video clip file on a networked drive and link it to the mail message, however, each member of your workgroup can access that same linked object. Sending the embedded object requires 50 MB of space to send a 5 MB message to 10 persons, whereas the linked object requires just over 5 MB of space. If your object is small, however, embedding the object in the mail message is much easier.

Using OLE

Now that you have a background on what OLE is and what it can do, you can learn how to use it in Word for Windows 95.

Creating an OLE Link

To create an OLE link between Word and another application, follow these steps:

1. Open the source application, and copy the text, graphics, or other material into the clipboard.

2. Switch to Word 95.

3. Place your insertion point where you want the information to be located, and select Paste Special from the Edit menu. The Paste Special dialog box opens (see fig. 20.2).

4. Select Paste Link to establish the link.

5. If you have a choice, select the application you want the linked object to be connected with, in the As box.

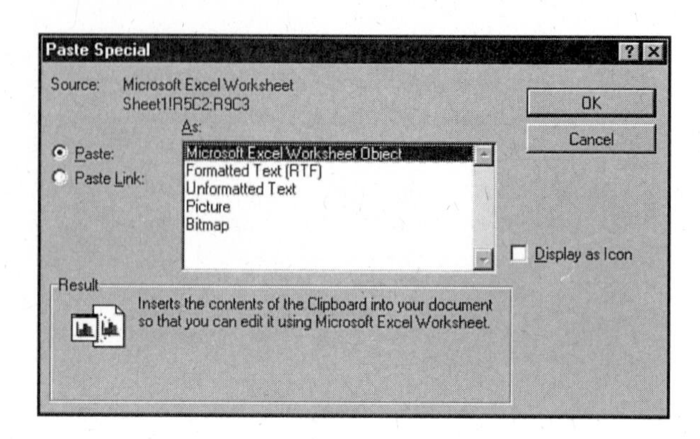

Figure 20.2

The Paste Special dialog box.

When you view field codes, your linked text or image is replaced by a code like the following:

```
{ LINK Excel.Sheet.5 "D:\\WordBook\\results1.xls" "Sheet1!R5C2:R9C3"
\a \p }
```

In this example, Excel.Sheet.5 specifies the source application, Microsoft Excel, and that the source file is a worksheet. D:\\WordBook\\results1.xls specifies the file name and path to the file; Sheet1!R5C2:R9C3 specifies the cells to be included.

Finally, \a tells Word to update the link automatically whenever it changes; \p tells Word that this link is in "picture" format. Of course, the Excel worksheet object isn't really a picture; this just means you're viewing a representation of the file or its contents, as opposed to another. To edit this data in Excel, double-click on it.

Managing Links

By default, Word automatically updates links whenever it opens a document or whenever a linked document changes during the active session for the Word document linked to it. You can, however, control how any Word link behaves. Select the linked object, and then choose Lin**k**s from the **E**dit menu to open the Links dialog box (see fig. 20.3).

The first decision you have to make is simply this: Do you want the link Updates to be **A**utomatic, as this chapter has described? Would you prefer **M**anual links that only update when you choose **U**pdate Now in this dialog box? Or how about Loc**k**ed links that don't update at all until you unlock them?

Or you can break the link altogether by clicking on the **B**reak Link button. This commonly is done for archival reasons, when you want a document to retain the linked information in the form it existed when you sent it.

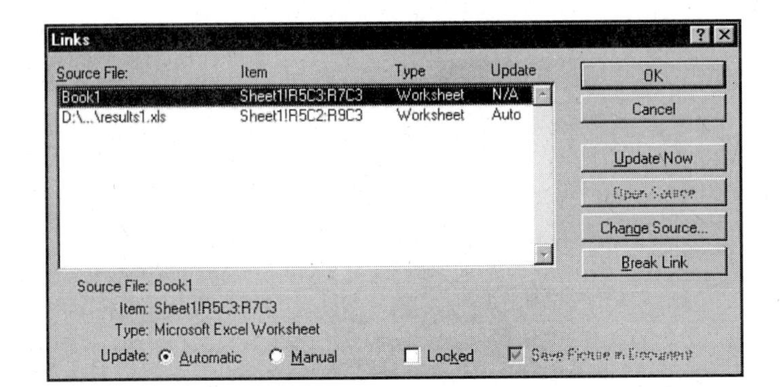

Figure 20.3

The Links dialog box.

Open Source enables you to open the source application, so you can edit the linked text or image directly. Change Source opens the dialog box shown in figure 20.4, in which you can select a new source file or a new part of the same source file. This means you could use Change Source to display a different image, or different cells within the same spreadsheet.

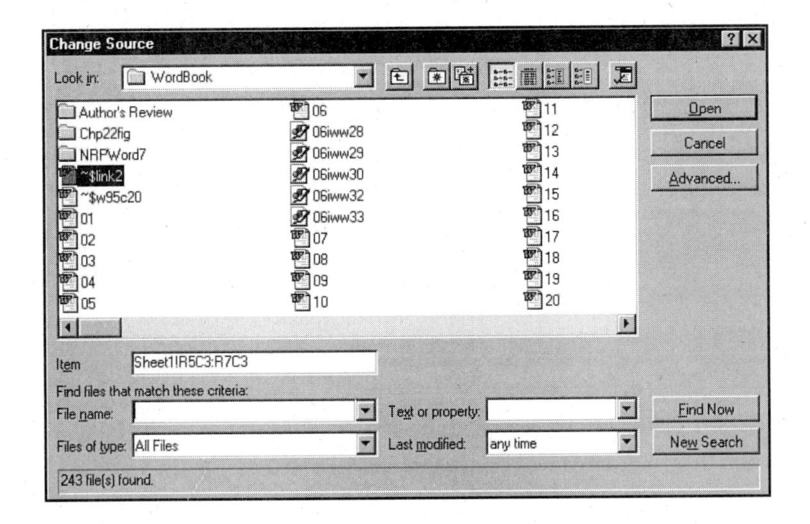

Figure 20.4

The Change Source dialog box.

The Change Source dialog box resembles the File Open dialog box. You can browse to find the new file and insert it in the File name box. If necessary, change folders or drives. Then, if necessary, edit Item to reflect the new range of cells or pixels in the object you want to link. (If you've linked the entire object, you don't need to do this.)

Because you can't see the new source when you work in Change Source, you might sometimes find simply deleting the existing link (and creating a new one) more practical. To do so, just open the source application and choose the source directly.

Creating a New Object from Scratch

To embed a *new* object, choose **O**bject from the **I**nsert menu to open the Object dialog box, which reveals the **C**reate New tab (see fig. 20.5).

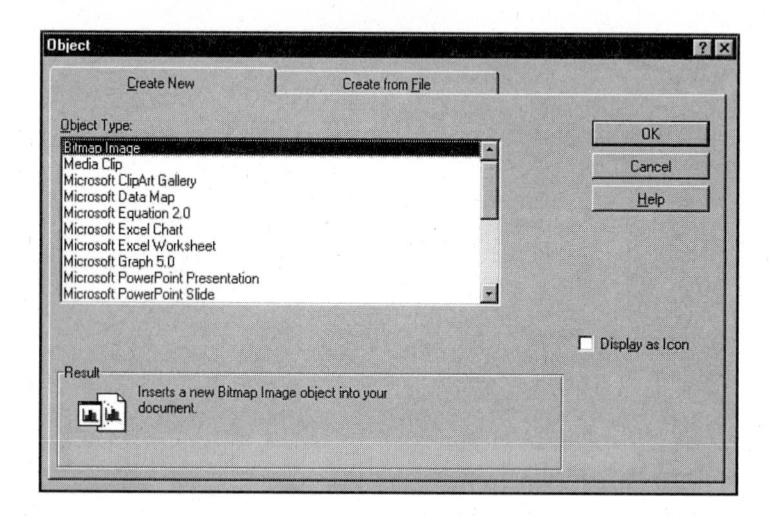

Figure 20.5
Object dialog box with the Create New tab showing.

The **C**reate New tab presents you with a list of all programs on your computer that are registered to perform object embedding. Select one. If you want to embed the object to appear in your document as an icon, as shown in figure 20.6, enable the Displ**a**y as Icon check box. (If you display the object as an icon, it also prints as an icon.)

Figure 20.6
Displaying an object as an icon.

Occasionally, you might have a program that can embed objects but isn't listed on the Create New tab. This might mean the program wasn't installed properly; reinstalling it often solves the problem.

Now the source application opens. Create the contents of the object here. After you finish, choose **E**xit (which sometimes might be called **E**xit and Return or something similar). If prompted to update your document, choose **Y**es.

The embedded object appears in your document, in its original form or as an icon. If you embed a sound object, such as a voice annotation recorded by microphone, a small speaker appears (see fig. 20.7). You can always double-click on the object to edit it.

Please listen to the voice annotation by double-clicking this box:

Figure 20.7

Speaker icon indicates a sound object is embedded.

Embedding an Existing File

Often, you might want to embed all or part of an existing file. To embed an entire file:

1. Choose Object from the Insert menu.
2. Choose the Create from File tab (see fig. 20.8).

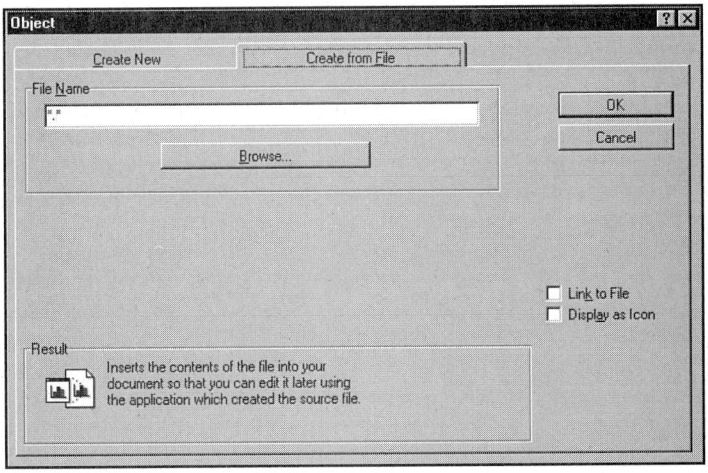

Figure 20.8

The Create from File tab.

3. If you know the name and path associated with the file you want, enter the file name; otherwise, choose **Browse** and select the file from the Browse dialog box.
4. If you want the file to display as an icon, enable the Display as Icon check box.
5. Choose OK.

To embed part of a file:

1. Place the insertion point where you want to embed the object.
2. Open the source file in the source application; select the part you want to embed.

3. Copy it to the Clipboard.
4. Choose Paste Special, as if you were creating a link.
5. Choose Paste.
6. When you select the object type in the As box, select the first option that includes the word object.
7. If you want the file to display as an icon, enable the Display as Icon check box.

Editing and Converting Objects

Once in a while you create an object in one application and then want to edit it in another. You can do so in the following instances:

- You purchase a new version of your software.
- You receive a file that contains an object created by software you don't own.
- You decide you prefer a different spreadsheet or graphics program from the one in which you created it.
- You've imported a graphic you can edit within Word and you want to shrink your file size. (In this case, you can convert your object to a Word Picture. It'll be smaller, but afterward, you can't convert it back to its original application format.)

To convert an object, use the following steps:

1. Select the object.
2. Choose Object from the Edit menu. Note that this menu option changes depending on the type of object you select. If you choose a picture object rather than a sound object, for example, this menu item appears as Picture Object instead of Wave Object.
3. Choose Convert to open the Convert dialog box (see fig. 20.9).
4. In Object Type, select the type of object you want your object to become.
5. You now have two choices: You can convert this object permanently to the new type of object by choosing Convert To. Or, you can open every object like this one as if it were the new kind of object without actually converting the object (choose Activate As).
6. Choose OK.

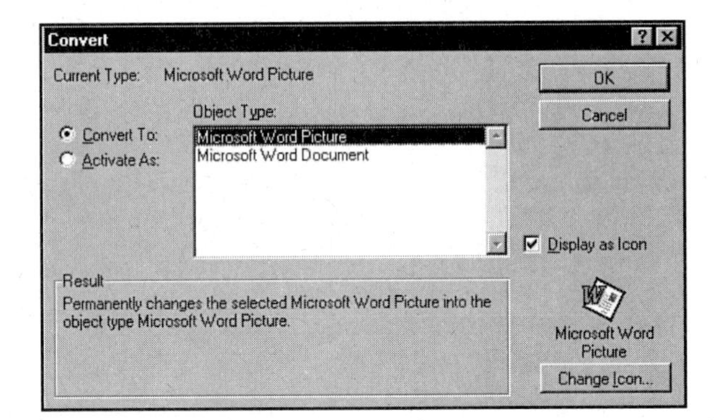

Figure 20.9
The Convert dialog box.

In-Place Editing with OLE 2.0

Version 2.0 of OLE, first incorporated in Word 6 and now included in Word 95 and the other Office 95 applications, offers even better integration among applications. Before OLE 2.0, double-clicking on an object would open the software used to create that object in a new window. You would revise the object in that software, and after you finished, you would exit that software, updating the object.

In contrast, when you click on an OLE 2.0 object, the menus from its source application appear in place of Word's menus. You can double-click on the Excel worksheet embedded in your Word document and work on it just as if you were in Excel; then click on the text next to it and work on that in Word.

To insert a Microsoft Excel worksheet object in a Word document, use the following steps:

1. Click on the Insert Microsoft Excel Worksheet button on the Standard toolbar.
2. Select the number of rows and columns you want in your Excel spreadsheet.

For OLE 2.0 objects, opening and exiting applications becomes a thing of the past. All your tools appear to be part of one big application in which the tools that appear are the ones you just happen to need at the moment.

It's a nifty vision, and many vendors have announced support for it. But announcing support and delivering products are two different things. OLE 2.0 is complex. So the age of *total* integration isn't quite here yet—but it's fast approaching.

Importing Databases

In Chapter 19, you learn how a Word mail merge can retrieve data directly from Microsoft Access. But you often might want to retrieve data from another database application—not just for mail merges. Word offers a command, **I**nsert **D**atabase, designed specifically for accomplishing this deed.

If you've read Chapter 19, "Automating Mail Merge Tasks," some of this will sound familiar.

The most basic database retrieval simply gathers all the information in a database file and inserts it into a Word table, at which point you can edit it. To accomplish that, do the following:

1. Choose **D**atabase from the **I**nsert menu. The Database dialog box appears (see fig. 20.10).

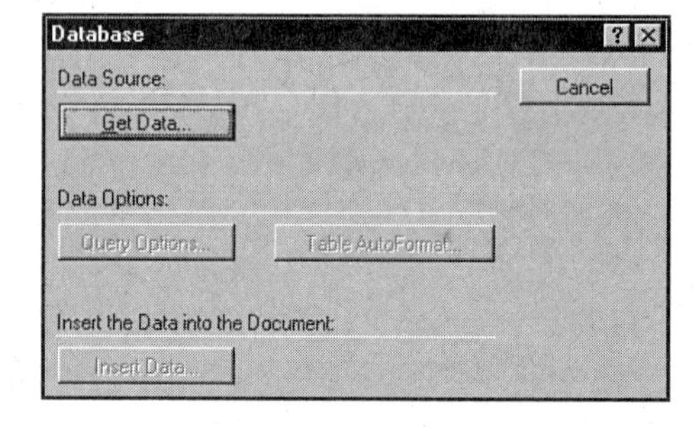

Figure 20.10
The Database dialog box.

2. Choose **G**et Data. The Open Data Source dialog box appears (see fig. 20.11).

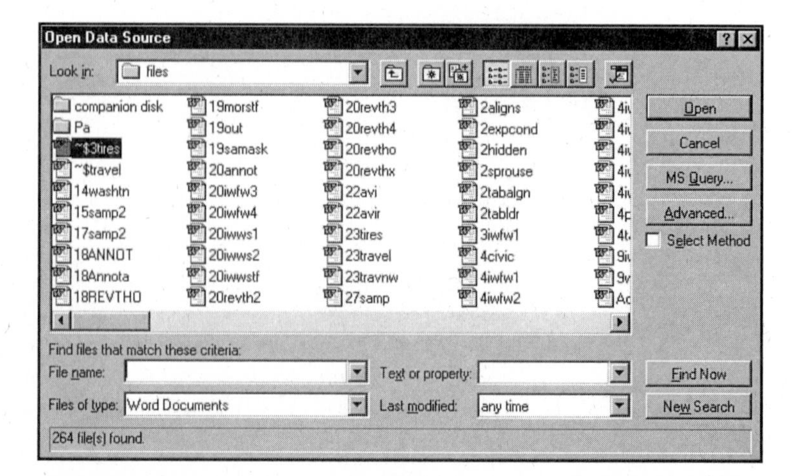

Figure 20.11
The Open Data Source dialog box.

3. Select the type of database file you want to open from the Files of type list box. Word's available choices are listed in table 20.1. If your file doesn't show up here, select All Files.

TABLE 20.1
Types of Database Files Word Can Open without Assistance

Document	Extension
Word Documents	(*.doc)
Rich Text Format	(*.rtf)
Text Files	(*.txt)
Microsoft Access Databases	(*.mdb)
Microsoft Excel Databases	(*.xls)
Microsoft FoxPro Files	(*.dbf)
Microsoft Query Files	(*.qry)
dBASE Files	(*.dbf)
Paradox Files	(*.db)

Word can successfully retrieve data from Microsoft Access, FoxPro, Borland Paradox 3.x, and dBASE IV because it comes with Open Database Connectivity (ODBC) drivers for these products.

If you have another database, find out if that database supports ODBC. If not, you can still use that database's data by exporting it to a file format Word can understand, such as comma- or tab-delimited files.

4. Select the file you want. You might need to change **Directories** or Drives, or use Find File.
5. If you want Word to prompt you to confirm file conversion attempts, check Confirm Conversions.
6. Choose OK.

After you reach the data, you need to decide which data you want. If you use Microsoft Access, you can select from a table or query built into your Access table, as covered in Chapter 19. Otherwise, you need to return to the Insert Database dialog box.

7. Choose **Q**uery Options to open the Query Options dialog box.

   You now have three choices:

   a. In the **F**ilter Records tab of the Query Options dialog box (see fig. 20.12), you can filter the records for only the information that meets certain criteria (covered in detail in Chapter 19, "Automating Mail Merge Tasks").

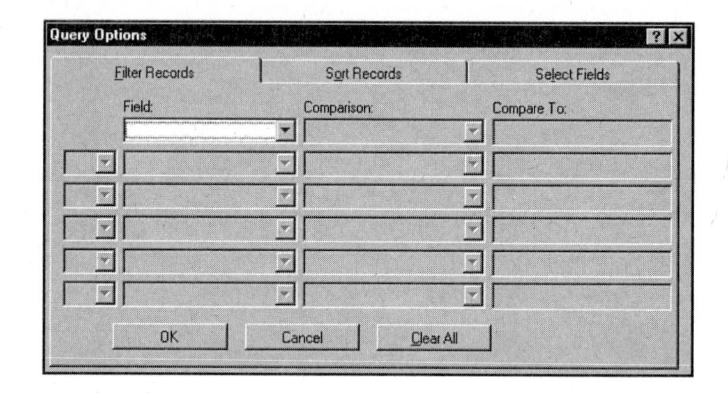

Figure 20.12
The Filter Records Tab.

   To do this:

   i. Select a field from the list of fields Word found in your database. (If you use a table or tab-delimited file, Word assumes that the top line contains your fields.)

   ii. Then make a comparison, using one of the options Word provides.

   iii. Generally, you need to provide text or a number to which Word can compare.

   b. On the S**o**rt Records tab in the Query Options dialog box (see fig. 20.13), specify the order in which you want to sort the records (covered in detail in Chapter 19).

   c. On the Se**l**ect Fields tab in the Query Options dialog box (see fig. 20.14), tell Word from which fields you want to retrieve information.

   Word assumes you want them all. To delete one, select it in the Selec**t**ed Fields list box, then choose **R**emove. To delete them all, choose R**e**move All.

   To *add* a field, select it in the Fields in **D**ata Source list box, then choose **S**elect. To add them all, choose S**e**lect All.

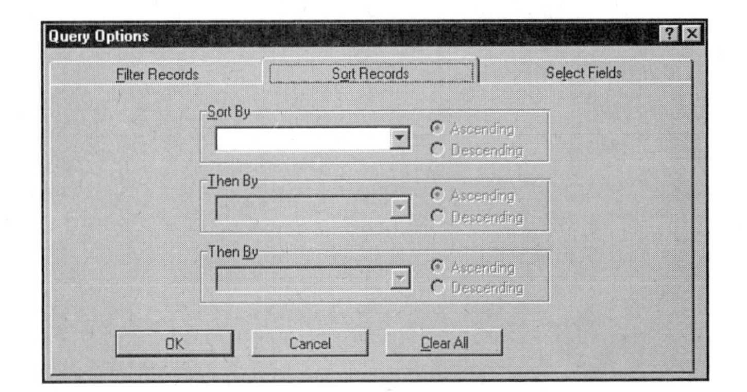

Figure 20.13
The Sort Records tab.

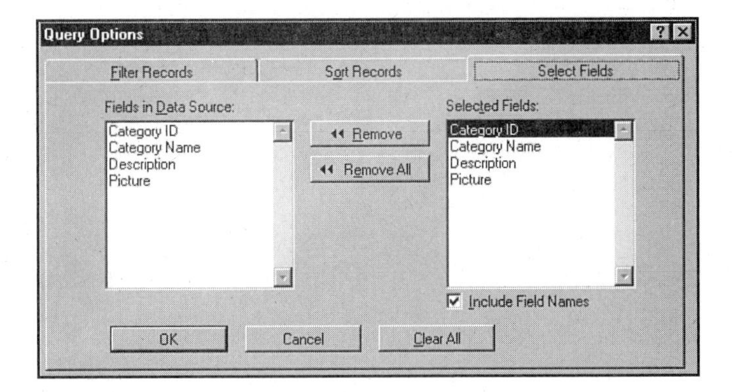

Figure 20.14
The Select Fields tab.

By default, Word adds the field names at the top row of the data table being imported. You might not want them, though. (If you do a mail merge later, you might be providing a separate header source.) To not include them, deselect Include Field Names.

To finish, click on OK.

8. You now have a table. To automatically format it, choose Table AutoFormat from the Database dialog box, select a format, and choose OK (optional).

9. After you're done, choose Insert Data to open the Insert Data dialog box (see fig. 20.15).

   Simply choosing OK inserts all the information. You can select only certain records by specifying the starting and ending record numbers in the From and To box.

Figure 20.15
The Insert Data dialog box.

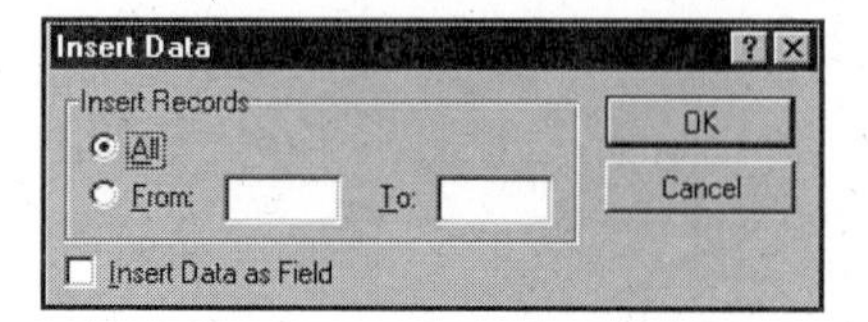

If you plan to update the information regularly, specify **I**nsert Data as Field. This places the information in the document in the form of a {DATABASE} field that you can update to reflect changes in the original database document at any time by selecting it and pressing F9.

Note The {DATABASE} field works only if the file used by the original application still contains the information, *and* if the original application still resides on your system. If you have to export it to a separate tab-delimited file that the original application no longer directly uses, {DATABASE} doesn't work.

Merging with Other Databases

Word still can use data from other database programs even if they don't have this luxurious level of interactivity. Word can recognize text files exported from your database program as a tab-delimited or comma-delimited text file.

Note A *delimiter* is a character that separates one field or record from another.

Occasionally, you might have to perform some cleanup. Your goal, of course, is to come up with something as close to a Word database table as possible.

If Word isn't sure about the contents of your file, it requests help by opening the Header Record Delimiters dialog box, shown in figure 20.16.

Figure 20.16
The Header Record Delimiters dialog box.

You can tell Word the characters you want it to use to separate (delimit) fields, and which ones to use to separate records. Of course, these should be different; otherwise, Word would think everything is part of one gigantic record. Word previews the results of your choices in the box at the bottom of the screen; you can scroll this box through the entire document.

If this dialog box appears, however, you might want to check out the condition of your database manually before you let Word make any conversions.

You might find some simple problem that you can fix with a global Replace command, which allows Word to recognize your database and open it relatively cleanly. (Remember, Word's Edit Replace feature can search and replace tabs, paragraph marks, and many other special characters.)

Using Advanced Searches

If you're not sure where to find your database information, Word 95's Open Data Source and Advanced Find dialog boxes provide the same advanced search capabilities you've seen in the new File, Open dialog box.

1. Choose Database from the Insert menu, which opens the Database dialog box.
2. Choose Get Data, which opens the Open Data Source dialog box.
3. Choose Advanced, which opens the Advanced Find dialog box.
4. Perform a search following the same procedures discussed in Chapter 6, "File Management." (Searches are covered there at length, starting in the section "Using File, Open to Manage and Locate Files," and continuing through the section "Performing Advanced Searches.")

Using Binders to Combine Multiple Documents

Occasionally, you might have related documents you would like to work with together; perhaps Word documents, as well as worksheets created in Excel or presentations created in PowerPoint. If you came by Microsoft Word as part of Microsoft Office, you have access to Microsoft Binder, a program that enables you to assemble multiple files from different Office programs and work with them from a single location. You can even integrate the page numbering among documents in the same binder, even if they were created using different Office programs.

You can use Binder to pull together existing files, create new files and place them in empty binders, or use one of four built-in Binders that already include Word, Excel, and PowerPoint templates.

Microsoft Binder is shown in figure 20.17. To create a new binder, choose New Binder from the File menu. The New Binder window opens. To start from a blank binder, choose Blank Binder and then OK. To select from among the built-in binder templates, choose the Binders tab, highlight a binder, and choose OK.

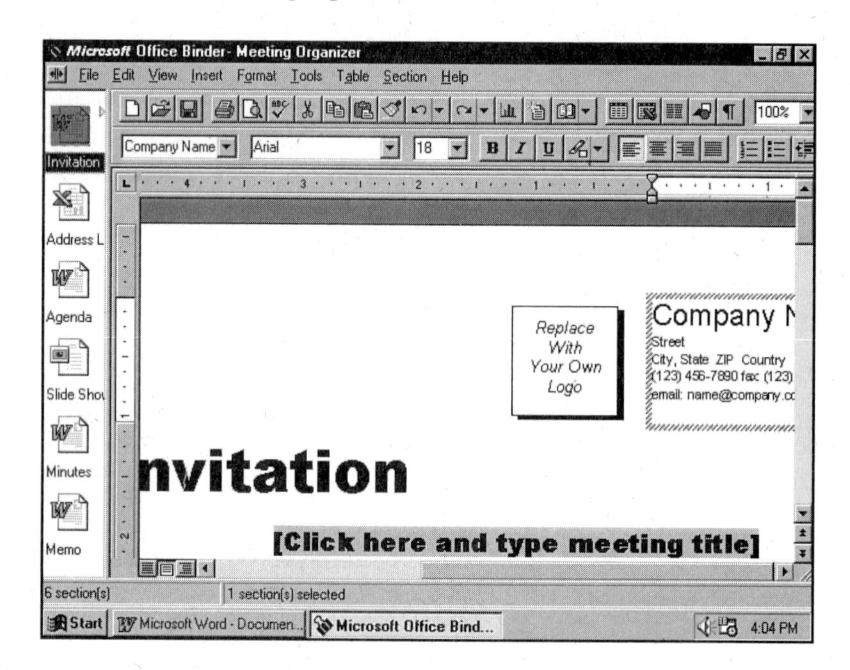

Figure 20.17
Microsoft Binder.

The following list describes the built-in binders:

- **Client Billing.** Includes an Excel file that contains a wizard that walks you through the billing process; Word templates for fax cover sheets, cover letters, and attachments; and Excel templates for an Invoice and Timecard.
- **Meeting Organizer.** Includes Word templates for invitations, agendas, minutes, and memos; an Excel template for address lists; and a PowerPoint slide show template.
- **Proposal and Marketing Plan.** Includes Word templates for cover letters, referrals, details, and follow-ups; Excel template for quotes; and a PowerPoint slide show template.

- **Report.** Includes Word templates for cover letters, executive summaries, and analyses; an Excel template for supporting data; and a PowerPoint slide show template.

Working with Binders

After you open a binder, the files in that binder appear as icons along the left-hand side of your screen. To open a file, double-click on its icon; the file opens in whatever application it requires, with all the application's capabilities. You might not immediately notice the change, because the title bar still says Microsoft Office Binder—and because Microsoft Office applications share all but one menu, as well as many of the same toolbar buttons. (This is an example of what Microsoft means by document-centric computing—documents become more prominent than the applications that display them.)

If you want to dedicate the entire screen to the document you're working on, click on the left/right arrow button to the left of the **File** menu.

Managing Your Binder

When you work in Binder, several new Binder commands appear in the **File** menu, as shown in figure 20.18.

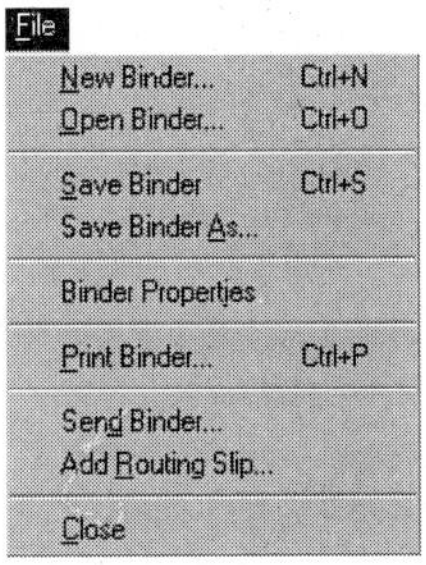

File
New Binder... Ctrl+N
Open Binder... Ctrl+O
Save Binder Ctrl+S
Save Binder As...
Binder Properties
Print Binder... Ctrl+P
Send Binder...
Add Routing Slip...
Close

Figure 20.18

Microsoft Office Binder's File menu.

A new menu also appears, called **Section** (see fig. 20.19). A set of File commands that enable you to manage the binder as a whole replaces your normal **File** commands. The **Section** commands enable you to manage, add, and remove binder sections, and control some elements of individual sections formerly controlled from the **File** menu. The **Section** menu, for example, provides commands for managing a section's Page Set**u**p, for Prin**t**ing a section, and for viewing Section Propert**i**es. From within the Binder, each section looks and behaves like a separate document file, even though they are *not* separate files—they're all part of one Binder file, stored with an OBD extension.

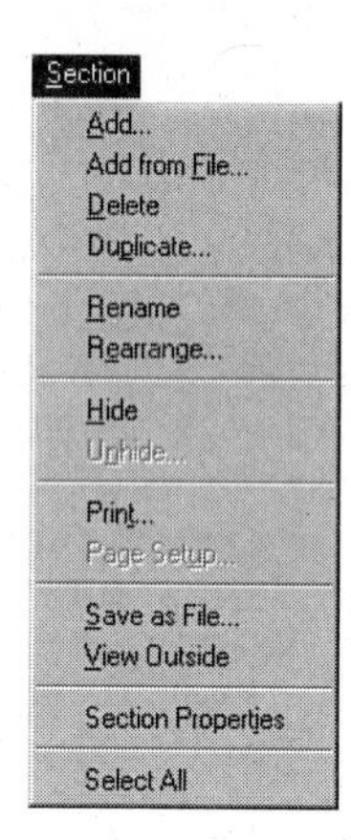

Figure 20.19

The Section menu in Microsoft Office Binder.

Adding New Blank Binder Sections

To add a new blank section to an existing binder, choose Add from the Section menu to open the Add Section dialog box (see fig. 20.20). Choose the Office application in which you want the new file to be created. Choose OK. The new file is created with a generic name, such as Section 1. To rename the file, click in its file name, and after the rectangle appears, enter the new file name.

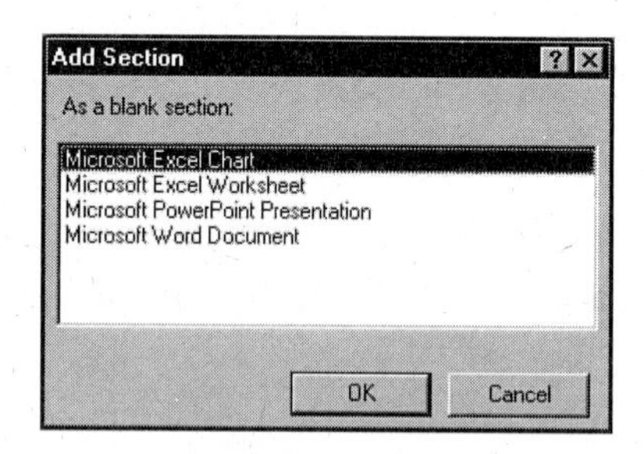

Figure 20.20

The Add Section dialog box in Microsoft Office Binder.

Incorporating an Existing File in a Binder

To include an existing file in an Office binder, choose Add from File from the Section menu to open the Add From File dialog box, which works like the File Open dialog box: locate the file you want to include and choose Add. When you add a file to your binder, you create a duplicate copy of it. Changes you make in the copy within the Binder aren't reflected in the original copy, nor are changes you make in the original copy reflected in the Binder.

Rearranging Files in a Binder

To rearrange the files in a binder, position the mouse pointer on the small yellow arrow to the top right of its Binder icon (see fig. 20.21), and drag it to the location you prefer, or choose Rearrange from the Section menu, select the section you want to move, and use the Move Up and Move Down buttons to relocate the section where you want it.

Figure 20.21

Moving a section within a Microsoft Office Binder.

Viewing a Section from Outside the Binder

You occasionally might want to view a document from inside Word itself rather than from inside Microsoft Binder. For example, you can't run Word's Print Preview command from inside a Binder. To open a section inside Word itself, display the section, and then choose View Outside from the Section menu.

Keep in mind that the section still isn't a separate file. You can, however, create a separate file that contains the section. If you already are viewing the file from outside the Binder, choose Save Copy As from the File menu. (As you might already have noticed, when you view a section from outside the Binder, the File menu changes yet again.)

Save Copy As essentially acts the same as Word's Save As command, and creates a separate copy of the file that exists only outside the Binder. After you use Save Copy As, however, the original section remains open, so the changes you make in your current session are stored in the Binder, not in the new duplicate file. After you use Save Copy As, changes you make in the Binder section aren't reflected in the duplicate file, or vice versa. If, however, you later update the duplicate file, you can always remove the original section from the Binder and insert the revised copy.

To simply update the Binder file that includes the section you're editing, choose Update from the File menu, the equivalent of the File, Save command. In fact, the keyboard shortcut Ctrl+S updates a binder section just as it normally would save a file. To update not only the current section but any other binder sections that have been changed since the last save, choose Save and Update All from the File menu.

After you finish working outside the Binder, you can return to the Binder by choosing Close and Return to from the File menu.

Using the Microsoft Office Shortcut Bar

If you purchase Word with Microsoft Office, another bonus you get is the Microsoft Office Shortcut Bar (OSB). If you've installed it, the OSB gives you a quick way to create or open documents, open other programs, or perform tasks built into Microsoft Schedule+, such as making an appointment. To view the OSB, click the Start button on the Windows 95 Taskbar, and choose Microsoft Office Shortcut Bar from the Programs menu. The Shortcut bar appears on your Word title bar, as shown in figure 20.22.

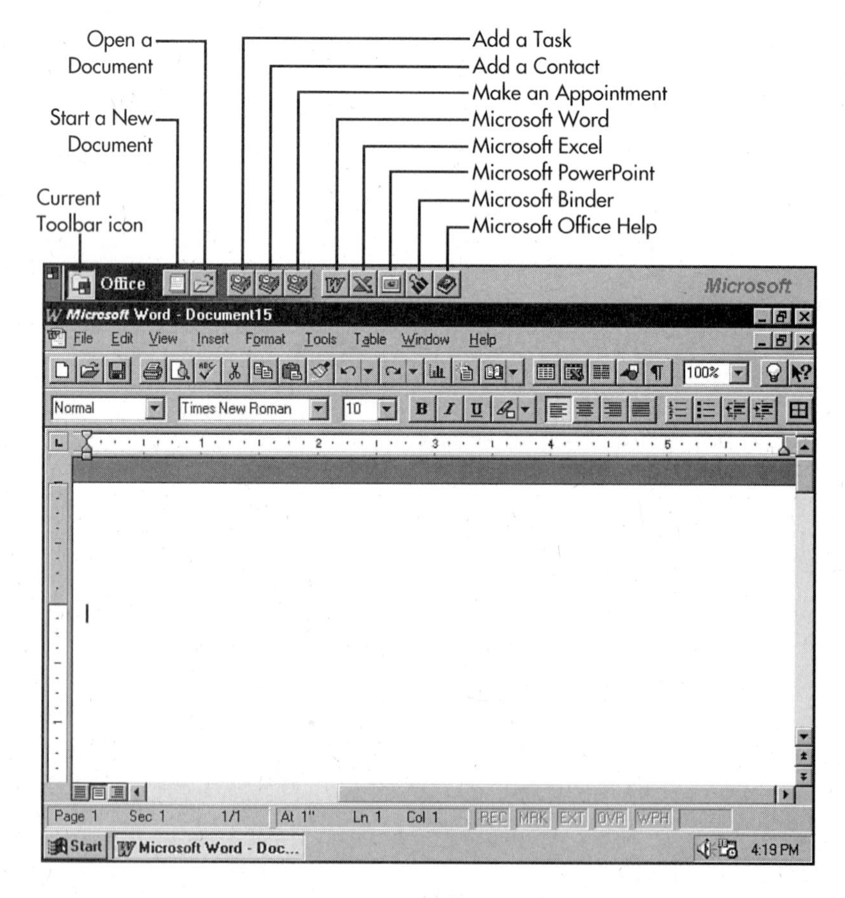

Figure 20.22

The Microsoft Office Shortcut Bar.

If you don't want to use the Office Shortcut Bar, you can add program icons to one of your existing Word toolbars, using the Tools, Customize features discussed in Chapter 24. If you use Microsoft Office, you might want to start with the Microsoft toolbar, which includes several icons for Office programs. You also can write macros that open specific files or new files based on specific templates, and then attach those macros to toolbar buttons.

Choosing an Office Shortcut Bar

You can choose among several predefined shortcut toolbars:

- **Office.** Shows the Office programs, as illustrated by figure 20.22.
- **Desktop.** Shows all the program icons that currently appear on your Windows desktop. You can use Desktop as an alternative to minimizing Word and viewing the desktop.
- **Favorites.** Displays the files you store in the Favorites folder (as discussed in Chapter 6)—generally, the files you use most often.
- **msn.** Shows the Microsoft Network startup icon and any Microsoft Network shortcuts added to your Windows 95 desktop.
- **Programs.** Displays Microsoft Office programs; major components of Windows 95, such as Windows Explorer, Microsoft Exchange, The Microsoft Network, and an MS-DOS prompt; and other programs available from the desktop.
- **Accessories.** Shows Windows 95 accessory programs, such as Paint and WordPad.

You choose an OSB toolbar the same way you choose a Word toolbar: right-click on an empty space on the toolbar and choose from the pop-up menu, as shown in figure 20.23.

Moving an Office Shortcut Bar

You can drag the Office Shortcut Bar anywhere you want: click on an empty portion of the OSB toolbar and drag. Some users like to keep the shortcut bar along the right edge of the screen, to the right of the scroll bars, as shown in figure 20.24. If you have a large monitor, you might even let it float in an otherwise empty space, as shown in figure 20.25. The Word window resizes automatically to accommodate the shortcut bar on the top or side of the screen.

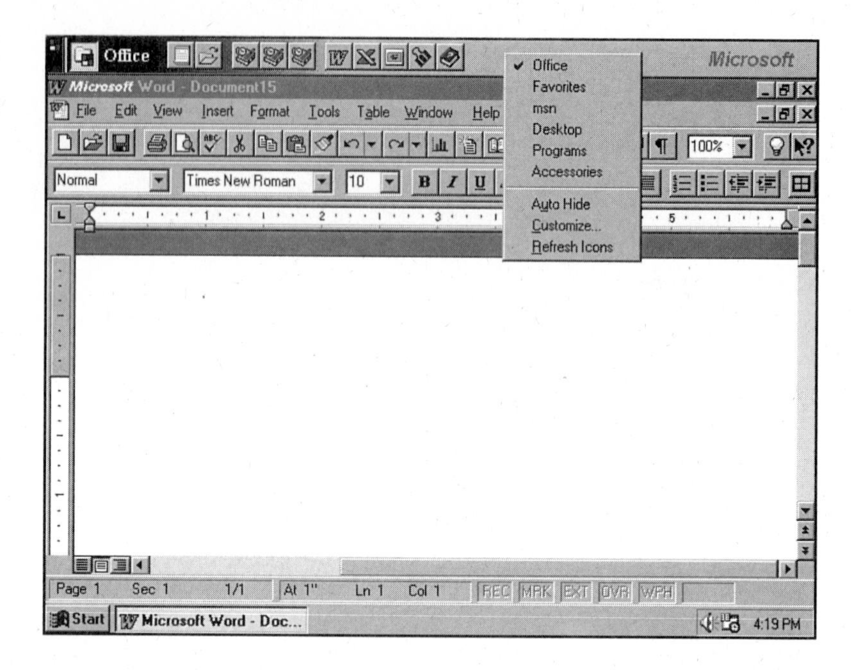

Figure 20.23
Choosing an OSB toolbar.

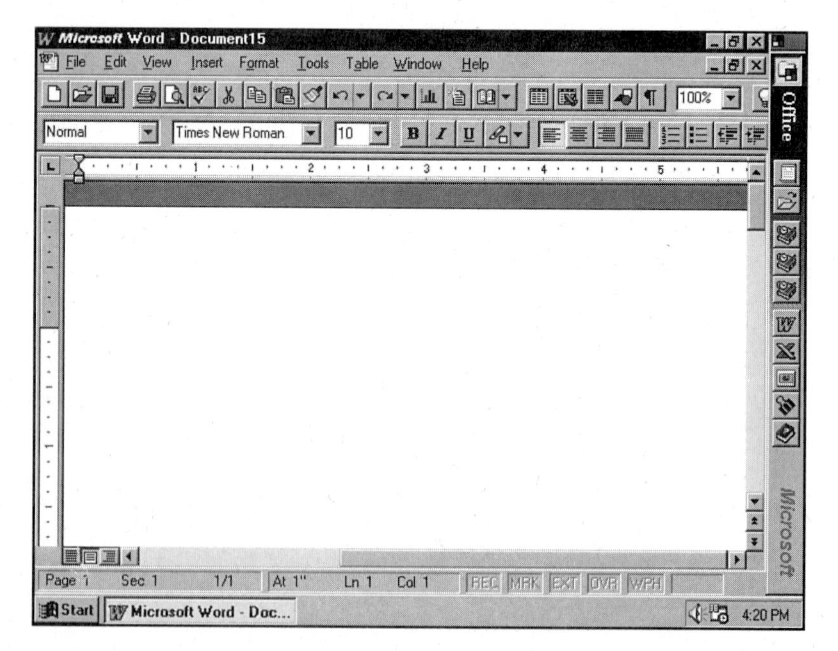

Figure 20.24
OSB toolbar along right-edge of screen.

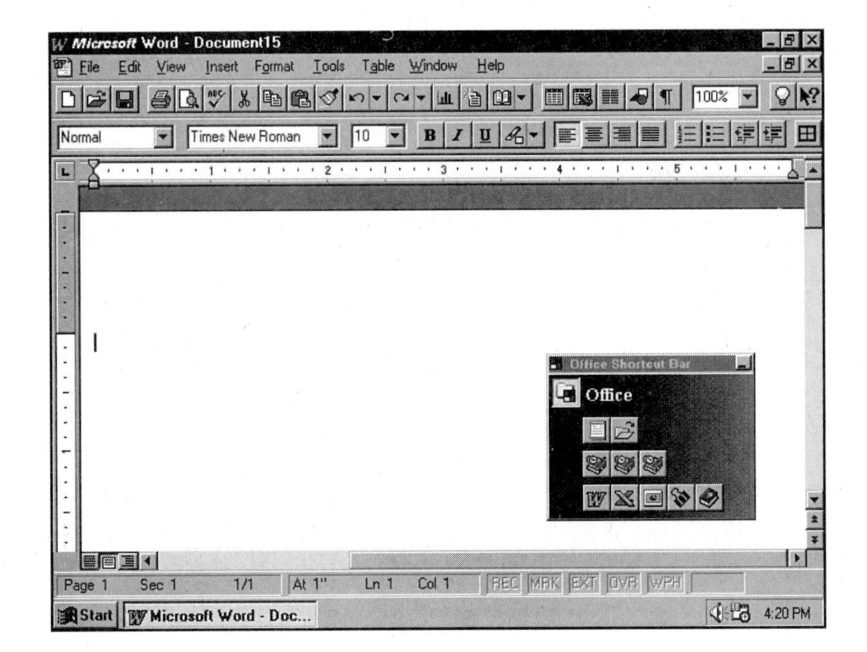

Figure 20.25
Floating OSB toolbar.

Customizing the Office Shortcut Bar

You can customize any open toolbar by right-clicking on the Office Shortcut Bar menu button at the left edge of the Microsoft Office Shortcut Bar and choosing Customize from the pop-up menu. The Customize dialog box appears; it contains the following four tabs:

- **View.** Allows you to customize the color and appearance of the toolbar itself, whether it uses small or large buttons, and several other aspects of toolbar behavior. For example, you can choose to Animate Toolbars and use Sound whenever you click a button.

- **Buttons.** Lets you check or clear boxes to display or hide buttons for each program or file available on an open toolbar. (You can't check or clear boxes in a toolbar you haven't displayed.) You also can add buttons for additional programs or folders by clicking on Add File or Add Folder. Finally, you can move toolbar buttons within a toolbar by using the up- and down-arrow Move buttons.

- **Toolbars.** Enables you to specify which toolbars to display and to create new toolbars. After you display a toolbar here, you can use the other tabs to customize it. Creating new toolbars is especially useful if you use an eclectic group of programs and files—not simply the ones Microsoft sells!
- **Settings.** Controls where Office stores templates for individual users and for your workgroup.

To create a new toolbar, follow these steps:

1. Choose Customize from the Tools menu. The Customize tabbed dialog box appears.
2. Choose the Toolbars tab.
3. Choose Add Toolbar to open the Add Toolbar dialog box (see fig. 20.26).

Figure 20.26
The Add Toolbar dialog box.

4. Click Create a new, blank Toolbar, and enter the name of the toolbar.
5. Choose OK.
6. The next step is to populate your new toolbar with buttons. Choose the Buttons tab, and choose Add File. Locate the program or file icon you want to add, and choose Add.
7. Repeat step 5 for each program or file icon you want to add.
8. Choose OK.

Using the Office Shortcut Bar to Install or Remove Word Program Components

Somewhere along the line, you might need to install or remove a component of Word. You might, for example, begin to receive files in an unusual format that requires you to use an import filter you never needed. This requires you to run the Office Setup program again. If you installed Microsoft Office Shortcut Bar and the Office Setup program when you installed Office, finding and running Office Setup is much easier.

Simply choose Add/Remove Office Programs from the Office Shortcut Bar menu. If you have installed several Microsoft programs, you are prompted for which one you want to install or uninstall. Choose the program; if you want to install new components to Word, choose Office. The Office setup program runs; from there you can specify which Word, Excel, PowerPoint, or other Office components you want to add or remove.

Desktop Publishing and Drawing

What program comes with the capability to import graphics from any Windows application, create multicolumn layouts, use drop caps, embed TrueType fonts for delivery to a typesetting machine, and also provides built-in brochure and newsletter designs, 14 fonts, 100 clip-art images, and built-in drawing and font effects software? You've got it. It's Word 95.

Word isn't quite a desktop publishing (DTP) program—no color separations here. But if you know your way around Word, you can do a pretty fair newsletter or brochure. In this chapter, you learn about several features you can use in any document, but that are most frequently used in newsletters, brochures, and other DTP documents.

In this chapter:

- Using Word as a desktop publishing program
- Working in Page Layout view
- Working with multiple columns

- Using borders and shading
- Using frames
- Importing pictures
- Drawing in Word
- Using WordArt 2.5

Working in Page Layout View

If you're planning to create a publication with multiple columns, or with graphics and wrap-around text, you'll quickly find yourself in Page Layout view. (Many of the Word drawing tools that you'll see later in this chapter won't work unless you're in Page Layout view.)

To enter Page Layout view, select the Page Layout View button to the left of the horizontal scroll bar (see fig. 21.1). Figure 21.2 shows a document in Page Layout view.

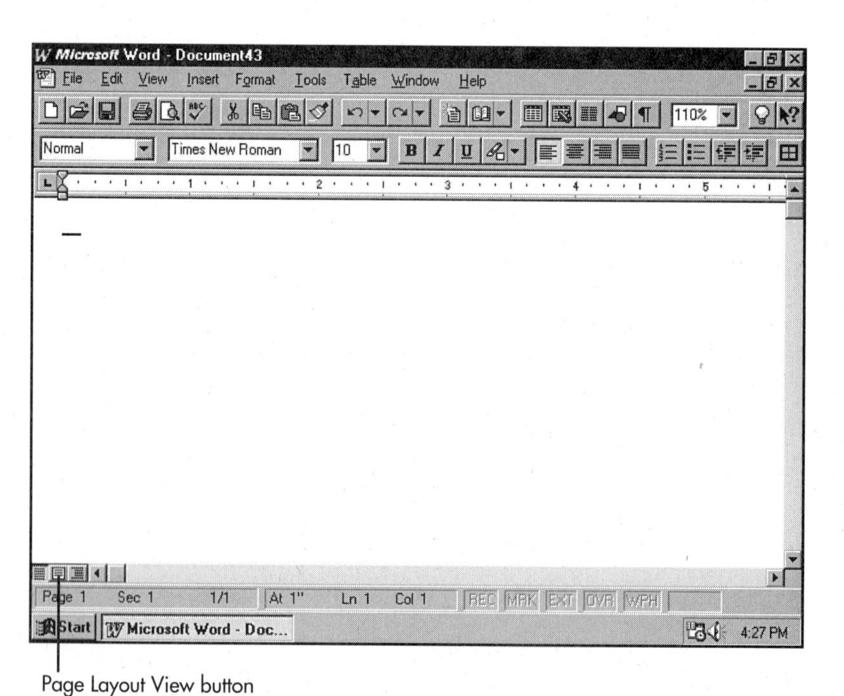

Figure 21.1
The Page Layout View button.

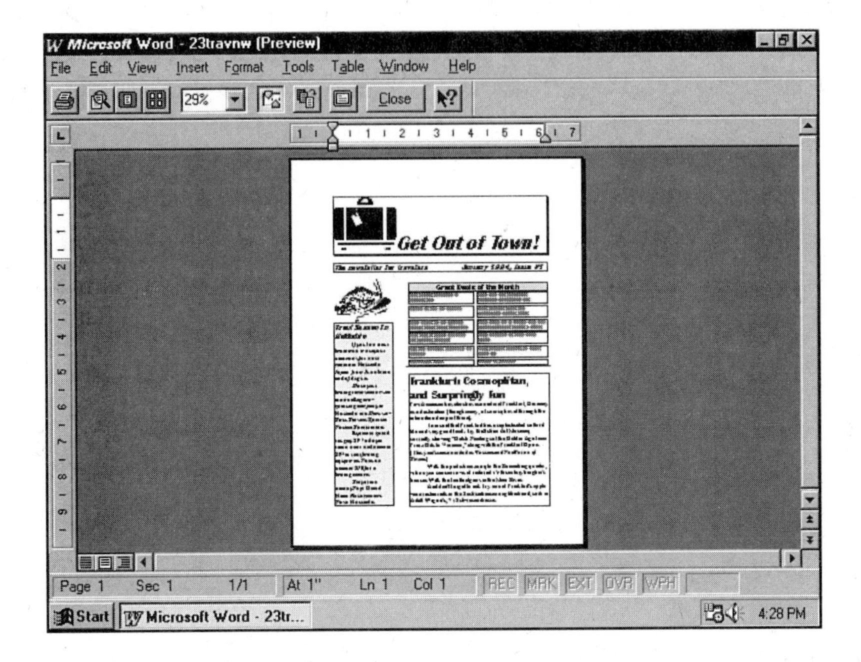

Figure 21.2

A sample page in Page Layout view.

Working with Multiple Columns

Word gives you extensive control over columns. You can create uneven columns, specifying exact widths for each. You also can add a new column to existing columns.

If you simply want to create multiple columns of the same size, click on the Columns toolbar button. (If you want to create multiple columns for only part of the document, select the text you want to split into columns, and then choose the Columns toolbar button.)

When you choose Columns, a box appears, displaying four columns (see fig. 21.3). Click on the box and drag across until the number of columns you want is highlighted. Then release the mouse button.

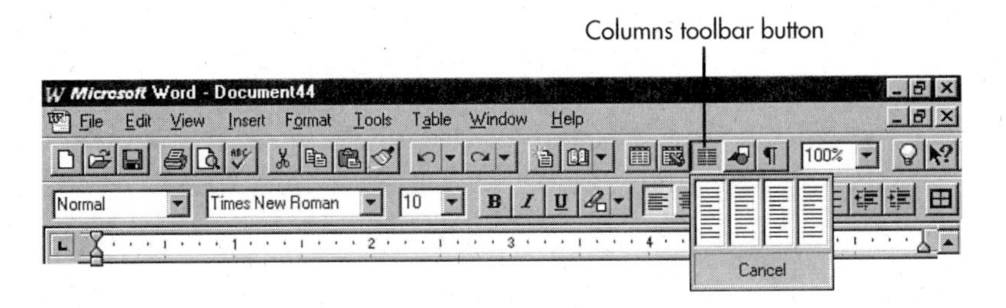

Figure 21.3

The Columns toolbar button.

If you are creating multiple columns for only a portion of your document, Word inserts section breaks before and after the text you've selected.

Although the Columns button displays four columns when you open it, you can use it to create up to six columns.

The accompanying CD-ROM contains a file you can use to practice some of the procedures in this chapter: IWMS21A.DOC.

Getting More Control from Format Columns

You may want more control than the Columns button can give you. You might want columns of different sizes, for example. You might want to change the exact spacing between individual columns, or add a line between columns. To do any of these things, choose **C**olumns from the F**o**rmat menu. The Columns dialog box opens (see fig. 21.4).

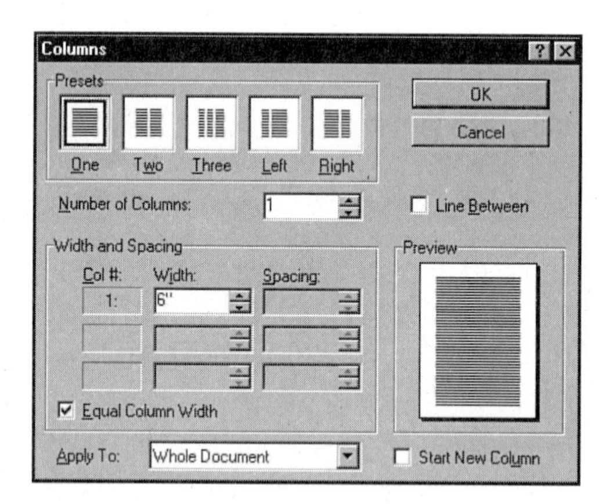

Figure 21.4
The Columns dialog box.

Columns comes with five preset column formats: basic **O**ne column, T**w**o column, and **T**hree column formats, as well as two-column formats in which the **L**eft or **R**ight column is larger.

You also can specify the number of columns directly, using the **N**umber of Columns spin box. Word won't create columns narrower than 0.5 inch, so if you're using Word's default formatting of 1.25-inch left and right margins on an 8.5-inch page, you can specify up to 12 columns. Check Line **B**etween to tell Word to place a line between each column.

In the Apply To box, choose whether you want your column settings to apply to the Whole Document or from This Point Forward. If you choose This Point Forward, Word inserts a section break at your insertion point if you are not at the start of a new section.

If you've selected text before opening the Columns dialog box, your choices here are Selected Text or Whole Document. As already mentioned, if you create columns for selected text, section breaks are added before and after the text.

As you make changes, Word shows their effects in the Preview box.

Changing a Column Width Using the Ruler

To change a column width from the Ruler, switch to Page Layout view. Notice the column markers that appear in the horizontal ruler (see fig. 21.5).

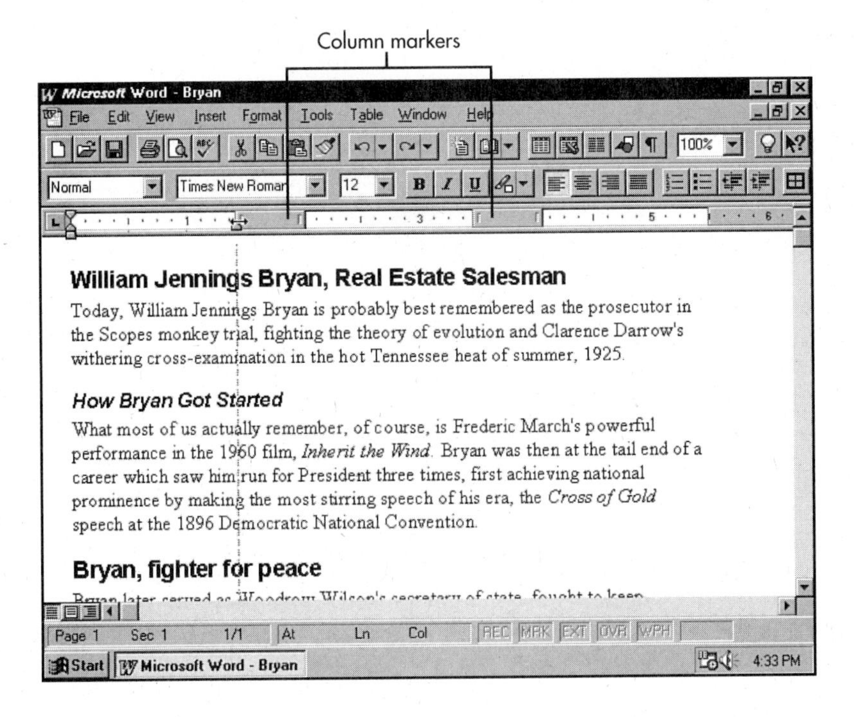

Figure 21.5

Changing column widths using the Ruler.

To change a column width, drag the column marker to where you want it. If all your columns are equally wide, this changes them all. If your columns vary in width, this changes only your current column.

You can't drag one column marker into the space reserved for another column. You have to narrow that column first.

Getting More Control over Individual Column Widths

You can set precise column widths in the Format, Columns dialog box. If your current settings are for columns of equal width, first clear the Equal Column Width check box. This enables you to work on any column listed in the Width and Spacing area.

Then for each column, set Width and Spacing. (You can move from one box to the next by pressing Tab.) If you have more than three columns, a scroll bar appears to the left of the Col. # list; use it to scroll to the columns you want to set.

Starting a New Column

To begin a new column at your insertion point, either:

1. Select Break from the Insert menu.
2. Select Column Break.
3. Click on OK.

Or:

1. Select Columns from the Format menu.
2. Check the Start New Column box.
3. Click on OK.

Evening the Bottoms of Columns

Sometimes you'll want a document in which all the bottom columns line up. This is called *balancing* your columns, and it isn't always easy to do in a way consistent with your paragraph pagination commands. If you've specified that two paragraphs must stay together (Keep With Next), for example, you limit Word's capability to move a few lines around to even things out.

To tell Word to balance the columns on a page, choose a **C**ontinuous Section Break at the end of the column you want to balance. (Use **I**nsert, **B**reak.) This allows Word to end the section wherever necessary to balance the columns.

Using Borders and Shading

You can apply borders or shading to any paragraph in a Word document—or to table cells, frames, WordArt type effects, and graphics. To border or shade text, first select it, and then apply the bordering or shading you want.

The easiest way to reach Word's bordering and shading features is to click on the Border button at the far right of the Formatting toolbar (see fig. 21.6). When you do, the Borders toolbar opens (see fig. 21.7).

Figure 21.6

The Border button.

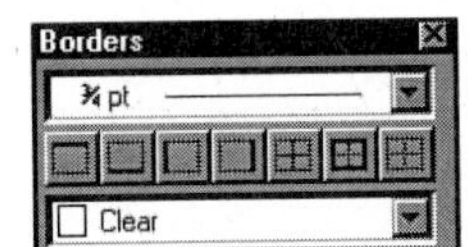

Figure 21.7

The Borders floating toolbar.

At the top, the toolbar contains a list box that enables you to choose the line that will be used in your border. By clicking on the down arrow, you get a list of choices, as shown in figure 21.8.

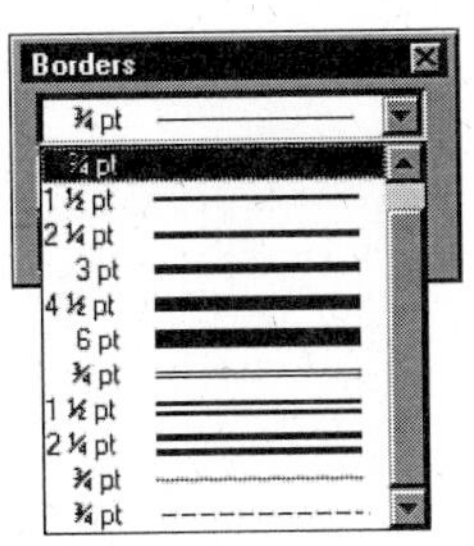

Figure 21.8

The Border line choices.

The buttons at the center specify which part of the rectangle you've selected will be bordered, as shown in table 21.1. If a border already exists, clicking on the button switches it off.

Table 21.1
Borders Toolbar Buttons

Button	What It Does
Top	Switches bordering of the top of selected text
Bottom	Switches bordering of the bottom of selected text
Left	Switches bordering of the left edge of selected text
Right	Switches bordering of the right edge of selected text
Inside Cells	Switches inside bordering of every cell in a selection, or between each selected paragraph
Box	Borders all four corners of selected text
Remove Box	Removes all borders from selected text

If you're bordering a table, you have to click two boxes to create bordering that covers every cell in a matrix: the *Box* button to get the outside border, and the *Inside Cells* border to get the inside borders. The button at the far right clears any border you might have already assigned.

The list box at the bottom controls shading; the default is Clear—no shading. Click on the right arrow to see your choices (see fig. 21.9).

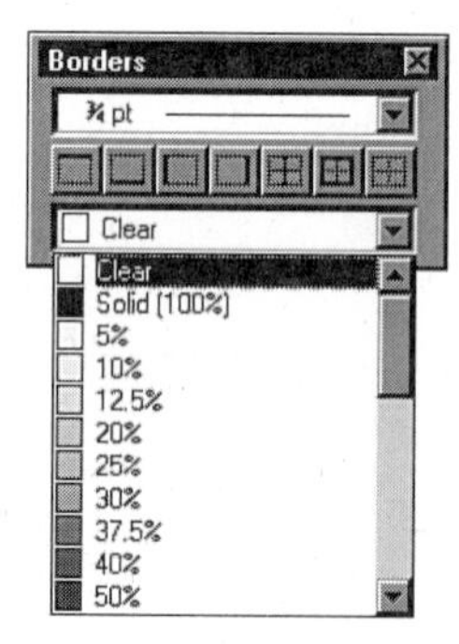

Figure 21.9
Shading choices.

Many of these border choices, such as the patterns, should rarely, if ever, be used over text. They're ideal, however, for blocking off empty space to help the eye move across the page.

To close the Borders toolbar, either click on its control box or click on the Borders button again.

Setting Shadows, Colors, and Other Border Elements

For more control over your borders and shading, choose Borders and Shading from the Format menu. The dialog box shown in figure 21.10 opens. Choose the Borders tab if it's not already open.

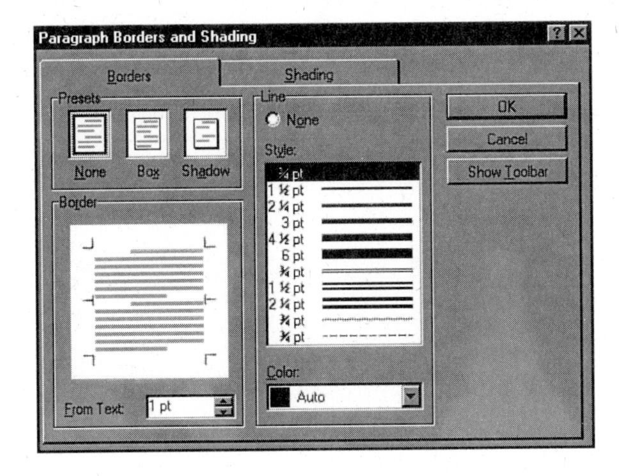

Figure 21.10

The Paragraph Borders and Shading dialog box.

Word offers three preset borders: None and Box, which are also available through the Borders toolbar; and Shadow, which isn't. Shadow creates a shadow effect by using a slightly wider border on the bottom and right edges of a box.

In the Border box, you can choose exactly which edges of a box, including any table cells or individual paragraphs within it, will be bordered. Click on the edge you want to border; triangles mark that border and the currently selected line style is applied.

If you want to change an edge's border line, select it (make sure that the triangles are showing) and choose another border line from the Style box.

You also can choose a color from the Color list box. Your choices are shown in figure 21.11. Finally, in the From Text spin box, you can specify how far from text your border lines will appear. As you make changes, the Border previews them.

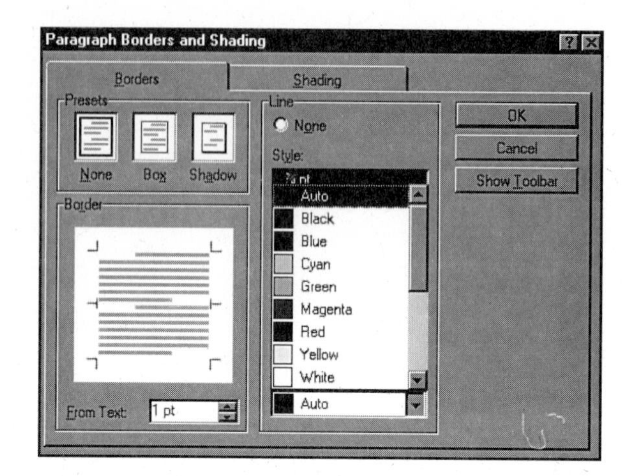

Figure 21.11
Color choices.

Using the Shading Dialog Box

To set shading, choose the **S**hading tab of the Paragraph Borders and Shading dialog box (see fig. 21.12).

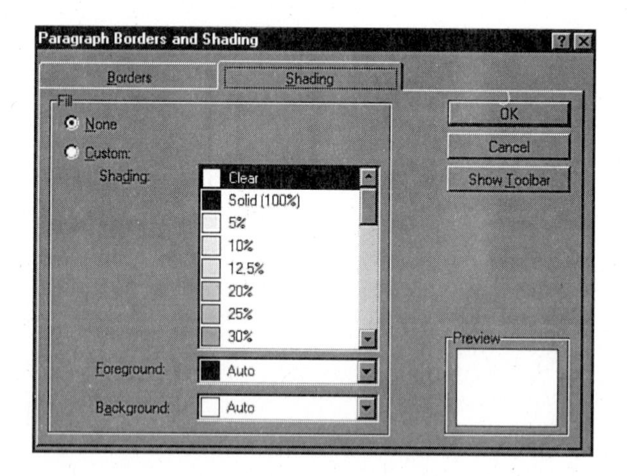

Figure 21.12
The Shading tab.

Normally, when you create text, your text is black against a white background. When you set a shading pattern, such as 50%, Word creates the shading by adding dots against a white background. The higher the percentage, the more dots are visible, and the less background you can see. Similarly, when you use a pattern border, the pattern appears as black, and the background remains white.

To change the background color, choose a new color from the B**a**ckground box. To change the foreground color—the dots or lines Word displays against the background—choose a new color from the **F**oreground box.

You can use borders and shading together to create a sidebar—a chunk of text that discusses material relevant to the main discussion, but which might interrupt the flow of that discussion. For best control of sidebar placement, place them within a frame.

You're looking at a sidebar now.

Using Frames

Normally, when you work in Word, your text adjusts up, down, or sideways when you make other editing changes. But sometimes you want something—either text, a graphic, a table, or some other document element—to stay put no matter what. That's what *frames* are for.

You can create a new, empty frame. You might do this to set aside space for an illustration or text that is to be added later. Or, you can select an existing item or selection of text and frame it. Then, having done so, you can move the frame to any position you want, and it will stay there.

Creating a New Frame

To create a new frame, choose Frame from the Insert menu. Word asks you to switch to page layout view if you're not already in page layout view (see fig. 21.13).

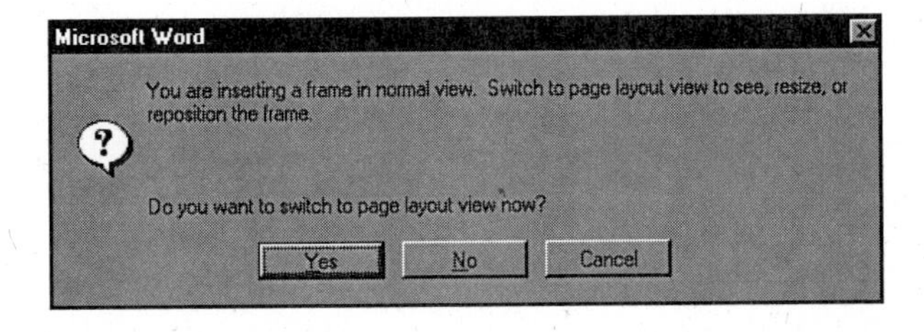

Figure 21.13

Switch to page layout view.

If you don't choose Yes, Word inserts the frame, but you won't be able to work with it. Most of the time, then, Yes seems to be the appropriate choice.

Page layout view appears, and your mouse pointer changes to crosshairs. Click on where you want the frame's top left corner to be; then drag across and down to set the frame's borders. A dotted line appears as you drag the frame (see fig. 21.14). When you're finished, a box with a shaded border appears (see fig. 21.15). That's your frame.

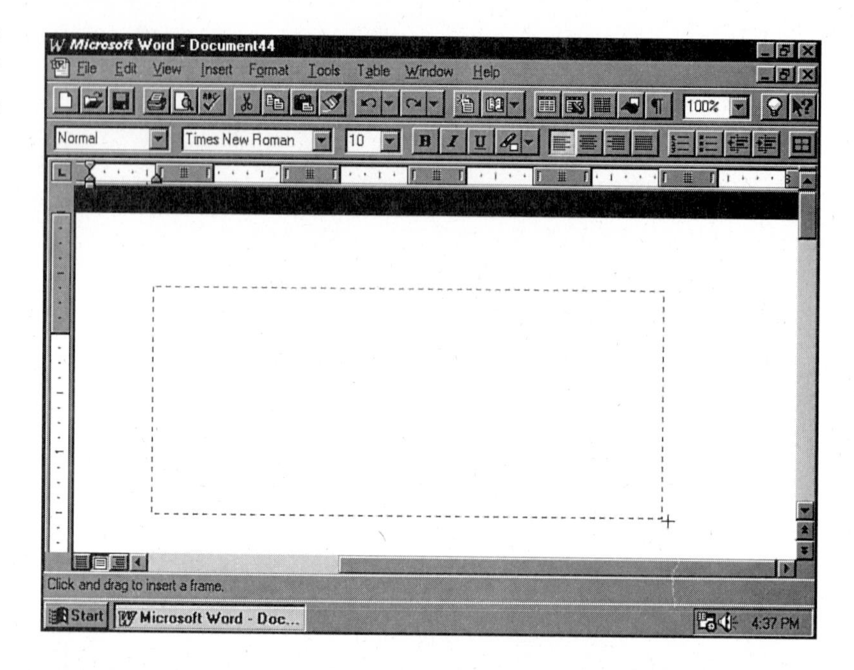

Figure 21.14

Dragging the new frame into place.

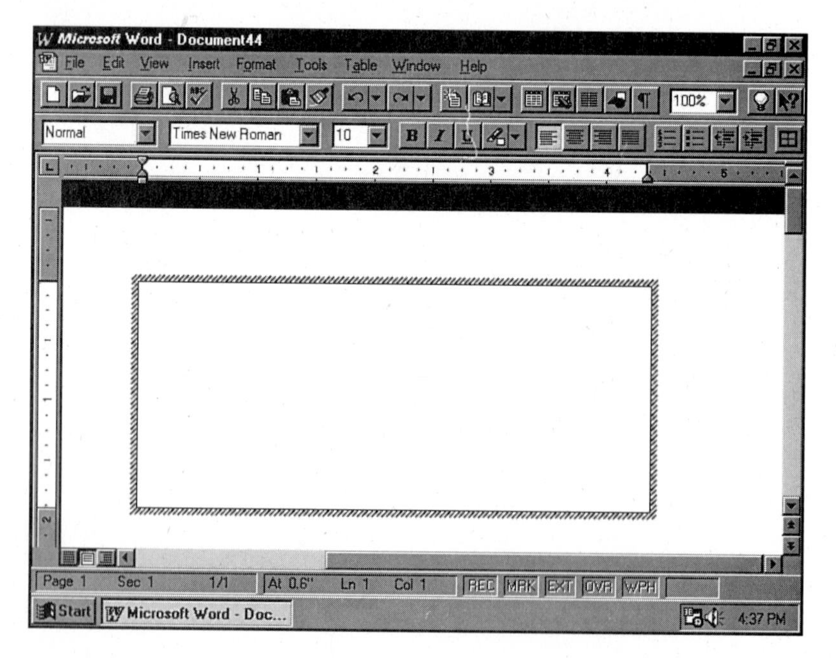

Figure 21.15

The completed new frame.

Now that you have the frame, you can type in it using any of Word's formatting techniques. You can copy text into or out of it. You also can copy a graphic into it.

To frame existing material, select the material, select Frame from the Insert menu, and choose Yes when you're asked to go into Page Layout view. Word creates a frame that fits the material you've selected. If you select a paragraph, for example, the frame appears *around* the paragraph.

In Word, frames are automatically bordered with a 3/4-point line border. This border prints unless you remove it with the Borders commands discussed earlier in this chapter.

Moving and Resizing Frames

Now that you have a border, Word provides tools to help you place it where you want.

First, select the frame. If its border isn't visible, click within the frame to make its cross-hatched edges appear. To move a frame, position the mouse pointer on any of the cross-hatched edges, and drag it where you want it.

When you select the frame, eight small squares appear on its edges. These are *sizing handles*, which you can use to resize a frame. When you click and drag a sizing handle, the frame extends in the direction you're dragging it.

You can always tell which directions a sizing handle can take your frame by positioning your mouse pointer on it and looking at the new mouse pointer icon, as in figure 21.16. (The diagonal mouse pointer is in the lower-left corner of the frame.)

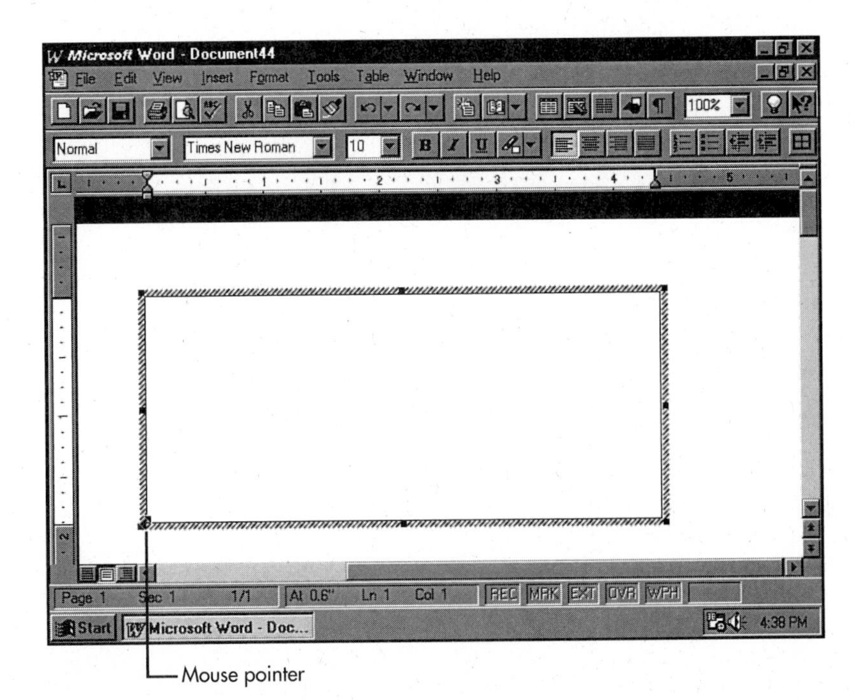

Figure 21.16

The diagonal mouse pointer icon and frame borders.

Getting Better Control over Your Frames

If you want exact control over your frame, select it and choose Fra<u>m</u>e from the F<u>o</u>rmat menu. The Frame dialog box opens (see fig. 21.17).

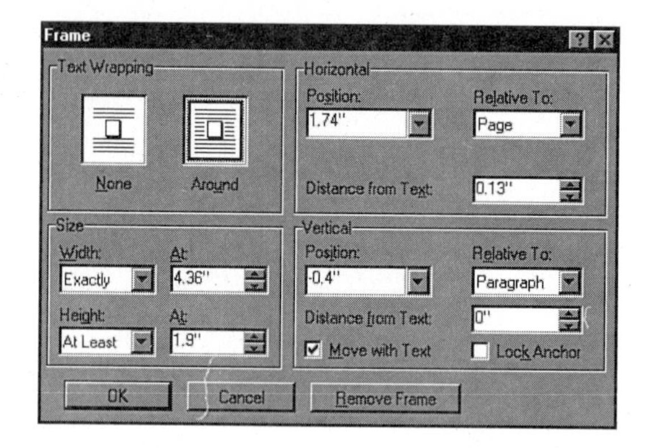

Figure 21.17
The Frame dialog box.

Wrapping Text

By default, Word assumes that you want any document text to wrap around your frame, as in the following example (see fig. 21.18).

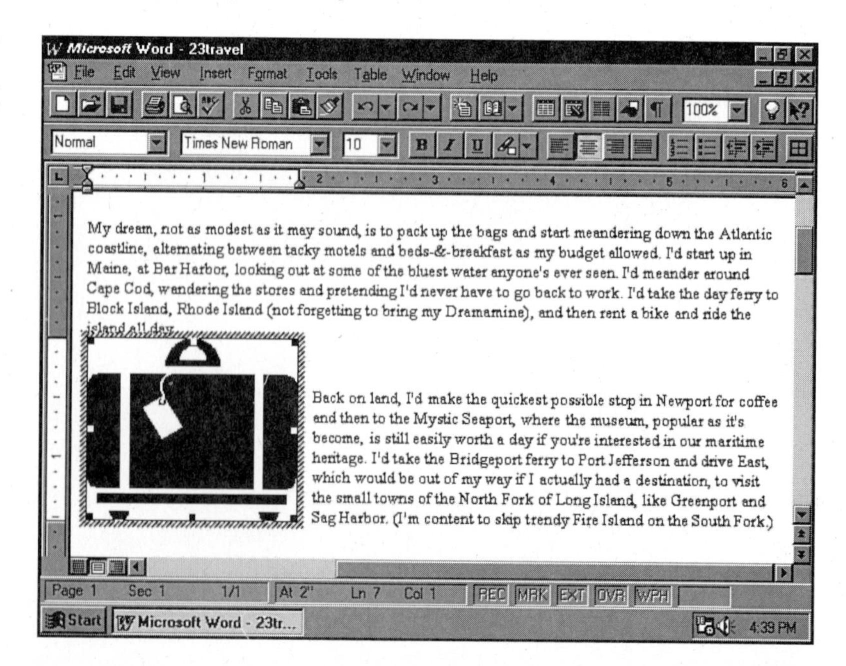

Figure 21.18
Text wrapping around a frame.

Sometimes, you may not. Choose None in the Text Wrapping box, and the frame appears on a line of its own, with any text that follows it starting on the next line.

Specifying the Precise Size of a Frame

By default, Word extends your frame from the left to the right margins, unless you've set it differently when you inserted it, either by dragging the borders or by framing something that didn't extend to both margins, such as an imported graphic. (Most often, you'll encounter these automatic left-to-right-margin frames when you frame paragraphs.)

In either case, you can specify the exact size of the frame using the Width and Height boxes in Size. Specify Exactly, and then set a size in the appropriate At box.

Specifying the Exact Position of a Frame

Next, you can specify exactly where a frame appears. In doing so, you establish horizontal and vertical *reference points*—the starting locations from where Word can mark off the distance you specify.

You can create *horizontal* reference points that tell Word to measure from the margin, page, or column. These each affect your frame differently, as shown in figure 21.19. To choose a horizontal reference point, choose from the Relative To list box in the Horizontal area.

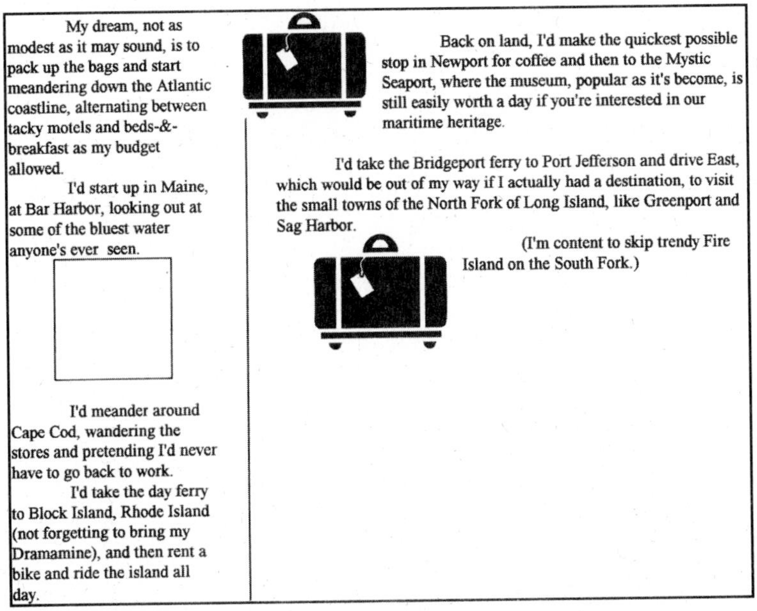

My dream, not as modest as it may sound, is to pack up the bags and start meandering down the Atlantic coastline, alternating between tacky motels and beds-&-breakfast as my budget allowed.

I'd start up in Maine, at Bar Harbor, looking out at some of the bluest water anyone's ever seen.

I'd meander around Cape Cod, wandering the stores and pretending I'd never have to go back to work.

I'd take the day ferry to Block Island, Rhode Island (not forgetting to bring my Dramamine), and then rent a bike and ride the island all day.

Back on land, I'd make the quickest possible stop in Newport for coffee and then to the Mystic Seaport, where the museum, popular as it's become, is still easily worth a day if you're interested in our maritime heritage.

I'd take the Bridgeport ferry to Port Jefferson and drive East, which would be out of my way if I actually had a destination, to visit the small towns of the North Fork of Long Island, like Greenport and Sag Harbor.

(I'm content to skip trendy Fire Island on the South Fork.)

Figure 21.19

Frames set relative to the margin, page, and column.

You also can set a frame's *vertical* reference point. Here, your choices are Paragraph, Margin, and Page; Paragraph is the default setting.

After you've set the reference point in the Relative To list box, it's easy to specify the actual Position—how far from the reference point Word should place the frame. Your frame's current settings appear in these boxes; you can change them, and your frame will move.

Understanding How Frames Anchor to Paragraphs

By default, every Word frame is *anchored* to the nearest paragraph. If the paragraph moves, the frame moves with it. You can see which paragraph a frame is anchored to by selecting the frame and clicking the Show/Hide Paragraph button; an anchor appears next to the paragraph connected to your frame (see fig. 21.20).

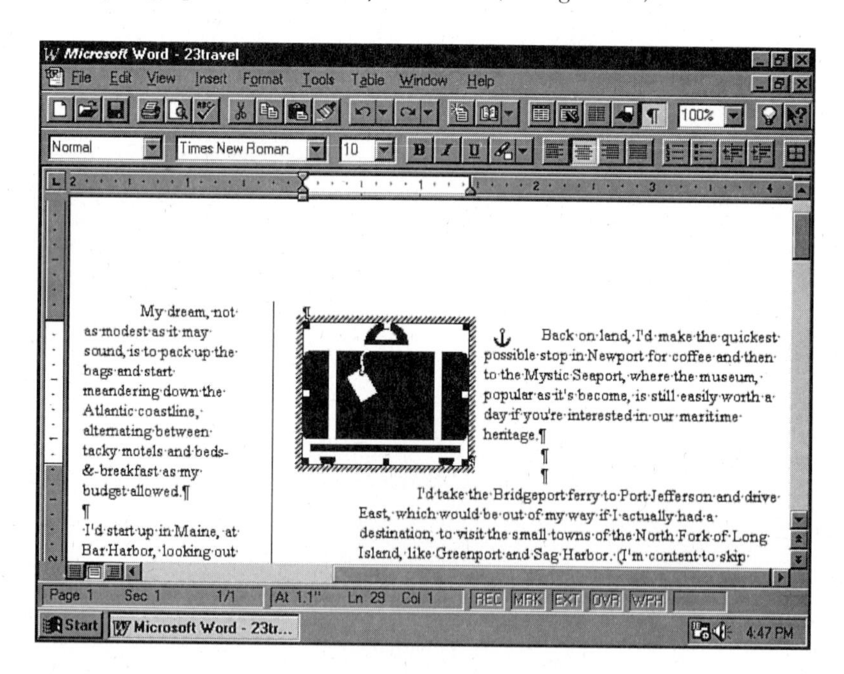

Figure 21.20
Paragraph showing anchor icon.

This anchoring arrangement is ideal for some tasks. Let's say that you've created a side heading, such as that shown in figure 21.21.

Or, say that you're framing a graphic that needs to stay near its text reference.

If you're framing a graphic that needs to stay with a caption, such as one you can create with Insert, Caption, place both the graphic and the caption in the same frame.

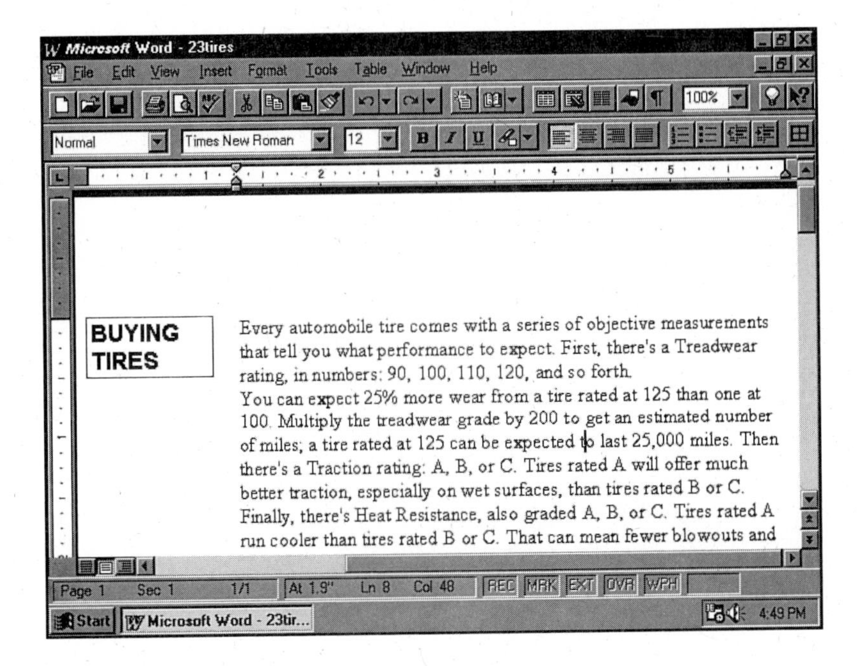

Figure 21.21
A typical side heading.

Many desktop-published documents, however, require that a page element stay in the same location, no matter what's going on around it. That's pretty fundamental page design. And that's what you were promised when you started this section.

To make a frame stay put, position the frame *not* relative to a paragraph, but instead relative to the *page*. Choose Page in the Relative To box in the Vertical group. When you do, the Move with Text box clears; the frame now stays in the same location on the same page.

Note The keyboard shortcut for Vertical's Relative To is **E**; the keyboard shortcut for Horizontal's Relative To is **L**. Word does something like this whenever a dialog box contains two settings with the same name.

Locking Anchor

You've made sure that the frame stays in the same location no matter where the text goes. But what if you'd like the frame to always appear on the same location on the page, and always appear on the same page with the text to which it refers?

Word handles this through a feature called *Lock Anchor*. Check the Lock Anchor box, and the frame moves to any new page where the paragraph to which it's anchored goes. When you use Lock Anchor on a frame, the Locked Anchor icon appears next to the paragraph to which it's locked (see fig. 21.22).

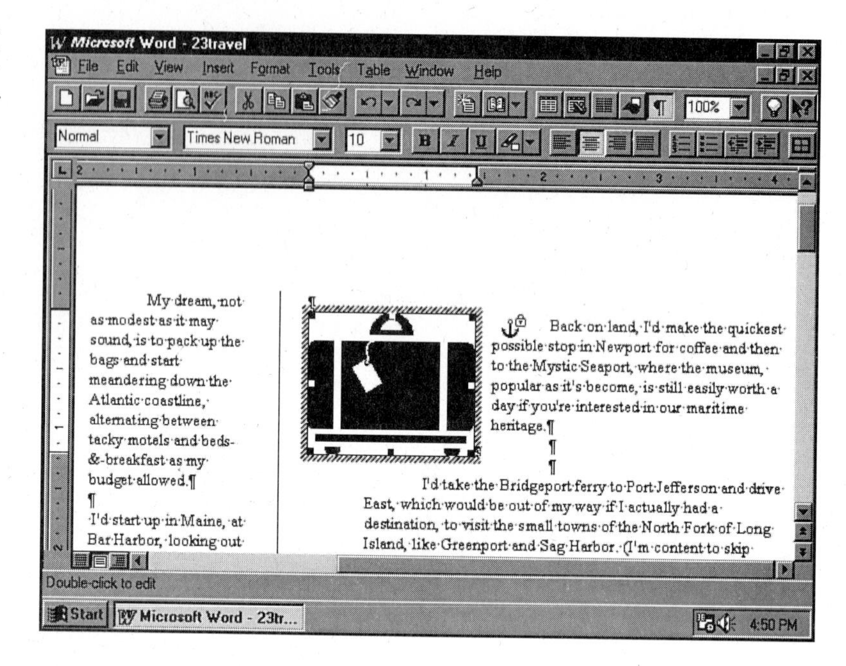

Figure 21.22
The locked anchor icon.

Tip You can change the paragraph to which a frame is anchored by dragging the icon (either the anchor or locked anchor icon) to a new paragraph.

Removing a Frame

You can delete a frame by selecting it and pressing Delete, or by choosing **R**emove Frame from the F**o**rmat **F**rame dialog box.

Stop Deleting a frame deletes all text or graphics contained within it.

Working with Graphics

This book has frequently alluded to adding graphics to your document. There are two ways to do this:

- Import a graphic from another application
- Create your own graphic, using Word's powerful drawing tools

Importing Pictures

Word now comes with its own clip-art library, contained in the directory \winword\clipart or \office95\clipart (assuming you've installed it). There are 100 Windows Metafile (WMF) images here; a list of them appears in table 21.2.

Table 21.2
Clip Art That Ships with Word

File Name	Description
1stplace.wmf	First-place ribbon
anchor.wmf	Ship anchor
artist.wmf	Artist painting on canvas
atomengy.wmf	Stylized atom with spinning electrons
banner.wmf	Scroll (18th-century woodcarving style)
bearmrkt.wmf	Bear
books.wmf	Open book sitting on closed book; ink quill pen nearby
bullmrkt.doc	Bull
buttrfly.doc	Monarch butterfly
cakeslic.wmf	Slice of layer cake (stylized)
cat.wmf	Silhouette of cat (side view)
celtic.wmf	Celtic symbol
checkmrk.wmf	Reversed check mark in square
cityscpe.wmf	Generic city skyline mirrored in water
coffee.wmf	Silhouette of steaming coffee cup
compass.wmf	Compass
computer.wmf	Computer monitor in foreground; silhouette of individuals working at computer in background
conductr.wmf	Orchestra conductor with raised baton
continen.wmf	Outlined Mercator projection

continues

Table 21.2, Continued
Clip Art That Ships with Word

File Name	Description
dancers.wmf	Silhouetted ballroom dancers
deco.wmf	Art deco symbol
dinner1.wmf	Stylized silhouette of wine and cheese platter
dinner2.wmf	Stylized silhouette of whole fish on plate with napkin underneath
diploma.wmf	Diploma with seal
disk.wmf	Stylized silhouette of 3.5-inch floppy disk
divider1.wmf	Simple page divider containing diamond shape
divider2.wmf	Simple page divider containing triangle shape
divider3.wmf	Simple page divider containing string-knot shape
drama.wmf	Traditional two-masks drama symbol
drink.wmf	Silhouette of Caribbean-style drink
easter.wmf	Easter plant
elephant.wmf	Silhouette of elephant in grass, facing view
fall.wmf	Falling leaves over a picket fence
film.wmf	Reel of movie film
flourish.wmf	Decorative flourish
flyace.wmf	Red Baron-style pilot, trailing empty message banner
fyi.wmf	Styled F.Y.I. heading logo
gavel.wmf	Gavel and stand
golf.wmf	Stylized golf club about to hit ball on tee
hangle.wmf	Simple frame
hcorner.wmf	Frame with simple decorative corners
hdecobox.wmf	Art-deco style frame
heart.wmf	Stylized greeting-card-style heart
hmedeval.wmf	Fancy-bordered frame
horse.wmf	Silhouette of galloping horse
houses.wmf	Stylized row houses
hplaque.wmf	Plaque

File Name	Description
hpresbox.wmf	Simple empty frame
jazz.wmf	Image of jazz instruments
jet.wmf	Stylized jet taking off
label1.wmf	Ribbon
label2.wmf	Ribbon
label3.wmf	Label
lblkdiam.wmf	Ribbon (diamond-shaped)
ldiamond.wmf	Ribbon (diamond-shaped)
lightblb.wmf	Light bulb
luggage.wmf	Silhouette of luggage
mail.wmf	Various envelopes, one opened letter
medstaff.wmf	Traditional "staff" physician's emblem
motorcrs.wmf	Racing flags
movie.wmf	Symbols of movies: love scene, popcorn, strip of film
music.wmf	String of musical notes
nosmoke.wmf	No-smoking symbol
notes.wmf	Stylized musical notes flying into distance
nouveau1.wmf	Art nouveau decoration
nouveau2.wmf	Art nouveau decoration
nouvflwr.wmf	Art nouveau flowered decorative border
office.wmf	Symbols of office: paper clip, pens, folders, pads
ornamnt1.wmf	Ornament
ornamnt2.wmf	Ornament
ornamnt3.wmf	Ornament
ornamnt4.wmf	Ornament
ornate.wmf	Ornate pattern
party.wmf	Party balloons
pharmacy.wmf	Traditional pharmacist's emblem
phone.wmf	Pushbutton phone
pizza.wmf	Stylized pizza slice

continues

Table 21.2, Continued
Clip Art That Ships with Word

File Name	Description
present.wmf	Wrapped and ribboned box
realest.wmf	Silhouetted rooftops of houses
recycle.wmf	Recycling symbol
rose.wmf	Silhouetted rose
sail.wmf	Boat's wheel
scales.wmf	Scales of justice
server.wmf	Tuxedoed waiter bringing covered dish
splat.wmf	Splatter image
sports.wmf	Sports images: helmets, sneakers, bats and balls
spring.wmf	Spring image: flowers blooming
star.wmf	Star
summer.wmf	Summer image: boat on lake
tennis.wmf	Stylized images of tennis balls, racquets, nets
theatre.wmf	Drama icon against stage backdrop
travel.wmf	Travel images
vbevbox.wmf	Bevelled border
vcontbox.wmf	Modern border
vprisbox.wmf	Modern border
vwind.wmf	Border
wheelchr.wmf	Wheelchair-accessible symbol
wine.wmf	Stylized wine glass and grapes
winter.wmf	Winter image: snowflakes and icicles
woodcut.wmf	Woodcut border

To open one, choose Picture from the Insert dialog box (see fig. 21.23). Notice that the dialog box automatically opens to the \winword6\clipart directory. To choose a picture, click on it; Word shows the picture in the Preview box if Preview Picture is marked.

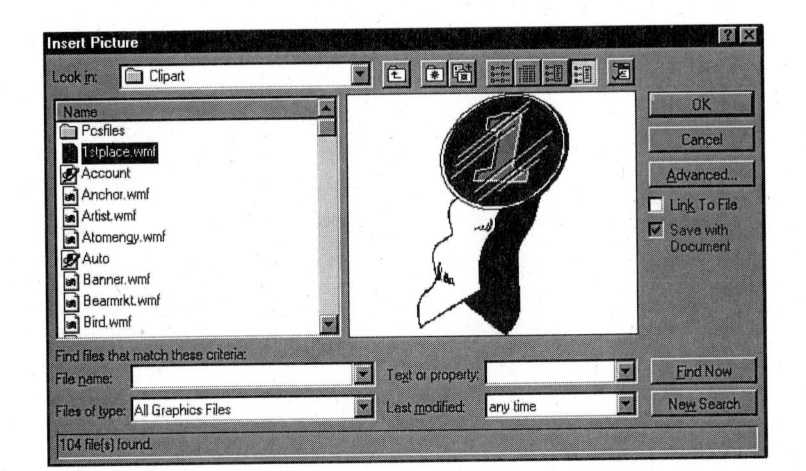

Figure 21.23

The Insert Picture dialog box.

If you know exactly what you're looking for, double-click on the picture to open it, or clear **P**review Picture to save the time it would take for Word to display the picture here.

If you have other graphics files on disk, you can open them by selecting their drive and directory. Word can import files in the following formats:

AutoCAD (*.dxf) format
AutoCAD Plot files (*.plt)
Computer Graphics Metafile (*.cgm)
CorelDRAW! (*.cdr)
Encapsulated PostScript (*.eps)
HP Graphic Language (*.hgl)
Lotus 1-2-3 graphics (*.pic)
Micrografx Designer and Draw (*.drw)
PC Paintbrush (*.pcx)
PICT (Macintosh graphics run through a Windows PICT Filter) (*.pct)
Tagged Image Format (*.tif)
Windows Bitmaps (*.bmp)
Windows Metafiles (*.wmf)—Word's clip art format
WordPerfect/DrawPerfect (*.wpg)

One format that unfortunately is missing is GIF, the format used for exchanging graphics on CompuServe.

If you have Microsoft Office for Windows 95, you can also access the graphics collection that accompanies Microsoft PowerPoint, by installing these graphics in the Microsoft Clip Art Gallery application and inserting the graphics from there.

Linking Graphics

If you're using a graphic created in or compatible with another Windows program, you might want to check the Link To File box in Insert, Picture.

This creates a link with the graphic's native program. With a link established, when you double-click on the graphic, that program opens and you can easily edit it.

Graphics are huge—and Word files have a way of constantly getting larger. If you've created a link to your graphic's original program, you can tell Word to keep only the link in your document, not the file itself. To do this, *after* checking the Link To File check box, clear the Save with Document check box.

There are always tradeoffs: in exchange for a smaller file size, your graphic may display more slowly. And if you move the graphic without reestablishing the link, the graphic disappears from your document, to be replaced by an empty box. Unlike frames, graphics come into Word without a border. You can, however, add one using the Borders toolbar or choose Format, Borders and Shading.

You also can select a graphic and place it in a frame. Word creates a frame the same size as the graphic you're framing.

If you're just editing text, you may not want to see the graphics at all. They actually slow down Word quite a bit. To replace graphics with empty boxes, open the Tools, Options, View dialog box, and check Picture Placeholders.

Resizing and Cropping Imported Pictures

To resize a graphic you've brought into Word, click on it. A cross-hatched border and sizing handles appear, like the ones mentioned earlier in the frames discussion (see fig. 21.24).

The diagonal sizing handles increase or decrease the size of the graphic without changing its proportion. The middle sizing handles on the left and right of the box widen or narrow the image. The top and bottom sizing handles in the middle of the box make the graphic taller or shorter.

These *scaling* controls stretch the image like Silly Putty, but so far none of them deletes any part of it. To cut out some of the image—*crop it,* as graphics professionals say—press the Shift key while you drag a sizing handle toward the center of the graphic. While you crop the image, the mouse pointer changes shape, as shown in figure 21.25.

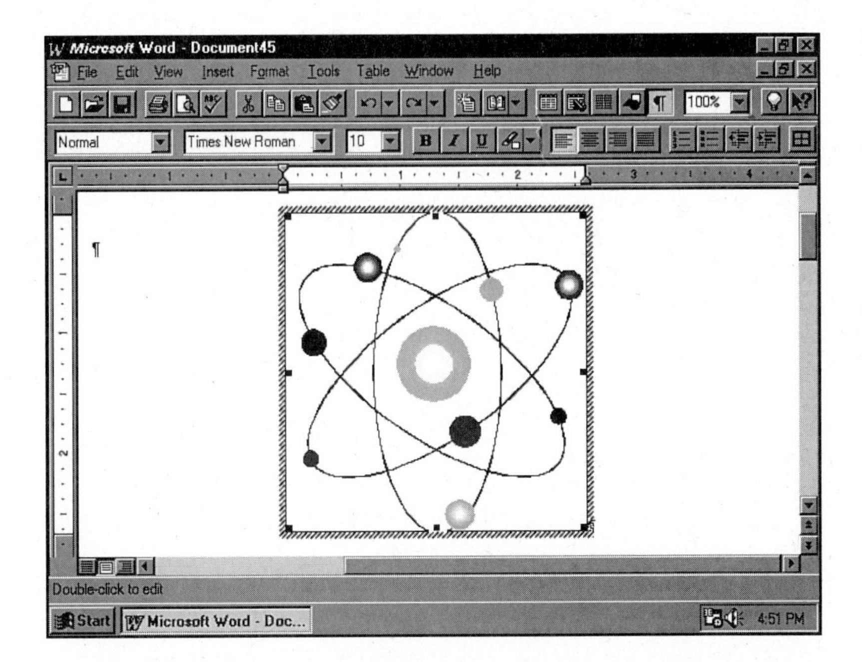

Figure 21.24
Selecting a picture.

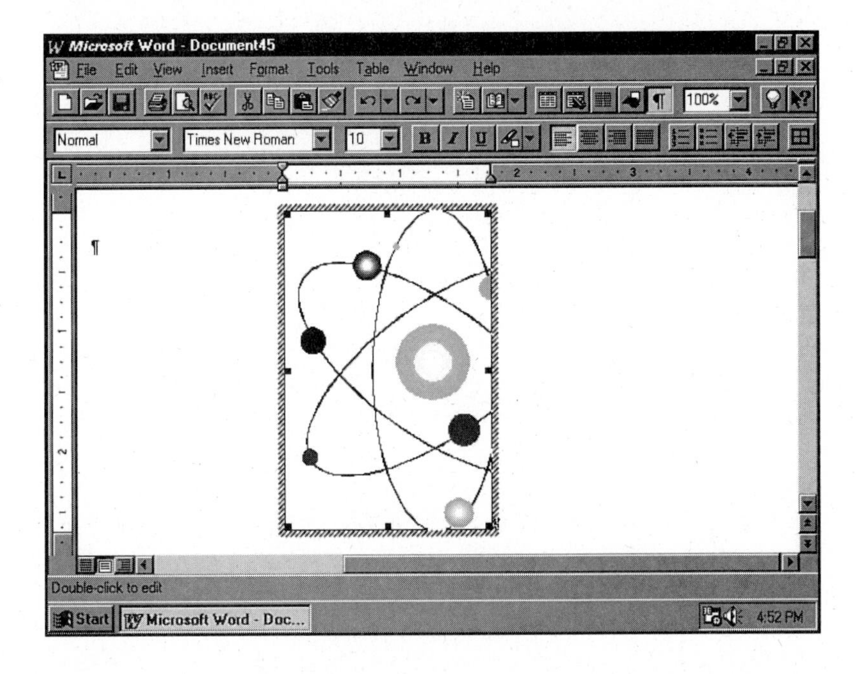

Figure 21.25
Cropping an image.

You also can add *white space* around a graphic by pressing Shift and moving a handle away from the center of the graphic (see fig. 21.26).

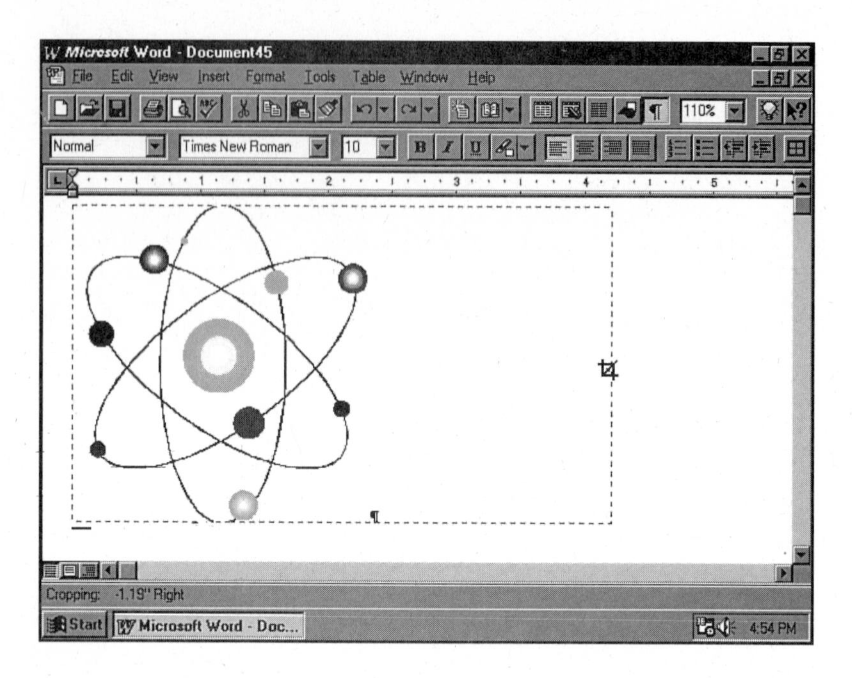

Figure 21.26

Adding white space around a graphic.

Tip: You can't add shading to a graphic, nor to the white space you add to the graphic with the cropping tool. You can, however, place the graphic inside a frame, enlarge the frame, and shade the portion of the frame that doesn't contain the graphic.

Using the Format, Picture Command

As with frames, you can take more precise control over your picture size, scaling, and cropping through a F**o**rmat menu item. In this case, it's F**o**rmat, **P**icture (see fig. 21.27).

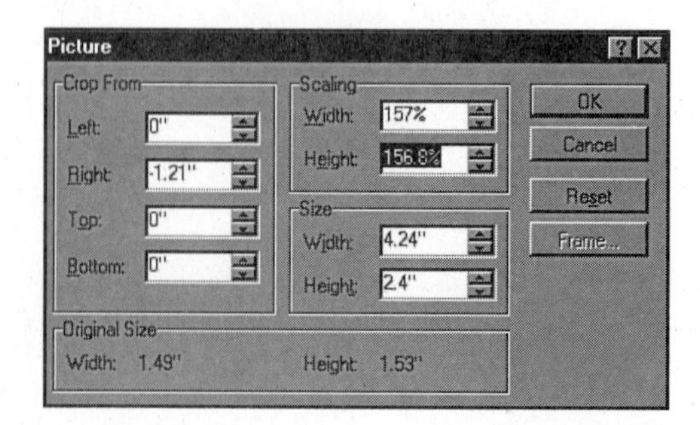

Figure 21.27

The Picture dialog box.

In the Original Size box, Word displays the original size of the picture when it came into Word. In the Crop From boxes, you can specify Left, Right, Top, and Bottom crop amounts, to 1/100th of an inch. Negative crop amounts add white space around the image.

Four equal corners. Word's sizing handles don't provide a good way of adding equal amounts of white space to all four edges of a picture, but you can do that easily here by specifying the same amount in each Crop From box.

Restoring ancient artwork. Format, Picture stores information about your original picture, so if you crop a picture and want to restore some of it later, you can do that here.

You also can control Scaling to 1/100th of an inch, by specifying Width and Height in percentages. A Width below 100% tells Word to make the image narrower, as if you were trying to squeeze it through a tight alleyway. Likewise, a Height above 100%. (Think of Stan Laurel.)

Conversely, a Width above 100% and a Height below 100% gives you a short, squat image. (Think of Oliver Hardy.)

Finally, you can control the overall image size by changing the Width and Height boxes in the Size area. (If you change the proportions here, the boxes automatically change in scaling, and vice versa.)

To reset the image to its original size and shape, choose Reset. To change aspects of a frame surrounding the image, choose Frame, and the Frame dialog box opens.

Drawing in Word

It's all well and good to import an illustration if you already have one that will do the job. But sometimes you need to create a new one. That's where Word's drawing features come in handy.

Word 2 came with a separate drawing program, Microsoft Draw. No more; Word's drawing tools were not only improved, but Microsoft also incorporated them directly into the Word application.

Word is a *drawing* program, which means it builds its images from lines. (Sometimes drawing programs are called *vector* programs.) This contrasts with *bitmapped* painting programs that splash dots across the screen as you create your image.

You already own a painting program—Microsoft Paint, which comes with Windows 95. (This is the successor program to Microsoft Paintbrush, which came with Windows 3.1.) With Word's drawing features, you can draw as well. Painting programs are traditionally a bit easier to work with, but drawing programs create images that can be printed on any kind of printer at any resolution.

Using Word to Edit Graphics from Other Programs

Because Word is a drawing program, you can use it to edit imported drawings that come from other Windows drawing programs. First make sure that Microsoft Word is selected as the Picture Editor in the Edit tab of the Tools, Options dialog box. (This is the default setting.) Then double-click on the graphic to edit it.

If you're already comfortable with another drawing program, you can select that one instead from the Picture Editor list of the Windows picture-editing programs you have.

If you want, you also can change the image so that it can only be edited by Microsoft Word. Import the image as an object, using Insert Object's Create from File tab. Then select the object, and choose Object from the Edit menu. Select Convert, and choose Microsoft Word from the list. This permanently converts the object to a Microsoft Word picture that can only be edited from Word.

Importing Files with or without Their Native Formats

By default, when you import a file from another graphics program, Word preserves that program's formatting information as well as its own. That takes plenty of disk space. If you don't intend to export the file back, you can tell Word only to save the Word format, as follows:

1. Choose Options from the Tools menu.
2. Choose the Save tab.
3. Check the Save Native Picture Formats Only box.
4. Click on OK.

Using Imported Encapsulated PostScript Graphics

Encapsulated PostScript (EPS) files contain the PostScript code that a high-end laser printer needs to print out your image at high resolution, and a bitmapped (PICT) version you can use to view it on-screen. When you import an EPS file, make sure that you get both.

Here's how: Copy the graphic into the Windows Clipboard from your graphics program, but when you select Copy, also press and hold down the Ctrl key. Then when you paste the graphic into Word, you'll have both screen and printer versions.

The Drawing Toolbar

To draw in Word, first display the Drawing toolbar (see fig. 21.28). To show the Drawing toolbar, right-click on the Show/Hide Paragraph Marks button, or anywhere on the toolbar, and a Toolbar menu appears; choose Drawing.

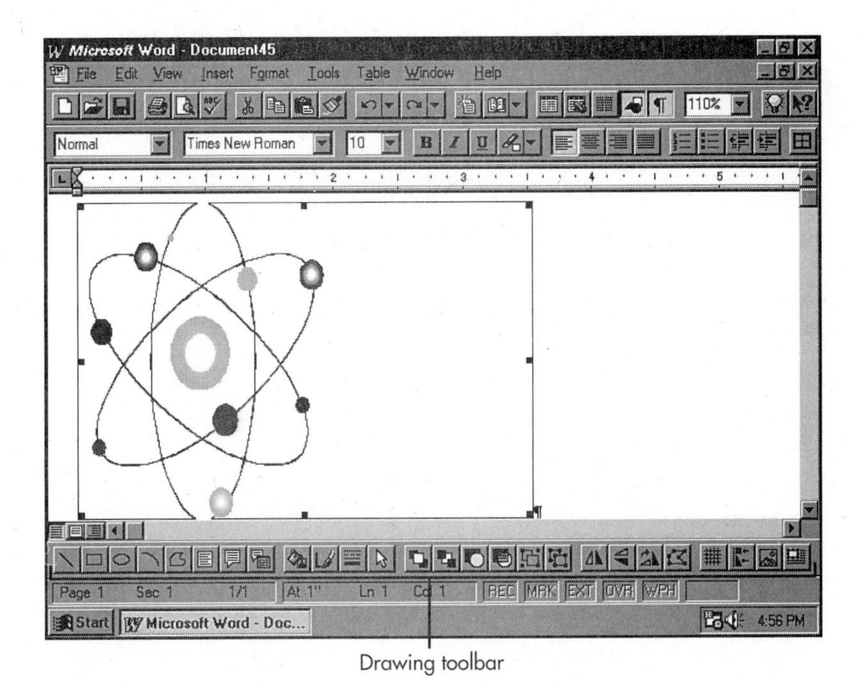

Figure 21.28
The Drawing toolbar.

The Drawing toolbar contains Word's tools for drawing. You'll find some of these—such as callouts—valuable even if you never create an image from scratch. Table 21.3 lists and describes Word's drawing tools.

TABLE 21.3
Word's Drawing Tools

Button	What It Does
Line tool	Draws straight lines
Rectangle/ Square tool	Draws boxes
Ellipse/Circle tool	Draws curved lines
Arc tool	Draws arcs and creates pie wedge shapes
Freeform tool	Draws freeform shapes
Text box	Enables you to insert text
Callout	Enables you to insert a callout
Format callout	Enables you to choose a callout style
Fill color	Enables you to choose a fill color
Line color	Enables you to choose a line color
Line style	Enables you to choose a line style
Select drawing objects	Selects one or more objects for editing
Bring to front	Moves drawing object to foreground
Move to back	Moves drawing object to background
Bring in front of text	Moves drawing object in front of text
Send behind text	Moves drawing object behind text
Group	Connects objects in a group, so that they all can be edited or moved at once
Ungroup	Separates objects in a group so that they can be edited or moved individually
Flip horizontal	Flips a drawing left-to-right
Flip vertical	Flips a drawing upside down
Rotate right	Rotates selected drawing 90° to the right
Reshape	Reshapes selected freeform object
Snap to grid	Creates a grid that objects can adhere to so that you can position them more precisely

Button	What It Does
Align drawing	Lines up one or more drawing objects with each other, or with the page
Create picture	Inserts a Word Picture drawing container
Frame	Inserts a frame

To draw, you need to be in page layout view. If you're not in page layout view and you choose a drawing tool from the Drawing toolbar, Word reminds you (see fig. 21.29).

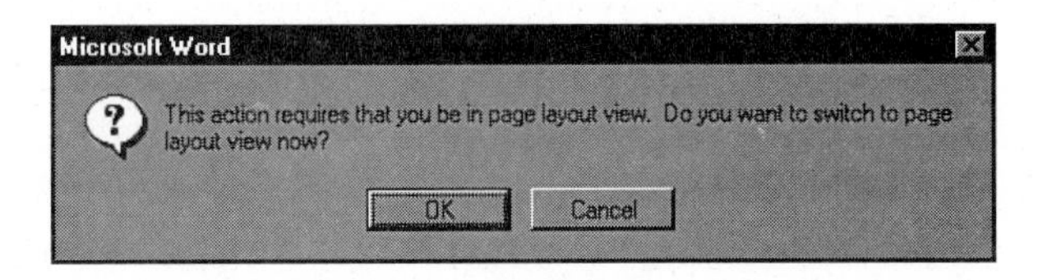

Figure 21.29

Your invitation to page layout view.

Click on OK. To create a line or shape, choose the drawing tool you want, and click where you want the shape to begin. (Your mouse pointer now looks like a crosshair.) Then drag the drawing tool to where you want the shape to end (see fig. 21.30). When you release the mouse button, the shape appears.

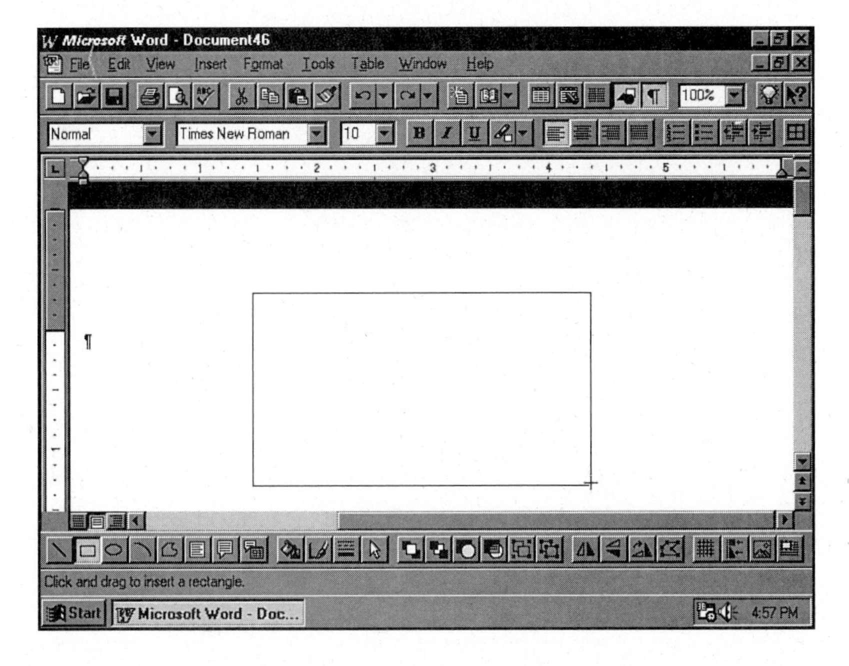

Figure 21.30

Dragging a drawing tool.

You'll see small square boxes (*handles*) at the ends or corners of the shape. These indicate the shape is *active*. You can delete an active shape by pressing Backspace. You can move the entire shape by dragging it. You can move one end, shrinking or enlarging the shape, by dragging its handle. You also can add color to the line or the inside of the shape, add patterns, and change the line style.

Changing Line Style and Drawing Arrows

You've already seen how to draw a line. Wouldn't it be neat if that line had an arrow at the end of it? Then you could draw a pointer connected to anything you wanted.

Word offers this feature. Click on the Line Style button, and a variety of line styles appear, including several thicknesses of regular lines, dotted lines, and broken lines—along with several arrows going in either or both directions (see fig. 21.31).

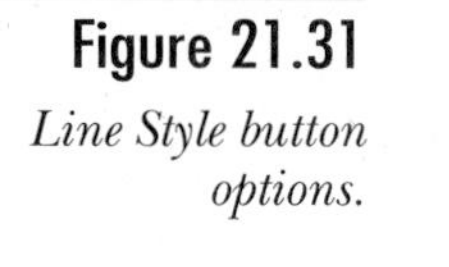

Figure 21.31

Line Style button options.

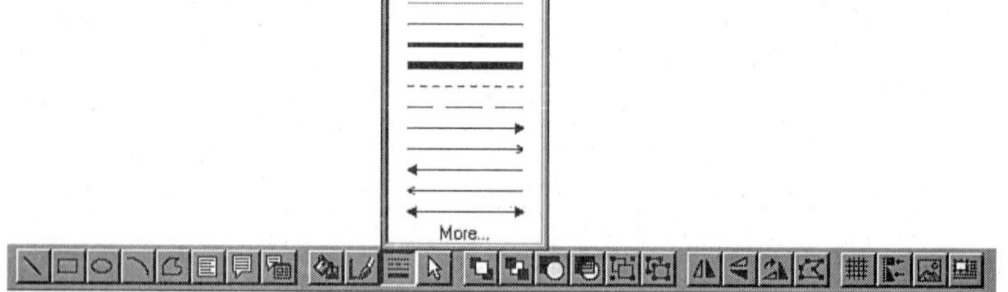

You can choose one of these, and then choose the Line button to insert the line or arrow. Or, to get more control over your line or arrow, choose More. The Drawing Defaults dialog box opens, showing the Line tab (see fig. 21.32).

Figure 21.32

The Line tab.

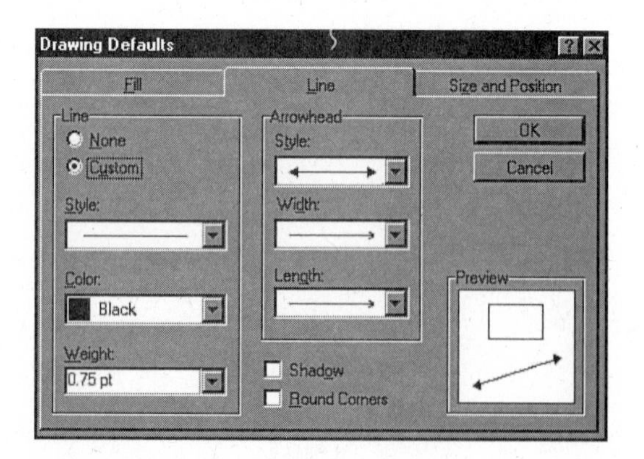

From here, you can specify a line color and weight (defaults are 35% gray, 0.75 point). Additional line styles also are available. If you're creating an arrow, choose Style, Width, and Length in the Arrowhead box. If you've already drawn a line or box, you might find that it doesn't look quite like you expect.

First of all, Word's default settings include a shadow. When you draw a line, you get both a gray line and a black one. Second, your rectangles have rounded borders. These are not real rectangles. Word's default settings specify round corners.

These defaults are much easier to change than to rationalize. In the **L**ine tab, clear Shad**o**w and/or **R**ound Corners. You'll probably also want to reset your line **C**olor from 35% gray to black or a solid color while you're at it.

Now your lines are *lines*, and your rectangles are *rectangles*!

To change the color of a line (or the edges of a shape), you also can click on the Line Color button. Select a color from the palette that appears.

Making Exact Squares, Circles, and Angles

It's rarely been easy to draw an exact square or circle using typical drawing tools. Word offers a shortcut. If you want an exact square or circle, choose the rectangle or ellipse button and press Shift while you drag the mouse.

The same Shift key works to make straight lines that are precisely horizontal, vertical, or diagonal. If you press Shift while you drag the Line tool, you're limited to the following angles: vertical, horizontal, and 30°, 45°, and 60° angles in all four quadrants.

If you're creating a shape with the Freeform tool, click and drag to draw the first part of the shape (see figs. 21.33 and 21.34); after completing the drawing, double-click or press Esc.

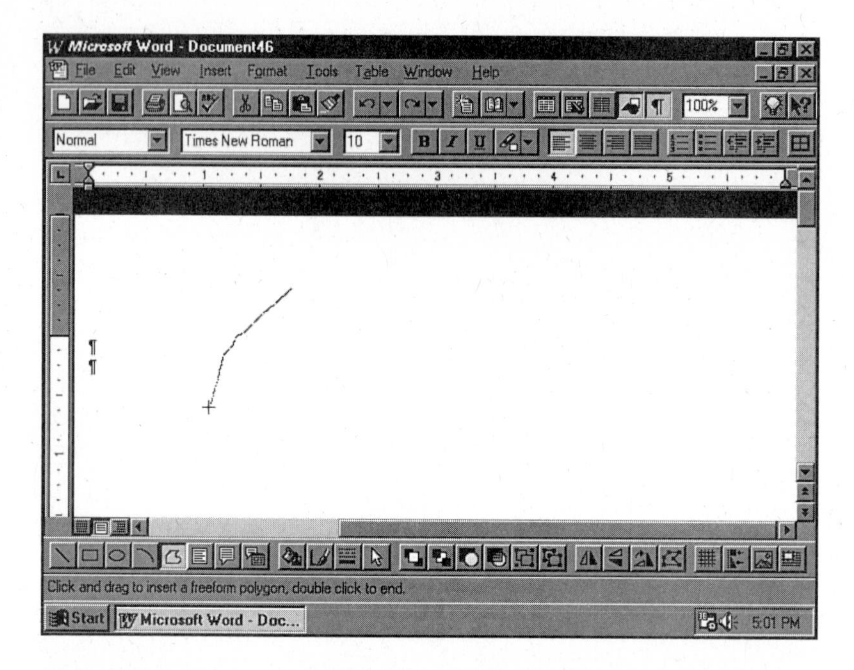

Figure 21.33

Starting a freeform object.

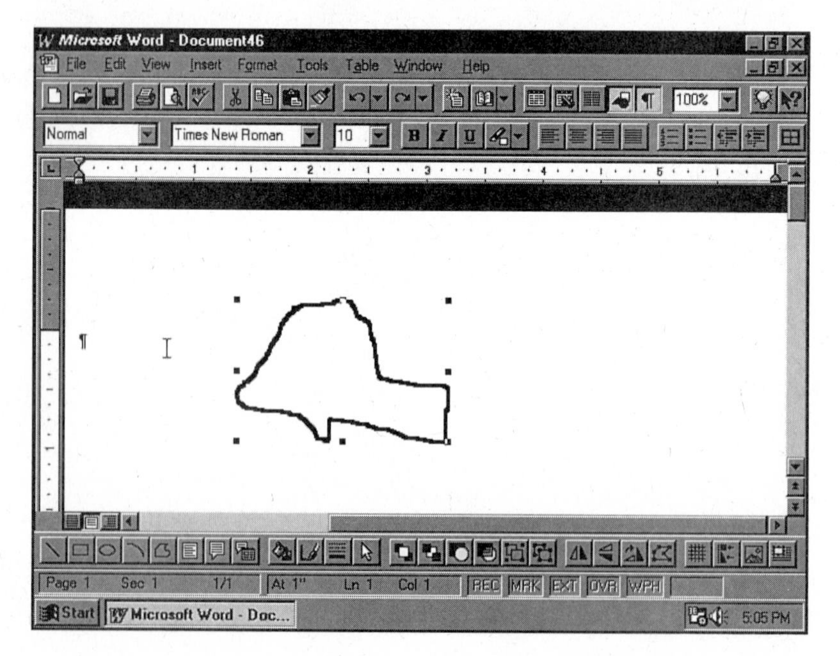

Figure 21.34

Continuing the freeform object.

Changing the Fill Color of a Drawing Object

Shapes, like free time, exist to be filled. You can tell Word to fill a shape with a solid color or pattern by selecting the shape to be filled, clicking the Fill Color button, and choosing a color from the available palette (see fig. 21.35).

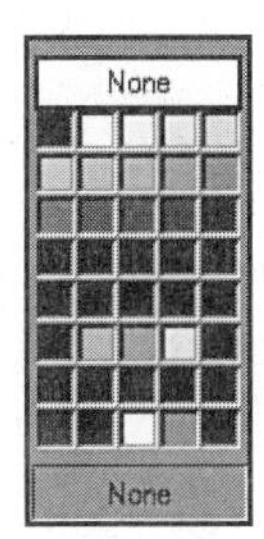

Figure 21.35

The Fill Color palette.

Controlling Color through Format Drawing Objects

As with Line, Word offers a dialog box that controls fill colors and patterns. Select the shape you want to fill. Then select Drawing Objects from the Format menu; choose Fill. The Fill tab of the Drawing Defaults dialog box appears (see fig. 21.36).

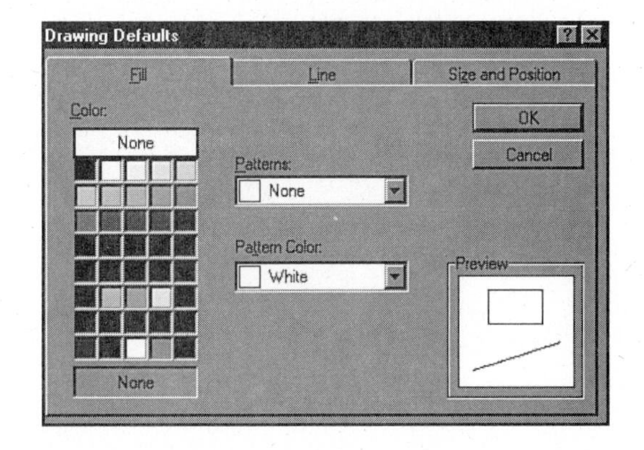

Figure 21.36

The Fill tab within the Drawing Defaults dialog box.

On the left is the same Color palette you've just seen. There are, however, also list boxes for Patterns and Pattern Color. Make selections here, preview them in the Preview box, and then click on OK.

Using Text Boxes

You might want to include text in your drawing. To do so, choose the Text Box button. Click and drag where you want the text box to appear (see fig. 21.37).

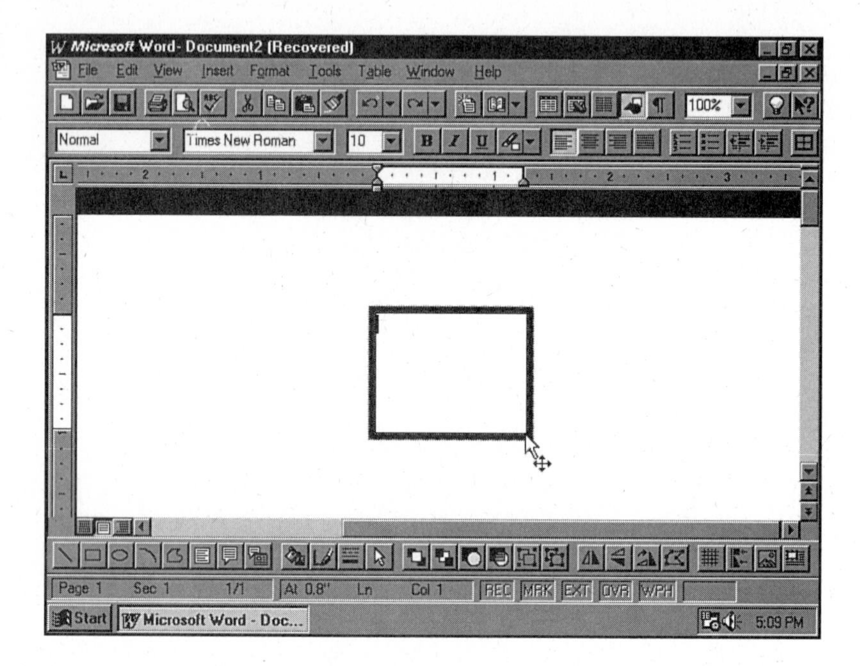

Figure 21.37
The text box.

The text box appears, surrounded by a gray border. An insertion point appears. You can edit and format inside a text box as you can anywhere else in Word. You also can copy material into a text box.

If your text extends beyond the text box, it won't all be visible. But you can expand the text box by clicking on its border to select it, and then dragging its sizing handles.

Creating Callouts

Arrows plus text boxes equal callouts. So Word has added a Callout button that you can use whenever you want to add a pointer containing information.

To add a callout, choose the Callout button, and click on the spot where you want the arrow or line to begin. Then drag the crosshair mouse pointer to where you want to type the callout. Release the mouse button; a text box appears there.

If you move the text box, the callout line still ends at the same spot where you put it, unless you select it and move it manually.

Getting More Control over Your Callouts

Callouts have their own dialog box. To view it, click on the Format Callout button, or do the following:

1. Choose Drawing Object from the Format menu.
2. Select the Size and Position tab.
3. Choose Callout. The Format Callout dialog box appears (see fig. 21.38).

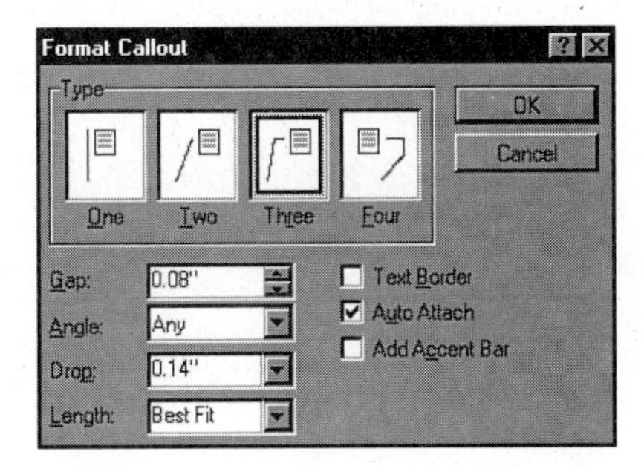

Figure 21.38

The Format Callout dialog box.

You can choose one of four callout styles in the Type box. You can then specify any of the following:

- The Gap between the callout line and the callout text
- The Angle Word can use in drawing the line from the item you're calling out
- The Drop—the space between the top of callout text and the beginning of the first part of the callout line
- The Length of the first part of the callout line

Checking the Text Border dialog box tells Word to place a border around the callout text. Checking Auto Attach, which is on by default, makes sure that the callout line doesn't overlap the callout text. Checking Add Accent Bar places a vertical line next to the callout text.

Specifying an Exact Location for Your Drawing

You can resize or move a drawing by selecting and dragging it. You also can set exact locations and size with a dialog box:

1. Select the object.
2. Select Drawing Objects from the Format menu.
3. Select the Size and Position tab (see fig. 21.39).

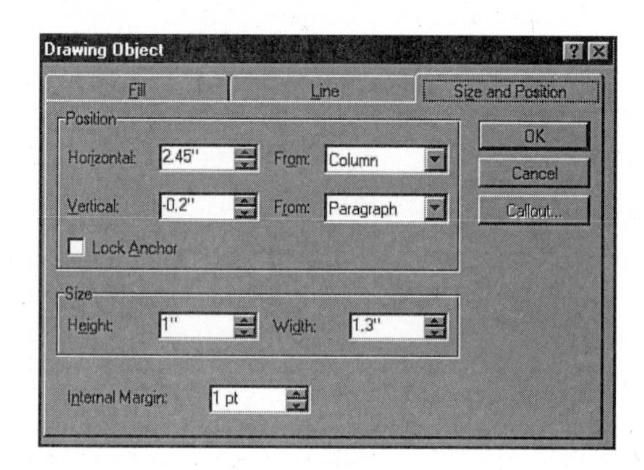

Figure 21.39

The Size and Position tab.

This is similar to the Format, Frame dialog box you saw earlier in this chapter. You can set the object's height and width—reshaping its proportions if you want. You also can set its Horizontal and Vertical position, counted from the Margin, edge of Page, Column, and Paragraph.

You also can set a text box Internal Margin—the space between the edges of the text box and the text contained within it.

Grouping and Ungrouping

At some point, you might have several shapes and lines you'd like to move, style, or remove together. To select them, choose the Select Drawing Objects button, and extend a rectangle around them. Then move or restyle them, or press Backspace to delete them.

Most individual drawings are made up of several components, grouped together. A drawing of a house, for example, might include a grouping for each window, another for the door, another for the chimney, and so on. To edit a part of this drawing, you'll first want to separate the part—ungroup it—from the rest. To ungroup part of an image, select it using the Select Drawing Objects button, and then click on the Ungroup button.

Conversely, you may want to group several objects together, making them easier and faster to move and display. To group drawing objects, select them and click on the Group button.

Layering Your Drawing

Word enables you to create layers in your drawing. The document text you create most of the time is one layer. There's another layer "in front of" your text, and a third layer "behind" your text. You can see these in figure 21.40.

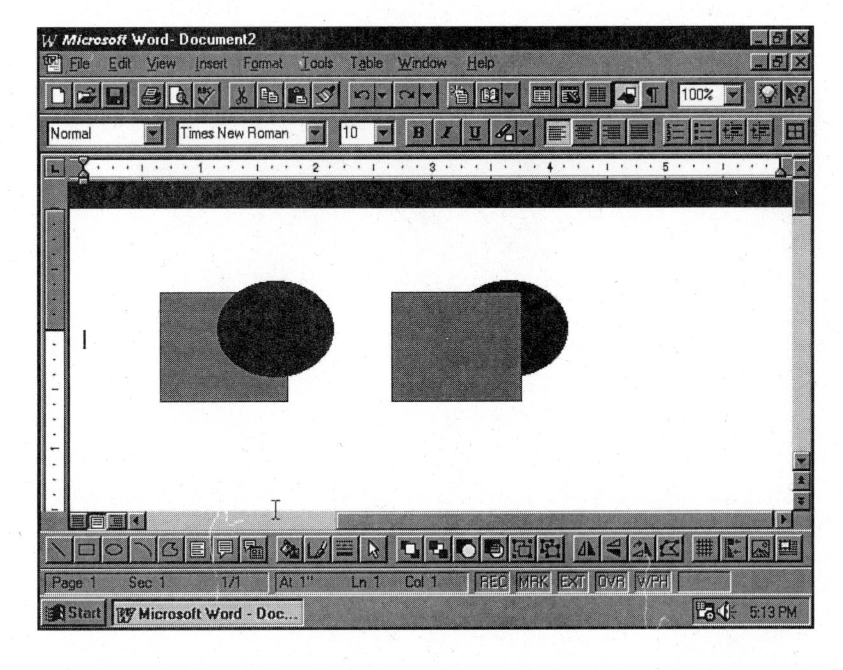

Figure 21.40

Examples of Word's layering.

To specify whether a shape, line, or text box appears in the front or back, select it and then choose either the Bring to Front or Send to Back button.

Rotating Your Illustration

Word offers features for rotating a shape or an illustration. To flip an illustration from left to right (mirror image), choose the Flip Horizontal button. To flip an illustration from top to bottom, choose Flip Vertical. To turn an image 90 degrees to the right, choose Rotate Right.

You can rotate a text box, but the text in it will stay right side up. Use WordArt to create upside-down and sideways text. You learn how later in this chapter.

Aligning Elements of Your Drawing

Often, you'll want to line up two or more elements of your drawing. Word provides an easy way to do this. Select them, and click on the Align Drawing Objects button. The Align dialog box opens (see fig. 21.41).

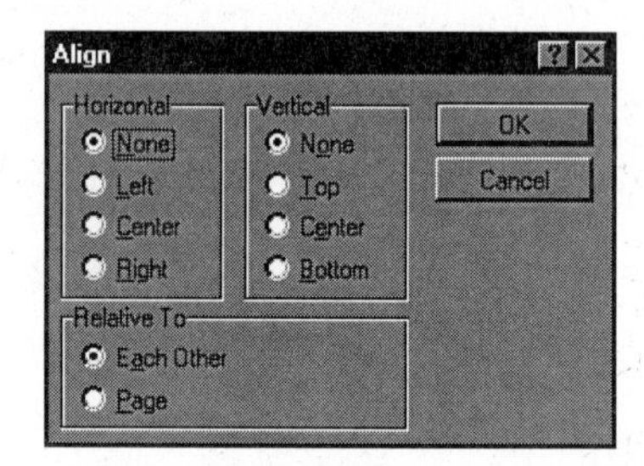

Figure 21.41
The Align dialog box.

Choose how the objects will align horizontally and vertically, and specify whether they will line up with Each Other or the Page.

Using Create Picture

Sometimes, while you're working on a document in Page Layout view, you might want to leave space for a picture that you'll work on later. To do so, place your insertion point where you'll want the picture, and then click on Create Picture. A separate window opens where you can edit the picture (see fig. 21.42). You can use any of Word's drawing tools here, or you can choose Close Picture on the Picture toolbar, and come back to it later.

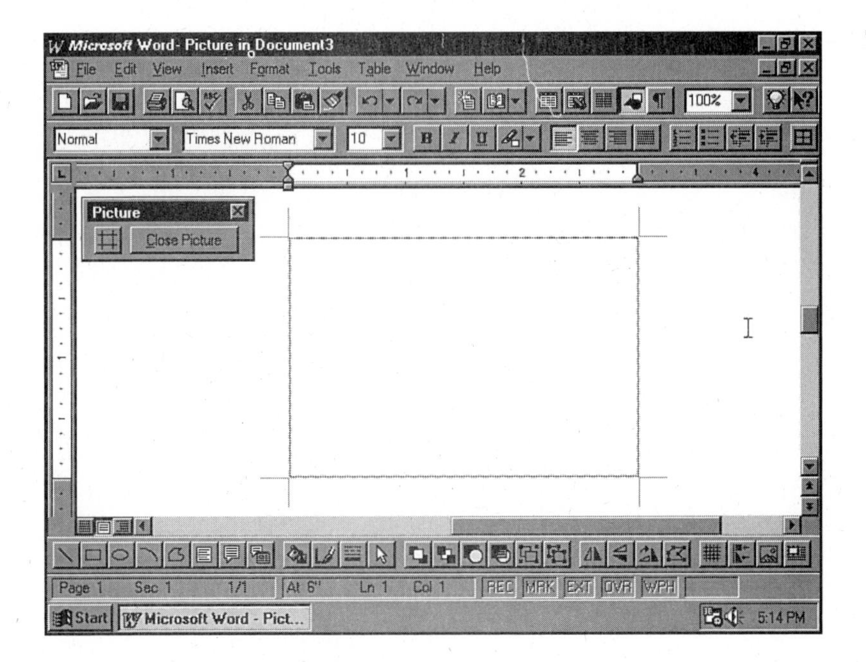

Figure 21.42

The Picture editing window.

Snap to Grid

Word contains a built-in invisible grid that aligns drawing objects to the nearest 1/10th inch. This makes it much easier to line up objects. You can change the fineness of the grid, or turn it off altogether, by choosing the Snap to Grid button. The Snap to Grid dialog box opens (see fig. 21.43).

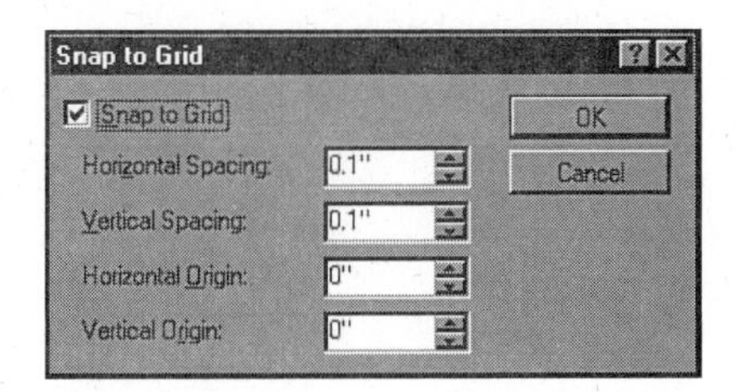

Figure 21.43

The Snap to Grid dialog box.

You can change the Horizontal or Vertical Spacing. You also can change what Word calls the Horizontal Origin and the Vertical Origin. These set the grid's beginning point; in other words, you can specify no grid on part of your screen, and a grid on the rest of it. To turn off the grid entirely, clear the Snap to Grid check box.

Using WordArt 2.5

Word for Windows 95 also comes with a built-in program, WordArt 2.5, which allows you to manipulate fonts in practically any way you like—stretch them, squeeze them, bend them into shapes, add shadows, borders, and a variety of other effects. WordArt 2.5 supports OLE 2.0, so you can move back and forth between WordArt and Word much more easily than before. In fact, WordArt 2.5 works from within any OLE 2.0-compliant application, including Microsoft Excel and PowerPoint for Windows 95, and an increasing number of other applications.

Note WordArt 2.5 is essentially the same program as WordArt 2.0, which shipped with Word 6.0; however, it has been updated to run under Windows 95.

WordArt also supports all TrueType fonts; the version of WordArt that shipped with Word 2.0 only supported 19 oddball fonts named after Washington State towns.

To use WordArt 2.5, choose **O**bject from the **I**nsert menu. The **O**bject dialog box opens (see fig. 21.44).

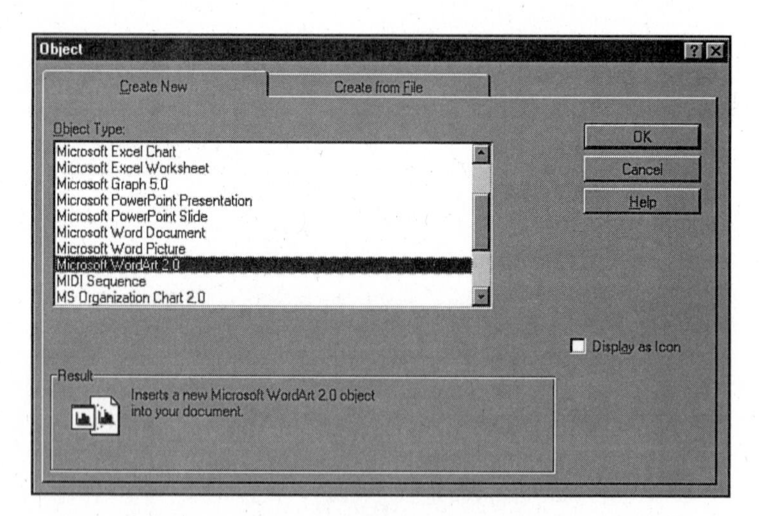

Figure 21.44
Inserting a WordArt 2.5 object.

First, position your insertion point where you want the WordArt object to appear. Then, in the **C**reate New tabbed dialog box, choose Microsoft WordArt 2.5 from the **O**bject Type box. Click on OK, and WordArt opens (see fig. 21.45).

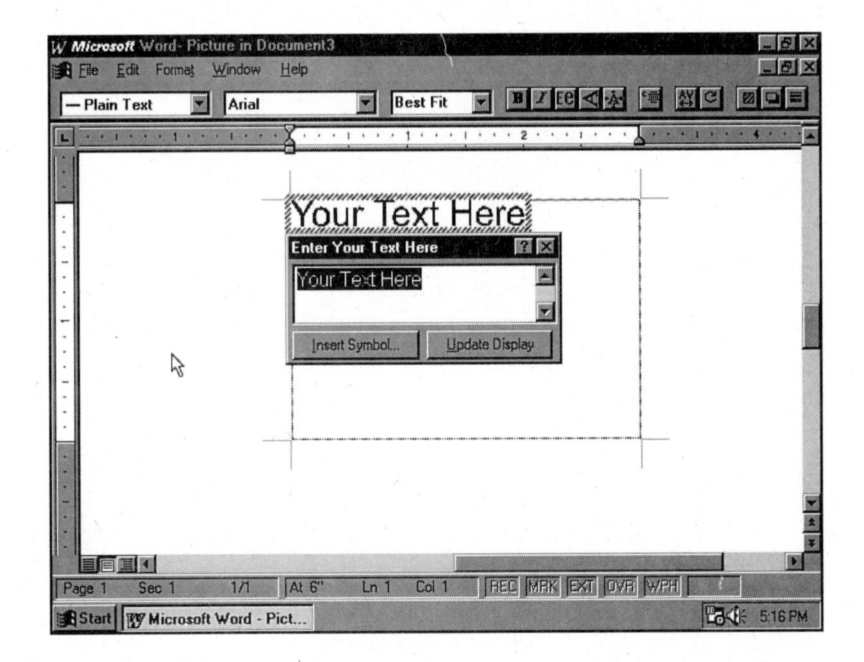

Figure 21.45
The WordArt 2.5 opening screen.

You'll notice immediately that your menus and toolbars change. The replacement menus are the WordArt menus. (This is a feature of OLE 2.0. When you click in the area containing WordArt, the WordArt menus and toolbars appear; the rest of the time, the Word menus and toolbars are at your service.)

Meanwhile, a box with a shaded border appears in your document, and the Enter Your Text Here dialog box appears. Press Enter to delete that text, and type the text you want to work with. Although you can select text to edit it, you can't select text for formatting. The formatting commands you apply affect all the text in the box.

To include a symbol, click on the Insert Symbol button; Word displays the Insert Symbol dialog box (see fig. 21.46). Choose a symbol to insert, and click on OK. To Update your WordArt box to reflect your most recent changes, choose Update Display.

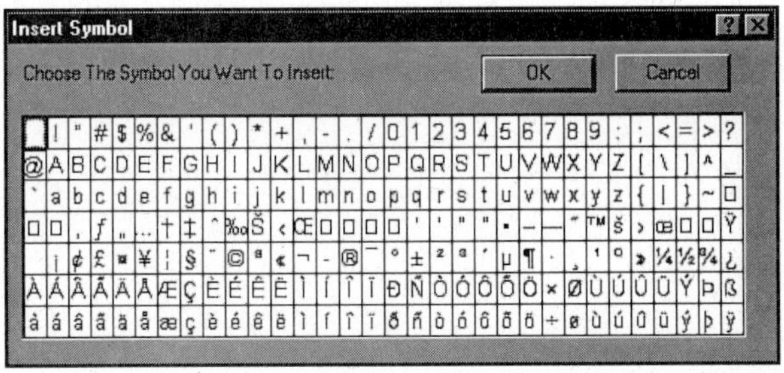

Insert Symbol
Choose The Symbol You Want To Insert:
OK
Cancel

Figure 21.46
WordArt's Insert Symbol dialog box.

WordArt has its own separate Help system, available by choosing **C**ontents from the **H**elp menu while you're working in WordArt.

You'll do most of your text manipulation from the WordArt toolbar, which contains most of WordArt's features, including Line and Shape, Font, Font Size, Bold, Italic, Even Height, Flip, Stretch, Alignment, Character Spacing, Special Effects, Shading, Shadow, and Border.

The Line and Shape box, which resembles Word's style box, can reshape your text into any of these forms (see fig. 21.47). Figure 21.48 shows an example of what changing Line and Shape can do to your text.

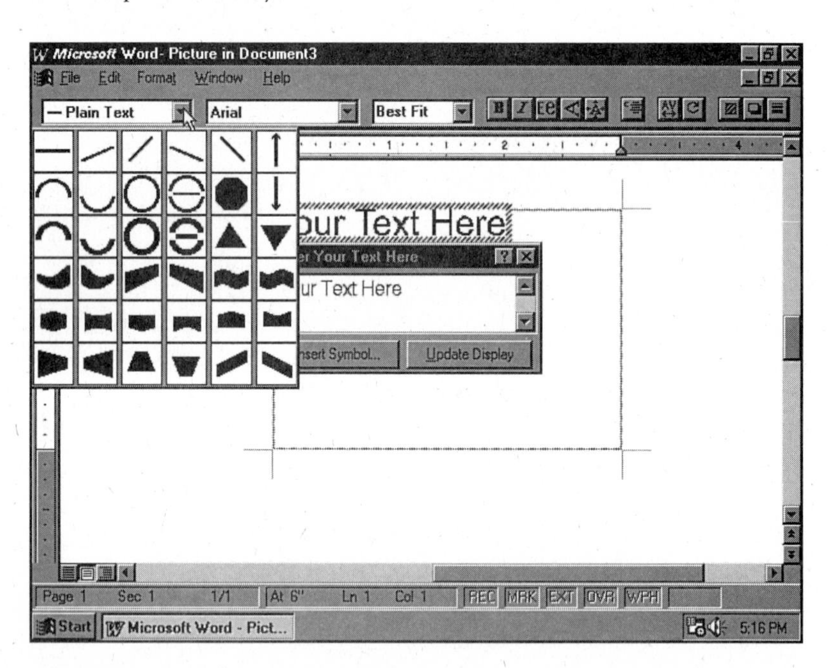

Figure 21.47
Line and Shape options.

If you've chosen a Shape you want to clear, choose the top left straight line. That returns your text to its normal left-to-right style.

The next two boxes control Font and Font Size, the same as in Word itself. WordArt's default font size, however, is Best Fit, which means Word uses what it thinks is the best possible size for all the letters you've typed into the space that's available.

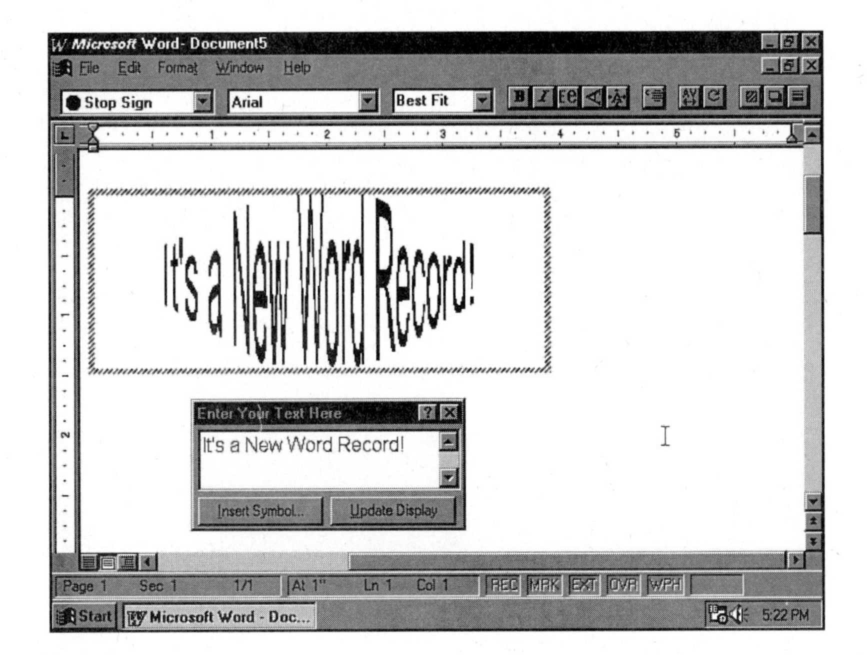

Figure 21.48
WordArt Line and Shape samples.

You can change the size of a WordArt box as follows:

1. Switch to Page Layout view.
2. Click outside the WordArt box to see the Word menus.
3. The WordArt box displays sizing handles. Move them to increase or decrease the box size.

The Bold and Italic buttons do the same thing they do in Word itself—make your text bold and/or italic. The next button, Even Height, shrinks capital letters to the same size as lowercase letters (see fig. 21.49). Clicking on the Flip button turns your text on its side, looking up at the stars (see fig. 21.50).

Clicking on the Stretch button fills the entire box with your text, stretching your text if necessary. Clicking on the Alignment button opens a menu that enables you to choose how to align your WordArt (see fig. 21.51).

Clicking on the Spacing Between Characters button opens a dialog box that enables you to set the tightness of the letterspacing ("tracking") among your characters (see fig. 21.52).

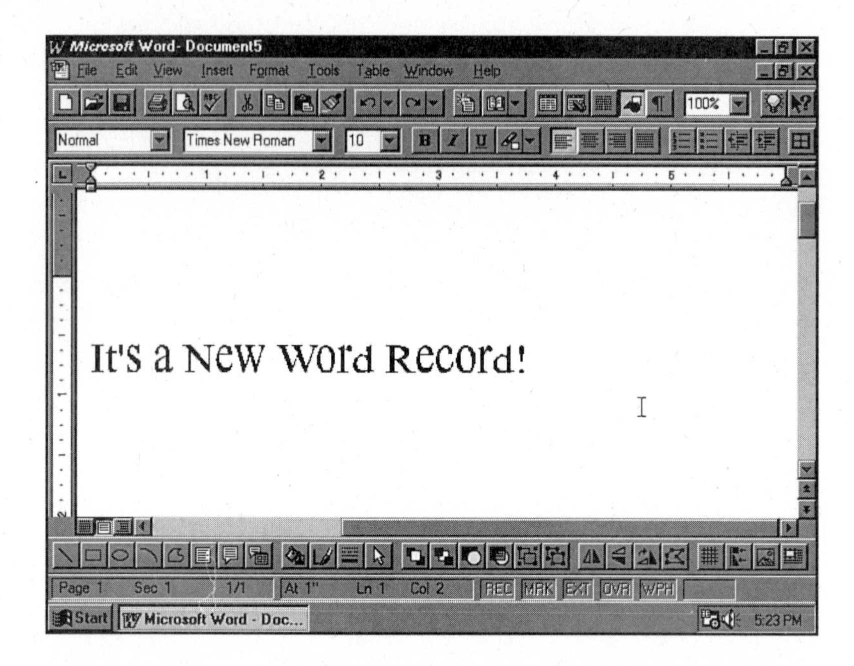

Figure 21.49

Using Even Height.

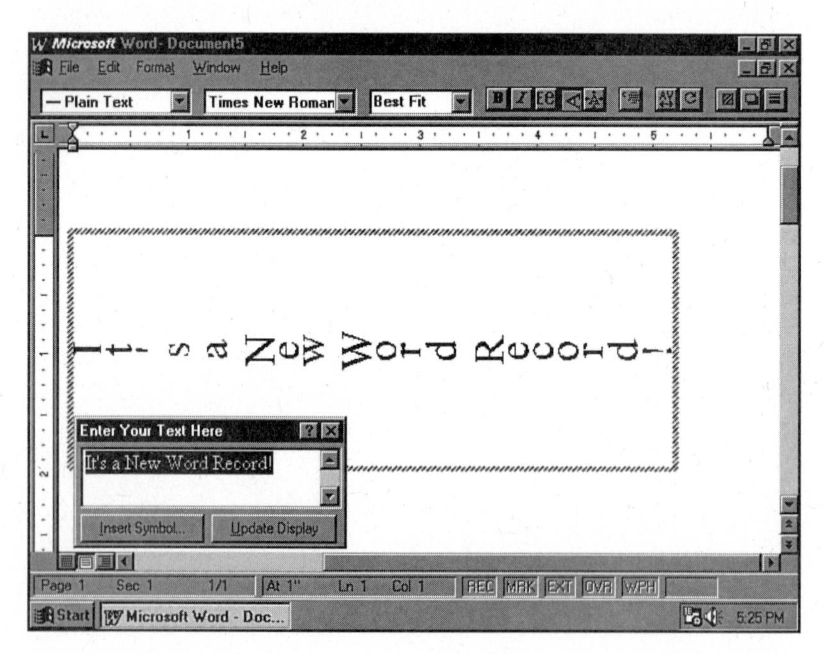

Figure 21.50

Using Flip.

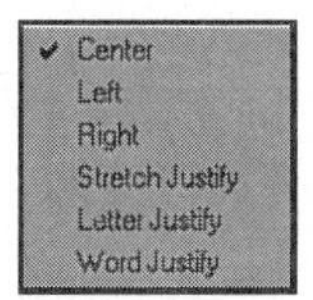

Figure 21.51

The Alignment menu.

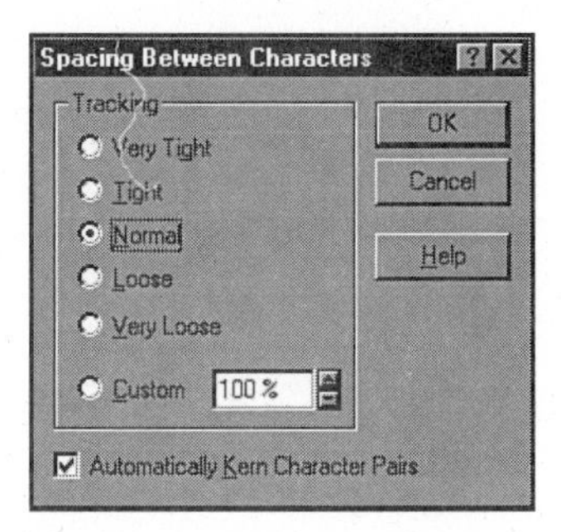

Figure 21.52

The Spacing Between Characters dialog box.

Make your selection and click on OK. Notice that you can set Custom tracking. Also notice that, by default, Word *kerns* (squeezes together) character pairs that need it. You can clear this box if you've created a text effect that doesn't lend itself to kerning.

Rotation and Effects opens the Special Effects dialog box (see fig. 21.53). Rotation sets the angle at which the text appears—from a default setting of 0° to 360°. Slider leans the type forward or back. The default setting is 50%—straight up. A setting of 0% leans the text forward (similar to italic, or more precisely, oblique). 100% leans the text back on its heels. If you've selected an arc shape, you can also control the Arc Angle.

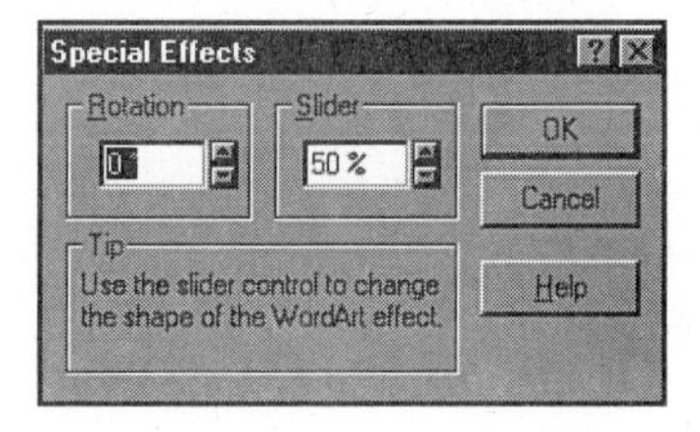

Figure 21.53

The Special Effects dialog box.

Clicking on the Shading button opens the Shading dialog box, which offers a wide variety of shading patterns and colors (see fig. 21.54). Click on the Shadow button to open the Shadow dialog box (see fig. 21.55). Here, you can choose a shadow effect, and if you want, choose a Shadow Color from the drop-down box.

Finally, you can create a Border for your WordArt text. Click on Border, and the Border dialog box opens. What's neat here is that you can choose a colored border to surround black text. The colors are pretty cool, too—and they're not all the same colors used by Word.

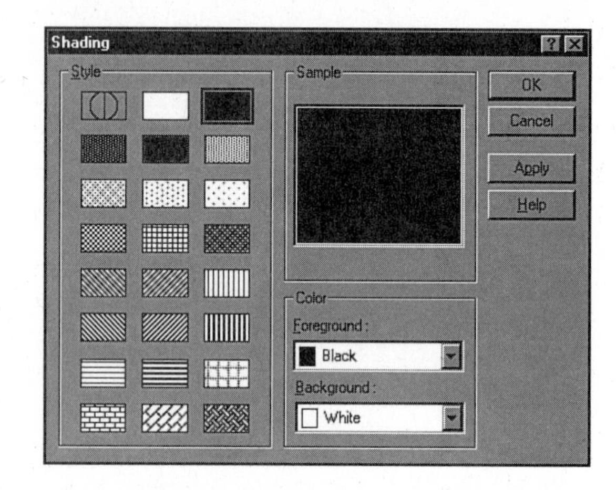

Figure 21.54 *The Shading dialog box.*

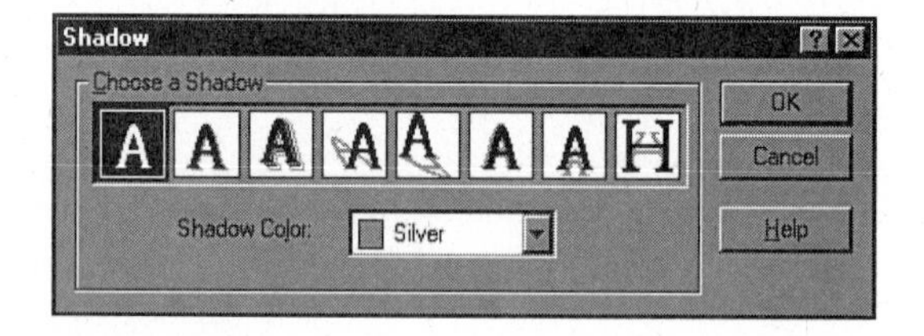

Figure 21.55 *The Shadow dialog box.*

Using Menus in WordArt

While you're in WordArt, the File and Window menus are the same as in Word. This means, for example, that you can switch among open files while you're using WordArt. If the other file isn't in WordArt, the standard Word menus open there.

Edit includes only one item: Edit WordArt Text. Format (keyboard shortcut Alt+T) can get you to several of the same dialog boxes already shown:

- Spacing Between Characters
- Border
- Shading
- Shadow
- Stretch to Frame
- Rotation and Effects

Finally, Help includes specific help for WordArt. (To use standard Word help, click in the document outside the WordArt box, and then choose Help.)

Using Word's Graphing Features

Word makes it easy to integrate business graphs and charts in your documents. Word and the other Microsoft Office applications share a powerful, newly enhanced graph-making program called *Microsoft Graph 5.* Microsoft Graph 5, combined with the new Graph Wizard, makes it significantly easier to create graphs than in previous versions of Word. You can create your data in Word—or use Excel data—then run the Graph Wizard, and finally, adjust your graph's formatting any way you like from within Microsoft Graph.

In this chapter:

- Using graphs and charts
- What is Microsoft Graph 5?
- Using the ChartWizard
- Formatting charts manually
- Inserting new chart elements
- Changing chart types

- Working with the datasheet
- Revising a chart
- Using 3D charts
- OLE and chart embedding
- AutoFormatting charts
- Creating custom AutoFormats
- Adding arrows, titles, and labels

Using Graphs and Charts

Considerable merit attaches to the old idea of a picture being worth more than a thousand words. This is just as true about figures. Tables or columns of numbers often appear dry, uninteresting, and difficult to understand—but a chart that shows a graphical representation of the same information can impart instant understanding.

Suppose you look at sales figures for a company with four regional offices over four financial quarters. Discerning who is doing well and who isn't is not always easy. Put the same figures into a comparative 3D bar chart and you see patterns instantly that reveal which offices deserve credit and which offices need to pull up their socks.

Microsoft uses the terms graph and chart interchangeably throughout Microsoft Graph. These include a wide variety of graph and chart types—including bar, pie, line, area, and 3D charts, along with column and XY graphs.

The accompanying CD-ROM contains two files you can use to practice some of the procedures in this chapter: IWMS22A.DOC and IWMS22B.DOC.

Using Microsoft Graph

Charts and graphs have been used quite commonly to design reports in spreadsheet packages, but recently they have become a feature of word-processing applications. Word for Windows was one of the first mainstream PC word-processing applications to include a charting/graphing module, called Microsoft Graph. Microsoft Office 95 includes an updated version of Microsoft Graph, Release 5.0, which makes it easier

than ever to create and edit your charts. The charting capabilities provided by Microsoft Graph to Word are also available from Microsoft Excel and PowerPoint.

Restoring the Microsoft Graph Toolbar Button

You might have noticed that the Microsoft Graph icon that appeared on the Standard toolbar in Word 6 has been removed. If you do much charting, you may want to put it back—either on the Standard toolbar or another toolbar you use regularly.

The Microsoft Graph button can still be found on the Word for Windows 2.0 toolbar. In the following example, you copy it to the Borders toolbar, which has room for it, and which many people like to display anyway:

1. Open the Borders toolbar by clicking on the Borders button at the far right of the Formatting toolbar.
2. Choose Customize from the Tools menu (see fig. 22.1). If the dialog box obscures the Borders toolbar, to which you're copying the Insert Graph button, drag the dialog box out of the way.

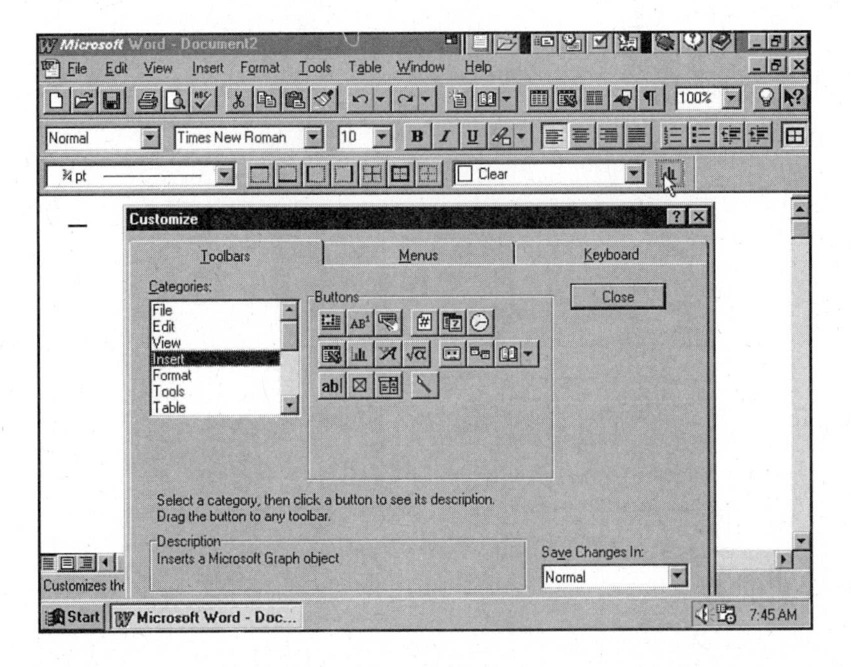

Figure 22.1

Dragging the Insert Graph button from the Word for Windows 2.0 toolbar to the Borders toolbar.

3. Choose the Insert option from the Categories list.
4. Drag the Insert Graph button from the Customize dialog box to the location you choose on the Borders toolbar. If you want to copy the button rather than move it, press Ctrl as you drag it.
5. Close the Customize dialog box.

Creating Data to Be Graphed

The easiest way to create data in Word for charting by Microsoft Graph is to start by setting up a Word table and entering the data there, as shown in figure 22.2.

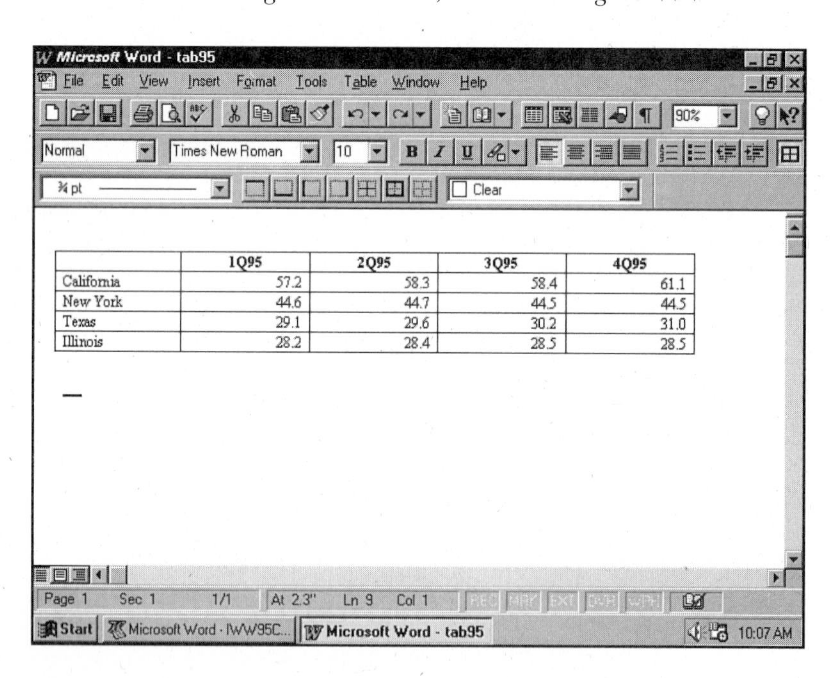

	1Q95	2Q95	3Q95	4Q95
California	57.2	58.3	58.4	61.1
New York	44.6	44.7	44.5	44.5
Texas	29.1	29.6	30.2	31.0
Illinois	28.2	28.4	28.5	28.5

Figure 22.2
A Word table containing data to be charted.

If you created your data with neatly lined up tabs, this also will work, but if Word cannot interpret the information you want it to graph, it opens Microsoft Graph and displays a chart with dummy data instead of running the ChartWizard.

When you select cells, you rarely want to select a row or column containing totals. Doing so skews the scale that Microsoft Graph uses by making all the other data points look small in relation to the single data point that contains the total. If you're creating a pie chart, exactly half the pie will contain your total. This probably is not the result you had in mind.

Once you create the table, the next step is to run Word's ChartWizard:

1. Select the table—or the portion of a table—that you want to chart.
2. Select Object from the Insert menu, select Microsoft Graph 5.0 Chart from the Object Type window, and choose OK. (If you've reinstalled the Insert Graph toolbar button, you can just click on that instead.)

   The ChartWizard appears, as shown in figure 22.3.

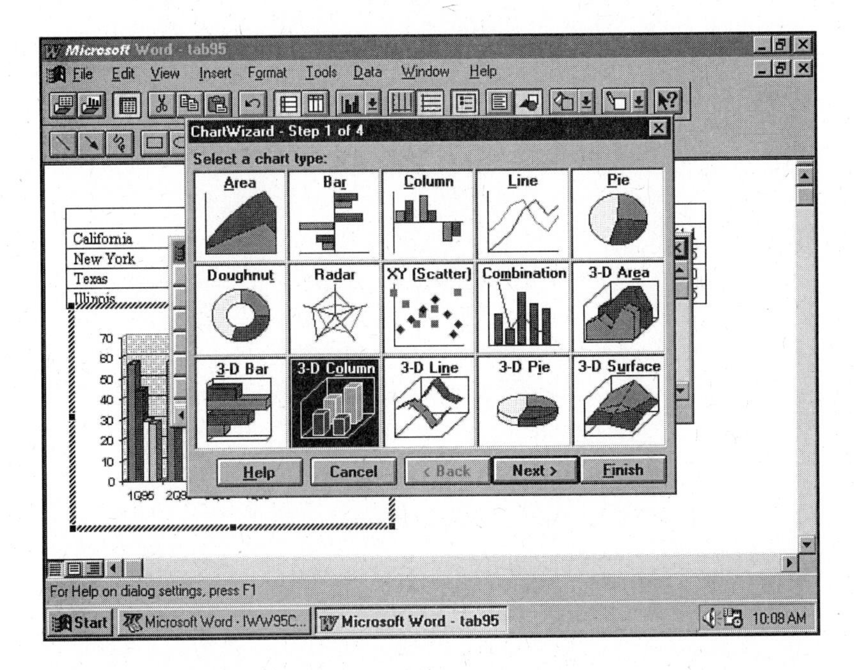

Figure 22.3

ChartWizard's opening window.

ChartWizard Step 1: Selecting a Chart Type

The ChartWizard walks you through the process of building a chart. In the Step 1 of 4 window, a 3D column graph is highlighted. If you're satisfied with the ChartWizard's default options and you don't want any additional titles or labels, just click on Finish and you're done. The ChartWizard inserts a graph immediately beneath the table containing the cells you selected. You can make changes in the chart later, by selecting it or elements of it.

If you prefer another type of chart, select it from the window and click on Next.

Later, you learn how to change the default chart used by the ChartWizard.

ChartWizard Chart Types

A wide variety of chart types is supported within Microsoft Graph. Each type is particularly suited for a given set of data, although you can display any single set of data in several ways:

- **Area graph.** The area graph shows data as areas of the graph that are filled with different colors or patterns (see fig. 22.4). It is best-suited for graphs that do not have large numbers of data points and that use several data series. Area graphs look particularly dramatic in 3D form.

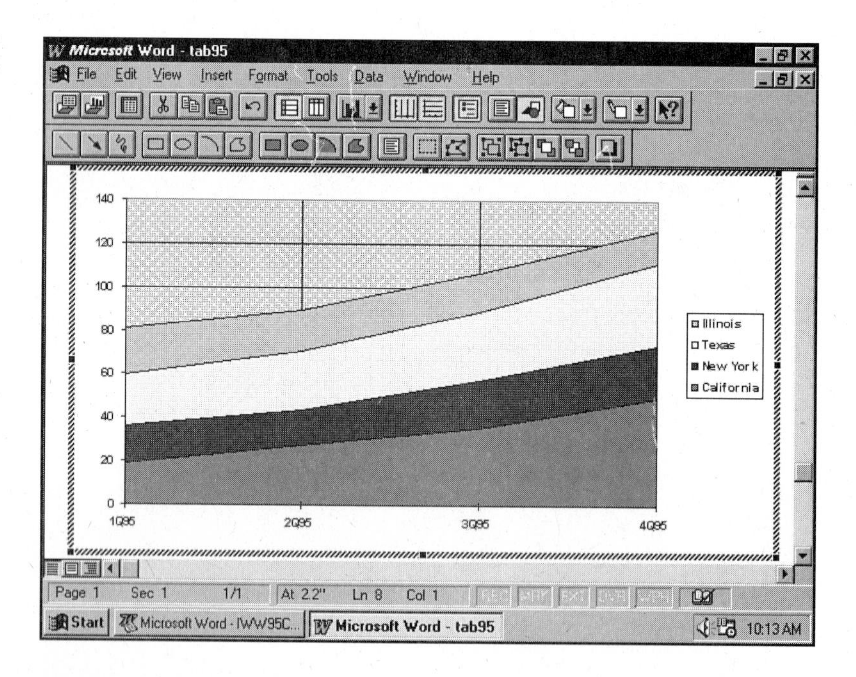

Figure 22.4
Area graph.

- **Bar graph.** Probably the most popular type of graph, the bar graph shows data as a series of horizontal bars (see fig. 22.5). It can be used effectively with three or four series of data over a period of time (such as monthly sales figures from four different regions).

- **Column graph.** A column graph is the same as a bar graph, only it has vertical bars (see fig. 22.6).

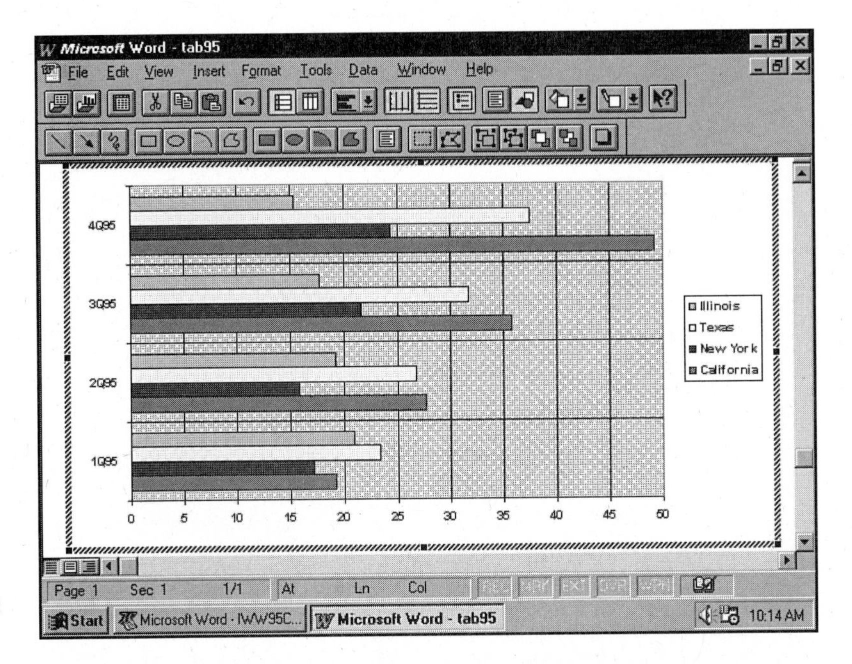

Figure 22.5

Bar graph.

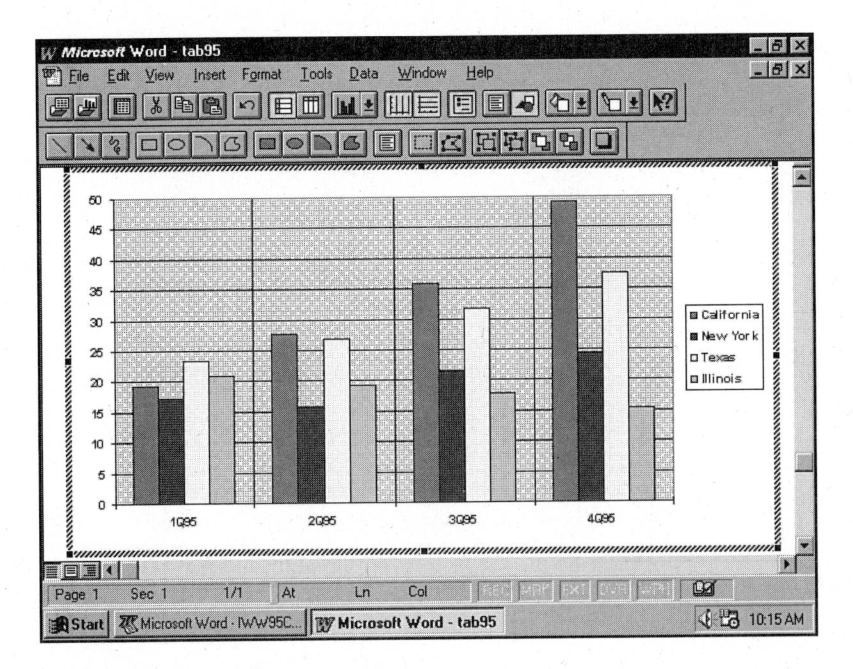

Figure 22.6

Column graph.

- **Line graph.** The line graph is most useful for graphs that have large numbers of data points and several series. Data appears as a series of points connected by a single line (see fig. 22.7).

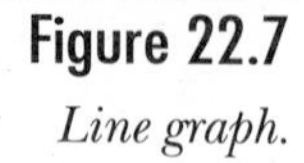

Figure 22.7

Line graph.

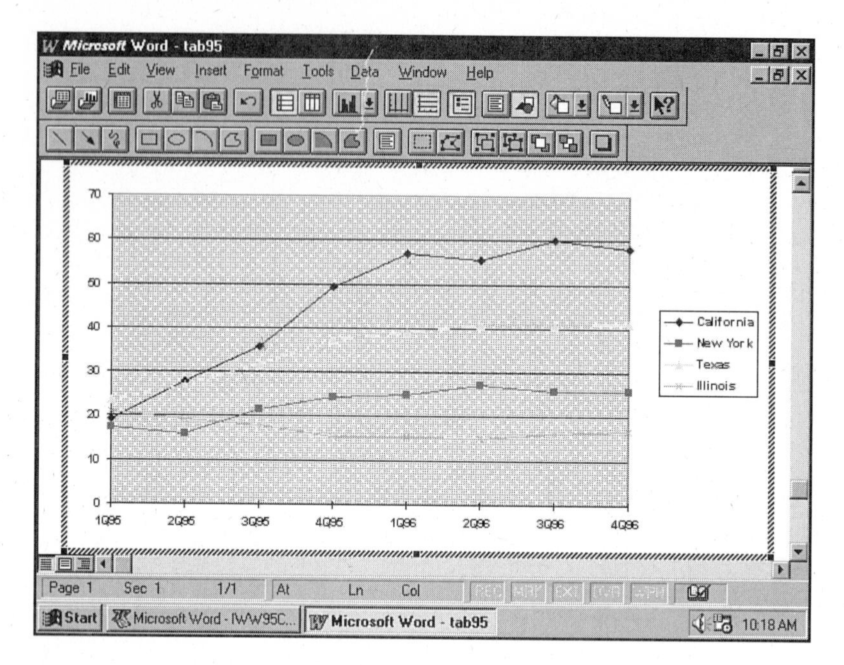

◆ **Pie chart.** The pie chart can be used only with a single series of data, but is particularly well-suited for showing the percentage distribution of expenses, revenues, or any other single-series data (see fig. 22.8).

Figure 22.8

Pie chart.

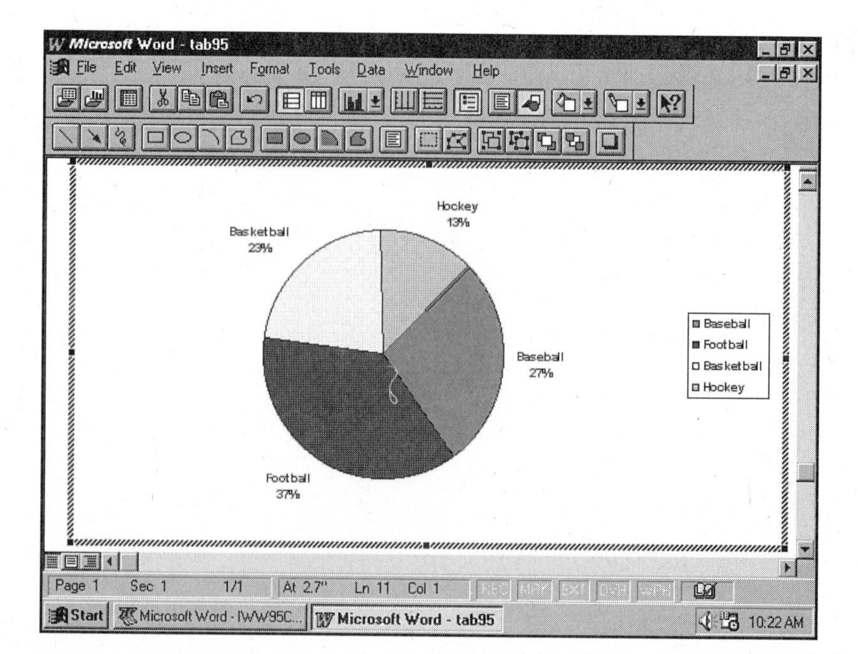

◆ **XY (Scatter) graph.** The scatter graph is particularly useful for showing the relationship or degree of relationship between numeric values in separate groups of data (see fig. 22.9). You can use a scatter graph to find patterns or trends and determine whether variables are dependent on or affect one another.

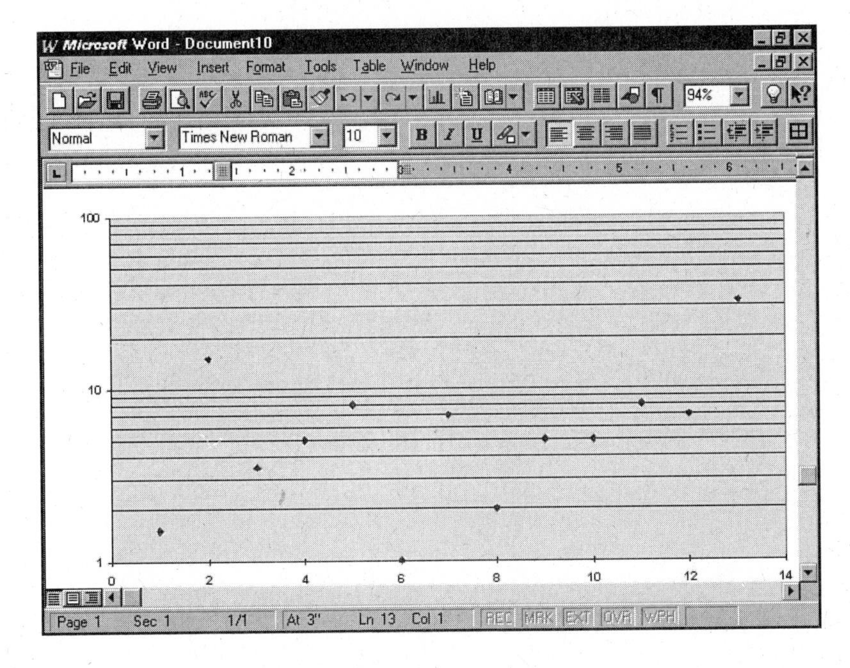

Figure 22.9
XY (Scatter) graph.

◆ **Combination graph.** If you combine something like a bar graph and a line graph (where one series of data, for example, appears as vertical bars and another as a line), you can more easily highlight the differences in the data (see fig. 22.10). Graph enables you to combine up to two different graphs (called *main* and *overlay charts*) to form a combination graph.

There are also 3D versions of the most commonly used charts: 3D Area, 3D Bar, 3D Column, 3D Line, and 3D Pie charts.

Finally, Word also provides a 3D Surface Chart (see fig. 22.11), which resembles a rubber sheet stretched over a 3D column chart. 3D surface charts can help show relationships between large amounts of data; colors or patterns show areas sharing the same value. Use this for finding the best combinations between two sets of data.

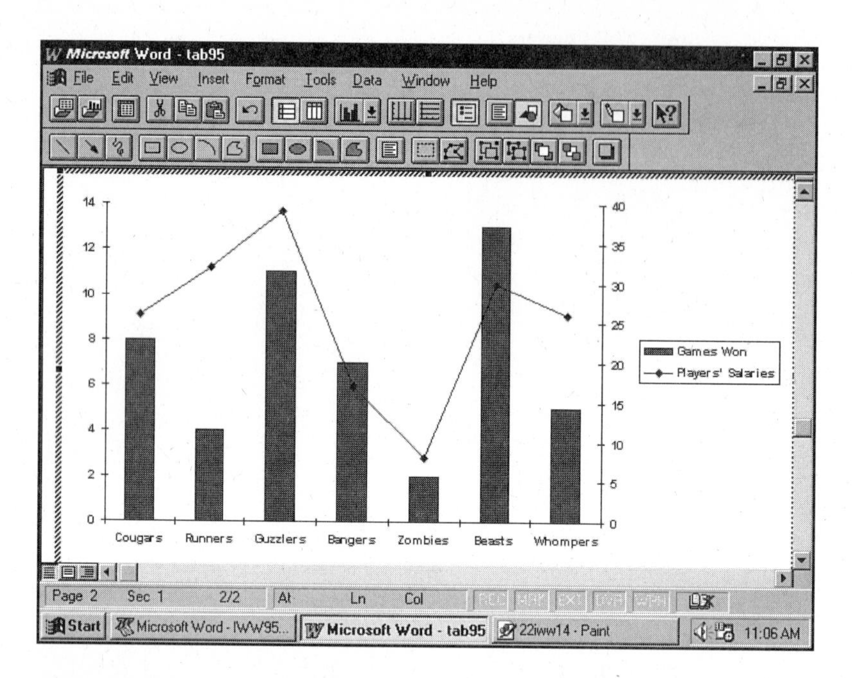

Figure 22.10
Combination graph.

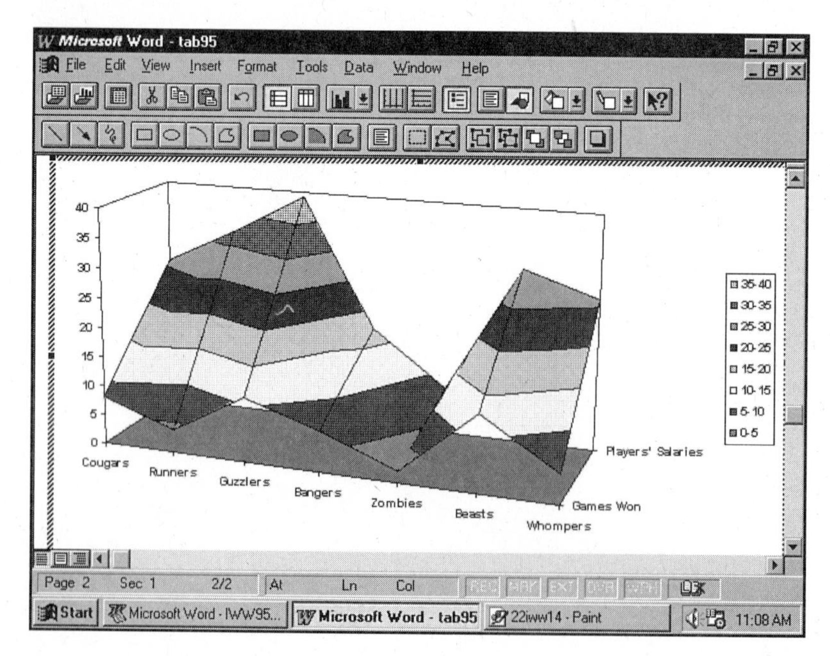

Figure 22.11
3D Surface Chart.

ChartWizard Step 2: Selecting a Chart Format

Once you select a chart type, click on Next or press Enter. The ChartWizard now displays the library of formats that it has available for that chart, as shown in figure 22.12.

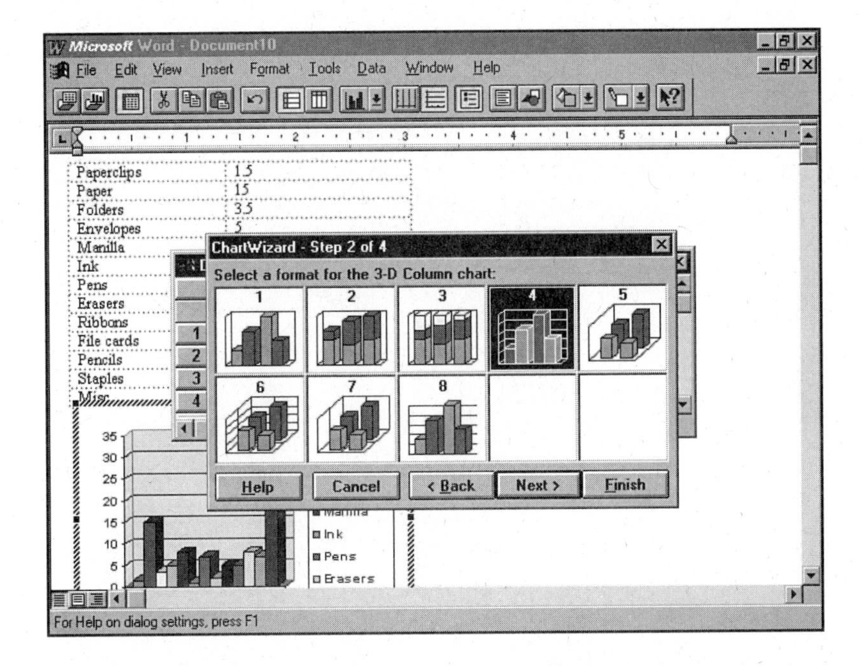

Figure 22.12

Selecting a chart format.

ChartWizard Step 3: Setting First Column, Row, and Data Series

Once you select a chart type, click on Next or press Enter. As shown in figure 22.13, the ChartWizard then presents Step 3, where you can approve or change default settings for the following:

- Contents of the first row of the chart
- Contents of the first column of the chart
- Whether data series appear in **Rows** (the default) or **Columns**

Your specific options for the contents of the first row and column vary depending on the chart you choose. When you make a change, the effects of that change appear in the sample chart shown to the left.

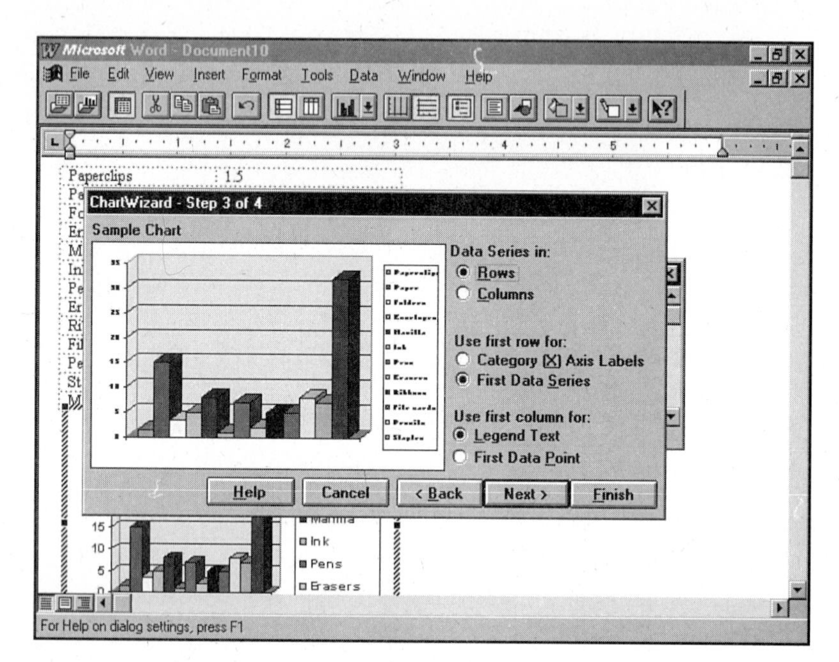

Figure 22.13

Establishing some chart settings.

ChartWizard Step 4: Annotating the Chart

Click on Next or press Enter to continue to the last step of the ChartWizard (see fig. 22.14). Here you can annotate the chart with a title, a legend, and titles for each individual chart axis, depending on the number of axes the chart has. Again, the effects of each change appear in the sample chart.

When you're finished, click on Finish or press Enter; the ChartWizard places a chart in your document directly under the table containing the cells you used.

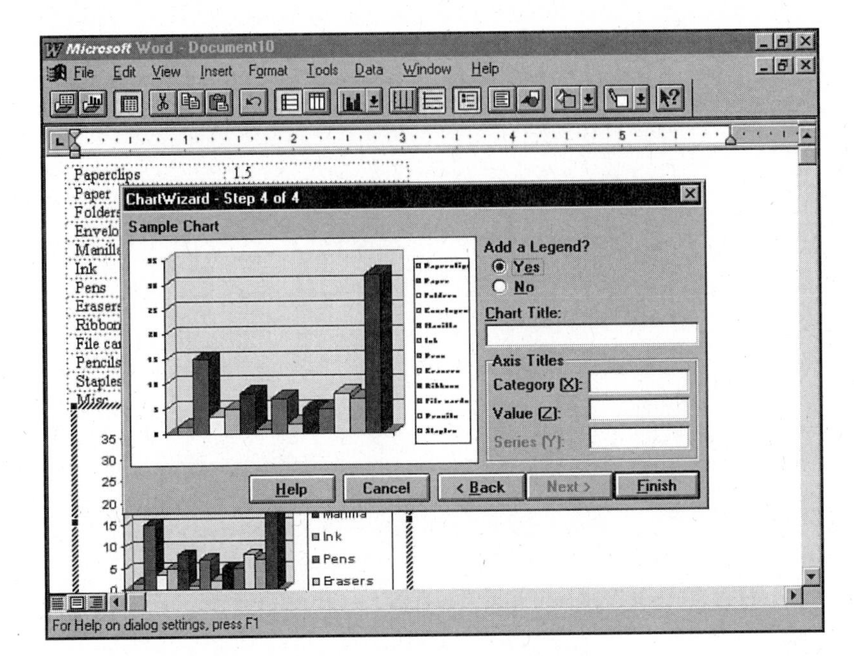

Figure 22.14

A finished chart displayed in a document.

Inspecting a Word Chart

Figure 22.15 shows a typical 3D column chart. This chart contains several elements, each of which can be changed to suit your data needs. These elements include the *plot area* (the main part of the chart), which is bounded by the axes—the X-axis, a Y-axis, and possibly a Z-axis in some three-dimensional charts.

Within the plot area, the chart depicts one or more data series, each representing a set of data from your Word table or other source. The individual bars, columns, or other elements representing each data point within the data series are called *data markers*. The plot area can also contain several optional text elements, such as *axis titles* that describe what each access is measuring and *data labels* that show exact values (or names) for each data marker. *Gridlines* are used to help the eye keep track of multiple lines.

A *chart title* appears at the top of the chart (assuming you added one in Step 4 of the Wizard). In this example, the Y-axis is the scale Microsoft Graph uses to generate the chart. This is true with most charts, with the notable exception of pie charts. If all your data points are beneath 500, for example, Graph places 0 at the bottom of the scale and 500 at the top.

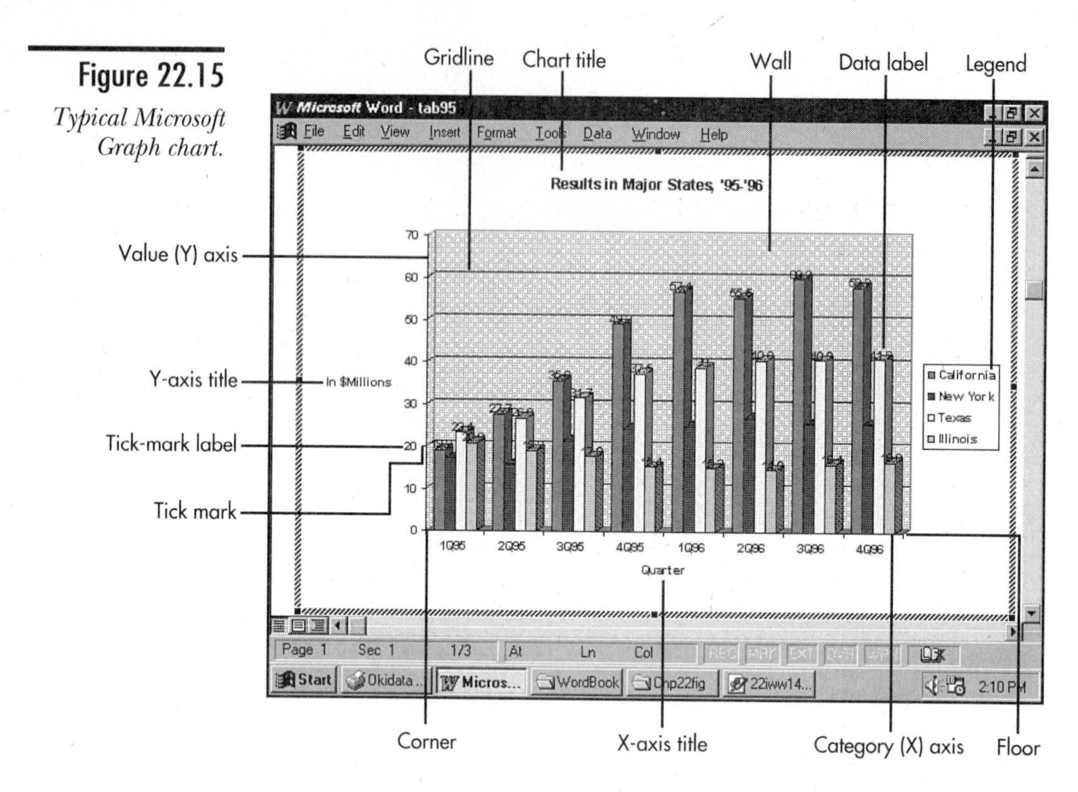

Figure 22.15

Typical Microsoft Graph chart.

Each increment on the Y-axis is called a *tick mark*. Graph also features a *Y-axis title* that you use to tell your audience what you're measuring. Some examples might be: *Profit, in millions of dollars; Commissions, by percentage; Hard disk speed, in milliseconds; Land, in square miles.*

The X-axis normally tells which data series is being measured. Often, the X-axis displays the passage of time; for example, it might show four quarters in a year or monthly results. It might show results from various locations or divisions.

By default, Graph displays each data series in a different color, with like information displayed in the same color. Graph maintains contrast between adjacent bars, pie slices, and so on. This contrast enables you to understand the data clearly, even when it's printed in black and white. As you'll see, however, you can change color, add patterns, or change the background Graph normally uses.

In 3D charts such as the one shown in figure 22.15, Graph also includes a *wall, corner,* and *floor,* which make up the 3D background to the "room" where the chart appears. Walls and floors can each be formatted separately.

Finally, most charts (except those that use only one data series) also contain a *legend*—the explanation of what each color or pattern represents. Graph inserts a legend by default.

Editing a Chart from Word

After you create a chart, you can *activate* it for editing by double-clicking on it in your Word document. Squares and a thick shaded border appear around your chart as Microsoft Graph opens; your menu selections and toolbar change as well, as shown in figure 22.16.

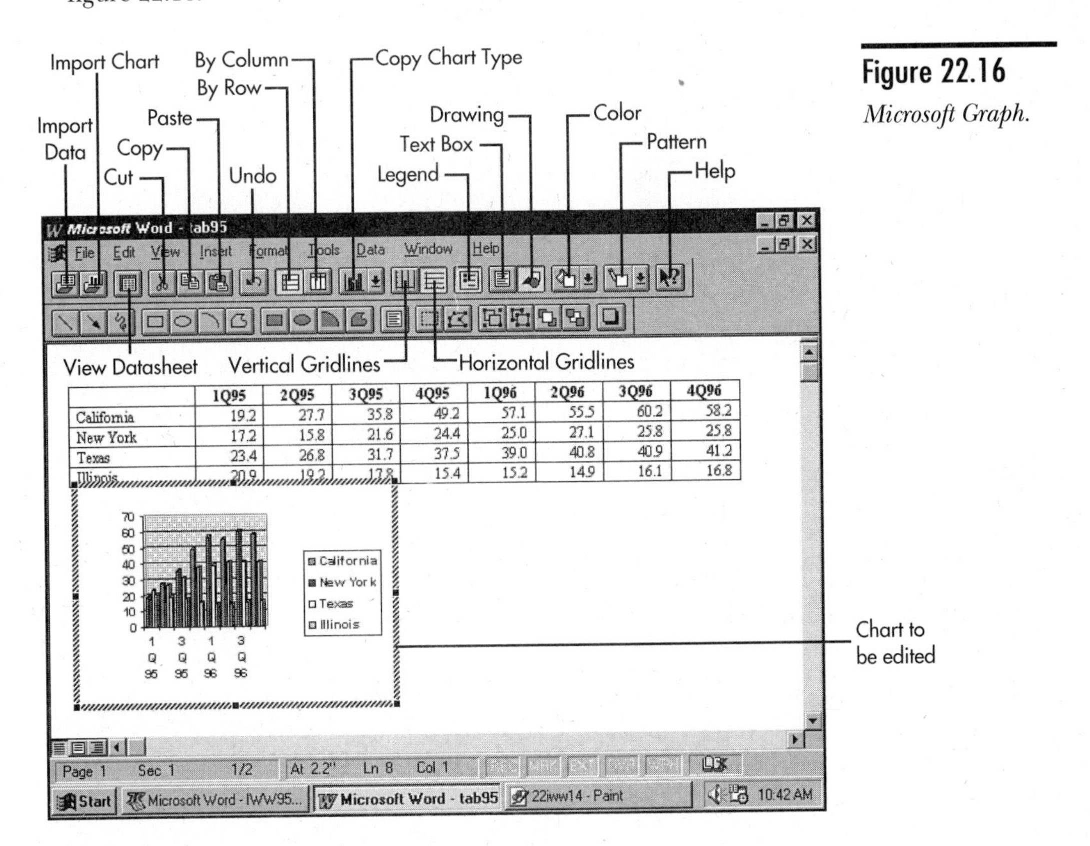

Figure 22.16

Microsoft Graph.

Reformatting Chart Elements

To reformat an existing element of the chart, double-click on it. Graph presents a dialog box with your options for that chart element. For example, if you want to edit a data series, double-click on one of the data markers in that data series. The Format Data Series dialog box appears, as shown in figure 22.17.

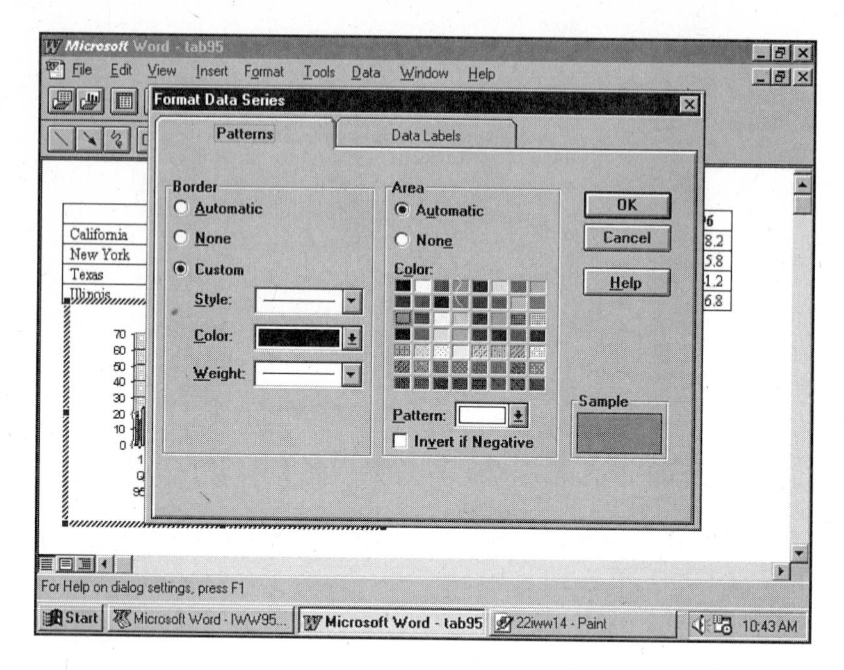

Figure 22.17

Format Data Series dialog box.

This dialog box has two tabs:

- **Patterns—**Enables you to set the colors, borders, and patterns of all the data markers in that series
- **Data Labels—**Enables you to specify whether each data marker will be accompanied by a value or by its label

Accompany each data marker with a value when you want your audience to know precise values, not just the rough values that might be inferred from viewing a bar, column, or other chart element.

To format an individual data point, click on it once to select the entire data series; then click on it once more to select only the data point; then double-click and the Format Data Point dialog box opens.

Similar formatting dialog boxes are available for many chart elements, as shown in table 22.1.

Table 22.1
Chart Elements and Their Dialog Box Formatting Controls

Chart Element	Formatting Controls
Axis	Patterns, Scale, Font, Number, Alignment
Chart Area	Patterns, Font
Plot Area	Patterns
Data Point	Patterns, Data Labels
Data Series	Patterns, Data Labels
Gridlines	Patterns, Scale
Chart Title	Patterns, Font, Alignment
Error Bars	Patterns, Y Error Bars
Legend	Patterns, Font, Placement
Legend Entry	Font
Plot Area	Patterns
Trendline	Patterns, Type, Options

You can also control the contents of a chart element by right-clicking on it to display the pop-up menu associated with that element, as shown in figure 22.18.

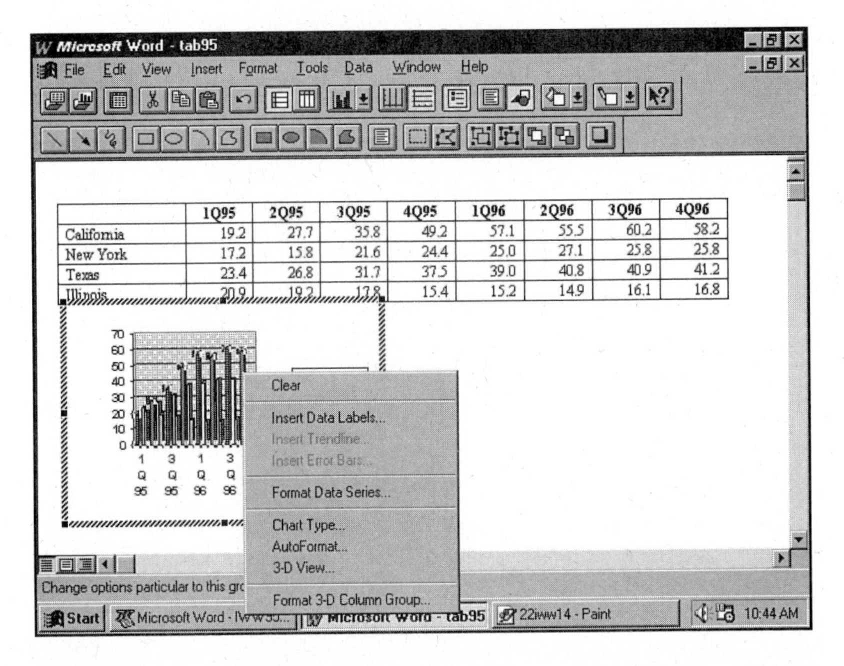

Figure 22.18

Pop-up menu associated with a Data Series chart element.

If you print a color graph to a black-and-white printing device (such as a standard monochrome inkjet or laser printer), you might want to pay special attention to the pattern option under Format. Although Word does try to ensure that grayscale printing of colors differentiates parts of the graph, you can improve the look by selecting appropriate contrasting patterns.

AutoFormatting a Chart

Windows 95

Rather than formatting a chart one element at a time, you can AutoFormat it using one of Microsoft Graph's library of chart formats. To do so, select the chart by clicking on the corner of the chart area. Choose AutoFormat from the Format menu. The AutoFormat dialog box opens. In the Galleries box, choose the chart type you want. Then, in the Format box, choose the chart that most closely resembles what you're seeking. Choose OK, and Graph AutoFormats the chart.

Creating a Custom AutoFormat

Windows 95

Your organization may standardize on a certain custom look for charts. Is there an easy way to make all your charts look the same without manually reformatting every one? Yes, by creating a custom AutoFormat. Here's how:

1. Format a chart the way you want it.
2. Choose AutoFormat from the Format menu.
3. Choose the User-Defined button. (If you're doing this for the first time, there will be no User-Defined AutoFormats.) Choose Customize.
4. The User-Defined AutoFormats dialog box opens (see fig. 22.19). Choose Add.

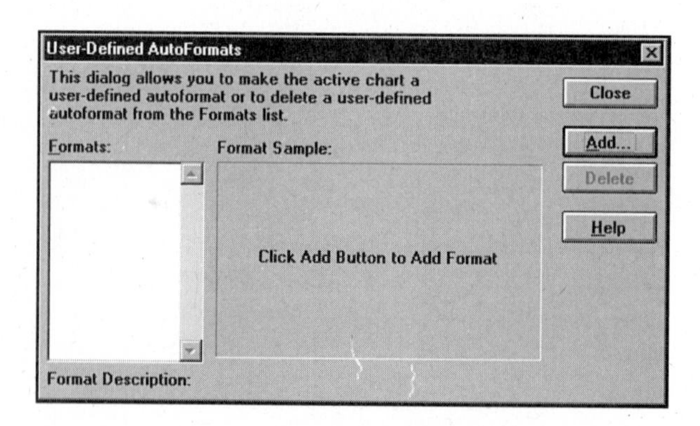

Figure 22.19
User-Defined AutoFormats dialog box.

5. The Add Custom AutoFormats dialog box opens (see fig. 22.20). Enter a Format Name and a Description of no more than 31 characters. Choose OK.

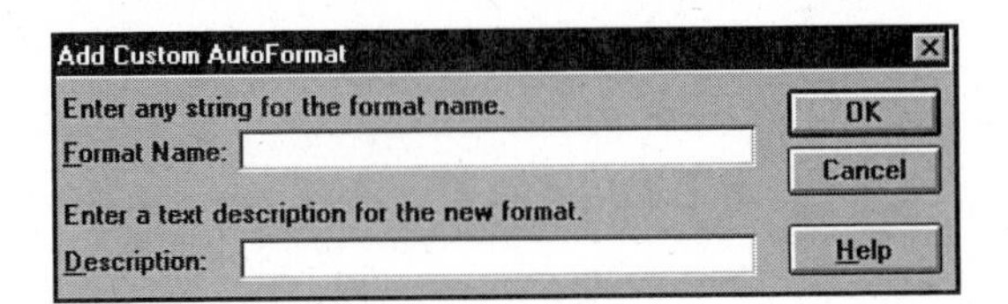

Figure 22.20
Add Custom AutoFormat dialog box.

6. The custom format name and a thumbnail sketch now appear in the User-Defined AutoFormats box. Choose Close.

Inserting New Chart Elements

What if you have created a chart and now decide that you want to add a new element, such as a legend or a title? Choose the element you want to add from the Insert menu: Titles, Data Labels, Legends, Axes, or Gridlines. (Legends and both Horizontal and Vertical Gridlines can also be toggled on and off with Microsoft Graph toolbar buttons.)

Inserting a New Title

If you choose Titles, Graph displays the Titles dialog box (see fig. 22.21), where you can specify which titles you wish to add: a chart title and titles for one or more axes. Choose the titles you wish to add, and choose OK. Graph then displays boxes in the chart where you can edit the titles you've added, as shown in figure 22.22.

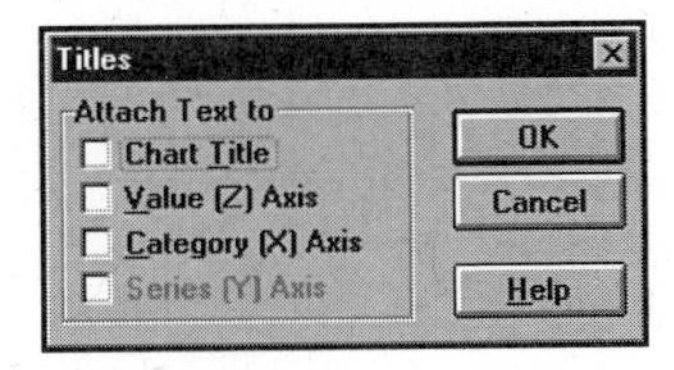

Figure 22.21
Titles dialog box.

Inserting New Data Labels

If you choose Data Labels, the Data Labels dialog box opens (see fig. 22.23). You can either display the value associated with each selected data series or data point (Show Value) or the name of that data series or data point (Show Label). For pie charts, you also have the option of displaying a percentage (Show Percent).

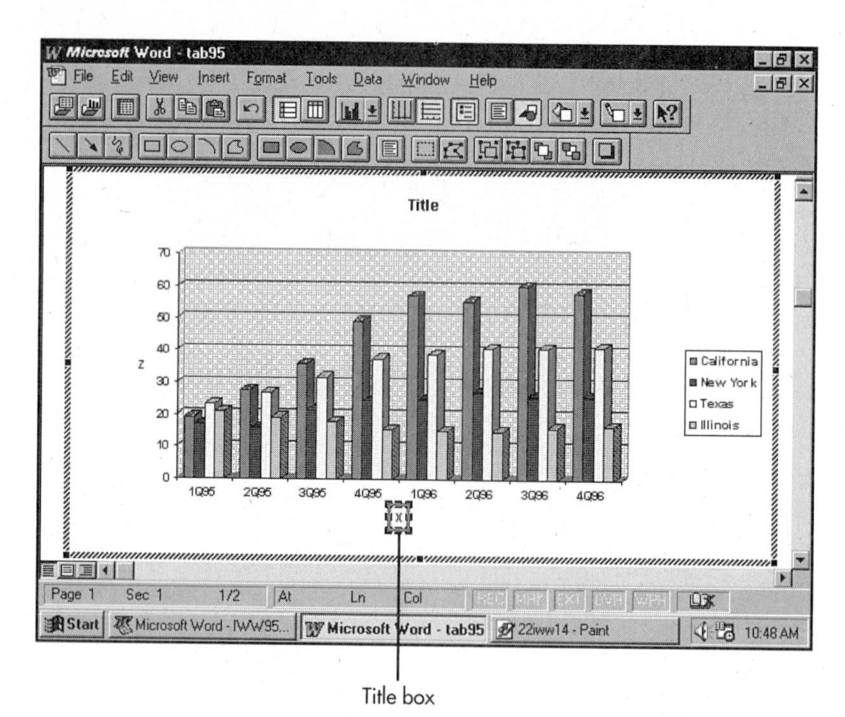

Figure 22.22

Editing a title in the chart.

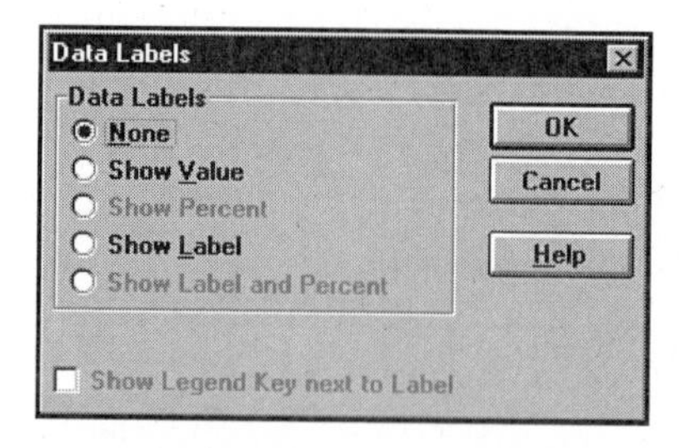

Figure 22.23

The Data Labels dialog box.

Inserting New Gridlines

Recall that you can toggle vertical or horizontal gridlines on and off using toolbar buttons. If you want more control over your gridlines, however, choose Gridlines from the Insert menu. The Gridlines dialog box opens (see fig. 22.24).

By default, Graph places gridlines perpendicular to the data being charted at the same points where values are shown along the axis. For example, if you use a bar graph where the columns appear horizontally, the value axis is the X-axis, and the gridlines are displayed vertically from that axis, as shown in figure 22.25).

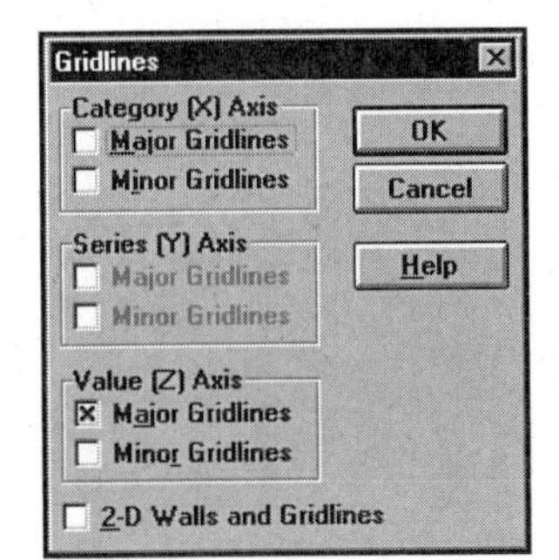

Figure 22.24

Gridlines dialog box.

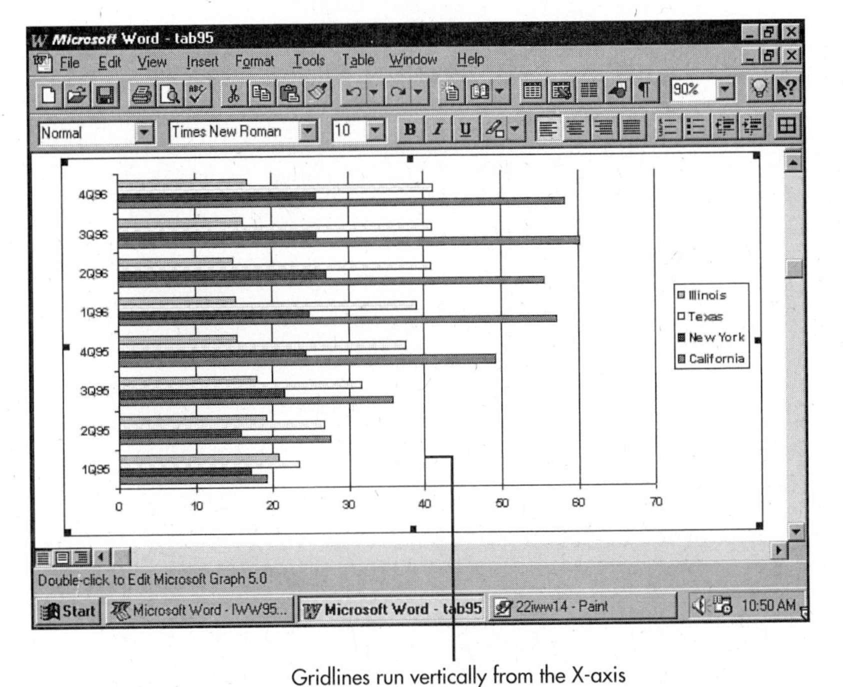

Figure 22.25

Default gridlines for a horizontal bar graph.

Gridlines placed at the same points as values are called Major Gridlines. If you want additional gridlines to appear between major gridlines, add Minor Gridlines.

By default, Graph does not display gridlines parallel to the data being charted, but you can add these as well—both major and minor gridlines.

Adding Text Boxes, Arrows, and Other Drawing Elements

Windows 95

Sometimes you want to annotate a chart to call attention to a specific data point. Most of the Word drawing tools you learned about in Chapter 21 are available from within Graph; just click the Drawing button on the toolbar to display them. Graph makes it even easier to use text boxes by placing the Text Box button on the main Graph toolbar.

To create a text box in a chart, click on the Text Box button; then click in the chart and drag the mouse pointer to make the text box as large as you want it. An editing cursor appears at the beginning of the text box; enter the text you want to include.

Once you have a text box, you may want to add an arrow directed at the data point you're referencing. Click on the Drawing button, and Microsoft Graph's Drawing toolbar appears. Notice that it's quite similar to Word's Drawing toolbar. Click on the Arrow button, place the mouse pointer in your chart, and drag from where you want the tail of the arrow to where you want the head of the arrow. Figure 22.26 shows a chart with text box and arrow pointing to a data point.

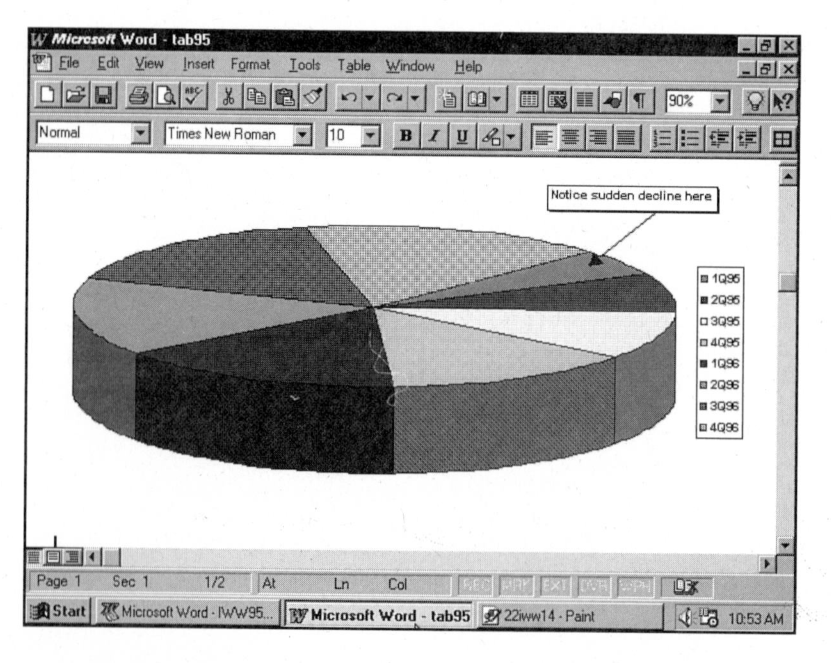

Figure 22.26
Chart with text box and arrow.

Changing a Chart Type

If you create a chart and later decide that a different type of chart will communicate your information more accurately, Graph gives you several ways to make the change.

If you want an entirely different kind of chart, activate the chart you want to change, click on the down-arrow next to the Chart Type button, and choose the chart you want. If you want more control, choose Chart Type from the Format menu. The Chart Type dialog box opens (see fig. 22.27).

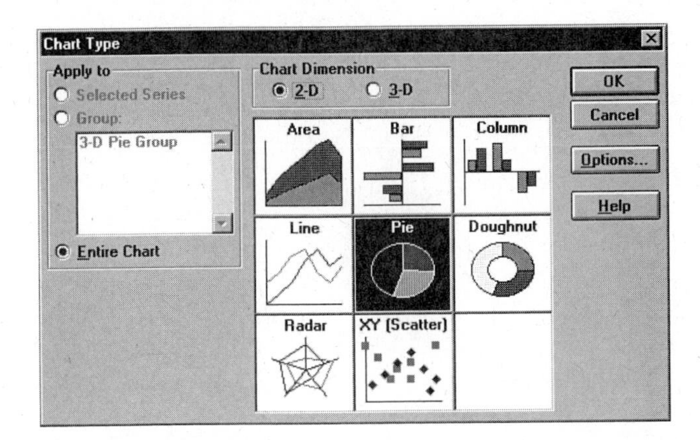

Figure 22.27

Chart Type dialog box.

If you want to reformat the entire chart, check **E**ntire Chart. Then, in Chart Dimension, check **2**-D or **3**-D to specify the group of charts from which you want to choose. Then highlight a specific type of chart, such as Bar or Column. If you're satisfied with a generic chart, choose OK, and Graph will reformat your chart accordingly. If you want more control, check **O**ptions. The Format 3-D Bar Group dialog box opens (see fig. 22.28). The options in the dialog box vary depending on the chart type you've chosen. Figure 22.28 shows the options available for 3D bar charts.

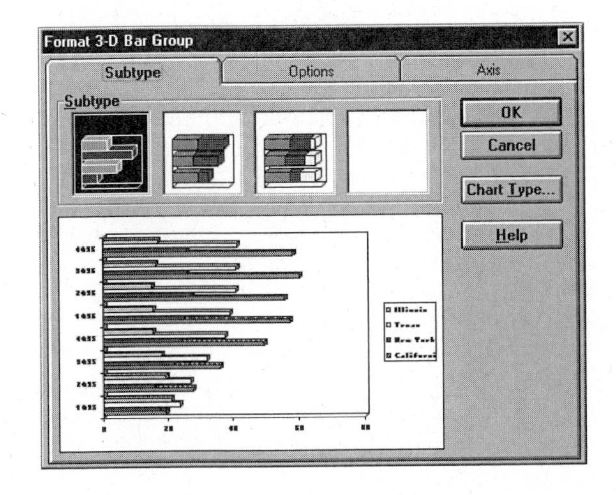

Figure 22.28

Format 3-D Bar Group dialog box.

The *Subtype* tab presents the chart appearance options Microsoft Graph has available within the Chart type you choose. For example, if you choose a bar chart, Graph gives you the option of using a stacked bar chart wherein all data points for the same time period are stacked on the same bar, as shown in figure 22.29.

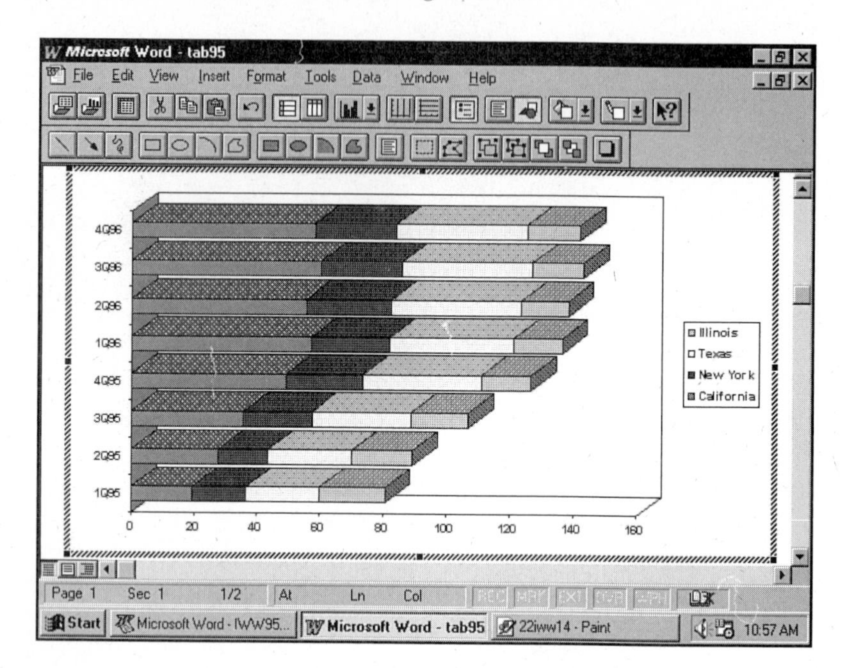

Figure 22.29
Stacked bar chart.

The *Options* tab enables you to control spacing of elements in your chart. For example, in 3D charts, you can specify the angle at which they appear; in 2D charts, you can specify whether they overlap. The *Axis* tab enables you to specify whether the chart is plotted on a primary or secondary axis; this option is available for only a few types of charts.

Using Trendlines and Error Bars

Trendlines and error bars are statistical tools that help your audience evaluate the meaning and implications of your data. Trendlines show apparent trends in a data series, and Microsoft Graph can map these trends into the future by using regression analysis techniques. Error bars show degrees of uncertainty relative to each data marker in a series, and they are often used in engineering applications.

To create a trendline, select a data series and choose Trendline from the Insert menu. The Trendline dialog box opens, as shown in fig. 22.30. Choose the type of trendline you want, set any options, and choose OK.

Similarly, to create an error bar, select a data series and choose Error Bar from the Insert menu. The Error Bar dialog box opens (see fig. 22.31). Choose the type of error bar you want, set any options, and choose OK.

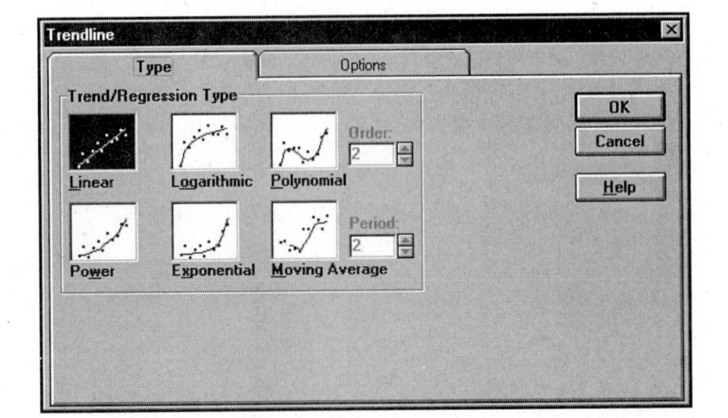

Figure 22.30

Trendline dialog box.

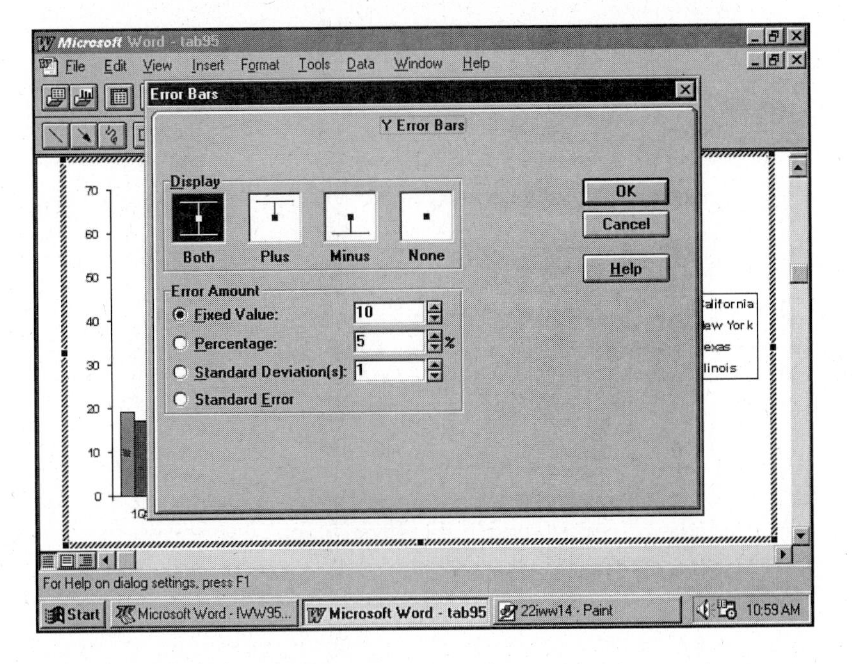

Figure 22.31

Error Bars dialog box.

Working in the Datasheet Window

At some point, you may want to change manually the values your chart is based on while you're working in Microsoft Graph. Graph includes a datasheet window for this purpose. The datasheet acts much like a basic spreadsheet, except that you can enter only numbers and letters in it. It does not use cell references and cannot handle formulas. The only purpose of the datasheet is to control the data that creates a chart in Microsoft Graph. To view the datasheet, click on the View Datasheet button or choose Datasheet from the View menu (see fig. 22.32).

Figure 22.32

The datasheet.

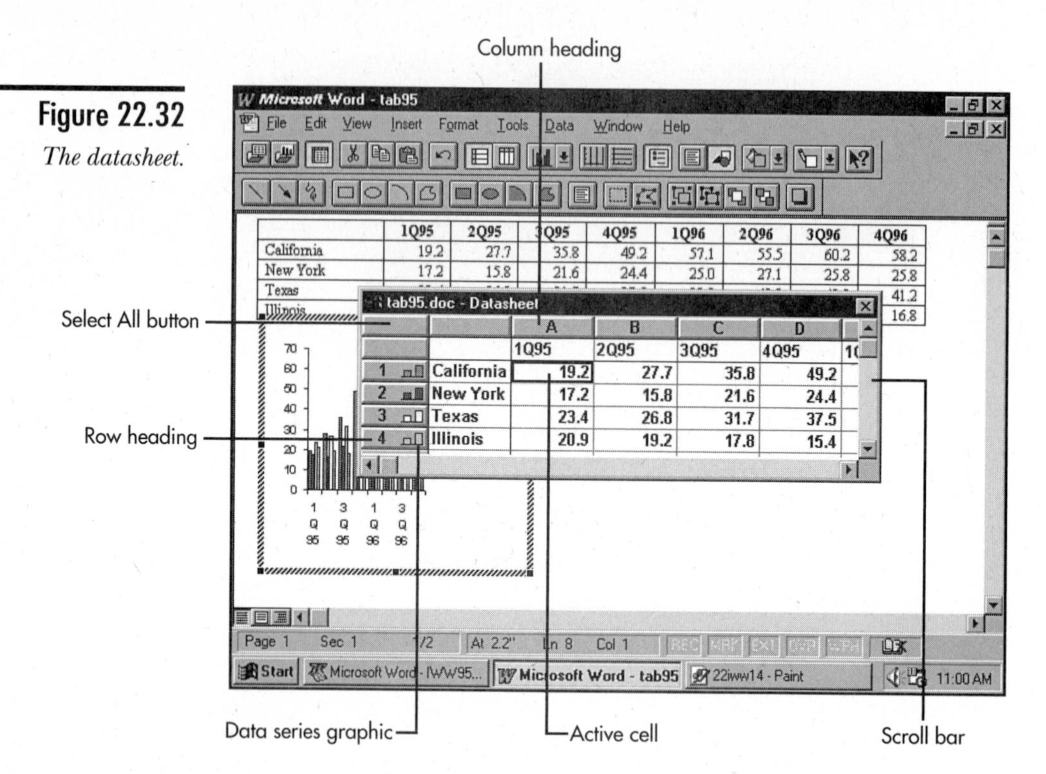

If you create your chart from data in a Word document, that data also appears in the datasheet when you open it. To change a value, click in its cell and enter the new value. When you change a value in the datasheet, the chart reflects the change immediately.

Stop

Keep in mind that changes you make in the datasheet are not automatically reflected in the table or Word text you used as the original source for the chart. If you make changes in the datasheet, your chart can be based on different values than the data appearing next to it in your document.

To link the values in your document to the contents of your chart automatically, see "Establishing an OLE Link between Word and Graph" later in this chapter.

Notice that each row of the datasheet also contains a *data series graphic*, a chart icon showing the color and pattern of the corresponding data series as it now appears in the chart.

Moving Data in the Datasheet

If you've used Excel, working in the datasheet will seem familiar. You can select a row by clicking on the row number box to its left; you can select a column by clicking on the column letter above it. You can select the entire datasheet by clicking on the gray box at the top left. You have access to pop-up menus for cutting, pasting, copying, and deleting cells, rows, and columns. (Keyboard shortcuts and toolbar buttons are also available for cutting, copying, and pasting.)

You can also use drag-and-drop to move data from one location in the datasheet to another. If drag-and-drop doesn't work, choose Options from the Tools menu and make sure Allow Cell Drag and Drop is checked.

Formatting Data in the Datasheet

Although the text formatting of the datasheet generally doesn't affect the formatting of either the chart or your original Word document, you do have the ability to change fonts, font size, and column widths. Select the cells, rows, or columns you want to change, and choose Font from the Format menu or the pop-up menu. A Font dialog box opens, much like the one in Word itself; from there you can choose fonts, font styling, font size, and other font formatting.

To change column width, select the column(s) you want to adjust and choose Column Width from the Format or pop-up menu. You also can position the mouse pointer above the column, at the edge of the next column, and drag the pointer until the column is the width you want.

In one case, the formatting you apply in the datasheet *does* affect the chart. You can use Format, Number or choose Number from the pop-up menu to specify how numbers are formatted. The Number Format dialog box appears (see fig. 22.33). Microsoft Graph enables you to specify a wide variety of number formats. For example, you can specify that numbers be formatted as dollars and cents, or with scientific notation, or precisely to a specific number of decimal places. As soon as you make a change in Number formatting, that change is reflected in the chart as well.

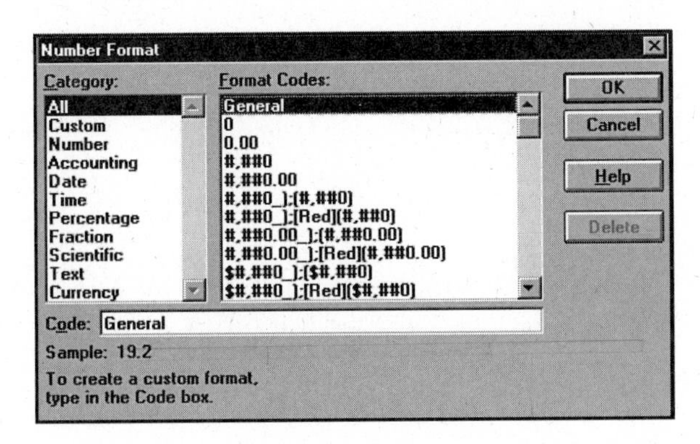

Figure 22.33
Number Format dialog box.

Revising Charts

If the data used to create a chart changes—as it often does when you report on fluid business situations—you need to be able to alter your charts quickly. Microsoft Graph is well-suited to enable you to make quick changes, because it holds the data for the chart in the datasheet. If you change the information in the datasheet, you update the chart accordingly.

You can make your changes by entering new data directly into the Datasheet and overwriting the old data in the process; or, if the data is held in a spreadsheet that is continually revised, you can reimport the spreadsheet data every time it changes. If you want your chart to update automatically when you make a change in your document, however, there's another solution: OLE links.

Establishing an OLE Link between Word and Graph

If you want tight and permanent links between your chart and your Word document, so that the chart changes when data changes in your document, establish an OLE link between the Word document's original chart data and the contents of the chart itself. Then, when you open the chart, it updates to reflect changes you may have made in the document. Here's how to do this:

1. Select and copy the Word data you want to graph.
2. Open Microsoft Graph.
3. If the datasheet does not appear, click on the View Datasheet button to view it.
4. Click your insertion point in the top left cell of the datasheet.
5. Choose Paste Link from the Edit menu.
6. If you are importing only a small number of cells, make sure that Graph has overwritten all the generic data that appeared in the datasheet previously. If not, delete them yourself.
7. Graph displays the ChartWizard window where you can specify whether the data series should be in columns or rows, and how data in the first column and row should be plotted. Make your selections and choose OK.

Establishing a Link with Microsoft Excel

Essentially the same procedure can be used to establish a link with Microsoft Excel and other programs that support Microsoft's OLE 2.0 specification. To create an OLE

link between an Excel worksheet and a Microsoft Graph chart appearing in a Microsoft Word document, follow these steps:

1. In Excel, open the Excel worksheet you want to link.
2. Copy the cells you want to include in a chart in Word.
3. Open or switch to Word, and open the document where you want the chart.
4. Place your insertion point where you want the chart.
5. Open Microsoft Graph by choosing it in **I**nsert, **O**bject or clicking on the Insert Chart button.
6. If the datasheet does not appear, click on the View Datasheet button to view it.
7. Click your insertion point in the top left cell of the datasheet.
8. Choose Paste Li**n**k from the **E**dit menu.
9. If you are importing only a small number of cells, make sure that Graph has overwritten all the generic data that appeared in the datasheet previously. If not, delete them yourself.
10. Graph displays the ChartWizard window where you can specify whether the data series should be in columns or rows, and how data in the first column and row should be plotted. Make your selections and choose OK.

Now, when a change is made in the Excel worksheet, that change is reflected in the Word chart as well.

If you close both the Word and Excel documents, when you reopen the Word document containing the chart, you may need to double-click on the chart to update it.

Word as a Forms Program

You'd think the PC would be a natural for creating forms. After all, both form design and form filling are well within a PC's technical capabilities. But until recently, surprisingly few people responsible for forms have used the PC as well as they might have. And they've had their reasons.

Using the PC to create forms often meant purchasing a separate program designed especially for forms. And *filling in* the forms was probably still a paper task—unless you provided a form-filling program to everyone likely to use them.

But now Word—a program with wide distribution—has sophisticated forms capabilities. You can create forms that enable users to choose from lists of options. Forms that provide on-line help. Forms that guide the user from beginning to end. Best of all, users can fill in these forms—without changing the underlying form itself. And if you're networked, you can use your network server rather than some distant warehouse as a central repository for forms.

All in all, maybe it's time to take another look at how you handle forms.

In this chapter:

- Using Word features to create a form framework
- Using the Forms toolbar
- Using the Forms shortcut menu
- Adding check boxes and list boxes
- Adding fill-in fields
- Adding on-line help
- Using macros
- Protecting a form from unwanted change
- Filling in on-line forms
- Creating printed forms
- Printing just the data
- Distributing your forms

Using Word Features to Create a Form

The first step when you create a form is to create a new template, which should contain the basic information you want to include in every form. Include any list boxes, check boxes, dialog boxes, and Help features you might add to the form. Finally, the template should contain any macros and AutoText entries you can create to streamline filling out the forms later.

As you learned in Chapter 10, you create a new template by choosing New from the File menu. Click on the Template button in the New dialog box (see fig. 23.1), and click on OK.

You then use Word's formatting techniques to lay out the basic elements of the form. You'll probably find tables, frames, borders, and shading especially useful here.

If you already have the basic contents of a form in a file, you can save that file as a template.

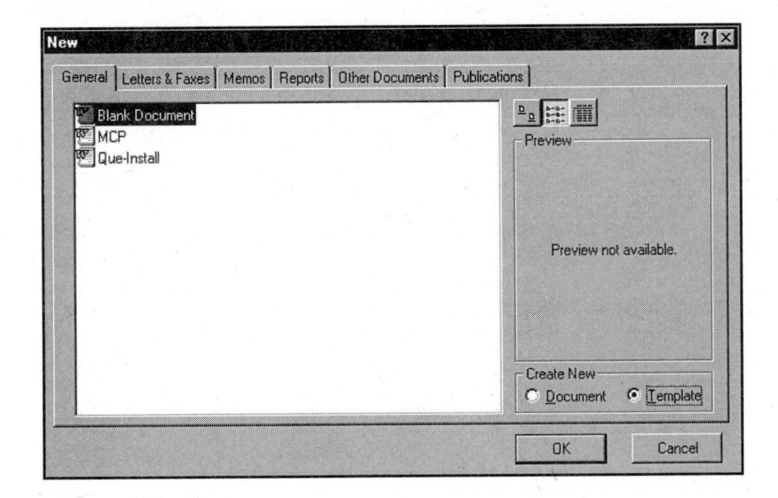

Figure 23.1

Creating a new template.

The accompanying CD-ROM contains a file you can use to practice some of the procedures in this chapter: IWMS23A.DOT.

When you create a new template, your form is unprotected, which means you can make any changes you want. But if you need to revise an existing form, its original designer probably has protected it from changes.

To unprotect the form, choose Unprotect Document from the Tools menu, choose Forms, and choose OK. The section "Protecting a Form from Unwanted Change," later in this chapter, covers protecting and unprotecting forms in more detail.

At this stage, you don't include any of the options used to fill out the form. You just put the structure in place, as in figure 23.2.

Figure 23.2

The first step in creating a form: blocking out where everything will fit.

Scott Petrozzini's Pizza Joint
Specializing in Corporate Catering since 1882

556 Hackensack Street
Hasbrouck Heights, New Jersey 07604
201-555-1750
Fax Orders Welcome at 201-555-1752

Invoice #:		**Attn:**
P.O. #:		
Date:		

Product	**Unit Price**	**Quantity**	**Total Cost**
		Subtotal	
		Tax	
		Total	

Payment is due upon receipt. Thank you very much. We hope to serve you again!
If you have any questions about this invoice, call us at 1-800-555-2004.

Un-Advertised Special, Just For Our Best Customers...

Using the Forms Toolbar

As you read through the following sections on creating form fields, keep in mind that Word also provides a nifty shortcut for building forms: the Forms toolbar (see fig. 23.3). You can display it from any form options dialog box. Or you can right-click on an empty part of a toolbar and then choose Forms from the shortcut menu that appears.

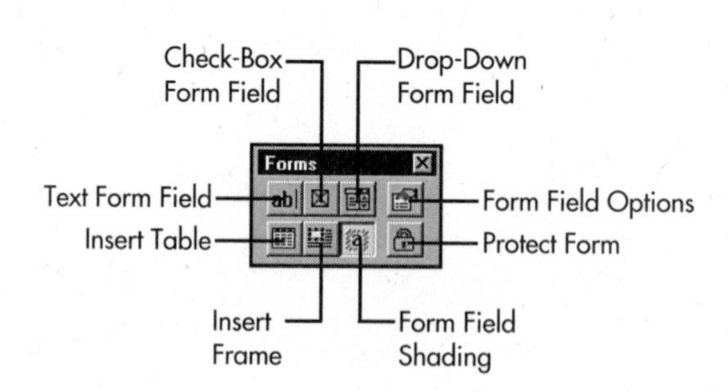

Figure 23.3

The Forms toolbar.

Tip

When you construct a form, you might want to display both the Forms and Borders toolbars. The Forms toolbar helps you to add and edit your form's elements. The Borders toolbar helps you refine your form's look and feel.

Text Form Field, Check-Box Form Field, and *Drop-Down Form Field* correspond to the three radio buttons in the Type box in the Form Field dialog box, which enables you to choose the type of form field to insert.

Form Field Options opens the Options dialog box for the current form field. (You have to select a form field before you can use this tool.)

Insert Table and *Insert Frame* give you a quick way to reach tables and frames, two of the most important formatting elements in most forms. (Insert Table behaves identically to its twin on the Formatting toolbar.)

Form Field Shading is the only toolbar function not available elsewhere. By default, Word shades all form fields gray so users can easily see the spaces they're expected to fill in. Clicking on the Change Shading button toggles shading on and off.

Finally, *Protect Form* turns document protection on and off.

Inserting Form Fields

Now you want to specify exactly where users may enter text. To do so, place your insertion point at the location, and then choose Insert, Form Field to insert a form field. The dialog box shown in figure 23.4 appears.

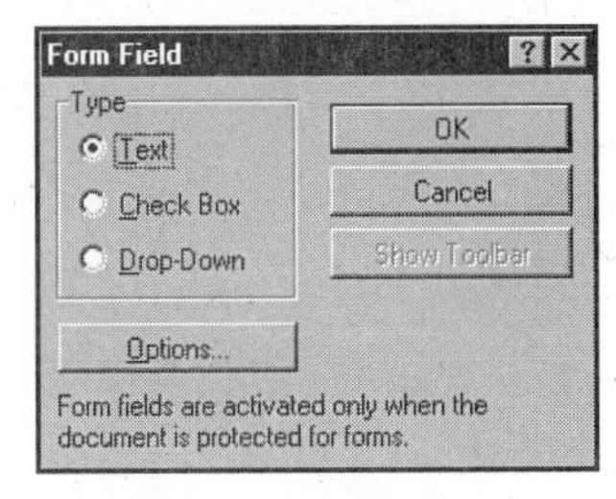

Figure 23.4
The Form Field dialog box.

You can choose one of three kinds of form fields in the Type area:

- **Text.** Text form fields accept text, numbers, symbols, and spaces—as well as preprogrammed dates and calculations.
- **Check Box.** Check box form fields place a check box in your form, as shown in figure 23.5.
- **Drop-Down.** Drop-down form fields enable you to give your user a list of alternatives, as shown in figure 23.6.

Each form field has different options associated with it.

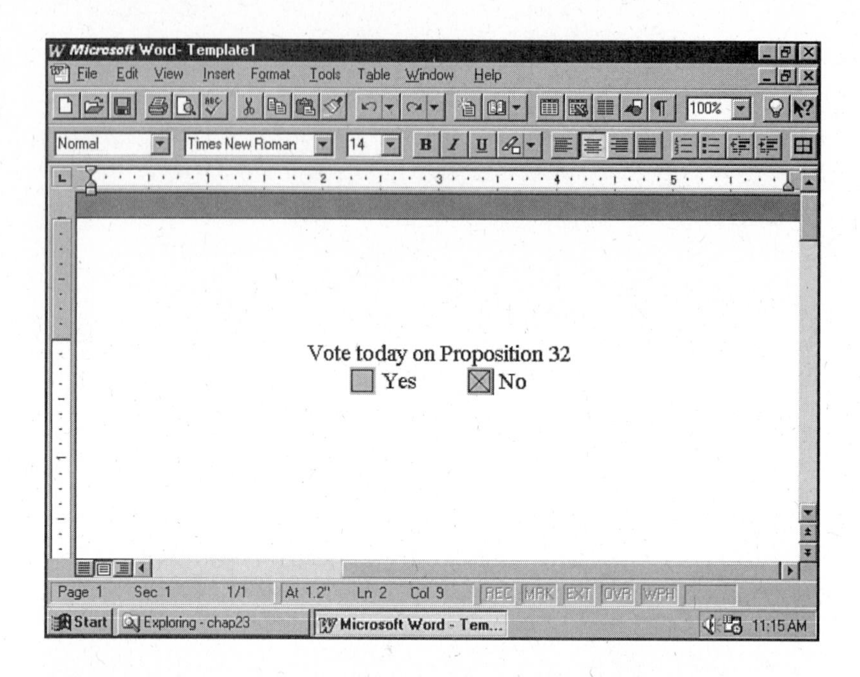

Figure 23.5

A check-box form field.

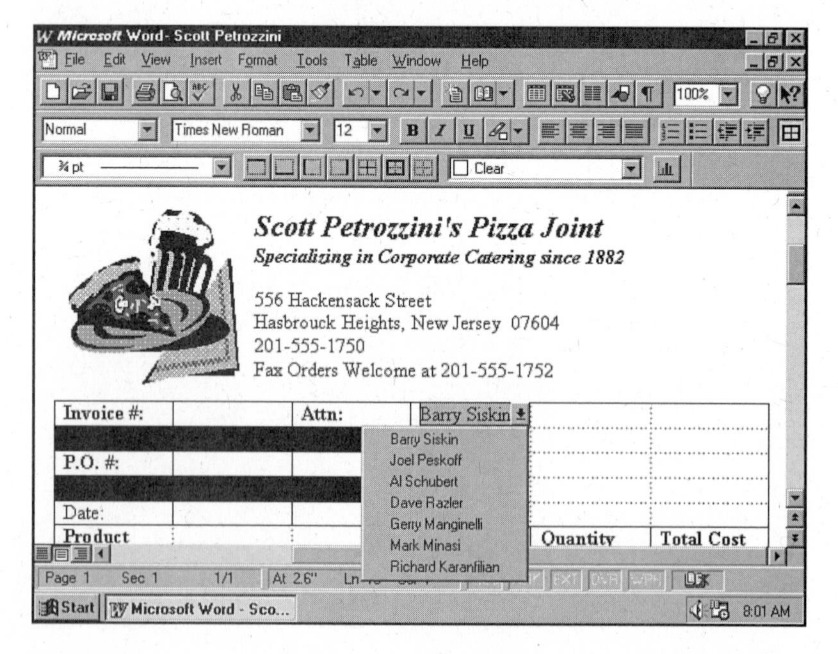

Figure 23.6

A drop-down (list box) form field.

Adding Text Form Fields

To enter a standard text form field—one that enables users to enter any text at all—choose Insert, Form Field, choose the Text option (unless already selected as the default choice), and click on OK. The form field's location appears shaded in the document.

Often, however, you want to refine your text field a little more. To do so, choose Options. The Text Form Field Options dialog box appears, as shown in figure 23.7.

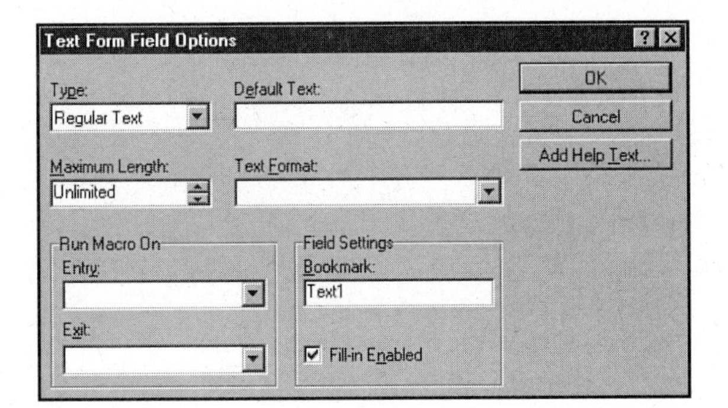

Figure 23.7

The Text Form Field Options dialog box.

Word also provides a context-sensitive shortcut menu with some "likely" commands to help in forms design (see fig. 23.8).

You can right-click on the text field to view it, and choose Form Field Options to open the Text Form Field Options dialog box.

Placing a Number, Date, or Time in a Text Form Field

The first aspect of the text form field you can control is whether it should be text at all. You can use the Type drop-down list box in the Text Form Field Options dialog box to specify several alternatives.

One of the most useful options is Number. Specifying Number takes you one small step toward data integrity: nobody can fill in alphabetic characters, for example, in a field that requires a dollar amount.

If you choose Number, you also can specify the format in which the number appears. Make a choice from the Number Format list box. (The format drop-down list box, second down on the right in the dialog box, changes its title depending on the format you choose.) Then, even if the user enters another format, Word automatically changes it to be consistent with all the other forms you're collecting.

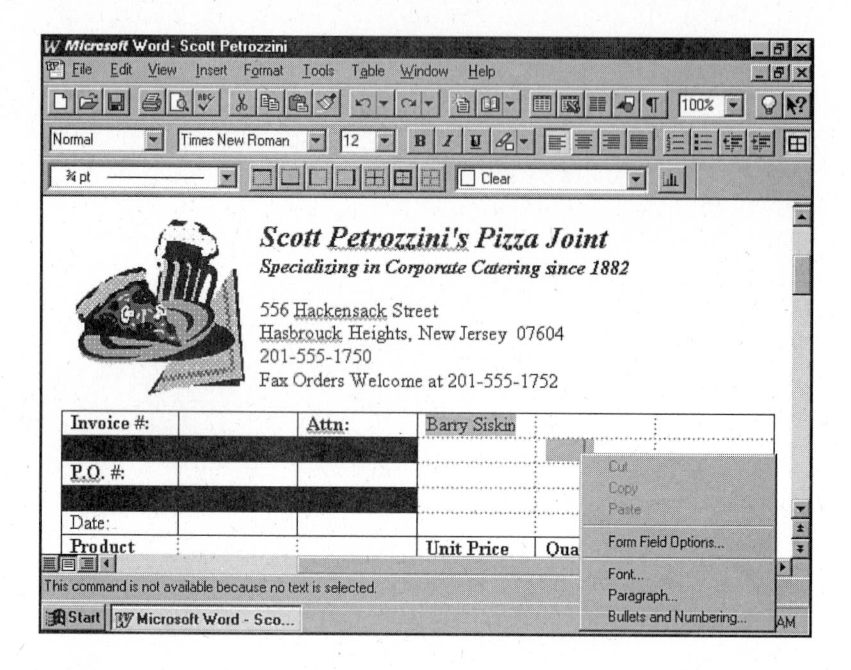

Figure 23.8

The Form Creation shortcut menu.

In the example invoice shown in the figures in this chapter, Number form fields have been added to each of the table cells under Unit Price. Because unit prices are in dollars and cents, that default formatting has been specified (see fig. 23.9).

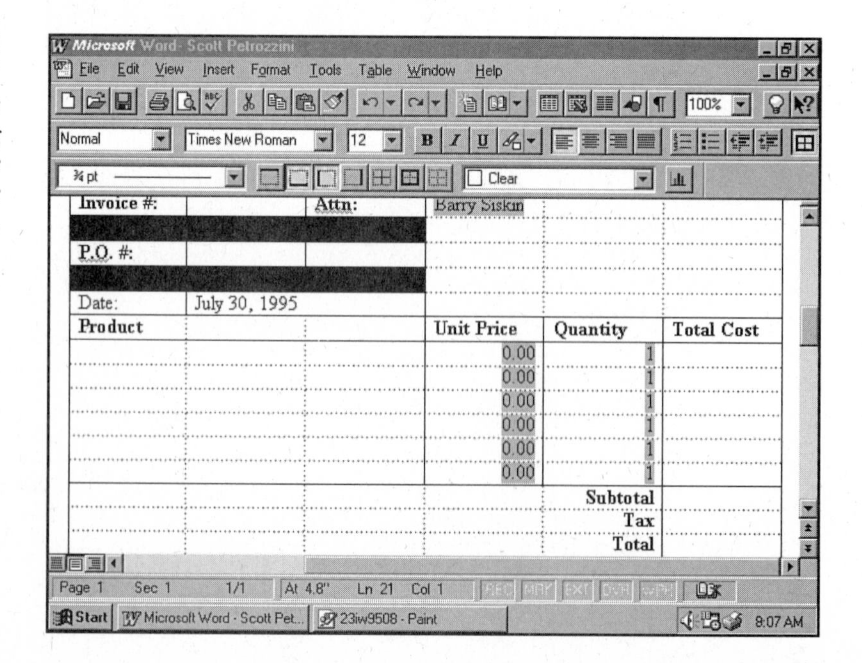

Figure 23.9

Dollars-and-cents formatting appears in the Unit Price column.

You can go beyond standard numeric formats by adding a numeric picture in the Number Format box, as you might in Insert Field. The numeric picture "###.###", for example, tells Word to round off any entry to thousandths. Chapter 10 covers numeric picture formatting.

Another useful option is *time stamping*. You can specify that the form field automatically display the date when the form is filled out. Alternatively, you can specify that it always display the current date or current time. You can choose a date/time format from the Date Format list box, or use Word's date/time picture feature to create your own (see Chapter 10 for more information).

When users work with this form later, they can't change the date simply by typing it, because Word sets this information.

If you're really concerned about the chronological accuracy of your forms, remember that a user can circumvent your time and date settings by resetting the system clock, thereby making it appear a form was filled out at a different time than it really was.

You might think that you could use Word's standard date and time fields here, but you can't. They don't update when you use them in a form. When you place a text form field in your template, Word places a new kind of field there—one unavailable from Insert Field:

```
{FORMTEXT}
```

When you specify the date, Word creates a nested field:

```
{FORMTEXT {DATE}}
```

You can see these fields in your template if you choose to view field codes (check the Field Codes box in Tools Options View).

You theoretically can use Ctrl+F9 to create them directly, but working with Insert Form Fields is much easier.

Whether you insert text, a number, or a date, you can provide default information that appears in the form unless a user changes it. Enter the default information in the Default text box (top right in the Options dialog box). The name of this text box changes as you change the type of the data for the control to accept.

In the invoice example, users generally purchase one of an item, so **1** has been specified as the default number in each cell under Quantity (see fig. 23.10).

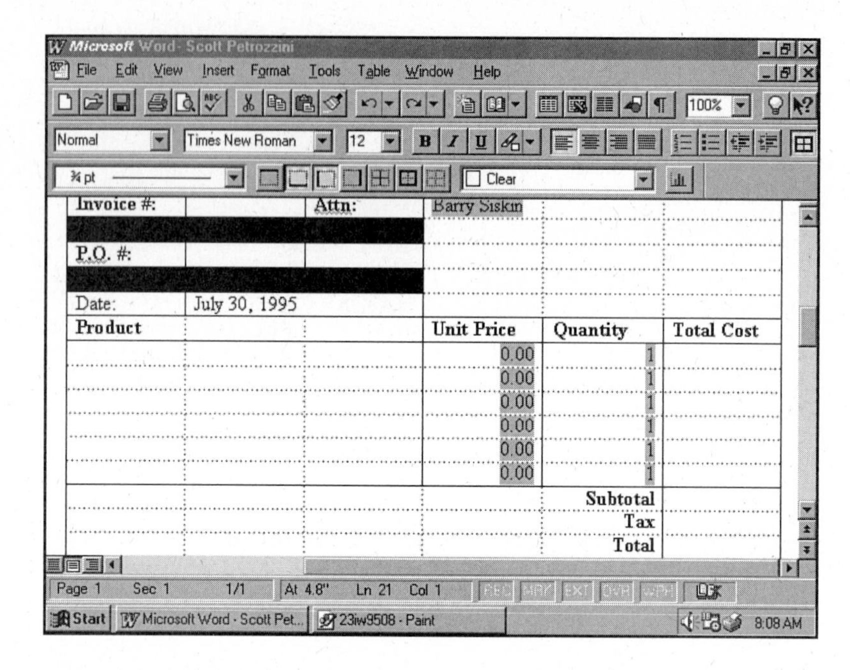

Figure 23.10

Here, the default number "1" appears in each cell in the Quantity column.

In this example, it is assumed that each entry under Invoice # will be no longer than four digits, so that value has been specified in the Maximum Length option in the Text Form Field Options dialog box. (Your form field can be up to 255 characters.)

Tip By the way, you can't select several cells and insert form fields into all of them from the Insert, Form Fields box. But you can create one form field and then copy it into any other location where you want an identical field.

Finally, you can insert a calculation in your form by choosing Calculation from the Type box. The Default Text option changes to Expression, and an equals sign appears in the Expression text box.

Here, you can create a calculation just as you might in Table Formula or Insert Field. Again, however, a calculation doesn't work in a form unless you build the calculation in the Text Form Field Options dialog box.

In the example shown in figure 23.10, a calculation field has been inserted to multiply automatically a product's Unit Price by the Quantity purchased to arrive at the Total Cost in each row. Then these values are added together to arrive at a Subtotal; 7 percent tax is added; and a Total is created.

Calculations also appear in the document as nested field codes, such as

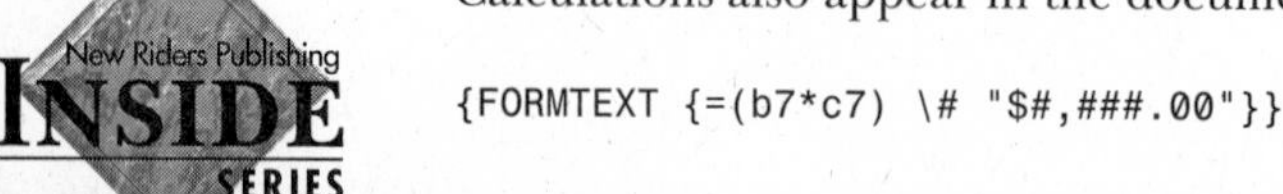

```
{FORMTEXT {=(b7*c7) \# "$#,###.00"}}
```

You can see the sample invoice's field codes in figure 23.11.

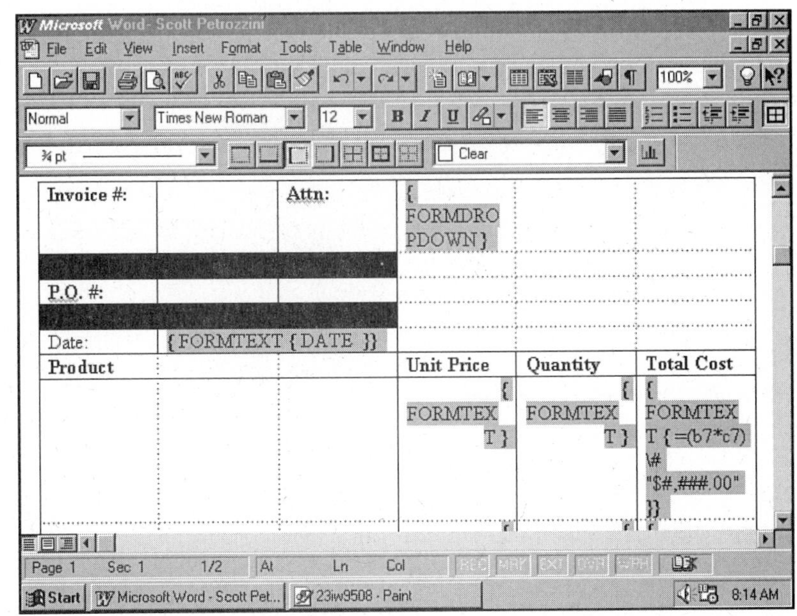

Figure 23.11
Field codes displayed in document.

You have to create these fields one at a time, because they're all different—they reference different cells. Unlike Excel, Word has no Fill Down feature.

If you ever need to insert consecutive numbers in a table, use the Table Number macro in the TABLES.DOT template included with Word. The macros in this template are described in Chapter 11.

Adding Character Formatting to a Text Field

You also can specify the character formatting that appears in a form field. Select the field, and choose Font from the Format menu. The Font tabbed dialog box appears. Choose the font, style, size, effects, and/or color you want. Click the Character Spacing tab to choose options like spacing and kerning. After you have what you want in the field, click on OK.

Be sure to select fonts that are available on all the computers that will use this form; otherwise you'll face the dreaded font-substitution monster. The best solution is to limit yourself to the Windows default fonts and the 14 fonts that ship with Word.

Adding Check-Box Form Fields

By using check-box form fields, a user can select as many options as appropriate (in contrast to *option* buttons, which accept only one choice from a list).

You could, for example, build a list of options as shown in figure 23.12. To insert a simple check box with no options, choose Insert, Form Field. Then choose Check Box in the Form Field dialog box, and click on OK.

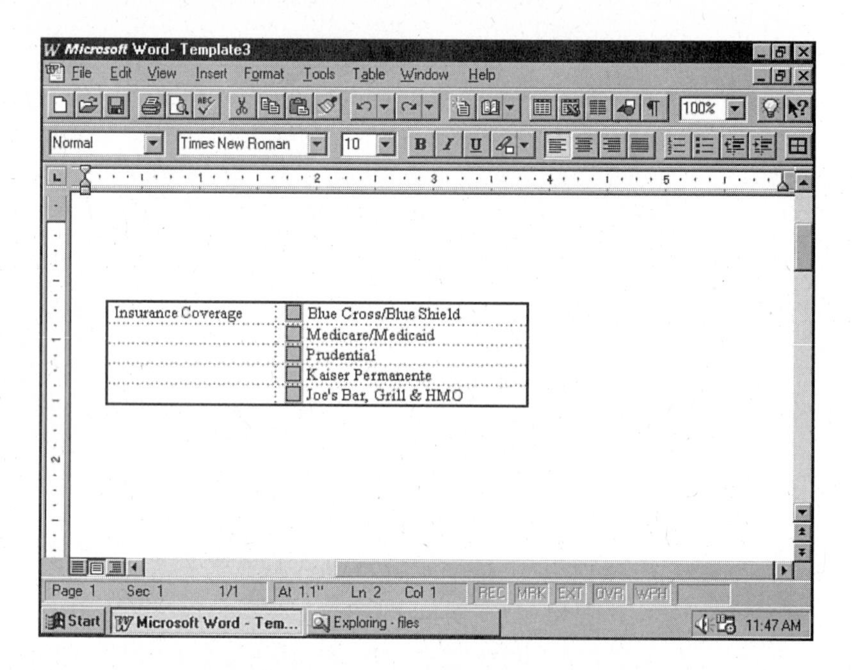

Figure 23.12
Sample of check boxes used in a form.

By default, Word displays boxes unchecked. If you want a box to appear checked, choose Insert, Form Field, choose Check Box, and choose Options. The dialog box shown in figure 23.13 appears.

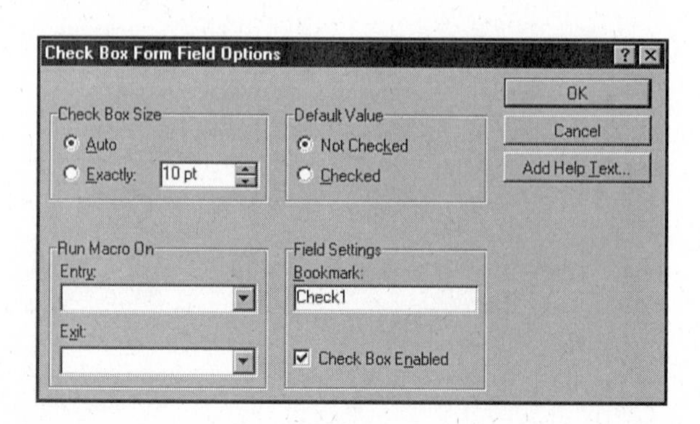

Figure 23.13
The Check Box Form Field Options dialog box.

In the Default Value box, choose Checked. By default, Word keeps your check box the same size as the text that follows it. The Check Box Form Fields Options dialog box, however, enables you to change the size of the check box *without* changing the size of any surrounding text. You could enlarge a box for emphasis, for example, as in figure 23.14.

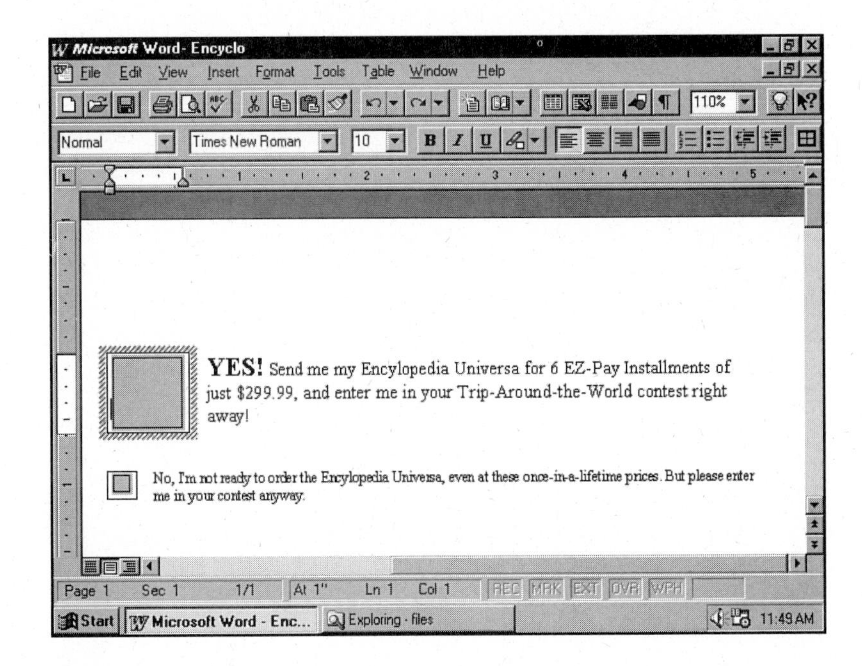

Figure 23.14
Enlarging a check box for emphasis.

In the example shown in figure 23.14, the second boxes around the check boxes are frames, which hold the check boxes in place while the promotional copy "wraps around" them. Frames are covered in more detail in Chapter 21.

To change the size of a form field check box, choose the **E**xactly option button in the Check Box Size area, then enter the new size in points in the text box.

Occasionally, you might want to display a box checked or unchecked but prevent users from changing the setting. Select the initial state of the check box using the option buttons in the Default Value area.

Adding Drop-Down Form Fields

You also can add drop-down list boxes to a form to give your users a set of choices (see fig. 23.15).

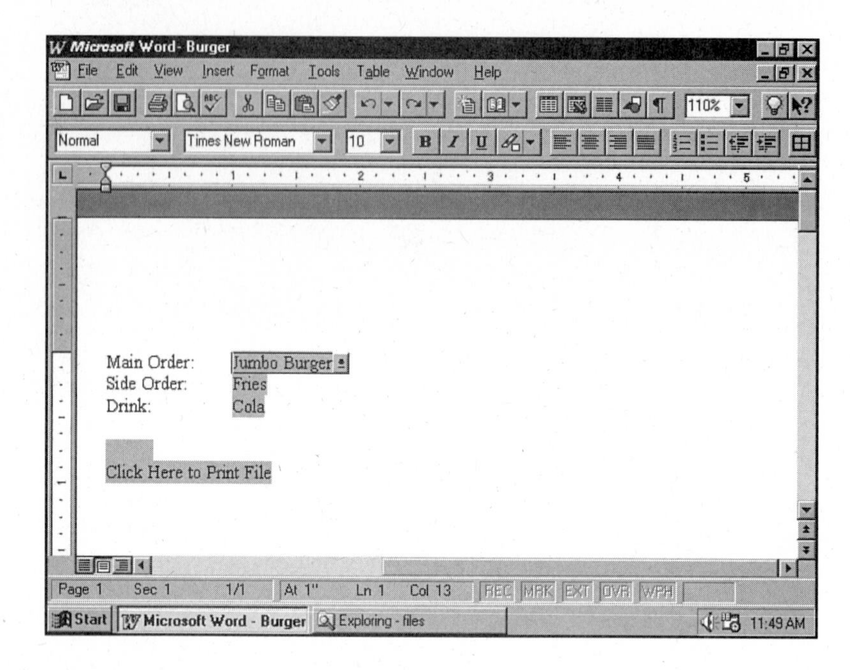

Figure 23.15

Sample list boxes.

Note Unlike some Word drop-down lists, list boxes don't enable a user to type a selection that's not on the list.

To add a drop-down list box to a form, choose **I**nsert, For**m** Field. Choose **D**rop-Down in the Type area. To place a list of choices in the drop-down list box, choose **O**ptions. The Drop-Down Form Field Options dialog box appears, as shown in figure 23.16.

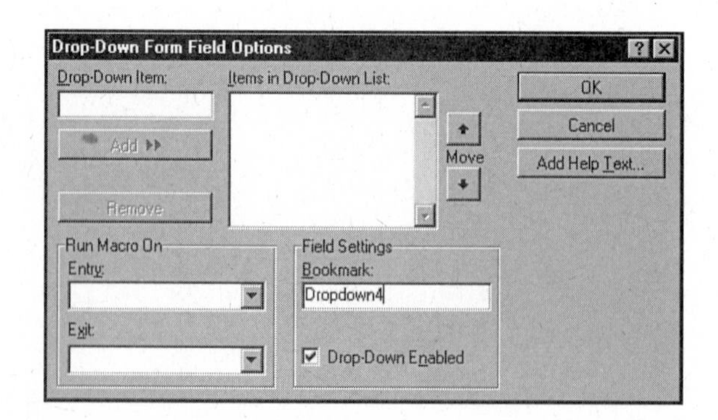

Figure 23.16

The Drop-Down Form Field Options dialog box.

To add an item, type it in the **D**rop-Down Item text box and choose **A**dd. The item then appears in the **I**tems in Drop-Down List list box. You can place up to 50 items in a drop-down box.

Word treats the first item in your list as your default choice—it appears selected in the form when the user opens it.

To change the order of a list, select the item you want to move, and click on the Move up-arrow or down-arrow button. You also can reach these arrows with the Tab (forward) and Shift+Tab (backward) keyboard combinations, as with other dialog box elements.

Suppose that America really jumps off the diet bandwagon, and nobody's buying SkinnyBurgers. You can delete this item from your list by selecting it and choosing Remove.

Adding Help to Your Forms

If you're in charge of helping people fill out their forms, you can cut down dramatically on the time you spend by adding built-in help to your on-line forms. Built-in help can provide more explanation of the options you offer or the information you want. It also can explain how to use the form itself.

You should give at least basic help in the form itself, where the help is visible for people who don't know how to look for it. Include language like this:

To get help about any item, move to it with the mouse or the keyboard and press F1.

Otherwise, your users probably won't know how to get the help you've worked so hard to include.

To add help text, create the form field, and in the Options dialog box for that type of field, choose Add Help Text. The dialog box shown in figure 23.17 appears.

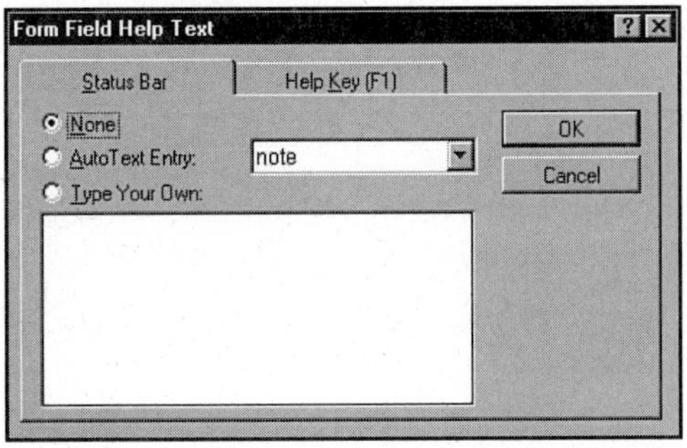

Figure 23.17

The Form Field Help Text dialog box.

You now have two sets of choices to make: where your help message appears and where it comes from. You can display your help message for a field in the status bar (choose Status Bar), where the message appears automatically whenever a user selects that field. This setting is the default. Or you can choose Help Key (F1), as shown in figure 23.18, to display a tabbed Help dialog box.

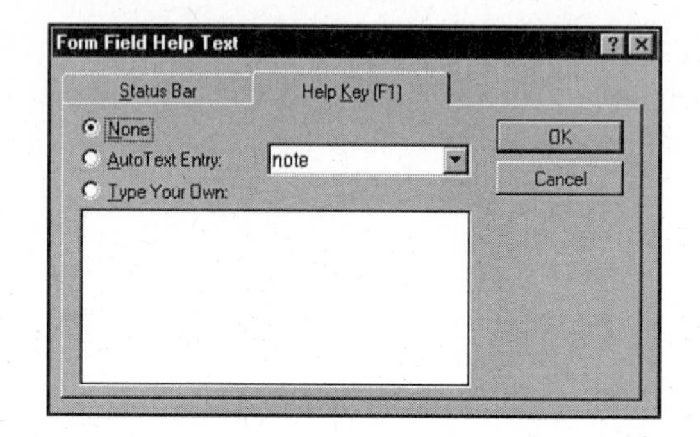

Figure 23.18

The Help Key (F1) tab in the Form Field Help Text dialog box.

The special Help dialog box for a form field appears only when a user selects the field and presses the Help key, F1. The Help dialog box appears as shown in figure 23.19.

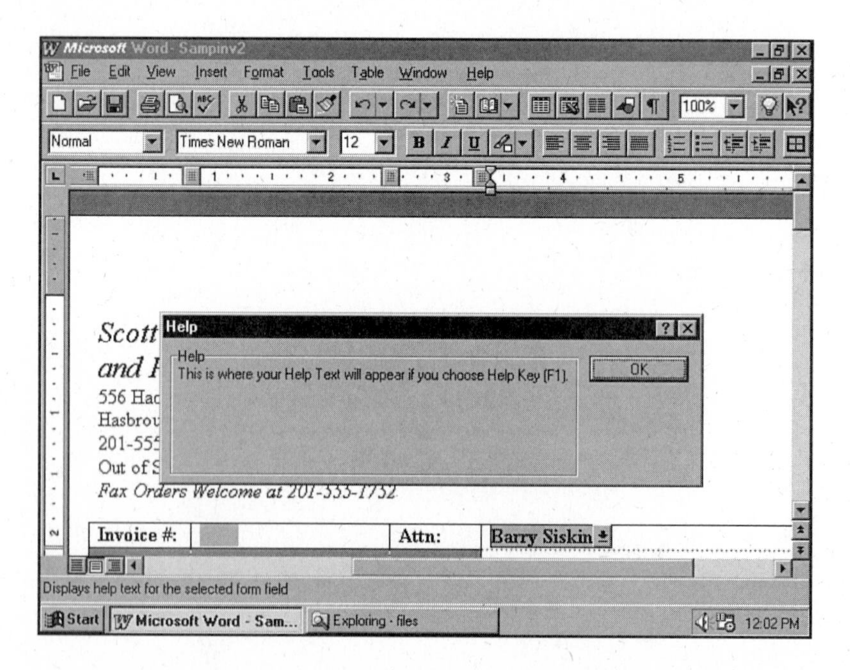

Figure 23.19

The Help dialog box.

Next, you can decide in the Form Field Help Text dialog box whether the help message comes from an AutoText entry you have already created, or from a message you insert here, by choosing Type Your Own and then typing the message in the box.

To select an AutoText entry, choose the AutoText Entry list box and select from the available AutoText entries.

Chances are, though, you'll want to type your own message—for two reasons. First of all, neither the Help dialog box nor the status bar displays graphics or tables, even though AutoText entries store them. Using the AutoText entry might mean you lose your graphical information and tables when the help message appears. Second, finding the help message is easier if you type it in the Type Your Own box, because the entry isn't mixed in with the text in the AutoText entry.

Exploring Other Options Available from any Form Field

In addition to creating help, you can perform three other actions in any kind of form field:

- Run a macro
- Set a form field as a bookmark
- Set a form field to display specific information all the time

You can instruct Word to run a macro when a user enters or leaves a field. In either case, you can select from all macros available in this template. (Of course, you'll probably be creating the macro within the new template, and saving the macro there.)

A simple example of how you might use this feature is shown in figure 23.20. In this example, a macro, PrintForm, has been recorded. PrintForm simply sends the file to your default printer. When you click in the Click Here to Print File field—that is, when you enter the field—the file prints automatically.

One drawback to this example is you can't protect this field from revision. The user can select only fields he or she can actually edit.

You also can set a form field as a bookmark that a Word macro can recognize and act upon. (Simply use the controls in the Run Macro On group in the Options dialog box for the form field you are using to set the macro you want.) You could, for example, create a macro that checks the current contents of a bookmark and, based on what Word finds, places corresponding contents in other fields.

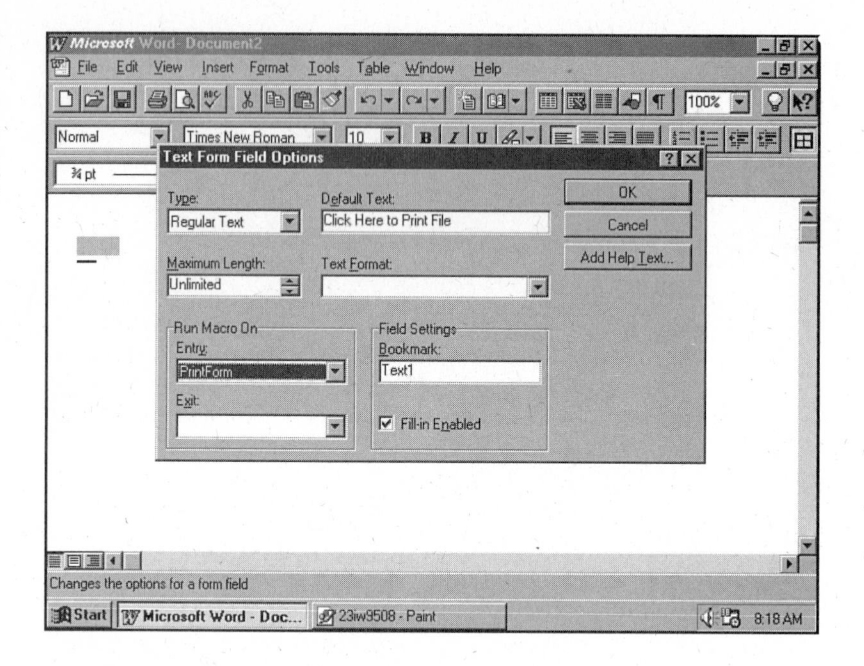

Figure 23.20 *Using Run Macro On Entry to place a print command in the document.*

This feature has many applications. When you insert a name, the form could automatically insert a corresponding company and address. When you insert a check box, the macro could fill in information in other locations.

Finally, you can set a form field to display specific information all the time. This information is read-only—the user can't edit it.

You might, for example, require customers to purchase one specific item before they become eligible to buy other products. You would insert a checked check box for that item and not allow changes.

To make sure that a field always displays its default text, item, or value, open the field's Options dialog box and uncheck the Enabled box in Field Settings. (This box is called Fill-in Enabled in a text field, Check Box Enabled in a check box field, and Drop-Down Enabled in a drop-down list box field.)

Changing a Form Field

You can't change a form field from a document based on your form template. You have to change the form field from within the template itself. To do so, follow these steps:

1. Open the template. (After you choose File, Open, you need to specify Document Templates in the List Files of Type box.)

2. Unprotect the document so you can edit it. Choose Unprotect Document from the Tools menu.

3. Double-click on the form field. The Options dialog box for the field you've chosen appears.

4. Make your changes.

5. Click on OK.

Protecting a Form from Unwanted Change

This chapter briefly mentions protecting and unprotecting form templates. Word gives you extremely tight control over the changes that can be made to a form. When you protect a template, a user can't make any changes in documents based on that template, except where you've inserted form fields. In fact, a form doesn't behave like a form until you protect it.

When you protect a form, some form fields that provide specific information can't be changed either. In a text form field that makes a calculation, for example, the user can't override the calculation. And, as you've seen, unchecking the Enabled check box in the Options dialog box also prevents a user from making changes in that field.

To protect a form, first open the form and then choose Tools, Protect Document. The dialog box shown in figure 23.21 appears.

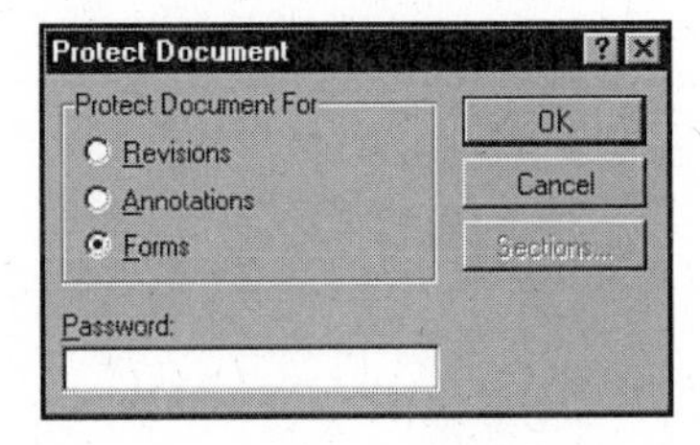

Figure 23.21

Protecting a form.

If you want, you can add a password. Including one probably makes sense if your form will be used in a large organization where someone might feel like editing it inappropriately. (You don't want sabbaticals in Tahiti added to your benefits option form.)

Unlike protecting an entire document, form passwords don't encrypt the document. Users can still *open* a password-protected form template; they just can't unprotect and edit it. When a user does try to unprotect such a document, the Unprotect Document Password dialog box opens, as shown in figure 23.22.

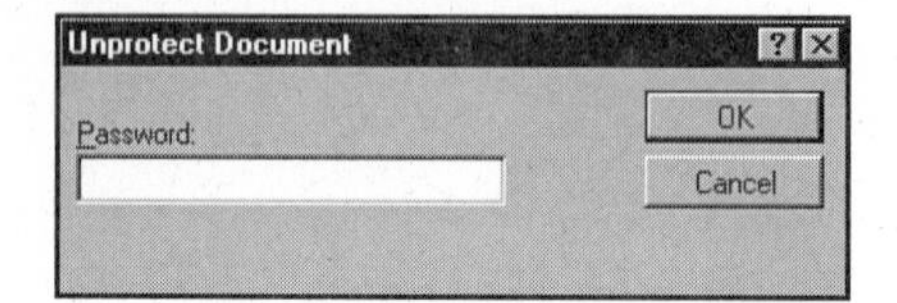

Figure 23.22
The Unprotect Document Password dialog box.

All the usual password safeguards apply. Choose a password you'll remember but nobody else can figure out. Don't write it down and leave it in an obvious location. And remember, after you create and confirm a password, you have *no* way to unprotect the document without the password.

To remove a password, first open the document (using its password). Then unprotect it using the Unprotect Document option on the Tools menu. Then protect it again by choosing Protect Document from the Tools menu. Choose Forms in the Protect Document dialog box. No password appears in the Password box. If no password is what you want, choose OK. When you save the file, it no longer requires a password. (If you want a new password, type it and confirm it. After you save the file, the new password goes into effect.)

Saving a Form

After you create a form, save it as a template under a new name, preferably a descriptive one. If your organization numbers its forms, you might include the new form number in the name.

Filling In On-Line Forms

To fill in an on-line form, create a new document based on the template that contains the form. Each form field is shaded in gray. The first field is shaded in deeper gray. That's where your insertion point is (see fig. 23.23).

Unless you specify a maximum length, each text field can grow to 255 characters. The gray area extends as you type. If the field is located in a text cell, the text simply wraps when you reach the end of the cell.

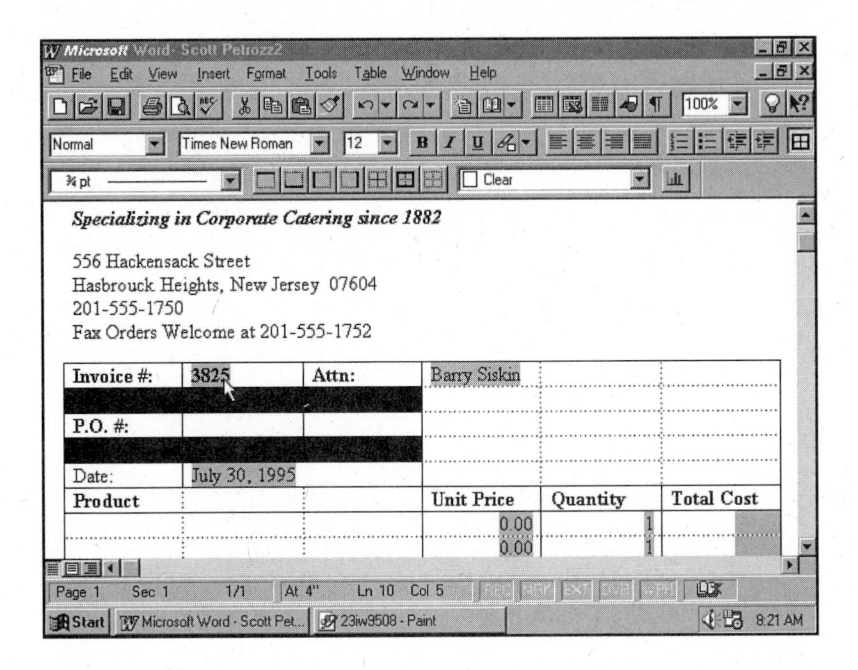

Figure 23.23
Filling in a form.

This word wrap can wreak havoc with a form design. That's one reason to set a maximum length when you create the form, especially if you ultimately plan to print it.

After you fill in a form field, press Enter, Tab, or the down-arrow key—they all move you to the next form field in which you may make an entry. (Word skips over form fields that it automatically calculates and fields in which you disable user input.)

Table 23.1 shows Word's editing and navigation keys for editing forms. As you can see, some keys work a little differently in forms compared with other documents.

Table 23.1
Word's Form-Editing Commands

To Do This	Use This Key or Combination
Move to the next editable field	Enter, Tab, or down arrow
Move to the previous editable field	Shift+Tab or up arrow

continues

Table 23.1, Continued
Word's Form-Editing Commands

To Do This	Use This Key or Combination
Show the contents of a drop-down list	F4 or Alt+down arrow
Move up or down in a drop-down list	Up arrow or down arrow
Make a selection in a drop-down list	Enter
Mark or unmark a check box	Space bar or X
Show help for a form	F1 (unless you have specified the help field, it always displays in the status bar)
Insert a tab	Ctrl+Tab

The mouse works the way it normally does. And Word also provides a fairly limited context-sensitive shortcut menu you can use as you fill in forms (see fig. 23.24). Click the right mouse button.

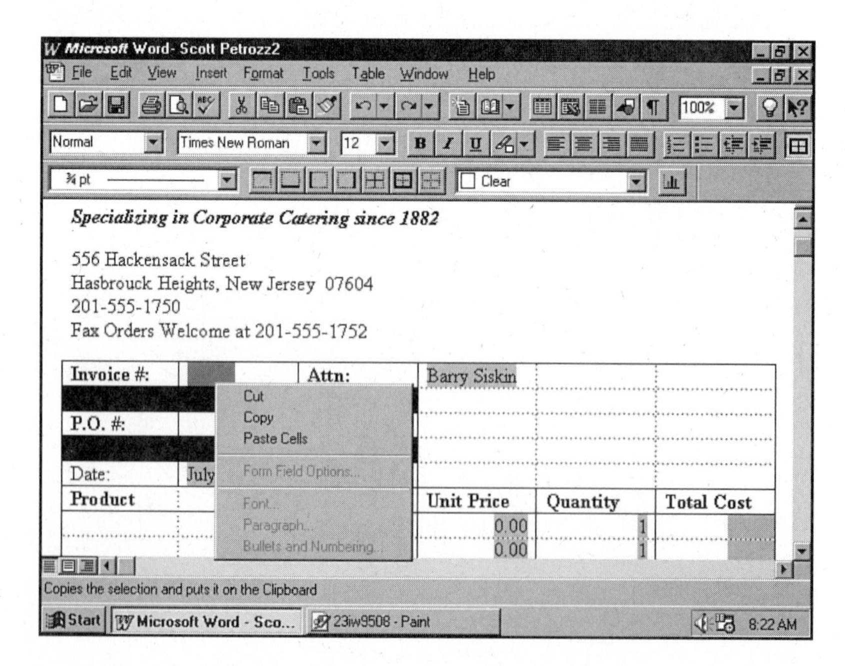

Figure 23.24

Context-sensitive shortcut menu for filling in forms.

One oddity: Cut and Paste work with text fields, but if you cut an entire form field, you can't put anything back in its place. This is a good time to remember that Word's Undo feature can let you reach back into the past to undo this action.

Creating Printed Forms

Your users often need hard copies of blank forms, which are easy to generate. Simply print the template or an empty document based on the template.

Sometimes, you might want to print only the data in the form—not the form itself. To print only the data, follow these steps:

1. Choose **T**ools, **O**ptions.
2. Choose the **P**rint tab.
3. In the Options for Current Document Only box, choose **P**rint Data Only for Forms.
4. Click on OK.

Print a copy of the data you've added to your new document.

Distributing Your Forms

You have several choices concerning the way you distribute your forms. The simplest is to use Word primarily as an easy way to create paper forms. This method enables you to print forms only as needed and to revise them quickly, rather than store large quantities of forms that risk obsolescence as your needs change.

One step forward is to compile all your forms on a floppy disk and provide a copy of the disk to everyone who shares your forms. This approach has the advantage of largely eliminating printed forms (well, at least in theory). Of course, it assumes everyone is running Word. Previous versions of Word don't understand form fields.

Before you distribute your forms electronically, you should seriously consider password protecting them. If you're networked, you can place your protected form templates in a common subdirectory available to everyone on the network.

If you have a form that you want everyone to fill out, you can send the template as an attachment on your electronic mail network. (Remember to add instructions on what to do with the form.)

If you happen to be using Microsoft Exchange or another MAPI or VIM compatible e-mail system, sending forms is especially easy. Word has already added two commands to your **F**ile menu: **S**end and Add **R**outing Slip.

Send is ideal for sending the template to one or two individuals. Add **R**outing Slip makes sending the template to as many people on the network as necessary easy—either one at a time or all at once.

Personalizing Word

You might need to be convinced to read this chapter and take it seriously. Until recently, most programs have been immutable objects. You did things their way. And if you didn't, you risked disaster. By now, you've all learned that lesson in the same way cats learn not to jump on hot stoves. You've been burned. So you figure: Word can do just about anything as it is. Wouldn't it be easier for me to learn how Word does it, than to figure out how to make Word do it my way?

Not anymore. First of all, Word 95 makes customization easy. And it's also easier to restore Word's default settings if you don't like your changes. So the risks are nil. Second, you can use customization to turn nearly any task you perform into a one-step process accessible from a toolbar, a menu, or the keyboard.

You've already learned how templates, macros, styles, AutoText, and other Word features can cut the amount of time required to perform specific tasks—often by 90 percent or more. In a sense, customization completes this process, because it enables you to bring your shortcuts to the surface, where you can get at them right away.

The following are a few examples:

Suppose that you often have to alphabetize lists. Put the Sort A-Z button on your Standard toolbar, and suddenly it's a one-button command. (A Sort A-Z button is already available. You just have to put it where you can see it.)

Or suppose that you often insert index entries. That's currently a several-step process, even in Word 95. But you could record a macro that selects your current word to be indexed, opens the appropriate dialog box, and marks the entry. If you then assign that macro to a button on your toolbar, indexing, too, becomes a one-button process.

Or suppose that you're a salesperson. Your Normal (NORMAL.DOT) template could include pushbuttons to create or open each of the documents you use most (see fig. 24.1). You can add access to the programs you use most in addition to Word (your Excel spreadsheets, for instance), the print envelope routine you use to direct mail to clients, and the file-sorting routine that helps you to sort through the various memos you have sent to clients.

Figure 24.1

A sample template for a salesperson.

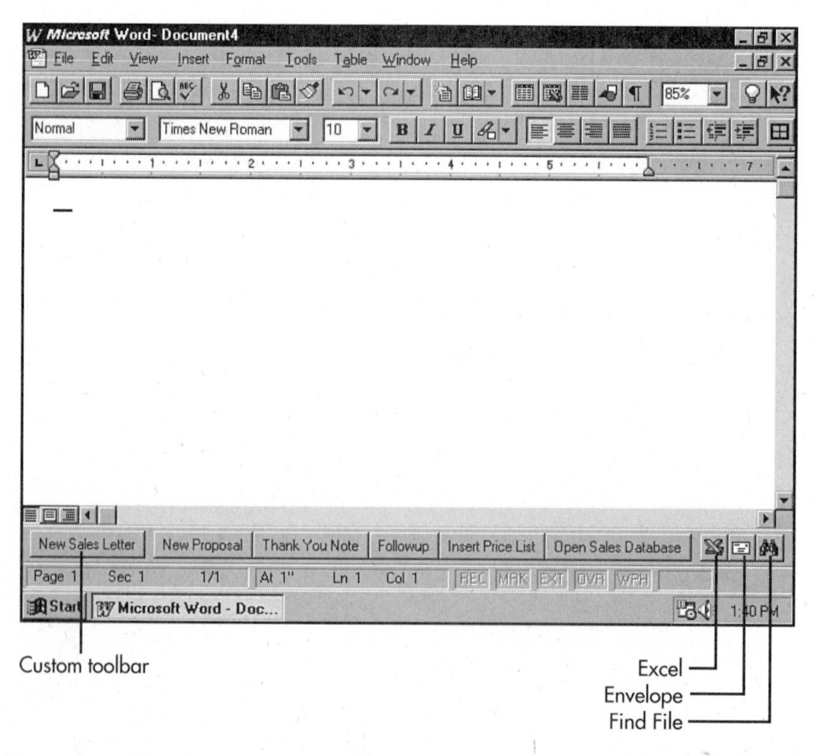

Or suppose that you're in charge of your organization's personnel policies. You could customize everyone's copy of Word to add a menu containing your forms and

(read-only) personnel manual. A user might then see what's shown in figure 24.2. The custom company menu can provide direct and immediate access to the information your employees need the most regarding personnel policies, requisitions, and benefits.

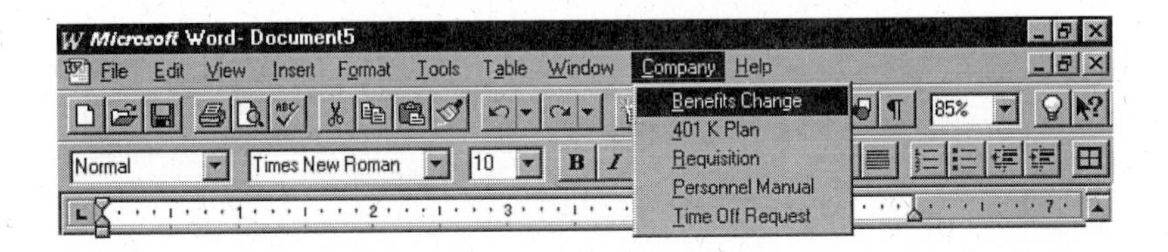

Figure 24.2
A new menu addition.

Customization offers a lot of potential, after you get past the notion that Word is not to be messed with. This chapter starts with a few basic techniques for automating the way Word runs when you load it in the morning. Then you go on to the heart of the chapter: customizing the way Word presents itself to you so that you can get more done, more quickly.

Finally, you learn about some options for making Word a more comfortable place to be. Chances are, you'll be spending a lot of time there—you might as well get comfortable.

In this chapter:

- Starting Word automatically
- Customizing a toolbar
- Adding your own toolbar
- Customizing a menu
- Adding your own menus
- Adding keyboard shortcuts
- Hiding parts of the interface
- Working with a blank screen
- Simulating WordPerfect
- Changing view options
- Changing general options
- Changing editing options

Starting Word Automatically

Windows 95

If Word is your primary application, you might want to start it automatically every time you turn on your computer. Here's how:

1. Click on Start on the Taskbar and position the mouse pointer over **S**ettings.
2. Choose Taskbar. The Taskbar Properties dialog box opens.
3. Click on the Start Menu Programs tab (see fig. 24.3).

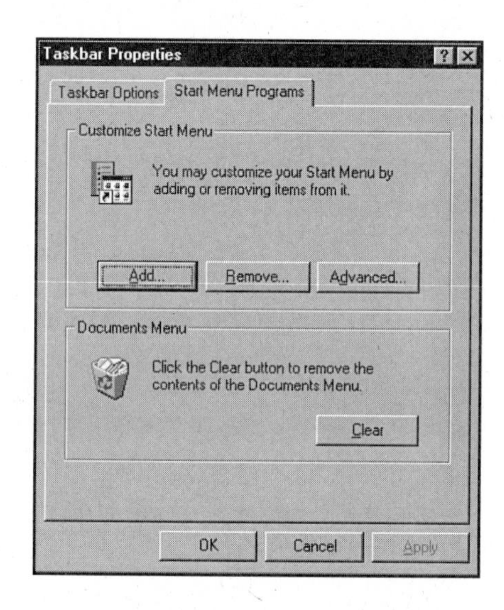

Figure 24.3
The Taskbar Properties dialog box, with the Start Menu Programs tab selected.

4. Click on **A**dd. The Create Shortcut window opens (see fig. 24.4).

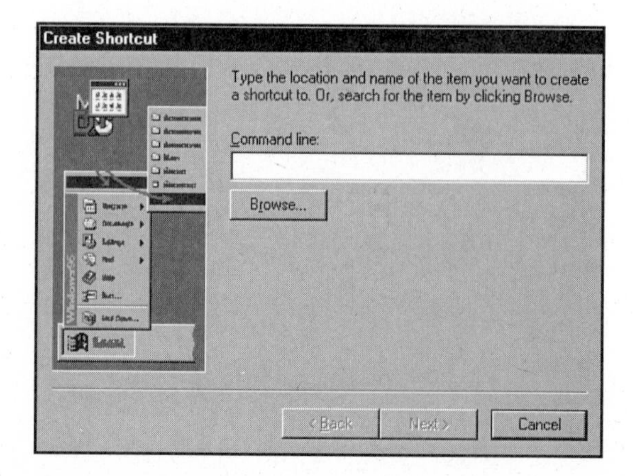

Figure 24.4
The Create Shortcut dialog box.

5. Click Browse to find your Word program file. The Browse window opens (see fig. 24.5). It's similar to the File, Open window you've been working with. Microsoft Word is probably in your Office95 or Winword folder.

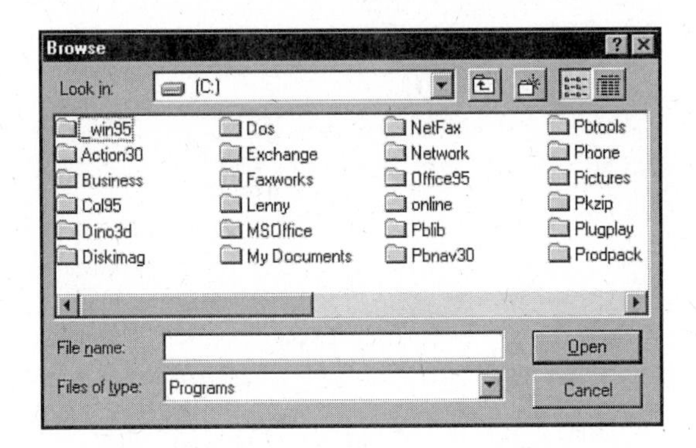

Figure 24.5

The Browse dialog box.

6. When you find Word, click on it, and choose Open. You're returned to the Create Shortcut window.

7. Choose Next. The Select Program Folder dialog box opens (see fig. 24.6).

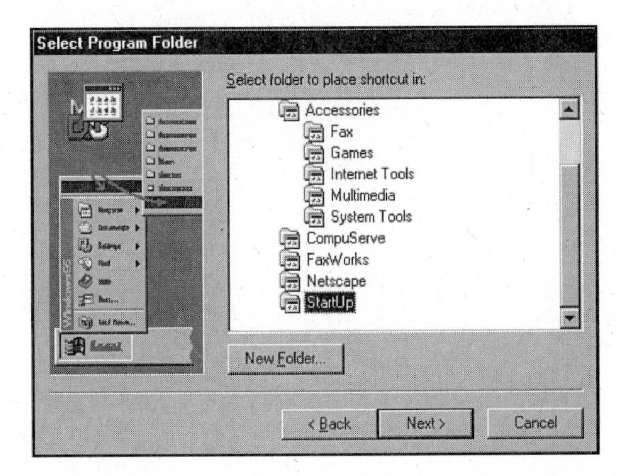

Figure 24.6

The Select Program Folder dialog box.

8. Click on the StartUp folder, and select Next.

9. The Select a Title for the Program window opens; if the name Microsoft Word is acceptable to you, click on OK. (Otherwise, edit the name.)

10. Click on OK to close the Taskbar Properties dialog box.

Starting Word with a Particular Task

Now take it a step farther. Suppose that you use Word almost exclusively to write sales letters. You've created a template for sales letters that includes substantial boilerplate text, along with AutoText entries that you can use to fill out the letter with specifics.

Now record a macro that opens your sales letter template, and name the macro AutoExec. If you use this special macro name, whenever you run Word it automatically creates a new sales letter document. (This feature is covered in more detail in Chapter 11, "Macros.")

If you looked under the hood, you'd find that AutoExec is actually a short macro. Just substitute your template name for Letter1 in the following:

```
Sub MAIN

FileNew .Template = "Letter1",
.NewTemplate = 0

End Sub
```

Another idea for AutoExec is to open automatically the last document you worked on. Just record a macro that selects 1 from the **F**ile menu, as in

```
Sub MAIN
FileList 1
End Sub
```

Taking Stock of Word's Customization Features

Now changing any Word toolbar, menu, or keyboard shortcut is almost easy. You can even add your own menus and toolbars.

What can you put in them?

- Any of the 210 Word buttons already assigned to specific tasks. (Many already appear on one or another of Word's toolbars, but quite a few don't.)

- Any of Word's more than 500 WordBasic commands, corresponding to any individual task Word can perform. These commands include every Word menu item and most Word formatting options.
- Any macro you've recorded, or written in WordBasic.
- Any font available on your computer. (In other words, you can create a toolbar entry that reformats in a specific font text you select.)
- Any AutoText entry you've created. (So that your custom toolbar entries or menu selections can add specific boilerplate text.)
- Any style you've created or any built-in Word style.

You can customize the Normal template—in which case all documents display your customized menus unless you specify otherwise. Or you can customize a specific template. Thus, you can create different working environments for different situations.

Suppose that three people share a computer. Joe has poor eyesight; the Joe template automatically displays enlarged buttons and text magnified to 150 percent. Diane is part-time office manager; the Diane template includes toolbar buttons for sending e-mail, creating purchase orders, and compiling quarterly reports on office activity. Kevin is a salesperson who's on the road most of the time; the Kevin template duplicates the customized template in his notebook PC.

On his notebook PC, Kevin can automatically load new documents based on the Kevin template by recording an AutoNew macro that does this job. The AutoNew macro runs each time Kevin starts a new file using this template. That makes things easier to manage, because he'll be using the same template (Kevin) on both the notebook and the desktop PC.

The NRP template, NRP.DOT, has already been customized with toolbars and menu items that might be useful to you (see fig. 24.7).

You can use this template by copying it to your template subdirectory, most likely C:\OFFICE95\TEMPLATE. (To find out where your templates are stored, choose Tools, Options, File Locations to open the File Locations tabbed dialog box.)

A description of NRP.DOT appears as an AutoText entry in that template. To view it, type **help** and press F3, or choose About NRP.DOT in the Help menu.

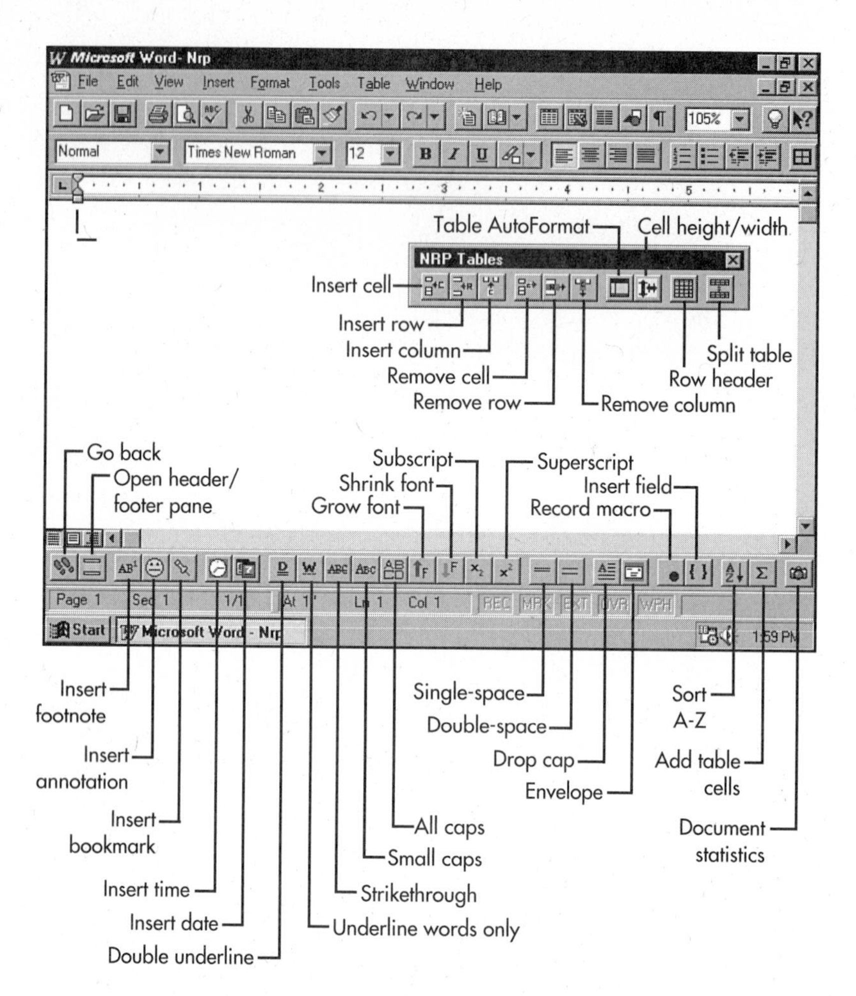

Figure 24.7

The NRP.DOT template.

Customizing the Toolbars

You can drag any toolbar to a new location and reshape how the toolbar appears at that location by dragging the corner of the toolbar, as shown in figure 24.8. But you can control many other elements of toolbars. In this section, you learn how to change the way the buttons appear on-screen; how to control which buttons appear on which toolbar; and how to add commands, macros, and other options to toolbars.

Figure 24.8
Moving toolbar buttons.

Changing the Appearance of Toolbar Buttons

To control other elements of the toolbar, choose View, Toolbars. The dialog box shown in figure 24.9 appears.

By default, the Standard and Formatting toolbars are checked as open. Word also might have opened others if you previously used their capabilities. If you insert a picture and then open it for editing, for example, Word displays the Drawing toolbar at the bottom of the screen.

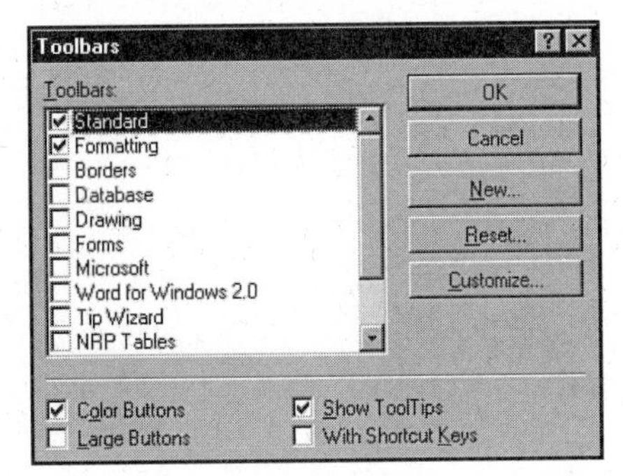

Figure 24.9
The Toolbars dialog box.

You can open or close any toolbar here by checking or unchecking its box. You have two more immediate choices as well:

- **Color Buttons.** By default, Word displays buttons in color even if you don't use a color monitor. If you have a monochrome monitor, you might find the display slightly clearer if you display buttons in black and white. Also, a few people might find color buttons distracting.

  In any event, you can choose to display them in black and white by clearing the Color Buttons box.

- **Large Buttons.** This option enlarges the size of all buttons on all your toolbars. Large buttons are most helpful when you are working at higher screen resolutions, such as 1024 x 768. Some commands on some toolbars might not be visible at lower screen resolutions. To use the large buttons option, check the Large Buttons box.

If you prefer large buttons, you might want to collect your most used buttons on a single toolbar and float it onto the screen while hiding Word's Standard and Formatting toolbars. (You learn how soon.) An example of this strategy is shown in figure 24.10.

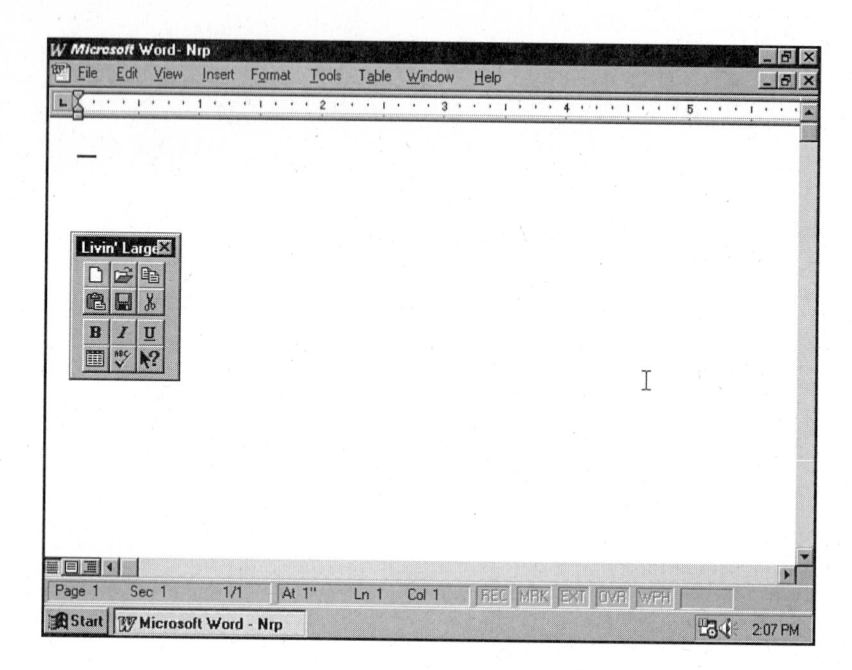

Figure 24.10

One approach to using large buttons.

If all you want to do is open or close a toolbar, right-click any toolbar in a space not covered by a button. A toolbar's list appears. Check or uncheck the toolbar you want to display or hide.

This method opens only toolbars available from where you're working.

In Word 95, you have two more options. By default, when you hover the mouse pointer over a button in a Word toolbar, Word shows you a brief description of the button. These descriptions are called *ToolTips.* If you prefer not to see ToolTips, clear the **S**how ToolTips check box. If you like ToolTips, you can make them even more useful by telling Word to display the equivalent keyboard shortcuts. Displaying keyboard shortcuts is a good way to learn the keyboard shortcuts you're most likely to use. To display keyboard shortcuts, check the With Shortcut **K**eys check box.

Adding or Changing Preformatted Toolbar Buttons

You can add, change, or delete buttons on any of Word's 16 toolbars. To change the buttons on a toolbar, choose View, Toolbars, and then choose Customize. Examine the plethora of possibilities in figure 24.11.

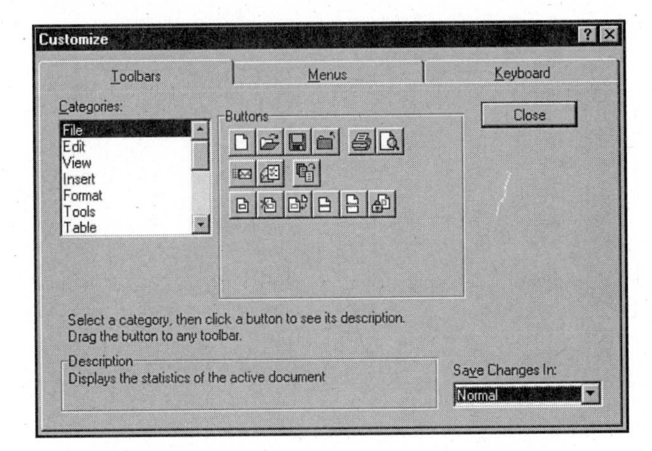

Figure 24.11
The Customize dialog box.

As you can see, the Customize dialog box also contains tabs for customizing the menus and the keyboard. You get to those later; for now, focus on the Toolbars tab.

The elements that you can add to a toolbar are divided into categories. Word organizes most of its existing buttons the same way it organizes menus: File, Edit, View, Insert, Format, Tools, Table, and the combined category Window and Help. Three more categories, Drawing, Borders, and Mail Merge, correspond to Word context-specific toolbars. These, too, contain buttons you can add or move.

When you choose one of these categories, the preformatted buttons associated with this aspect of Word appear in the Buttons box. Notice that many of these buttons have no equivalent on any menu, even the menu under which they might be listed.

Quite a few buttons don't appear on any built-in toolbar. (In other words, you have plenty of new one-button choices you can't get at any other way.)

The following table lists some examples of features that have preassigned buttons not found on any toolbar. If you use these features extensively, you might want to place their buttons on your own custom toolbar—or replace buttons on the Standard toolbar that you don't use much. (Or you can use the NRP.DOT toolbar, which contains many of these features.)

Button	Feature	Category
	Send E-mail	File
	Footnote	Insert
	Double-space	Format
	Double underline	Format
	Small caps	Format
	Add drop cap	Format
	Superscript	Format
	Subscript	Format
	Inserts one or more cells	Table

And here are some more features that do appear on toolbars but aren't typically displayed by default:

Button	Feature	Category
	Date	Insert
	Time	Insert
	Page number	Insert
	Envelope	Tools
	Record macro	Tools

	Open another Microsoft program (FoxPro)	Tools
	Sort list A-Z	Table
	Sort list Z-A	Table

To add a button to an existing toolbar, follow these steps:

1. Open the toolbar if it isn't already open. You can do so by choosing it in the View, Toolbars dialog box or by opening the part of the document that displays the toolbar.

   (You can view the Header and Footer toolbar, for example, only by choosing View, Header and Footer.)

2. Open the Customize dialog box. (Choose Tools, Customize; or if you're already in the Toolbars dialog box, choose Customize.)

3. In the Categories list, select the category you want.

4. In the Buttons box, select the button you want to add. (To see what a button does, click on it; a description of what it does appears in the Description box.)

5. Make sure that the change is being made where you want. Changes are made in the global template Normal unless you are working in a document based on another template. Then, the changes are made in that template, unless you choose Normal from the Save Changes In box.

If you want to make changes to a specific template, open a document based on that template first.

6. Drag the button to its new location. (You might have to drag the Customize dialog box out of the way first.)

Make sure not to drop the button on top of another button—unless you want to replace that button.

7. Click on Close. The change takes effect immediately.

If you've opened the template and made changes directly to it, these changes aren't locked in until you specifically save them. You see a dialog box like the one in figure 24.12 when you save or close the file.

Word's Standard and Formatting toolbars are already as wide as can be displayed on-screen. If you add buttons to these toolbars, they won't be visible unless you "float" them in two or more rows somewhere else on-screen. (Note: If you are using higher screen resolutions than the standard 640 x 480, you might be able to see more buttons on your toolbars without floating them.)

You have two alternatives:

1. Replace buttons you don't use much.
2. Create an entirely new custom toolbar. (You learn how shortly.)

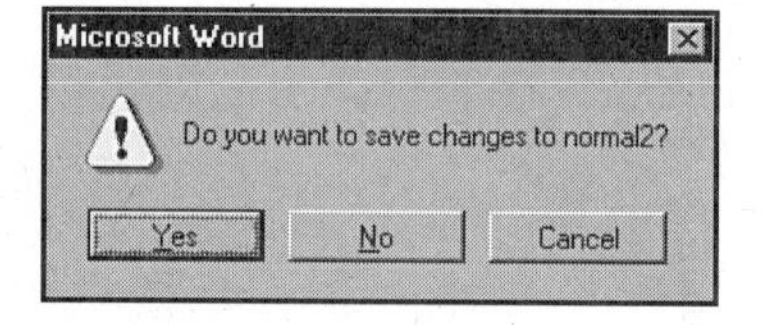

Figure 24.12
Dialog box asking for confirmation that you want to save changes to the template.

Adding Commands, Macros, and Other Toolbar Options

As mentioned previously, you can add many other elements to a Word toolbar. These elements appear in the Categories list of the Toolbars tab of the Customize dialog box, after the ones mentioned in the preceding section.

They include the following:

◆ Commands

◆ Macros

◆ Fonts

◆ AutoText

◆ Styles

To add any of these items to a toolbar, start by following the same steps described in the preceding section:

1. Open the toolbar.
2. Open the Customize dialog box.
3. Choose the category. (The list box next to it changes its name to reflect the category.)
4. Choose the template in which you want to make the change.
5. Choose the item and drag it—the highlighted text in the list box—to its new location.

Now, you have an added step: you have to define how your button should look. The Custom Button dialog box opens, as shown in figure 24.13. (Click with the right mouse button on any toolbar and select the Customize option from the resulting menu to open the dialog box.)

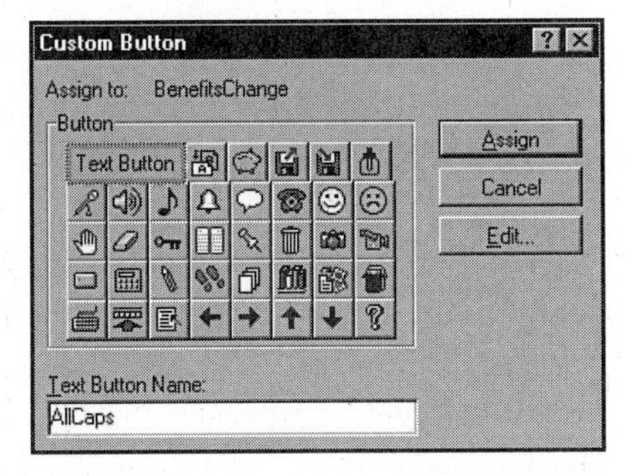

Figure 24.13

The Custom Button dialog box.

If you want, you can choose from Word's library of 37 generic buttons by clicking on the one you want.

The smiley-face button doesn't insert "Have a Nice Day" in your text, but you could easily assign it to an AutoText entry that would.

Or you can type text in the Text Button Name box. (Word assumes that you want to name your button after the command, macro, font, AutoText entry, or style you've chosen, but you can call the button anything you want.)

Note One thing you can't do is add the & symbol anywhere; as you see later, Word uses that symbol for a specific purpose in menu commands.

Editing and Creating Buttons

If you're really ambitious, you can edit an existing button or even manufacture a new one—one pixel (dot) at a time. To edit a button, choose it, and then choose **E**dit. The Button Editor dialog box opens, as shown in figure 24.14.

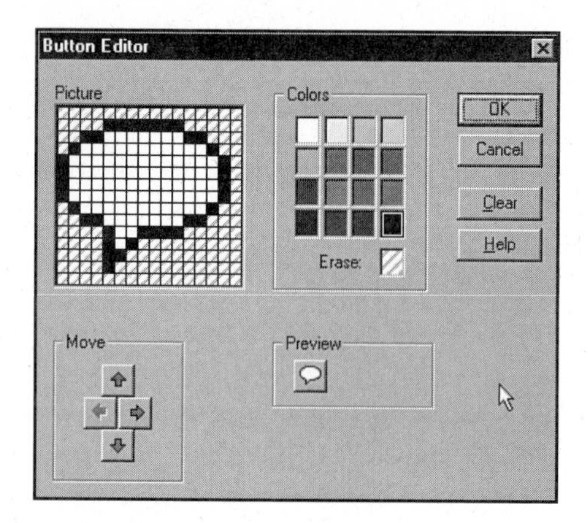

Figure 24.14

The Button Editor dialog box.

You can click on any black pixel to make it match the background color, and click on any white pixel to turn it black. To use a color in your picture, click on the color in the Colors box, and then click on the individual pixels you want to color.

As you change pixels, the button image changes; you can see your changes in the Preview box.

Tip To mark several pixels quickly, left-click and drag the mouse pointer across the pixels you want to change.

You also can move button images slightly within the button square by using the Move buttons. (You can't move the edge of an image beyond the square.)

To create an altogether new button image, choose **E**dit in the Custom Button dialog box *without* choosing a button image first. The Button Editor dialog box opens with a blank gray picture, which you can customize from scratch.

Importing a Button Image

Unless you're an artist blessed with patience, you might find that creating your own button image from scratch with the Button Editor is difficult. You do have an alternative: you can import an image from a clip-art library or graphics program.

Unfortunately, relatively few clip art images, including Word's, were designed to be clear at 1/8 inch-square. But if you want to try to import art, follow these steps:

1. Open the application containing the artwork.
2. Copy the artwork you want into the Clipboard. If you have a choice, copy it as a bitmap.
3. Switch back to Word.
4. Make sure that the toolbar button you want to change is visible.
5. Choose Tools, Customize.
6. With the dialog box open, right-click on the button you want to change. The Button shortcut menu opens, as shown in figure 24.15.
7. Choose Paste Button Image.

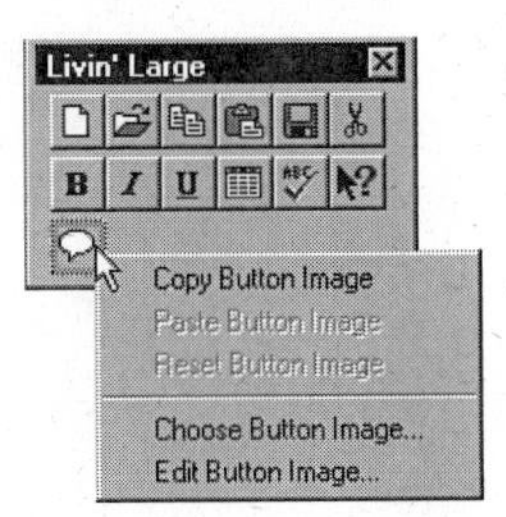

Figure 24.15

The Button shortcut menu.

Word's clip art. If you're still interested in Word's clip art as a source for button images, try the clip art image (CHECKMRK.WMF).

Importing Word clip art onto a button isn't as straightforward as it might seem. These are Windows Metafiles, and your buttons need bitmapped images. If you simply copy the artwork into the Clipboard from Word, and then paste it onto a button, it doesn't work.

continues

The work-around involves Microsoft Paint, an accessory program that comes with Windows 95. Follow these steps:

1. Choose **I**nsert, **P**icture.
2. Choose an image, and preview it. (Check the Preview Picture box.) By the way, you can open other Windows Metafile (WMF) images this way, too.
3. When you have the image you want, click on OK to open it.
4. Copy the image to the Clipboard.
5. To open Paint, click the Start button; then choose Programs, Accessories, and Paint.
6. Paste the image.
7. Copy the part of the image you want back into the Clipboard (see fig. 24.16).
8. Switch back to Word by clicking the Word icon in the Taskbar.
9. Now that you're back in Word, follow the steps for pasting an image into a toolbar button.

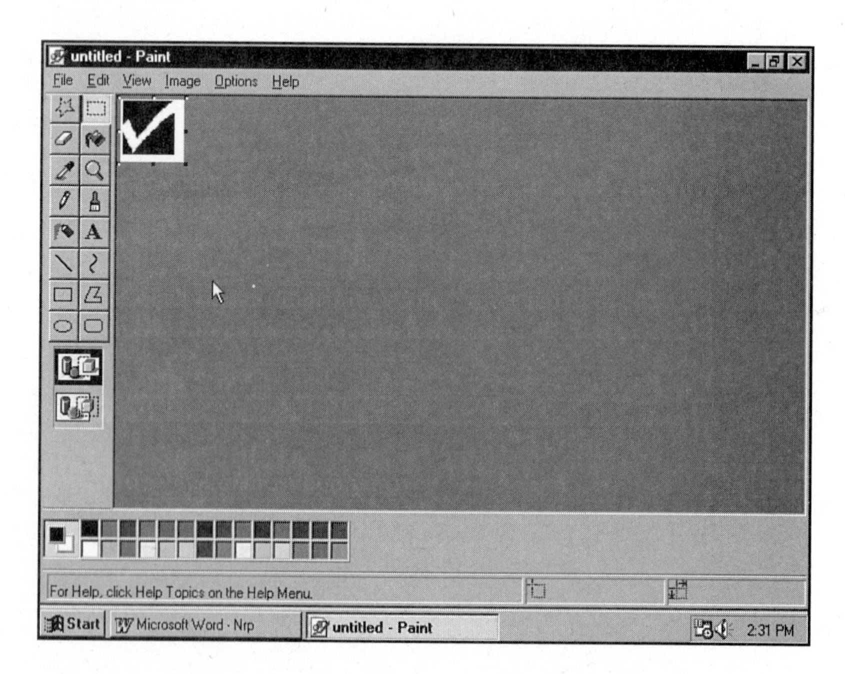

Figure 24.16

Using Microsoft Paint to cut an image into the Clipboard.

Editing Existing Button Images

One possible solution to the clip art problem is to import from another source and then edit the imported art in the Button Editor. What you want, ultimately, is an image with strong outlines and not much internal detail except for shading.

To edit an image, paste it onto a button. Then, with the Customize dialog box still open, right-click to reopen the Button shortcut menu, and choose Edit Button Image.

You can use Edit Button Image, Paste Button Image, and the rest of the Button shortcut menu only when the Customize dialog box is open to the Toolbars tab. The same story goes for moving buttons between toolbars with the mouse and some other features covered later.

You don't have to use the dialog box for anything—it just has to be open.

Widening Boxes

Several of the items you can place in toolbars are boxes, not buttons—such as the style list, font list, and zoom box. You can change the width of these boxes. If you use long style names, for example, you might lengthen the style box. Otherwise, you might shrink the style box or font list box to accommodate another button.

Choose Tools, Customize, and choose Toolbars to open the Toolbars tab. Click on the box you want to modify and point to its right edge. Your mouse pointer changes to the sizing arrow (the same one you may have seen if you changed the width of table cells). Drag the right edge of the box to narrow or widen it.

Moving and Copying Buttons among Toolbars

You also can move or copy buttons among toolbars. The Word for Windows 2.0 toolbar, for example, contained an Envelope button. If you prepare envelopes regularly, you might miss it.

To move a toolbar icon, choose Tools, Customize, and drag the button from its current location to its new location. To copy a toolbar icon, follow the same procedure, but hold down the Ctrl key while you drag the button.

Giving Your Toolbar Buttons Breathing Room

You might have noticed that most Word toolbars group their related buttons, leaving a little space between the groupings. This design makes the toolbars easier to understand and use. You can add space between any two toolbar buttons.

Suppose, for example, that you have the three buttons shown in figure 24.17. Now assume that you want to move button 2 away from button 1. First, open the Toolbars tabs of the Customize dialog box. Then drag button 2 so that it partly overlaps button 3. Let go, and Word leaves a space between buttons 1 and 2 (see fig. 24.18). Keep in mind, though, that dragging button 2 away from button 1 also pushes button 3 to the right. To *eliminate* the space, drag button 2 back partway over button 1.

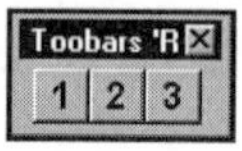

Figure 24.17

A sample three-button toolbar.

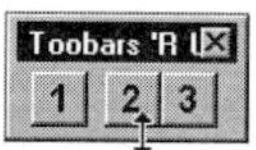

Figure 24.18

The results of adjusting the space between two buttons.

Adding Your Own Toolbar

Because the Standard and Formatting toolbars already have no vacancies, you might consider building your own custom toolbar. Then you can fill it with the supplemental buttons you use most and still leave the Standard and Formatting toolbars alone.

Note This way, your documentation, including this book and Word's Help, will still be accurate when discussing the buttons available on the Standard and Formatting toolbars.

To create a new custom toolbar, follow these steps:

1. Choose View, Toolbars.
2. Choose New. The New Toolbar dialog box opens.
3. Type a new name for the toolbar in the Toolbar Name box.
4. Choose whether you want the toolbar available to all documents (the Normal template) or to a specific open template. (The template must be open before you can choose it.)
5. Click on OK. A new, empty toolbar appears, and so does the Customize dialog box (see fig. 24.19).

Figure 24.19

A new, empty custom toolbar.

You now can drag new toolbar items into the empty toolbar as you've already learned. When you finish, choose Close in the Customize dialog box. Then decide where to place the toolbar. You can either float it on-screen or pull it to one of the edges.

Changing, Renaming, or Deleting a Custom Toolbar

After you create a custom toolbar, it appears in the Toolbars tab of the Customize dialog box, so you can easily display or hide the toolbar.

An even easier way to display or hide Word's most commonly used toolbars is with the toolbar shortcut menu. Right-click any buttonless area of a toolbar, and the shortcut menu opens (see fig. 24.20). Then just check or uncheck the toolbar you want to show or hide.

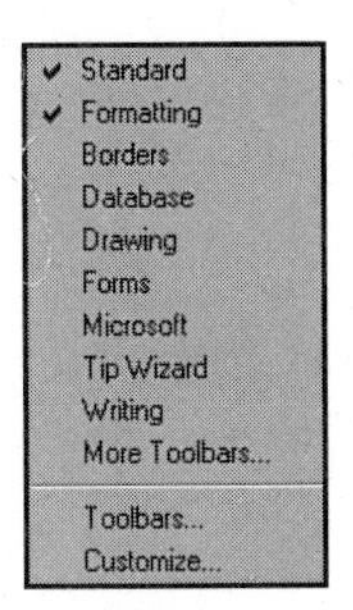

Figure 24.20

The toolbar shortcut menu.

You can change your custom toolbar the same way you change any other toolbar: by opening the Customize dialog box and moving buttons in or out.

You can rename the toolbar in Word's Organizer. (Perhaps not where you expected.) Follow these steps:

1. Choose File, Templates.

2. Choose Organizer.

3. Choose **T**oolbars.
4. Select the toolbar to be renamed.
5. Choose **R**ename.
6. Type the new name.
7. Click on OK.
8. Choose Close.

If you know that you don't need a custom toolbar anymore, you can delete it. (But you might simply want to hide it instead. You never know.) Deleting a custom toolbar doesn't require the Organizer. Follow these steps:

1. Choose **V**iew, **T**oolbars.
2. Choose the custom toolbar on the list by clicking on it.
3. Choose **D**elete. (You can't delete a built-in Word toolbar.)
4. Choose Yes to confirm.
5. Click on OK.

After you delete a custom toolbar, it's just about gone. You can't reset it like you can a built-in toolbar. Even Undo can't bring it back. Your only option is to close the document without saving changes to the template. You lose all your other changes, too, but at least you still have the custom toolbar.

Restoring Toolbars to Their Original Settings

You might find that you're not satisfied with the toolbar changes you've made—or maybe you simply don't need them any more. To change a built-in toolbar back to its original setting, follow these steps:

1. Choose **V**iew, **T**oolbars.
2. Choose the toolbar to be reset.

3. Choose **R**eset.

4. Choose the template where you want the toolbar to be restored to its original settings.

5. Click on OK twice.

Many context-sensitive toolbars, such as Headers and Footers, don't appear on the View toolbars list unless you display them first.

Customizing the Menus

You have just as much control over menus as you do over toolbars. You can add or delete items and even can create new custom menus. To customize a menu, first choose **T**ools, **C**ustomize. Then choose **M**enus to open the Menus tabbed dialog box shown in figure 24.21.

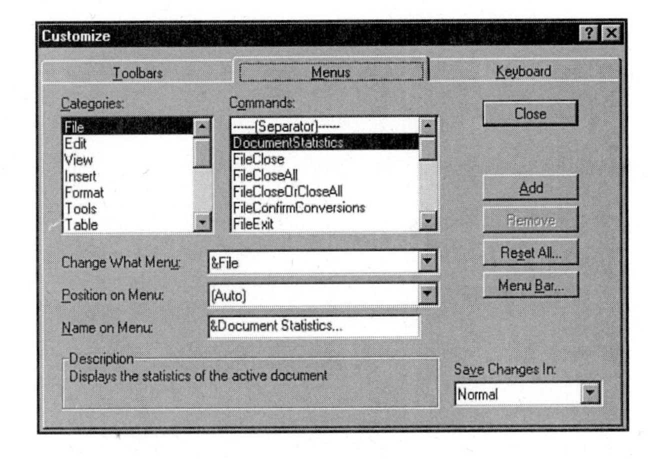

Figure 24.21

The Menus tab of the Customize dialog box.

If you've used the Toolbars dialog box, the **C**ategories list here will look familiar. You can add the same categories to menus as you can to toolbars, including WordBasic commands, custom macros or those provided with Word, fonts, AutoText entries, and styles.

As with the Toolbars box, many commands are organized similarly to Word's own menu structure. And each command contains a description, which appears in the Description box when you select the command.

Adding a Command to an Existing Menu

To add a command to an existing menu, follow these steps:

1. Choose a category from the Categories list.

2. Choose an item from the list box to the right of Categories (Commands, Macros, Fonts, AutoText, or Styles).

3. In Change What Menu, choose the menu where you want this command to go.

   Word has preassigned each command or other item to the menu it considers most appropriate. If you choose a font, for example, Word believes that you'll probably want to place it in the Format menu. Ninety-nine percent of the time, Word's guesses are good—unless of course, you create an altogether new menu.

4. In Position on Menu, choose where you want the item to appear. You have several choices:

Auto	Places new menu choice with any similar choices already on the same menu.
At top or at bottom	Places item at the top or the bottom of the menu.
In a specific location	Choose a current menu item; the new item appears after it.

5. In the Name on Menu box, either accept Word's default name or enter your own.

You've noticed that each Word menu item has a shortcut key. You can add a shortcut key to your new menu item by placing the **&** symbol in front of the letter you want to assign, as in the following example:

```
Mark &Citation
```

Tip: If you want to use "&" as a character in a menu name, type **&&** in the menu name. The doubling of the character tells Word that you meant the character to appear in the menu name, not to cause the next character in the name to be underlined.

Note: Notice that Word commands and macros, which normally require a one-word title, can have a menu name of more than one word.

Adding a Separator

If you're adding several similar items to a menu—for example, several fonts—you might want to separate them from the rest of the menu. To do so, add a *separator*, a line that Word provides for this purpose. Each category listing contains a separator. You choose it and then follow the same procedure already described for placing any other item on a menu. But note one difference: you can't name the separator (see fig. 24.22).

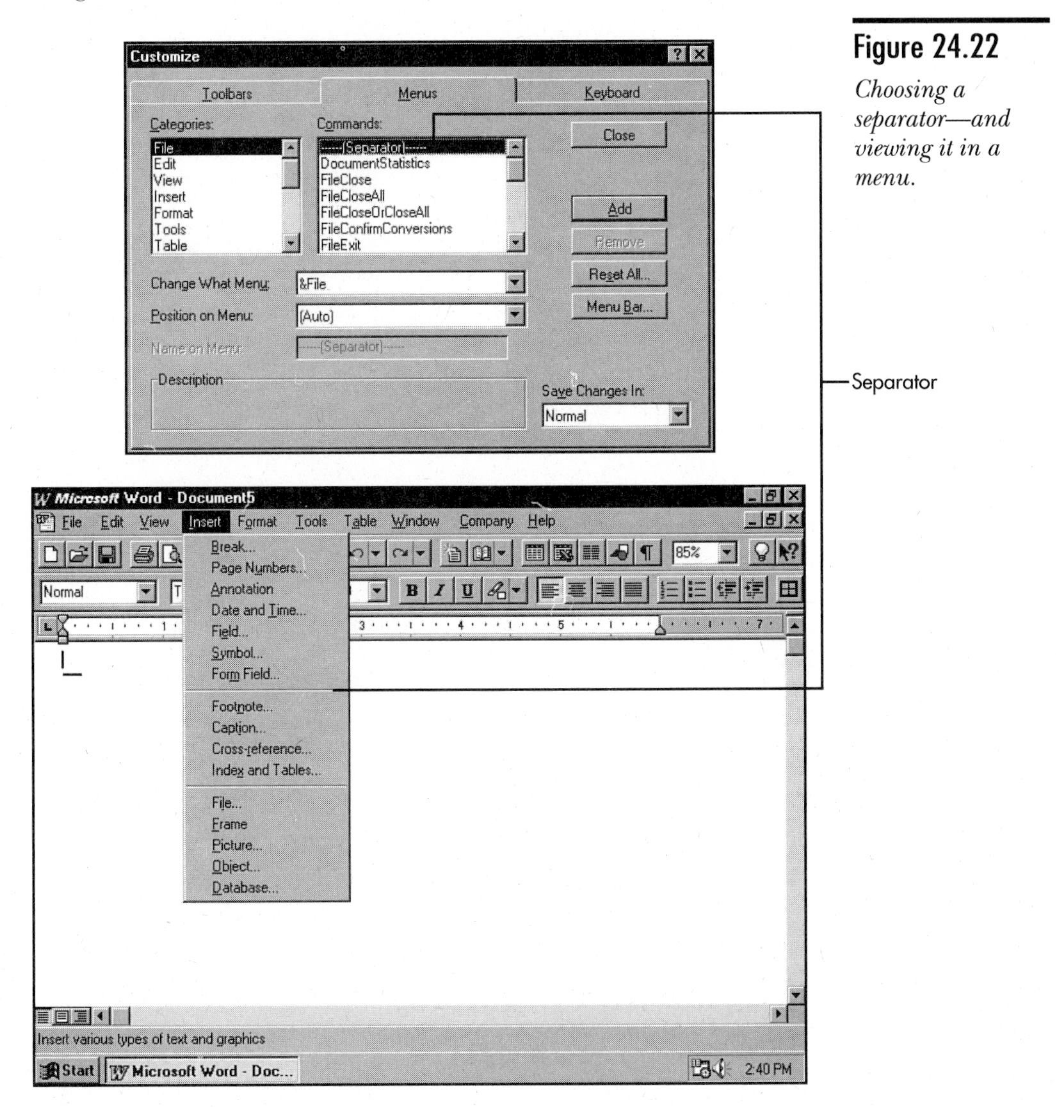

Figure 24.22

Choosing a separator—and viewing it in a menu.

Removing a Command

You can remove a command by choosing it in the Customize Menus tabbed dialog box and then choosing **R**emove. But Word provides a nifty keyboard shortcut. Follow these steps:

1. Press Ctrl+Alt+minus sign. The insertion point becomes a thick horizontal line, as shown in figure 24.23.

2. Choose the menu item you want to delete. Instead of performing the action specified by the menu item, Word deletes the menu item.

To move a menu item from one menu to another, delete the item from the first menu and add it to the other.

Figure 24.23

Removing a menu item with Ctrl+Alt+minus sign.

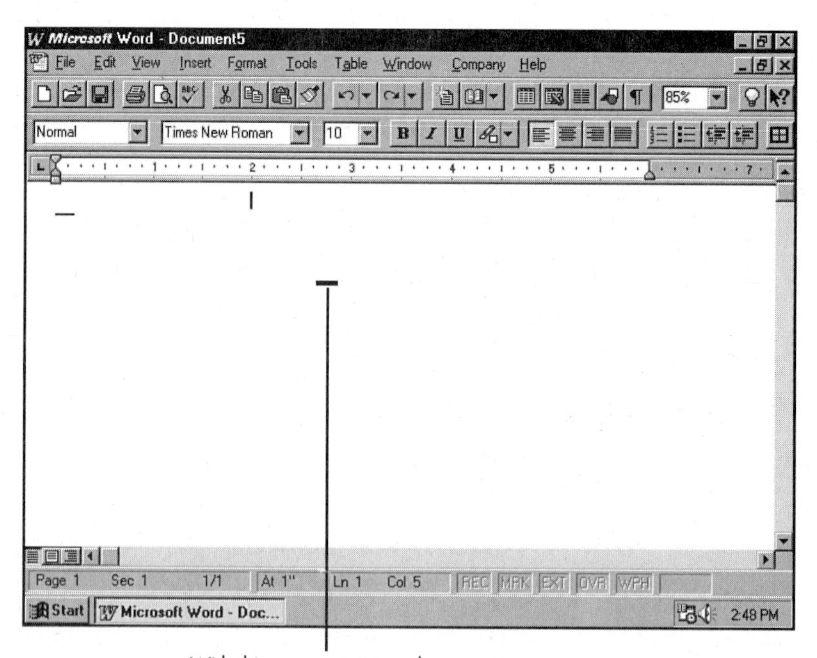

Resetting Menus You've Changed

As with Toolbars, Word "remembers" its original menu settings in case you need them again. To reset all your built-in menus, eliminating any changes you've made, follow these steps:

1. Choose Tools, Customize.
2. In the Customize dialog box, choose Menus to open the Menus tab.
3. Specify which template's changes you want to undo in the Save Changes In drop-down list box (lower-right corner of the dialog box).
4. Choose Reset All.
5. Choose Yes to confirm the change; then choose Close.

Adding Your Own Menus

You also can add an entirely new Word menu. Earlier in this chapter, for example, you read about a suggested special Company menu that loads forms and (read-only) procedure manuals. You can create menus for many other applications. For example:

- Indexing and tables of contents, figures, and authorities could use a menu of their own. (Right now, they're all buried deep in the Insert, Index and Tables menu selection.)
- If you have several commonly used AutoText entries or macros, you can create a new AutoText menu and a customized macro menu.

Theoretically, you can add up to 20 menus. But where would they all fit?

To add a new menu, follow these steps:

1. Choose Tools, Customize.
2. Choose Menus to open the Menus tab.
3. Specify whether you want to save the changes in the Normal global template or in another template that's already open.

4. Choose Menu **B**ar. The Menu Bar dialog box opens, as shown in figure 24.24.
5. Type the name of the new menu in the **N**ame on Menu Bar text box. Place an **&** symbol before the letter you want as your shortcut letter.
6. Place the **M**enu name on the menu bar by clicking on the position you want in the **P**osition on Menu Bar list box. As with placing menu items, you have some choices:

First	Choose **(First)**.
Last	Choose **(Last)**.
Specific location	Choose an existing menu; the new menu will follow it.

7. Choose Close twice. Your new menu appears. You can now add menu items to it the same way you can to any other menu (see "Adding a Command to an Existing Menu" earlier in this chapter).

Choosing Re**s**et All in the Menus tabbed dialog box deletes custom menus, too.

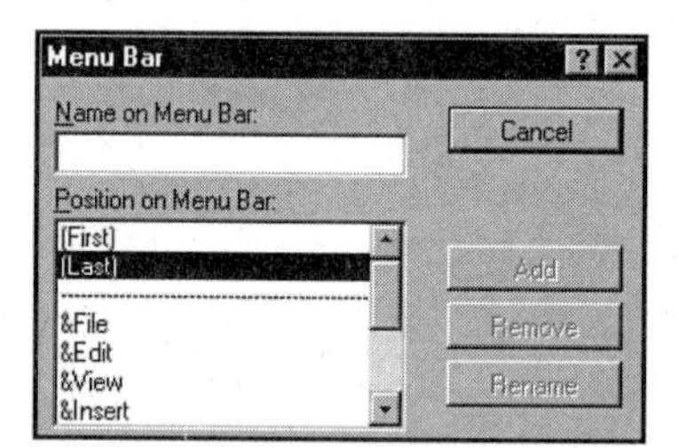

Figure 24.24
The Menu Bar dialog box.

Renaming a Built-In or Custom Menu

You can rename either a custom menu or a built-in menu by following these steps:

1. Choose **T**ools, **C**ustomize.
2. Choose **M**enus to open the Menus tab.
3. Specify whether you want to display the new name in the Normal global template or in another template that's already open.

4. Choose Menu **B**ar.

5. In the **P**osition on Menu Bar box, choose the menu to be renamed.

6. Type the new name in the **N**ame on Menu Bar box.

7. Choose **R**ename.

8. Choose Close twice.

Adding Keyboard Shortcuts

Out of the box, Word comes with more than 250 keyboard shortcuts. Many tasks have more than one keyboard shortcut. What more could you want?

Well, you might be switching to Word from another word processor. Maybe you're used to its keyboard commands, and you find yourself constantly pressing the wrong keys in Word. You can redefine some of the more annoying commands so that they work the way you've come to expect.

And, notwithstanding all the built-in shortcuts, many aspects of Word have few or no keyboard shortcuts at all. Three good examples are drawing, tables, and forms. If you use these features regularly, you might want to assign them keyboard shortcuts.

Adding Keyboard Shortcuts to Commands on Existing Menus or Buttons

To assign a new keyboard shortcut to a task that's already on a button or menu, follow these steps:

1. Press Alt+Ctrl+plus sign. (Use the + on the numeric keypad.) Your mouse pointer changes to the command symbol, as shown in figure 24.25.

2. Click on the toolbar button, or choose the menu item you want to give a keyboard shortcut. (If you're using a toolbar button, make sure that the toolbar is displayed first.)

3. The Customize Keyboard tabbed dialog box appears, showing the command you've chosen in the C**o**mmands box, as shown in figure 24.26. A description of the task appears in the Description box.

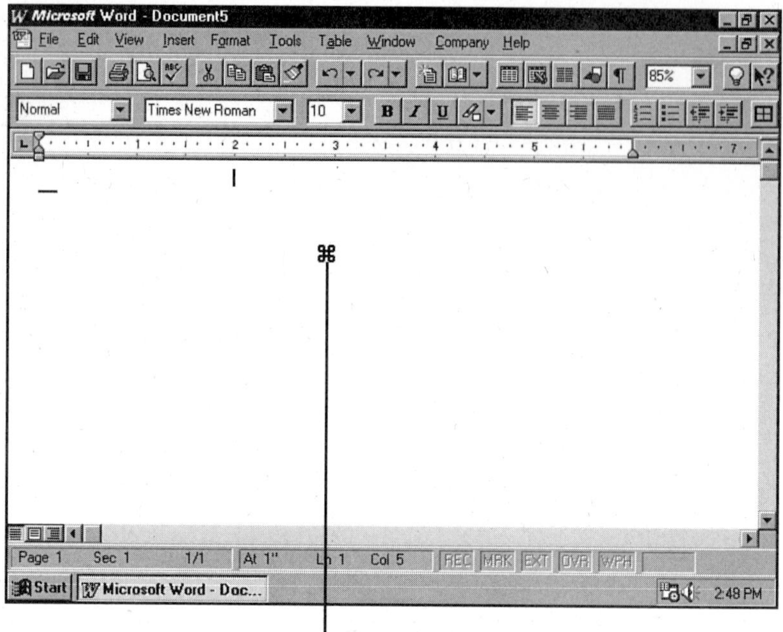

With this mouse pointer, choose the button or menu selection to which you want to assign a keyboard shortcut.

Figure 24.25

The command mouse pointer.

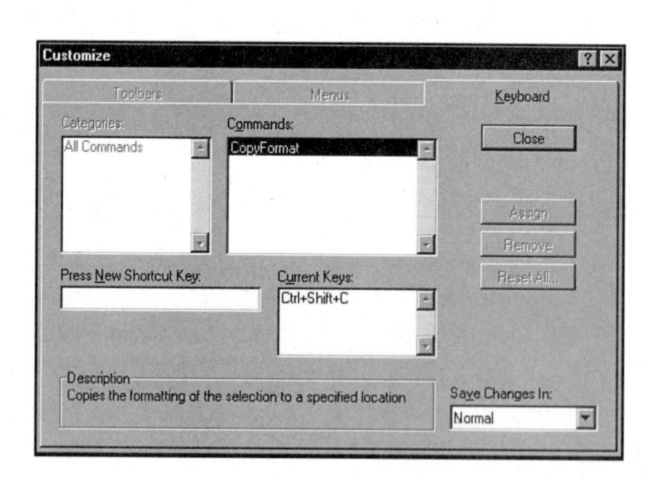

Figure 24.26

The Keyboard tab, accessed from the command mouse pointer.

4. Now move the mouse pointer to Press New Shortcut Key, and press the key or combination you want to associate with this task. Your keystroke or combination of keystrokes appears in the box.

   If the shortcut key you indicate is already associated with a task, that task appears in the Currently Assigned To area (see fig. 24.27).

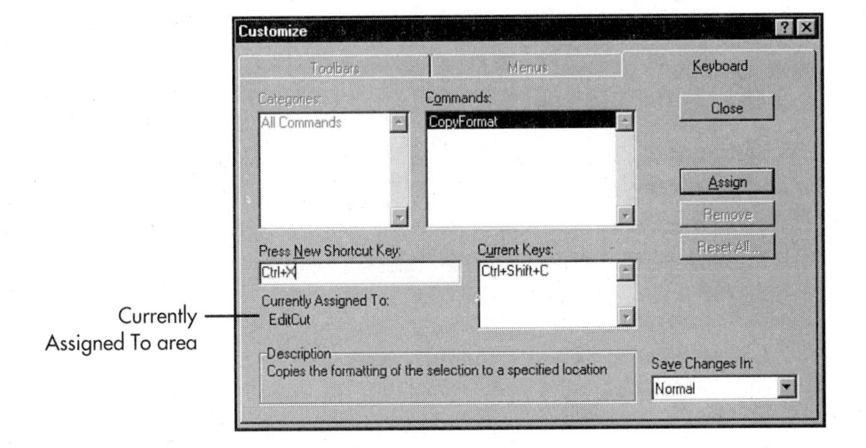

Figure 24.27
Viewing the Currently Assigned To area.

5. If you want to reassign this key combination, choose **Assign**. The new key combination appears in Current Keys, beneath the name Commands list box.

   If you prefer to assign another combination, backspace to erase the combination in Press New Shortcut Key, and try another combination.

Keeping track of Word's keyboard combinations can be difficult. If you're going to start changing them, you need a reference. Appendix A contains a complete list, arranged by function. But what you really need is an alphabetical list of all the commands, with all the Alt+function key combinations together, all the Ctrl+Shift combinations together, and so on. That way you'll know in advance which combinations are available.

The companion disk that accompanies this book includes such a list, called KEYBLIST.DOC. You can use it to print and distribute new lists if you dramatically revamp the keyboard settings built into Word.

Tip: Don't re-sort KEYBLIST.DOC; some adjustments in alphabetical order were made to improve its usefulness.

Adding Keyboard Shortcuts to Other Commands

Most of the commands built into Word don't have menu or toolbar equivalents. And neither do macros, fonts, AutoText entries, or styles, unless you've added them yourself. You can provide or change keyboard shortcuts for these, too.

You also can use the following technique to simplify the convoluted finger-stretches required to type characters such as _ or ñ.

To create or change a keyboard shortcut for one of these elements, follow these steps:

1. Choose **T**ools, **C**ustomize.
2. Choose **K**eyboard. The Keyboard tabbed dialog box appears—this time, containing all possible commands for which you can create a keyboard shortcut (see fig. 24.28).

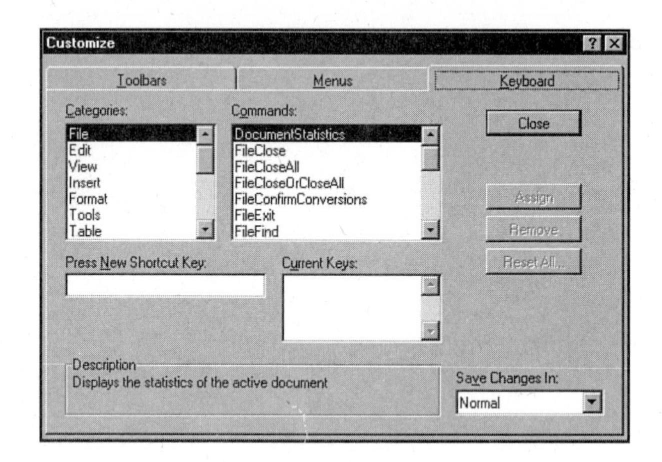

Figure 24.28

The Keyboard tab, ready for assigning a keyboard shortcut.

3. Narrow your search for the command you want by choosing a category from the **C**ategories list.

   This list is the same one available in the Toolbars and Menus tabs, with one addition: Common Symbols.

   Common Symbols includes Word's default keyboard shortcuts for many foreign language characters and a few other special characters, such as ellipses, trademark and copyright symbols, and curly quotation marks.

4. Choose a command or other element from the detailed list to the right of **C**ategories. This list is named C**o**mmands, Macr**o**s, F**o**nts, Aut**o**Text, St**y**les, or C**o**mmon Symbols, depending on your choice in step 3.
5. As in the earlier example, move the mouse pointer to Press **N**ew Shortcut Key, and press the key or combination you want to associate with this task. You see your keystrokes in the box; if you've chosen a combination that's already assigned, Word notifies you in the Currently Assigned To area.
6. To reassign this key combination, choose **A**ssign. To assign another combination, backspace to erase the combination in Press **N**ew Shortcut Key and try again.

Removing or Resetting Key Combinations

You can tell Word to remove a specific key combination or to reset all key combinations to what they were when you installed the software. (Resetting also eliminates other key combinations you might have assigned earlier to new macros.) Follow these steps:

1. Choose **T**ools, **C**ustomize.
2. Choose **K**eyboard.
3. To remove a specific keyboard combination, select it, and choose **R**emove.
4. To reset all key combinations, choose Re**s**et All. The dialog box shown in figure 24.29 appears.
5. Choose **Y**es to reset.

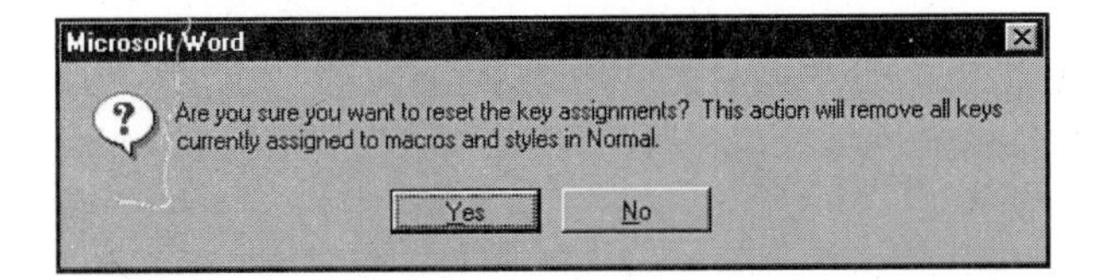

Figure 24.29

Resetting key assignments.

Using Add-In Programs

For years, several small companies made a living marketing *add-ons* to Word. These programs have generally been specialized WordBasic macros or document templates that simplify special tasks.

Now, Word also supports *add-ins*. These are programs that load into Word and become part of it. (If you're involved in desktop publishing, you might be familiar with this concept. You can supplement Quark XPress with third-party programs called Quark Xtensions, and Aldus PageMaker now has the equivalent Aldus Additions.)

Superficially, they're similar to WordBasic macros, but add-ins run faster. Like WordBasic macros, add-ins can be added to toolbar commands, assigned menu selections, and given keyboard shortcuts.

And, according to Microsoft, you often can adapt add-ins from existing code written in the popular computer language C. Thus some pretty sophisticated add-in programs could be around the corner.

To load an add-in program, follow these steps:

1. Choose File, Templates.
2. Choose the add-in you want from the Global Templates and Add-ins box.
3. Choose Add.
4. Click on OK.

To remove an add-in program, follow the preceding steps 1 and 2, but then choose Remove and OK.

Add-ins written for Word 6 may need to be updated for Windows 95.

Hiding Parts of the Interface

You've learned how to add toolbars to the interface. But what if you find the Word interface cluttered as it is? Answer: You can delete some or all of it.

You've already seen that you can hide toolbars by right-clicking the Toolbar shortcut menu and unchecking the toolbars you want to hide. And you know that you can hide the ruler by choosing Ruler from the View menu and unchecking that option.

You can hide the status bar, the horizontal scroll bar, or the vertical scroll bar by following these steps:

1. Choose Tools, Options.
2. Choose View to open the View tabbed dialog box.
3. In the Window group, uncheck the screen element you want to hide.

Working with a Blank Screen

The ultimate interface is none at all, and Word will oblige. Choose Full Screen from the View menu. Everything goes away except your text and the Full Screen toolbar, shown in figure 24.30.

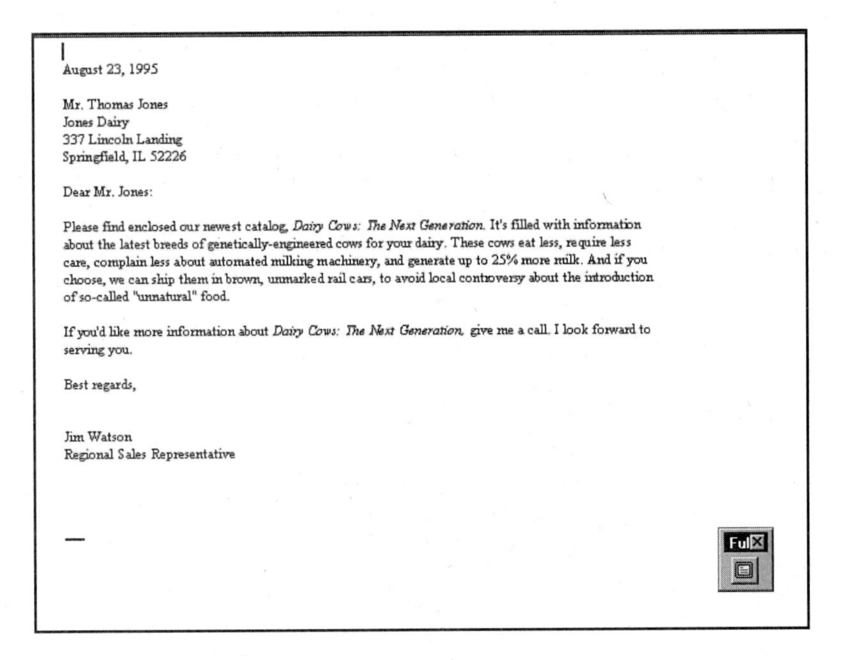
August 23, 1995

Mr. Thomas Jones
Jones Dairy
337 Lincoln Landing
Springfield, IL 52226

Dear Mr. Jones:

Please find enclosed our newest catalog, *Dairy Cows: The Next Generation*. It's filled with information about the latest breeds of genetically-engineered cows for your dairy. These cows eat less, require less care, complain less about automated milking machinery, and generate up to 25% more milk. And if you choose, we can ship them in brown, unmarked rail cars, to avoid local controversy about the introduction of so-called "unnatural" food.

If you'd like more information about *Dairy Cows: The Next Generation*, give me a call. I look forward to serving you.

Best regards,

Jim Watson
Regional Sales Representative

Figure 24.30

Word with no user interface, except the Full Screen toolbar.

Click on the Full Screen button to return to your previous interface. Or you can click on the top left corner of the toolbar to make even the Full Screen toolbar go away. In that case, pressing Esc returns Word to its normal interface.

Any appropriate shortcut menus, such as the Table shortcut menu, are still available when you're in full screen.

Simulating WordPerfect

If you're moving from WordPerfect 5.1, you may feel more comfortable knowing that Word can simulate its bare look. Step 1 is to use white type on a blue background. Follow these steps to change the type and background color:

1. Choose Tools, Options.
2. Choose General to open the General tab.
3. Check Blue Background, White Text.
4. Click on OK.

Step 2 is to use a draft font—the built-in system font that you'd normally use to have Word run a little more quickly. Follow these steps to use the draft font:

1. Choose **O**ptions from the **T**ools menu.
2. Choose **V**iew to open the View tab.
3. Check **D**raft Font in the Show box.

And Step 3 is to choose **V**iew, **F**ull Screen. The results, shown in figure 24.31, are fairly convincing.

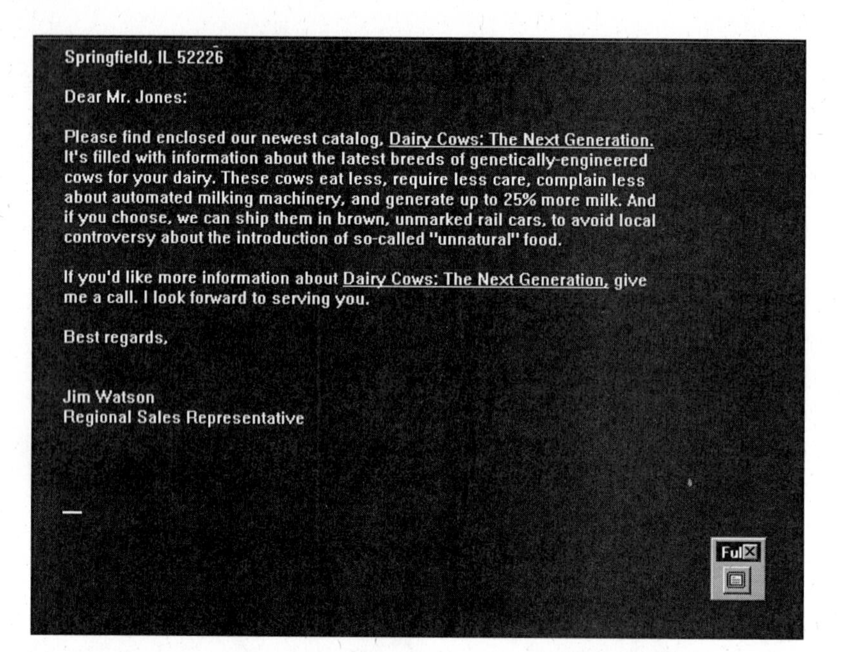
Springfield, IL 52226

Dear Mr. Jones:

Please find enclosed our newest catalog, Dairy Cows: The Next Generation. It's filled with information about the latest breeds of genetically-engineered cows for your dairy. These cows eat less, require less care, complain less about automated milking machinery, and generate up to 25% more milk. And if you choose, we can ship them in brown, unmarked rail cars, to avoid local controversy about the introduction of so-called "unnatural" food.

If you'd like more information about Dairy Cows: The Next Generation, give me a call. I look forward to serving you.

Best regards,

Jim Watson
Regional Sales Representative

Figure 24.31

Running "WordPerfect style."

Changing Word Options

In this chapter and throughout the book, you've learned about many aspects of Word that you can adjust in the tabbed dialog boxes available through **T**ools, **O**ptions. Some of these changes fall into the category of personalizing Word, so they are covered here.

Note Some of these options also make Word run a little bit faster.

Changing View Options

You've already visited the View tabbed dialog box (accessed via Tools, Options, View) twice in this chapter. (The dialog box is shown in fig. 24.32.)

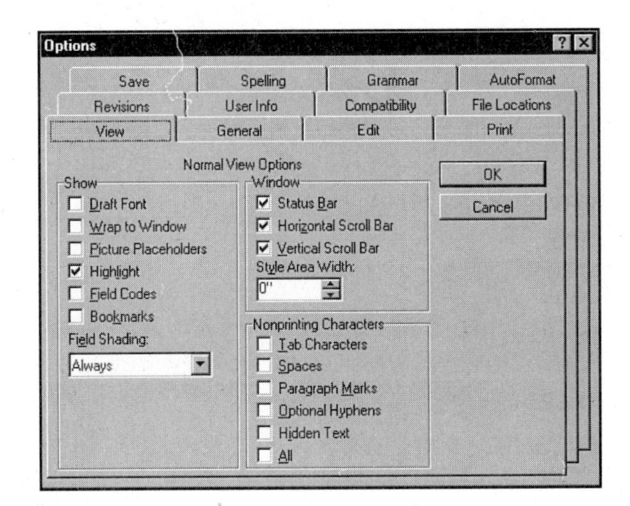

Figure 24.32

The View tab of the Options dialog box.

As mentioned previously, using the draft font (Draft Font), at least while you're doing routine editing, can speed up Word on a slow system.

Another kick in the pants for a sluggish system is Picture Placeholders. This option tells Word not to waste energy displaying graphics all the time—just show a blank box where they're located.

The third item worth covering here doesn't speed up your computer, but it could make your life much more convenient. It's called Wrap to Window.

Suppose, for example, that you use wide margins or you like to magnify your document above 100 percent (perhaps to preserve your eyesight). Often, then, not all your text fits on-screen at once. You find yourself moving from left to right as if you were watching a Ping-Pong match. *Annoying.*

You could change your margins—but that affects many aspects of your document, and you have to remember to change them back. Or you could choose the Page Width option in the View, Zoom dialog box. But that defeats the purpose of enlarging your text. Neither of these is an ideal solution.

Check Wrap to Window, however, and your text fits within your screen; all your pagination remains as it should be; and your text remains as large as you want.

If you use Wrap to Window regularly, you might find that you no longer need your horizontal scroll bar.

Changing General Options

Next you need to know about a few general options for personalizing your system that haven't been covered elsewhere in the book. Look at the General tab, which you access by choosing Tools, Options, and then General (see fig. 24.33).

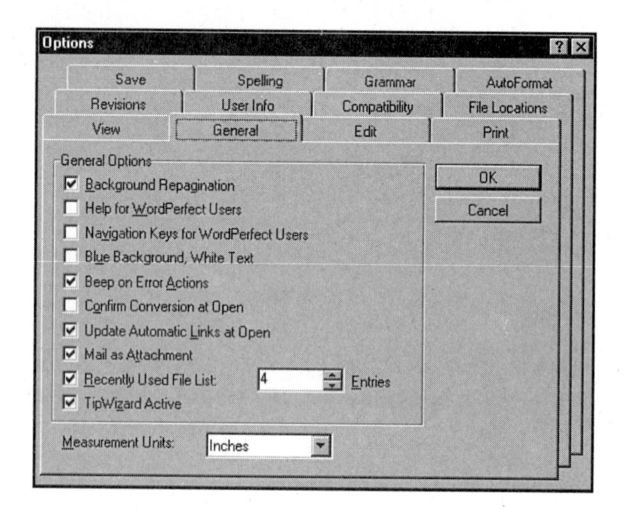

Figure 24.33
The General tab of the Options dialog box.

Background Repagination, normally set to on, automatically repaginates your document while you work. To pick up a little speed, you can turn it off while you work in Normal or Outline view. Word still repaginates when you go into Print Preview or Page Layout view, when you print, or when you ask for a word count.

Beep on Error Actions, also normally set to on, is fairly straightforward: when you make a mistake, Word beeps. If you hate to be beeped at, uncheck it.

Recently Used File List tells Word how many of the files you've closed lately should be listed in the File menu. The list is provided so that you can conveniently restart where you left off. Typically, it's four. You can choose any number from zero to nine.

Finally, as mentioned before, you can tell Word to display its ruler and dialog-box measurements not in inches but in centimeters, points, or picas. Choose your new measuring system from the Measurement Units list box.

Changing Editing Options

One more Tools, Options dialog box is available: Edit (see fig. 24.34).

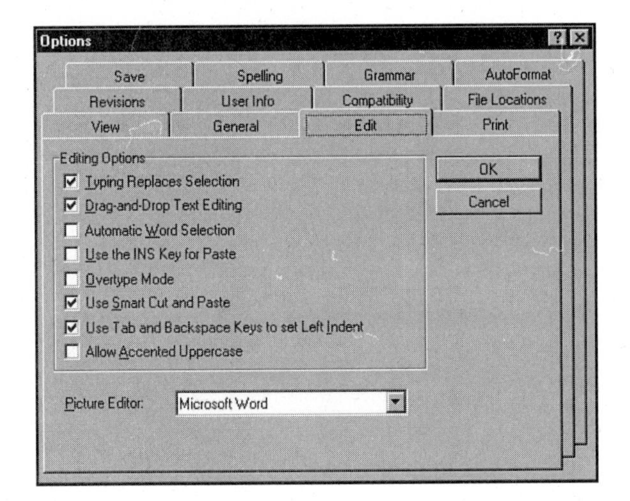

Figure 24.34

The Tools, Options, Edit dialog box.

The first option, checked by default, is Typing Replaces Selection. If you've noticed, when you select text, that text disappears as soon as you start typing over it. Most people find that a useful shortcut. Some people—maybe you're one of them—find that it deletes text they intended to preserve. If you prefer, uncheck it.

Similarly, Drag-and-Drop Text Editing enables you to select text and drag it to a new location. Some people find themselves inadvertently dragging text they didn't intend to move. You can turn off the feature here if you choose.

The next three editing options—Automatic Word Selection, Use the INS Key for Paste, and Overtype Mode—are off by default.

With Automatic Word Selection enabled, if you've already selected one word and you click again in the next, that entire word is also selected.

Use the INS Key for Paste enables you to use the Insert key to paste text or graphics, as is the case with some other word processors. With this feature on, pressing Insert no longer switches you to Overtype mode. Also, INS rather than Ctrl+V is listed as the shortcut for Paste on the Edit menu (though both shortcuts work).

Choosing Overtype Mode tells Word to type over existing text, replacing it instead of moving it to the right. (You also can enter Overtype mode temporarily by pressing Insert, unless you've enabled the Use the INS key for Paste option.)

The next Word feature, Use Smart Cut and Paste, is turned on by default. With this option, if you cut a word from one location and paste the word into another location, Word makes sure that one space—no more, no less—falls between the pasted word and the words before and after it. You might not even notice that the feature is on; you might just find yourself doing less cleanup. If, however, you find the feature disconcerting, you can turn it off.

Allow Accented Uppercase is specifically targeted for text you format as French (by using Format, Language). It is turned off by default. The option enables Word's Format, Change Case feature and its French proofing tools (if you have them) to suggest adding accents to uppercase letters when appropriate.

Windows 95

Finally, Word 95 adds one more editing option: Use Tab and Backspace Keys to Set Left Indent. This option, which is turned on by default, affects paragraphs that are being AutoFormatted, such as numbered lists. For example, with this box checked, if you insert three .5-inch tabs before the first item in a numbered list, all the items that follow will also be indented 1.5 inch.

Part V

Command Reference

New Riders Publishing
INSIDE
SERIES

WordBasic Command Reference

Abs()

Purpose

Returns the absolute (positive) value of a number, whether that number is positive or negative.

Syntax

```
x=Abs(number)
```

Parameters

number
Any positive or negative value or function that results in a positive or negative value.

Returns

A positive number.

See Also

Int()
Format
Rnd ()
Sgn ()

Activate

Purpose

Activates (moves to the front) a document window.

Syntax

```
Activate Window$, [PaneNumber]
```

Parameters

Window$
The name of the window to be activated. Also can be the full path

and name of the document. The document must already be open.

PaneNumber
The number of the pane to activate_1 or 2 for Top pane; 3 or 4 for Bottom pane.

See Also

DocSplit
NextWindow
OtherPane
PrevWindow
WindowList
WindowName$()
WindowNumber
WindowPane()

ActivateObject

Purpose

Performs the same function as double-clicking on an object in a document. (The object must already be selected or indicated by the insertion point.)

Syntax

```
ActivateObject
```

See Also

EditGoTo
EditObject

AddAddress

Purpose

Adds a new address to the Microsoft Exchange Personal Address Book you choose. (Available only if Microsoft Exchange or Schedule+ are installed.)

Syntax

```
AddAddress AddressProperties$()
```

Parameters

AddressProperties$()
A two-dimensional array containing the information for the new address you want to add. Create the array first, using the DIM statement, as in the following example:

```
dim addresstext(2,1)
```

The first dimension of the two-dimensional array is used to identify the property where new information will be placed. In the preceding example, the number 2 means that the array will be 3 rows deep: 0, 1, and 2.

The second dimension is used to specify the text to be included. The number 1 means that the array will be 2 rows wide: 0 and 1.

Next, populate the array, as in the following example:

```
addresstext$(0,0) = PR_GIVEN_NAME
addresstext$(1,0) = PR_SURNAME
addresstext$(1,1) = Flacker
addresstext$(2,0) = PR_COMPANY_NAME
addresstext$(2,1) = Record World
```

Finally, use AddAddress to move the contents of the array into your default Microsoft Exchange Personal Address Book:

```
AddAddress addresstext$()
```

Here is a list of properties you can use to define addressee information to be placed in a Microsoft Exchange Personal Address Book:

PR_ADDRTYPE
Type of E-mail address

PR_BEEPER_TELEPHONE_NUMBER
Beeper number

PR_BUSINESS_FAX_NUMBER
Business fax number

PR_CAR_TELEPHONE_NUMBER
Car phone number

PR_CELLULAR_TELEPHONE_NUMBER
Cellular phone number

PR_COMMENT
Text on Notes tab for address entry

PR_COMPANY_NAME
Company name

PR_COUNTRY
Country

PR_DEPARTMENT_NAME
Department

PR_DISPLAY_NAME
Name displayed in Address Book dialog box

PR_EMAIL_ADDRESS
E-mail address

PR_GIVEN_NAME
First name

PR_HOME_FAX_NUMBER
Home fax number

PR_INITIALS
Initials

PR_LOCALITY
City or locality

PR_LOCATION
Building/room location (Building number, then room number)

PR_OFFICE_LOCATION
Office location

PR_OFFICE_TELEPHONE_NUMBER
Office phone number

PR_OFFICE2_TELEPHONE_NUMBER
Second office phone

PR_OTHER_TELEPHONE_NUMBER
Alternate phone number

PR_POSTAL_CODE
Postal or ZIP Code

PR_PRIMARY_FAX_NUMBER
Primary fax number

PR_PRIMARY_TELEPHONE_NUMBER
Primary phone number

PR_RADIO_TELEPHONE_NUMBER
Radiophone number

PR_STATE_OR_PROVINCE
State or province

PR_STREET_ADDRESS
Street address

PR_SURNAME
Last name

PR_TITLE
Job title

See Also

GetAddress($)
InsertAddress
ToolsCreateEnvelope
ToolsCreateLabels

AddAddIn or AddAddIn()

Purpose

Adds a template or DLL/WLL to the list of global templates and add-ins.

Syntax

```
AddAddIn DLLName$, [Load]
```

or

```
x = AddAddIn(DLLName$ [,Load]
```

Parameters

DLLName$
: The full path and file name of the dynamic link library add-in.

Load
: 0: Do not load add-in;1: Load add-in.

Returns

Returns the position of the template or add-in in the list.

See Also

AddInState()
ClearAddIns
CountAddIns()
CountMacros()
DeleteAddIn
Format
GetAddInID()
GetAddInName$
()MacroName$()

AddButton

Purpose

Adds a button to a toolbar.

Syntax

```
AddButton Toolbar$, Position, Category, Name$ [, ButtonTextOrImageNum][, Context][, CommandValue$]
```

Parameters

Toolbar$
: The name of the toolbar.

Position
: The position in the toolbar to assign to the new tool.

Category
The type of item:
1 or omitted: Built-in commands
2: Macros
3: Fonts
4: AutoText entries
5: Styles

Name$
: The name of the command, macro, etc.

ButtonTextOrImageNum
: The text to appear on the button, or the number of an image.

Context
: 0: Normal template.
1: Active template.

CommandValue$
: Additional text required by the command.

See Also

ChooseButtonImage
CopyButtonImage
DeleteButton
EditButtonImage
Format
MoveButton
PasteButtonImage
ResetButtonImage

AddDropDownItem

Purpose

Adds an item to a drop-down form field (up to 25 items).

Syntax

```
AddDropDownItem BookmarkName$,
ItemText$
```

Parameters

BookmarkName$
The name of the bookmark that marks the drop-down form field.

ItemText$
The item to add to the drop-down form field.

See Also

DropDownFormField
RemoveAllDropDownItems
RemoveDropDownItem

AddInState

Purpose

Loads or unloads the add-in.

Syntax

```
AddInState DLLName, Load
```

or

```
x = AddInState(DLLName)
```

Parameters

DLLName
Can be a number or a string.

Number:
Identifies the add-in in the File|Templates menu.

String:
Identifies the path and file name of the add-in.

Load
0: Do not load add-in.
1: Load add-in.

Returns

Additive values:

0: None of the following
1: Add-in is loaded
2: Add-in is a dynamic-link library
4: Add-in loads automatically

See Also

AddAddIn
ClearAddIns
CountAddIns()

DeleteAddIn
GetAddInID()
GetAddInName$()

AllCaps or AllCaps()

Purpose

Converts the selection to all uppercase letters or removes the AllCaps formatting from the selection.

Syntax

```
AllCaps [Action]
```

or

```
x = AllCaps()
```

Parameters

Action

1: Formats the selection.
0: Removes AllCaps formatting from selection.
omitted: Toggles AllCaps formatting.

Returns

-1: Only part of the selection is in AllCaps format.
0: None of the selection is in AllCaps format.
1: All the selection is in AllCaps format.

See Also

FormatFont

AnnotationRef FromSel$()

Purpose

Returns the annotation mark immediately after the insertion point.

Syntax

```
x$ = AnnotationRefFromSel$()
```

Returns

The annotation mark, or "[0]" if none.

See Also

EditGoTo
GoToAnnotationScope
GoToNextItem
GoToPreviousItem
ShowAnnotationBy

AppActivate

Purpose

Activates (brings to the front) Window$ in another application (not Word).

Syntax

```
AppActivate Window$, [When]
```

Parameters

Window$

The name of the window to be activated; also can be the full path and name of the document. The document must already be open. (NOTE: Some applications may append the name of the open working file to their window name, especially if the application is maximized.)

When:

0: If Word is not active, Word's title bar flashes and waits until Word is activated before activating Window$.

1: Word immediately activates Window$, regardless of Word's status.

See Also

AppClose
AppGetNames
AppIsRunning()
MicrosoftAccess
MicrosoftExcel
MicrosoftFox
MicrosoftMail
MicrosoftPowerPoint
MicrosoftProject
MicrosoftPublisher
MicrosoftSchedule
Shell

AppClose

Purpose

Closes the application.

Syntax

```
AppClose [AppName$]
```

Parameters

AppName$
The name of the application.

See Also

AppActivate
AppIsRunning()
Shell

AppCount()

Purpose

Returns the number of open applications.

Syntax

```
x = AppCount()
```

Returns

The number of open applications.

See Also

AppGetNames

AppGetNames or AppGetNames()

Purpose

Fills a string array with the names of all open applications.

Syntax

```
AppGetNames Array$()
```

Parameters

Array$
A previously defined array.

Returns

The names of all open applications, in Array$. The function form returns the number of open applications.

See Also

AppActivate
AppClose
AppCount()
AppIsRunning()

AppHide

Purpose

Hides the application and removes its window from the Task List.

Syntax

```
AppHide [WindowName$]
```

Parameters

WindowName$
An open application.

See Also

AppClose
AppShow

AppInfo$()

Purpose

Returns information about the current state of Microsoft Word.

Syntax

```
AppInfo$(InfoNumber)
```

Parameters

InfoNumber
A code indicating the type of information to return:

TRUE = -1, FALSE = 0 (NOTE: available memory can vary due to disk swapping.)

1 The (Windows) environment string

2 Word's version number string

3 Is Word in a special mode (e.g. MoveText): Returns TRUE or FALSE

4 X Position of the Word window, in points from the left of the screen (Maximized = -3)

5 Y Position of the Word window, in points from the left of the screen (Maximized = -3)

6 Width in points of the active document workspace

7 Height in points of the active document workspace

8 Is Word Maximized: Returns TRUE or FALSE

9 Total conventional memory (returns 0 in Windows 95)

10 Total conventional memory available (returns 0 in Windows 95)

11 Total expanded memory

12 Total expanded memory available

13 Is math coprocessor installed: Returns TRUE or FALSE

14 Is mouse present: Returns TRUE or FALSE

15 Total disk space available

16 The language version of Word

17 The list separator setting in WIN.INI

18 The decimal setting in WIN.INI

19 The thousands separator setting in WIN.INI

20 The currency symbol setting in WIN.INI

21 The clock format setting in WIN.INI

22 The a.m. string setting in WIN.INI

23 The p.m. string setting in WIN.INI

24 The time separator setting in WIN.INI

25 The date separator setting in WIN.INI

26 Returns 0 in Windows 95

Returns

TRUE=1
FALSE=0, or a number string

See Also

AppGetNames
GetSystemInfo

AppIsRunning()

Purpose

Indicates if a given application is running.

Syntax

```
x = AppIsRunning()
```

Returns

TRUE (-1): Application currently is running.
FALSE (0): Application currently is not running.

See Also

AppActivate
AppClose

AppMaximize or AppMaximize()

Purpose

Maximizes or restores an application window.

Syntax

```
AppMaximize [AppName$][,.State]
```

or

```
x = AppMaximize([AppName$])
```

Parameters

AppName$
The name of the application. If omitted, Word is assumed.

State
The action to perform on the application.
omitted: Toggles maximize/restore.
0: Restores the application.
1: Maximizes the application.

Returns

TRUE (-1): Maximized
FALSE (0): Not maximized

See Also

AppMinimize
AppMove
AppRestore
AppSize
DocMaximize

AppMinimize or AppMinimize()

Purpose

Minimizes or restores an application window.

Syntax

```
AppMinimize [AppName$][,.State]
```

or

```
x = AppMinimize([AppName$])
```

Parameters

AppName$
The name of the application. If omitted, Word is assumed.

State
The action to perform on the application.
omitted: Toggles minimize/restore.
0: Restores the application.
1: Minimizes the application.

Returns

TRUE (-1): Minimized
FALSE (0): Not minimized

See Also

AppMaximize
AppMove
AppRestore
AppSize
DocMinimize

AppMove

Purpose

Enables you to move an application window (if it is not maximized).

Syntax

```
AppMove [AppName$,] XPosition, YPosition
```

Parameters

AppName$
The name of the application. If omitted, Word is assumed.

XPosition, Yposition
The destination coordinates of the upper-left corner of the Word window, measured from the upper-left corner of the screen.

See Also

AppRestore
AppSize
AppWindowPosLeft
AppWindowPosTop
DocMove

AppRestore or AppRestore()

Purpose

Restores an application window from minimized or maximized.

Syntax

```
AppRestore [AppName$]
```

or

```
x = AppRestore ([AppName$])
```

Parameters

AppName$
The name of the application. If omitted, Word is assumed.

Returns

TRUE (-1): Restored
FALSE (0): Not restored

See Also

AppMaximize
AppMinimize
AppMove
AppSize
DocRestore
Format

AppSendMessage

Purpose

Sends a Windows message and its associated parameters to an application.

Syntax

```
AppSendMessage [AppName$,] Message, WParam, LParam
```

Parameters

AppName$
The name of the application. If omitted, Word is assumed.

Message, WParam, LParam
Parameters of the message.

See Also

AppActivate
AppIsRunning
DDEExecute
DDEPoke

AppShow

Purpose

Reverses AppHide.

Syntax

```
AppShow [WindowName$]
```

Parameters

WindowName$
An open application.

See Also

AppActivate
AppHide

AppSize

Purpose

Enables the resizing of an application window (if it is not maximized or minimized).

Syntax

```
AppSize [AppName$,] Width, Height
```

Parameters

AppName$
The name of the application. If omitted, Word is assumed.

Width, Height
The dimensions in pixels of the Word window.

See Also

AppMove
AppRestore
AppWindowHeight
AppWindowWidth
DocSize

AppWindowHeight or AppWindowHeight()

Purpose

Adjusts the height of an application window.

Syntax

```
AppWindowHeight [AppName$,] Height
```

or

```
x = AppWindowHeight [AppName$]
```

Parameters

AppName$
The name of the application. If omitted, Word is assumed.

Height
The desired window height in points.

Returns

The current height of the application window in points.

See Also

AppSize
AppWindowPosLeft
AppWindowPosTop
AppWindowWidth

AppWindowPosLeft or AppWindowPosLeft()

Purpose

Enables moving an application window horizontally.

Syntax

```
AppWindowPosLeft [AppName$,]
HorizPosition
```

or

```
x = AppWindowPosLeft [AppName$]
```

Parameters

AppName$
The name of the application. If omitted, Word is assumed.

HorizPosition
The desired window horizontal position, in points from the left edge of the screen.

Returns

The current horizontal position of the application window in points.

See Also

AppMove
AppWindowHeight
AppWindowPosTop
AppWindowWidth

AppWindowPosTop or AppWindowPosTop()

Purpose

Enables moving an application window horizontally.

Syntax

```
AppWindowPosTop [AppName$,]
VertPosition
```

or

```
x = AppWindowPosTop [AppName$]
```

Parameters

AppName$
The name of the application. If omitted, Word is assumed.

VertPosition
The desired window vertical position, in points from the top edge of the screen.

Returns

The current vertical position of the application window in points.

See Also

AppMove
AppWindowHeight
AppWindowPosLeft
AppWindowWidth

AppWindowWidth or AppWindowWidth()

Purpose

Adjusts the width of an application window.

Syntax

```
AppWindowWidth [AppName$,] Width
```

or

```
x = AppWindowWidth [AppName$]
```

Parameters

AppName$
The name of the application. If omitted, Word is assumed.

Width
The desired window width, in points.

Returns

The current width of the application window in points.

See Also

AppSize
AppWindowHeight
AppWindowPosLeft
AppWindowPosTop

Asc()

Purpose

Returns the ANSI value of the first character in a string.

Syntax

```
x = Asc(string$)
```

Parameters

string$
Any string variable or function that results in a string.

Returns

A number indicating the ANSI value of the first character in string$.

See Also

Chr$()
Len()

AtEndOfDocument()

Purpose

Checks the position of the insertion point for the end of the document; does not move the insertion point.

Syntax

```
x = AtEndOfDocument()
```

Returns

TRUE (-1): Insertion point is at end of the document.
FALSE (0): Insertion point is not at end of the document.

See Also

AtStartOfDocument()

EndOfDocument

AtStartOfDocument()

Purpose

Checks the position of the insertion point for the start of the document; does not move the insertion point.

Syntax

```
x = AtStartOfDocument()
```

Returns

TRUE (-1): Insertion point is at start of document.
FALSE (0): Insertion point is not at start of document.

See Also

AtEndOfDocument()
StartOfDocument

AutoMarkIndex Entries

Purpose

Indexes the active document using a concordance file.

Syntax

```
AutoMarkIndexEntries Concordance$
```

Parameters

Concordance$
A file containing a list of words to index.

See Also

MarkIndexEntry

AutomaticChange

Purpose

Makes an AutoFormatting change when the Tip Wizard suggests one.

Syntax

```
AutomaticChange
```

See Also

TipWizard
ShowMe

AutoText

Purpose

Inserts an AutoText entry in place of the selection, through a dialog box.

Syntax

```
AutoText
```

See Also

AutoTextName$()
CountAutoTextEntries()
EditAutoText
GetAutoText$()
InsertAutoText
SetAutoText

AutoTextName$()

Purpose

Returns the name of an AutoText entry.

Syntax

```
x$ = AutoTextName$(Count [, Context])
```

Parameters

Count
The number of the AutoText entry.

Context
0: Normal template.
1: Active template (not the Normal template).

Returns

The name of an AutoText entry.

See Also

AutoText
CountAutoTextEntries()
EditAutoText
GetAutoText$()
InsertAutoText
SetAutoText

Beep

Purpose

Causes the computer's speaker to beep.

Syntax

```
Beep [Type]
```

Parameters

Type
Currently ignored; Value can be 1 (or omitted), 2, 3, or 4.

BeginDialog... EndDialog

Purpose

Begins and ends a dialog box definition.

Syntax

```
BeginDialog UserDialog [X, ] [Y, ]
dX, dY [, Title$] [, .Identifier]
EndDialog
```

Parameters

DialogName
: The name of the dialog. Used in Dimensioning to distinguish multiple dialog box definitions in the same macro.

X, Y
: The coordinates of the upper-left corner of the dialog box, measured in fractions of the system font size. If omitted, the dialog box is centered on the screen.

dX, dY
: The width and height of the dialog box, measured in fractions of the system font size.

Title$
: The title appearing in the title bar of the dialog.

.Identifier
: A control extension used to access the dialog box dynamically from within a function of the same name.

See Also

CancelButton
CheckBox
ComboBox
Dialog
Dim
DropListBox
FilePreview
GroupBox
ListBox
OKButton
OptionButton
OptionGroup
Picture
PushButton
Text
TextBox

Bold or Bold()

Purpose

Converts the selection to all bold letters, or removes the Bold formatting from the selection.

Syntax

```
Bold [Action]
```

or

```
x = Bold([Action])
```

Parameters

Action
: 1: Formats the selection.
0: Removes Bold formatting from selection.
omitted: Toggles Bold formatting.

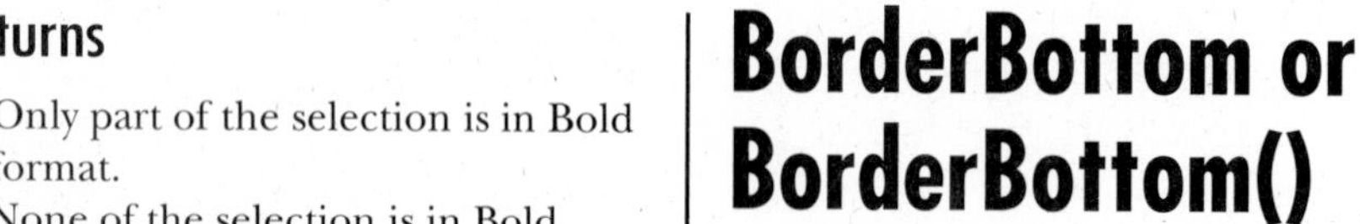

Returns

-1: Only part of the selection is in Bold format.
0: None of the selection is in Bold format.
1: All the selection is in Bold format.

See Also

FormatFont

BookmarkName$()

Purpose

Returns the name of the specified bookmark.

Syntax

```
x$ = BookmarkName$(BookmarkNumber)
```

Parameters

BookmarkNumber
The number of the bookmark. This number is the location of the bookmark in the sequential list of bookmarks and can change when a bookmark is deleted.

Returns

The name of the bookmark given by BookmarkNumber.

See Also

CountBookmarks()
GetBookmark$()

BorderBottom or BorderBottom()

Purpose

Turns on or off a bottom border for a paragraph(s), table, or graphic.

Syntax

```
BorderBottom [Action]
```

or

```
x = BorderBottom([Action])
```

Parameters

Action

1: Applies the border.
0: Removes the border.
omitted: Toggles the border.

Returns

0: Some or none of the selection has a bottom border.
1: All the selection has a bottom border.

See Also

BorderInside
BorderLeft
BorderLineStyle
BorderNone
BorderOutside
BorderRight
BorderTop
FormatBordersAndShading
ShadingPattern

BorderInside or BorderInside()

Purpose

Turns on or off an inside border for a paragraph(s) or a table.

Syntax

```
BorderInside [Action]
```

or

```
x = BorderInside([Action])
```

Parameters

Action
- 1: Applies the border.
- 0: Removes the border.
- omitted: Toggles the border.

Returns

0: Some or none of the selection has a border.
1: All the selection has a border.

See Also

BorderBottom
BorderLeft
BorderLineStyle
BorderNone
BorderOutside
BorderRight
BorderTop
FormatBordersAndShading
ShadingPattern

BorderLeft or BorderLeft()

Purpose

Turns on or off a left border for a paragraph(s), table, or graphic.

Syntax

```
BorderLeft [Action]
```

or

```
x = BorderLeft([Action])
```

Parameters

Action
- 1: Applies the border.
- 0: Removes the border.
- omitted: Toggles the border.

Returns

0: Some or none of the selection has a left border.
1: All the selection has a left border.

See Also

BorderBottom
BorderInside
BorderLineStyle
BorderNone
BorderOutside
BorderRight
BorderTop
FormatBordersAndShading
ShadingPattern

BorderLineStyle or BorderLineStyle()

Purpose

Sets the line style for subsequent border commands.

Syntax

`BorderLineStyle Style`

or

`x = BorderLineStyle([Style])`

Parameters

Style
One of 12 line styles, or 0 = no line.

See Also

BorderBottom
BorderInside
BorderLeftBorderNone
BorderOutside
BorderRight
BorderTop
FormatBordersAndShading
ShadingPattern

BorderNone or BorderNone()

Purpose

Removes or applies all borders for a selected paragraph(s), table, or graphic.

Syntax

`BorderNone [Remove]`

or

`x = BorderNone([Remove])`

Parameters

Remove
0: Apply borders.
1 or omitted: Remove borders.

Returns

0: At least one border
1: No borders in selection

See Also

BorderBottom
BorderInside
BorderLeft
BorderLineStyle
BorderOutside
BorderRight
BorderTop
FormatBordersAndShading
ShadingPattern

BorderOutside or BorderOutside()

Purpose

Turns on or off an outside border for a paragraph(s), table, or graphic.

Syntax

```
BorderOutside [Action]
```

or

```
x = BorderOutside([Action])
```

Parameters

Action
1: Applies the border.
0: Removes the border.
omitted: Toggles the border.

Returns

0: Some or none of the selection has a border.
1: All the selection has a border.

See Also

BorderBottom
BorderInside
BorderLeft
BorderLineStyle
BorderNone
BorderRight
BorderTop
FormatBordersAndShading
ShadingPattern

BorderRight or BorderRight()

Purpose

Turns on or off a right border for a paragraph(s), table, or graphic.

Syntax

```
BorderRight [Action]
```

or

```
x = BorderRight([Action])
```

Parameters

Action
1: Applies the border.
0: Removes the border.
omitted: Toggles the border.

Returns

0: Some or none of the selection has a right border.
1: All the selection has a right border.

See Also

BorderBottom
BorderInside
BorderLeft
BorderLineStyle
BorderNone
BorderOutside
BorderTop
FormatBordersAndShading
ShadingPattern

BorderTop or BorderTop()

Purpose

Turns on or off a top border for a paragraph(s), table, or graphic.

Syntax

```
BorderTop [Action]
```

or

```
x = BorderTop([Action])
```

Parameters

Action

1: Applies the border.
0: Removes the border.
omitted: Toggles the border.

Returns

0: Some or none of the selection has a top border.
1: All the selection has a top border.

See Also

BorderBottom
BorderInside
BorderLeft
BorderLineStyle
BorderNone
BorderOutside
BorderRight
FormatBordersAndShading
ShadingPattern

Call

Purpose

Transfers program control to a defined subroutine.

Syntax

```
Call SubName [Parameter List]
```

Parameters

SubName

The name of a defined subroutine. The subroutine name is the same as defined in Sub...End Sub, if it is located in the same macro. If the subroutine is located in a different macro, the format of SubName is RemoteMacroName.SubroutineName. Program execution is slightly slower using the latter method. The Call keyword is optional.

Parameter List

A list of parameter values to be passed to the subroutine. The parameters are passed to SubName in the same order as they are defined, not necessarily in the order of the same variable names.

See Also

Sub...End Sub

Cancel

Purpose

Terminates a special Word mode (for example, ExtendSelection).

Syntax

```
Cancel
```

See Also

ColumnSelect
CopyFormat
CopyText
ExtendSelection

IconBarMode
OK
RulerMode

CancelButton

Purpose

Defines a Cancel button within a dialog box definition.

Syntax

```
CancelButton X, Y, dX, dY
[,.Identifier]
```

Parameters

X, Y
The coordinates of the upper-left corner of the Cancel button, relative to the upper-left corner of the dialog box, measured in fractions of the system font size.

dX, dY
The width and height of the Cancel button, measured in fractions of the system font size.

.Identifier
Can be used by statements in a dialog function.

See Also

Begin Dialog...End Dialog
Dialog
Err
Error
OKButton
On Error
PushButton

CenterPara or CenterPara()

Purpose

Centers the selected or indicated paragraph(s).

Syntax

```
CenterPara
```

or

```
x = CenterPara()
```

Returns

-1: Only part of the selection is centered.
0: None of the selection is centered.
1: All the selection is centered.

See Also

FormatParagraph
JustifyPara
LeftPara
RightPara

ChangeCase or ChangeCase()

Purpose

Changes the selected text to all uppercase, all lowercase, or to initial caps. Character formats (such as Bold, AllCaps) are unchanged.

Syntax

```
ChangeCase [Set]
```

or

```
x = ChangeCase()
```

Parameters

Set

Sets the type of case to change:

omitted: Toggles between case types

0: Sets selection to all lowercase.

1: Sets selection to all uppercase.

2: Capitalizes the first letter of each word.

3: Capitalizes the first letter of each selected sentence.

4: Capitalizes the first letter of the selection.

5: Toggles case of each letter selected.

Returns

0: None of the selection is in upper case.
1: All the selection is in uppercase.
2: Only part of the selection is in uppercase.

See Also

AllCaps
LCase$()
SmallCaps
UCase$()

CharColor

Purpose

Sets the selection to the specified character color.

Syntax

```
CharColor Color
```

Parameters

Color A color code:

0	Auto color
1	Black
2	Blue
3	Cyan
4	Green
5	Magenta
6	Red
7	Yellow
8	White
9	Dark Blue
10	Cyan
11	Green
12	Magenta
13	Red
14	Yellow
15	Gray
16	Light Gray

Returns

The color code of the selection or the current insertion color. Returns -1 if the selection is not all the same color.

See Also

FormatFont
SelectCurColor

CharLeft or CharLeft()

Purpose

Moves the insertion point to the left by the given number of characters.

Syntax

```
CharLeft [Count,] [Select]
```

or

```
x = CharLeft([Count,] [Select])
```

Parameters

Count
The number of characters to move past. If 0 or omitted, 1 is default. Negative signs are ignored.

Select
If nonzero, the selection is extended by Count characters.

Returns

0: The action cannot be performed.
-1: The action can be performed, even if only partially.

See Also

CharRight
SentLeft
SentRight
WordLeft
WordRight

CharRight or CharRight()

Purpose

Moves the insertion point to the right by the given number of characters.

Syntax

```
CharRight [Count,] [Select]
```

or

```
x = CharRight([Count,] [Select])
```

Parameters

Count
The number of characters to move past. If 0 or omitted, 1 is default. Negative signs are ignored.

Select
If nonzero, the selection is extended by Count characters.

Returns

0: The action cannot be performed.
-1: The action can be performed, even if only partially.

See Also

CharLeft
SentLeft
SentRight
WordLeft
WordRight

ChDefaultDir

Purpose

Sets a default directory to the given path for current session.

Syntax

```
ChDefaultDir Path$, Type
```

Parameters

Path$
The full pathname for the directory.

Type
Refers to the default directory to set:

0: document path

1: picture path

2: user .DOT path

3: workgroup .DOT path

4: .INI path

5: autosave path

6: tools path

7: CBT path

8: startup path

15: style gallery-template path (disregarded in Windows 95)

See Also

ChDir
DefaultDir$()
Files$()
GetDirectory$()
ToolsOptionsFileLocations

ChDir

Purpose

Sets the current directory to the given drive and directory.

Syntax

```
ChDir Path$
```

Parameters

Path$
A string indicating the new path from a drive, the root directory of the current drive, or the current directory downward.

See Also

Connect
CountDirectories()
Files$()
GetDirectory$()
MkDirRmDir

CheckBox

Purpose

Defines a Check Box within a dialog box definition.

Syntax

```
CheckBox X, Y, dX, dY, Text$,
.Identifier
```

Parameters

X, Y
: The coordinates of the upper-left corner of the Check Box, relative to the upper-left corner of the dialog box, measured in fractions of the system font size.

dX, dY
: The width and height of the Check Box and its associated text, measured in fractions of the system font size.

Text$
: The text accompanying the Check Box, positioned immediately to the right of the box. An ampersand preceding a character in the text sets Alt+Character to a hot key to toggle the Check Box values.

.Identifier
: A control extension used to set or access the value of the Check Box from outside the dialog box definition.

Returns

When the dialog containing the Check Box is accessed by the syntax x = Dialog.Identifier, the value returned is:

-1: The Check Box is grayed.
0: The Check Box is not checked.
1: The Check Box is checked.

See Also

Begin Dialog...End Dialog

CheckBoxFormField

Purpose

Inserts a check box form field at the insertion point.

Syntax

```
CheckBoxFormField
```

See Also

DropDownFormField
InsertFormField
TextFormField

ChooseButtonImage

Purpose

Changes the text or image of a toolbar button.

Syntax

```
ChooseButtonImage [.Face =
ButtonFace][,.Button =
ButtonNum][,.Context =
Context][,.Text = ButtonText$][,]
.Toolbar = Toolbar$
```

Parameters

ButtonFace
The image number.

ButtonNum
The button position in the toolbar.

Context
0: Normal template.
1: Active template.

ButtonText$
The text to appear on the button.

Toolbar$
The name of the toolbar.

See Also

AddButton
CopyButtonImage
DeleteButton
EditButtonImage
MoveButton
PasteButtonImage
ResetButtonImage

Chr$()

Purpose

Returns the character of the given ANSI character code.

Syntax

```
Chr$(number)
```

Parameters

number
An ANSI character code.

Returns

The ANSI character given by number.

See Also

Asc()
Str$()

CleanString$()

Purpose

Changes most non-printing characters in a string to spaces.

Syntax

```
x$ = CleanString$(Source$)
```

Parameters

Source$
Any string variable or function that results in a string; the source string to clean.

Returns

A clean string, with the exception of ANSI characters 1-29, 31, 160, 172, 176, 182, 183.

See Also

LTrim$()
RTrim$()

ClearAddIns

Purpose

Unloads all add-ins.

Syntax

```
ClearAddIns Remove
```

Parameters

Remove

0: Unload but keep in list.
1: Unload and remove from list.

See Also

AddAddIn
AddInState()
CountAddIns()
DeleteAddIn
GetAddInID()
GetAddInName$()

ClearFormField

Purpose

In a protected form document, clears the text in a text form field.

Syntax

```
ClearFormField
```

See Also

SetFormResult
TextFormField

Close

Purpose

Closes an open data file.

Syntax

```
Close [#StreamNum]
```

Parameters

StreamNum
The stream number of an open data file. If omitted, all open data files are closed. StreamNum can also be a variable separated from the pound sign (#) by a space.

See Also

Eof()
Input
Input$()
Line Input
Lof()
Open
Print
Read
Seek
Write

ClosePane

Purpose

Closes only the lower pane of a split-screen Word document.

Syntax

```
ClosePane
```

See Also

DocSplit
OtherPane
WindowPane()

ClosePreview

Purpose

Returns the active document from Print Preview to the prior view.

Syntax

```
ClosePreview
```

See Also

FilePrintPreview

CloseUpPara

Purpose

Resets the Spacing Before paragraph formatting of the current selected or indicated paragraph (sets to 0 pt.).

Syntax

```
CloseUpPara
```

See Also

FormatParagraph
OpenUpPara

CloseViewHeader Footer

Purpose

Closes the header/footer editing pane.

Syntax

```
CloseViewHeaderFooter
```

See Also

GoToHeaderFooter
ShowNextHeaderFooter
ShowPrevHeaderFooter
ViewFooter
ViewHeader

CmpBookmarks()

Purpose

Compares the location of two bookmarks.

Syntax

```
x = CmpBookmarks(Bookmk1$, Bookmk2$)
```

Parameters

Bookmk1$, Bookmk2$
Any two bookmark names.

Returns

0: Bookmk1$ = Bookmk2$.
1: Bookmk1$ is entirely below Bookmk2$.
2: Bookmk1$ is entirely above Bookmk2$.
3: Bookmk1$ is below and inside Bookmk2$.
4: Bookmk1$ is above and inside Bookmk2$.
5: Bookmk1$ encloses Bookmk2$.
6: Bookmk2$ encloses Bookmk1$.
7: Bookmk1$ and Bookmk2$ begin at the same point, but Bookmk1$ is longer.
8: Bookmk1$ and Bookmk2$ begin at the same point, but Bookmk2$ is longer.
9: Bookmk1$ and Bookmk2$ end at the same point, but Bookmk1$ is longer.
10: Bookmk1$ and Bookmk2$ end at the same point, but Bookmk2$ is longer.
11: Bookmk1$ is below and adjacent to Bookmk2$.
12: Bookmk1$ is above and adjacent to Bookmk2$.
13: Bookmk1$ and/or Bookmk2$ do(es) not exist.

See Also

CopyBookmark
EditBookmark
EmptyBookmark

ColumnSelect

Purpose

Starts column selection mode. (Cancel, OK ends it.)

Syntax

```
ColumnSelect
```

See Also

Cancel
ExtendSelection

ComboBox

Purpose

Defines a Combo Box within a dialog box definition.

Syntax

```
ComboBox X, Y, dX, dY, Array$(),
.Identifier
```

Parameters

X, Y
The coordinates of the upper-left corner of the Combo Box, relative to the upper-left corner of the dialog box, measured in fractions of the system font size.

dX, dY
The width and height of the Combo Box and its associated text, measured in fractions of the system font size.

Array$()
A string array containing the text entries to be listed in the Combo Box.

.Identifier
A control extension used to set or access the value of the Combo Box from outside the dialog box definition.

Returns

When the dialog containing the Combo Box is accessed by the syntax x$ = Dialog.Identifier, the value returned is the string appearing in the upper region of the Combo Box.

See Also

Begin Dialog...End Dialog
Dialog
Dim

CommandValid()

Purpose

Checks the availability of a dialog box equivalent.

Syntax

```
x = CommandValid(CmdName$)
```

Parameters

CmdName$
A Word command.

Returns

TRUE (-1) if CmdName$ is available in its current context.

See Also

IsMacro()

Connect

Purpose

Connects to a network drive.

Syntax

```
Connect [.Drive = DriveNum,] .Path = PathName$ [,.Password = Pswd$]
```

Parameters

DriveNum
The given drive letter that is DriveNum past the next available drive letter.

PathName$
The full pathname for the network drive.

Pswd$
The password for network drive access.

See Also

ChDir
CountDirectories()
GetDirectory$()

ControlRun

Purpose

Runs an application listed in the Run dialog box.

Syntax

```
ControlRun .Application = number
```

Parameters

number
The number of the application, as listed in the Control|Run dialog box. (0: Clipboard, 1: Control Panel).

See Also

Shell

Converter$()

Purpose

Returns the class name of a file format.

Syntax

```
x$ = Converter$(FormatNum)
```

Parameters

FormatNum
The number of a file format, as listed in the Save File As Type box in the FileSaveAs dialog box.

Returns

The class name of the specified file format.

See Also

ConverterLookup()
FileSaveAs

ConverterLookup()

Purpose

Returns the list number of a file format.

Syntax

```
x = ConverterLookup(FormatName$)
```

Parameters

FormatName$
The class name of the specified file format.

Returns

The number of a file format, as listed in the Save File As Type box in the FileSaveAs dialog box. -1: Does not exist.

See Also

Converter$()
FileSaveAs

ConvertObject

Purpose

Converts the selected object from one class to another.

Syntax

```
ConvertObject [.IconNumber =
IconNum][,.ActivateAs =
Convert][,.IconFilename =
IconFile$][,.Caption =
Capt$][,.Class =
Class$][,.DisplayIcon = DispIcon]
```

Parameters

IconNum
The number of the icon in the program file.

Convert
0: Converts the object.
1: Uses server application to edit object.

IconFile$
The program file where icons are stored.

Capt$
The caption of the icon to be displayed.

Class$
The class name to convert to.

DispIcon
0 or omitted: Do not display object as icon.
1: Display object as icon.

See Also

EditObject
InsertObject

CopyBookmark

Purpose

Sets one bookmark equal to another.

Syntax

```
CopyBookmark Bookmk1$, Bookmk2$
(Sets Bookmk2$ equal to Bookmk1$)
```

Parameters

Bookmk1$, Bookmk2$
Valid bookmark names.

See Also

CmpBookmarks()
EditBookmark
SetEndOfBookmark
SetStartOfBookmark

CopyButtonImage

Purpose

Copies the toolbar button image to the Clipboard.

Syntax

```
CopyButtonImage ToolbarName$, Tool
[,Context]
```

Parameters

ToolbarName$
The name of the toolbar, as it appears in the View menu.

Tool
The number of the tool, counting from right to left.

Context
0 or omitted: Copy Normal template button face.
1: Copy currently displayed button face.

See Also

AddButton
ChooseButtonImage
EditButtonImage
MoveButton
PasteButtonImage
ResetButtonImage

CopyFile

Purpose

Copies a file to another directory.

Syntax

```
CopyFile File$, Path$
```

Parameters

File$
The file to copy.

Path$
The full pathname of the destination directory.

See Also

FileSaveAs
Kill
Name

CopyFormat

Purpose

Sets the special Word mode to copy the format of the current selection to another place in the document. After a selection is made, CopyFormat initializes the Word mode to copy formatting to another place in the document. After issuing the CopyFormat command, change the selection to the destination text and issue the OK command.

Syntax

```
CopyFormat
```

See Also

Cancel
OK
PasteFormat

CopyText

Purpose

Sets the special Word mode to copy the text of the current selection to another place in the document. After a selection is made, CopyText initializes the Word mode to copy text to another place in the document. After issuing the CopyText command, change the insertion point to the destination and issue the OK command.

Syntax

```
CopyText
```

See Also

Cancel
MoveText
OK

CountAddIns

Purpose

Returns the number of add-ins currently loaded.

Syntax

```
x = CountAddIns()
```

Returns

The number of add-ins currently loaded.

See Also

AddAddIn
AddInState()
ClearAddIns
DeleteAddIn
GetAddInID()
GetAddInName$()

CountAutoCorrectExceptions()

Purpose

Windows 95

Returns a number corresponding to the number of AutoCorrect exceptions you have specified in either the First Letter or Initial Caps tabbed dialog box (in AutoCorrect).

Syntax

```
CountAutoCorrectExceptions(Tab)
```

Parameters

Tab

0 (zero): Returns number of exceptions from First Letter tab.

1: Returns number of exceptions from INitial CAps tab.

Returns

Number of exceptions listed in the tab you specify.

See Also

GetAutoCorrectException$()
IsAutoCorrectException()
ToolsAutoCorrectExceptions

CountAutoText Entries()

Purpose

Returns the number of AutoText entries for the given context.

Syntax

```
x = CountAutoTextEntries([Context$])
```

Parameters

Context$

0: Normal template.
1: Active template.

Returns

The number of AutoText entries for the given context.

See Also

AutoTextName$()
GetAutoText$()

CountBookmarks()

Purpose

Returns the number of bookmarks defined in the active document.

Syntax

```
x = CountBookmarks()
```

Returns

The number of bookmarks defined in the active document.

See Also

BookmarkName$()
EditBookmark

CountDirectories()

Purpose

Returns the number of subdirectories within the given (or current) directory.

Syntax

```
x =
CountDirectories([DirectoryName$])
```

Parameters

DirectoryName$
The full path name to a directory to examine. If omitted, the current directory is assumed.

Returns

The number of subdirectories within the given (or current) directory.

See Also

Files$()
GetDirectory$()

CountDocument Properties()

Windows 95

Purpose

Counts the built-in and custom document properties specified in the current document

Syntax

```
x = CountDocumentProperties()
```

Returns

Total number of built-in and custom styles contained in the active document.

See Also

DocumentPropertyName$()
GetDocumentProperty()

CountDocumentVars()

Purpose

Returns the number of document variables defined in the active document.

Syntax

```
x = CountDocumentVars()
```

Returns

The number of document variables set in the active document.

See Also

GetDocumentVar$()
GetDocumentVarName$()
SetDocumentVar

CountFiles()

Purpose

Returns the number of file names in the File menu files list.

Syntax

```
x = CountFiles()
```

Returns

The number of file names that are in the file list on the bottom of the File menu.

See Also

FileList
FileName$()
FileNumber

CountFonts()

Purpose

Returns the number of fonts available. (Note: This number can change for different printers.)

Syntax

```
x = CountFonts()
```

Returns

The number of fonts available for the currently active printer.

See Also

Font

CountFoundFiles()

Purpose

Returns the number of files found in the last File|Find search.

Syntax

```
x = CountFoundFiles()
```

Returns

The number of files found in the last File|Find search.

See Also

FileFind
FoundFileName$()

CountKeys()

Purpose

Returns the number of key assignments that differ from the default.

Syntax

```
x = CountKeys([Context])
```

Parameters

Context
0: Global (default).
1: Template.

Returns

The number of currently defined key assignments that differ from the default.

See Also

KeyCode()
KeyMacro$()
ToolsCustomizeKeyboard

CountLanguages()

Purpose

Returns the number of languages available.

Syntax

```
x = CountLanguages()
```

Returns

The number of languages in the Format|Language dialog box.

See Also

FormatLanguage
Language
ToolsLanguage

CountMacros()

Purpose

Returns the number of macros defined for the context.

Syntax

```
x =- CountMacros([Context][,All]
[,Global])
```

Parameters

Context
0: Global (default).
1: Template.

All
If 1, Word commands are included in the count.

Global
If 1, only add-in macro commands are counted.

Returns

The number of macros defined for the given context.

See Also

AddAddIn
AddInState()
ClearAddIns
CountAddIns()
DeleteAddIn
GetAddInID()
GetAddInName$()
MacroName$()

CountMenuItems()

Purpose

Returns the number of menu item assignments that differ from the default.

Syntax

```
x = CountMenuItems(Menu$, Type,
[Context])
```

Parameters

Menu$
The name of the menu to count.

Type
The type of menu item:
1: Menus when a document is open.
2: Menus when no document is open.
3: Shortcut menus.

Context
0: Global (default),
1: Template.

Returns

The number of currently defined menu item assignments that differ from the default.

See Also

MenuItemMacro$()
MenuItemText$()

CountMenus()

Purpose

Returns the number of menus of the given type.

Syntax

```
CountMenus(Type, [Context])
```

Parameters

Type
The type of menu item:
1: Menus when a document is open.
2: Menus when no document is open.
3: Shortcut menus.

Context
0: Global (default)
1: Template.

Returns

The number of menus of the given type.

See Also

CountMacros()
CountMenuItems()
MenuText$()

CountMergeFields()

Purpose

Returns the number of fields associated with the active merge document.

Syntax

```
x = CountMergeFields()
```

Returns

The number of fields contained in the header file or the header record of the data file, associated with the active merge document. Returns 0 if active document is not a main document, data file, or header file.

See Also

InsertMergeField
MergeFieldName$()

CountStyles()

Purpose

Returns the number of styles defined for the context.

Syntax

```
x = CountStyles([Context,] [All])
```

Parameters

Context
0: Active document (default).
1: Template.

All
If nonzero, unused standard styles are included in the count.

Returns

The number of styles defined for the given context.

See Also

StyleName$()

CountToolbarButtons()

Purpose

Returns the number of tool buttons on a toolbar.

Syntax

```
x = CountToolbarButtons(Toolbar$,
[, Context])
```

Parameters

Toolbar$
The name of the toolbar.

Context
0 or omitted: Count Normal template buttons.
1: Count currently available buttons.

Returns

The number of tool buttons on a toolbar (including spaces and list boxes).

See Also

CountToolbars()
ToolbarButtonMacro$()
ToolbarName$()

CountToolbars()

Purpose

Returns the number of toolbars currently available.

Syntax

```
x = CountToolbars([Context])
```

Parameters

Context
0 or omitted: Count Normal template toolbars.
1: Count currently available toolbars.

Returns

The number of toolbars currently available.

See Also

CountToolbarButtons()
ToolbarButtonMacro$()
ToolbarName$()

CountToolsGrammarStatistics()

Purpose

Returns the number of statistics stored when grammar checking.

Syntax

```
x = CountToolsGrammarStatistics()
```

Returns

The number of statistics stored when grammar checking.

See Also

ToolsGrammar
ToolsGrammarStatisticsArray
ToolsOptionsGrammar

CountWindows()

Purpose

Returns the number of open windows.

Syntax

```
x = CountWindows()
```

Returns

The number of open windows, listed at the bottom of the Window menu.

See Also

WindowName$()
WindowNumber

CreateSubdocument

Purpose

Converts the selected outline headings into subdocuments.

Syntax

```
CreateSubdocument
```

See Also

InsertSubdocument
MergeSubdocument
OpenSubdocument
RemoveSubdocument
SplitSubdocument
ViewMasterDocument

Date$()

Purpose

Returns the current date.

Syntax

```
x$ = Date$([DateNum])
```

Parameters

DateNum
A date corresponding to number given. DateNum is the number of days that follow December 30, 1899.

Returns

The date given by DateNum, or current day's date if omitted, in the format set in the International selection of the Windows Control Panel.

See Also

DateSerial()
DateValue()

Day()
GetPrivateProfileString$()
Month()
Now()
SetPrivateProfileString$()
Time$()
TimeSerial()
Today()
Year()

DateSerial()

Purpose

Returns the number of days from December 30, 1899 for the date you specify.

Syntax

```
x = DateSerial(Year, Month, Day)
```

Parameters

Year
The year, from 100 to 9999. For years from 1900 to 1999, you only need the last two digits.

Month
The month, numbered between 1 and 12.

Day
The day, numbered between 1 and 31.

Returns

The number of days from December 30, 1899 corresponding to the date given.

See Also

Date$()
DateValue()
Day()
Month()
Now()
TimeSerial()
Time$()
Today()
Year()

DateValue()

Purpose

Returns the number of the specified date, in number of days from December 30, 1899.

Syntax

```
x = DateValue(DateString$)
```

Parameters

DateString$
A string that indicates valid date, in a valid date format.

Returns

The number of days from December 30, 1899 corresponding to the date given.

See Also

Date$()
DateSerial()
Day()
Month()

Now()
Time$()
TimeSerial()
Today()
Year()

Day()

Purpose

Returns the day of the month that corresponds to the date serial number given.

Syntax

```
x = Day(DateNum)
```

Parameters

DateNum
A date that corresponds to the number given. DateNum is the number of days that follow December 30, 1899.

Returns

The integer day of the month that corresponds to the date serial number given.

See Also

Date$()
DateSerial()
DateValue()
Day()
Hour()
Minute()
Month()
Now()
Second()
Today()
Weekday()
Year()

Days360()

Purpose

Returns the number of days between two given dates, based on a 360-day year (useful for such activities as accounting, for example).

Syntax

```
x = Days360(StartDate[$],
EndDate[$])
```

Parameters

StartDate
A string or date serial number that represents the starting date.

EndDate
A string or date serial number that represents the ending date.

Returns

The number of days between two given dates, based on a 360-day year.

See Also

Date$()
DateSerial()
DateValue()
Day()

DDEExecute

Purpose

Sends a command over an established DDE channel.

Syntax

```
DDEExecute Channel, Command$
```

Parameters

Channel
A DDE channel, obtained by the return value from DDEInitiate().

Command$
A command sent to another application, using DDE. The command is only valid to the receiving application, and does not have to have any meaning to Word.

See Also

DDEExecute
DDEInitiate()
DDEPoke
DDERequest$()
DDETerminate
DDETerminateAll

DDEInitiate()

Purpose

Opens a DDE channel to an application.

Syntax

```
x = DDEInitiate(Application$, Topic$)
```

Parameters

Application$
The name of the desired application.

Topic$
Describes something in the desired application (for example, a document to open).

Returns

The DDE channel number, to be used by subsequent DDE commands.

See Also

DDEExecute
DDEPoke
DDERequest$()
DDETerminate
DDETerminateAll

DDEPoke

Purpose

Transmits data over an established DDE channel.

Syntax

```
DDEPoke Channel, Item$, Data$
```

Parameters

Channel
A DDE channel, obtained by the return value from DDEInitiate().

Item$
The item within the application to which the data is sent.

Data$
The data to transmit.

See Also

DDEExecute
DDEInitiate()
DDERequest$()
DDETerminate
DDETerminateAll

DDERequest$()

Purpose

Requests information from an established DDE channel.

Syntax

```
x$ = DDERequest$(Channel, Item$)
```

Parameters

Channel
A DDE channel, obtained by the return value from DDEInitiate().

Item$
The item within the application from which the data is requested.

Returns

Text data, or a null string if unsuccessful. Pictures or RTF-format text cannot be transferred.

See Also

DDEExecute
DDEInitiate()
DDEPoke
DDETerminate
DDETerminateAll

DDETerminate

Purpose

Closes a DDE channel.

Syntax

```
DDETerminate Channel
```

Parameters

Channel
A DDE channel, obtained by the return value from DDEInitiate().

See Also

DDEExecute
DDEInitiate()
DDEPoke
DDERequest$()
DDETerminateAll

DDETerminateAll

Purpose

Closes all open DDE channels opened by Word.

Syntax

```
DDETerminateAll
```

See Also

DDEExecute
DDEInitiate()
DDEPoke
DDERequest$()
DDETerminate

Declare

Purpose

Declares an external library function as a defined WordBasic subroutine or function.

Syntax

```
Declare Sub SubroutineName Lib
LibraryName [(ParameterList As
{String/Integer/Double/Long})][Alias
ModuleName]
```

or

```
Declare Function FunctionName[$] Lib
LibraryName [(ParameterList)][Alias
ModuleName] As {String/Integer/
Double/Long}
```

Parameters

SubroutineName or *FunctionName*
The name of the routine as called from WordBasic.

LibraryName
The library name where the routine resides.

ParameterList
The list of parameters to be passed to the routine.

ModuleName
The name of the routine to be accessed.

See Also

Dim

DefaultDir$()

Purpose

Returns one of the current default directories.

Syntax

```
x$ = DefaultDir$(Type)
```

Parameters

Type Refers to the default directory to set:

0: document path
1: picture path
2: user .DOT path
3: workgroup .DOT path
4: INI path
5: autosave path

6: tools path
7: CBT path
8: startup path
9: program file path
10: graphics filter path
11: text converter path
12: proofing tools path
13: temporary file path
14: current directory
15: style gallery-template path (disregarded in Word 95)

Returns

One of the current default directories.

See Also

ChDefaultDir
ChDir

DeleteAddIn

Purpose

Removes an add-in from the list.

Syntax

```
DeleteAddIn AddIn
```

Parameters

AddIn
The list number of the add-in, or the path and file name of the add-in.

See Also

AddAddIn
AddInState()
ClearAddIns
CountAddIns()
GetAddInID()
GetAddInName$()

DeleteBackWord

Purpose

Clears the word that immediately precedes the selection. The Clipboard is unaffected.

Syntax

```
DeleteBackWord
```

See Also

DeleteWord
EditClear
EditCut
WordLeft

DeleteButton

Purpose

Removes a button, list box, or space from a toolbar.

Syntax

```
DeleteButton Toolbar$, Count
[,Context]
```

Parameters

Toolbar$
The name of the toolbar.

Count
The position of the button in the toolbar.

Context
0 or omitted: Normal template.
1: Active template.

See Also

AddButton
ChooseButtonImage
CopyButtonImage
EditButtonImage
MoveButton
PasteButtonImage
ResetButtonImage

DeleteDocumentProperty

Windows 95

Purpose

Deletes an existing custom property that has previously been specified in the Custom Properties tabbed dialog box (within File, Properties)

Syntax

```
DeleteDocumentProperty Name$
```

See Also

DocumentPropertyExists()
GetDocumentProperty()
IsCustomDocumentProperty()
SetDocumentProperty()

DeleteWord

Purpose

Clears the word that immediately follows the selection. The Clipboard is unaffected.

Syntax

```
DeleteWord
```

See Also

DeleteBackWord
EditClear
EditCut
WordLeft

DemoteList

Purpose

Demotes the selected paragraph(s) by one level.

Syntax

```
DemoteList
```

See Also

FormatBulletsAndNumbering
PromoteList

DemoteToBodyText

Purpose

Applies the Normal style to headings, thus demoting them.

Syntax

```
DemoteToBodyText
```

See Also

OutlineDemote
OutlineMoveDown
OutlinePromote

Dialog or Dialog()

Purpose

Displays a predefined dialog box.

Syntax

Dialog *DialogVariable* [,.*DefaultButton*][,.*TimeOut*]

or

x = Dialog(*DialogVariable* [,.*DefaultButton*][,.*TimeOut*])

Parameters

DialogVariable
A variable that has been previously dimensioned to a user-defined or Word-defined dialog box.

.DefaultButton
The default command button:
-2: None
-1: OK button
0: Cancel button
>0: Pushbuttons, by order of definition.

.TimeOut
The amount of time in milliseconds that the dialog box is displayed. 0 = no time out period.

Returns

-1: the OK Button was chosen.
0: the Cancel Button was chosen.
>0: a Push Button was chosen.

The order of the push buttons in the dialog definition dictates the integer number returned (for example, the first push button listed in the dialog definition returns a 1, the second a 2, and so on).

See Also

Begin Dialog...End Dialog
DialogEditor
Dim
GetCurValues

DialogEditor

Purpose

Activates the Word Dialog Editor (starting it if necessary).

Syntax

```
DialogEditor
```

See Also

Begin Dialog...End Dialog

Dim

Purpose

Allocates memory space for a variable or array.

Syntax

```
Dim [Shared] VariableList
```

or

```
Dim DialogVariable As DefinedDialog
```

Parameters

Shared
Sets the variable as global; the same variable can be used by all subroutines within the same macro.

VariableList
A list of variables, single or array, to which to allocate memory space. All arrays must be explicitly declared with a Dim statement. All arrays begin with element "0".

DialogVariable
A variable used to hold all attributes of a dialog box.

DefinedDialog
The name of a Word-defined or user-defined ("UserDialog") dialog box.

See Also

Declare
Dialog
Let
Redim

DisableAutoMacros

Purpose

Disables the AutoMacros (AutoNew, AutoOpen, AutoClose, AutoExit) from executing, until enabled later. AutoExec cannot be disabled.

Syntax

```
DisableAutoMacros Disable
```

Parameters

Disable

0: Enable AutoMacros;
1 or omitted: Disable AutoMacros.

DisableInput

Purpose

Sets the effect of the ESC key and the mouse within a macro.

Syntax

```
DisableInput Disable
```

Parameters

Disable

0: Enable ESC key and mouse.
1 or omitted: Disable ESC key from macro; ESC key cancels dialog box.
2: completely disables ESC key.
3: Disables mouse.
4: Disables ESC key and mouse.
5: Enables ESC key.
6: Enables mouse.

DlgControlId()

Purpose

Returns the numeric identifier of the dialog box control. Using the numeric identifier instead of the string can speed up processing of dialog box functions.

Syntax

```
DlgControlId(Ident$)
```

Parameters

Ident$
A dialog box control.

Returns

The numeric identifier of the dialog box control.

See Also

DlgFocus
DlgValue

DlgEnable

Purpose

Enables or disables a dialog box control dynamically.

Syntax

```
DlgEnable Identifier[$]
[, On]
```

Parameters

Identifier
The string or numeric dialog box control identifier.

On
omitted: Toggles the control.
0: Disables the control.
1: Enables the control.

Returns

TRUE (-1): Control is enabled.
FALSE (0): Control is disabled.

See Also

DlgVisible

DlgFilePreview or DlgFilePreview()

Purpose

Allows a document to be previewed from within a dialog function. The preview is placed in a separate window.

Syntax

```
DlgFilePreview Identifier[$]
[,FileName$]
```

or

```
x$ = DlgFilePreview$()
```

Parameters

Identifier
The string or numeric dialog box control identifier.

FileName$
The path and file name to preview. If omitted, the active document is assumed.

Returns

The path and file name of the document being previewed.

See Also

DlgSetPicture
FilePreview
Picture

DlgFocus or DlgFocus()

Purpose

Sets the focus to a dialog box control within a dialog box function.

Syntax

```
DlgFocus Identifier[$]
```

or

```
x$ = DlgFocus$()
```

Parameters

Identifier
The string or numeric dialog box control identifier.

Returns

The dialog box identifier name.

See Also

DlgEnable
DlgVisible

DlgListBoxArray or DlgListBoxArray()

Purpose

Fills a list box, drop-down list box, or combo box dynamically within a dialog box function.

Syntax

```
DlgListBoxArray Identifier[$]
[,Array$()]
```

or

```
x = DlgListBoxArray(Identifier[$]
[,Array$()])
```

Parameters

Identifier
The string or numeric dialog box control identifier.

Array$()
The items to be displayed within the box.

Returns

The number of entries in Array$(). In the function form, Array$() is filled with the contents of the box.

See Also

DlgEnable
DlgFocus
DlgText

DlgSetPicture

Purpose

Places a graphic dynamically in the dialog box within a dialog box function.

Syntax

```
DlgSetPicture Identifier[$], Name$,
Stored$
```

Parameters

Identifier
The string or numeric dialog box control identifier.

Name$
The name of the picture to be displayed within the box.

Stored$
The way the picture is stored:
0: as a file
1: in an AutoText entry
2: as a bookmark
3: in the Clipboard (Name$ is irrelevant).

See Also

Picture

DlgText or DlgText()

Purpose

Sets the text to a dialog box control within a dialog box function.

Syntax

```
DlgText Identifier[$], Text$
```

or

```
x$ = DlgText$(Identifier[$])
```

Parameters

Identifier
The string or numeric dialog box control identifier.

Text$
The new text to be displayed with the dialog box control.

Returns

The text or label of the dialog box control specified by Identifier.

See Also

DlgValue

DlgUpdateFilePreview

Purpose

Updates a file preview box within a dialog box function.

Syntax

```
DlgUpdateFilePreview [Identifier]
```

Parameters

Identifier
: The string or numeric dialog box control identifier. This is optional, because a dialog box can have only one file preview box.

See Also

DlgFilePreview
FilePreview

DlgValue or DlgValue()

Purpose

Sets a numeric value associated with a dialog box control, dynamically within a dialog box function.

Syntax

```
DlgValue Identifier[$], Value
```

or

```
x = DlgValue(Identifier[$])
```

Parameters

Identifier
: The string or numeric dialog box control identifier.

Value
: The new value to be set with the dialog box control.

Returns

The current numeric value of a dialog box control.

See Also

DlgText

DlgVisible or DlgVisible()

Purpose

Hide or unhide a dialog box control within a dialog box function.

Syntax

```
DlgVisible Identifier[$] [, On]
```

or

```
x = DlgVisible(Identifier[$])
```

Parameters

Identifier
: The string or numeric dialog box control identifier.

On
: omitted: Toggles the control.
0: Hides the control.
1: Shows the control.

Returns

TRUE (-1): control is visible
FALSE (0): control is hidden.

See Also

DlgEnable
DlgFocus
DlgText

DocClose

Purpose

Closes only the active document window or pane.

Syntax

```
DocClose SaveCmd
```

Parameters

SaveCmd

0 or omitted: Prompts the user if needed
1: Saves without prompting
2: Closes without saving

See Also

ClosePane
FileClose

DocMaximize or DocMaximize()

Purpose

Maximizes the active document window. (NOTE: If the window is already maximized, DocMaximize will restore the document window.)

Syntax

```
DocMaximize
```

or

```
x = DocMaximize()
```

Returns

Maximized = TRUE (-1) or FALSE (0)

See Also

AppMaximize
DocMinimize
DocRestore

DocMinimize or DocMinimize()

Purpose

Minimizes the active document window. (Note: If the window is already minimized, DocMinimize Restores the document window.)

Syntax

```
DocMinimize
```

or

```
x = DocMinimize()
```

Returns

Minimized = TRUE (-1) or FALSE (0)

See Also

AppMinimize
DocMaximize
DocRestore

DocMove

Purpose

Enables you to move the active document window (if the window is not maximized).

Syntax

```
DocMove XPosition, YPosition
```

Parameters

XPosition, Yposition
The destination coordinates of the upper-left corner of the document window, measured from the upper-left corner of the Word workspace.

See Also

AppMove
DocSize
DocWindowPosLeft
DocWindowPosTop

DocRestore

Purpose

Restores the active document window from minimized or maximized.

Syntax

```
DocRestore
```

Returns

Restored = TRUE (0) or FALSE (any nonzero value).

See Also

AppRestore
DocMaximize
DocMinimize

DocSize

Purpose

Enables you to resize the active document window (if the window is not maximized or minimized).

Syntax

```
DocSize Width, Height
```

Parameters

Width, Height
The dimensions in pixels of the document window.

See Also

AppInfo$()
AppSize
DocWindowHeight
DocWindowWidth

DocSplit or DocSplit()

Purpose

Splits the active document window into two panes.

Syntax

```
DocSplit Percent
```

or

```
x = DocSplit()
```

Parameters

Percent
: The percentage of the Word workspace that the top pane occupies.

Returns

The percent value (0 to 100) by which the document window is split. 0 indicates not split.

See Also

ClosePane
OtherPane
WindowPane()

DocumentHasMisspellings()

Purpose

Tells whether a document has been spell checked, and if so, whether it contains misspellings.

Syntax

```
x = DocumentHasMisspellings()
```

Returns

-1: Automatic spell checking is turned off or spell checking is already in progress.
0 (zero): The document has been checked and has no spelling errors, or is empty.
1: The document has been checked and contains one or more misspellings.

See Also

NextMisspelling
ToolsGetSpelling
ToolsLanguage
ToolsOptionsSpelling

DocumentPropertyExists()

Purpose

Returns 1 if the property you specify exists; otherwise returns 0.

Syntax

```
x = DocumentPropertyExists(Name$)
```

Returns

1: Name$ is the name of an existing property.
0: Name$ is not the name of an existing property.

See Also

DeleteDocumentProperty
DocumentPropertyName$()
DocumentPropertyType()
IsCustomDocumentProperty()

DocumentProperty Name$()

Purpose

Returns the name of a document property you specify.

Syntax

```
x =
DocumentPropertyName$(PropertyNumber)
```

Parameters

PropertyNumber
The number of the property as it appears in Word's list of document properties; built-in properties appear first, followed by custom properties.

Returns

The name of a document property. The following are Word's built-in document properties; you can also add any other property you choose:

Title	Document title
Subject	Document subject
Author	Document author
Manager	Manager of document's author
Company	Company name
Category	Document category
Keywords	Keyword document identifiers
Comments	Comments about document
Template	Document template (read-only)
CreateTime	Creation date/time (read-only)
LastSavedBy	Who last saved the document (read-only)
LastSavedTime	Date document was last saved (read-only)
LastPrinted	Date document was last printed (read-only)
RevisionNumber	Number of times document has been saved (read-only)
TotalEditingTime	Time document has been open (read-only)
Pages	Number of pages (read-only)

Paragraphs	Number of paragraphs (read-only)
Lines	Number of lines (read-only)
Words	Number of words (read-only)
Characters	Number of characters (read-only)
Bytes	Document size, in bytes (read-only)
NameOf-Application	Name of associated application (read-only)
Security	Level of document protection (read-only)

See Also

CountDocumentProperties()
DocumentPropertyType()
GetDocumentProperty()
IsDocumentPropertyReadOnly()
SetDocumentProperty

DocumentPropertyType()

Purpose

Identifies the type of property you specified.

Syntax

```
x = DocumentPropertyType(Name$)
```

Returns

0: string
1: number
2: date
3: Yes or No value

See Also

DocumentPropertyExists()
DocumentPropertyName$()
IsCustomDocumentProperty()
IsDocumentPropertyReadOnly()

DocumentProtection()

Purpose

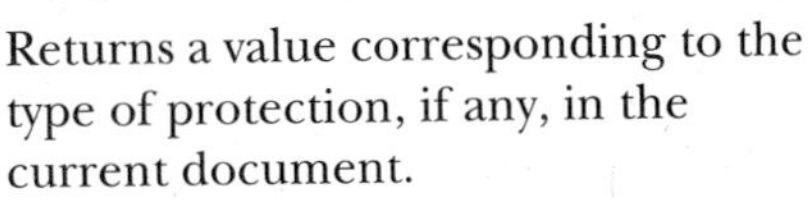

Returns a value corresponding to the type of protection, if any, in the current document.

Syntax

```
x = DocumentProtection()
```

Returns

0: No protection.
1: Protected for forms. (Users can only select and edit text in form fields.)
2: Protected for annotations. (Users can only annotate a document.)
3: Users can select and edit text, but their changes are tracked with revision marks.

See Also

ToolsProtectDocument
ToolsUnprotectDocument

DocumentStatistics

Purpose

Enables you to retrieve the active document statistics.

Syntax

```
DocumentStatistics .Stat = value$, ...
```

Parameters

.Stat

A Statistics argument:

.FileSize	The document size
.FileName	The document name
.Directory	The document directory's full path
.Template	The document template's full path
.Title	The document's title
.Created	The document's creation date and time
.LastSaved	The date and time when last saved
.LastSavedBy	The document's author
.Revision	The current revision count
.Time	Total document's editing time
.Printed	The date and time when last printed
.Pages	The number of pages in the document
.Words	The number of words in the document
.Characters	The number of characters in document
.Paragraphs	The number of paragraphs in the document
.Lines	The number of lines in the document

value$

The information about that argument.

Returns

Values that are automatically updated when the command is invoked.

See Also

FileSummaryInfo
SelInfo()

DocWindowHeight or DocWindowHeight()

Purpose

Sets the active document window to a specified height.

Syntax

```
DocWindowHeight Height
```

or

```
x = DocWindowHeight()
```

Parameters

Height

The window height, in points.

Returns

The height of the active document window, in points.

See Also

AppWindowHeight
DocSize
DocWindowWidth

DocWindowPosLeft or DocWindowPosLeft()

Purpose

Positions the active document from the left edge of the Word workspace.

Syntax

```
DocWindowPosLeft Position
```

or

```
x = DocWindowPosLeft()
```

Parameters

Position
The window position from the left edge of the Word workspace, in points.

Returns

The position of the active document window from the left edge of the Word workspace, in points.

See Also

AppWindowPosLeft
DocMove
DocSize
DocWindowHeight
DocWindowPosTop
DocWindowWidth

DocWindowPosTop or DocWindowPosTop()

Purpose

Positions the active document from the top edge of the Word workspace.

Syntax

```
DocWindowPosTop Position
```

or

```
x = DocWindowPosTop()
```

Parameters

Position
The window position from the top edge of the Word workspace, in points.

Returns

The position of the active document window from the top edge of the Word workspace, in points.

See Also

AppWindowPosTop
DocMove
DocSize
DocWindowHeight
DocWindowPosLeft
DocWindowWidth

DocWindowWidth or DocWindowWidth()

Purpose

Sets the active document window to a specified width.

Syntax

```
DocWindowWidth Width
```

or

```
x = DocWindowWidth()
```

Parameters

Width
The window width, in points.

Returns

The width of the active document window, in points.

See Also

AppWindowWidth
DocSize
DocWindowHeight

DoFieldClick

Purpose

Simulates a mouse double-click. This is useful when the insertion point is positioned within a GOTOBUTTON or MACROBUTTON field.

Syntax

```
DoFieldClick
```

DOSToWin$()

Purpose

Translates a string from the OEM character set to Windows character set.

Syntax

```
x$ = DOSToWin$(XlateString$)
```

Parameters

XlateString$
Any string in the OEM (that is, MS-DOS) character set to translate.

Returns

A translated string.

See Also

WinToDOS$()

DottedUnderline or DottedUnderline()

Purpose

Adds or removes dotted-underline character formatting.

Syntax

```
DottedUnderline [Action]
```

or

```
x = DottedUnderline()
```

Parameters

Action

1: Sets selection to double underline
0: Removes double underlining from selection.
omitted: Toggles double underlining.

Returns

-1: only part of the selection is dotted underline.
0: none of the selection is dotted underline.
1: all of the selection is dotted under line.

See Also

DoubleUnderline
FormatBordersAndShading
FormatFont
Underline

DoubleUnderline or DoubleUnderline()

Purpose

Converts the selection to all underline letters, or removes the double-underline formatting from the selection.

Syntax

```
DoubleUnderline [Action]
```

or..

```
x = DoubleUnderline([Action])
```

Parameters

Action

1: Sets selection to double underline.
0: Removes double underlining from selection.
omitted: Toggles double underlining.

Returns

-1: Only part of the selection is double underlined.
0: None of the selection is double underlined.
1: All of the selection is double underlined.

See Also

DottedUnderline
FormatBordersAndShading
FormatFont
Underline

DrawAlign

Purpose

Aligns selected drawing objects.

Syntax

```
DrawAlign [.Horizontal =
number][,.Vertical =
number][,.RelativeTo = number]
```

Parameters

number
Horizontal:

0 or omitted: Preserve existing alignment
1: Left
2: Center
3: Right

Vertical:
0 or omitted: Preserve existing alignment
1: Top
2: Center
3: Bottom

RelativeTo: (what objects are aligned with)
0 or omitted: Each other
1: Page

See Also

DrawCount()
DrawExtendSelect
DrawSelect
DrawSetRange
FormatDrawingObject

DrawArc

Purpose

Switches to Page Layout view and adds a default arc in front of the text layer.

Syntax

```
DrawArc
```

See Also

DrawEllipse
DrawFlipHorizontal
DrawFlipVertical
DrawGetType()
DrawLine
DrawRotateLeft
DrawRotateRight
FormatDrawingObject

DrawBringForward

Purpose

Moves the selected drawing object forward in the drawing stack. Does not move an object around text.

Syntax

```
DrawBringForward
```

See Also

DrawBringInFrontOfText
DrawBringToFront
DrawSendBackward
DrawSendBehindText
DrawSendToBack

DrawBringInFront OfText

Purpose

Moves the selected object from behind text to in front of text.

Syntax

```
DrawBringInFrontOfText
```

See Also

DrawBringForward
DrawBringToFront
DrawSendBackward
DrawSendBehindText
DrawSendToBack

DrawBringToFront

Purpose

Brings an object to the top of the drawing stack. Does not move an object around text.

Syntax

```
DrawBringToFront
```

See Also

DrawBringForward
DrawBringInFrontOfText
DrawSendBackward
DrawSendBehindText
DrawSendToBack

DrawCallout

Purpose

Inserts a callout in front of the current text layer.

Syntax

```
DrawCallout
```

See Also

DrawGetCalloutTextbox
DrawSetCalloutTextbox
DrawTextbox
FormatCallout
FormatDrawingObject

DrawClearRange

Purpose

Clears a drawing range.

Syntax

```
DrawClearRange
```

See Also

DrawSetRange

DrawCount()

Purpose

Returns the number of objects whose anchors are in the set range.

Syntax

```
x = DrawCount()
```

Returns

The number of objects whose anchors are in the set range (by DrawSetRange).

See Also

DrawGetType()
DrawSetRange

DrawCountPolyPoints()

Purpose

Returns the number of points in a freeform drawing object.

Syntax

```
x = DrawCountPolyPoints([Object])
```

Parameters

Object

0: the selected object.
>0: an object whose anchor is in the set range.

Returns

The number of points in a freeform drawing object.

See Also

DrawFreeformPolygon
DrawGetPolyPoints
DrawSetPolyPoints

DrawDisassemble Picture

Purpose

Converts the selected object into a group of drawing objects.

Syntax

```
DrawDisassemblePicture
```

See Also

DrawGroup
DrawUngroup

DrawEllipse

Purpose

Switches to Page Layout view and adds a default ellipse in front of the text layer.

Syntax

```
DrawEllipse
```

See Also

DrawGetType()
DrawRoundRectangle
FormatDrawingObject

DrawExtendSelect

Purpose

Extend selection to an object whose anchor is in the set range.

Syntax

```
DrawExtendSelect Layer
```

Parameters

Layer
The position of the selection relative to the text layer.

See Also

DrawGroup
DrawSelect

DrawFlipHorizontal

Purpose

Flips the drawing object from left to right (does not work on embedded objects).

Syntax

```
DrawFlipHorizontal
```

See Also

DrawFlipVertical
DrawRotateLeft
DrawRotateRight

DrawFlipVertical

Purpose

Flips the drawing object from top to bottom (does not work on embedded objects).

Syntax

```
DrawFlipVertical
```

See Also

DrawFlipHorizontal
DrawRotateLeft
DrawRotateRight

DrawFreeformPolygon

Purpose

Switches to Page Layout view and adds a default freeform object in front of the text layer.

Syntax

```
DrawFreeformPolygon
```

See Also

DrawCountPolyPoints()
DrawGetPolyPoints
DrawSetPolyPoints
FormatDrawingObject

DrawGetCallout Textbox

Purpose

Fills an array with position and size describing the callout.

Syntax

```
DrawGetCalloutTextbox Array$(,)
[,Object]
```

Parameters

Array$(,)
: A two-dimensional array. Can be 2´2 to get positions and sizes.

Object
: Specifies a drawing object: omitted: the selected drawing object.
: >0: an object whose anchor is in the set range.

See Also

DrawCallout
DrawSetCalloutTextbox
DrawSetInsertToTextbox

DrawGetPolyPoints

Purpose

Fills an array with coordinates of the endpoints of a specified freeform object.

Syntax

```
DrawGetPolyPoints Array$(,)
[,Object]
```

Parameters

Array$(,)
: A two-dimensional array. Can be 2´2 to get both coordinates.

Object
: Specifies a drawing object: omitted: the selected drawing object
: >0: an object whose anchor is in the set range.

See Also

DrawCountPolyPoints()
DrawFreeformPolygon
DrawSetPolyPoints

DrawGetType()

Purpose

Returns a number corresponding to the type of the specified object.

Syntax

```
DrawGetType(ObjNum)
```

Parameters

ObjNum
: The number of the drawing object.

Returns

The type of drawing object:

0: No object selected.

1: More than one object selected.
2: Object is a line.
3: Object is a text box.
4: Object is a rectangle.
5: Object is an ellipse.
6: Object is an arc.
7: Object is a freeform shape.
8: Object is a callout.

See Also

DrawCount()
DrawSelect
DrawSetRange

DrawGroup

Purpose

Groups the selected objects. You can manipulate groups as a single object.

Syntax

```
DrawGroup
```

See Also

DrawDisassemblePicture
DrawExtendSelect
DrawSelect
DrawSetRange
DrawUngroup

DrawInsertWordPicture

Purpose

Enables you to draw and embed a drawing object into the active document.

Syntax

```
DrawInsertWordPicture
```

See Also

InsertDrawing
InsertObject
InsertPicture

DrawLine

Purpose

Adds a default linear object in front of the text layer.

Syntax

```
DrawLine
```

See Also

DrawArc
DrawEllipse
DrawFlipHorizontal
DrawFlipVertical
DrawFreeformPolygon
DrawGetType()
DrawRotateLeft
DrawRotateRight
FormatDrawingObject

DrawNudgeDown

Purpose

Moves the selected object down by one interval. The interval is either 7.5 points, or the Vertical Spacing in Snap To Grid.

Syntax

```
DrawNudgeDown
```

See Also

DrawNudgeDownPixel
DrawNudgeLeft
DrawNudgeLeftPixel
DrawNudgeRight
DrawNudgeRightPixel
DrawNudgeUp
DrawNudgeUpPixel
DrawSnapToGrid

DrawNudgeDownPixel

Purpose

Moves the selected object down by one pixel.

Syntax

```
DrawNudgeDownPixel
```

See Also

DrawNudgeDown
DrawNudgeLeft
DrawNudgeLeftPixel
DrawNudgeRight
DrawNudgeRightPixel
DrawNudgeUp
DrawNudgeUpPixel
DrawSnapToGrid

DrawNudgeLeft

Purpose

Moves the selected object left by one interval. The interval is either 7.5 points, or the Horizontal Spacing in Snap To Grid.

Syntax

```
DrawNudgeLeft
```

See Also

DrawNudgeDown
DrawNudgeDownPixel
DrawNudgeLeftPixel
DrawNudgeRight
DrawNudgeRightPixel
DrawNudgeUp
DrawNudgeUpPixel
DrawSnapToGrid

DrawNudgeLeftPixel

Purpose

Moves the selected object left by one pixel.

Syntax

```
DrawNudgeLeftPixel
```

See Also

DrawNudgeDown
DrawNudgeDownPixel
DrawNudgeLeft
DrawNudgeRight

DrawNudgeRightPixel
DrawNudgeUp
DrawNudgeUpPixel
DrawSnapToGrid

DrawNudgeRight

Purpose

Moves the selected object right by one interval. The interval is 7.5 points, or the Horizontal Spacing in Snap To Grid.

Syntax

```
DrawNudgeRight
```

See Also

DrawNudgeDown
DrawNudgeDownPixel
DrawNudgeLeft
DrawNudgeLeftPixel
DrawNudgeRightPixel
DrawNudgeUp
DrawNudgeUpPixel
DrawSnapToGrid

DrawNudgeRightPixel

Purpose

Moves the selected object right by one pixel.

Syntax

```
DrawNudgeRightPixel
```

See Also

DrawNudgeDown
DrawNudgeDownPixel
DrawNudgeLeft
DrawNudgeLeftPixel
DrawNudgeRight
DrawNudgeUp
DrawNudgeUpPixel
DrawSnapToGrid

DrawNudgeUp

Purpose

Moves the selected object up by one interval. The interval is 7.5 points, or the Vertical Spacing in Snap To Grid.

Syntax

```
DrawNudgeUp
```

See Also

DrawNudgeDown
DrawNudgeDownPixel
DrawNudgeLeft
DrawNudgeLeftPixel
DrawNudgeRight
DrawNudgeRightPixel
DrawNudgeUpPixel
DrawSnapToGrid

DrawNudgeUpPixel

Purpose

Moves the selected object up by one pixel.

Syntax

```
DrawNudgeUpPixel
```

See Also

DrawNudgeDown
DrawNudgeDownPixel
DrawNudgeLeft
DrawNudgeLeftPixel
DrawNudgeRight
DrawNudgeRightPixel
DrawNudgeUp
DrawSnapToGrid

DrawRectangle

Purpose

Adds a default rectangular object in front of the text layer.

Syntax

```
DrawRectangle
```

See Also

DrawFreeformPolygon
DrawRoundRectangle
DrawTextBox
FormatDrawingObject

DrawResetWordPicture

Purpose

Resets the boundaries in a Word Picture object.

Syntax

```
DrawResetWordPicture
```

See Also

DrawInsertWordPicture
FileClosePicture

DrawReshape

Purpose

Toggles the handles on the selected freeform drawing shape, so you can manipulate the bounds or the vertices.

Syntax

```
DrawReshape
```

See Also

DrawFreeformPolygon
DrawGetType()
DrawSelect

DrawRotateLeft

Purpose

Rotates the selected object 90 degrees counterclockwise (will not work on embedded objects).

Syntax

```
DrawRotateLeft
```

See Also

DrawFlipHorizontal
DrawFlipVertical
DrawRotateRight

DrawRotateRight

Purpose

Rotates the selected object 90 degrees clockwise (does not work on embedded objects).

Syntax

```
DrawRotateRight
```

See Also

DrawFlipHorizontal
DrawFlipVertical
DrawRotateLeft

DrawRoundRectangle

Purpose

Adds a default rectangular object with rounded corners in front of the text layer.

Syntax

```
DrawRoundRectangle
```

See Also

DrawEllipse
DrawFreeformPolygon
DrawRectangle
DrawTextBox
FormatDrawingObject

DrawSelect or DrawSelect()

Purpose

Selects the specified object and deselects all others.

Syntax

```
DrawSelect Object
```

or

```
x = DrawSelect(Object)
```

Parameters

Object
A drawing object whose anchor is in the set range.

Returns

TRUE (-1): Select successful.
FALSE (0): Select not successful.

See Also

DrawExtendSelect
DrawSetRange

DrawSelectNext

Purpose

Changes the selection to the next drawing object in the drawing stack.

Syntax

```
DrawSelectNext
```

See Also

DrawExtendSelect
DrawSelect
DrawSelectPrevious

DrawSelectPrevious

Purpose

Changes the selection to the previous drawing object in the drawing stack.

Syntax

```
DrawSelectPrevious
```

See Also

DrawExtendSelect
DrawSelect
DrawSelectNext

DrawSendBackward

Purpose

Moves the selected drawing object backward in the drawing stack. Does not move an object around text.

Syntax

```
DrawSendBackward
```

See Also

DrawBringForward
DrawBringInFrontOfText
DrawBringToFront
DrawSendBehindText
DrawSendToBack

DrawSendBehind Text

Purpose

Moves the selected object from in front of text to behind text.

Syntax

```
DrawSendBehindText
```

See Also

DrawBringForward
DrawBringInFrontOfText
DrawBringToFront
DrawSendBackward
DrawSendToBack

DrawSendToBack

Purpose

Moves an object to the bottom of the drawing stack. Does not move an object around text.

Syntax

```
DrawSendToBack
```

See Also

DrawBringForward
DrawBringInFrontOfText
DrawBringToFront
DrawSendBackward
DrawSendBehindText

DrawSetCallout Textbox

Purpose

Sets the position and size, stored in an array, of the specified callout.

Syntax

```
DrawSetCalloutTextbox
Array$(,) [,Object]
```

Parameters

Array$(,)
A two-dimensional array. Can be 2´2 to get positions and sizes.

Object
Specifies a drawing object:
omitted: the selected drawing object.
>0: an object whose anchor is in the set range.

See Also

DrawCallout
DrawGetCalloutTextbox
DrawSetInsertToTextbox

DrawSetInsert ToAnchor

Purpose

Moves the insertion point to the beginning of the paragraph to which the specified object is anchored.

Syntax

```
DrawSetInsertToAnchor [Object]
```

Parameters

Object
Specifies a drawing object: omitted: the selected drawing object
>0: an object whose anchor is in the set range.

See Also

DrawSetInsertToTextbox

DrawSetInsert ToTextbox

Purpose

Moves the insertion point to the specified text box or callout.

Syntax

```
DrawSetInsertToTextbox [Object]
```

Parameters

Object
Specifies a drawing object:
omitted: the selected drawing object
>0: an object whose anchor is in the set range.

See Also

DrawCallout
DrawSelect
DrawSetInsertToAnchor
DrawTextBox

DrawSetPolyPoints

Purpose

Applies the coordinates in an array to the specified freeform object.

Syntax

```
DrawSetPolyPoints NumPoints,
Array$(,) [,Object]
```

Parameters

NumPoints
Number of drawing points to be set in the freeform shape. NumPoints must be less than or equal to the size of *Array*$(,).

Array$(,)
A two-dimensional array, holding coordinates for the freeform shape.

Object
Specifies a drawing object:
omitted: the selected drawing object.
>0: an object whose anchor is in the set range.

See Also

DrawCountPolyPoints()
DrawFreeformPolygon
DrawGetPolyPoints
DrawReshape

DrawSetRange or DrawSetRange()

Purpose

Sets the drawing range specified by a given bookmark.

Syntax

```
DrawSetRange BookmarkName$
```

or

```
x = DrawSetRange(BookmarkName$)
```

Parameters

BookmarkName$
Sets the drawing range.

Returns

TRUE (-1): Range was set.
FALSE (0): Range was not set.

See Also

DrawClearRange
DrawCount()
DrawSelect

DrawSnapToGrid

Purpose

Sets a grid that governs where you can place objects.

Syntax

```
DrawSnapToGrid .SnapToGrid = number
[,.XGrid = number/text ][,.YGrid =
number/text ][,.XOrigin = number/
text ][,.YOrigin = number/text ]
```

Parameters

.SnapToGrid
0: snap off;
1: snap on.

.XYGrid
The distance between horizontal/vertical gridlines.

.XYOrigin
The distance from the left edge of the page to the start of the grid.

See Also

DrawAlign
DrawNudgeDown
DrawNudgeLeft
DrawNudgeRight
DrawNudgeUp

DrawTextBox

Purpose

Adds a default bounded area of text to the drawing layer in front of the current text layer.

Syntax

```
DrawTextBox
```

See Also

DrawCallout
DrawRectangle
DrawSetInsertToAnchor
DrawSetInsertToTextBox
FormatDrawingObject

DrawUngroup

Purpose

Removes the group attribute of an object so that you can manipulate the component objects independently.

Syntax

```
DrawUngroup
```

See Also

DrawExtendSelect
DrawGroup
DrawSelect

DrawUnselect

Purpose

Deselects the currently selected object.

Syntax

```
DrawUnselect
```

See Also

DrawExtendSelect
DrawSelect
DrawSelectNext
DrawSelectPrevious

DropDownFormField

Purpose

Inserts a drop-down form field at the insertion point.

Syntax

```
DropDownFormField
```

See Also

AddDropDownItem
CheckBoxFormField
InsertFormField
RemoveAllDropDownItems
RemoveDropDownItem
TextFormField

DropListBox

Purpose

Defines a drop-down list box within a dialog box definition.

Syntax

```
DropListBox X, Y, dX, dY, Array$(),
.Identifier
```

Parameters

X, Y
The coordinates of the upper-left corner of the drop-down list box, relative to the upper-left corner of the dialog box, measured in fractions of the system font size.

dX, dY
The width and height of the drop-down list box and the associated text, measured in fractions of the system font size.

Array$()
A string array that contains the text entries to be listed in the drop-down list box.

.Identifier
A control extension used to set or access the value of the drop-down list box from outside of the dialog box definition.

Returns

When the dialog that contains the drop-down list box is accessed by the syntax 'x = Dialog.Identifier', the value returned is the entry number in the drop-down list box.

See Also

Begin Dialog...EndDialog
ComboBox
DlgListBoxArray
ListBox

EditAutoText

Purpose

Inserts, adds, or deletes an AutoText entry.

Syntax

```
EditAutoText .Name = Name$
[,.Context = Template] [,.InsertAs =
formatting][,.Insert][,.Add][,.Delete]
```

Parameters

Name$
The name of the AutoText entry.

Template
0: Normal template.
1: Active template.

formatting
governs how the text is inserted.
0: Inserted with formatting.
1: Inserted as plain text.

See Also

AutoText
AutoTextName$()
CountAutoTextEntries
GetAutoText$()
InsertAutoText
SetAutoText

EditBookmark

Purpose

Adds, deletes, selects the specified bookmark.

Syntax

```
EditBookmark .Name = Name$ [,.SortBy
= Sort] [,.Add][,.Delete][,.Goto]
```

Parameters

Name$
The name of the bookmark.

Sort
0: By name; 1: By location.

.Goto:
Moves the selection point to the specified bookmark.

See Also

BookmarkName$()
CmpBookmarks()
CopyBookmark
CountBookmarks()
EditGoTo
EditBookmark
EmptyBookmark()
ExistingBookmark()

GetBookmark$()
SetEndOfBookmark
SetStartOfBookmark

EditButtonImage

Purpose

Allows editing of a toolbar button image.

Syntax

```
EditButtonImage Toolbar$, Tool
[,Context]
```

Parameters

Toolbar$
The name of the toolbar, as it appears in the View menu.

Tool
The number of the tool, counting from right to left.

Context
0 or omitted: Normal template.
1: Active template.

See Also

AddButton
ChooseButtonImage
CopyButtonImage
MoveButton
PasteButtonImage
ResetButtonImage

EditClear

Purpose

Deletes the selection or a specified number of characters. Can also delete the selection plus one less than the specified number of characters, to the right or the left. The Clipboard is unaffected.

Syntax

```
EditClear [Count]
```

Parameters

Count
the number of characters to delete:

<0: deletes Count characters left.
0: deletes the selection or one character right.
>0: deletes Count characters right.

See Also

EditCut

EditConvertAll Endnotes

Purpose

Converts all endnotes to footnotes in the active document.

Syntax

```
EditConvertAllEndnotes
```

See Also

EditConvertAllFootnotes
EditConvertNotes
EditSwapAllNotes

EditConvertAllFootnotes

Purpose

Converts all footnotes to endnotes in the active document.

Syntax

```
EditConvertAllFootnotes
```

See Also

EditConvertAllEndnotes
EditConvertNotes
EditSwapAllNotes

EditConvertNotes

Purpose

Converts all footnotes to endnotes or endnotes to footnotes in the active pane of the active document.

Syntax

```
EditConvertNotes
```

See Also

EditConvertAllEndnotes
EditConvertAllFootnotes
EditSwapAllNotes

EditCopy

Purpose

Copies the selection to the Clipboard.

Syntax

```
EditCopy
```

See Also

EditCut
EditPaste
EditPasteSpecial

EditCut

Purpose

Cuts the selection to the Clipboard.

Syntax

```
EditCut
```

See Also

EditCopy
EditPaste
EditPasteSpecial
Spike

EditFind

Purpose

Searches through the active document for given text.

Syntax

```
EditFind .Attrib = number
```

Parameters

.Attrib—An EditFind attribute:

.Find =	The text to search
.Direction =	The search direction: 0: Up; 1: Down
.WholeWord =	The search text is a whole word only
.MatchCase =	Find search text in the same case
.Pattern =	If =1, wild cards ("*", "?") can be used in the *.Find* string
.SoundsLike =	Checks the SoundsLike check box
.Format =	0: ignores, 1: searches for formatting
.Wrap =	Determines search action when end of document is reached: 0: the search ends 1: the search automatically wraps 2: the search wraps, with prompt

value

The information about that argument.

See Also

EditFindClearFormatting
EditFindFont
EditFindFound()
EditFindLang
EditFindPara
EditFindStyle
EditReplace

EditFindClear Formatting

Purpose

Clears the formatting used in EditFind.

Syntax

```
EditFindClearFormatting
```

See Also

EditFind
EditFindFont
EditFindLang
EditFindPara
EditFindStyle
EditReplace
EditReplaceClearFormatting

EditFindFont

Purpose

Defines the character format used in EditFind.

Syntax

```
EditFindFont .Format = value
```

Parameters

.Format—A character format:

.Points =	The character's point size
.Underline =	Underline format ting
.Color =	The character's color
.Strikethrough =	Strikethrough formatting
.Superscript =	Superscript formatting
.Subscript =	Subscript format ting
.Hidden =	Hidden character
.SmallCaps =	Small caps format ting
.AllCaps =	All Caps formatting
.Spacing =	The character's spacing
.Position =	The character's position in the line
.Kerning =	The character's kerning size
.KerningMin =	The character's minimum kerning
.Default =	Use default settings (no value)
.Tab =	Tab stops
.Font =	The character's font
.Bold =	Bold formatting
.Italic =	Italic formatting

value

The information about that argument, .Strikethrough, .Superscript, .Subscript, .Hidden, .SmallCaps, .AllCaps, .Kerning, .Bold, .Italic:

-1: find text regardless of formatting
0: find text that does not have the formatting
1: find text that does have the formatting

Note: Descriptions in quotes indicate that the value is a string.

See Also

EditFind
EditFindClearFormatting
EditFindLang
EditFindPara
EditFindStyle
EditReplace
EditReplaceFont
FormatFont

EditFindFound()

Purpose

Indicates whether the last EditFind was successful.

Syntax

```
x = EditFindFound()
```

Returns

TRUE (-1): The last EditFind was successful.
FALSE (0): The last EditFind was not successful.

See Also

EditFind
EditReplace
While...Wend

EditFindHighlight

Windows 95

Purpose

Finds highlighted text of any color (when followed by an EditFind or EditReplace instruction including the argument .Format = 1)

Syntax

```
EditFindHighlight
```

See Also

EditFind
EditFindNotHighlight
EditReplace
EditReplaceHighlight
EditReplaceNotHighlight

EditFindNotHighlight

Purpose

Finds text that is not highlighted (when followed by an EditFind or EditReplace instruction including the argument .Format = 1)

Syntax

```
EditFindNotHighlight
```

See Also

EditFind
EditFindHighlight
EditReplace
EditReplaceHighlight
EditReplaceNotHighlight

EditFindLang

Purpose

Defines the language format used in EditFind.

Syntax

```
EditFindLang .Language = Lang$
```

Parameters

Lang$
The language formatting of the text to find.

See Also

EditFind
EditFindFont
EditFindPara
EditFindStyle
EditReplace
EditReplaceLang
Language
ToolsLanguage

EditFindPara

Purpose

Defines the paragraph formatting used in EditFind.

Syntax

```
EditFindPara .Format = value
```

Parameters

.Format—A paragraph format:

.LeftIndent =	The paragraph's left indent point
.RightIndent =	The paragraph's right indent point
.Before =	The paragraph's spacing before
.After =	The paragraph's spacing after
.LineSpacing =	The paragraph's line spacing
.Alignment =	The paragraph's justification
.WidowControl =	How the paragraph treats widows
.KeepWithNext =	Keep paragraph with next paragraph
.KeepTogether =	Keep paragraph together
.PageBreak =	Page break before the paragraph
.NoLineNum =	Suppress line numbers
.DontHyphen =	The paragraph's hyphen attribute
.Tab =	The paragraph's tab stops
.FirstIndent =	The paragraph's first indent point

value

The information about that argument .WidowControl, .KeepWithNext, .KeepTogether, .PageBreak, .NoLineNum, .DontHyphen:

-1: find text regardless of formatting

0: find text that does not have the formatting

1: find text that does have the formatting

Note: Descriptions in quotes indicate that the value is a string.

See Also

EditFind
EditFindFont
EditFindLang
EditFindStyle
EditReplace
EditReplacePara
FormatParagraph

EditFindStyle

Purpose

Defines the style used in EditFind.

Syntax

```
EditFindStyle .Style = style
```

Parameters

style

The name of a style. A null string indicates no style to search.

See Also

EditFind
EditFindFont
EditFindLang
EditFindPara
EditReplace
EditReplaceStyle
FormatStyle

EditGoTo

Purpose

Moves the selection to the specified bookmark or string.

Syntax

```
EditGoTo .Destination = string$
```

Parameters

string$
An existing bookmark or goto command string.

The goto command string uses the following keys:

number: a line, page, or section number
"" : bookmark
"a": annotation
"e": endnote
"q": equation
"d": field
"f": footnote
"g": graphic
"l": line
"o": object
"p": page
"s": section
"t": table
"%": percent of document.
Example: "l-5": go 5 lines back in the document,
Example: "s2p5": goto Section 2, Page 5,
Example: "%25": goto 25% down in the document.

See Also

EditFind
GoBack
GoToNextItem
GoToPreviousItem
NextField
NextObject
PrevField
PrevObject
PrevPage
RepeatFind

EditLinks

Purpose

Sets parameters for the specified links.

Syntax

```
EditLinks .Attrib = number
```

Parameters

.Attrib—An attribute:

.UpdateMode =	1: Automatic, 2: Manual
.Locked =	0: Unlocks, 1:Locks
.SavePictureInDoc =	Saves a copy of the linked object in the document
.UpdateNow =	Update link now
.OpenSource =	Open source
.KillLink =	Remove link
.Link =	The name of the link
.Application =	The applica tion name making link
.Item =	The item making the link
.Filename =	The file name of the item

value
The information about that argument.

Note: Descriptions in quotes indicate that the value is a string.

Note: Only descriptions with equal signs need values.

See Also

EditPasteSpecial
InsertField
LockFields
UnlinkFields
UnlockFields

EditObject

Purpose

Opens the selected object for editing, in the object's editor.

Syntax

```
EditObject
```

See Also

ActivateObject
EditGoTo
InsertObject

EditPaste

Purpose

Inserts the contents of the Clipboard at the insertion point.

Syntax

```
EditPaste
```

See Also

CopyText
EditCopy
EditCut
EditPasteSpecial
MoveText

EditPasteSpecial

Purpose

Inserts information from the Clipboard at the insertion point.

Syntax

```
EditPasteSpecial [.IconNumber =
IconNum][,.Link =
LinkNum][,.DisplayIcon =
DispNum][,.Class = Class$][.DataType
= DType$][,.IconFilename =
IconFile$][,.Caption = Capt$]
```

Parameters

IconNumber
: The number of the icon in the icon file.

LinkNum
: 0 or omitted: no link created 1: link created

DispNum
: 0 or omitted: link not displayed as an icon
: 1: link displayed as an icon

Class$
: The object class of the contents of the Clipboard.

Dtype$
The format of the data:

Text	Unformatted text
RTF	Rich Text Format
PICT	Windows Metafile (.WMF)
Bitmap	Windows Bitmap (.BMP)
Object	OLE object
DIB	Windows Device Independent Bitmap

IconFile$
The icon's path and file name.

Capt$
The caption of the icon to be displayed.

See Also

EditCopy
EditCut
EditLinks
EditPaste
InsertField

EditPicture

Purpose

Activates Microsoft Draw to edit the selected object.

Syntax

```
EditPicture
```

See Also

EditObject
FormatPicture
InsertPicture
Picture

EditRedo

Purpose

Restores the last action that was undone.

Syntax

```
EditRedo
```

See Also

EditRepeat
EditUndo

EditRepeat

Purpose

Repeats the last editing operation.

Syntax

```
EditRepeat
```

See Also

EditRedo
EditUndo

EditReplace

Purpose

Searches through the active document for given text and replaces it.

Syntax

```
EditReplace .Attrib = number
```

Parameters

.Attrib—An EditReplace attribute:

.Find=	The text to search
.Replace =	The text to replace
.Direction =	The search direction: 0: Up, 1: Down
.WholeWord =	The search text is a whole word only
.MatchCase =	Find search text in the same case
.PatternMatch =	If =1, wildcards ("*", "?") can be used in the .Find string
.SoundsLike =	Checks the SoundsLike check box
.FindNext =	Repeats for the next text
.ReplaceOne =	Replace the first occurrence only
.ReplaceAll-	Replace all occurrences
.Format =	0: ignores, 1: searches for formatting
.Wrap	Determines search action when end of document is reached: 0: the search ends 1: the search automatically wraps 2: the search wraps, with prompt.

value

The information about that argument.

See Also

EditFind
EditReplaceClearFormatting
EditReplaceFont
EditReplaceLang
EditReplacePara
EditReplaceStyle

EditReplaceClear Formatting

Purpose

Clears the formatting used in EditReplace.

Syntax

```
EditReplaceClearFormatting
```

See Also

EditFindClearFormatting
EditReplace
EditReplaceFont
EditReplaceLang
EditReplacePara
EditReplaceStyle

EditReplaceFont

Purpose

Defines the character format used in EditReplace.

Syntax

```
EditReplaceFont .Format = value
```

Parameters

.Format—A character format:

.Points =	The character's point size
.Underline =	Underline format ting
.Color =	The character's color
.Strikethrough =	Strikethrough formatting
.Superscript =	Superscript formatting
.Subscript =	Subscript format ting
.Hidden =	Hidden character
.SmallCaps =	Small caps format ting
.AllCaps =	All Caps format ting
.Spacing =	The character's spacing
.Position =	The character's position in the line
.Kerning =	The character's kerning size
.KerningMin =	The character's minimum kerning
.Default =	Use default settings (no value)
.Tab =	Tab stops
.Font =	The character's font
.Bold =	Bold formatting
.Italic =	Italic formatting

value

The information about that argument .Strikethrough, .Superscript, .Subscript, .Hidden, .SmallCaps, .AllCaps, .Kerning, .Bold, .Italic:

-1: find text regardless of formatting
0: find text that does not have the formatting
1: find text that does have the formatting

Note: Descriptions in quotes indicate that the value is a string.

See Also

EditFindFont
EditReplace
EditReplaceClearFormatting
EditReplaceLang
EditReplacePara
EditReplaceStyle

EditReplaceHighlight

Purpose

Windows 95

Replaces highlighted text (when followed by an EditFind or EditReplace instruction including the argument .Format = 1).

Syntax

```
EditReplaceHighlight
```

See Also

EditFind
EditReplace
EditFindHighlight
EditFindNotHighlight
EditReplaceNotHighlight

EditReplaceNot Highlight

Purpose

Replaces text that is not highlighted (when followed by an EditFind or EditReplace instruction including the argument .Format = 1).

Syntax

```
EditReplaceNotHighlight
```

See Also

EditFind
EditReplace
EditFindHighlight
EditFindNotHighlight
EditReplaceHighlight

EditReplaceLang

Purpose

Defines the language format used in EditReplace.

Syntax

```
EditReplaceLang .Language = Lang$
```

Parameters

Lang$
The language formatting of the text to find.

See Also

EditFindLang
EditReplace
EditReplaceClearFormatting
EditReplaceFont
EditReplacePara
EditReplaceStyle
ToolsLanguage

EditReplacePara

Purpose

Defines the paragraph formatting used in EditReplace.

Syntax

```
EditReplacePara .Format = value
```

Parameters

.Format—A paragraph format:

.LeftIndent =	The paragraph's left indent point
.RightIndent =	The paragraph's right indent point
.Before =	The paragraph's spacing before
.After =	The paragraph's spacing after
.LineSpacing =	The paragraph's line spacing
.Alignment =	The paragraph's justification
.WidowControl =	How the paragraph treats widows
.KeepWithNext =	Keep paragraph with next paragraph

.KeepTogether =	Keep paragraph together
.PageBreak =	Page break before the paragraph
.NoLineNum =	Suppress line numbers
.DontHyphen =	The paragraph's hyphen attribute
.Tab =	The paragraph's tab stops
.FirstIndent =	The paragraph's first indent point

value

The information about that argument .WidowControl, .KeepWithNext, .KeepTogether, .PageBreak, .NoLineNum, .DontHyphen:
-1: find text regardless of formatting
0: find text that does not have the formatting
1: find text that does have the formatting

Note: Descriptions in quotes indicate that the value is a string.

See Also

EditFindPara
EditReplace
EditReplaceClearFormatting
EditReplaceFont
EditReplaceLang
EditReplaceStyle
FormatParagraph

EditReplaceStyle

Purpose

Defines the style used in EditReplace.

Syntax

```
EditReplaceStyle .Style = style
```

Parameters

style

The name of a style. A null string indicates no style to search.

See Also

EditFindStyle
EditReplace
EditReplaceClearFormatting
EditReplaceFont
EditReplaceLang
EditReplacePara
FormatStyle

EditSelectAll

Purpose

Selects the entire active document.

Syntax

```
EditSelectAll
```

EditSwapAllNotes

Purpose

Converts all footnotes to endnotes or endnotes to footnotes in the active document.

Syntax

```
EditSwapAllNotes
```

See Also

EditConvertAllEndnotes
EditConvertAllFootnotes
EditConvertNotes

EditTOACategory

Purpose

Modifies the name of a category of citations.

Syntax

```
EditTOACategory .Category =
Category, .CategoryName = CatName$
```

Parameters

Category
The category to modify, numbered consecutively in the list.

CatName$
The new name for the category of citations.

See Also

InsertTableOfAuthorities
MarkCitation

EditUndo

Purpose

Reverses the last action(s) (in most cases).

Syntax

```
EditUndo
```

See Also

EditRedo
EditRepeat

EmptyBookmark()

Purpose

Determines whether a given bookmark is an insertion point or a selection.

Syntax

```
x = EmptyBookmark(BookmarkName$)
```

Parameters

BookmarkName$
The name of a bookmark to check.

Returns

TRUE (-1): Bookmark is an insertion point ("empty").
FALSE (0): Bookmark is a selection.

See Also

BookmarkName$()
CmpBookmarks()
CountBookmarks()
EditBookmark
ExistingBookmark()
GetBookmark$()

EnableFormField

Purpose

Allows or prevents changes to the given form field while the form is being filled in.

Syntax

```
EnableFormField BookmkName$, Enable
```

Parameters

BookmkName$
The name of the bookmark marking the form field.

Enable
0: cannot be changed; 1: can be changed.

See Also

InsertFormField

EndOfColumn or EndOfColumn()

Purpose

Moves the insertion point to the last column of the current row of a table.

Syntax

```
EndOfColumn [Select]
```

or

```
x = EndOfColumn([Select])
```

Parameters

Select
0: do not extend selection.
nonzero: extend selection.

Returns

TRUE (-1): The action was performed.
FALSE (0): The action was not performed; the insertion point was already at the end of a column.

See Also

EndOfRow
StartOfColumn

EndOfDocument or EndOfDocument()

Purpose

Moves the insertion point to the end of the active document.

Syntax

```
EndOfDocument [Select]
```

or

```
x = EndOfDocument([Select])
```

Parameters

Select
0: do not extend selection.
nonzero: extend selection.

Returns

TRUE (-1): The action was performed.
FALSE(0): The action was not performed; the insertion point was already at the end of the document.

See Also

AtEndOfDocument()
StartOfDocument

EndOfLine or EndOfLine()

Purpose

Moves the insertion point to the end of the current line.

Syntax

```
EndOfLine [Select]
```

or

```
x = EndOfLine([Select])
```

Parameters

Select
0: do not extend selection.
nonzero: extend selection.

Returns

TRUE (-1): The action was performed.
FALSE(0): The action was not performed; the insertion point was already at the end of the line.

See Also

EndOfRow
ParaDown
StartOfLine

EndofRow or EndofRow()

Purpose

Moves the insertion point to the last row of the current column of a table.

Syntax

```
EndofRow [Select]
```

or

```
x = EndOfRow([Select])
```

Parameters

Select
0: do not extend selection, nonzero: extend selection.

Returns

TRUE (-1): The action was performed.
FALSE(0): The action was not performed; the insertion point was already at the end of a row.

See Also

EndOfColumn
EndOfLine
StartOfRow

EndOfWindow or EndOfWindow()

Purpose

Moves the insertion point to the lower right corner of the current window.

Syntax

```
EndOfWindow [Select]
```

or

```
x = EndOfWindow([Select])
```

Parameters

Select
: 0: do not extend selection
nonzero: extend selection.

Returns

TRUE (-1): The action was performed.
FALSE(0): The action was not performed; the insertion point was already at the end of the window.

See Also

EndOfDocument
StartOfWindow

Environ$()

Purpose

Returns the current setting of an MS-DOS environment variable.

Syntax

```
x$ = Environ$(EnvVariable$)
```

Parameters

EnvVariable$
: An existing environment variable set in MS-DOS.

Returns

The current setting of the given MS-DOS environment variable.

See Also

AppInfo$()
GetProfileString$()
GetSystemInfo$()

Eof()

Purpose

Determines whether the end of an open data file has been reached.

Syntax

```
x = Eof(Stream)
```

Parameters

Stream
: The stream number of the open file.

Returns

TRUE (-1): At end of file.
FALSE (0): Not at end of file.

See Also

Close
Input
Input$()
Line Input
Lof()
Open
Print
Read
Seek
Write

Err

Purpose

This variable contains the error code for the most recent error.

If error-trapping is used, Err must be set to 'Err = 0' before returning from the error trapping routine, to reset error trapping. 'Err = 0' should be used only at the end of the error trapping routine, or repeated error trapping may unexpectedly occur prior to returing to the main routine.

Syntax

```
x = Err
```

or

```
Err = x
```

or

```
Error Err
```

Parameters

Err is a WordBasic variable.

See Also

Error
Goto
On Error

Error

Purpose

Generates an error condition. Useful in testing routines.

Syntax

```
Error ErrorCode
```

Parameters

ErrorCode
A given error code to test.

See Also

Err
Goto
On Error

ExistingBookmark()

Purpose

Tests for the existence of a given bookmark.

Syntax

```
x = ExistingBookmark(BookmarkName$)
```

Parameters

BookmarkName$
A bookmark name to test.

Returns

TRUE (-1): The bookmark exists.
FALSE (0): The bookmark does not exist.

See Also

BookmarkName$()
CmpBookmarks()
CountBookmarks()
EditBookmark
EmptyBookmark()
GetBookmark$()

ExitWindows

Purpose

Closes all open applications and logs the current user off Windows. WARNING: all unsaved work in Word will be lost, though dialog boxes will prompt you to save unsaved files in other applications.

Syntax

```
ExitWindows
```

See Also

FileExit

ExtendMode()

Purpose

Checks if extend mode is in effect.

Syntax

```
x = ExtendMode()
```

Returns

TRUE (-1): Extend mode is in effect.
FALSE (0): Extend mode is not in effect.

See Also

Cancel
ColumnSelect
ExtendSelection

ExtendSelection

Purpose

Sets Extend Mode.

Syntax

```
ExtendSelection [Character$]
```

Parameters

Character$
The character to which the selection is extended.

See Also

Cancel
ColumnSelect
ExtendMode()
ShrinkSelection

FieldSeparator or FieldSeparator$()

Purpose

Sets the separator character you use when you convert text to a table.

Syntax

```
FieldSeparator Separator$
```

or

```
x$ = FieldSeparator$()
```

Parameters

Separator$
The character used to separate cells when you convert text to a table.

Returns

The current separator character.

See Also

TextToTable

FileClose

Purpose

Closes the active file and its associated windows.

Syntax

```
FileClose [SaveCmd]
```

Parameters

SaveCmd

0 or omitted: Prompts the user if needed.
1: Saves without prompting.
2: Closes without saving.

See Also

ClosePane
DocClose
FileCloseAll
FileExit
IsDocumentDirty()
SetDocumentDirty

FileCloseAll

Purpose

Closes all open document windows.

Syntax

```
FileCloseAll [SaveCmd]
```

Parameters

SaveCmd

0 or omitted: Prompts the user if needed.
1: Saves without prompting.
2: Closes without saving.

See Also

DocClose
FileClose
FileExit

FileClosePicture

Purpose

Closes the picture editor and (re)embeds a Picture object in the active document.

Syntax

```
FileClosePicture [SaveCmd]
```

See Also

DrawResetWordPicture

FileConfirm Conversions or FileConfirm Conversions()

Purpose

Governs display of a confirmation box used during FileOpen for conversion from one file format to another.

Syntax

```
FileConfirmConversions [Display]
```

or

```
x = FileConfirmConversions()
```

Parameters

Display

omitted: Toggles between display/no display.
0: Does not display confirmation box.
1: Displays confirmation box.

Returns

TRUE (-1): Set to display box.
FALSE (0): Set to not display box.

See Also

FileOpen
MailMergeAskToConvertChevrons

FileExit

Purpose

Exits Word.

Syntax

```
FileExit [SaveCmd]
```

Parameters

SaveCmd

0 or omitted: Prompts the user if needed.
1: Saves without prompting.
2: Exits without saving.

See Also

AppClose
ExitWindows
FileCloseAll

FileFind

Purpose

Finds files based on given criteria.

Syntax

```
FileFind .Attrib = value
```

Parameters

.Attrib—A FileFind attribute:

.SearchName =	A group of search criteria
.SearchPath =	The path(s) to search
.Name =	The file names to search
.SubDir =	If 1, subdirectories are searched
.Title =	The summary title to search
.Author =	The summary author to search
.Subject =	The summary subject to search
.Keywords =	The summary keywords to search
.MatchCase =	0: Find search text in any case 1: Find search text in the same case
.Text =	The search text within documents
.PatternMatch =	If 1, allows wildcards
.SavedBy =	Name who last saved
.DateCreated From =	Earliest creation date
.DateCreated To =	Latest creation date
.DateSaved From =	Earliest save date
.DateSavedTo =	Latest save date
.View =	Display in the dialog box: 0: File information 1: Preview selected file 2: Summary info for selected file
.SortBy =	How documents are sorted: 0: Alphabetically by author 1: By receding creation date 2: Alphabetically by LastSavedName

	3: By receding last saved date
	4: Alphabetically by file name
	5: By increasing size
.ListBy =	0: File name
	1: Title
.SelectedFile =	Returns list number of last selected file.
.Add	Stores group of search criteria.
.Delete	Removes group of search criteria.
.Options =	0: Create a new list
	1: Add to existing file list.
	2: Search only in the existing list.

value
The information about that argument.

Note: Descriptions in quotes indicate that the value is a string.

See Also

CountFoundFiles()
FoundFileName$()

FileList

Purpose

Opens a file listed at the bottom of the File menu.

Syntax

```
FileList ListNum
```

Parameters

ListNum
A number in the file list of the File menu corresponding to the file name to be opened.

See Also

CountFiles()
FileName$()
FileNumber
FileOpen

FileName$()

Purpose

Returns the name of the active document or the most recently opened document.

Syntax

```
x$ = FileName$([FileList])
```

Parameters

FileList
The number in the file list of the File menu corresponding to the file name.

Returns

The file name as a string.

See Also

CountFiles()
FileList
FileNameFromWindows$()
FileNumber

Files$()
WindowName$()

FileNameFromWindows$()

Purpose

Returns the path and file name of the document in a window.

Syntax

```
FileNameFromWindows$
([WindowNum])
```

Parameters

WindowNum
The list number of the window in the Window menu.

Returns

Returns the path and file name of the active document.

See Also

CountWindows()
FileName$()
WindowName$()

FileNameInfo$()

Purpose

Returns specified parts of a path/file name.

Syntax

```
FileNameInfo$(FileName$, InfoType)
```

Parameters

FileName$
The path and file name of a document.

InfoType
The information to return:
1: The full path and file name.
2: The file name only, if in current directory.
3: The file name only.
4: The file name, stripped of extension.
5: The full path only.
6: The network path and file name.

Returns

Specified parts of a path/file name as a string.

See Also

FileName$()
FileNameFromWindows$()

FileNew

Purpose

Opens a new document.

Syntax

```
FileNew [.NewTemplate =
number],[.Template = TemplateName$]
```

Parameters

number

0: Creates a new document.

1: Creates a new template.

TemplateName$

The name of the template to attach or upon which to base the new template.

See Also

FileNewDefault
FileOpen

FileNewDefault

Purpose

Creates a new document, based on the Normal template.

Syntax

```
FileNewDefault
```

See Also

FileNew

FileNumber

Purpose

Opens a given file name in the File menu file list.

Syntax

```
File1, or File2, or ... File9.
```

See Also

CountFiles()
FileList
FileName$()
WindowNumber

FileOpen

Purpose

Opens an existing document.

Syntax

```
FileOpen .Name = FileName$
[,.ConfirmConversions =
Confirm][,.ReadOnly =
ReadOnly][,.AddToMru =
MostRecUsed][,.PasswordDoc =
DocPass$][,.PasswordDot =
DotPass$][,.Revert =
Revert][,.WritePasswordDoc =
DocPassWr$][,.WritePasswordDot =
DotPassWr$]
```

Parameters

FileName$

The name of the file to open.

Confirm

1: Displays the Convert File dialog box.

ReadOnly

1: Opened read-only, 0: opened for writing.

MostRecUsed
1: adds file name to the bottom of the file list in the File menu.

DocPass$
The document password.

DotPass$
The template password.

Revert
If *FileName$* is open:
0: the open document is activated.
1: closes the document (no save), and reopens it.

DocPassWr$
The document write-protect password.

DotPassWr$
The template write-protect password.

See Also

FileConfirmConversions
FileFind
FileNew

FilePageSetup

Purpose

Sets the page setup for the current or all sections of the active document.

Syntax

```
FilePageSetup .Format = value
```

Parameters

.Format	A page setup format:
.Tab =	Tab to modify page setup: 0: Margins 1: Size & Orientation 2: Paper Source 3: Page Layout
.ApplyPropsTo=	Where to apply page properties: 0: Current selection 1: This point forward 2: Selected sections 3: Selected text 4: Whole document
.TopMargin=	Distance top of page to text
.BottomMargin=	Distance text to bottom of page
.LeftMargin=	Distance left page to text
.RightMargin=	Distance right page to text
.Gutter=	Distance allowed for binding
.HeaderDistance=	Distance from top of page
.FooterDistance=	Distance from bottom of page
.FacingPages=	(Re)Sets the Facing Pages setting
.PageWidth=	Width of the page
.PageHeight=	Height of the page
.Orientation=	0: Portrait, 1: Landscape
.FirstPage=	Sets method of printing first page 0: Default tray 1: Upper tray 4: Manual feed 5: Envelope
.OtherPages=	Sets method of printing pages 0: Default tray 1: Upper tray 4: Manual feed

	5: Envelope
.SectionStart=	Sets type of section break 0: Continuous 1: New Column 2: New Page 3: Even Page 4: Odd Page
.VertAlign=	Sets alignment of section on page 0: Top 1: Center 2: Justified
.OddAndEven Pages=	Different odd/even pages
.DifferentFirst Page=	Sets different first page
.Endnotes=	Suppresses end notes
.LineNum=	Adds line numbering
.StartingNum=	The number to begin line numbering
.FromText=	line number spacing from text
.CountBy=	line number increment
.NumMode=	Sets how lines are numbered 0: Restart at each page 1: Restart at each section 2: Continuous
.Default—	Makes the settings the default.

value

The information about that argument.

Note: Descriptions in quotes indicate that the value is a string.

See Also

FormatColumns
FormatSectionLayout

FilePost

Purpose

Posts the active document to a Microsoft Exchange public folder.

Syntax

```
FilePost Destination
```

Parameters

Destination

The Microsoft Exchange public folder where you want the document posted.

Returns

What the statement returns.

See Also

FileRoutingSlip
FileSendMail

FilePreview

Purpose

Defines a preview box within a dialog box definition.

Syntax

```
FilePreview X, Y, dX, dY,
.Identifier
```

Parameters

X, Y

The coordinates of the upper-left corner of the preview box, relative to the upper-left corner of the dialog box, measured in fractions of the system font size.

dX, dY

The width and height of the preview box and its associated text, measured in fractions of the system font size.

.Identifier

A control extension used to set or access the value of the preview box from outside of the dialog box definition.

See Also

DlgFilePreview
DlgUpdateFilePreview
Picture

FilePrint

Purpose

Prints all or a portion of the active document.

Syntax

```
FilePrint .Attrib = value
```

Parameters

.Attrib—A print attribute:

.Background=	If 1, print in background
.AppendPrFile	0: Overwrite; 1: Append
.PrToFile Name =	File to print to
.Type =	The text to search 0: Document 1: Summary Information 2: Annotations 3: Styles 4: AutoText Entries 5: Key Assignments
.NumCopies =	Number of copies to print
.From	Starting page number in range
.To	Ending page num ber in range
.Range	Set page range 0: prints entire document 1: prints selection or current page 2: prints currently active page 3: prints range of pages
.Pages	Page numbers to print
.Order	Specifies range of pages to print 0: All pages in range 1 Odd pages in range 2: Even pages in range
.PrintToFile	1: Yes
.Collate	Collate output yes/no
.FileName	The specified file is printed

value

The information about that argument.

Note: Descriptions in quotes indicate that the value is a string.

See Also

FilePrintDefault
FilePrintSetup
ToolsOptionsPrint

FilePrintDefault

Purpose

Prints the active document, using the current default settings.

Syntax

```
FilePrintDefault
```

See Also

FilePrint
FilePrintSetup
ToolsOptionsPrint

FilePrintPreview or FilePrintPreview()

Purpose

Toggles the Print Preview window.

Syntax

```
FilePrintPreview [On]
```

or

```
x = FilePrintPreview([On])
```

Parameters

On

omitted: Toggles preview.
0: Turns off preview.
1: Turns on preview.

Returns

TRUE (-1): Preview is on.
FALSE (0): Preview is off.

See Also

ClosePreview
FilePrintPreviewFullScreen
FilePrintPreviewPages
ViewZoom

FilePrintPreview FullScreen

Purpose

Governs display of tools, rulers, and horizontal scroll bar in Print Preview.

Syntax

```
FilePrintPreviewFullScreen [Clean]
```

Parameters

Clean

omitted: Toggles screen elements.
0: Displays screen elements.
1: Hides screen elements.

See Also

ClosePreview
FilePrintPreview
ToolsOptionsView

FilePrintPreview Pages

Purpose

Toggles display in Print Preview between one and two pages.

Syntax

```
FilePrintPreviewPages [Pages]
```

or

```
x = FilePrintPreviewPages()
```

Parameters

*Pages_*

0 or omitted: Toggles text margins.
1: Displays one page.
2: Displays two pages.

Returns

TRUE (-1): One page is displayed.
FALSE (0): Two pages are displayed.

See Also

ClosePreview
FilePrintPreview
ViewPage
ViewZoom

FileProperties

Purpose

Display's the active document's Properties dialog box.

Syntax

```
FileProperties
```

Parameters

None

Returns

Displays property dialog box.

See Also

DocumentPropertyName$()
CountDocumentProperties()
DeleteDocumentProperty
DocumentPropertyExists()
DocumentPropertyName$()
DocumentPropertyType()
GetDocumentProperty(),
GetDocumentProperty$()
IsCustomDocumentProperty()
IsDocumentPropertyReadOnly()
SetDocumentProperty
SetDocumentPropertyLink

FilePrintSetup

Purpose

Changes printing options for the active document.

Syntax

```
FilePrintSetup [.Printer =
PrinterName$][,.Options]
```

Parameters

PrinterName$
The name of the printer to be activate.

.Options
Displays a dialog box to present the user with the setup options.

See Also

FilePrint
ToolsOptionsPrint

FileRoutingSlip

Purpose

Edits the routing slip for the active document.

Syntax

```
FileRoutingSlip .Attrib = value
```

Parameters

.Attrib—A routing slip attribute:

.Subject =	The subject line of the mail
.Message =	The message to precede the icon
.AllAtOnce =	How recipient receives document: 0: Send only to first recipient 1: Send to all at same time
.Return WhenDone=	Sends doc back as confirmation
.TrackStatus=	Sends message to sender whenever document is forwarded
.Protect =	Sets level of protection 0: No protection 1: All changes have revision marks 2: Add annotations only 3: Enter in form fields only
.AddSlip =	Adds a routing slip to active doc
.Route Document =	Routes the active doc
.AddRecipient =	Add to list of recipients
.OldRecipient =	Add to list only if not routed
.ResetSlip =	Prepares document for rerouting
.ClearSlip =	Removes routing slip
.ClearRecipients =	Removes all routing addresses
.Address =	The address of a recipient

value
The information about that argument.

Note: Descriptions in quotes indicate that the value is a string.

See Also

FileSendMail

Files$()

Purpose

Finds a file name that matches, in the current directory.

Syntax

```
x$ = Files$(FileName$)
```

Parameters

FileName$
The file to find. If omitted, the last *Files$()* *FileName$* is used to find the next file.

Returns

The file name if *FileName$* is found. A null string is returned if it was not found.

See Also

FileFind

FileSave

Purpose

Saves the active document.

Syntax

FileSave

See Also

FileSaveAll
FileSaveAs
IsDocumentDirty()
IsTemplateDirty()

FileSaveAll

Purpose

Saves all changed files.

Syntax

```
FileSaveAll [SaveCmd] [, OrigFormat]
```

Parameters

SaveCmd
0 or omitted: prompts the user if needed.
1: saves without prompting.

OrigFormat
If file cannot be saved in original format:
0: Saves document in Word format.
1: Saves document in original format.
2 or omitted: Prompts to save in Word format.

See Also

FileSave
FileSaveAs
IsDocumentDirty()
IsTemplateDirty()

FileSaveAs

Purpose

Saves the active document with a new name/format.

Syntax

```
FileSaveAs .Attrib = value
```

Parameters

.Attrib—A FileSaveAs attribute:

.Name = New name for the file

.Format = Sets the new format for the file
0: Word format
1: Document template
2: ANSI text
3: ANSI text with line breaks
4: (PC-8) IBM PC character set text
5: (PC-8) IBM PC text with breaks
6: Rich Text Format (RTF)

.LockAnnot = Locks document for annotations

.Password = Sets a document password

.WritePassword = Sets a write-protect password

.AddToMru = 1: Adds name to the File menu list

.RecommendReadOnly_ 1: Suggest opening as read-only

.EmbedFonts = If 1, embeds True Type fonts

.FormsData =If 1, saves data in form

value
The information about that argument.

See Also

FileSave
FileSaveAll
Name
ToolsOptionsSave
ToolsProtectDocument

FileSendMail

Purpose

Opens Microsoft Mail.

Syntax

```
FileSendMail
```

See Also

ToolsOptionsGeneral

FileSummaryInfo

Purpose

Sets the summary information and allows access to document statistics.

Syntax

```
FileSummaryInfo .Info = value, ...
```

Parameters

.Info

A SummaryInfo argument:

.Title=	The document's title
.Subject=	The document's subject
.Author=	The document's author
.Keywords=	The document's keywords
.Comments=	The document's comments
.Filename=	The document name
.Directory=	The document directory's full path
.Template=	The document template's full path
.CreateDate=	The document's creation date and time
.LastSavedDate=	The date and time when last saved
.LastSavedBy=	The document's author
.RevisionNumber=	The current revision count
.EditTime=	Total document's editing time
.LastPrintedDate=	Date and time when last printed
.NumPages=	The number ofpages in the document
.NumWords=	The number of words in the document
.NumChars=	The number of characters in document
.Update=	Updates .Pages, .Words, .Characters

value

The information about that argument.

See Also

DocumentStatistics

FileTemplates

Purpose

Changes the template attached to the active document.

Syntax

```
FileTemplates .Template = Template$,
.LinkStyles = Context
```

Parameters

Template$

The template name to attach.

Context

If 1, styles in active document are linked to the active template.

See Also

AddAddIn
AddInState
DeleteAddIn
FileNew
Organizer

Font or Font$()

Purpose

Applies a font to the selection.

Syntax

```
Font Name$, [Size]
```

or

```
x$ = Font$([Count])
```

Parameters

Name$
The font name to apply.

Size
The point size of the font to apply.

Count
The name of the Count font in the total list of fonts (given by CountFonts()). If omitted, returns the font of the selection. If more than one font is selected, a null string is returned.

Returns

The font name of the selection if Count is omitted. If Count is supplied, the name of the font given by that number (in the font list) is returned.

See Also

CountFonts()
FontSize
FormatFont

FontSize or FontSize()

Purpose

Sets the point size of the selection.

Syntax

```
FontSize Size
```

or

```
x = FontSize()
```

Parameters

Size
The size in points to make the font.

Returns

The point size of the selection. If multiple point sizes are in the selection, returns 0.

See Also

Font
FontSizeSelect
FormatFont
FontSizeSelect

FontSizeSelect

Purpose

Moves the focus to the Font Size in the toolbar, else opens the Font dialog box.

Syntax

```
FontSizeSelect
```

See Also

Font
FontSize
FormatFont

FontSubstitution

Purpose

Sets font mapping options for the active document.

Syntax

```
FontSubstitution .UnavailableFont = FontFrom$, .SubstituteFont = FontTo$
```

Parameters

FontFrom$
The unavailable font.

FontTo$
An available font to map to *FontFrom$*.

See Also

ToolsOptionsCompatibility

For...Next

Purpose

Sets a program loop structure.

Syntax

```
For Counter = Start To End [Step Stepsize]...Next [Counter]
```

Parameters

Counter
The loop counter variable.

Start
The initial value of *Counter*.

End
The last value of *Counter* for which the loop will execute. After the loop is finished, *Counter* = End + 1.

Stepsize
The amount by which *Counter* will increment each time through the loop. The default is +1. Stepsize can be fractional or negative.

See Also

Goto
If...Then...Else
Select Case
While...Wend

FormatAddrFonts

Purpose

Sets character formatting for addresses on envelopes.

Syntax

```
FormatAddrFonts .Format = value
```

Parameters

.Format—A character format:

.Points =	The character's point size
.Underline =	Underline formatting
.Color =	The character's color
.Strikethrough =	Strikethrough formatting
.Superscript =	Superscript formatting

.Subscript =	Subscript formatting
.Hidden =	Hidden character
.SmallCaps =	Small caps format ting
.AllCaps =	All Caps formatting
.Spacing =	The character's spacing
.Position =	The character's position in the line
.Kerning =	The character's kerning size
.KerningMin =	The character's minimum kerning
.Default =	Use default settings (no value)
.Tab =	Tab stops
.Font =	The character's font
.Bold =	Bold formatting
.Italic =	Italic formatting

value

The information about that argument.

Note: Descriptions in quotes indicate that the value is a string.

See Also

FormatFont
FormatRetAddrFonts
ToolsCreateEnvelope

FormatAutoFormat

Purpose

Automatically formats a document with the selected style. Displays a dialog box when complete.

Syntax

```
FormatAutoFormat
```

See Also

FormatStyleGallery
ToolsOptionsAutoFormat

FormatBordersAndShading

Purpose

Sets border and shading formats for paragraphs, tables, and pictures.

Syntax

```
FormatBordersAndShading .Attrib = value
```

Parameters

.Attrib—A FormatBorder attribute:

.FromText =	Distance to adjacent text
.Shading =	Specifies a shading pattern
.Foreground =	Specifies foreground shading color
.Background =	Specifies background shading color
.Tab =	0: Borders tab; 1: Shading tab
.ApplyTo =	Border applies to: 0: Paragraphs 1: Pictures 2: Cells 3: Whole table
.Shadow =	Apply a shadow to the borders: 0: None 1: Shadow

.TopBorder =	Specifies top border
.LeftBorder =	Specifies left border
.BottomBorder =	Specifies bottom border
.RightBorder =	Specifies right border
.HorizBorder =	Specifies inside horizontal border
.VertBorder =	Specifies inside vertical border
.TopColor =	Specifies top border color
.LeftColor =	Specifies left border color
.BottomColor =	Specifies bottom border color
.RightColor =	Specifies right border color
.HorizColor =	Specifies inside horiz border color
.VertColor =	Specifies inside vert border color
.FineShading =	Specifies shading pattern by 2.5%

value
The information about that argument.

Note: Descriptions in quotes indicate that the value is a string.

See Also

BorderBottom
BorderInside
BorderLeft
BorderLineStyle
BorderNone
BorderOutside
BorderRight
BorderTop
ShadingPattern

FormatBullet

Purpose

Adds bullets to selected paragraphs.

Syntax

```
FormatBullet [.Points = number]
[.Color = number] [,.Alignment =
number] [,.Indent = number or text]
[,.Space = number or text] [,.Hang =
number] [,.CharNum = number] [,.Font
= text]
```

Parameters

.Points
Bullet size, in points.

.Color
Of bullets (use list shown in CharColor, earlier in this command reference).

.Alignment
Alignment for bullets within space between left indent and first line of text (disregarded unless .Space = 0).
0 or omitted: Left
1: Centered
2: Right

.Indent
Distance between left indent and first line of text, in points or text measurement.

.Space
Distance between bullet and first line of text, in points or text measurement.

.Hang
If 1, applies a hanging indent.

.CharNum
Identifies a symbol to be used as the bullet, as follows: 31+ number corresponding to position of symbol in the Insert Symbol dialog box, counting from left to right.

.Font
Name of font containing the symbol chosen in *.Symbol.*

See Also

CharColor
FormatBulletsAndNumbering
FormatBulletDefault
FormatHeadingNumber
FormatMultilevel
FormatNumber

FormatBulletDefault or FormatBulletDefault()

Purpose

Adds or removes default bullets from the selected paragraphs.

Syntax

```
FormatBulletDefault [Add]
```

or

```
x = FormatBulletDefault()
```

Parameters

Add
omitted: Toggles bullets.
0: Removes bullets.
1: Adds bullets.

Returns

-1: Not all selected paragraphs bulleted or numbered.
0: None of selected paragraphs bulleted or numbered.
1: All selected paragraphs bulleted or numbered.

See Also

FormatBulletsAndNumbering
FormatNumberDefault
SkipNumbering

FormatBulletsAnd Numbering

Purpose

Adds or removes bullets or numbers in selected paragraphs.

Syntax

```
FormatBulletsAndNumbering
[.Remove][,.Hang = Hang][,.Tab=
Tab][,.Preset = Preset]
```

Parameters

Hang

If 1, applies hanging indent to selection.

Tab

Specified tab to select when using a user-defined dialog box.
0: Bulleted tab
1: Numbered tab
2: Multilevel tab

Preset

Sets a scheme for bullets:
1-6: Bulleted tab schemes
7-12: Numbered tab schemes
13-18: Multilevel tab schemes

See Also

FormatBulletDefault
FormatNumberDefault
RemoveBulletsNumbers
SkipNumbering

FormatCallout

Purpose

Sets options for callout drawing objects.

Syntax

```
FormatCallout .Attrib = value
```

Parameters

.*Attrib*—A FormatCallout attribute:

.Type = Sets type of callout
0: One line segment (V or H)
1: One line segment (V, H, or Diag)
2: Two line segments
3: Three line segments

.Gap = Specifies distance between callout line and text area

.Angle = Specifies callout line angle
0: Automatically adjusts
1: 30 degrees
2: 45 degrees
3: 60 degrees
4: 90 degrees

.Drop = Starting position of callout line
Top: Top of text area
Center: Center of text area
Bottom: Bottom of text area

.Length = The length of the first line segment

.Border = If 1, puts border around callout text

.AutoAttach = Auto change starting position

.Accent = If 1, add vertical line next to text

value

The information about that argument.

Note: Descriptions in quotes indicate that the value is a string.

See Also

DrawCallout
DrawGetCalloutTextbox
DrawSetCalloutTextbox
DrawTextbox
FormatDrawingObject

FormatChangeCase

Purpose

Changes the case of the selection.

Syntax

```
FormatChangeCase [.Type = TypeNum]
```

Parameters

TypeNum

Type of capitalization to apply:
0: Caps first character in each sentence.
1: Change selection to lowercase.
2: Change selection to uppercase.
3: Change selection to initial caps.
4: Toggles case for each letter in selection.

See Also

AllCaps
LCase$()
SmallCaps
UCase$

FormatColumns

Purpose

Sets the column width and spacing for the current section (using multiple text columns).

Syntax

```
FormatColumns .Format = value
```

Parameters

.Format—A column format:

.Columns = The number of columns to set

.ColumnNo = The number of the column to change

.ColumnWidth = Width of the specified column

.ColumnSpacing = The spacing between columns

.EvenlySpaced = If 1, makes all columns same width

.ApplyColsTo = Apply column format to:
0: the active section
1: from insertion point forward
2: selected section
3: selected text
4: whole document.

.ColLine = Set/Remove line between columns

.StartNewCol = Section starts in new column

value

The information about that argument.

Note: Descriptions in quotes indicate that the value is a string.

See Also

TableColumnWidth

FormatDefineStyle Borders

Purpose

Sets border and shading formats for paragraphs, tables, and pictures.

Syntax

```
FormatDefineStyleBorders .Attrib = value
```

Parameters

.Attrib—A FormatBorder attribute:

.FromText =	Distance to adjacent text
.Shading =	Specifies a shading pattern
.Foreground =	Specifies foreground shading color
.Background =	Specifies background shading color
.Tab_	0: Borders tab; 1: Shading tab
.ApplyTo =	Border applies to: 0: Paragraphs 1: Pictures 2: Cells 3: Whole table
.Shadow =	Apply a shadow to the borders: 0: None 1: Shadow
.TopBorder =	Specifies top border
.LeftBorder =	Specifies left border
.BottomBorder =	Specifies bottom border
.RightBorder =	Specifies right border
.HorizBorder =	Specifies inside horizontal border
.VertBorder =	Specifies inside vertical border
.TopColor =	Specifies top border color
.LeftColor =	Specifies left border color
.BottomColor =	Specifies bottom border color
.RightColor =	Specifies right border color
.HorizColor =	Specifies inside horizontal border color
.VertColor =	Specifies inside vertical border color

value

The information about that argument.

Note: Descriptions in quotes indicate that the value is a string.

See Also

FormatBordersAndShading
FormatDefineStyleFont
FormatDefineStylePara
FormatStyle

FormatDefineStyle Font

Purpose

Sets character formatting in the current or specified style.

Syntax

```
FormatDefineStyleFont .Format =
value
```

Parameters

.Format—A character format:

.Points =	The character's point size
.Underline =	Underline formatting
.Color =	The character's color
.Strikethrough =	Strikethrough formatting
.Superscript =	Superscript formatting
.Subscript =	Subscript formatting
.Hidden =	Hidden character
.SmallCaps =	Small caps formatting
.AllCaps =	All Caps formatting
.Spacing =	The character's spacing
.Position =	The character's position in the line
.Kerning =	The character's kerning size
.KerningMin =	The character's minimum kerning
.Default =	Use default settings (no value)
.Tab =	Tab stops
.Font =	The character's font
.Bold =	Bold formatting
.Italic =	Italic formatting

value

The information about that argument.

Note: Descriptions in quotes indicate that the value is a string.

See Also

FormatFont
FormatStyle

FormatDefineStyleFrame

Purpose

Sets frame formats for the active style.

Syntax

```
FormatDefineStyleFrame .Format =
value
```

Parameters

.Format—A frame format:

.Wrap = wraps text	Wraps/Not around frame
.WidthRule =	Exact/Auto frame width
.FixedWidth =	Exact frame width
.HeightRule =	0: Auto, 1: At least, 2: Exactly
.FixedHeight =	Frame height
.PositionHorz =	Absolute horizontal position
.PositionHorzRel =	to: 0: Margin, 1: Page, 2: Column
.DistFromText =	Distance of frame from text
.PositionVert =	Absolute vertical position

.PositionVertRel =to:
0: Margin,
1: Page,
2: Column
.DistVertFromText = Distance of frame from text
.MoveWithText = Move frame with text
.RemoveFrame = Remove the frame formatting.

value
The information about that argument.

Note: Descriptions in quotes indicate that the value is a string.

See Also

FormatDefineStyleFont
FormatDefineStylePara
FormatFrame
FormatStyle

FormatDefineStyle Lang

Purpose

Sets language formats for the active style.

Syntax

```
FormatDefineStyleLang .Language = Lang$ [,.Default]
```

Parameters

Lang$
The language name.

.Default
Sets the language as default.

See Also

FormatDefineStyleFont
FormatDefineStylePara
FormatStyle
ToolsLanguage

FormatDefineStyle Numbers

Purpose

Sets number formatting in the current or specified style.

Syntax

```
FormatDefineStyleNumbers .Format = value
```

Parameters

.Format—A number format:
.Points= The size of the numbers in points
.Color = The color of the numbers
.Type = Type of numbering:
0: 1, 2, 3, 4
1: I, II, III, IV
2: i, ii, iii, iv
3: A, B, C, D
4: a, b, c, d
.StartAt = Start numbering at number
.Alignment =Alignment within left margin:
0 or omitted: Left
1: Centered
2: Right

.RightWidth = Distance between number and text
.Hang = if 1, applies hanging indent
.Before = Text to appear before the number
.After = Text to appear after the number
.Level = The heading level
.CharNum = Character position in Symbol font
.Font = The font name

value
The information about that argument.

Note: Descriptions in quotes indicate that the value is a string.

See Also

FormatBullet
FormatDefineStyleFont
FormatDefineStylePara
FormatMultilevel
FormatNumber
FormatStyle

FormatDefineStyle Para

Purpose

Sets paragraph formats for the active style.

Syntax

```
FormatDefineStylePara .Format = value
```

Parameters

.Format—A paragraph format:

.Alignment = The paragraph's justification
.LeftIndent = The paragraph's left indent point
.RightIndent = The paragraph's right indent point
.FirstIndent = The paragraph's first indent point
.Before = The paragraph's spacing before
.After = The paragraph's spacing after
.LineSpacingRule = Determines line spacing
0 or omitted: Single
1: 1.5 Lines
2: Double
3: At Least
4: Exactly
5: Multiple
.LineSpacing = The paragraph's line spacing
.PageBreak = Page break before the paragraph
.KeepTogether = Keep paragraph together
.KeepWithNext = Keep paragraph with next paragraph
.NoLineNum = Suppress line numbers

value
The information about that argument.

Note: Descriptions in quotes indicate that the value is a string.

See Also

FormatParagraph
FormatStyle

FormatDefineStyle Tabs

Purpose

Sets tab stops for the active style.

Syntax

```
FormatDefineStyleTabs .Format = value
```

Parameters

.Format—A tab format:

.Position=	Position of the tab stop
.DefTabs =	Position of default tab stops
.Align =	Alignment of tab stops 0: Left 1: Centered 2: Right 3: Decimal
.Leader =	Leader character for the tab stop 0: None 1: Dot 2: Dash 3: Underline
.Set	Set tab stop
.Clear	Clear tab stop
.ClearAll	Clear all tab stops.

value

The information about that argument.

Note: Descriptions in quotes indicate that the value is a string.

See Also

FormatDefineStyleFont
FormatDefineStylePara
FormatStyle
FormatTabs

FormatDrawingObject

Purpose

Sets formatting for the selected drawing object(s).

Syntax

```
FormatDrawingObject .Format  = value
```

Parameters

.Format—A drawing format:

.Tab=	Tab to select 0: Fill tab 1: Line tab 2: Size and Position tab.
.FillColor =	Specifies a fill color Color < 0 is % gray /2.
.LineColor =	Specifies a line color
.FillPatternColor =	Specifies the pattern color
.FillPattern =	Specifies the fill pattern
.LineType =	0: Hides the line; 1: Shows the line.
.LineStyle =	Specifies a line style

.LineWeight =	Specifies a line width
.ArrowStyle =	Specifies the arrow style
.ArrowWidth =	Specifies the arrow width 0: Narrow 1: Medium 2: Thick
.ArrowLength =	Specifies the arrow length
.Shadow =	If 1, applies shadow effect
.RoundCorners =	If 1, rounds corners
.HorizontalPos =	Distance: reference to object
.HorizontalFrom =	Specifies reference 0: Margin 1: Page 2: Column
.VerticalPos =	Distance: reference to object
.VerticalFrom =	Specifies reference 0: Margin 1: Page 2: Column
.Height =	Height of drawing object
.Width =	Width of drawing object
.InternalMargin =	Between text box and callout.

value
The information about that argument.

Note: Descriptions in quotes indicate that the value is a string.

See Also

DrawAlign
DrawReshape
DrawSnapToGrid

FormatDropCap

Purpose

Modifies the formatting of the first character of the current paragraph to become a dropped capital letter.

Syntax

```
FormatDropCap [.Position =
WhereDropped][,.Font =
Font$][,.DropHeight =
Height][,.DistFromText = Dist]
```

Parameters

WhereDropped
Specifies positioning
0: No dropped cap formatting.
1: Dropped in line.
2: In margin.

Font$
Specifies the dropped cap font.

Height
The height of the dropped cap.

Dist
The distance between the dropped cap and the rest of the paragraph.

See Also

FormatFrame
InsertFrame

FormatFont

Purpose

Applies character formatting to the selection.

Syntax

```
FormatFont .Format = value
```

Parameters

.Format—A character format:

.Points=	The character's point size
.Underline =	Underline formatting
.Color =	The character's color
.Strikethrough =	Strikethrough formatting
.Superscript =	Superscript formatting
.Subscript =	Subscript formatting
.Hidden =	Hidden character
.SmallCaps =	Small caps formatting
.AllCaps =	All Caps formatting
.Spacing =	The character's spacing
.Position =	The character's position in the line
.Kerning =	The character's kerning size
.KerningMin =	The character's minimum kerning
.Default =	Use default settings (no value)
.Tab =	Tab stops
.Font =	The character's font
.Bold =	Bold formatting
.Italic =	Italic formatting

value
The information about that argument.

Note: Descriptions in quotes indicate that the value is a string.

See Also

AllCaps
Bold
CharColor
DottedUnderline
DoubleUnderline
EditFindFont
EditReplaceFont
Font
FontSize
FormatChangeCase
FormatDefineStyleFont
GrowFont
Hidden
Italic
ResetChar
ShrinkFont
SmallCaps
Strikethrough
Subscript
Superscript
Underline
WordUnderline

FormatFrame

Purpose

Sets frame formats for the active style.

Syntax

```
FormatFrame .Format = value
```

Parameters

.Format—

A frame format:

.Wrap =	Wraps/Not wraps text around frame
.WidthRule =	Exact/Auto frame width
.FixedWidth =	Exact frame width
.HeightRule =	0: Auto, 1: At least 2: Exactly
.FixedHeight =	Frame height
.PositionHorz =	Absolute horizontal position
.PositionHorzRel =	to: 0: Margin 1: Page 2: Column
.DistFromText =	Distance of frame from text
.PositionVert =	Absolute vertical position
.PositionVertRel =	to: 0: Margin 1: Page 2: Column
.DistVertFromText =	Distance of frame from text
.MoveWithText =	Move frame with text
.LockAnchor =	If 1, locks frame anchor
.RemoveFrame =	Remove the frame formatting.

value

The information about that argument.

Note: Descriptions in quotes indicate that the value is a string.

See Also

FormatDefineStyleFrame
InsertFrame
RemoveFrames

FormatHeader FooterLink

Purpose

Replaces current header or footer in pane with previous header or footer.

Syntax

```
FormatHeaderFooterLink
```

See Also

ShowNextHeaderFooter
ShowPrevHeaderFooter
ToggleHeaderFooterLink
ViewHeader

FormatHeading Number

Purpose

Applies numbers for heading level(s) in the active document.

Syntax

```
FormatHeadingNumber .Format = value
```

Parameters

.Format
A number format:

.Points =
The size of the numbers in points

FormatHeading Numbering

Purpose

Adds or removes numbers for headings in selection.

Syntax

```
FormatHeadingNumbering [.Preset =
PresetNum][,.Remove]
```

Parameters

PresetNum
A number from the Heading Numbering dialog.

.Remove
Removes numbering in selection.

See Also

FormatBulletsAndNumbering
FormatHeadingNumbers

FormatMultilevel

Purpose

Applies multilevel list numbers to selected paragraphs, or changes numbering options for a specific heading level.

Syntax

```
FormatMultilevel [.Points = number]
[,.Color = number] [,.Before = text]
[,.Type = number] [,After = text]
[,.StartAt = number] ],.Include =
number] [,.Alignment = number]
[,.Indent = number or text] [,.Space
= number or text] [,.Hang = number]
[,.Level = number] [,.Font = text]
[,.Striketrhough = number] [,.Bold =
number] [,.Italic =
number][,.Underline = number]
```

Parameters

.Level
Heading level from 1 through 9 (however, if you specify level, options for formatting multilevel headings do not apply).

.Points
The character's point size.

.Color
The character's color, based on numbering scheme in CharColor.

.Font
The character's font.

.Bold
Bold formatting.

.Italic
Italic formatting.

.Underline
Underline formatting.

.Strikethrough
1 = Strikethrough formatting.

.Indent
Distance between indent and text.

.Hang
If 1, applies hanging indent.

.Before
Text to appear before the number.

.After
Text to appear after the number.

.Space
Distance between number and text.

.Alignment
Alignment for numbers within space between left-indent and first line of text (ignored unless .Space = 0):
0 or omitted: Left
1: Centered
2: Right

.Type
Type of numbering:
0: 1, 2, 3, 4
1: I, II, III, IV
2: i, ii, iii, iv
3: A, B, C, D
4: a, b, c, d
5: 1st, 2nd
6: One, Two
7: First, Second

.StartAt
Start numbering at heading number

.Include
Whether to include numbers and position options for previous headings:
0: Don't include numbers or position options
1: Precede specified level with a series of numbers from higher-level headings.
2: Include both higher-level heading numbering and position options

See Also

FormatBullet
FormatBulletsAndNumbering
FormatHeadingNumber
FormatNumber

FormatNumber

Purpose

Sets number formatting for the active style.

Syntax

```
FormatNumbers .Format = value
```

Parameters

.Format—A number format:

.Points =	The size of the numbers in points
.Color =	The color of the numbers
.Type =	Type of numbering: 0: 1, 2, 3, 4 1: I, II, III, IV 2: i, ii, iii, iv 3: A, B, C, D 4: a, b, c, d
.StartAt =	Start numbering at number
.Alignment =	Alignment within left margin: 0 or omitted: Left 1: Centered 2: Right

.Indent =	Distance between indent and text
.Hang =	If 1, applies hanging indent
.Before =	Text to appear before the number
.After =	Text to appear after the number
.Space =	Distance between number and text
.Font =	The font name

value

The information about that argument.

Note: Descriptions in quotes indicate that the value is a string.

See Also

FormatBullet
FormatBulletsAndNumbering
FormatHeadingNumbers
FormatMultilevel
FormatNumberDefault
FormatStyle

FormatNumberDefault or FormatNumberDefault()

Purpose

Adds or removes numbers from selected paragraph(s).

Syntax

```
FormatNumberDefault [On]
```

or

```
x = FormatNumberDefault()
```

Parameters

On

0: Removes numbers.
1: Adds numbers.

Returns

-1: Not all selected paragraphs numbered or bulleted.
0: None of selected paragraphs numbered or bulleted.
1: All selected paragraphs numbered or bulleted.

See Also

FormatBullet
FormatBulletDefault
FormatBulletsAndNumbering
FormatNumber
SkipNumbering

FormatPageNumber

Purpose

Defines the page number format for the current section.

Syntax

```
FormatPageNumber [.NumFormat =
Format][,.Level = Level][.Separator
= SepChar][,.NumRestart =
DiffStNum][,.StartingNum = PgNum$]
```

Parameters

Format
The page numbering format:
0: 1 2 3 ...
1: a b c ...
2: A B C ...
3: i ii iii ...
4: I II III ...

Level
The heading level of the first paragraph in each chapter.

SepChar
Separator between chapter number and page number.

DiffStNum
0: Continue from previous section,
1: Begin at .StartingNum

PgNum$
The starting page number.

See Also

InsertPageNumbers

FormatParagraph

Purpose

Sets paragraph formats for the active style.

Syntax

```
FormatParagraph .Format = value
```

Parameters

.Format—A paragraph format:

.LeftIndent =	The paragraph's left indent point
.RightIndent =	The paragraph's right indent point
.Before =	The paragraph's spacing before
.After =	The paragraph's spacing after
.LineSpacing =	The paragraph's line spacing
.Alignment =	The paragraph's justification
.WidowControl =	How the paragraph treats widows
.KeepWithNext =	Keep paragraph with next para graph
.KeepTogether =	Keep paragraph together
.PageBreak =	Page break before the paragraph
.NoLineNum =	Suppress line numbers
.DontHyphen =	The paragraph's hyphen attribute
.Tab =	The paragraph's tab stops
.FirstIndent =	The paragraph's first indent point

value
The information about that argument.

Note: Descriptions in quotes indicate that the value is a string.

See Also

EditFindPara
EditReplacePara

FormatBordersAndShading
FormatDefineStylePara
FormatStyle
FormatTabs
ParaKeepLinesTogether
ParaKeepWithNext
ParaPageBreakBefore
ParaWidowOrphanControl
Style

FormatPicture

Purpose

Applies picture formatting to selected picture.

Syntax

```
FormatPicture .Format = value
```

Parameters

.Format—A picture format:

.SetSize =	0: Use ScaleXY, 1: Use SizeXY
.CropTop =	Amount to crop top of picture
.CropLeft =	Amount to crop left of picture
.CropBottom =	Amount to crop bottom of picture
.CropRight =	Amount to crop right of picture
.ScaleX =	% to scale X
.ScaleY=	% to scale Y
.SizeX =	Size in points of horizontal of picture
.SizeY =	Size in points of vertical of picture.

value
The information about that argument.

Note: Descriptions in quotes indicate that the value is a string.

See Also

InsertPicture

FormatRetAddrFonts

Purpose

Sets character formatting for return addresses on envelopes.

Syntax

```
FormatRetAddrFonts .Format = value
```

Parameters

.Format—A character format:

.Points =	The character's point size
.Underline =	Underline formatting
.Color =	The character's color
.Strikethrough =	Strikethrough formatting
.Superscript =	Superscript formatting
.Subscript =	Subscript formatting
.Hidden =	Hidden character
.SmallCaps =	Small caps formatting
.AllCaps =	All Caps formatting
.Spacing =	The character's spacing

.Position =	The character's position in the line
.Kerning =	The character's kerning size
.KerningMin =	The character's minimum kerning
.Default =	Use default settings (no value)
.Tab =	Tab stops
.Font =	The character's font
.Bold =	Bold formatting
.Italic =	Italic formatting

value

The information about that argument.

Note: Descriptions in quotes indicate that the value is a string.

See Also

FormatAddrFonts
FormatFont
ToolsCreateEnvelope

FormatSectionLayout

Purpose

Applies section formatting to the selected sections.

Syntax

```
FormatSectionLayout .Format = value
```

Parameters

.Format—A section format:

.SectionStart =	Sets type of section break

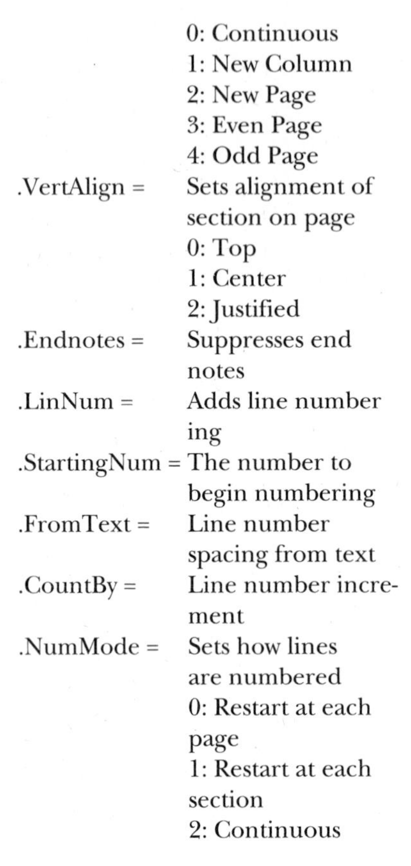

	0: Continuous 1: New Column 2: New Page 3: Even Page 4: Odd Page
.VertAlign =	Sets alignment of section on page 0: Top 1: Center 2: Justified
.Endnotes =	Suppresses end notes
.LinNum =	Adds line numbering
.StartingNum =	The number to begin numbering
.FromText =	Line number spacing from text
.CountBy =	Line number increment
.NumMode =	Sets how lines are numbered 0: Restart at each page 1: Restart at each section 2: Continuous

value

The information about that argument.

Note: Descriptions in quotes indicate that the value is a string.

See Also

FileSetup

FormatStyle

Purpose

Defines a style or applies the style to the selection.

Syntax

```
FormatStyle .Format = value
```

Parameters

.Format—A style format:

.Name =	The name of the style
.NewName =	A new name for the style
.AddToTemplate =	0: Doc only, 1: Doc & Template
.BasedOn =	Style to base current formatting
.NextStyle =	Style applied after new paragraph
.Type =	0 or omitted: Paragraph; 1: Character
.FileName =	A style to be merged (doc/template)
.Source =	Direction to merge: 0: From active document to file 1: From file to active document
.Rename =	Renames a style
.Merge =	Merges a style
.Define =	Adds a style
.Apply =	Applies the style
.Delete =	Deletes a style

value
The information about that argument.

Note: Descriptions in quotes indicate that the value is a string.

See Also

CountStyles()
FormatDefineStyleBorders
FormatDefineStyleFont
FormatDefineStyleFrame
FormatDefineStyleLang
FormatDefineStyleNumbers
FormatDefineStylePara
FormatDefineStyleTabs
NormalStyle
Organizer
Style
StyleName$()

FormatStyleGallery

Purpose

Copies styles from the given template into the active document.

Syntax

```
FormatStyleGallery .Template =
Source$
```

Parameters

Source$
The source template for the styles.

See Also

FormatAutoFormat
FormatStyle
ToolsOptionsAutoFormat

FormatTabs

Purpose

Sets tab stops for the active style.

Syntax

```
FormatTabs .Format = value
```

Parameters

.Format—A tab format:

.Position =	Position of the tab stop
.DefTabs =	Position of default tab stops
.Align =	Alignment of tab stops 0: Left 1: Centered 2: Right 3: Decimal 4: Bar
.Leader =	Leader character for the tab stop 0: None 1: Period 2: Hyphen 3: Underline
.Set =	Set tab stop
.Clear =	Clear tab stop
.ClearAll =	Clear all tab stops

value

The information about that argument.

Note: Descriptions in quotes indicate that the value is a string.

See Also

FormatDefineStyleTabs
NextTab()
PrevTab()
TabLeader$()
TabType

FormFieldOptions

Purpose

Changes the attributes of a selected form field.

Syntax

```
FormFieldOptions .Attrib = value
```

Parameters

.Attrib—A form field attribute:

.Entry =	The macro that runs when the form field received focus
.Exit =	The macro that runs when the form field loses focus
.Name =	Name of bookmark marking form field
.Enable =	if 1, allows form field to be changed
.TextType =	Specifies the type: 0: Regular Text 1: Number 2: Date 3: Current Date 4: Current Time 5: Calculation
.TextDefault =	The default text
.TextWidth =	0: Unlimited; >0: Maximum width
.TextFormat =	Uppercase Lowercase First Capital Title Case
.CheckSize =	0: Auto size; 1: Exact size
.CheckWidth	if 1, width is as specified
.CheckDefault	Default 0: Cleared; 1: Selected
.Type =	Type of form field 0: Text 1: Check box 2: Drop-down
.OwnHelp =	if 1, enables .HelpText

.HelpText =	Custom help text
.OwnStat =	If 1, enables .StatText
.StatText =	Custom status bar text

value
The information about that argument.

Note: Descriptions in quotes indicate that the value is a string.

See Also

EnableFormField
InsertFormField

FormShading or FormShading()

Purpose

Sets shading for form fields in the active document.

Syntax

```
FormShading [On]
```

or

```
x = FormShading()
```

Parameters

On

omitted: Toggles form-field shading
0:No form-field shading
1:Shade form-fields

Returns

TRUE (-1): Form fields are shaded.
FALSE (0): Form fields are not shaded.

See Also

FormFieldOptions

FoundFileName$()

Purpose

Returns the name of a found file.

Syntax

```
x$ = FoundFileName$(n)
```

Parameters

n
A number from 1 to CountFoundFiles().

Returns

The filename of the found file.

See Also

CountFoundFiles()
FileFind

Function...End Function

Purpose

Defines a function.

Syntax

```
Function Name([Parameter List])...End Function
```

Parameters

Name
The name of the function. In the main routine, it is called by 'x = *Name*()'.

Parameter List
A list of variables to be passed into and out of the function, separated by commas. WordBasic assumes all variables are local unless specifically stated by using 'Dim Shared'. *Parameter List* cannot contain values, only variables.

See Also

Sub...End Sub

GetAddInID()

Purpose

Returns given add-in's position.

Syntax

```
x = GetAddInID(AddInName$)
```

Parameters

AddInName$
Path and file name of template or DLL/WLL.

Returns

The position of the given add-in in the list under Global Templates And Add-Ins.

See Also

AddAddIn
AddInState
ClearAddIns
CountAddIns
DeleteAddIn
GetAddInName$()

GetAddInName$()

Purpose

Returns the path and file name of the given add-in.

Syntax

```
GetAddInName$(AddInID)
```

Parameters

AddInID
The position of the given add-in in the list under Global Templates And Add-Ins.

Returns

The path and file name of the given template or DLL/WLL.

See Also

AddAddIn
AddInState
ClearAddIns
CountAddIns
DeleteAddIn
GetAddInID()

GetAddress$()

Purpose

Retrieves an address stored in a Microsoft Exchange Personal Address Book or Schedule+ Contact List. (Available only if Microsoft Exchange or Schedule+ 2.0 is installed.)

Syntax

```
GetAddress$()[Name$],[AddressProperties$],
[UseAutoText],[DisplaySelectDialog],
[SelectDialog],[CheckNamesDialog],
[MRUChoice], [UpdateMRU]
```

Parameters

Name$
Address name specified in the address book's Search Name dialog box

AddressProperties$
If UseAutoText = 1, this specifies the name of an AutoText entry defining a sequence of address book properties. If UseAutoText = 0 or is omitted, *AddressProperties$* defines a custom layout. To specify custom layouts, specify the MAPI (official) field names you want, within brackets. These fieldnames are listed under AddAddress, earlier in this Command Reference. You can combine address book field name references with other functions such as Chr$(), which returns a character from the ASCII command set.

UseAutoText
Specifies a value for use by *AddressProperties$*:
0 (or omitted): Tells AddressProperties$ to define a custom layout
1: Tells AddressProperties$ to find a layout in a specific AutoText entry

DisplaySelectDialog
Determines whether to display Select Name dialog box:
0: Does not display dialog box
1 (or omitted): Does display dialog box
2: Does not display dialog box, and does not search for specific names either. Returns previously selected address.

SelectDialog
Determines how to display SelectName dialog box:
0: In Browse mode
1: In Compose mode, with To: box only
2: In Compose mode, with To: and CC: boxes

CheckNamesDialog
Determines whether to display the Check Names dialog box if Name$ does not provide a specific enough value
0: Check Names box not displayed
1 (or omitted): Check Names box is displayed.

MRUChoice
Chooses list of most-recently used addresses to use in address list:
0 (or omitted): Delivery addresses
1: Return addresses

UpdateMRU
Determines whether new address is added to list of most-recently used addresses (ignored if SelectDialog is set to 1 or 2):
0 (or omitted): Not added
1: Added
Returns An address from the default address book.

See Also

AddAddress
AutoText
InsertAddress
ToolsCreateEnvelope
ToolsCreateLabels

GetAttr()

Purpose

Returns the file attributes of a file.

Syntax

```
GetAttr(FileName$)
```

Parameters

FileName$
The path and file name of a file to examine.

Returns

A sum of the following:

0: No attributes selected
1: Read Only attribute selected
2: Hidden attribute selected
4: System attribute selected
32: Archive attribute selected

See Also

SetAttr

GetAutoCorrect$()

Purpose

Returns the AutoCorrect replacement text for a string.

Syntax

```
x$ = GetAutoCorrect$(Entry$)
```

Parameters

Entry$
An AutoCorrect entry.

Returns

The replacement text for a given AutoCorrect entry.

See Also

ToolsAutoCorrect

GetAutoCorrect Exception$()

Purpose

Returns the text of an AutoCorrect Exception you have previously specified.

Syntax

```
x = GetAutoCorrectException$
(Tab,EntryNumber)
```

Parameters

Tab
: 0: First Letter tab
: 1: INitial CAps tab

EntryNumber
: A number corresponding to the exception's position in the exception list. Number cannot exceed the number of exceptions, as returned by CountAutoCorrectExceptions()

Returns

Text of the exception corresponding to EntryNumber in the tab you specify.

See Also

CountAutoCorrectExceptions()
IsAutoCorrectException()
ToolsAutoCorrectExceptions

GetAutoText$()

Purpose

Returns the given AutoText entry.

Syntax

```
x$ = GetAutoText$(Name$, Context)
```

Parameters

Name$
: The name of the AutoText entry.

Context
: 0 or omitted: Normal template; 1: Active template.

Returns

The unformatted text of the given AutoText entry.

See Also

AutoText
AutoTextName$()
CountAutoTextEntries()
EditAutoText
InsertAutoText
SetAutoText

GetBookmark$()

Purpose

Returns the text marked by a bookmark.

Syntax

```
x$ = GetBookmark$(BookmarkName$)
```

Parameters

BookmarkName$
: The name of a bookmark.

Returns

The unformatted text marked by the specified bookmark.

See Also

BookmarkName$()
CountBookmarks()
EditBookmark

GetCurValues

Purpose

Stores the current values of a dialog box in a given dialog variable.

Syntax

```
GetCurValues dlgVariable
```

Parameters

dlgVariable
A dimensioned dialog record.

See Also

Dialog
Dim

GetDirectory$()

Purpose

Returns a subdirectory name.

Syntax

```
x$ = GetDirectory$(DirName$, Count)
```

Parameters

DirName$
The path name of the parent directory.

Count
The number of the subdirectory within the parent directory.

Returns

The name of the given subdirectory.

See Also

CountDirectories()

GetDocument Property(), GetDocument Property$()

Purpose

Windows 95

Returns a number or a string representation of a document property you specify that is defined in the active document.

Syntax

```
GetDocumentProperty(Name$),
(CustomOrBuiltIn)
or
GetDocumentProperty$(Name$),
(CustomOrBuiltIn)
```

Parameters

Name$
Property name

CustomOrBuiltIn:
0 (or omitted): Word searches both built-in and custom properties and returns the first matching value it finds.
1: Word searches the list of built-in properties only.

2: Word searches the list of custom properties only.

Returns

GetDocumentProperty() returns a numeric value of the *Name$* property you choose. Yes properties are returned as 1; No as 0.

GetDocumentProperty$() returns a string of text representing the *Name$* property you choose, or an error message if *Name$* is a number or undefined. Date properties return in default date format. Yes returns as Y; No returns as N.

See Also

DocumentPropertyName$()
DocumentPropertyType()
SetDocumentProperty

GetDocumentVar$()

Purpose

Returns the string associated with a document variable.

Syntax

```
x$ = GetDocumentVar$(VblName$)
```

Parameters

VblName$
A document variable.

Returns

The string associated with the given document variable.

See Also

GetDocumentVarName$()
SetDocumentVar

GetDocumentVar Name$()

Purpose

Returns the name associated with a document variable.

Syntax

```
x$ = GetDocumentVarName$(VblNum)
```

Parameters

VblNum
The list number of a document variable.

Returns

The name associated with the given document variable.

See Also

CountDocumentVars()
GetDocumentVar$()
SetDocumentVar

GetFieldData$()

Purpose

Returns data stored in a MACRO field. The insertion point must be within the MACRO field.

Syntax

```
x$ = GetFieldData$()
```

Returns

Data stored in a MACRO field.

See Also

PutFieldData

GetFormResult()

Purpose

Returns the setting of a check-box form field or a drop-down form field.

Syntax

```
x = GetFormResult(BookmkName$)
```

or

```
x$ = GetFormResult$(BookmkName$)
```

Parameters

BookmkName$
The name of the bookmark marking the form field.

Returns

Integer form
Check box:
0: Cleared; 1: Selected
Drop-down: (Item number selected) - 1

String form:
Check box: “0”: Cleared;
“1”: Selected
Drop-down: Item selected

See Also

SetFormResult

GetMergeField$()

Purpose

Returns the contents of a merge field.

Syntax

```
x$ = GetMergeField$(Name$)
```

Parameters

Name$
The name of the merge field.

Returns

The contents of the specified merge field.

See Also

CountMergeFields()
MergeFieldName$()

GetPrivateProfile String$()

Purpose

Returns a setting in a private .INI file.

Syntax

```
x$ = GetPrivateProfileString$
(Section$, Option$, FileName$)
```

Parameters

Section$
The section name (appearing inside "[]" in the .INI file_do not include brackets in *Section$*).

Option$
The option to retrieve (preceding the "=").

FileName$
The file name of the private .INI file.

Returns

A given setting in a private .INI file.

See Also

GetProfileString$()
SetPrivateProfileString
SetProfileString

GetProfileString$()

Purpose

Returns a setting in the WIN.INI file.

Syntax

```
GetProfileString$ ([Section$],
Option$)
```

Parameters

Section$
The section name (appearing inside "[]" in the .INI file_do not include brackets in *Section$*). If omitted, "Microsoft Word" is assumed.

Option$
The option to retrieve (preceding the "=")

Returns

A given setting in the WIN.INI file.

See Also

GetPrivateProfileString$()
SetPrivateProfileString
SetProfileString

GetSelEndPos()

Purpose

Returns the character position of the end of the current selection relative to the start of the document.

Syntax

```
x = GetSelEndPos()
```

Returns

The character position of the end of the current selection, relative to the start of the document. All characters are included in the count.

See Also

GetSelStartPos()
GetText$()
SetSelRange

GetSelStartPos()

Purpose

Returns the character position of the beginning of the current selection relative to the start of the document.

Syntax

```
x = GetSelStartPos()
```

Returns

The character position of the beginning of the current selection, relative to the start of the document. All characters are included in the count.

See Also

GetSelEndPos()
GetText$()
SetSelRange

GetSystemInfo or GetSystemInfo()

Purpose

Fills an array with information about Word's operating environment.

Syntax

```
GetSystemInfo Array$()
```

or

```
x = GetSystemInfo(Type)
```

Parameters

Array$()
The array into which the information is to be deposited.

Type
The information to be returned:
21: The environment name
22: Type of CPU
23: MS-DOS version number (not meaningful in Windows 95)
24: Windows version number
25: Percent of system resources available (not meaningful in Windows 95)
26: Amount of available disk space, in bytes
27: The current Windows mode (not meaningful in Windows 95)
28: Math coprocessor installed (Yes/No)
29: Country setting
30: Language setting
31: Vertical display resolution
32: Horizontal display resolution.

Returns

Fills an array with information, or returns one piece of information from the function form, about Word's operating environment.

See Also

AppInfo$()

GetText$()

Purpose

Returns the text between two character positions.

Syntax

```
x$ = GetText$(Position1, Position2)
```

Parameters

Position1
The starting character position, counting from the start of the document.

Position2
The ending character position, counting from the start of the document.

Returns

The unformatted text (except hidden characters) between two given character positions.

See Also

GetSelEndPos()
GetSelStartPos()
SetSelRange

GoBack

Purpose

Cycles the insertion point between the last four editing locations.

Syntax

```
GoBack
```

See Also

EditGoTo

Goto

Purpose

Allows jumping within a macro program.

Syntax

```
Goto Label
```

Parameters

Label
A program label.

See Also

For...Next
If...Then...Else
Select Case
While...Wend

GoToAnnotationScope

Purpose

Select the range of text associated with an annotation.

Syntax

```
GoToAnnotationScope
```

See Also

GoToNextItem
GoToPreviousItem
OtherPane
ViewAnnotations()
WindowPane()

GoToHeaderFooter

Purpose

Moves the insertion point between a header and a footer.

Syntax

```
GoToHeaderFooter
```

See Also

CloseViewHeaderFooter
ShowNextHeadereFooter
ShowPrevHeaderFooter
ViewFooter
ViewHeader

GoToNextItem

Purpose

Moves the insertion point to the next specified item.

Syntax

```
GoToNextItem
```

Parameters

Item
"Annotation", "Endnote", "Foot-note", "Page", "Section", "Subdocument".

See Also

EditGoTo
GoToHeaderFooter
GoToPreviousItem

GoToPreviousItem

Purpose

Moves the insertion point to the previous specified item.

Syntax

```
GoToPreviousItem
```

Parameters

Item
"Annotation", "Endnote", "Foot-note", "Page", "Section", "Subdocument".

See Also

EditGoTo
GoBack
GoToHeaderFooter
GoToNextItem

GroupBox

Purpose

Defines a Group Box within a dialog box definition.

Syntax

```
GroupBox X, Y, dX, dY, Label$, .Identifier
```

Parameters

X, Y
The coordinates of the upper-left corner of the Group Box, relative

to the upper-left corner of the dialog box, measured in fractions of the system font size.

dX, dY
The width and height of the Group Box and its associated text, measured in fractions of the system font size.

Label$
The label displayed in the upper left corner of the Group Box. An ampersand for a shortcut key is legal in *Label$*.

.Identifier
A control extension used to set or access the value of the Group Box from outside of the dialog box definition.

See Also

Begin Dialog...End Dialog
DlgText
OptionGroup

GrowFont

Purpose

Increases the font size of the selection to the next size supported by the printer.

Syntax

```
GrowFont
```

See Also

FontSize
FormatFont
GrowFontOnePoint
ShrinkFont
ShrinkFontOnePoint

GrowFontOnePoint

Purpose

Increases the font size of the selection by one point.

Syntax

```
GrowFontOnePoint
```

See Also

FontSize
FormatFont
GrowFont
ShrinkFont
ShrinkFontOnePoint

HangingIndent

Purpose

Applies a hanging indent to the selected paragraph(s), or increases the current hanging indent to the next tab stop.

Syntax

```
HangingIndent
```

See Also

Indent
UnHang
UnIndent

Help

Purpose

Displays Word Help Contents, or help for the selected context.

Syntax

```
Help
```

See Also

HelpActiveWindow
HelpTool

HelpAbout

Purpose

Returns information from HelpAbout.

Syntax

```
HelpAbout .Attrib = value$
```

Parameters

.Attrib:

.AppName = The name and version of Word

.AppCopyright = The copyright notice

.AppUserName = The name to whom licensed

.AppOrganization = The org name during install

.AppSerialNumber = The serial number of Word

.ConventionalMemory = Per-centages of available

.MathCoprocessor = Present or None

.DiskSpace = Amount of available disk space

value$

Used in a dimensioned dialog record.

Returns

Read-only text values through a dimensioned dialog record.

See Also

AppInfo$()
DocumentStatistics
GetSystemInfo$()

HelpActiveWindow

Purpose

Displays help associated with the active view or pane.

Syntax

HelpActiveWindow

See Also

Help
HelpTool

HelpContents

Purpose

Displays Word Help Topics dialog box.

Syntax

```
HelpContents
```

See Also

Help
HelpIndex

HelpExamplesAndDemos

Purpose

Allows access to all examples and demonstrations in Help.

Syntax

```
HelpExamplesAndDemos
```

See Also

HelpQuickPreview

HelpIndex

Purpose

Displays the Help Index.

Syntax

```
HelpIndex
```

See Also

Help
HelpContents

HelpKeyboard

Purpose

Displays help topics for keyboard and mouse
shortcuts.

Syntax

```
HelpKeyboard
```

HelpMSN

Purpose

Displays The Microsoft Network sign-in box to connect the user to a Word help forum there. (If the computer has already defined shortcuts to other areas of Microsoft Help on MSN, a dialog box appears first, asking where to go.)

Syntax

```
HelpMSN
```

See Also

HelpPSSHelp

HelpPSSHelp

Purpose

Displays Word support services Help.

Syntax

```
HelpPSSHelp
```

See Also

HelpMSN

HelpQuickPreview

Purpose

Starts Word's introductory tutorial.

Syntax

```
HelpQuickPreview
```

See Also

HelpExamplesAndDemos

HelpSearch

Purpose

Allows a keyword search in Help.

Syntax

```
HelpSearch
```

HelpTipOfTheDay

Purpose

Sets to display the Tip Of The Day dialog box when Word is started.

Syntax

```
HelpTipOfTheDay .StartupTips =
TipsOn
```

Parameters

TipsOn
: If 1, displays the Tip Of The Day dialog box when Word is started.

See Also

HelpTool

HelpTool

Purpose

Changes the mouse to a question mark, and allows context-sensitive help by clicking on an element of the Word screen.

Syntax

```
HelpTool
```

See Also

Help
HelpActiveWindow

HelpUsingHelp

Purpose

Displays a list of Help topics describing how to use Help.

Syntax

```
HelpUsingHelp
```

HelpWordPerfect Help

Purpose

Used with Dialog or Dialog() instruction, displays Help for WordPerfect Users dialog box.

Syntax

```
HelpWordPerfectHelp
```

HelpWordPerfect HelpOptions

Purpose

Sets options for WordPerfect Users Help.

Syntax

```
HelpWordPerfectHelpOptions .Attrib = value
```

Parameters

.Attrib:

.CommandKeyHelp= If 1, WP keystrokes used

.DocNavKeys = If 1, PgUp, PgDn, Home, End, ESC keys function as in WP

.MouseSimulation = If 1, Help controls mouse

.DemoGuidance = If 1, help text given during user prompts

.DemoSpeed = 0: Fast; 1: Medium; 2: Slow

.HelpType = 0: Help text; 1: Demonstration.

Hidden or Hidden()

Purpose

Adds or removes the hidden character format for the current selection.

Syntax

```
Hidden [Set]
```

or

```
x = Hidden()
```

Parameters

Set

Sets the type of case to change: omitted: Toggles hidden formatting.

0: Removes hidden formatting.
1: Sets hidden formatting.

Returns

-1: Part of the selection is hidden.
0: None of the selection is hidden.
1: All of the selection is hidden.

See Also

FormatFont

Highlight

Purpose

Highlights or removes highlighting from selected text

Syntax

```
Highlight
```

See Also

HighlightColor

HighlightColor or HighlightColor()

Purpose

Selects a highlight color for selected text, or reports the highlight color used by selected text that is already highlighted.

Syntax

```
HighlightColor (Color)
```

or

```
x = HighlightColor()
```

Parameters

Color

A number corresponding to the highlight color, as follows:

0	Auto color
1	Black
2	Blue
3	Cyan
4	Green
5	Magenta
6	Red
7	Yellow
8	White
9	Dark Blue
10	Cyan
11	Green
12	Magenta
13	Red
14	Yellow
15	Gray
16	Light Gray

Returns

-1: Text has varying highlight colors.
0: Text has no highlighting.
n: A number corresponding to the selected text's highlight color, from 1 to 16.

See Also

EditFindHighlight
EditReplaceHighlight
Highlight
ToolsOptionsRevisions

HLine

Purpose

Scrolls the active document horizontally (via the scroll arrow).

Syntax

```
HLine [Count]
```

Parameters

Count

The amount to scroll
omitted: One line to the right
<0: scrolls *Count* lines left.
>0: scrolls *Count* lines right.

See Also

HPage
HScroll
VLine

Hour()

Purpose

Returns a number corresponding to the hours of a serial number.

Syntax

```
x= Hour(SerNo)
```

Parameters

SerNo

A decimal representation of date, time, or both.

Returns

An integer between 0 and 23.

See Also

DateSerial()
Day()
Minute()
Month()
Now()
Second()
Today()
Weekday()
Year()

HPage

Purpose

Scrolls the active document horizontally (via the scroll bar).

Syntax

```
HPage [Count]
```

Parameters

Count

The amount to scroll omitted: One line to the right
<0: scrolls *Count* widths left
>0: scrolls *Count* widths right.

See Also

HLine
HScroll
VLine

HScroll or HScroll()

Purpose

Scrolls the active document horizontally by the given percentage of the document width.

Syntax

```
HScroll Percent
```

or

```
x = HScroll()
```

Parameters

Percent
An integer from 0 to 100.

Returns

The current horizontal scroll position as a percentage of the document width.

See Also

HLine
HPage
VScroll

If...Then...Else (ElseIf...End If)

Purpose

Conditionally executes instructions.

Syntax

```
If Condition Then CommandTrue Else
CommandFalse End If
```

Parameters

Condition
A statement that returns TRUE (not = 0) or FALSE (= 0).

CommandTrue
A command or series of commands executed if *Condition* is TRUE.

CommandFalse
A command or series of commands executed if *Condition* is FALSE.

See Also

For...Next
Goto
Select Case
While...Wend

Indent

Purpose

Moves the left indent of the selected paragraph(s) to the next tab stop.

Syntax

```
Indent
```

See Also

FormatParagraph
HangingIndent
UnIndent

Input

Purpose

Takes string or numeric values from an open sequential file or from user input.

Syntax

```
Input [#StreamNumber]or[Prompt$],
VariableList
```

Parameters

#StreamNumber
The number used in the Open statement; specifies the open file. The "#" must be included for Word to recognize this as a Stream Number and not a prompt.

Prompt$
A prompt appearing to the user in the status bar, followed by a question mark. The statement waits for user input in the status bar before continuing.

VariableList
The variable(s) to be filled from the file or user input.

Returns

String or numeric values taken from an open sequential file or from user input.

See Also

Close
Eof()
Input$()
InputBox$()
Line Input
Lof()
Open
Print
Read
Seek
Write

Input$()

Purpose

Reads characters from an open sequential file.

Syntax

```
x$ = Input$(NumChar,
[#]StreamNumber)
```

Parameters

NumChar
The number of characters to read from the file.

StreamNumber
The number used in the Open statement; specifies the open file.

Returns

A string of characters read from an open sequential file.

See Also

Close
Eof()
Input
InputBox$()
Line Input
Lof()
Open
Print
Read
Seek
Write

InputBox$()

Purpose

Posts a default dialog box for user input.

Syntax

```
x$ = InputBox$(Prompt$ [, Title$][,
Default$]))
```

Parameters

Prompt$
The prompt displayed in the dialog box.

Title$
The text displayed in the title bar of the dialog box.

Default$
The default text in the text box of the dialog box. Upon initiating the InputBox, the default text is highlighted.

Returns

The text within the text box of the dialog box when OK is chosen.

See Also

Begin Dialog...End Dialog
Input
MsgBox
On Error
Val()

Insert

Purpose

Inserts text at the insertion point of the active document.

Syntax

```
Insert Text$
```

Parameters

Text$
Text to insert

See Also

Chr$()
InsertPara
LTrim$()
Str$()

InsertAddCaption

Purpose

Adds a new caption label to the list.

Syntax

```
InsertAddCaption .Name = Label$
```

Parameters

Label$
The name for the new caption.

See Also

InsertAutoCaption
InsertCaption
InsertCaptionNumbering

InsertAddress

Purpose

Opens the default Microsoft Exchange Personal Address Book and inserts an address selected by the user into the current location in a Word document.

Syntax

```
InsertAddress
```

See Also

AddAddress
GetAddress$()
ToolsCreateEnvelope
ToolsCreateLabels

InsertAnnotation

Purpose

Inserts an annotation mark at the insertion point in the active document and opens the annotation pane for entry.

Syntax

```
InsertAnnotation
```

See Also

GoToAnnotationScope
InsertFootnote
ShowAnnotationBy
ViewAnnotations
WindowPane()

InsertAutoCaption

Purpose

Specifies a caption to automatically insert when a given type of object is inserted into the active document.

Syntax

```
InsertAutoCaption
[.Clear][,.ClearAll][,.Object =
```

```
ObjType$][,.Label =
Caption$][,.Position = CaptPos]
```

Parameters

ObjType$
The name of the object type to set AutoCaption.

Caption$
The caption to insert automatically.

CaptPos
Caption is placed:
0: Above; 1: Below item

See Also

InsertAddCaption
InsertCaption
InsertCaptionNumbering

InsertAutoText

Purpose

Attempts to insert an AutoText entry based on the current selection or text surrounding the insertion point.

Syntax

```
InsertAutoText
```

See Also

AutoText
AutoTextName$()
CountAutoTextEntries()
EditAutoText
GetAutoText
SetAutoText

InsertBreak

Purpose

Inserts a page, column, or section break at the insertion point in the active document.

Syntax

```
InsertBreak [.Type = BreakType]
```

Parameters

BreakType
The type of break to insert:
0 or omitted: Page break
1: Column break
2: Next Page Section break
3: Continuous Section break
4: Even Page Section break
5: Odd Page Section break

See Also

InsertColumnBreak
InsertPageBreak
InsertSectionBreak
ParaPageBreakBefore
TableSplit

InsertCaption

Purpose

Inserts a caption to an object.

Syntax

```
InsertCaption [.Label =
Label$][,.TitleAutoText =
AutoEntry$][,.Title =
```

```
Caption$][,.Delete][,.Position =
CaptPos]
```

Parameters

Label$
The caption label to insert.

AutoEntry$
The AutoText entry to insert after the label in the caption.

Caption$
The text to insert after the label in the caption (unless an *AutoEntry$* has been defined).

CaptPos
Caption is placed:
0: Above;
1: Below item

See Also

InsertAddCaption
InsertAutoCaption
InsertCaptionNumbering

InsertCaption Numbering

Purpose

Defines a format for numbering captions.

Syntax

```
InsertCaptionNumbering [.Label =
Label$][,.FormatNumber =
FormatNum][,.ChapterNumber =
ChaptNum][,.Level =
Level][,.Separator = Separator$]
```

Parameters

Label$
The caption label to define numbering.

FormatNum
Type of numbering:

0: 1, 2, 3, 4
1: a, b, c, d
2: A, B, C, D
3: i, ii, iii, iv
4: I, II, III, IV

ChaptNum
If 1, a chapter number is included in the caption.

Level
The heading level of the caption.

Separator$
The separator character between the chapter number and the caption sequence number.

See Also

InsertAddCaption
InsertAutoCaption
InsertCaption

InsertChart

Purpose

Starts Microsoft Graph for user editing to embed a chart in the active document.

Syntax

```
InsertChart
```

See Also

InsertDrawing
InsertExcelTable
InsertObject

InsertColumnBreak

Purpose

Inserts a column break at the insertion point.

Syntax

```
InsertColumnBreak
```

See Also

InsertBreak
InsertPageBreak
InsertSectionBreak
TableSplit

InsertCrossReference

Purpose

Inserts a cross-reference.

Syntax

```
InsertCrossReference [.ReferenceType
= RefType$][.ReferenceKind =
RefKind$][.ReferenceItem = RefItem$]
```

Parameters

RefType$

The type of item to insert a cross-reference.

RefKind$

The number of the cross-reference information to cross-reference to:

Heading:
0: Heading text
7: Page number
8: Heading number

Bookmark:
1: Bookmark text
7: Page number
9: Paragraph number

Footnote:
5: Footnote number
7: Page number

Endnote:
6: Endnote number
7: Page number

An Item:
2: Entire caption
3: Only label and number
4: Only caption text
7: Page number

RefItem$

The number of the cross-reference item referred to in the For Which Heading box.

See Also

InsertCaption

InsertDatabase

Purpose

Inserts data, read from a database, at the insertion point of the active document.

Syntax

```
InsertDatabase .Attrib = value
```

Parameters

.Attrib—

A database attribute:

.LinkToSource=	If 1, establishes a link
.Connection=	The connection string
.SQLStatement=	An SQL query string
.PasswordDoc=	The document password
.PasswordDot=	The template password
.DataSource=	Path/file name of the data source
From=	The first data record number
.To=	The last data record number
.Format=	The format list number
.Style=	The sum of the following: 0: None 1: Borders 2: Shading 4: Font 8: Color 16: Best Fit 32: Heading Rows 64: Last Row 128: First Column 256: Last Column
.IncludeFields	If 1, field names placed in the first row of new table

value

The information about that argument

Note: Descriptions in quotation marks indicate that the value is a string.

See Also

InsertExcelTable
MailMergeCreateDataSource

InsertDateField

Purpose

Inserts a Date field at the insertion point.

Syntax

```
InsertDateField
```

See Also

InsertDateTime
InsertField
InsertPageField
InsertTimeField

InsertDateTime

Purpose

Inserts a date and time field at the insertion point.

Syntax

```
InsertDateTime [.InsertAsField =
AsField][,.DateTimePic = Format$]
```

Parameters

AsField

Specifies insertion of TIME field:
omitted: Uses Insert|DateAndTime settings.
0: Inserts time as text.
1: Inserts time as TIME field.

Format$

Describes the format of the date and time to be inserted.

See Also

InsertDateField
InsertField
InsertPageField
InsertTimeField

InsertDrawing

Purpose

Starts Microsoft Draw for user editing to embed a drawing in the active document.

Syntax

```
InsertDrawing
```

See Also

InsertChart
InsertEquation
InsertExcelTable
InsertObject
InsertPicture
InsertSound
InsertWordArt

InsertEquation

Purpose

Starts Microsoft Equation for user editing to embed an equation in the active document.

Syntax

```
InsertEquation
```

See Also

InsertChart
InsertDrawing
InsertExcelTable
InsertObject
InsertWordArt

InsertExcelTable

Purpose

Starts Microsoft Excel for user editing to embed a spreadsheet in the active document.

Syntax

```
InsertExcelTable
```

See Also

InsertChart
InsertDrawing
InsertDatabase
InsertObject
InsertWordArt

InsertField

Purpose

Inserts a field at the insertion point.

Syntax

```
InsertField .Field = FieldStmt$
```

Parameters

FieldStmt$
The specific field to insert

See Also

InsertFieldChars

InsertFieldChars

Purpose

Inserts field characters at the insertion point. The insertion point is left positioned between the field characters.

Syntax

```
InsertFieldChars
```

See Also

InsertField

InsertFile

Purpose

Inserts the contents of a file at the insertion point.

Syntax

```
InsertFile .Name = FileName$
[,.Range =
Range$][,.ConfirmConversions =
Conv][,.Link = LinkNum]
```

Parameters

FileName$
The path and file name to insert

Range$
A bookmark in the file to insert or a range of cells in a spreadsheet

Conv
If 1, displays the Convert File dialog box if necessary

LinkNum
If 1, inserts an INCLUDETEXT field instead of the file contents

See Also

InsertDatabase
InsertField

InsertFootnote

Purpose

Inserts a footnote or endnote reference mark at the insertion point and opens the footnote or endnote pane for editing.

Syntax

```
InsertFootnote [.Reference = RefMark$][,.NoteType = NoteType]
```

Parameters

RefMark$
A custom reference mark

NoteType
The type of note to insert:
omitted: The most recently inserted type
0: Footnote
1: Endnote

See Also

InsertAnnotation
NoteOptions
ViewFootnoteArea
ViewFootnotes

InsertFormField

Purpose

Inserts a form field at the insertion point.

Syntax

```
InsertFormField .Attrib = value
```

Parameters

.Attrib—A form field attribute:

.Entry=	The macro that runs when the form field receives focus
Exit=	The macro that runs when the form field loses focus
.Name=	Name of bookmark marking form field
.Enable=	If 1, allows form field to be changed
.TextType=	Specifies the type: 0: Regular Text 1: Number 2: Date 3: Current Date 4: Current Time 5: Calculation
.TextDefault=	The default text
.TextWidth=	0: Unlimited; >*0*: Maximum width
.TextFormat=	Uppercase Lowercase First Capital Title Case
.CheckSize=	0: Auto size; 1: Exact size
.CheckWidth=	If 1, width is as specified

.CheckDefault=	Default 0: Cleared; 1: Selected
.Type=	Type of form field 0: Text 1: Check box 2: Drop-down
.OwnHelp=	If 1, enables .HelpText
.HelpText=	Custom help text
.OwnStat=	If 1, enables .StatText
.StatText=	Custom status bar text

value
The information about that argument.

Note: Descriptions in quotation marks indicate that the value is a string.

See Also

AddDropDownItem
CheckBoxFormField
DropDownFormField
EnableFormField
FormFieldOptions
RemoveAllDropDownItems
RemoveDropDownItem
TextFormField

InsertFrame

Purpose

Inserts an empty frame at the insertion point or frames the selected object.

Syntax

```
InsertFrame
```

See Also

FormatFrame
RemoveFrames

InsertIndex

Purpose

Compiles and inserts an index at the insertion point.

Syntax

```
InsertIndex .Attrib = value
```

Parameters

.Attrib—An index attribute:

.HeadingSeparator=	0 or omitted: None 1: Blank line 2: Letter
.Replace=	Governs replacing existing index 0: Do not replace 1: Replace existing index
.Type=	Type of index: 0 or omitted: Indented 1: Run-in
.RightAlignPageNumbers=	If 1, aligns page numbers with the right edge of column

.Columns=	Number of columns in index

value
The information about that argument.

Note: Descriptions in quotation marks indicate that the value is a string.

See Also

AutoMarkIndexEntries
MarkIndexEntry

InsertMergeField

Purpose

Inserts a MERGEFIELD at the insertion point.

Syntax

```
InsertMergeField .MergeField = Field$
```

Parameters

Field$
A merge field name.

See Also

InsertField
MailMergeInsertAsk
MailMergeInsertFillin
MailMergeInsertIf
MailMergeInsertMergeRec
MailMergeInsertMergeSeq
MailMergeInsertNext
MailMergeInsertNextIf
MailMergeInsertSet
MailMergeInsertSkipIf

InsertObject

Purpose

Starts an OLE application for user editing, and inserts an EMBED field at the insertion point.

Syntax

```
InsertObject .Attrib = value
```

Parameters

.Attrib—An object attribute:

.IconNumber=	The list number of the icon
.FileName=	The object path and file name
.Link=	If 1, create link .DisplayIcon= 0: Link not displayed as icon 1: Link displayed as icon
.Tab=	Tab to select in custom dialog: 0: Create New tab 1: Create From File tab
.Class=	Class name of new object
.IconFilename=	Icon path and file name
.Caption=	Caption of icon

value
The information about that argument.

Note: Descriptions in quotation marks indicate that the value is a string.

See Also

ActivateObject
EditObject
InsertChart
InsertDrawing
InsertExcelTable

InsertPageBreak

Purpose

Inserts page break at insertion point.

Syntax

```
InsertPageBreak
```

See Also

InsertBreak
InsertColumnBreak
InsertSectionBreak
ParaPageBreakBefore
TableSplit

InsertPageField

Purpose

Inserts a PAGE field at the insertion point.

Syntax

```
InsertPageField
```

See Also

InsertDateField
InsertField
InsertPageNumbers
InsertTimeField

InsertPageNumbers

Purpose

Inserts a PAGE field inside a frame in the header or footer.

Syntax

```
InsertPageNumbers [.Type = HeadFoot][,.Position = NumPos][,.FirstPage = FirstPage]
```

Parameters

HeadFoot
Where to add:
0: Header; 1: Footer

NumPos
Position of framed PAGE field:
0: Left
1: Center
2: Right
3: Inside
4: Outside

FirstPage
If 1, field included on first page.

See Also

FormatPageNumber
InsertPageField
ViewHeader
ViewFooter

InsertPara

Purpose

Inserts a paragraph mark at the insertion point. Preferred over `Insert Chr$()` characters to break paragraphs.

Syntax

```
InsertPara
```

See Also

Chr$()
Insert

InsertPicture

Purpose

Inserts a graphic object at the insertion point.

Syntax

```
InsertPicture .Name = PicName$
[,.LinkToFile = Link][,.New]
```

Parameters

PicName$
The path and file name of the graphic.

Link
Governs insertion:
0 or omitted: Inserts graphic
1: Inserts INCLUDEPICTURE field and saves graphic in document
2: Inserts INCLUDEPICTURE field and prevents saving graphic in document

New
Inserts a default graphic, surrounded by a border.

See Also

InsertDrawing
InsertFile
InsertObject

InsertSectionBreak

Purpose

Inserts section break with formatting identical to the section where the insertion point is.

Syntax

```
InsertSection
```

See Also

InsertBreak
InsertColumnBreak
InsertPageBreak

InsertSound

Purpose

Starts Sound Recorder for user editing to embed a sound in the active document.

Syntax

```
InsertSound
```

See Also

InsertChart
InsertDrawing
InsertExcelTable
InsertObject

InsertSpike

Purpose

Inserts contents of the Spike at the insertion point and clears the Spike. The Spike is a special AutoText entry.

Syntax

```
InsertSpike
```

See Also

EditAutoText
InsertAutoText
Spike

InsertSubdocument

Purpose

Inserts a file as a subdocument at the insertion point.

Syntax

```
InsertSubdocument .Name = FileName$
[,.ConfirmConversions =
Confirm][,.ReadOnly = ReadOnly]
[,.PasswordDoc =
DocPass$][,.PasswordDot =
DotPass$][,.Revert =
Revert][,.WritePasswordDoc =
DocPassWr$][,.WritePasswordDot =
DotPassWr$]
```

Parameters

FileName$
The name of the file to open

Confirm
1: displays the Convert File dialog.

ReadOnly
1: opened read-only, 0: opened for writing.

DocPass$
The document password.

DotPass$
The template password.

Revert
If *FileName$* is open,
0: the open document is activated
1: closes the document (no save), and reopens it

DocPassWr$
The document write-protect password.

DotPassWr$
The template write-protect password.

See Also

CreateSubdocument
FileOpen
MergeSubdocument
OpenSubdocument
RemoveSubdocument
SplitSubdocument
ViewMasterDocument

InsertSymbol

Purpose

Inserts a symbol at the insertion point. (This is different from Word 2.0 InsertSymbol functionality.)

Syntax

```
InsertSymbol .Font = SymFont$,
.CharNum = Char
```

Parameters

SymFont$
The name of the symbol's font.

Char
The position of the symbol in the table of symbols.

See Also

Chr$()

InsertTableOf Authorities

Purpose

Inserts a Table of Authorities field at the insertion point, and collects all Table of Authorities Entry field contents.

Syntax

```
InsertTableOfAuthorities [.Replace =
Replace][,.Passim =
Passim][,.KeepFormatting =
Format][,.Category = Cat]
```

Parameters

Replace
Replace previous TOA:
0: Do not replace.
1: Replace existing TOA.

Passim
If 1, five or more different page refs to the same authority are replaced with "passim".

Format
If 1, document formatting is kept in TOA.

Cat
The type of citations to collect.

See Also

InsertTableOfContents
InsertTableOfFigures
MarkCitation

InsertTableOf Contents

Purpose

Inserts a Table of Contents field at the insertion point and collects all heading entries or Table of Contents Entry field contents.

Syntax

```
InsertTableOfContents .Attrib =
value
```

Parameters

.Attrib—A form field attribute:

.Outline=	If 1, collects from headings
.Fields=	If 1, collects from TC fields
.From=	Highest level of heading style
.To=	Lowest level of heading style
.TableId=	TC field entry identifier
.AddedStyles=	Styles to collect in addition to the heading styles

.Replace=
Governs replacement of existing TOC:
0 or omitted: Not replaced
1: Existing TOC replaced

.RightAlignPageNumbers=
If 1, aligns page numbers with right margin.

value
The information about that argument.

Note: Descriptions in quotation marks indicate that the value is a string.

See Also

InsertTableOfAuthorities
InsertTableOfFigures
MarkTableOfContentsEntry

InsertTableOfFigures

Purpose

Inserts a Table of Figures field at the insertion point and collects all captions with a given label.

Syntax

```
InsertTableOfFigures [.Caption =
Caption$][,.Label =
LabelNum][,.RightAlignPageNumbers =
PageNum][,.Replace = Replace]
```

Parameters

Caption$
The label identifying the items.

LabelNum
If 1, includes labels and sequence numbers.

PageNum
If 1, aligns page numbers with right margin.

Replace
Governs replacement of existing TOF:
0 or omitted: Not replaced.
1: Existing TOF is replaced.

See Also

InsertAutoCaption
InsertCaption
InsertTableOfAuthorities
InsertTableOfContents

InsertTimeField

Purpose

Inserts a TIME field at the insertion point.

Syntax

```
InsertTimeField
```

See Also

InsertDateField
InsertDateTime
InsertField
InsertPageField

InsertWordArt

Purpose

Starts Microsoft WordArt for user editing to embed a WordArt object in the active document.

Syntax

```
InsertWordArt
```

See Also

ActivateObject
EditObject
InsertChart
InsertDrawing
InsertEquation
InsertExcelTable
InsertObject

InStr()

Purpose

Finds a substring within a string.

Syntax

```
x = InStr([Index,] Source$, Search$)
```

Parameters

Index
The character position within *Source$* at which to begin the search.

Source$
The string to be searched.

Search$
The string to find within *Source$*.

Returns

The position of the first character of the search string within the source string.

See Also

Left$()
Len()
LTrim$()
Mid$()
Right$()
RTrim$()

Int()

Purpose

Returns the integer portion of a number.

Syntax

```
x = Int(number)
```

Parameters

number
Any positive or negative value or function that results in a positive or negative value; Value must be between -32,769 and +32,768.

Returns

An integer.

See Also

Abs()
Rnd()
Sgn()

IsAutoCorrect Exception()

Purpose

Returns 1 if a text string is in the list of AutoCorrect exceptions; otherwise returns 0.

Syntax

```
x =
IsAutoCorrectException(Tab,Exception$)
```

Parameters

Tab
The exception tab Word searches for the text you specify
0: First letter
1: INitial CAps

Exception$
The text of the exception you are looking for.

Returns

-1: The text you specified appeared on the exception list you specified.
0: The text you specified did not appear on the exception list you specified.

See Also

CountAutoCorrectExceptions()
GetAutoCorrectException$()
ToolsAutoCorrectExceptions

IsCustomDocument Property()

Purpose

Checks whether a Property is a custom property.

Syntax

```
IsCustomDocumentProperty(Name$)
```

Parameters

Name$
The Property name you want to check.

Returns

1: Property is custom.
2: Property is not custom or does not exist.

See Also

CountDocumentProperties()
DocumentPropertyExists()
DocumentPropertyType()
IsDocumentPropertyReadOnly()

IsCustomPropertyReadOnly()

Purpose

Returns 1 if a property you specify is read-only; otherwise returns 0.

Syntax

```
x = IsCustomPropertyReadOnly(Name$,
CustomOrBuiltIn)
```

Parameters

Name$
The property's name.

CustomOrBuiltIn:
0 (or omitted): Custom property unless appearing on the list of built-in properties
1: Built-in property
2: Custom property, even if a built-in property with the same name exists

Returns

1: Property is read-only.
0: Property is not read-only.
Error: Name$ is not a valid property.

See Also

DocumentPropertyExists()
DocumentPropertyName$()
DocumentPropertyType()
IsCustomDocumentProperty()

IsDocumentDirty()

Purpose

Indicates whether the active document has been changed since last save. (This command was renamed from IsDirty in Word 2.0.)

Syntax

```
x = IsDocumentDirty()
```

Returns

TRUE (-1): Document has changed since last save.
FALSE (0): Document has not changed since last save.

See Also

IsTemplateDirty()
SetDocumentDirty
SetTemplateDirty

IsExecuteOnly()

Purpose

Indicates whether a macro is execute-only.

Syntax

```
x = IsExecuteOnly([MacroName$])
```

Parameters

MacroName$
The name of a macro to check. If omitted, the active macro is assumed.

Returns

TRUE (-1): Macro is execute-only.
FALSE (0): Macro is not execute-only.

See Also

IsMacro()
MacroCopy

IsMacro()

Purpose

Indicates whether a window is a macro editing window.

Syntax

```
x = IsMacro([WindowNum])
```

Parameters

WindowNum
Specifies a window in the Window menu to check.

Returns

TRUE (-1): Window is a macro editing window.
FALSE (0): Window is not a macro editing window.

See Also

IsExecuteOnly
MacroFileName$()
MacroNameFromWindows
SelInfo()

IsTemplateDirty()

Purpose

Indicates whether the active template has been changed since last save.

Syntax

```
x = IsTemplateDirty()
```

Returns

TRUE (-1): Template has changed since last save.
FALSE (0): Template has not changed since last save.

See Also

IsDocumentDirty()
SaveTemplate
SetDocumentDirty
SetTemplateDirty

Italic or Italic()

Purpose

Converts the selection to all italic letters or removes the italic formatting from the selection.

Syntax

```
Italic [Action]
```

or

```
x = Italic()
```

Parameters

Action

1: Formats the selection
0: Removes italic formatting from selection.
omitted: Toggles italic formatting.

Returns

-1: Only part of the selection is in italic format.
0: None of the selection is in italic format.
1: All the selection is in italic format.

See Also

FormatFont

JustifyPara or JustifyPara()

Purpose

Justifies the paragraphs selected, or returns their justification.

Syntax

```
JustifyPara
```

or

```
x = JustifyPara()
```

Returns

-1: Only part of the selection is justi fied.
0: None of the selection is justified.
1: All the selection is justified.

See Also

CenterPara
FormatParagraph
LeftPara
RightPara

KeyCode()

Purpose

Returns a number representing a key assignment. This is given only if the assignment differs from the default assignment.

Syntax

```
x = KeyCode(Count [, Context][,
FirstOrSecond)
```

Parameters

Count
The key code.

Context
0 or omitted: Normal template;
1: Active template

FirstOrSecond
Specifies the key combination to return a code:
1: The first key combination in the sequence
2: The second key combination in the sequence

Returns

A number representing a key assignment different from the default key assignment.

See Also

CountKeys()
KeyMacro$()

KeyMacro$()

Purpose

Returns the name of a macro or command having a key assignment. This is given only if the assignment differs from the default assignment.

Syntax

```
x$ = KeyMacro$(Count [, Context])
```

Parameters

Count
The key code.

Context
0 or omitted: Normal template
1: Active template

Returns

The name of a macro or comment having a key assignment different from the default key assignment.

See Also

CountKeys()
KeyCode
MenuItemMacro$()

Kill

Purpose

Deletes a file.

Syntax

```
Kill FileName$
```

Parameters

FileName$
The path and file name to delete.

See Also

CopyFile

Language or Language$()

Purpose

Identifies the selection as a specific language.

Syntax

```
Language LangName$
```

or

```
x$ = Language$([Count])
```

Parameters

LangName$
A valid language.

Count
The list number of the language.

Returns

If *Count* = 0, returns the language format of the first character of the selection.
If *Count* > 0, returns the name of the language indicated by *Count*.

See Also

CountLanguages()
ToolsLanguage

LCase$()

Purpose

Converts a string to all lowercase.

Syntax

```
x$ = LCase$(string$)
```

Parameters

string$
Any string variable or function that results in a string.

Returns

string$: As all lowercase letters.

See Also

ChangeCase
UCase$()

Left$()

Purpose

Returns the leftmost portion of a string.

Syntax

```
x$ = Left$(string$, Length)
```

Parameters

string$
Any string variable or function that results in a string.

Length
The number of characters to return, counting from the beginning of the string.

Returns

The leftmost *Length* characters of *string$*.

See Also

InStr()
Len()
LTrim$()
Mid$()
Right$()
RTrim$()

LeftPara or LeftPara()

Purpose

Aligns the selected paragraph(s) with the left indent.

Syntax

```
LeftPara
```

or

```
x = LeftPara()
```

Returns

-1: Only part of the selection is Left-justified.
0: None of the selection is Left-justified.
1: All the selection is Left-justified.

See Also

CenterPara
FormatParagraph
JustifyPara
RightPara

Len()

Purpose

Returns the length of a string.

Syntax

```
x = Len(string$)
```

Parameters

string$
Any string variable or function that results in a string.

Returns

The length of a given string.

See Also

InStr()
Left$()
LTrim$()
Mid$()
Right$()
RTrim$()

Let

Purpose

Assigns a value to a variable. (Let is optional.)

Syntax

```
[Let] Variable = Expression
```

Parameters

Variable
Any single or array variable.

Expression
Any value or function that results in a value.

See Also

Dim

Line Input

Purpose

Reads a line from an open file.

Syntax

```
Line Input
[#StreamNumber]or[Prompt$],
Variable$
```

Parameters

#StreamNumber
The number used in the Open statement; specifies the open file. The "#" must be included for Word to recognize this as a stream number and not a prompt.

Prompt$
A prompt appearing to the user in the status bar, followed by a question mark. The statement waits for user input in the status bar before continuing.

Variable
The variable to be filled from the file or user input.

Returns

A string taken from an open sequential file or from user input.

See Also

Close
Eof()
Input()
Input$()
Lof()
Open
Print
Read
Seek
Write

LineDown or LineDown()

Purpose

Moves the insertion point down in the active document.

Syntax

```
LineDown [Count][, Select]
```

or

```
x = LineDown ([Count] [, Select])
```

Parameters

Count
The number of lines to move down. If this is omitted, *Count* = 1 is assumed.

Select
How to select text:
0 or omitted: Move without extending selection.
nonzero: Extend selection *Count* lines down.

Returns

-1: LineDown was partially or fully successful.
0: LineDown failed.

See Also

LineUp
ParaDown
ParaUp

LineUp or LineUp()

Purpose

Moves the insertion point up in the active document.

Syntax

```
LineUp [Count][, Select]
```

or

```
x = LineUp ([Count] [, Select])
```

Parameters

Count
The number of lines to move up. If this is omitted, *Count* = 1 is assumed.

Select
How to select text:
0 or omitted: Move without extending selection.
nonzero: Extend selection *Count* lines up.

Returns

-1: LineUp was partially or fully successful.
0: LineUp failed.

See Also

LineDown
ParaDown
ParaUp

ListBox

Purpose

Defines a list box within a dialog box definition.

Syntax

```
ListBox X, Y, dX, dY, Array$(),
.Identifier
```

Parameters

X, Y
The coordinates of the upper left corner of the list box, relative to

the upper left corner of the dialog box, measured in fractions of the system font size.

dX, dY
: The width and height of the list box and its associated text, measured in fractions of the system font size.

Array$()
: A string array containing the text entries to be listed in the list box.

.Identifier
: A control extension used to set or access the value of the list box from outside of the dialog box definition.

Returns

When the dialog containing the list box is accessed by the syntax `x$ = Dialog.Identifier`, the value returned is the string selected in the list box.

See Also

Begin Dialog...End Dialog
ComboBox
Dialog
Dim
DlgListBoxArray
DropListBox

LockDocument or LockDocument()

Purpose

Adds or removes read-only protection for a master document or subdocument.

Syntax

```
LockDocument[Lock]
```

or

```
LockDocument()
```

Parameters

Lock:
: Value specifying whether document is to be locked
: 0: Removes read-only protection (if you remove read-only protection for a master document, all subdocuments are also unlocked)
: 1: Adds read-only protection
: Omitted: Toggles read-only protection

Returns

LockDocument()returns:
-1: Document is read-only.
0: Document is not read-only.

See Also

ToolsProtectDocument
ToolsProtectSection
ToolsUnprotectDocument

LockFields

Purpose

Prevents a field(s) from being updated.

Syntax

```
LockFields
```

See Also

UnlinkFields
UnlockFields
UpdateFields

Lof()

Purpose

Returns the length in bytes of the open sequential file.

Syntax

```
x = Lof([#]StreamNumber)
```

Parameters

StreamNumber
The number used in the Open statement; specifies the open file.

Returns

The length in bytes of the open sequential file.

See Also

Close
Eof()
Input()
Input$()
Line Input
Open
Print
Read
Seek
Write

LTrim$()

Purpose

Removes leading spaces from a string.

Syntax

```
x$ = LTrim$(string$)
```

Parameters

string$
Any string variable or function that results in a string.

Returns

string$ without leading spaces.

See Also

InStr()
Left$()
Mid$()
Right$()
RTrim$()

MacroCopy

Purpose

Copies one macro to another; can be used to copy macros between different templates.

Syntax

```
MacroCopy MacroName1$, MacroName2$
[, ExecuteOnly]
```

Parameters

MacroName1$
The name of the macro to copy from. This can indicate a different template by using the form `TemplateName.MacroName`.

MacroName2$
The name of the macro to copy to. This can indicate a different template by using the form `TemplateName.MacroName`.

ExecuteOnly
If 1, makes the copy into execute only; the copy cannot be edited. Note: the ExecuteOnly feature cannot be reversed.

See Also

IsExecuteOnly()

MacroDesc$()

Purpose

Returns the description of a macro.

Syntax

```
x$ = MacroDesc$(MacroName$)
```

Parameters

MacroName$
The name of the macro. This can indicate a different template by using the form `TemplateName.MacroName`.

Returns

The description associated with the given macro.

See Also

CountMacros()
KeyMacro$()
MacroName$()
MenuItemMacro$()
ToolsMacro

MacroFileName$()

Purpose

Returns the path and file name of the template containing a macro.

Syntax

```
x$ = MacroFileName$(MacroName$)
```

Parameters

MacroName$
The name of the macro. This can indicate a different template by using the form `TemplateName.MacroName`.

Returns

The path and file name of the template containing the given macro.

See Also

MacroDesc$()
MacroName$()
MacroNameFromWindow$()

MacroName$()

Purpose

Returns the name of a macro.

Syntax

```
MacroName$(Count [, Context][,
All][, Global])
```

Parameters

Count
The list number of the desired macro.

Context
0: Normal template; 1: Active template.

All
If 1, all available macros and commands are listed.

Global
If 1, only global macros and add-ins are listed.

Returns

The the name of the given macro.

See Also

CountMacros()

MacroName FromWindows$()

Purpose

Returns the name of the macro currently in an editing window.

Syntax

```
MacroNameFromWindows$ (WindowNum)
```

Parameters

WindowNum
The list number of the window, as listed in the Window menu.

Returns

The name of the macro currently in the given editing window.

See Also

IsMacro()
MacroFileName$()
MacroName$()

Magnifier or Magnifier()

Purpose

Toggles the mouse pointer between the standard pointer and a magnifying glass in print preview.

Syntax

```
Magnifier [On]
```

or

```
x = Magnifier()
```

Parameters

On:

omitted: Toggles the mouse pointer.
0: Displays the standard pointer.
1: Displays the magnifying glass pointer.

Returns

TRUE (-1): Pointer is a magnifying glass.
FALSE (0): Pointer is the standard pointer.

See Also

FilePrintPreview
ViewZoom

MailCheckNames

Purpose

Checks the addresses in an active WordMail message. (Available only if Microsoft Exchange is installed.)

Syntax

```
MailCheckNames
```

See Also

MailHideMessageHeader
MailSelectNames

MailHide MessageHeader

Purpose

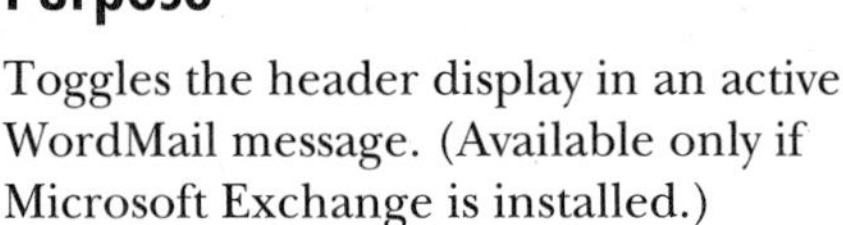

Toggles the header display in an active WordMail message. (Available only if Microsoft Exchange is installed.)

Syntax

```
MailHideMessageHeader
```

See Also

MailCheckNames
MailSelectNames

MailMerge

Purpose

Sets options for mail merge, and/or merges main document with data.

Syntax

```
MailMerge .Attrib = value
```

Parameters

.Attrib—A mail merge attribute:

.CheckErrors=	How to check and report errors: 0: Simulates merge, reports errors in a new document 1: Performs merge, reports errors interactively 2: Performs merge, reports errors in a new document
.Destination=	Where to send merged documents: 0: New document 1: Printer 2: Electronic mail 3: Fax
.MergeRecords=	Merge all or a subset: 0: Merges all records 1: Merges a range of data
.From=	Number of first record to merge
.To=	Number of last record to merge
.Suppression=	How to print empty fields: 0: Not print blank lines 1: Print blank lines
.MailMerge=	Performs mail merge
.MailSubject=	Subject text (for e-mail)
.MailAsAttachment=	If 1, sends merged as attach.
.MailAddress=	Name of field with address

value
The information about that argument.

Note: Descriptions in quotation marks indicate that the value is a string.

See Also

MailMergeCheck
MailMergeQueryOptions
MailMergeToDoc
MailMergeToPrinter

MailMergeAskToConvertChevrons or MailMergeAskToConvertChevrons()

Purpose

Asks to convert text enclosed by chevrons (from a Word for Macintosh document) into merge fields.

Syntax

```
MailMergeAskToConvertChevrons
[Prompt]
```

or

```
x = MailMergeAskToConvertChevrons()
```

Parameters

Prompt
omitted: Toggles display prompt option
0: Does not prompt
1: Prompts to convert

Returns

TRUE (-1): Option set to display prompt.
FALSE (0): Option set to not prompt.

See Also

MailMergeConvertChevrons

MailMergeCheck

Purpose

Check for errors in mail merging.

Syntax

```
MailMergeCheck .CheckErrors = Action
```

Parameters

Action
Governs performing a mail merge when error checking:
0: Simulates merge, reports errors in a new document
1: Performs merge, reports errors interactively
2: Performs merge, reports errors in a new document

See Also

MailMerge

MailMergeConvert Chevrons()

Purpose

Sets conversion of text enclosed by chevrons (from a Word for Macintosh document) into merge fields.

Syntax

```
MailMergeConvertChevrons [Convert]
```

or

```
x = MailMergeConvertChevrons()
```

Parameters

Prompt
omitted: Toggles conversion option
0: Does not convert chevrons
1: Sets option to convert chevrons

Returns

TRUE (-1): Option set to convert chevrons.
FALSE (0): Option set to not convert chevrons.

See Also

MailMergeAskToConvertChevrons

MailMerge CreateDataSource

Purpose

Creates a Word document to store data for a mail merge.

Syntax

```
MailMergeCreateDataSource .Attrib =
value
```

Parameters

.Attrib—A database attribute:

.FileName=	Path/file name of new data source
.PasswordDoc=	The data source password
.HeaderRecord=	Field names for header
.MSQuery=	Uses MSQuery to retrieve data
.SQLStatement=	An SQL query string
.Connection=	The connection string
.LinkToSource=	If 1, establishes a link

value
The information about that argument.

Note: Descriptions in quotation marks indicate that the value is a string.

See Also

MailMergeCreateHeaderSource
MailMergeEditDataSource
MailMergeOpenDataSource

MailMerge CreateHeaderSource

Purpose

Creates a Word document to store a header record for a mail merge. This header record supersedes the header in the data source.

Syntax

```
MailMergeCreateHeaderSource .Attrib
= value
```

Parameters

.Attrib—A database attribute:

.FileName =	Path/file name of new header source
.PasswordDoc =	The header source password
.HeaderRecord=	Field names for header

See Also

MailMergeCreateDataSource
MailMergeEditDataSource
MailMergeOpenDataSource

MailMergeDataForm

Purpose

Enables user entry of a new mail merge data record through the Data Form dialog box.

Syntax

```
MailMergeDataForm
```

See Also

MailMergeEditDataSource

MailMerge DataSource$()

Purpose

Returns information about the mail merge data source and other data.

Syntax

```
x = MailMergeDataSource$(Type)
```

Parameters

Type

0: The path/file name of the data source
1: The path/file name of the header source
2: A number indicating how data is supplied
3: A number indicating how header is supplied
4: The connection string for data source
5: The SQL query string

Returns

A string, or the following for Type = 2 or Type = 3:
0: From Word document or Word file converter
1: DDE from Microsoft Access
2: DDE from Microsoft Excel
3: DDE from Microsoft Query
4: Open Database Connectivity (ODBC)

See Also

MailMergeCreateDataSource
MailMergeEditDataSource
MailMergeOpenDataSource

MailMerge EditDataSource

Purpose

Enables editing of the mail merge data source in its native application.

Syntax

```
MailMergeEditDataSource
```

See Also

MailMergeCreateDataSource
MailMergeEditMainDocument
MailMergeOpenDataSource

MailMergeEdit HeaderSource

Purpose

Enables editing of the mail merge header source document.

Syntax

```
MailMergeEditHeaderSource
```

See Also

MailMergeCreateHeaderSource
MailMergeEditDataSource
MailMergeOpenHeaderSource

MailMergeEdit MainDocument

Purpose

Enables editing of the mail merge main document.

Syntax

```
MailMergeEditMainDocument
```

See Also

MailMergeEditDataSource

MailMergeFindRecord

Purpose

Finds the first data record matching the given text, and displays its associated merge document.

Syntax

```
MailMergeFindRecord .Find = SearchText$, .Field = FieldName$
```

Parameters

SearchText$
Text to find

FieldName$
Specifies a field name to limit the search

See Also

MailMergeFirstRecord
MailMergeFoundRecord()
MailMergeGotoRecord
MailMergeLastRecord
MailMergeNextRecord
MailMergePrevRecord
MailMergeViewData

MailMergeFirstRecord

Purpose

Displays the associated merge document for the first data record in a main document.

Syntax

```
MailMergeFirstRecord
```

See Also

MailMergeFindRecord
MailMergeGotoRecord
MailMergeLastRecord
MailMergeNextRecord
MailMergePrevRecord
MailMergeViewData

MailMerge FoundRecord()

Purpose

Indicates the success of the most recent MailMergeFindRecord.

Syntax

```
x = MailMergeFoundRecord()
```

Returns

TRUE (-1): MailMergeFindRecord was successful.
FALSE (0): MailMergeFindRecord was not successful.

See Also

MailMergeFindRecord

MailMerge GotoRecord or MailMerge GotoRecord()

Purpose

Displays the associated merge document for a given data record in a main document.

Syntax

```
MailMergeGotoRecord RecNumber
```

or

```
x = MailMergeGotoRecord()
```

Parameters

RecNumber
The position of the record in the query result (not necessarily the position of the record in the data source).

Returns

The number of the data record currently displayed.

See Also

MailMergeFindRecord
MailMergeFirstRecord

MailMergeLastRecord
MailMergeNextRecord
MailMergePrevRecord
MailMergeViewData

MailMergeHelper

Purpose

Displays a dialog box to assist in mail merging; used with custom-designed dialog boxes.

Syntax

```
MailMergeHelper
```

See Also

MailMerge

MailMergeInsertAsk

Purpose

Inserts an Ask field at the insertion point.

Syntax

```
MailMergeInsertAsk .Name =
BookmarkName$ [,.Prompt =
Prompt$][,.DefaultBookmarkText =
DefText$][,.AskOnce = Ask]
```

Parameters

BookmarkName$
The name of the bookmark to assign to the entered text.

Prompt$
The dialog box prompt.

DefText$
The default text in the dialog box.

Ask
If 1, user is prompted only at beginning of merge. If 0, user is prompted at each data record.

See Also

InsertField
MailMergeInsertFillin
MailMergeInsertSet

MailMergeInsertFillin

Purpose

Inserts a Fillin field at the insertion point.

Syntax

```
MailMergeInsertFillin [,.Prompt =
Prompt$] [,.DefaultFillinText =
DefText$][,.AskOnce = Ask]
```

Parameters

Prompt$
The dialog box prompt.

DefText$
The default text in the dialog box.

Ask
If 1, user is prompted only at beginning of merge. If 0, user is prompted at each data record.

See Also

InsertField
MailMergeInsertAsk
MailMergeInsertSet

MailMergeInsertIf

Purpose

Inserts an IF field at the insertion point.

Syntax

```
MailMergeInsertIf .Attrib = value
```

Parameters

.Attrib—A mail merge attribute:

.MergeField=	Name of the merge field to compare
.Comparison=	Comparison operator: 0: = 1: <> 2: < 3: > 4: <= 5: >= 6: = "" 7: <> ""
.CompareTo=	Compare to merge field
.TrueAutoText=	AutoText to insert if True
.TrueText=	Text to insert if True
.FalseAutoText=	AutoText to insert if False
.FalseText=	Text to insert if False

value
The information about that argument.

Note: Descriptions in quotation marks indicate that the value is a string.

See Also

InsertField
MailMergeInsertNext
MailMergeInsertNextIf
MailMergeInsertSkipIf

MailMerge InsertMergeRec

Purpose

Inserts a MERGEREC field at the insertion point.

Syntax

```
MailMergeInsertMergeRec
```

See Also

InsertField
MailMergeInsertMergeSeq

MailMerge InsertMergeSeq

Purpose

Inserts a MERGESEQ field at the insertion point.

Syntax

```
MailMergeInsertMergeSeq
```

See Also

InsertField
MailMergeInsertMergeRec

MailMerge InsertNext

Purpose

Inserts a NEXT field at the insertion point.

Syntax

```
MailMergeInsertNext
```

See Also

InsertField
MailMergeInsertNextIf

MailMerge InsertNextIf

Purpose

Inserts a NEXTIF field at the insertion point.

Syntax

```
MailMergeInsertNextIf .Attrib = value
```

Parameters

.Attrib—A mail merge attribute:

.MergeField=	Name of merge field to compare
.Comparison=	Comparison operator: 0: = 1: <> 2: < 3: > 4: <= 5: >= 6: = " " 7: <> " "
.CompareTo=	Compare to merge field

See Also

InsertField
MailMergeInsertIf
MailMergeInsertNext
MailMergeInsertSkipIf

MailMergeInsertSet

Purpose

Inserts a SET field at the insertion point.

Syntax

```
MailMergeInsertSet .Attrib = value
```

Parameters

.Attrib—A mail merge attribute:

.Name=	Name of bookmark to define
.ValueText=	Text to which to assign bookmark
.ValueAutoText=	AutoText to which to assign bookmark

See Also

InsertField
MailMergeInsertAsk
MailMergeInsertFillin

MailMerge InsertSkipIf

Purpose

Inserts a SKIPIF field at the insertion point.

Syntax

```
MailMergeInsertSkipIf .Attrib = value
```

Parameters

.Attrib—A mail merge attribute:

.MergeField=	Name of merge field to compare
.Comparison=	Comparison operator: 0: = 1: <> 2: < 3: > 4: <= 5: >= 6: = "" 7: <> ""
.CompareTo=	Compare to merge field

See Also

InsertField
MailMergeInsertIf
MailMergeInsertNext
MailMergeInsertNextIf

MailMerge LastRecord

Purpose

Displays the associated merge document for the last data record in a main document.

Syntax

```
MailMergeLastRecord
```

See Also

MailMergeFindRecord
MailMergeFirstRecord
MailMergeGotoRecord
MailMergeNextRecord
MailMergePrevRecord
MailMergeViewData

MailMergeMainDocumentType or MailMergeMainDocumentType$()

Purpose

Makes the active window the main mail merge document.

Syntax

```
MailMergeMainDocumentType Type
```

or

```
x = MailMergeMainDocumentType$()
```

Parameters

Type
The type of merged document to create:
0 or omitted: Form letters
1: Mailing labels
2: Envelopes
3: Catalog documents

Returns

TRUE (-1): The active document is a main document.
FALSE (0): The active document is not a main document.

See Also

MailMergeCreateDataSource
MailMergeOpenDataSource
MailMergeReset

MailMerge NextRecord

Purpose

Displays the associated merge document for the next record in the current query result.

Syntax

```
MailMergeNextRecord
```

See Also

MailMergeFindRecord
MailMergeFirstRecord
MailMergeGotoRecord
MailMergeLastRecord
MailMergePrevRecord
MailMergeViewData

MailMerge OpenDataSource

Purpose

Attaches a data source to the active document.

Syntax

```
MailMergeOpenDataSource .Attrib = value
```

Parameters

.Attrib—A database attribute:

.Name=	Name of the data source file
.ConfirmConversions=	If 1, displays the Convert File dialog
.ReadOnly=	1: opened read-only, 0: opened for writing
.LinkToSource=	If 1, establishes a link
.AddToMru=	1: adds file name to the bottom of the file list in the File menu
.PasswordDoc=	The document password
.PasswordDot=	The template password
.Revert=	If *FileName$* is open, 0: the open document is activated 1: closes the document (no save), and reopens it
.WritePasswordDoc=	The document write password
.WritePasswordDot=	The template write password
.Connection=	The connection string
.SQLStatement=	An SQL query string

value
The information about that argument

Note: Descriptions in quotation marks indicate that the value is a string.

See Also

FileOpen
MailMergeCreateDataSource
MailMergeEditDataSource
MailMergeOpenHeaderSource

MailMerge OpenHeaderSource

Purpose

Attaches a header source to the active document.

Syntax

```
MailMergeOpenHeaderSource .Attrib = value
```

Parameters

.Attrib—A database attribute:

.Name=	Name of the data source file
.ConfirmConversions=	If 1, displays the Convert File dialog.
.ReadOnly=	1: opened read-only, 0: opened for writing
.AddToMru=	1: adds file name to the bottom of the file list in the File menu
.PasswordDoc=	The document password
.PasswordDot=	The template password
.Revert=	If *FileName$* is open, 0: the open document is activated 1: closes the document (no save), and reopens it.
.WritePasswordDoc=	The document write password
.WritePasswordDot=	The template write password

value
The information about that argument.

Note: Descriptions in quotation marks indicate that the value is a string.

See Also

MailMergeCreateHeaderSource
MailMergeEditHeaderSource
MailMergeOpenDataSource

MailMerge PrevRecord

Purpose

Displays the associated merge document for the previous record in the current query result.

Syntax

```
MailMergePrevRecord
```

See Also

MailMergeFindRecord
MailMergeFirstRecord
MailMergeGotoRecord
MailMergeLastRecord
MailMergeNextRecord
MailMergeViewData

MailMerge QueryOptions

Purpose

Specifies query options for a mail merge.

Syntax

```
MailMergeQueryOptions .SQLStatement
= Statement$
```

Parameters

Statement$
An SQL query string.

See Also

MailMergeCreateDataSource
MailMergeOpenDataSource

MailMergeReset

Purpose

Resets the active mail merge main document to a regular Word document.

Syntax

```
MailMergeReset
```

See Also

MailMergeMainDocumentType

MailMergeState()

Purpose

Returns some information about the current state of a mail merge setup.

Syntax

```
x = MailMergeState(Type)
```

Parameters

Type
Returns the following for each type:

0: About the active document:
0: Regular Word document
1: Main doc, no header source attached
2: Main doc, data source attached
3: Main doc, header source attached
4: Main doc, data & header sources attached
5: Data or header source file(s) open

1: The type of main document:
0: Form letters
1: Mailing labels
2: Envelopes
3: Catalog

2: Mail merge options:
0: No blank-line suppress nor query options
1: Blank-line suppression enabled
2: Query options enabled
3: Blank-line suppress and query options

3: Mail merge destination:
0: New document
1: Printer
2: Electronic mail
3: Fax

See Also

MailMergeMainDocumentType

MailMergeToDoc

Purpose

Merges data records into main mail merge document and sends resulting merge to a new Word document.

Syntax

```
MailMergeToDoc
```

See Also

MailMerge
MailMergeToPrinter

MailMergeToPrinter

Purpose

Merges data records into main mail merge document and sends resulting merge to the printer.

Syntax

```
MailMergeToPrinter
```

See Also

MailMerge
MailMergeToDoc

MailMergeUse AddressBook

Windows 95

Purpose

Specifies a Microsoft Exchange Personal Address Book as the data source for a Word mail merge. (Available only if Microsoft Exchange is installed.)

Syntax

```
MailMergeUseAddressBook
.AddressBookType = text
```

Parameters

.AddressBookType
Specifies the type of address book you want to use:
scd: Schedule+ Contact List
pab: Microsoft Exchange Personal Address Book

See Also

AddAddress
GetAddress$()

MailMergeViewData or MailMergeViewData()

Purpose

Controls the display of merge fields in a main document.

Syntax

```
MailMergeViewData [Display]
```

or

```
x = MailMergeViewData()
```

Parameters

Display:
- 0: Merge field names
- 1: Return information from current data record

Returns

0: Merge field names displayed.
1: Information from current data record displayed.

See Also

MailMergeEditDataSource

MailMessageDelete

Purpose

Deletes an active WordMail message. (Available only if Microsoft Exchange is installed.)

Syntax

```
MailMessageDelete
```

(d)See Also

MailMessageMove
MailMessageNext
MailMessagePrevious

MailMessageForward

Purpose

Opens a new WordMail message that will forward the active WordMail message to another recipient. (Available only if Microsoft Exchange is installed.)

Syntax

```
MailMessageForward
```

See Also

MailMessageReply
MailMessageReplyAll

MailMessageMove

Purpose

Moves an active WordMail message to a folder in a message store currently available in Microsoft Exchange. (Available only if Microsoft Exchange is installed.)

Syntax

```
MailMessageReply
```

See Also

MailMessageDelete
MailMessageNext
MailMessagePrevious

MailMessageNext

Purpose

Closes an active WordMail message and displays the next message, if any. (Available only if Microsoft Exchange is installed.)

Syntax

```
MailMessageNext
```

See Also

MailMessageDelete
MailMessageMove
MailMessagePrevious

MailMessagePrevious

Purpose

Closes an active WordMail message and displays the previous message, if any. (Available only if Microsoft Exchange is installed.)

Syntax

```
MailMessagePrevious
```

See Also

MailMessageDelete
MailMessageMove
MailMessageNext

MailMessage Properties

Purpose

Opens the Properties dialog box associated with an active WordMail message. (Available only if Microsoft Exchange is installed.)

Syntax

```
MailMessageProperties
```

See Also

MailMessageDelete
MailMessageMove
MailMessageNext
MailMessagePrevious

MailMessageReply

Purpose

Opens a new WordMail message window for replying to an active message. (Available only if Microsoft Exchange is installed.)

Syntax

```
MailMessageReply
```

See Also

MailMessageForward
MailMessageReplyAll

MailMessageReplyAll

Purpose

Opens a new WordMail message window for replying to both the sender and all other recipients of an active message. (Available only if Microsoft Exchange is installed.)

Syntax

```
MailMessageReplyAll
```

See Also

MailMessageForward
MailMessageReply

MailSelectNames

Purpose

Allows a user to add addresses to an active, unsent WordMail message. (Available only if Microsoft Exchange is installed.)

Syntax

```
MailSelectNames
```

See Also

MailCheckNames
MailHideMessageHeader

MarkCitation

Purpose

Inserts TA (Table of Authorities) entry next to selection or next to every instance of selection text.

Syntax

```
MarkCitation .Attrib = value
```

Parameters

.Attrib—A database attribute:

.LongCitation=	Citation to TA
.LongCitationAutoText=	AutoText name to TA
.Category=	List number of category

.ShortCitation=	Citation to list
.NextCitation=	Finds next .ShortCitation
.Mark=	Insert TA field next to selection
.MarkAll=	Insert TA field by all text instances

value
The information about that argument.

Note: Descriptions in quotation marks indicate that the value is a string.

See Also

InsertTableOfAuthorities
MarkIndexEntry
MarkTableOfContentsEntry

MarkIndexEntry

Purpose

Inserts XE (Index Entry) field next to selection or next to every instance of selection text.

Syntax

```
MarkIndexEntry .Attrib = value
```

Parameters

.Attrib—A database attribute:

.MarkAll=	Insert XE field by all text instances
.Entry=	The text to appear in index
.EntryAutoText=	AutoText entry to index
.CrossReferenceAutoText=	AutoText for crossref
.CrossReference=	The text for crossref
.Range=	Bookmark name of pages to index
.Bold=	If 1, page numbers bold in index
.Italic=	If 1, page numbers italic in index

value
The information about that argument.

Note: Descriptions in quotation marks indicate that the value is a string.

See Also

InsertIndex
MarkCitation
MarkTableOfContentsEntry

MarkTableOfContentsEntry

Purpose

Inserts TC (Table of Contents Entry) field next to selection.

Syntax

```
MarkTableOfContentsEntry .Attrib = value
```

Parameters

.Attrib—A database attribute:

.Entry =	"The text to appear in TOC"
.EntryAutoText =	"AutoText entry to TOC"
.TableId =	"One-char ID for type of item"
.Level =	"Level for entry in TOC"

value
The information about that argument.

Note: Descriptions in quotation marks indicate that the value is a string.

See Also

InsertTableOfContents
MarkCitation
MarkIndexEntry

MenuItemMacro$()

Purpose

Returns the name of the macro or command associated with a menu item. This command was formerly MenuMacro$ in Word 2.0.

Syntax

```
x$ = MenuItemMacro$(Menu$, Type, Item [, Context])
```

Parameters

Menu$
A menu name. An ampersand is optional.

Type
Type of menu:
0: Menus when document is open
1: Menus when no document is open
2: Shortcut menus

Item
The item's numerical position in the menu.

Context
The menu assignment:
0 or omitted: Menus when Normal template active
1: Current menus

Returns

The name of the macro or command associated with a menu item.

See Also

CountMacros()
KeyMacro$()
MacroDesc$()
MacroName$()
MenuItemText$()
ToolsCustomizeMenus

MenuItemText$()

Purpose

Returns the menu text associated with a macro or command. This command was formerly MenuText$() in Word 2.0.

Syntax

```
x$ = MenuItemText$(Menu$, Type, Item
[, Context])
```

Parameters

Menu$
A menu name. An ampersand is optional.

Type
Type of menu:
0: Menus when document is open
1: Menus when no document is open
2: Shortcut menus

Item
The item's numerical position in the menu.

Context
The menu assignment:
0 or omitted: Menus when Normal template active
1: Current menus

Returns

The menu text associated with a macro or command.

See Also

CountMenuItems()
CountMenus()
MenuItemMacro$()
MenuText$()
ToolsCustomizeMenus

MenuMode

Purpose

Activates the menu bar.

Syntax

```
MenuMode
```

MenuText$()

Purpose

Returns the name of a menu. Note: the function of this command has changed from Word 2.0.

Syntax

```
x$ = MenuText$(Type, MenuNum [,
Context])
```

Parameters

Type
Type of menu:
0: Menus when document is open
1: Menus when no document is open
2: Shortcut menus

MenuNum
The position of the menu, numbered from left to right.

Context
The menu assignment:
0 or omitted: Normal template
1: Active template

Returns

The name of a given menu.

See Also

CountMenuItems()
CountMenus()
MenuItemMacro$()
MenuItemText$()
ToolsCustomizeMenus

MergeFieldName$()

Purpose

Returns a field name in a data or header source for a mail merge document.

Syntax

```
x$ = MergeFieldName$(Count)
```

Parameters

Count
The sequential number of the desired field name.

Returns

A selected field name in a data or header source for a mail merge document.

See Also

CountMergeFields()
InsertMergeField

MergeSubdocument

Purpose

Merges selected subdocuments of a master document into one subdocument.

Syntax

```
MergeSubdocument
```

See Also

CreateSubdocument
InsertSubdocument
OpenSubdocument
RemoveSubdocument
SplitSubdocument
ViewMasterDocument

MicrosoftAccess

Purpose

Starts Microsoft Access.

Syntax

```
MicrosoftAccess
```

See Also

AppActivate
AppIsRunning()

MicrosoftExcel
MicrosoftFox
MicrosoftMail
MicrosoftPowerPoint
MicrosoftProject
MicrosoftPublisher
MicrosoftSchedule

MicrosoftExcel

Purpose

Starts Microsoft Excel.

Syntax

```
MicrosoftExcel
```

See Also

AppActivate
AppIsRunning()
MicrosoftAccess
MicrosoftFox
MicrosoftMail
MicrosoftPowerPoint
MicrosoftProject
MicrosoftPublisher
MicrosoftSchedule

MicrosoftFox

Purpose

Starts Microsoft FoxPro.

Syntax

```
MicrosoftFox
```

See Also

AppActivate
AppIsRunning()
MicrosoftAccess
MicrosoftExcel
MicrosoftMail
MicrosoftPowerPoint
MicrosoftProject
MicrosoftPublisher
MicrosoftSchedule

MicrosoftMail

Purpose

Starts Microsoft Mail.

Syntax

```
MicrosoftMail
```

See Also

AppActivate
AppIsRunning()
MicrosoftAccess
MicrosoftExcel
MicrosoftFox
MicrosoftPowerPoint
MicrosoftProject
MicrosoftPublisher
MicrosoftSchedule

MicrosoftPowerPoint

Purpose

Starts Microsoft PowerPoint.

Syntax

```
MicrosoftPowerPoint
```

See Also

AppActivate
AppIsRunning()
MicrosoftAccess
MicrosoftExcel
MicrosoftFox
MicrosoftMail
MicrosoftProject
MicrosoftPublisher
MicrosoftSchedule

MicrosoftProject

Purpose

Starts Microsoft Project.

Syntax

```
MicrosoftProject
```

See Also

AppActivate
AppIsRunning()
MicrosoftAccess
MicrosoftExcel
MicrosoftFox
MicrosoftMail
MicrosoftPowerPoint
MicrosoftPublisher
MicrosoftSchedule

MicrosoftPublisher

Purpose

Starts Microsoft Publisher.

Syntax

```
MicrosoftPublisher
```

See Also

AppActivate
AppIsRunning()
MicrosoftAccess
MicrosoftExcel
MicrosoftFox
MicrosoftMail
MicrosoftPowerPoint
MicrosoftProject
MicrosoftSchedule

MicrosoftSchedule

Purpose

Starts Microsoft Schedule+.

Syntax

```
MicrosoftSchedule
```

See Also

AppActivate
AppIsRunning()
MicrosoftAccess
MicrosoftExcel
MicrosoftFox
MicrosoftMail
MicrosoftPowerPoint

MicrosoftProject
MicrosoftPublisher

MicrosoftSystemInfo

Purpose

Starts Microsoft System Info.

Syntax

```
MicrosoftSystemInfo
```

See Also

AppInfo$()
GetSystemInfo

Mid$()

Purpose

Returns a portion of a string, beginning at a given character position.

Syntax

```
x$ = Mid$(Source$, Start [, Count])
```

Parameters

Source$
Any string variable or function that results in a string.

Start
The character position in *Source$* to begin returning.

Count
The number of characters to return. If omitted, the rest of *Source$* beginning at *Start* is returned.

Returns

A substring of *Source$*.

See Also

InStr()
Left$()
Len()
LTrim$()
Right$()
RTrim$()

Minute()

Purpose

Returns the minute from the date serial number.

Syntax

```
x = Minute(DateNum)
```

Parameters

DateNum
The minute corresponding to number given. *DateNum* is the number of days following December 30, 1899.

Returns

The minute given by *DateNum* as an integer between 0 and 59, in the format set in the International selection of the Windows Control Panel.

See Also

DateSerial()
Day()
Hour()
Month()
Now()
Second()
Time$()
TimeSerial()
Today()
Weekday()
Year()

MkDir

Purpose

Creates a subdirectory.

Syntax

```
MkDir DirName$
```

Parameters

DirName$
A valid subdirectory name

See Also

ChDir
CountDirectories()
Files$()
GetDirectory$()
Name
RmDir

Month()

Purpose

Returns the month from a number.

Syntax

```
x$ = Month(DateNum)
```

Parameters

DateNum
The month corresponding to number given. *DateNum* is the number of days following December 30, 1899.

Returns

The month given by *DateNum* as an integer between 1 and 12, in the format set in the International selection of the Windows Control Panel.

See Also

DateSerial()
Day()
Hour()
Minute()
Now()
Second()
Time$()
TimeSerial()
Today()
Weekday()
Year()

MoveButton

Purpose

Move or copy a toolbar item.

Syntax

```
MoveButton SourceTBar$, SourcePos,
DestTBar$, DestPos [, Copy][,
Context]
```

Parameters

SourceTBar$
The name of the toolbar containing the item to move or copy

SourcePos
The sequential position of the item, counting from left to right

DestTBar$
The name of the destination toolbar

DestPos
The sequential position of the item's destination, counting from left to right

Copy
If 1, copies item; else moves item

Context
0 or omitted: Normal template.
1: Active template.

See Also

AddButton
ChooseButtonImage
CopyButtonImage
DeleteButton
EditButtonImage
PasteButtonImage
ResetButtonImage

MoveText

Purpose

Moves selected text without affecting the Clipboard.

Syntax

```
MoveText
```

See Also

Cancel
CopyFormat
CopyText
ExtendSelection
OK

MoveToolbar

Purpose

Moves a toolbar.

Syntax

```
MoveToolbar ToolbarName$, Anchor,
HorizPos, VertPos
```

Parameters

ToolbarName$
The name of the toolbar to move.

Anchor
Specifies how toolbar is to be anchored:

0: Floats over document window
1: Anchored at top of Word window
2: Anchored at left of Word window
3: Anchored at right of Word window
4: Anchored at bottom of Word window

HorizPos, VertPos
If toolbar is floating, the distance in pixels between the upper left corner of the Word window and the upper left corner of the toolbar

See Also

ToolbarName$()
ToolbarState()
ViewToolbars

MsgBox or MsgBox()

Purpose

Displays a message in a default dialog box.

Syntax

```
MsgBox Message$ [, Title$][, Type]
```

or

```
x = MsgBox(Message$ [, Title$]
[, Type])
```

Parameters

Message$
The message to be displayed in the dialog box

Title$
The text displayed in the title bar of the dialog box

Type
The sum of the following:
0 or omitted: OK button only, no symbol, first button is default
1: OK, Cancel buttons
2: Abort, Retry, Ignore buttons
3: Yes, No, Cancel buttons
4: Yes, No buttons
5: Retry, Cancel buttons
16: Stop symbol
32: Question symbol
48: Attention symbol
64: Information symbol
256: Second button default
512: Third button default

Returns

-1: First (left) button.
0: Second (middle) button.
1: Third (right) button.

See Also

InputBox$()
Print

Name...As

Purpose

Renames or moves a file.

Syntax

```
Name OldName$ As NewName$
```

Parameters

OldName$
The current name of the file.

NewName$
The new name of the file.

See Also

ChDir
CopyFile
FileSaveAs
Kill
MkDir
RmDir

NewToolbar

Purpose

Adds a toolbar to the current or Normal template

Syntax

```
NewToolbar .Name = ToolbarName$
[,.Context = Context]
```

Parameters

ToolbarName$
The name for the new toolbar.

Context
0: Normal template.
1: Active template.

See Also

AddButton
CountToolbars()
MoveButton
ToolbarName$()
ViewToolbars

NextCell or NextCell()

Purpose

Selects the next table cell (equivalent to pressing the Tab key when positioned in a table).

Syntax

```
NextCell
```

or

```
x = NextCell()
```

Returns

TRUE (-1): Operation was successful.
FALSE (0): Operation was not successful.

See Also

PrevCell

NextField or NextField()

Purpose

Selects the next field. Skips over hidden fields.

Syntax

```
NextField
```

or

```
x = NextField()
```

Returns

1: Operation was successful.
0: Operation was not successful.

See Also

PrevField

NextMisspelling

Purpose

Goes to the next misspelled word in the active document.

Syntax

```
NextMisspelling
```

See Also

DocumentHasMisspelling()
ToolsGetSpelling
ToolsLanguage
ToolsOptionSpelling

NextObject

Purpose

Moves to the next object.

Syntax

```
NextObject
```

See Also

PrevObject

NextPage or NextPage()

Purpose

Scrolls forward one page.

Syntax

```
NextPage
```

or

```
x = NextPage()
```

Returns

1: Operation was successful.
0: Operation was not successful.

See Also

EditGoTo
PageDown
PrevPage
ViewPage
VPage

NextTab()

Purpose

Returns the position of the tab stop to the right of a position.

Syntax

```
x = NextTab(Position)
```

Parameters

Position
The position to start searching for a tab stop.

Returns

The position of the tab stop to the right of *Position*.

See Also

FormatTabs
PrevTab()
TabLeader$()
TabType()

NextWindow

Purpose

Activates the next window in the window list.

Syntax

```
NextWindow
```

See Also

Activate
ChDir
PrevWindow
Window()
WindowList
WindowName$()
Window*Number*

NormalFontPosition

Purpose

Removes superscript or subscript formatting from the selection.

Syntax

```
NormalFontPosition
```

See Also

FormatFont
NormalFontSpacing

NormalFontSpacing

Purpose

Removes expanded or condensed font spacing from the selection.

Syntax

```
NormalFontSpacing
```

See Also

FormatFont
NormalFontPosition

NormalStyle

Purpose

Applies Normal style to the selection.

Syntax

```
NormalStyle
```

See Also

FormatStyle
ResetPara
Style
StyleName$()

NormalView HeaderArea

Purpose

Opens the header/footer pane and sets options for headers and footers.

Syntax

```
NormalViewHeaderArea .Attrib =
number
```

Parameters

.Attrib—A note option:

.Type =	Display header or footer
.FirstPage =	Allows a different first page header or footer
.OddAndEvenPages =	If 1, sets a different header and footer for odd and even pages
.HeaderDistance =	Distance from top of page to header
.FooterDistance =	Distance from bottom of page to footer

number

The information about that argument.

See Also

InsertFootnote

NoteOptions

Purpose

Sets options for formatting and placing notes.

Syntax

```
NoteOptions .Attrib = number
```

Parameters

.Attrib—A note option:

.FootnotesAt =	Where to place footnotes: 0: Bottom of page 1: Beneath text
FootNumberAs =	Format of footnote references: 0: 1, 2, 3, 4 1: a, b, c, d 2: A, B, C, D 3: i, ii, iii, iv 4: I, II, III, IV 5: special
.FootStartingNum =	Starting number for footnotes
.FootRestartNum =	Numbering after page breaks: 0: Continuous 1: Restart Each Section 2: Restart Each Page
.EndnotesAt =	Where to place endnotes: 0: End of section 1: End of document
.EndNumberAs =	Formatting for endnote refs
.EndStartingNum =	Starting number for endnotes
.EndRestartNum =	Numbering after page breaks: 0: Continuous 1: Restart Each Section

number

The information about that argument.

See Also

InsertFootnote

Now()

Purpose

Returns the current day's date.

yntax

```
x = Now()
```

Returns

The current day's date.

See Also

Date$()
DateSerial()
DateValue()
Today()

OK

Purpose

Completes a special operation.

Syntax

```
OK
```

See Also

Cancel
CopyText
MoveText

OKButton

Purpose

Defines an OK button within a dialog box definition.

Syntax

```
OKButton X, Y, dX, dY [,.Identifier]
```

Parameters

X, Y
The coordinates of the upper left corner of the OK button, relative to the upper left corner of the dialog box, measured in fractions of the systemfont size

dX, dY
The width and height of the OK button, measured in fractions of the system font size

.Identifier
Can be used by statements in a dialog function

See Also

Begin Dialog...End Dialog
Dialog
CancelButton
PushButton

On Error

Purpose

Sets the error handler.

Syntax

```
On Error Action
```

Parameters

Action:

"Goto *Label*"	Jumps to an error handling routine indicated in the program by the line "Label:", in which Label can be any nonmeasured alphanumeric string

"Resume Next"	Continues on the statement following the statement where the error occurred
"Goto 0"	Disables error trapping

See Also

Err
Error
Goto
Select Case

OnTime

Purpose

Runs a macro at a specified time. Word must be running at the specified time.

Syntax

```
OnTime Time[$], MacroName$
[, Tolerance]
```

Parameters

Time$
The time in 24-hour format or as a date serial number

MacroName$
The name of the macro to be run.

Tolerance
The tolerance of time in starting the macro.

See Also

Date$()
DateSerial()
DateValue()
Day()
Month()
Now()
Time$()
TimeSerial()
Today()
Year()

Open (...For...As)

Purpose

Opens a sequential file for input or output.

Syntax

```
Open Name$ For Mode$ As
[#]StreamNumber
```

Parameters

Name$
The name of the file to open.

Mode$
The mode to open the file: Input, Output, Append.

StreamNumber
A number to assign to the file (1 to 4)

See Also

Close
Eof()
Input

Input$()
Line Input
Lof()
Print
Read
Seek
Write

OpenSubdocument

Purpose

Opens the subdocument based at the insertion point.

Syntax

```
OpenSubdocument
```

See Also

CreateSubdocument
FileOpen
InsertSubdocument
MergeSubdocument
RemoveSubdocument
SplitSubdocument
ViewMasterDocument

OpenUpPara

Purpose

Sets Spacing Before Paragraph to "12 pt."

Syntax

```
OpenUpPara
```

See Also

CloseUpPara
FormatParagraph

OptionButton

Purpose

Defines an option button within a dialog box definition.

Syntax

```
OptionButton X, Y, dX, dY, Label$
[,.Identifier]
```

Parameters

X, Y
: The coordinates of the upper left corner of the option button, relative to the upper left corner of the dialog box, measured in fractions of the system font size.

dX, dY
: The width and height of the option button, measured in fractions of the system font size.

Label$
: The label displayed next to the option button.

.Identifier
: Can be used by statements in a dialog function.

See Also

CheckBox
GroupBox

OptionGroup
PushButton

OptionGroup

Purpose

Defines a group for option buttons.

Syntax

```
OptionGroup .Identifier
```

Parameters

.Identifier
Returns the number of the option button selected, in the order listed in the dialog box definition.

Returns

When referenced as the syntax `dlg.Identifier`, the number of the option button selected is returned.

See Also

Begin Dialog...End Dialog
GroupBox
ListBox
OptionButton

Organizer

Purpose

Allows organization of styles, AutoText, toolbars, and macros.

Syntax

```
Organizer .Attrib = value
```

Parameters

.Attrib—An attribute:

.Copy =	Copies an item
.Delete =	Deletes an item
.Rename =	Renames an item
.Source =	The file name containing the item
.Destination =	The destination file name
.Name =	The name of the item
.NewName =	"The new name for the item
.Tab =	The kind of item 0: Styles 1: AutoText 2: Toolbars 3: Macros

value
The information about that argument.

Note: Descriptions in quotes indicate that the value is a string.

See Also

EditAutoText
FileTemplates
FormatStyle
NewToolbar
ToolsMacro

OtherPane

Purpose

Activates the other open pane.

Syntax

```
OtherPane
```

See Also

ClosePane
DocSplit
WindowPane()

OutlineCollapse

Purpose

Collapses one level of selected heading or text.

Syntax

```
OutlineCollapse
```

See Also

OutlineExpand
ShowAllHeadings

OutlineDemote

Purpose

Demotes the selected heading by one level.

Syntax

```
OutlineDemote
```

See Also

OutlineMoveDown
OutlinePromote

OutlineExpand

Purpose

Expands one level of selected heading or text.

Syntax

```
OutlineExpand
```

See Also

OutlineCollapse
ShowAllHeadings

OutlineLevel()

Purpose

Returns the heading level of the selected paragraph(s).

Syntax

```
x = OutlineLevel()
```

Returns

The heading level of the selected paragraph(s).

See Also

FormatStyle
StyleName$()

OutlineMoveDown

Purpose

Moves the selected paragraph level(s) below the next paragraph level.

Syntax

```
OutlineMoveDown
```

See Also

OutlineDemote
OutlineMoveUp

OutlineMoveUp

Purpose

Moves the selected paragraph level(s) below the next paragraph level.

Syntax

```
OutlineMoveUp
```

See Also

OutlineMoveDown
OutlinePromote

OutlinePromote

Purpose

Promotes the selected heading by one level.

Syntax

```
OutlinePromote
```

See Also

OutlineDemote
OutlineMoveUp

OutlineShowFirstLine or OutlineShowFirstLine()

Purpose

Controls the display of body text in Outline view.

Syntax

```
OutlineShowFirstLine [On]
```

or

```
x = OutlineShowFirstLine()
```

Parameters

On

0: All body text is displayed.
1 or omitted: Display only first line.

Returns

TRUE (-1): Only first line of body text displayed.
FALSE (0): All lines of body text displayed.

See Also

OutlineCollapse
OutlineShowFormat

OutlineShowFormat

Purpose

Toggles display of character formatting.

Syntax

```
OutlineShowFormat
```

See Also

OutlineShowFirstLine
ViewDraft

Overtype or Overtype()

Purpose

Switches between overtype and insert modes.

Syntax

```
Overtype [On]
```

or

```
x = Overtype()
```

Parameters

On

omitted: Toggles between overtype and insert.
0: Switches to insert mode.
1: Switches to overtype mode.

Returns

TRUE (-1): Overtype mode on
FALSE (0): Insert mode on

See Also

ToolsOptionsGeneral

PageDown or PageDown()

Purpose

Moves the insertion point down by screens.

Syntax

```
PageDown [Count][, Select]
```

or

```
x = PageDown([Count][, Select])
```

Parameters

Count

The number of screens to move down. If omitted, 1 is assumed.

Select
0:Do not extend selection
nonzero: Extend selection

Returns

TRUE (-1): Operation was successful.
FALSE (0): Operation was not successful.

See Also

EditGoTo
HPage
HScroll
NextPage
PageUp
VPage
VScroll

PageUp or PageUp()

Purpose

Moves the insertion point up by screens.

Syntax

```
PageUp [Count][, Select]
```

or

```
x = PageUp([Count][, Select])
```

Parameters

Count
The number of screens to move up. If omitted, 1 is assumed.

Select
0: Do not extend selection
nonzero: Extend selection

Returns

TRUE (-1): Operation was successful.
FALSE (0): Operation was not successful.

See Also

EditGoTo
HPage
HScroll
PageDown
PrevPage
VPage
VScroll

ParaDown or ParaDown()

Purpose

Moves the insertion point down by paragraphs.

Syntax

```
ParaDown [Count][, Select]
```

or

```
x = ParaDown([Count][, Select])
```

Parameters

Cout
The number of paragraphs to move down. If omitted, 1 is assumed.

Select
0: Do not extend selection
nonzero: Extend selection

Returns

TRUE (-1): Operation was successful.
FALSE (0): Operation was not successful.

See Also

LineDown
PageDown
ParaUp

ParaKeepLinesTogether or ParaKeepLinesTogether()

Purpose

Sets paragraph formatting to keep all lines of the paragraph on the same page.

Syntax

```
ParaKeepLinesTegether [On]
```

or

```
x = ParaKeepLinesTegether()
```

Parameters

On

omitted: Toggles formatting.
0: Removes formatting.
1: Sets formatting.

Returns

-1: Not all selected paragraphs kept together.
0: None of selected paragraphs kept together.
1: All selected paragraphs kept together.

See Also

FormatParagraph
ParaKeepWithNext
ParaPageBreakBefore

ParaKeepWithNext or ParaKeepWithNext()

Purpose

Sets paragraph formatting to keep the current paragraph on the same page with the following paragraph.

Syntax

```
ParaKeepWithNext [On]
```

or

```
x = ParaKeepWithNext()
```

Parameters

On

omitted: Toggles formatting.
0: Removes formatting.
1: Sets formatting.

Returns

-1: Not all selected paragraphs kept with next.
0: None of selected paragraphs kept with next.
1: All selected paragraphs kept with next.

See Also

FormatParagraph
ParaKeepLinesTogether
ParaPageBreakBefore

ParaPage BreakBefore or ParaPage BreakBefore()

Purpose

Sets paragraph formatting to always insert a page break before the current paragraph.

Syntax

```
ParaPageBreakBefore [On]
```

or

```
= ParaPageBreakBefore()
```

Parameters

On
omitted: Toggles formatting.
0: Removes formatting.
1: Sets formatting.

Returns

-1: Not all selected paragraphs with page break before.
0: one of selected paragraphs with page break before.
1: All selected paragraphs with page break before.

See Also

FormatParagraph
ParaKeepLinesTogether
ParaKeepWithNext

ParaUp or ParaUp()

Purpose

Moves the insertion point up by paragraphs.

Syntax

```
ParaUp [Count][, Select]
```

or

```
x = ParaUp([Count][, Select])
```

Parameters

Count
The number of paragraphs to move up. If omitted, 1 is assumed.

Select
0: Do not extend selection
nonzero: Extend selection

Returns

TRUE (-1): Operation was successful.
FALSE (0): Operation was not successful.

See Also

LineUp
PageUp
ParaDown

ParaWidow OrphanControl or ParaWidow OrphanControl()

Purpose

Sets paragraph formatting to add or remove the Widow/Orphan control to the current paragraph.

Syntax

```
ParaWidowOrphanControl [On]
```

or

```
x = ParaWidowOrphanControl()
```

Parameters

On
omitted: Toggles formatting.
0: Removes formatting.
1: Sets formatting.

Returns

-1: Not all selected paragraphs with Widow/Orphan control.
0: None of selected paragraphs with Widow/Orphan control.
1: All selected paragraphs with Widow/Orphan control.

See Also

FormatParagraph
ParaKeepLinesTogether
ParaKeepWithNext
ParaPageBreakBefore

PasteButtonImage

Purpose

Copies the face of a toolbar button from the Clipboard.

Syntax

```
PasteButtonImage Toolbar$, ToolNum
[, Context]
```

Parameters

Toolbar$
The name of the toolbar.

ToolNum
The button number, counted from left to right.

Context
0: Normal template.
1: Active template.

See Also

ChooseButtonImage
CopyButtonImage
EditButtonImage
ResetButtonImage

PasteFormat

Purpose

Applies formatting to selection copied using CopyFormat.

Syntax

```
PasteFormat
```

See Also

CopyFormat
ResetChar
ResetPara

PathFromMacPath$()

Purpose

Converts a Macintosh path and file name to a valid path and file name in the current operating system.

Syntax

```
x$ = PathFromMacPath$(Path$)
```

Parameters

Path$
A Macintosh path name.

PauseRecorder

Purpose

Stops and restarts the macro recorder.

Syntax

```
PauseRecorder
```

Picture

Purpose

Displays a graphic in a user-defined dialog box.

Syntax

```
Picture X, Y, dX, dY, PicName$,
Type, .Identifier
```

Parameters

X, Y
The coordinates of the upper left corner of the picture, relative to the upper left corner of the dialog box, measured in fractions of the system font size.

dX, dY
The width and height of the picture and its associated text, measured in fractions of the system font size.

PicName$
The name of the picture

Type
How the graphic is stored:
0: A graphics file
1: An AutoText entry
2: A bookmark
3: In the Clipboard

.Identifier
A control extension used to set or access the value of the combo box from outside of the dialog box definition.

See Also

DlgSetPicture

PrevCell or PrevCell()

Purpose

Selects the contents of the previous cell in a table.

Syntax

```
PrevCell
```

or

```
x = PrevCell()
```

Returns

TRUE (-1): Operation was successful.
FALSE (0): Operation was not successful.

See Also

NextCell

PrevField or PrevField()

Purpose

Selects the field previous to the insertion point. Hidden fields are ignored.

Syntax

```
PrevField
```

or

```
x = PrevField()
```

Returns

TRUE (1): Operation was successful.
FALSE (0): Operation was not successful.

See Also

NextField

PrevObject

Purpose

Moves to the previous object.

Syntax

```
PrevObject
```

See Also

NextObject

PrevPage or PrevPage()

Purpose

Scrolls back one page.

Syntax

```
PrevPage
```

or

```
x = PrevPage()
```

Returns

TRUE (1): Operation was successful.
FALSE (0): Operation was not successful.

See Also

EditGoTo
NextPage
PageUp
ViewPage
VPage

PrevTab()

Purpose

Returns the position of the tab stop to the left of a position.

Syntax

```
x = PrevTab(Position)
```

Parameters

Position
The position from which to start searching for a tab stop.

Returns

The position of the tab stop to the left of *Position*.

See Also

FormatTabs
NextTab()
TabLeader$()
TabType()

PrevWindow

Purpose

Activates the previous window in the window list.

Syntax

```
PrevWindow
```

See Also

Activate
ChDir
NextWindow
Window()
WindowList
WindowName$()
WindowNumber

Print

Purpose

Displays a message to the status bar or sends information to a file.

Syntax

```
Print [#StreamNumber], VariableList
```

Parameters

#StreamNumber
The number used in the Open statement; specifies the open file.

VariableList
The variables to be filled from the file or user input.

See Also

Close
Eof()
Input
Input$()
Line Input
Lof()
MsgBox
Open
Print
Read
Seek
Write

PromoteList

Purpose

Promotes the selected paragraph(s) by one level.

Syntax

```
PromoteList
```

See Also

DemoteList
FormatBulletsAndNumbers

PushButton

Purpose

Defines a pushbutton within a dialog box definition.

Syntax

```
PushButton X, Y, dX, dY, Label$
[,.Identifier]
```

Parameters

X, Y
The coordinates of the upper left corner of the pushbutton, relative to the upper left corner of the dialog box, measured in fractions of the system font size.

dX, dY
The width and height of the push button, measured in fractions of the system font size.

Label$
The text to appear on the face of the push button.

.Identifier
Can be used by statements in a dialog function.

See Also

Begin Dialog...End Dialog
CancelButton
Dialog
OKButton
OptionButton

PutFieldData

Purpose

Stores text data in a MACRO field. The insertion point must be within a MACRO field.

Syntax

```
PutFieldData Text$
```

Parameters

Text$
The text to store in the field.

See Also

GetFieldData$()

Read

Purpose

Takes string or numeric values from an open sequential file.

Syntax

```
Read #StreamNumber, VariableList
```

Parameters

#StreamNumber
The number used in the Open statement; specifies the open file. The "#" must be included for Word to recognize this as a Stream Number and not a prompt.

VariableList
The variables to be filled from the file or user input.

Returns

String or numeric values taken from an open sequential file.

See Also

Close
Eof()
Input
Input$()
Line Input
Lof()
Open
Print
Seek
Write

RecordNextCommand

Purpose

Records a WordBasic instruction for the next command performed and inserts the instruction in an open macro editing window.

Syntax

```
RecordNextCommand
```

Redim

Purpose

Reallocates memory space for a variable or array. All re-dimensioned variables are cleared.

Syntax

```
ReDim [Shared] VariableList
```

or

```
ReDim DialogVariable As
DefinedDialog
```

Parameters

Shared
Sets the variable as global; the same variable can be used by all subroutines within the same macro.

VariableList
A list of variables, single or array, to which memory space is to be allocated. All arrays must be explicitly declared with a Dim statement. All arrays begin with element "0".

DialogVariable
A variable used to hold all attributes of a dialog box.

DefinedDialog
The name of a Word-defined or user-defined ("UserDialog") dialog box.

See Also

Dim
Let

REM

Purpose

Reserves the current line in the program listing as a comment line.

Syntax

```
Rem comment
```

or

```
'comment
```

RemoveAll DropDownItems

Purpose

Removes all items from a drop-down form field.

Syntax

```
RemoveAllDropDownItems BookmarkName$
```

Parameters

BookmarkName$
The name of the bookmark marking the drop-down form field.

See Also

AddDropDownItem
CheckBoxFormField
DropDownFormField
InsertFormField
RemoveDropDownItem
TextFormField

RemoveBullets Numbers

Purpose

Removes bullet/numbering formatting from the selected paragraph(s)

Syntax

```
RemoveBulletsNumbers
```

See Also

FormatBulletsAndNumbers
SkipNumbering

RemoveDrop DownItem

Purpose

Removes an item from a drop-down form field.

Syntax

```
RemoveDropDownItem
BookmarkName$,Item$
```

Parameters

BookmarkName$
The name of the bookmark marking the drop-down form field.

Item$
The item to remove.

See Also

AddDropDownItem
CheckBoxFormField
DropDownFormField
InsertFormField
RemoveAllDropDownItems
TextFormField

RemoveFrames

Purpose

Removes all frames in selection.

Syntax

```
RemoveFrames
```

See Also

FormatBordersAndShading
FormatFrame
InsertFrame

RemoveSubdocument

Purpose

Merges contents of the subdocument into the master document.

Syntax

```
RemoveSubdocument
```

See Also

CreateSubdocument
InsertSubdocument

MergeSubdocument
OpenSubdocument
SplitSubdocument
ViewMasterDocument

RenameMenu

Purpose

Renames a menu.

Syntax

```
RenameMenu MenuName$, NewName$, Type
[, Context]
```

(d)Parameters

MenuName$
The current name of the menu.

NewName$
The new name for the menu.

Type
0: Menus when a document is open.
1: Menus when no document is open.

Context
0: Normal template;
1: Active template

See Also

MenuText$()
ToolsCustomizeMenus

RepeatFind

Purpose

Repeats the most recent EditFind or EditGoTo.

Syntax

```
RepeatFind
```

See Also

EditFind
EditGoTo
EditRepeat

ResetButtonImage

Purpose

Resets the face of a toolbar button.

Syntax

```
ResetButtonImage Toolbar$, ToolNum
[, Context]
```

Parameters

Toolbar$
The name of the toolbar.

ToolNum
The button number, counted from left to right.

Context
0:Normal template.
1: Active template.

See Also

ChooseButtonImage
CopyButtonImage
EditButtonImage
PasteButtonImage
ViewToolbars

ResetChar or ResetChar()

Purpose

Removes manual character formatting from the selection.

Syntax

```
ResetChar
```

or

```
x = ResetChar()
```

Returns

1: Manual character formatting not present.
0: Manual character formatting present.

See Also

FormatFont
ResetPara

ResetNote SepOrNotice

Purpose

Resets the separator, continuation notice, or continuation separator for footnotes or endnotes.

Syntax

```
ResetNoteSepOrNotice
```

See Also

NoteOptions
ViewEndnoteContNotice
ViewEndnoteContSeparator
ViewEndnoteSeparator
ViewFootnoteContNotice
ViewFootnoteContSeparator
ViewFootnoteSeparator

ResetPara or ResetPara()

Purpose

Removes manual paragraph formatting from the selection.

Syntax

```
ResetPara
```

or

```
x = ResetPara()
```

Returns

1: Manual paragraph formatting not present.
0: Manual paragraph formatting present.

See Also

FormatParagraph
NormalStyle
ResetChar

Right$()

Purpose

Returns the rightmost portion of a string.

Syntax

```
x$ = Right$(string$, Length)
```

Parameters

string$
Any string variable or function that results in a string.

Length
The number of characters to return, counting from the end of the string.

Returns

The rightmost *Length* characters of *string$*.

See Also

InStr()
Left$()
Len()
LTrim$()
Mid$()
RTrim$()

RightPara or RightPara()

Purpose

Aligns the selected paragraph(s) with the right indent.

Syntax

```
RightPara
```

or

```
x = RightPara()
```

Returns

-1: Only part of the selection is right-justified.
0: None of the selection is right-justified.
1: All the selection is right-justified.

See Also

CenterPara
FormatParagraph
JustifyPara
LeftPara

RmDir

Purpose

Removes a subdirectory. The directory must be empty in order to be removed.

Syntax

```
RmDir
```

See Also

ChDir
Files$()
Kill
MkDir

Rnd()

Purpose

Returns a random number.

Syntax

```
x = Rnd()
```

Returns

A random number between 0 and 1.

See Also

Abs()
Int()
Sgn()

RTrim$()

Purpose

Removes trailing spaces from a string.

Syntax

```
x$ = RTrim$(string$)
```

Parameters

string$
Any string variable or function that results in a string.

Returns

string$ without trailing spaces.

See Also

InStr()
Left$()
LTrim$()
Mid$()
Right$()

RunPrintManager

Purpose

Starts the Print Manager.

Syntax

```
RunPrintManager
```

See Also

AppActivate
AppIsRunning()
ControlRun

SaveTemplate

Purpose

Saves changes to the active template.

Syntax

```
SaveTemplate
```

See Also

FileSave
FileSaveAll

ScreenRefresh

Purpose

Updates the current display; best used after restoring ScreenUpdating.

Syntax

```
ScreenRefresh
```

See Also

ScreenUpdating

ScreenUpdating or ScreenUpdating()

Purpose

Controls display changes while a macro is running. Interaction with the user through dialogs and messages is unaffected.

Syntax

```
ScreenUpdating [On]
```

or

```
ScreenUpdating()
```

Parameters

On

omitted: Toggles screen updating
0: Screen does not update while macro is running
1: Screen updates while macro is running

Returns

TRUE (-1): Screen updating turned on.
FALSE (0): Screen updating turned off.

See Also

ScreenRefresh

Second()

Purpose

Returns the seconds from the date serial number.

Syntax

```
x = Second(DateNum)
```

Parameters

DateNum
The second corresponding to number given. *DateNum* is the number of days following December 30, 1899.

Returns

The second given by *DateNum* as an integer between 0 and 59, in the format set in the International selection of the Windows Control Panel.

See Also

DateSerial()
Day()
Hour()
Minute()
Month()
Now()
Time$()
TimeSerial()
Today()
Weekday()
Year()

Seek or Seek()

Purpose

Controls where data is transferred to or from an open sequential file.

Syntax

```
Seek [#]StreamNumber, Count
```

or

```
x = Seek([#]StreamNumber)
```

Parameters

StreamNumber
The number used in the Open statement; specifies the open file.

Count
The character position where data transfer occurs.

Returns

The character position in the open sequential file.

See Also

Close
Eof()
Input
Input$()
Line Input
Lof()
Open
Print
Read
Write

Select Case...Case Else...End Select

Purpose

Runs one of a series of instructions based on a value.

Syntax

```
Select Case Condition Then CaseNum
Commands Case Else CaseNum Commands
End Select
```

Parameters

Condition
A statement that returns a number.

CaseNum
A number to which *Condition* could evaluate.

Command
A series of commands to be executed when *Condition* = *CaseNum*.

See Also

For...Next
Goto
If...Then...Else
While...Wend

SelectCurAlignment

Purpose

Extends the selection forward until a different paragraph alignment is reached.

Syntax

```
SelectCurAlignment
```

See Also

CenterPara
FormatParagraph
JustifyPara
LeftPara
RightPara
SelectCurIndent
SelectCurSpacing
SelectCurTabs

SelectCurColor

Purpose

Extends the selection forward until a different color is reached.

Syntax

```
SelectCurColor
```

See Also

CharColor
FormatFont
SelectCurFont

SelectCurFont

Purpose

Extends the selection forward until a different font or font size is reached.

Syntax

```
SelectCurFont
```

See Also

Font
FontSize
FormatFont
SelectCurColor

SelectCurIndent

Purpose

Extends the selection forward until a different paragraph indent is reached.

Syntax

```
SelectCurIndent
```

See Also

FormatParagraph
Indent
SelectCurAlignment
SelectCurSpacing
SelectCurTabs
UnIndent

SelectCurSentence

Purpose

Selects the entire current sentence, including the trailing space(s).

Syntax

```
SelectCurSentence
```

See Also

SelectCurWord
SentLeft
SentRight

SelectCurSpacing

Purpose

Extends the selection forward until a different paragraph line spacing is reached.

Syntax

```
SelectCurSpacing
```

See Also

FormatParagraph
SelectCurAlignment
SelectCurIndent
SelectCurTabs
SpacePara1
SpacePara15
SpacePara2

SelectCurTabs

Purpose

Extends the selection forward until a different paragraph with different tab stops is reached.

Syntax

```
SelectCurTabs
```

See Also

FormatTabs
SelectCurAlignment
SelectCurIndent
SelectCurSpacing

SelectCurWord

Purpose

Selects the entire current word without the trailing space(s).

Syntax

```
SelectCurWord
```

See Also

SelectCurSentence
WordLeft
WordRight

SelectDrawingObjects

Purpose

Toggles the mouse pointer between the standard mouse pointer and the pointer for selecting drawing objects.

Syntax

```
SelectDrawingObjects
```

See Also

DrawExtendSelect
DrawSelect

Selection$()

Purpose

Returns the unformatted text of the selection.

Syntax

```
x$ = Selection$()
```

Returns

The current selection as unformatted text.

See Also

ExtendSelection
SelInfo()
SelType
ShrinkSelection

SelectionFileName$()

Purpose

Returns the full path and file name of the active document (if saved).

Syntax

```
x$ = SelectionFileName$()
```

Returns

The full path and file name of the active document (if the document has been saved).

See Also

FileName$()
FileNameInfo$()
GetDirectory$()

SelInfo()

Purpose

Returns information about the selection.

Syntax

```
x = SelInfo(Type)
```

Parameters

Type

Types of information to return about the selection:

1: Number of page with end of selection
2: Number of section with end of selection
3: Number of page from start of document with end of selection
4: Number of pages in document
5: Horizontal position (Page Layout)
6: Vertical position (Page Layout)
7: Horizontal position from boundary (Page Layout)
8: Vertical position from boundary (Page Layout)
9: Position of first character in selection
10: Line number of first character in selection
11: TRUE if selection is entire frame
12: TRUE if selection is within a table
13: (Table): Row number with start of selection
14: (Table): Row number with end of selection
15: (Table): Number of rows in table
16: (Table): Column number with start of selection
17: (Table): Column number with end of selection
18: (Table): Greatest number of columns in table
19: % Zoom
20: Current selection mode
21: TRUE if Caps Lock
22: TRUE if Num Lock
23: TRUE if Overtype mode
24: TRUE if revision marking in effect
25: TRUE if in footnote
26: TRUE if in annotation pane
27: TRUE if in macro editing window
28: TRUE if in header or footer
29: Number of bookmark with start of selection
30: Number of last bookmark in selection
31: TRUE if at end-of-row mark in table
32: Position of selection, as returned below

Returns

Type = 32 returns the following:

-1: Selection includes a note reference (footnote, endnote, or annotation).
0: Selection does not include a note reference.
1: Selection is in a footnote reference.

2: Selection is in an endnote reference.
3: Selection is in an annotation reference.
All other Types return values as stated.

See Also

Selection$()
SelType

SelType or SelType()

Purpose

Specifies how the insertion point is indicated.

Syntax

```
SelType Type
```

or

```
x = SelType()
```

Parameters

Type The type of cursor:

1: Solid insertion point (default)
2: Solid selection (default)
4: Dotted selection and insertion point
5: Dotted insertion point (CopyText/MoveText)
6: Dotted selection (CopyText/MoveText)

Returns

A value indicating how the insertion point is currently indicated.

See Also

Selection$()
SelInfo()

SendKeys

Purpose

Sends keystrokes to an active application, mimicking keyboard typing to the application.

Syntax

```
SendKeys Keys$, Wait
```

Parameters

Keys$
A key sequence. Nonprinting keys are listed as follows:

"{backspace}", "{bs}", or "{bksp}"
"{break}"
"{capslock}"
"{clear}"
"{delete}" or "{del}"
"{down}"
"{end}"
"{enter}" or "~"
"{escape}" or "{esc}"
"{help}"
"{home}"
"{insert}"
"{left}"
"{numlock}"
"{pgdn}"
"{pgup}"
"{prtsc}"
"{right}"
"{tab}"
"{up}"

"{Fn}" (all function keys, where *n* is key number)
:Shift key: "+"
:Alt key: "%"
:Ctrl key: "^".

Wait
-1: waits for all keys to be processed before continuing.

See Also

AppActivate
DDEExecute
DDEInitiate()
DDEPoke

SentLeft or SentLeft()

Purpose

Moves the insertion point to the left by the given number of sentences

Syntax

```
SentLeft [Count,] [Select]
```

or

```
x = SentLeft([Count,] [Select])
```

Parameters

Count
The number of sentences to move past. If 0 or omitted, 1 is default. Negative signs are ignored.

Select
If nonzero, the selection is extended by *Count* sentences.

Returns

0: The action cannot be performed.
-1: The action can be performed, even if only partially.

See Also

CharLeft
ParaUp
SelectCurSentence
SentRight
StartOfLine
WordLeft

SentRight or SentRight()

Purpose

Moves the insertion point to the right by the given number of sentences.

Syntax

```
SentRight [Count,] [Select]
```

or

```
x = SentRight([Count,] [Select])
```

Parameters

Count
The number of sentences to move past. If 0 or omitted, 1 is default. Negative signs are ignored.

Select
If nonzero, the selection is extended by *Count* sentences.

Returns

0: The action cannot be performed.
-1: The action can be performed, even if only partially.

See Also

CharRight
EndOfLine
ParaDown
SelectCurSentence
SentLeft
WordRight

SetAttr

Purpose

Sets file attributes for a file

Syntax

```
SetAttr FileName$, Attribute
```

Parameters

FileName$
The path and file name of the file to set attributes.

Attribute
The sum of the following:

0: Clears all attributes
1: Read only
2: Hidden
4: System
32: Archive

See Also

GetAttr()

SetAutoText

Purpose

Defines a text-only AutoText entry.

Syntax

```
SetAutoText Name$, EntryText$
[, Template]
```

Parameters

Name$
The name of the new AutoText entry.

EntryText$
The text associated with the new entry.

Template
0: Normal template.
1: Active template.

See Also

AutoText
AutoTextName$()
CountAutoTextEntries()
EditAutoText
GetAutoText$()
InsertAutoText

SetDocumentDirty

Purpose

Controls whether Word recognizes that a document was changed since last saving (formerly SetDirty in Word 2.0).

Syntax

```
SetDocumentDirty [Dirty]
```

Parameters

Dirty

0: The document is treated as "clean"

1: The document is treated as "dirty"

See Also

IsDocumentDirty()
IsTemplateDirty()
SetTemplateDirty

SetDocumentProperty

Purpose

Specifies a document property in an active document.

Syntax

```
SetDocumentProperty Name$, Type,
Value[$], CustomOrBuiltIn
```

Parameters

Name$

Property name

Type

0: String
1: Number
2: Date
3: Yes or No

Value[$]

Property value

CustomOrBuiltIn

0 or omitted: Custom property unless it appears in the list of built-in properties; f it does, SetDocumentProperty updates the built-in property
1: Must be built-in property
2: Must be custom property

Returns

If *Name$*, *Type*, and/or *Value[$]* do not match, an error is returned.

See Also

DocumentPropertyExists()
GetDocumentProperty()
IsCustomDocumentProperty()
IsDocumentPropertyReadOnly()
SetDocumentPropertyLink

SetDocument PropertyLink

Purpose

Specifies a custom document property for an active document and links that property to an existing bookmark in the document.

Syntax

```
SetDocumentPropertyLink
Name$,Source$
```

Parameters

Name$

Property name (either built-in or custom).

Source$
Bookmark name (must already exist in the document).

See Also

GetDocumentProperty()
SetDocumentProperty

SetDocumentVar

Purpose

Sets a document variable value.

Syntax

```
SetDocumentVar VblName$, VblText$
```

or

```
X = SetDocumentVar(VblName$,
VblText$)
```

Parameters

VblName$
The name of a document variable.

VblText$
The value to assign to the document variable.

See Also

GetDocumentVar$()

SetEndOfBookmark

Purpose

Extends the end of a bookmark to another bookmark.

Syntax

```
SetEndOfBookmark BookmarkName1$,
BookmarkName2$
```

Parameters

BookmarkName1$
The name of the bookmark to extend.

BookmarkName2$
The destination bookmark.

See Also

CopyBookmark
EditBookmark
SetStartOfBookmark

SetFormResult

Purpose

Sets the result of a form field marked by a bookmark.

Syntax

```
SetFormResult BookmarkName$, Result
[, DefaultResult]
```

Parameters

BookmarkName$
The name of the bookmark.

Result
The result of the form field.

DefaultResult
If 1, *Result* becomes the default result for the form.

See Also

GetFormResult()

SetPrivate ProfileString or SetPrivate ProfileString()

Purpose

(Re)defines a setting in a private .INI file.

Syntax

```
SetPrivateProfileString Section$,
Option$, Setting$, FileName$
```

or

```
x =
SetPrivateProfileString(Section$,
Option$, Setting$, FileName$)
```

Parameters

Section$
The section name (appearing within "[]" in the .INI file; do not include brackets in *Section$*).

Option$
The option to write (preceding the "=").

Setting$
The setting to write (after the "=").

FileName$
The file name of the private .INI file.

Returns

TRUE (-1): The action was successful.
FALSE (0): The action was not successful.

See Also

GetPrivateProfileString$()
GetProfileString$()
SetProfileString
ToolsAdvancedSettings

SetProfileString

Purpose

(Re)defines a setting in WIN.INI

Syntax

```
SetProfileString Section$, Option$,
Setting$
```

or

```
x = SetProfileString(Section$,
Option$, Setting$)
```

Parameters

Section$
The section name (appearing within "[]" in the .INI file; do not include brackets in *Section$*).

Option$
The option to write (preceding the "=").

Setting$
The setting to write (after the "=").

Returns

TRUE (-1): The action was successful.
FALSE (0): The action was not successful.

See Also

GetPrivateProfileString$()
GetProfileString$()
SetPrivateProfileString
ToolsAdvancedSettings

SetSelRange

Purpose

Selects characters between two given character positions.

Syntax

```
SetSelRange Position1, Position2
```

Parameters

Position1
Character position of start of selection, counted from start of document.

Position2
Character position of end of selection, counted from start of document.

See Also

GetSelEndPos()
GetSelStartPos()
GetText$()

SetStartOfBookmark

Purpose

Extends the start of a bookmark to another bookmark.

Syntax

```
SetStartOfBookmark BookmarkName1$,
BookmarkName2$
```

Parameters

BookmarkName1$
The name of the bookmark to extend.

BookmarkName2$
The destination bookmark.

See Also

CopyBookmark
EditBookmark
SetEndOfBookmark

SetTemplateDirty

Purpose

Controls whether Word recognizes that a template has been changed since last saving.

Syntax

```
SetTemplateDirty [Dirty]
```

Parameters

Dirty
0: The template is treated as "clean."
1: The template is treated as "dirty."

See Also

IsDocumentDirty()
IsTemplateDirty()
SetDocumentDirty

Sgn()

Purpose

Returns the sign (positive, negative, zero) of a number.

Syntax

```
x = Sgn(number)
```

Parameters

number
A positive or negative number.

Returns

-1: *number* is negative.
0: *number* is zero.
1: *number* is positive.

See Also

Abs()
Int()
Rnd()

ShadingPattern or ShadingPattern()

Purpose

Applies a shading format to the selection.

Syntax

```
ShadingPattern Type
```

or

```
x = ShadingPattern()
```

Parameters

Type
One of 26 shading types.

Returns

-1: None of the selection is shaded.
0: Some of the selection is shaded.
1-25: The shading pattern of the entire selection.

See Also

FormatBordersAndShading

Shell

Purpose

Starts another application.

Syntax

```
Shell AppName$ [, WindowDisp]
```

Parameters

AppName$
The path and file name of the application.

WindowDisp
How the window should be displayed:

0: Minimized window (icon)
1: Normal window
2: Minimized window (for MS Excel)
3: Maximized window
4: Deactivated window

See Also

AppActivate
DDEInitiate()
Environ$()

ShowAll or ShowAll()

Purpose

Governs the display of all nonprinting characters.

Syntax

```
ShowAll [On]
```

or

```
x = ShowAll()
```

Parameters

On
omitted: Toggles display
0: Hides nonprinting characters
1: Displays nonprinting characters

Returns

TRUE (-1): Show All is off.
FALSE (0): Show All is on.

See Also

ToolsOptionsView

ShowAllHeadings

Purpose

Toggles between showing all text and showing only headings, in Outline view.

Syntax

```
ShowAllHeadings
```

See Also

OutlineCollapse
OutlineExpand
OutlineShowFirstLine
ShowHeading*Number*

ShowAnnotationBy

Purpose

Displays a given reviewer's annotations.

Syntax

`ShowAnnotationBy` *`ReviewerName$`*

Parameters

ReviewerName$
The name of a reviewer of the document.

See Also

ViewAnnotations

ShowHeadingNumber

Purpose

Shows all headings up to a given heading level in Outline view.

Syntax

```
ShowHeadingNumber
```

See Also

OutlineCollapse
OutlineExpand
OutlineShowFirstLine
ShowAllHeadings

ShowMe

Purpose

Shows the online help window or, if available, a Word Assistant dialog box that can show a user how a procedure is performed.

Syntax

```
ShowMe
```

See Also

AutomaticChange
Help

ShowNext HeaderFooter

Purpose

Moves to the next header/footer within the current section or to the first header/footer within the following section.

Syntax

```
ShowNextHeaderFooter
```

See Also

CloseViewHeaderFooter
FormatHeaderFooterLink
GoToHeaderFooter
ShowPrevHeaderFooter
ToggleHeaderFooterLink
ViewFooter
ViewHeader

ShowPrev HeaderFooter

Purpose

Moves to the previous header/footer within the current section or to the first header/footer within the preceding section.

Syntax

```
ShowPrevHeaderFooter
```

See Also

CloseViewHeaderFooter
FormatHeaderFooterLink
GoToHeaderFooter
ShowNextHeaderFooter
ToggleHeaderFooterLink
ViewFooter
ViewHeader

ShowVars

Purpose

Displays a dialog with a list of variables and their current values; useful in debugging macros.

Syntax

```
ShowVars
```

See Also

MsgBox()
Print
Stop

ShrinkFont

Purpose

Decreases the font size of the selection to the next size supported by the printer.

Syntax

```
ShrinkFont
```

See Also

Font
FontSize
FormatFont
GrowFont
GrowFontOnePoint
ShrinkFontOnePoint

ShrinkFontOnePoint

Purpose

Decreases the font size of the selection by one point.

Syntax

```
ShrinkFontOnePoint
```

See Also

Font
FontSize
FormatFont
GrowFont
GrowFontOnePoint
ShrinkFont

ShrinkSelection

Purpose

Reduces the selection to the next unit of text.

Syntax

```
ShrinkSelection
```

See Also

Cancel
ExtendMode()
ExtendSelection

SizeToolbar

Purpose

Sizes a floating toolbar.

Syntax

```
SizeToolbar ToolbarName$, Width
```

Parameters

ToolbarName$
The name of the toolbar.

Width
The desired width of the toolbar, in pixels.

See Also

MoveToolbar

SkipNumbering or SkipNumbering()

Purpose

Skips bullets or numbers in the selected paragraphs for a list.

Syntax

```
SkipNumbering
```

or

```
SkipNumbering()
```

Returns

-1: Some selected paragraphs are skipped.
0: The selected paragraphs are not skipped.
1: The selected paragraphs are all skipped.

See Also

DemoteList
FormatBulletsAndNumbers
PromoteList
RemoveBulletsNumbers

SmallCaps or SmallCaps()

Purpose

Adds or removes Small Caps formatting from the selection.

Syntax

```
SmallCaps [On]
```

or

```
x = SmallCaps()
```

Parameters

On
omitted: Toggles Small Caps formatting.
0:Removes Small Caps formatting.
1:Sets Small Caps formatting.

Returns

-1: Only part of the selection is in Small Caps.
0: None of the selection is in Small Caps.
1: All the selection is in Small Caps.

See Also

AllCaps
ChangeCase
FormatFont
UCase$()

SortArray

Purpose

Performs a sort on an array.

Syntax

```
SortArray
```

Parameters

ArrayName$()
Array to be sorted. A maximum of two-dimensional arrays can be sorted.

Order
0: Ascending;
1: Descending.

From
The element in the array to begin sorting.

To
The element in the array to end sorting.

SortType
The type of sort (two-dimensional arrays):

0: Sort the rows in the array.
1: Sort the columns in the array.

SortKey
Specifies the column or row to define the sort.

See Also

Dim
TableSort

SpacePara1

Purpose

Formats the selected paragraph(s) with single line spacing.

Syntax

```
SpacePara1
```

Returns

-1: Only part of the selection is single-spaced.
0: None of the selection is single-spaced.
1: All the selection is single-spaced.

See Also

CloseUpPara
FormatParagraph
OpenUpPara
SpacePara15
SpacePara2

SpacePara15 or SpacePara15()

Purpose

Formats the selected paragraph(s) with 1.5 line spacing.

Syntax

```
SpacePara15
```

or

```
x = SpacePara15()
```

Returns

-1: Only part of the selection is in 1.5 spacing.
0: None of the selection is in 1.5 spacing.
1: All the selection is in 1.5 spacing.

See Also

CloseUpPara
FormatParagraph
OpenUpPara
SpacePara1
SpacePara2

SpacePara2

Purpose

Formats the selected paragraph(s) with double-line spacing.

Syntax

```
SpacePara2
```

Returns

-1: Only part of the selection is double-spaced.
0: None of the selection is double-spaced.
1: All the selection is double-spaced.

See Also

CloseUpPara
FormatParagraph
OpenUpPara
SpacePara1
SpacePara15

SpellChecked, SpellChecked()

Purpose

Returns 1 if selected text has been spell checked; otherwise returns 0.

Syntax

```
SpellChecked [On]
```

or

```
SpellChecked()
```

Parameters

On

Specifies whether to identify text as checked for spelling errors or not checked.

1: Identifies text as checked.
0: Identifies text as not checked.
Omitted: Toggles current setting.

Returns

0: If not spell checked.
1: If completely checked.
-1: If partly checked.

See Also

ToolsSpelling
DocumentHasMisspellings()

Spike

Purpose

Adds the selection to the special AutoText entry and deletes the selection from the text.

Syntax

```
Spike
```

See Also

EditAutoText
EditCut
InsertSpike

SplitSubdocument

Purpose

Divides the current subdocument into two subdocuments.

Syntax

```
SplitSubdocument
```

See Also

CreateSubdocument
InsertSubdocument
MergeSubdocument
OpenSubdocument
RemoveSubdocument
ViewMasterDocument

StartOfColumn or StartOfColumn()

Purpose

Moves the insertion point to the beginning of a table column.

Syntax

`StartOfColumn [Select]`

or

`x = StartOfColumn([Select])`

Parameters

Select
If nonzero, extends selection.

Returns

TRUE (-1): The selection was moved.
FALSE (0): The selection was not moved.

See Also

EndOfColumn
StartOfRow

StartOfDocument or StartOfDocument()

Purpose

Moves the insertion point to the beginning of the active document.

Syntax

`StartOfDocument [Select]`

or

`x = StartOfDocument([Select])`

Parameters

Select
If nonzero, extends selection.

Returns

TRUE (-1): The selection was moved.
FALSE (0): The selection was not moved.

See Also

AtStartOfDocument()
EndOfDocument

StartOfLine or StartOfLine()

Purpose

Moves the insertion point to the beginning of the current line.

Syntax

```
StartOfLine [Select]
```

or

```
x = StartOfLine([Select])
```

Parameters

Select
If nonzero, extends selection.

Returns

TRUE (-1): The selection was moved.
FALSE (0): The selection was not moved.

See Also

EndOfLine
ParaUp
StartOfRow

StartOfRow or StartOfRow()

Purpose

Moves the insertion point to the beginning of a table row.

Syntax

```
StartOfRow [Select]
```

or

```
x = StartOfRow([Select])
```

Parameters

Select
If nonzero, extends selection.

Returns

TRUE (-1): The selection was moved.
FALSE (0): The selection was not moved.

See Also

EndOfRow
StartOfColumn
StartOfLine

StartOfWindow or StartOfWindow()

Purpose

Moves the insertion point to the upper-left corner of the active document window.

Syntax

```
StartOfWindow [Select]
```

or

```
x = StartOfWindow([Select])
```

Parameters

Select
If nonzero, extends selection.

Returns

TRUE (-1): The selection was moved.
FALSE (0): The selection was not moved.

See Also

EndOfWindow
StartOfDocument

Stop

Purpose

Stops a running macro.

Syntax

```
Stop [NoMessage]
```

Parameters

NoMessage
If -1, no message is posted that the macro was interrupted.

See Also

ShowVars

Str$()

Purpose

Returns the string representation of a number.

Syntax

```
x$ = Str$(number)
```

Parameters

number
Any number.

Returns

number: represented as a string.

See Also

Chr$()
InStr()
Left$()
LTrim$()
Mid$()
Right$()
RTrim$()
String$()
Val()

Strikethrough or Strikethrough()

Purpose

Adds or removes Strikethrough character formatting to the selection (formerly Strikeout in Word 2.0).

Syntax

```
Strikethrough [On]
```

or

```
x = Strikethrough()
```

Parameters

On
omitted: Toggles Strikethrough formatting.
0: Removes Strikethrough formatting.
1: Sets Strikethrough formatting.

Returns

-1: Only part of the selection is in Strikethrough.
0: None of the selection is in Strikethrough.
1: All the selection is in Strikethrough.

See Also

FormatFont
ToolsRevisions

String$()

Purpose

Returns the first character in a source string, repeated a given number of times.

Syntax

```
x$ = String$(Count, Source$)
```

or

```
x$ = String$(Count, CharCode)
```

Parameters

Count
The number of times to repeat a character.

Source$
The character to repeat.

CharCode
The ANSI character code to repeat.

Returns

A string with *Count* repeated characters.

See Also

Asc()
Chr$()
InStr()
Str$()

Style

Purpose

Applies a style to the selected paragraph(s).

Syntax

```
StyleStyleName$
```

Parameters

StyleName$
The name of the style to apply.

See Also

FormatStyle
NormalStyle
StyleName$()

StyleDesc$()

Purpose

Returns the description of a style.

Syntax

```
x$ = StyleDesc$(StyleName$)
```

Parameters

StyleName$
The name of a style.

Returns

The description of a style.

See Also

CountStyles()
FormatStyle
StyleName$()

StyleName$()

Purpose

Returns the name of a style.

Syntax

```
x$ =
StyleName$([Count,][Context,][All])
```

Parameters

Count
The list number of the style.

Context
0:Active document; 1: Active template.

All
If 1, include built-in styles in list.

Returns

The name of the specified style.

See Also

CountStyles()
FormatStyle
StyleDesc$()

Sub...End Sub

Purpose

Defines a subroutine.

Syntax

```
Sub SubroutineName (Arguments)...End
Sub
```

Parameters

SubroutineName
The name of the subroutine; the main subroutine is always entitled MAIN.

Arguments
The variables to be passed into and out of the subroutine. All variables are by default local, unless dimensioned as Shared variables.

See Also

Call
Function...End Function

Subscript or Subscript()

Purpose

Adds or removes Subscript character formatting to the selection.

Syntax

```
Subscript [On]
```

or

```
x = Subscript()
```

Parameters

On

omitted: Toggles Subscript formatting.
0: Removes Subscript formatting.
1: Sets Subscript formatting.

Returns

-1: Only part of the selection is subscripted.
0: None of the selection is subscripted.
1: All the selection is subscripted.

See Also

FormatFont
Superscript

Superscript or Superscript()

Purpose

Adds or removes Superscript character formatting to the selection.

Syntax

```
Superscript [On]
```

or

```
x = Superscript()
```

Parameters

On

omitted: Toggles Superscript formatting.
0: Removes Superscript formatting.
1: Sets Superscript formatting.

Returns

-1: Only part of the selection is superscripted.
0: None of the selection is superscripted.
1: All the selection is superscripted.

See Also

FormatFont
Subscript

SymbolFont

Purpose

Formats the selection with the Symbol font or inserts Symbol text at the insertion point.

Syntax

```
SymbolFont [InsertText$]
```

Parameters

InsertText$
The text to insert at the insertion point (in Symbol font).

See Also

FormatFont
InsertSymbol

TabLeader$()

Purpose

Returns the leader character of a custom tab stop.

Syntax

```
x$ = TabLeader$(Position)
```

Parameters

Position
Position of a tab stop in points.

Returns

The leader character of a custom tab stop.

See Also

FormatTabs
NextTab()
PrevTab()
TabType()

TableAutoFormat

Purpose

Applies predefined formats to a table.

Syntax

```
TableAutoFormat .Attrib = value
```

Parameters

.Attrib—A table attribute:

.Format =	The list number of the format
.Borders =	If 1, applies border formatting
.Shading =	If 1, applies shading formatting
.Font =	If 1, applies font formatting
.Color =	If 1, applies color formatting
.AutoFit =	If 1, sizes table columns to fit

.HeadingRows =	If 1, applies heading-row formatting
.FirstColumn =	If 1, applies first column formatting
.LastRow =	If 1, applies last row formatting
.LastColumn =	If 1, applies last column formatting

value

The information about that argument.

See Also

TableColumnWidth
TableHeadings
TableRowHeight
TableUpdateAutoFormat

TableAutoSum

Purpose

Inserts a formula field.

Syntax

```
TableAutoSum
```

See Also

TableFormula

TableColumnWidth

Purpose

Sets the column sizing for the selected columns.

Syntax

```
TableColumnWidth .Attrib = value
```

Parameters

.Attrib—A table attribute:

.ColumnWidth =	The width of the columns
.SpaceBetweenCols =	Space between text in columns
.PrevColumn =	Selects previous column after actions
.NextColumn =	Selects next column after actions
.AutoFit =	Makes columns just wide enough to fit
.RulerStyle =	How Word adjusts table: 0: Only selected cells changed 1: Preserves row width all cells 2: Preserves row width adjacent 3: Preserves row width uniform 4: Only selected cells changed

value
The information about that argument.

See Also

SelInfo()
TableDeleteColumn
TableRowHeight
TableSelectColumn

TableDeleteCells

Purpose

Deletes selected cells.

Syntax

```
TableDeleteCells .ShiftCells = ShiftWhere
```

Parameters

ShiftWhere
Direction to shift remaining cells:

0 or omitted: Shift cells left
1: Shift cells up
2: Delete entire row
3: Delete entire column

See Also

SelInfo()
TableDeleteColumn
TableDeleteRow

TableDeleteColumn

Purpose

Deletes the entire table column containing the insertion point.

Syntax

```
TableDeleteColumn
```

See Also

SelInfo()
TableDeleteCells
TableDeleteRow

TableDeleteRow

Purpose

Deletes the entire table row containing the insertion point.

Syntax

```
TableDeleteRow
```

See Also

SelInfo()
TableDeleteCells
TableDeleteColumn

TableFormula

Purpose

Inserts a formula field at the insertion point.

Syntax

```
TableFormula [.Formula = Formula$][,.NumFormat = Format$]
```

Parameters

Formula$
The mathematical formula.

Format$
A format for the result of the formula field.

See Also

InsertField
TableAutoSum
ToolsCalculate

TableGridlines or TableGridlines()

Purpose

Governs display of table gridlines.

Syntax

```
TableGridlines [On]
```

or

```
x = TableGridlines()
```

Parameters

On
omitted: Toggles table gridline display.
0: Hides table gridlines.
1: Displays table gridlines.

Returns

TRUE (-1): Table gridlines displayed.
FALSE (0): Table gridlines hidden.

See Also

ToolsOptionsView

TableHeadings or TableHeadings()

Purpose

Adds or removes the table heading format for the selected rows.

Syntax

```
TableHeadings [On]
```

or

```
x = TableHeadings()
```

Parameters

On
omitted: Toggles table heading formatting.
0: Removes table heading formatting.
1: Sets table heading formatting.

Returns

-1: Only part of the selection has table headings.
0: None of the selection has table headings.
1: All the selection has table headings.

See Also

TableRowHeight

TableInsertCells

Purpose

Insert cells in a table. Cells are inserted above or to the left of the selected cells.

Syntax

```
TableInsertCells .ShiftCells = ShiftWhere
```

Parameters

ShiftWhere
Direction to shift remaining cells:

0 or omitted: Shift cells left
1: Shift cells up.
2: Insert entire row.
3: Insert entire column.

See Also

SelInfo()
TableInsertColumn
TableInsertRow

TableInsertColumn

Purpose

Inserts a column in a table. The column is inserted to the left of the insertion point.

Syntax

```
TableInsertColumn
```

See Also

TableInsertCells
TableInsertRow

TableInsertRow

Purpose

Inserts a row in a table. The row is inserted above the insertion point.

Syntax

```
TableInsertRow .NumRows = NumRows
```

Parameters

NumRows
Number of rows to insert. If omitted, the number of rows inserted is governed by the number of rows selected.

See Also

TableInsertCells
TableInsertColumn

TableInsertTable

Purpose

Converts the selected paragraph(s) into a table. If there is no selection, inserts a blank table.

Syntax

```
TableInsertTable .Attrib = value
```

Parameters

.Attrib—A table attribute:

.ConvertFrom =	Character used to separate 0: Paragraph marks 1: Tab characters 2: Commas
.NumColumns =	Number of columns in table
.NumRows =	Number of rows in table
.InitialColWidth =	Initial width for each column
.Wizard =	Runs Table Wizard
.Format =	Number of a predefined format
.Apply =	Attributes to apply: 0: None 1: Borders 2: Shading 4: Font 8: Color 16: Best Fit 32: Heading Rows 64: Last Row 128: First Column 256: Last Column

value

The information about that argument.

See Also

TableAutoFormat
TableToText
TextToTable

TableMergeCells

Purpose

Merges selected cells into a single cell. Cells to merge must be on the same row.

Syntax

```
TableMergeCells
```

See Also

TableSplitCells

TableRowHeight

Purpose

Sets the row sizing for the selected rows.

Syntax

```
TableRowHeight .Attrib = value
```

Parameters

.Attrib—A table attribute:

.RulerStyle =	How Word adjusts table: 0: Moves cells right 1: Preserves right edge all cells 2: Preserves right edge first column cells 3: Preserves eight edge uniform 4: Only selected cells changed.
.LineSpacingRule =	Determine height of rows: 0: Auto 1: At Least 2: Exactly
.LineSpacing =	Height of rows
.LeftIndent =	Spacing from text to left margin
.Alignment =	Alignment of rows: 0: Left 1: Center 2: Right
.AllowRowSplit=	If 1, allows page break in row
.PrevRow=	Selects previous row for formatting
.NextRow=	Selects next row for formatting

value
The information about that argument.

See Also

TableColumnWidth
TableHeadings
TableSelectRow

TableSelectColumn

Purpose

Selects the table column containing the insertion point.

Syntax

```
TableSelectColumn
```

See Also

TableSelectRow
TableSelectTable

TableSelectRow

Purpose

Selects the table row containing the insertion point.

Syntax

```
TableSelectRow
```

See Also

TableSelectColumn
TableSelectTable

TableSelectTable

Purpose

Selects the entire table that contains the insertion point.

Syntax

```
TableSelectTable
```

See Also

TableSelectColumn
TableSelectRow

TableSort

Purpose

Sorts the selected paragraph(s) or table rows.

Syntax

```
TableSort .Attrib = value
```

Parameters

.Attrib—A sort attribute:

.DontSortHdr =	If 1, header not sorted
.FieldNum =	The number of the fields to sort by
.Type =	Sort types: 0: Alphanumeric 1: Numeric 2: Date
.Order =	0:Ascending; .1: Descending
.FieldNum2 =	Same as .FieldNum
.Type2 =	Same as .Type
.Order2 =	Same as .Order
.FieldNum3 =	Same as .FieldNum
.Type3 =	Same as .Type
.Order3 =	Same as .Order
.Separator =	Type of separator 0: Comma 1: Tab 2: Other (specified)
.SortColumn =	If 1, sorts only selected column
.CaseSensitive =	If 1, does case-sensitive sort

value
The information about that argument.

See Also

TableSortAToZ
TableSortZToA

TableSortAToZ

Purpose

Sorts the paragraphs or table rows in ascending alphanumeric order.

Syntax

```
TableSortAToZ
```

See Also

MailMergeEditDataSource
TableSort
TableSortZToA

TableSortZToA

Purpose

Sorts the paragraphs or table rows in descending alphanumeric order.

Syntax

```
TableSortZToA
```

See Also

MailMergeEditDataSource
TableSort
TableSortAToZ

TableSplit

Purpose

Inserts an empty paragraph above the current row in a table.

Syntax

```
TableSplit
```

See Also

TableSplitCells

TableToText

Purpose

Converts the selected rows to normal text.

Syntax

```
TableToText .ConvertTo = SepChar
```

Parameters

SepChar
The character used to separate the contents of each cell:

0: Paragraph marks
1: Tab characters
2: Commas
3: Other (specified)

See Also

TableInsertTable
TextToTable

TableSplitCells

Purpose

Splits each selected table cell.

Syntax

```
TableSplitCells .NumColumns = NumCells$
```

Parameters

NumCells$
The number of cells to generate from the split.

See Also

TableMergeCells
TableSplt

TableUpdate AutoFormat

Purpose

Updates the current table with a predefined table format.

Syntax

```
TableUpdateAutoFormat
```

See Also

TableAutoFormat

TabType()

Purpose

Returns the alignment of a tab stop.

Syntax

```
x = TabType(Position)
```

Parameters

Position
Position of a tab stop in points.

Returns

The alignment of a tab stop, in points.

See Also

FormatTabs
NextTab()
PrevTab()
TabLeader$()

Text

Purpose

Defines a fixed area of text within a dialog box definition.

Syntax

```
Text X, Y, dX, dY, Label$
[, .Identifier]
```

Parameters

X, Y
The coordinates of the upper-left corner of the text, relative to the upper-left corner of the dialog box, measured in fractions of the system font size.

dX, dY
The width and height of the text, measured in fractions of the system font size.

Label$
The text to appear on the dialog box.

.Identifier
A control extension used to set or access the value of the text from outside of the dialog box definition.

Returns

When the dialog containing the text is accessed by the syntax `x$ = Dialog.Identifier`, the value returned is the text string.

See Also

Begin Dialog...End Dialog
Dialog
TextBox

TextBox

Purpose

Defines a text box within a dialog box definition.

Syntax

```
TextBox X, Y, dX, dY,
[.Identifier][, Multiline]
```

Parameters

X, Y
The coordinates of the upper-left corner of the text box, relative to the upper-left corner of the dialog box, measured in fractions of the system font size.

dX, dY
The width and height of the text box and its associated text, measured in fractions of the system font size.

.Identifier
A control extension used to set or access the value of the text box from outside of the dialog box definition.

Multiline
Specifies a single-line or multi-line text box:

0: Single-line
1: Multiple-line

Returns

When the dialog box containing the text box is accessed by the syntax `x$ = Dialog.Identifier`, the value returned is the string appearing in the text box.

See Also

Begin Dialog...End Dialog
Dialog
Text

TextFormField

Purpose

Inserts a text form field at the insertion point.

Syntax

```
TextFormField
```

See Also

CheckBoxFormField
DropDownFormField
InsertFormField

TextToTable

Purpose

Converts the selected paragraph(s) into a table.

Syntax

```
TextToTable .Attrib = value
```

Parameters

.*Attrib*—A table attribute:

.ConvertFrom =	Character used to separate 0: Paragraph marks 1: Tab characters 2: Commas
.NumColumns =	Number of columns in table
.NumRows =	Number of rows in table
.InitialColWidth =	Initial width for each column
.Format =	Number of a predefined format
.Apply =	Attributes to apply: 0: None 1: Borders 2: Shading 4: Font 8: Color 16: Best Fit 32: Heading Rows 64: Last Row 128: First Column 256: Last Column

value
The information about that argument.

See Also

TableAutoFormat
TableInsertTable
TableToText

Time$()

Purpose

Returns the time based on the time serial number; if omitted, returns the current time.

Syntax

```
x$ = Time$([TimeNum])
```

Parameters

TimeNum
A time serial number.

Returns

The time given by *TimeNum* or current day's date if omitted, in the format set in the International selection of the Windows Control Panel.

See Also

Date$()
DateSerial()
GetPrivateProfileString$()
Hour()
Minute()
Now()
Second()
SetPrivateProfileString$()
TimeSerial()
TimeValue()

TimeSerial()

Purpose

Returns the serial number of the specified time.

Syntax

```
x = TimeSerial(Hour, Minute, Second)
```

Parameters

Hour
The hour, numbered between 0 and 23.

Minute
The minute, numbered between 0 and 59.

Second
The second, numbered between 0 and 59.

Returns

The time serial number, from 0 to approximately 1.

See Also

DateSerial()
Day()
Month()
Now()
Time$()
TimeValue()
Today()
Year()

TimeValue()

Purpose

Returns the serial number of the specified time.

Syntax

```
x = TimeValue(TimeString$)
```

Parameters

TimeString$
A string indicating a valid time, in a valid time format.

Returns

The serial number of the specified time.

See Also

DateSerial()
DateValue()

Day()
Month()
Now()
Time$()
TimeSerial()
Today()
Year()

TipWizard

Purpose

Displays or hides the Tip Wizard.

Syntax

```
TipWizard
```

See Also

Help
ShowMe

Today()

Purpose

Returns a time serial number representing the current date.

Syntax

```
x = Today()
```

Returns

A time serial number representing the current date.

See Also

Date$()
DateSerial()
DateValue()
Day()
Month()
Now()
Time$()
TimeSerial()
TimeValue()
Year()

ToggleFieldDisplay

Purpose

Toggles modes between display of field codes and display of field results.

Syntax

```
ToggleFieldDisplay
```

See Also

ViewFieldCodes

ToggleFull

Purpose

Toggles full screen mode.

Syntax

```
ToggleFull
```

See Also

ToolsOptionsView
ViewToolbars

ToggleHeader FooterLink

Purpose

Toggles the link between the current header/footer and the previous header/footer.

Syntax

```
ToggleHeaderFooterLink
```

See Also

FormatHeaderFooterLink
ShowNextHeaderFooter
ShowPrevHeaderFooter
ViewHeader

ToggleMainTextLayer

Purpose

Toggles display of main text layer when headers/footers are displayed.

Syntax

```
ToggleMainTextLayer
```

See Also

ViewHeader

TogglePortrait

Purpose

Toggles section(s) between protrait and landscape page orientations.

Syntax

```
TogglePortrait
```

See Also

FilePageSetup

ToggleScribbleMode

Purpose

Toggles hand annotation mode; for use with Windows for Pen only.

Syntax

```
ToggleScribbleMode
```

ToolbarButton Macro$()

Purpose

Returns the name of the macro or command assigned to a toolbar button.

Syntax

```
x$ = ToolbarName$()
```

Parameters

ToolbarName$
The name of the toolbar.

Position
The number of the toolbar button, counted from left to right.

Context
0: Normal template; 1 or omitted: current template

Returns

The name of the macro or command assigned to a given toolbar button.

See Also

CountToolbarButtons()
CountToolbars()
ToolbarName$()

ToolbarName$()

Purpose

Returns the name of a toolbar.

Syntax

```
x$ = ToolbarName$(ToolbarName$,
Context)
```

Parameters

ToolbarName$
The name of the toolbar.

Context
0: Normal template; 1 or omitted: current template

Returns

The name of a given toolbar.

See Also

CountToolbarButtons()
CountToolbars()
ToolbarButtonMacro$()

ToolbarState()

Purpose

Returns the display state of a toolbar.

Syntax

```
X$ = ToolbarState(ToolbarName$)
```

Parameters

ToolbarName$
The name of the toolbar.

Returns

TRUE (-1): The toolbar is displayed.
FALSE (0): The toolbar is not displayed.

See Also

ToolbarName$()
ViewRibbon
ViewRuler
ViewStatusBar
ViewToolbars

ToolsAdd RecordDefault

Purpose

Adds an empty record to the end of a data source.

Syntax

```
ToolsAddRecordDefault
```

See Also

MailMergeEditDataSource
ToolsRemoveRecordDefault

ToolsAdvanced Settings

Purpose

Changes options in an initialization file.

Syntax

```
ToolsAdvancedSettings .Attrib = value
```

Parameters

.Attrib—An advanced settings attribute:

.Application =	Name of an .INI section
.Option =	The option to set
.Setting =	The new setting for the option
.Delete =	Deletes the option
.Set =	Sets the option

value
The information about that argument.

See Also

GetPrivateProfileString$()
GetProfileString$()
SetPrivateProfileString
SetProfileString
ToolsOptionsFileLocations

ToolsAutoCorrect

Purpose

Sets AutoCorrect options.

Syntax

```
ToolsAutoCorrect .Attrib = value
```

Parameters

.Attrib—An advanced settings attribute:

.SmartQuotes =	If 1, inserts smart quotes
.InitialCaps =	If 1, corrects first two caps
.SentenceCaps =	If 1, caps first letter in sentence
.Days =	If 1, caps day of the week
.ReplaceText =	Activate auto text replacement
.Formatting =	If 1, auto text replaces with format
.Replace =	"Text to remove"
.With =	"Text to substitute"
.Add =	Adds entry in auto replace list

.Delete = Deletes entry in auto replace list

value
The information about that argument.

See Also

ToolsAutoCorrectDays
ToolsAutoCorrectInitialCaps
ToolsAutoCorrectReplaceText
ToolsAutoCorrectSentenceCaps
ToolsAutoCorrectSmartQuotes

ToolsAutoCorrect CapsLockOff, ToolsAutoCorrect CapsLockOff()

Purpose

Toggles the Word AutoCorrect feature that automatically fixes accidental usage of the CAPS LOCK key, or reports whether the feature is on or off.

Syntax

```
ToolsAutoCorrectCapsLockOff [On]
```

or

```
x = ToolsAutoCorrectCapsLockOff()
```

Parameters

On
Turns AutoCorrect Caps Lock feature on.

Returns

0: AutoCorrect Caps Lock is turned off.
-1: AutoCorrect Caps Lock is turned on.

See Also

ToolsAutoCorrect
ToolsAutoCorrectInitialCaps
ToolsAutoCorrectReplaceText
ToolsAutoCorrectSentenceCaps
ToolsAutoCorrectSmartQuotes

ToolsAuto CorrectDays or ToolsAuto CorrectDays()

Purpose

Sets automatic capitalization of names of days.

Syntax

```
ToolsAutoCorrectDays [On]
```

or

```
X = ToolsAutoCorrectDays()
```

Parameters

On

omitted: Toggles capitalization.
0: Clears capitalization.
1: Sets capitalization.

Returns

TRUE (-1): Capitalization is set.
FALSE (0): Capitalization is not set.

See Also

ToolsAutoCorrect

ToolsAutoCorrectExceptions

Purpose

Adds or removes words from the AutoCorrect exceptions list.

Syntax

```
ToolsAutoCorrectExceptions [.Tab = Number] [,.Name = text] [,.AutoAdd = Number] [,.Add] [,.Delete]
```

Parameters

.Tab

The tab where you want to add or remove the exception:
0: First Letter tab
1: INitial CAps tab

.Name

Text of list entry to be added or removed.

.AutoAdd

1: Include in the exception list any word the user changes back to its original spelling or capitalization after Word has automatically corrected it.

.Add

Adds the specified .Name to the exception list set in .Tab.

.Delete

Deletes the specified name from the exception list set in .Tab.

Returns

What the statement returns.

See Also

CountAutoCorrectExceptions()
GetAutoCorrectException$()
IsAutoCorrectException()

ToolsAutoCorrectInitialCaps or ToolsAutoCorrectInitialCaps()

Purpose

Sets to automatically correct two initial capital letters of a word.

Syntax

```
ToolsAutoCorrectInitialCaps [On]
```

or

```
X = ToolsAutoCorrectInitialCaps()
```

Parameters

On

omitted: Toggles correction.
0: Clears correction.
1: Sets correction.

Returns

TRUE (-1): Correction is set.
FALSE (0): Correction is not set.

See Also

ToolsAutoCorrect
ToolsAutoCorrectDays

ToolsAutoCorrectReplaceText or ToolsAutoCorrectReplaceText()

Purpose

Sets to automatically correct typing. If set, erroneously typed words are corrected immediately.

Syntax

```
ToolsAutoCorrectReplaceText [On]
X = ToolsAutoCorrectReplaceText()
```

Parameters

On

omitted: Toggles correction.
0: Clears correction.
1: Sets correction.

Returns

TRUE (-1): Correction is set.
FALSE (0): Correction is not set.

See Also

ToolsAutoCorrect
ToolsAutoCorrectDays

ToolsAutoCorrectSentenceCaps or ToolsAutoCorrectSentenceCaps()

Purpose

Sets to automatically correct sentences to add an initial capital letter real-time with typing.

Syntax

```
ToolsAutoCorrectSentenceCaps [On]
```

or

```
X = ToolsAutoCorrectSentenceCaps()
```

Parameters

On

omitted: Toggles correction.
0: Clears correction.
1: Sets correction.

Returns

TRUE (-1): Correction is set.
FALSE (0): Correction is not set.

See Also

ToolsAutoCorrect
ToolsAutoCorrectDays

ToolsAutoCorrectSmartQuotes or ToolsAutoCorrectSmartQuotes()

Purpose

Sets to automatically include "smart quotes" real-time with typing.

Syntax

```
ToolsAutoCorrectSmartQuotes [On]
```

or

```
X = ToolsAutoCorrectSmartQuotes()
```

Parameters

On

omitted: Toggles smart quotes.
0: Sets straight quotes.
1: Sets smart quotes.

Returns

TRUE (-1): Smart quotes are set.
FALSE (0): Straight quotes are set.

See Also

ToolsAutoCorrect
ToolsAutoCorrectDays

ToolsBulletListDefault

Purpose

Adds bullets, tabs, and hanging indents to selected paragraph(s).

Syntax

```
ToolsBulletListDefault
```

See Also

FormatBulletDefault
FormatBulletsAndNumbers
FormatNumberDefault
ToolsBulletsNumbers
ToolsNumberListDefault

ToolsBulletsNumbers

Purpose

Sets formatting for bulleted and numbered paragraphs.

Syntax

```
ToolsBulletsNumbers .Attrib = value
```

Parameters

.Attrib—A format attribute:

.Font =	Font for bullets or numbers
.CharNum =	ANSI Character to use as bullet
.Type =	Type of list: 0: Bulleted list 1: Numbered list 2: Outline-numbered list
.FormatOutline =	Numbering outline formats: Legal, Outline, Sequence, Learn, Outline All
.AutoUpdate =	If 1, fields auto update
.FormatNumber =	Numbering format: 0: 1, 2, 3, 4 1: I, II, III, IV 2: i, ii, iii, iv 3: A, B, C, D 4: a, b, c, d.
Punctuation	Separator char in list
.StartAt	Starting number or letter for list
.Points	Size of bullet, in points
.Hang	If 1, sets hanging indent for list
.Indent	Width of left indent in points
.Remove	Removes existing bullets/numbers
.Replace	Replace existing with new

value

The information about that argument.

See Also

FormatBulletDefault
FormatBulletsAndNumbers
FormatNumberDefault
ToolsBulletListDefault
ToolsNumberListDefault

ToolsCalculate or ToolsCalculate()

Purpose

Evaluates the selection as a mathematical expression. The result is placed in the Clipboard and displayed in the status bar.

Syntax

```
ToolsCalculate
```

or

```
x = ToolsCalculate([Expression$])
```

Parameters

Expression$

A mathematical expression to be evaluated.

See Also

TableAutoSum
TableFormula

ToolsCompareVersions

Purpose

Displays revision marks.

Syntax

```
ToolsCompareVersions .Name = CompareDoc$
```

Parameters

CompareDoc$
The path and file name of the document to be compared to the active document.

See Also

ToolsOptionsRevisions
ToolsRevisions

ToolsCreateEnvelope

Purpose

Creates an envelope.

Syntax

```
ToolsCreateEnvelope .Attrib = value
```

Parameters

.Attrib—An envelope attribute:

.ExtractAddress =	0: Not use 'EnvelopeAddress' bookmark 1: Use 'EnvelopeAddress' bookmark
.EnvAddress =	"Recipient address"
.EnvOmitReturn =	0: Return address not omitted 1: Return address omitted
.EnvReturn =	"Return address"
.PrintBarCode =	If 1, print POSTNET barcode
.EnvWidth =	Width of envelope
.EnvHeight =	Height of envelope
.EnvPaperSize =	List number of envelope size
.PrintFIMA =	If 1, add Facing ID Mark (FIM A)
.UseEnvFeeder =	The envelope source number
.AddrFromLeft =	Left distance to address
.AddrFromTop =	Top distance to address
.RetAddrFromLeft =	Left distance to return address

.RetAddrFromTop = Top distance to return address

.PrintEnvLabel = Prints the envelope

.AddToDocument = Adds addresses to document

value
The information about that argument.

See Also

FormatAddrFonts
FormatRetAddrFonts
ToolsCreateLabels

ToolsCreateLabels

Purpose

Creates mailing labels.

Syntax

```
ToolsCreateLabels .Attrib = value
```

Parameters

.Attrib—An envelope attribute:

.LabelListIndex = An item in the label products

.LabelIndex = An item in the product number

.LabelDotMatrix = 0: Laser; 1: Dot matrix

.LabelTray = The label tray

.LabelAcross = Number of labels in row

.LabelDown = Number of labels in column

.SingleLabel = If 1, print single label

.LabelRow = The row containing the label to print

.LabelColumn = The column containing the label

.LabelAutoText= AutoText entry for label text

.LabelText = The text on the label

.PrintEnvLabel = Prints the label

.AddToDocument = Makes labels on new document

.LabelTopMargin = Width of top margin

.LabelSideMargin = Width of side margin

.LabelVertPitch = Vertical space between labels

.LabelHorPitch = Horiz space between labels

.LabelHeight = Height of labels

.LabelWidth = Width of labels

value
The information about that argument.

See Also

ToolsCreateEnvelope

ToolsCustomize

Purpose

Displays the Customize dialog box.

Syntax

```
ToolsCustomize [.Tab = TabNum]
```

Parameters

TabNum

The tab to open:
0: Toolbars
1: Menus
2: Keyboard

See Also

AddButton
ToolsCustomizeKeyboard
ToolsCustomizeMenuBar
ToolsCustomizeMenus

ToolsCustomize Keyboard

Purpose

Assigns shortcut keys.

Syntax

```
ToolsCustomizeKeyboard .Attrib = value
```

Parameters

.*Attrib*—A keyboard attribute:

.KeyCode =	ANSI code for a key combination
.KeyCode2 =	ANSI code for second key combination
.Category =	Type of item to assign: 1 or omitted: Built-in commands 2: Macros 3: Fonts 4: AutoText entries 5: Styles 6: Common symbol
.Name =	The name of the macro, command,...
.Add =	Adds the key assignment
.Remove =	Remove the key assignment
ResetAll =	Resets all key assignments to default
.CommandValue =	More text needed by command
.Context =	0:Normal template; 1:Active template

value

The information about that argument.

See Also

CountKeys()
KeyCode()
KeyMacro$()

ToolsCustomize MenuBar

Purpose

Enables modification of the menus on the menu bar.

Syntax

```
ToolsCustomizeMenuBar .Attrib =
value
```

Parameters

.Attrib—A menu attribute:

.Context =	0: Normal template; 1: Active template
.Position =	Where to add new menu, from left
.MenuType =	Menu bar to change: 0 or omitted: Open document 1: No open document
.MenuText =	New name for menu
.Menu =	Name of menu to change
.Add =	Adds the menu
.Remove =	Remove the menu
.Rename =	Renames the menu

value
The information about that argument.

See Also

ToolsCustomizeMenus

ToolsCustomizeMenus

Purpose

Changes menu assignments for menu items.

Syntax

```
ToolsCustomizeMenus .Attrib = value
```

Parameters

.Attrib—A menu attribute:

.Context =	0: Normal template; 1: Active template
.Position =	Position on menu: -1 or omitted: Auto position -2: Add to bottom
n:	Add in specified position
.Category =	Type of item: 1 or omitted:

	Built-In commands 2: Macros 3: Fonts 4: AutoText entries 5: Styles
.MenuType =	Menu bar to change: 0 or omitted: Open document 1: No open document 2: Shortcut menus
.MenuText =	"New text for menu item"
.Menu =	Name of menu to change
.AddBelow =	Add item below specified item
.Add =	Adds the menu
.Remove =	Remove the menu
.ResetAll =	Resets all menu assignments
.Rename =	Renames the menu

value
The information about that argument.

See Also

CountMenuItems()
MenuItemMacro$()
MenuText$()
ToolsCustomizeMenuBar

ToolsGetSpelling or ToolsGetSpelling()

Purpose

Fills an array with suggested replacements for a misspelled word.

Syntax

```
ToolsGetSpelling Array$()
[, Word$][, MainDict$][, SupplDict$]
[, Mode]
```

or

```
x = ToolsGetSpelling(Array$()
[, Word$][, MainDict$][, SupplDict$]
[, Mode])
```

Parameters

Array$()
Array to fill with suggestions.

Word$
Possible misspelled word.

MainDict$
Name of main dictionary for language.

SupplDict$
Path and file name of custom dictionary.

Mode:
0 or omitted: Returns suggestions.
1: Returns suggestions based on wild cards.
2: Returns anagrams for search word.

Returns

The number of replacements suggested. Correct spelling returns a zero.

See Also

ToolsGetSynonyms
ToolsLanguage
ToolsOptionsSpelling

ToolsGetSynonyms or ToolsGetSynonyms()

Purpose

Fills an array with synonyms for a word.

Syntax

```
ToolsGetSynonyms Array$()
[, Word$][, MainDict$]
```

or

```
x = ToolsGetSpelling(Array$()
[, Word$][, MainDict$])
```

Parameters

Array$()
Array to fill with synonyms.

Word$
Word to find synonyms.

MainDict$
Name of main dictionary for language.

Returns

TRUE (-1): Synonyms found.
FALSE (0): No synonyms found.

See Also

ToolsGetSpelling

ToolsGrammar

Purpose

Displays Grammar dialog box.

Syntax

```
ToolsGrammar
```

See Also

ToolsSpelling

ToolsGrammar StatisticsArray

Purpose

Performs a grammar check, then fills an array with statistics.

Syntax

```
ToolsGrammarStatisticsArray
2DArray$(,)
```

Parameters

2DArray$
Two-dimensional array to fill with name counts, averages, and indexes.

See Also

CountToolsGrammarStatistics()

ToolsHyphenation

Purpose

Hyphenates the document.

Syntax

```
ToolsHyphenation .Attrib = value
```

Parameters

.Attrib—A hyphenation attribute:

.AutoHyphenation = If 1, no prompt for hyphen

.HyphenateCaps = If 1, hyphenate all-caps words

.HyphenationZone = Max space on right side

.LiitConsecutiveHyphens = Max number of consecutive lines with hyphens

value
The information about that argument.

See Also

ToolsHyphenationManual

ToolsHyphenationManual

Purpose

Hyphenates the document, with user assistance.

Syntax

```
ToolsHyphenationManual
```

See Also

ToolsHyphenation

ToolsLanguage

Purpose

Sets the language format for the selection.

Syntax

```
ToolsLanguage .Language = LangName$
[,.Default]
```

Parameters

LangName$
The name of the language.

See Also

CountLanguages()
FormatDefineStyleLang
Language

ToolsMacro

Purpose

Enables access to macros.

Syntax

```
ToolsMacro .Attrib = value
```

Parameters

.Attrib—A hyphenation attribute:

.Name=	The name of the macro
.Show=	The context: omitted: Search for macro 0: All available macros 1: Macros in Normal template 2: Built-in commands 3: Macros in active template >3: Macros in global templates
.Description=	A new description
.Run=	Runs macro
.Edit=	Opens macro edit window
.Delete=	Delete macro
.Rename=	Rename macro
.NewName=	New name for macro
.SetDesc=	Set new description for macro

value

The information about that argument.

See Also

CountMacros()
IsMacro()
KeyMacro$()
MacroDesc$()
MacroFileName$()
MacroNameFromWindows
MenuItemMacro$()
Organizer
PauseRecorder

ToolsManageFields

Purpose

Allows changes to a field name in a mail merge data source or header source.

Syntax

```
ToolsManageFields .Attrib = value
```

Parameters

.Attrib—A menu attribute:

.FieldName =	The field name
.Add =	Adds the field name
.Remove =	Remove the field name
.Rename =	Renames the field name
.NewName =	A new name for the field

value
The information about that argument.

See Also

MailMergeEditDataSource

ToolsMergeRevisions

Purpose

Merges revision marks from the active document into another document.

Syntax

```
ToolsMergeRevisions .Name = FileName$
```

Parameters

FileName$
The path and file name of the document to merge into.

See Also

ToolsCompareVersions
ToolsOptionsRevisions
ToolsReviewRevisions
ToolsRevisions

ToolsNumber ListDefault

Purpose

Add numbers, tabs, and hanging indents to selected paragraph(s).

Syntax

```
ToolsNumberListDefault
```

See Also

FormatBulletDefault
FormatBulletsAndNumbers
FormatNumberDefault
ToolsBulletListDefault
ToolsBulletsNumbers

ToolsOptions

Purpose

Displays the ToolsOptions dialog box, with a tab selected.

Syntax

```
ToolsOptions .Tab = OptionNum
```

Parameters

OptionNum
The tab to select:

0: View
1: General
2: Edit
3: Print
4: Save
5: Spelling
6: Grammar
7: AutoFormat
8: Revisions
9: UserInfo
10: Compatibility
11: File locations

See Also

ToolsCustomize

ToolsOptionsAutoFormat

Windows 95

Note new Word 95 parameters.

Purpose

Sets automatic formatting options.

Syntax

```
ToolsOptionsAutoFormat .Attrib = value
```

Parameters

.Attrib—An AutoFormat attribute:

.ShowOptionsFor =	Specifies which set of options are set by Tools OptionsAuto
Format:	0 = AutoFormat As You Type options 1 or omitted = Format AutoFormat statement (Available only in Word 95)
.PreserveStyles =	If 1, keeps previous styles (Word 95 ignores this argument if
.ShowOptionsFor = 0)	
.PreserveIndentLevels =	If 1, keeps indents
.ApplyStylesHeadings =	If 1, applies auto style heading
.ApplyStylesLists =	If 1, applies auto style lists (Word 95 ignores this argument if .
ShowOptionsFor = 0)	
.ApplyStylesOtherParas =	If 1, applies auto style paragraphs (Word 95 ignores this argument if .
ShowOptionsFor = 0)	
.AdjustParaMarks =	If 1, applies auto styles to inside addresses and salutations
.AdjustTabsSpaces =	If 1, auto adjust tab sets
.AdjustEmptyParas =	If 1, remove extra para marks
.ReplaceQuotes =	If 1, use smart quotes
.ReplaceSymbols =	If 1, use Symbols
.ReplaceBullets =	If 1, replaces with bullets If -1, uses setting in . ApplyBulletedLists

.ApplyBulletedLists = If 1, replaces bullet characters with bullets used in Bullets and Numbering dialog box, using symbols where appropriate (available only in Word 95)

.ReplaceOrdinals = If 1, replaces 1st with 1st, 2nd with 2nd, and so on

ReplaceFractions = If 1, replaces typed fractions such as 1/2 with fraction symbols from current character set, such as _

.ApplyBorders = If 1, replaces three or more minus signs (—), equal signs (===) or underlines (___) with the corresponding Word border (Available only in Word 95; ignored if .ShowOptionsFor equals 1 or is omitted)

.ApplyNumberedLists = If 1, interprets and reformats paragraphs as numbered lists, following the numbering scheme currently set in the Format, Bullets and Numbering dialog box (Available only in Word 95; ignored if .ShowOptionsFor equals 1 or is omitted)

See Also

ToolsAutoCorrect
FormatAutoFormat

ToolsOptions Compatibility

Note new Word 95 parameters that enable improved compatibility with WordPerfect and Microsoft Word 5.x for the Macintosh.

Purpose

Adjusts display of the active document to mimic other word processors.

Syntax

```
ToolsOptionsCompatibility .Attrib = value
```

Parameters

.Attrib—A compatibility attribute:

.Product =	The name of the product to mimic
.Default =	If 1, makes settings default.
NoTabHangIndent =	If 1, a tab stop not added to a hanging indent
.NoSpaceRaiseLower=	If 1, extra line spacing not added for super/subscript
.PrintColBlack =	If 1, all colors print black
.WrapTrailSpaces =	If 1, spaces at end of line wrap to next line
.NoColumnBalance =	If 1, text columns not balanced above continuous section breaks
.ConvMailMergeEsc =	If 1, interprets "\" from Word 2.x mail merge
.SuppressSpBfAfterPgBrk =	If 1, space before/after hard page and column breaks removed
.SuppressTopSpacing =	If 1, extra line spacing at top of page is removed
.OrigWordTableRules =	If 1, table borders combined as in Macintosh
TransparentMetafiles =	If 1, area behind metafile pictures is not blanked (new in Word 95)
.ShowBreaksInFrames =	If 1, displays hard page and column breaks in frames that contain them (new in Word 95)
.SwapBordersFacingPages =	If 1, prints a left paragraph border, not a box, on the right on odd-numbered pages, assuming either the Different Odd and Even or Mirror Margins checkboxes in the PageSetup dialog box are checked
.SuppressTopSpacingMac5 =	If 1, handles extra line spacing at the top of the page as Word

for the Macintosh 5.x did

.SpacingInWholePoints = If 1, rounds character spacing measurements to nearest integer

.PrintBodyTextBeforeHeader = If 1, prints main text layer before header/footer layer, thereby processing PostScript codes in the same order as Word for the Macintosh 5.x

.NoLeading = If 1, displays text lines without leading as Word for the Macintosh 5.x did

.NoSpaceForUL = If 1, adds no extra space for underlines (new in Word 95)

.MWSmallCaps = If 1, Word creates slightly larger small caps, as did Word for the Macintosh 5.x

.NoExtraLineSpacing = If 1, handles line spacing like WordPerfect 5.x

.TruncateFontHeight = If 1, font size rounded up or down as in WordPerfect 6.x for Windows (new in Word 95)

.SubFontBySize= If 1, fonts are substituted based on font size as in WordPerfect 6.x (new in Word 95)

See Also

FontSubstitution

ToolsOptionsEdit

Purpose

Sets editing options.

Syntax

```
ToolsOptionsEdit .Attrib = value
```

Parameters

.Attrib—an Edit option:

.ReplaceSelection = If 1, typing replaces selection

DragAndDrop = If 1, allows drag-and-drop

.AutoWordSelection = If 1, drag selects one word instead of one character

.InsForPaste = If 1, allows INS key for paste

.Overtype = If 1, enables overtype mode

.SmartCutPaste = If 1, auto adjusts spacing between words and punctuation during cut and paste

.AllowAccentedUppercase = If 1, Word can accent uppercase letters

.PictureEditor = App name to edit pictures

value
The information about that argument.

See Also

Overtype

ToolsOptions FileLocations

Purpose

Sets default directories.

Syntax

```
ToolsOptionsFileLocations .Path = PathName$, .Setting = Setting$
```

Parameters

PathName$
A Word pathname: DOC-PATH, PICTURE-PATH, USER-DOT-PATH, WORKGROUP-DOT-PATH, INI-PATH, AUTOSAVE-PATH, TOOLS-PATH, CBT-PATH, STARTUP-PATH

Setting$
The path for the default directory.

See Also

SetPrivateProfileString

ToolsOptionsGeneral

Note new Word 95 parameters for opening non-Word files and for controlling the Tip Wizard.

Purpose

Sets general options.

Syntax

```
ToolsOptionsGeneral .Attrib = value
```

Parameters

.Attrib—an Edit option:

.Pagination = If 1, allows background repagination

.WPHelp = If 1, enables WordPerfect Help

.WPDocNavKeys =If 1, enables WP document navigation keys

.BlueScreen =	If 1, sets white chars on blue
.ErrorBeeps =	If 1, enable beeps on error
.UpdateLinks =	If 1, auto update links on open
.SendMailAttach =	If 1, send active document as attachment instead of text, in e-mail
.RecentFiles =	If 1, list recently used files above Exit command on File menu
.RecentFileCount =	If 1, number of files to list
.Units =	If 1, default unit of measurement 0: Inches 1: Centimeters 2: Points 3: Picas
.ButtonFieldClicks =	Sets number of clicks required to run a MACROBUTTON field
.ConfirmConversions =	If 1, displays Convert File dialog box when opening files not in Word format (new in Word 95)
.TipWizardActive =	If 1, activates Tip Wizard; if Tip Wizard is active, resets it (new in Word 95)

See Also

Beep
CountFiles()
HelpWPHelpOpt
ToolsRepaginate

ToolsOptions Grammar

Purpose

Sets grammar checking options.

Syntax

```
ToolsOptionsGrammar [.Options =
Rules][,.CheckSpelling =
Spell][,.ShowStatistics = Stats]
```

Parameters

Rules

Specifies set of grammar rules:

0: All rules
1: Business writing
2: Casual writing
3: Custom 1
4: Custom 2
5: Custom 3

Spell

If 1, checks spelling during grammar checks.

Stats

If 1, displays readability statistics when complete.

See Also

ToolsGrammar

ToolsOptionsPrint

Purpose

Sets printing options.

Syntax

```
ToolsOptionsPrint .Attrib = value
```

Parameters

.Attrib—a Print option:

.Draft =	If 1, prints draft output
.Reverse =	If 1, prints in reverse order
.UpdateFields =	If 1, updates fields when printed
.UpdateLinks =	If 1, updates links when printed
.Background =	If 1, allows background printing
.Summary =	If 1, prints summary info with doc
.ShowCodes =	If 1, prints field codes (no results)
.Annotations =	If 1, prints annotations
.ShowHidden =	If 1, prints all hidden text
.EnvFeederInstalled =	If 1, envelope feeder OK
.DrawingObjects =	If 1, prints Word drawing objects
.FormsData =	If 1, print only data entered in form
.DefaultTray =	Default paper tray

value

The information about that argument.

See Also

FilePrint
FilePrintSetup

ToolsOptions Revisions

Note new Word 95 parameters for controlling highlight color in revisions.

Purpose

Sets revision marking options.

Syntax

```
ToolsOptionsRevisions .Attrib = value
```

Parameters

Attrib—a revisions option:

.InsertedTextMark Format for inserted text:
0: None
1: Bold
2: Italic
3: Underline
4: Double underline

.InsertedTextColor = Color for inserted text

.DeletedTextMark = Format for deleted text:
0: Hidden
1: Strikethrough

.DeletedTextColor = Color for deleted text

.RevisedLinesMark = Position for revised text:
0: None
1: Left border
2: Right border
3: Outside border

.RevisedLinesColor = Color for revised text

.HighlightColor = The color to be used for highlighting. Remains current color unless you specify a different one from the following list:
0: Transparent
1: Black
2: Blue
3: Cyan
4: Green
5: Magenta
6: Red
7: Yellow
8: White
9: Dark Blue
10: Cyan
11: Green
12: Magenta
13: Red
14: Yellow
15: Gray
16: Light Gray

(Highlighting parameter is new in Word 95.)

See Also

ToolsCompareVersions
ToolsRevisions
Highlight

ToolsOptionsSave

Purpose

Sets save options.

Syntax

```
ToolsOptionsSave .Attrib = value
```

Parameters

.Attrib—a Save option:

.CreateBackup = If 1, create backup every save

.FastSaves = If 1, allow fast saves

.SummaryPrompt = If 1, prompt for summary info

.GlobalDotPrompt = If 1, prompt to save changes to Normal template.

NativePictureFormat = If 1, saves only Windows version of imported graphics

.EmbedFonts = If 1, embeds TrueType fonts

.FormsData = If 1, saves data tab-delimited

.AutoSave = If 1, allows automatic save

.SaveInterval = Save interval

.Password = Read password

.WritePassword = Write password .RecommendReadOnly=If 1, displays dialog recommended open as read-only

value
The information about that argument.

See Also

FileSave
FileSaveAll
FileSaveAs

ToolsOptionsSpelling

Windows 95

Note new Word 95 parameters for managing automatic spell checking.

Purpose

Sets options for checking spelling.

Syntax

```
ToolsOptionsSpelling .Attrib = value
```

Parameters

.Attrib—a Spelling option:

.AlwaysSuggest = If 1, always give replacement

.SuggestFromMainDictOnly = If 1, draws from main dictionary only

.IgnoreAllCaps = If 1, ignores words in all caps

.IgnoreMixedDigits = If 1, ignores words that contain numbers

.ResetIgnoreAll = Reset IgnoreAll setting

.Type = If 1, Type of dictionary:
 0: Normal
 2: Complete
 3: Medical
 4: Legal

.CustomDict*n* = Path and file name of custom

.AutomaticSpellChecking = If 1, turns on automatic spell checking for the current document (new in Word 95)

.HideSpellingErrors= If 1, hides underlining of spelling errors in current document (new in Word 95)

.RecheckDocument= If 1, rechecks entire docuemnt for spelling errors, making sure previously reviewed and corrected words are double-checked (new in Word 95)

value
The information about that argument.

See Also

ToolsSpelling
ToolsSpellSelection
DocumentHasMisspellings
NextMisspelling

ToolsOptionsUserInfo

Purpose

Allows access to user information.

Syntax

```
ToolsOptionsUserInfo [.Name =
UserName$][,.Initials =
UserInitials$][,.Address =
UserAddr$]
```

Parameters

UserName$
The name of the current user

UserInitials$
The initials of the current user

UserAddr$
The mailing address of the current user

See Also

DocumentStatistics
FileSummaryInfo

ToolsOptionsView

Note new Word 95 parameters for viewing highlighting.

Purpose

Sets display options.

Syntax

```
ToolsOptionsView .Attrib = value
```

Parameters

.Attrib—a View option:

.DraftFont =	If 1, display all text in same font
.WrapToWindow =	If 1, wraps text in doc windows
.Drawings =	If 1, hides drawing objects .Anchors = If 1, display anchors
.TextBoundaries =	If 1, display text boundaries
.PicturePlaceHolders =	If 1, display placeholder graphics
.FieldCodes =	If 1, display field codes
.BookMarks =	If 1, display bold brackets
.FieldShading =	If 1, When to display shading: 0: Never 1: Always 2: When selected
.StatusBar =	If 1, display status bar
.Hscroll =	If 1, display horiz scroll bar
.Vscroll =	If 1, display vert scroll bar
.Vruler =	If 1, display vert ruler
.StyleAreaWidth =	Sets width of style area
.Tabs =	If 1, display tab marks
.Spaces =	If 1, display space marks
.Paras =	If 1, display paragraph marks
.Hyphens =	If 1, display optional hyphens
.Hidden =	If 1, display hidden text
.ShowAll =	If 1, display nonprinting characters
.Highlight =	If 1, displays highlight formatting (new in Word 95)

See Also

Highlight
ShowAll
TableGridlines
ToggleFull
ToolsOptionsCompatibility
ViewDraft
ViewRibbon
ViewRuler
ViewStatusBar

ToolsProtectDocument

Purpose

Protects the document from changes.

Syntax

```
ToolsProtectDocument
[.DocumentPassword =
DocPass$][,.NoReset =
NoReset][,.Type = Type]
```

Parameters

DocPass$
The document password.

NoReset
Cannot reset fields if form is protected.

Type
Type of protection:
0 or omitted: Revision marks only.
1: Add annotations only.
2: Modify text in form fields only.

See Also

FileSaveAs
ToolsOptionsSave
ToolsProtectSection
ToolsUnprotectDocument

ToolsProtectSection

Purpose

(Re)Sets protection for sections with a document.

Syntax

```
ToolsProtectSection .Section =
SectionNum [,.Protect = Protection]
```

Parameters

SectionNum
The section number to enable or disable protection.

Protection
0: Disables;
1: Enables protection

See Also

ToolsProtectDocument
ToolsUnprotectDocument

ToolsRemove RecordDefault

Purpose

Removes data record containing insertion point.

Syntax

```
ToolsRemoveRecordDefault
```

See Also

MailMergeEditDataSource
ToolsAddRecordDefault

ToolsRepaginate

Purpose

Forces repagination of entire document; (formerly ToolsRepaginateNow in Word 2.0).

Syntax

```
ToolsRepaginate
```

See Also

ToolsOptionsGeneral

ToolsReviewRevisions

Purpose

Searches for revision marks or accepts/rejects selected revisions.

Syntax

```
ToolsReviewRevisions .Attrib = value
```

Parameters

.*Attrib*—a revision option:

.ShowMarks =	Displays revision marks
.HideMarks =	Hides revision marks
.Wrap =	Controls action at end of document: 0 or omitted: Search ends 1: Search automatically wraps 2: Search wraps, with prompt
.FindPrevious =	Finds the prior text with revisions
.FindNext =	Finds the next text with revisions
.AcceptRevisions =	Accepts revisions to the text
.RejectRevisions =	Rejects revisions to the text

value

The information about that argument.

See Also

ToolsCompareVersions
ToolsOptionsRevisions
ToolsRevisions
ToolsRevisionType()

ToolsRevisionAuthor$()

Purpose

Returns the name of the person who made the selected revision.

Syntax

```
x$ = ToolsRevisionAuthor$()
```

Returns

The name of the person who made the selected revision.

See Also

ToolsReviewRevisions
ToolsRevisionsDate$()
ToolsRevisions
ToolsRevisionType()

ToolsRevisionDate$()

Purpose

Returns the date and time the selected revision was made.

Syntax

```
x$ = ToolsRevisionDate$()
```

Returns

The date and time the selected revision was made.

See Also

ToolsReviewRevisions
ToolsRevisionAuthor$()
ToolsRevisionDate()
ToolsRevisions
ToolsRevisionType()

ToolsRevisionDate()

Purpose

Returns a date serial number representing the date and time the selected revision was made.

Syntax

```
x = ToolsRevisionDate()
```

Returns

A date serial number.

See Also

ToolsReviewRevisions
ToolsRevisionAuthor$()
ToolsRevisionDate$()
ToolsRevisions
ToolsRevisionType()

ToolsRevisions

Purpose

Sets how revisions are marked and reviewed in the active document.

Syntax

```
ToolsRevisions .Attrib = value
```

Parameters

.Attrib—a revision option:

.MarkRevisions =	If 1, activates revision marks
.ViewRevisions =	If 1, revision marks appear
.PrintRevisions =	Include marks in print: 0: Revision marks do not appear 1: Revision marks appear
.AcceptAll=	Accepts revisions to the document
.RejectAll =	Rejects revisions to the document

value
The information about that argument.

See Also

ToolsCompareVersions
ToolsMergeRevisions
ToolsOptionsRevisions
ToolsReviewRevisions
ToolsRevisionType()

ToolsRevisionType()

Purpose

Returns the type of revision made.

Syntax

```
x = ToolsRevisionType()
```

Returns

0: Selection contains no revisions.
1: All/part of selection contains inserted text.
2: All/part of selection contains deleted text.
3: All/part of selection contains replacement text.
4: Selection contains more than one revision.

See Also

ToolsReviewRevisions
ToolsRevisionAuthor$()
ToolsRevisionDate$()
ToolsRevisionDate()
ToolsRevisions

ToolsShrinkToFit

Purpose

Attempts to decrease the font size of the text to try to fit the active document on fewer pages.

Syntax

```
ToolsShrinkToFit
```

See Also

ViewZoomWholePage

ToolsSpelling

Purpose

Checks spelling in the current selection or from the insertion point to the end of the document.

Syntax

```
ToolsSpelling
```

See Also

ToolsOptionsSpelling
ToolsSpellSelection

ToolsSpelling RecheckDocument

Purpose

Completely rechecks a document for spelling errors.

Syntax

```
ToolsSpellingRecheckDocument
```

See Also

DocumentHasMisspellings()
NextMisspelling
SpellChecked
ToolsSpelling
ToolsSpellSelection

ToolsSpellSelection

Purpose

Checks spelling in the current selection; used to check spelling of one word.

Syntax

```
ToolsSpellSelection
```

See Also

ToolsOptionsSpelling
ToolsSpelling

ToolsThesaurus

Purpose

Displays the Thesaurus dialog box.

Syntax

```
ToolsThesaurus
```

See Also

ToolsGetSynonyms

ToolsUnprotect Document

Purpose

Removes protection from the active document.

Syntax

```
ToolsUnprotectDocument
[.DocumentPassword = DocPass$]
```

Parameters

DocPass$
The document password. Note: passwords are case-sensitive.

See Also

ToolsProtectDocument
ToolsProtectSection

ToolsWordCount

Purpose

Counts the number of characters, words, lines, paragraphs, and pages in the active document.

Syntax

```
ToolsWordCount [.CountFootnotes =
][,.Pages = ][,.Words = ]
[,.Characters = ][,.Paragraphs = ]
[,.Lines = ]
```

Parameters

CountFoot
If 1, text in footnotes and endnotes is included in the count.

Pages$
The number of pages in the document.

Words$
The number of words in the document.

Chars$
The number of characters in the document.

Paras$
The number of paragraphs in the document.

Lines$
The number of lines in the document.

Returns

All attributes are read-only and must be read through a Dialog variable.

See Also

DocumentStatistics
FileSummaryInfo

UCase$()

Purpose

Converts a string to all uppercase.

Syntax

```
x$ = UCase$(string$)
```

Parameters

string$
Any string variable or function that results in a string.

Returns

string$: as all uppercase letters.

See Also

ChangeCase
LCase$()

Underline or Underline()

Purpose

Adds or removes underline formatting from the selection.

Syntax

```
Underline [Action]
```

or

```
x = Underline()
```

Parameters

Action

1: Sets selection to underline.
0: Removes underlining from selection.
omitted: Toggles underlining.

Returns

-1: Only part of the selection is under lined.
0: None of the selection is underlined.
1: All the selection is underlined.

See Also

DottedUnderline
DoubleUnderline
FormatFont
WordUnderline

UnHang

Purpose

Removes a hanging indent from the selected paragraph(s).

Syntax

```
UnHang
```

See Also

HangingIndent
UnIndent

UnIndent

Purpose

Moves the left indent of the selected paragraph(s) to the previous tab stop.

Syntax

```
UnIndent
```

See Also

Indent
UnHang

UnlinkFields

Purpose

Replaces selected fields with their most recent results. Once executed, this command cannot be reversed.

Syntax

```
UnlinkFields
```

See Also

LockFields
UnlockFields
UpdateFields

UnlockFields

Purpose

Allows selected, previously locked fields to be updated; reverses LockFields.

Syntax

```
UnlockFields
```

See Also

LockFields
UnlinkFields
UpdateFields

UpdateFields

Purpose

Updates selected fields.

Syntax

```
UpdateFields
```

See Also

LockFields
UnlinkFields
UnlockFields

UpdateSource

Purpose

Saves changes made to an INCLUDETEXT field into the source document.

Syntax

```
UpdateSource
```

See Also

UpdateFields

Val()

Purpose

Returns the numeric value of a string.

Syntax

```
x = Val(string$)
```

Parameters

string$
Any string variable or function that results in a string.

Returns

The numeric value of a string.

See Also

Str$()

ViewAnnotations or ViewAnnotations()

Purpose

Controls display of the annotation pane.

Syntax

```
ViewAnnotations [Action]
```

or

```
x = ViewAnnotations()
```

Parameters

Action

1: Closes the annotation pane
0: Opens the annotation pane
omitted: Toggles the annotation pane

Returns

TRUE (-1): The annotation pane is open.
FALSE (0): The annotation pane is closed.

See Also

InsertAnnotation
ViewEndnoteArea
ViewFootnoteArea
ViewFootnotes

ViewBorderToolbar

Purpose

Toggles the display of the Borders toolbar.

Syntax

```
ViewBorderToolbar
```

See Also

ViewDrawingToolbar
ViewToolbars

ViewDraft or ViewDraft()

Purpose

Controls draft mode for the active document.

Syntax

```
ViewDraft [Action]
```

or

```
x = ViewDraft()
```

Parameters

Action

1: Turns on draft mode.
0: Turns off draft mode.
omitted: Toggles draft mode.

Returns

TRUE (-1): Draft mode is on.
FALSE (0): Draft mode is off.

See Also

ToolsOptionsView

ViewDrawingToolbar

Purpose

Toggles display of the Drawing toolbar.

Syntax

```
ViewDrawingToolbar
```

See Also

ViewBorderToolbar
ViewToolbars

ViewEndnoteArea or ViewEndnoteArea()

Purpose

Controls display of the endnote pane or moves to or from the endnote area in Page Layout view.

Syntax

```
ViewEndnoteArea [Action]
```

or

```
x = ViewEndnoteArea()
```

Parameters

Action

0: Closes the endnote pane.
1: Opens the endnote pane.
omitted: Toggles the endnote pane.

Returns

TRUE (-1): The endnote pane is open.
FALSE (0): The endnote pane is closed.

See Also

ViewAnnotations
ViewFootnoteArea
ViewFootnotes

ViewEndnoteContNotice

Purpose

Opens a pane containing the endnote continuation notice (indicates that an endnote is continued on the following page).

Syntax

```
ViewEndnoteContNotice
```

See Also

ResetNoteSepOrNotice
ViewEndnoteContSeparator

ViewEndnoteSeparator
ViewFootnoteContNotice

ViewEndnote ContSeparator

Purpose

Opens a pane containing the endnote continuation separator (indicates that an endnote is continued from the previous page).

Syntax

```
ViewEndnoteContSeparator
```

See Also

ResetNoteSepOrNotice
ViewEndnoteContNotice
ViewEndnoteSeparator
ViewFootnoteContNotice

ViewEndnote Separator

Purpose

Opens a pane containing the endnote separator (separates an endnote from the document's text).

Syntax

```
ViewEndnoteSeparator
```

See Also

ResetNoteSepOrNotice
ViewEndnoteContNotice
ViewEndnoteContSeparator
ViewFootnoteSeparator

ViewFieldCodes or ViewFieldCodes()

Purpose

Controls the display of either field statements or field results for the active document.

Syntax

```
ViewFieldCodes [Action]
```

or

```
x = ViewFieldCodes()
```

Parameters

Action
1: Displays all field statements.
0: Displays all field results.
omitted: Toggles the display of fields.

Returns

TRUE (-1): Field statements are displayed.
FALSE (0): Field results are displayed.

See Also

ToggleFieldDisplay
ToolsOptionsView

ViewFooter or ViewFooter()

Purpose

Switches the active document to Page Layout view and moves the insertion point to the footer area.

Syntax

```
ViewFooter
```

or

```
x = ViewFooter()
```

Returns

TRUE (-1): The insertion point is in the footer area.
FALSE (0): The insertion point is not in footer area.

See Also

CloseViewHeaderFooter
ViewHeader

ViewFootnoteArea or ViewFootnoteArea()

Purpose

Toggles display of the footnote pane in the active document.

Syntax

```
ViewFootnoteArea [Action]
```

or

```
x=ViewFootnoteArea()
```

Parameters

Action
0: Closes the footnote pane.
1: Opens the footnote pane.
omitted: Toggles the footnote pane.

Returns

TRUE (-1): The footnote pane is open.
FALSE (0): The footnote pane is closed.

See Also

ViewAnnotations
ViewEndnoteArea
ViewFootnotes

ViewFootnote ContNotice

Purpose

Opens a pane containing the footnote continuation notice (indicates that a footnote is continued on the following page).

Syntax

```
ViewFootnoteContNotice
```

See Also

ResetNoteSepOrNotice
ViewEndnoteContSeparator
ViewEndnoteSeparator
ViewFootnoteContNotice

ViewFootnote ContSeparator

Purpose

Opens a pane containing the footnote continuation separator (indicates that a footnote is continued from the previous page).

Syntax

```
ViewFootnoteContSeparator
```

See Also

ResetNoteSepOrNotice
ViewEndnoteContNotice
ViewEndnoteSeparator
ViewFootnoteContNotice

ViewFootnotes or ViewFootnotes()

Purpose

Controls the display of the footnote or endnote pane in the active document.

Syntax

```
ViewFootnotes
```

or

```
x = ViewFootnotes()
```

Returns

TRUE (-1): A footnote or endnote pane is open.
FALSE (0): The footnote and endnote panes are closed.

See Also

ViewEndnoteArea
ViewFootnoteArea

ViewFootnote Separator

Purpose

Opens a pane containing the footnote separator (separates a footnote from the document's text).

Syntax

```
ViewFootnoteSeparator
```

See Also

ResetNoteSepOrNotice
ViewEndnoteSeparator
ViewFootnoteContNotice
ViewFootnoteContSeparator

ViewHeader or ViewHeader()

Purpose

Switches the active document to Page Layout view and moves the insertion point to the header area.

Syntax

```
ViewHeader
```

or

```
x = ViewHeader()
```

Returns

TRUE (-1): The insertion point is in the header area.
FALSE (0): The insertion point is not in header area.

See Also

ViewFooter

ViewMasterDocument or ViewMasterDocument()

Purpose

Switches the active document to Master Document view.

Syntax

```
ViewMasterDocument
```

or

```
x = ViewMasterDocument()
```

Returns

TRUE (-1): The document is in the master doc view.
FALSE (0): The document is not in master doc view.

See Also

ViewOutline
ViewToggleMasterDocument

ViewMenus()

Purpose

Indicates which menu bar is displayed.

Syntax

```
x = ViewMenus()
```

Returns

0: The full menu bar is displayed.
1: Only File, Help, and Control menus are displayed.

See Also

ToolsCustomizeMenus
ToolsCustomizeMenuBar

ViewNormal or ViewNormal()

Purpose

Switches the active document to Normal view.

Syntax

```
ViewNormal
```

or

```
x = ViewNormal()
```

Returns

TRUE (-1): The document is in Normal view.
FALSE (0): The document is not in Normal view.

See Also

FilePrintPreview
ViewDraft
ViewMasterDocument
ViewOutline
ViewPage

ViewOutline or ViewOutline()

Purpose

Switches the active document to Outline view.

Syntax

```
ViewOutline
```

or

```
x = ViewOutline()
```

Returns

TRUE (-1): The document is in Outline view.
FALSE (0): The document is not in Outline view.

See Also

FilePrintPreview
ViewDraft
ViewMasterDocument
ViewNormal
ViewPage

ViewPage or ViewPage()

Purpose

Switches the active document to Page Layout view.

Syntax

```
ViewPage
```

or

```
x = ViewPage()
```

Returns

TRUE (-1): The document is in Page Layout view.

FALSE (0): The document is not in Page Layout view.

See Also

FilePrintPreview
ViewDraft
ViewMasterDocument
ViewNormal
ViewOutline

ViewRibbon or ViewRibbon()

Purpose

Controls the display of the Formatting Ribbon.

Syntax

```
ViewRibbon [Action]
```

or

```
x = ViewRibbon()
```

Parameters

Action

1: Displays the Ribbon.
0: Hides the Ribbon.
omitted: Toggles display of the Ribbon.

Returns

TRUE (-1): The Ribbon is displayed.
FALSE (0): The Ribbon is not displayed.

See Also

ToolsOptionsView
ViewRuler
ViewStatusBar
ViewToolbars

ViewRuler or ViewRuler()

Purpose

Controls the display of the Rulers.

Syntax

```
ViewRuler [Action]
```

or

```
x = ViewRulers()
```

Parameters

Action

1: Displays the rulers.
0: Hides the rulers.
omitted: Toggles display of the rulers.

Returns

TRUE (-1): The rulers are displayed.
FALSE (0): The rulers are not displayed.

See Also

ToolsOptionsView
ViewRibbon
ViewStatusBar
ViewToolbars

ViewStatusBar or ViewStatusBar()

Purpose

Controls the display of the status bar.

Syntax

```
ViewStatusBar [Action]
```

or

```
x = ViewStatusBar()
```

Parameters

Action

1: Displays the status bar.
0: Hides the status bar.
omitted: Toggles display of the status bar.

Returns

TRUE (-1): The status bar is displayed.
FALSE (0): The status bar is not displayed.

See Also

ToolsOptionsView
ViewRibbon
ViewRuler
ViewToolbars

ViewToggle MasterDocument

Purpose

Toggles the active document between Outline view and Master Document view.

Syntax

```
ViewToggleMasterDocument
```

See Also

ViewMasterDocument
ViewOutline

ViewToolbars

Purpose

Sets options for viewing toolbars (formerly the ViewToolbar command in Word 2.0).

Syntax

```
ViewToolbars .Attrib = value
```

Parameters

.Attrib—a toolbar attribute:

.Toolbar =	The name of the toolbar
.Context =	0: Normal template; 1: Active template

.ColorButtons =	If 1, displays color tools
.LargeButtons =	If 1, displays large tools
.ToolTips =	If 1, displays tool tips by pointer
.Reset =	If 1, restores default toolbar
.Delete =	If 1, deletes the toolbar
.Show =	If 1, displays the tolbar
.Hide =	If 1, hides the toolbar

value
The information about that argument.

See Also

NewToolbar
ToolsOptionsView
ViewRibbon
ViewRuler
ViewStatusBar

ViewZoom

Purpose

Changes the magnification for the active document and all documents later created.

Syntax

```
ViewZoom .Attrib = value
```

Parameters

.Attrib—a toolbar attribute:

.BestFit =	Sets zoom to entire page width
.TwoPages =	Sets zoom so two pages are visible
.FullPage =	Sets zoom so full page is visible
.NumColumns =	Number of columns in grid of pages
.NumRows =	Number of rows in grid of pages
.ZoomPercent =	Percent magnification

value
The information about that argument.

See Also

ViewZoom100
ViewZoom200
ViewZoom75
ViewZoomPageWidth
ViewZoomWholePage

ViewZoom100

Purpose

Switches to Normal view and sets magnification to 100 percent. This command is valid for the active document and all documents later created.

Syntax

```
ViewZoom100
```

See Also

ViewZoom
ViewZoom200
ViewZoom75
ViewZoomPageWidth
ViewZoomWholePage

ViewZoom200

Purpose

Switches to Normal view and sets magnification to 200 percent. This command is valid for the active document and all documents later created.

Syntax

```
ViewZoom200
```

See Also

ViewZoom
ViewZoom100
ViewZoom75
ViewZoomPageWidth
ViewZoomWholePage

ViewZoom75

Purpose

Switches to Normal view and sets magnification to 75 percent. This command is valid for the active document and all documents later created.

Syntax

```
ViewZoom75
```

See Also

ViewZoom
ViewZoom100
ViewZoom200
ViewZoomPageWidth
ViewZoomWholePage

ViewZoom PageWidth

Purpose

Sets the magnification so that the entire width of the page is visible.

Syntax

```
ViewZoomPageWidth
```

See Also

ViewZoom
ViewZoom100
ViewZoom200
ViewZoom75
ViewZoomWholePage

ViewZoom WholePage

Purpose

Sets the magnification so that the entire page is visible in Page Payout view.

Syntax

```
ViewZoomWholePage
```

See Also

ViewZoom
ViewZoom100
ViewZoom200
ViewZoom75
ViewZoomPageWidth

VLine

Purpose

Scrolls the active document vertically (via the scroll arrow).

Syntax

```
VLine [Count]
```

Parameters

Count
The amount to scroll
omitted: One line down.
<0: scrolls *Count* lines up.
>0: scrolls *Count* lines down.

See Also

HLine
VPage
VScroll

VPage

Purpose

Scrolls the active document vertically (via the scroll bar).

Syntax

VPage [*Count*]

Parameters

Count
The amount to scroll
omitted: One line down.
<0: scrolls *Count* screens up.
>0: scrolls *Count* screens down.

See Also

HPage
VLine
VScroll

VScroll or VScroll()

Purpose

Scrolls the active document vertically by the given percentage of the document length.

Syntax

```
VScroll Percent
```

or

```
x = VScroll()
```

Parameters

Percent
An integer from 0 to 100. The current vertical scroll position as a percentage of the document width.

See Also

HScroll
VLine
VPage

WaitCursor

Purpose

Toggles the cursor between a regular cursor and an hourglass.

Syntax

```
WaitCursor Cursor
```

Parameters

Cursor
0: The current pointer
1: The hourglass

Weekday()

Purpose

Returns the number of the day of the week, represented by a date serial number.

Syntax

```
x = Weekday(SerialNumber)
```

Parameters

SerialNumber
A date serial number.

Returns

An integer between 1 and 7; 1 is Sunday.

See Also

DateSerial()
Day()
Hour()
Minute()
Month()
Now()
Second()
Today()
Year()

While...Wend

Purpose

Repeats a series of instructions while a condition(s) is true.

Syntax

```
While Condition
...Instructions...Wend
```

Parameters

Condition
An expression returning a logical true/false value (nonzero = TRUE).

Instructions
The set of instructions to be repeated while.

Condition
Evaluates TRUE.

See Also

For...Next
Goto
If...Then...Else
Select Case

Window()

Purpose

Returns the list number of the active Word window (as listed in the Window menu).

Syntax

```
x = Window()
```

Returns

The list number of the active window (as listed in the Window menu), beginning with 1.

See Also

WindowList
WindowName$()
WindowNumber
WindowPane()

WindowArrangeAll

Purpose

Arranges all open Word windows in the Word workspace so that there is no overlap.

Syntax

```
WindowArrangeAll
```

See Also

DocMove
DocRestore
DocSize

WindowList

Purpose

Activates a Word window.

Syntax

```
WindowList Number
```

Parameters

Number
The list number of the window.

See Also

CountWindows()
Window()
WindowName$()
WindowNumber
WindowPane()

WindowName$()

Purpose

Returns the title of an open Word window.

Syntax

```
x$ = WindowName$(WindowNumber)
```

Parameters

WindowNumber
The list number of the window.

Returns

The title of an open Word window. If omitted, the title of the active window is returned.

See Also

CountWindows()
Window()
WindowList()
Window*Number*
WindowPane()

WindowNewWindow

Purpose

Opens a new window with a copy of the active document.

Syntax

```
WindowNewWindow
```

See Also

DocSplit
WindowArrangeAll
WindowName$()

WindowNumber

Purpose

Activates a Word window.

Syntax

```
WindowNumber
```

Parameters

Number is a number from 1 to 9.

See Also

Activate
CountWindows()
Window()
WindowList()
WindowName$()
WindowPane()

WindowPane()

Purpose

Returns status of the window panes.

Syntax

```
x = WindowPane()
```

Returns

1: If a) the active window is not split, or b) the insertion point is in the top pane of the active window
3: If the insertion point is in the bottom pane of the active window

See Also

DocSplit
OtherPane
ViewAnnotations()
ViewFootnoteArea()

WinToDOS$()

Purpose

Translates a string from the Windows character set to the OEM character set.

Syntax

```
x$ = WinToDOS$(string$)
```

Parameters

string$
Any string variable or function that results in a string.

Returns

string$: translated into the OEM character set.

See Also

DOSToWin$()

WordLeft or WordLeft()

Purpose

Moves the insertion point to the left by the given number of words.

Syntax

```
WordLeft [Count,] [Select]
```

or

```
x = WordLeft([Count,] [Select])
```

Parameters

Count
The number of words to move past. If 0 or omitted, 1 is default. Negative signs are ignored.

Select
If nonzero, the selection is extended by *Count* words.

Returns

0: The action cannot be performed.
-1: The action can be performed, even if only partially.

See Also

CharLeft
SelectCurWord
SentLeft
WordRight

WordRight or WordRight()

Purpose

Moves the insertion point to the right by the given number of words.

Syntax

```
WordRight [Count,] [Select]
```

or

```
x = WordRight([Count,] [Select])
```

Parameters

Count
The number of words to move past. If 0 or omitted, 1 is default. Negative signs are ignored.

Select
If nonzero, the selection is extended by *Count* words.

Returns

0: The action cannot be performed.
-1: The action can be performed, even if only partially.

See Also

CharRight
SelectCurWord
SentRight
WordLeft

WordUnderline or WordUnderline()

Purpose

Adds or removes word underline formatting from the selection.

Syntax

```
WordUnderline [Action]
```

or

```
x = WordUnderline()
```

Parameters

Action
1: Sets selection to underline words only.
0: Removes word underlining from selection.
omitted: Toggles word underlining.

Returns

-1: Only part of the selection is word underlined.
0: None of the selection is word underlined.
1: All the selection is word underlined.

See Also

DottedUnderline
DoubleUnderline
FormatFont
Underline

Write

Purpose

Writes string or numeric values to an open sequential file.

Syntax

```
Write #StreamNumber, VariableList
```

Parameters

#StreamNumber
: The number used in the Open statement; specifies the open file.

VariableList
: The variables to be written to the file.

See Also

Close
Eof()
Input
Input$()
Line Input
Lof()
Open
Print
Read
Seek

Year()

Purpose

Returns the year of a date serial number.

Syntax

```
x = Year(SerialNumber)
```

Parameters

SerialNumber
: A date serial number.

Returns

An integer year between 1899 and 4095.

See Also

DateSerial()
Day()
Hour()
Minute()
Month()
Now()
Second()
Today()
Weekday()

Part VI

Appendixes

New Riders Publishing
INSIDE
SERIES

Keyboard Shortcuts

In Word for Windows 95, just about anything you can do with a mouse you also can do with the keyboard. And often, the keyboard is faster and easier. This appendix provides a complete list of Word keyboard shortcuts.

You also find an alphabetized list of Word's keyboard shortcuts, KEYBLIST.DOC, on the disk that comes with this book. By the way, suggestions for the 18 most useful keyboard shortcuts appear in Chapter 1.

Working with Menus and Dialog Boxes

Task	Keyboard Combination
Activate menu bar	F10 or Alt
Perform action	Enter
Cancel	Esc
Show Shortcut Menu	Shift+F10

Working with Files

Task	Keyboard Combination
New file	Ctrl+N
Open existing file	Ctrl+O or Ctrl+F12 or Alt+Ctrl+F2
Print	Ctrl+P or Ctrl+Shift+F12
Print Preview	Ctrl+F2 or Alt+Ctrl+I
Save	Shift+F12 or Ctrl+S or Alt+Shift+F2
Save As	F12
Exit Word (request to save documents)	Alt+F4

Getting Help

Task	Keyboard Combination
Go to Help System	F1
Activate Help button	Shift+F1 (then click on what you need help with)

Editing

Task	Keyboard Combination
Overtype/Insert Mode (toggle)	Ins
Delete character to the left	Backspace
Delete character to the right	Delete
Copy	Ctrl+C or Ctrl+Ins
Cut	Ctrl+X or Shift+Del
Cut to Spike	Ctrl+F3
Delete previous word	Ctrl+Backspace
Delete next word	Ctrl+Delete
Find	Ctrl+F
Find Again	Shift+F4 or Alt+Ctrl+Y
Move text	F2
Paste	Ctrl+V or Shift+Ins
Redo Undone Action	Alt+Shift+Backspace
Repeat Last Action	F4 or Ctrl+Y or Alt+Enter
Replace	Ctrl+H
Undo	Ctrl+Z or Alt+Backspace

Moving around a Document

Task	Keyboard Combination
Go to a specific location	Arrow keys
Go To	F5 or Ctrl+G
Previous Insertion Point	Shift+F5 or Alt+Ctrl+Z
Beginning of document	Ctrl+Home
End of document	Ctrl+End
Top of window	Ctrl+PageUp

continues

Task	Keyboard Combination
Bottom of window	Ctrl+PageDown
Next screen	PageDown
Previous screen	PageUp
Next page	Alt+Ctrl+PageDown
Previous page	Alt+Ctrl+PageUp
Next paragraph	Ctrl+Down
Previous paragraph	Ctrl+Up
Previous field	Shift+F11 or Alt+Shift+F1
Previous object	Alt+Up
Previous window	Ctrl+Shift+F6 or Alt+Shift+F6
Beginning of column	Alt+PageUp or Alt+Shift+PageUp
End of column	Alt+PageDown or Alt+Shift+PageDown
Beginning of line	Home
End of line	End
Next line	Down arrow
Previous line	Up arrow
Beginning of row	Alt+Home or Alt+Shift+Home
Last cell in row	Alt+End or Alt+Shift+End
Left one word	Ctrl+Left
Right one word	Ctrl+Right
Left one character	Left arrow
Right one character	Right arrow
Next annotated text	Alt+F11
Previous field	Shift+F11
Next field	F11 or Alt+F1
Previous frame or object	Alt+UpArrow
Next frame or object	Alt+DownArrow
Previous column in table	Ctrl+UpArrow
Next column in table	Ctrl+DownArrow
Next misspelling	Alt+F7

Selecting Text

Task	Keyboard Combination
Start extending selection	F8
Select entire document	Ctrl+NumPad or Ctrl+A
Select headers, footers, annotations, footnotes, or endnotes	Ctrl+NumPad5 (with insertion point in pane)
Select entire table	Alt+NumPad5
Select vertical column or block of cells	Ctrl+Shift+F8

Extend Selection	Keyboard Combination
To beginning of document	Ctrl+Shift+Home
To end of document	Ctrl+Shift+End
To top of window	Ctrl+Shift+PageUp
To bottom of window	Ctrl+Shift+PageDown
Down one page	Shift+PageDown
Up one page	Shift+PageUp
Down one paragraph	Ctrl+Shift+Down
Up one paragraph	Ctrl+Shift+Up
Up one line	Shift+Up arrow
Down one line	Shift+Down arrow
To beginning of line	Shift+Home
To end of line	Shift+End
Left one word	Ctrl+Shift+Left
Right one word	Ctrl+Shift+Right
Left one character	Shift+Left arrow
Right one character	Shift+Right arrow

Viewing the Document

Task	Keyboard Combination
Normal View	Alt+Ctrl+N
Outline View	Alt+Ctrl+O
Page Layout View	Alt+Ctrl+P
Show/Hide All Nonprinting Characters	Ctrl+*

Inserting

Task	Keyboard Combination
Annotation	Alt+Ctrl+A
AutoText	F3, Alt+Ctrl+V
Bookmark	Ctrl+Shift+F5
Citation	Alt+Shift+I
Column Break	Ctrl+Shift+Enter
Date	Alt+Shift+D
Endnote	Alt+Ctrl+E
Field	Ctrl+F9
Footnote	Alt+Ctrl+F
Index Entry	Alt+Shift+X
Line Break	Shift+Enter
Non-Breaking Hyphen	Ctrl+Shift+Hyphen
Non-Breaking Space	Ctrl+Shift+Spacebar
Page Break	Ctrl+Enter
Page Number	Alt+Shift+P
Spiked text	Ctrl+Shift+F3
Table of Contents Entry	Alt+Shift+O
Time	Alt+Shift+T

Formatting Characters

Task	Keyboard Combination
Clear manual character formatting	Ctrl+Spacebar or Ctrl+Shift+Z
Copy Formatting	Ctrl+Shift+C
Paste Formatting	Ctrl+Shift+V
Change Case	Shift+F3
All Caps	Ctrl+Shift+A
Bold	Ctrl+B
Hidden Text	Ctrl+Shift+H
Italic	Ctrl+I
Small caps	Ctrl+Shift+K
Subscript	Ctrl+EqualSign
Superscript	Ctrl+PlusSign
Symbol Font	Ctrl+Shift+Q
Underline	Ctrl+U
Underline words only (not spaces)	Ctrl+Shift+W
Double Underline	Ctrl+Shift+D
Kern more	Ctrl+Shift+]
Kern less	Ctrl+Shift+[
Font Formatting/Spacing	Ctrl+D
Font List Box	Ctrl+Shift+F
Font Size	Ctrl+Shift+P
Grow font 1 point	Ctrl+]
Grow font to next available size	Ctrl+>
Shrink font 1 point	Ctrl+[
Shrink font to next available size	Ctrl+<
Shrink selection	Shift+F8

Formatting Paragraphs

Task	Keyboard Combination
Apply Style	Ctrl+Shift+S
Normal Style	Ctrl+Shift+N
Clear manual paragraph formatting	Ctrl+Q
Run AutoFormat	Ctrl+K
Heading 1 Style	Alt+Ctrl+1
Heading 2 Style	Alt+Ctrl+2
Heading 3 Style	Alt+Ctrl+3
Left-align Paragraph	Ctrl+L
Justify Paragraph	Ctrl+J
Right-align Paragraph	Ctrl+R
Center Paragraph	Ctrl+E
Add/Remove 1/2 Line Before Paragraph	Ctrl+0
Single-space paragraph	Ctrl+1
1.5-line space paragraph	Ctrl+5
Double-space paragraph	Ctrl+2
Indent	Ctrl+M
Unindent	Ctrl+Shift+M
Hanging indent	Ctrl+T
Decrease hanging indent	Ctrl+Shift+T
List bullet	Ctrl+Shift+L

Using Headers and Footers

Task	Keyboard Combination
Link header/footer to preceding section	Alt+Shift+R

Proofing

Task	Keyboard Combination
Spell check	F7
Thesaurus	Shift+F7

Using Tables

Task	Keyboard Combination
Update table formatting (with Autoformat)	Alt+Ctrl+U

Outlining

Task	Keyboard Combination
Collapse Outline	Alt+Underline or Alt+Shift+NumPadHyphen
Promote one level heading	Alt+Shift+Left
Demote one level heading	Alt+Shift+Right
Demote to Body Text	Ctrl+N
Move above next item	Alt+Shift+Up
Move beneath next item	Alt+Shift+Down
Display additional level heading	Alt+Plus or Alt+Shift+NumPadPlus
Shows heading levels 1–2	Alt+@
Shows heading level 1	Alt+!
Shows heading levels 1–3	Alt+#
Shows heading levels 1–4	Alt+$
Shows heading levels 1–5	Alt+%

continues

Task	Keyboard Combination
Shows heading levels 1–6	Alt+^
Shows heading levels 1–7	Alt+&
Shows heading levels 1–8	Alt+*
Shows heading levels 1–9	Alt+(
Show all headings	Alt+Shift+A
Show first line of body text (toggle)	Alt+Shift+L
Show/Hide all character formatting	NumPad/ (Slash key on numeric keypad)

Fields and Links

Task	Keyboard Combination
View Field Codes	Alt+F9
Show/Hide Field Codes	Shift+F9
Click on field button (perform action)	Alt+Shift+F9
Lock Field	Ctrl+3 or Ctrl+F11
Unlink Field	Ctrl+6 or Ctrl+Shift+F9
Unlock Field	Ctrl+4 or Ctrl+Shift+F11
Update Fields	F9 or Alt+Shift+U
Update Source Document	Ctrl+Shift+F7

Using Mail Merge

Task	Keyboard Combination
Check for Errors	Alt+Shift+K
Insert Merge Field	Alt+Shift+F
Merge to Document	Alt+Shift+N

Task	Keyboard Combination
Merge to Printer	Alt+Shift+M
Open Data Source	Alt+Shift+E

Managing Word Windows

Task	Keyboard Combination
Next window	Ctrl+F6 or Alt+F6
Previous window	Ctrl+Shift+F6
Switch panes	F6 or Shift+F6
Maximize Word window	Alt+F10
Restore Word window	Alt+F5
Close window	Alt+Shift+C
Maximize document window	Ctrl+F10
Move document window	Ctrl+F7
Resize document window	Ctrl+F8
Restore document window	Ctrl+F5
Split document window horizontally	Alt+Ctrl+S

Customizing Word

Task	Keyboard Combination
Add menu item	Alt+Ctrl+EqualSign
Remove menu item	Alt+Ctrl+MinusSign (then choose menu item)
Add keyboard shortcut	Alt+Ctrl+NumPadPlusSign
Remove keyboard shortcut	Alt+Ctrl+NumPadMinusSign

Common Symbols

When a comma appears between symbols, type the characters consecutively. When a key you must type is in uppercase, use the Shift key.

Character	Keyboard Combination
... (Ellipsis)	Alt+Ctrl+.
‘ (Single opening quote)	Ctrl+`,`
’ (Single closing quote)	Ctrl+’,’
“ (Double opening quote)	Ctrl+`,”
” (Double closing quote)	Ctrl+’,”
– (En dash)	Ctrl+NumPadMinus
— (Em dash)	Alt+Ctrl+NumPadMinus
™ (Trademark)	Alt+Ctrl+T
- (Nonbreaking hyphen)	Ctrl+Underline
© (Copyright)	Alt+Ctrl+C
- (Optional hyphen)	Ctrl+Hyphen
® (Registered trademark)	Alt+Ctrl+R
(Nonbreaking space)	Ctrl+Shift+Spacebar
à	Ctrl+‘,a
À	Ctrl+‘,A
á	Ctrl+’,a
Á	Ctrl+’,A
â	Ctrl+^,a
Â	Ctrl+^,A
ã	Ctrl+~,a
Ã	Ctrl+~,A
ä	Ctrl+:,a
Ä	Ctrl+:,A
å	Ctrl+@,a
Å	Ctrl+@,A
æ	Ctrl+&,a

Character	Keyboard Combination
Æ	Ctrl+&,A
ç	Ctrl+,,c (insert one comma, then press c)
Ç	Ctrl+,,C
´d	Ctrl+’,d
D	Ctrl+’,D
è	Ctrl+‘,e
È	Ctrl+‘,E
é	Ctrl+’,e
É	Ctrl+’,E
ê	Ctrl+^,e
Ê	Ctrl+^,E
ë	Ctrl+:,e
Ë	Ctrl+:,E
ì	Ctrl+‘,i
Ì	Ctrl+‘,I
í	Ctrl+’,i
Í	Ctrl+’,I
î	Ctrl+^,i
Î	Ctrl+^,I
ï	Ctrl+:,i
Ï	Ctrl+:,I
ñ	Ctrl+~,n
Ñ	Ctrl+~,N
ò	Ctrl+‘,o
Ò	Ctrl+‘,O
ó	Ctrl+’,o
Ó	Ctrl+’,O
ô	Ctrl+^,o
Ô	Ctrl+^,O

continues

Character	Keyboard Combination
õ	Ctrl+~,o
Õ	Ctrl+~,O
ö	Ctrl+:,o
Ö	Ctrl+:,O
ø	Ctrl+/,o
Ø	Ctrl+/,O
œ	Ctrl+&,o
Œ	Ctrl+&,O
s	Alt+Ctrl+^,s
S	Alt+Ctrl+^,S
ß	Ctrl+&,s
ù	Ctrl+‘,u
Ù	Ctrl+‘,U
ú	Ctrl+’,u
Ú	Ctrl+’,U
û	Ctrl+^,u
Û	Ctrl+^,U
ü	Ctrl+:,u
Ü	Ctrl+:,U
y	Ctrl+’,y
Y	Ctrl+’,Y
ÿ	Ctrl+:,y
Ÿ	Ctrl+:,Y

Mouse Shortcuts and Toolbars

This appendix summarizes the primary shortcuts Word for Windows 95 provides for getting the job done: text selection shortcuts, drag-and-drop, scroll bars, rulers, toolbars, and other buttons.

In this appendix:

- Mouse shortcuts for selecting text
- Drag-and-drop
- Vertical and horizontal scroll bars
- Standard toolbar
- Formatting toolbar
- Borders toolbar
- Database toolbar
- Drawing toolbar

- Forms toolbar
- Microsoft toolbar
- Word for Windows 2.0 toolbar
- Macro toolbar
- Mail Merge toolbar
- Master Document toolbar
- Outlining toolbar
- Picture toolbar
- View buttons
- Equation Editor palettes

Using Mouse Shortcuts to Select Text

Table B.1 shows the mouse shortcuts you can use to select text in Word 95.

Table B.1
Mouse Shortcuts

To Select	Do This
Specific text	Click at the beginning of the text you want to select, and drag the mouse pointer to the end of the text you want to select. Or, place the insertion point at the beginning of the text you want to select, press Shift, and left-click. Then place the insertion point at the end of the text you want to select and left-click again. This highlights the selected text.
A word	Double-click anywhere in the word.
A sentence	Press Ctrl and left-click anywhere in the sentence.
A paragraph	Triple-click anywhere in the paragraph. Or double-click in the far left of the screen, in the "selection bar" (see fig. B.1).
A table cell	Left-click on the left edge of the cell.

To Select	Do This
More text than you can see on the screen	Place the insertion point at the beginning of the text you want to select, and left-click. Then hold down the left mouse button and move the insertion point above or below the editing window. Word scrolls the text until you reach the end of the text you want to select.
The whole document	Press Ctrl and left-click anywhere in the left-edge selection bar.

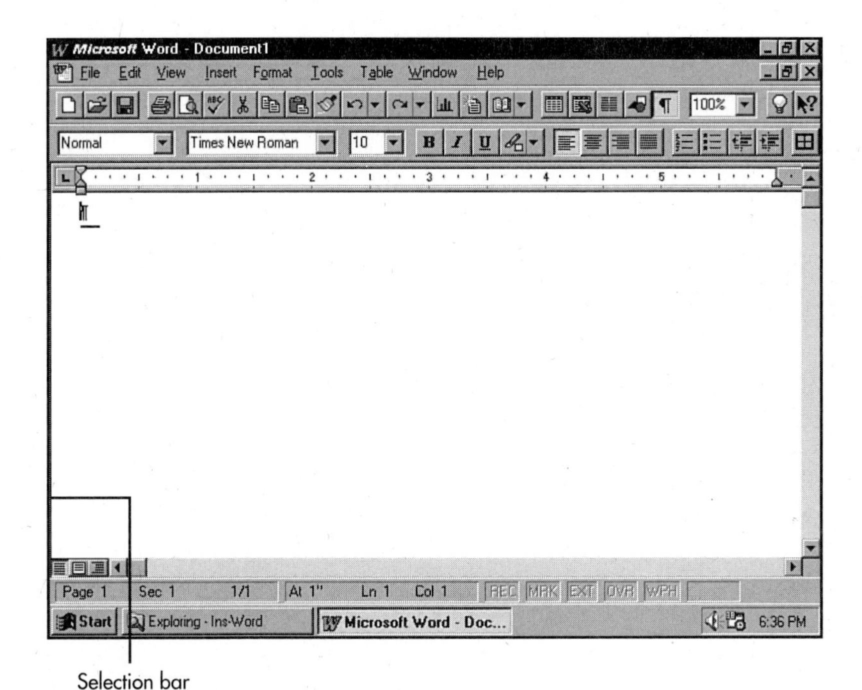

Figure B.1

The selection bar.

Using Drag-and-Drop

To move text, select it and left-click. Keeping the left mouse button pressed down, move the insertion point to the new text location.

In Windows 95, you also can drag-and-drop text to the Desktop; when you do, the "scrap" of text appears on the Desktop with its own icon. You can later drag that scrap into any other document or Windows file.

Using Vertical and Horizontal Scroll Bars

You can use Word's vertical and horizontal scroll bars (see fig. B.2) to move quickly throughout your document. The scroll box marks your current location.

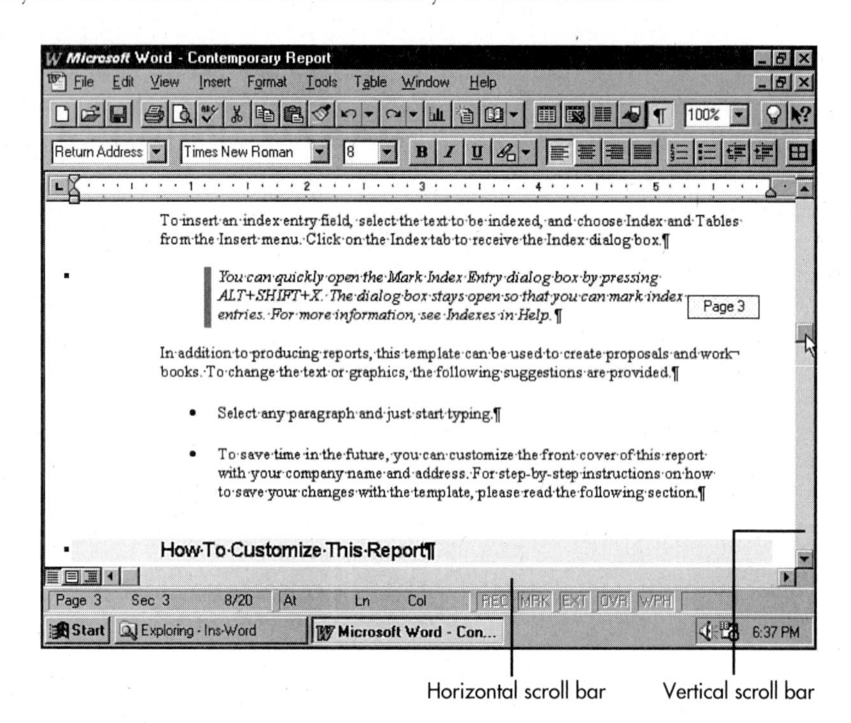

Figure B.2 *The vertical and horizontal scroll bars.*

Windows 95

New in Word 95: When you click on the vertical scroll bar, Word displays what page you're on, and as you drag the scroll bar, Word shows where you are in the document, which makes scrolling to the correct location much easier.

To scroll throughout your document a line at a time, left-click on the scroll-bar arrow key for the direction you want to go. Press the left mouse button until you arrive at your destination.

To scroll a page at a time, click on the vertical or horizontal scroll bar in the direction you want to go. To go to a specific portion of the document, left-click on the scroll box and drag it where you want to go.

Using Main Toolbars

The following toolbars may be viewed any time a Word text window is displayed (although not all toolbar buttons work in every context).

Standard Toolbar

Figure B.3 shows the Standard toolbar, which contains buttons for the Word features Microsoft expects you to use most often, including creating, opening, saving, and printing files, as well as basic editing shortcuts.

Figure B.3

The Standard toolbar.

Table B.2 describes the buttons in the Standard toolbar.

TABLE B.2
Standard Toolbar Buttons

Button	What It Does
New	Creates a new file using the default template (usually Normal).
Open	Displays the File Open dialog box, which enables you to open a file.
Save	Saves an existing file; for new files, opens Save As so you can choose a file name and location.
Print	Prints document to default printer with default settings.
Print Preview	Displays document in Print Preview.
Spell Check	Begins spell check from current location.
Cut	Cuts text or other material to Clipboard.
Copy	Copies text or other material to Clipboard.
Paste	Pastes text or other material from Clipboard.
Format Painter	Copies formats of selected text to any text you select.
Undo	Enables you to undo most recent events, up to 100.

continues

Table B.2, Continued
Standard Toolbar Buttons

Button	What It Does
Redo	Enables you to redo an event recently undone, up to 100 events.
AutoFormat	Formats document based on built-in Word styles.
Insert Address	Inserts an address from your Microsoft Exchange Address Book.
Table	Displays a matrix of rows and columns; choose the number of rows and columns you want, and Word inserts a table.
Insert Excel Worksheet	Inserts an Excel worksheet.
Text Columns	Displays a matrix of columns; choose the number you want, and Word creates a new section with that number of columns.
Draw	Turns the Drawing toolbar on or off.
Show Paragraph Marks	Shows paragraph marks and other nonprinting characters.
Show/Choose Zoom	Shows current magnification of document; change it by typing a new number in the box or selecting a preset option by clicking on the down arrow.
Tip Wizard	Displays or hides the Tip Wizard that presents suggestions on how to perform Word tasks or tells you about AutoFormat changes Word has made.
Help	Gives help on any button or screen area you select.

Formatting Toolbar

Figure B.4 shows the Formatting toolbar, which contains buttons for Word's most common formatting commands, including specifying font, font size, font attributes, alignment, highlighting, indenting, bullets and indents, and styles.

Table B.3 describes the buttons in the Formatting toolbar.

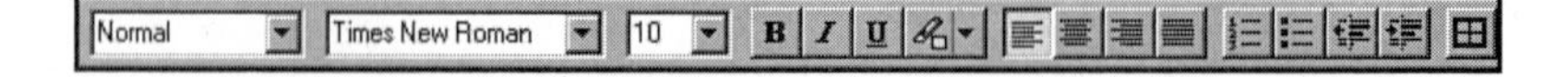

Figure B.4
The Formatting toolbar.

TABLE B.3
Formatting Toolbar Buttons

Button	What It Does
Style List Box	Enables you to choose or redefine a style.
Font List Box	Enables you to choose an available font.
Font Size List Box	Enables you to choose an available font size.
Boldface	Turns boldface on or off.
Italics	Turns italics on or off.
Underline	Turns underline on or off.
Highlight	Enables you to choose a highlight color for selected text.
Left Align	Left-aligns selected paragraphs.
Center Align	Center-aligns selected paragraphs.
Right Align	Right-aligns selected paragraphs.
Justify	Spreads ("justifies") selected paragraphs from left to right margin.
Numbered List	Creates a numbered list from selected text, using the default settings.
Bulleted List	Creates a bulleted list from selected text, using the default settings.
Unindent	Moves selected indented text to the left 0.5 inch.
Indent	Indents selected text by 0.5 inch.
Borders	Turns the Borders toolbar on or off.

Borders Toolbar

Figure B.5 shows the Borders toolbar, which contains buttons for creating borders, specifying thickness and location of borders, and adding shading.

Table B.4 describes the buttons in the Borders toolbar.

Figure B.5
The Borders toolbar.

Table B.4
Borders Toolbar Buttons

Button	What It Does
Border Line Style Box	Borders selected text. Press the down arrow to choose the thickness and type of border line.
Top Border	Turns border at top of selected text on or off.
Bottom Borders	Turns border at bottom of selected text on or off.
Left Border	Turns border at left edge of selected text on or off.
Right Border	Turns border at right edge of selected text on or off.
Inside Border	Turns inside bordering of every cell in a selection, or between each selected paragraph, on or off.
Outside Border	Borders all four corners of selected text.
No Border	Removes all borders from selected text.
Shading Box	Applies shading within borders of selected text. Press the down arrow to choose type of shading.

Database Toolbar

Figure B.6 shows the Database toolbar, which contains buttons for working with database information you want to include in a Word document.

Figure B.6
The Database toolbar.

Table B.5 describes the buttons in the Database toolbar.

Table B.5
Database Toolbar Buttons

Button	What It Does
Data Form	Enables you to edit a list or table in a form.
Manage Fields	Adds/deletes a database field.

Button	What It Does
Add New Record	Adds a new record to a database at the insertion point.
Delete Record	Deletes a selected record from a database.
Sort Ascending	Sorts records in A-Z and/or 0-9 (ascending).
Sort Descending	Sorts records in Z-A and/or 9-0 (descending) order.
Insert Database	Gets information from elsewhere and places it in the current document.
Update Fields	Updates the results of fields you select.
Find Record	Locates a specific record in a mail merge data source.
Mail Merge Main Document	Readies a main document to be merged with a data document.

Drawing Toolbar

Figure B.7 shows the Drawing toolbar, which contains buttons for Word's drawing features, including lines, boxes, text boxes, callouts, and pictures.

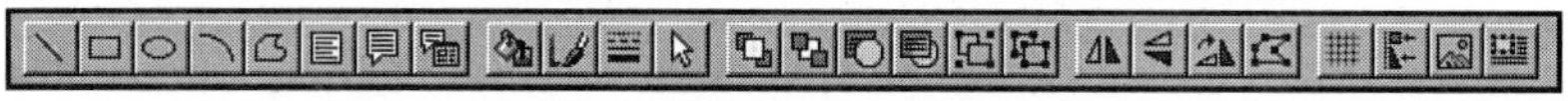

Figure B.7

The Drawing toolbar.

Table B.6 describes the buttons in the Drawing toolbar.

Table B.6
Drawing Toolbar Buttons

Button	What It Does
Line tool	Draws straight lines.
Rectangle tool	Draws boxes.
Ellipse tool	Draws round lines.
Arc tool	Draws arcs and creates pie-wedge shapes.
Freeform tool	Draws freeform shapes.
Text Box	Enables you to insert text.

continues

Table B.6, Continued
Drawing Toolbar Buttons

Button	What It Does
Callout	Enables you to insert a callout.
Format Callout	Enables you to choose a callout style.
Fill Color	Enables you to choose a fill color.
Line Color	Enables you to choose a line color.
Line Style	Enables you to choose a line style.
Select Drawing Objects	Selects one or more objects for drawing.
Bring to Front	Moves drawing object to foreground.
Send to Back	Moves drawing object to background.
Bring in Front of Text	Moves drawing object in front of text.
Send Behind Text	Moves drawing object behind text.
Group	Connects objects in a group so you can edit or move them all at once.
Ungroup	Separates objects in a group so you can edit or move them individually.
Flip Horizontal	Flips a drawing left-to-right.
Flip Vertical	Flips a drawing upside down.
Rotate Right	Rotates selected drawing 90 degrees to the right.
Reshape	Reshapes selected freeform object.
Snap to Grid	Creates a grid to which objects can adhere, so you can position them more precisely.
Align Drawing Objects	Lines up one or more drawing objects with each other, or with the page.
Create Picture	Inserts a Word Picture drawing container.
Insert Frame	Inserts a frame.

Forms Toolbar

Figure B.8 shows the Forms toolbar, which contains buttons for creating and working with Word's forms feature, including buttons for adding a variety of form fields that can be filled in by users of the forms you create.

Figure B.8

The Forms toolbar.

Table B.7 describes the buttons in the Forms toolbar.

TABLE B.7
Forms Toolbar Buttons

Button	What It Does
Text Form Field	Inserts a text form field that enables you to enter any text.
Check Box Form Field	Inserts a check box form field with an unchecked box.
Drop-Down Form Field	Inserts a drop-down list form field with no entries in it.
Form Field Options	Opens the Form Field Options box for the selected form field.
Insert Table	Displays a matrix of rows and columns; choose the number of rows and columns you want and Word inserts a table.
Insert Frame	Inserts a frame and asks if you want to view it in Page Layout View.
Form Field Shading	Turns shading on or off for all form fields in the document.
Form Protect	Turns document's form protection on or off (if the form is protected by a password, you also must enter the password).

Microsoft Toolbar

You can use the Microsoft toolbar buttons (see fig. B.9) as shortcuts for opening other Microsoft programs. But occasionally, the buttons can't find installed Microsoft programs and you must open the other programs normally. After you open a program, you can use the toolbar button to switch back and forth.

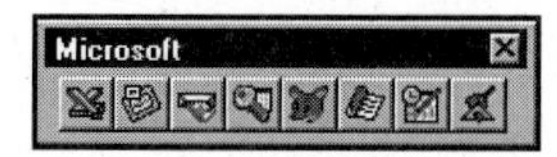

Figure B.9

The Microsoft toolbar.

Table B.8 describes the buttons in the Microsoft toolbar.

Table B.8
Microsoft Toolbar Buttons

Button	What It Does
Microsoft Excel	Opens or switches to Microsoft Excel spreadsheet program.
Microsoft PowerPoint	Opens or switches to Microsoft PowerPoint presentation graphics program.
Microsoft Mail	Opens or switches to Microsoft Mail electronic mail program. If Microsoft Exchange is running on your computer, it opens the Microsoft Exchange Inbox window.
Microsoft Access	Opens or switches to Microsoft Access database program.
Microsoft FoxPro	Opens or switches to Microsoft FoxPro database program.
Microsoft Project	Opens or switches to Microsoft Project project-management program.
Microsoft Schedule+	Opens or switches to Microsoft Schedule+ scheduling program.
Microsoft Publisher	Opens or switches to Microsoft Publisher desktop publishing program.

Word for Windows 2.0 Toolbar

The Word for Windows 2.0 toolbar (see fig. B.10) displays the toolbar that appears in Word 2, with one change: Word's new multilevel Undo list box replaces the old Undo erase button.

Figure B.10
The Word for Windows 2.0 toolbar.

Table B.9 describes the buttons in the Word for Windows 2.0 toolbar.

TABLE B.9
Word for Windows 2.0 Toolbar Buttons

Button	What It Does
New	Creates a new file using the default template (usually Normal).
Open	Displays the File Open dialog box, so you can open a file.
Save	Saves an existing file (for new files, opens Save As so you can choose a file name and location).
Cut	Cuts text or other material to the Clipboard.
Copy	Copies text or other material to the Clipboard.
Paste	Pastes text or other material from the Clipboard.
Undo	Displays a list of the most recent events you can undo, up to 100.
Numbering	Creates a numbered list from selected text, using the default settings.
Bullets	Creates a bulleted list from selected text, using the default settings.
Decrease Indent	Moves selected indented text to the left 0.5 inch.
Increase Indent	Indents selected text by 0.5 inch.
Insert Table	Displays a matrix of rows and columns; choose the number you want, and Word inserts a table.
Columns	Displays a matrix of columns; choose the number you want, and Word creates a new section with that number of columns.
Insert Frame	Inserts a frame and asks if you want to view it in Page Layout View.
Drawing	Turns the Drawing toolbar on or off.
Graph	Opens Microsoft Graph so you can insert a Graph object.
Create Envelope	Creates or prints an envelope.
Spelling	Begins spell check from current location.
Print	Prints document.
One Page	Shrinks page to fit on-screen.
Zoom 100%	Displays page full size.
Zoom Page Width	Shrinks page to fit entire width on-screen.

Using Specialized Toolbars

The following toolbars appear only when you perform specific tasks.

Full Screen Toolbar

This toolbar (see fig. B.11) enables you to switch back to normal Word menus and toolbars after you choose Full Screen display.

Figure B.11
The Full Screen toolbar.

Table B.10 describes the button in the Full Screen toolbar.

Table B.10
Full Screen Toolbar Button

Button	What It Does
Full Screen	Returns to normal display after using Full Screen.

Header and Footer Toolbar

Figure B.12 shows the Header and Footer toolbar, which contains the buttons shown in the Header and Footer window, including buttons for managing headers and footers, and for adding page numbers, dates, and times.

Figure B.12
The Header and Footer toolbar.

Table B.11 describes the buttons in the Header and Footer toolbar.

TABLE B.11
Header and Footer Toolbar Buttons

Button	What It Does
Switch Between Header and Footer	Turns header or footer on and off.
Show Previous	Shows header associated with preceding section.
Show Next	Shows header associated with next section.
Same as Previous	Links or unlinks a header from preceding section.
Page Numbers	Inserts a page field.
Date	Inserts a date field; uses the date format you choose in Insert Date and Time.
Time	Inserts a time field.
Page Setup	Opens Page Setup dialog box so you can change margins, paper size, paper source, or document layout.
Show/Hide Document Text	Switches between displaying light-gray body text in the background and showing no text in the background.
Close	Closes the Header or Footer window.

Macro Toolbar

This toolbar (see fig. B.13) appears only when you edit a WordBasic macro.

Figure B.13
The Macro toolbar.

Table B.12 describes the buttons in the Macro toolbar.

Table B.12
Macro Toolbar Buttons

Button	What It Does
Active Macro	Lists macros you can edit.
Record	Turns macro recording on or off.
Record Next Command	Records only the next command executed.
Start	Runs the macro that appears in the editing window.
Trace	Highlights each statement as it executes.
Continue	Starts running paused macro from the highlighted statement.
Stop	Stops running or recording a macro.
Step	Runs macro one step at a time, and steps through subroutines one step at a time.
Step Subs	Runs macro one step at a time, but treats each subroutine as a single step.
Show Variables	Lists variables in the current macro.
Add/Remove REM	Inserts/deletes REM statements at the beginning of line(s) you select.
Macro	Opens the organizer, from where you can run, create, delete, or edit a macro.
Dialog Editor	Opens macro dialog editor.

Mail Merge Toolbar

The Mail Merge toolbar (see fig. B.14) is available only in a mail merge main document.

Figure B.14
The Mail Merge toolbar.

Table B.13 describes the buttons in the Mail Merge toolbar.

TABLE B.13
Mail Merge Toolbar Buttons

Button	What It Does
Insert Merge Field	Inserts your choice of existing merge fields from the document with which you intend to merge.
Insert Word Field	Inserts your choice of these Word fields: Ask, Fill-in, If...Then...Else, Merge Record#, Merge Sequence#, Next Record, Next Record If, Set Bookmark, and/or Skip Record If.
View Merged Data	Displays the merge document as it will appear after you merge it.
First Record	Shows the first record in the data source.
Previous Record	Shows the previous record in the data source.
Go to Record box	Shows the current record in the data source; type a new number to go to another record.
Next Record	Shows the next record in the data source.
Last Record	Shows the final record in the data source; readies a main document to be merged with a data document.
Mail Merge Helper	Opens main Mail Merge Helper window that helps you manage the overall mail merge process.
Check for Errors	Checks for mail merge errors.
Merge to New Document	Merges data source and main document to a new file that appears on-screen.
Merge to Printer	Merges data source and main document and prints the results.
Mail Merge	Opens Merge dialog box, in which you specify where to merge the document to (including e-mail) and select from many other options.
Find Record	Finds records that contain specific information you can choose, in any field you choose.
Edit Data Source	Switches to data form so you can edit records.

Master Document Toolbar

To display this toolbar (see fig. B.15), choose Master Document from the View menu, or select Outline view and click on the Master Document toolbar button on the Outlining toolbar.

The Master Document toolbar is available only in Master Document view.

Figure B.15
The Master Document toolbar.

Table B.14 describes the buttons in the Master Document Toolbar.

TABLE B.14
Master Document Toolbar Buttons

Button	What It Does
Create Subdocument	Turns selected outline items into individual subdocuments.
Remove Subdocument	Removes a subdocument from a master document.
Insert Subdocument	Opens a subdocument and inserts it in the current master document.
Merge Subdocument	Combines two or more subdocuments into one subdocument.
Split Subdocument	Splits one subdocument into two.
Lock Document	Locks master document or subdocument so it cannot be edited.

Outlining Toolbar

The Outlining toolbar (see fig. B.16) is available only in Outline view.

Figure B.16
The Outlining toolbar.

Table B.15 describes the buttons in the Outlining toolbar.

TABLE B.15
Outlining Toolbar Buttons

Button	What It Does
Promote	Raises a heading one level (making it more important).
Demote	Lowers a heading one level (making it less important).
Demote to Body Text	Changes the contents of a heading to body text.
Move Up	Moves the current outline element (headings or body text) ahead of the previous one.
Move Down	Moves the current outline element after the next one.
Expand	Completely expands any outline elements you select.
Collapse	Completely collapses any outline elements you select.
Show Heading 1	Shows only 1st-level headings.
Show Heading 2	Shows only 1st- and 2nd-level headings.
Show Heading 3	Shows heading levels 1–3.
Show Heading 4	Shows heading levels 1–4.
Show Heading 5	Shows heading levels 1–5.
Show Heading 6	Shows heading levels 1–6.
Show Heading 7	Shows heading levels 1–7.
Show Heading 8	Shows heading levels 1–8.
All	Shows all heading levels.
Show First Line Only	Switches between displaying all body text in selected paragraphs, or just the first line of text in each paragraph.
Show Formatting Character	Switches between displaying all formatting, including Word styles, or just a draft font.

Picture Toolbar

This toolbar (see fig. B.17) is available only when you work on a drawing.

Figure B.17
The Picture toolbar.

Table B.16 describes the buttons in the Picture toolbar.

Table B.16
Picture Toolbar Buttons

Button	What It Does
Reset Picture Boundary	Resets page margins wide enough to enclose all drawing objects.
Close Picture	Closes active picture document.

Print Preview Toolbar

Figure B.18 shows the Print Preview toolbar, which appears only when you have chosen Print Preview. Among the shortcuts included in this toolbar are buttons for zooming in and out, and for showing more or fewer pages at once.

Figure B.18
The Print Preview toolbar.

Table B.17 describes the buttons in the Print Preview toolbar.

Table B.17
Print Preview Toolbar Buttons

Button	What It Does
Print	Prints one copy of the current document to the current printer.
Magnifier	Switches between zooming in to 100 percent and zooming out, normally to 34 percent.
One Page	Reduces page so you can see it in entirety.

Button	What It Does
Multiple Pages	Displays from one to six pages.
Zoom Control	Shows/changes percentage page is scaled up or down.
View Ruler	Switches the ruler on or off.
Shrink to Fit	Tries to squeeze your document into one less page.
Full Screen	Hides menus and most other items so you can enlarge the text somewhat.
Close	Closes Print Preview, returning to previous view.
Help	Displays help on screen areas and buttons you select.

Using View Buttons

Figure B.19 shows the View buttons that appear at the bottom left of the screen, above the status bar, and which enable you to control your view of the document.

Figure B.19

The view buttons on the horizontal scroll bar.

Table B.18 describes the View buttons.

Table B.18
View Buttons

Button	What It Does
Normal view	Displays current document in Normal view.
Page Layout view	Displays current document in Page Layout view.
Master Document view	Displays current document in Outline view.

Using Microsoft Equation 2.0 Symbol Palettes

These palettes (see fig. B.20) are available when you use the Insert Object menu to open Microsoft Equation 2.0. (Greek letters also are available when you use Insert Symbol, even if you don't use Microsoft Equation 2.0.)

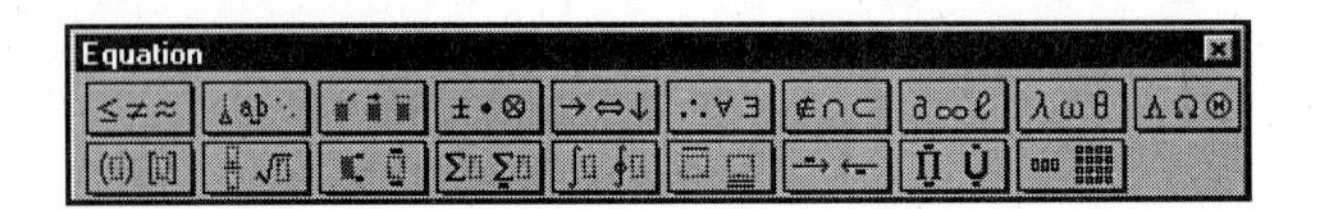

Figure B.20
The Microsoft Equation 2.0 symbol palettes.

Table B.19 describes the buttons available from Microsoft Equation 2.0 symbol palettes.

TABLE B.19
Equation Editor Symbol Palettes

Palette	What It Does
Relational Symbols	Enables you to insert a relational symbol.
Spaces and Ellipsis	Enables you to insert a symbol or ellipsis.
Embellishments	Enables you to insert an embellishment.
Operator Symbols	Enables you to insert an operator symbol.
Arrow Symbols	Enables you to insert an arrow symbol.
Logical Symbols	Enables you to insert a logical symbol.
Set Theory Symbols	Enables you to insert a set theory symbol.
Miscellaneous Symbols	Enables you to insert a miscellaneous symbol that doesn't fit into any other category.
Lowercase Greek Characters	Enables you to insert any lowercase Greek character.
Uppercase Greek Characters	Enables you to insert any uppercase Greek character.

Using the Microsoft Graph Toolbar

Figure B.21 shows the Microsoft Graph toolbar, which contains buttons for controlling graphs in Word and other Microsoft Office documents.

Figure B.21
The Microsoft Graph toolbar.

Table B.20 describes the buttons on the Microsoft Graph toolbar.

Table B.20
Microsoft Graph Toolbar Buttons

Button	What It Does
Import Data	Imports data from another application.
Import Chart	Imports a Microsoft Excel chart.
View Datasheet	Views the information the graph is based on.
Cut	Cuts selected material to Clipboard.
Copy	Copies selected material to Clipboard.
Paste	Pastes selected material from Clipboard.
Undo	Undoes previous action.
By Row	Specifies a data series by row.
By Column	Specifies a data series by column.
Chart Type	Enables you to choose from any of Microsoft Graph's available chart types.
Vertical Gridlines	Toggles vertical gridlines on or off.
Horizontal Gridlines	Toggles horizontal gridlines on or off.
Legend	Adds or removes a legend.
Text Box	Inserts a text box at the location you specify.
Drawing	Displays or hides the Drawing toolbar.
Color	Adds color to whatever you've selected.
Pattern	Adds a pattern to whatever you've selected.
Help	Displays context-sensitive help.

Inside the Word for Windows 95 CD-ROM

The *Word for Windows 95* CD-ROM contains tools to help you hone not only your Word skills, but also your Microsoft Excel skills. On it you'll find the *New Riders' Professional Solutions Guides for Word and Excel,* and sample files that enable you to practice the Word techniques you learn in the book.

To learn how to reach New Riders' Internet and CompuServe sites, see the section "New Riders Publishing Online," at the end of this appendix.

The New Riders' Professional Solutions Guides for Word and Excel

The CD-ROM that accompanies this book contains a set of documents called *The New Riders' Professional Solutions Guides for Word and Excel.* These documents, included as both MS Word (DOC) and MS Write (WRI) files, contain approximately 300 problems and solutions covering the following topics:

For Word:

Element	Title	File Name
Chapter 1	Setting Up Word	01word.*
Chapter 2	Using Word to Perform Advanced Tasks	02word.*
Chapter 3	Managing Files	03word.*
Chapter 4	Formatting Word Documents	04word.*
Chapter 5	Linking and Embedding Objects in Word	05word.*
Chapter 6	Working with Tables	06word.*
Chapter 7	Using Document Templates	07word.*
Chapter 8	Working with Master Documents	08word.*
Chapter 9	Proofing Word Documents	09word.*
Chapter 10	Printing Documents	10word.*
Chapter 11	Customizing Word	11word.*
Chapter 12	Creating Macros	12word.*
Chapter 13	Using Word on a Network	13word.*
Chapter 14	Using Word with Other Applications	14word.*
Chapter 15	Troubleshooting Word	15word.*
Appendix A	WordBasic Commands: New and Obsolete	aaword.*

For Excel:

Element	Title	File Name
Chapter 1	Cell Formatting	excelcd01.*
Chapter 2	Printing	excelcd02.*
Chapter 3	Toolbars and Buttons	excelcd03.*
Chapter 4	Pivot Tables	excelcd04.*
Chapter 5	Names and Links	excelcd05.*
Chapter 6	Importing Objects	excelcd06.*
Chapter 7	Managing Files	excelcd07.*
Chapter 8	Creating and Using Functions	excelcd08.*
Chapter 9	Creating Dialog Boxes	excelcd09.*
Chapter 10	Working with Lotus 1-2-3	excelcd10.*
Chapter 11	VBA Solutions Explored	excelcd11.*
Chapter 12	Analysis Goal Seek, Solver, Scenarios, and ToolPak	excelcd12.*
Chapter 13	Statistics	excelcd13.*
Chapter 14	Miscellaneous Solutions	excelcd14.*

Sample Files

The CD-ROM also contains a set of sample files you can use to try the procedures in this book. The file names indicate which chapter each file was designed to be used with; and references to the files appear throughout this book.

Installing the Disk

Refer to the README files on the CD-ROM for installation instructions.

New Riders Publishing Online

In addition to the contents of this disk, you can always get the latest information about Microsoft Word and Windows 95 by visiting the Macmillan Publishing Internet World Wide Web site:

```
http://www.mcp.com
```

Much of the information on our World Wide Web site also is available on our CompuServe forum. To get there, sign on to CompuServe and type **GO MACMILLAN**.

Index

Symbols

A

B

D

E

F

H

K

L

M

N

O

P

Q–R

S

T

U

V

W

X–Y–Z

Name ______________________ Title ______________________

Company ______________________ Type of business ______________________

Address ______________________

City/State/ZIP ______________________

Have you used these types of books before? ☐ yes ☐ no

If yes, which ones? ______________________

____

How many computer books do you purchase each year? ☐ 1–5 ☐ 6 or more

How did you learn about this book? ______________________

Where did you purchase this book? ______________________

Which applications do you currently use? ______________________

____

Which computer magazines do you subscribe to? ______________________

____

What trade shows do you attend? ______________________

____

Comments: ______________________

____

____

Would you like to be placed on our preferred mailing list? ☐ yes ☐ no

☐ **I would like to see my name in print!** You may use my name and quote me in future New Riders products and promotions. My daytime phone number is: ______________________

New Riders Publishing 201 West 103rd Street ◆ Indianapolis, Indiana 46290 USA

Fax to **317-581-4670** Orders/Customer Service **1-800-653-6156** Source Code **NRP95**

Fold Here

NO POSTAGE
NECESSARY
IF MAILED
IN THE
UNITED STATES

FIRST-CLASS MAIL PERMIT NO. 9918 INDIANAPOLIS IN

POSTAGE WILL BE PAID BY THE ADDRESSEE

NEW RIDERS PUBLISHING
201 W 103RD ST
INDIANAPOLIS IN 46290-9058